FINANCIAL ACCOUNTING PRINCIPLES

Sarah Teh

986-0089

BFIN 141

FINANCIAL ACCOUNTING PRINCIPLES

SECOND CANADIAN EDITION

KERMIT D. LARSON
University of Texas-Austin

PAUL B. W. MILLER
University of Colorado-Colorado Springs

MICHAEL ZIN
University of Windsor

MORTON NELSON
Wilfrid Laurier University

Homewood, IL 60430
Boston, MA 02116

All chapter and appendix openers photographed by *Sharon Hoogstraten*. Styled by *Anne Dawson*.

Cover photo: © Image Bank/Chicago

© RICHARD D. IRWIN, INC., 1991 and 1993

Senior sponsoring editor:	*Roderick T. Banister*
Marketing manager:	*David J. Collinge*
Project editor:	*Margaret Haywood*
Production manager:	*Diane Palmer*
Designer:	*Michael Warrell*
Cover designer:	*Amy Osborne*
Art coordinator:	*Mark Malloy*
Compositor:	*York Graphic Services, Inc.*
Typeface:	*10/12 Times Roman*
Printer:	*Von Hoffmann Press*

ISBN 0-256-13415-4

Library of Congress Catalog Number: 92–75982

Printed in the United States of America
1 2 3 4 5 6 7 8 9 0 VH 0 9 8 7 6 5 4 3

Preface

The tradition of *Financial Accounting Principles* includes clear explanations of accounting concepts and practices with closely related assignment material. Recent editions also reflect an educational philosophy we call *action learning*. We are firmly convinced that students learn most effectively when their study activities are designed to emphasize active behaviour. The second Canadian edition continues this focus on the effective use of student study time.

By providing a wide variety of action-oriented items in the text and in support of the text, we hope to encourage student involvement within the classroom as well as during out-of-class study. Newly developed and thoroughly revised assignment materials provide an extensive basis for varied assignments that stimulate interest, promote a sense of accomplishment, show the real-world relevance of the subject matter, and sharpen the analytical and communications ability of each student. In addition, the study guide and the computerized tutorial give students a number of action-learning opportunities.

The *Financial Accounting Principles* package provides a fully integrated system for the first two-semester course at the college and university level. The system helps instructors and students meet the course objectives, which include providing a strong foundation for future courses in business and finance and initiating course work leading to a major and career in accounting. Both objectives are also served by the continuous development of the concepts that guide financial and managerial accounting practices.

The second edition of *Financial Accounting Principles* reflects a concise yet conceptually thorough writing style and provides a rich source of assignment material that includes a wide range of questions, multiple-choice questions, mini discussion cases, exercises, problems, alternate problems, provocative problems, analytical and review questions, and As a Matter of Record cases. Specific features in and changes to the second edition that contribute to the process of learning through active student involvement are presented on the next page.

New Features

"As a Matter of Fact" Articles. Several chapters contain newly selected excerpts from relevant articles that originally appeared in the financial press, such as the *Globe and Mail.*

"As a Matter of Ethics" Cases. Each chapter that contains a case entitled As a Matter of Ethics also includes a provocative problem requiring students to analyze and discuss the case. These problems are identified as As a Matter of Ethics: Essay.

"As a Matter of Opinion" Interviews. A new feature in this edition, these inserts provide professional testimony about the relevance of the topical coverage to real-world decisions. Brief biographical sketches of the interviewees disclose the variety of career paths that relate to accounting.

Expanded Use of Visual Learning Aids. A significant number of new graphical illustrations have been created to appeal to today's students. These diagrams focus the readers' attention on relationships among concepts, actions, and financial measures.

Computer Systems and Assignments. Chapter 6 includes a new introduction to the computerized accounting systems used in today's businesses. In addition, a large number of homework assignments throughout the text are preloaded on the spreadsheet (SPATS) software package that is available with the text.

Excerpts and Assignments from Annual Reports. Most chapters contain a question and a problem assignment related to the annual report of Bombardier Inc. in Appendix I.

Analytical Essays Each chapter includes questions that require students to write a brief analytical essay explaining the effect(s) of accounting actions.

Synonymous Terms A glossary of synonymous terms has been added to the end of most chapters.

Multiple Choice Answers The answers to the multiple choice questions are included at the end of each chapter.

GST Accounting for the collection and payment of GST is included in Chapter 6 along with the section on specialized journals and in Chapter 12 on liabilities.
     Other changes include an expanded discussion of information systems in Chapter 6 and a new learning unit (Part V). These are discussed more fully in the section dealing with specific chapters.

Features Retained

Features about which our adopters have expressed enthusiasm have been retained in this second edition. These include the effective use of colour, chapter and part introductions, the various forms of problem material, the comprehensive review problems, acetate overlays, chapter glossaries, demonstration problems with solutions, integrated learning objectives, illustrative diagrams, and the comprehensive accounting cycle illustration.

Other Important Changes that Affect Several Chapters

In addition to the changes above, several chapters have had specific improvements including the following:

- Essentially all of the sections in Chapter 1 have been thoroughly rewritten. We believe the revision is more interesting, more informative, and more effective in helping students prepare for the changing environment of accounting and business.
- The definitions in Chapters 1 to 5 have been simplified and a continuous problem runs from Chapter 2 through Chapter 5.
- Chapter 5's Appendix D on Accounting Principles and Financial Statement Concepts has been taken from the chapter and moved to Part V (new).
- New coverage on information systems and converage of GST has been added to Chapter 6. Appendix E from the sixth edition has been deleted.
- In Chapter 8, the three days of grace has been eliminated from the material on discounting notes receivable. We now use a 365-day year for short-term interest calculations. Coverage of investments in equity securities has been moved to new Appendix E (Chapter 8) from the old Chapter 19, which has been deleted.
- The new title, "Capital Assets," reflecting the recent changes to the *CICA Handbook* has been used for Chapters 10 and 11. The terminology has been changed in most places to amortization instead of depreciation. We have removed coverage of the sum-of-the years'-digits method of amortization due to its lack of use in Canada.
- Part V is a new stand-alone section covering accounting principles, the conceptual framework, and alternative valuation methods. Its placement between Chapters 14 and 15 facilitates its use as a capstone for the first semester or as a lead-in to the second semester.
- Accounting for treasury stock has been moved from the body of Chapter 16 to Appendix F at the end of that chapter.

Appendixes and End-of-Text Items

To provide instructors flexibility in planning course content, the second edition includes several appendixes. Those that clearly relate to a single chapter are placed at the end of the chapter. Others appear at the end of the book. Appendixes E, F, and H are new to this edition.

Appendix H. Located at the end of the book, this appendix explains accounting for deferred income taxes. It reflects the most basic requirements of Section 3470 of the *CICA Handbook*.

Comprehensive List of Accounts Used in Exercises and Problems. This list provides students with the large variety of accounts that companies use and that are needed to solve the exercises and problems provided in the text. This list is located at the end of this text.

For the Instructor

The support package for *Financial Accounting Principles* includes many items to assist the instructor. They include the following:

- A *Solutions Manual* that has more extensive supporting calculations in this edition.

- Solution transparencies that include all exercises, problems, alternate problems, and comprehensive problems. These transparencies are now printed in boldface in a new, exceptionally large typeface so that visibility from a distance is strikingly improved.

- An expanded set of Teaching Transparencies, many of which are now in colour.

- Computerized Teaching Transparencies that are designed to support teaching the course using a computer, data display, and an overhead projector.

- Video tapes that are available upon adoption. The tapes reinforce important topics and procedures. They may be used in the classroom or media lab.

- *Spreadsheet Applications Template Software (SPATS),* a software package developed for use with the text by J. Russell Curtis and Minta Berry. SPATS includes a Lotus® 1-2-3® tutorial and innovatively designed templates that may be used with Lotus® 1-2-3® to solve many of the exercises and problems in the text. Upon adoption, this package is available to instructors for classroom or laboratory use.

- *Tutorial Software* by J. Russell Curtis and Leland Mansuetti. This software package includes glossary reviews, journalizing problems, multiple-choice exercises, and analyses of financial statements. Upon adoption, these computerized tutorials are available to instructors for classroom or laboratory use.

- A dramatically expanded test bank to accompany the second edition. The new bank includes a much greater variety of multiple-choice and true/false questions.

- *Computest III,* an improved test generator program that allows editing of questions, provides up to 99 different versions of each test, and allows question selection based on type of question, level of difficulty, or learning objectives.

- *Teletest,* which is a system for obtaining laser-printed tests by telephoning the publisher and specifying the questions to be drawn from the test bank.

- The *Instructor's Resource Manual* by Ray F. Carroll includes sample course syllabi, suggested homework assignments, a series of lecture outlines, demonstration problems, suggested points for emphasis, and background materials for discussion of ethics in accounting.

■ *Solutions Manual to accompany the practice sets* that will include detailed solutions to all of the practice sets accompanying the text.

For the Student

In addition to the text, the package of support items for the student includes the following:

■ *Working Papers, Chapters 1–19*. These include working papers for the exercises, problems, alternate problems, and comprehensive problems, with additional forms that may be adapted for the provocative problems.

■ The *Study Guide,* which provides a basis for independent study and review, has been expanded to include multiple-choice and true/false questions as well as several additional problems with solutions for each chapter and appendix.

■ Check Figures for the problems and alternate problems.

■ *Barns Bluff Camping Equipment,* by Barrie Yackness and Terrie Kroshus, a manual, single proprietorship practice set with business papers that may be assigned after Chapter 7.

■ *Student's Name Book Centre,* by Harvey C. Freedman, a manual, single proprietorship practice set covering a one month accounting cycle. The set includes business papers and can be assigned after Chapter 7.

Acknowledgments

We are indebted to those adopters who maintained diaries as the basis for their thoughtful reviews and to several other reviewers who provided insight and extremely helpful criticisms. Many of the improvements in the second edition are based on the input from these reviewers. In addition, numerous adopters, students, and professional colleagues have made a variety of significant contributions and constructive suggestions. These individuals include:

David Carr, *Dawson College*

Janet Falk, *The University College of the Fraser Valley*

John Fitzgerald, *Red River Community College*

Diane Fletcher, *Seneca College of Applied Arts and Technology*

Harvey C. Freedman, *Humber College of Applied Arts and Technology*

Cliff Harrison, *Saskatchewan Institute of Applied Science and Technology*

Peter Henderson, *Douglas College*

Rod Tilley, *Mount Saint Vincent University*

Barrie Yackness, *British Columbia Institute of Technology*

We also want to recognize and thank the important group of people who checked every problem and solution for accuracy. Their efforts, coupled with our own accuracy check and that of a professional proofreader, should make the text "error-free." They include:

Margaret Briscall, *British Columbia Institute of Technology*

Ray F. Carroll, *Dalhousie University*

Harvey C. Freedman, *Humber College of Applied Arts and Technology*

Cliff Harrison, *Saskatchewan Institute of Applied Science and Technology*

Richard Wright, *Fanshawe College of Applied Arts and Technology*

Last but not least, we gratefully acknowledge the contribution from the faculty members and secretarial staff at the University of Windsor and Wilfrid Laurier University, especially Sharon Roth and Sandra J. Berlasty.

Michael Zin
Morton Nelson

Contents in Brief

Contents

Processing Accounting Data 68

Accounting for Assets   356

PART

IV

Accounting for Liabilities and
Partnerships   608

PART V

Accounting Principles, Conceptual Framework, and Alternative Valuation Methods   731

PART VI

Accounting for Corporations, Long-Term Installment Notes, and Bonds 758

PART

Financial Statements: Interpretation and Modifications   898

Appendixes

FINANCIAL
ACCOUNTING
PRINCIPLES

Introduction

In one form or another, accounting touches everyone's life. Young people add and subtract figures to decide how to spend their weekly allowances. Newspaper carriers keep records of payments by their customers. Students determine where the money for their education is coming from and how to spend it. Taxpayers account for their taxable income and deductions. And businesses account for what they own and owe, and the profits they make from their operations. In fact, all of us use accounting information to make financial decisions of one kind or another.

As you study this text, a new world of understanding and knowledge will unfold for you. Because of what you learn about accounting, you will be better prepared to earn a living and to live on what you earn. You will also find more meaning in news stories about such things as a company that has achieved record high sales and profits or another that faces bankruptcy. In other words, what you learn will give you useful and productive skills that will help you understand much more about the business world and the role accounting information plays in our economy.

Part I of *Fundamental Accounting Principles* consists of:

To the Student Reader

Fundamental Accounting Principles is designed to get you actively involved in the learning process so that you will learn quickly and more thoroughly. The more time you spend expressing what you are learning, the more effectively you will learn. In accounting, you do this primarily by answering questions and solving problems. However, you can also express your ideas by using the wide margins for taking notes, summarizing a phrase, or writing down a question that remains unanswered in your mind. These notes will assist in your later review of the material, and the simple process of writing them will help you learn.

As you read the text, you will learn many important new terms. In addition to being defined and discussed in the chapter, these terms are defined in a glossary at the end of each chapter. You will find these terms printed in teal in the glossary and in the text where they are defined. The glossary is a good place to begin your review of important concepts. You can also find the key terms in the index at the back of the book.

To guide your study, learning objectives are listed at the beginning of each chapter, repeated in the margins next to the related topics throughout the chapter, and used as the basis for summarizing the chapter. The exercises and problems are also coded in terms of these objectives.

Other special features of the book include excerpts from news articles entitled "As a Matter of Fact" and "As a Matter of Record Cases." These relate real-world events to the material in the chapter. You also will find brief cases entitled "As a Matter of Ethics," which will help you think about the ethical aspects of accounting. In brief inserts called "As a Matter of Opinion," business and community leaders tell how they use accounting in their decisions.

The use of colour in the book has been carefully planned to facilitate your learning. All of the textual headings are printed in teal, as are important new terms where they are being defined. Teal also identifies the learning objectives. The colours in the illustrations have been selected to help you distinguish between different types of concepts and graphical entities. A cream background identifies the "As a Matter of Ethics," "As a Matter of Fact," and "As a Matter of Opinion" elements. The ethics cases are set off with a small blue box at the top, the fact cases with a green box, and the opinions with a purple. All financial reports, which are the output of the accounting process, are cream. A soft, noninterruptive teal colour is used as a background in the illustrations and the end-of-chapter material. A light cream background identifies the comprehensive problems.

Each chapter contains a demonstration problem and related solution that illustrate many of the issues discussed in the chapter. There is also a short section entitled "Objective Review" that contains a series of multiple-choice questions related to the learning objectives. Answer them as a quick test of your learning. Then check your answers against the correct ones listed at the end of the chapter.

Ethics: The Most Fundamental Accounting Principle

"Each person capable of making moral decisions is responsible for making his [her] own decisions. The ultimate locus of moral responsibility is in the individual."[1]

As students, you no doubt realize that ethics and ethical behaviour are important features of civilized society. Ethical considerations abound in daily life, both privately and professionally. The media often remind us of the importance of ethics to society. These reminders come in the form of news stories about such things as civil rights violations, fraudulent attempts to rip off the elderly, credit card scams, parents who fail to make child support payments, children who ignore or abuse their elderly parents, politicians who fail to disclose past instances of misconduct, the alleged bribery of government officials, and security dealers who use inside information for personal gain.

The Meaning of Ethics

As a discipline of study, ethics deals "with what is good and bad or right and wrong or with moral duty and obligation." In practice, ethics is the "principles of conduct that govern an individual or a profession."[2] Some unethical actions are unlawful. Other actions may be within the law but, nevertheless, are widely recognized as being ethically wrong. In addition, some actions are not clearly right or wrong but are ethically questionable.

Many of the issues we face in school, in the workplace, and beyond have ethical dimensions; they are unavoidable aspects of life. How well we deal with ethical matters influences how we feel about ourselves, how we are perceived by others, and in the aggregate, the quality of our society. But why begin an accounting text with a prologue on ethics? How does ethics relate to business and, more specifically, to the discipline of accounting?

Ethics in Business

To answer the question of why we begin this text with a prologue on ethics, we must recognize that ethical standards in business and accounting are a matter of public concern. In recent years, many people have expressed concern about deteriorating ethical standards in business. For example, a recently conducted opinion survey on business ethics included over 1,100 business executives,

---

[1] Harold H. Titus and Morris Keeton, *Ethics for Today*, 4th ed. (New York: American Book–Stratford Press, 1966), p. 131.

[2] *Webster's Third New International Dictionary of the English Language, Unabridged* (Springfield, Mass.: G. & C. Merriam Co., 1971), p. 780.

deans of business schools, and members of the U.S. Congress. Of those in the survey, 94% agreed that "the business community is troubled by ethical problems."[3] Ironically, those surveyed also believed that companies that are successful over the long run seem to have high ethical standards. You may infer from this that "ethics is good business." Ethical business practices can help create loyal customers and suppliers, trustworthy and productive employees, and a solid reputation.

Because of the widespread public interest in business ethics, many banks, insurance companies, and other businesses have recently revised or written new codes of ethics. Companies generally use these codes as public statements of their commitment to ethical business practices and also as guides for employees to follow.

Ethics in Accounting

In accounting, many professional organizations such as the Provincial Institutes of Chartered Accountants, the Provincial Associations of Certified General Accountants, and the Society of Management Accountants have had codes of ethics for years. Most of these codes have been re-evaluated and revised in recent years. Ethics is important in accounting because accountants often are required to make decisions that have ethical implications. The activities performed by accountants have a profound impact on many individuals, businesses, and other institutions. An accountant's decisions can affect such things as the amount of money a corporation distributes to its shareholders; the price a buyer pays for a business enterprise; the compensation levels of managers and executives; the success or failure of specific products and divisions; and the amount of taxes paid by an individual or a business.

To see how an accountant's decisions can have an ethical dimension, consider the following example. Assume that Smith and Jones agreed to be partners in a business venture that would last two years. Because the original idea for the business venture was Smith's, they agreed that Smith

would receive 75% of the first year's profits and Jones would receive 25%. In the second year, however, their agreement was that Smith and Jones would split the profits evenly. At the end of the first year, their accountant discovers that there are two alternative methods for recording a recent transaction. If method A is used, a profit of $100,000 will be recognized in year 1. If method B is used, the profit of $100,000 will not be recognized until year 2. Clearly, the accountant's decision about which method should be used will affect each partner's compensation. If method A is used, Smith will receive $75,000 of the profit and Jones will receive $25,000. But if method B is used, each partner will receive $50,000.

In this example, more information is needed to help the accountant choose between methods A and B. As an ethical matter, however, the accountant's decision should not be influenced by the fact that method A is more favourable to Smith and method B is more favourable to Jones.

The preceding example is not unusual. Accountants are frequently called on to choose between alternative methods for recognizing profits. These decisions cannot be made lightly because, as the example shows, the decisions may shift wealth from one party to another.

Another aspect of accounting that illustrates the importance of ethical behaviour involves the issue of confidentiality. Accountants, by the very nature of their duties, frequently work with private, confidential information. For example, accountants have access to individual salary records, future business plans and budgets, and a variety of information about the financial status of their clients or employers. As an ethical matter, accountants must respect and maintain the confidentiality of this information.

The Ethical Challenge

As you proceed in your study of accounting, you will encounter many other situations in which ethical considerations are important. We encourage you to seek out and explore any ethical issues that may arise. Accounting must be done ethically if it is to be an effective tool in the service of society. This is, perhaps, the most fundamental principle of accounting.

---

[3] Touche Ross & Co., *Ethics in American Business* (New York, 1988), pp. 1–2.

AS A MATTER OF
Opinion

James S. Clark, FCA

Mr. Clark received his university education at Assumption College of the University of Western Ontario. He joined the Canadian Peat Marwick firm in 1965 and served as the managing partner of its Windsor, Ontario, office from 1971 until his retirement in 1991. He was a member of its Committee on Professional Practice (Audit) from 1975 to 1978. A member of the ICAO, he received his C.A. designation in 1958 and F.C.A. in 1985.

The accounting profession is charged with the maintenance of an important public trust in the preservation and application of the highest possible standards of ethics and conduct. These standards apply to all professional accountants and in every area of service to the public including teaching and research, government, industry, and the public practice of the profession.

You will come to appreciate and understand that members of the profession are faced with ongoing pressures and challenges to the maintenance of this public trust. To those entering the profession, ethical standards are and will remain one of the foundations upon which individual success will be dependent and measured both by one's peers and by the public. That success will bring deserving recognition not only to the individual but to the profession as well.

Ethical decisions and the development of ethical standards are areas in your life where you are in control. Each of us as an individual is free to shape his or her own moral positions. Adapting a phrase originally spoken by Supreme Court Justice Earl Warren in reference to the law: ''In civilized life, [accounting] floats on a sea of ethics.'' It is your choice how you elect to navigate this sea.

Accounting: An Introduction to Its Concepts

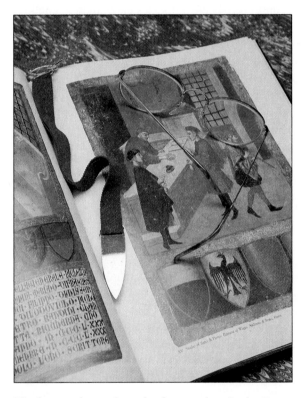

The factors that reshaped culture and art in the Renaissance also brought rapid advances to commerce and banking. Further progress was spurred when Luca Pacioli, an Italian cleric and mathematician, described double-entry accounting in the late 1400s. We still collect useful information with this system, despite five centuries of change.

Y our study of accounting begins in this chapter with the questions: What is accounting? and Why study accounting? Because many of you will either become accountants or work closely with them, this chapter also describes the accounting profession and the kinds of information that accountants provide in financial statements. We then discuss some general principles accountants follow in producing these statements and some of the organizations that govern or influence accounting practices. Next, we explain the different ways that businesses are organized. Finally, we introduce you to the way accountants analyze the effects of business transactions.

Learning Objectives

After studying Chapter 1, you should be able to:

1. Describe the function of accounting and the nature and purpose of the information it provides.
2. List the main fields of accounting and the activities carried on in each field.
3. Describe the information contained in the financial statements of a business and be able to prepare simple financial statements.
4. Briefly explain the accounting principles introduced in the chapter and describe the process by which generally accepted accounting principles are established.
5. Briefly explain the differences between a single proprietorship, a partnership, and a corporation, comparing the differing responsibilities of their owners for the debts of the business.
6. Recognize and be able to indicate the effects of transactions on the elements of the accounting equation.
7. Define or explain the words and phrases listed in the chapter glossary.

What Is Accounting?

LO 1 Describe the function of accounting and the nature and purpose of the information it provides.

The function of **accounting** is to communicate useful information to people who make rational investment, credit, and similar decisions.[1] In effect, accountants *serve* decision makers by providing them with financial information to help them reach better decisions. The decision makers include present and potential investors, lenders, and other users. Other users include the managers of businesses and those who sell to or buy from businesses.

In addition to providing information about profit-oriented businesses, accountants also account for not-for-profit organizations. Some examples of entities that are not operated for profit are churches, hospitals, museums, schools, and various government agencies. Accounting information about these entities is used by people who manage them. The information is also

---

[1] *CICA Handbook,* "Financial Statement Concepts," par, 1000.12

used by people who donate to, pay taxes to, or use the services of these organizations.

In making decisions about an economic entity, people generally begin by asking questions about it. The answers are often found in accounting reports. For example, owners and managers of businesses look to accounting for help in answering questions like these:

- What resources (items the business owns and uses to earn income) does the business have?
- What debts does it owe?
- How much income is it earning?
- Are the expenses appropriate for the amount of sales?
- Is the right amount of merchandise being kept on hand?
- Are customers' accounts being collected promptly?
- Can the company's debts be paid on time?
- Should additional resources be acquired to expand operations?
- Should a new product be introduced?
- Should selling prices be increased?

Individual investors also use financial reports when they make decisions about buying, keeping, or selling their investments.

Banks and suppliers who loan money (grant credit) to a business use accounting information to answer questions like these:

- Should the company be granted additional credit now?
- Does it have good prospects for future earnings?
- Does it have the ability to pay its current debts?
- Has it promptly paid its debts in the past?

In addition, many government agencies use accounting information in carrying out their activities. These activities may include delivering public services, regulating businesses, or collecting taxes. Employees and labor unions also use accounting information when they negotiate contracts with businesses.

The Difference between Accounting and Bookkeeping

Some people mistakenly confuse accounting and bookkeeping by thinking that they are the same thing. While bookkeeping is critical to accounting, it is only the clerical part of the accounting process. That is, **bookkeeping** is the part of accounting that records transactions and other events, either manually or with computers. Accounting, on the other hand, is concerned with identifying how transactions and events should be described in financial reports. It is also concerned with designing bookkeeping systems that make it easy to produce useful reports and to control the operations of the business. Thus, the work of the accountant is much broader than bookkeeping. Accounting involves more professional expertise and judgment than bookkeeping because the accountant must analyze complex and unusual events. Also, the accountant must be able to interpret the information contained in accounting reports.

Initially, your study of accounting requires you to learn some basic book-keeping practices. This knowledge of bookkeeping helps you understand how accountants gather financial data and use it to produce useful reports.

Accounting and Computers

Since computers became available in the 1950s, they have spread throughout our everyday lives and the business world. From the beginning, accounting and bookkeeping have been popular applications of computer technology. Computers are widely used in accounting because they are able to efficiently store, process, and summarize large quantities of financial data. Furthermore, computers perform these functions very rapidly and with little or no human intervention. Thus, using computers has reduced the time, effort, and cost of processing data. It has also improved clerical accuracy. As a result of these advantages, most accounting systems are now computerized. Even so, manual accounting systems are still used by small businesses.

To practice accounting in today's world, you should understand the important role computers now play in most accounting systems. Specifically, computers are important tools used by accountants to produce the information that users need. The coming of computers and the huge growth in their numbers has changed the way that accountants work. However, computers have not eliminated the need for people educated in accounting. A strong demand exists for individuals who can design accounting systems, supervise the operation of those systems, analyze complex transactions, and interpret the reports. While computers have taken over many routine accounting and bookkeeping tasks, they are not substitutes for qualified people.

Why Study Accounting?

Given the wide range of questions that you can answer with accounting information, you will almost certainly use accounting in your future career. To use it effectively, you need to understand the words and terms unique to accounting and the concepts that guide the preparation of accounting reports. You also should understand the procedures used to gather accounting information and to summarize it in financial reports.

Your study of accounting will also make you aware of its limitations. For example, you will learn that to a great extent much accounting information is not based on precise measurements. In fact, a lot of the information is based on estimates and predictions.

Another very good reason for studying accounting is to make it the basis for an interesting and highly rewarding career. The next sections of this chapter describe in more detail what accountants do. When you read these sections, you will learn more about the different kinds of accounting information. You will also learn about some of the career opportunities that exist for accountants.

Mr. Chant received his B.A. in economics from Michigan State University and his Ph.D. in accounting and information systems from Northwestern University. He was a member of the faculty of management at McGill University from 1974 to 1980 and has worked in the national office of Deloitte and Touche since 1980. He became a partner there in 1985 and is involved in the application of accounting standards to the reporting of complex and innovative transactions. Mr. Chant has been a member of the Accounting Standards Board, CICA, since 1991.

Peter D. Chant

highly subjective process in which investments do not always turn out as planned, and, in fact, the results may not always be known. The motives of managers, investors, and accountants often conflict in these circumstances. I have found that accounting requires mental discipline and a broad perspective not only of accounting and finance, but of all aspects of human behaviour. This includes the abilities to discriminate right from wrong and to convince others of the merits of your position. I doubt that there are many other endeavours that can challenge an individual in so many dimensions.

I find the practice of accounting a fascinating blend of the science of finance and the art of portraying the financial conditions of an enterprise. The business environment is often a highly uncertain,

---

One way to classify different types of accountants is to identify the kinds of organizations for which they work. The three types are:

The Types of Accountants

1. Accountants who work for a private company.
2. Accountants who offer their services to the public.
3. Accountants who work for a government agency.

Another way to classify accountants is to identify the kinds of work they do. In general, accountants work in three broad fields. These fields involve providing different kinds of information to various types of users. The fields of accounting are

1. Financial accounting.
2. Managerial accounting.
3. Tax accounting.

In the following paragraphs, we provide more information about the three types of accountants and their work within these fields.

Most accountants are **private accountants.** Private accountants work for a single employer, which is usually a business.

Many other accountants are **public accountants.** Public accountants provide their services to many different clients. They are called *public account-*

ants because they offer their services to the public. Some public accountants are self-employed. Many others work for public accounting firms. These firms may have only a few employees, or as many as several thousand employees.

Government accountants are employed by government agencies at local, provincial, and federal levels. Some government accountants perform accounting services for their employers. Other government accountants are involved with business regulation. Still others investigate violations of the law.

Accounting is considered to be a profession like law and medicine because accountants have special abilities and responsibilities. The professional status of an accountant is often indicated by one or more certificates.

Professional Certification

In Canada, there are a number of accounting organizations providing education and professional training. These include the provincial Institutes of Chartered Accountants, the Certified General Accountants' Association of Canada, and the Society of Management Accountants (SMA). Successful completion of the prescribed courses of instruction and practical experience lead to the following appellations:

Chartered Accountant (CA).
Certified General Accountant (CGA).
Certified Management Accountant (CMA).

An activity of the three accounting organizations that has shaped accounting thought has been the education and the publication program. Each has an extensive educational program and has maintained the publication of journals which enjoy wide readership.

In the past decade reliance on post-secondary accounting education has become a significant part of the educational process and complements the extensive correspondence, university distance study and lecture programs of the Certified General Accountants' Association of Canada. The provincial bodies of the Canadian Institute of Chartered Accountants (CICA) and the Society of Management Accountants generally require a university degree with specified courses.

Accountancy is the fastest growing of the professions. This growth is in response to the expansion and complexity of the economy, the increasing involvement of the accountant in the process of management decision making, and a growing number of financial reporting activities.

The Fields of Accounting

LO 2 List the main fields of accounting and the activities carried on in each field.

Accountants practice in three fields of accounting—financial accounting, managerial accounting, and tax accounting. The actual work done by an accountant depends on both the field and whether the person is a private, public, or government accountant. Illustration 1–1 identifies the specific activities of the three types of accountants within these fields.

ILLUSTRATION 1–1

Activities of Accountants

Types of Accountants	Fields of Accounting		
	Financial Accounting	Managerial Accounting	Tax Accounting
Private accountants	Preparing financial statements	General accounting Cost accounting Budgeting Internal auditing	Preparing tax returns Planning
Public accountants	Auditing financial statements	Providing managerial advisory services	Preparing tax returns Planning
Government accountants	Preparing financial statements Reviewing financial reports Writing regulations Assisting companies Investigating violations	General accounting Cost accounting Budgeting Internal auditing	Reviewing tax returns Assisting taxpayers Writing regulations Investigating violations

Financial Accounting

Financial accounting provides information to decision makers who are not involved in the day-to-day operations of an organization. These decision makers include investors, lenders, and others. The information is distributed primarily through general purpose financial statements. Financial statements describe the condition of the organization and the events that happened during the year. The most common financial statements are described later in this chapter.

The Financial Accounting column of Illustration 1–1 shows that financial statements are prepared by a company's private accountants. However, many companies issue their financial statements only after they have been subjected to an **audit.** Audits are performed by independent public accountants.

The purpose of an audit is to add credibility to the financial statements. For example, banks require audits of the financial statements of companies applying for large loans. Also, the law requires companies to have audits before their securities (shares and bonds) can be sold to the public. Thereafter, their financial statements must be audited as long as the securities are traded.

In performing an audit, the auditors examine the statements and the accounting records used to prepare them. During the audit, the auditors decide whether the statements reflect the company's financial position and operating results in accordance with **generally accepted accounting principles (GAAP).** These principles are the rules adopted by the accounting profession as guides in measuring, recording, and reporting the financial affairs and activities of a business. We discuss the purposes and origins of GAAP in a later section of this chapter. We also describe specific requirements of GAAP in many of the succeeding chapters.

When the audit is completed, the auditors prepare a report that states their professional opinion about the financial statements. The auditor's report must accompany the financial statements when they are distributed.

Some government accountants are also involved in financial accounting. In the bottom section of Illustration 1–1, the first column shows that some government accountants prepare financial statements. These statements describe the financial status of government agencies and results of events occurring during the year. The financial statements are published to allow voters to know more about the condition of the agencies and the performance of the elected or appointed officials who administer them. The statements are also distributed to lenders when, for example, local governments need to borrow money. Usually the financial statements of governmental bodies are audited by public accountants.

Accountants who work for regulatory agencies, such as the Board of Transport Commissioners and the Ontario Securities Commission, may review reports filed by businesses that are subject to the agencies' authority. Government accountants also help write regulations concerning financial accounting. Because the regulations can be complex, government accountants also assist the companies in understanding and following the regulations.

Some government accountants investigate possible violations of laws and regulations. For example, accountants who work for the provincial securities commissions investigate crimes related to securities. The RCMP and provincial police forces employ accountants who assist in detecting financial frauds and other white-collar crimes.

Managerial Accounting

The field of managerial accounting involves providing information to the managers of organizations. Managerial accounting reports often include much of the same information provided through financial accounting. However, managerial accounting reports also include information not reported outside the company.

In Illustration 1–1, look at the first and third sections of the Managerial Accounting column. Note that private and government accountants have the same four major activities. The second section of the Managerial Accounting column shows that public accountants also perform activities related to managerial accounting. All of these managerial accounting activities are described next.

General Accounting.   The task of recording transactions, processing the recorded data, and preparing reports for managers of businesses and government agencies is called **general accounting.** General accounting also includes preparing the financial statements presented to investors, lenders, and others. Accountants who work for an organization design the accounting information system, usually with help from a public accountant. The clerical and data processing staff work under the supervision of a chief accounting officer, who is often called the organization's **controller.** This title stems from the fact that a primary use of accounting data is to control the operations of an organization.

Cost Accounting. One managerial accounting activity is called **cost accounting** because it is designed to help managers identify, measure, and control operating costs. Cost accounting information is also useful for assessing the performance of managers who are responsible for controlling costs. Cost accounting may involve accounting for the costs of producing a given product or service or of performing some other specific activity. Good management requires knowledge of costs so that they can be controlled. Therefore, a large company may have a number of accountants engaged in cost accounting.

Budgeting. The process of developing formal plans for future business and government activities is called **budgeting.** A primary goal of budgeting is to provide managers with a clear understanding of the activities to be undertaken and completed to accomplish the company's objectives. Then, after the budget plan has been put into effect, it provides a basis for evaluating actual performance. Large companies and government agencies have many accountants who devote all their time to budgeting.

Internal Auditing. Just as independent auditing adds credibility to financial statements, **internal auditing** adds credibility to reports produced and used within an organization. Internal auditors not only evaluate the record-keeping processes but also assess whether managers throughout the organization are following established operating procedures. Internal auditors also evaluate the efficiency of the operating procedures. Almost all large companies and government agencies employ internal auditors.

Managerial Advisory Services. Public accountants participate in managerial accounting when they provide **managerial advisory services** to their clients. Independent auditors gain an intimate knowledge of a client's accounting and operating procedures. Thus, the auditors are in an excellent position to offer suggestions for improving the company's procedures. Clients often expect these suggestions as a useful by-product of the audit. Other advisory services may have nothing to do with the audit. For example, public accountants often help companies design and install new accounting systems. Many times, this effort includes offering advice on selecting new computer systems. Other advice might relate to budgeting or choosing employee benefit plans.

Tax Accounting

Income taxes raised by federal and provincial governments are based on the income earned by taxpayers. These taxpayers include both individuals and corporate businesses. The amount of taxes is based on what the tax laws define to be income. Tax accountants help taxpayers comply with these laws by preparing their tax returns. Another **tax accounting** activity involves planning future transactions to minimize the amount of tax to be paid. The Tax Accounting column of Illustration 1–1 identifies the activities of tax accountants.

Large companies usually have their own private accountants who are responsible for preparing tax returns and doing tax planning. However, a large company may consult with a public accountant when special tax expertise is

ILLUSTRATION 1–2

Income Statement for Jerry Dow, Lawyer

JERRY DOW, LAWYER
Income Statement
For Month Ended December 31, 1993

Revenues:		
Legal fees earned		$3,900
Operating expenses:		
Salaries expense.	$ 700	
Rent expense	1,000	
Total operating expenses		1,700
Net income		$2,200

needed. Almost all smaller companies rely on public accountants for their tax work.

Many accountants are employed on the government side of the tax process. For example, **Revenue Canada** employs numerous tax accountants to fulfill its duty to collect income taxes and otherwise enforce the income tax laws. Many Revenue Canada accountants review tax returns filed by taxpayers, while others offer assistance to taxpayers and help write tax regulations. Still others investigate possible violations of the tax laws.

Financial Statements

LO 3 Describe the information contained in the financial statements of a business and be able to prepare simple financial statements.

Financial statements communicate accounting information to managers and other decision makers. These statements are the primary product of the accounting process. Thus, financial statements are a good place to start your study of accounting. We begin by looking at two widely used financial statements: the income statement and the balance sheet.

The Income Statement

An example of an **income statement** appears in Illustration 1–2. The income statement is considered by many people to be the most important financial statement. The income statement is important because it shows whether the business earned a profit (also called *net income*), which is one of its primary operating objectives. A **net income** is earned if the company's revenues exceed its expenses; a **net loss** is incurred if the expenses exceed the revenues. The example in Illustration 1–2 shows that the income statement does not simply report the amount of net income or net loss. Instead, it lists the types and amounts of the revenues and expenses. This detailed information is more useful for decisions than just a single number for the profit or loss.

Revenues are inflows of cash or other assets received in exchange for providing goods or services to customers. Revenue may also occur from a decrease in a liability, for example, providing goods and services for which payment was received in advance.

ILLUSTRATION 1–3

Balance Sheet for Jerry Dow, Lawyer

JERRY DOW, LAWYER
Balance Sheet
December 31, 1993

Assets		Liabilities	
Cash	$ 1,100	Accounts payable	$ 760
Law library	2,880	**Owner's Equity**	
Office equipment	6,880	Jerry Dow, capital	10,100
		Total liabilities and	
Total assets	$10,860	owner's equity	$10,860

The income statement in Illustration 1–2 shows that the business of Jerry Dow, Lawyer, had $3,900 of revenues from providing legal services to clients during the month of December. Examples of revenues that other businesses might have include sales of products and amounts earned from rent, dividends, and interest.

Expenses are costs incurred by a firm in the process of earning revenue and are measured by the cost of goods and services consumed in the operation of the business. The income statement in Illustration 1–2 shows that the business, Jerry Dow, Lawyer, used an employee's services. This cost is reported as salaries expense of $700. The business also used services in the form of office space rented to the business by the owner of a building. This cost is reported in Illustration 1–2 as rent expense of $1,000.

Note from Illustration 1–2 that the heading of an income statement begins with the name of the business. The heading also shows the time period covered by the statement. Knowledge of the time period is important for judging if the company's performance is satisfactory. For example, to evaluate the $3,900 of legal fees earned by Jerry Dow, you must know that they were earned during a one-month period.

The Balance Sheet

The purpose of the **balance sheet** is to provide information that helps users understand the financial *status* of the business. In fact, the balance sheet is often called the **statement of financial position.** The balance sheet describes financial position by listing the types and amounts of assets, liabilities, and equity of the business. (Owner's equity is the difference between a company's assets and its liabilities.)

Illustration 1–3 presents the balance sheet for Jerry Dow, Lawyer, as of December 31, 1993. The heading of the balance sheet begins with the company's name. The balance sheet describes conditions that exist at a point in time. Thus, the heading also shows the date on which the assets are identified and measured. The amounts in the balance sheet are understood to be stated as of the close of business on that date.

The balance sheet in Illustration 1–3 shows that the business owned three different assets at the close of business on December 31, 1993. The assets were cash, a law library, and office equipment. The total dollar amount for these assets was $10,860. The balance sheet also shows that there were liabilities of $760. Owner's equity was $10,100. This amount is the difference between the assets and the liabilities.

Observe that the total amounts on the two sides of the balance sheet are equal. This equality is the source of the name *balance sheet*. The name also reflects the fact that the statement reports the balances of the assets, liabilities, and equity on a given date.

Assets, Liabilities, and Owner's Equity

In general, the assets of a business are the items (economic resources) owned by the business and expected to benefit future operations. One familiar asset is cash. Another asset consists of amounts owed to the business by its customers for goods and services sold to them on credit. This asset is called accounts receivable. In general, individuals who owe amounts to the business are called debtors. Other assets owned by businesses include merchandise held for sale, supplies, equipment, buildings, and land. Assets also can be intangible rights, such as those granted by a patent or copyright.

The liabilities of a business are its debts. These debts normally require future payment in assets or the rendering of services or both. One common liability consists of amounts owed for goods and services bought on account. This liability is called accounts payable. Other liabilities are salaries and wages owed to employees, taxes payable, notes payable, and interest payable.

A liability represents a claim against a business. In general, those who have the right to receive payments from a company are called its creditors. From the creditor's side, a liability is the right to be paid by a business. If a business fails to pay its debts, the law gives the creditors the right to force the sale of the business's assets to obtain the money to meet their claims. If the assets are sold under these conditions, the creditors are paid first, up to the full amount of their claims, with the remainder (the residual) going to the owner of the business.

Creditors often use a balance sheet to help them decide whether to loan money to a business. They use the balance sheet to compare the amounts of the existing liabilities and assets. A loan is less risky if the liabilities are small in comparison to the assets. There is less risk because there is a larger cushion if the assets cannot be sold at the amount shown on the balance sheet. On the other hand, a loan is more risky if the liabilities are large compared to the assets. The risk is greater because it is more likely that the assets cannot be sold for enough cash to pay all the debts.

Equity is the amount remaining of the assets after deducting the liabilities. Equity is also called net assets.

If a business is owned by one person, the owner's equity is commonly shown on a balance sheet by listing that person's name, followed by the word *capital*. The amount of equity is then shown. This practice is used in Illustration 1–3 for Jerry Dow. The use of the word *capital* comes from the idea that the owner furnished the business with resources, or capital, equal to the amount of the equity. A later section in this chapter briefly describes the accounting practices used when the business has more than one owner.

With this background on the balance sheet and income statement in place, we can now go on to explain more about financial accounting. In the next sections of the chapter, you will learn about the principles that guide financial accounting.

On page 15, you learned that financial accounting is governed by a set of rules called *generally accepted accounting principles,* or *GAAP.* Some knowledge of GAAP is essential for all who use or prepare financial statements.

The primary purpose of GAAP is to help accountants provide relevant and comparable information. In other words, financial accounting practices should produce information that is relevant to the decisions made by financial statement users. The information should also allow them to compare companies. These comparisons are more likely to be useful if all companies use the same practices. GAAP identify uniform practices that make financial statements more understandable and useful.

Generally Accepted Accounting Principles (GAAP)

LO 4 Briefly explain the accounting principles introduced in the chapter and describe the process by which generally accepted accounting principles are established.

The Development of GAAP

From the earliest days of accounting up through the first third of the 20th century, GAAP were developed through common usage. In other words, a practice was considered good if it was acceptable to most accountants. This history is still reflected in the phrase, *generally accepted.* A principle became generally accepted as accountants came to agree that it would provide useful and dependable information. However, as the accounting profession grew and the world of business became more complex, many people were not satisfied with the rate of progress toward improved financial reporting.

Many professional accountants, managers, and the government wanted to bring more uniformity to practice. Thus, in the 1930s, they began to give authority for defining accepted principles to small groups of experienced people. Since then, there have been several authoritative bodies with different structures and procedures. The power to prescribe acceptable principles also has been greatly increased. We will presently describe the current arrangement for establishing GAAP.

Broad and Specific Accounting Principles

You should understand that GAAP consist of both broad and specific principles. *Broad* principles are rooted in long-used practices. More *specific* principles usually result from the work of authoritative bodies. These specific principles are described in the official pronouncements published by these bodies.

You will benefit from knowing about both broad and specific principles. Thus, we describe both kinds in this book. The broad principles are especially

ILLUSTRATION 1–4

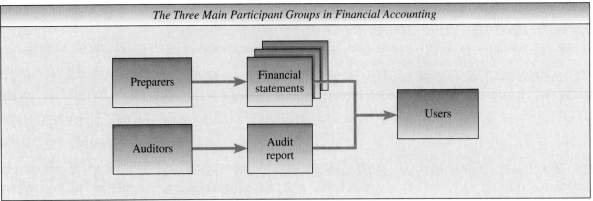

The Three Main Participant Groups in Financial Accounting

helpful for learning accounting. For this reason, they are emphasized in the beginning chapters of this book. The specific principles are also important. They are described throughout the book and summarized in Part V.[2]

Accounting Principles, Auditing Standards, and Financial Accounting

Generally accepted accounting principles are not natural laws like the laws of physics or other sciences. GAAP are identified in response to needs of users and others affected by accounting. Thus, GAAP are subject to change as needs change. Current GAAP have developed through the experience and thinking of public, private, and government accountants, as well as accounting professors and others. In today's world, a formal system has been developed to allow these groups to get together to find a consensus.

This system reflects the fact that three groups are most affected by financial reporting. These groups are identified in Illustration 1–4 as *preparers, auditors,* and *users.* Private accountants prepare the financial statements. Auditors examine the statements and attach the audit report to the statements. The statements and the audit report are then distributed to the users.

Illustration 1–5 shows how accounting principles and auditing standards relate to the financial reporting process. First, Illustration 1–5 shows that GAAP are applied in preparing the financial statements. Preparers use GAAP in deciding which procedures to follow as they account for business transactions and put the statements together.

Second, Illustration 1–5 shows that audits are performed in accordance with **generally accepted auditing standards (GAAS).** GAAS are the rules

---

[2] A problem arises in describing accounting principles because different writers have used different words to mean the same thing. For example, broad principles also have been called *concepts, theories, assumptions,* and *postulates.* For simplicity's sake, we have decided to call them *principles* in this book. Don't be confused if you see them called by other names in other books.

ILLUSTRATION 1–5

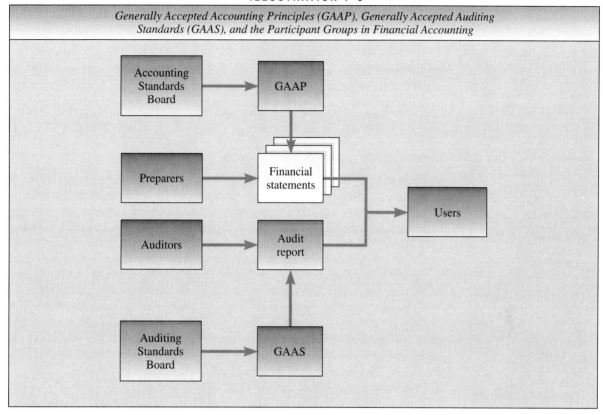

Generally Accepted Accounting Principles (GAAP), Generally Accepted Auditing Standards (GAAS), and the Participant Groups in Financial Accounting

adopted by the accounting profession as guides in conducting audits of financial statements. GAAS tell auditors what they must do in their audits.

Third, Illustration 1–5 identifies two organizations as the primary sources of GAAP and GAAS.

The primary source of GAAP is the Accounting Standards Board. The board members, supported by a research staff, use their collective knowledge to identify problems in financial accounting and to find ways to solve them. The board also seeks advice from groups and individuals affected by GAAP. The advice comes via comments on the board's "exposure drafts" on specific issues. The finalized recommendations are published as part of the *CICA Handbook*.

The Accounting Standards Board gains its authority from both law and the members of the Canadian Institute of Chartered Accountants. Under the regulations of the Canada Business Corporations Act, the accounting standards for external reporting set out in the *CICA Handbook* have the force of law. Also, in 1969 the CICA adopted paragraph 1500.06, which states:

How Accounting Principles Are Established

> Where the accounting treatment or statement presentation does not follow the recommendations of this *Handbook,* the practice used should be explained in notes to the financial statements with an indication of the reason why the recommendation concerned was not followed.

A number of other professional organizations support the Accounting Standards Board's process by providing input. In summary, the Accounting Standards Board's job is to improve financial reporting while balancing the interests of the affected groups.

International Accounting Standards

For many reasons, people in different countries engage in business with each other more easily than in the past. Some reasons are improved systems of communication, cheaper transportation, and political changes such as the breakup of the Soviet Union. These changes have opened up many international business opportunities. For example, a company in Canada might sell its products in countries all over the world. Another company in Singapore might raise cash by selling shares to Canadian, U.S., and Japanese investors. At the same time, it might borrow from creditors in Saudi Arabia and Germany.

The global nature of business creates a major accounting problem. The problem is that each country has its own unique accounting standards. Consider the impact of the problem on the Singapore company in the previous paragraph. Should it comply with Singapore accounting standards, or the standards used in Canada, the United States, Japan, Saudi Arabia, or Germany? Should it have to prepare five different sets of reports?

Accounting organizations from around the world responded to this problem by forming the International Accounting Standards Committee (IASC). The IASC was created in 1973 and has its headquarters in London. The IASC identifies preferred accounting practices and encourages that they be adopted worldwide. By narrowing the range of alternatives, the IASC hopes to create more harmony among the accounting practices of different countries.

In many countries, the bodies that set accounting standards have encouraged the IASC. However, the IASC does not have the authority to impose its standards. Although some advances have occurred since 1987, progress has been slow. In both Canada and the United States, there is a growing interest in moving toward the IASC's preferred practices. The authority to make such changes continues to rest with the Accounting Standards Board, the FASB, and the SEC.

Understanding Generally Accepted Accounting Principles

Recall the first sentence of this chapter. It states that the function of accounting is to communicate useful information to people who make rational investment, credit, and similar decisions. In fact, this description of the function of accounting is paraphrased from "Financial Statement Concepts," section 1000 of the *CICA Handbook.* This statement of concepts also defines a number of terms used by accountants. For example, we relied on the conceptual framework when we defined revenue, expense, asset, liability, and equity.

AS A MATTER OF

Fact

PW Chief Makes Pitch for Global Standards

Washington—In a speech before the Financial Executives Institute's Washington chapter, Shaun O'Malley [Price Waterhouse's chairman] said today's international business community needs a revamped financial reporting system that provides truly comparable financial statements and greater disclosure of risks and uncertainties. This new system, he said, would better protect investors and managers alike from the kind of unpleasant surprises associated with unforeseen business failures or financial setbacks.

"The advent of more intense foreign competition, plus today's more rapid pace of technology and more volatile economic and political conditions, all have added new complexities to judgments management must make."

*   *   *

To help users of financial statements better assess future adverse effects that might result from management's decisions, O'Malley proposed the adoption of internationally comparable financial statements that incorporate greater disclosure of risks and uncertainties. Such statements would better protect investors and would help companies in such activities as conducting competitive surveillance, extending credit to customers, evaluating alternative suppliers and potential partners for international alliances and joint ventures, raising capital abroad, and investing in foreign securities.

O'Malley emphasized that there are several courses of action to take in his proposed solution. For one, he suggested that the national standard-setting bodies of the world, such as FASB, could take the initiative in reaching agreement on accounting treatments.

Another possibility, he said, would be for the securities regulators of the world to agree to acknowledge the authority of a transnational organization in international standard setting, which would most likely be the International Accounting Standards Committee. Finally, he called on financial executives to develop solutions of their own.

The ultimate standards developed, said O'Malley, must be broad. They must provide the harmonization without constraint of local standard-setters and must find a way to assign priorities, perhaps giving top priorities to those principles that currently receive the most diverse treatment on an international basis, such as accounting for pensions, leases, and business combinations, he said.

Excerpted by permission from *Accounting Today,* October 7, 1991. Copyright Lebhar-Friedman, Inc., 425 Park Avenue, New York, NY 10022.

Another purpose of the conceptual framework was to describe the characteristics that make accounting information useful. In particular, the conceptual framework expresses the commonsense idea that information is useful only if it has both *relevance* and *reliability*. Information is relevant if it is capable of making a difference in a decision. For example, the amount of cash reported on the balance sheet is relevant to statement users who make decisions that depend on knowing whether the company can pay its bills within a short time period.

However, relevant information is useful only if users can rely on it to be what it is supposed to be. If they cannot trust the amount of cash reported on the balance sheet, that information is not useful. The need for reliability is also

LO 4 Briefly explain the accounting principles introduced in the chapter and describe the process by which generally accepted accounting principles are established.

reflected in the requirement that financial statements be audited. The statements would not be as useful without the reliability provided by the audit.

Now that you have some understanding of how accounting principles are developed, we can begin to describe some of these broad principles.

Business Entity Principle

The **business entity principle** requires every business to be accounted for separately and distinctly from its owner or owners. This principle also requires us to account separately for other entities that might be controlled by the same owner. The reason behind this principle is that separate information for each business is relevant to decision makers.

To illustrate, suppose that an owner of a business wants to see how well the business is doing. To be useful, the financial statements for the business should not mix the owner's personal transactions with the business transactions. For example, since the owner's personal expenses do not contribute to the success of the business, they should not be subtracted from the revenues of the business on its income statement. Thus, the business's statements should not report such things as the owner's personal entertainment expenses. Otherwise, the net income of the business would be understated and the business would appear less profitable than is really the case.

To conclude, the records and reports of a business should not include either the transactions, assets, and liabilities of another business or the personal transactions, assets, and liabilities of its owner or owners. If this principle were not followed carefully, the reported financial position and net income of the business would be distorted.

Objectivity Principle

The **objectivity principle** requires the information in financial statements to be supported by evidence other than someone's imagination or opinion. The reason behind this principle is that information is not reliable if it is based only on what the statement preparer thinks might be true. This information may not be reliable because the preparer may be too optimistic or too pessimistic. In the worst case, an unethical preparer might try to mislead users of the financial statements by deliberately misrepresenting the truth. The objectivity principle is intended to make financial statements useful by ensuring that they present reliable information.

Cost Principle

The **cost principle** requires the information in financial statements to be based on costs incurred in business transactions. Sales and purchases are examples of **business transactions.** Business transactions are completed exchanges of economic consideration between two parties. The consideration may be such things as goods, services, money, or rights to collect money. In applying the cost principle, cost is measured on a cash or cash equivalent basis. If the consideration given for an asset or service is cash, the cost of the asset or service is measured as the entire cash outlay. If the consideration is something other than cash, cost is measured as the cash equivalent value of what was given up or of the item received, whichever is more clearly evident. For example, if a machine that can be readily sold for $15,000 is exchanged for a parcel of land, the $15,000 is the equivalent value or the cost of the land.

The cost principle is acceptable because it puts relevant information in the financial statements. Cost is the amount initially sacrificed to purchase an asset or service. Cost also represents the market value at the time of purchase of what was received. Information about the amount sacrificed and the initial market value of what was received is generally assumed to be relevant to decision makers. The cost principle provides this information.

The cost principle also is generally accepted because it is consistent with the objectivity principle. Most accountants believe that information based on actual costs is more likely to be objective than information based on estimates of value. For example, reporting purchases of assets and services at cost is more objective than reporting the manager's estimate of their value. Thus, financial statements based on costs are more reliable because the information is more objective.

To illustrate, assume that a business pays $50,000 for land to be used in carrying on its operations. The cost principle tells us to record the purchase at $50,000. It would make no difference if the buyer and several independent appraisers think that the land is worth at least $60,000. The cost principle requires the acquisition to be recorded at the cost of $50,000.

Going-Concern Principle

The **going-concern principle** (also called the **continuing-concern principle**) requires accountants to prepare financial statements under the assumption that the business will continue operating instead of being put up for sale or closed. Thus, a business's operating assets to be held for the long term are not reported in the balance sheet at their liquidation or market values. Instead, the amounts reported for these assets are based on their cost. Usually, most decisions made about a business are made with the expectation that it will continue to exist in the future. Therefore, accountants generally conclude that the going-concern principle leads to reporting relevant information.

However, the going-concern principle must be ignored if the company is expected to fail or be liquidated. In these cases, the going-concern principle and the cost principle do not apply to the financial statements. Instead, estimated market values are thought to be more relevant than costs.

Applying the cost and going-concern principles means that a company's balance sheet seldom describes what the company is worth. Thus, if a company is to be bought or sold, the buyer and seller are well advised to obtain additional information from other sources.

This section of the chapter continues your introduction to accounting by describing three legal forms for business organizations. Some differences occur in financial statements depending on the form the company takes. The three forms are *single* (or *sole*) *proprietorships*, *partnerships*, and *corporations*.

Legal Forms of Business Organizations

LO 5 Briefly explain the
differences between a
single proprietorship, a
partnership, and a
corporation, comparing
the differing
responsibilities of their
owners for the debts of the
business.

Single Proprietorships

A **single proprietorship** (or **sole proprietorship**) is owned by one person and is
not organized under federal or provincial laws as a corporation, which we
discuss shortly. Small retail stores and service enterprises are commonly operated as single proprietorships. No special legal requirements must be met to
start this kind of business. As a result, single proprietorships are the most
numerous of all types of businesses.

Legally, a single proprietorship does not have a separate existence apart
from its owner. Thus, for example, a court can order the owner's personal
assets to be sold to pay the proprietorship's debts. Also, a court can force the
proprietorship's assets to be sold to pay the owner's personal debts. Nevertheless, the *business entity principle* applies in accounting for a single proprietorship. That is, the business is treated as separate and distinct from its owner.

Partnerships

A **partnership** is owned by two or more people, called *partners,* and is not
organized as a corporation. Like a single proprietorship, no special legal requirements must be met in starting a partnership. All that is required is for the
partners to agree to operate a business together. The agreement can be either
oral or written. However, a written partnership agreement is better because it
helps the partners avoid later disagreements.

For accounting, a partnership is treated under the *business entity principle*
as separate and distinct from its partners. However, just as with a single proprietorship, no *legal* distinction is made between the partnership and its owners with respect to its debts. That is, a court may order the personal assets of
the partners to be sold to pay the business's debts. In fact, the personal assets
of a partner may be ordered sold by a court to satisfy *all* the debts of the
partnership, even if this amount exceeds his or her equity in the partnership.
This unlimited liability aspect of partnerships can be an important disadvantage of organizing a business with this form.

Corporations

A **corporation** is a separate legal entity formed, or incorporated, under the laws
of a province or the federal government. Unlike a single proprietorship or
partnership, a corporation is legally separate and distinct from its owners.

The corporation's equity is divided into units called shares. Therefore, the
owners of a corporation are called **shareholders** or **stockholders.** For example,
a corporation that has issued 1,000 shares has divided its equity into 1,000
units. A shareholder who owns 500 shares owns 50% of the equity.

Perhaps the most important characteristic of a corporation is its status as a
separate legal entity. This characteristic means that the corporation is responsible for its own acts and its own debts. This arrangement relieves the shareholders of liability for these acts and debts. This limited liability is a major
advantage of corporations over proprietorships and partnerships.

The separate legal status of a corporation means that it can enter into contracts for which it is solely responsible. For example, a corporation can buy, own, and sell property in its own name. It also can sue and be sued in its own name. In short, the separate legal status enables a corporation to conduct its business affairs with all the rights, duties, and responsibilities of a person, including paying income tax on its taxable income. Of course, a corporation lacks a physical body, and must act through its managers, who are its legal agents.

The separate legal status of a corporation also means that its life is not limited by its owners' lives or by a need for them to remain owners. Thus, a shareholder can sell or transfer shares to another person without affecting the operations of the corporation.

Even though there are fewer corporations than proprietorships in Canada, corporations dominate in the sense that they control more economic wealth than proprietorships. This is because the corporation offers greater advantages for accumulating and managing capital resources.

Accounting Differences

Despite the legal differences among the three forms of businesses, there are only a few accounting differences. One difference is found in the equity section of the balance sheet. A proprietorship usually lists the capital balance of the single owner beside his or her name. Partnerships do the same, unless there are too many owners for their names to fit in the allotted space. The names of a corporation's shareholders are not listed in the balance sheet. Instead, the total shareholders' equity is divided into contributed capital and retained earnings. Contributed capital is the equity created through investments by the shareholders. A corporation's retained earnings is the equity that has resulted from its profitable activities.

Another difference occurs in accounting for the amounts paid to the managers of the business. If the owner of a single proprietorship is also its manager, no salary expense is reported on the income statement. Instead, the owner achieves income only if the proprietorship earns a profit. The same is true for a partnership. However, salaries paid to managers of a corporation are reported as expenses on the income statement.

To keep things simple while you are beginning to learn accounting, the early examples in this book are based on single proprietorships. More is said about partnerships in Chapters 4 and 14, and details about corporate accounting are found in Chapters 4, 15, and 16.

Recall that *owner's equity* is defined as the difference between a business entity's assets and liabilities. The definition of equity can be stated as the following equation:

The Balance Sheet Equation

$$\text{Assets} - \text{Liabilities} = \text{Owner's Equity}$$

LO 6 Recognize and be able to indicate the effects of transactions on the elements of the accounting equation.

Like any equation, this one can be modified by moving the terms. The following form of the equation is called the **balance sheet equation:**

$$\text{Assets} = \text{Liabilities} + \text{Owner's Equity}$$

The balance sheet equation is also known as the **accounting equation.** The following section shows you how this equation can be used to keep track of changes in the amounts of assets, liabilities, and owner's equity.

Effects of Transactions on the Accounting Equation

A *business transaction* was defined earlier as a completed exchange of economic consideration, such as goods, services, money, or rights to collect money. Because these exchanged items are assets and liabilities, business transactions affect the components of the accounting equation. It is important for you to see that every transaction always leaves the equation in balance. In other words, the total assets always equal the sum of the liabilities and the equity.

To demonstrate how this equality is maintained, we use the transactions of Jerry Dow's law practice as examples. Dow's business is organized as a single proprietorship.

Transaction 1. On December 1, 1993, Jerry Dow began a new law practice by investing $9,000 of his personal cash in the business. The money was then deposited in a bank account opened in the name of the business: "Jerry Dow, Lawyer." After this investment, the cash (an asset) and the owner's equity each equal $9,000. Thus, the accounting equation is in balance:

$$\text{Assets} \quad = \quad \text{Owner's Equity}$$

$$\underbrace{\text{Cash, \$9,000}} \quad \underbrace{\text{Jerry Dow, Capital, \$9,000}}$$

The equation shows that the business has one asset, cash, equal to $9,000. It has no liabilities, and Dow's equity in the business is $9,000.

Transactions 2 and 3. The second business transaction was to use $2,500 of the business cash to purchase books for a law library. Next, in transaction 3, $5,600 of the business cash was used to buy office equipment. Transactions 2 and 3 are both exchanges of cash for other assets. The purchases merely changed the form of the assets from cash to books and equipment.

The effects of these transactions are shown in colour in Illustration 1–6. Observe that the decreases in cash were exactly equalled by the increases in the law library and the equipment. Therefore, the equation remains in balance after each transaction.

Transaction 4. Dow decided that the law practice needed additional equipment and more library items for the office. The items to be purchased would have a total cost of $1,660. However, as shown on the last line of the first column in Illustration 1–6, the business had only $900 in cash. Because there was not enough cash on hand to make these purchases, Dow arranged to purchase them on credit from Equip-it Company. That is, he agreed to take delivery of

ILLUSTRATION 1–6

The Effect on the Balance Sheet Equation of Asset Purchases for Cash

	Assets			=	Owner's Equity	
	Cash +	Law Library +	Office Equipment	=	Jerry Dow, Capital	Explanation of Change
(1)	$9,000				$9,000	Investment
(2)	−2,500	+$2,500				
Bal.	$6,500	$2,500			$9,000	
(3)	−5,600		+$5,600			
Bal.	$ 900 +	$2,500 +	$5,600	=	$9,000	

the items and promised to pay for them later. The books cost $380, the equipment cost $1,280, and the total liability to Equip-it is $1,660.

The effects of this purchase are reflected in Illustration 1–7 as transaction 4. Notice that the purchase increased total assets by $1,660 and liabilities (called *accounts payable*) increased by the same amount.

Transaction 5. A primary objective of a business is to increase the wealth of its owner. This goal is met when the business produces a profit (also called *net income*). A net income increases the owner's equity in the business. Dow's law practice seeks to produce net income by providing legal services to its clients for fees. The business will produce a net income only if these fees are greater than the expenses incurred in earning them. The acts of earning legal fees and incurring expenses change the accounting equation.

Watch how the accounting equation is affected by transaction 5. In transaction 5, the law firm provided legal assistance to a client on December 10 and immediately collected $2,200 cash for the services. Illustration 1–8 shows that this event increased cash by $2,200 and increased equity by $2,200. This event is identified in the last column as a revenue because it increased the business's assets and the owner's equity as a result of providing services. This information is used later in preparing the income statement.

Transactions 6 and 7. Also on December 10, the law practice paid $1,000 rent for the office to the owner of the building. Paying this amount allowed Dow to occupy the space for the entire month of December. The effects of this event are shown in Illustration 1–8 as transaction 6. On December 12, Dow paid the $700 salary of the office secretary. This event is reflected in Illustration 1–8 as transaction 7.

Both transactions 6 and 7 produced expenses for the business. That is, they used up cash for the purpose of providing services to clients.[3] Unlike the asset purchases in transactions 2 and 3, the cash payments in transactions 6

---

[3] Instead of immediate cash outflows, expenses also may occur as increases in liabilities. For example, an unpaid telephone bill would cause an increase in the liabilities and an equal decrease in owner's equity.

ILLUSTRATION 1–7

The Effect on the Balance Sheet Equation of Asset Purchases on Credit

		Assets		= Liabilities +	Owner's Equity	
	Cash +	Law + Library	Office Equipment	= Accounts Payable	+ Jerry Dow, Capital	Explanation of Change
Bal.	$900	$2,500	$5,600		$9,000	
(4)		+ 380	+1,280	+$1,660		
Bal.	$900 +	$2,880 +	$6,880	= $1,660 +	$9,000	

ILLUSTRATION 1–8

The Effect on the Balance Sheet Equation of Revenues Received in Cash and Expenses Paid in Cash

		Assets		= Liabilities +	Owner's Equity	
	Cash +	Law + Library	Office Equipment	= Accounts Payable	+ Jerry Dow, Capital	Explanation of Change
Bal.	$ 900	$2,880	$6,880	$1,660	$ 9,000	
(5)	+2,200				+ 2,200	Revenue
Bal.	$3,100	$2,880	$6,880	$1,660	$11,200	
(6)	−1,000				−1,000	Expense
Bal.	$2,100	$2,880	$6,880	$1,660	$10,200	
(7)	− 700				− 700	Expense
Bal.	$1,400 +	$2,880 +	$6,880	= $1,660 +	$ 9,500	

and 7 acquired services. The benefits of these services did not last beyond the end of the month. The equations in Illustration 1–8 show that both transactions reduced cash and owner's equity. Thus, the equation remains in balance after each event. The last column in Illustration 1–8 notes that these decreases were expenses. This information is useful when the income statement is prepared.

Summary. We said before that a business produces a net income when its revenues exceed its expenses. Net income is reflected as an increase in owner's equity. If expenses had exceeded the revenues, the company's equity would have been decreased, and a net loss would have resulted. You should understand that the amount of net income or loss is not affected by transactions completed between the business and its owners. Thus, Jerry Dow's initial investment of $9,000 is not income to the business, even though it increased the equity.

To keep things simple, and to emphasize the concept that revenues and expenses produce changes in equity, the illustrations in this first chapter add the revenues directly to Dow's equity and subtract the expenses from the equity. In actual practice, however, the revenues and expenses are accumulated separately and then added to or subtracted from equity at the end of the accounting period. We discuss this process further in Chapters 2, 3, and 4.

Because of the importance of revenue for achieving net income, we are going to briefly interrupt the description of the law practice's transactions to describe the revenue recognition principle that accountants follow in determining when to record a company's revenue.

Revenue Recognition Principle

History shows that managers and auditors need guidance to know when to recognize revenue. (*Recognize* means to record an event for the purpose of reporting its effects in the financial statements.) For example, if revenue is recognized too early, the income statement reports income sooner than it should and the business looks more profitable than it really is. On the other hand, if the revenue is not recognized on time, the income statement shows lower amounts of revenue and net income than it should and the business looks less profitable than it really is.

LO 4 Briefly explain the accounting principles introduced in the chapter and describe the process by which generally accepted accounting principles are established.

The question of when revenue should be recognized on the income statement is answered by the **revenue recognition principle** (also called the **realization principle**). This principle includes three important guidelines:

1. *Revenue should be recognized at the time, but not before, it is earned.* Theoretically, revenue is earned throughout the entire performance of a service or throughout the whole process of securing goods for sale, taking a customer's order, and delivering the goods. However, the amount of revenue to be recognized usually cannot be determined reliably until all these steps are completed and the business obtains the right to collect the sales price. Therefore, in most cases, revenue should not be recognized until the earnings process is essentially complete. For most businesses, this occurs at the time services are rendered or at the time the seller transfers title (legal ownership) of goods sold to the buyer. Thus, no revenue has been earned if a customer pays in advance of taking delivery of a good or service. The seller must actually perform a revenue-earning act before recognizing the revenue. This approach is known as the *sales basis of revenue recognition.*

2. *The inflow of assets associated with revenue does not have to be in the form of cash.* The most common noncash asset received in a revenue transaction is an account receivable from the customer. These transactions, called *credit sales,* occur because it is convenient for the customer to get the goods or services now and pay for them later. As long as there is objective evidence that the seller has the right to collect the account receivable, the seller should recognize the revenue. When the cash is collected later, no additional revenue is recognized. Instead, collecting the cash simply changes the form of the asset from a receivable to cash.

3. *The amount of revenue recognized should be measured as the cash received plus the cash equivalent value (fair market value) of any other asset or assets received.* For example, if the transaction creates an account receivable, the seller should recognize revenue equal to the value of the receivable, which is usually the amount of cash to be collected.

ILLUSTRATION 1–9

		Assets			= Liabilities +	Owner's Equity	
	Cash +	Accounts + Receivable	Law + Library	Office Equipment	= Accounts Payable	+ Jerry Dow, Capital	Explanation of Change
Bal.	$1,400		$2,880	$6,880	$1,660	$ 9,500	
(8)		+$1,700				+ 1,700	Revenue
Bal.	$1,400	$1,700	$2,880	$6,880	$1,660	$11,200	
(9)	+1,700	−1,700					
Bal.	$3,100 +	$ –0– +	$2,880 +	$6,880	= $1,660 +	$11,200	

The Effect on the Balance Sheet Equation of Noncash Revenues and the Later Receipt of Cash

ILLUSTRATION 1–10

The Effect on the Balance Sheet Equation of Debt Repayments and Withdrawals by the Owner

		Assets			= Liabilities +	Owner's Equity	
	Cash +	Accounts + Receivable	Law + Library	Office Equipment	= Accounts Payable	+ Jerry Dow, Capital	Explanation of Change
Bal.	$3,100	$ –0–	$2,880	$6,880	$1,660	$11,200	
(10)	− 900				− 900		
Bal.	$2,200	$ –0–	$2,880	$6,880	$ 760	$11,200	
(11)	−1,100					− 1,100	Withdrawal
Bal.	$1,100 +	$ –0– +	$2,880 +	$6,880	= $ 760 +	$10,100	

Understanding the Effects of Transactions

To show how the revenue recognition principle works, we now return to the example of Jerry Dow, Lawyer.

Transactions 8 and 9. Assume that the Jerry Dow law practice completed legal work and billed the client $1,700 for the services. This event is identified in Illustration 1–9 as transaction 8. Ten days later, in transaction 9, the client paid the Dow law practice the full $1,700.

In Illustration 1–9, observe that transaction 8 created a new asset, the account receivable from the client. The $1,700 increase in assets was accompanied by an equal increase in owner's equity. Notice that the increase in equity is labeled in the last column of Illustration 1–9 as a revenue.

Transaction 9 changed the receivable into cash. Because transaction 9 did not increase the total amount of assets, there was no change in equity. Thus, this transaction did not involve revenue. The revenue was generated when Dow rendered the services, not when the cash was collected. This emphasis on the earning process instead of collection is the goal of the revenue recognition principle.

Transaction 10. To demonstrate another effect on the accounting equation, assume that Jerry Dow's law practice paid $900 to Equip-it Company on December 24 as partial repayment of the account payable. Illustration 1–10 identifies

ILLUSTRATION 1–11

The Effect on the Balance Sheet Equation of All Transactions

	Cash	+ Accounts Receivable	+ Law Library	+ Office Equipment	= Accounts Payable	+ Jerry Dow, Capital	Explanation of Change
(1)	$9,000					$ 9,000	Investment
(2)	−2,500		+$2,500				
Bal.	$6,500		$2,500			$ 9,000	
(3)	−5,600			+$5,600			
Bal.	$ 900		$2,500	$5,600		$ 9,000	
(4)			+380	+1,280	+$1,660		
Bal.	$ 900		$2,880	$6,880	$1,660	$ 9,000	
(5)	+2,200					+2,200	Revenue
Bal.	$3,100		$2,880	$6,880	$1,660	$11,200	
(6)	−1,000					−1,000	Expense
Bal.	$2,100		$2,880	$6,880	$1,660	$10,200	
(7)	− 700					− 700	Expense
Bal.	$1,400		$2,880	$6,880	$1,660	$ 9,500	
(8)		+$1,700				+1,700	Revenue
Bal.	$1,400	$1,700	$2,880	$6,880	$1,660	$11,200	
(9)	+1,700	−1,700					
Bal.	$3,100	$ –0–	$2,880	$6,880	$1,660	$11,200	
(10)	−900				−900		
Bal.	$2,200	$ –0–	$2,880	$6,880	$ 760	$11,200	
(11)	−1,100					−1,100	Withdrawal
Bal.	$1,100 +	$ –0– +	$2,880 +	$6,880 =	$ 760 +	$10,100	

this event as transaction 10. The illustration shows that this transaction decreased the law practice's cash by $900 and its liability to Equip-it by the same amount. Notice that there was no reduction in equity. This event is not an expense, even though cash flowed out of the company.

Transaction 11. Another type of event, the owner's withdrawal of assets from the business, is identified in Illustration 1–10 as transaction 11. In this case, Jerry Dow took $1,100 out of the business bank account for his own use. In accordance with the *business entity principle,* this transaction was not an expense of the business, even though its assets were decreased. As we said earlier, the owner of a single proprietorship does not earn a salary but receives income only if the business achieves a net profit. Thus, the last column in the illustration labels transaction 11 as a withdrawal instead of an expense.[4]

Illustration 1–11 presents the effects of the entire series of 11 transactions for Jerry Dow's law practice. Take time now to see that the equation remained in balance after each transaction. This result occurred because the effects of each transaction are always in balance. Transactions 1, 5, and 8 increased total

_____

[4] For corporations, payments to the owners are called *dividends.* Dividends are not a factor in determining the corporation's net income.

ILLUSTRATION 1–12

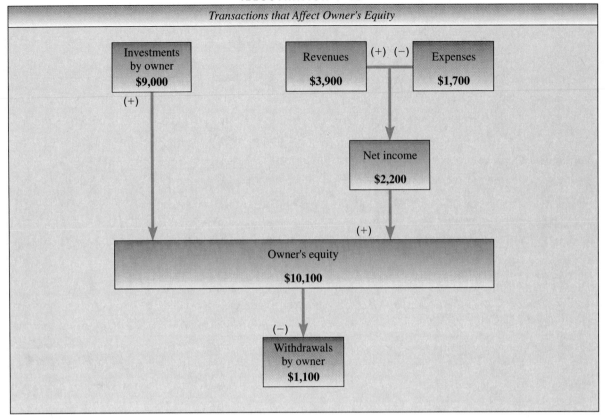

Transactions that Affect Owner's Equity

assets and equity by the same amount. Transactions 2, 3, and 9 increased one asset while decreasing another by the same amount. Transaction 4 increased total assets and a liability by the same amount. Transactions 6, 7, and 11 decreased assets and equity by the same amount. Finally, transaction 10 decreased total assets and a liability by the same amount. The equality of these effects is central to the working of *double-entry accounting*. You will learn more about double-entry accounting in the next chapter.

Illustration 1–12 shows how owner's equity is affected by different types of transactions. Recall that equity is the residual that remains after subtracting the company's liabilities from its assets. Equity is also a residual in the sense that it is what is left over from the owner's investments and net income after deducting the owner's withdrawals. Illustration 1–12 shows these changes in equity. It shows that equity was increased by the $9,000 investment from Jerry Dow and the $2,200 net income. It also shows that the $2,200 net income is the difference between the revenues of $3,900 and the expenses of $1,700. Finally, Illustration 1–12 shows that the $1,100 withdrawal reduced equity. These events leave a residual balance of $10,100 in equity at the end of the month.

The function of accounting is to provide useful information to people who make rational investment, credit, and similar decisions. This information is communicated to its users through the financial statements. Accountants prepare the financial statements from data gathered about transactions and other events. Although the record-keeping system described in this chapter is simpler than what is really used in practice, it is adequate for preparing the financial statements of the law practice of Jerry Dow, Lawyer.

Up to this point, you have learned about only two financial statements: the income statement and the balance sheet. GAAP also require that two other statements be reported. They are the statement of changes in owner's equity and the statement of changes in financial position.

Preparing the Financial Statements

LO 3 Describe the information contained in the financial statements of a business and be able to prepare simple financial statements.

The Income Statement

The top section of Illustration 1–13 shows the income statement for Jerry Dow's law practice. It is based on the information about revenues and expenses recorded in the Owner's Equity column of Illustration 1–11.

Notice that the heading of the income statement identifies the time period covered by the statement, that is, the month ended December 31, 1993. Next, note that the income statement lists total revenues of $3,900. This amount is the result of transactions 5 and 8. The revenues are identified as legal fees earned. If the business had earned other kinds of revenues, they would have been listed separately. The income statement then lists the salaries and rent expenses incurred in transactions 7 and 6. The types of expenses are usually identified to help users form a more complete picture of the events of the time period. Finally, the income statement presents the amount of net income earned during the month.

The Statement of Changes in Owner's Equity

The **statement of changes in owner's equity** presents information about what happened to equity during a time period. The statement shows the beginning amount of equity, the events that increased it (new investments and net income), and the events that decreased it (net loss, if any, and withdrawals).

The middle section of Illustration 1–13 shows the statement of changes in owner's equity for Jerry Dow. The heading refers to the month of December 1993 because the statement describes events that happened during that time period. The beginning balance of equity is zero because the business did not exist before December 1. The statement shows that $9,000 of equity came from Dow's initial investment. It also shows $2,200 of net income for the month. This item links the income statement and the statement of changes in owner's equity. The statement also reports Jerry Dow's withdrawal of $1,100 from the business and his $10,100 equity at the end of the month.

The Balance Sheet

The bottom section of Illustration 1–13 presents the balance sheet for Jerry Dow's law practice. The heading shows that the statement describes the company's financial condition at the close of business on December 31, 1993.

ILLUSTRATION 1–13

ILLUSTRATION 1–13

Financial Statements for Jerry Dow, Lawyer

JERRY DOW, LAWYER
Income Statement
For Month Ended December 31, 1993

Revenues:		
Legal fees earned		$3,900
Operating expenses:		
Salaries expense.	$ 700	
Rent expense	1,000	
Total operating expenses		1,700
Net income		$2,200

JERRY DOW, LAWYER
Statement of Changes in Owner's Equity
For Month Ended December 31, 1993

Jerry Dow, capital, November 30,1993		$ –0–
Plus: Investments by owner	$9,000	
Net income	2,200	11,200
Total.		$11,200
Less withdrawals by owner		1,100
Jerry Dow, capital, December 31, 1993		$10,100

JERRY DOW, LAWYER
Balance Sheet
December 31, 1993

Assets		Liabilities	
Cash.	$ 1,100	Accounts payable.	$ 760
Law library	2,880	**Owner's Equity**	
Office equipment	6,880	Jerry Dow, capital	10,100
		Total liabilities and	
Total assets	$10,860	owner's equity	$10,860

The left side of the balance sheet lists the assets of the business. In this case, they are cash, law library, and office equipment. It shows the balance of cash and the costs of the other two assets. The right side of the balance sheet shows that $760 is owed on accounts payable. If any other liabilities had existed (such as bank loans), they would have been listed in this section. Because the business is a single proprietorship, the equity section identifies only one item, Jerry Dow's capital. The $10,100 balance is the difference between the assets and liabilities. Notice that this amount equals the last line of the statement of changes in owner's equity. Thus, it links these two statements.

The Statement of Changes in Financial Position

The fourth financial statement is the **statement of changes in financial position,** which describes where cash came from and where it went during the period. The statement also shows how much cash was on hand at the beginning of the

ILLUSTRATION 1–14

A Schedule of Cash Changes for Jerry Dow, Lawyer

JERRY DOW, LAWYER
Schedule of Cash Changes
For Month Ended December 31, 1993

Cash inflows:		
Investment by owner	$9,000	
Receipts from customers	$3,900	
Total cash inflows		$12,900
Cash outflows:		
Payment to employee	$ 700	
Payment of rent	1,000	
Purchase of office equipment	5,600	
Purchase of law library	2,500	
Repayment of debt	900	
Withdrawal by owner	1,100	
Total cash outflows		11,800
Increase in cash		$ 1,100
Cash balance, November 30, 1993 . . .		–0–
Cash balance, December 31, 1993 . . .		$ 1,100

period, and how much was left at the end. This information is important because good cash management is essential if a business is to prosper or even survive.

The statement of changes in financial position, covered in Chapter 18, has complexities that you do not have the background to grasp at this stage of your course. You should, however, be able to prepare a schedule of cash changes during the period. Illustration 1–14 shows the schedule of cash changes for Jerry Dow's law practice. The information reported in the schedule was taken from the first column (labeled Cash) of Illustration 1–11. The heading identifies December as the time period covered by the statement.

Summary of the Chapter in Terms of Learning Objectives

LO 1. The function of accounting is to communicate useful information to people who make rational investment, credit, and similar decisions. In effect, accountants serve decision makers by providing them with financial information to help them reach better decisions. The decision makers include the owners and creditors of a business. Other users include business managers and those who sell to or buy from businesses. Financial reports are used to describe the activities and financial status of many different organizations in addition to businesses.

LO 2. Accountants work as private accountants, public accountants, and government accountants. All three groups have members who work in the fields of financial accounting, managerial accounting, and tax accounting. Financial accounting involves preparing and auditing financial statements that are distributed to people who are not involved in day-to-day management. Managerial accounting provides information to those who are involved in day-to-day management. Activities related to this field include general accounting, cost accounting, budgeting, internal auditing, and management advisory services. Tax accounting is concerned with determining the proper amount of income taxes to be paid, preparing tax returns, and tax planning.

LO 3. The income statement shows a business's revenues, expenses, and net income or loss. The balance sheet lists a business's assets, liabilities, and owner's equity. The statement of changes in owner's equity shows the increase in owner's equity from investments by the owner, the decrease from withdrawals, and the increase from net income or the decrease from a net loss. The statement of changes in financial position shows the events that caused cash to change. You should note that in Appendix I such a statement classifies cash changes resulting from operating activities, financing activities, and investing activities. At this stage, only a schedule of cash changes was covered, an understanding of which will aid in the preparation and understanding of the statement of changes in financial position covered in Chapter 18.

LO 4. Accounting principles are intended to help accountants produce relevant and reliable information. Broad accounting principles include the business entity principle, the objectivity principle, the cost principle, the going-concern principle, and the revenue recognition principle. Specific accounting principles for financial accounting are established in Canada primarily by the Accounting Standards Board. The recommendations of the board are published as part of the *CICA Handbook*. The International Accounting Standards Committee (IASC) identifies preferred practices and encourages their adoption throughout the world. However, the IASC does not have the authority to impose its standards.

LO 5. A single (or sole) proprietorship is an unincorporated business owned by one individual. A partnership differs from a single proprietorship in that it has more than one owner. Proprietors and partners are personally responsible for the debts of their businesses. A corporation is a separate legal entity. As such, its owners (called *shareholders*) are not personally responsible for its debts.

LO 6. The accounting equation states that Assets = Liabilities + Owner's Equity. Business transactions always have at least two effects on the elements in the accounting equation. The accounting equation is always in balance when business transactions are properly recorded.

Demonstration Problem

After planning for several months, Barbara Schmidt decided to start her own haircutting business, The Cutlery. During its first month of operation, The Cutlery completed the following transactions:

a. On August 1, 1993, Schmidt put $2,000 of her savings into a chequing account in the name of The Cutlery.

b. On August 2, The Cutlery bought store supplies for $600 cash.

c. On August 3, The Cutlery paid $500 rent for the month of August for a small store.

d. On August 5, Schmidt furnished the store, installing new fixtures sold to The Cutlery on account by the supplier for $1,200. This amount is to be repaid in three equal payments at the end of August, September, and October.

e. The Cutlery opened August 12, and in the first week of business ended August 16, cash receipts from haircutting amounted to $825.

f. On August 17, The Cutlery paid $125 to an assistant for working during the business's grand opening.

g. Cash receipts from haircutting during the two-week period ended August 30 amounted to $1,930.

h. On August 31, The Cutlery paid the first installment on the fixtures.

i. On August 31, Schmidt withdrew $900 cash for her personal expenses.

Required

1. Arrange the following asset, liability, and owner's equity titles in an equation like the one in Illustration 1–11: Cash, Store Supplies, Store Equipment (for the fixtures), Accounts Payable, and Barbara Schmidt, Capital. Show by additions and subtractions the effects of each of the preceding transactions on the equation.

2. Prepare an income statement for The Cutlery for the month ended August 31, 1993.

3. Prepare a statement of changes in owner's equity for the month ended August 31, 1993.

4. Prepare a schedule of cash changes for the month ended August 31, 1993.

5. Prepare an August 31, 1993, balance sheet for the business.

Planning the Solution

■ Set up a table with the appropriate columns, including a final column in which to describe the events that involve revenues and expenses.

■ Analyze each transaction and show its effects as increases or decreases in the appropriate columns of the table, being sure that the accounting equation remains in balance after each event.

■ To prepare the income statement, find the revenues and expenses in the last column. Then list those items on the statement, calculate the difference, and label the result as *net income* or *net loss*.

■ Prepare the statement of changes in owner's equity using the information shown in the owner's equity column.

■ Prepare a schedule of cash changes.

■ Finally, use the information on the last row of the table to prepare the balance sheet.

Solution to
Demonstration
Problem

1.

	Assets			= Liabilities +	Owner's Equity	
	Cash +	Store + Supplies	Store Equip.	= Accounts + Payable	Barbara Schmidt, Capital	Explanation of Change
a.	$2,000				$2,000	Investment
b.	− 600	+$600				
Bal.	$1,400	$600			$2,000	
c.	− 500				− 500	Expense
Bal.	$ 900	$600			$1,500	
d.			+$1,200	+$1,200		
Bal.	$ 900	$600	$1,200	$1,200	$1,500	
e.	+ 825				+ 825	Revenue
Bal.	$1,725	$600	$1,200	$1,200	$2,325	
f.	− 125				− 125	Expense
Bal.	$1,600	$600	$1,200	$1,200	$2,200	
g.	+1,930				+1,930	Revenue
Bal.	$3,530	$600	$1,200	$1,200	$4,130	
h.	− 400			− 400		
Bal.	$3,130	$600	$1,200	$ 800	$4,130	
i.	− 900				− 900	Withdrawal
Bal.	$2,230 +	$600 +	$1,200 =	$ 800 +	$3,230	

2.

THE CUTLERY
Income Statement
For Month Ended August 31, 1993

Revenues:		
Haircutting revenue.		$2,755
Operating expenses:		
Rent expense	$500	
Wages expense	125	
Total operating expenses		625
Net income		$2,130

3.

THE CUTLERY
Statement of Changes in Owner's Equity
For Month Ended August 31, 1993

Barbara Schmidt, capital, July 31, 1993		$ –0–
Plus: Investments by owner.	$2,000	
Net income	2,130	4,130
Total		$4,130
Less withdrawals by owner.		(900)
Barbara Schmidt, capital, August 31, 1993		$3,230

4.

THE CUTLERY
Schedule of Cash Changes
For Month Ended August 31, 1993

Cash inflows:
    Investment by owner $2,000
    Receipts from customers 2,755
    Total cash inflows $4,755

Cash outflows:
    Payment of rent . . . . $ 500
    Payment of wages 125
    Purchase of store supplies 600
    Repayment of debt 400
    Withdrawals by owner 900
    Total cash outflows 2,525
Increase in cash $2,230
Cash balance, July 31, 1993 . . . . . –0–
Cash balance, August 31, 1993 . . . . $2,230

5.

THE CUTLERY
Balance Sheet
August 31, 1993

Assets		**Liabilities**	
Cash	$2,230	Accounts payable	$ 800
Store supplies	600	**Owner's Equity**	
Store equipment	1,200	Barbara Schmidt, capital	3,230
		Total liabilities and	
Total assets	$4,030	owner's equity	$4,030

Glossary

Accounting a service-oriented activity that communicates useful information to people who make rational investment, credit, and similar decisions to help them reach better decisions. pp. 10–12

Accounting equation an expression in dollar amounts of the relationship between the assets and the liabilities and equity of an enterprise; stated as Assets = Liabilities + Owner's Equity; also called the *balance sheet equation*. p. 30

Accounts payable liabilities resulting from the purchase of goods or services on credit. p. 20

Accounts receivable amounts owed to a business by its customers for goods or services sold to them on credit. p. 20

Assets the properties or economic resources owned by the business and expected to benefit future periods. p. 20

Audit an examination of an entity's accounting records and statements designed to determine whether the statements fairly reflect the company's financial position and operating results in accordance with generally accepted accounting principles; an audit is designed to add credibility to the information in the financial statements. p. 15

Balance sheet a financial statement providing information that helps users understand the financial status of the business; it lists the types and amounts of assets, liabilities, and equity as of a specific date. Also called the *statement of financial position*. pp. 19–20, 37–38

Balance sheet equation another name for the *accounting equation*. pp. 29–30

Bookkeeping the part of accounting that records transactions and other events, either manually or with computers. pp. 11–12

Budgeting the process of developing formal plans for future business and government activities, which then serve as a basis for evaluating actual accomplishments. p. 17

Business entity principle the principle that requires every business to be accounted for separately and distinctly from its owner or owners; based on the goal of providing relevant information about the business. p. 26

Business transaction a completed exchange between two parties of economic consideration, such as goods, services, money, or rights to collect money. p. 30

CA chartered accountant. p. 14

CGA certified general accountant.

CGA-Canada Certified General Accountants' Association of Canada. p. 14

CICA Canadian Institute of Chartered Accountants. p. 14

CMA certified management accountant. p. 14

Continuing-concern principle another name for the *going-concern principle*. p. 27

Controller the chief accounting officer of a business. p. 16

Corporation a business established as a separate legal entity (*incorporated*) under the laws of the provincial or federal government. pp. 28–29

Cost accounting a type of accounting designed to help managers identify, measure, and control operating costs. p. 17

Cost principle the accounting principle that requires the financial statements to present information based on costs incurred in a transaction; it requires assets, services, and liabilities to be recorded initially at the cash or cash-equivalent amount given in exchange. p. 26

Creditors individuals or organizations entitled to receive payments from a company. p. 20

Debtors individuals or organizations that owe an amount to a business. p. 20

Equity the difference between a company's assets and its liabilities; more precisely, it is the residual interest in the assets of an entity that remains after deducting its liabilities; also called *net assets*. p. 20

Expenses costs incurred by a firm in the process of earning revenue; expenses are measured by the cost of goods and services consumed in operation of the business. p. 19

GAAP the abbreviation for *generally accepted accounting principles*. pp. 21–22

GAAS the abbreviation for *generally accepted auditing standards*. pp. 22–23

General accounting the field of accounting that deals primarily with recording transactions, processing the recorded data, and preparing financial reports for management, investors, creditors, and others. p. 16

Generally accepted accounting principles rules adopted by the accounting profession as guides in measuring, recording, and reporting the financial affairs and activities of a business; GAAP include both broad and specific principles. pp. 21–22

Generally accepted auditing standards rules adopted by the accounting profession as guides in conducting audits of financial statements. pp. 22–23

Going-concern principle the rule that requires accountants to prepare financial statements under the assumption that the business will continue operating instead of being put up for sale or closed, unless evidence shows that it will not continue. p. 27

Government accountants accountants who are employed by government agencies at local, provincial, and federal levels. p. 14

IASC International Accounting Standards Committee; a committee that attempts to create harmony among the accounting practices of different countries by identifying preferred practices and encouraging their adoption throughout the world. p. 24

Income statement the financial statement that shows whether the business earned a profit; it also lists the types and amounts of the revenues and expenses. pp. 18–19

Internal auditing the use of a business's own accounting employees to check records and operating procedures for the purpose of making sure that established accounting procedures and management directives are being followed. Also includes evaluations of operating efficiency. p. 17

Liabilities debts owed by a business or organization; normally requiring future payment in assets or the rendering of services or both. p. 20

Managerial advisory services the activity in which public accountants provide advice to managers; the services may include designing and installing an accounting system, advice on selecting a new computer system, or help with budgeting or selecting employee benefit plans. p. 17

Net assets another name for *equity*. p. 20

Net income the excess of revenues over expenses. p. 18

Net loss the excess of expenses over revenues. p. 18

Objectivity principle the accounting rule that wherever possible the amounts used in recording transactions be based on verifiable evidence such as business transactions between independent parties. p. 26

Partnership a business that is owned by two or more people and is not organized as a corporation. p. 28

Private accountants accountants who work for a single employer, usually a business. p. 13

Public accountants accountants who offer their services to the public. p. 13

Realization principle another name for the *revenue recognition principle*. pp. 33–34

Revenue Canada the federal agency that has the duty of collecting income taxes and otherwise enforcing the income tax laws. p. 18

Revenue recognition principle the rule that states: (1) revenue should be reported when it is earned and not before, (2) the inflow of assets associated with revenue does not have to be in the form of cash, and (3) the amount of revenue should be measured as the cash received plus the cash equivalent value of any noncash assets received from customers in exchange for goods or services. pp. 33–34

Revenues inflows of cash or other properties received in exchange for providing goods or services to customers; may also occur as a result of decreases in liabilities as well as inflows of assets. p. 18

Shareholders the owners of a corporation; also called *stockholders*. p. 28

Single proprietorship a business owned by one individual, not organized as a corporation. p. 28

SMA Society of Management Accountants. p. 14

Sole proprietorship another name for a single proprietorship. p. 28

Statement of changes in financial position a financial statement that describes where the business's cash came from and where it went during the period; the cash flows are classified as being associated with operations, investing activities, and financing activities. pp. 38–39

Statement of changes in owner's equity a financial statement that presents information about what happened to equity during a time period; it shows the beginning amount of equity, the events that increased it (new investments and net income), and the events that decreased it (net loss, if any, and withdrawals). p. 37

Statement of financial position another name for the *balance sheet*. p. 37

Stock equity of a corporation divided into units or shares. p. 19

Stockholders another name for *shareholders*. p. 28

Tax accounting the field of accounting that includes preparing tax returns and planning future transactions to minimize the amount of tax that has to be paid; involves private, public, and government accountants. pp. 17–18

Synonymous Terms

Accounting equation balance sheet equation.

Balance sheet statement of financial position; position statement.

Economic resources assets

Equity net assets; owner's equity.

Going-concern principle continuing-concern principle.

Revenue recognition principle realization principle.

Shareholders stockholders.

Single proprietorship sole proprietorship.

Answers to the following questions are listed at the end of this chapter. Be sure that you decide which is the one best answer to each question *before* you check the answers.

LO 1 The primary function of accounting is:

a. To provide the information that the managers of an economic entity need to control its operations.
b. To provide information that the creditors of an economic entity can use in deciding whether to make additional loans to the entity.
c. To measure the periodic net income of economic entities.
d. To provide financial information that is useful in making rational investment, credit, and similar decisions.
e. To measure the resources owned by economic entities and the financial obligations of economic entities.

LO 2 Accountants who are employed in public accounting generally work in one or more of the following fields:

a. Tax services, managerial advisory services, and auditing.
b. Internal auditing, income tax services, and managerial advisory services.
c. General accounting, auditing, and budgeting.
d. Government accounting, private accounting, and auditing.
e. Income tax services, cost accounting, and budgeting.

LO 3 The financial statements usually presented to the owner of a business and to other outside parties are the:

a. Revenues, expenses, assets, liabilities, and owner's equity.
b. Income statement, balance sheet, and statement of changes in financial position.
c. Income statement and balance sheet.
d. Income statement, statement of changes in owner's equity, and balance sheet.
e. Balance sheet, statement of changes in financial position, income statement, and statement of changes in owner's equity.

LO 4 At present, generally accepted accounting principles in Canada usually are established by:

a. The CICA, subject to the legal authority of Parliament.
b. Public accounting firms, subject to the recommended auditing standards.
c. The Canadian Business Corporations Act, subject to the review of the CICA.
d. The Accounting Standards Board.
e. The CICA, subject to the oversight of various regulatory commissions.

LO 5   Compared to a partnership or corporation, the nature of a single proprietor-ship is such that:

a.   Its owner holds all the shares of stock issued by the business.
b.   It is not a separate legal entity but is owned by more than one person.
c.   It is a separate legal entity.
d.   The debts of the business are the responsibility of the business but not of the owner.
e.   It is not a separate legal entity and it has only one owner who is personally re-sponsible for its debts.

LO 6   A new business has the following transactions: (1) the owner invested $3,600; (2) $2,600 of supplies were purchased for cash; (3) $2,300 was received in payment for services rendered by the business; (4) a salary of $1,000 was paid to an em-ployee; and (5) $3,000 was borrowed from the bank. After these transactions are completed, the total assets, total liabilities, and total owner's equity of the business are:

a. $ 7,900; $5,300; $2,600.
b. $ 7,900; $3,000; $4,900.
c. $10,500; $5,600; $4,900.
d. $ 7,900; $ –0– ; $7,900.
e. $ 7,900; $4,300; $3,600.

LO 7   The rule that helps accounting information be reliable is called:

a.   The objectivity principle.
b.   The going-concern principle.
c.   Accounting.
d.   Budgeting.
e.   Equity.

Questions for Class Discussion

1.   What is the function of accounting?
2.   What are three or four examples of questions that a business owner or manager might try to answer by looking to accounting information?
3.   What is the difference between accounting and bookkeeping?
4.   Why is the study of accounting necessary for someone who uses a computer to process accounting data?
5.   Why do most provinces license public accountants?
6.   What are three fields of accounting?
7.   What is the purpose of an audit? What do public accountants do when they per-form an audit?
8.   What are some examples of management advisory services typically provided by public accountants?
9.   What information is presented in an income statement?
10.   What information is presented in a balance sheet?
11.   Define (*a*) assets, (*b*) liabilities, (*c*) equity, and (*d*) net assets.
12.   What is the primary purpose of generally accepted accounting principles?

13. Why is a business treated as a separate entity for accounting purposes?
14. Why is there a need for objectivity in accounting?
15. What is required by the cost principle? Why is this principle needed?

Mini Discussion
Cases

In order to realize a lifelong dream, Judy Edelman decides to open a video and audio rental and sales business. Judy worked for such a business on a part-time basis while attending school and learned much about the operation of such a business. However, she needs help setting up the business—especially with determining available sources of financing because her own resources are insufficient to provide for the necessary assets to start such a business.

Case 1–1

Required

Prepare for Judy a possible balance sheet that will show the necessary assets to start the business and the proposed sources of these assets. Support your proposal.

Studies indicate that 50% of small businesses fail within the first two years of their life. These studies also indicate that the failure rate would be substantially reduced if serious planning preceded the starting of a business.

Case 1–2

Required

Discuss the type of preplanning indicated by the balance sheet, income statement, and a statement of changes in financial position.

Joseph Strum located a business he was interested in and started negotiations with the owner, Robert Wargo, for its purchase. Wargo supplied Strum with a balance sheet. The balance sheet, which Wargo had prepared personally, listed four assets, two liabilities, and the owner's capital account. The listed assets were cash, accounts receivable, merchandise, and building and equipment.

Case 1–3

The purchase was completed, and Joseph Strum took over with satisfaction and enthusiasm. Sales the first month of operations were up to Strum's expectation. But prior to the end of the month, Strum received a disturbing letter from Doris Wargo, which he turned over to a lawyer. A couple of days later he learned from the lawyer that Doris Wargo was indeed the sole owner of the building. Strum was certain he had purchased the building since it was listed on the balance sheet Robert Wargo had given him.

Required

Discuss the GAAP applicable to the situation and what Strum should have done prior to concluding the purchase.

Exercises

Exercise 1–1
Balance sheet for a single proprietorship
(LO 3, 5, 6)

On April 30, 1993, the accounting equation for Sue's Shoes, a single proprietorship, showed the following:

Cash	$ 4,000
Other assets	75,000
Accounts payable	40,000
Sue Hahn, Capital	39,000

On that date, Sue Hahn sold the "other assets" for $50,000 cash in preparation for ending and liquidating the business of Sue's Shoes.

Required

1. Prepare a balance sheet for the shop as it would appear immediately after the sale of the assets.
2. Tell how the shop's cash should be distributed in ending the business and why.

Exercise 1–2
The accounting equation
(LO 6)

Determine the missing amount on each of the following lines:

	Assets	= Liabilities +	Owner's Equity
a.	$57,600	$10,500	?
b.	$47,700	?	$29,700
c.	?	$ 9,800	$36,900

Exercise 1–3
Effects of transactions on the accounting equation
(LO 6)

The effects of five transactions on the assets, liabilities, and owner's equity of Mike Levin in his dental practice are shown in the following equation with each transaction identified by a letter. Write a short sentence or phrase describing the probable nature of each transaction.

	Cash	+ Accounts Receivable	+ Office Supplies	+ Land	= Accounts Payable	+ Mike Levin, Capital
	Assets				**= Liabilities +**	**Owner's Equity**
	$12,300		$6,360	$ 3,200		$21,860
a.	−11,000			+11,000		
	$ 1,300		$6,360	$14,200		$21,860
b.			+ 560		+$560	
	$ 1,300		$6,920	$14,200	$ 560	$21,860
c.		+$860				+860
	$ 1,300	$860	$6,920	$14,200	$ 560	$22,720
d.	− 560				− 560	
	$ 740	$860	$6,920	$14,200	$–0–	$22,720
e.	+ 860	− 860				
	$ 1,600 +	$–0–	+ $6,920 +	$14,200 =	$–0– +	$22,720

Exercise 1–4
Use of the accounting equation
(LO 6)

Determine:

a. The equity of the owner in a business having $156,300 of assets and owing $23,900 of liabilities.
b. The liabilities of a business having $110,300 of assets and in which the owner has a $79,300 equity.

c. The assets of a business with $10,500 of liabilities and in which the owner has a $48,600 equity.

On October 1, Roy Devon began operating a new travel agency. After each of the agency's first five transactions, the accounting equation for the agency showed the following balances. Analyze the equations and describe the probable nature of the five transactions with their amounts.

Exercise 1–5
Analyzing the accounting equation
(LO 6)

Balances after Transaction	Cash	+ Accounts Receivable	+ Office Supplies	+ Office Furniture	= Accounts Payable	+ Roy Devon, Capital
1	$25,000	$ –0–	$ –0–	$ –0–	$–0–	$25,000
2	23,800	–0–	2,000	–0–	800	25,000
3	13,800	–0–	2,000	10,000	800	25,000
4	13,800	2,300	2,000	10,000	800	27,300
5	12,100	2,300	2,800	10,900	800	27,300

A business had the following assets and liabilities at the beginning and at the end of a year:

Exercise 1–6
Determination of net income
(LO 3, 6)

	Assets	Liabilities
Beginning of the year	$ 86,000	$34,000
End of the year	100,000	23,000

Determine the net income or net loss of the business during the year under each of the following unrelated assumptions:

a. The owner of the business made no additional investments in the business and no withdrawals of assets from the business during the year.
b. The owner made no additional investments in the business during the year but withdrew $2,900 per month to pay personal living expenses.
c. During the year, the owner made no withdrawals but made a $40,000 additional investment in the business.
d. The owner withdrew $3,500 from the business each month to pay personal living expenses and near the year-end invested an additional $15,000 in the business.

Irina Orman began the practice of pediatrics on November 1 and will prepare financial statements at the end of each month. During November, Dr. Orman completed these transactions:

Exercise 1–7
Effects of transactions on the accounting equation
(LO 6)

a. Invested $15,700 in cash and medical equipment having a $3,500 fair market (cash equivalent) value.
b. Paid the rent on the office space for November, $2,500.
c. Purchased additional medical equipment on credit, $7,600.
d. Completed medical work for a patient and immediately collected $260 cash for the work.
e. Completed medical work for a patient on credit, $2,800.
f. Purchased additional medical equipment for cash, $590.
g. Paid the medical assistant's wages for November, $1,900.
h. Collected $2,000 of the amount owed by the patient of transaction e.
i. Paid for the equipment purchased in transaction c.

Required

Arrange the following asset, liability, and equity titles in an equation form like Illustration 1–11: Cash; Accounts Receivable; Medical Equipment; Accounts Payable; and Irina Orman, Capital. Then, show by additions and subtractions the effects of the transactions on the elements of the equation. Show new totals after each transaction.

Exercise 1–8
Analysis of transaction effects on the accounting equation
(LO 6)

For each of the following five pairs of changes in components of the accounting equation, provide an example of a transaction that will produce the described effects:

a. Increase an asset and decrease an asset.
b. Increase an asset and increase a liability.
c. Decrease an asset and decrease a liability.
d. Decrease a liability and increase a liability.
e. Increase an asset and increase equity.
f. Decrease an asset and decrease equity.

Exercise 1–9
An income statement for a single proprietorship
(LO 3)

On March 1, 1993, Lynn Lyonne began the practice of tax accounting under the name of Lynn Lyonne, Accountant. On March 31, her record showed the following assets, liabilities, owner's investments, owner's withdrawals, revenues, and expenses:

Cash	$ 600	Owner's withdrawals	$3,000
Accounts receivable	400	Tax fees earned	4,900
Office supplies	800	Miscellaneous expense	75
Professional library	4,000	Rent expense	700
Office equipment	2,600	Salaries expense	1,000
Accounts payable	2,775	Telephone expense	500
Owner's investments	6,000		

From the preceding information, prepare a March 1993 income statement for the business.

Exercise 1–10
A statement of changes in owner's equity for a single proprietorship
(LO 3)

Based on the facts provided in Exercise 1–9, prepare a March 1993 statement of changes in owner's equity for the business of Lynn Lyonne, Accountant.

Exercise 1–11
A balance sheet for a single proprietorship
(LO 3)

Based on the facts provided in Exercise 1–9, prepare a March 31, 1993, balance sheet for the business of Lynn Lyonne, Accountant.

Exercise 1–12
Identifying the information in each financial statement
(LO 3)

Linda Tomas is in the business of managing commercial real estate. Examine each of the following items related to the business and state with the appropriate letter (a, b, c, or d) whether the item should appear on (a) an income statement, (b) a statement of changes in owner's equity, (c) a balance sheet, or (d) a schedule of cash changes. If an item should appear on two statements, list both letters.

1. Management fees earned.
2. Accounts receivable.

3. Investments of cash by owner.
4. Cash received from customers.
5. Rent expense paid in cash.
6. Cash withdrawals by owner.
7. Office supplies.
8. Accounts payable.

Calculate the missing item in each of the following independent cases:

	a	b	c	d
Owner's equity, January 1, 1993	$ –0–	$ –0–	$ –0–	$ –0–
Owner's investments during 1993. . . .	25,000	32,000	47,000	?
Owner's withdrawals during 1993 . . .	4,000	?	13,000	6,000
Net income (loss) in 1993.	?	16,000	(22,000)	25,000
Owner's equity, December 31, 1993 . .	36,000	40,000	?	53,000

Problems

Daisy Pell secured her broker's license and opened a real estate office. During a short period, she completed these transactions for the agency:

Problem 1–1
Effects of transactions on
the accounting equation
(LO 6)

a. Sold a personal investment in BCE shares for $52,640, and deposited $50,000 of the proceeds in a bank account opened in the name of the business, Daisy Pell, Realtor.

b. Purchased for $125,000 a small building to be used as an office. Paid $45,000 in cash and signed a note payable promising to pay the balance over a period of years.

c. Took office equipment from home for use in the business. The equipment had a $900 fair value.

d. Purchased office supplies for cash, $425.

e. Purchased office equipment on credit, $7,000.

f. Completed a real estate appraisal on credit and billed the client $720 for the work done.

g. Paid a local newspaper $150 for a notice of the opening of the agency.

h. Sold a house for a client and collected a $12,000 cash commission on completion of the sale.

i. Made a $700 installment payment on the equipment purchased in transaction e.

j. The client of transaction f paid $500 of the amount he owed.

k. Paid the office secretary's wages, $850.

l. Daisy Pell withdrew $400 from the bank account of the business to pay personal living expenses.

Required

1. Arrange the following asset, liability, and owner's equity titles in an equation like Illustration 1–11: Cash; Accounts Receivable; Office Supplies; Office Equipment; Building; Accounts Payable; Notes Payable; and Daisy Pell, Capital. Leave space for an Explanation column to the right of Daisy Pell, Capital.

2. Show by additions and subtractions the effects of each transaction on the elements of the equation. Show new totals after each addition or subtraction. Next to each change in Daisy Pell, Capital, state whether it was caused by an investment, a revenue, an expense, or a withdrawal.

Problem 1-2
Preparation of balance sheet and income statement
(LO 3, 6)

Isaac Trou graduated from university in May 1993 with a degree in architecture. On July 1, he invested $5,600 in a new business under the name Isaac Trou, Architect. Financial statements for the business will be prepared at the end of each month. The following transactions occurred during July:

July 1　Rented the furnished office and equipment of an architect who was retiring, paying $1,000 cash for July's rent.

　　　1　Purchased drafting supplies for cash, $120.

　　　3　Paid $175 for July's janitorial expense.

　　　6　Completed architectural work for a client and immediately collected $450 cash.

　　　9　Completed architectural work for Jacks Realty on credit, $1,275.

　　16　Paid the draftsman's salary for the first half of July, $825.

　　19　Received payment in full for the work completed for Jacks Realty on July 9.

　　21　Completed architectural work for Western Contractors on credit, $1,750.

　　22　Purchased additional drafting supplies on credit, $200.

　　24　Completed architectural work for Bob Urick on credit, $1,200.

　　28　Purchased on credit the service of copying blueprints; the copies were delivered to clients. The cost was $220.

　　29　Received payment in full from Western Contractors for the work completed on July 21.

　　30　Paid for the drafting supplies purchased on July 22.

　　31　Paid the July telephone bill, $150.

　　31　Paid the July utilities expense, $125.

　　31　Paid the draftsman's salary for the second half of July, $825.

　　31　Purchased insurance protection for the next 12 months (beginning August 1) by paying a $2,100 premium. Since none of this insurance protection had been used up on July 31, it was at that time an asset called Prepaid Insurance.

　　31　Trou withdrew $1,000 from the business for his personal use.

Required

1. Arrange the following asset, liability, and owner's equity titles in an equation like Illustration 1-11: Cash; Accounts Receivable; Prepaid Insurance; Drafting Supplies; Accounts Payable; and Isaac Trou, Capital. Include an Explanation column for changes in owner's equity.

2. Show the effects of the transactions on the elements of the equation by recording increases and decreases in the appropriate columns. Indicate an increase with a + and a decrease with a − before the amount. Do not determine new totals for the items of the equation after each transaction. Next to each change in Isaac Trou, Capital, state whether it was caused by an investment, a revenue, an expense, or a withdrawal.

3. After recording the final transaction, calculate and insert on the next line the ending total for each item of the equation and determine if the equation is in balance.

4. Analyze (classify) the items in the last column of the equation and prepare a July income statement for the practice.

5. Prepare a July statement of changes in owner's equity.

6. Prepare a July 31 balance sheet.

The accounting records of Caren Cox's medical practice show the following assets and liabilities as of the end of 1992 and 1993:

Problem 1–3
Preparation of balance sheet; calculation of net income
(LO 3, 6)

	December 31	
	1992	**1993**
Cash	$10,700	$ 2,200
Accounts receivable (OHIP)	6,800	8,000
Office supplies	1,200	900
Automobiles	7,500	7,500
Office equipment	20,100	24,150
Land		85,000
Building.		127,500
Accounts payable.	1,500	2,000
Notes payable.		152,500

Late in December 1993 (just before the amounts in the second column were calculated), Dr. Cox purchased a small office building in the name of the practice, Caren Cox, M.D., and moved the practice from rented quarters to the new building. The building and the land it occupies cost $212,500. The practice paid $60,000 in cash and a note payable was signed for the balance. Dr. Cox had to invest an additional $50,000 in the practice to enable it to pay the $60,000. The practice earned a satisfactory net income during 1993, which enabled Dr. Cox to withdraw $5,000 per month from the practice to pay personal living expenses.

Required

1. Prepare two balance sheets for the business, as of the end of 1992 and the end of 1993. (Remember that the owner's equity equals assets less liabilities.)

2. By comparing the owner's equity amounts from the balance sheets, and using the additional information just presented, prepare a calculation to show the net income earned by the business during 1993.

Harry Moss began a new law practice and completed these transactions during June 1993:

Problem 1–4
Analyzing transactions and preparing financial statements
(LO 3, 6)

June 1 Transferred $7,000 from his personal savings account to a chequing account opened in the name of the law practice, Harry Moss, Lawyer.

1 Rented the furnished office of a lawyer who was retiring, and paid cash for June's rent, $2,000.

1 Purchased the law library of the retiring lawyer for $5,000, paying $3,000 in cash and agreeing to pay the balance in six months.

2 Purchased office supplies for cash, $300.

7 Completed legal work for a client and immediately collected $750 in cash for the work done.

June 10   Purchased office equipment on credit, $500.

     13   Completed legal work for Central Bank on credit, $2,765.

     17   Purchased office supplies on credit, $50.

     20   Paid for the office equipment purchased on June 10.

     23   Completed legal work for Orr Realty on credit, $1,300.

     25   Received $2,765 from Central Bank for the work completed on June 13.

     30   Paid the office secretary's salary, $1,500.

     30   Paid the monthly utility bills, $140.

     30   Harry Moss took $2,100 out of the business for his personal use.

Required

1. Arrange the following asset, liability, and owner's equity titles in an equation like Illustration 1–11: Cash; Accounts Receivable; Office Supplies; Professional Library; Office Equipment; Accounts Payable; and Harry Moss, Capital. Leave space for an Explanation column to the right of Harry Moss, Capital.

2. Show by additions and subtractions the effects of each transaction on the items of the equation. Show new totals after each transaction. Next to each change in Harry Moss, Capital, state whether it was caused by an investment, a revenue, an expense, or a withdrawal.

3. Analyze (classify) the increases and decreases in the last column of the equation and prepare a June income statement for the practice.

4. Prepare a June statement of changes in owner's equity.

5. Prepare a June 30 balance sheet.

Problem 1–5
Calculating financial statement amounts
(LO 3)

The following financial statement information is known about five unrelated companies:

	Company 1	Company 2	Company 3	Company 4	Company 5
December 31, 1992:					
Assets	$35,000	$39,000	$46,000	$29,000	$63,000
Liabilities	27,000	30,000	30,000	20,000	?
December 31, 1993:					
Assets	37,000	48,000	75,000	?	88,000
Liabilities	23,800	?	36,000	27,000	40,000
During 1993:					
Owner investments	4,600	7,000	?	23,000	–0–
Net income	?	6,000	20,000	10,000	23,000
Owner withdrawals	2,000	2,600	4,000	5,000	7,000

Required

1. Answer the following questions about Company 1:
   a. What was the owner's equity on December 31, 1992?
   b. What was the owner's equity on December 31, 1993?
   c. What was the net income for 1993?

2. Answer the following questions about Company 2:
   a. What was the owner's equity on December 31, 1992?
   b. What was the owner's equity on December 31, 1993?
   c. What was the amount of liabilities owed on December 31, 1993?

3. For Company 3, calculate the amount of owner investments during 1993.

4. For Company 4, calculate the amount of assets on December 31, 1993.

5. For Company 5, calculate the amount of liabilities owed on December 31, 1992.

Identify how each of the following 14 transactions affects the company's financial statements. For the balance sheet, identify how each transaction affects total assets, total liabilities, and owner's equity. For the income statement, identify how each transaction affects net income. For the schedule of cash changes, identify how each transaction affects cash changes. If there is an increase, place a + in the column or columns. If there is a decrease, place a − in the column or columns. If there is both an increase and a decrease, place +/− in the column or columns.

The lines for the first two transactions are completed as examples.

Problem 1–6
Identifying effects of transactions on the financial statements
(LO 3, 6)

	Transaction	Balance Sheet			Income Statement	Schedule of Cash Changes
		Total Assets	Total Liabilities	Equity	Net Income	Cash
1	Owner invests cash	+		+		+
2	Purchases supplies on credit	+	+			
3	Owner invests equipment					
4	Pays wages with cash					
5	Sells services on credit					
6	Sells services for cash					
7	Buys office equipment for cash					
8	Acquires services on credit					
9	Owner withdraws cash					
10	Sells extra equipment for cash (at cost)					
11	Buys land with note payable					
12	Borrows cash with note payable					
13	Pays rent with cash					
14	Collects receivable from (5)					

Problem 1–7
Analytical essay
(LO 3, 4)

Review the facts presented in Problem 1–1, and focus on transactions *f* and *j*. Indicate which of these transactions involves a revenue and explain why that transaction is a revenue and why the other transaction is not. Also review transactions *d* and *k*. Indicate which one of these transactions involves an expense and explain why that transaction is an expense and why the other is not.

Problem 1–8
Analytical essay
(LO 2, 6)

Review the facts presented in Problem 1–4. Now assume that all of the business's revenue transactions had been for cash and none had been for credit. Also assume that all of the expense transactions had been paid in cash and none were on credit. Describe the differences, if any, these assumptions would make in the appearance of the income statement, the statement of changes in owner's equity, and the balance sheet. Describe the differences in general terms without calculating actual dollar amounts of difference. Also explain why each statement is affected or not affected by the preceding assumptions.

Alternate Problems

Problem 1–1A
Effects of transactions on the accounting equation
(LO 6)

Patsy Dane opened a dental practice and during a short period completed these transactions on behalf of the practice:

a. Sold a personal investment in Imperial Oil shares for $90,000 and deposited $85,000 of the proceeds in a bank account opened in the name of the practice, Patsy Dane, D.D.S.

b. Purchased for $140,000 a small building to be used as an office. Paid $50,000 in cash and signed a note payable promising to pay the balance over a period of years.

c. Purchased office equipment for cash, $13,300.

d. Took office equipment from home for use in the practice. The equipment had a $620 fair value.

e. Purchased on credit office supplies for $300 and office equipment for $7,000.

f. Paid the local paper $150 for a notice announcing the opening of the practice.

g. Completed dental work and billed the patient $550, which is to be paid later.

h. Performed dental services and received $250 cash.

i. Patsy Dane withdrew $3,000 from the business to pay personal expenses.

j. The patient paid for the services of transaction *g*.

k. Made a $4,500 installment payment on the amount owed from transaction *e*.

l. Paid the dental assistant's wages, $1,400.

Required

1. Arrange the following asset, liability, and owner's equity titles in an equation like Illustration 1–11: Cash; Accounts Receivable; Office Supplies; Office Equipment; Building; Accounts Payable; Notes Payable; and Patsy Dane, Capital. Leave space for an Explanation column to the right of Patsy Dane, Capital.

2. Show by additions and subtractions the effects of each transaction on the elements of the equation. Show new totals after each transaction. Next to each change in Patsy Dane, Capital, state whether it was caused by an investment, a revenue, an expense, or a withdrawal.

Sam Henry graduated from university, completed his internship, and on September 1, 1993, began an engineering practice by investing $9,000 in the practice. Financial statements for the business will be prepared at the end of each month. The following transactions occurred during September:

Problem 1–2A
Preparation of balance
sheet and income
statement
(LO 3, 6)

Sept. 1 Rented the office and equipment of an engineer who was retiring, paying $2,100 cash for September's rent.

1 Paid $225 for janitorial expense during September.

2 Purchased engineering supplies for cash, $75.

4 Completed an engineering engagement for a client and immediately collected $3,200 cash.

7 Purchased additional engineering supplies on credit, $175.

9 Completed engineering work for Berk Contractors on credit, $2,600.

15 Paid the assistant's salary for September 1–15, $1,200.

16 Paid for the engineering supplies purchased on September 7.

19 Received payment in full from Berk Contractors for the work completed on September 9.

21 Completed engineering work for Younger Realtors on credit, $2,100.

25 Purchased additional engineering supplies on credit, $150.

29 Completed additional architectural work for Berk Contractors on credit, $1,350.

30 Paid the assistant's salary for September 16–30, $1,200.

30 Paid the September telephone bill, $65.

30 Paid the September hydro bill, $210.

30 Purchased liability insurance protection for the next year (beginning October 1) by paying a premium of $3,000. Since none of this insurance protection had been used up on September 30, it was at that time an asset called *prepaid insurance*.

30 Henry withdrew $2,800 from the business's chequing account to pay for some personal items.

Required

1. Arrange the following asset, liability, and owner's equity titles in an equation like Illustration 1–11: Cash; Accounts Receivable; Prepaid Insurance; Engineering Supplies; Accounts Payable; and Sam Henry, Capital. Include an Explanation column for changes in owner's equity.

2. Show the effects of the transactions on the elements of the equation by recording increases and decreases in the appropriate columns. Indicate an increase with a + and a decrease with a − before the amount. Do not determine new totals for the items of the equation after each transaction. Next to each change in Sam Henry, Capital, state whether it was caused by an investment, a revenue, an expense, or a withdrawal.

3. After recording the final transaction, determine and enter on the next line the ending total for each item and determine if the equation is in balance.

4. Analyze the items in the last column of the equation and prepare a September income statement for the practice.

5. Prepare a September statement of changes in owner's equity.

6. Prepare a September 30 balance sheet.

Problem 1–3A
Preparation of balance sheet; calculation of net income
(LO 3, 6)

The accounting records of Wendy Stone's real estate office show the following assets and liabilities as of the end of 1992 and 1993:

	December 31	
	1992	**1993**
Cash	$10,700	$ 2,700
Accounts receivable	6,800	8,000
Office supplies	2,000	900
Automobiles	5,900	5,900
Office equipment	19,600	24,300
Land		80,000
Building		130,000
Accounts payable.	2,500	2,700
Notes payable		150,000

During the last week of December 1993 (just before the amounts in the second column were calculated), Stone purchased a small building in the name of the realty office, Stone Realtors, and moved her business from rented quarters to the new building. The building and the land it occupies cost $210,000; the business paid $60,000 in cash and signed a note payable for the balance. Stone had to invest an additional $50,000 in the business to enable it to pay the $60,000. The business earned a satisfactory net income during 1993, which enabled Stone to withdraw $4,100 per month from the business to pay personal living expenses.

Required

1. Prepare two balance sheets for the business, as of the end of 1992 and the end of 1993. (Remember that the owner's equity equals assets less liabilities.)
2. Using the information just presented and by comparing the owner's equity amount from the balance sheets, prepare a calculation to show the net income earned by the business during 1993.

Problem 1–4A
Analyzing transactions and preparing financial statements
(LO 3, 6)

James Bell completed his studies in May 1993, and on June 1 began private practice as a public accountant by investing $6,000 in cash in the practice. He also transferred to the business some office equipment having a cash value of $9,600. Then, he completed these additional transactions during June:

June 1 Rented the office of a public accountant who was retiring and paid the rent for June, $900.

1 Moved accounting books required in university from home to the office. (In other words, invested the books in the practice.) The books had a $500 fair value.

2 Purchased office supplies for cash, $130.

4 Purchased additional accounting books costing $1,500. Paid $500 in cash and promised to pay the balance within 90 days.

5 Completed accounting work for a client and immediately collected $600.

10 Completed accounting work for Village Store on credit, $1,600.

15 Purchased additional office supplies on credit, $70.

20 Received $1,600 from Village Store for the work completed on June 10.

25 Completed accounting work for Olson Realty on credit, $1,400.

30 Made a $400 installment payment on the accounting books purchased on June 4.

June 30 Paid the June telephone bill, $80.

     30 Paid the office secretary's wages, $1,300.

     30 James Bell took $1,500 out of the business for his personal use.

Required

1. Arrange the following asset, liability, and owner's equity titles in an equation like Illustration 1–11: Cash; Accounts Receivable; Office Supplies; Professional Library; Office Equipment; Accounts Payable; and James Bell, Capital. Leave space for an Explanation column to the right of James Bell, Capital.

2. Show by additions and subtractions the effects of each transaction on the elements of the equation. Show new totals after each transaction. Next to each change in James Bell, Capital, state whether it was caused by an investment, a revenue, an expense, or a withdrawal.

3. Analyze the items in the last column of the equation and prepare a June income statement for the practice.

4. Prepare a June statement of changes in owner's equity.

5. Prepare a June 30 balance sheet.

The following financial statement information is known about five unrelated companies:

Problem 1–5A
Calculating financial statement amounts
(LO 3)

	Company A	Company B	Company C	Company D	Company E
December 31, 1992:					
Assets	$73,000	$69,000	$30,000	$67,000	$83,000
Liabilities	57,000	52,000	25,000	49,000	?
December 31, 1993:					
Assets	80,000	97,000	?	83,000	96,000
Liabilities	?	60,000	29,000	43,000	50,000
During 1993:					
Owner investments	8,000	19,000	21,000	?	10,000
Net income	24,000	?	8,600	17,500	17,000
Owner withdrawals	3,000	5,000	3,600	–0–	6,000

Required

1. Answer the following questions about Company A:
   a. What was the owner's equity on December 31, 1992?
   b. What was the owner's equity on December 31, 1993?
   c. What was the amount of liabilities owed on December 31, 1993?

2. Answer the following questions about Company B:
   a. What was the owner's equity on December 31, 1992?
   b. What was the owner's equity on December 31, 1993?
   c. What was the net income for 1993?

3. For Company C, calculate the amount of assets on December 31, 1993.

4. For Company D, calculate the amount of owner investments during 1993.

5. For Company E, calculate the amount of liabilities owed on December 31, 1992.

Identify how each of the 14 transactions on page 62 affects the company's financial statements. For the balance sheet, identify how each transaction affects total assets, total liabilities, and owner's equity. For the income statement, identify how each transaction affects net income. For the schedule of cash changes, identify how each transaction affects cash. If there is an increase, place a + in the column or columns. If there is

Problem 1–6A
Identifying effects of transactions on the financial statements
(LO 3, 6)

	Transaction	Balance Sheet			Income Statement	Schedule of Cash Changes
		Total Assets	Total Liabilities	Equity	Net Income	Cash
1	Owner invests cash	+		+		+
2	Pays wages with cash	−		−	−	−
3	Buys store equipment for cash					
4	Purchases supplies on account					
5	Owner invests supplies					
6	Owner withdraws cash					
7	Sells services on account					
8	Sells extra equipment for cash (at cost)					
9	Acquires services on account					
10	Sells services for cash					
11	Borrows cash with note payable					
12	Pays rent with cash					
13	Collects receivable from (7)					
14	Buys land with note payable					

a decrease, place a − in the column or columns. If there is both an increase and a decrease, place +/− in the column or columns. The lines for the first two transactions are completed as examples.

Review the facts presented in Problem 1–1A, and focus on transactions *g* and *j*. Indicate which of these transactions involves a revenue and explain why that transaction is a revenue and why the other transaction is not. Also review transactions *f* and *k*. Indicate which of these transactions involves an expense and explain why that transaction is an expense and why the other transaction is not.

Problem 1–7A
Analytical essay
(LO 3, 4)

Review the facts presented in Problem 1–4A. Now assume that all of the business's revenue transactions had been on credit and none had been for cash. Also assume that the expense transactions had been on credit and the resulting accounts payable were not paid prior to the end of the period. Describe the differences, if any, these assumptions would make in the appearance of the income statement, the statement of changes in owner's equity, and the balance sheet. Describe the differences in general terms without calculating actual dollar amounts of difference. Also explain why each statement is affected or not affected by the preceding assumptions.

Problem 1–8A
Analytical essay
(LO 2, 6)

Provocative Problems

On September 5, 1993, Norma Clay invested $500 cash in a short-term enterprise that participated in a local farmers' market set up in her rural community especially for the Labour Day weekend. She paid $200 for a spot in the market to sell homegrown vegetables and homemade jams and jellies. She bought paper sacks (supplies) at a cost of $55. She also paid a neighbor $85 for materials to construct a stand, which would not have any value at the end of the weekend. Norma purchased her vegetables and jams from several neighbors at a total cost of $450; because she had only $160 in cash, she could not pay in full for everything. However, her neighbors knew Norma's credit was good, and agreed to accept $150 in cash and the promise that she would pay the $300 balance the day after the market closed. During the weekend, she collected $1,120 in cash from sales and paid a young person $60 for helping her with the sales. Norma estimated a $25 value for her unsold goods, which she thought could be sold in the future. None of the sacks were left.

She wanted to decide whether she should look for similar opportunities elsewhere and continue her enterprise, which she called Norma Clay's Homegrown Goods. Assemble the information and prepare an income statement for the three-day market period, which ended on September 7. Then prepare a statement of changes in owner's equity for the same period and a balance sheet dated September 7. Finally, prepare a schedule of cash changes for the three days.

Provocative Problem 1–1
Weekend farmers' market
(LO 3, 6)

Joe Sterling ran out of money at the end of the first semester of his sophomore year in university. He looked for work but could not find a satisfactory job. Since he had a set of drums, Joe decided to hire himself out to bands. Consequently, billing himself as Joe Rockhead, he began his enterprise with no assets other than the drums, which had a fair market value of $1,500. He kept no accounting records. Now, at the year-end, he has engaged you to determine the net income that he earned during the year. You find that Joe's business has a $650 year-end bank balance plus $25 of undeposited cash. A local

Provocative Problem 1–2
Joe's rock band
(LO 3)

band owes Joe $125 for his last job. In the last week of the year, Joe sold his drums for $950 and used some of the cash proceeds to help buy a new set of drums that cost $4,200. Joe still owes a finance company $3,000 as a result of the purchase. Joe also borrowed $650 from his father to help make the down payment. This loan made to Joe's business was interest-free and has not been repaid. Finally, since Joe's enterprise has been profitable from the beginning, Joe has withdrawn $150 of its earnings each week for the 52 weeks of its existence to pay personal living expenses. Determine the amount of net income earned by the business during the first year of its operations. Show your calculation in a form that will be understandable by others.

Provocative Problem 1–3
Inglis Limited
(LO 4)

Inglis Limited is a major manufacturer of household appliances. In a recent annual report, the notes to the financial statements included the following comments:

9. Related party transactions

During the year, the Company made sales to and acquired goods and services on normal trade terms from Whirlpool Corporation and its associated companies of $3,816,000 and $24,022,000 respectively. An amount receivable of $108,000 is outstanding from Whirlpool Corporation at the year end. In addition, a subordinated demand promissory note in the amount of $3,792,000 is outstanding to Whirlpool Corporation at the year end, and included in loans and advances.

During the year, Sears Canada Inc. (Sears) sold its equity interest in the Company. At the time of sale, sales to Sears amounted to approximately 30% of the Company's sales to date and this level continued throughout the year.

Why do you think Inglis included the preceding comments in its annual report? What accounting principle might be compromised by related-party transactions?

Provocative Problem 1–4
Bombardier Inc.
(LO 3)

Bombardier Inc. is a Canadian company principally engaged in manufacturing and marketing transportation equipment. The financial statements and related financial information disclosed in Bombardier's 1992 annual report are shown in Appendix I. From your inspection of Bombardier's 1992 financial statements, answer the following questions:

1. What is the closing date of Bombardier's annual accounting period?
2. What amount of net earnings (net income) was earned by Bombardier during the 1992 accounting period?
3. How much cash (plus cash equivalents) was held by the company on January 31st 1992?
4. What was the net amount of cash provided or used from financing activities during 1992?
5. Did the company's investing activities during 1992 result in a net cash inflow or outflow? By what amount?
6. In Bombardier's consolidated statement of financial position, the dollar amounts are rounded to what amount?
7. Comparing 1991 to 1992, did the company's total revenues increase or decrease? By what amount?
8. What amount was reported as shareholders' equity at the end of the 1992 accounting period?
9. Compare 1991 to 1992. What was the change in net income?

Arnold Miller began his Auto Repair Shop the first part of this month. The balance sheet, prepared by an inexperienced part-time bookkeeper is shown below: **A&R Problem 1–1**

MILLER AUTO REPAIR SHOP
Balance Sheet
November 30, 1993

Assets		Liabilities and Owner's Equity	
Cash.	$ 3,600	Parts and supplies	$ 6,300
Accounts payable	19,800	Accounts receivable.	27,000
Equipment.	12,600	Prepaid rent	1,800
Arnold Miller, capital	15,300	Mortgage payable	16,200
Total assets	$51,300	Total equities	$51,300

Required

1. Prepare a correct balance sheet.
2. Explain why the incorrect balance sheet can be in balance.

Marjorie Cahill began the practice of law the first day of October with an initial investment of $5,000 in cash. After completing the first month of practice, the financial statements were being prepared by John Gilbert, the secretary/bookkeeper Ms. Cahill had hired. The statements were completed, and Ms. Cahill almost burst out laughing when she saw them. She had completed a course in legal accounting in law school and knew the statements prepared by Mr. Gilbert left much to be desired. Consequently, she asks you to revise the statements. The Gilbert version is presented below: **A&R Problem 1–2**

MARJORIE CAHILL, LAWYER
Balance Sheet
October 31, 1993

Assets		Owner's Equity	
Cash	$1,800	M. Cahill, capital	$3,500
Prepaid rent.	1,000		
Supplies expense	200		
Accounts payable.	500		
	$3,500		$3,500

MARJORIE CAHILL, LAWYER
Income Statement
For the Month Ended October 31, 1993

Revenues:		
Legal fees.	$5,500	
Accounts receivable	1,000	$6,500
Expenses:		
Salaries expense	$1,400	
Telephone expense	100	
Rent expense	1,000	
Supplies	500	
Law library.	4,000	7,000
Loss		$ 500

Required

Prepare the corrected financial statements for Marjorie Cahill.

As a Matter of
Record

Record Case 1-1

Margaret Philip reports the following in her article "Firm Seeks $14.6 Million, Cars, Phones and Paintings" (*Globe and Mail*, May 25, 1991, p. B1):

> Campeau Corp., the company Robert Campeau founded and ran for more than four decades, is suing him for $14.6 million in cash as well as for the return of paintings, cars, and telephone equipment he used in his capacity as company chairman.
>
> Cash-strapped Campeau is demanding that its ousted chairman promptly return eight works of art—appraised last year at a total of $1.33-million—that have hung on the walls of his Toronto mansion for the past 11 years.
>
> Mr. Campeau and his wife, Ilse, are being asked as well to turn over the keys of a 1984 blue Cadillac, valued at $9,000, and a white Pontiac Safari, valued at $6,000, that they drove while Mr. Campeau was at the company's helm. The lawsuit demands the return of $6,140 of telephone equipment currently installed in Mr. Campeau's home, right down to the jacks.
>
> In two separate lawsuits, Mr. Campeau has been called to repay $14.6 million of overdue loans from the company, some of it borrowed to finance the building of a lavish château on 15.5 acres in the Austrian Alps outside of Salzburg.
>
> A $10 million interest-free and unsecured loan Mr. Campeau borrowed from the company two years ago fell due at the end of January, but remains unpaid. Campeau is seeking repayment of a further 4.6 million in loans—money that was lavished on the Austrian hideaway.

Required

Discuss the accounting principle(s) implicit in the situation described above.

Record Case 1-2

"Ethical Standards Begin at the Top" by Michael Stern (*Globe and Mail*, November 11, 1991, p. B4) is partially reproduced below:

> Scandals at Japanese securities dealers, money-laundering at international banks, misrepresentation at blue-chip brokerage giant Salomon Brothers Inc., fraud and forgery charges against a partner at an Ontario law firm.
>
> Based on the headlines, it is no wonder Decima Research last year found that 45 percent of Canadians consider business leaders unprincipled, compared with 20 percent 10 years ago.
>
> Despite this poor showing, extensive contact with a wide range of business executives indicates to me that companies are quietly adopting higher ethical standards—although they will never be as lily-white as some reformers, academics, or journalists might like.
>
> As a Toronto marketing executive put it: the overriding principle is no longer doing whatever you can get away with. You have to be able to look at yourself in the mirror that next morning.
>
> The pressures vary in each industry, but across Canada, businesses are taking ethical behaviour more seriously. The temptation to bend the rules is always there—but on an individual basis, more executives are struggling with the dilemma and trying to do the right thing.
>
> Helping companies recruit new senior managers puts a search consultant in a good position to trace this shift. Recruitment is the process through which a company finds new executives who share its ideals and values. Before executive search consultants can start looking, they must understand a client firm's corporate culture—and its ethics.
>
> These days, when clients are asked what qualities they value most in a job candidate, the ability to get results is still primary. However, even in confidential con-

versations, it is apparent that we have gone well beyond the day when companies are looking for people who can land a sale at any cost. . . .

One of the best reasons for staying honest is to set the right example. When a company condones lying about its products or overcharging a customer, it virtually invites its employees to rip it off, too. In the end, the best way to discourage cheaters is to demonstrate that they never prosper.

Required

What is your perception of ethics in Canadian business? Support your answer with personal experiences and citations from media reports.

LO 1 *(d)*	LO 4 *(d)*	LO 6 *(b)*	Answers to Objective
LO 2 *(a)*	LO 5 *(e)*	LO 7 *(a)*	Review Questions
LO 3 *(e)*			

Processing Accounting Data

In the next five chapters, we describe the accounting process that starts with an analysis of a business's transactions and ends with the periodic preparation of financial statements. Your careful study of these chapters will pay great dividends. It will make the later parts of the book much easier to understand.

Recording Transactions

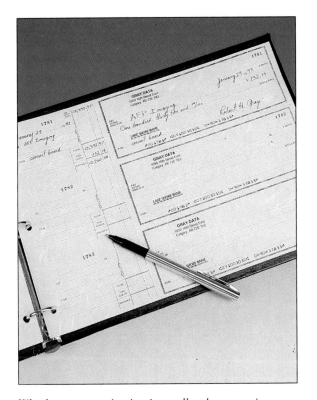

Whether an organization is small or large, an important key to gathering useful information is a system that records the effects of transactions as soon as they occur. Double-entry accounting serves this purpose very well.

*I*n Chapter 1, you were introduced to the accounting equation (Assets = Liabilities + Owner's Equity) and the effect of business transactions on the accounting equation. Now you will learn how the effects of business transactions are recorded and stored in the accounting records. You can use the procedures you learn in this chapter to record the effects of any type of business transactions you may encounter. No matter how unique or complex the business is, you can use these procedures to successfully record its transactions.

We begin this chapter with a discussion of business papers that provide evidence of transactions. Next, we explain how accounts are used to store information and describe several commonly used accounts. We then describe the rules of debit and credit and illustrate how a variety of transactions affect the accounts. With this background in place, we then describe the actual process of recording transactions.

Learning Objectives

After studying Chapter 2, you should be able to:

1. Describe the nature of the events that are recorded in accounting and the importance of business papers in recording those events.

2. Describe the use of accounts to record and store the effects of business transactions, the use of a number to identify each account, and the meaning of the words *debit* and *credit* in relation to T-accounts.

3. State the rules of debit and credit and use those rules to analyze transactions and show their effects on the accounts.

4. Record transactions in a General Journal, describe balance column accounts, and post entries from the journal to the accounts.

5. Prepare and explain the use of a trial balance to discover and correct errors.

6. Define or explain the words and phrases listed in the chapter glossary.

The Accounting Process Starts by Analyzing Economic Events

LO 1 Describe the nature of the events that are recorded in accounting and the importance of business papers in recording those events.

In Chapter 1, we said that accounting provides quantitative (primarily financial) information about economic entities. This information is intended to be useful in economic decision making. The accounting process involves (1) analyzing the economic events of an entity and recording the effects of those events; and (2) classifying and summarizing the recorded effects in reports or financial statements that individuals find useful in making economic decisions about the entity. This process is presented graphically in Illustration 2–1.

Business Transactions

In Illustration 2–1, note that economic events consist of business transactions and other (internal) events. Remember from Chapter 1 that business transactions are completed exchanges of economic consideration between two or more parties. Whenever an entity engages in a business transaction, the trans-

ILLUSTRATION 2–1

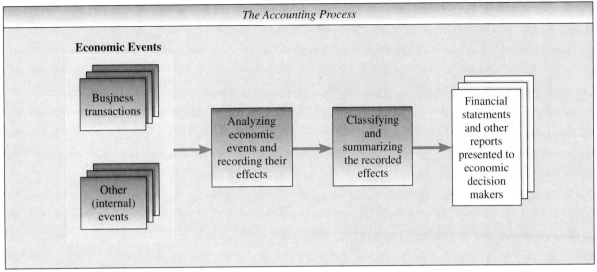

The Accounting Process

Economic Events

Business transactions

Other (internal) events

→ Analyzing economic events and recording their effects

→ Classifying and summarizing the recorded effects

→ Financial statements and other reports presented to economic decision makers

action affects the entity's accounting equation. The accounting process begins by analyzing an entity's transactions to determine their effects on the accounting equation. Then, those effects are recorded in the accounting records, which are sometimes referred to as *the books*. Because business transactions are between the entity and some other (outside) party, they are sometimes called **external transactions.**

Other (Internal) Events

Some economic events affect an entity's accounting equation even though they are not transactions with outside parties. For example, a business uses a machine in its operations. As a result, the remaining usefulness of the machine is decreased. That is, the economic benefit of the machine is partially used up. The using up of the machine's economic benefit is an economic event that decreases the assets and decreases the owner's equity in the business. Internal economic events of this sort are not transactions between two or more parties. Nevertheless, because they affect the accounting equation, they are sometimes called **internal transactions.** The analysis and recording of internal economic events is the central topic of Chapter 3.

Many years ago, most companies used pen and ink to manually record and process the data resulting from transactions. Today, only very small companies use this method. Now, large and small companies use computers in recording transactions and in processing the recorded data. A few companies still use electric bookkeeping machines. These machines were developed years ago as an early step in the path of progress from manual to computerized systems.

Nevertheless, you will begin your study of accounting by learning to process accounting data manually. By manually processing the data, you can more readily understand the importance of each step in the accounting process. Also, the general concepts you learn through manual methods apply equally well to computerized accounting systems.

While taking classes toward her undergraduate degree in accounting, Karen Muñoz accepted a part-time job at a busy fast-food restaurant in a downtown mall. As a new employee, she was trained by the restaurant's assistant manager. Included in the training were instructions about how to operate the cash register. The assistant manager explained that the formal policy is to ring up each sale when an order is placed and the cash is received. But, because of the pressure of the noon-hour rush, it is easier to accept the cash and make change without ringing up the sales.

The assistant manager explained that it is more important to serve the customers promptly so they won't go to another restaurant in the mall. Then, after two o'clock, the assistant manager adds up the cash in the drawer and rings up sufficient sales to equal the amount collected. In this way, the tape in the register always comes out right and there are no problems to explain when the manager arrives at four o'clock to handle the dinner traffic.

Muñoz sees the advantages in this shortcut but wonders whether something is wrong with it. She also wonders what will happen if the manager comes in early and observes her taking this shortcut.

Business Papers

The printed documents that businesses use in the process of completing transactions are called **business papers.** They include such things as sales slips or invoices, cheques, purchase orders, customer billings, employee earnings records, and bank statements. Because they provide evidence of business transactions and are the basis for accounting entries, business papers are also called **source documents.**

For example, if you buy a pocket calculator on your charge account, two or more copies of an invoice or sales ticket are prepared. One copy is given to you. The other is sent to the store's accounting department and becomes the basis for an entry to record the sale. On the other hand, if you pay cash for the calculator and do not charge it, the sale typically is rung up on a cash register that records and stores the amount of each sale. Some cash registers print the amount of each sale on a paper tape locked inside the register and some store the data electronically. In either case, the proper keyboard commands at the end of the day cause the cash register to calculate and print the total cash sales for that day. This printed total becomes the basis for an entry to record the sales.

Business papers such as sales invoices often are used by both the seller and the buyer as a basis for recording the transaction in their accounting records. For example, if you bought the calculator for use in your business, your copy of the invoice or sales ticket would provide the information you would need to record the transaction in the accounting records of your business.

To summarize, business papers are the starting point in the accounting process. Furthermore, verifiable business papers, especially those that originate outside the business, provide objective evidence of completed transactions and the amounts at which they should be recorded. As you learned in Chapter 1, this type of evidence is important because of the *objectivity principle.*

In accounting for an entity, the different effects of its business transactions must be recorded and stored in separate locations so that they can be sorted and combined when financial reports are prepared. These locations in the accounting system are called **accounts.** A number of accounts are normally required. A separate account summarizes the increases and decreases in each asset, liability, and owner's equity item that appears on the balance sheet. Further, a separate account is used for each revenue and expense item that appears on the income statement.

The specific accounts a business uses depend on the assets owned, the debts owed, and the information it needs to obtain from the accounting records. While different businesses use a variety of accounts, the following accounts are widely used.

Storing Information in Accounts

LO 2 Describe the use of accounts to record and store the effects of business transactions, the use of a number to identify each account, and the meaning of the words *debit* and *credit* in relation to T-accounts.

Asset Accounts

If the accounting system is to provide useful information about the different assets of a company, you must keep a separate account for each kind of asset owned. Generally, accounts are maintained for the following common assets.

Cash. Increases and decreases in cash are recorded in a Cash account. The cash of a business consists of money or any medium of exchange that a bank accepts at face value for deposit. Cash includes coins, currency, cheques, and postal and bank money orders. The balance of the Cash account shows both the cash on hand in the store or office and the cash on deposit in the bank.

Accounts Receivable. Goods and services are commonly sold to customers on the basis of oral or implied promises of future payment. Such sales are called *charge sales* or *sales on account,* and the oral or implied promises to pay are called *accounts receivable.* Accounts receivable are increased by charge sales and are decreased by customer payments. Since a company must know the amount currently owed by each customer, a separate record must be kept of each customer's purchases and payments. We discuss this separate record in a later chapter. For the present, however, all increases and decreases in accounts receivable are recorded in a single Accounts Receivable account.

Notes Receivable. A **promissory note** is an unconditional written promise to pay a definite sum of money on demand or on a defined future date (or dates). When amounts due from others are evidenced by promissory notes, the notes are known as *notes receivable.* Depending on how soon it comes due, it is recorded in the Short-Term Notes Receivable account or in the Long-Term Notes Receivable account.

Prepaid Insurance. Insurance contracts normally require payment in advance for protection against fire, liability, or other losses. The amount paid is called a *premium* and the protection lasts for a period of time such as one year or even as much as three years. As a result, a large portion of the premium may be an asset for a considerable time after payment. Since the unexpired amount represents a future benefit to the organization in the protection it provides, the amount is properly classified as an asset.

When an insurance premium is paid in advance, the payment normally is recorded in an asset account called Prepaid Insurance. Thereafter, whenever financial statements are prepared, the cost of the insurance that has expired is calculated and recorded as an expense, and the balance of the Prepaid Insurance account is reduced accordingly.

Office Supplies. Stamps, stationery, paper, pencils, and similar items are called *office supplies*. They are assets when purchased and continue to be assets until used up. As the supplies are used up, their cost becomes an expense. Increases and decreases in the asset are commonly recorded in an Office Supplies account.

Store Supplies. Wrapping paper, cartons, bags, tape, and similar items used by a store to package products for delivery to their customers are called *store supplies*. Increases and decreases in such items are recorded in a Store Supplies account.

Other Prepaid Expenses. When payments are made for economic benefits that do not expire until later, the payments create assets called **prepaid expenses.** Then, as the economic benefits are used up or expire, the assets become expenses. As a practical matter, if a purchased benefit will fully expire before the next income statement is prepared, the payment usually is recorded as an expense. When purchased benefits will not be used up or will not fully expire in the current time period, the payments are recorded in asset accounts as prepaid expenses. Examples of prepaid expenses already mentioned include prepaid insurance, office supplies, and store supplies. Rent that is paid for more than one period in advance is another example. Others include legal fees and management fees paid in advance of receiving the legal or management services. Each type of prepaid expense is accounted for in a separate asset account.

Equipment. Increases and decreases in physical assets such as typewriters, desks, chairs, and office machines are commonly recorded in an Office Equipment account. In a similar manner, physical assets used in the selling operations of a store—for example, counters, showcases, and cash registers—are recorded in a Store Equipment account.

Buildings. A building used by a business in carrying on its operations may be a store, garage, warehouse, or factory. Such assets are commonly recorded in a Buildings account. If several buildings are owned, a separate account may be kept for each building.

Land. A Land account is commonly used to record increases and decreases in the land owned by a business. However, land does not include buildings located on the land. Although the land and the buildings may be physically inseparable, the buildings wear out, or depreciate, while the land on which they are placed does not. Therefore, the land and the buildings must be recorded in separate accounts.

Liability Accounts

Recall from Chapter 1 that liabilities are present obligations to transfer assets or provide services to other entities in the future. A business may have several different liabilities, each of which requires a separate account. The following are common.

Accounts Payable. When purchases are made on the basis of oral or implied promises to pay, the amounts owed are called *accounts payable*. The items purchased on account may be merchandise, supplies, equipment, or services. Since a business must know the amount owed to each creditor, a separate record must be kept of the purchases from and the payments to each creditor. We discuss this individual record in a later chapter. For the present, however, all increases and decreases in accounts payable are recorded in a single Accounts Payable account.

Notes Payable. When an entity makes a formal written promise to pay a definite sum of money on a defined future date (or dates), the liability is called a *note payable*. Depending on how soon the liability must be repaid, it is recorded in a Short-Term Notes Payable account or in a Long-Term Notes Payable account.

Unearned Revenues. As you learned in Chapter 1, the revenue recognition principle states that you should not report revenues on the income statement until the revenues are earned. This rule raises the question of how you should record a cash receipt from a customer for products or services to be delivered at some future date. Because receipts such as this are received in advance of being earned, they are called **unearned revenues.**

An unearned revenue is a liability that will be satisfied by delivering the product or service that was paid for in advance. Examples are subscriptions collected in advance by a magazine publisher, rent collected in advance by a building owner, and legal fees collected in advance by a lawyer. On receipt, the amounts collected are recorded in liability accounts such as Unearned Subscriptions, Unearned Rent, and Unearned Legal Fees. When the products or services are delivered, the amounts earned are transferred to the revenue accounts: Subscriptions Earned, Rent Earned, and Legal Fees Earned.

Other Short-Term Payables. Other examples of short-term payables include wages payable, taxes payable, and interest payable. Each of these items must be recorded in a separate account.

Owner's Equity, Withdrawals, Revenue, and Expense Accounts

In Chapter 1, we illustrated four different types of transactions that affected the owner's equity in a proprietorship. They are (1) investments by the owner, (2) withdrawals of cash or other assets by the owner, (3) revenues, and (4) expenses. Recall that in the illustrations of Chapter 1, all such transactions were entered in a column under the name of the owner. This procedure was used to show the effect of transactions on the accounting equation. However, when we prepared an income statement and a statement of changes in owner's equity in Chapter 1, we had to analyze the items entered in the owner's column. Now you can see that such an analysis is not necessary. All that you need is a separate account for the owner's capital, for the owner's withdrawals, and for each revenue and each expense. Then, as each transaction affecting owner's equity is completed, it is recorded in the proper account. We describe these accounts in the following paragraphs.

Capital Account. When a person invests in his or her own proprietorship, the investment is recorded in an account that carries the owner's name and the word *Capital*. For example, an account called Jerry Dow, Capital, is used to record the investment of Jerry Dow in his law practice. In addition to the original investment, the **capital account** is used for any additional increases or decreases in owner's equity that are expected to be relatively permanent.

Withdrawals Account. Perhaps the most obvious reason why a person might invest in a business is to earn an income. If the business earns an income, the net assets of the business increase. The owner may choose to leave the additional assets invested in the business or may, from time to time, withdraw assets from the business. As the owner withdraws assets for personal uses, both the assets and the owner's equity of the business are reduced.

To record the withdrawal of assets by an owner, use an account that has the name of the owner and the word *Withdrawals*. For example, an account called Jerry Dow, Withdrawals, is used to record the withdrawals of cash by Jerry Dow from his law practice. The **withdrawals account** is also known as the **personal account** or **drawing account.**

In many cases, the owner of an unincorporated business plans to withdraw a fixed amount each week or month. The owner may even think of these withdrawals as a salary. However, in a legal sense, they are not a salary because an unincorporated business is not legally separate from its owner and one cannot contract with oneself. In other words, one cannot hire oneself or pay oneself a salary. Therefore, according to law, such *withdrawals are neither a salary nor an expense of the business; they are simply the opposite of investments by the owner.*

Revenue and Expense Accounts. When you prepare an income statement for an entity, you need to know the amount of each kind of revenue earned and each kind of expense incurred during the period covered by the statement. To accumulate this information, a business may need to use a wide variety of revenue and expense accounts. Furthermore, various businesses may have very different kinds of revenues and expenses. As a result, we cannot possibly list all of the possible revenue and expense accounts that are used. Nevertheless, common examples of revenue accounts are Commissions Earned, Legal Fees Earned, Rent Earned, and Interest Earned. Common examples of expense accounts are Advertising Expense, Store Supplies Expense, Office Salaries Expense, Office Supplies Expense, Rent Expense, Utilities Expense, and Insurance Expense. Note that the title of each account generally indicates the kind of revenue or expense that should be recorded in the account.

To get an idea of the variety of accounts that may be used, you will find a long list of accounts at the back of this text. It is a comprehensive list of all the accounts we have used in writing the exercises and problems in this book.

The Ledger and the Chart of Accounts

The size of a business generally affects the number of accounts that it uses to record its transactions. A small company may get by with as few as two dozen accounts, while a large company may use several thousand accounts. Depending on the accounting system, the accounts may take different forms. In a computerized system, each account is stored on a disk or on a tape. In a manual system, each account is placed on a separate page in a bound or loose-leaf book, or on a separate card in a tray of cards.

Regardless of the physical form the accounts of a business may take, the collection of accounts is called the **ledger.** If the accounts are kept in a book, the book is the ledger. If they are kept on cards in a file tray, the tray of cards is the ledger. In other words, a ledger is simply a group of accounts.

All companies should follow a systematic method of assigning identifying numbers to their accounts. A list of all the accounts used by a company, showing the identifying number assigned to each account, is called a **chart of accounts.** One example of a system that service businesses might use in developing a chart of accounts is to assign numbers as follows (normal order of accounts in the ledger):

Asset accounts, 101 through 199.

Liability accounts, 201 through 299.

Owner's equity accounts, 301 through 399.

Revenue accounts, 401 through 499.

Operating expense accounts, 501 through 699.

Observe that the first (or hundreds) digit of the numbers assigned to asset accounts is 1. The first (or hundreds) digit of the numbers assigned to liability accounts is 2, and so on. In each case, the first digit of an account's number tells its balance sheet or income statement classification. The second and third digits further identify the account. We describe this type of account numbering system more completely in the next chapter.

Using T-Accounts

In its simplest form, an account looks like the letter **T**, as follows:[1]

(Place for the Name of the Item Recorded in This Account)

(Left side)	(Right side)

---

[1] The T-account is used as a convenient tool to illustrate and solve problems. In practice, the balance column account (see Illustration 2–5) is normally used.

Given its shape, this simple form of account is called a *T-account*. Note that the **T** format gives the account a left side, a right side, and a place for the name of the account. The name indicates the type of items or effects to be stored in this particular account. For example, the *Cash* account is the location where all cash increases and decreases are recorded and stored.

When a **T-account** is used to record increases and decreases in an item, the increases are placed on one side of the account and the decreases on the other. By convention, some types of accounts will have the increases recorded on the left side while others will have increases recorded on the right side. For example, recall the transactions of Jerry Dow's law practice discussed in Chapter 1. Many of those transactions affected cash. When the increases and decreases in the cash of Jerry Dow's law practice are recorded in a T-account, they appear as follows:

Cash

Investment	9,000	Purchase of law books	2,500
Legal fees earned	2,200	Purchase of office equipment	5,600
Collection of account receivable	1,700	Rent payment	1,000
		Payment of salary	700
		Payment of account payable	900
		Withdrawal by owner	1,100

Calculating the Balance of an Account

Putting the increases on one side and the decreases on the other makes it easy to determine the balance of an account. To do so, you simply add the increases shown on one side, separately add the decreases on the other side, and then subtract the sum of the decreases from the sum of the increases. Regardless of the type of account, the **account balance** is the difference between its increases and decreases. Thus, the balance of an asset account is the amount of that asset owned by the entity on the date the balance is calculated. The balance of a liability account is the amount owed by the entity on the date of the balance.

In the Cash account for Jerry Dow's law practice, the total increases were $12,900, the total decreases were $11,800, and the account balance is $1,100, as follows:

Cash

Investment	9,000	Purchase of law books	2,500
Legal fee earned	2,200	Purchase of office equipment	5,600
Collection of account receivable	1,700	Rent payment	1,000
		Payment of salary	700
		Payment of account payable	900
		Withdrawal by owner	1,100
Total increases	12,900	Total decreases	11,800
Less decreases	−11,800		
Balance	1,100		

Debits and Credits

Note again that a T-account has a left side and a right side. In accounting, the left side is called the **debit** side, abbreviated "Dr."; and the right side is called the **credit** side, abbreviated "Cr."[2] When amounts are entered on the left side of an account, they are called *debits,* and the account is said to be *debited.* When amounts are entered on the right side, they are called *credits,* and the account is said to be *credited.* The difference between the total debits and the total credits recorded in an account is the *account balance.* The balance may be either a *debit balance* or a *credit balance.* It is a debit balance when the sum of the debits exceeds the sum of the credits. It is a credit balance when the sum of the credits exceeds the sum of the debits.

The words *to debit* and *to credit* should not be confused with *to increase* and *to decrease.* To debit means to enter an amount on the left side of an account. To credit means to enter an amount on the right side. Whether a debit (or credit) is an increase or a decrease depends on the type of account. For example, notice the way in which the investment of Jerry Dow is recorded in the Cash and capital accounts:

Cash		Jerry Dow, Capital	
Investment 9,000			Investment 9,000

When Dow invested $9,000 in his law practice, both the cash of the business and Dow's equity increased. Observe in the accounts that the increase in cash is recorded on the left or debit side of the Cash account, while the increase in owner's equity is recorded on the right or credit side. The transaction is recorded in this manner because of the mechanics of **double-entry accounting,** which we explain in the next section.

In double-entry accounting, every transaction affects and is recorded in two or more accounts. Also, in *recording each transaction, the total amount debited must equal the total amount credited.* Since every transaction is recorded with total debits equal to total credits, the sum of the debit account balances in the ledger should equal the sum of the credit balances. If the sum of the debit balances does not equal the sum of the credit balances, an error has been made. Thus, one by-product of having equal debits and credits is that many errors are easy to detect.

In double-entry accounting, increases in assets are recorded on the debit side of asset accounts. Why do assets have debit balances? There is no specific reason; it is simply a matter of convention. However, since assets have debit balances, we can reason that increases in liabilities and owner's equity must be recorded as credits. This results from the accounting equation, $A = L + OE$, and from the requirement that debits equal credits. In other words, if assets

The Rules of Debit and Credit in Double-Entry Accounting

LO 3 State the rules of debit and credit and use those rules to analyze transactions and show their effects on the accounts.

---

[2] These abbreviations are remnants of 18th-century English practices, when the terms used were *Debitor* and *Creditor.* The abbreviations take the first and last letters from the words, just as is done for *Mister* (Mr.) and *Doctor* (Dr.).

have debit balances, equal debits and credits are possible only if increases in liabilities and owner's equity are recorded on the opposite or credit side. Therefore, increases and decreases in all balance sheet accounts have to be recorded as follows:

Assets		=	Liabilities		+	Owner's Equity	
Debit for increases	Credit for decreases		Debit for decreases	Credit for increases		Debit for decreases	Credit for increases

As pictured in these T-accounts, the rules for recording transactions under a double-entry system may be expressed as follows:

1. Increases in assets are debited to asset accounts; therefore, decreases in assets must be credited.
2. Increases in liability and owner's equity items are credited to liability and owner's equity accounts; therefore, decreases in liabilities and owner's equity must be debited.

Recall from Chapter 1 that owner's equity is increased by the owner's investment and by revenues. Owner's equity is decreased by expenses and by withdrawals. Because of these facts, we offer these additional rules:

3. Investments by the owner of a business are credited to the owner's capital account.
4. Since the owner's withdrawals of assets decrease owner's equity, they are debited to the owner's withdrawals account.
5. Since revenues increase owner's equity, they are credited in each case to a revenue account that shows the kind of revenue earned.
6. Since expenses decrease owner's equity, they are debited in each case to an expense account that shows the kind of expense incurred.

At this stage, you will find it helpful to memorize these rules. You will apply them over and over in the course of your study. Eventually, the rules will become second nature to you.

Transactions Illustrating the Rules of Debit and Credit

The following transactions for Jerry Dow's law practice illustrate how to apply the rules of debit and credit while recording transactions in the accounts. The number before each transaction is used throughout the illustration so that you can identify the transaction in the accounts. Note that the first 11 transactions were used in Chapter 1 to illustrate the effects of transactions on the accounting equation. Five additional transactions (12 through 16) are presented in this chapter.

   To record a transaction, first analyze it to determine which items were increased or decreased. The rules of debit and credit are then applied to determine the debit and credit effects of the increases or decreases. An analysis of each of the following transactions is given to demonstrate the process.

1. On December 1, Jerry Dow invested $9,000 in a new law practice.

Cash		
(1)	9,000	

Jerry Dow, Capital		
	(1)	9,000

Analysis of the transaction: The transaction increased the cash of the practice. At the same time, it increased Dow's equity in the business. Increases in assets are debited, and increases in owner's equity are credited. Therefore, to record the transaction, Cash should be debited and Jerry Dow, Capital, should be credited for $9,000.

2. Purchased books for a law library, paying cash of $2,500.

Cash			
(1)	9,000	(2)	2,500

Law Library		
(2)	2,500	

Analysis of the transaction: The law library is an asset that is increased by the purchase of books; and cash is an asset that is decreased. Increases in assets are debited, and decreases are credited. Therefore, to record the transaction, debit Law Library and credit Cash for $2,500.

3. Purchased office equipment for cash, $5,600.

Cash			
(1)	9,000	(2)	2,500
		(3)	5,600

Office Equipment		
(3)	5,600	

Analysis of the transaction: The asset office equipment is increased, and the asset cash is decreased. Debit Office Equipment and credit Cash for $5,600.

4. Purchased on account from Equip-it Company law library items, $380, and office equipment, $1,280.

Law Library		
(2)	2,500	
(4)	380	

Office Equipment		
(3)	5,600	
(4)	1,280	

Accounts Payable		
	(4)	1,660

Analysis of the transaction: This transaction increased the assets, law library and office equipment, but it also created a liability. Increases in assets are debits, and increases in liabilities are credits. Therefore, debit Law Library for $380 and Office Equipment for $1,280, and credit Accounts Payable for $1,660.

5. Completed legal work for a client and immediately collected a $2,200 fee.

Cash			
(1)	9,000	(2)	2,500
(5)	2,200	(3)	5,600

Legal Fees Earned			
		(5)	2,200

Analysis of the transaction: This revenue transaction increased both assets and owner's equity. Increases in assets are debits, and increases in owner's equity are credits. Since revenues increase owner's equity, revenue accounts are increased with credits. Therefore, debit Cash to record the increase in assets. Credit Legal Fees Earned to increase owner's equity and accumulate information for the income statement.

6. Paid the office rent for December, $1,000.

Cash			
(1)	9,000	(2)	2,500
(5)	2,200	(3)	5,600
		(6)	1,000

Rent Expense			
(6)	1,000		

Analysis of the transaction: The cost of renting the office during December is an expense, the effect of which is to decrease owner's equity. Since decreases in owner's equity are debits, expenses are recorded as debits. Therefore, debit Rent Expense to decrease owner's equity and to accumulate information for the income statement. Also, credit Cash to record the decrease in assets.

7. Paid the secretary's salary for the two weeks ended December 12, $700.

Cash			
(1)	9,000	(2)	2,500
(5)	2,200	(3)	5,600
		(6)	1,000
		(7)	700

Salaries Expense			
(7)	700		

Analysis of the transaction: The secretary's salary is an expense that decreased owner's equity. Debit Salaries Expense to have the effect of decreasing owner's equity and to accumulate information for the income statement. Also, credit Cash to record the decrease in assets.

8. Completed legal work for a client on account and billed the client $1,700 for the services rendered.

Accounts Receivable			
(8)	1,700		

Legal Fees Earned			
		(5)	2,200
		(8)	1,700

Analysis of the transaction: This revenue transaction gave the law practice the right to collect $1,700 from the client, and thus increased assets and owner's equity. Therefore, debit Accounts Receivable for the increase in assets and credit Legal Fees Earned to increase owner's equity and at the same time accumulate information for the income statement.

9. The client paid the $1,700 legal fee billed in transaction 8.

Cash			
(1)	9,000	(2)	2,500
(5)	2,200	(3)	5,600
(9)	1,700	(6)	1,000
		(7)	700

Analysis of the transaction: One asset was increased, and the other decreased. Debit Cash to record the increase in cash, and credit Accounts Receivable to record the decrease in the account receivable, or the decrease in the right to collect from the client.

Accounts Receivable			
(8)	1,700	(9)	1,700

10. Paid Equip-it Company $900 of the $1,660 owed for the items purchased on account in transaction 4.

Cash			
(1)	9,000	(2)	2,500
(5)	2,200	(3)	5,600
(9)	1,700	(6)	1,000
		(7)	700
		(10)	900

Analysis of the transaction: Payments to creditors decrease in equal amounts both assets and liabilities. Decreases in liabilities are debited, and decreases in assets are credited. Debit Accounts Payable and credit Cash.

Accounts Payble			
(10)	900	(4)	1,660

11. Jerry Dow withdrew $1,100 from the law practice for personal use.

Cash			
(1)	9,000	(2)	2,500
(5)	2,200	(3)	5,600
(9)	1,700	(6)	1,000
		(7)	700
		(10)	900
		(11)	1,100

Analysis of the transaction: This transaction reduced in equal amounts both assets and owner's equity. Cash is credited to record the asset reduction; and the Jerry Dow, Withdrawals, account is debited to decrease owner's equity and to accumulate information for the statement of changes in owner's equity.

Jerry Dow, Withdrawals			
(11)	1,100		

12. Signed a contract with Chemical Supply to do its legal work on a fixed-fee basis for $500 per month. Received the fee for the first six months in advance, $3,000.

Cash			
(1)	9,000	(2)	2,500
(5)	2,200	(3)	5,600
(9)	1,700	(6)	1,000
(12)	3,000	(7)	700
		(10)	900
		(11)	1,100

Analysis of the transaction: The $3,000 receipt of cash increased assets but is not a revenue until earned. Receipt of cash before it is earned creates a liability that will be satisfied by doing the client's legal work over the next six months. Record the asset increase by debiting Cash. Record the liability increase by crediting Unearned Legal Fees.

Unearned Legal Fees			
		(12)	3,000

13. Paid a $2,400 premium for liability insurance protection that lasts two years.

Cash

(1)	9,000	(2)	2,500
(5)	2,200	(3)	5,600
(9)	1,700	(6)	1,000
(12)	3,000	(7)	700
		(10)	900
		(11)	1,100
		(13)	2,400

Analysis of the transaction: The advance payment of an insurance premium creates an asset by decreasing another asset. The new asset is recorded with a debit to Prepaid Insurance, and the payment is recorded with a credit to Cash.

Prepaid Insurance

(13)	2,400

14. Purchased office supplies for cash, $120.
15. Paid the December utilities bill for hydro and water, $230.
16. Paid the secretary's salary for the two weeks ended December 26, $700.

Cash

(1)	9,000	(2)	2,500
(5)	2,200	(3)	5,600
(9)	1,700	(6)	1,000
(12)	3,000	(7)	700
		(10)	900
		(11)	1,100
		(13)	2,400
		(14)	120
		(15)	230
		(16)	700

Analysis of the transactions: These transactions are alike because each decreased cash; but they differ in that office supplies are assets while the utilities and secretary's services have been used up and are expenses. The cost of the supplies should be debited to an asset account, while the utilities and the salary should be debited to separate expense accounts. Each transaction involves a credit to Cash.

Office Supplies

(14)	120

Utilities Expense

(15)	230

Salaries Expense

(16)	700

The Accounts and the Equation

Illustration 2–2 shows the accounts of the Dow law practice after the transactions have been recorded in them. The accounts are classified according to the elements of the accounting equation.

ILLUSTRATION 2-2

The Ledger for Jerry Dow, Lawyer

	Assets Cash			=	Liabilities Accounts Payable			+	Owner's Equity Jerry Dow, Capital	
(1)	9,000	(2)	2,500	(10)	900	(4)	1,660		(1)	9,000
(5)	2,200	(3)	5,600	Total	900	Total	1,660			
(9)	1,700	(6)	1,000				−900			
(12)	3,000	(7)	700			Balance	760		**Jerry Dow, Withdrawals**	
		(10)	900						(11) 1,100	
		(11)	1,100							
		(13)	2,400		**Unearned Legal Fees**					
		(14)	120			(12)	3,000		**Legal Fees Earned**	
		(15)	230						(5)	2,200
		(16)	700						(8)	1,700
Total	15,900	Total	15,250						Balance	3,900
	−15,250									
Balance	650									

Jerry Dow, Withdrawals

(11)	1,100

Legal Fees Earned

		(5)	2,200
		(8)	1,700
		Balance	3,900

Accounts Receivable

(8)	1,700	(9)	1,700

Salaries Expense

(7)	700		
(16)	700		
Balance	1,400		

Office Supplies

(14)	120		

Rent Expense

(6)	1,000		

Prepaid Insurance

(13)	2,400		

Utilities Expense

(15)	230		

Law Library

(2)	2,500		
(4)	380		
Balance	2,880		

The accounts in this box involve increases and decreases in owner's equity and are reported on the income statement or the statement of changes in owner's equity.

Office Equipment

(3)	5,600		
(4)	1,280		
Balance	6,880		

In the previous pages, we used the rules of debit and credit to show how a variety of transactions affected the accounts. As a learning exercise, this process of analyzing transactions and recording their effects directly in the accounts is helpful. However, if you use a manual accounting system in the real world, you should not record transactions directly in the accounts. If you attempt to record the effects directly in the accounts and you make errors, the

Transactions Should First Be Recorded in a Journal

ILLUSTRATION 2–3

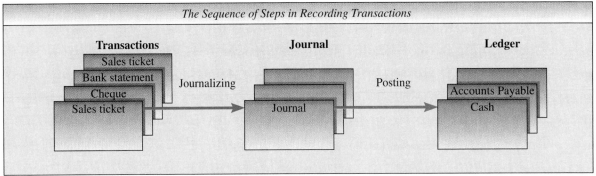

The Sequence of Steps in Recording Transactions

LO 4 Record transactions in a General Journal, describe balance column accounts, and post entries from the journal to the accounts.

errors will be very difficult to locate. Even with a transaction that has only one debit and one credit, the debit is entered on one ledger page or card and the credit on another, and there is nothing to link the two together.

Therefore, *before transactions are recorded in the accounts, they are first entered in a* **journal.** This practice links together the debits and credits of each transaction and provides in one place a complete record of each transaction. Remember this rule: all transactions should be recorded first in a journal. Then, after the transactions are entered in a journal, the debit and credit information about each transaction is copied from the journal to the ledger accounts. These procedures reduce the likelihood of errors. And, if errors are made, the journal record makes it possible to trace the debits and credits into the accounts for the purpose of locating the errors.

The process of recording transactions in a journal is called *journalizing transactions.* The process of copying journal entry information from a journal to a ledger is called **posting.** Remember the sequence of these steps, as shown in Illustration 2–3. Since transactions are first journalized and then posted to the ledger, a journal is called a **book of original entry** and a ledger a **book of final entry.**

The General Journal

The simplest and most flexible type of journal is a **General Journal.** The General Journal is designed so that it can be used to record any kind of transaction. For each transaction, it provides places for recording:

1. The transaction date.
2. The names of the accounts involved.
3. The amount of each debit and credit.
4. An explanation of the transaction.

And, when the amounts are copied from the journal to the accounts in the ledger, the General Journal provides:

5. A column in which to mark the identifying numbers of the accounts to which the debit(s) and credit(s) were copied.

Illustration 2–4 shows a typical general journal page on which the first four transactions of the Dow law practice have been recorded.

ILLUSTRATION 2–4

A General Journal Showing Transactions of Jerry Dow, Lawyer

		GENERAL JOURNAL				Page 1	
Date		**Account Titles and Explanation**	**PR**	**Debit**		**Credit**	
1993 Dec.	1	Cash		9,000	00		
		Jerry Dow, Capital				9,000	00
		Investment by owner.					
	2	Law Library		2,500	00		
		Cash				2,500	00
		Purchased law books for cash.					
	3	Office Equipment		5,600	00		
		Cash				5,600	00
		Purchased office equipment for cash.					
	6	Law Library		380	00		
		Office Equipment		1,280	00		
		Accounts Payable				1,660	00
		Purchased supplies and equipment on credit.					

The last entry in Illustration 2–4 records the credit purchase of law books and office equipment. Note that three accounts are involved in this transaction. When a transaction involves three or more accounts, it is recorded in the General Journal with a **compound journal entry.** That is, a compound journal entry involves three or more accounts.

Recording Transactions in a General Journal

Use the following procedures to record transactions in a General Journal:

1. Write the year in small figures at the top of the first column.
2. Write the month on the first line in the first column. The year and the month are not repeated except at the top of a new page or at the beginning of a new month or year.
3. Write the day of each transaction in the second column on the first line of the transaction.
4. Write the names of the accounts to be debited and credited and an explanation of the transaction in the Account Titles and Explanation column. *The names of the accounts debited are written first, beginning at*

ILLUSTRATION 2–5

A Cash Account Formatted as a Balance Column Account

	Cash				Account No. 101	

Date		Explanation	PR	Debit	Credit	Balance
1993 Dec.	1		G1	9,000 00		9,000 00
	2		G1		2,500 00	6,500 00
	3		G1		5,600 00	900 00
	10		G1	2,200 00		3,100 00

the left margin of the column. *The names of the accounts credited are written on the following lines, indented about one inch.* The explanation is placed on the next line, indented about a half inch from the left margin. The explanation should be short but sufficient to explain the transaction and set it apart from other transactions.

5. Write the debit amount in the Debit column on the same line as the name of the account to be debited. Write the credit amount in the Credit column on the same line as the account to be credited.

6. Skip a single line between each journal entry to keep the entries separate.

When transactions are first recorded in the General Journal, nothing is entered in the **Posting Reference (PR) column.** However, when the debits and credits are copied from the journal to the ledger, the account numbers of the ledger accounts to which the debits and credits are copied are entered in this column. The Posting Reference column is sometimes called the **Folio column.**

Balance Column Accounts

T-accounts like the ones shown so far are used only in textbook illustrations and in accounting classes for demonstrations. In both cases, their use eliminates details and lets you concentrate on ideas. In real-world accounting systems, however, T-accounts are not used. Instead, accounts like the one in Illustration 2–5 are generally used.

The account in Illustration 2–5 is called a **balance column account.** It differs from a T-account because it has columns for specific information about each debit and credit entered in the account. Also, its Debit and Credit columns are placed side by side, and it has a third Balance column. In this Balance column, the account's new balance is entered each time the account is debited or credited. As a result, the last amount in the column is the account's current balance. For example, on December 1, the illustrated Cash account was debited for the $9,000 investment of Jerry Dow, which caused it to have a $9,000 debit balance. It was then credited for $2,500, and its new $6,500 balance was entered. On December 3, it was credited again for $5,600, which reduced its balance to $900. Then, on December 10, it was debited for $2,200, and its balance was increased to $3,100.

When a balance column account like that of Illustration 2–5 is used, the heading of the Balance column does not tell whether the balance is a debit balance or a credit balance. However, this should not create a problem. You should be able to determine the normal balance of any account by reading the account title and recognizing what type of account it is. The following normal balances result from the rules of debit and credit:

Account Classification	Since Increases Are Recorded as:	The Normal Balance Is:
Asset	Debits	Debit
Liability	Credits	Credit
Owner's equity:		
Capital	Credits	Credit
Withdrawals	Debits	Debit
Revenue	Credits	Credit
Expense	Debits	Debit

When an unusual transaction causes an account to have a balance opposite from its normal kind of balance, this abnormal balance is indicated in the account by circling the amount or by indicating the balance as debit or credit. Also, a –0– or 0.00 is written in the Balance column when a debit or credit entered in an account causes the account to have no balance.

Posting Transaction Information

The process of posting journal entry information from the journal to the ledger may be done daily, weekly, or as time permits. In any case, posting should be done without undue delay, and all transactions must be posted before financial statements can be prepared at the end of each accounting period.

In the posting procedure, journal debits are copied and become ledger account debits and journal credits are copied and become ledger account credits. Illustration 2–6 shows the posting procedures for a journal entry. As shown in the illustration, the procedures to post a journal entry are as follows:

For the debit:

1. In the ledger, find the account named in the debit of the journal entry.
2. Enter in the account the date of the entry as shown in the journal.
3. In the Debit column of the account, write the debit amount shown in the journal.
4. Enter the letter *G* and the journal page number from which the entry is being posted in the Posting Reference column of the account. The letter *G* indicates that the amount was posted from the General Journal. We discuss other journals later in the text, and each is identified by its own letter.

ILLUSTRATION 2–6

Procedures to Follow in Posting a General Journal Entry

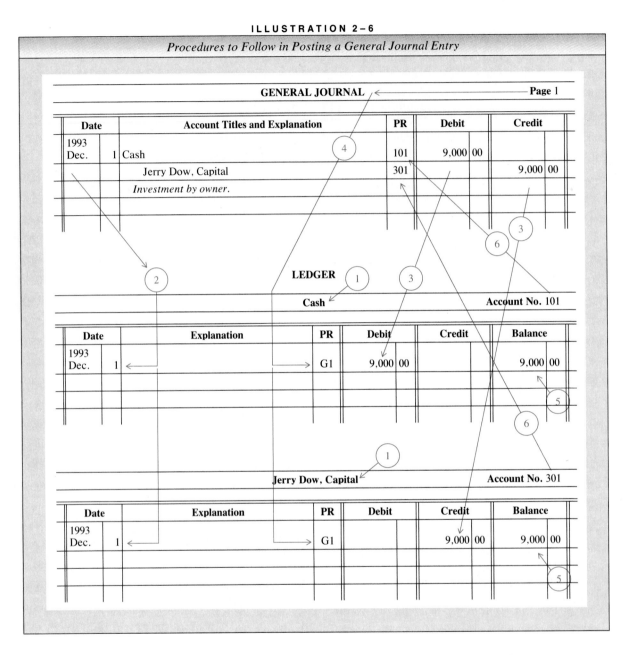

5. Determine the effect of the debit on the account balance and enter the new balance.

6. Enter in the Posting Reference column of the journal the account number of the account to which the amount was posted.

For the credit:

Repeat the preceding steps. However, the credit amount is entered in the Credit column and has a credit effect on the account balance.

ILLUSTRATION 2–7

Trial Balance Drawn from the Ledger of Jerry Dow, Lawyer

JERRY DOW, LAWYER
Trial Balance
December 31, 1993

Cash	$ 650	
Office supplies	120	
Prepaid insurance	2,400	
Law library.	2,880	
Office equipment.	6,880	
Accounts payable		$ 760
Unearned legal fees		3,000
Jerry Dow, capital		9,000
Jerry Dow, withdrawals	1,100	
Legal fees earned.		3,900
Salaries expense	1,400	
Rent expense.	1,000	
Utilities expense	230	
Totals.	$16,660	$16,660

Observe that the last step (step 6) in the posting procedure for either the debit or the credit of an entry is to insert the account number in the Posting Reference column of the journal. Inserting the account number in this column serves two purposes: (1) The account number in the journal and the journal page number in the account act as a cross-reference when you want to trace an amount from one record to the other. (2) Writing the account number in the journal as a last step in posting indicates that posting is completed. If posting is interrupted, the bookkeeper can examine the journal's Posting Reference column to see where posting stopped.

Preparing a Trial Balance

LO 5 Prepare and explain the use of a trial balance to discover and correct errors.

Recall that in a double-entry accounting system, every transaction is recorded with equal debits and credits. As a result, you know that an error has been made if the total of the debits in the ledger does not equal the total of the credits. Also, when the balances of the accounts are determined, the sum of the debit balances must equal the sum of the credit balances; otherwise, you know an error has been made. This equality is tested by preparing a **trial balance**. Preparing a trial balance requires five steps:

1. Determine the balance of each account in the ledger.
2. List the accounts (in order of appearance on the ledger with balances other than zero, with the debit balances in one column and the credit balances in another (see Illustration 2–7).
3. Add the debit balances.
4. Add the credit balances.
5. Compare the sum of the debit balances with the sum of the credit balances.

The trial balance in Illustration 2–7 was prepared from the accounts in Illustration 2–2 on page 87. Note that its column totals are equal; in other words, the trial balance is in balance. Therefore, debits equal credits in the ledger.

The Evidence of Accuracy Offered by a Trial Balance

When a trial balance does not balance, one or more errors have been made. The error(s) may have been in journalizing the transactions, in posting to the ledger, in determining the account balances, in copying the balances to the trial balance, or in adding the columns of the trial balance. On the other hand, if the trial balance balances, the accounts are probably free of those errors that cause an inequality in debits and credits.

However, a trial balance that balances is not proof of complete accuracy. Some errors do not affect the equality of the trial balance columns. For example, you may record a correct debit amount to the wrong account. This error will not cause a trial balance to be out of balance. Another example would be to record a wrong amount with an equal debit and credit. Because errors of this sort do not affect the equality of debits and credits, a trial balance that balances does not prove recording accuracy. It does, however, provide evidence that several types of errors have not been made.

Locating Errors

When a trial balance does not balance, one or more errors have been made. To locate the error or errors, check the journalizing, posting, and trial balance preparation steps in their reverse order. First check the addition of the columns in the trial balance to see that no addition errors were made. Then check to see that the account balances were correctly copied from the ledger. Note that if a debit (or credit) balance was incorrectly listed in the trial balance as a credit (or debit), the difference between total debits and total credits would be twice the amount of the incorrectly listed amount.

Next, recalculate the account balances. If the error or errors are not found at this stage, check the posting and then the original journalizing of the transactions. A common error to look for involves transposing numbers. For example, a $691 debit may have been posted as $619. As a result, total debits would be larger than total credits by $72. That is, $691 − $619 = $72. To test for a transposing error, note that all transposing errors are divisible evenly by nine. Note that 72 is divisible by 9, or 72/9 = 8. Note as well that the numbers reversed are 8 digits apart.

Correcting Errors

When an error is discovered in either the journal or the ledger, it must be corrected. The method of correction depends on the nature of the error and the stage in the accounting procedures at which it is discovered.

If an error is discovered in a journal entry before the error is posted, it may be corrected by ruling a single line through the incorrect amount or account name and writing the correct amount or account name above. Likewise, if a correctly journalized amount was posted incorrectly as a different (wrong) amount, you may correct it in the same manner. However, if a journal entry to the wrong account has been posted to that account, you should correct the error with a new journal entry. The correcting journal entry should transfer the change from the wrong account to the proper account. For example, the following journal entry to record the purchase of office supplies was made and posted:

Oct.	14	Office Equipment	160.00	
		Cash.		160.00
		To record the purchase of office supplies.		

Obviously, the debit of the entry is to the wrong account; therefore, the following entry is needed to correct the error:

Oct.	17	Office Supplies	160.00	
		Office Equipment		160.00
		To correct the entry of October 14 in which the Office Equipment account was debited in error for the purchase of office supplies.		

The debit of the second entry correctly records the purchase of supplies, and the credit cancels the error of the first entry. Note the full explanation of the correcting entry. Such an explanation should always be full and complete so that anyone can see exactly what occurred.

Bookkeeping Techniques

When amounts are entered in a journal or a ledger, it is not necessary to use commas indicating thousands of dollars or decimal points to separate dollars and cents. The ruled lines accomplish this. However, when statements are prepared on unruled paper, you should use decimal points and commas.

Dollar signs are not used in journals or ledgers; however, you should use them on financial reports prepared on unruled paper. On such reports, place a dollar sign (1) before the first amount in each column of figures and (2) before the first amount appearing after a ruled line that indicates an addition or a subtraction. Examine Illustration 3–6, page 142, for examples of the use of dollar signs on a financial report.

When an amount to be entered in a ledger or a journal is an amount of dollars and no cents, some bookkeepers save time by using a dash in the cents column in the place of two zeros to indicate that there are no cents. On financial reports, however, two zeros are preferred.

To save space and simplify some of the illustrations, we often use exact dollar amounts in this text. In such cases, neither zeros nor dashes are used.

Summary of the
Chapter in Terms of
Learning Objectives

LO 1. The economic events recorded in accounting include business transactions and other (internal) events that have an effect on the assets, liabilities, and owner's equity of the entity. Business papers provide evidence of completed transactions and the amounts that should be used to record the transactions.

LO 2. In an accounting system, the different effects of business transactions are stored in separate locations called *accounts*. Commonly used asset accounts include Cash, Notes Receivable, Accounts Receivable, Prepaid Insurance, Office Supplies, Store Supplies, Equipment, Buildings, and Land. Commonly used liability accounts include Notes Payable, Accounts Payable, and Unearned Revenue. The owner's investments in a proprietorship and other relatively permanent changes in the owner's equity are recorded in the owner's capital account. Revenue, expense, and withdrawal accounts are used to accumulate changes in owner's equity.

The collection of accounts used by a business is called a ledger. Each account in the ledger is assigned a unique number to identify the account. The chart of accounts for a business lists all the account titles (and the account numbers) that are used in recording the transactions of the business.

In the accounts, debits record increases in assets, withdrawals, and expenses. Decreases in liabilities, the owner's capital account, and revenues are also recorded with debits. Credits record increases in liabilities, the owner's capital account, and revenues. Credits are also used to record decreases in assets, withdrawals, and expenses.

LO 3. To understand the effects of a transaction on a business, first analyze the transaction to determine what accounts were increased or decreased. Every transaction affects two or more accounts and the sum of the debits always equals the sum of the credits. As a result, the effects of business transactions never violate the accounting equation, Assets = Liabilities + Owner's Equity.

LO 4. A transaction is first recorded in a journal so that all of the transaction's effects on the accounts are shown in one place. The equality of total debits and credits on each page is confirmed. Then, each effect is posted (copied) to the appropriate account in the ledger so that the accounts classify and summarize the effects of all transactions. After each amount is posted, the account number is recorded in the journal and the journal page number is recorded in the account as a cross-reference to assist in the discovery of errors.

LO 5. To prepare a trial balance, list the ledger accounts that have balances, showing the debit and credit balances in separate columns. The columns are totaled to show that the sum of all debit account balances in the ledger equals the sum of all credit account balances. If the totals are not equal, search for the errors that were made and then make appropriate corrections.

This demonstration problem is based on the same facts as the demonstration problem presented at the end of Chapter 1. During its first month of operation, Barbara Schmidt's haircutting business (The Cutlery) completed the following transactions:

a. On August 1, 1993, Schmidt put $2,000 of her savings into a chequing account in the name of The Cutlery.

b. On August 2, The Cutlery bought $600 of supplies for the shop.

c. On August 3, The Cutlery paid $500 rent for the month of August for a small store.

d. On August 5, Schmidt furnished the store, installing new fixtures that the supplier sold to The Cutlery for $1,200. This amount was to be repaid in three equal payments at the end of August, September, and October.

e. The Cutlery opened August 12, and in the first week of business ended August 16, cash receipts from haircutting amounted to $825.

f. On August 17, Schmidt paid $125 to an assistant for working during the business's grand opening.

g. Cash receipts from haircutting during the two-week period ended August 30 amounted to $1,930.

h. On August 31, The Cutlery paid the first installment on the fixtures.

i. On August 31, Schmidt withdrew $900 cash for her personal expenses.

Required

1. Prepare general journal entries to record the preceding transactions.
2. Open the following accounts: Cash, 101; Store Supplies, 125; Store Equipment, 165; Accounts Payable, 201; Barbara Schmidt, Capital, 301; Barbara Schmidt, Withdrawals, 302; Haircutting Services Revenue, 403; Wages Expense, 623; and Rent Expense, 640.
3. Post the journal entries to the proper ledger accounts.
4. Prepare a trial balance for The Cutlery.

Planning the Solution

■ Analyze each transaction to determine which accounts are affected by the transaction and the amount of each effect.

■ Use the rules of debit and credit to prepare a journal entry for each transaction.

■ Transfer each debit and each credit in the journal to the appropriate ledger accounts and cross-reference each posted amount in the Posting Reference columns of the journal and the account.

■ Calculate each account balance and list the accounts with their balances on a trial balance.

■ As evidence of error-free work, observe that total debits equal total credits on the trial balance.

1.

Page 1

	Date		Account Titles and Explanations	PR	Debit	Credit
a.	1993 Aug.	1	Cash. . . . . Barbara Schmidt, Capital . . . . *Invested $2,000 in business.*	101 301	2,000.00	 2,000.00
b.		2	Store Supplies . . . . Cash . . . . *Purchased store supplies.*	125 101	600.00	 600.00
c.		3	Rent Expense . . . . Cash . . . . *Paid rent for August.*	640 101	500.00	 500.00
d.		5	Store Equipment. . . . . Accounts Payable. . . . . *Purchased fixtures on credit.*	165 201	1,200.00	 1,200.00
e.		16	Cash . . . . Haircutting Services Revenue . . . . *Cash sales to customers.*	101 403	825.00	 825.00
f.		17	Wages Expense . . . . Cash . . . . *Paid wages to assistant.*	623 101	125.00	 125.00
g.		30	Cash . . . . Haircutting Services Revenue . . . . *Two weeks' sales to customers.*	101 403	1,930.00	 1,930.00
h.		31	Accounts Payable . . . . Cash . . . . *Paid first payment on store equipment purchase of August 5.*	201 101	400.00	 400.00
i.		31	Barbara Schmidt, Withdrawals . . . . Cash . . . . *Withdrew cash for personal use.*	302 101	900.00	 900.00

2, 3.

Cash **Account No. 101**

Date		Explanation	PR	Debit	Credit	Balance
1993 Aug.	1		G1	2,000		2,000
	2		G1		600	1,400
	3		G1		500	900
	16		G1	825		1,725
	17		G1		125	1,600
	30		G1	1,930		3,530
	31		G1		400	3,130
	31		G1		900	2,230

Store Supplies   Account No. 125

Date		Explanation	PR	Debit	Credit	Balance
1993 Aug.	2		G1	600		600

Store Equipment   Account No. 165

Date		Explanation	PR	Debit	Credit	Balance
1993 Aug.	5		G1	1,200		1,200

Accounts Payable   Account No. 201

Date		Explanation	PR	Debit	Credit	Balance
1993 Aug.	5		G1		1,200	1,200
	31		G1	400		800

Barbara Schmidt, Capital   Account No. 301

Date		Explanation	PR	Debit	Credit	Balance
1993 Aug.	1		G1		2,000	2,000

Barbara Schmidt, Withdrawals   Account No. 302

Date		Explanation	PR	Debit	Credit	Balance
1993 Aug.	31		G1	900		900

Haircutting Services Revenue   Account No. 403

Date		Explanation	PR	Debit	Credit	Balance
1993 Aug.	16		G1		825	825
	30		G1		1,930	2,755

Wages Expense   Account No. 623

Date		Explanation	PR	Debit	Credit	Balance
1993 Aug.	17		G1	125		125

Rent Expense   Account No. 640

Date		Explanation	PR	Debit	Credit	Balance
1993 Aug.	3		G1	500		500

4.

THE CUTLERY
Trial Balance
August 31, 1993

Cash	$2,230	
Store supplies.	600	
Store equipment	1,200	
Accounts payable.		$ 800
Barbara Schmidt, capital		2,000
Barbara Schmidt, withdrawals	900	
Haircutting services revenue		2,755
Wages expense	125	
Rent expense	500	
Totals	$5,555	$5,555

Glossary

Account balance the difference between the increases and decreases recorded in an account. p. 80

Accounts separate locations in an accounting system each one of which is used to store the increases and decreases in a different type of revenue, expense, asset, liability, or owner's equity item. p. 75

Balance column account an account that has debit and credit columns for entering changes in the account and a third column for entering the new account balance after each debit or credit is posted to the account. pp. 90–91

Book of final entry a ledger in which amounts are posted from a journal. p. 88

Book of original entry a journal in which transactions are first recorded. p. 88

Business papers printed documents that businesses use in the process of completing business transactions and that provide evidence of the transactions; sometimes called *source documents*. p. 74

Capital account an account used to record the owner's investments in the business plus any more or less permanent changes in the owner's equity. p. 78

Chart of accounts a list of all the accounts used by a company, showing the identifying number assigned to each account. p. 79

Compound journal entry a journal entry that has more than one debit and/or more than one credit. p. 89

Credit the right side of an account, or entries that decrease asset and expense accounts, or increase liability, owner's equity, and revenue accounts. pp. 81–82

Debit the left side of an account, or entries that increase asset and expense accounts, or decrease liability, owner's equity, and revenue accounts. pp. 81–82

Double-entry accounting a system of accounting in which each transaction affects and is recorded in two or more accounts with total debits equal to total credits. p. 81

Drawing account another name for the *withdrawals account*. p. 78

External transactions completed exchanges of economic consideration between the entity being accounted for and some other outside parties. p. 73

Folio column another name for the *Posting Reference column*. p. 90

General Journal a book of original entry designed flexibly so that it can be used to record any type of transaction. pp. 88–90

Internal transactions a name sometimes given to economic events that have an effect on an entity's accounting equation but that do not involve transactions with outside parties. p. 73

Journal a book of original entry in which a complete record of transactions is first recorded and from which transaction amounts are posted to the ledger accounts. p. 88

Ledger a group of accounts used by a business in recording its transactions. p. 79

Personal account another name for the *withdrawals account*. p. 78

Posting transcribing the debit and credit amounts from a journal to the ledger accounts. p. 88

Posting Reference (PR) column a column in a journal and in each account that is used for cross-referencing amounts that have been posted from a journal to the account. Also called a *folio column*. p. 90

Prepaid expenses assets created by payments for economic benefits that do not expire until some later time; then, as the benefits expire or are used up, the assets become expenses. p. 76

LO 6 Define or explain the words and phrases listed in the chapter glossary.

Promissory note a formal written promise to pay a definite sum of money on demand or at a fixed or determinable future date. p. 75

Source documents another name for *business papers*. p. 74

T-account a simple form of account that is widely used in accounting education to illustrate the debits and credits required in recording a transaction. pp. 79–81

Trial balance a list of the accounts that have balances in the ledger, the debit or credit balance of each account, the total of the debit balances, and the total of the credit balances. p. 93

Unearned revenues liabilities created by the receipt of cash from customers in payment for products or services that have not yet been delivered to the customers; the liabilities will be satisfied by delivering the product or service. p. 77

Withdrawals account the account used to record the transfers of assets from a business to its owner; also known as *personal account* or *drawing account*. p. 78

Synonymous Terms

Business papers source documents.

Journal book of original entry.

Ledger book of final entry.

Posting Reference column folio column.

Withdrawals account drawing account; personal account.

Objective Review

Answers to the following questions are listed at the end of this chapter. Be sure that you decide which is the one best answer to each question *before* you check the answers.

LO 1 Examples of the source documents used in accounting are:

a. Journals and ledgers.

b. Income statements and balance sheets.

c. External transactions and internal transactions.

d. Bank statements and sales slips.

e. All of the above.

LO 2 The following are commonly used accounts: (1) Prepaid Rent, (2) Unearned Legal Fees, (3) Buildings, (4) Owner, Capital, (5) Wages Payable, (6) Owner, Withdrawals, (7) Office Supplies. These accounts should be classified as assets, liabilities, or owner's equity as follows:

	Assets	Liabilities	Owner's Equity
a.	1,3,7	2,5	4,6
b.	1,3,7	2,5,6	4
c.	1,3,7	5,6	2,4
d.	1,7	5,6	2,3,4
e.	1,7	2,5	3,4,6

LO 3 The requirements of double-entry accounting are such that:

a. All transactions that involve debits to asset accounts must also involve credits to liability or owner's equity accounts.

b. Each transaction is recorded with total debits equal to total credits.

c. The total debits of all recorded transactions equal the total credits of all re-corded transactions.

d. The effects on the balance sheet equation of external transactions can be re-corded but the effects of other economic events, sometimes called internal transactions, cannot be recorded.

e. Both (*b*) and (*c*) are correct.

LO 4 When David Shipman started his business, he invested $15,000 cash plus some land that had a fair market value of $23,000. Also, the business assumed re-sponsibility for a note payable of $18,000 that was issued to finance the purchase of the land. In recording Shipman's investment:

a. The entry will consist of one debit and one credit.

b. The entry will consist of two debits and one credit.

c. The entry will consist of two debits and two credits.

d. The entry will consist of debits that total $38,000 and credits that total $33,000.

e. None of the above answers is correct.

LO 5 A trial balance shows total debits of $14,000 and total credits of $17,000. Which of the following errors would explain this situation?

a. A journal entry that debited Wages Expense for $1,500 was incorrectly posted to the ledger account as a credit.

b. A journal entry that debited Wages Expense for $3,000 was incorrectly posted to the ledger account as a credit.

c. A journal entry that credited Services Fees Earned for $1,500 was incorrectly posted to the ledger account as a debit.

d. A journal entry that credited Services Fees Earned for $3,000 was incorrectly posted to the ledger account as a debit.

e. None of the above is correct.

LO 6 A list of all the accounts used by a company, showing the identifying number assigned to each account, is called:

a. A journal.

b. A ledger.

c. A trial balance.

d. A source document.

e. A chart of accounts.

Questions for Class Discussion

1. What two types of economic events affect an entity's accounting equation?

2. What are the two fundamental steps in the accounting process?

3. Why are business papers called *source documents?*

4. Why is the evidence provided by business papers important to accounting?

5. What is an account? What is a ledger?

6. What types of transactions increase the owner's equity in a business? What types decrease owner's equity?

7. Does debit always mean increase and credit always mean decrease?

8. If a transaction has the effect of decreasing an asset, is the decrease recorded as a debit or as a credit? If the transaction has the effect of decreasing a liability, is the decrease recorded as a debit or as a credit?

9. Why are some accounting systems called *double-entry* accounting systems?

10. What entry (debit or credit) would you make to (*a*) increase a revenue, (*b*) decrease an expense, (*c*) record an owner's withdrawals, and (*d*) record an owner's investment?

11. Why are the rules of debit and credit the same for both liability and owner's equity accounts?

12. Why is a trial balance prepared?

13. What kinds of errors would cause the column totals of a trial balance to be unequal? What are some examples of errors that would not be revealed by a trial balance?

14. Should transactions be recorded first in a journal or first in the ledger? Why?

15. What is the purpose of posting reference numbers that are entered in the journal at the time entries are posted to the accounts?

Mini Discussion Case

Case 2-1

Jessica and Andrew, students in accounting class, were overheard discussing problems they encountered in the first test after Chapter 2. Their problem centered around their inability to understand the rules of debit and credit. They just could not understand why, when they deposit their allowances at the Campus Bank, their accounts are credited, reflecting an increase in the amount of money they have on deposit. When they withdraw money from the bank their accounts are debited, reflecting a decrease in the amount of money they have left on deposit. Yet in their class and in their textbook they are told just the opposite.

The two students decided to go to their instructor for a resolution of their dilemma. The instructor welcomed them and began to explain their apparent problem.

Required

Put yourself in the position of the instructor and explain to Jessica and Andrew the source of their problem and why the rules of debit and credit are correct as stated in the textbook.

Exercises

Exercise 2-1
Increases, decreases, and normal balances of accounts
(LO 2, 3)

Prepare the following columnar form. Then enter the word *debit* or *credit* in each of the last three columns to indicate the action necessary to increase the account, to indicate the action necessary to decrease the account, and to show the normal balance of the account.

Kind of Account	Increases	Decreases	Normal Balance
Asset			
Liability			
Owner's capital			
Owner's withdrawals			
Revenue			
Expense			

Indicate the necessary action (debit or credit) to increase or decrease each of the following accounts:

a. To decrease Cash.

b. To increase owner's withdrawals account.

c. To decrease Rent Expense.

d. To increase Accounts Payable.

e. To decrease the owner's capital account.

f. To decrease Prepaid Insurance.

g. To decrease Unearned Legal Fees.

h. To increase Rent Earned.

i. To increase Office Equipment.

Exercise 2–2
Actions to increase or decrease different accounts
(LO 2, 3)

On March 12, Karen Tucker billed a client $40,000 for construction consulting services. The client did not have enough cash to pay the bill and asked Ms. Tucker to accept ownership of a building valued at $75,000 and to assume responsibility for a $35,000 note payable. Ms. Tucker agreed. The effects of the March 12 transaction on Ms. Tucker's accounts would include which of the following:

a. A $40,000 increase in an asset account.

b. A $75,000 increase in Ms. Tucker's capital account.

c. A $35,000 increase in a revenue account.

d. A $75,000 increase in a revenue account.

e. A $35,000 increase in a liability account.

Exercise 2–3
Analyzing the effect of a transaction on the accounts
(LO 3)

Place the following T-accounts on a sheet of notebook paper: Cash; Accounts Receivable; Office Supplies; Office Equipment; Accounts Payable; J. J. Wright, Capital; Services Revenue; and Utilities Expense. Then record these transactions by entering debits and credits directly in the accounts. Use the transaction letters to identify amounts entered in the accounts.

a. J. J. Wright began a service business, called N. E. Time, by investing $3,500 in the business.

b. Purchased office supplies for cash, $90.

c. Purchased office equipment on account, $2,800.

d. Received $500 cash for services provided to a customer.

e. Paid for the office equipment purchased in transaction *c.*

f. Billed a customer $400 for services provided to the customer.

g. Paid the monthly utility bills, $60.

h. Collected $200 of the amount owed by the customer of transaction *f.*

Exercise 2–4
Showing the effect of transactions on T-accounts
(LO 3)

Exercise 2-5
Preparing a trial balance
(LO 5)

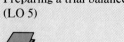

After recording the transactions of Exercise 2–4, prepare a trial balance for N. E. Time. Use the current date.

Exercise 2-6
Trial balance errors
(LO 5)

Prepare a form with the following three column headings: (1) Error, (2) Amount Out of Balance, and (3) Column Having Larger Total. Then for each of the following errors: (1) in the first column list the error by letter, (2) in the second column show the difference in the trial balance column totals that will result from the error, and (3) in the third column indicate which trial balance column (debit or credit) will have the larger total as a result of the error. If the error does not affect the trial balance, write *none* in each of the last two columns.

a. A $500 debit to Prepaid Rent was debited to Rent Expense.
b. A $230 debit to Automobiles was debited to Accounts Payable.
c. A $90 credit to Cash was credited to the Cash account twice.
d. A $128 debit to Utilities Expense was posted as a $120 debit.
e. A $25 debit to Office Supplies was not posted.
f. A $440 credit to Fees Earned was posted as a $400 credit.

Exercise 2-7
Analyzing a trial balance
error
(LO 5)

A trial balance does not balance. In looking for the error, you notice that Office Equipment has a debit balance of $15,600. However, you discover that a transaction for the purchase of a computer for $1,100 had been recorded with a $1,100 credit to Office Equipment and a $1,100 credit to Accounts Payable. Answer each of the following questions, giving the dollar amount of the misstatement, if any.

a. Was the balance of the Office Equipment account overstated, understated, or correctly stated in the trial balance?
b. Was the balance of the Accounts Payable account overstated, understated, or correctly stated in the trial balance?
c. Was the debit column total of the trial balance overstated, understated, or correctly stated?
d. Was the credit column total of the trial balance overstated, understated, or correctly stated?
e. If the debit column total of the trial balance was $142,000 before the error was corrected, what was the total of the credit column?

Exercise 2-8
Preparing a corrected trial
balance
(LO 5)

A careless bookkeeper prepared the following trial balance, which does not balance, and you have been asked to prepare a corrected trial balance. In examining the records of the concern you discover the following: (1) The debits to the Cash account total $62,850, and the credits total $57,120. (2) A $280 receipt of cash from a customer in payment of the customer's account was not posted to Accounts Receivable. (3) A $70 purchase of shop supplies on account was entered in the journal but was posted only to Accounts Payable. (4) The bookkeeper made a transposition error in copying the balance of the Services Revenue account in the trial balance. The correct amount was $40,270.

WANDA'S WELDING SHOP
Trial Balance
December 31, 1993

Cash.	$ 5,930	
Accounts receivable.		$ 6,660
Shop supplies	2,800	
Shop equipment.	11,200	
Accounts payable	1,800	
Wanda Wong, capital	12,930	
Wanda Wong, withdrawals	19,800	
Services revenue		42,070
Rent expense		7,800
Advertising expense.	1,220	
Totals	$55,680	$56,530

1. During the month of February, Sun Company had cash receipts of $37,000 and cash disbursements of $36,500. The February 28 cash balance was $8,400. Calculate the beginning (January 31) cash balance.

2. On January 31, Sun Company had an Accounts Receivable balance of $16,000. During the month of February, total credits to Accounts Receivable were $20,000, which resulted from customer payments. The February 28 Accounts Receivable balance was $24,000. Calculate the amount of credit sales during February.

3. Fred Dukes, the owner of Sun Company, had a capital account balance of $40,000 on January 31 and $34,000 on February 28. Net income for the month of February was $11,000. Calculate the owner's withdrawals during February.

Exercise 2–9
Analyzing account entries and balances
(LO 2, 3)

The following accounts contain seven transactions keyed together with letters. Write a short explanation of each transaction with the amount or amounts involved.

Exercise 2–10
Analyzing transactions from T-accounts
(LO 2, 3)

Cash			
(a)	3,500	(b)	1,800
(e)	1,250	(c)	300
		(f)	1,200
		(g)	350

Camera Equipment		
(a)	2,800	
(d)	4,700	

Carol Reed, Capital		
	(a)	11,800

Photography Supplies		
(c)	300	
(d)	100	

Darkroom Equipment		
(a)	5,500	

Photography Fees Earned		
	(e)	1,250

Prepaid Rent		
(b)	1,800	

Accounts Payable			
(f)	1,200	(d)	4,800

Advertising Expense		
(g)	350	

Prepare a form like Illustration 2–4 and then prepare general journal entries to record the following transactions. Omit the year in the journal date column.

Exercise 2–11
General Journal entries
(LO 4)

Mar. 1   Tom Waits invested $5,000 in cash and an automobile having a $35,000
          fair value in a limousine service he called Star Limousines.
      1   Rented furnished office space and paid for six months in advance, $1,200.
      2   Purchased a cellular phone for the limo for cash, $900.
      15 Chauffeured clients for two weeks and collected $2,500 in fees.
      31 Paid for gas and oil used in the limousine during March, $260.

Exercise 2–12
T-accounts and the trial
balance
(LO 3, 5)

1. Open T-accounts for each of the following items: Cash; Prepaid Rent; Automo-
    biles; Equipment; Tom Waits, Capital; Fees Earned; and Gas and Oil Expense.
2. Post the transactions of Exercise 2–11 to the T-accounts. Omit posting reference
    numbers.
3. Prepare a trial balance of the T-accounts.

Exercise 2–13
Analyzing and journalizing
revenue transactions
(LO 5)

Examine each of the following transactions and prepare general journal entries to record only the revenue transactions. Explain why the remaining transactions are not
revenue transactions.

a.   Received $1,500 cash for orthodontic services provided to customer.
b.   Received $2,500 cash from Robin Walker, the owner of the business.
c.   Received $300 from a customer in partial payment of his account receivable.
d.   Rendered orthodontic services to a customer on credit, $600.
e.   Borrowed $10,000 from the bank by signing a promissory note.
f.   Received $1,600 from a customer in payment for services to be rendered next
       year.

Exercise 2–14
Analyzing and journalizing
expense transactions
(LO 4)

Examine each of the following transactions and prepare general journal entries to record only the expense transactions. Explain why the remaining transactions are not
expense transactions.

a.   Paid $1,500 cash for shop equipment.
b.   Paid $2,400 in partial payment for supplies purchased 30 days previously.
c.   Paid utility bill of $310.
d.   Paid $900 to owner of the business for his personal use.
e.   Paid $750 wages of shop employee.

Problems

Problem 2–1
Recording transactions in
T-accounts; preparing a
trial balance
(LO 2, 3, 5)

April Stewart opened an advertising business and during a short period as an agent
completed these business transactions:

a.   Invested $50,000 in cash and office equipment with a $20,000 fair value in an
       advertising agency she called Stewart Advertising.
b.   Purchased land valued at $60,000 and a small office building valued at
       $230,000, paying $43,500 cash and signing a long-term note payable to pay the
       balance over a period of years.
c.   Purchased office supplies on account, $480.

d. Stewart contributed her personal automobile, which had a $17,200 fair value, for exclusive use in the business.

e. Purchased additional office equipment on account, $2,500.

f. Paid the office secretary's salary, $800.

g. Sold an advertisement and collected a $3,500 cash fee on the sale.

h. Paid $450 for a magazine advertisement that had already appeared.

i. Paid for the supplies purchased on account in transaction *c*.

j. Purchased a new typewriter for the business, paying $1,000 cash plus an old typewriter carried in the accounting records at $200.

k. Completed a marketing research assignment on account and billed the client $1,300.

l. Paid the secretary's salary, $800.

m. Received payment in full for the marketing research of transaction *k*.

n. Stewart withdrew $1,800 from the business to pay personal expenses.

Required

1. Open the following T-accounts: Cash; Accounts Receivable; Office Supplies; Automobiles; Office Equipment; Building; Land; Accounts Payable; Long-Term Notes Payable; April Stewart, Capital; April Stewart, Withdrawals; Advertising Fees Earned; Marketing Research Fees Earned; Office Salaries Expense; and Advertising Expense.

2. Show the effects of the transactions on the accounts by entering debits and credits directly in the accounts. Use the transaction letters to identify each debit and credit amount.

3. Determine the balance of each account in the ledger and prepare a trial balance using the current date.

Alan Meaken began business as a surveyor and during a short period completed these business transactions:

Problem 2–2
Recording transactions in T-accounts; preparing a trial balance
(LO 2, 3, 5)

a. Began business by investing cash, $20,000; office equipment, $3,000; and surveying equipment, $45,000.

b. Purchased land for an office site, $19,000. Paid $3,800 in cash and signed a long-term note payable for the balance.

c. Purchased for cash a used prefabricated building and moved it onto the land for use as an office, $8,000.

d. Prepaid the annual premium on two insurance policies, $4,800.

e. Completed a surveying job and collected $800 cash in full payment.

f. Purchased additional equipment costing $3,700. Gave $700 in cash and signed a long-term note payable for the balance.

g. Completed a surveying job on account for Kilmer Contractors, $2,100.

h. Purchased additional office equipment on account, $250.

i. Completed a surveying job for Valley Hospital on account, $3,150.

j. Received and recorded as an account payable a bill for rent on special machinery used on the Valley Hospital job, $150.

k. Received $2,100 from Kilmer Contractors for the work of transaction *g*.

l. Paid the wages of the surveying assistant, $840.

m. Paid for the office equipment purchased in transaction *h*.

n. Paid $350 cash for repairs to a piece of surveying equipment.

o. Alan Meaken wrote a $260 cheque on the bank account of the business to pay for repairs to his personal automobile. (The car is not used for business purposes.)

p. Paid the wages of the surveying assistant, $880.

q. Paid fee to county for surveying permits, $150.

Required

1. Open the following T-accounts: Cash; Accounts Receivable; Prepaid Insurance; Office Equipment; Surveying Equipment; Building; Land; Accounts Payable; Long-Term Notes Payable; Alan Meaken, Capital; Alan Meaken, Withdrawals; Surveying Fees Earned; Wages Expense; Machinery Rental Expense; Permits Expense; and Repairs Expense, Surveying Equipment.

2. Record the transactions by entering debits and credits directly in the accounts. Use the transaction letters to identify each debit and credit. Prepare a trial balance using the current date and titled Alan Meaken, Surveyor.

Problem 2–3
Posting from General Journal entries; preparing a trial balance
(LO 4, 5)

Kay Martinez, Public Accountant, completed these business transactions during June of the current year:

June 1 Began a public accounting practice by investing $5,700 in cash and office equipment having an $8,100 fair value.

1 Prepaid three months' rent in advance on suitable office space, $2,250.

2 Purchased on account office equipment, $800, and office supplies, $300.

4 Completed accounting work for a client and immediately received payment of $350 cash.

8 Completed accounting work on account for Bank One, $1,700.

10 Paid for the items purchased on account on June 2.

14 Paid the annual $2,400 premium on an insurance policy.

18 Received payment in full from Bank One for the work completed on June 8.

24 Completed accounting work on account for Turner Construction, $400.

28 Martinez withdrew $1,000 cash from the practice to pay personal expenses.

29 Purchased additional office supplies on account, $120.

30 Paid the June utility bills, $210.

Required

1. Open the following accounts: Cash; Accounts Receivable; Office Supplies; Prepaid Insurance; Prepaid Rent; Office Equipment; Accounts Payable; Kay Martinez, Capital; Kay Martinez, Withdrawals; Accounting Fees Earned; and Utilities Expense.

2. Prepare General Journal entries to record the transactions.

3. Post to the accounts.

4. Prepare a trial balance. Title the trial balance Kay Martinez, Public Accountant.

Mike Leaman completed these business transactions during April of the current year:

Problem 2–4
Journalizing, posting, and
preparing a trial balance
(LO 4, 5)

Apr. 1 Began an engineering firm by investing cash, $25,000; drafting supplies, $700; and office and drafting equipment, $18,500.

1 Prepaid two months' rent in advance on suitable office space, $3,100.

3 Paid the annual premium on an insurance policy taken out in the name of the business, $2,400.

4 Purchased drafting equipment, $680, and drafting supplies, $90, on credit.

9 Delivered a set of plans to a contractor and collected $4,000 cash in full payment.

15 Paid the draftsman's salary, $960.

16 Completed and delivered a set of plans to the City of North York on account, $7,800.

18 Purchased drafting supplies on account, $40.

19 Paid for the equipment and supplies purchased on Apr. 4.

26 Received $7,800 from the city of North York for the plans delivered on Apr. 16.

27 Mike Leaman withdrew $2,000 from the business for personal use.

28 Paid for the supplies purchased on Apr. 18.

29 Completed engineering work for Acme Construction on credit, $1,400.

30 Paid the draftsman's salary, $960.

30 Paid the April utility bill, $170.

30 Paid the blueprinting expenses incurred in April, $110.

Required

1. Open the following accounts: Cash; Accounts Receivable; Drafting Supplies; Prepaid Insurance; Prepaid Rent; Office and Drafting Equipment; Accounts Payable; Mike Leaman, Capital; Mike Leaman, Withdrawals; Engineering Fees Earned; Salaries Expense; Blueprinting Expense; and Utilities Expense.

2. Prepare and post General Journal entries to record the transactions. Prepare a trial balance, titling it Mike Leaman, Engineer.

Colin Wong completed these business transactions during November of the current year:

Problem 2–5
Journalizing, posting,
and preparing financial
statements
(LO 4, 5)

Nov. 1 Began a new veterinary practice by investing $27,000 in cash and medical equipment having a $20,500 fair value.

1 Rented the furnished office of a veterinarian who was retiring because of illness, and paid the rent (expense) for November, $1,600.

1 Took out a malpractice insurance policy giving one year's protection and paid the premium (expense) for the month of November, $1,500.

3 Purchased medical supplies on account, $580.

9 Completed work and immediately collected $2,400 cash for the work.

13 Paid for the medical supplies purchased on November 3.

16 Completed work for Ed Albe on account, $700.

23 Completed work for Pat Gillespie on account, $200.

26 Received $700 from Ed Albe for the work completed on Nov. 16.

28 Colin Wong wrote a $70 cheque on the bank account of the practice to pay his home telephone bill.

Nov. 29   Purchased additional medical supplies on account, $340.

    30   Paid the November telephone bill of the office, $80.

    30   Paid the salaries of the receptionist and assistant, $2,350.

    30   Prepaid the rent on the office for December and January, $3,200.

    30   Prepaid the malpractice insurance premium for the next three months, $4,500.

Required

1. Open the following accounts: Cash; Accounts Receivable; Medical Supplies; Prepaid Insurance; Prepaid Rent; Medical Equipment; Accounts Payable; Colin Wong, Capital; Colin Wong, Withdrawals; Veterinary Fees Earned; Salaries Expense; Insurance Expense; Rent Expense; and Telephone Expense.

2. Prepare general journal entries to record the transactions, post to the accounts, and prepare a trial balance titled Colin Wong, DVM.

3. Prepare an income statement for the month ended November 30.

4. Prepare a statement of changes in owner's equity for the month ended November 30.

5. Prepare a balance sheet dated November 30.

Problem 2–6
Analytical essay
(LO 3)

Review the facts provided in Problem 2–2 and focus on transactions *h* and *o*. Explain how the effects of transaction *h* on the balance sheet, income statement, and statement of changes in owner's equity differ from the effects of transaction *o*. Also discuss how your explanation would be changed if Meaken had used the $260 from transaction *o* to pay for renting a machine that was used in the business.

Problem 2–7
Analytical essay
(LO 3, 5)

Review the facts provided in Problem 2–3 and assume that certain mistakes had been made in journalizing and posting the transactions. Explain the effects of each of the following errors on the account balances listed in the trial balance and on the trial balance column totals:

a. The June 1 investment by Martinez was journalized correctly but the debit to Cash was posted to the Cash account as $7,500.

b. The June 4 transaction was incorrectly recorded as a receipt of cash for work that was to be done the next year.

c. In journalizing the June 14 transaction, the account that should have been debited was credited and the account that should have been credited was debited.

d. In posting the June 29 transaction, the debit was correctly posted but the credit was not posted.

e. The $210 payment on June 30 was incorrectly journalized as a $120 payment.

Alternate Problems

Problem 2–1A
Recording transactions in T-accounts; preparing a trial balance
(LO 2, 3, 5)

April Stewart completed these agency transactions during a short period:

a. Opened an advertising agency by investing the following assets at their fair values: cash, $15,000; office equipment, $5,500; automobile, $9,000; land, $27,500; and building, $120,000. The business should also assume responsibility for a $100,000 long-term promissory note that was given to the bank to finance the purchase of the land and building.

b. Purchased office supplies, $100, and additional office equipment, $700, on account.

c. Collected a $6,500 fee for an advertising campaign for a client.

d. Purchased additional office equipment on account, $1,100.

e. Paid for advertising that had appeared in a national magazine, $1,800.

f. Traded the agency's automobile and $10,000 in cash for a new automobile.

g. Paid the office secretary's salary, $850.

h. Paid for the supplies and equipment purchased in transaction b.

i. Completed a marketing research assignment for a client on account, $800.

j. Collected a $2,950 fee from the sale of an advertisement for a client.

k. The client of transaction i paid $400 of the amount owed.

l. Paid the secretary's salary, $850.

m. Paid $475 for a magazine advertisement that had already appeared.

n. Stewart withdrew $1,500 from the business for personal use.

Required

1. Open the following T-accounts: Cash; Accounts Receivable; Office Supplies; Automobiles; Office Equipment; Building; Land; Accounts Payable; Long-Term Notes Payable; April Stewart, Capital; April Stewart, Withdrawals; Advertising Fees Earned; Marketing Research Fees Earned; Office Salaries Expense; and Advertising Expense.

2. Record the transactions by entering debits and credits directly in the accounts. Use the transaction letters to identify the amounts in the accounts.

3. Determine the balance of each account in the ledger and prepare a trial balance under the name Stewart Advertising and using the current date.

Alan Meaken completed these business transactions during a short period:

Problem 2–2A
Recording transactions in T-accounts; preparing a trial balance
(LO 2, 3, 5)

a. Began business as a surveyor by investing cash, $18,000; office equipment, $2,800; and surveying equipment, $19,200.

b. Purchased for $24,000 land to be used as an office site. Paid $4,800 in cash and signed a long-term promissory note for the balance.

c. Purchased additional surveying equipment costing $13,950. Paid $4,650 in cash and signed a long-term promissory note for the balance.

d. Paid $5,400 cash for a used prefabricated building and moved it on the land for use as an office.

e. Completed a surveying job and immediately collected $2,300 in cash for the work.

f. Prepaid the premium on an insurance policy giving one year's protection, $660.

g. Completed a $1,650 surveying job for Ace Contractors on account.

h. Paid the wages of the surveying assistant, $890.

i. Paid $190 cash for repairs to surveying equipment.

j. Received $1,650 from Ace Contractors for the work of transaction g.

k. Completed a $750 surveying job for Benton Real Estate Company on account.

l. Received and recorded as an account payable a $130 bill for the rental of special machinery used on the Ace Contractors job.

m. Purchased additional office equipment on account, $500.

n. Alan Meaken withdrew $350 from the business for personal use.

o. Paid the wages of the surveying assistant, $740.

p. Paid the $130 account payable resulting from renting the machine of transaction *l.*

q. Paid for surveying permits acquired from the county, $260.

Required

1. Open the following T-accounts: Cash; Accounts Receivable; Prepaid Insurance; Office Equipment; Surveying Equipment; Building; Land; Accounts Payable; Long-Term Notes Payable; Alan Meaken, Capital; Alan Meaken, Withdrawals; Surveying Fees Earned; Wages Expense; Machinery Rental Expense; Permits Expense; and Repairs Expense, Surveying Equipment.

2. Record the transactions by entering debits and credits directly in the accounts. Use the transaction letters to identify each debit and credit. Prepare a trial balance using the current date and headed Alan Meaken, Surveyor.

Problem 2–3A
Posting from General Journal entries; preparing a trial balance
(LO 4, 5)

Kay Martinez began a public accounting practice and completed these business transactions during September of the current year:

Sept. 1 Invested $5,000 in a public accounting practice begun this day.

1 Rented suitable office space and prepaid two months' rent in advance, $1,600.

2 Purchased office supplies, $140, and office equipment, $4,750, on account.

4 Paid the annual premium on a liability insurance policy, $900.

6 Completed accounting work for a client and immediately collected $580 in cash for the work done.

12 Completed accounting work for Toronto Savings on account, $1,400.

16 Purchased additional office supplies on account, $35.

22 Received $1,400 from Toronto Savings for the work completed on September 12.

25 Kay Martinez withdrew $600 from the accounting practice to pay personal expenses.

29 Completed accounting work for Alice's Restaurant on account, $700.

30 Made an installment payment of $1,000 on the equipment and supplies purchased on September 2.

30 Paid the September utility bills of the accounting practice, $180.

Required

1. Open the following accounts: Cash; Accounts Receivable; Office Supplies; Prepaid Insurance; Prepaid Rent; Office Equipment; Accounts Payable; Kay Martinez, Capital; Kay Martinez, Withdrawals; Accounting Fees Earned; and Utilities Expense.

2. Prepare General Journal entries to record the transactions.

3. Post to the accounts.

4. Prepare a trial balance titled Kay Martinez, Public Accountant.

Mike Leaman completed these business transactions during July of the current year:

Problem 2–4A
Journalizing, posting, and
preparing a trial balance
(LO 4, 5)

July 1 Began an engineering firm by opening a bank account in the name of the business, Mike Leaman, Engineer, and deposited $14,700 therein.

1 Rented suitable office space and prepaid six months' rent in advance, $4,800.

2 Purchased for $6,500 office and drafting equipment under an agreement calling for a $1,500 down payment and the balance in monthly installments. Paid the down payment and recorded the account payable.

4 Purchased drafting supplies for cash, $270.

8 Completed and delivered a set of plans to a contractor and immediately received $2,900 cash in full payment.

12 Paid the annual premium on a liability insurance policy, $1,500.

14 Purchased on account additional drafting supplies, $60, and drafting equipment, $230.

15 Paid the salary of the draftsman, $750.

17 Completed and delivered a set of plans to Ridgemont School District on account, $2,000.

21 Paid in full for the supplies and equipment purchased on July 14.

25 Completed additional engineering work for Ridgemont School District on account, $900.

27 Received $2,000 from Ridgemont School District for the plans delivered on July 17.

28 Mike Leaman withdrew $1,300 cash from the business to pay personal expenses.

31 Paid the salary of the draftsman, $750.

31 Paid the July utility bills, $90.

31 Paid $80 cash for blueprinting expense.

Required

1. Open the following accounts: Cash; Accounts Receivable; Drafting Supplies; Prepaid Insurance; Prepaid Rent; Office and Drafting Equipment; Accounts Payable; Mike Leaman, Capital; Mike Leaman, Withdrawals; Engineering Fees Earned; Salaries Expense; Blueprinting Expense; and Utilities Expense.

2. Prepare General Journal entries to record the transactions, post to the accounts, and prepare a trial balance.

Colin Wong completed these business transactions in August of the current year:

Problem 2–5A
Journalizing, posting, and
preparing financial
statements
(LO 4, 5)

Aug. 1 Began a veterinary practice by investing $10,000 in cash and medical equipment having a $4,200 fair value.

1 Rented the furnished office of a veterinarian who was retiring and paid the rent (expense) for August, $1,000.

2 Purchased medical equipment costing $6,600 under an agreement calling for a $2,000 down payment and the balance in monthly installments. Paid the down payment and recorded the remaining $4,600 as an account payable.

5 Purchased medical supplies on account, $1,760.

6 Took out a malpractice insurance policy giving one year's protection and paid the premium (expense) for the month of August, $900.

Aug. 8   Completed work for clients and immediately collected $1,350 for the work done.

12   Paid for the medical supplies purchased on account on August 5.

16   Completed work for Richard Tuck on account, $550.

22   Colin Wong wrote a $300 cheque on the bank account of the practice to pay for plumbing repairs of his personal residence.

24   Received $550 from Richard Tuck for the work completed July 16.

26   Completed work for clients on account, $3,440.

30   Paid the telephone bill of the practice, $210.

31   Paid the salary of the office receptionist, $1,200.

31   Prepaid the rent on the office for September and October, $2,000.

31   Prepaid the malpractice insurance premium for the next two months, $1,800.

Required

1. Open the following accounts: Cash; Accounts Receivable; Medical Supplies; Prepaid Insurance; Prepaid Rent; Medical Equipment; Accounts Payable; Colin Wong, Capital; Colin Wong, Withdrawals; Veterinary Fees Earned; Salaries Expense; Insurance Expense; Rent Expense; and Telephone Expense.

2. Prepare general journal entries to record the transactions, post to the accounts, and prepare a trial balance titled Colin Wong, DVM.

3. Prepare an income statement for the month ended August 31.

4. Prepare a statement of changes in owner's equity for the month ended August 31.

5. Prepare a balance sheet dated August 31.

Problem 2–6A
Analytical essay
(LO 3)

Review the facts provided in Problem 2–2A and focus on transactions *n* and *o*. Explain how the effects of transaction *n* on the balance sheet, income statement, and statement of changes in owner's equity differ from the effects of transaction *o*. Also discuss how your explanation would be changed if Meaken had used the $350 from transaction *n* to purchase equipment for use in the office.

Problem 2–7A
Analytical essay
(LO 3, 5)

Review the facts provided in Problem 2–3A and assume that certain mistakes had been made in journalizing and posting the transactions. Explain the effects of each of the following errors on the account balances listed in the trial balance and on the trial balance column totals:

a. The September 1 investment of $5,000 by Martinez was incorrectly recorded as a $3,000 investment.

b. The September 6 transaction was incorrectly recorded as work done on credit.

c. In journalizing the September 16 transaction, the account that should have been debited was credited and the account that should have been credited was debited.

d. In posting the September 29 transaction, the debit was correctly posted but the credit was not posted.

e. The $180 payment on September 30 was incorrectly journalized as an $18 payment.

(This problem is continued in Chapters 3, 4, and 5. Do not assign this problem unless the Working Papers are being used.)

On October 1, 1993, John Conard started a computer service company named Precision Computer Services. Precision is organized as a single proprietorship, with Conard doing consulting services, computer system installations, and computer program development to meet specific customer needs. Conard expects to prepare financial statements for the first time on December 31, 1993. To begin accounting for the business, Conard opened the following general ledger accounts.

Accounts	Number
Cash	101
Accounts receivable	106
Computer supplies	126
Prepaid insurance	128
Prepaid rent	131
Office equipment	163
Computer equipment	167
Accounts payable	201
John Conard, capital	301
John Conard, withdrawals	302
Computer services revenue	403
Wages expense	623
Advertising expense	655
Mileage expense	676
Miscellaneous expenses	677
Repairs expense, computer	684
Telephone expense	688
Utilities expense	690

Required

Journalize and post the following transactions completed by Precision Computer Services during October and November.

Oct. 1 John Conard invested $5,000 personal cash in the business, along with a $3,000 computer and $340 of office equipment.

2 Rented office space in the Town Hall Shopping Centre for $225 per month and paid four months' rent in advance.

3 Purchased computer supplies on account for $50 from Ajax Supply Company.

4 Paid one year's premium on a fire/theft and liability insurance policy, $195.

5 Billed Ball Company $500 for work this week installing a new computer.

8 Paid for the computer supplies purchased from Ajax Supply.

10 Hired an assistant, Ann White, for $70 a day, as needed. She will start on October 15 and will be paid every other Friday.

12 Withdrew $600 for personal expenses.

12 Worked this week again at Ball Company and billed them for $750.

15 Received $500 from Ball Company for work performed the first week of October.

17 Purchased $25 of parts to repair Precision's computer, which was damaged in the move to the new office.

Oct. 18   Billed AB Company for computer services performed this week, $1,000.

19   Paid $15 for an advertisement in the Shopper Newspaper announcing Precision's grand opening.

22   Received the $750 billed to Ball Company on October 12.

23   Received $250 cash from Dog Enterprise for computer services.

24   Completed work for Ear Hearing and billed them $425.

25   Paid Ann White for six days' work.

25   Purchased on account from Ajax Supply additional computer supplies for $55.

28   Billed Call Company for computer services, $725.

30   Paid the hydro bill for the month, $47, and the telephone bill, $115.

30   Paid $600 to John Conard for personal use.

Nov. 1   Reimbursed Ann White's business car mileage, 150 km at $0.24 per km.

1   Reimbursed John Conard's business car mileage, 450 km at $0.24 per km.

4   Received $425 from Ear Hearing for work done on October 24.

5   Received $300 cash from Dog Enterprise for computer services.

6   Received $1,000 from AB Company, billed on October 18.

7   Purchased an additional $45 of computer supplies from Ajax Supply. Paid for both this purchase and the one on October 25.

8   Billed Farm Research for services, $895.

8   Paid Ann White for five days' work.

11   Notified by AB Company that Precision's bid of $1,500 was accepted and began work this day.

13   Received a notice from Republic Bank that a $4 service charge had been deducted from Precision's chequing account.

15   Paid John Conard $600 as a withdrawal.

18   Paid John Conard's home water bill, $35.

20   Received $500 from Call Company against the bill dated October 28.

22   Gave a $10 donation to the Canadian Cancer Society on behalf of Precision.

22   Paid Ann White for six days' work.

25   Completed work begun on November 11 for AB Company and billed them for the amount due.

27   Sent another bill to Call Company for the past due amount of $225 related to billing on October 28.

28   Paid the hydro bill for the month, $49, and the telephone bill, $118.

28   Paid $650 to John Conard as a withdrawal.

29   Reimbursed Ann White's business car mileage, 200 km at $0.24 per km.

29   Reimbursed John Conard's business car mileage, 500 km at $0.24 per km.

Sheila Lyon operates a landscape architecture business. Through the month of October, the accounting records for the business had been maintained by a public accountant. Those records showed that Lyon's October 31 capital balance was $25,000. However, Lyon believed that the public accountant had overcharged for her work in the past. As a result, Lyon decided to keep her own records. At the end of November, she prepared the following statements. She was shocked to discover how unprofitable her business had become, and asked you to review the statements. You should prepare new financial statements, including a statement of changes in owner's equity.

Provocative Problem 2–1
Sheila Lyon, Landscape
Architect
(LO 2)

SHEILA LYON, LANDSCAPE ARCHITECT
Income Statement
For Month Ended November 30, 19--

Revenue:

Unearned landscape architecture fees		$ 2,000
Investments by owner		1,000
Total		$ 3,000

Operating expenses:

Rent expense	$ 700	
Telephone expense	200	
Professional library	1,800	
Utilities expense	100	
Withdrawals by owner	2,000	
Travel and entertainment expense	1,400	
Insurance expense	300	
Total operating expenses		6,500
Net income (loss)		$(3,500)

SHEILA LYON, LANDSCAPE ARCHITECT
Balance Sheet
November 30, 19--

Assets		Liabilities	
Cash	$ 1,300	Accounts payable	$ 800
Accounts receivable	900	Landscape architecture	
Prepaid insurance	600	fees earned	6,000
Prepaid rent	1,400	Short-term notes payable	16,000
Office supplies	100	Total liabilities	$22,800
Buildings	27,000		
Land	12,000	**Owner's Equity**	
Salaries expense	1,000	Sheila Lyon, capital	21,500
		Total liabilities and	
Total assets	$44,300	owner's equity	$44,300

Paul Jensen opened a new business as a computer instructor and completed a number of transactions during April, the first month of operation. He recorded all transactions with double entries in just two accounts, Cash and Income Summary. At the end of the first month, he asks you to review his records and improve his ledger. Based on the following information, you should present a compound General Journal entry dated April 30 to show your corrections and improvements.

Provocative Problem 2–2
Jensen's Computer
Classes
(LO 2, 4)

Cash   Acct. No. 101

Date		Explanation	PR	Debit	Credit	Balance
Apr.	1	Investment by owner.	G1	6,000		6,000
	1	Purchased computer equipment.	G1		4,200	1,800
	1	Purchased office equipment.	G1		1,000	800
	5	Signed short-term note payable				
		to bank.	G1	2,000		2,800
	11	Paid for April office rental.	G1		400	2,400
	14	Received cash for lessons given.	G1	600		3,000
	14	Paid wages of assistant.	G1		270	2,730
	27	Received cash for May lessons.	G1	1,200		3,930
	28	Purchased computer supplies.	G1		200	3,730
	29	Received cash for lessons given.	G1	800		4,530
	29	Paid wages of assistant.	G1		230	4,300
	30	Withdrew cash for personal use.	G1		800	3,500

Income Summary   Acct. No. 901

Date		Explanation	PR	Debit	Credit	Balance
Apr.	1		G1		6,000	6,000
	1		G1	4,200		1,800
	1		G1	1,000		800
	5		G1		2,000	2,800
	11		G1	400		2,400
	14		G1		600	3,000
	14		G1	270		2,730
	27		G1		1,200	3,930
	28		G1	200		3,730
	29		G1		800	4,530
	29		G1	230		4,300
	30		G1	800		3,500

Provocative Problem 2–3
Wind Jammin'
(LO 4, 5)

Barry Young, a graduate student, has just completed the first summer's operation of a concession on Paradise Lake, where he rents sailboats and sells T-shirts, caps, and sunglasses. He began the summer's operation with $7,000 in cash and a five-year lease on a boat dock and a small concession building on the lake. The lease requires a $1,800 annual rental, although the concession is open only from June 1 through August 31. On opening day, Barry paid the first year's rent and purchased three sailboats at $900 each, paying cash.

During the summer, he purchased T-shirts, caps, and sunglasses costing $5,750, all of which were paid for by summer's end, except for T-shirts purchased for $180 during the last week's operation. By summer's end, he had paid utility bills, $220, and wages of a part-time helper, $1,000. He had also withdrawn $160 of earnings of the concession each week for 12 weeks for personal expenses.

He took in $5,460 in sailboat rentals during the summer and sold $8,340 worth of T-shirts, caps, and sunglasses. All of this was collected in cash, except $200 owed by The Captain's Club for T-shirts for its members.

On August 31, when he closed for the summer, Barry was able to return to the sunglasses company several pairs of sunglasses for which he received a $150 cash refund. However, he had to take home for personal consumption a number of T-shirts and caps that cost $90 and that could have been sold for $135. He then sold the three sailboats to a used sporting goods dealer for $300 each.

Prepare an income statement showing the results of the summer's operations, a statement of changes in owner's equity, and an August 31 balance sheet. Head the statements Wind Jammin'. (T-accounts may be helpful in organizing the data.)

On graduation from high school last summer, Cliff Sands needed a job to earn a portion of his first-year university expenses. He was unable to find anything satisfactory and decided to go into the construction cleanup business. He had $160 in a savings account that he used to buy a wheelbarrow, tools, and supplies. However, to haul the debris from the construction site to a dump, he needed a truck. Consequently, he borrowed $2,400 from a bank by signing a short-term promissory note that had an interest rate of 1% per month in exchange for a secondhand truck.

　From the beginning, he had as much work as he could do, and after two months, he repaid the bank loan plus two months' interest. On August 28, he ended the business after exactly three months' operations. Throughout the summer, he followed the practice of depositing in the bank all cash received from customers. An examination of his chequebook record showed he had deposited $4,050. He had written cheques to pay $180 for gas, oil, and lubricants used in the truck, and a $90 cheque for dumping fees. A notebook in the truck contained copies of credit card tickets that showed the business owed $40 for additional gas and oil used in the truck. The notebook also showed that customers owed Cliff $150 for services. He decided to give his equipment and tools to his parents, and estimated they had a fair value of $100. He received a good offer on the truck and sold it for $2,500. Under the assumption that Cliff had withdrawn $300 from the business during the summer for spending money and to buy clothes, prepare an income statement showing the results of the summer's operations. Also prepare a statement of changes in owner's equity and an August 28 balance sheet. Head the statements Cliff's Clean Up Service. (T-accounts should be helpful in organizing the data.)

Provocative Problem 2–4
Cliff's Clean Up Service
(LO 4, 5)

Debra Widmark began a real estate agency, and completed seven transactions. The transactions included a cash investment by Widmark, a purchase on account, and other cash transactions. After completing these transactions, she prepared the trial balance that follows. Analyze the trial balance and prepare a list describing each transaction and its amount. (Hint: T-accounts may help.)

Provocative Problem 2–5
Widmark Real Estate Agency
(LO 2, 5)

DEBRA WIDMARK, REALTOR
Trial Balance
November 7, 1993

Cash	$ 4,620	
Office supplies	230	
Prepaid insurance	1,400	
Office equipment.	5,000	
Accounts payable		$ 5,000
Debra Widmark, capital		6,110
Debra Widmark, withdrawals	13,000	
Commissions earned		15,890
Advertising expense	2,750	
Totals	$27,000	$27,000

The financial statements and related financial information disclosed in Bombardier's 1992 annual report are shown in Appendix I. Based on your examination of those statements, answer the following questions:

Provocative Problem 2–6
Bombardier Inc.

1. Bombardier reported different types of revenue. What were they?
2. Bombardier's current asset account balances reported different items. What were they?
3. The current liability account balances reported different items. What were they?
4. How much provision for income tax expense was recorded by Bombardier in 1992? In 1991?

Provocative Problem 2–7
As a Matter of Ethics:
Essay

Ethics

Review the "As a Matter of Ethics" case on page 74. Discuss the nature of the problem faced by Karen Muñoz and evaluate the alternative courses of action she should consider.

Analytical and Review Problems

A&R Problem 2–1

Mary Pearson just dismissed her inexperienced bookkeeper and asked you to help out until she finds a replacement. Since you had a few days off during your winter break, you agreed to see Pearson through a proper trial balance. Pearson was grateful for your offer and turned over all the accounting records. You found that the trial balance prepared by the bookkeeper (shown below) was nothing more than a listing of account balances.

PEARSON COMPANY
Trial Balance
December 31, 1993

Cash.	$ 2,820
Accounts receivable.	23,660
Supplies.	1,830
Prepaid rent	2,000
Accounts payable	1,530
M. Pearson, capital	12,000
M. Pearson, withdrawals	5,940
Service revenue	33,200
Salaries expense.	8,900
Insurance expense.	600
Miscellaneous expenses.	420
Total.	$92,900

After classifying the accounts into debit and credit balances, you found that the trial balance did not balance. Consequently, you examined the accounting records. In searching back through the accounting records, you discovered that the accounts as listed had normal balances and that the following errors were made by the bookkeeper.

a. An entire entry was not posted. It included a debit to Cash and a credit to Accounts Receivable for $220.

b. In computing the balance of Accounts Payable, a credit of $100 was omitted from the computation.

c. In copying Pearson's Capital account, the bookkeeper entered $12,000 instead of $11,400, the correct amount in the ledger.

d. A withdrawal of $30 by Pearson was posted as a credit to Pearson's withdrawal account.

e. Supplies of $200 were debited to Prepaid Rent when purchased.

Required

Prepare a corrected trial balance for the Pearson Company as of December 31, 1993.

Brandon Russo opened Russo's Sports Consulting business on October 1, 1993, with a cash investment of $10,000. He relied on a student to do his bookkeeping. The student properly journalized all of the October entries; however, because of inexperience and interruptions, the student made posting errors and ommissions. The following T-accounts represent Russo's ledger as of October 31, 1993:

A&R Problem 2–2

Cash*					Accounts Receivable			
Oct. 1	10,000	Oct. 1	1,200		Oct. 15	2,000	Oct. 25	1,000
8	1,400	14	800		29	2,400		
22	1,500	18	3,000					
		28	800					

Supplies			Prepaid Rent	
		Oct. 3	400	Oct. 1	12,000

Accounts Payable				Consulting Revenue		
Oct. 3	400	Oct. 18	300		Oct. 8	1,400
					15	2,000
					22	1,500
					29	2,400

Wages Expense	
Oct. 14	800
28	800

* Cash count on October 31 showed a $10,800 balance.

Required

1. Identify the probable errors and omissions the student bookkeeper made.
2. Prepare a trial balance on the assumption that the errors and omissions you identified in (1) above are corrected.

LO 1 (*d*)	LO 3 (*e*)	LO 5 (*a*)
LO 2 (*a*)	LO 4 (*c*)	LO 6 (*e*)

Answers to Objective
Review Questions

3

Adjusting the Accounts and Preparing the Statements

Although most economic events that affect an organization occur as external transactions, other kinds of events also change its assets, liabilities, and net income. The adjusting process records these events so that the financial statements present more useful information.

A t the beginning of Chapter 2, we recognized that an entity's accounting equation is affected by business transactions and by other (internal) economic events. The primary focus of Chapter 2 was to teach the double-entry process of recording the effects of business transactions. This process involves journalizing the transactions in a book of original entry and then posting to the accounts. In studying Chapter 3, you will learn that some of the account balances that result from recording business transactions must be adjusted. These adjustments are recorded so that the entity's internal economic events will be reflected in the account balances.

Learning Objectives

After studying Chapter 3, you should be able to:

1. Explain why the life of a business is divided into accounting periods of equal length and why unrecorded economic events require adjustments at the end of each period.
2. Explain why adjustments are required by the revenue recognition and matching principles and why the accrual basis of accounting is preferred to a cash basis.
3. Prepare adjusting entries for prepaid expenses, amortization, unearned revenues, accrued expenses, and accrued revenues.
4. Show the effects of making adjustments by preparing a schedule that reconciles the unadjusted and adjusted trial balances and by preparing financial statements from the adjusted trial balance.
5. Prepare entries to record cash receipts and cash disbursements of items that were recorded at the end of the previous period as accrued expenses and accrued revenues.
6. Define each asset and liability classification appearing on a balance sheet, classify balance sheet items, and prepare a classified balance sheet.
7. Define or explain the words and phrases listed in the chapter glossary.

After studying Appendix A at the end of Chapter 3, you should be able to:

8. Explain why some companies record prepaid and unearned items in income statement accounts and prepare adjusting entries when this procedure is used.

LO 1 Explain why the life of a business is divided into accounting periods of equal length and why unrecorded economic events require adjustments at the end of each period.

The life of a business often spans many years, during which its activities go on without interruption. However, decision makers such as managers and investors cannot wait for the business to conclude its operations before they evaluate its financial progress. Instead, they expect a business to provide financial reports periodically. To accomplish this, the accounting process is based on a **time period principle.** In other words, the activities of a business are identified as occurring during specific time periods such as months or three-month periods or years. Then, financial reports that show the results of operations are prepared for each period. Since this division of the life of a business into time periods is done for accounting purposes, the time periods are called **accounting periods.** The primary accounting period used by most businesses is one year, for which they prepare annual financial statements. However, businesses also prepare **interim financial reports** based on one-month or three-month accounting periods.

Businesses do not always adopt the calendar year ending December 31 as the annual accounting period. They may adopt a period of any 12 consecutive months. The specific 12-month period that a business adopts as its annual accounting period is called the **fiscal year.** In choosing a fiscal year, businesses that do not have much seasonal fluctuation in their sales volume often choose the calendar year. Those that have wide fluctuations in volume tend to choose their **natural business year,** which ends when business activities are at their lowest ebb. For example, in department stores, the natural business year begins on February 1, after the Christmas and January sales, and ends the following January 31. Therefore, the annual accounting periods of department stores commonly begin on February 1 and end the following January 31. The Oshawa Group Limited uses 52- or 53-week fiscal periods; thus, the last three fiscal periods (1992, 1991, and 1990) ended on January 25, 26, and 27.

Need for Adjustments at the End of an Accounting Period

At the end of an accounting period, after all transactions are recorded, several of the accounts in a company's ledger typically do not show proper end-of-period balances for presentation in the financial statements. This occurs even though all transactions were recorded correctly. The balances must be updated for statement purposes, not because errors have been made, but because internal economic events have occurred and have not yet been recorded.

One event of this type involves costs that expire with the passage of time. For example, the third item on the trial balance of Dow's law practice, as prepared in Chapter 2 and reproduced again as Illustration 3–1, is "Prepaid insurance, $2,400." This $2,400 represents the insurance premium for two years. The insurance protection began on December 1. However, by December 31, $2,400 is not the correct balance sheet amount for this asset. During December, one month's insurance ($2,400/24 = $100) was used up, or expired, and became an expense. Only $2,300, or ($2,400 − $100), remains as an asset. Likewise, the $120 balance in Office Supplies includes the cost of some supplies that have been used up and become an expense during December. Also, the items in the law library have a limited useful life and part of their usefulness expired during December. Therefore, part of the $2,880 cost of the law library should be reported as expense during December. Likewise, the office equipment has begun to wear out and some of its cost should be charged to December. Because of these events, the balances of the Prepaid Insurance, Office Supplies, Law Library, and Office Equipment accounts are not the proper amounts to appear on the December 31 balance sheet. These items must be *adjusted* before financial statements are prepared.

ILLUSTRATION 3–1

Trial Balance Drawn from the Ledger of Jerry Dow, Lawyer

JERRY DOW, LAWYER
Trial Balance
December 31, 1993

Cash	$ 650	
Office supplies	120	
Prepaid insurance	2,400	
Law library	2,880	
Office equipment	6,880	
Accounts payable		$ 760
Unearned legal fees		3,000
Jerry Dow, capital		9,000
Jerry Dow, withdrawals	1,100	
Legal fees earned		3,900
Salaries expense	1,400	
Rent expense	1,000	
Utilities expense	230	
Totals	$16,660	$16,660

Some of the other accounts in the trial balance of Dow's law practice also must be adjusted before financial statements are prepared. They include Office Salaries Expense, Unearned Legal Fees, and Legal Fees Earned.

The Adjustment Process

LO 2 Explain why adjustments are required by the revenue recognition and matching principles and why the accrual basis of accounting is preferred to a cash basis.

The adjustment process is based on two accounting principles, the *revenue recognition principle* and the **matching principle.** As explained in Chapter 1, the *revenue recognition principle* requires that revenue be reported in the income statement when it is earned, not before and not after. For most firms, revenue is earned at the time a service is rendered or a product is sold to the customer.

For example, if a lawyer renders legal services to a client during December, the legal fees are earned during December. According to the *revenue recognition principle,* the lawyer must report these legal fees as revenue on the December income statement, even though the cash receipt from the client may take place in November or January. In cases such as this, the adjustment process assigns the revenue to December, when it was earned.

The *matching principle* requires reporting expenses on the income statement in the same accounting period as the revenues that were earned as a result of the expenses. For example, assume that a business uses an office to earn revenues during December. According to the *revenue recognition principle,* the business must report the revenues on the December income statement. One expense the business incurred in the pursuit of those December revenues was the December office rent. Therefore, the *matching principle* requires reporting the rent for December on the December income statement. This must be done even if the December rent was paid in November (or in January). In such cases, the adjustment process is used to match the cost of December's rent with the revenues earned during December.

When the adjustment process is used to assign revenues to the periods in which they are earned and to match expenses with revenues, the accounting system is described as **accrual basis accounting.** The accrual basis reflects the understanding that the economic effect of a revenue generally occurs when it is earned, not when cash is received.

Expenses involve the expiration or using up of assets and generally are assumed to produce revenues during the period in which the assets expire. Thus, to match expenses with revenues, the accrual basis reports expenses in the period the assets expire, not when cash is paid.

An alternative to accrual basis accounting is the **cash basis of accounting.** Under the cash basis, revenues are reported when cash is received and expenses are reported when cash is paid. For example, if revenue is earned in December but cash from the customer is not received until January, an adjustment is *not* made to report the revenue in December. Instead, the revenue is reported in January. Because revenues are reported when cash is received and expenses are deducted when cash is paid, net income is calculated as the difference between revenue receipts and expense disbursements.

The conclusion of "Financial Statement Concepts" is: "Items recognized in financial statements are accounted for in accordance with the accrual basis of accounting. The accrual basis of accounting recognizes the effect of transactions and events in the period in which the transactions and events occur, regardless of whether there has been a receipt or payment of cash or its equivalent."[1] Some concerns use a cash basis, but it is acceptable only if the amount of prepaid, unearned, and accrued items is unimportant.

One important benefit of accrual accounting is that it makes the information on accounting statements comparable from period to period. For example, in December 1993, the Dow law practice paid $2,400 for two years of insurance coverage beginning December 1. Under accrual accounting, insurance expense of $100 is reported on the December 1993 income statement. Twelve hundred dollars will be reported as expense during 1994 ($100 each month if monthly income statements are prepared), and $1,100 will be reported as expense during 1995 ($100 each month for the first 11 months). This allocation of the insurance cost is shown graphically in Illustration 3–2.

In contrast, a cash basis income statement for December 1993 would show insurance expense of $2,400; and the income statements related to the next 23 months would show $–0– expense. If you compare monthly income statements for the 24 months of insurance coverage, the accrual basis correctly shows that all 24 months incurred the expense of insurance coverage. The cash basis would suggest that December 1993 was much less profitable than the following 23 months.

Accrual Basis Accounting versus Cash Basis Accounting

The process of adjusting the accounts is essentially the same as the process of analyzing and recording business transactions. Each account balance and the economic events that affect that account are analyzed to determine whether an

Adjusting the Accounts

---

[1] *CICA Handbook,* par. 1000.41.

ILLUSTRATION 3–2

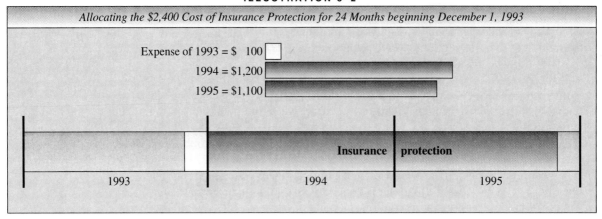

Allocating the $2,400 Cost of Insurance Protection for 24 Months beginning December 1, 1993

Expense of 1993 = $ 100
1994 = $1,200
1995 = $1,100

Insurance | protection

1993   1994   1995

LO 3 Prepare adjusting entries for prepaid expenses, amortization, unearned revenues, accrued expenses, and accrued revenues.

adjustment is needed. If an adjustment is required, an **adjusting entry** is prepared to bring the asset or liability account balance up to date. This process also brings the related expense or revenue account balance up to date. After the adjusting entries are journalized, they are posted to the accounts. In the following paragraphs, we explain why adjusting entries are needed to account for prepaid expenses, amortization, unearned revenues, accrued expenses, and accrued revenues.

Prepaid expenses, amortization, and unearned revenues involve previously recorded assets and liabilities. However, since they were first recorded, economic events or simply the passage of time have affected these assets and liabilities and adjusting entries must be made to record the effects. Accrued expenses and accrued revenues, on the other hand, involve assets and liabilities that have not yet been recorded. Adjusting entries are used to record these assets and liabilities as well as the related expenses and revenues.

Prepaid Expenses

As the name implies, a prepaid expense is an economic benefit that has been paid for in advance of its use. At the time of payment, an asset is acquired that will expire or be used up. As it is used up, it becomes an expense.

For example, recall Jerry Dow's December prepayment of $2,400 for two years' insurance protection. Although the payment was made on December 26, the policy went into effect on December 1. The allocation of this cost to 1993, 1994, and 1995 is shown in Illustration 3–2. As each day of December went by, the benefit of insurance protection expired, or was used up; thus, a portion of the prepaid insurance became an expense. On December 31, one month's insurance, valued at $\frac{1}{24}$ of the cost of $2,400, or $100, had expired. Therefore, the following adjusting entry is required so that the accounts reflect proper asset and expense amounts on December 31:

Adjustment (a)

Dec.	31	Insurance Expense	100.00	
		Prepaid Insurance		100.00
		To record the expired insurance.		

Posting the adjusting entry has the following effect on the accounts:

Prepaid Insurance				**Insurance Expense**		
Dec. 26	2,400	Dec. 31	100	Dec. 31	100	

After the entry is posted, the $2,300 balance in Prepaid Insurance and the $100 balance in Insurance Expense are proper statement amounts.

In looking at Illustration 3–2, you should recognize that adjusting entries will be required to allocate $1,200, or ($2,400/24) × 12, to 1994, and to allocate $1,100, or ($2,400/24) × 11, to 1995.

Another prepaid expense item that requires an adjustment is office supplies. For example, during December, the Dow law practice purchased some office supplies and placed them in the office for use. In the following days, the secretary used some of the supplies. The amount used was an expense that reduced the supplies on hand. However, the daily reductions were not recognized in the accounts because day-by-day information about amounts used and remaining was not needed. Also, labour is saved by making only one entry to record the total cost of all supplies used during the month.

Therefore, for the accounts to reflect proper statement amounts on December 31, the dollar amount of office supplies used during the month must be determined and recorded. To learn the amount used, you must count, or take an inventory of, the remaining supplies. Then, deduct the cost of the remaining supplies from the cost of the supplies purchased. If, for example, $75 of supplies remain, $45 ($120 − $75 = $45) of supplies were used and became an expense. The following adjusting entry records the using up of the supplies:

Adjustment (b)

Dec.	31	Office Supplies Expense	45.00	
		Office Supplies		45.00
		To record the supplies used.		

The effect of the adjusting entry on the accounts is:

Office Supplies				**Office Supplies Expense**		
Dec. 26	120	Dec. 31	45	Dec. 31	45	

Unlike the two previous examples, some items that are prepaid expenses at the time of purchase are both bought and fully used up within a single accounting period. For example, a company might pay its rent in advance on the first day of each month. Each month, the amount paid results in a prepaid expense that fully expires before the month's end and before the end of the accounting period. In such cases, you should ignore the fact that an asset results from each prepayment because an adjustment can be avoided if each prepayment is originally recorded as an expense.

Amortization[2]

Tangible, long-lived assets held for use in the production or sale of other assets or services are called **capital assets.** They include assets such as land, buildings, machines, professional libraries, and automobiles. All items of capital assets, except for land, eventually wear out or lose their usefulness. Therefore, the cost of these assets must be charged to expense over their useful lives. This process of allocating the cost of these items to expense is called **amortization.** Amortization is recorded with adjusting entries similar to those used for prepaid expenses.

For example, the Dow law practice owns a law library that cost $2,880. Dow estimates that beginning December 1, 1993, the items in this library will be useful for three years, after which they will have to be discarded and replaced. Based on this estimate, the amortization expense for December is calculated as $2,880/36 months = $80. You record this expense with the following adjusting entry:

		Adjustment (c)		
Dec.	31	Amortization Expense, Law Library	80.00	
		Accumulated Amortization, Law Library		80.00
		To record amortization for December.		

The effect of the entry on the accounts is:

Law Library			Amortization Expense, Law Library	
Dec. 2	2,500		Dec. 31	80
6	380			

Accumulated Amortization, Law Library	
Dec. 31	80

After the entry is posted, the Law Library account and its related Accumulated Amortization, Law Library, account together show the December 31 balance sheet amounts for this asset. The Amortization Expense, Law Library, account shows the amount of amortization expense that should appear on the December income statement.

---

[2] In 1990, the revised *CICA Handbook,* section 3060, recommended use of the term *amortization* instead of *depreciation,* but the use of *depreciation* was not ruled out. Also, *fixed assets* was replaced by *capital assets.* It may take several years for the new terminology to be widely implemented by companies; thus, *depreciation* and *depletion* may continue in use for some time.

In most cases, a decrease in an asset is recorded with a credit to the account in which the asset is recorded. However, note in the illustrated accounts that this procedure is not followed in recording amortization. Rather, amortization is recorded in a **contra account.** (A contra account's balance is subtracted from the balance of an associated account to show a more proper amount for the item recorded in the associated account.) In the present case, the contra account is Accumulated Amortization, Law Library.

Why are contra accounts used to record amortization? Contra accounts allow balance sheet readers to observe both the original cost of the asset and the estimated amount of amortization that has been charged to expense. Knowing both the original cost and the accumulated amortization, readers are better able to evaluate the productive capacity and the potential need to replace the company's assets. For example, if the balance sheet for Jerry Dow's law practice shows both the $2,880 original cost of the law library and the $80 balance in the accumulated amortization contra account, readers can better judge the size of the library and can see that it is almost new.

Note the words **accumulated amortization** in the title of the contra account. This emphasizes the fact that amortization taken in all prior periods is recorded in this account. For example, if monthly financial statements are prepared for Dow's law practice, the Law Library account and its related accumulated amortization account at the end of February 1994 appear as follows:

Law Library		Accumulated Amortization, Law Library	
Dec. 2	2,500	Dec. 31	80
6	380	Jan. 31	80
		Feb. 28	80

And the law library's cost and three months' accumulated amortization are shown on its February 28 balance sheet thus:

Law library.	$2,880	
Less accumulated amortization	240	$2,640

The office equipment of Dow's law practice is another type of capital assets that must be amortized. Early in December, Dow made two purchases of office equipment for $5,600 and $1,280. For convenience, assume that all of the items purchased are estimated to have a four-year useful life. Also, Dow estimates that at the end of the four-year useful life, the business will be able to sell the equipment for $880. Therefore, the cost that will expire over the 48-month life is $6,880 − $880, or $6,000. Amortization expense for each month is $6,000/48 = $125 and the entry to record amortization for December is:

		Adjustment (d)		
Dec.	31	Amortization Expense, Office Equipment.	125.00	
		Accumulated Amortization, Office Equipment.		125.00
		To record amortization for December.		

The effects of posting this entry to the accounts appear as follows:

Office Equipment			Amortization Expense, Office Equipment		
Dec. 3	5,600		Dec. 31	125	
6	1,280				

Accumulated Amortization, Office Equipment		
	Dec. 31	125

Accumulated amortization accounts are sometimes titled *Allowance for Amortization*. However, the word *accumulated* better describes the amortization procedure than does *allowance*.

Unearned Revenues

An unearned revenue results when payment for goods or services is received in advance of delivering the goods. For instance, Jerry Dow entered into an agreement with Chemical Supply to do its legal work on a fixed-fee basis of $500 per month, beginning December 15. On December 26, Dow received $3,000 in payment for providing legal services for the six-month period beginning December 15. This entry records the fee:

Dec.	26	Cash.	3,000.00	
		Unearned Legal Fees.		3,000.00
		Received a legal fee in advance.		

Receiving the fee in advance increased the cash of the law practice and created a liability, the obligation to do Chemical Supply's legal work for the next six months. However, by December 31, the law practice has discharged $250 of the liability and earned that much revenue. According to the *revenue recognition principle,* the $250 that has been earned should appear on the December income statement. Therefore, on December 31, the following adjusting entry is required:

		Adjustment (e)		
Dec.	31	Unearned Legal Fees	250.00	
		Legal Fees Earned ($500 × ½)		250.00
		Earned legal fees that had been received in advance.		

Posting the entry has this effect on the accounts:

Unearned Legal Fees				Legal Fees Earned		
Dec. 31	250	Dec. 26	3,000		Dec. 10	2,200
					12	1,700
					31	250

The effect of the entry is to transfer the $250 earned portion of the fee from the liability account to the revenue account. It reduces the liability and records as a revenue the $250 that has been earned.

Accrued Expenses

Most expenses are recorded at the time they are paid. That is because when the cash payment is recorded, the credit to Cash is balanced by a debit to the expense account. However, at the end of an accounting period, some expenses incurred during the period may remain unrecorded because payment is not due. Incurred expenses that are unpaid and therefore unrecorded are called **accrued expenses.** One common example is unpaid wages to employees for work that has already been done.

For example, the Dow law practice has a secretary who earns $70 per day or $350 for a week that begins on Monday and ends on Friday. The secretary's wages are due and payable every two weeks on Friday. During December, these wages were paid on the 12th and 26th and were recorded as follows:

Cash			Salaries Expense		
Dec. 12	700		Dec. 12	700	
26	700		26	700	

Notice on the calendar shown in the margin that December included three workdays after the December 26 payment of wages. As a result, at the close of business on Wednesday, December 31, the secretary has earned three days' wages for which payment is not yet due. Because payment has not been made, the wages have not yet been recorded. However, this $210 of earned but unpaid wages is as much a part of the December expenses as the $1,400 of wages that have been paid. Also, on December 31, the unpaid wages are a liability. Therefore, for the accounts to show the correct salary expense for December and all liabilities owed on December 31, you must make the following adjusting entry:

December						
S	M	T	W	T	F	S
	1	2	3	4	5	6
7	8	9	10	11	12	13
14	15	16	17	18	19	20
21	22	23	24	25	26	27
28	29	30	31			

		Adjustment (f)		
Dec.	31	Salaries Expense	210.00	
		Salaries Payable		210.00
		To record accrued wages.		

The effect of the entry on the accounts is:

Salaries Expense			Salaries Payable		
Dec. 12	700			Dec. 31	210
26	700				
31	**210**				

Another typical accrued expense that requires an adjusting entry at the end of the period is interest incurred on outstanding notes payable. (Some accounts payable also bear interest.) Interest expense is incurred with the

Bill Pena is the accountant for Cryer Company. Just before Pena prepared the adjusting entries to record accrued expenses at the end of the company's first year of operations, he was called into the company president's office. The president asked about the accrued expenses and then told Pena not to make the adjustments. Although Pena expressed concern about these instructions, the president said that because the bills will not be received until January, they should not be reported as expenses until the next year.

In addition, the president asked how much this year's revenues will be increased by the purchase order recently received from Broker Company. Pena explained that there will be no effect on sales until January because Broker Company will not take delivery until after the first of the year. The president was exasperated and pointed out that the order had already been received and Cryer was ready to make the deliveries. Even though Broker Company's order indicated that the merchandise should not be delivered until late January, the president told Pena to record the sale in December.

Pena knows that the combination of recording the sale to Broker Company and not accruing the expenses will increase the reported income by a large amount and is not sure what to do. He also wonders what reaction the company's auditors will have when they review the adjustments. What should Pena do?

passage of time. Therefore, unless the interest has been paid and recorded on the last day of the accounting period, some additional interest will have accrued since the last payment date. Record this accrued interest with an adjusting entry similar to the preceding entry to record accrued salaries.

Accrued Revenues

Many revenues are recorded when cash is received. Others are recorded at the time the goods or services are sold on credit and a bill is given to the customer. However, at the end of an accounting period, some revenues may remain unrecorded even though they have been earned. Earned revenues that are unrecorded because payment has not been received are called **accrued revenues.** For example, on December 20, Jerry Dow agreed to do Guaranty Bank's legal work for a fixed fee of $600 per month. The fee was to be paid on the 20th of each month for work completed in the preceding 30 days. Therefore, by December 31, the law practice has earned one third of a month's fee, or $200. According to the *revenue recognition principle,* this revenue should be reported on the December income statement. To record the amount that has been earned, make the following adjusting entry:

		Adjustment (g)		
Dec.	31	Accounts Receivable	200.00	
		Legal Fees Earned		200.00
		To record accrued legal fees.		

ILLUSTRATION 3-3

The December 31, 1993, Unadjusted and Adjusted Trial Balances for Jerry Dow, Lawyer

	Unadjusted Trial Balance		Adjustments		Adjusted Trial Balance	
	Dr.	Cr.	Dr.	Cr.	Dr.	Cr.
Cash	650				650	
Office supplies	120			(b) 45	75	
Prepaid insurance	2,400			(a) 100	2,300	
Law library.	2,880				2,880	
Office equipment.	6,880				6,880	
Accounts payable		760				760
Unearned legal fees.		3,000	(e) 250			2,750
Jerry Dow, capital		9,000				9,000
Jerry Dow, withdrawals	1,100				1,100	
Legal fees earned.		3,900		(e) 250		4,350
				(g) 200		
Salaries expense	1,400		(f) 210		1,610	
Rent expense.	1,000				1,000	
Utilities expense	230				230	
Totals.	16,660	16,660				
Insurance expense			(a) 100		100	
Office supplies expense			(b) 45		45	
Amortization expense, law library			(c) 80		80	
Accumulated amortization, law library.				(c) 80		80
Amortization expense, office equipment			(d) 125		125	
Accumulated amortization, office equipment. . .				(d) 125		125
Salaries payable				(f) 210		210
Accounts receivable			(g) 200		200	
Totals.			1,010	1,010	17,275	17,275

Posting the entry has this effect on the accounts:

Accounts Receivable					Legal Fees Earned	
Dec. 12	1,700	Dec. 22	1,700		Dec. 10	2,200
31	**200**				12	1,700
					31	250
					31	**200**

We mentioned earlier that interest was a typical example of an accrued expense that requires an adjusting entry. Interest is also a typical example of an accrued revenue. If a company has outstanding notes receivable or accounts receivable that bear interest, you must make an adjusting entry to record any accrued interest earned since the last cash receipt.

A trial balance prepared before adjustments have been recorded is called an **unadjusted trial balance.** By comparison, an **adjusted trial balance** shows the account balances after the adjusting entries have been posted. Illustration 3-3

The Adjusted Trial Balance

LO 4 Show the effects of making adjustments by preparing a schedule that reconciles the unadjusted and adjusted trial balances and by preparing financial statements from the adjusted trial balance.

shows the December 31, 1993, unadjusted trial balance, the adjustments, and the adjusted trial balance for the law practice of Jerry Dow. Note that in the adjustments columns, letters identify debits and credits with the adjusting entries explained earlier in the chapter.

Preparing Statements from the Adjusted Trial Balance

An adjusted trial balance shows proper balance sheet and income statement amounts. Therefore, you can use it to prepare the financial statements. When this is done, the income statement is prepared first because the net income, as calculated on the income statement, is needed to complete the statement of changes in owner's equity.

Illustration 3–4 shows how the revenues and expenses of Dow's law practice are arranged into an income statement and a statement of changes in owner's equity. In preparing the statement of changes in owner's equity, refer back to the ledger to determine how much of the owner's capital account balance existed at the beginning of the period and how much resulted from the owner's investments during the current period.

Illustration 3–5 shows how the asset, liability, and owner's equity items are drawn from the adjusted trial balance and arranged into a balance sheet. The balance sheet is prepared last because the owner's equity is calculated in the statement of changes in owner's equity.

Disposing of Accrued Items

Accrued Expenses

Earlier in this chapter, we recorded the December 29, 30, and 31 accrued wages of the secretary as follows:

LO 5 Prepare entries to record cash receipts and cash disbursements of items that were recorded at the end of the previous period as accrued expenses and accrued revenues.

Dec.	31	Salaries Expense	210.00	
		Salaries Payable		210.00
		To record accrued wages.		

When these wages are paid on Friday, January 9, you must make the following entry:

Jan.	9	Salaries Payable....................	210.00	
		Salaries Expense	490.00	
		Cash		700.00
		Paid two weeks' wages.		

The first debit in the January 9 entry cancels the liability for the three days' wages accrued on December 31. The second debit records the wages of January's first seven working days as an expense of the January accounting period. The credit records the total amount paid to the secretary.

ILLUSTRATION 3–4

Preparing the Income Statement and Statement of Changes in Owner's Equity from the Adjusted Trial Balance

JERRY DOW, LAWYER
Adjusted Trial Balance
December 31, 1993

Cash	$ 650	
Office supplies	75	
Prepaid insurance	2,300	
Law library	2,880	
Office equipment	6,880	
Accounts payable		$ 760
Unearned legal fees		2,750
Jerry Dow, capital		9,000
Jerry Dow, withdrawals	1,100	
Legal fees earned		4,350
Salaries expense	1,610	
Rent expense	1,000	
Utilities expense	230	
Insurance expense	100	
Office supplies expense	45	
Amortization expense, law library	80	
Accumulated amortization, law library		80
Amortization expense, office equipment	125	
Accumulated amortization, office equipment		125
Salaries payable		210
Accounts receivable	200	
Totals	$17,275	$17,275

JERRY DOW, LAWYER
Income Statement
For Month Ended December 31, 1993

Revenues:		
Legal fees earned		$4,350
Operating expenses:		
Salaries expense	$1,610	
Rent expense	1,000	
Utilities expense	230	
Insurance expense	100	
Office supplies expense	45	
Amortization expense, law library	80	
Amortization expense, office equipment	125	
Total operating expenses		3,190
Net income		$1,160

JERRY DOW, LAWYER
Statement of Changes in Owner's Equity
For Month Ended December 31, 1993

Jerry Dow, capital, November 30, 1993		$9,000
Plus:		
Investments by owner	$ –0–	
Net income	1,160	10,160
Total		$10,160
Less:		
Withdrawals by owner		1,100
Jerry Dow, capital, December 31, 1993		$ 9,060

ILLUSTRATION 3–5

Preparing the Balance Sheet from the Adjusted Trial Balance

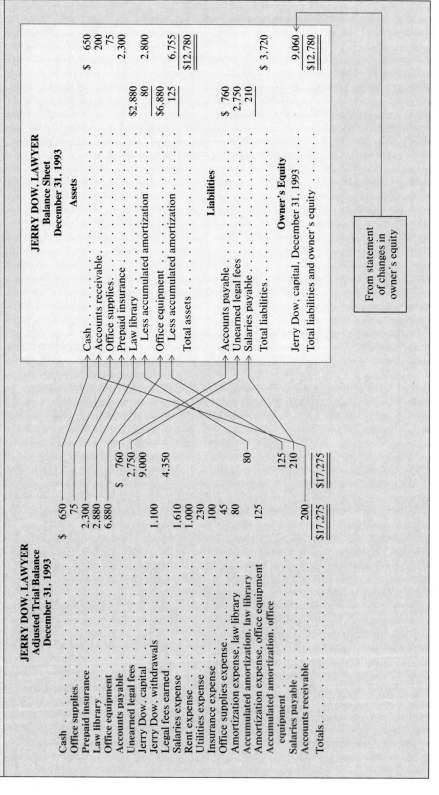

JERRY DOW, LAWYER
Adjusted Trial Balance
December 31, 1993

Cash	$ 650	
Office supplies	75	
Prepaid insurance	2,300	
Law library	2,880	
Office equipment	6,880	
Accounts payable		$ 760
Unearned legal fees		2,750
Jerry Dow, capital		9,000
Jerry Dow, withdrawals	1,100	
Legal fees earned		4,350
Salaries expense	1,610	
Rent expense	1,000	
Utilities expense	230	
Insurance expense	100	
Office supplies expense	45	
Amortization expense, law library	80	
Accumulated amortization, law library		80
Amortization expense, office equipment	125	
Accumulated amortization, office equipment		125
Salaries payable		210
Accounts receivable	200	
Totals	$17,275	$17,275

JERRY DOW, LAWYER
Balance Sheet
December 31, 1993

Assets

Cash		$ 650
Accounts receivable		200
Office supplies		75
Prepaid insurance		2,300
Law library	$2,880	
Less accumulated amortization	80	2,800
Office equipment	$6,880	
Less accumulated amortization	125	6,755
Total assets		$12,780

Liabilities

Accounts payable	$ 760	
Unearned legal fees	2,750	
Salaries payable	210	
Total liabilities		$ 3,720

Owner's Equity

Jerry Dow, capital, December 31, 1993		9,060
Total liabilities and owner's equity		$12,780

From statement
of changes in
owner's equity

Accrued Revenues

On December 20, Jerry Dow agreed to do Guaranty Bank's legal work on a fixed-fee basis for $600 per month. On December 31, the following adjusting entry was made to record one third of a month's revenue earned under this contract:

Dec.	31	Accounts Receivable	200.00	
		Legal Fees Earned		200.00
		To record accrued legal fees.		

When payment of the first month's fee is received on January 20, you should make the following entry:

Jan.	20	Cash.	600.00	
		Accounts Receivable		200.00
		Legal Fees Earned		400.00
		Received cash for accrued and earned legal fees.		

The first credit in the January 20 entry records the collection of the fee accrued at the end of December. The second credit records as revenue the fee earned during the first 20 days of January.

Classification of Balance Sheet Items

The balance sheets that we have presented up to this point (for example, see Illustration 3–5) are **unclassified balance sheets.** This means that we did not attempt to divide the assets or liabilities into classes. However, a balance sheet becomes more useful when its assets and liabilities are classified into meaningful groups. Readers of such **classified balance sheets** can better judge the adequacy of the different assets used in the business. Also, they can better estimate the probable availability of funds to meet the various liabilities as they become due.

LO 6 Define each asset and liability classification appearing on a balance sheet, classify balance sheet items, and prepare a classified balance sheet.

Businesses do not all use the same system of classifying assets and liabilities on their balance sheets. However, most businesses classify them as shown in Illustration 3–6. Assets are classified as (1) current assets, (2) investments, (3) plant and equipment, and (4) intangible assets. Liabilities are either (1) current liabilities or (2) long-term liabilities. We explain the nature of these classes next.

Current Assets

Current assets are cash and other assets that are reasonably expected to be realized in cash or to be sold or consumed within one year or within the normal **operating cycle of the business,** whichever is longer. In addition to cash, current assets typically include temporary investments in marketable securities, accounts receivable, notes receivable, products held for resale (merchandise inventory), and prepaid expenses.

ILLUSTRATION 3–6

A Classified Balance Sheet

NATIONAL ELECTRICAL SUPPLY
Balance Sheet
December 31, 1993

Assets

Current assets:		
Cash	$ 1,050	
Temporary investments	2,145	
Accounts receivable	3,961	
Notes receivable	600	
Merchandise inventory	10,248	
Prepaid expenses	405	
Total current assets		$ 18,409
Investments:		
Chrysler Corporation common shares	$ 2,400	
Land held for future expansion	8,000	
Total investments		10,400
Plant and equipment:		
Store equipment	$ 3,200	
Less accumulated amortization	800	$ 2,400
Buildings	$70,000	
Less accumulated amortization	18,400	51,600
Land		24,200
Total plant and equipment		78,200
Intangible assets:		
Franchise		10,000
Total assets		$117,009

Liabilities

Current liabilities:		
Accounts payable	$ 2,715	
Wages payable	480	
Notes payable	3,000	
Current portion of long-term liabilities	1,200	
Total current liabilities		$ 7,395
Long-term liabilities:		
Notes payable	48,800	
Total liabilities		$ 56,195

Owner's Equity

Bruce Brown, capital	60,814
Total liabilities and owner's equity	$117,009

The operating cycle of a business depends on the nature of its activities. For a business that sells services, the operating cycle is the average time between the payment of salaries to the employees who perform the services and the receipt of cash from customers in payment for those services. For a business that sells merchandise, the operating cycle is the average time between

ILLUSTRATION 3–7

The Operating Cycle of a Business

Service Business

Cash

Cash is paid as salaries to employees who perform services

Receivables are converted into cash by customer payments

Services are sold to customers in exchange for receivables

Merchandising Business

Cash

Cash is paid to purchase merchandise inventory

Receivables are converted into cash by customer payments

Merchandise is sold to customers in exchange for receivables

the payment of cash to purchase merchandise and the receipt of cash from customers in payment for the merchandise. Illustration 3–7 shows typical operating cycles for service businesses and merchandising businesses.

Most companies have an operating cycle that is less than one year. As a result, these companies use a one-year period to decide whether assets should be reported as current assets. Some companies, however, have an operating cycle that is longer than one year. For example, wine distributors may age some products for several years before the products are ready for sale. In such companies, the average length of the operating cycle should be used to decide whether assets satisfy the current asset definition.

Return to Illustration 3–6 and note that current assets are listed first. This is because they are more easily converted into cash than are other types of assets. In other words, current assets are said to be more *liquid* than other assets. Also, within the current asset category, the items are listed in the order of their liquidity, the most liquid first and the least liquid last. Note that prepaid expenses are listed last among the current assets. Unlike other current assets, prepaid expenses will not be converted into cash. Nevertheless, prepaid expenses substitute for future cash payments that would be required if the expenses had not been prepaid. Therefore, prepaid expenses are listed as current assets until their benefits expire or they are used up.

The prepaid expenses of a business, as a total, are seldom a major item on its balance sheet. As a result, instead of listing them individually, they often are totaled and shown as a single item called *prepaid expenses*. Therefore, the "Prepaid expenses" in Illustration 3–6 may include several items such as prepaid insurance, office supplies, and store supplies.

Investments

The second balance sheet classification is investments. This includes stocks, bonds, and promissory notes that do not qualify as current assets. Generally, this means that they will be held for more than one year or one operating cycle. Investments also include such things as land held for future expansion but not now being used in the business operations. In Illustration 3–6, observe that temporary investments of cash are not listed in the investments category. Instead, they appear as current assets. We explain the differences between temporary investments and long-term investments more completely in a later chapter.

Capital Assets

Earlier in this chapter, we described capital assets as tangible, long-lived assets held for use in the production or sale of other assets or services. Examples include equipment, buildings, and land. The key words in the definition are *long-lived* and *held for use in the production or sale of other assets or services*. Land held for future expansion is not a plant asset because it is not being used to produce or sell other assets, goods, or services.

The words **plant and equipment** are commonly used as a balance sheet caption. Alternative captions are *property, plant, and equipment,* or *land, buildings, and equipment,* or simply *plant assets. Fixed assets,* a caption that was widely used, has been replaced by the current terminology, *capital assets.* The order in which plant assets are listed within the balance sheet classification varies from one business to another.

Intangible Assets

Economic benefits or resources that do not have a physical substance are called **intangible assets.** Their value stems from the privileges or rights that accrue to their owner. Examples of intangible assets are goodwill, patents, trademarks, copyrights, and franchises.

Current Liabilities

Obligations that are due to be paid or liquidated within one year or one operating cycle of the business, whichever is longer, are classified as **current liabilities.** Current liabilities usually are satisfied by paying current assets or by incurring new current liabilities. Common current liabilities are accounts payable, notes payable, wages payable, taxes payable, interest payable, and unearned revenues. Also, since long-term liabilities often require periodic payments, the portion of long-term liabilities that is due to be paid within one year or one operating cycle must be classified as a current liability. Illustration 3–6 shows how this item usually is described. The order in which current liability items are listed is not uniform.

Unearned revenues are classified as current liabilities because current assets normally are required in their liquidation. For example, advance receipts for future delivery of merchandise will be earned and the liability liquidated by delivering merchandise, which is a current asset.

Long-Term Liabilities

The second liability classification is **long-term liabilities.** Liabilities that are not due to be paid within one year or the current operating cycle are listed under this classification. Common long-term liability items are notes payable and bonds payable. Because businesses may owe both long-term notes payable and notes payable that are current liabilities, they often use two different accounts: Short-Term Notes Payable and Long-Term Notes Payable.

The equity section of a balance sheet differs depending on whether the business is organized as a single proprietorship, a partnership, or a corporation.

Owner's Equity on the Balance Sheet

Single Proprietorships and Partnerships

When a business is organized as a single proprietorship, the equity section of the balance sheet is presented as a single line that reports the owner's equity as of the date of the balance sheet. Thus, Illustration 3–5 shows "Jerry Dow, capital, December 31, 1993 . . . 9,060." In the unusual case where total liabilities exceed total assets, the negative (or debit) equity amount is shown in parentheses and subtracted from total liabilities.

When a business is organized as a partnership, separate capital accounts and withdrawals accounts are maintained for each partner. Changes in the partners' equities are reported in a statement of changes in partners' equities similar to the statement of changes in owner's equity. In the equity section of the balance sheet, the equity of each partner is listed as follows:

Partners' Equities		
Shirley Tucker, capital	$17,300	
Mark Jackman, capital	24,800	
Total equities of the partners		$42,100

Corporations

Corporations are established under provincial or federal laws. These laws generally distinguish between the amounts a corporation receives from its shareholders through investments, and the increase or decrease in shareholders' equity due to net incomes, net losses, and **dividends.** (A dividend is a distribution, generally of cash, made by a corporation to its shareholders. A cash dividend reduces the assets and the equity of a corporation in the same way a withdrawal reduces the assets and equity of a proprietorship.)

The amounts shareholders have invested are classified as **contributed capital.** The equity that represents the corporation's cumulative net income less net losses and dividends is called **retained earnings.** Therefore, shareholders' equity is shown on a corporation balance sheet as follows:

Shareholders' Equity

Contributed capital:
    Common shares $400,000
    Retained earnings.   124,400
    Total shareholders' equity $524,400

If a corporation issues only one kind of shares (others are discussed later), they are called **common shares** or sometimes *share capital—common*. The $400,000 amount of common shares shown is the amount originally contributed to the corporation by its shareholders through the purchase of the corporation's shares. The $124,400 of retained earnings represents the increase in the shareholder's equity resulting from cumulative net income that exceeded any net losses and any dividends paid to the shareholders.

Alternative Balance Sheet Arrangements

The balance sheet in Illustration 1–3 (p. 19), with the liabilities and owner's equity placed to the right of the assets, is called an **account form balance sheet**. Such an arrangement emphasizes that assets equal liabilities plus owner's equity. Alternatively, when balance sheet items are arranged vertically, such as in Illustration 3–5, the format is called a **report form balance sheet**. Both forms are commonly used, and neither is preferred over the other.

Identifying Accounts by Number

We introduced a typical three-digit account numbering system in Chapter 2. In such a system, the number assigned to an account usually identifies the account and its balance sheet or income statement classification of the account. For example, in the following system, the first digit in an account's number tells its primary balance sheet or income statement classification. A first digit of 1 indicates an asset account. Liability accounts are assigned numbers with first digits of 2. The accounts in each balance sheet and income statement classification of a concern selling merchandise are numbered as follows:

101 to 199 are assigned to asset accounts.
201 to 299 are assigned to liability accounts.
301 to 399 are assigned to owner's equity accounts.
401 to 499 are assigned to sales or revenue accounts.
501 to 599 are assigned to cost of goods sold accounts.
601 to 699 are assigned to operating expense accounts.
701 to 799 are assigned to accounts that reflect unusual and/or infrequent gains.
801 to 899 are assigned to accounts that reflect unusual and/or infrequent losses.

In a system like this, the second digit of each account number can be used to identify the subclassification of the account, as follows:

101 to 199. Asset accounts
    101 to 139. Current asset accounts (second digits of 0, 1, 2, or 3)
    141 to 149. Long-term investment accounts (second digit is 4)

151 to 179. Plant asset accounts (second digits of 5, 6, or 7)

181 to 189. Natural resources (second digit is 8)

191 to 199. Intangible asset accounts (second digit is 9)

201 to 299. Liability accounts

201 to 249. Current liability accounts (second digits of 0, 1, 2, 3, or 4)

251 to 269. Long-term liability accounts (second digits of 5 or 6)

Finally, a third digit is assigned so that each account is uniquely identified by its number. For example, specific current asset accounts might be assigned numbers as follows:

101 to 199. Asset accounts

101 to 139. Current asset accounts

101. Cash

106. Accounts Receivable

110. Rent Receivable

128. Prepaid Insurance

The preceding three-digit account numbering system would be adequate for many simple businesses. For more complex businesses, however, the account numbering system may use four, five, or more digits. Chapter 5 discusses the sales and cost of goods sold accounts listed in the previous account numbering system. Note that the numbering system of the ledger accounts coincides with the order in which the accounts appear on the balance sheet and income statement.

LO 1. The life of a business is divided into accounting periods so that periodic financial reports can be prepared and used to evaluate the financial progress of the business. Adjustments at the end of each period are necessary to update some of the asset, liability, expense, and revenue accounts and to show the effects of previously unrecorded internal economic events of the business.

LO 2. When revenues are earned and the related cash is received in different periods, the revenue recognition principle requires that adjusting entries be made as necessary to report the revenues in the period they are earned. And when assets expire or are used up in one period but are paid for in another period, the matching principle requires that adjusting entries be made to report expenses in the period the assets expire.

These principles are the essence of accrual accounting, which is preferred because it reports revenues and expenses when they have an economic impact on the entity. In contrast to accrual basis accounting, cash basis accounting reports revenues when cash is received and reports expenses when cash is paid. Hence, the cash basis of accounting does not require adjustments.

LO 3. Adjusting entries are used (*a*) to charge the expired portion of prepaid expenses to expense, (*b*) to charge the expired portion of plant and equipment cost to amortization expense, (*c*) to recognize as revenues the earned portion of unearned revenue liabilities, (*d*) to accrue expenses and

Summary of the Chapter in Terms of Learning Objectives

record the related liabilities, and (*e*) to accrue revenues and record the related assets.

LO 4. A six-column schedule can show the effects of the adjustments on the accounts by listing the unadjusted trial balance in the first two columns, the debits and credits of the adjusting entries in the next two columns, and the adjusted trial balance in the last two columns. The adjusted trial balance shows all of the ledger accounts with balances, including revenues, expenses, withdrawals, assets, liabilities, and owner's equity. Hence, it contains all of the account balance information needed to prepare the income statement, then the statement of changes in owner's equity, and finally the balance sheet.

LO 5. When accrued expenses are paid early in a new accounting period, the entry to record the payment includes a debit to the previously recorded liability and a debit to expense for the portion incurred during the new period. When payment of accrued revenues is received, the entry includes a credit to the previously recorded asset and a credit to revenue for the portion earned during the new period.

LO 6. Classified balance sheets usually report four classes of assets: current assets, investments, plant and equipment, and intangible assets. Liabilities are either current liabilities or long-term liabilities. The equity of a single proprietorship is reported on one line, while a separate capital account is reported for each partner in a partnership. Corporations report the investments of its shareholders as contributed capital; the equity from net income less net losses and dividends is reported as retained earnings.

Demonstration Problem	The following data relates to Best Plumbing Company on December 31, 1993. The company prepares financial statements on a calendar-year basis.

  a. Best Plumbing Company's weekly payroll is $2,800, paid every Friday for a five-day workweek. At the 1993 year-end, the employees have worked Monday through Wednesday.

  b. On December 1, 1993, the company borrowed $45,000 from a local bank for 90 days at 12% interest.

  c. During December, the company advertised in the local paper at a cost of $600, which remains unpaid and unrecorded.

  d. Equipment that cost $10,000 and has no salvage value was purchased on July 1, 1992. It has a five-year useful life.

  e. At the beginning of the year, office supplies amounted to $210. During the year, $650 of supplies were purchased and charged to the asset account. At year-end, there were $280 of supplies on hand.

  f. On October 1, 1993, Best Plumbing Company contracted to install plumbing for a new housing project. The contract was for $144,000 to install plumbing in 24 new houses. The $144,000 was received on October 1, 1993, and credited to Unearned Plumbing Revenue. As of December 31, 1993, 18 houses have been completed.

  g. On September 1, 1993, a one-year insurance policy was purchased for $1,200 and was debited to Prepaid Insurance.

h. The previous year, on December 1, 1992, the company had purchased a one-year policy for $900. The portion of the cost that relates to 1993 exists in the Prepaid Insurance account.

Required

1. Prepare the necessary adjusting journal entries on December 31, 1993.
2. Complete the following schedule:

Entry	Account	Amount of Adjustment	Amount That Will Appear on Balance Sheet	Classification of Account on Balance Sheet*
a	Wages payable	$	$	
b	Interest payable			
c	Accounts payable			
d	Accumulated amortization			
e	Office supplies			
f	Unearned plumbing revenue			
g and *h*	Prepaid insurance			

* Indicate whether current asset, plant and equipment, current liability, or long-term liability.

3. State whether the effect of each adjustment was to increase, or decrease, or leave unchanged each of the following: net income, total assets, total liabilities.

Planning the Solution

■ Analyze the information related to each potential adjustment to determine which accounts need to be updated.

■ Calculate the amount of adjustment required for each item and prepare the necessary journal entries.

■ Enter the amount of each adjustment in the table, calculate the resulting account balance that will appear on the balance sheet, and determine the balance sheet classification of the account.

■ Review the debit and credit of each adjusting entry to determine the entry's overall effect on net income, and total assets or total liabilities.

1. Adjusting journal entries:

Solution to
Demonstration
Problem

a.	Dec.	31	Wages Expense	1,680.00	
			Wages Payable		1,680.00
			To accrue wages for the last three days of the year (³⁄₅ × $2,800).		
b.		31	Interest Expense	450.00	
			Interest Payable		450.00
			To accrue wages for one month ($45,000 × .12 × ¹⁄₁₂).		
c.		31	Advertising Expense	600.00	
			Accounts Payable.		600.00
			To record advertising expense.		

d.	31	Amortization Expense, Equipment . . . . Accumulated Amortization, Equipment . . . . *To record amortization expense for the year* *($10,000/5 = $2,000).*	2,000.00	2,000.00
e.	31	Office Supplies Expense . . . . Office Supplies . . . . *To record office supplies used* *($210 + $650 − $280).*	580.00	580.00
f.	31	Unearned Plumbing Revenue . . . . Plumbing Services Revenue . . . . *To recognize plumbing revenues earned* *($144,000 × $^{18}/_{24}$).*	108,000.00	108,000.00
g.	31	Insurance Expense . . . . Prepaid Insurance . . . . *To adjust for the expired portion of insurance* *($1,200 × $^{4}/_{12}$).*	400.00	400.00
h.	31	Insurance Expense . . . . Prepaid Insurance . . . . *To record the expiration of insurance* *($900 × $^{11}/_{12}$).*	825.00	825.00

2.

Entry	Account	Amount of Adjustment	Amount that Will Appear on Balance Sheet	Classification of Account on Balance Sheet
a	Wages payable	$ 1,680	$ 1,680	Current liability
b	Interest payable	450	450	Current liability
c	Accounts payable	600	600	Current liability
d	Accumulated amortization	2,000	3,000	Plant and equipment
e	Office supplies	(580)	280	Current asset
f	Unearned plumbing revenue	(108,000)	36,000	Current liability
g and h	Prepaid insurance	(1,225)	800*	Current asset

* $825 + $1,200 − $825 − $400 = $800.

3.

Entry	Net Income Increase (Decrease)	Total Assets Increase (Decrease)	Total Liabilities Increase (Decrease)
a	$ (1,680)	$ –0–	$ 1,680
b	(450)	–0–	450
c	(600)	–0–	600
d	(2,000)	(2,000)	–0–
e	(580)	(580)	–0–
f	108,000	–0–	(108,000)
g	(400)	(400)	–0–
h	(825)	(825)	–0–

Recording Prepaid and Unearned Items in Income Statement Accounts

Prepaid Expenses

LO 8 Explain why some companies record prepaid and unearned items in income statement accounts and prepare adjusting entries when this procedure is used.

The discussion in Chapter 3 emphasized the fact that prepaid expenses are assets at the time they are purchased. Therefore, at the time of purchase, we recorded prepaid expenses with debits to asset accounts. Then, at the end of the accounting period, adjusting entries transferred the expired cost to expense accounts. In the chapter, we also recognized that some prepaid expenses will fully expire before the end of the accounting period. When this is expected, it is easier to charge prepaid expenses to expense accounts at the time of purchase. Then, no adjusting entry is necessary.

Some companies record all prepaid expenses by debiting expense accounts. Then, at the end of the accounting period, if any amounts remain unused or unexpired, adjusting entries are made to transfer the cost of the unused portions from the expense accounts to prepaid expense (asset) accounts. This practice is perfectly acceptable. The reported financial statements are exactly the same under either procedure.

Recall that on December 26, the Dow law practice purchased office supplies for $120. We recorded that purchase with a debit to an asset account but could have recorded a debit to an expense account. The alternatives are as follows:

		Purchase Recorded as Asset		Purchase Recorded as Expense	
Dec. 26	Office Supplies	120.00			
	Cash		120.00		
26	Office Supplies Expense			120.00	
	Cash				120.00

At the end of the accounting period (December 31), an inventory of the office supplies on hand revealed unused supplies that cost $75. That means $120 − $75 = $45 of office supplies were used and became an expense of December. The required adjusting entry depends on how the original purchase was recorded. The alternative adjustments are:

		Purchase Recorded as Asset		Purchase Recorded as Expense	
Adjusting entries:					
Dec. 31	Office Supplies Expense	45.00			
	Office Supplies		45.00		
31	Office Supplies			75.00	
	Office Supplies				

When these entries are posted to the accounts, you can see that the two alternative procedures give the same results. Regardless of which procedure is followed, the December 31 adjusted account balances show office supplies of $75 and office supplies expense of $45.

Purchase Recorded as Asset				Purchase Recorded as Expense		
Office Supplies				**Office Supplies**		
Dec. 26	120 −45	Dec. 31	45	Dec. 31	75	
Bal.	75					

Office Supplies Expense				**Office Supplies Expense**		
Dec. 31	45			Dec. 26	120 −75	Dec. 31 75
				Bal.	45	

To continue the example for another month, assume that during January Dow's law practice purchased $150 of supplies. On January 31, an inventory showed $100 of supplies on hand. As you can see in the preceding accounts, the December 31 balance in the Office Supplies account was $75, regardless of which procedure is used. Therefore, the total of supplies available for use during January was $75 + $150 = $225. Since $100 of supplies remain unused on January 31, the adjusting entry on January 31 must be designed to report a supplies asset of $100 and a supplies expense of $225 − $100 = $125. Depending on how the purchases were recorded, the alternative adjusting entries are:

	Purchase Recorded as Asset	Purchase Recorded as Expense
Adjusting entries:		
Jan. 31 Office Supplies Expense.	125.00	
Office Supplies	125.00	
31 Office Supplies		25.00
Office Supplies Expense		25.00

Note that if the purchases of supplies are debited to an expense account, the required adjusting entry increases the Office Supplies account balance $25, from $75 to $100. The credit in the entry reduces the Office Supplies Expense account debit balance from $150 to $125.

Unearned Revenues

The procedures for recording unearned revenues are similar to those used to record prepaid expenses. Receipts of unearned revenues may be recorded with credits to liability accounts (as described in Chapter 3) or they may be recorded with credits to revenue accounts. The adjusting entries at the end of the period are different, depending on which procedure is followed. Nevertheless, either procedure is acceptable. The amounts reported in the financial statements are exactly the same, regardless of which procedure is used.

To illustrate the alternative procedures of recording unearned revenues, recall that on December 26, the Dow law practice received $3,000 in payment for legal services to be provided over the six-month period beginning December 15. In Chapter 3, that receipt was recorded with a credit to a liability account. The alternative would be to record it with a credit to a revenue account. Both alternatives follow:

	Receipt Recorded as a Liability	Receipt Recorded as a Revenue
Dec. 26 Cash	3,000.00	3,000.00
Unearned Legal Fees.	3,000.00	
26 Cash		3,000.00
Legal Fees Earned		3,000.00

By the end of the accounting period (December 31), the Dow law practice had earned $250 of these legal fees. That means $250 of the liability had been satisfied. Depending on how the original receipt was recorded, the required adjusting entry is as follows:

	Receipt Recorded as a Liability	Receipt Recorded as a Revenue
Adjusting entries:		
Dec. 31 Unearned Legal Fees	250.00	
Legal Fees Earned	250.00	
31 Legal Fees Earned		2,750.00
Unearned Legal fees		2,750.00

Posting these entries shows that the two alternative procedures give the same results. Regardless of which procedure is followed, the December 31 adjusted account balances show unearned legal fees of $2,750 and legal fees earned of $250.

Receipt Recorded as a Liability				Receipt Recorded as a Revenue			
Unearned Legal Fees				**Unearned Legal Fees**			
Dec. 31	250	Dec. 31	3,000 −250			Dec. 31	2,750
		Bal.	2,750				

Legal Fees Earned				**Legal Fees Earned**			
		Dec. 31	250	Dec. 31	2,750	Dec. 26	3,000 −2,750
						Bal.	250

LO 8. Because many prepaid expenses expire during the same period in which they are purchased, some companies choose to charge all prepaid expenses to expense accounts at the time they are purchased. When this is done, end-of-period adjusting entries are required to transfer any unexpired amounts from the expense accounts to appropriate asset accounts. Also, unearned revenues may be credited to revenue accounts at the time cash is received. If so, end-of-period adjusting entries are required to transfer any unearned amounts from the revenue accounts to appropriate unearned revenue accounts.

Summary of
Appendix A in Terms
of Learning Objective

Glossary

LO 7 Define or explain the words and phrases listed in the chapter glossary.

Account form balance sheet a balance sheet that is arranged so that the assets are listed on the left and the liability and owner's equity items are listed on the right. p. 146

Accounting period the length of time into which the life of a business is divided for the purpose of preparing periodic financial statements. p. 127

Accrual basis of accounting a system of accounting in which the adjustment process is used to assign revenues to the periods in which they are earned and to match expenses with revenues. pp. 129–30

Accrued expenses expenses incurred during an accounting period but that, prior to end-of-period adjustments, remain unrecorded because payment is not due. pp. 135–36, 138

Accrued revenues revenues earned during an accounting period but that, prior to end-of-period adjustments, remain unrecorded because payment has not been received. pp. 136–37, 141

Accumulated amortization the total amount of amortization recorded against an asset or group of assets during the entire time the asset or assets have been owned. pp. 133–34

Adjusted trial balance a trial balance that shows the account balances after they have been revised to reflect the effects of end-of-period adjustments. pp. 137–38

Adjusting entry a journal entry made at the end of an accounting period for the purpose of assigning revenues to the period in which they are earned, assigning expenses to the period in which the expiration of benefit is incurred, and to update related liability and asset accounts. p. 130

Amortization the expiration of the usefulness of capital assets (plant, equipment, and intangibles), and the related process of allocating the cost of such assets to expense of the periods during which the assets are used. pp. 132–34

Capital assets tangible, long-lived assets held for use in the production or sale of other assets or services. p. 132

Cash basis of accounting an accounting system in which revenues are reported in the income statement when cash is received and expenses are reported when cash is paid. p. 129

Classified balance sheet a balance sheet that shows assets and liabilities grouped in meaningful subclasses. pp. 141–45

Common shares the name given to a corporation's shares when it issues only one kind or class of shares. p. 146

Contra account an account the balance of which is subtracted from the balance of an associated account to show a more proper amount for the item recorded in the associated account. pp. 133–34

Contributed capital the portion of a corporation's equity that represents investments in the corporation by its shareholders. p. 145

Current assets cash or other assets that are reasonably expected to be realized in cash or to be sold or consumed within one year or one operating cycle of the business, whichever is longer. p. 141

Current liabilities obligations due to be paid or liquidated within one year or one operating cycle of the business, whichever is longer. p. 144

Dividends a distribution, generally of assets, made by a corporation to its shareholders. p. 145

Fiscal year any 12 consecutive months used by a business as its annual accounting period. p. 127

Intangible assets economic benefits or resources without physical substance, the value of which stems from the privileges or rights that accrue to their owner. p. 150

Interim financial reports financial reports of a business that are based on one-month or three-month accounting periods. p. 127

Long-term liabilities obligations not due to be paid within one year or the current operating cycle of the business. p. 145

Matching principle accounting requirement that expenses be reported in same accounting period as the revenues that were earned as a result of the expenses. p. 128

Natural business year the 12-month period that ends when the activities of a business are at their lowest point. p. 127

Operating cycle of a business the average time a business takes to pay cash for salaries of employees or to pay for merchandise and then to receive cash from customers in exchange for the sale of the services or merchandise. pp. 141–44

Plant and equipment same as capital assets. p. 144

Report form balance sheet a balance sheet with a vertical format that shows the assets above the liabilities and the liabilities above the owner's equity. p. 146

Retained earnings the portion of a corporation's equity that represents its cumulative net income, less net losses and dividends. p. 145

Time period principle identifying the activities of a business as occurring during specific time periods such as months, or three-month periods, or years so that periodic financial reports of the business can be prepared. pp. 126–27

Unadjusted trial balance trial balance before adjustments have been recorded. p. 137

Unclassified balance sheet a balance sheet that presents a single list of assets and a single list of liabilities with no attempt to divide them into classes. p. 141

Synonymous Terms

Accumulated amortization allowance for amortization

Amortization depreciation

Capital assets property, plant, and equipment; land, buildings, and equipment; plant assets; fixed assets

Common shares capital stock

Objective Review

Answers to the following questions are listed at the end of this chapter. Be sure you decide which is the best answer to each question *before* you check the answers.

LO 1 For purposes of preparing financial statements, the act of dividing the life of a business into equal time periods:

a. Results in an annual accounting period called the fiscal year.
b. Always is done so that the annual accounting period ends at the close of the natural business year.
c. Results in annual financial reports called interim financial reports.
d. Always is done so that the annual accounting period ends at the close of the calendar year.
e. None of the above is correct.

LO 2 On April 1, 1993, Collier Company paid $2,400 for two years' insurance coverage. In accounting for this item:

a. Under the cash basis of accounting, 1994 insurance expense will be $–0–.
b. Under the accrual basis of accounting, 1993 insurance expense will be $2,400.

c. Under the cash basis of accounting, 1995 insurance expense will be $300.

d. Under the accrual basis of accounting, an adjusting entry for insurance will not be required at the end of 1994.

e. Under the cash basis of accounting, 1993 insurance expense will be $900.

LO 3 On December 31, 1993, Colony Company failed to make an adjustment for $200 of accrued service revenues earned and also failed to record the expiration of $700 of insurance premiums that had been debited to Prepaid Insurance. As a result of these errors, on the 1993 income statement:

a. Net income will be understated by $200.

b. Revenues will be overstated $200 and expenses will be understated $700.

c. Revenues will be overstated $200 and expenses will be overstated $700.

d. Revenues will be understated $200 and expenses will be overstated $700.

e. Revenues will be understated $200 and expenses will be understated $700.

LO 4 Selected information from B. Jones Company's unadjusted and adjusted trial balances follows:

	Unadjusted Trial Balance		Adjusted Trial Balance	
	Debit	Credit	Debit	Credit
Prepaid insurance	6,200		5,900	
Salaries payable				1,400
Office supplies	900		800	

The adjusting entries included which of the following:

a. A $300 debit to Prepaid Insurance, a $1,400 credit to Salaries Payable, and a $100 credit to Office Supplies.

b. A $300 credit to Prepaid Insurance, a $1,400 debit to Salaries Payable, and a $100 credit to Office Supplies.

c. A $300 credit to Insurance Expense, a $1,400 debit to Salaries Expense, and a $100 debit to Office Supplies Expense.

d. A $300 debit to Insurance Expense, a $1,400 credit to Salaries Payable, and a $100 debit to Office Supplies.

e. A $300 debit to Insurance Expense, a $1,400 debit to Salaries Expense, and a $100 debit to Office Supplies Expense.

LO 5 On December 31, 1993, Holland Photo Company made an entry to record $1,600 of accrued salaries. The next payment of salaries, on January 5, was $8,000. Related to these transactions only:

a. You can be sure that Holland Photo Company is using the cash basis of accounting.

b. The entry on January 5 will include a $6,400 credit to Cash.

c. The salaries expense charged to 1994 will be $8,000.

d. The salaries expense charged to 1994 will be $6,400.

e. The salaries expense charged to 1993 will be $6,400.

LO 6 A company owns the following items:

1. Land used in the operations of the business.

2. Office supplies.

3. Receivables from customers due in 10 months.

4. A three-year note receivable from the purchaser of land previously owned by the company.
5. The right to receive insurance protection for the next nine months.
6. Land held in case expanded operations require it.
7. Trucks used in servicing customers.
8. Trademarks used in selling the company's services.

These items should be classified as follows:

	Current Assets	Investments	Plant and Equipment	Intangible Assets
a.	2	4,6	1,7	3,5,8
b.	2,3,4	6	1,7	5,8
c.	2,3	4,6	1,7	5,8
d.	2,3,5	4	1,6,7	8
e.	2,3,5	4,6	1,7	8

LO 7 A distribution, generally of assets, made by a corporation to its shareholders is called:

a. A dividend.
b. Paid-out capital.
c. Retained earnings.
d. An intangible asset.
e. A withdrawal.

LO 8 Blalock Consulting Company records prepaid and unearned items in income statement accounts. In preparing adjusting entries at the end of the company's first operating period:

a. The accrual of unpaid salaries will require a debit to Prepaid Salaries and a credit to Salaries Expense.
b. The entry to recognize the existence of unused office supplies will require a debit to Supplies Expense and a credit to Office Supplies.
c. The entry to record the fact that some cash receipts for services remain unearned will require a debit to Consulting Fees Earned and a credit to Unearned Consulting Fees.
d. The accrual of earned but unbilled consulting fees will require a debit to Unearned Consulting Fees and a credit to Consulting Fees Earned.
e. None of the above is correct.

A letter [A] *identifies the questions, exercises, and problems based on Appendix A at the end of the chapter.*

---

1. Why is the life of a business divided into time periods of equal length?
2. In selecting a fiscal year, what types of businesses are most apt to select their natural business year instead of the calendar year?
3. Why would you expect some account balances of a concern to require updating at the end of an accounting period even though all transactions were correctly recorded?
4. What purposes are served by making end-of-period adjustments?
5. A prepaid expense is an asset at the time of its purchase or prepayment. When is it best to ignore this and record the prepayment as an expense? Why?

Questions for Class Discussion

6. What contra account is used to record amortization? Why is such an account used?

7. If a building is purchased for $100,000 and amortization of $2,500 is taken each year, what amount of accumulated amortization will appear in the balance sheet at the end of five years?

8. What is an accrued expense? Give an example.

9. How does an unearned revenue arise? Give an example.

10. What is an accrued revenue? Give an example.

11. When financial statements are prepared from an adjusted trial balance, why should the income statement be prepared first? What statement is prepared next?

12. Which accounting principles provide the basis for the adjustment process?

13. What is meant by the matching principle?

14. What is the difference between the cash and accrual bases of accounting?

A15. Bee Company records revenues received in advance with credits to liability accounts, while Cee Company records revenues received in advance with credits to revenue accounts. Will these companies have differences in their financial statements because of this difference in their procedures? Why or why not?

Mini Discussion Cases

Case 3–1

The president of Impatient Company called in the controller to personally express his displeasure with the length of time the accounting department took to produce the monthly financial statements. The controller replied that he appreciated the president's frustration; however, the month-end adjustments did require time, which was reduced to the absolute minimum. The president responded that he did not know why these adjustments were necessary. In fact, in his opinion, the time spent on adjustments was nothing more than a make-work procedure. It was unnecessary since these adjustments were repetitions of the same items which, if left alone, would cancel out the effects and result in financial statements that were just as accurate. For example, the president continued, with accrued wages payable at the end of each month, why then waste time on adjustments?

Required

Discuss whether the president's underlying assumptions are realistic and apply equally to all types of adjustments normally encountered at the end of each period.

Case 3–2

Short-Cut Company's president believed that the monthly executive meetings, which considered the results of previous month's activity, could be pushed ahead a couple of days if the financial statements were available. After a discussion with the controller, the president found out that the month-end adjustments were the cause of delays. Consequently, he is contemplating asking the controller to speed up month-end statement preparation without the benefit of month-end adjustments. However, before taking such a step, he asks you to evaluate such an alternative.

Required

Discuss the short-comings of unadjusted financial statements. Focus your discussion on (*a*) compliance with GAAP, (*b*) treatment of such items as supplies and insurance, and (*c*) manipulation of results.

Exercises

Ora Company's two employees each earn $90 per day for a four-day week that begins on Monday and ends on Thursday. They were paid for the week ended Thursday, December 27, and both worked a full day on Monday, December 31. January 1 of the next year was an unpaid holiday, but the employees all worked on Wednesday and Thursday, January 2 and 3. Journalize the year-end adjusting entry to record the accrued wages and the entry to pay the employees on January 3.

Exercise 3–1
Adjusting entries for accrued expenses (LO 3)

Prepare adjusting journal entries on December 31, 1993, prior to the preparation of annual financial statements, for the following independent situations:

a. The Supplies account had a $470 debit balance on January 1, 1993; $330 of supplies were purchased during the year; and a year-end inventory showed $100 of supplies on hand.

b. The Prepaid Insurance account had a $1,700 debit balance at the end of the accounting period before adjustment for expired insurance. An examination of insurance policies showed $1,360 of insurance had expired.

c. The Prepaid Insurance account had a $640 debit balance at the end of the accounting period before adjustment for expired insurance. An examination of insurance policies showed $440 of unexpired insurance.

d. Amortization on equipment was estimated at $3,470 for the accounting period.

e. Six months' property taxes, estimated at $1,260, have accrued but are unrecorded and unpaid at the accounting period end.

Exercise 3–2
Adjusting entries for expenses (LO 3)

Assume that the required adjustments of Exercise 3–2 were not made at the end of the accounting period. For each adjustment, tell the effect of its omission on the income statement and balance sheet prepared at that time.

Exercise 3–3
Omission of adjusting entries (LO 1, 4)

Determine the amounts indicated by the question marks in the following columns. The amounts in each column constitute a separate problem.

Exercise 3–4
Missing data in calculations of supplies (LO 3)

	(a)	(b)	(c)	(d)
Supplies on hand on January 1.	$180	$410	$745	$?
Supplies purchased during the year	230	390	?	645
Supplies remaining at the year-end	80	?	115	560
Supplies expense for the year	?	320	850	425

Prepare adjusting journal entries dated March 31 for the following items. Then prepare journal entries to record the April payments.

a. Employees are paid total salaries of $2,400 each Friday after they complete a five-day workweek. As of March 31, the employees had worked three days since the last payment. The next payment date is April 2.

b. The company owes a $90,000 note payable, which requires that 1% interest be paid each month on the 10th of the month. The interest was paid March 10 and the next payment is due April 10.

c. On March 1, the company retained a lawyer at a monthly fee of $300 payable on the 15th of the following month.

Exercise 3–5
Adjustments and payments of accrued items (LO 3, 5)

Exercise 3–6
Cash basis versus accrual basis expense amounts
(LO 2, 4)

Tote Company paid the $4,860 premium on a three-year insurance policy on September 1, 1993. The policy gave protection beginning on that date.

a. Assuming the accrual basis of accounting, how many dollars of the premium will appear as an expense on the annual income statement for 1993? for 1994? for 1995? for 1996?

b. Assuming the accrual basis, how many dollars of the premium will appear as an asset on each December 31 balance sheet for 1993? for 1994? for 1995? for 1996?

c. Assuming the cash basis of accounting, how many dollars of the premium will appear as an expense on the annual income statement for 1993? for 1994? for 1995? for 1996?

d. Assuming the cash basis, how many dollars of the premium will appear as an asset on each December 31 balance sheet for 1993? for 1994? for 1995? for 1996?

Exercise 3–7
Unearned and accrued revenues
(LO 2, 4)

The owner of an office building prepares annual financial statements based on a calendar-year accounting period.

a. A tenant rented space in the building on September 1 at $1,600 per month, paying six months' rent in advance. The receipt was credited to Unearned Rent. Give the December 31 adjusting entry of the building owner, prior to the preparation of annual financial statements.

b. Another tenant rented space in the building at $760 per month on November 1. The tenant paid the November rent on the first day of November, but by December 31 the December rent had not yet been paid. Give the December 31 adjusting entry of the building owner.

c. Assume the tenant in (*b*) paid the rent for December and January on January 3 of the new year. Give the entry to record the receipt of the $1,520.

Exercise 3–8
Classified balance sheet
(LO 6)

The adjusted trial balance that follows was taken from the ledger of Anthony Joseph, Photographer. Calculate the amount of owner's equity on December 31, 1993, and prepare a classified balance sheet for the business.

ANTHONY JOSEPH, PHOTOGRAPHER
Adjusted Trial Balance
December 31, 1993

Cash	$ 6,700	
Accounts receivable	4,100	
Photography supplies	1,950	
Prepaid insurance	2,050	
Investment in Geffen Corporation common shares	2,200	
Photography equipment	42,400	
Accumulated amortization, photography equipment		$ 20,750
Building	85,000	
Accumulated amortization, building		31,600
Land	70,000	
Salaries payable		400
Unearned photography fees		2,800
Long-term notes payable		108,500
Anthony Joseph, capital		56,350
Anthony Joseph, withdrawals	47,000	
Photography fees earned		80,300
Operating expenses (combined)	39,300	
Totals	$300,700	$300,700

An inexperienced bookkeeper prepared the income statement shown below in columns 1 and 2, but he forgot to adjust the accounts before its preparation. The accountant discovered the oversight and prepared the statement shown in columns 3 and 4. Analyze the statements and prepare the adjusting journal entries made between the preparation of the two statements. Assume that one fourth of the additional property management fees resulted from recognizing accrued fees and three fourths resulted from previously recorded unearned fees earned by the date of the statements.

Exercise 3–9
Analyzing statements for adjusting entries
(LO 3, 4)

SAMSON REALTY
Income Statements
For Year Ended December 31, 1993

	Prepared without Adjustments	Prepared after Adjustments
Revenues:		
Property management fees earned	$ 6,400	$ 7,800
Commissions earned	89,050	89,050
Total revenues	$95,450	$96,850
Operating expenses:		
Amortization expense, automobiles.		$ 4,000
Amortization expense, office equipment . .		1,400
Salaries expense	$16,500	17,700
Insurance expense		1,800
Rent expense	13,500	13,500
Office supplies expense		200
Advertising expense	3,750	3,750
Utilities expense	1,900	1,900
Total operating expenses	35,650	44,250
Net income	$59,800	$52,600

A corporation had $3 million of common shares issued and outstanding during all of 1993. It began the year with $650,000 of retained earnings, and it declared and paid $255,000 of cash dividends to its shareholders. It also earned a $640,000 1993 net income. Prepare the equity section of the corporation's year-end balance sheet.

Exercise 3–10
Balance sheet equity section for a corporation
(LO 6)

Calculate the missing item in each of the following cases:

Exercise 3–11
Calculating elements of change in owner's equity
(Review exercise)

	Case 1	Case 2	Case 3	Case 4	Case 5
The Owner, capital, January 1, 1993 . .	$45,000	$72,000	$ (c)	$89,300	$56,000
Total revenues during 1993	29,200	(b)	26,500	47,700	38,300
Total expenses during 1993	31,700	43,400	19,900	(d)	29,600
Withdrawals during the year	18,500	24,000	7,800	15,000	(e)
The Owner, capital, December 31, 1993	(a)	65,900	21,300	52,100	44,500

Calculate the missing item in each of the following cases:

Exercise 3–12
Calculating statement of changes in owner's equity amounts
(Review exercise)

	Case 1	Case 2	Case 3	Case 4
The Owner, capital, January 1, 1993	$37,000	$53,800	$ (c)	$66,600
Owner's investments during the year . .	12,500	(b)	26,500	17,700
Net income (loss) during 1993	14,000	32,500	(9,400)	(d)
Owner's withdrawals during the year . .	(a)	20,000	11,000	14,500
The Owner, capital, December 31, 1993	22,000	66,300	84,200	47,300

^AExercise 3–13
Adjustments for prepaid
items recorded in expense
and revenue accounts
(LO 8)

Alderan Consulting was organized on December 1 and follows the procedure of debiting expense accounts when it records prepayments of expenses; also, revenue accounts are credited when unearned revenues are received. Prepare adjusting journal entries on December 31 for the following items:

a. Shop Supplies were purchased during December for $840. A December 31 inventory showed that $505 of supplies were on hand.

b. The company paid insurance premiums of $660 during December. On December 31, an examination of the insurance policies showed that $110 of insurance had expired.

c. During December, the business received $3,500 from one client for two consulting projects. As of December 31, only one project, for which the client was charged $2,700, had been completed.

d. Late in December, the business received $800 from a second client for consulting services to be performed in January.

^AExercise 3–14
Adjustments for supplies
when purchases were
recorded as expenses
(LO 8)

Ritz-Carlton Company prepares monthly financial statements. On September 30, the balance in the Office Supplies account was $350. During October, $490 of supplies were purchased and debited to Office Supplies Expense.

a. Prepare an adjusting journal entry on October 31 to account for the supplies, assuming an October 31 inventory of supplies showed that $120 of supplies were on hand.

b. Prepare an adjusting journal entry on October 31 to account for the supplies, assuming an October 31 inventory of supplies showed that $510 of supplies were on hand.

Problems

Problem 3–1
Adjusting journal entries
(LO 3, 5)

The following information for adjustments was available on December 31, 1993, the end of Ming Company's annual accounting period.

a. The Office Supplies account had an $80 debit balance at the beginning of the year, $490 of supplies were purchased during the year, and the inventory of supplies at year-end totaled $140.

b. An examination of insurance policies showed three policies, as follows:

Policy	Date of Purchase	Life of Policy	Cost
1	September 1, 1992	3 years	$2,700
2	March 1, 1993	2 years	3,480
3	July 1, 1993	1 year	540

Prepaid Insurance was debited for the cost of each policy at the time of its purchase. Expired insurance was correctly recorded at the end of 1992.

c. The company's three employees earn $60 per day, $70 per day, and $120 per day, respectively. They are paid each Friday for a five-day workweek that begins on Monday. This year, December 31 fell on Thursday, and the employees all worked on Monday, Tuesday, Wednesday, and Thursday. The next payment for five days' work will be on January 1.

d. The company purchased a building on June 1, 1993. The building cost $396,000, has an estimated 30-year life, and is not expected to have any salvage value at the end of that time.

e. The company occupies most of the space in its building, and it also rents space. One tenant rented a small amount of space on October 1 at $540 per month. The tenant paid the rent on the first day of October and November, and the amounts paid were credited to Rent Earned. However, the tenant did not pay the December rent until January 15, 1994, at which time he also paid the rent for January.

f. Another tenant agreed on November 1 to rent a small amount of space at $750 per month, and on that date paid three months' rent in advance. The receipt was credited to Unearned Rent.

Required

1. Given the preceding information, journalize adjusting entries dated December 31, 1993, prior to the preparation of annual financial statements.

2. Prepare journal entries to record the January payments and receipts that involve amounts accrued on December 31.

Community Technical School's unadjusted trial balance on December 31, 1993, the end of its annual accounting period, is as follows:

Problem 3–2
Adjusting entries and the
adjusted trial balance
(LO 3, 4, 6)

COMMUNITY TECHNICAL SCHOOL
Trial Balance
December 31, 1993

Cash	$ 7,200	
Office supplies	4,300	
Prepaid insurance	8,100	
Professional library	19,800	
Accumulated amortization, professional library		$ 8,490
Equipment	43,300	
Accumulated amortization, equipment		14,900
Accounts payable		860
Unearned extension fees		2,400
Kay Perry, capital		55,950
Kay Perry, withdrawals	15,000	
Enrollment fees earned		43,400
Salaries expense	16,800	
Rent expense	9,600	
Advertising expense	500	
Utilities expense	1,400	
Totals	$126,000	$126,000

Required

1. Set up accounts for the items in the trial balance plus these accounts: Accounts Receivable; Salaries Payable; Extension Fees Earned; Amortization Expense, Equipment; Amortization Expense, Professional Library; Insurance Expense; and Office Supplies Expense. Enter the trial balance amounts in the accounts.

2. Use the following information to prepare and post adjusting entries:
    a. An examination of insurance policies shows $900 of expired insurance.
    b. An inventory shows $1,670 of office supplies on hand.
    c. Estimated annual amortization on the equipment is $3,300.
    d. Estimated annual amortization on the professional library is $1,320.
    e. Community Technical School offers extended services to those in need of training beyond the campus. On November 1, the company agreed to in-home tutoring for a client. The contract calls for a $600 monthly fee, and the client paid the first four months' fees in advance at the time the contract was signed. The amount paid was credited to Unearned Extension Fees.
    f. On October 15, the school agreed to teach a three-month computer class for a local business for $1,080 per month payable at the end of the class. Extension fees for two and one half months have accrued.

g. The one employee is paid weekly; and on December 31, three days' wages at $70 per day have accrued.

3. After posting the adjusting entries, prepare an adjusted trial balance, an income statement, a statement of changes in owner's equity, and a classified balance sheet. Perry did not make additional investments in the business during the year.

Problem 3–3
Adjusting entries and the adjusted trial balance
(LO 3, 4, 6)

The unadjusted trial balance of Eden's Garden follows:

EDEN'S GARDEN
Trial Balance
December 31, 1993

Cash	$ 3,000	
Accounts receivable	1,400	
Landscaping supplies	1,680	
Prepaid insurance	3,200	
Investment in Sierra, Inc., common shares (long-term) . .	6,000	
Trucks	42,000	
Accumulated amortization, trucks.		$ 17,000
Landscaping equipment	5,700	
Accumulated amortization, landscaping equipment		1,900
Building	68,000	
Accumulated amortization, building		19,800
Land	16,000	
Franchise	30,000	
Unearned landscape architecture fees		1,050
Long-term notes payable		75,600
Eve Adams, capital		49,270
Eve Adams, withdrawals	27,000	
Landscape architecture fees earned		12,250
Landscaping services revenue		84,000
Office salaries expense	14,200	
Landscape wages expense	31,950	
Interest expense	6,800	
Gas, oil, and repairs expense	3,940	
Totals	$260,870	$260,870

Required

1. Set up accounts for the items in the trial balance plus these additional accounts: Wages Payable; Amortization Expense, Building; Amortization Expense, Trucks; Amortization Expense, Landscaping Equipment; Insurance Expense; and Landscaping Supplies Expense. Enter the trial balance amounts in the accounts. Journalize and post adjusting entries given the following information:
    a. Insurance premiums of $2,220 expired during the year.
    b. An inventory showed $410 of unused landscaping supplies on hand.
    c. Estimated amortization on the landscaping equipment, $820.
    d. Estimated amortization on the trucks, $6,600.
    e. Estimated amortization on the building, $3,020.
    f. Of the $1,050 credit balance in Unearned Landscape Architecture Fees, $750 was earned by the year-end.
    g. Accrued landscape architecture fees earned but unrecorded at year-end totaled $480.
    h. There were $630 of earned but unrecorded landscape wages at the year-end.

2. Prepare an adjusted trial balance, an income statement for the year, a statement of changes in owner's equity, and a classified year-end balance sheet. Adams's capital account balance reflects the December 31, 1992, balance plus a January 1, 1993, investment of $12,000. A $9,000 installment on the note payable is due within one year.

Cherokee Campground's unadjusted trial balance is as follows:

Problem 3–4
Adjusting entries and the
adjusted trial balance
(LO 3, 4, 6)

CHEROKEE CAMPGROUND
Trial Balance
December 31, 1993

Cash.	$ 2,850	
Office supplies.	180	
Prepaid insurance	1,470	
Office equipment	3,400	
Accumulated amortization, office equipment . .		$ 2,300
Buildings.	174,500	
Accumulated amortization, buildings		28,750
Land.	48,000	
Unearned fees		1,300
Long-term notes payable		155,750
John Eagle, capital.		30,260
John Eagle, withdrawals.	12,000	
Fees earned		51,640
Wages expense.	8,700	
Interest expense	13,470	
Property taxes expense	3,100	
Utilities expense.	2,330	
Totals	$270,000	$270,000

Required

1. Set up accounts for the items in the trial balance plus these additional accounts: Accounts Receivable; Interest Payable; Wages Payable; Estimated Property Taxes Payable; Amortization Expense, Buildings; Amortization Expense, Office Equipment; Insurance Expense; and Office Supplies Expense. Enter the trial balance amounts in the accounts.

2. Use the following information to prepare adjusting journal entries:
   a. An insurance policy examination showed $1,100 of expired insurance.
   b. An inventory showed $60 of office supplies on hand.
   c. Estimated amortization expense on office equipment, $680.
   d. Estimated amortization on buildings, $7,200.
   e. By year-end, $840 of the Unearned Fees account balance was earned.
   f. A camper is in arrears on fee payments, and this $90 of accrued revenue was unrecorded at the time the trial balance was prepared.
   g. The one employee of the campground works a five-day workweek at $40 per day. The employee was paid last week but has worked three days this week for which he has not been paid.
   h. Three months' property taxes, totaling $780, have accrued. This additional amount of property tax expense has not been recorded.
   i. One month's interest on the note payable, $1,120, has accrued but is unrecorded.

3. Post the adjusting entries and prepare an adjusted trial balance, an income statement for the year, a statement of changes in owner's equity, and a classified balance sheet. Eagle's capital account balance has not been increased by investments during 1993. A $9,000 installment on the note payable is due within one year.

Problem 3–5
Comparing the unadjusted
and adjusted trial balances
(LO 3, 4)

Foster Company's unadjusted trial balance and adjusted trial balance on December 31, 1993, the end of its annual accounting period, appear as follows:

	Unadjusted Trial Balance		Adjusted Trial Balance	
Cash.	$ 15,450		$ 15,450	
Accounts receivable			3,050	
Office supplies.	1,320		480	
Prepaid insurance	2,400		1,200	
Office equipment	8,700		8,700	
Accumulated amortization, office equipment .		$ 1,600		$ 2,400
Accounts payable		720		1,130
Interest payable				1,230
Salaries payable				1,500
Unearned consulting fees		6,750		3,670
Long-term notes payable		7,300		7,300
Frank Foster, capital		8,470		8,470
Frank Foster, withdrawals.	44,040		44,040	
Consulting fees earned.		93,130		99,260
Amortization expense, office equipment . . .			800	
Salaries expense.	28,100		29,600	
Interest expense.			1,230	
Insurance expense.			1,200	
Rent expense	13,500		13,500	
Office supplies expense			840	
Advertising expense.	4,460		4,870	
Totals	$117,970	$117,970	$124,960	$124,960

Required

Examine Foster Company's unadjusted and adjusted trial balances and prepare the year-end adjusting journal entries that Foster must have made. Your adjusting entries should explain the differences between the two trial balances.

Problem 3–6
Accrual basis income
statement
(LO 2, 3, 5)

Andrea Perkins purchased Four Seasons, an eight-unit apartment building, last September 1, and she has operated it four months without keeping formal accounting records. However, she has deposited all receipts in the bank and has kept an accurate chequebook record of payments. An analysis of the cash receipts and payments follows:

	Receipts	Payments
Investment	$114,000	
Purchased Four Seasons:		
Office equipment		$ 2,620
Buildings		156,000
Land		89,000
Total		$247,620
Less long-term note payable signed . .		148,500
Cash paid.		$ 99,120
Wages paid		7,380
Insurance premium paid		4,200
Office supplies purchased		500
Property taxes paid.		2,100
Utilities paid		800
Owner's withdrawals of cash		3,200
Apartment rentals collected	16,000	
Totals.	$130,000	$117,300
Cash balance, December 31		12,700
Totals.	$130,000	$130,000

Ms. Perkins wants you to prepare an accrual basis income statement for the apartment for the four-month period she has operated the business, a statement of changes in owner's equity, and a December 31 classified balance sheet. You ascertain the following (T-accounts may be helpful in organizing the data):

The building was estimated to have a 20-year remaining life when purchased and at the end of that time will be wrecked. It is estimated that the sale of salvaged materials will just pay the wrecking costs and the cost of clearing the site. The office equipment is in good condition. At the time of purchase, Ms. Perkins estimated she would use the equipment for three years and would then trade it in on new equipment of like kind. She thought $100 was a fair estimate of what she would receive for the old equipment when she traded it in at the end of three years.

The $4,200 payment for insurance was for a policy taken out on September 1. The policy's protection was for one year beginning on that date. Ms. Perkins estimates that one half of the office supplies purchased have been used. She also says that the one employee of the apartment earns $50 per day for a five-day week that ends on Friday. The employee was paid last week but has worked three days, December 29 through 31, for which he has not been paid.

Included in the $16,000 of apartment rentals collected is $1,500 received from a tenant for three months' rent beginning on December 1. Also, a tenant has not paid his $500 rent for the month of December.

The long-term note payable requires an annual payment of 10 per cent interest on the beginning principal balance plus a $7,500 annual payment on the principal. The first payment is due next September 1. The property tax payment was for one year's taxes that were paid on October 1 for the tax year beginning on September 1, the day Ms. Perkins purchased the business.

Masquerade Company debits expense accounts when recording prepaid expenses; it credits revenue accounts when recording unearned receipts. The following information was available on December 31, 1993, the end of the company's annual accounting period.

^A**Problem 3–7**
Recording prepayments and unearned items in income statement accounts
(LO 2, 8)

a. The Store Supplies account had a $740 debit balance at the beginning of the year, $1,600 of supplies were purchased during the year, and an inventory of unused supplies at the year-end totaled $520.

b. An examination of insurance policies showed two policies, as follows:

Policy	Date of Purchase	Life of Policy	Cost
1	April 1, 1991	3 years	$3,240
2	August 1, 1993	2 years	960

Insurance Expense was debited for the cost of each policy at the time of its purchase. However, the correct amount of Prepaid Insurance was recorded during the adjustment processes at the end of 1991 and 1992.

c. On November 15, 1993, Masquerade Company agreed to provide consulting services to a client and received an advance payment of $4,200. At year-end, the client agreed that two thirds of the services had been provided.

d. The company occupies most of the space in its building but it also rents space to one tenant. The tenant agreed on November 1 to rent a small amount of space at $400 per month, and on that date paid three months' rent in advance.

e. The Office Supplies account had a $320 debit balance at the beginning of the year and $650 of supplies were purchased during the year. A year-end inventory of office supplies indicated that supplies amounting to $710 had been used during the year.

Required

Prepare adjusting journal entries dated December 31, 1993, prior to the preparation of annual financial statements. For item *b*, prepare a separate adjusting entry for each insurance policy.

Problem 3-8
Analytical essay
(LO 3, 4, 5)

Review the information presented in Problem 3-3 and focus on the adjustment information described in requirement 1. Then describe the effects of each of the following assumptions on the 1993 income statement; the December 31, 1993, balance sheet; the 1994 income statement; and the December 31, 1994, balance sheet.

1. Assume that the company failed to record the estimated 1993 amortization of $6,600 on the trucks. This error was not discovered during 1993 or 1994.

2. Assume that the company failed to record the $480 of accrued landscape architecture fees at the end of 1993. Instead, these fees were recorded as earned when the cash was received during 1994.

3. Assume that the December 31, 1993, adjusting entry to record the $630 of accrued landscape wages was incorrectly made for $360. Then, when the correct amount of wages was paid in 1994, $360 was removed from Wages Payable and the rest of the payment was charged to Landscape Wages Expense.

ᴬProblem 3-9
Analytical essay
(LO 3, 4, 8)

On October 1, 1993, Able Company and Bravo Company each paid $3,600 for two-year insurance policies. Able recorded its payment with a debit to Prepaid Insurance and Bravo recorded its payment with a debit to Insurance Expense. Explain the differences between the adjusting entries the two companies should make on December 31, 1993, the end of their annual accounting periods. Also explain how the difference in the two companies' procedures affect the financial statements.

Alternate Problems

Problem 3-1A
Adjusting journal entries
(LO 3, 5)

The following information for preparing adjusting entries was available on December 31, 1993, the end of Sherwood Company's annual accounting period:

a. The Office Supplies account had a $240 debit balance at the beginning of the year, $760 of supplies were purchased during the year, and the inventory of supplies at year-end totaled $190.

b. An examination of insurance policies showed three policies, as follows:

Policy	Protection Began on	Life of Policy	Cost
1	April 14, 1991	3 years	$1,440
2	July 1, 1991	2 years	1,800
3	October 1, 1993	1 year	420

Prepaid Insurance was debited for the cost of each policy at the time of purchase. Expired insurance was correctly recorded at the end of 1991 and 1992.

c. The company's two employees earn $45 per day and $80 per day, respectively. They are paid each Friday for a five-day workweek that begins on Monday. December 31 fell on Tuesday, and the employees both worked on Monday and Tuesday but have not been paid. The next payment for five days' work will be on January 3.

d. The company purchased a building on May 1, 1993. The building cost $472,500, has an estimated 25-year life, and is not expected to have any salvage value at the end of its life.

e. The company occupies most of the space in its building, and it also rents space. One tenant rented a small amount of space on September 1 at $650 per month. The tenant paid the rent on the first day of each month, September through November, and the amounts paid were credited to Rent Earned. However, the tenant did not pay the December rent until January 12, at which time she also paid the rent for January.

f. Another tenant agreed on November 1 to rent a small amount of space at $490 per month and on that date paid three months' rent in advance. The amount paid was credited to Unearned Rent.

Required

1. Given the preceding information, journalize adjusting entries dated December 31, 1993, prior to the preparation of annual financial statements.

2. Prepare journal entries to record the January payments and receipts that involve amounts accrued on December 31.

Landscape Design School's unadjusted trial balance on December 31, 1993, the end of its annual accounting period, is as follows:

Problem 3–2A
Adjusting entries and the adjusted trial balance
(LO 3, 4, 6)

LANDSCAPE DESIGN SCHOOL
Trial Balance
December 31, 1993

Cash	$ 7,200	
Office supplies	4,300	
Prepaid insurance.	8,100	
Professional library.	19,800	
Accumulated amortization, professional library . .		$ 8,490
Equipment	43,300	
Accumulated amortization, equipment		14,900
Accounts payable.		860
Unearned extension fees		2,400
Kay Perry, capital		55,950
Kay Perry, withdrawals	15,000	
Enrollment fees earned.		43,400
Salaries expense	16,800	
Rent expense.	9,600	
Advertising expense	500	
Utilities expense	1,400	
Totals.	$126,000	$126,000

Required

1. Set up accounts for the items in the trial balance plus these additional accounts: Accounts Receivable; Salaries Payable; Extension Fees Earned; Amortization Expense, Equipment; Amortization Expense, Professional Library; Insurance Expense; and Office Supplies Expense. Enter the trial balance amounts in the accounts.

2. Use the information that follows to prepare and post adjusting entries:
   a. An examination of insurance policies shows $2,025 of expired insurance.
   b. An inventory shows $1,075 of supplies on hand.
   c. Estimated annual amortization on the equipment is $3,830.
   d. Estimated annual amortization on the library is $2,800.

e. The December utilities bill arrived after the trial balance was prepared, and its $420 amount was not included in the trial balance amounts. Also, a $120 bill for newspaper advertising that had appeared in December was not included in the trial balance amounts.

f. A client who was landscaping his office building signed a contract with Landscape Design School for consulting assistance through the extension services offered. The contract calls for a $150 monthly fee and services began on December 1. The client paid three months' fees in advance, and the amount paid was credited to the Unearned Extension Fees account.

g. Landscape Design School agreed to hold a seminar, through the extension services, on xeriscape design for the City Environmental Services Department for $400 per month payable at the end of three months. The contract was signed on November 15, and one and one half months' fees have accrued.

h. The one employee is paid weekly, and on December 31, four days' wages at $80 per day have accrued.

3. After posting the adjusting entries, prepare an adjusted trial balance, an income statement, a statement of changes in owner's equity, and a classified balance sheet. Perry's capital account balance of $55,950 consists of a $48,950 balance on December 31, 1992, plus a $7,000 investment during 1993.

Problem 3–3A
Adjusting entries and the adjusted trial balance
(LO 3, 4, 6)

The unadjusted trial balance of Tejas Landscape follows:

TEJAS LANDSCAPE
Trial Balance
December 31, 1993

Cash	$ 3,000	
Accounts receivable	1,400	
Landscaping supplies	1,680	
Prepaid insurance	3,200	
Investment in Sierra, Inc., common shares (long-term)	6,000	
Trucks	42,000	
Accumulated amortization, trucks		$ 17,000
Landscaping equipment	5,700	
Accumulated amortization, landscaping equipment		1,900
Building	68,000	
Accumulated amortization, building		19,800
Land	16,000	
Franchise	30,000	
Unearned landscape architecture fees		1,050
Long-term notes payable		75,600
Eve Adams, capital		49,270
Eve Adams, withdrawals	27,000	
Landscape architecture fees earned		12,250
Landscaping services revenue		84,000
Office salaries expense	14,200	
Landscape wages expense	31,950	
Interest expense	6,800	
Gas, oil, and repairs expense	3,940	
Totals	$260,870	$260,870

Required

1. Set up accounts for the items in the trial balance plus these additional accounts: Wages Payable; Amortization Expense, Building; Amortization Expense, Trucks; Amortization Expense, Landscaping Equipment; Insurance Expense; and Landscaping Supplies Expense. Enter the trial balance amounts in the accounts.

2. Use the information that follows to prepare and post adjusting entries:
   a. Insurance premiums of $960 expired during the year.
   b. An inventory shows $990 of unused landscaping supplies on hand.
   c. Amortization on the landscaping equipment, $1,400.
   d. Amortization on the trucks, $8,300.
   e. Amortization on the building, $3,800.
   f. Of the $1,050 balance in the Unearned Landscape Architecture Fees account, $350 was earned by the year-end.
   g. Accrued landscape architecture fees earned but unrecorded at year-end totaled $1,000.
   h. There were $720 of earned but unrecorded landscape wages at the year-end.

3. Prepare an adjusted trial balance, an income statement for the year, a statement of changes in owner's equity, and a classified year-end balance sheet. Adams's $49,270 capital balance reflects the December 31, 1992, balance plus a January 15, 1993, investment of $15,000. A $9,450 installment on the long-term note payable is due within one year.

Great Outdoors' unadjusted trial balance, at the end of its annual accounting period, follows:

Problem 3–4A
Adjusting entries and the adjusted trial balance
(LO 3, 4, 6)

GREAT OUTDOORS
Trial Balance
December 31, 1993

Cash	$ 2,850	
Office supplies	180	
Prepaid insurance	1,470	
Office equipment	3,400	
Accumulated amortization, office equipment . .		$ 2,300
Buildings	174,500	
Accumulated amortization, buildings		28,750
Land	48,000	
Unearned fees		1,300
Long-term notes payable		155,750
John Eagle, capital		30,260
John Eagle, withdrawals	12,000	
Fees earned		51,640
Wages expense	8,700	
Interest expense	13,470	
Property taxes expense	3,100	
Utilities expense	2,330	
Totals	$270,000	$270,000

Required

1. Set up accounts for the items in the trial balance plus these additional accounts: Accounts Receivable; Interest Payable; Wages Payable; Estimated Property Taxes Payable; Amortization Expense, Buildings; Amortization Expense, Office Equipment; Insurance Expense; and Office Supplies Expense. Enter the trial balance amounts in the accounts.

2. Use the information that follows to prepare adjusting journal entries:
   a. An insurance policy examination shows $490 of expired insurance.
   b. An inventory shows $50 of office supplies on hand.
   c. Estimated amortization of office equipment, $600.
   d. Amortization of buildings, $8,100.
   e. An examination reveals that $550 of the Unearned Fees balance was earned by the year-end.

      f. One camper is in arrears on fee payments, and this $150 of accrued revenue was unrecorded at the time the trial balance was prepared.

      g. Four months' property tax expense, estimated at $1,040, has accrued but was not recorded at the time the trial balance was prepared.

      h. The one employee of the campground works a five-day week at $50 per day. He was paid last week but has worked four days this week for which he has not been paid.

      i. Three months' interest on the note payable, $3,900, has accrued but is unpaid on the trial balance date.

3. Post the adjusting entries and prepare an adjusted trial balance, an income statement for the year, a statement of changes in owner's equity, and a classified balance sheet. Eagle's capital account balance has not been increased by investments during 1993. A $7,800 payment on the long-term note payable is due within one year.

Problem 3–5A
Comparing the unadjusted and adjusted trial balances
(LO 3, 4)

Northside Management's unadjusted trial balance and adjusted trial balance on December 31, the end of its annual accounting period, appear as follows:

	Unadjusted Trial Balance		Adjusted Trial Balance	
Cash	$ 23,515		$ 23,515	
Accounts receivable			2,220	
Office supplies	960		320	
Prepaid insurance	12,000		8,000	
Office equipment	13,220		13,220	
Accumulated amortization, office equipment		$ 4,250		$ 6,120
Building	195,000		195,000	
Accumulated amortization, building		45,600		58,400
Land	65,000		65,000	
Accounts payable		1,750		3,790
Interest payable				8,560
Estimated property taxes payable				6,400
Unearned management fees		15,270		7,190
Long-term notes payable		92,700		92,700
Susan Rain, capital		22,775		22,775
Susan Rain, withdrawals	52,200		52,200	
Management fees earned		261,750		272,050
Amortization expense, building			12,800	
Amortization expense, office equipment . .			1,870	
Wages expense	54,800		54,800	
Interest expense			8,560	
Insurance expense			4,000	
Office supplies expense			640	
Advertising expense	21,660		23,700	
Property taxes expense			6,400	
Utilities expense	5,740		5,740	
Totals	$444,095	$444,095	$477,985	$477,985

Required

Examine Northside Management's unadjusted and adjusted trial balances and prepare the year-end adjusting journal entries that must have been entered. Your entries should explain the differences between the two trial balances.

David Pittard, a lawyer, has always kept his records on a cash basis; at the end of 1993, he prepared the following cash basis income statement:

DAVID PITTARD, LAWYER
Income Statement
For Year Ended December 31, 1993

Revenues	$256,000
Expenses	80,450
Net income	$175,550

In preparing the statement, he ignored the following amounts of prepaid, unearned, and accrued items at the end of 1992 and 1993:

	End of	
	1992	**1993**
Prepaid expenses	$12,600	$14,200
Accrued expenses	6,120	5,800
Unearned revenues	10,400	7,500
Accrued revenues	12,000	14,900

Required

Under the assumptions that the 1992 prepaid expenses were consumed or expired in 1993, the 1992 unearned revenues were earned in 1993, and the 1992 accrued items were either paid or received in cash in 1993, prepare a 1993 accrual basis income statement for David Pittard's law practice. Attach to your statement calculations showing how you arrived at each 1993 income statement amount.

In recording prepaid expenses and unearned revenues, Major League Company debits the disbursements to expense accounts and credits the receipts to revenue accounts. The following information was available on December 31, 1993, the end of Major League Company's annual accounting period:

^AProblem 3–7A
Recording prepayments
and unearned items in
income statement
accounts
(LO 2, 8)

a. The Store Supplies account had a $400 debit balance at the beginning of the year, $1,150 of supplies were purchased during the year, and an inventory of unused supplies at the year-end totaled $1,250.

b. An examination of insurance policies showed two policies, as follows:

Policy	Date of Purchase	Life of Policy	Cost
1	July 1, 1991	3 years	$3,420
2	October 1, 1993	2 years	8,640

Insurance Expense was debited for the cost of each policy at the time of its purchase. However, the correct amount of Prepaid Insurance was recorded during the adjustment processes at the end of 1991 and 1992.

c. On September 17, 1993, Major League Company agreed to provide consulting services to a client and received an advance payment of $9,450. At year-end, the client agreed that two thirds of the services had been provided.

d. The company occupies most of the space in its building, and it also rents space to one tenant. The tenant agreed on October 1 to rent a small amount of space at $750 per month, and on that date paid six months' rent in advance.

e. The Office Supplies account had a $220 debit balance at the beginning of the year and $540 of supplies were purchased during the year. A year-end inventory of office supplies indicated that supplies amounting to $400 had been used during the year.

Required

Prepare adjusting journal entries dated December 31, 1993, prior to the preparation of annual financial statements. For item *b,* prepare a separate adjusting entry for each insurance policy.

Problem 3–8A
Analytical essay
(LO 3, 4, 5)

Review the information presented in Problem 3–3A and focus on the adjustment information described in requirement 2. Then describe the effects of each of the following assumptions on the 1993 income statement; the December 31, 1993, balance sheet; the 1994 income statement; and the December 31, 1994, balance sheet.

1. Assume that the company incorrectly recorded the $8,300 estimated 1993 amortization on the trucks as $3,800. This error was not discovered during 1993 or 1994.

2. Assume that the company failed to record the fact that $350 of the $1,050 balance in the Unearned Landscape Architecture Fees account had been earned by the end of the 1993 year. Instead, when the adjusting entries were made on December 31, 1994, these fees were recorded as earned during 1994.

3. Assume that the company failed to record the $720 of accrued landscape wages on December 31, 1993. Then, when the correct amount of wages was paid in 1994, the entire payment was recorded as wages expense.

^A**Problem 3–9A**
Analytical essay
(LO 3, 4, 8)

On September 1, 1993, Delta Company and Echo Company each received $5,400 for consulting services to be provided over the next several months. Delta recorded its receipt with a credit to Unearned Consulting Services Revenue and Echo recorded its receipt with a credit to Consulting Services Revenue. As of December 31, 1993, each company had earned $1,200 of the amount received in advance. Explain the differences between the adjusting entries the two companies should make on December 31, 1993, the end of their annual accounting periods. Also explain how the difference in the two companies' procedures affects the financial statements.

Serial Problem

Precision Computer Services

(This problem should not be assigned unless the working papers are being used. This is the second segment of a serial problem that started in Chapter 2 and continues in Chapters 4 and 5. If you did not complete the solution in Chapter 2, you can begin the problem at this point. However, you may need to review some of the facts presented in the Chapter 2 segment of the problem. See page 122).

Precision Computer Services has had a successful two months of business since it started on October 1, 1993. At the request of John Conard, the owner, you already recorded the transactions that occurred during October and November. (This was done in Chapter 2.) Now, before making the December entries, several additional accounts have been added to the General Ledger, as shown on page 175.

Accounts	Number
Accumulated Amortization, Office Equipment	164
Accumulated Amortization, Computer Equipment . .	168
Wages Payable	210
Unearned Computer Fees	233
Amortization Expense, Office Equipment	612
Amortization Expense, Computer Equipment	613
Insurance Expense	637
Rent Expense	640
Computer Supplies Expense	652

Required

1. Journalize and post the following December transactions and end-of-period adjusting entries:

Dec. 2 Paid $300 to the Town Hall Shopping Centre for Precision's share of advertising that benefited all businesses in the centre.

3 Paid $76 to repair the company's computer.

5 Received total amount due from AB Company as a result of the transaction on November 25.

6 Paid Ann White for four days' work at her regular daily rate of $70.

9 Received notice from AB Company that Precision's bid of $1,850 for computer services was accepted. An advance of $450 was received.

11 Purchased on credit from Ajax Supply additional computer supplies, $85.

12 Sent a second bill to Farm Research for services originally recorded on November 8.

13 Received notice that Republic had deducted a $4 service charge from the chequing account.

16 Paid Shopper Newspaper $15 for newspaper advertisement.

18 Completed work for Dog Enterprise and received $495.

20 Paid John Conard $675 for personal use.

20 Ann White did not work during the last two weeks.

22–26 Took the week off for Christmas holiday.

29 Received a $450 payment from Farm Research on their outstanding account balance that resulted from a November 8 transaction.

30 Paid hydro bill of $51 and telephone bill of $110.

31 Reimbursed Ann White's business car use, 50 km at $0.24 per km.

31 Reimbursed John Conard's business car use, 300 km at $0.24 per km.

31 In anticipation of preparing financial statements for the three-month period since the business started, gathered the following information related to adjusting entries:

a) Computer Supplies ending inventory, $17.

b) Three months' insurance has expired.

c) December 31 falls on Wednesday, and Ann White has worked three days, but will not be paid until Friday, January 2.

d) The computer is expected to have a three-year useful life with no salvage value.

e) The office equipment is expected to have a four-year useful life with no salvage value.

f) Recalled that four months' rent had been paid in advance early in October.

2. After you have journalized and posted these transactions and adjusting entries, prepare an adjusted trial balance; an income statement for the last three months of 1993; a statement of changes in owner's equity for the last three months of 1993; and a December 31, 1993, balance sheet.

Provocative Problems

Provocative Problem 3–1
Landmark Property Services
(LO 3, 4)

The 1992 and 1993 balance sheets of Landmark Property Services show the following assets and liabilities at the end of each of the years:

	December 31	
	1992	**1993**
Accounts receivable	$ 4,450	$ 3,180
Prepaid insurance	5,720	2,600
Interest payable	14,625	11,700
Unearned property management fees	5,200	6,460

The company's records show the following amounts of cash disbursed and received for these items during 1993:

Cash disbursed to pay insurance premiums	$ 4,470
Cash disbursed to pay interest	18,750
Cash received for managing property	76,200

Present calculations to show the amounts to be reported on Landmark Property Services' 1993 income statement for (*a*) insurance expense, (*b*) interest expense, and (*c*) property management fees earned.

Provocative Problem 3–2
AAA Appliance Repair
(LO 2, 3, 4, 6)

Arthur McNair began AAA Appliance Repair, a new business, on January 2, 1993. After one year's operation, McNair believes the business has done a lot of work. However, the bank has begun to dishonour AAA's cheques. Creditors are billing the company for amounts it is unable to pay, and McNair is concerned that the business has not been profitable. He would like to determine whether or not to continue operations. Consequently, he has asked your help in evaluating the first year's operations.

You find that the service's accounting records, such as they are, have been kept by McNair's son, who has no formal training in record-keeping. However, he has prepared for your inspection the following statement of cash receipts and disbursements:

AAA APPLIANCE REPAIR
Cash Receipts and Disbursements
For Year Ended December 31, 1993

Receipts:		
Owner's investment	$25,000	
Received from customers for services	45,900	$70,900
Disbursements:		
Rent expense	$ 5,590	
Repair equipment purchased	22,750	
Service truck expense	13,100	
Wages expense	17,500	
Insurance expense	3,000	
Repair parts and supplies	9,290	71,230
Bank overdraft		$ (330)

There were no errors in the statement, and you learn these additional facts:

1. The lease contract for the shop space runs for five years and requires rent payments of $430 per month, with the first and last month's rent to be paid in advance. All required payments were made on time.

2. The repair equipment has an estimated five-year life, after which it will be valueless. It has been used a full year.

3. The service truck expense consists of $11,500 paid for the truck on January 2, plus $1,600 paid for gas, oil, and repairs. McNair expects to use the truck five years, after which he expects to get $2,000 for it as a trade-in on a new truck.

4. The wages expense consists of $4,000 paid the repair service's one employee who was hired on September 1, plus $13,500 of personal withdrawals by McNair. Also, the one employee is owed $190 of earned but unpaid wages.

5. The $3,000 of insurance expense resulted from paying premiums on two insurance policies on January 2. One policy cost $840 and gave protection for one year. The other policy cost $2,160 for two years' protection.

6. In addition to the $9,290 of repair parts and supplies paid for during the year, creditors have billed the business $430 for parts and supplies purchased and delivered but not paid for. Also, an inventory shows $1,660 of parts and supplies on hand.

7. McNair reports that the business does most of its work for cash, but customers owe $620 for repair work done on credit.

Prepare an accrual basis income statement for the year, a statement of changes in owner's equity, and a classified balance sheet showing its year-end financial position. (The bank overdraft represents a current obligation of the service business to the bank.)

During the first week of January 1993, Sheila Lyon began a jewelry design and repair business, Benchmark Design and Goldsmith. She has kept no accounting records, but she does keep any unpaid invoices in a box near her workbench. She has kept a good record of the year's receipts and payments, which follows:

Provocative Problem 3–3
Benchmark Design and Goldsmith
(LO 2, 3, 4, 6)

	Receipts	Payments
Investment.	$18,000	
Shop equipment		$ 8,200
Repair parts and supplies.		10,600
Rent payments		5,850
Insurance premiums paid.		720
Newspaper advertising paid		1,470
Utility bills paid		1,020
Part-time helper's wages paid		5,200
Sheila Lyon for personal use.		16,500
Revenue from repairs	34,150	
Subtotals.	$52,150	$49,560
Cash balance, December 31, 1993		2,590
Totals	$52,150	$52,150

Lyon would like to know how much the business actually earned during its first year. Therefore, she would like you to prepare an accrual basis income statement, a statement of changes in owner's equity, and a year-end classified balance sheet for the shop.

The shop equipment has an estimated eight-year life, after which it will be worthless. There is a $980 unpaid invoice in the box near Lyon's workbench for supplies received, and an inventory shows $1,740 of supplies on hand. The shop space rents for

$450 per month on a five-year lease. The lease contract requires payment of the first and last months' rents in advance, which were paid. The insurance premiums were for two policies taken out on January 2. The first is a one-year policy that cost $300. The second is a two-year policy that cost $420. There are $120 of earned but unpaid wages owed the helper, and customers owe the shop $1,650 for services they have received.

Provocative Problem 3–4
Bombardier Inc.
(LO 6)

The financial statements and related financial information disclosed in Bombardier's 1992 annual report are shown in Appendix I. From your inspection of Bombardier's 1992 financial statements, including the Notes that follow the statements, answer the following questions:

1. Is the Consolidated Balance Sheet a classified balance sheet?
2. How many classes of shares does Bombardier have? What are they?
3. What is the total amount of accumulated amortization (depreciation) on January 31, 1992?
4. How many Class B shares did Bombardier have outstanding as of January 1992?
5. What amount of Bombardier's long-term debt in January 1992 was payable within one year?

Provocative Problem 3–5
As a Matter of Ethics:
Essay

Ethics

Review the "As a Matter of Ethics" case on page 136. Discuss the problem faced by Pena and evaluate the alternative courses of action Pena might take. Also explain how your answer would differ given the following assumptions: (*a*) Pena knows that the company's financial statements are not going to be audited; (*b*) Pena knows that the president's bonus depends on the amount of income reported in the first year; (*c*) Pena's job depends on complying with the president's wishes.

Analytical and Review Problems

A&R Problem 3–1

The Salaries Payable account of Hudson Bay Company Limited appears below:

Salaries Payable			
Entries during 1993	194,560	Bal. Jan. 1, 1993	11,260
		Entries during 1993	194,420

The company records the salary expense and related liability at the end of each week and pays the employees on the last Friday of the month.

Required

Calculate:

1. Salary expense for 1993.
2. How much was paid to employees in 1993 for work done in 1992?
3. How much was paid to employees in 1993 for work done in 1993?
4. How much will be paid to employees in 1994 for work done in 1993?

Robert Butler, a local dentist, asked you to help him prepare an income statement that would be acceptable by Revenue Canada. Butler's secretary/nurse maintained all the records and had developed the following statement for the year ended December 31, 1993.

A&R Problem 3–2

DR. ROBERT BUTLER
Income and Expense Statement
1993

Dental fees collected		155,800
Expenses paid:		
Rent for office	$ 12,000	
Rent for dental equipment	30,000	
Utilities.	600	
Telephone	360	
Supplies	3,500	
Wages of secretary/nurse.	26,000	72,460
Profit for the year.		$83,340

Since the statement was prepared on a 100% cash basis you realized that it would not be acceptable by Revenue Canada. Consequently, you conducted an investigation of records of the current year as well as of the previous year. You discovered the following:

a. Of the $155,800 of fees collected in 1993, $2,800 was for work performed in 1992.

b. On December 31, 1993, uncollected fees for work performed during 1993 were $6,600.

c. When Butler started his dental practice in 1992 he entered into a 10-year agreement with Universal Dental Supply, Inc. Under the agreement Butler obtained all the necessary equipment for a monthly rental of $2,500. The payments are made on the 15th of each month.

d. Office rent is paid at the rate of $1,000 on the 1st of each month.

e. On December 31, 1993, a count of supplies indicated $300 were on hand. It was estimated that on January 1, 1993, supplies of $100 were on hand.

f. The secretary/nurse started working in February 1993 and on December 31, 1993, wages amounting to $600 remained unpaid.

g. Unpaid utilities and telephone for December 1993 were expected to be greater by $40 and $30 respectively than for December 1992.

Required

Prepare an income statement for 1993 on an accrual basis. Support all changes in amounts from the statement prepared by the secretary/nurse.

As a Matter of
Record

The following report, "New Accounting May Boost Firms' Costs; CICA Studies Retirement Benefits," by Margot Gibb-Clark, Workplace Reporter, appeared in *The Globe and Mail,* November 12, 1991, page B8:

Record Case 3–1

Canadian companies could face higher costs if this country follows the U.S. approach to accounting for retiree health-care benefits.

Adopting an "accrual basis" for the cost of postretirement benefits could be four times as expensive as the current way of handling the issue, according to predictions in a recent study by the Financial Executives Institute Canada.

And the Canadian Institute of Chartered Accountants is about to embark on a project to look at new methods of accounting for the retiree benefits.

Currently, the vast majority of Canadian companies account for the obligation toward their retirees on a pay-as-you-go basis, FEIC president Al Jameson said.

"Pay as you go simply means covering what you are incurring today," he said. It does not look at companies' future obligations for the people now on staff once they are retired.

The accrual method recognizes costs now for future obligations. With inflation and rising health costs, they are likely to be expensive.

Ron Salole, the CICA's assistant director of accounting standards, said the institute is just about to develop standards for accounting for the retiree benefits—Canada so far has none.

The project, expected to take 12 to 18 months, came about as a result of a study done for the FEIC by Coopers & Lybrand consultants. That study showed retiree benefits are an issue, particularly for large companies, Mr. Salole said.

One reason for this is that medium to large companies are much more likely to offer postretirement benefits to former employees, Mr. Jameson said. Of those companies responding to the joint survey, 115 of 233 offered such benefits.

Mr. Salole said the CICA will try to pick up U.S. standards and modify them for Canadian use. In the case of pensions, accounting rules are quite similar, he noted.

Required

Discuss whether the issue is higher costs or simply the recording or nonrecording of the existing costs and the implicit liability.

Answers to Objective Review Questions

LO 1 (*a*)	LO 4 (*e*)	LO 7 (*a*)
LO 2 (*a*)	LO 5 (*d*)	LO 8 (*c*)
LO 3 (*e*)	LO 6 (*e*)	

The Work Sheet and Closing the Accounts of Proprietorships, Partnerships, and Corporations

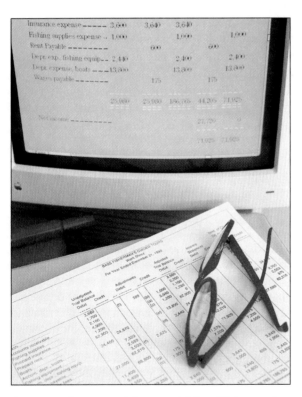

A systematic approach is essential for efficient and accurate processing of large amounts of information. Whether work sheets are on paper or computerized, they help provide this structure. Proprietorships, partnerships, and corporations all use similar work sheets.

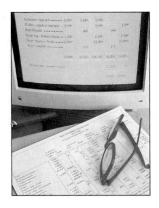

Y our study of Chapter 4 will focus on some of the procedures performed at the end of each accounting period. You will learn to use a work sheet to show the effects of the adjustments and to organize the data prior to preparing financial statements. Also, you will learn the necessary steps to get the accounts ready for use in the following accounting period.

Learning Objectives

After studying Chapter 4, you should be able to:

1. Explain why a work sheet is prepared and be able to prepare a work sheet for a service business.

2. Prepare closing entries for a service business and explain why it is necessary to close the temporary accounts at the end of each accounting period.

3. Prepare a post-closing trial balance and explain its purpose.

4. Explain the nature of a corporation's retained earnings and their relationship to the declaration of dividends.

5. Prepare entries to record the declaration and payment of a dividend and to close the temporary accounts of a corporation.

6. List the steps in the accounting cycle in the order they are completed and perform each step.

7. Define or explain the words and phrases listed in the chapter glossary.

After studying Appendix B at the end of Chapter 4, you should be able to:

8. Prepare reversing entries and explain when and why they are used.

Using a Work Sheet at the End of Each Accounting Period

LO 1 Explain why a work sheet is prepared and be able to prepare a work sheet for a service business.

In the process of organizing the data that go into the formal financial reports given to managers and other interested parties, accountants prepare numerous memoranda, analyses, and informal papers. These analyses and memoranda are called **working papers** and are invaluable tools of the accountant. One important example of such working papers is the **work sheet** described in this chapter. The work sheet for a business is not given to the business owner or manager. It is prepared solely for the accountant's use to assemble data for the preparation of financial statements.

Recall the end-of-period procedures discussed in Chapter 3. After all transactions were recorded, an unadjusted trial balance was prepared and adjusting entries were entered in the journal and posted to the accounts. Then an adjusted trial balance was prepared and used as a basis for preparing the financial statements.

For a very small business, these procedures are satisfactory. However, if a company has more than a few accounts and adjustments, you will make fewer errors by inserting an additional step into the procedures. The additional step is to prepare a work sheet. A work sheet is prepared before the adjusting entries are journalized or posted to the accounts.

On the work sheet, the accountant (1) shows the unadjusted trial balance, (2) shows the effects of the adjustments on the account balances, (3) shows the adjusted trial balance, and (4) sorts the adjusted amounts into columns according to whether the accounts are used in preparing the income statement or the statement of changes in owner's equity or balance sheet. Also, the amount of net income is calculated on the work sheet. After the work sheet is completed, the work sheet information is used to prepare the financial statements and to journalize the adjusting entries and the closing entries. (We discuss closing entries later in this chapter.)

Preparing a Work Sheet

Illustration 4–1 shows the multicolumn form used to prepare a work sheet. Note that this form provides two columns each for the unadjusted trial balance, the adjustments, the adjusted trial balance, the income statement, and the statement of changes in owner's equity or balance sheet. A work sheet could contain two separate columns for the statement of changes in owner's equity and two separate columns for the balance sheet. However, because the statement of changes in owner's equity includes only a few items, this usually is not done. Instead, most work sheets provide only two columns for both statements, as Illustration 4–1 shows.

When you use a work sheet, do not prepare the unadjusted trial balance on a separate form. Instead, the first step in preparing the work sheet is to prepare the unadjusted trial balance in the first two money columns of the work sheet form. Turn the first transparency overlay to see Illustration 4–2, which shows this first step in preparing the work sheet for Jerry Dow, Lawyer. This is the same example that we used in Chapters 1 through 3.

Remember that Dow's law practice completed a number of transactions during December 1993. The unadjusted trial balance in Illustration 4–2 reflects the account balances after these December transactions were recorded but *before any adjusting entries were journalized or posted.*

In Illustration 4–2, a blank line was left after the Legal Fees Earned account. Based on past experience, the accountant may realize that more than one line will be needed to show the adjustments to a particular account. When you turn the second transparency overlay, you will see in Illustration 4–3 that Legal Fees Earned is an example. Another alternative is to squeeze two adjustments on one line or to combine the effects of two or more adjustments in one amount.

The next step in preparing a work sheet is to enter the adjustments in the columns labeled Adjustments, as shown in Illustration 4–3. The adjustments shown in Illustration 4–3 are the same ones that we discussed in Chapter 3. Notice that an identifying letter relates the debit and credit of each adjustment. After preparing a work sheet, you still have to enter the adjusting entries in the journal and post them to the ledger. At that time, the identifying letters help you to match correctly the debit and credit of each adjusting entry.

Explanations of the adjustments on the illustrated work sheet are as follows:

Adjustment (*a*): To adjust for expired insurance.
Adjustment (*b*): To adjust for the office supplies used.

Adjustment (*c*): To adjust for amortization of the law library.

Adjustment (*d*): To adjust for amortization of the office equipment.

Adjustment (*e*): To adjust for unearned revenue.

Adjustment (*f*): To adjust for accrued salaries.

Adjustment (*g*): To adjust for accrued revenue.

Most of the adjustments on the illustrated work sheet required one or two additional accounts to be written in below the original trial balance. These accounts did not have balances when the trial balance was prepared. Therefore, they were not listed in the trial balance. If you anticipate that additional accounts will be required, however, you may list them in the process of preparing the unadjusted trial balance.

After the adjustments are entered in the Adjustments columns, the columns are totaled to prove the equality of the debit and credit adjustments. Then proceed to prepare the adjusted trial balance. To do so, each amount in the Unadjusted Trial Balance columns is combined with its adjustments in the Adjustments columns, if any, and is entered in the Adjusted Trial Balance columns.

For example, in Illustration 4–3, the Prepaid Insurance account has a $2,400 debit balance in the Unadjusted Trial Balance columns. This $2,400 debit is combined with the $100 credit in the Adjustments columns to give Prepaid Insurance a $2,300 debit in the Adjusted Trial Balance columns. Insurance Expense has no balance in the Unadjusted Trial Balance columns, but it has a $100 debit in the Adjustments columns. Therefore, no balance combined with a $100 debit gives Insurance Expense a $100 debit in the Adjusted Trial Balance columns. Cash, Office Equipment, and several other accounts have trial balance amounts that were not adjusted. As a result, their unadjusted trial balance amounts are carried unchanged into the Adjusted Trial Balance columns.

After carrying the combined amounts to the Adjusted Trial Balance columns, add the Adjusted Trial Balance columns to prove their equality. Then sort the amounts in these columns to the proper financial statement columns, as shown in Illustration 4–4. (Turn the next transparency overlay.) Sort expense items to the Income Statement Debit column, and revenues to the Income Statement Credit column. Then sort assets and the owner's withdrawals to the Statement of Changes in Owner's Equity or Balance Sheet Debit column. Liability items and the owner's capital account are sorted to the Statement of Changes in Owner's Equity or Balance Sheet Credit column. This easy task requires answers to only two questions: (1) Is the item to be sorted a debit or a credit? and (2) On which statement does it appear?

After sorting the amounts to the proper columns, total the columns as shown in Illustration 4–5. (Turn the last transparency overlay.) At this point, the difference between the totals of the Income Statement columns is the net income or loss. The difference is the net income or loss because revenues are entered in the Credit column and expenses in the Debit column. If the Credit column total exceeds the Debit column total, the difference is a net income. If the Debit column total exceeds the Credit column total, the difference is a net loss. In the illustrated work sheet, the Credit column total exceeds the Debit column total, and the result is a $1,160 net income.

After calculating the net income in the Income Statement columns, add it to the Statement of Changes in Owner's Equity or Balance Sheet Credit column. In that final column, the $9,000 balance of the capital account does not yet reflect the increase in capital that resulted from net income. Therefore, adding the net income to this column has the effect of adding it to the capital account.

Had there been a loss, it would have been necessary to add the loss to the Debit column. This is because losses decrease owner's equity, and adding the loss to the Debit column has the effect of subtracting it from the capital account.

When the net income or net loss is added to the appropriate Statement of Changes in Owner's Equity or Balance Sheet column, the totals of the last two columns should balance. If they do not balance, one or more errors were made in constructing the work sheet. The error or errors may have been mathematical or an amount may have been sorted to a wrong column.

Although balancing the last two columns is done in an effort to discover errors, the fact that they balance is not proof that the work sheet is free from error. These columns balance even when certain types of errors have been made. For example, if you incorrectly carry an asset amount into the Income Statement Debit column, the columns still balance. Or if you carry a liability amount into the Income Statement Credit column, the columns still balance. Either error causes the net income amount to be incorrect, but the columns are in balance. Therefore, exercise care in sorting the adjusted trial balance amounts into the correct financial statement columns.

Preparing Adjusting Entries from the Work Sheet

Entering the adjustments in the Adjustments columns of a work sheet does not get these adjustments into the ledger accounts. Therefore, after completing the work sheet, you must prepare adjusting journal entries like the ones described in Chapter 3. The adjusting entries must be entered in the General Journal and posted to the accounts in the ledger. The work sheet makes this easy, because its Adjustments columns provide the information for these entries. All that is needed is an entry for each adjustment that appears in the columns. If you prepare adjusting entries from the information in Illustration 4–5, you will see that they are the same adjusting entries we discussed in the last chapter.

Preparing Financial Statements from the Work Sheet

A work sheet is not a substitute for the financial statements. The work sheet is nothing more than a supporting tool that the accountant uses at the end of an accounting period to help organize the data. However, as soon as it is completed, the accountant uses the work sheet to prepare the financial statements. The items in the Income Statement columns provide the information necessary to prepare the formal income statement. Next, information is taken from the last two columns to prepare the statement of changes in owner's equity and the balance sheet. The financial statements prepared from the information in Illustration 4–5 are shown in Illustration 4–6.

ILLUSTRATION 4–1

Preparing a Work Sheet at the End of the Accounting Period

The heading should identify the entity, the nature of the document, and the time period

JERRY DOW, LAWYER
Work Sheet for Month Ended December 31, 1993

Account Titles	Unadjusted Trial Balance		Adjustments		Adjusted Trial Balance		Income Statement		Statement of Changes in Owner's Equity or Balance Sheet	
	Dr.	Cr.	Dr.	Cr.	Dr.	Cr.	Dr.	Cr.	Dr.	Cr.

The multicolumn work sheet can be prepared manually or with a computer spreadsheet program

The work sheet collects and summarizes the information used to prepare financial statements and to journalize adjusting and closing entries

ILLUSTRATION 4–6

Financial Statements Prepared from the Work Sheet

JERRY DOW, LAWYER
Income Statement
For Month Ended December 31, 1993

Revenues:		
Legal fees earned		$ 4,350
Operating expenses:		
Salaries expense	$1,610	
Rent expense	1,000	
Utilities expense	230	
Insurance expense	100	
Office supplies expense	45	
Amortization expense, law library	80	
Amortization expense, office equipment	125	
Total operating expenses		3,190
Net Income		$ 1,160

JERRY DOW, LAWYER
Statement of Changes in Owner's Equity
For Month Ended December 31, 1993

Jerry Dow, capital, November 30, 1993		$ –0–
Plus:		
Investments by owner.	$9,000	
Net income	1,160	10,160
Total.		$10,160
Less withdrawals by owner		1,100
Jerry Dow, capital, December 31, 1993		$ 9,060

JERRY DOW, LAWYER
Balance Sheet
December 31, 1993

Assets			Liabilities		
Cash		$ 650	Accounts payable	$ 760	
Accounts receivable		200	Unearned legal fees	2,750	
Prepaid insurance		2,300	Salaries payable	210	
Office supplies		75	Total liabilities		$ 3,720
Law library.	$2,880				
Less accumulated amortization . . .	80	2,800			
Office equipment.	$6,880		**Owner's Equity**		
Less accumulated amortization . . .	125	6,755	Jerry Dow, Capital.		9,060
			Total liabilities and		
Total assets.		$12,780	owner's equity.		$12,780

Closing Entries— What They Involve and Why They Are Made

LO 2 Prepare closing entries for a service business and explain why it is necessary to close the temporary accounts at the end of each accounting period.

After the work sheet and statements are completed and the adjusting entries are recorded, you must journalize and post **closing entries.** As shown in Illustration 4–7, closing entries are designed to transfer the end-of-period balances in the revenue accounts, the expense accounts, and the withdrawals account to a balance sheet equity account. To close the revenue and expense accounts, transfer their balances first to a summary account called **Income Summary.** Then, for a single proprietorship, transfer the Income Summary account balance (the net income or loss) to the owner's capital account. Finally, transfer the owner's withdrawals account to the owner's capital account. After the closing entries are posted, the revenue, expense, and withdrawals accounts have zero balances. Thus, these accounts are said to be closed or cleared.

One reason why closing entries are prepared at the end of each accounting period is to update the owner's capital account. The transfers of the revenue, expense, and withdrawals account balances to the owner's capital account are necessary because:

1. Revenues increase owner's equity, while expenses and withdrawals decrease owner's equity.
2. During an accounting period, these increases and decreases are temporarily accumulated in revenue, expense, and withdrawals accounts rather than in the owner's capital account.
3. By transferring the effects of revenues, expenses, and withdrawals from the revenue, expense, and withdrawals accounts to the owner's capital account, closing entries install the correct, end-of-period balance in the owner's capital account.

Also, closing entries cause the revenue, expense, and withdrawals accounts to begin each new accounting period with zero balances. This is necessary because:

1. An income statement reports the revenues earned and expenses incurred during one accounting period and is prepared from information recorded in the revenue and expense accounts.
2. The revenue and expense accounts are not discarded at the end of each accounting period but are used to record the revenues and expenses of succeeding periods.
3. Because these accounts should reflect only one period's revenues and expenses, the accounts must begin each period with zero balances.
4. Since the statement of changes in owner's equity reports the owner's withdrawals during only one period, the withdrawals account also must begin each period with a zero balance.

Closing Entries Illustrated

At the end of December, after its adjusting entries were posted but before its accounts were closed, the revenue, expense, withdrawals, and capital accounts of Dow's law practice had the balances shown in Illustration 4–8. (As a rule, an account's Balance column heading does not tell whether the balance is debit or credit. However, in Illustration 4–8, and in the illustrations that immediately follow, the nature of each account's balance is shown as a study aid.)

In Illustration 4–8, notice that Dow's Capital account shows only the $9,000 investment by Dow made on December 1. This is not the amount of Dow's equity on December 31. Closing entries are required to make this account show the December 31 equity.

ILLUSTRATION 4–7

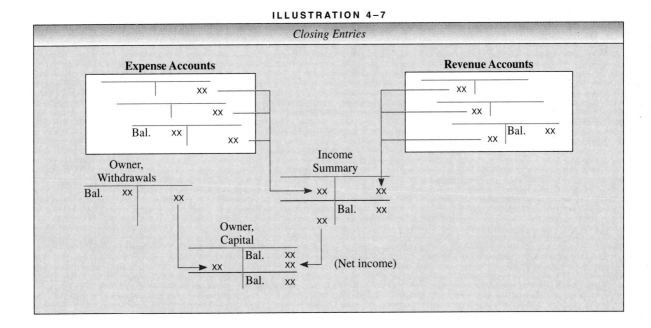

Closing Entries

Notice also the last account in Illustration 4–8, the Income Summary account. This account is used only at the end of the accounting period to summarize and clear the revenue and expense accounts.

Closing Revenue Accounts

Before closing entries are posted, revenue accounts have credit balances. Therefore, to close revenue accounts, you must debit each revenue account and credit Income Summary.

The Dow law practice has only one revenue account, and the entry to close it is:

Dec.	31	Legal Fees Earned	4,350.00	
		Income Summary.		4,350.00
		To close the revenue account.		

Posting this entry has the following effect on the accounts:

Legal Fees Earned

Date		Explanation	Debit	Credit	Balance
Dec.	10			2,200	2,200
	12			1,700	3,900
	31			250	4,150
	31			200	4,350
	31		4,350		–0–

Income Summary

Date		Explanation	Debit	Credit	Balance
Dec.	31			4,350	4,350

ILLUSTRATION 4–8

Revenue, Expense, Withdrawals, and Capital Accounts of Jerry Dow, Lawyer

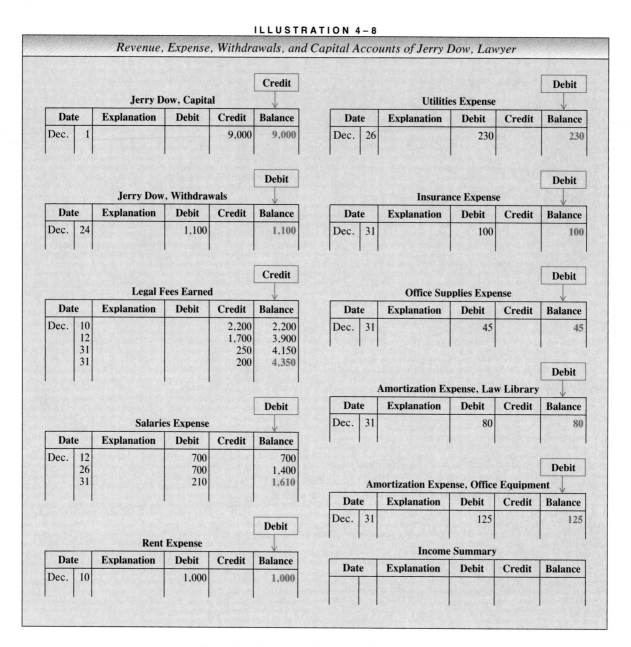

Note that the entry clears the revenue account by transferring its balance as a credit to the Income Summary account. It also causes the revenue account to begin the new accounting period with a zero balance.

Closing Expense Accounts

Before closing entries are posted, expense accounts have debit balances. Therefore, to close a concern's expense accounts, debit the Income Summary account and credit each individual expense account. The Dow law practice has seven expense accounts, and the compound entry to close them is:

Dec.	31	Income Summary	3,190.00	
		Salaries Expense		1,610.00
		Rent Expense.		1,000.00
		Utilities Expense		230.00
		Insurance Expense		100.00
		Office Supplies Expense		45.00
		Amortization Expense, Law Library		80.00
		Amortization Expense, Office Equipment		125.00
		To close the expense accounts.		

Posting the entry has the effect shown in Illustration 4–9. In that illustration, notice that the entry clears the expense accounts of their balances by transferring the balances as a debit to the Income Summary account. Also, the entry causes the expense accounts to begin the new period with zero balances.

Closing the Income Summary Account

After a business's revenue and expense accounts are closed to Income Summary, the balance of the Income Summary account is equal to the net income or loss. When revenues exceed expenses, there is a net income and the Income Summary account has a credit balance. On the other hand, when expenses exceed revenues, there is a loss and the account has a debit balance. Regardless of the nature of its balance, the Income Summary account must be closed by transferring its balance to the capital account. The Dow law practice earned $1,160 during December. Therefore, after its revenue and expense accounts are closed, its Income Summary account has a $1,160 credit balance. Transfer this balance to the Jerry Dow, Capital account with this entry:

Dec.	31	Income Summary	1,160.00	
		Jerry Dow, Capital		1,160.00
		To close the Income Summary account.		

Posting this entry has the following effect on the accounts:

Income Summary   Credit

Date		Explanation	Debit	Credit	Balance
Dec.	31			4,350	4,350
	31		3,190		1,160
	31		1,160		–0–

Jerry Dow, Capital   Credit

Date		Explanation	Debit	Credit	Balance
Dec.	1			9,000	9,000
	31			1,160	10,160

Notice that the entry clears the Income Summary account, transferring its balance, the amount of the net income in this case, to the capital account.

ILLUSTRATION 4–9

The Entry to Close the Expense Accounts

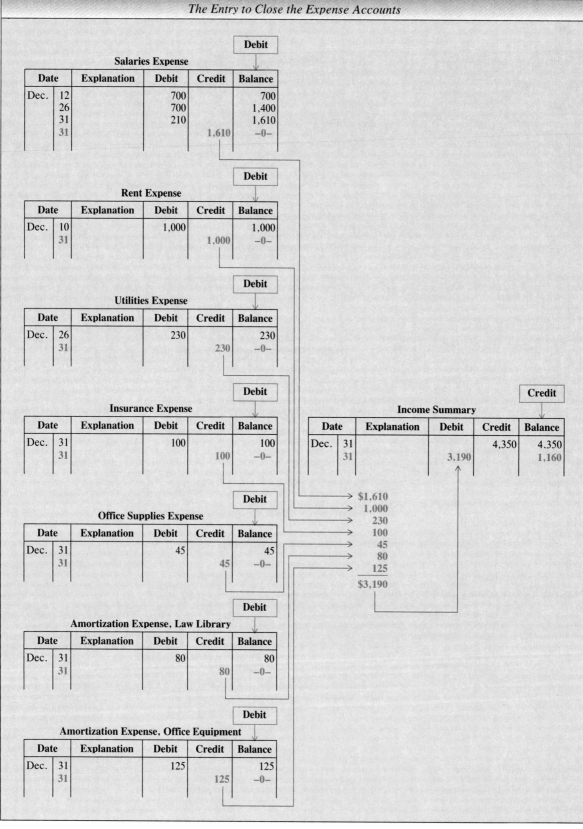

Closing the Withdrawals Account

At the end of an accounting period, the withdrawals account shows the decrease in the owner's equity due to the owner's withdrawals. To close the account, transfer its debit balance to the capital account with this entry:

Dec.	31	Jerry Dow, Capital	1,100.00	
		Jerry Dow, Withdrawals		1,100.00
		To close the withdrawals account.		

Posting the entry has this effect on the accounts:

Debit

Jerry Dow, Withdrawals

Date		Explanation	Debit	Credit	Balance
Dec.	24		1,100		1,100
	31			1,100	–0–

Credit

Jerry Dow, Capital

Date		Explanation	Debit	Credit	Balance
Dec.	1			9,000	9,000
	31			1,160	10,160
	31		1,100		9,060

After you post the entry to close the withdrawals account, notice that the two reasons for making closing entries are accomplished: (1) all revenue, expense, and withdrawals accounts have zero balances; (2) the net effect of the period's revenue, expense, and withdrawals transactions on the owner's equity is shown in the capital account.

Temporary (Nominal) Accounts and Permanent (Real) Accounts

Revenue accounts, expense accounts, withdrawals accounts, and the Income Summary account are often called **temporary accounts** or **nominal accounts.** We use these terms because amounts are stored in these accounts only temporarily. Such accounts are closed at the end of each accounting period. By contrast, accounts that appear in the balance sheet are often called **permanent accounts** or **real accounts,** because they remain open as long as the asset, liability, or owner's equity items recorded in the accounts continue in existence.

Information for closing entries may be taken from the individual revenue and expense accounts. However, the work sheet provides this information in a more convenient form. Look at the work sheet in Illustration 4–5. Every account that has a balance in the Income Statement columns must be closed. In addition, the withdrawals account must be closed.

Sources of Closing Entry Information

The Accounts after Closing

After both adjusting and closing entries are posted, the Dow law practice accounts appear as in Illustration 4–10. Observe that the asset, liability, and owner's capital accounts show their end-of-period balances. Also, note that the revenue and expense accounts have zero balances and are ready to be used when revenues and expenses are recorded in the next accounting period.

The Post-Closing Trial Balance

LO 3 Prepare a post-closing trial balance and explain its purpose.

Because errors may have been introduced in the process of adjusting and closing the accounts, a new trial balance is prepared after all adjusting and closing entries have been posted. This **post-closing trial balance** is prepared to retest the equality of the accounts. The post-closing trial balance for Dow's law practice appears in Illustration 4–11.

Compare Illustration 4–11 with the accounts that have balances in Illustration 4–10. Note that only asset, liability, and the owner's capital accounts have balances in Illustration 4–10. Note also that these are the only accounts that appear on the post-closing trial balance. The revenue and expense accounts have been cleared and have zero balances at this stage.

Accounting for Partnerships and Corporations

Partnership Accounting

Accounting for a partnership is like accounting for a single proprietorship except for transactions that directly affect the partners' capital and withdrawals accounts. These transactions require a capital account and a withdrawals account for each partner. To close the Income Summary account, make a compound entry that allocates to each partner his or her share of the net income or loss such as the following:

Dec.	31	Income Summary	7,000.00	
		Julie Ehlers, Capital		3,000.00
		Megan Brinkoeter, Capital		4,000.00
		To close the Income Summary account.		

Corporate Accounting

LO 4 Explain the nature of a corporation's retained earnings and their relationship to the declaration of dividends.

Accounting for a corporation also differs from that of a single proprietorship for transactions that affect the equity accounts of the corporation. The accounts of a corporation are designed to distinguish between equity resulting from amounts invested in the corporation by its shareholders and equity resulting from earnings. This distinction is important because a corporation generally cannot pay a legal dividend unless it has shareholders' equity resulting from earnings. In making the distinction, two kinds of shareholders' equity accounts are kept: (1) *contributed capital accounts* and (2) *retained earnings accounts*. Amounts invested in a corporation (contributed) by its shareholders are shown in contributed capital accounts such as the Common Share account. Shareholders' equity resulting from earnings is shown in a retained earnings account.

ILLUSTRATION 4-10

The General Ledger for Jerry Dow, Lawyer

Cash   Acct. No. 101

Date		Explanation	PR	Debit		Credit		Balance	
1993 Dec.	1		G1	9,000	00			9,000	00
	2		G1			2,500	00	6,500	00
	3		G1			5,600	00	900	00
	10		G1	2,200	00			3,100	00
	10		G1			1,000	00	2,100	00
	12		G1			700	00	1,400	00
	22		G1	1,700	00			3,100	00
	24		G2			900	00	2,200	00
	24		G2			1,100	00	1,100	00
	26		G2	3,000	00			4,100	00
	26		G2			2,400	00	1,700	00
	26		G2			120	00	1,580	00
	26		G2			230	00	1,350	00
	26		G2			700	00	650	00

Accounts Receivable   Acct. No. 106

Date		Explanation	PR	Debit		Credit		Balance	
1993 Dec.	12		G1	1,700	00			1,700	00
	22		G2			1,700	00	–0–	
	31		G3	200	00			200	00

Office Supplies   Acct. No. 124

Date		Explanation	PR	Debit		Credit		Balance	
1993 Dec.	26		G2	120	00			120	00
	31		G3			45	00	75	00

ILLUSTRATION 4–10

(continued)

Prepaid Insurance — Acct. No. 128

Date		Explanation	PR	Debit		Credit		Balance	
1993 Dec.	26		G2	2,400	00			2,400	00
	31		G3			100	00	2,300	00

Law Library — Acct. No. 159

Date		Explanation	PR	Debit		Credit		Balance	
1993 Dec.	2		G1	2,500	00			2,500	00
	6		G1	380	00			2,880	00

Accumulated Amortization, Law Library — Acct. No. 160

Date		Explanation	PR	Debit		Credit		Balance	
1993 Dec.	31		G3			80	00	80	00

Office Equipment — Acct. No. 163

Date		Explanation	PR	Debit		Credit		Balance	
1993 Dec.	3		G1	5,600	00			5,600	00
	6		G1	1,280	00			6,880	00

Accumulated Amortization, Office Equipment — Acct. No. 164

Date		Explanation	PR	Debit		Credit		Balance	
1993 Dec.	31		G3			125	00	125	00

ILLUSTRATION 4-10

(continued)

Accounts Payable — Acct. No. 201

Date		Explanation	PR	Debit		Credit		Balance	
1993 Dec.	6		G1			1,660	00	1,660	00
	24		G2	900	00			760	00

Salaries Payable — Acct. No. 209

Date		Explanation	PR	Debit		Credit		Balance	
1993 Dec.	31		G3			210	00	210	00

Unearned Legal Fees — Acct. No. 231

Date		Explanation	PR	Debit		Credit		Balance	
1993 Dec.	26		G2			3,000	00	3,000	00
	31		G3	250	00			2,750	00

Jerry Dow, Capital — Acct. No. 301

Date		Explanation	PR	Debit		Credit		Balance	
1993 Dec.	1		G1			9,000	00	9,000	00
	31		G3			1,160	00	10,160	00
	31		G3	1,100	00			9,060	00

Jerry Dow, Withdrawals — Acct. No. 302

Date		Explanation	PR	Debit		Credit		Balance	
1993 Dec.	24		G2	1,100	00			1,100	00
	31		G3			1,100	00	−0−	

ILLUSTRATION 4-10

(continued)

Legal Fees Earned — Acct. No. 401

Date		Explanation	PR	Debit		Credit		Balance	
1993 Dec.	10		G1			2,200	00	2,200	00
	12		G1			1,700	00	3,900	00
	31		G3			250	00	4,150	00
	31		G3			200	00	4,350	00
	31		G3	4,350	00			–0–	

Amortization Expense, Law Library — Acct. No. 610

Date		Explanation	PR	Debit		Credit		Balance	
1993 Dec.	31		G3	80	00			80	00
	31		G3			80	00	–0–	

Amortization Expense, Office Equipment — Acct. No. 612

Date		Explanation	PR	Debit		Credit		Balance	
1993 Dec.	31		G3	125	00			125	00
	31		G3			125	00	–0–	

Salaries Expense — Acct. No. 622

Date		Explanation	PR	Debit		Credit		Balance	
1993 Dec.	12		G1	700	00			700	00
	26		G2	700	00			1,400	00
	31		G3	210	00			1,610	00
	31		G3			1,610	00	–0–	

ILLUSTRATION 4–10

(concluded)

Insurance Expense　　　　　　　　　　　　Acct. No. 637

Date		Explanation	PR	Debit		Credit		Balance	
1993 Dec.	31		G3	100	00			100	00
	31		G3			100	00	–0–	

Rent Expense　　　　　　　　　　　　Acct. No. 640

Date		Explanation	PR	Debit		Credit		Balance	
1993 Dec.	10		G1	1,000	00			1,000	00
	31		G3			1,000	00	–0–	

Office Supplies Expense　　　　　　　　　　　　Acct. No. 650

Date		Explanation	PR	Debit		Credit		Balance	
1993 Dec.	31		G3	45	00			45	00
	31		G3			45	00	–0–	

Utilities Expense　　　　　　　　　　　　Acct. No. 690

Date		Explanation	PR	Debit		Credit		Balance	
1993 Dec.	26		G2	230	00			230	00
	31		G3			230	00	–0–	

Income Summary　　　　　　　　　　　　Acct. No. 901

Date		Explanation	PR	Debit		Credit		Balance	
1993 Dec.	31		G3			4,350	00	4,350	00
	31		G3	3,190	00			1,160	00
	31		G3	1,160	00			–0–	

ILLUSTRATION 4–11

The Post-Closing Trial Balance

JERRY DOW, LAWYER
Post-Closing Trial Balance
December 31, 1993

Cash	$ 650	
Accounts receivable	200	
Office supplies	75	
Prepaid insurance	2,300	
Office equipment	6,880	
Accumulated amortization, office equipment		$ 125
Law library	2,880	
Accumulated amortization, law library		80
Accounts payable		760
Salaries payable		210
Unearned legal fees		2,750
Jerry Dow, capital		9,060
Totals	$12,985	$12,985

To demonstrate corporate accounting, assume that five persons secured a certificate of incorporation for a new corporation. Each invested $10,000 in the corporation by buying 1,000 of its common shares. The corporation's entry to record their investments is

Jan.	5	Cash	50,000.00	
		Common Shares		50,000.00
		Issued 5,000 common shares for cash.		

If during its first year the corporation earned $20,000, the entry to close its Income Summary account is

Dec.	31	Income Summary	20,000.00	
		Retained Earnings		20,000.00
		To close the Income Summary account.		

If these are the only entries that affected the Common Shares and Retained Earnings accounts during the first year, the corporation's year-end balance sheet will show the shareholders' equity as follows:

Shareholders' Equity

Share capital–common: 5,000 shares outstanding	$50,000	
Retained earnings	20,000	
Total shareholders' equity		$70,000

Because a corporation is a separate legal entity, the names of its share-holders usually are of little interest to a balance sheet reader and are not shown in the equity section. However, in this case, the section does show that the net assets or equity of the corporation is $70,000. Of this amount, $50,000 resulted from the issuance of shares to the shareholders and $20,000 was the result of net income that has not been paid out as dividends.

Perhaps the concept of retained earnings would be clearer if the balance sheet item were labeled "Shareholders' equity resulting from earnings." However, the retained earnings caption is commonly used; it does not repre-sent a specific amount of cash or any other asset. These are shown in the asset section of the balance sheet. Retained earnings represent the shareholders' equity resulting from earnings.

To continue, assume that on January 10 of the corporation's second year, its board of directors met and by vote declared a $1 per share dividend payable on February 1 to the January 25 shareholders of record (shareholders accord-ing to the corporation's records). The entry to record the declaration of the dividend is as follows:

LO 5 Prepare entries to record the declaration and payment of a dividend and to close the temporary accounts of a corporation.

Jan.	10	Cash Dividends Declared	5,000.00	
		Common Dividend Payable.		5,000.00
		Declared a $1 per share dividend.		

The **Cash Dividends Declared**[1] account is a temporary account that serves the same function for a corporation as does a withdrawals account for a propri-etorship. At the end of each period, the Cash Dividends Declared account is closed to Retained Earnings. The entry to record the payment of the dividend is as follows:

Feb.	1	Common Dividend Payable	5,000.00	
		Cash		5,000.00
		Paid the dividend declared on January 10.		

Note from the two entries that the dividend declaration reduces share-holders' equity and increases liabilities, while the payment of the dividend reduces the corporation's assets and liabilities. The net result is to reduce assets and shareholders' equity just as a withdrawal of cash by the owner of a single proprietorship reduces assets and the owner's equity.

A cash dividend is normally paid by mailing cheques to the shareholders. Also, as in this case, three dates are normally involved in a dividend declara-tion and payment. They are (1) the date of declaration, (2) the date of record,

---

[1] Some corporations prefer to debit retained earnings directly at the time of dividend dec-laration. The Cash Dividend Declared account is used to illustrate the parallelism in account-ing for withdrawals in proprietorships and partnerships and dividends in corporate accounting.

and (3) the date of payment. On the date of declaration, the dividend becomes a liability of the corporation. However, if some shareholders sell their shares to new investors in time for the new shareholders to be listed in the corporation's records on the date of record, the new shareholders will receive the dividend on the date of payment. Otherwise, the dividend will be paid to the old shareholders.

A dividend must be formally voted by a corporation's board of directors. Also, courts have generally held that the board is the final judge of when a dividend should be paid. Therefore, shareholders have no right to a dividend until it is declared. However, as soon as a cash dividend is declared, it becomes a liability of the corporation, normally a current liability, and must be paid. Furthermore, shareholders have the right to sue and force payment of a cash dividend once it is declared.

If during its second year (1994) the corporation suffered a $7,000 net loss, the entries to close its Income Summary and Dividends Declared accounts are:

1994				
Dec.	31	Retained Earnings.	7,000.00	
		Income Summary.		7,000.00
		To close the Income Summary account.		
	31	Retained Earnings.	5,000.00	
		Cash Dividends Declared.		5,000.00
		To close the Cash Dividends Declared account.		

Now assume that during 1995, the corporation paid no dividends but suffered a net loss of $14,000. The entry to close the Income Summary account at the end of 1995 is

1995				
Dec.	31	Retained Earnings.	14,000.00	
		Income Summary.		14,000.00
		To close the Income Summary account.		

Posting these entries has the following effects on the Retained Earnings account:

Retained Earnings						**Acct. No.** 318
Date		**Explanation**	**PR**	**Debit**	**Credit**	**Balance**
1993						
Dec.	31	Net income	G4		20,000.00	20,000.00
1994						
Dec.	31	Net loss	G5	7,000.00		13,000.00
	31	Cash dividends declared	G7	5,000.00		8,000.00
1995						
Dec.	31	Net loss	G9	14,000.00		6,000.00 Dr.

Fact

Dividends Declared

Compiled by The Financial Post Information Service
for the week ending November 21, 1991

Details	Dividend amount	Pay date	Record date
REGULAR			
BET plc, ADR	e.3852	Jan 31	Dec 5
BMTC Group, cl A.	.025	Jan 10	Dec 31
British Gas, ADR	e.8632175	Apr 4	Feb 14
British Steel, ADR	e.80	Jan 24	Dec 6
Budd Canada, com	.25	Dec 31	Dec 13
Cda Malting, com	.125	Dec 16	Nov 29
Cdn Util, ser P pf.	.50	Mar 1	Feb 12
Cdn Util, 7.1% pf N	.44375	Mar 1	Feb 12
Cdn Util, 7.08% pf M . . .	.4425	Mar 1	Feb 12
Cdn Util, 7.7% pf L	.48125	Mar 1	Feb 12
Cdn Util, 7.8% pf K	.4875	Mar 1	Feb 12
Cdn Util, 8.74% pf I	.54625	Feb 1	Jan 10
Cdn Util, 7.3% pf C	.45625	Feb 1	Jan 10
Cdn Util, 6% pf	1.50	Feb 1	Jan 10
Cdn Util, 5% pf	1.25	Feb 15	Jan 24
Cdn Util, 4.25% pf	1.0625	Feb 15	Jan 24
Citadel Cap, pf A.	.48125	Dec 15	Dec 1
Consumer Gas, 7.69% . . .	.480625	Jan 1	Dec 5
Consumer Gas, 7.60% . . .	.475	Jan 1	Dec 5
Consumer Gas, pf A&B . . .	1.375	Jan 1	Dec 5
Derlan Ind, 9.5% pf	.2019	Dec 30	Dec 13
Derlan Ind, com	.07	Dec 6	Nov 26
Echo Bay Mines, com . . .	u.0375	Dec 31	Dec 16
Elders IXL Cda 7.75% . . .	.484375	Dec 31	Dec 16
First Australia, ord.	.11	Dec 13	Nov 29
Greyhound Lines, com. . . .	.30	Dec 31	Dec 10
Gulf Cda Res, sr pf.	e.028	Dec 12	Nov 29
Haley Inds, com	.025	Dec 16	Nov 29
Lac Minerals, com	.11	Dec 19	Dec 6
Lakewood Energy, Rty Un.	.26	Nov 30	Nov 22
Lessard Beaucage com. . .	.025	Dec 10	Nov 27
MICC Inv, 10% pf	.625	Dec 15	Dec 3

Details	Dividend amount	Pay date	Record date
MICC Inv, 8.625% pf . . .	.53907	Dec 31	Dec 13
MacMillan Bl B pf 10. . . .	e.17813	Dec 12	Nov 29
Maple Leaf Food, com. . .	.095	Dec 31	Dec 6
Maple Leaf Gard, com . . .	.20	Jan 15	Dec 31
Maritime Life, pf A	e.4113	Dec 31	Dec 2
Molson, cl A & B com . . .	.18	Jan 1	Dec 4
Nat'l Sea, cl D pf.	.1375	Jan 2	Dec 12
Nat'l Sea, cl C pf.	.1375	Jan 2	Dec 12
Nth Cdn Oils, com	.10	Dec 31	Dec 15
Nth Cdn Oils, B pf 7	.46875	Dec 31	Dec 15
Nth Cdn Oils, B pf 6	.50	Dec 31	Dec 15
Nthwstn Utilities pf	1.00	Feb 1	Jan 10
Orbit O&G, 8.5% pf	.2125	Dec 31	Dec 13
Orbit O&G, 7.5% pf . . .	.1875	Dec 31	Dec 13
PWA Corp, $2.4375 pf . . .	.6094	Dec 31	Dec 6
Pac Nat'l Fin, cl A	.015	Dec 27	Dec 11
Quebec-Tel, 7.75% pf . . .	.3875	Jan 1	Dec 2
Quebec-Tel, 5% pf	.25	Jan 1	Dec 2
Quebec-Tel, 4.75% pf . . .	.2375	Jan 1	Dec 2
Royal Bank, 1st pf E	e.5339	Dec 12	Nov 29
Seagram, com	u.50	Dec 13	Dec 2
Shell Canada, cl A	.45	Dec 13	Nov 30
Strathfield 1st pf C	.175	Dec 31	Dec 23
TD Bank, cl B pf 1	e.505875	Dec 12	Nov 29
Trilon, cl A com	.225	Dec 31	Dec 12
Trilon, cl II pf 2	.466	Dec 12	Nov 30
Triton Cda, 10% pf.	.25	Jan 31	Jan 21
Triton Cda, 9.25% pf	.4625	Dec 31	Dec 15
Triton Cda, pf ser B	.30	Dec 31	Dec 15
Unicorp Energy, pf C	.50	Dec 31	Dec 16
Unicorp Energy, pf B	.2925	Dec 31	Dec 16
Unigesco, cl A & B	.07	Dec 31	Dec 6
Unigesco, 1st pf 2	.1625	Dec 31	Dec 6
Union Carb Cda Eq un . . .	.53125	Dec 31	Dec 5
West Kootenay, pf 2	.49375	Nov 29	Nov 25
Xerox Cda, exch cl B . . .	e.28245	Jan 1	Dec 6
DECREASE			
H Paulin & Co, cl B	.04	Dec 19	Dec 3
H Paulin & Co, cl A	.04	Dec 19	Dec 3
Samuel Manu-Tech com . .	.06	Jan 15	Dec 30

Details	Dividend amount	Pay date	Record date
INCREASE			
Quebec-Tel, com	.29	Jan 1	Dec 2
INITIAL			
Meriden Energy, cl A . . .	.0075	Dec 21	Dec 1

Dividends Payable

For the week ending November 29, 1991

Details	Dividend amount	Pay date	Record date
BC Sugar, cl B	.20	Nov 25	Nov 1
BC Sugar, cl A	.20	Nov 25	Nov 1
Bk of Mtl, cl B pf 1 . . .	.5625	Nov 25	Nov 8
Bk of Mtl, cl A pf 4 . . .	.5625	Nov 25	Nov 8
Bk of Mtl, com	.53	Nov 28	Nov 8
Bk of Mtl, cl A pf 3 . . .	.53125	Nov 25	Nov 8
CGC Inc, com	.21	Nov 27	Nov 14
CHUM Ltd, cl B	.02	Nov 29	Nov 18
Flet Chall Inv, Ser 2. . .	1.41	Nov 29	Nov 15
Flet Chall Inv II, B . . .	1.41	Nov 29	Nov 15
Global Gov't, com . . .	u.045	Nov 29	Nov 15
Goodfellow, com	.05	Nov 29	Nov 15
Hubbard Holding, com .	.10	Nov 29	Nov 19
MRRM Inc, com	.50	Nov 29	Nov 8
NCE Petrofund, unit . . .	.0225	Nov 29	Nov 15
Phillips Pete, com. . . .	u.28	Nov 29	Nov 8
Royal LePage, com . . .	.175	Nov 26	Nov 12
SR Telecom, com	.03	Nov 29	Nov 15
Tuckahoe Fin, cl A . . .	.03	Nov 29	Nov 15
United Cdn Shs, com . .	.125	Nov 29	Nov 15
Vitran Corp, cl A	.03	Nov 29	Nov 20
West Kootenay, pf 2 . .	.49375	Nov 29	Nov 25
e = estimate.			
u = U.S. funds.			

Due to the dividend and the net losses, the Retained Earnings account has a $6,000 debit balance. A debit balance in a Retained Earnings account indicates a negative amount of retained earnings. A corporation with a negative amount of retained earnings is said to have a **deficit.** A deficit may be shown on a corporation's balance sheet as follows:

Shareholders' Equity		
Share capital–common: 5,000 shares outstanding . .	$50,000	
Deduct retained earnings deficit	(6,000)	
Total shareholders' equity		$44,000

In most jurisdications, a corporation with a deficit is not allowed to pay a cash dividend. This legal requirement is intended to protect the creditors of the corporation. Because a corporation is a separate legal entity, it is responsible for its own debts. However, the corporation's shareholders normally are not responsible for the corporation's debts. Therefore, if a corporation's creditors are to be paid, they must be paid from the corporation's assets. By making dividends illegal when there is a deficit, a corporation in financial difficulty is prevented from paying its assets in dividends and leaving nothing for payment of its creditors.

The Accounting Cycle

LO 6 List the steps in the accounting cycle in the order they are completed and perform each step.

In Chapters 2, 3, and 4, we have discussed all of the accounting procedures that must be completed during each accounting period, beginning with the recording of transactions in a journal and ending with a post-closing trial balance. Since these steps are repeated each period, they are called the **accounting cycle.** Illustration 4–12 shows the steps in the order of their occurrence. Review this illustration to be sure that you understand how to perform each step in the proper sequence. To assist your review, we briefly describe each step as follows:

1. **Journalizing** . . . . . Analyzing and recording transactions in a journal.

2. **Posting** . . . . Copying the debits and credits of the journal entries into the ledger accounts.

3. **Preparing an un-adjusted trial balance** . . . . Summarizing the ledger accounts and testing the recording accuracy.

4. **Completing the work sheet** . . . . Gaining the effects of the adjustments before entering the adjustments in the accounts. Then sorting the account balances into the proper financial statement columns and calculating the net income or net loss.

5. **Adjusting the ledger accounts** . . . . . . Preparing adjusting journal entries from information in the Adjustments columns of the work sheet and posting the entries to bring the account balances up to date.

6. **Preparing the statements** . . . . . . Using the information on the work sheet to prepare an income statement, a statement of changes in owner's equity, a balance sheet, and a statement of changes in financial position. (You will learn more about preparing the statement of changes in financial position in Chapter 14.)

7. **Closing the temporary accounts** . . . . Preparing and posting journal entries to close the temporary accounts and to transfer the net income or loss to the capital account or accounts in a single proprietorship or partnership or to the Retained Earnings account in a corporation.

ILLUSTRATION 4-12

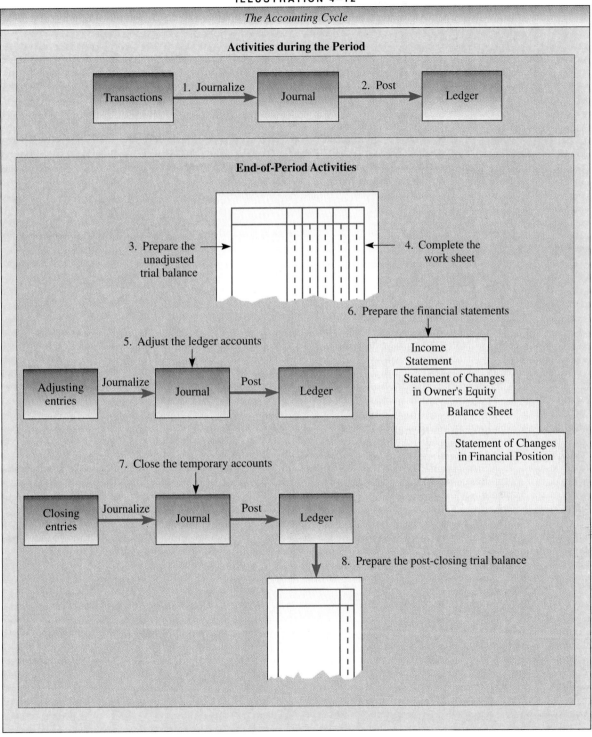

The Accounting Cycle

Activities during the Period

Transactions → 1. Journalize → Journal → 2. Post → Ledger

End-of-Period Activities

3. Prepare the unadjusted trial balance →

← 4. Complete the work sheet

6. Prepare the financial statements

5. Adjust the ledger accounts

Adjusting entries → Journalize → Journal → Post → Ledger

Income Statement
Statement of Changes in Owner's Equity
Balance Sheet
Statement of Changes in Financial Position

7. Close the temporary accounts

Closing entries → Journalize → Journal → Post → Ledger

8. Prepare the post-closing trial balance

8. **Preparing a post-
   closing trial balance**   . Proving the accuracy of the adjusting and
                              closing procedures.

   In practice, steps 1–6 are completed monthly, while steps 7 and 8 are
   completed only at the end of the fiscal year.

Summary of the Chapter in Terms of Learning Objectives

LO 1. A work sheet is a tool the accountant uses at the end of an accounting period to show the effects of the adjustments and to organize the data for use in preparing financial statements and recording the adjusting and closing entries.

LO 2. Closing the temporary accounts at the end of each accounting period serves to transfer the effects of these accounts to the proper owner's equity account that appears on the balance sheet. It also gives the revenue, expense, and withdrawals or Cash Dividends Declared accounts zero balances, preparing them for use in the following period.

LO 3. A post-closing trial balance tests the equality of debits and credits in the ledger after the adjusting and closing entries have been posted. It also confirms the fact that all temporary accounts have been closed.

LO 4. Retained earnings are the total amount of net incomes a corporation has earned since it was organized, less (*a*) the total amount of net losses it has incurred and (*b*) the total amount of dividends it has declared.

LO 5. Cash dividend declarations are recorded with a debit to a temporary account called Cash Dividends Declared and a credit to a liability account. When paid in cash, the liability account is debited and Cash is credited.

LO 6. The steps in the accounting cycle are to journalize and post transactions, prepare a trial balance and complete the work sheet, record the adjustments, prepare the financial statements, close the temporary accounts, and prepare a post-closing trial balance.

The December 31, 1993, adjusted trial balance of Westside Appliance Repair, Inc., is as follows:

Demonstration Problem

Cash.	$ 83,300	
Accounts receivable.	45,000	
Notes receivable	60,000	
Prepaid insurance	19,000	
Prepaid rent	5,000	
Equipment	165,000	
Accumulated amortization, equipment . .		$ 52,000
Accounts payable		37,000
Income taxes payable		21,500
Long-term notes payable		58,000
Common shares		55,000
Retained earnings		99,000
Cash dividends declared.	75,000	
Repair services revenue.		420,000
Interest earned		6,500
Amortization expense, equipment.	26,000	
Wages expense	179,000	
Rent expense	47,000	
Insurance expense.	7,000	
Interest expense.	4,700	
Income taxes expense.	33,000	
	$749,000	$749,000

Required

1. Prepare closing entries for Westside Appliance Repair, Inc.
2. Prepare a post-closing trial balance for the business.
3. Set up a Retained Earnings account, and post all necessary amounts to the account.

Planning the Solution

Solution to Demonstration Problem

■ Examine the adjusted trial balance and identify all of the nominal accounts that must be closed.

■ Prepare entries to close the revenue accounts to Income Summary, to close the expense accounts to Income Summary, to close Income Summary to Retained Earnings, and to close Cash Dividends Declared to Retained Earnings.

■ List the permanent accounts with their balances on the post-closing trial balance, using the post-closing balance for the Retained Earnings account.

■ In the Retained Earnings account, enter the balance shown on the adjusted trial balance and post the closing entries to the account.

Requirement 1:

Closing entries:

1993				
Dec.	31	Repair Services Revenue	420,000.00	
		Interest Earned	6,500.00	
		Income Summary.		426,500.00
	31	Income Summary	296,700.00	
		Amortization Expense, Equipment.		26,000.00
		Wages Expense.		179,000.00
		Interest Expense		4,700.00
		Insurance Expense		7,000.00
		Rent Expense.		47,000.00
		Income Taxes Expense		33,000.00
	31	Income Summary	129,800.00	
		Retained Earnings		129,800.00
	31	Retained Earnings.	75,000.00	
		Cash Dividends Declared.		75,000.00

Requirement 2:

WESTSIDE APPLIANCE REPAIR, INC.
Post-Closing Trial Balance
December 31, 1993

Cash.	$ 83,300	
Accounts receivable.	45,000	
Notes receivable	60,000	
Prepaid insurance	19,000	
Prepaid rent	5,000	
Equipment	165,000	
Accumulated amortization, equipment . .		$ 52,000
Accounts payable		37,000
Income taxes payable		21,500
Long-term notes payable		58,000
Common shares		55,000
Retained earnings		153,800
Totals	$377,300	$377,300

Requirement 3:

Retained Earnings

Date		Explanation	PR	Debit	Credit	Balance
1993						
Jan.	1	Beginning balance			99,000	99,000
Dec.	31	Close Income Summary			129,800	228,800
	31	Close Cash Dividends Declared		75,000		153,800

B

Reversing Entries

In this appendix, we explain some optional entries accountants may use in accounting for accrued items. These optional entries, called **reversing entries,** make the bookkeeping process easier.

In accounting for Jerry Dow's law practice, the December 31, 1993, adjusting entries included an accrual of the secretary's salary. This entry was as follows:

LO 8 Prepare reversing entries and explain when and why they are used.

1993				
Dec.	31	Salaries Expense	210.00	
		Salaries Payable		210.00
		To record accrued wages.		

Then, on December 31, the Salaries Expense account was closed to Income Summary.

Since the secretary is paid every two weeks, the next payment is on January 9, and is recorded as follows:

Jan.	9	Salaries Payable.	210.00	
		Salaries Expense	490.00	
		Cash		700.00
		Paid wages for two weeks.		

To make the January 9 entry correctly, the bookkeeper must remember that part of the cash payment is of accrued salaries and part is expense of the current period. Since the accrual is easy to forget, you can avoid the need to remember by preparing and posting entries to reverse any end-of-period adjustments of accrued items. These reversing entries are made after the adjusting and closing entries are posted and are normally dated the first day of the new accounting period.

Also, Appendix A at the end of Chapter 3 explained that some companies follow the practice of recording prepaid and unearned items in income statement accounts. When that is the practice, the end-of-period adjusting entries transfer the unused or unearned portions to asset and liability accounts. Thereafter, reversing entries may be used to transfer the prepaid asset and unearned liability account balances back into the expense and revenue accounts.

To reverse the accrual of wages, make the following entry:

Jan.	1	Salaries Payable.	210.00	
		Salaries Expense		210.00
		To reverse the accrual of salaries.		

Observe that the reversing entry is the exact opposite of the original, December 31 adjusting entry. After the adjusting, closing, and reversing entries are posted, the Salaries Expense and Salaries Payable accounts appear as follows:

Salaries Expense

Date		Explanation	Debit	Credit	Balance
Dec.	12	Paid wages	700		700
	26	Paid wages	700		1,400
	31	Accrued wages	210		1,610
	31	Closing		1,610	–0–
1994					
Jan.	1	Reversal		210	210 Cr.

Salaries Payable

Date		Explanation	Debit	Credit	Balance
Dec.	31	Accrued wages		210	210
1994					
Jan.	1	Reversal	210		–0–

Notice that the reversing entry cancels the $210 of salaries that appeared in the Salaries Payable account. It also causes the accrued salaries to appear in the Salaries Expense account as a $210 credit. Therefore, due to the reversing entry, when the salaries are paid on January 9, you can record the transaction with this entry:

Jan.	9	Salaries Expense	700.00	
		Cash		700.00
		Paid wages for two weeks.		

The entry's $700 debit to Salaries Expense includes both the $210 salary incurred during 1993 and the $490 salary expense incurred during 1994. However, when the entry is posted, because of the previously posted reversing entry with the resulting credit balance of $210, the balance of the Salaries Expense account shows only the $490 expense of the current period, as follows:

Salaries Expense

Date		Explanation	Debit	Credit	Balance
Dec.	12	Paid wages	700		700
	26	Paid wages	700		1,400
	31	Accrued wages	210		1,610
	31	Closing		1,610	–0–
1994					
Jan.	1	Reversal		210	210 Cr.
	9	Paid wages	700		490

LO 8. Reversing entries may be applied to all accrued items, such as accrued interest earned, accrued interest expense, accrued taxes, and accrued salaries and wages. Reversing entries also may be used for prepaid and unearned items if (and only if) the business records prepaid expenses with debits to expense accounts, and records unearned revenues with credits to revenue accounts (as explained in Appendix A at the end of Chapter 3). In any case, reversing entries are not required. The financial statements appear exactly the same whether or not reversing entries are used. Reversing entries are used as a convenience in bookkeeping.

Summary of
Appendix B in Terms
of Learning Objective

Glossary

LO 7 Define or explain
the words and phrases
listed in the chapter
glossary.

Accounting cycle the recurring accounting steps performed each accounting period beginning with the recording of transactions and proceeding through posting the recorded amounts, preparing an unadjusted trial balance and completing a work sheet, journalizing and posting adjusting entries, preparing the financial statements, journalizing and posting closing entries, and preparing a post-closing trial balance. pp. 202–04

Cash Dividends Declared a temporary account that serves the same function for a corporation as does a withdrawals account for a proprietorship, and which is closed to Retained Earnings at the end of each accounting period. p. 199

Closing entries entries made at the end of each accounting period to establish zero balances in the temporary accounts and to transfer the temporary account balances to a capital account or accounts or to the Retained Earnings account. pp. 186–91

Date of declaration the date on which a dividend is declared by vote of a corporation's board of directors. p. 199

Date of payment the date on which a dividend liability of a corporation is satisfied by mailing cheques to the shareholders. p. 200

Date of record the date on which the shareholders who are listed in a corporation's records are determined to be those who will receive a dividend. p. 199

Deficit a negative amount (debit balance) of retained earnings. pp. 201–202

Income Summary the account used in the closing process to summarize the amounts of revenues and expenses, and from which the amount of the net income or loss is transferred to the owner's capital account in a single proprietorship, or to the partners' capital accounts in a partnership, or to the Retained Earnings account in a corporation. p. 186

Nominal accounts another name for *temporary accounts*. p. 191

Permanent accounts accounts that remain open as long as the asset, liability, or owner's equity items recorded in the accounts continue in existence; therefore, accounts that appear on the balance sheet. p. 191

Post-closing trial balance a trial balance prepared after all adjusting and closing entries have been posted. p. 192

Real accounts another name for *permanent accounts*. p. 191

Reversing entries optional entries that transfer the balances in balance sheet accounts which arose as a result of certain adjusting entries (usually accruals) to income statement accounts. pp. 207–208

Shareholders of record the shareholders of a corporation as reflected in the records of the corporation. p. 199

Temporary accounts accounts that are closed at the end of each accounting period; therefore, the revenue, expense, Income Summary, and withdrawals accounts. p. 191

Working papers the memoranda, analyses, and other informal papers prepared by accountants in the process of organizing the data that go into the formal financial reports given to managers and other interested parties. p. 182

Work sheet a working paper on which the accountant shows the unadjusted trial balance, shows the effects of the adjustments on the account balances, calculates the net income or loss, and sorts the adjusted amounts according to the financial statements on which the amounts appear. pp. 182–86

Permanent accounts   real accounts; balance sheet accounts.

Temporary accounts   nominal accounts.

Synonymous Terms

Answers to the following questions are listed at the end of this chapter. Be sure that you decide which is the one best answer to each question *before* you check the answers.

Objective Review

LO 1   In preparing a work sheet at the end of the annual accounting period, Ritz Company's accountant incorrectly extended a $9,400 salaries expense amount from the adjusted trial balance to the Statement of Changes in Owner's Equity or Balance Sheet Debit column. As a result of this error:

a. The adjusted trial balance columns will not balance.

b. The net income calculated on the work sheet will be understated.

c. The net income calculated on the work sheet will be overstated.

d. On the bottom row of the work sheet, the totals of the last two columns will not be equal.

e. Both (*b*) and (*d*) are correct.

LO 2   Related to the process of preparing closing entries:

a. Expenses, revenues, and the withdrawals account are closed to Income Summary.

b. All expense accounts are first closed to the revenue accounts, which are then closed to Income Summary.

c. After the process is completed, the Income Summary account balance equals net income or net loss for the period.

d. After the process is completed, all temporary accounts have zero balances.

e. None of the above is correct.

LO 3   A post-closing trial balance:

a. Includes the balances of all accounts that appear on the financial statements.

b. Is one of the important financial statements presented to the owner of a business and other outside parties.

c. Must be prepared as the first step in the end-of-period procedures that lead to the preparation of financial statements.

d. Should include the balances of accounts that appear on the income statement and on the balance sheet.

e. Should include only balances of accounts that appear on the balance sheet.

LO 4   The retained earnings of a corporation:

a. Will be reported as a deficit if the sum of all prior net losses plus all dividend declarations exceeds the sum of all prior net incomes.

b. Less any contributed capital amounts equals the total shareholders' equity of the corporation.

c. Represent cash balances the corporation has available to pay dividends.

d. Will be reported as a positive amount if net income for the current period exceeds dividend declarations during the period.

e. Include the sum of all past net incomes (less net losses) of the corporation plus any dividends that have been declared but not paid.

LO 5 In accounting for cash dividends that a corporation declares and pays:

a. The Cash Dividends Declared account is reported on the balance sheet as a liability.

b. No entry is required on the date of record.

c. A dividend declaration is debited to Retained Earnings and credited to Cash Dividends Declared.

d. The Cash Dividends Declared account is closed to Income Summary.

e. A payment of a previously recorded dividend declaration is debited to Cash Dividends Declared and credited to Cash.

LO 6 The steps in the accounting cycle:

a. Are the eight procedures followed in preparing a work sheet.

b. Begin with the preparation of an unadjusted trial balance.

c. Are completed once during the life of each business.

d. Are concluded with the preparation of a post-closing trial balance.

e. All of the above are correct.

LO 7 The date on which the shareholders listed in a corporation's records are determined to be those who will receive dividends is the:

a. Date of transfer.

b. Date of declaration.

c. Date of record.

d. Date of payment.

e. Closing date.

LO 8 Reversing entries:

a. Must be used by all companies that have an accrual accounting system.

b. Are journalized and posted at the end of the accounting period after the adjusting entries are posted and prior to posting the closing entries.

c. Have the effect of deferring the reporting of accrued expenses from one period to the next.

d. Have no effect on the amounts reported on the financial statements.

e. None of the above is correct.

A letter ^B *identifies the questions, exercises, and problems based on Appendix B at the end of the chapter.*

Questions for Class Discussion

1. What is the difference between working papers and a work sheet?
2. What tasks are performed on a work sheet?
3. Is it possible to complete the statements and adjust and close the accounts without preparing a work sheet? What is gained by preparing a work sheet?

4. At what stage in the accounting process is a work sheet prepared?

5. Where do you obtain the amounts that are entered in the Unadjusted Trial Balance columns of a work sheet?

6. Why are the adjustments in the Adjustments columns of a work sheet keyed together with letters?

7. What is the result of combining the amounts in the Unadjusted Trial Balance columns with the amounts in the Adjustments columns of a work sheet?

8. Why must you exercise care in sorting the items in the Adjusted Trial Balance columns to the proper Income Statement or Balance Sheet columns?

9. In extending the items in the Adjusted Trial Balance columns of a work sheet, what would be the effect on the net income of extending (*a*) an expense to the Statement of Changes in Owner's Equity or Balance Sheet Debit column, (*b*) a liability to the Income Statement Credit column, and (*c*) a revenue to the Statement of Changes in Owner's Equity or Balance Sheet Debit column? Which, if any, of these errors would be detected automatically on the work sheet? Why would they be detected?

10. Why are revenue and expense accounts called *temporary accounts?* Are there any other temporary accounts?

11. What two purposes are accomplished by recording closing entries?

12. What accounts are affected by closing entries? What accounts are not affected?

13. Explain the difference between adjusting and closing entries.

14. What is the purpose of the Income Summary account?

[B]15. If one company uses reversing entries and another does not, what differences between the two companies will show up on the financial statements?

Mini Discussion Case

In the days of exploration and in quest of finding alternate routes to the new world, group-financed individual ventures were the order of the day. A venture lasted for two, three, or more years, and once completed involved a windup. Financial statements were prepared with precision without the need for adjusting entries. Closing entries were, however, required to close out the profit on the venture and the capital accounts to complete the windup.

Case 4–1

Required

Discuss the similarities and differences between venture accounting of yesteryear and present-day accounting for similar ventures that would be required under GAAP.

Exercises

The balances of the following accounts appeared in the Adjusted Trial Balance columns of a work sheet. Copy the account numbers in a column on a sheet of notepaper, and beside each number indicate by letter the Income Statement or Balance Sheet column to which the account's balance would be sorted in completing the work sheet. Use the letter *a* to indicate the Income Statement Debit column, *b* to indicate the Income State-

Exercise 4–1
Sorting account balances
on a work sheet
(LO 1)

ment Credit column, *c* to indicate the Statement of Changes in Owner's Equity or Balance Sheet Debit column, and *d* to indicate the Statement of Changes in Owner's Equity or Balance Sheet Credit column.

1. Donna Munnerlyn, Withdrawals.
2. Machinery.
3. Amortization Expense, Machinery.
4. Office Supplies.
5. Prepaid Insurance.
6. Rent Expense.
7. Service Revenue.

8. Accounts Receivable.
9. Donna Munnerlyn, Capital.
10. Wages Expense.
11. Accounts Payable.
12. Accumulated Amortization, Machinery.
13. Cash.
14. Utilities Expense.

Exercise 4–2
Preparing adjusting entries from work sheet information
(LO 1)

The following item amounts are from the adjustments columns of a work sheet. Use this information to prepare adjusting journal entries dated December 31.

		Adjustments		
		Debit		Credit
Prepaid insurance			(*a*)	2,475
Office supplies.			(*b*)	360
Accumulated amortization, office equipment . .			(*c*)	1,670
Accumulated amortization, plant equipment. . .			(*d*)	8,200
Office salaries expense	(*e*)	780		
Insurance expense, office equipment	(*a*)	625		
Insurance expense, plant equipment.	(*a*)	1,850		
Office supplies expense	(*b*)	360		
Amortization expense, office equipment.	(*c*)	1,670		
Amortization expense, plant equipment	(*d*)	8,200		
Salaries payable			(*e*)	780
Totals		13,485		13,485

Exercise 4–3
Using T-account information to prepare closing entries
(LO 2)

On a sheet of paper, copy the following T-accounts and their end-of-period balances. Below the accounts, prepare entries to close the accounts. Post to the T-accounts.

Rita Ivy, Capital				Rent Expense	
	Dec. 31	19,700	Dec. 31	5,400	

Rita Ivy, Withdrawals			Salaries Expense		
Dec. 31	22,500		Dec. 31	4,200	

Income Summary			Supplies Expense		
			Dec. 31	9,775	

Fees Earned				Amortization Expense, Equipment	
	Dec. 31	38,100	Dec. 31	3,600	

The following items appeared in the Income Statement columns of a December 31 work sheet prepared for Alfred Dole, an accountant. Assume that Dole withdrew $32,000 from his accounting practice during the year and prepare entries to close the accounts.

Exercise 4–4
Using work sheet
information to prepare
closing entries
(LO 2)

	Income Statement	
	Debit	**Credit**
Accounting fees earned		71,000
Office salaries expense	18,000	
Rent expense	9,600	
Insurance expense	3,360	
Office supplies expense	580	
Amortization expense, office equipment . .	2,300	
	33,840	71,000
Net income	37,160	
	71,000	71,000

Open the following T-accounts on notepaper for a corporation that does word processing for other companies. Below the T-accounts prepare entries to close the accounts. Post to the T-accounts.

Exercise 4–5
Preparing and posting
closing entries for a
corporation
(LO 2, 5)

Common Shares		Rent Expense	
	Dec. 31 50,000	Dec. 31 7,800	

Retained Earnings		Salaries Expense	
	Dec. 31 6,800	Dec. 31 33,280	

Income Summary		Insurance Expense	
		Dec. 31 1,500	

Services Revenue		Amortization Expense, Equipment	
	Dec. 31 62,400	Dec. 31 7,600	

Cash Dividends Declared	
Nov. 15 8,750	

A corporation debited Cash Dividends Declared for $50,000 during the year ended December 31. The items that follow appeared in the Income Statement columns of the work sheet prepared at year-end. Prepare closing journal entries for the corporation.

Exercise 4–6
Closing entries for a
corporation
(LO 2)

| | Income Statement | |
	Debit	Credit
Services revenue		285,700
Office salaries expense	187,000	
Rent expense	18,000	
Insurance expense	4,400	
Office supplies expense	400	
Amortization expense, office equipment . .	5,100	
	214,900	285,700
Net income	70,800	
	285,700	285,700

Exercise 4–7
Recording corporate
transactions in T-accounts
(LO 4, 5)

1. On a sheet of notepaper, open the following T-accounts: Cash, Accounts Receivable, Equipment, Notes Payable, Common Dividend Payable, Common Shares, Retained Earnings, Income Summary, Cash Dividends Declared, Services Revenue, and Operating Expenses.

2. Record directly in the T-accounts these transactions of a new corporation:
    a. Issued common shares for $150,000 cash.
    b. Purchased equipment for $146,500 cash.
    c. Sold and delivered $30,000 of services on credit.
    d. Collected $27,000 of accounts receivable.
    e. Paid $18,000 of operating expenses.
    f. Declared cash dividends of $7,500.
    g. Paid the dividends declared in (*f*).
    h. Purchased $12,000 of additional equipment, giving $5,000 in cash and a $7,000 promissory note.
    i. Closed the revenue accounts, (*j*) the expense accounts, (*k*) Income Summary, and (*l*) Cash Dividends Declared.

3. Answer these questions:
    a. Does the corporation have retained earnings?
    b. Does it have any cash?
    c. If the corporation has retained earnings, why does it not also have cash?
    d. Can the corporation legally declare additional cash dividends?
    e. Can it pay additional cash dividends?
    f. What does the balance of the Notes Payable account tell the financial statement reader about the makeup of the corporation's assets?
    g. Explain what the balance of the Common Shares account represents.
    h. Explain what the balance of the Retained Earnings account represents.

Exercise 4–8
Preparing a work sheet
(LO 1)

Following is an alphabetical list of Ware Printing Company's accounts and their unadjusted balances. All are normal balances. To save you time, the balances are in one- and two-digit numbers.

Trial Balance Accounts and Balances

Accounts payable	$ 2	Rent expense	$ 7
Accounts receivable.	5	Printing services revenue . . .	24
Accumulated amortization,		Uby Ware, capital	30
printing equipment	12	Uby Ware, withdrawals	8
Cash.	4	Printing equipment	30
Notes payable	3	Printing supplies.	6
Prepaid insurance	2	Wages expense	9

Required

1. Prepare a work sheet form and enter the trial balance accounts and amounts on the work sheet.
2. Complete the work sheet using the following information:
   a. Estimated amortization of printing equipment, $4.
   b. Expired insurance, $1.
   c. Unused printing supplies per inventory, $3.
   d. Earned but unpaid wages, $1.

The unadjusted trial balance of Frame Factory, Inc., as of December 31, 1993, (the end of its annual accounting period) follows:

Exercise 4–9
Preparing a work sheet
(LO 1)

Cash	$ 15,500	
Prepaid insurance	1,400	
Framing supplies.	24,300	
Framing equipment	28,000	
Accumulated amortization, framing equipment . .		$ 6,500
Common shares		30,000
Retained earnings		7,000
Cash dividends declared	5,000	
Services revenue.		82,900
Salaries expense	42,000	
Rent expense	10,200	
Totals	$126,400	$126,400

Required

1. Prepare a work sheet form on notepaper and enter the trial balance.
2. Complete the work sheet using the information that follows:
   a. Expired insurance, $800.
   b. Unused framing supplies per inventory, $5,100.
   c. Estimated amortization of framing equipment, $1,300.
   d. Earned but unpaid salaries, $500.

Prepare adjusting and closing journal entries for the corporation of Exercise 4–9.

Exercise 4–10
Adjusting and closing
entries
(LO 5)

List the letters identifying the following steps in the accounting cycle in the order the steps are performed:

a. Preparing a post-closing trial balance.
b. Journalizing and posting adjusting entries.
c. Completing the work sheet.
d. Preparing an unadjusted trial balance.
e. Journalizing and posting closing entries.
f. Journalizing transactions.
g. Posting the entries to record transactions.
h. Preparing the financial statements.

Exercise 4–11
The steps in the
accounting cycle
(LO 6)

^BExercise 4–12
Reversing entries
(LO 8)

On December 31, adjusting entry information for Laredo Company is as follows:

a. Amortization on office equipment, $3,400.
b. Eight hundred dollars of the Prepaid Insurance balance has expired.
c. Employees have earned salaries of $1,700 that have not been paid.
d. The Unearned Service Fees account balance includes $2,100 that has been earned.
e. The company has earned $4,900 of service fees that have not been collected or recorded.

Required

List the letters that identify adjustments for which reversing entries should be made. Assuming the appropriate adjusting entries have been recorded, prepare the reversing entries.

^BExercise 4–13
Reversing entries
(LO 8)

The following information relates to Lomas Company on December 31, 1993, the end of its annual accounting period:

a. Lomas rents office space for $6,200 per month. The company failed to pay the rent for December until January 6, at which time it paid the rent for December and January.
b. Because Lomas does not use all of its office space, it subleases space to a tenant for $800 per month. The tenant failed to pay the December rent until January 8, at which time it paid the rent for December and January.

Required

1. Assuming that Lomas does not use reversing entries, prepare adjusting journal entries dated December 31. Also prepare entries to record Lomas's payment of rent in January and the receipt of rent in January from Lomas's tenant.
2. Assuming that Lomas uses reversing entries, prepare adjusting journal entries dated December 31 and reversing entries dated January 1. Also prepare entries to record Lomas's payment of rent in January and the receipt of rent in January from Lomas's tenant.

Problems

Problem 4–1
The work sheet; financial statements and closing entries
(LO 1, 2)

At the end of its annual accounting period, a trial balance from the ledger of Dunhill Employment Services appeared as follows:

DUNHILL EMPLOYMENT SERVICES
Unadjusted Trial Balance
December 31, 1993

Cash.	$ 4,850	
Office supplies.	1,100	
Prepaid insurance	2,120	
Office equipment	27,860	
Accumulated amortization, office equipment . .		$11,630
Accounts payable		890
B. K. Dunhill, capital		16,380
B. K. Dunhill, withdrawals	22,500	
Employment fees earned.		56,400
Wages expense.	18,220	
Rent expense	7,500	
Utilities expense.	1,150	
Totals	$85,300	$85,300

Required

1. Enter the trial balance on a work sheet form and complete the work sheet using the information that follows:
   a. Expired insurance, $1,410.
   b. An office supplies inventory showed $460 of supplies on hand.
   c. Estimated amortization on office equipment, $2,800.
   d. Wages earned by the one employee but unpaid and unrecorded, $220.

2. Journalize the adjusting entries and the closing entries.

3. From the work sheet prepare an income statement, a statement of changes in owner's equity, and a classified balance sheet. Dunhill did not make additional investments in the business during 1993.

The accounts of Mesa Surveying Company, showing balances as of the end of its annual accounting period, appear in the booklet of working papers that accompanies this text, and a trial balance of its ledger is reproduced on a work sheet form provided there. The trial balance has the items that follow:

Problem 4–2
End-of-period accounting procedures
(LO 1, 2, 3)

MESA SURVEYING COMPANY
Unadjusted Trial Balance
December 31, 1993

Cash	$ 2,740	
Surveying supplies	1,930	
Prepaid insurance	3,500	
Surveying equipment.	85,365	
Accumulated amortization, surveying equipment . .		$ 35,460
Accounts payable		900
Long-term notes payable.		12,000
Lisa Garza, capital		34,680
Lisa Garza, withdrawals	21,000	
Surveying fees earned		58,400
Wages expense.	16,820	
Interest expense	720	
Rent expense.	5,400	
Property taxes expense	2,470	
Repairs expense, equipment	535	
Utilities expense	960	
Totals	$141,440	$141,440

Required

1. Enter the unadjusted trial balance on a work sheet form and complete the work sheet using the information that follows:

    a. Surveying supplies inventory, $840.

    b. Expired insurance, $1,600.

    c. Estimated amortization on surveying equipment, $6,300.

    d. The December hydro bill for the office arrived in the mail after the trial balance was prepared. Its $85 amount was unrecorded.

    e. Wages earned but unpaid and unrecorded, $210.

    f. The lease contract on the office calls for total annual rent equal to 10% of the annual revenue, with $450 payable each month on the first day of the month. The $450 was paid each month and debited to the Rent Expense account.

    g. Maintenance expenses on the surveying equipment amounting to $620 have accrued but are unrecorded and unpaid.

    h. The long-term note payable was signed on September 1, and interest on the debt is at a 12% annual rate or $120 per month. The note calls for payment in advance of $360 interest every three months. Payments are recorded in the Interest Expense account. Interest payments were made on September 1 and December 1. A $1,200 payment on the note principal is due next September 1.

2. Journalize and post the adjusting entries. (Omit posting if you are not using the working papers.)

3. Prepare an income statement, a statement of changes in owner's equity, and a classified balance sheet. Garza did not make additional investments in the business during 1993.

4. Journalize and post the closing entries and prepare a post-closing trial balance. (Omit this requirement if you are not using the working papers.)

Problem 4–3
End-of-period accounting
procedures
(LO 1, 2, 3)

The unadjusted trial balance of Tower Window Cleaning is as follows:

TOWER WINDOW CLEANING
Unadjusted Trial Balance
December 31, 1993

Cash	$ 890	
Accounts receivable	1,400	
Cleaning supplies	470	
Prepaid insurance	2,100	
Prepaid rent	350	
Trucks	18,235	
Accumulated amortization, trucks		$ 7,295
Cleaning equipment	4,930	
Accumulated amortization, cleaning equipment		1,970
Accounts payable		985
Unearned cleaning services revenue		800
Marian Stone, capital		10,115
Marian Stone, withdrawals	15,000	
Cleaning services revenue		52,850
Office salaries expense	9,600	
Cleaning wages expense	15,840	
Rent expense	3,500	
Gas, oil, and repairs expense	1,220	
Telephone expense	480	
Totals	$74,015	$74,015

Required

1. Enter the unadjusted trial balance on a work sheet form and complete the work sheet using the information that follows:
    a. Insurance expired on the cleaning equipment, $130, and on the truck, $1,450.
    b. An inventory showed $265 of cleaning supplies on hand.
    c. Estimated amortization on the cleaning equipment, $495.
    d. Estimated amortization on the truck, $3,650.
    e. In December 1992, the company had prepaid the January 1993 rent for garage and office space occupied by the window cleaning service. This amount appears as the balance of the Prepaid Rent account. Rents for February through November were paid each month and debited to the Rent Expense account. As of the trial balance date, the December 1993 rent had not been paid.
    f. Three office buildings signed contracts with Tower, agreeing to pay a fixed fee for the cleaning services. Two of the office buildings made advance payments on the contracts, and the amounts received were credited to the Unearned Cleaning Services Revenue account. An examination of the contracts shows $600 of the $800 received was earned by the end of the accounting period. The third building's contract provides for a $250 monthly fee to be paid at the end of each month's service. It was signed on December 15, and one half of a month's revenue has accrued but is unrecorded.
    g. A $45 December telephone bill and a $190 bill for repairs to the truck used in the business arrived in the mail on December 31. Neither bill was paid or recorded before the trial balance was prepared.
    h. Office salaries, $145, and cleaning wages, $255, have accrued but are unpaid and unrecorded.
2. Journalize and post the adjusting entries. (Omit posting if you are not using the working papers.)
3. Prepare an income statement, a statement of changes in owner's equity, and a classified balance sheet. Stone did not make additional investments in the business during 1993.
4. Journalize and post the closing entries and prepare a post-closing trial balance. (Omit this requirement if you are not using the working papers.)

Melton Realty Company's unadjusted trial balance on December 31, 1993, (the end of its annual accounting period) is as follows:

^BProblem 4–4
Reversing entries
(LO 2, 8)

MELTON REALTY COMPANY
Unadjusted Trial Balance
December 31, 1993

Cash.	$ 12,450	
Notes receivable.	63,000	
Office supplies.	1,100	
Building	480,000	
Unearned commissions		$ 15,000
Notes payable		290,000
J. Melton, capital		150,820
J. Melton, withdrawals	180,000	
Commissions earned.		288,000
Rent earned		57,600
Interest earned.		6,930
Salaries expense.	38,000	
Interest expense.	26,100	
Insurance expense.	7,700	
Totals	$808,350	$808,350

Information necessary to prepare adjusting entries is as follows:

a. Employees, who are paid $3,270 every two weeks, have earned $1,960 since the last payment. The next payment of $3,270 will be on January 4.

b. Melton rents office space to several tenants, of whom one has paid only $500 of the $1,000 rent for December. On January 10, the tenant will pay the remainder along with the rent for January.

c. An inventory of office supplies discloses $550 of supplies on hand.

d. Premiums for medical insurance for employees are paid monthly. The $700 premium for December will be paid January 12.

e. Melton owes $290,000 on a note payable that requires quarterly payments of accrued interest. The quarterly payments of $8,700 each are made on the 15th of January, April, July, and October.

f. An analysis of Melton's sales contracts with customers shows that $5,200 of the amount customers have prepaid remains unearned.

g. Melton has a $63,000 note receivable on which interest of $315 has accrued. On January 15, the note and the total accrued interest of $630 will be repaid to Melton.

h. Melton has earned but not yet recorded revenue of $9,000 for commissions from a customer who will pay for the work on January 25. At that time, the customer will also pay $1,800 for sales services Melton will perform in early January.

Required

1. Prepare adjusting journal entries.
2. Prepare closing journal entries.
3. Prepare reversing entries.
4. Prepare journal entries to record the January 1994 cash receipts and cash payments identified in the preceding information.

Problem 4–5
Closing entries for partnerships and corporations
(LO 2, 4, 5)

Carol Boyce, Sarah Reed, and John Hudson started a business on January 7, 1992, and each invested $75,000 in the business. During 1992, the business lost $30,240, and during 1993, it earned $83,550. On January 5, 1994, the three owners agreed to pay out to themselves $36,000 of the accumulated earnings of the business. On January 9, 1994, the $36,000 was paid out.

Required

1. Assume that the business is a partnership and the partners share net incomes and net losses equally. Give the entries to record the investments and to close the Income Summary account at the end of 1992 and again at the end of 1993. Also assume that the partners shared equally in the $36,000 of earnings paid out. Give the entry to record the withdrawals.

2. Assume that the business is organized as a corporation and that each owner invested $75,000 in it by buying 7,500 of its common shares. Give the entry to record the investments. Also, give the entries to close the Income Summary account at the end of 1992 and again at the end of 1993 and to record the declaration and payment of the $1.60 per share dividend. (Ignore corporate income taxes and assume that the three owners are the corporation's board of directors.)

Ted Dey opened a financial consulting business, Dey Financial Services. During June, he completed these transactions:

Problem 4-6
All steps in the accounting
cycle (covers two
accounting cycles)
(LO 1, 2, 3, 4, 6)

June 3   Invested in the business $70,000 in cash and an automobile having an $18,000 fair value.

     3   Rented furnished office space and paid one month's rent, $1,250.

     4   Purchased office supplies for cash, $680.

     8   Paid the premium on a one-year insurance policy, $1,080.

   14   Paid the salary of the office secretary for two weeks, $750.

   16   Provided consulting services and collected a $2,700 fee.

   28   Paid the salary of the office secretary for two weeks, $750.

   30   Paid the June telephone bill, $320.

   30   Paid for gas and oil used in the automobile during June, $90.

Required Work for June

1. Open these accounts: Cash; Office Supplies; Prepaid Insurance; Automobiles; Accumulated Amortization, Automobiles; Salaries Payable; Ted Dey, Capital; Ted Dey, Withdrawals; Consulting Fees Earned; Amortization Expense, Automobiles; Salaries Expense; Insurance Expense; Rent Expense; Office Supplies Expense; Gas, Oil, and Repairs Expense; Telephone Expense; and Income Summary.

2. Prepare and post journal entries to record the transactions.

3. Prepare an unadjusted trial balance on a work sheet form and complete the work sheet using the following information:
   a. Two thirds of a month's insurance has expired.
   b. An inventory shows $640 of office supplies remaining.
   c. Estimated amortization on the automobile, $375.
   d. Earned but unpaid salary of the office secretary, $150.

4. Journalize and post the adjusting entries.

5. Prepare an income statement and a statement of changes in owner's equity for June, and prepare a June 30 classified balance sheet.

6. Journalize and post the closing entries.

7. Prepare a post-closing trial balance.

During July, Ted Dey completed these business transactions:

July 1   Paid the July rent on the office space, $1,250.
      3   Purchased additional office supplies for cash, $35.
     11   Paid the salary of the office secretary for two weeks, $750.
     15   Withdrew $2,000 cash from the business for personal use.
     18   Provided consultation and collected a $4,200 fee.
     25   Paid the salary of the office secretary for two weeks, $750.
     31   Paid for gas and oil used in the automobile during July, $70.
     31   Paid the July telephone bill, $190.

Required Work for July

1. Prepare and post journal entries to record the transactions.
2. Prepare an unadjusted trial balance on a work sheet form and complete the work
   sheet using the following information:
   a. One month's insurance has expired.
   b. An office supplies inventory shows $580 of supplies on hand.
   c. Estimated amortization on the automobile, $375.
   d. Earned but unpaid secretary's salary, $300.
3. Journalize and post the adjusting entries.
4. Prepare an income statement and a statement of changes in owner's equity for
   July and prepare a July 31 classified balance sheet.
5. Journalize and post the closing entries.
6. Prepare a post-closing trial balance.

Problem 4–7
Analytical essay
(LO 1)

Refer to the information presented in Problem 4–2 and describe the incorrect amounts
that would appear on the work sheet as a result of each of the following assumptions:

1. In adjusting the surveying supplies inventory, $840 was debited to Surveying
   Supplies Expense and credited to Surveying Supplies.
2. In making the adjustment for the accrual of maintenance expenses on the surveying equipment, $620 was debited to Surveying Equipment and credited to
   Estimated Property Taxes Payable.
3. In extending the combined unadjusted trial balance amounts and the adjustment
   amounts, the Cash balance was extended to the Credit column of the adjusted
   trial balance.
4. In extending the adjusted trial balance amounts to the financial statement columns, the Prepaid Insurance was extended to the Income Statement Debit
   column.

^BProblem 4–8
Analytical essay
(LO 8)

In preparing adjusting entries on December 31, 1993, Castillo Company and Barnum
Company each recorded a $5,000 accrual of wages payable and a $2,400 accrual of
interest earned. The next date on which both companies pay wages is January 4, at
which time both will pay wages of $14,000. The accrued interest will be received in cash
on February 24, as part of a total receipt of $3,700.
  Describe the differences in the entries Castillo Company and Barnum Company
will make when the wages are paid and when the interest is received if Barnum follows a
practice of making reversing entries and Castillo Company does not make reversing
entries. Explain why these differences exist and also describe any differences in the
two companies' financial statements that result from the differences in the procedures
used by the two companies.

Alternate Problems

A trial balance of the ledger of Bass Fisherman's Guided Tours at the end of its annual accounting period appeared as follows:

Problem 4–1A
The work sheet; financial statements and closing entries
(LO 1, 2)

BASS FISHERMAN'S GUIDED TOURS
Unadjusted Trial Balance
December 31, 1993

Cash	$ 3,680	
Accounts receivable	1,700	
Fishing supplies.	2,100	
Prepaid insurance.	4,920	
Prepaid rent.	1,200	
Boats	82,900	
Accumulated amortization, boats.		$ 24,870
Fishing equipment	24,400	
Accumulated amortization, fishing equipment . .		7,320
Accounts payable.		2,550
Unearned tour fees		3,500
Bill Mayes, capital		62,210
Bill Mayes, withdrawals	27,000	
Tour fees earned		68,800
Wages expense	11,400	
Rent expense	5,400	
Gas, oil, and repairs expense	4,550	
Totals.	$169,250	$169,250

Required

1. Enter the trial balance on a work sheet form and complete the work sheet using the information that follows:
   a. Expired insurance, $3,640.
   b. An inventory of fishing supplies showed $1,100 of supplies on hand.
   c. The fishing guide service rents equipment storage and garage space. At the beginning of the year, two months' rent was prepaid as shown by the debit balance of the Prepaid Rent account. Rents for March through November were paid on the first day of each month and debited to the Rent Expense account. The December 1993 rent was unpaid on the trial balance date.
   d. Estimated amortization on the fishing equipment, $2,440.
   e. Estimated amortization on the boats, $13,800.
   f. On November 15, Bass Fisherman's Guided Tours contracted and began guided tours for the Galvan Resort for $1,750 per month. The resort company paid for two months' service in advance, and the amount paid was credited to the Unearned Tour Fees account. Bass also entered into a contract and conducted tours for Traveler's International on December 15. By the month's end, a half month's revenue, $500, had been earned on this contract but was unrecorded.
   g. Employee's wages amounting to $175 had accrued but were unrecorded on the trial balance date.

2. Journalize the adjusting entries and the closing entries.

3. Prepare an income statement, a statement of changes in owner's equity, and a classified balance sheet for the business. Mayes did not make additional investments in the business during 1993.

Problem 4–2A
End-of-period accounting procedures
(LO 1, 2, 3)

The accounts of Mesa Surveying Company, showing balances as of the end of its annual accounting period, appear in the booklet of working papers that accompanies this text, and a trial balance of its ledger is reproduced on a work sheet form provided there. The trial balance has the items that follow:

MESA SURVEYING COMPANY
Unadjusted Trial Balance
December 31, 1993

Cash	$ 2,740	
Surveying supplies	1,930	
Prepaid insurance	3,500	
Surveying equipment	85,365	
Accumulated amortization, surveying equipment . .		$ 35,460
Accounts payable		900
Long-term notes payable		12,000
Lisa Garza, capital		34,680
Lisa Garza, withdrawals	21,000	
Surveying fees earned		58,400
Wages expense	16,820	
Interest expense	720	
Rent expense	5,400	
Property taxes expense	2,470	
Repairs expense, equipment	535	
Utilities expense	960	
Totals	$141,440	$141,440

Required

1. Enter the unadjusted trial balance on a work sheet form and complete the work sheet using the information that follows:
    a. Surveying supplies inventory, $630.
    b. Expired insurance, $2,400.
    c. Estimated amortization on surveying equipment, $7,100.
    d. The December hydro bill for the office arrived in the mail after the trial balance was prepared. Its $140 amount was unrecorded.
    e. Wages earned but unpaid and unrecorded, $330.
    f. The lease contract on the office calls for total annual rent equal to 10% of the annual revenue, with $450 payable each month on the first day of the month. The $450 was paid each month and debited to the Rent Expense account.
    g. Additional property taxes amounting to $460 have accrued but are unrecorded and unpaid.
    h. The long-term note payable was signed on September 1, and interest on the debt is at a 12% annual rate or $120 per month. The note calls for payment in advance of $360 interest every three months. Payments are recorded in the Interest Expense account. Interest payments were made on September 1 and December 1. A $3,000 payment on the note principal is due next September 1.

2. Journalize and post adjusting entries. (Omit the posting if you are not using the working papers.)

3. Prepare an income statement, a statement of changes in owner's equity, and a classified balance sheet. Garza did not make additional investments in the business during 1993.

4. Journalize and post closing entries and prepare a post-closing trial balance. (Omit this requirement if you are not using the working papers.)

The unadjusted trial balance of Tower Window Cleaning is as follows:

Problem 4–3A
End-of-period accounting
procedures
(LO 1, 2, 3)

TOWER WINDOW CLEANING
Unadjusted Trial Balance
December 31, 1993

Cash	$ 890	
Accounts receivable	1,400	
Cleaning supplies	470	
Prepaid insurance	2,100	
Prepaid rent	350	
Trucks	18,235	
Accumulated amortization, trucks		$ 7,295
Cleaning equipment	4,930	
Accumulated amortization, cleaning equipment		1,970
Accounts payable		985
Unearned cleaning services revenue		800
Marian Stone, capital		10,115
Marian Stone, withdrawals	15,000	
Cleaning services revenue		52,850
Office salaries expense	9,600	
Cleaning wages expense	15,840	
Rent expense	3,500	
Gas, oil, and repairs expense	1,220	
Telephone expense	480	
Totals	$74,015	$74,015

Required

1. Enter the unadjusted trial balance on a work sheet form and complete the work sheet using the information that follows:
    a. Insurance expired on the cleaning equipment, $150, and on the truck, $1,200.
    b. An inventory showed $160 of cleaning supplies on hand.
    c. Estimated amortization on the cleaning equipment, $1,020.
    d. Estimated amortization on the truck, $2,850.
    e. In December 1992, the company had prepaid the January 1993 rent for garage and office space occupied by the window cleaning service. This amount appears as the balance of the Prepaid Rent account. Rents for February through November were paid each month and debited to the Rent Expense account. As of the trial balance date, the December 1993 rent had not been paid.
    f. Three office buildings signed contracts with Tower, agreeing to pay a fixed fee for the cleaning services. Two of the office buildings made advance payments on their contracts, and the amounts received were credited to the Unearned Cleaning Services Revenue account. An examination of the contracts shows $400 of the $800 received was earned by the end of the accounting period. The third building's contract provides for a $400 monthly fee to be paid at the end of each month's service. It was signed on December 15, and one half of a month's revenue has accrued but is unrecorded.
    g. A $50 December telephone bill and a $320 bill for repairs to the truck used in the business arrived in the mail on December 31. Neither bill was paid or recorded before the trial balance was prepared.
    h. Office salaries, $200, and cleaning wages, $280, have accrued but are unpaid and unrecorded.
2. Journalize and post adjusting entries. (Omit posting if you are not using the working papers.)

3. Prepare an income statement, a statement of changes in owner's equity, and a classified balance sheet. Stone did not make additional investments in the business during 1993.

4. Journalize and post closing entries and prepare a post-closing trial balance. (Omit this requirement if you are not using the working papers.)

^B**Problem 4–4A**
Reversing entries
(LO 2, 8)

Ogletree Design Associates' unadjusted trial balance on December 31, 1993 (the end of its annual accounting period), is as follows:

OGLETREE DESIGN ASSOCIATES
Unadjusted Trial Balance
December 31, 1993

Cash	$ 14,120	
Notes receivable	17,500	
Office supplies	1,700	
Building	290,000	
Land	375,000	
Unearned design fees		$ 7,800
Notes payable		471,100
M. Ogletree, capital		67,950
M. Ogletree, withdrawals	120,000	
Design fees earned		367,400
Rent earned		17,250
Interest earned		1,500
Salaries expense	77,600	
Interest expense	31,800	
Insurance expense	5,280	
Totals	$933,000	$933,000

Information necessary to prepare adjusting entries is as follows:

a. Employees, who are paid $3,040 every two weeks, have earned $1,440 since the last payment. The next payment of $3,040 will be on January 6.

b. Ogletree rents office space to a tenant who has paid only $750 of the $1,500 rent for December. On January 10, the tenant will pay the remainder along with the rent for January.

c. An inventory of supplies discloses $650 of supplies on hand.

d. Premiums for employees' medical insurance are paid monthly. The $480 premium for December will be paid January 12.

e. Ogletree owes $471,100 on a note payable that requires quarterly payments of accrued interest. The quarterly payments of $10,600 each are made on the 15th of January, April, July, and October.

f. An analysis of Ogletree's service contracts with customers shows that $4,300 of the amount customers have prepaid remains unearned.

g. Ogletree has a $17,500 note receivable on which interest of $50 has accrued. On January 22, the note and the total accrued interest of $125 will be repaid to Ogletree.

h. Ogletree has earned but unrecorded fees of $20,000 for design work provided to a customer who will pay for the work on January 24. At that time, the customer will also pay $3,500 for design work Ogletree will perform in early January.

Required

1. Prepare adjusting journal entries.
2. Prepare closing journal entries.
3. Prepare reversing entries.
4. Prepare journal entries to record the January 1994 cash receipts and cash payments identified in the preceding information.

On January 7, 1992, John Aspen, Sarah Khan, and Paul Glen started a business in which John Aspen invested $10,000, Sarah Khan invested $20,000, and Paul Glen invested $40,000. During 1992, the business lost $7,000; and during 1993, it earned $24,500. On January 5, 1994, the three business owners agreed to pay out to themselves $14,000 of the accumulated earnings of the business, and on January 10, the $14,000 was paid out.

Problem 4–5A
Closing entries for partnerships and corporations
(LO 2, 4, 5)

Required

1. Assume that the business is a partnership and that the partners share net incomes and net losses in proportion to their investments. Give the entries to record the investments and to close the Income Summary account at the end of 1992 and again at the end of 1993. Also assume that the partners paid out the accumulated earnings in proportion to their investments. Give the entry to record the withdrawals.
2. Assume that the business is organized as a corporation and that the owners invested in the corporation by buying its common shares at $5 per share, with John Aspen buying 2,000 shares, Sarah Khan buying 4,000 shares, and Paul Glen buying 8,000 shares. Give the entry to record the investments. Also, give the entries to close the Income Summary account at the end of 1992 and again at the end of 1993. Then give the entries to record the declaration and payment of the $1 per share dividend. (Ignore corporation income taxes and assume the investors are the corporation's board of directors.)

Ted Dey opened a financial consulting business, Dey Financial Services. During June, he completed these transactions:

Problem 4–6A
All steps in the accounting cycle (covers two accounting cycles)
(LO 1, 2, 3, 4, 6)

June 3 Invested in the business $40,000 in cash and an automobile having a $16,000 fair value.
      3 Rented furnished office space and paid one month's rent, $900.
      4 Purchased office supplies for cash, $750.
      7 Provided consulting services and collected a $3,200 fee.
     14 Paid the premium on a one-year insurance policy, $840.
     14 Paid the salary of the office secretary for two weeks, $700.
     16 Provided consulting services and collected a $1,800 fee.
     28 Paid the salary of the office secretary for two weeks, $700.
     30 Paid the June telephone bill, $240.
     30 Paid for gas and oil used in the business car during June, $80.

Required Work for June

1. Open these accounts: Cash; Office Supplies; Prepaid Insurance; Automobiles; Accumulated Amortization, Automobiles; Salaries Payable; Ted Dey, Capital; Ted Dey, Withdrawals; Consulting Fees Earned; Amortization Expense, Auto-

mobiles; Salaries Expense; Insurance Expense; Rent Expense; Office Supplies Expense; Gas, Oil, and Repairs Expense; Telephone Expense; and Income Summary.

2. Prepare and post journal entries to record the transactions.

3. Prepare an unadjusted trial balance on a work sheet form and complete the work sheet using the following information:
   a. One half of a month's insurance has expired.
   b. An inventory shows $670 of office supplies remaining.
   c. Estimated amortization on the automobile, $200.
   d. Earned but unpaid salary of the office secretary, $70.

4. Journalize and post the adjusting entries.

5. Prepare an income statement and a statement of changes in owner's equity for June, and prepare a June 30 classified balance sheet.

6. Journalize and post the closing entries.

7. Prepare a post-closing trial balance.

During July, Ted Dey completed these transactions:

July 1   Paid the July rent on the office space, $900.
      3   Purchased additional office supplies for cash, $30.
      12 Paid the salary of the office secretary for two weeks, $700.
      15 Ted Dey withdrew $2,000 cash from the business for personal use.
      18 Provided consultation and collected a $2,400 fee.
      26 Paid the salary of the office secretary for two weeks, $700.
      31 Paid for gas and oil used in the business car during July, $100.
      31 Paid the July telephone bill, $170.

Required Work for July

1. Prepare and post journal entries to record the transactions.

2. Prepare an unadjusted trial balance on a work sheet form and complete the work sheet using the following information:
   a. One month's insurance has expired.
   b. An office supplies inventory shows $610 of supplies on hand.
   c. Estimated amortization on the automobile, $200.
   d. Earned but unpaid secretary's salary, $210.

3. Journalize and post the adjusting entries.

4. Prepare an income statement and a statement of changes in owner's equity for July and prepare a July 31 classified balance sheet.

5. Journalize and post the closing entries.

6. Prepare a post-closing trial balance.

Problem 4–7A
Analytical essay
(LO 1)

Refer to the information in Problem 4–2A and describe the incorrect amounts that would appear on the work sheet as a result of each of the following assumptions:

1. In adjusting the Prepaid Insurance account, $1,100 was debited to Insurance Expense and credited to Prepaid Insurance.

2. In making the adjustment for rent expense, $440 was debited to Rent Expense and credited to Surveying Fees Earned.

3. On the work sheet, the company failed to record the adjustment for property taxes.

4. In extending the adjusted trial balance amounts to the financial statement columns, the Utilities Expense balance was extended to the Statement of Changes in Owner's Equity or Balance Sheet Debit column.

In preparing adjusting entries on December 31, 1993, Craven Company and Luong Company each recorded an $8,500 accrual of interest payable and a $4,600 accrual of consulting services revenue. The next date on which both companies pay interest is March 1, at which time both will pay interest of $27,000. The accrued consulting services revenue will be received in cash on January 30, as part of a total receipt of $52,600.

Describe the differences in the entries Craven Company and Luong Company will make when the interest is paid and when the consulting services revenue is received if Luong follows a practice of making reversing entries and Craven Company does not make reversing entries. Explain why these differences exist and also describe any differences in the two companies' financial statements that will result from the differences in the procedures used by the two companies.

^BProblem 4–8A
Analytical essay
(LO 8)

Serial Problem

Precision Computer Services

(This problem should not be assigned unless the working papers are being used. This is the third segment of a serial problem that started in Chapter 2, was continued in Chapter 3, and will be continued in Chapter 5. If you did not complete the solutions in Chapters 2 and 3, you can begin the problem at this point. However, you may need to review some of the facts presented in the Chapter 2 and Chapter 3 segments of the problem on pages 117 and 174.)

After being in business for the last three months of 1993, John Conard, the owner of Precision Computer Services, is preparing to begin the new year. In fulfilling the requirements of the problem in Chapters 2 and 3, all transactions that occurred during October, November, and December 1993 have been journalized and posted, as have been the December 31 adjusting entries. Also, financial statements for the three-month period ended December 31 have been prepared.

In anticipation of closing the books, an Income Summary account (Acct. No. 901) has been added to the General Ledger. To complete the accounting cycle, you should journalize and post the closing entries. Also, prepare a post-closing trial balance.

Provocative Problems

Provocative Problem 4–1
Galaxy Cleaners
(review problem)

During his second year in college, Daniel Rusk inherited Galaxy Cleaners when his father died. He immediately dropped out of school and took over management of the business. At the time he took over, Rusk recognized he knew little about accounting. However, he reasoned that since the business performed its services strictly for cash, if the cash of the business increased, the business was doing all right. Therefore, he was pleased as he watched the cash balance grow from $3,700 when he took over to $24,780 at year-end. Furthermore, since he had withdrawn $25,000 from the business to buy a new car and to pay personal expenses, he reasoned that the business must have earned $46,080 during the year. He arrived at the $46,080 by adding the $21,080 increase in cash to the $25,000 he had withdrawn from the business. Daniel was shocked when he received the following income statement and learned that the business had earned only slightly more than the amount withdrawn.

GALAXY CLEANERS
Income Statement
For Year Ended December 31, 1993

Cleaning services revenue		$73,750
Operating expenses:		
Amortization expense, building	$ 5,750	
Amortization expense, trucks	6,000	
Amortization expense, cleaning equipment . .	7,400	
Wages expense.	12,100	
Insurance expense.	1,310	
Cleaning supplies expense	6,040	
Gas, oil, and repairs expense	1,745	
Property taxes expense	4,235	
Utilities expense.	2,760	
Total operating expenses.		47,340
Net income.		$26,410

After thinking about the statement for several days, Rusk asked you to explain how, in a year in which the cash increased $21,080 and he withdrew $25,000, the business earned only $26,410. In examining the accounts of the business, you note that accrued wages payable at the beginning of the year were $235 but increased to $475 at year's end. Also, the accrued property taxes payable were $860 at the beginning of the year but had increased to $950 at year-end. Also, the balance of the Prepaid Insurance account was $180 more and the balance of the Cleaning Supplies account was $370 less at the end of the year than at the beginning. However, except for the changes in these accounts, the change in cash, and the changes in the balances of the accumulated amortization accounts, there were no other changes in the balances of the concern's asset and liability accounts between the beginning of the year and the end. Back your explanation with a calculation that accounts for the increase in the business's cash.

Provocative Problem 4–2
Louise O'Connor, Lawyer
(LO 2)

During the first year-end closing of the accounts of Louise O'Connor's law practice, the office bookkeeper became seriously ill and entered the hospital, unable to have visitors. O'Connor is certain the bookkeeper prepared a work sheet and complete financial statements, but she has only the income statement and cannot find the work sheet or remaining statements. She does have the unadjusted trial balance. She has asked you to take the information she has and prepare adjusting and closing entries. She also wants you to prepare a statement of changes in owner's equity and a classified balance sheet. She says the $5,000 of unearned legal fees on the trial balance represents a retainer fee paid by First City Bank. The bank retained Louise O'Connor on November 1 to do its legal work, and agreed to pay her $1,250 per month for her services. She says she has also agreed with Goodwin Realty to do its legal work on a fixed-fee basis. The agreement calls for a $750 monthly fee payable at the end of each three months. The agreement was signed on December 1, and one month's fee has accrued but has not been recorded. O'Connor did not make any additional investments in the business during the year.

LOUISE O'CONNOR, LAWYER
Unadjusted Trial Balance
December 31, 1993

Cash.	$ 8,320	
Legal fees receivable	3,500	
Office supplies.	300	
Prepaid insurance	4,450	
Office equipment	27,900	
Accounts payable		$ 1,810
Unearned legal fees		5,000
Short-term notes payable		6,000
Louise O'Connor, capital		19,220
Louise O'Connor, withdrawals	38,000	
Legal fees earned		83,400
Salaries expense.	22,400	
Rent expense	9,000	
Telephone expense	1,560	
Totals	$115,430	$115,430

LOUISE O'CONNOR, LAWYER
Income Statement
For Year Ended December 31, 1993

Revenue:		
Legal fees earned		$86,650
Operating expenses:		
Amortization expense, office equipment . .	$ 2,790	
Salaries expense	22,560	
Interest expense.	720	
Insurance expense	3,900	
Rent expense	9,000	
Office supplies expense.	200	
Telephone expense	1,560	
Total operating expenses		40,730
Net income		$45,920

The balance sheet that follows was prepared for Mark Mitchell Graphic Design at the end of its annual accounting period:

Provocative Problem 4–3
Mark Mitchell Graphic
Design
(LO 1)

MARK MITCHELL GRAPHIC DESIGN
Balance Sheet
December 31, 1993

Assets

Current assets:			
Cash.		$ 4,845	
Office supplies		530	
Prepaid insurance		670	
Total current assets			$ 6,045
Plant and equipment:			
Automobiles.	$24,500		
Less accumulated amortization. . . .	14,700	$ 9,800	
Office equipment	$52,700		
Less accumulated amortization. . . .	29,860	22,840	
Total plant and equipment.			32,640
Total assets			$38,685

Liabilities

Current liabilities:

Accounts payable	$1,090	
Salaries payable	335	
Unearned illustration fees	500	
Total liabilities		$1,925

Owner's Equity

Mark Mitchell, capital, December 31, 1993 . .		36,760
Total liabilities and owner's equity		$38,685

After completing the balance sheet, Mark Mitchell Graphic Design's accountant prepared and posted the following adjusting and closing entries for the concern:

Dec.	31	Insurance Expense	1,100.00	
		Prepaid Insurance		1,100.00
	31	Office Supplies Expense	740.00	
		Office Supplies		740.00
	31	Amortization Expense, Office Equipment	5,400.00	
		Accumulated Amortization, Office Equipment		5,400.00
	31	Amortization Expense, Automobiles	5,880.00	
		Accumulated Amortization, Automobiles		5,880.00
	31	Unearned Illustration Fees	1,000.00	
		Illustration Fees Earned		1,000.00
	31	Salaries Expense	335.00	
		Salaries Payable		335.00
	31	Graphic Design Fees Earned	58,850.00	
		Illustration Fees Earned	7,200.00	
		Income Summary		66,050.00
	31	Income Summary	37,720.00	
		Amortization Expense, Automobiles		5,880.00
		Amortization Expense, Office Equipment		5,400.00
		Salaries Expense		15,000.00
		Insurance Expense		1,100.00
		Rent Expense		7,500.00
		Office Supplies Expense		740.00
		Gas, Oil, and Repairs Expense		1,270.00
		Telephone Expense		830.00
	31	Income Summary	28,330.00	
		Mark Mitchell, Capital		28,330.00
	31	Mark Mitchell, Capital	24,000.00	
		Mark Mitchell, Withdrawals		24,000.00

Enter the relevant information from the balance sheet and the adjusting and closing entries on a work sheet form and complete the work sheet by working backward to the items that appeared in its Unadjusted Trial Balance columns.

Bombardier's January 31, 1992, consolidated statement of financial position is presented in Appendix I. Assuming that a ledger account exists for each item in that statement, prepare a January 31, 1992, post-closing trial balance for Bombardier. (Express amounts in millions of dollars.)

BBD

Analytical and Review Problems

The partially completed work sheet for the current fiscal year of Linda's Delivery Service appears below:

A&R Problem 4–1

Required

1. Complete the work sheet.
2. Journalize the adjusting and closing entries (omit narratives).

LINDA'S DELIVERY SERVICE
Work Sheet
For the Year Ended December 31, 1993

Account Titles	Trial Balance Dr.	Trial Balance Cr.	Adjustments Dr.	Adjustments Cr.	Adjusted Trial Balance Dr.	Adjusted Trial Balance Cr.	Income Statement Dr.	Income Statement Cr.	Balance Sheet Dr.	Balance Sheet Cr.
Cash	10,650									
Accounts receivable	5,200				6,000					
Supplies on hand	1,400								200	
Prepaid insurance	2,400									
Prepaid rent	1,200									
Delivery trucks					40,000					
Accounts payable		3,130				3,130				
Unearned delivery fees		4,500								2,000
Linda Orseti, capital, Dec. 31, 1993		50,000								
Linda Orseti, drawing	3,000									
Delivery service revenue		10,700								
Advertising expense	50									
Gas and oil expense	680									
Salaries expense	3,600									
Utilities expense	150									
	68,330	68,330								
Insurance expense							800			
Rent expense					600					
Supplies expense										
Amortization expense—delivery trucks										
Accumulated amortization—delivery trucks										1,000
Accrued salaries payable										300
Net income										

A&R Problem 4–2

Fred Sui operates a management consulting firm and uses a cash basis for recording transactions. The trial balance presented below reflects the operations for the first year of business.

ELITE MANAGEMENT CONSULTING SERVICES
Trial Balance
December 31, 1993

Cash	$ 3,600	
Office equipment expense	28,000	
F. Sui, capital.		$ 11,000
Management consulting fees		108,000
Office salaries expense	31,000	
Telephone expense	1,000	
Insurance expense	3,000	
Office supplies expense.	800	
F. Sui, withdrawals	51,600	
Totals	$119,000	$119,000

Additional information

a. Amount of office supplies still on hand at the end of the year was $500.

b. The office equipment was estimated to have a 10-year useful life with no salvage value.

c. Consulting services rendered for which no payment has been received amounted to $4,000.

d. Telephone bill for the month of December 1993 was paid in January 1994, $150.

e. Advertising expenses incurred but not yet paid, $800.

f. Golden, Ltd., paid $2,000 consulting fee for services to be performed in 1994.

Required

1. Prepare all necessary adjusting entries (omit narratives) to reflect Sui's operation on an accrual basis of accounting.

2. Prepare a trial balance on the accrual basis of accounting.

3. What is the difference in net income between the cash and the accrual bases of accounting for Sui's business?

4. Which basis, in your opinion, more realistically reflects the operations of Sui? Why?

5. What are the similarities and dissimilarities between the adjusting entries to convert a cash basis to an accrual basis and the adjusting entries for an accrual basis?

As a Matter of Record

Record Case 4–1

The following appeared in hundreds of newspapers all over the world under this headline: "BCCI Manager Charged."

> British prosecutors charged a former Bank of Credit and Commerce International account manager on Friday with false accounting for $179.4 million. BCCI, with operations in about 70 countries, had a total of 1.25 million depositors and $20 billion in liabilities when international bank regulators seized it on July 5.

Required

Between now and the end of your accounting course, peruse the financial pages of your newspaper and list the reported irregularities in the accounting records of companies.

Following is the November 30, 1993, unadjusted trial balance of Paramount Moving and Storage, which is owned by George Sanders. The temporary account balances represent the results of entries recorded during the first 11 months of 1993; the balance in George Sanders's capital account has not changed since December 31, 1992.

Paramount Moving and Storage
(Review of Chapters 1–4)

PARAMOUNT MOVING AND STORAGE
Unadjusted Trial Balance
November 30, 1993

	Acct. No.	Debits	Credits
Cash.	101	$ 51,610	
Office supplies.	124	450	
Moving supplies.	126	8,700	
Prepaid insurance	128	7,475	
Trucks.	153	350,000	
Accumulated amortization, trucks. . . .	154		$200,000
Building	173	185,000	
Accumulated amortization, building. . .	174		29,120
Accounts payable	201		2,350
Interest payable	203		–0–
Wages payable.	210		–0–
Unearned storage fees.	233		700
Long-term notes payable	251		245,000
George Sanders, capital	301		42,205
George Sanders, withdrawals	302	26,500	
Moving fees earned	401		179,600
Storage fees earned	402		26,750
Amortization expense, building	606	–0–	
Amortization expense, trucks	611	–0–	
Wages expense	623	41,700	
Interest expense.	633	–0–	
Insurance expense.	637	–0–	
Office supplies expense	650	–0–	
Moving supplies expense	652	–0–	
Advertising expense.	655	5,900	
Gas, oil, and repairs expense	669	31,510	
General and administrative expenses . .	672	16,880	
Income summary	901		–0–
		$725,725	$725,725

The following transactions occurred during the month of December 1993:

Dec. 2 Received $180 as advance payments on storage rental.

  5 Paid accounts payable of $720.

  6 Paid insurance premiums of $8,100 in advance.

  7 Deposited $8,700 of moving fee receipts.

  10 Purchased $1,560 of moving supplies on credit.

  12 Acquired additional truck worth $56,000 by paying $6,000 cash and giving a long-term note payable for the balance.

Dec. 14   Paid wages of $2,700 for the period December 1–14.

  17   Purchased $130 of office supplies on credit.

  21   Deposited $6,260 from moving fee receipts and $1,600 from storage fee receipts.

  24   Paid $860 for repairs to truck for damages sustained in an accident.

  28   Paid wages of $2,850 for the period December 15–28.

  30   Paid $900 to a magazine for advertisements that appeared in December.

  31   Deposited $4,700 from moving fee receipts and $800 from storage fee receipts.

Required

1. Set up accounts for the items listed in the November 30 trial balance and enter the November 30 balances in them.

2. Prepare and post journal entries to record the December transactions previously listed.

3. Prepare a 10-column work sheet and enter the December 31 unadjusted balances from the accounts. Also enter adjusting entries for the following items, and complete the work sheet:

   a. Unpaid wages were $610 as of December 31.
   b. The December 31 office supplies inventory was $180.
   c. The moving supplies inventory was $4,530 on December 31.
   d. The unexpired portion of the prepaid insurance was $9,475 as of December 31.
   e. Amortization for the year on the trucks was $50,350.
   f. Amortization for the year on the building was $7,400.
   g. Unearned storage fees balance at December 31 was $650.
   h. Sanders had withdrawn $1,600 cash on December 30, but he had not taken the time to record it.
   i. Interest expense on the notes payable for 1993 was $24,700.

4. Journalize and post the adjusting entries.

5. Prepare an income statement and a statement of changes in owner's equity for the year ended December 31, 1993, and a December 31, 1993, classified balance sheet.

6. Journalize and post the closing entries.

7. Prepare a post-closing trial balance.

Answers to Objective
Review Questions

LO 1 (*c*)	LO 4 (*a*)	LO 7 (*c*)
LO 2 (*d*)	LO 5 (*b*)	LO 8 (*d*)
LO 3 (*e*)	LO 6 (*d*)	

Accounting for a Merchandising Concern

Whether they deal in roller blades or razor blades, many companies earn profits by buying merchandise and selling it to customers. Accounting helps managers determine the amount of income earned by these companies and the cost of the inventory they have on hand.

*I*n previous chapters, we used illustrations of businesses that provided services to their customers, such as law firms, accounting firms, and real estate agencies. In this chapter, we shift our attention to merchandising businesses. These entities buy goods or products and then resell them to their customers. Your study of this chapter will focus on the problem of accounting for the goods that merchandising companies purchase for resale. You will learn to identify the elements of cost of goods sold and to complete the end-of-period accounting procedures used by merchandising companies, whether they are organized as corporations or proprietorships.

Learning Objectives

After studying Chapter 5, you should be able to:

1. Analyze and record transactions that involve the purchase and resale of merchandise.
2. Explain the nature of each item entering into the calculation of cost of goods sold and gross profit from sales.
3. Prepare a work sheet and the financial statements for a merchandising business that uses a periodic inventory system and that is organized as a corporation or as a single proprietorship.
4. Prepare adjusting and closing entries for a merchandising business organized as either a corporation or a single proprietorship.
5. Define or explain the words and phrases listed in the chapter glossary.

After studying Appendix C at the end of Chapter 5, you should be able to:

6. Explain the adjusting entry approach to accounting for inventories and prepare a work sheet, adjusting entries, and closing entries according to the adjusting entry approach. Also, be aware that approaches other than those illustrated may be used.

The previous chapters have described the accounting records and financial statements of Jerry Dow, Lawyer, which is a service enterprise. Other examples of service enterprises are laundries, taxi companies, airlines, financial planners, hair salons, theatres, and golf courses. Each provides a service to its customers for a commission, fare, or fee, and its net income is the difference between the revenues earned and the operating expenses incurred.

On the other hand, a merchandising company, whether a wholesaler or a retailer, earns revenue by buying and selling goods called merchandise. In such a company, net income results when revenue from sales exceeds the cost of the goods sold and the operating expenses, as follows:

EASTSIDE HARDWARE STORE
Condensed Income Statement
For Month Ended July 31, 1993

Revenue from sales.	$100,000
Less cost of goods sold	60,000
Gross profit from sales	$ 40,000
Less operating expenses	25,000
Net income	$ 15,000

This income statement shows that Eastside Hardware Store sold goods to customers for $100,000. Eastside acquired the goods that were sold at a cost of $60,000. As a result, the company earned a $40,000 **gross profit,** which is the difference between the revenue and the cost of goods sold. Also, note that the company incurred operating expenses of $25,000 and achieved a $15,000 net income for the month.

The parts of this calculation are what make accounting for a merchandising company different from accounting for a service company. To account for a merchandising company, you must understand how to account for the two components of gross profit: revenue from sales and cost of goods sold.

Revenue from Sales

Revenue from sales consists of the gross or total proceeds from merchandise sales less returns, allowances, and discounts. Gross proceeds are called *gross sales.*

LO 1 Analyze and record transactions that involve the purchase and resale of merchandise.

Gross Sales

On the partial income statement (p. 243), the gross sales item is the total cash and credit sales made by the company during the year. Cash sales were rung up on the cash register as each sale was completed. At the end of each day, the register total showed the amount of that day's cash sales, which was recorded with an entry such as this:

Nov.	3	Cash.	1,205.00	
		Sales		205.00
		To record the day's cash sales.		

Also, an entry such as the following was used to record credit sales:

Nov.	3	Accounts Receivable	45.00	
		Sales		45.00
		Sold merchandise on credit.		

Sales Returns and Allowances

Most stores allow customers to return any unsatisfactory merchandise that they bought. Sometimes, customers are allowed to keep the unsatisfactory goods and are given an *allowance,* which is an amount off the sales price. Either way, returns and allowances involve dissatisfied customers. Therefore, management must know the amount of returns and allowances and their size in relation to sales. The Sales Returns and Allowances account supplies this information because each return or allowance is recorded as follows:

Nov.	4	Sales Returns and Allowances	20.00	
		Accounts Receivable (or Cash).		20.00
		Customer returned unsatisfactory merchandise.		

The Sales Returns and Allowances account is contra to the Sales account.

Sales Discounts

When goods are sold on credit, the terms of payment must be stated clearly to avoid any misunderstanding about the amount and time of the future payment or payments. These **credit terms** specify the amounts and timing of payments that a buyer agrees to make in return for being granted credit to purchase goods or services. The credit terms normally appear on the invoice or sales ticket and are part of the sales agreement. Exact terms usually depend on the custom of the trade. In some areas of business, it is customary for invoices to become due and payable 10 days after the end of the month **(EOM)** in which the sale occurred. These credit terms are stated on the sales invoices as ''n/10 EOM.'' In other lines of business, invoices become due and payable 30 days after the invoice date. These invoices are said to carry terms of ''n/30.''

When credit periods are long, creditors often grant a **cash discount** for early payment. Early payments bring the cash into the selling company more quickly, and thus make it easier for the firm's managers to carry on their activities. When cash discounts for early payment are granted, they are made part of the credit terms and appear on the invoice as, for example, ''Terms: 2/10, n/60.'' Terms of 2/10, n/60 mean that there is a 60-day **credit period,** which is the agreed period of time for which credit is granted. Although the payment is not due for 60 days, the debtor may deduct 2% from the invoice amount if payment is made within 10 days after the invoice date. The 10-day period is known as the **discount period.**

At the time of a sale, the merchandiser does not know if the customer will pay within the discount period and take advantage of a cash discount. As a result, a sales discount usually is not recorded until the customer pays. For example, on November 12, Sowa Sales, Incorporated, sold merchandise to a customer at a gross sales price of $100, subject to credit terms of 2/10, n/60. The sale was recorded as follows:

Nov.	12	Accounts Receivable	100.00	
		Sales		100.00
		Sold merchandise, terms 2/10, n/60.		

The customer has two alternative ways to satisfy this $100 obligation. One option is to pay $98 any time on or before November 22. Or the customer can wait up to 60 days, until January 11, and pay the full $100. If the customer elects to pay by November 22 and take advantage of the cash discount, Sowa Sales, Incorporated, records the receipt of the $98 as follows:

Nov.	22	Cash.	98.00	
		Sales Discounts	2.00	
		Accounts Receivable		100.00
		Received payment for the November 12 sale less the discount.		

Cash discounts granted to customers are called **sales discounts,** and are accumulated in the Sales Discounts account until the end of an accounting period. This account is contra, that is, a reduction, to the Sales account. In other words, the total discounts are deducted from gross sales in calculating net revenue from sales. Deducting discounts from sales makes sense because a sales discount is an amount off the regular price of goods that is granted for early payment. As a result, it reduces revenue from sales.

Revenue from sales may be reported on an income statement as follows:

SOWA SALES, INCORPORATED
Income Statement
For Year Ended December 31, 1993

Revenue from sales:		
Gross sales.		$306,200
Less: Sales returns and allowances . .	$1,900	
Sales discounts	4,300	6,200
Net sales		$300,000

Some businesses, such as automobile dealers or major appliance stores, make a limited number of sales each day. Therefore, they can easily refer to their records at the time of each sale and determine the cost of the car or appliance sold. On the other hand, a drugstore or a hardware store may find this task to be more difficult. For instance, if a drugstore clerk sells a customer a tube of toothpaste, a box of aspirin, and a magazine, the cash register can easily be used to record the sale of these items at their marked selling prices. However, with large-volume, low-priced items, it would be quite difficult to determine quickly the cost of each item so that the cost of goods sold could be recorded at

Periodic and Perpetual Inventory Systems

ILLUSTRATION 5-1

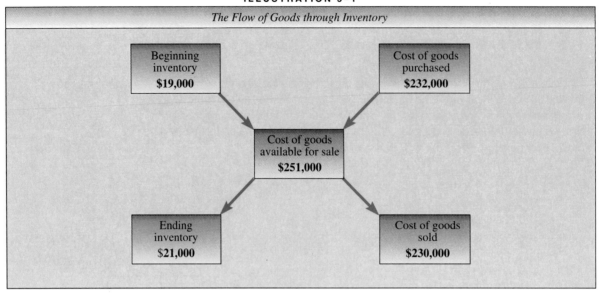

The Flow of Goods through Inventory

the time of sale. Some computerized systems allow this task to be done. Many stores that sell a large volume of low-priced items, however, make no effort to record the cost of goods sold at the time of each sale. Rather, they wait until the end of an accounting period to make the calculation. At that time, they count their **inventory,** which is the collection of goods on hand waiting to be sold. This counting process is called *taking a physical inventory.* This information plus data from the accounting records is then used to determine the cost of all goods sold during the period.

Drug, hardware, grocery, or similar stores often use **periodic inventory systems** to learn the cost of their inventories and the cost of goods sold. We describe and explain these periodic inventory systems in this chapter. An alternative approach to accounting for inventories and cost of goods sold involves recording the cost of goods sold each time a sale is made and keeping an up-to-date record of the goods on hand. These systems are called **perpetual inventory systems.** You will learn more about them when you study Chapter 9.

Cost of Goods Sold, Periodic Inventory System

LO 2 Explain the nature of each item entering into the calculation of cost of goods sold and gross profit from sales.

As we mentioned earlier, a store that uses a periodic inventory system does not record the cost of items sold at the time they are sold. Rather, it waits until the end of an accounting period and determines the cost of all the goods sold during the period. To do this, it must have information about (1) the cost of the merchandise on hand at the beginning of the period, (2) the cost of merchandise purchased during the period, and (3) the cost of unsold goods on hand at the end of the period. With this information, a store can calculate the cost of goods sold during a period by applying the flows represented in Illustration 5-1.

Illustration 5–1 shows that the company had $251,000 of goods available for sale during the period. This included $19,000 of goods on hand when the period started and $232,000 of goods newly purchased during the period. Some of the available goods were sold during the period and the rest remained on hand at the end of the period. Because $21,000 of goods were on hand at the end, $230,000 must have been sold. To summarize, calculate the cost of goods sold as follows:[1]

Cost of goods on hand at beginning of the period . .	$ 19,000
Cost of goods purchased during the period	232,000
Goods available for sale during the period.	$251,000
Less unsold goods on hand at the period end	21,000
Cost of goods sold during the period.	$230,000

The following paragraphs explain how to accumulate the information that you need to perform this calculation.

Merchandise Inventories

The merchandise on hand at the beginning of an accounting period is called *beginning inventory*. The merchandise on hand at the end is called *ending inventory*. Because a new accounting period starts as soon as the old period ends, the ending inventory of one period is automatically the beginning inventory of the next.

When a periodic inventory system is used, the dollar amount of the ending inventory is determined by (1) counting the unsold items on the shelves in the store and in the stockroom, (2) multiplying the counted quantity of each type of good by its cost, and (3) adding all the costs of the different types of goods.

After the cost of the ending inventory is determined in this manner, it is subtracted from the cost of the goods available for sale to arrive at cost of goods sold. Then, at the end of the accounting period, a journal entry is made to record the ending inventory amount in an asset account called *Merchandise Inventory*. This ending inventory amount remains as the balance in the Merchandise Inventory account during the next accounting period. Thus, throughout the new accounting period, the balance of the Merchandise Inventory account represents the cost of the inventory on hand at the end of the previous period, which is also the beginning inventory of the current period.

Other than to correct errors, entries are made in the Merchandise Inventory account *only* at the end of each accounting period. As time passes during an accounting period and merchandise is both purchased and sold, neither the

---

[1] Some accountants prefer to skip the determination of goods available for sale during the period and calculate cost of goods sold as:

Cost of goods purchased during the period . .	$232,000
Change in inventory.	(2,000)
Cost of goods sold during the period	$230,000

Also see the last paragraph of Appendix C.

purchases nor the cost of goods sold amounts are entered in the Merchandise Inventory account. Therefore, as soon as any goods are purchased or sold in the current period, the Merchandise Inventory account does not show the dollar amount of merchandise on hand. Rather, the account's balance reflects the beginning inventory of the period. Later in this chapter, we explain how the appropriate entry is made at the end of the period to update the account.

Cost of Merchandise Purchased

LO 1 Analyze and record transactions that involve the purchase and resale of merchandise.

To determine the cost of purchased merchandise, you must record the invoice price of goods purchased and subtract any cash discounts that were taken. You also need to record all returns and allowances for any unsatisfactory goods purchased. Then, add any freight or other transportation costs incurred by the purchaser to ship the goods from the supplier to the purchaser's place of business. The following paragraphs explain how these amounts are accumulated in the accounts.

Under a periodic inventory system, the cost of merchandise bought for resale is debited to an account called Purchases, as shown here:

Nov.	5	Purchases	1,000.00	
		Accounts Payable		1,000.00
		Purchased merchandise on credit, invoice dated November 2, terms 2/10, n/30.		

The purpose of the Purchases account is to accumulate the cost of all merchandise bought for resale during an accounting period. The Purchases account does not show at any time whether the merchandise is on hand or has been disposed of through sale or other means. It is just a temporary holding place for information that will be used later.

Because stores commonly buy merchandise on credit, merchants are often able to take advantage of cash discounts for payment within the discount period. The discounts on purchases are called **purchases discounts.** When payment is made within the discount period, the accounting system records a credit to the contra account called Purchases Discounts, as shown in the following entry:

Nov.	12	Accounts Payable	1,000.00	
		Purchases Discounts		20.00
		Cash		980.00
		Paid for the purchase of November 5 less the discount.		

When suppliers offer cash discounts, the total amount to be saved by the buyer is usually significant. The information in the Purchases Discounts account helps managers know whether the discounts are being taken.

To ensure that discounts are not missed, a company should set up a system to pay all invoices within any discount period described in the credit terms. On the other hand, good cash management requires that no invoice be paid until the *last* day of its discount period. To accomplish both objectives, a helpful system files every invoice in such a way that it automatically comes to the attention of the person responsible for its payment on the last day of its discount period. A simple manual system uses a file with 31 folders, one for each day in a month. After an invoice is recorded, it is placed in the file folder of the last day of its discount period. For example, if the last day of an invoice's discount period is November 12, it is filed in folder number 12. Then, on November 12, the invoice and any other invoices in the same folder are removed and paid. Computerized systems accomplish the same result by having the operator enter a code that identifies the last date in the discount period. When that date is reached, the computer provides a reminder that the account should be paid.

Sometimes, merchandise received from suppliers is not acceptable and must be returned. Or, the purchaser may keep defective merchandise because the supplier grants an allowance or reduction in its price. When merchandise is returned, the purchaser gets a refund or a reduction in the amount owed to the supplier. Even though there is no charge for the returned goods, the process of receiving, inspecting, evaluating, and returning defective merchandise creates costs that should be minimized. As a result, the amount of purchase returns or allowances must be controlled, and a purchaser may look for another supplier if purchased merchandise is frequently defective.

An important key to controlling the problem of defective merchandise purchases is information about the amount of returns and allowances. To get this information, returns and allowances on purchases are commonly recorded in a contra account called Purchases Returns and Allowances. This account is used to record a return of merchandise as follows:

Nov.	14	Accounts Payable.	65.00	
		Purchases Returns and Allowances.		65.00
		Returned defective merchandise.		

When an invoice for purchased goods is subject to a cash discount and a portion of the goods is returned before the invoice is paid, the discount applies only to the goods kept. For example, assume that you buy merchandise for $500, subject to a 2% cash discount. Then, you return $100 of the goods before the invoice is paid. When you pay the amount due before the discount period expires, the discount of 2% applies only to the remaining $400. In other words, you pay $392, which is the gross cost of $400 minus the discount of $8, or 2% of $400.

Sometimes a supplier assumes responsibility for the costs of transporting the sold goods to the merchandiser's place of business. In this case, the total cost of the goods to the purchaser is the amount the purchaser must pay to the supplier. In other situations, the purchaser must pay the transportation costs, called **transportation-in.** When these costs are incurred, they are properly added to the cost of the purchased goods and may be recorded with an additional debit to the Purchases account. However, more complete information is obtained if such costs are debited to a special account called Transportation-In. The balance of this account is eventually added to the Purchases account balance to get the total cost. The use of this account is shown in the following entry, which records a $22 charge for freight on incoming merchandise:

Nov.	24	Transportation-In	22.00	
		Cash		22.00
		Paid express charges on merchandise purchased.		

Note that freight paid on purchased goods coming from suppliers must be accounted for separately from freight paid on sold goods being sent to customers. The shipping cost of incoming goods should be included in the cost of goods sold, while the cost of shipping outgoing goods should be an expense of making sales.

When a purchase or sale involves transportation charges, the buyer and seller must understand which party is responsible for paying them. Because costs are involved, the responsibility for shipping should be part of the negotiations. Under one arrangement, called *free on board factory,* the seller transfers ownership of the goods to the buyer at the seller's place of business, and the buyer must pay the shipping charges. This arrangement is usually abbreviated as **FOB** *factory.* Alternatively, the terms of the purchase may be *FOB destination,* which means that ownership of the goods passes at the buyer's place of business. In this case, the seller is responsible for the shipping charges. As an example, a seller may quote a price of $300, FOB factory. A buyer who wants the seller to pay the freight (and assume the risk of loss in transit) tries to get terms of $300, FOB destination.

Even though the terms are FOB factory, a seller may agree to prepay the transportation costs as a service to the buyer. Of course, these charges are then added to the amount the buyer must pay. If the credit terms include a cash discount, the discount does not apply to the transportation charges. In other words, the purchaser must reimburse the seller for 100% of the transportation charges, even if the bill is paid within the discount period.

At the end of the period, the cost of the merchandise purchased during the period is determined by combining the balances of the Purchases, Purchases Returns and Allowances, Purchases Discounts, and Transportation-In accounts. This calculation may appear on the income statement of a merchandising company in the following form:

Purchases		$235,800	
Less: Purchases returns and allowances . .	$1,200		
Purchases discounts	4,100	5,300	
Net purchases.		$230,500	
Add transportation-in.		1,500	
Cost of goods purchased			$232,000

Cost of Goods Sold

The last item in the preceding calculation is the cost of the merchandise purchased during the accounting period. To calculate the cost of goods sold, you must combine this amount with the beginning and ending inventories, as follows:

AS A MATTER OF

Ethics

Renee Fleck was recently hired as an accountant for Printers, Inc., a medium-sized company that purchases most of its supplies on credit. Fleck's duties include managing cash and accounts payable. She overlapped for several days on the job with Martin Hull, the outgoing accountant, so that they could spend time together to help Fleck learn the ropes.

One of Fleck's responsibilities is to ensure that the accounts are paid promptly to maintain the company's credit standing with its suppliers and to take advantage of all cash discounts. Hull told Fleck that the system in place has accomplished both goals easily, and has also made another contribution to the company's profits. Hull explained that when credit purchases are made on terms that include a discount for early payment, the system has been to prepare cheques for the "net-of-discount" amounts. Then, the cheques are not mailed until *after* the end of the discount period. The cheques are dated the last day of the discount period, but are not mailed until four or five days later. Because the accounts are always paid, Printers, Inc., has had little difficulty with its creditors. "It's simple," Hull said, "we get the free use of the cash for an extra five days, and who's going to complain? Even if someone gripes, we can always blame the computer or the mail room."

Only a few days later, on April 18, Hull has departed and Fleck recognizes that the discount period on a $10,000 payable is about to lapse. The purchase was made on April 9, subject to terms of 2/10, n/30. Fleck is trying to decide whether she should pay the bill on the 19th or wait until April 23.

Cost of goods sold:			
Merchandise inventory, January 1, 1993 . . .			$ 19,000
Purchases.		$235,800	
Less: Purchases returns and allowances . .	$1,200		
Purchases discounts	4,100	5,300	
Net purchases		$230,500	
Add transportation-in.		1,500	
Cost of goods purchased			232,000
Goods available for sale			$251,000
Merchandise inventory, December 31, 1993 .			21,000
Cost of goods sold			$230,000

Notice that the sum of the beginning inventory and purchases is calculated and identified as the cost of *goods available for sale*. The ending inventory is deducted from the goods available for sale to arrive at the cost of goods sold.

Inventory Losses

Merchandising companies lose merchandise in a variety of ways, such as spoilage or shoplifting. When merchandise is lost, it is called *shrinkage*. A periodic inventory system automatically includes the cost of shrinkage in cost of goods sold. For example, assume that during a year shoplifters stole merchandise that cost $500 from a store. Because the stolen goods were not on hand at the end of the year when the inventory was counted, these thefts caused the store's year-end inventory to be $500 less than it otherwise would have been. And, since the year-end inventory was $500 smaller as a result of the loss, the number assigned to the cost of the goods sold was $500 larger.

Many merchandisers are troubled with shoplifting or other inventory losses. Unfortunately, a disadvantage of the periodic inventory system is its inability to provide clear information about the amount of such losses. Instead, the amount of the losses is hidden in the cost of goods sold figure. The perpetual inventory systems, described in Chapter 9, provide more complete information about merchandise losses. Chapter 9 also discusses a method of estimating inventory losses when using a periodic inventory system.

Income Statement of a Merchandising Company

A classified income statement for a merchandising company has (1) a revenue section, (2) a cost of goods sold section, and (3) an operating expenses section. Note in Illustration 5–2 how the first two sections are brought together to show gross profit from sales. (This example includes many details of the calculations not often found in statements presented to users outside the company.)

Also notice in Illustration 5–2 how operating expenses are classified as either selling expenses or general and administrative expenses. **Selling expenses** include expenses of storing and preparing goods for sale, promoting sales, actually making sales, and delivering goods to customers. **General and administrative expenses** support the overall management and operations of a business. Examples are the central office, accounting, personnel, and credit and collection expenses.

Sometimes an expenditure should be divided, or prorated, between selling expenses and general and administrative expenses. For example, as you can see in Illustration 5–2, Sowa Sales, Incorporated, divided the $9,000 rent on its store building between these categories. Ninety percent ($8,100) was selling expense, and the remaining 10% ($900) was general and administrative expense.[2] This division should be made on a logical basis such as the relationship between the rental values of space occupied for selling and for administration.

In Illustration 5–2, the last item subtracted is income taxes expense. This income statement was prepared for Sowa Sales, Incorporated, which is a corporation. Of the three kinds of business organizations, only corporations pay provincial and federal income taxes. Notice in Illustration 5–2 that the result of subtracting operating expenses from gross profit is called *income from operations*. Income taxes expense is determined to be $1,700, and then subtracted from income from operations to obtain net income.

Work Sheet of a Merchandising Company

The work sheet for a merchandising company is like the work sheet for a service company. In both cases, the work sheet serves as a tool to help bring together the information needed at the end of the period to prepare the finan-

---

[2] These expenses can be recorded in separate accounts in the ledger. Alternatively, they can be recorded in one account, and the classification can be done by the accountant before preparing the financial statements.

ILLUSTRATION 5–2

A Classified Income Statement for a Merchandising Company

SOWA SALES, INCORPORATED
Income Statement
For Year Ended December 31, 1993

Net Sales –
COGS = GP

Revenue from sales:			
Gross sales			$306,200
Less: Sales returns and allowances.		$ 1,900	
Sales discounts.		4,300	6,200
Net sales			$300,000
Cost of goods sold:			
Merchandise inventory, January 1, 1993		$ 19,000 I_B	
Purchases	$235,800		
Less: Purchases returns and allowances . . .	$1,200		
Purchases discounts	4,100	5,300	+
Net purchases.		$230,500	
Add transportation-in.		1,500	
Cost of goods purchased		232,000 P_c	
Goods available for sale.		$251,000	
Merchandise inventory, December 31, 1993. . .		21,000 I_E	
Cost of goods sold.			230,000
Gross profit from sales			$ 70,000
Operating expenses:			
Selling expenses:			
Amortization expense, store equipment . . .	$ 3,000		
Sales salaries expense	18,500		
Rent expense, selling space.	8,100		
Store supplies expense	400		
Advertising expense	700		
Total selling expenses.		$ 30,700	
General and administrative expenses:			
Amortization expense, office equipment . . .	$ 700		
Office salaries expense	25,800		
Insurance expense	600		
Rent expense, office space	900		
Office supplies expense.	200		
Total general and administrative expenses . .		28,200	
Total operating expenses			58,900
Income from operations			$ 11,100
Less income taxes expense (assumed 15%) . . .			1,700
Net income			$ 9,400

cial statements and prepare the adjusting and closing journal entries. Illustration 5–3 shows the work sheet for Sowa Sales, Incorporated.

Illustration 5–3 differs from the Chapter 4 work sheet in several places. Most notably, Illustration 5–3 does not have Adjusted Trial Balance columns. Experienced accountants frequently omit these columns from a work sheet to reduce the time and effort required for its preparation. They first enter the adjustments in the Adjustments columns. Then, in a single operation, they combine the adjustments with the unadjusted trial balance amounts and sort

LO 3 Prepare a work sheet and the financial statements for a merchandising business that uses a periodic inventory system and that is organized as a corporation or as a single proprietorship.

ILLUSTRATION 5–3

A Work Sheet for a Merchandising Company

SOWA SALES, INCORPORATED
Work Sheet
For Year Ended December 31, 1993

	Account Titles	Unadjusted Trial Balance Dr.	Cr.	Adjustments Dr.	Cr.	Income Statement Dr.	Cr.	Retained Earnings Statement or Balance Sheet Dr.	Cr.
1	Cash	8,200						8,200	
2	Accounts receivable	11,200						11,200	
3	Merchandise inventory*	19,000				19,000	21,000	21,000	
4	Prepaid insurance	900			(a) 600			300	
5	Office supplies	300			(b) 200			100	
6	Store supplies	600			(c) 400			200	
7	Office equipment	4,400						4,400	
8	Accum. amort., office equipment		600		(d) 700				1,300
9	Store equipment	29,100						29,100	
10	Accum. amort., store equipment		2,500		(e) 3,000				5,500
11	Accounts payable		3,600						3,600
12	Income taxes payable				(f) 100				100
13	Common shares		50,000						50,000
14	Retained earnings		8,600						8,600
15	Cash dividends declared	4,000						4,000	
16	Sales		306,200				306,200		
17	Sales returns and allowances	1,900				1,900			
18	Sales discounts	4,300				4,300			
19	Purchases	235,800				235,800			
20	Purch. returns and allowances		1,200				1,200		
21	Purchases discounts		4,100				4,100		
22	Transportation-in	1,500				1,500			
23	Amort. expense, store equipment			(e) 3,000		3,000			
24	Sales salaries expense	18,500				18,500			
25	Rent expense, selling space	8,100				8,100			
26	Store supplies expense			(c) 400		400			
27	Advertising expense	700				700			
28	Amort. expense, office equipment			(d) 700		700			
29	Office salaries expense	25,800				25,800			
30	Insurance expense			(a) 600		600			
31	Rent expense, office space	900				900			
32	Office supplies expense			(b) 200		200			
33	Income taxes expense	1,600		(f) 100		1,700			
34		376,800	376,800	5,000	5,000	323,100	332,500	78,500	69,100
35	Net income					9,400			9,400
36						332,500	332,500	78,500	78,500

* Some accountants prefer to use one line for the beginning inventory and another line for the ending inventory. The result is the same since the $19,000 will appear on one line and the $21,000 on another line.

the combined amounts directly to the proper financial statement columns. In summary, omitting the Adjusted Trial Balance columns in preparing a work sheet is a suitable shortcut.

The next three differences all relate to the fact that Illustration 5–3 was prepared for a corporation instead of a proprietorship. The first one is minor— it is simply the presence of the word *incorporated* in the company's name. Second, notice that the heading of the last two columns is Retained Earnings Statement or Balance Sheet. Later in this chapter, we explain how the **retained earnings statement** reports the changes in a corporation's retained earnings that occurred during an accounting period.

The third difference is on lines 13 and 14 in Illustration 5–3. Specifically, the corporation work sheet includes Common Shares and Retained Earnings accounts instead of the owner's capital account that would appear on a proprietorship work sheet. Notice that the balances of these two corporation accounts are carried unchanged from the Unadjusted Trial Balance Credit column into the Retained Earnings Statement or Balance Sheet Credit column. The remaining similarities and differences of Illustration 5–3 are best described column by column.

Account Titles Column

The Account Titles column of the work sheet in Illustration 5–3 lists several accounts that do not have unadjusted trial balance amounts. (For example, see Store supplies expense on line 26.) These accounts are needed in the financial statements and are listed in the order of their appearance in the ledger. They are debited and credited in making the adjustments. Entering their names on the work sheet in financial statement order at the time the work sheet is begun makes it easier to prepare the statements later. Of course, any accounts that were not listed may be entered below the unadjusted trial balance totals as was done in Chapter 4.

Unadjusted Trial Balance Columns

In Illustration 5–3, the amounts in the Unadjusted Trial Balance columns are the account balances as of December 31, 1993, the end of the annual accounting period of Sowa Sales, Incorporated. They were taken from the company's General Ledger after all transactions were recorded but before any end-of-period adjustments were made.

Note the $19,000 inventory amount that appears in the Unadjusted Trial Balance Debit column on line 3. This amount is the cost of inventory the company had on hand as of December 31, 1992. (As the ending inventory for 1992, this amount is also the beginning inventory for 1993.) Because the company uses the periodic system, the $19,000 was debited to the Merchandise Inventory account at the end of 1992 by using closing entries, explained later in this chapter, and remained in the account as its balance throughout 1993.

Adjustments Columns

Six adjustments appear on the illustrated work sheet. The first five are similar to those discussed in Chapter 4:

a. The Prepaid Insurance account included $600 of insurance expense.
b. A count of the office supplies showed that $100 was on hand.
c. A count of the store supplies showed that $200 was on hand.
d. Annual amortization expense on the office equipment was $700.
e. Annual amortization expense on the store equipment was $3,000.

The sixth adjustment for income taxes is new and deserves explanation.

A business organized as a corporation is subject to the payment of federal and provincial income taxes. Near the beginning of each year, a corporation must estimate the amount of income it expects to earn during the year. Then it estimates the amount of income tax the firm will have to pay. This estimated tax must be paid in a series of installment payments during the year. Each payment is debited to Income Taxes Expense and credited to Cash. Therefore, a corporation that expects to earn a profit reaches the end of the year with a debit balance in its Income Taxes Expense account. However, because the balance is an estimate (and usually less than the full amount of the tax), an adjustment must be made to get the proper amount of expense and liability recorded. Thus, adjusting entry (*f*) on lines 12 and 33 accrues the additional tax expense of $100 and the taxes payable of the same amount.

Combining and Sorting the Items

After all adjustments are entered and totaled on the work sheet, the amounts in the Unadjusted Trial Balance and Adjustments columns are combined and sorted to the proper financial statement columns. Revenue, cost of goods sold, and expense items are sorted to the Income Statement columns. Asset, liability, and shareholders' equity accounts (including Cash Dividends Declared) are sorted to the Retained Earnings Statement or Balance Sheet columns.

Income Statement Columns

Observe in Illustration 5–3 that revenue, cost of goods sold, and expense items maintain their debit and credit positions when sorted to the Income Statement columns. Because sales returns and sales discounts are contra to sales, they are entered in the Debit column. The effect is to subtract them from sales when the columns are totaled and the net income is determined. The same is true in reverse for purchases returns and purchases discounts; they are contra to purchases and appear in the credit column.

The Beginning Inventory Amount.   Look at the beginning inventory amount on line 3. Note that the $19,000 unadjusted trial balance amount is sorted to the Income Statement Debit column. It is put in this column simply because it has a debit balance. This placement also helps us calculate the cost of goods sold. That is, the cost of goods available for sale is calculated by adding the beginning inventory to net purchases (another debit remainder, consisting of purchases, minus purchases returns and allowances, minus purchases discounts, plus transportation-in).

The Ending Inventory Amount. Recall that when using the periodic inventory system, you must take a physical inventory of merchandise on hand at the end of each accounting period. The December 31, 1993, physical inventory of Sowa Sales, Incorporated, showed that it had a $21,000 ending inventory. This amount was determined by counting the items of unsold merchandise and multiplying the quantities by the cost of each item.

After all adjusted account balances are sorted to the proper work sheet columns, the next step in preparing a work sheet is to simply insert the ending inventory amount in the Income Statement *Credit* column. The ending inventory amount is placed in the Income Statement Credit column because it must be subtracted from cost of goods available for sale (beginning inventory plus net purchases) when cost of goods sold is calculated for the income statement. Next, the ending inventory amount is put in the Retained Earnings Statement or Balance Sheet *Debit* column. Thus, the ending balance of $21,000 will appear on the balance sheet as the cost of the merchandise owned on the balance sheet date. In Illustration 5–3, note that the $21,000 ending inventory was inserted in these columns on line 3 of the work sheet. (Later in this chapter, we describe how to make the journal entry to record the ending inventory in the accounts.)

The amounts used in the calculation of cost of goods sold are in colour in the Income Statement columns of Illustration 5–3. The beginning inventory, purchases, and transportation-in amounts appear in the Debit column. The amounts of the ending inventory, purchases returns and allowances, and purchases discounts appear in the Credit column. Note in the following calculations that the sum of the three debit items minus the sum of the three credit items equals the $230,000 cost of goods sold shown in the income statement of Illustration 5–2.

Cost of Goods Sold on the Work Sheet

Debits:	
Beginning inventory	$ 19,000
Purchases	235,800
Transportation-in.	1,500
Total debits.	$256,300
Credits:	
Ending inventory.	$ (21,000)
Purchases returns and allowances	(1,200)
Purchases discounts	(4,100)
Total credits	(26,300)
Cost of goods sold	$230,000

Therefore, the combined effect of entering the six components of the cost of goods sold calculation in the Income Statement columns is a net $230,000 debit.

Completing the Work Sheet and Preparing Financial Statements

LO 3 Prepare a work sheet and the financial statements for a merchandising business that uses a periodic inventory system and that is organized as a corporation or as a single proprietorship.

After all items are sorted to the proper columns and the ending inventory amount is entered, you complete a work sheet such as Illustration 5–3 by adding the columns and then determining and adding in the net income or loss. When the work sheet for a corporation is completed, it is used to prepare an income statement, a retained earnings statement, and a balance sheet.

Preparing the Income Statement

After the work sheet is completed, the items in the Income Statement columns are used to prepare an income statement. The classified income statement prepared from information in the Income Statement columns of Illustration 5–3 is shown in Illustration 5–2 on page 251.

Preparing the Retained Earnings Statement

The retained earnings statement reports the changes in the corporation's retained earnings during the period. Therefore, the statement describes the events that changed the amounts of retained earnings reported on two successive end-of-period balance sheets.

The last two columns of the work sheet contain the information you need to prepare the retained earnings statement. The beginning retained earnings balance appears on the line showing the Retained Earnings account. The net income (or net loss) appears on a line near the bottom of the work sheet and the amount of cash dividends declared also appears on a separate line.

Illustration 5–4 shows the retained earnings statement of Sowa Sales, Incorporated. The statement shows that the company began the year with $8,600 of retained earnings, which is also the amount of retained earnings reported on its previous year-end balance sheet. Its retained earnings balance was increased by the $9,400 net income and reduced by the declaration of $4,000 of cash dividends. The result is the final balance of $14,000, which is also reported on the December 31, 1993, balance sheet.

Preparing the Balance Sheet

The classified balance sheet for Sowa Sales, Incorporated, appears in Illustration 5–5. As a matter of convenience, all of the prepaid expense items (prepaid insurance, store supplies, and office supplies) have been combined and presented as a single item on the balance sheet. This shortcut is justified by the fact that each of them has a small balance. It might also be possible to combine the $100 of taxes payable with the accounts payable, but those two debts are not as similar as the prepaid expense items. Also note that the $14,000 retained earnings amount on the balance sheet is the same amount calculated on the retained earnings statement shown in Illustration 5–4.

Adjusting and Closing Journal Entries

After the work sheet and statements are completed, you must prepare and post adjusting and closing journal entries. Illustration 5–6 on page 258 shows the entries for Sowa Sales, Incorporated. Notice that they differ from previously illustrated adjusting and closing entries because an explanation for each entry

ILLUSTRATION 5-4

A Corporation's Retained Earnings Statement

SOWA SALES, INCORPORATED
Retained Earnings Statement
For Year Ended December 31, 1993

Retained earnings, January 1, 1993	$ 8,600
Add 1993 net income	9,400
Total	$18,000
Deduct cash dividends	4,000
Retained earnings, December 31, 1993	$14,000

ILLUSTRATION 5-5

A Corporation's Classified Balance Sheet

SOWA SALES, INCORPORATED
Balance Sheet
December 31, 1993

Assets

Current assets:			
Cash		$ 8,200	
Accounts receivable		11,200	
Merchandise inventory		21,000	
Prepaid expenses		600	
Total current assets			$41,000
Plant and equipment:			
Office equipment	$ 4,400		
Less accumulated amortization	1,300	$ 3,100	
Store equipment	$29,100		
Less accumulated amortization	5,500	23,600	
Total plant and equipment			26,700
Total assets			$67,700

Liabilities

Current liabilities:			
Accounts payable		$ 3,600	
Income taxes payable		100	
Total liabilities			$ 3,700

Shareholders' Equity

Share capital-common: 10,000 shares			
outstanding		$50,000	
Retained earnings		14,000	
Total shareholders' equity			64,000
Total liabilities and shareholders' equity . .			$67,700

ILLUSTRATION 5–6

Adjusting and Closing Entries for a Merchandising Corporation

Date		Account Titles and Explanation	PR	Debit	Credit
1993		Adjusting Entries			
Dec.	31	Insurance Expense		600.00	
		Prepaid Insurance			600.00
	31	Office Supplies Expense		200.00	
		Office Supplies			200.00
	31	Store Supplies Expense		400.00	
		Store Supplies			400.00
	31	Amortization Expense, Office Equipment.		700.00	
		Accumulated Amortization, Office Equipment			700.00
	31	Amortization Expense, Store Equipment		3,000.00	
		Accumulated Amortization, Store Equipment			3,000.00
	31	Income Taxes Expense		100.00	
		Income Taxes Payable			100.00
		Closing Entries			
	31	Income Summary		323,100.00	
		Merchandise Inventory.			19,000.00
		Sales Returns and Allowances			1,900.00
		Sales Discounts.			4,300.00
		Purchases.			235,800.00
		Transportation-In.			1,500.00
		Amortization Expense, Store Equipment.			3,000.00
		Sales Salaries Expense			18,500.00
		Rent Expense, Selling Space			8,100.00
		Store Supplies Expense.			400.00
		Advertising Expense			700.00
		Amortization Expense, Office Equipment			700.00
		Office Salaries Expense			25,800.00
		Insurance Expense			600.00
		Rent Expense, Office Space			900.00
		Office Supplies Expense			200.00
		Income Taxes Expense.			1,700.00
	31	Merchandise Inventory		21,000.00	
		Sales		306,200.00	
		Purchases Returns and Allowances		1,200.00	
		Purchases Discounts		4,100.00	
		Income Summary.			332,500.00
	31	Income Summary		9,400.00	
		Retained Earnings			9,400.00
	31	Retained Earnings.		4,000.00	
		Cash Dividends Declared.			4,000.00

LO 4 Prepare adjusting and closing entries for a merchandising business organized as either a corporation or a single proprietorship.

is not given. Individual explanations may be given but are not necessary. The words *Adjusting Entries* before the first adjusting entry and *Closing Entries* before the first closing entry are sufficient to explain why they were recorded.

As you learned in Chapter 4, the Adjustments columns of a work sheet provide the information needed to prepare a company's adjusting entries. Each adjustment in the Adjustments columns must be recorded in the journal and posted to the ledger. Thus, the adjusting entries in Illustration 5–6 are the same as the adjustments on the work sheet of Illustration 5–3.

The work sheet in Illustration 5–3 also contains the information you need to prepare closing journal entries. Look at the first closing entry of Illustration 5–6 and compare it with the items in the Income Statement Debit column of Illustration 5–3. Note that Income Summary is debited for the $323,100 column total and that each account with an amount in the column is credited. This entry removes the $19,000 beginning inventory amount from the Merchandise Inventory account. It also closes all the contra revenue, cost of goods sold, and expense accounts that have debit balances.

Now compare the second closing journal entry with the items in the Income Statement Credit column of Illustration 5–3. Note that each account with an amount in the credit column is debited and the Income Summary account is credited for the $332,500 column total. This entry closes the revenue and cost of goods sold accounts that have credit balances. It also enters the $21,000 ending inventory amount in the Merchandise Inventory account.

The third closing journal entry transfers the $9,400 net income from Income Summary to Retained Earnings. Finally, the fourth closing entry closes the Cash Dividends Declared account and reduces the balance of Retained Earnings.

Closing Entries and the Inventories

There is nothing new about the closing entries of a merchandising company except for the beginning and ending inventories. However, you should understand how the closing entries affect the Merchandise Inventory account.

Before closing entries for 1993 are posted, the Merchandise Inventory account of Sowa Sales, Incorporated, shows the $19,000 beginning inventory balance:

	Merchandise Inventory				Acct. No. 119
Date	**Explanation**	**PR**	**Debit**	**Credit**	**Balance**
1992 Dec. 31		G10	19,000		19,000

Then, when the first closing entry for 1993 is posted, its $19,000 credit to Merchandise Inventory clears the beginning inventory amount from the inventory account:

	Merchandise Inventory				Acct. No. 119
Date	**Explanation**	**PR**	**Debit**	**Credit**	**Balance**
1992 Dec. 31		G10	19,000		19,000
1993 Dec. 31		G20		19,000	–0–

When the second closing entry is posted, its $21,000 debit to Merchandise Inventory puts the amount of the ending inventory into the account:

Merchandise Inventory						Acct. No. 119
Date		Explanation	PR	Debit	Credit	Balance
1992 Dec.	31		G10	19,000		19,000
1993 Dec.	31		G20		19,000	–0–
	31		G20	21,000		21,000

The $21,000 debit balance of the inventory account remains throughout 1994 as a historical record of the amount of inventory at the end of 1993 and the beginning of 1994.

Other Inventory Methods

There are several ways to handle the inventories in the end-of-period accounting procedures. However, all have the same objectives of (1) removing the beginning inventory balance from the inventory account and charging (debiting) it to Income Summary, and (2) entering the ending inventory amount in the inventory account and crediting it to Income Summary. As we have just shown, these objectives can be achieved with closing entries. Alternatively, adjusting entries may be used to accomplish the same results. Either method is satisfactory. The adjusting entry method is explained in Appendix C at the end of this chapter.

Multiple-Step and Single-Step Income Statements

The income statement in Illustration 5–2 on page 251 is called a *classified* income statement because its items are classified in significant groups. (Note that selling expenses are separated from general and administrative expenses.) It is also a **multiple-step income statement** because cost of goods sold is subtracted to arrive at gross profit and the expenses are subtracted to get net income.

Illustration 5–7 shows another statement format, the **single-step income statement.** Note how cost of goods sold and the expenses are added together in the illustration and are then subtracted from net sales in one step to get net income. This format is commonly used in published statements. Also, note that the information in the income statement is condensed. For example, it does not show the various components of net sales and cost of goods sold. Published statements often condense data in this manner.

Combined Income and Retained Earnings Statement

Many corporations present their income and retained earnings statements as a single, combined statement. Such a statement may be prepared in either single-step or multiple-step form. Illustration 5–8 shows a combined single-step income and retained earnings statement.

ILLUSTRATION 5–7

A Single-Step Income Statement

SOWA SALES, INCORPORATED
Income Statement
For Year Ended December 31, 1993

Revenue from sales		$300,000
Expenses:		
Cost of goods sold	$230,000	
Selling expenses	30,700	
General and administrative expenses . .	28,200	
Income taxes expense	1,700	
Total expenses		290,600
Net income		$ 9,400

ILLUSTRATION 5–8

Combining the Income Statement and the Retained Earnings Statement

SOWA SALES, INCORPORATED
Statement of Income and Retained Earnings
For Year Ended December 31, 1993

Revenue from sales		$300,000
Expenses:		
Cost of goods sold	$230,000	
Selling expenses	30,700	
General and administrative expenses . .	28,200	
Income taxes expense	1,700	
Total expenses		290,600
Net income		$ 9,400
Add retained earnings, January 1, 1993 . .		8,600
Total		$ 18,000
Deduct cash dividends declared		4,000
Retained earnings, December 31, 1993. . .		$ 14,000

When they do business together, buyers and sellers sometimes find that they need to adjust the amount that is owed by one to the other. For example, merchandise purchased may not meet specifications, goods may be received that were not ordered, fewer goods may be received than were ordered and billed, and errors may occur in preparing billings.

In many cases, the adjustment can be accomplished by the buyer without a negotiation. An example is an error on an invoice. If the buying company makes the adjustment, it notifies the seller of its action by sending a **debit memorandum** or a **credit memorandum.** A debit memorandum is a business

Debit and Credit Memoranda

form that has spaces for the name and address of the recipient and words such as "We debit your account," followed by space for typing in the reason for the debit. A credit memorandum, on the other hand, would say "We credit your account." Illustration 5–9 shows the use of these documents.

To explain the use of a debit memorandum, assume that a buyer discovers an error that overstated the total bill by $10. The buyer notifies the seller of the mistake with a debit memorandum: "We have debited your account to correct a $10 error on your November 17 invoice." A *debit* memorandum is sent because the correction reduces an account payable on the books of the buyer, and a debit is required to reduce an account payable. If the error is discovered before the purchase is recorded, the buyer should mark the correction on the bill and attach a copy of the debit memorandum to show that the seller was notified. Then, the buyer should record an entry that debits Purchases and credits Accounts Payable for the correct amount. If the purchase has already been recorded in the accounts before the error is discovered, the buyer would make another entry debiting Accounts Payable for $10 and crediting Purchases for $10.

Other adjustments require negotiations between the buyer and the seller before they can be recorded. For example, a buyer's claim that merchandise does not meet specifications normally requires discussion with the seller. In this case, the buyer should debit Purchases and credit Accounts Payable for the full amount and then negotiate with the seller for a return or a price adjustment. If the seller agrees, it formally notifies the buyer with a credit memorandum. A *credit* memorandum is used because the return or adjustment reduces an account receivable on the books of the seller, and a credit is required to reduce an account receivable. When the credit memorandum is received, the buyer records it by debiting Accounts Payable and crediting Purchases Returns and Allowances because the purchase was originally recorded at the full invoice price.

As this discussion shows, a debit or a credit memorandum may originate with either party to a transaction. The memorandum gets its name from the action of the originator. If the originator debits an account receivable or payable, it issues a debit memorandum. If the originator credits an account receivable or payable, it issues a credit memorandum.

Trade (Catalogue) Discounts

LO 1 Analyze and record transactions that involve the purchase and resale of merchandise.

When a manufacturer or wholesaler prepares a catalogue of items for sale, each item is given a **list price,** which is also called a *catalogue price.* This amount is the *nominal* selling price of the item. A **trade (catalogue) discount** is a reduction (perhaps as much as 40% or more) in a list price that is applied to determine the actual sales price of the goods sold to a customer. Trade discounts are commonly used by manufacturers and wholesalers to change selling prices without republishing their catalogues. When the seller wants to change the selling prices, it can notify its customers merely by sending them a new set of trade (or catalogue) discounts to apply to the catalogue prices.

Trade discounts are accounted for differently from the cash discounts discussed earlier in this chapter. Specifically, *trade (or catalogue) discounts offered or taken are not entered in the accounts by either party to a sale.* Instead,

ILLUSTRATION 5–9

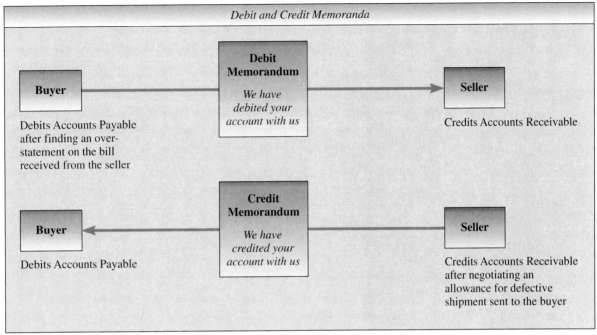

they are used only to calculate the sales price. For example, if a manufacturer deducts a 40% discount on an item listed in its catalogue at $100, the selling price is $60, which is computed as [$100 − (40% × $100)]. The seller records the credit sale as follows:

Dec.	10	Accounts Receivable	60.00	
		Sales		60.00
		Sold merchandise on credit.		

The buyer also records the purchase in its journal at $60. And, if a cash discount is allowed, it applies only to the amount of the purchase, $60.

LO 1. In determining the amount to record as a purchase (or sale), trade (catalogue) discounts are subtracted from list prices to calculate the invoice price, which is debited to Purchases (or credited to Sales). Purchases discounts, purchases returns and allowances, transportation-in, sales discounts, and sales returns and allowances are recorded in separate accounts.

LO 2. Sales discounts and sales returns and allowances are subtracted from sales to get net sales. The beginning inventory plus net purchases equals the cost of goods available for sale. The ending inventory is subtracted from the cost of goods available for sale to get cost of goods sold. The cost of goods sold is subtracted from net sales to get gross profit.

Summary of the
Chapter in Terms of
Learning Objectives

LO 3. When using the closing entry approach on the work sheet, the beginning inventory is sorted to the Income Statement Debit column and the ending inventory is inserted in the Income Statement Credit column and the Statement of Retained Earnings or Balance Sheet Debit column. This treatment of the inventory is used whether the company is a corporation or single proprietorship.

LO 4. With the closing entry approach, the beginning inventory is transferred from Merchandise Inventory to Income Summary in the closing process. Also, the ending inventory is debited to Merchandise Inventory and credited to Income Summary as part of a closing entry.

Demonstration Problem

The following partially completed work sheet was prepared for Continental Sales, Inc., as of December 31, 1993, the end of its annual accounting period.

CONTINENTAL SALES, INC.
Work Sheet
For Year Ended December 31, 1993

Account Titles	Unadjusted Trial Balance Dr.	Cr.	Adjustments Dr.	Cr.
Cash	19,000			
Merchandise inventory	52,000			
Store supplies	7,000			(a) 6,000
Equipment	40,000			
Accumulated amortization, equipment		11,000		(b) 5,500
Accounts payable		3,000		
Income taxes payable		6,000		(c) 1,000
Common shares		50,000		
Retained earnings		19,000		
Cash dividends declared	8,000			
Sales		320,000		
Sales discounts	20,000			
Purchases	147,000			
Purchases discounts		12,000		
Transportation-in	11,000			
Amortization expense			(b) 5,500	
Salaries expense	43,000			
Insurance expense	12,000			
Rent expense	24,000			
Store supplies expense			(a) 6,000	
Advertising expense	21,000			
Income taxes expense	17,000		(c) 1,000	
	421,000	421,000	12,500	12,500

Required

1. Complete the work sheet. (Ending inventory is $50,000.)
2. Prepare the 1993 income statement.
3. Prepare the 1993 retained earnings statement.
4. Prepare a balance sheet as of December 31, 1993.
5. Prepare closing entries.

Planning the Solution

- For all accounts, combine the unadjusted balances with any adjustments and sort to the appropriate columns in the work sheet. Enter the ending inventory in the Income Statement Credit column and the Balance Sheet Debit column. Take the totals of the Income Statement columns, find the net income for the year, and enter it in the Income Statement Debit column and the Balance Sheet Credit column.

- To prepare the income statement, first find the net sales by combining the sales accounts, and then find the cost of goods sold by combining the inventory related accounts. After computing gross profit, deduct the rest of the expenses.

- To prepare the retained earnings statement, list the beginning balance, net income, and cash dividends declared, and then find the ending balance.

- To prepare the balance sheet, use the amounts in the last two columns, being sure to substitute the ending balance of retained earnings from the statement of retained earnings.

- The first closing entry credits all accounts with debit balances in the income statement columns. The second closing entry debits all accounts with credit balances in the income statement columns. The third entry closes Income Summary to Retained Earnings. The fourth closing entry closes the Cash Dividends Declared account to Retained Earnings.

Solution to
Demonstration
Problem

1.

CONTINENTAL SALES, INC.
Work Sheet
For Year Ended December 31, 1993

Account Titles	Unadjusted Trial Balance		Adjustments		Income Statement		Retained Earnings Statement or Balance Sheet	
	Dr.	Cr.	Dr.	Cr.	Dr.	Cr.	Dr.	Cr.
Cash	19,000						19,000	
Merchandise inventory	52,000				52,000	50,000	50,000	
Store supplies	7,000			(a) 6,000			1,000	
Equipment	40,000						40,000	
Accumulated amortization, equipment		11,000		(b) 5,500				16,500
Accounts payable		3,000						3,000
Income taxes payable		6,000		(c) 1,000				7,000
Common shares		50,000						50,000
Retained earnings		19,000						19,000
Cash dividends declared	8,000						8,000	
Sales		320,000				320,000		
Sales discounts	20,000				20,000			
Purchases	147,000				147,000			
Purchases discounts		12,000				12,000		
Transportation-in	11,000				11,000			
Amortization expense			(b) 5,500		5,500			
Salaries expense	43,000				43,000			
Insurance expense	12,000				12,000			
Rent expense	24,000				24,000			
Store supplies expense			(a) 6,000		6,000			
Advertising expense	21,000				21,000			
Income taxes expense	17,000		(c) 1,000		18,000			
	421,000	421,000	12,500	12,500	359,500	382,000	118,000	95,500
Net income					22,500			22,500
					382,000	382,000	118,000	118,000

2.

CONTINENTAL SALES, INC.
Income Statement
For Year Ended December 31, 1993

Revenue from sales:			
Gross sales			$320,000
Less sales discounts			20,000
Net sales			$300,000
Cost of goods sold:			
Merchandise inventory, January 1, 1993		$ 52,000	
Purchases.	$147,000		
Less purchases discounts	12,000		
Net purchases	$135,000		
Plus transportation-in	11,000		
Cost of goods purchased		146,000	
Cost of goods available for sale.		$198,000	
Merchandise inventory, December 31, 1993		50,000	
Cost of goods sold			148,000
Gross profit from sales			$152,000
Operating expenses:			
Amortization expense		$ 5,500	
Salaries expense		43,000	
Insurance expense		12,000	
Rent expense.		24,000	
Store supplies expense		6,000	
Advertising expense		21,000	
Total operating expenses			111,500
Income from operations.			$ 40,500
Less income taxes expense.			18,000
Net income			$ 22,500

3.

CONTINENTAL SALES, INC.
Retained Earnings Statement
For Year Ended December 31, 1993

Retained earnings, January 1, 1993	$19,000
Add 1993 net income	22,500
Total	$41,500
Deduct cash dividends declared.	8,000
Retained earnings, December 31, 1993 . .	$33,500

4.

CONTINENTAL SALES, INC.
Balance Sheet
December 31, 1993

Assets

Current assets:

Cash		$19,000
Merchandise inventory		50,000
Store supplies		1,000
Total current assets.		$70,000
Equipment	$40,000	
Less accumulated amortization.	16,500	
Total equipment		23,500
Total assets		$93,500

Liabilities

Current liabilities:

Accounts payable.	$ 3,000	
Income taxes payable.	7,000	
Total liabilities		$10,000

Shareholders' Equity

Share capital: common	$50,000	
Retained earnings.	33,500	
Total shareholders' equity		83,500
Total liabilities and shareholders' equity . .		$93,500

5.

1993					
Dec.	31	Income Summary		359,500.00	
		Merchandise Inventory.			52,000.00
		Sales Discounts.			20,000.00
		Purchases.			147,000.00
		Transportation-In.			11,000.00
		Amortization Expense			5,500.00
		Salaries Expense			43,000.00
		Insurance Expense			12,000.00
		Rent Expense.			24,000.00
		Store Supplies Expense.			6,000.00
		Advertising Expense			21,000.00
		Income Taxes Expense			18,000.00
	31	Merchandise Inventory		50,000.00	
		Sales		320,000.00	
		Purchases Discounts		12,000.00	
		Income Summary.			382,000.00
	31	Income Summary		22,500.00	
		Retained Earnings			22,500.00
	31	Retained Earnings.		8,000.00	
		Cash Dividends Declared.			8,000.00

The Adjusting Entry Approach to Accounting for Merchandise Inventories

In the closing entries described in Chapter 5, we first transferred the amount of the beginning merchandise inventory to the Income Summary account. Then we recorded the ending inventory in the Merchandise Inventory account as part of a second closing entry. An alternative approach accomplishes these two transfers as adjustments on the work sheet; then they are recorded in the journal as adjusting entries.

Some accountants prefer the closing entry approach and others prefer the adjusting entry approach. Either accomplishes the same result, and the choice creates absolutely no difference in the financial statements. Some computerized accounting systems, however, prepare closing entries automatically. That is, the person who uses a computer system does not manually prepare closing entries. On receiving a single command of "close the accounts," the computer automatically closes all of the temporary accounts—but only the temporary accounts. Because the inventory account is not temporary, its balance is left unchanged by the automatic closing process. Thus, when using a system like this, you have to apply the adjusting entry approach to bring the Merchandise Inventory account balance up to date.

To illustrate the difference between the closing and adjusting entry approaches, we return to the example of Sowa Sales, Incorporated. In the closing entry approach used in Chapter 5, we removed the $19,000 beginning inventory balance from the Merchandise Inventory account and transferred it to the Income Summary account in the first closing entry. We recorded the $21,000 ending inventory in the Income Summary account in the second closing entry. This entry also put the $21,000 ending inventory balance in the Merchandise Inventory account.

In the adjusting entry approach, the first adjusting entry is prepared to transfer the beginning inventory out of the Merchandise Inventory account and into the Income Summary. A second adjusting entry records the ending inventory as a debit balance in the Merchandise Inventory account and as a credit to Income Summary. The adjusting and closing entries under both approaches are shown side by side in Illustration C–1. The entries to the inventory account are in colour.

Illustration C–1 shows that both approaches accomplish exactly the same changes in the Merchandise Inventory account. The beginning inventory of $19,000 was removed from the account with a credit, and the $21,000 ending inventory was added to the account with a debit. The only difference between the two approaches was whether the changes were made in a closing entry or an adjusting entry.

LO 6 Explain the adjusting entry approach to accounting for inventories and prepare a work sheet, adjusting entries, and closing entries according to the adjusting entry approach.

ILLUSTRATION C–1

Adjusting and Closing Entries for a Merchandising Corporation

		Closing Entry Approach		Adjusting Entry Approach	
1993	Adjusting Entries				
Dec. 31	Insurance Expense	600.00		600.00	
	Prepaid Insurance		600.00		600.00
31	Office Supplies Expense	200.00		200.00	
	Office Supplies		200.00		200.00
31	Store Supplies Expense	400.00		400.00	
	Store Supplies		400.00		400.00
31	Amortization Expense, Office Equipment	700.00		700.00	
	Accumulated Amortization, Office Equipment		700.00		700.00
31	Amortization Expense, Store Equipment	3,000.00		3,000.00	
	Accumulated Amortization, Store Equipment		3,000.00		3,000.00
31	Income Taxes Expense	100.00		100.00	
	Income Taxes Payable		100.00		100.00
31	Income Summary	—		19,000.00	
	Merchandise Inventory		—		19,000.00
31	Merchandise Inventory	—		21,000.00	
	Income Summary		—		21,000.00
	Closing Entries				
31	Income Summary	323,100.00		304,100.00	
	Merchandise Inventory		19,000.00		—
	Sales Returns and Allowances		1,900.00		1,900.00
	Sales Discounts		4,300.00		4,300.00
	Purchases		235,800.00		235,800.00
	Transportation-In		1,500.00		1,500.00
	Amortization Expense, Store Equipment		3,000.00		3,000.00
	Sales Salaries Expense		18,500.00		18,500.00
	Rent Expense, Selling Space		8,100.00		8,100.00
	Store Supplies Expense		400.00		400.00
	Advertising Expense		700.00		700.00
	Amortization Expense, Office Equipment		700.00		700.00
	Office Salaries Expense		25,800.00		25,800.00
	Insurance Expense		600.00		600.00
	Rent Expense, Office Space		900.00		900.00
	Office Supplies Expense		200.00		200.00
	Income Taxes Expense		1,700.00		1,700.00
31	Merchandise Inventory	21,000.00		—	
	Sales	306,200.00		306,200.00	
	Purchases Returns and Allowances	1,200.00		1,200.00	
	Purchases Discounts	4,100.00		4,100.00	
	Income Summary		332,500.00		311,500.00
31	Income Summary	9,400.00		9,400.00	
	Retained Earnings		9,400.00		9,400.00
31	Retained Earnings	4,000.00		4,000.00	
	Cash Dividends Declared		4,000.00		4,000.00

Also, both approaches produce exactly the same credit balance of $9,400 in the Income Summary account. Under the adjusting entry approach, the effects of the beginning and ending inventories on Income Summary are recorded with adjusting entries. And under the closing entry approach, these effects are recorded with closing entries.

The effect of the adjusting entry approach on the work sheet is depicted in Illustration C–2, which shows the work sheet for Sowa Sales, Incorporated. The transfer of the $19,000 beginning inventory from Merchandise Inventory to Income Summary is entered in the Adjustments columns of the work sheet as entry *g* on lines 3 and 15. The $21,000 ending inventory amount is debited to Merchandise Inventory and credited to Income Summary in the Adjustments columns as entry *h* on lines 3 and 15.

On line 3 of Illustration C–2, note that adjustment *g* removes the beginning inventory balance from the Merchandise Inventory account.

Adjustment *h* establishes the ending inventory amount in the account. Because the ending balance is an asset on December 31, 1993, it is carried directly to the Statement of Retained Earnings or Balance Sheet Debit column. Illustration C–2 also shows that the Income Summary account (line 15) was listed at the time the work sheet was first prepared. Note as well that the debit and credit adjustments *g* and *h* to this account are each carried into the Income Statement columns. Then, both these amounts are used to prepare the income statement. Therefore, you should *not* subtract one from the other and carry only the net amount over to the Income Statement columns. Rather, the $19,000 beginning inventory is extended to the Income Statement Debit column and the $21,000 ending inventory is extended to the Income Statement Credit column. Thus, the Income Statement columns end up being identical under the closing and adjusting entry approaches.

The remaining steps for completing the work sheet are exactly the same under either the adjusting entry approach or the closing entry approach, with one major exception. Specifically, the closing entries do not have a debit or credit for inventory. To see the work sheet differences between the two methods, compare Illustration C–2 (the adjusting entry approach) with Illustration 5–3 on p. 252 (the closing entry approach).

Notwithstanding the logic of what was stated above, remember that the work sheet is only a *tool* that facilitates and expedites the preparation of financial statements. In practice numerous variations are found, including doing what we stated above should not be done. Indeed, many accountants would adjust the beginning inventory, in Illustration C–2, by a debit to Merchandise Inventory and a credit to Income Summary for $2,000. Other variations of the adjusting method are also found in practice, all of which give the same final result. For problem-solving purposes, however, we identify the *adjusting method* as first discussed in this Appendix.

The Work Sheet under the Adjusting Entry Approach

LO 6. With the adjusting entry approach, adjusting entries update the Merchandise Inventory account and record the beginning and ending inventory elements of cost of goods sold in the Income Summary account. On the work sheet, these adjustments are entered in the Adjustments columns. Then, the ending inventory is extended to the Retained Earnings Statement or Balance Sheet Debit column. Both the debit and credit adjustments to Income Summary are individually extended to the Income Statement columns.

Summary of Appendix C in Terms of Learning Objective

ILLUSTRATION C–2

The Work Sheet when the Adjusting Entry Approach Is Used

SOWA SALES, INCORPORATED
Work Sheet
For Year Ended December 31, 1993

	Account Titles	Unadjusted Trial Balance Dr.	Cr.	Adjustments Dr.	Cr.	Income Statement Dr.	Cr.	Retained Earnings Statement or Balance Sheet Dr.	Cr.
1	Cash	8,200						8,200	
2	Accounts receivable	11,200						11,200	
3	Merchandise inventory	19,000		(h) 21,000	(g) 19,000			**21,000**	
4	Prepaid insurance	900			(a) 600			300	
5	Office supplies	300			(b) 200			100	
6	Store supplies	600			(c) 400			200	
7	Office equipment	4,400						4,400	
8	Accum. amort., office equipment		600		(d) 700				1,300
9	Store equipment	29,100						29,100	
10	Accum. amort., store equipment		2,500		(e) 3,000				5,500
11	Accounts payable		3,600						3,600
12	Income taxes payable				(f) 100				100
13	Common shares		50,000						50,000
14	Retained earnings		8,600						8,600
15	Income summary			(g) 19,000	(h) 21,000	19,000	21,000		
16	Cash dividends declared	4,000						4,000	
17	Sales		306,200				306,200		
18	Sales returns and allowances	1,900				1,900			
19	Sales discounts	4,300				4,300			
20	Purchases	235,800				235,800			
21	Purchases returns and allowances		1,200				1,200		
22	Purchases discounts		4,100				4,100		
23	Transportation-in	1,500				1,500			
24	Amort. expense, store equipment			(e) 3,000		3,000			
25	Sales salaries expense	18,500				18,500			
26	Rent expense, selling space	8,100				8,100			
27	Store supplies expense			(c) 400		400			
28	Advertising expense	700				700			
29	Amort. expense, office equipment			(d) 700		700			
30	Office salaries expense	25,800				25,800			
31	Insurance expense			(a) 600		600			
32	Rent expense, office space	900				900			
33	Office supplies expense			(b) 200		200			
34	Income taxes expense	1,600		(f) 100		1,700			
35		376,800	376,800	45,000	45,000	323,100	332,500	78,500	69,100
36	Net income					9,400			9,400
37						332,500	332,500	78,500	78,500

LO 5 Define or explain
the words and phrases
listed in the chapter
glossary.

Cash discount a deduction from the invoice price of goods that is granted if payment is made within a specified period of time. p. 242

Credit memorandum a memorandum sent to notify its recipient that the sender has credited the recipient's account in its records. p. 261

Credit period the agreed period of time for which credit is granted and at the end of which payment is expected. p. 242

Credit terms the specified amounts and timing of payments that a buyer agrees to make in return for being granted credit to purchase goods or services. p. 242

Debit memorandum a memorandum sent to notify its recipient that the sender has debited the recipient's account in its records. p. 261

Discount period the period of time during which, if payment is made, a cash discount may be deducted from the invoice price. p. 242

EOM an abbreviation for the words *end-of-month* that is sometimes used in expressing the credit terms of a sales agreement. p. 242

FOB the abbreviation for *free on board,* which is the legal arrangement for identifying the location (shipping point or destination) at which the seller transfers ownership of purchased goods to the buyer; if the terms are FOB factory (or shipping point), the buyer must pay the shipping costs; if the terms are FOB destination, the seller must pay the shipping costs. p. 248

General and administrative expenses expenses that support the overall management and operations of a business, such as central office, accounting, personnel, and credit and collection expenses. p. 250

Gross profit the difference between revenue and the cost of goods sold. p. 241

Inventory the collection of goods on hand waiting to be sold to customers. p. 244

List price the nominal price of an item from which any trade discount is deducted to determine the actual sales price; also known as the catalogue price. p. 262

Merchandise goods bought and sold to others. p. 240

Multiple-step income statement an income statement on which cost of goods sold and the expenses are subtracted in steps to get net income. p. 260

Periodic inventory system a method of accounting for inventories in which the inventory account is brought up to date once each period; requires the business to count the items on hand at the end of the period. p. 244

Perpetual inventory system a method of accounting for inventories in which cost of goods sold is recorded each time a sale is made and an up-to-date record of goods on hand is maintained. p. 244

Purchases discounts deductions from the invoice price of purchased items granted by suppliers in return for early payment; that is, cash discounts from suppliers. p. 246

Retained earnings statement a financial statement that reports the changes in a corporation's retained earnings that occurred during an accounting period. p. 253

Sales discount a deduction from the invoice price granted to customers in return for early payment; that is, cash discounts to customers. p. 243

Selling expenses the expenses of preparing and storing merchandise for sale, promoting sales, actually making sales, and delivering goods to customers. p. 250

Single-step income statement an income statement on which cost of goods sold and operating expenses are added together and subtracted from net sales in one step to get net income. p. 260

Trade (catalogue) discount a deduction from a list or catalogue price that is used to determine the actual sales price of goods. p. 262

Transportation-in costs incurred by a purchaser for transporting purchased merchandise to its place of business. p. 247

Synonymous Terms

Actual sales price invoice price
FOB factory FOB shipping point
Gross profit gross margin
List price catalogue price
Merchandise goods

Objective Review

Answers to the following questions are listed at the end of this chapter. Be sure that you decide which is the one best answer to each question *before* you check the answers.

LO 1 A deduction from the sales price of goods that is granted if payment is made within a specified period of time is a:

a. Trade discount.
b. Favored customer discount.
c. Credit discount.
d. Cash discount.
e. Merchandise discount.

LO 2 On the work sheet for a merchandising company that uses the closing entry approach to account for inventories:

a. The beginning inventory is extended from the trial balance to the Income Statement Credit column.
b. The ending inventory is inserted in the Income Statement Debit column and then extended to the Retained Earnings Statement or Balance Sheet Debit column.
c. The amount of cost of goods sold is calculated in the Adjustments columns.
d. The beginning inventory and ending inventory amounts appear in the Income Statement Debit and Income Statement Credit columns, respectively.
e. The components of the cost of purchases are extended to the Retained Earnings Statement or Balance Sheet Debit column.

LO 3 With a periodic inventory system, cost of goods sold:

a. Is subtracted from the cost of goods available for sale to determine gross profit from sales.
b. Plus the net cost of purchases equals the cost of goods available for sale.
c. Is calculated as the cost of the beginning inventory plus the cost of purchases less the cost of the ending inventory.
d. Is subtracted from gross sales to determine net sales.
e. Includes all operating expenses related to merchandising operations.

LO 4 In recording transactions that involve the purchase and resale of merchandise when a periodic inventory system is used:

a. The sales price of merchandise returned by customers is credited to Sales Returns and Allowances.

b. The purchase price of merchandise returned to a supplier is debited to Purchases Returns and Allowances.

c. The Sales account is credited for the cost of merchandise sold to customers.

d. The amount of any sales discounts taken by customers is debited to a Sales Discounts account.

e. The amount of any purchases discounts is debited to a Purchases Discounts account.

LO 5 When closing entries are used to account for merchandise inventories:

a. The closing entries include a credit to Merchandise Inventory for the cost of the beginning inventory.

b. The closing entries include a debit to Merchandise Inventory for the cost of the ending inventory.

c. The cost of goods sold is recorded in a separate Cost of Goods Sold account that is closed to Income Summary.

d. Cost of goods sold is calculated as the difference between the beginning and ending merchandise inventory amounts.

e. Both *(a)* and *(b)* are correct.

LO 6 When adjusting entries are used to account for merchandise inventories:

a. The adjusting entries include a debit to Merchandise Inventory for the cost of the beginning inventory.

b. The adjusting entries include a debit to Merchandise Inventory for the cost of the ending inventory.

c. The cost of goods sold is recorded in a separate Cost of Goods Sold account that is closed to Income Summary.

d. Cost of goods sold is calculated as the difference between the beginning and ending merchandise inventory amounts.

e. Both *(a)* and *(b)* are correct.

A letter ^{C} *identifies the questions, exercises, and problems that are based on Appendix C at the end of the chapter.*

---

1. What is gross profit?
2. Can a business earn a gross profit on its sales and still suffer a net loss? How?
3. Why should the manager of a business be interested in the amount of its sales returns and allowances?
4. Since sales returns and allowances are subtracted from sales on the income statement, why not save the effort of this subtraction by debiting all such returns and allowances directly to the Sales account?
5. What is a cash discount?
6. What is the difference between cash discounts offered as sales discounts and purchases discounts?

Questions for Class
Discussion

7. How and when is cost of goods sold determined in a store that uses a periodic inventory system?

8. Which of the following transactions would be debited to the Purchases account of a grocery store: (*a*) the purchase of a cash register, (*b*) the purchase of a refrigerated display case, (*c*) the purchase of advertising space in a newspaper, and (*d*) the purchase of a case of chicken soup?

9. If a business is allowed to return all unsatisfactory merchandise purchased and receive full credit for the purchase price, why should it be interested in controlling the amount of its returns?

10. At the end of an accounting period, does the beginning or ending inventory appear on the unadjusted trial balance of a company that uses a periodic inventory system?

11. How does a single-step income statement differ from a multiple-step income statement?

12. During the year, a company purchased merchandise that cost $165,000. What was the company's cost of goods sold if there were (*a*) no beginning or ending inventories? (*b*) a beginning inventory of $35,000 and no ending inventory? (*c*) a $30,000 beginning inventory and a $42,000 ending inventory? and (*d*) no beginning inventory and a $21,000 ending inventory?

13. In counting the merchandise on hand at the end of an accounting period, a clerk failed to count and consequently omitted from the inventory all the merchandise on one shelf. If the cost of the merchandise on that shelf was $150, what was the effect of the omission on (*a*) the balance sheet and (*b*) the income statement?

14. Suppose that the omission of the $150 from the inventory in the previous question was not discovered. What would be the effect on the balance sheet and income statement prepared at the end of the next accounting period?

^C15. What are the procedural differences between the adjusting entry and closing entry approaches to accounting for inventories?

Mini Discussion Cases

Case 5–1
The case of unrecorded invoices

Part 1. One month after purchasing a profitable wholesale plumbing distribution company, Mr. Gerald Laliberte realized he had a nightmare on his hands. The head accountant resigned after only two weeks with the new owner, and Gerald was getting calls from suppliers with regard to overdue accounts. He could not understand why because he had instructed the staff to pay all accounts as they became due.

Part 2. Gerald's wife, Gwen, offered to help. She had been the accountant for a family-owned firm, which had been sold about 15 years previously. With the aid of the assistant accountant, Gwen found a folder of unpaid and unrecorded invoices all dated prior to the purchase date. Further investigation and discussion with the former head accountant's secretary revealed that Gwen's discovery was nothing new. The secretary told the Labertes that her former boss told her that he delayed the recording of invoices in order to make the statements look good. He told her that no one was hurt, the goods went into inventory as they arrived, the invoices were eventually recorded, and the suppliers paid. She also informed them that the amount of $70,000 of the current unrecorded invoices was about $20,000 more than at the last year-end.

Required

If Mr. Laliberte could turn the clock back one month, what do you believe he would have done with regard to accounts payable prior to finalizing the purchase of the business?

Consider Part 2 of Case 5–1.

Case 5–2

Required

Discuss which statements were affected and how they were affected.

Exercises

Village Store purchased merchandise having a $7,000 invoice price, terms 2/10, n/60, from a manufacturer and paid for the merchandise within the discount period. Give (without dates) the journal entries made by the store to record the purchase and payment. Give (without dates) the entries made by the manufacturer to record the sale and collection. If Village Store borrowed sufficient money at a 12% annual rate of interest on the last day of the discount period to pay the invoice, how much did the store save by borrowing to take advantage of the discount?

Exercise 5–1
Analyzing and recording
purchases and purchases
discounts
(LO 1)

Prepare journal entries to record the following transactions of Harris General Store:

July 5 Purchased merchandise from Eastern Company subject to the following terms: $600 invoice price, 2/15, n/60, FOB factory.

    7 Paid Martin Trucking $65 for shipping charges on the purchase of July 5.

    9 Returned to Eastern Company unacceptable merchandise with a list price of $200.

  19 Sent Eastern Company a checque to pay for the July 5 purchase, net of discount and return.

  20 Purchased merchandise from Southern Company subject to the following terms: $900 list price, 2/10, n/30, FOB Southern Company factory. The invoice showed that Southern Company had paid the trucking company $70 to ship the merchandise to Harris.

  24 After advising Southern Company that some merchandise was damaged, received a credit memorandum granting Harris a $300 allowance on the July 20 purchase.

  30 Paid Southern Company for the July 20 purchase, net of the allowance, and the shipping charges prepaid by Southern.

Exercise 5–2
Journalizing merchandise
transactions
(LO 1)

On July 6, 1993, F Company received $7,000 of merchandise and an invoice dated July 5, terms of 2/10, n/30, FOB G Company's factory. On the day the goods were received, F Company paid Fast Freight Company $270 for shipping charges on the purchased merchandise. The next day, F Company returned to G Company $600 of defective goods and, on July 15, mailed G Company a cheque for the amount owed. Prepare general journal entries to record these transactions (*a*) on the books of F Company and (*b*) on the books of G Company. Assume that G Company recorded the return and the cheque the day after each was sent.

Exercise 5–3
Journal entries for
purchases and sales
and returns
(LO 1)

Exercise 5–4
Calculating expenses and income
(LO 2)

Copy the following tabulation and fill in the missing amounts. Indicate a loss by placing parentheses around the amount. Each horizontal row of figures is a separate situation.

Sales	Beginning Inventory	Purchases	Ending Inventory	Cost of Goods Sold	Gross Profit	Expenses	Net Income or Loss
$198,000	$144,000	$126,000	$?	$171,000	$?	$ 90,000	$?
333,000	117,000	?	135,000	144,000	?	99,000	90,000
270,000	90,000	?	54,000	?	153,000	81,000	72,000
?	135,000	198,000	108,000	?	180,000	72,000	?
288,000	108,000	171,000	?	189,000	?	126,000	?
90,000	27,000	?	45,000	54,000	?	?	9,000
?	207,000	396,000	234,000	?	252,000	?	90,000
144,000	?	90,000	63,000	?	54,000	?	18,000

Exercise 5–5
Multiple-step income statement for a proprietorship
(LO 3)

The Cottage is a single proprietorship business that ends its annual accounting period on December 31. The Income Statement columns of The Cottage's December 31, 1993, work sheet follow. Use the information in these columns to prepare a 1993 multiple-step income statement for The Cottage.

	Income Statement	
	Debit	**Credit**
Merchandise inventory	64,500	72,000
Sales.		360,000
Sales returns and allowances	2,250	
Sales discounts	2,700	
Purchases	216,000	
Purchases returns and allowances		1,500
Purchases discounts		4,500
Transportation-in	1,050	
Selling expenses.	54,000	
General and administrative expenses . .	37,500	
	378,000	438,000
Net income	60,000	
	438,000	438,000

Exercise 5–6
Preparing and posting proprietorship closing entries
(LO 4)

Part 1. Assume that The Cottage of Exercise 5–5 is owned by Carrie Black and prepare entries to close the temporary accounts of the business.

Part 2. Construct a Merchandise Inventory account in the form of a balance column account and enter the $64,500 beginning inventory of Exercise 5–5 as its balance on December 31, 1992. Then post to the account the portions of the closing entries that affect this account.

Exercise 5–7
Preparing an income statement from closing entries
(LO 3, 4)

The following two closing entries for Western Sales were made at the end of its 1993 annual accounting period. (Note that the individual expense accounts are combined to shorten the exercise.)

Dec.	Income Summary	475,200.00	
	Merchandise Inventory.		63,000.00
	Sales Returns and Allowances		3,600.00
	Sales Discounts.		5,400.00
	Purchases.		270,000.00
	Transportation-In.		7,200.00
	Selling Expenses		72,000.00
	General and Administrative Expenses		54,000.00
	Merchandise Inventory	82,500.00	
	Sales	450,000.00	
	Purchases Returns and Allowances	1,800.00	
	Purchases Discounts	3,600.00	
	Income Summary.		537,900.00

Required

Use the information in the closing entries to prepare an income statement for Western Sales.

The following items (with expenses condensed to conserve space) appeared in the last four columns of a work sheet prepared for Little Store, Incorporated, as of December 31, 1993, the end of its annual accounting period. Use this information to prepare a 1993 multiple-step income statement and a retained earnings statement for the corporation.

Exercise 5–8
Multiple-step income statement and retained earnings statement
(LO 3)

	Income Statement		Retained Earnings Statement or Balance Sheet	
	Debit	Credit	Debit	Credit
Merchandise inventory	71,000	90,000	90,000	
Other assets			225,000	
Common shares				111,500
Retained earnings				160,500
Cash dividends declared.			30,000	
Sales.		540,000		
Sales returns and allowances	2,700			
Sales discounts	5,400			
Purchases	324,000			
Purchases returns and allowances.		1,800		
Purchases discounts		4,500		
Transportation-in	900			
Selling expenses	81,000			
General and administrative expenses	63,900			
Income taxes expense	14,400			
	563,300	636,300	345,000	272,000
Net income	73,000			73,000
	636,300	636,300	345,000	345,000

Part 1. Prepare entries to close the temporary accounts of Little Store, Incorporated (Exercise 5–8).

Part 2. Construct a Merchandise Inventory account in the form of a balance column account and enter the $71,000 beginning inventory of Exercise 5–8 as its December 31, 1992, balance. Then post to the account those portions of the store's closing entries that affect its balance.

Exercise 5–9
Preparing and posting closing entries
(LO 4)

Exercise 5–10
Calculating operating
expenses and cost of
goods sold
(LO 2, 3)

The following information was taken from a single proprietorship's income statement:

Sales	$270,000	Purchases returns	
Sales returns	1,800	and allowances	$ 900
Sales discounts	3,600	Purchases discounts	2,700
Beginning inventory	72,000	Transportation-in	5,400
Purchases	171,000	Gross profit from sales	84,600
		Net loss	7,200

Required

Prepare calculations to determine (*a*) total operating expenses, (*b*) cost of goods sold, and (*c*) ending inventory.

Exercise 5–11
Preparing a work sheet for
a merchandising
corporation
(LO 3)

The following trial balance was taken from the ledger of Crown, Incorporated, at the end of its annual accounting period. (To simplify the exercise and save time, the account balances are in one- and two-digit numbers.)

CROWN, INCORPORATED
Unadjusted Trial Balance
December 31, 1993

Cash	$ 3	
Accounts receivable	11	
Merchandise inventory	9	
Store supplies	6	
Store equipment	15	
Accumulated amortization, store equipment . .		$ 4
Accounts payable		6
Salaries payable	—	—
Common shares		18
Retained earnings		15
Cash dividends declared	2	
Sales		63
Sales returns and allowances	3	
Purchases	28	
Purchases discounts		5
Transportation-in	3	
Amortization expense, store equipment	—	—
Salaries expense	17	
Rent expense	10	
Store supplies expense	—	—
Advertising expense	4	
Totals	$111	$111

Required

Prepare a work sheet for Crown, Incorporated (do not include columns for an adjusted trial balance). Copy the unadjusted trial balance onto the work sheet and complete the work sheet using the following information:

a. Ending store supplies inventory, $2.

b. Estimated amortization on the store equipment, $6.

c. Accrued salaries payable, $3.

d. Ending merchandise inventory, $10.

Use the information in Exercise 5–11 to prepare a work sheet according to the adjusting entry approach to accounting for merchandise inventories.

Use the adjusting entry approach to accounting for merchandise inventories and prepare adjusting journal entries and closing journal entries for Crown, Incorporated, the company described in Exercise 5–11.

The following trial balance was taken from the ledger of Martin Sales at the end of its annual accounting period. Jim Martin, owner of Martin Sales, did not make additional investments in the business during 1993. (To simplify the exercise and save time, the account balances are in one- and two-digit numbers.)

MARTIN SALES
Unadjusted Trial Balance
December 31, 1993

Cash	$ 12	
Accounts receivable	16	
Merchandise inventory	24	
Store supplies	14	
Accounts payable		$ 28
Salaries payable	—	
Jim Martin, capital		39
Jim Martin, withdrawals	9	
Sales		93
Sales returns and allowances	8	
Purchases	37	
Purchases discounts		6
Transportation-in	7	
Salaries expense	28	
Rent expense	11	
Store supplies expense	—	—
Totals	$166	$166

Required

Prepare a work sheet form (do not include columns for an adjusted trial balance). Copy the unadjusted trial balance onto the work sheet and complete the work sheet using the following information:

a. Ending store supplies inventory, $7.
b. Accrued salaries payable, $5.
c. Ending merchandise inventory, $32.

Use the information in Exercise 5–14 to prepare a work sheet according to the adjusting entry approach to accounting for merchandise inventories.

^CExercise 5–16
Updating the Merchandise
Inventory account;
adjusting entry approach
(LO 6)

Use the adjusting entry approach to accounting for merchandise inventories and prepare adjusting journal entries and closing journal entries for Martin Sales, the company described in Exercise 5–14.

Problems

Problem 5–1
Journal entries for
merchandising
transactions
(LO 1)

Prepare General Journal entries to record the following transactions of Ibis Sales Company:

Sept. 2   Purchased merchandise priced at $4,700 on account, terms 1/15, n/30, FOB the seller's factory.

 3   Purchased a new computer for office use on account for $10,000.

 3   Sold merchandise on account; terms 2/10, 1/30, n/60; $2,900.

 4   Paid $225 cash for freight charges on the shipment of merchandise purchased on September 2.

 8   Sold merchandise for cash, $470.

 10   Purchased merchandise on account; terms 2/15, n/30; $2,600.

 12   Received a $400 credit memorandum for merchandise purchased on September 10 and returned for credit.

 19   Sold merchandise on account; terms 2/10, n/30; $2,460.

 22   Issued a $335 credit memorandum to customer who had returned a portion of the merchandise purchased on September 19.

 23   Purchased office supplies on account, $295.

 24   Received a credit memorandum of $70 for unsatisfactory office supplies purchased on September 23 and returned for credit.

 25   Paid for the merchandise purchased on September 10, less the return and the discount.

 29   The customer who purchased merchandise on September 3 paid for the purchase of that date less the applicable discount.

 29   Received payment for the merchandise sold on September 19, less the return and applicable discount.

Oct. 1   Paid for the merchandise purchased on September 2.

Problem 5–2
Corporate income and
retained earnings
statements, and closing
entries
(LO 3)

On December 31, 1993, the end of Helgeson Sales Inc.'s annual accounting period, the financial statement columns of the company's work sheet were as follows:

	Income Statement		Retained Earnings Statement or Balance Sheet	
	Debit	**Credit**	**Debit**	**Credit**
Merchandise inventory	40,518	42,948	42,948	
Other assets			312,000	
Common shares				120,000
Retained earnings				223,284
Cash dividends declared			30,000	
Sales		396,612		
Sales returns and allowances	2,364			
Purchases	260,118			
Purchases returns and allowances		936		
Purchases discounts		3,906		
Transportation-in	1,686			
Amortization expense, store equipment . .	3,810			
Sales salaries expense	39,312			
Rent expense, selling space	19,440			
Store supplies expense	990			
Advertising expense	1,422			
Amortization expense, office equipment . .	954			
Office salaries expense	19,170			
Insurance expense	2,592			
Rent expense, office space	2,160			
Office supplies expense	390			
Telephone expense	1,026			
Income taxes expense	6,786			
	402,738	444,402	384,948	343,284
Net income	41,664			41,664
	444,402	444,402	384,948	384,948

Required

1. Prepare a 1993 classified, multiple-step income statement for the corporation, showing in detail the expenses and the items that make up cost of goods sold.

2. Prepare a 1993 retained earnings statement.

3. Prepare closing entries for the corporation.

4. Open a Merchandise Inventory account and enter a December 31, 1992, balance of $40,518. Then post the portions of the closing entries that affect this account.

5. Prepare a combined, single-step income and retained earnings statement. Condense each revenue and expense category into a single item.

A December 31, 1993, year-end, unadjusted trial balance from the ledger of The Window Store, a single proprietorship, is as follows:

Problem 5–3
Proprietorship work sheet and closing entries
(LO 3)

THE WINDOW STORE
Unadjusted Trial Balance
December 31, 1993

Cash	$ 2,400	
Merchandise inventory	61,152	
Office supplies	438	
Store supplies	1,410	
Prepaid insurance	3,276	
Office equipment	10,644	
Accumulated amortization, office equipment		$ 3,840
Store equipment	38,178	
Accumulated amortization, store equipment		15,372
Accounts payable		8,766
Ed Walker, capital		72,540
Ed Walker, withdrawals	32,400	
Sales		342,774
Sales returns and allowances	2,094	
Sales discounts	3,816	
Purchases	205,650	
Purchases returns and allowances		1,332
Purchases discounts		5,292
Transportation-in	1,158	
Amortization expense, store equipment	–0–	
Sales salaries expense	38,304	
Rent expense, selling space	23,220	
Store supplies expense	–0–	
Advertising expense	684	
Amortization expense, office equipment	–0–	
Office salaries expense	22,356	
Insurance expense	–0–	
Rent expense, office space	2,736	
Office supplies expense	–0–	
Totals	$449,916	$449,916

Required

1. Copy the unadjusted trial balance on a work sheet and complete the work sheet using the following information:
   a. Ending store supplies inventory, $240.
   b. Ending office supplies inventory, $150.
   c. Expired insurance, $2,682.
   d. Estimated amortization of store equipment, $3,816.
   e. Estimated amortization of office equipment, $690.
   f. Ending merchandise inventory, $62,784.

2. Prepare closing entries for the store.

3. Open a balance column Merchandise Inventory account and enter a December 31, 1992, balance of $61,152. Then post the portions of the closing entries that affect this account.

^cProblem 5–4
Adjusting entry approach to proprietorship work sheet, adjusting and closing entries
(LO 6)

Solve this problem using the information presented in Problem 5–3 for The Window Store. However, in satisfying the following requirements, use the adjusting entry approach to account for merchandise inventory.

Required

1. Copy the unadjusted trial balance on a work sheet and complete the work sheet. (Use the information presented in (1) of Problem 5–3.)

2. Prepare adjusting and closing entries for the store.

3. Open a balance column Merchandise Inventory account and enter a December 31, 1992, balance of $61,152. Then post those portions of the adjusting and closing entries that affect this account.

Following is the unadjusted trial balance of Honcho Shop, Incorporated, on December 31, 1993, the end of the annual accounting period:

Problem 5–5
Corporate work sheet, income and retained earnings statements, and closing entries (LO 3)

HONCHO SHOP, INCORPORATED
Unadjusted Trial Balance
December 31, 1993

Cash	$ 6,570	
Merchandise inventory	62,778	
Office supplies	570	
Store supplies	1,104	
Prepaid insurance	3,798	
Office equipment	15,192	
Accumulated amortization, office equipment . .		$ 1,662
Store equipment	66,954	
Accumulated amortization, store equipment . . .		6,372
Accounts payable		1,434
Salaries payable		–0–
Income taxes payable		–0–
Common shares, 7,200		72,000
Retained earnings		26,190
Cash dividends declared	18,000	
Sales		494,676
Sales returns and allowances	3,348	
Purchases	302,058	
Purchases returns and allowances		1,344
Purchases discounts		5,262
Transportation-in	3,930	
Amortization expense, store equipment	–0–	
Sales salaries expense	44,370	
Rent expense, selling space	18,900	
Store supplies expense	–0–	
Advertising expense	6,180	
Amortization expense, office equipment	–0–	
Office salaries expense	45,288	
Insurance expense	–0–	
Rent expense, office space	2,700	
Office supplies expense	–0–	
Income taxes expense	7,200	
Totals	$608,940	$608,940

Required

1. Copy the unadjusted trial balance on a work sheet and complete the work sheet using the information that follows:
   a. Ending store supplies inventory, $294.
   b. Ending office supplies inventory, $222.
   c. Expired insurance, $2,958.
   d. Amortization on the store equipment, $6,498.
   e. Amortization on the office equipment, $1,782.
   f. Accrued sales salaries payable, $402, and accrued office salaries payable, $288.
   g. Additional income taxes expense, $762.
   h. Ending merchandise inventory, $59,688.

2. Prepare a multiple-step classified income statement that shows in detail the expenses and the items that make up cost of goods sold.

3. Prepare a retained earnings statement.

4. Prepare closing entries for the corporation.

5. In addition to the preceding, prepare a single-step statement of income and retained earnings with the items condensed as they would be likely to appear in published statements.

^C**Problem 5–6**
Adjusting entry approach to corporate work sheet, income and retained earnings statements, adjusting and closing entries
(LO 6)

Use the information presented in Problem 5–5 for Honcho Shop, Incorporated, in solving this problem. However, in satisfying the following requirements, use the adjusting entry approach to accounting for merchandise inventories.

Required

1. Copy the unadjusted trial balance on a work sheet and complete the work sheet. (Use the adjustments information presented in requirement 1 of Problem 5–5.)

2. Prepare a multiple-step classified income statement that shows in detail the expenses and the items that make up cost of goods sold.

3. Prepare a retained earnings statement.

4. Prepare adjusting and closing entries for the corporation.

5. In addition to the preceding, prepare a single-step statement of income and retained earnings with the items condensed as they would be likely to appear in published statements.

Problem 5–7
Proprietorship work sheet, financial statements, and closing entries
(LO 4)

Following is the unadjusted trial balance of Comfort Clothes on December 31, 1993, the end of the annual accounting period:

COMFORT CLOTHES
Unadjusted Trial Balance
December 31, 1993

Cash	$ 12,330	
Accounts receivable	27,198	
Merchandise inventory	62,214	
Office supplies	930	
Store supplies	2,898	
Prepaid insurance	3,906	
Office equipment	15,012	
Accumulated amortization, office equipment		$ 3,390
Store equipment	74,376	
Accumulated amortization, store equipment		12,996
Accounts payable		9,972
Salaries payable		–0–
Trudy Geller, capital		127,218
Trudy Geller, withdrawals	18,000	
Sales		674,568
Sales returns and allowances	6,084	
Purchases	462,102	
Purchases returns and allowances		2,184
Purchases discounts		5,652
Transportation-in	6,150	
Amortization expense, store equipment	–0–	
Sales salaries expense	51,864	
Rent expense, selling space	24,300	
Store supplies expense	–0–	
Amortization expense, office equipment	–0–	
Office salaries expense	57,996	
Insurance expense	–0–	
Rent expense, office space	10,620	
Office supplies expense	–0–	
Totals	$835,980	$835,980

Required

1. Copy the unadjusted trial balance on a work sheet form and complete the work sheet using the information that follows:
   a. Ending store supplies inventory, $534.
   b. Ending office supplies inventory, $270.
   c. Expired insurance, $3,366.
   d. Amortization on the store equipment, $6,498.
   e. Amortization on the office equipment, $1,782.
   f. Accrued sales salaries payable, $533, and accrued office salaries payable, $252.
   g. Ending merchandise inventory, $65,238.

2. Prepare a multiple-step income statement that shows in detail the expenses and the items that make up cost of goods sold.

3. Prepare a statement of changes in owner's equity. On December 31, 1992, the Trudy Geller, Capital, account had a balance of $43,218. Early in 1993, Geller invested an additional $84,000 in the business.

4. Prepare a year-end classified balance sheet with the supplies and prepaid insurance combined and shown as a single item.

5. Prepare adjusting and closing entries.

In Problem 5–2, the first row of the work sheet shows the merchandise inventory amounts to be reported on the financial statements. Explain why merchandise inventory amounts are shown in both Income Statement columns and explain the work sheet procedures that resulted in the merchandise inventory amounts appearing as they do in the financial statement columns of the work sheet. Also describe the end-of-period journal entries that involve the merchandise inventory amounts shown on the work sheet.

Problem 5–8
Analytical essay
(LO 3, 4)

In Problem 5–2, the first row of the work sheet shows the merchandise inventory amounts to be reported on the financial statements. Explain how the presentation of these amounts in the work sheet would be different if Helgeson Sales, Inc. had used the adjusting entry approach to accounting for merchandise inventories. Include in your answer an explanation of the work sheet procedures and the end-of-period journal entries when the adjusting entry approach is used.

^C**Problem 5–9**
Analytical essay
(LO 3, 6)

Alternate Problems

Prepare general journal entries to record the following transactions of Taylor Merchandising:

Problem 5–1A
Journal entries for merchandising transactions
(LO 1)

Nov. 1 Purchased merchandise on account; terms 2/10, n/30; $8,640.

   3 Sold merchandise for cash, $900.

   8 Purchased merchandise on account; terms 2/10, n/30; $6,300, FOB the seller's factory.

   8 Paid $270 cash for freight charges on the merchandise shipment of the previous transaction.

   9 Purchased delivery equipment on credit, $14,400.

Nov. 13 Sold merchandise on account, terms 2/15, 1/30, n/60; $3,600.

   14 Received a $900 credit memorandum for merchandise purchased on November 8 and returned for credit.

   14 Purchased office supplies on account, $288, n/30.

   16 Sold merchandise on account, terms 2/10, 1/30, n/60; $2,520.

   16 Paid for the merchandise purchased on November 8, less the return and the discount.

   17 Received a credit memorandum for unsatisfactory office supplies purchased on November 14 and returned, $72.

   20 Issued a $252 credit memorandum to the customer who purchased merchandise on November 16 and returned a portion for credit.

   26 Received payment for the merchandise sold on November 16, less the return and applicable discount.

   28 The customer of November 13 paid for the purchase of that date, less the applicable discount.

Dec. 1 Paid for the merchandise purchased on November 1.

Problem 5–2A
Corporate income and retained earnings statements, and closing entries
(LO 3)

On December 31, 1993, the end of Pacific Sales Inc.'s annual accounting period, the financial statement columns of its work sheet appeared as follows:

	Income Statement		Retained Earnings Statement or Balance Sheet	
	Debit	Credit	Debit	Credit
Merchandise inventory	83,196	79,854	79,854	
Other assets.			585,342	
Common shares.				240,000
Retained earnings.				374,844
Cash dividends declared			60,000	
Sales		1,156,464		
Sales returns and allowances	6,858			
Sales discounts	17,496			
Purchases.	782,082			
Purchases returns and allowances		3,276		
Purchases discounts		10,764		
Transportation-in	11,046			
Amortization expense, store equipment . .	10,692			
Sales salaries expense	84,096			
Rent expense, selling space	39,600			
Store supplies expense	1,944			
Amortization expense, office equipment . .	3,312			
Office salaries expense	68,184			
Insurance expense	4,068			
Rent expense, office space	3,600			
Office supplies expense.	882			
Income taxes expense	22,950			
	1,140,006	1,250,358	725,196	614,844
Net income	110,352			110,352
	1,250,358	1,250,358	725,196	725,196

Required

1. Prepare a 1993 classified, multiple-step income statement for the corporation, showing in detail the expenses and the items that make up cost of goods sold.

2. Prepare a 1993 retained earnings statement.

3. Prepare closing entries for the corporation.

4. Open a Merchandise Inventory account and enter a December 31, 1992, balance of $83,196. Then post those portions of the closing entries that affect this account.

5. Prepare a combined, single-step income and retained earnings statement. Condense each revenue and expense category into a single item.

The December 31, 1993, year-end, unadjusted trial balance of the ledger of Ocean Store, a single proprietorship, follows:

Problem 5–3A
Proprietorship work sheet and closing entries
(LO 3)

OCEAN STORE
Unadjusted Trial Balance
December 31, 1993

Cash	$ 8,766	
Merchandise inventory	56,400	
Office supplies	774	
Store supplies	2,058	
Prepaid insurance	4,608	
Office equipment	16,956	
Accumulated amortization, office equipment		$ 4,404
Store equipment	69,282	
Accumulated amortization, store equipment		11,490
Accounts payable		5,616
B. J. Ocean, capital		112,302
B. J. Ocean, withdrawals	37,800	
Sales		574,620
Sales returns and allowances	3,822	
Sales discounts	6,228	
Purchases	397,578	
Purchases returns and allowances		2,214
Purchases discounts		5,670
Transportation-in	3,372	
Amortization expense, store equipment	–0–	
Sales salaries expense	41,652	
Rent expense, selling space	28,800	
Store supplies expense	–0–	
Advertising expense	1,464	
Amortization expense, office equipment	–0–	
Office salaries expense	33,156	
Insurance expense	–0–	
Rent expense, office space	3,600	
Office supplies expense	–0–	
Totals	$716,316	$716,316

Required

1. Copy the unadjusted trial balance on a work sheet form and complete the work sheet using the following information:
   a. Ending store supplies inventory, $462.
   b. Ending office supplies inventory, $216.
   c. Expired insurance, $3,318.
   d. Amortization on the store equipment, $7,038.
   e. Amortization on the office equipment, $2,106.
   f. Ending merchandise inventory, $58,776.

2. Prepare closing entries for the store.

3. Open a balance column Merchandise Inventory account and enter a December 31, 1992, balance of $56,400. Then, post those portions of the closing entries that affect this account.

CProblem 5–4A
Adjusting entry approach
to proprietorship work
sheet, adjusting and
closing entries
(LO 6)

Solve this problem using the information presented in Problem 5–3A for the Ocean Store. However, in satisfying the following requirements, use the adjusting entry approach to account for the merchandise inventory.

Required

1. Copy the unadjusted trial balance on a work sheet and complete the work sheet. (Use the adjustments information presented in requirement 1 of Problem 5–3A.)
2. Prepare adjusting and closing entries for the store.
3. Open a balance column Merchandise Inventory account and enter a December 31, 1992, balance of $56,400. Then post those portions of the adjusting and closing entries that affect this account.

Problem 5–5A
Corporate work sheet,
income and retained
earnings statements, and
closing entries
(LO 3, 4)

The unadjusted trial balance of Hilger Sales, Inc., on December 31, 1993, the end of the annual accounting period, follows:

HILGER SALES, INC.
Unadjusted Trial Balance
December 31, 1993

Cash.	$ 10,602	
Merchandise inventory	80,172	
Office supplies.	792	
Store supplies	1,752	
Prepaid insurance	5,208	
Office equipment	17,406	
Accumulated amortization, office equipment		$ 2,742
Store equipment.	78,084	
Accumulated amortization, store equipment.		11,220
Accounts payable		4,050
Salaries payable		–0–
Income taxes payable		–0–
Common shares, 9,000.		90,000
Retained earnings		16,746
Cash dividends declared.	9,000	
Sales.		641,772
Sales returns and allowances	3,816	
Purchases	422,814	
Purchases returns and allowances		2,598
Purchases discounts		5,916
Transportation-in	3,990	
Amortization expense, store equipment	–0–	
Sales salaries expense	50,574	
Rent expense, selling space	23,400	
Store supplies expense.	–0–	
Advertising expense.	6,594	
Amortization expense, office equipment.	–0–	
Office salaries expense	47,160	
Insurance expense.	–0–	
Rent expense, office space.	3,600	
Office supplies expense	–0–	
Income taxes expense	10,080	
Totals	$775,044	$775,044

Required

1. Copy the unadjusted trial balance on a work sheet and complete the work sheet using the information that follows:
   a. Ending store supplies inventory, $474.
   b. Ending office supplies inventory, $222.
   c. Expired insurance, $4,458.

d. Amortization on the store equipment, $7,668.

e. Amortization on the office equipment, $2,058.

f. Accrued sales salaries payable, $618, and accrued office salaries payable, $150.

g. Additional income taxes expense, $942.

h. Ending merchandise inventory, $77,166.

2. Prepare a multiple-step classified income statement that shows in detail the expenses and the items that make up cost of goods sold.

3. Prepare a retained earnings statement.

4. Prepare closing entries for the corporation.

5. In addition to the preceding, prepare a single-step statement of income and retained earnings with the items condensed as they would be likely to appear in published statements.

Solve this problem using the information presented in Problem 5–5A for Hilger Sales, Inc. However, in satisfying the following requirements, use the adjusting entry approach to accounting for the merchandise inventory.

Required

1. Copy the unadjusted trial balance on a work sheet and complete the work sheet. (Use the adjustments information presented in requirement 1 of Problem 5–5A.)

2. Prepare a multiple-step classified income statement that shows in detail the expenses and the items that make up cost of goods sold.

3. Prepare a retained earnings statement.

4. Prepare adjusting and closing entries for the corporation.

5. In addition to the preceding, prepare a single-step statement of income and retained earnings with the items condensed as they would be likely to appear in published statements.

^CProblem 5–6A
Adjusting entry approach
to corporate work sheet,
income and retained
earnings statements,
adjusting and closing
entries
(LO 6)

The unadjusted trial balance of Ingram's Designs on December 31, 1993, the end of the annual accounting period, follows:

Problem 5–7A
Proprietorship work sheet,
financial statements, and
closing entries
(LO 4)

INGRAM'S DESIGNS
Unadjusted Trial Balance
December 31, 1993

Cash	$ 12,204	
Accounts receivable	28,698	
Merchandise inventory	62,226	
Office supplies	1,008	
Store supplies	2,670	
Prepaid insurance	4,284	
Office equipment	14,262	
Accumulated amortization, office equipment . .		$ 3,300
Store equipment	67,536	
Accumulated amortization, store equipment . . .		11,004
Accounts payable		4,608
Salaries payable		–0–
Sally Ingram, capital		135,408
Sally Ingram, withdrawals	30,000	
Sales		662,112
Sales returns and allowances	5,382	
Purchases	458,424	
Purchases returns and allowances		2,304
Purchases discounts		5,178
Transportation-in	5,310	
Amortization expense, store equipment	–0–	
Sales salaries expense	47,430	
Rent expense, selling space	24,300	
Store supplies expense	–0–	
Amortization expense, office equipment	–0–	
Office salaries expense	50,280	
Insurance expense	–0–	
Rent expense, office space	9,900	
Office supplies expense	–0–	
Totals	$823,914	$823,914

Required

1. Copy the unadjusted trial balance on a work sheet and complete the work sheet using the following information:
   a. Ending store supplies inventory, $618.
   b. Ending office supplies inventory, $330.
   c. Expired insurance, $3,546.
   d. Amortization on the store equipment, $5,958.
   e. Amortization on the office equipment, $1,698.
   f. Accrued sales salaries payable, $582, and accrued office salaries payable, $330.
   g. Ending merchandise inventory, $64,602.

2. Prepare a multiple-step classified income statement that shows in detail the expenses and the items that make up cost of goods sold.

3. Prepare a statement of changes in owner's equity. On December 31, 1992, the Sally Ingram, Capital, account had a balance of $45,408. Early in the year, Ingram invested an additional $90,000 in the business.

4. Prepare a year-end classified balance sheet with the supplies and prepaid insurance combined and shown as a single item.

5. Prepare adjusting and closing entries.

Problem 5–8A
Analytical essay
(LO 3, 4)

In Problem 5–2A, the first row of the work sheet shows the merchandise inventory amounts to be reported on the financial statements. Since merchandise inventory is an asset, explain why merchandise inventory amounts are shown in the Income Statement columns. Also explain the work sheet procedures that resulted in the merchandise inventory amounts appearing as they do in the financial statement columns of the work sheet.

The fifth row of the work sheet shows $60,000 of cash dividends declared in the next to last column. Explain what this item represents and whether the $60,000 is likely to have been extended from the Unadjusted Trial Balance or from the Adjustments columns of the work sheet.

In Problem 5–2A, the first row of the work sheet shows the merchandise inventory amounts to be reported on the financial statements. Explain how the presentation of these amounts in the work sheet would be different if Pacific Sales Inc. had used the adjusting entry approach to accounting for merchandise inventories. Although the Adjustments columns of the work sheet are not shown in Problem 5–2A, describe the difference in the totals of the Adjustments columns that would have resulted if Pacific Sales, Inc., had used the adjusting entry approach to accounting for merchandise inventories.

^CProblem 5–9A
Analytical essay
(LO 3, 6)

Serial Problem

Precision Computer Services

(This problem should not be assigned unless the working papers are being used. This is the last segment of a serial problem that started in Chapter 2 and was continued in Chapters 3 and 4. If you did not complete the solutions in those chapters, you can begin the problem at this point. However, as you solve the problem in this chapter, you may need to review some of the facts presented in the Chapter 2, 3, and 4 segments of the problem. See pages 117, 174, and 231.)

John Conard started Precision Computer Services on October 1, 1993. Because the business had only a few credit customers during its first three months, the General Ledger included only one Accounts Receivable account. However, as business operations expanded, Conard decided that the General Ledger should be expanded to contain a separate Account Receivable for each credit customer. Although each general ledger account was originally assigned a three-digit number, Conard decided to add a fourth digit to the separate Account Receivable accounts. The Account Receivable accounts are as follows:

Account	Number
Account Receivable—AB Company	1060
Account Receivable—Ball Company	1061
Account Receivable—Call Company	1062
Account Receivable—Dog Enterprise . . .	1063
Account Receivable—Ear Hearing	1064
Account Receivable—Farm Research . . .	1065
Account Receivable—Goodall Limited . . .	1066
Account Receivable—Iceman, Inc..	1067
Account Receivable—Jackets and More . .	1068

Ever since Precision opened for business, customers have inquired repeatedly whether the company sells computer software and hardware. Conard has analyzed the market potential and decided to carry a limited inventory of some software programs and peripheral equipment. Precision's credit terms to all of its customers who purchase merchandise on credit is 1/10, n/30.

To account for Precision's expanded operations, several additional accounts have been added to the General Ledger. They are:

Account	Number
Merchandise Inventory	119
Sales	413
Sales Returns and Allowances	414
Sales Discounts	415
Purchases	505
Purchases Returns and Allowances	506
Purchases Discounts	507
Transportation-In	508

Precision does not use reversing entries. Journalize and post the following transactions for January, February, and March 1994:

Jan. 2 Paid Ann White for four days, three days last year and one day this year, at her normal rate of $70 per day.

5 Conard invested an additional $3,000 in the business to purchase merchandise inventory.

6 Purchased from DataMax merchandise inventory priced at $5,750 on credit terms of 1/10, n/30, FOB seller's warehouse.

7 Received $445 from Farm Research as final payment on its account. See transactions on November 8 (Chapter 2) and December 29 (Chapter 3).

9 Completed a $1,850 job for AB Company and billed $1,400, which is $1,850 less $450 previously received in advance. See transaction on December 9 (Chapter 3).

12 Sold merchandise on account to Dog Enterprise for $945.

13 Paid $138 for freight charges on the merchandise purchased on January 6.

14 Received notice that Nation Bank had deducted a $9 service charge from the chequing account balance.

15 Received $420 from Goodall Limited for computer services.

16 Paid DataMax for the January 6 purchase, net of the discount.

20 Dog Enterprise returned $125 of defective merchandise it had originally purchased on January 12.

21 Notified by Iceman, Inc., of acceptance of Precision's bid of $1,925 for computer services. Received a $500 advance payment.

22 Received balance due from Dog Enterprise as a result of the January 12 sale, net of the discount and the merchandise returned on January 20.

26 Returned defective merchandise to DataMax and accepted credit to apply against future purchases. Cost, less discount, was $95.

27 Sold $2,740 of merchandise on credit to Jackets and More.

28 Purchased an additional $895 of merchandise inventory on account from DataMax, terms 1/10, n/30, FOB seller's warehouse.

29 Received a $95 credit memo from DataMax acknowledging the return of merchandise on January 26.

30 Paid hydro bill of $62 and telephone bill of $105.

30 Paid Ann White for seven days' work.

Feb. 2 Paid $675 to Town Hall Shopping Centre for an additional three months' rent.

2 Completed job for Iceman, Inc., for which they had made a partial payment in advance on January 21. Billed them for the balance due.

Feb. 5 Paid DataMax for merchandise purchased on January 28, less the credit that resulted from the merchandise return on January 26, and less the discount.

9 Paid Shopper Newspaper $25 for advertisement.

10 Received amount due from AB Company as a result of the billing on January 9.

11 Completed work for Ball Company and billed them for $950.

14 Received notice that Nation Bank had deducted a $12 service charge from the chequing account balance.

14 Conard withdrew $650.

19 Received $520 from Ball Company in response to our February 11 billing.

20 Notified by AB Company of acceptance of Precision's bid of $2,125 for computer services. Received $600 in advance.

24 Sold merchandise, $1,285, on account to Goodall Limited.

26 Paid telephone bill, $108, and hydro bill, $58.

27 Paid Ann White for six days' work.

27 Reimbursed Ann White for business car mileage, 200 km at $0.24 per km.

27 Reimbursed Conard for business car mileage, 300 km at $0.24 per km.

Mar. 3 Received balance due from Ball Company (see transactions on February 11 and 19).

5 Completed job for AB Company and billed the balance due (see transaction on February 20).

8 Purchased $190 of computer supplies from Ajax Supply on account.

9 Received balance due from Goodall Limited as a result of the February 24 sale.

15 Replaced damaged parts on Precision's computer. Cost was $120.

16 Notified by Jackets and More of acceptance of Precision's bid of $2,450 for computer services and received $600 in advance.

19 Paid Ajax Supply balance due. See transactions on December 11 (Chapter 3) and on March 8.

24 Completed $850 worth of service work for Ball Company and billed them.

25 Sold $1,780 worth of merchandise on credit to Dog Enterprise.

30 Sold $290 worth of merchandise on credit to Ball Company.

30 Paid the hydro bill, $62, and the telephone bill, $110.

31 Paid Ann White's business car mileage, 100 km at $0.24 per km, and Conard's business car mileage, 200 km at $0.24 per km.

At the end of the first quarter of 1994, John Conard is interested in knowing how Precision is doing. Therefore, you need to prepare interim financial statements. Information necessary to prepare the work sheet, adjustments, and interim statements is as follows:

a. Computer supplies ending inventory, $19.

b. Three additional months of insurance has expired (a one-year policy was purchased on October 4 for $195).

c. Ann White has worked four days for which she has not been paid.

d. Three months of prepaid rent has expired.

e. Amortization on the office equipment for January through March is $21.25.

f. Amortization on the computer for January through March is $250.

g. Ending merchandise inventory, $2,167.

Do not prepare closing entries.

Provocative Problems

<table>
<tr><td>Provocative Problem 5–1
Jane's Workout Wear
(LO 3)</td><td>Jeff Frey and Jane Grey were partners in a store specializing in workout clothes. They had a major disagreement and decided to close the business and end their partnership. In settlement for her partnership interest, Jane Grey received an inventory of clothes having a $33,750 wholesale value. Because there was nothing practical she could do with the inventory except to open a new store, she did so by investing it and $27,000 in cash. She used $22,500 of the cash to buy store equipment and opened for business on June 1. During the succeeding seven months, she paid out $75,200 to creditors for additional inventory and $31,500 for operating expenses. She also withdrew $22,000 cash for personal expenses. At year-end, she prepared the following balance sheet:</td></tr>
</table>

JANE'S WORKOUT WEAR
Balance Sheet
December 31, 1993

Cash.		$13,325	Accounts payable (all		
Merchandise inventory		39,975	for merchandise)		$ 4,950
Equipment	$22,500		Jane Grey, capital		69,050
Less amortization . .	1,800	20,700			
			Total liabilities and		
Total assets		$74,000	owner's equity		$74,000

Based on the given information, calculate (*a*) the net income earned by the business, (*b*) the cost of goods sold, and (*c*) the amount of sales. Then prepare an income statement that shows the results of the store's operations during its first seven months (June 1, 1993, to December 31, 1993).

<table>
<tr><td>Provocative Problem 5–2
Westworld Store
(LO 3)</td><td>Wally West, the owner of Westworld Store, has not maintained an adequate accounting system and has asked you to help him prepare an income statement for 1993. Based on data that he has provided, the following balance sheet information is available:</td></tr>
</table>

	December 31	
	1992	**1993**
Cash.	$ 4,500	$ 14,580
Accounts receivable.	11,160	13,140
Merchandise inventory	54,720	51,300
Equipment (net after amortization)	44,640	37,080
Total assets	$115,020	$116,100
Accounts payable	$ 16,740	$ 14,760
Wages payable.	540	900
Wally West, capital	97,740	100,440
Total liabilities and owner's equity	$115,020	$116,100

Also, the store's records of cash receipts and disbursements provide the following information:

Collection of accounts receivable . .	$483,120
Payments for:	
Accounts payable	299,160
Employees' wages.	86,580
Other operating expenses	33,300
Wally West, withdrawals	54,000

Assume that the store makes all merchandise purchases and sales on credit, calculate the amounts of its sales, purchases, and wages expense for 1993. Then prepare an accrual basis income statement for 1993.

Larry Lowe worked in the Mountain Valley Store for 20 years, until his father died, leaving him a sizable estate. After sitting around long enough to get bored and see his bank balance start to dwindle, Lowe decided to open a lighting store. When he started the business on May 1, 1993, there were no other lighting stores in the town of Mountain Valley, and Lowe thought that the business would have a good chance to succeed.

Provocative Problem 5–3
Larry's Lights Fantastic
(LO 3)

On May 1, Lowe deposited $64,200 in a bank account under the name of Larry's Lights Fantastic. He then paid $14,400 cash for store equipment, which he expected to last 10 years before it became worthless. He also bought merchandise for $45,000 cash and paid $4,320 in advance for eight months' rent for the shop.

Lowe estimated that most lighting stores sold their lamps at prices averaging 40% above cost. For example, a lamp that cost $10 was sold for $14. To attract customers from other towns, Lowe decided to mark his merchandise for sale at only 35% above cost. Because his other operating costs would be low, he thought that this pricing strategy would leave a net income equal to at least a suitable 10% of sales.

On December 31, 1993, eight months after opening his store, Lowe has come to you for advice. He thinks business has been good. However, he doesn't quite understand why his cash balance has fallen to $4,000. He has not withdrawn any cash from the business.

In talking with Lowe and examining his records, you determine that the inventory was replaced three times during the eight months, each time at a cost of $45,000. All merchandise purchases have been paid in cash, except for one bill of $13,020, which is not yet due. A full stock of merchandise (cost of $45,000) is on hand and customers owe Lowe $39,110. In addition to the rent paid in advance, Lowe paid $17,640 for other expenses. There are no outstanding bills for expenses.

Prepare (*a*) an income statement for the business covering the eight-month period ended December 31, (*b*) a statement of changes in owner's equity, (*c*) a December 31, 1993, balance sheet, and (*d*) a schedule of cash changes that explains where the $4,000 cash balance came from by showing the cash receipts and cash disbursements during the eight months ended December 31.

For this problem, turn to the financial statements of Bombardier Inc. shown in Appendix I. Use the information presented in the consolidated statements of earnings and balance sheet and notes to consolidated financial statements to provide answers to these questions:

Provocative Problem 5–4
Bombardier Inc.
(LO 2)

1. Identify the divisions or segments and how much each contributed in 1992 to the total revenues.

2. Calculate the segment pretax income as a percentage of revenue for 1992 and 1991.

3. Identify which segment had the greatest, and which had the least, amount of growth between the two years.

4. Determine whether the 1992 total expenses, as a percentage of revenues, increased or decreased from 1991.

Provocative Problem 5–5
As a Matter of Ethics:
Essay

Review the ''As a Matter of Ethics'' case on page 249. Discuss the nature of the problem faced by Renee Fleck and evaluate her alternative courses of action.

Ethics

Analytical and Review Problems

A&R Problem 5–1

The partially completed work sheet of Incomplete Data Company appears below:

INCOMPLETE DATA COMPANY
Work Sheet for Year Ended December 31, 1993

Account Titles	Trial Balance Dr.	Trial Balance Cr.	Adjustments Dr.	Adjustments Cr.	Income Statement Dr.	Income Statement Cr.	Balance Sheet Dr.	Balance Sheet Cr.
Cash	2,780							
Accounts receivable							34,600	
Merchandise inventory					31,400	26,400		
Prepaid fire insurance	720						480	
Prepaid rent	4,800							
Office equipment							12,000	
Accumulated amortization—office equipment		4,500						
Accounts payable		8,000						
Clay Camp, capital		22,000						
Clay Camp, drawing							24,000	
Sales		300,000				302,400		
Sales returns and allowances					1,000			
Purchases	199,200							
Purchases returns and allowances						1,400		
Advertising expense	1,000							
Supplies expense	1,800							
Salaries expense	23,200							
Utilities expense	1,800							
Fire insurance expense								
Rent expense					3,600			
Amortization expense—office equipment					1,500			
Salaries payable								660

Required

Complete the work sheet for the year ended December 31, 1993.

The following are the selected data for the Allen Sales Company for the year ended December 31, 1994.

A&R Problem 5–2

a. Selected closing entries:

Income Summary	273,000	
Purchases Returns and Allowances	2,300	
Purchases		180,000
Transportation-In		4,000
Sales Salaries Expense		40,000
Advertising Expense		10,000
Rent Expense Office Space		8,000
Delivery Expense		4,800
Office Salaries Expense		26,000
Amortization, Office Equipment		2,000
Miscellaneous Expense		500
To close expense and other nominal accounts.		
G. Allen, Capital	30,000	
G. Allen, Withdrawals.		30,000
To close the withdrawals account.		

b. G. Allen follows the practice of withdrawing half of the annual net income from the business.

c. There were no sales returns and allowances for the year. However, sales discounts amounted to $2,000.

d. Inventories:
December 31, 1993—$20,000
December 31, 1994—$25,000

Required

1. Compute the amount of net income for 1994.

2. Compute the amount of sales for 1994.

3. Prepare a classified income statement for 1994.

As a Matter of Record

The following report, "OSC Issues Warning: Accounting Rules Can't Be Stretched," by Allan Robinson, appeared in *The Globe and Mail* January 15, 1992, page B9:

Record Case 5–1

The Ontario Securities Commission has warned Canada's major corporations not to mislead investors and creditors by using accounting rules to unfairly improve their income statement or balance sheet, although there is a temptation in the midst of a recession to do so.

The cornerstone principle of securities regulation is that companies should provide "full, fair, and plain disclosure," the OSC said.

No specific grades were given in the OSC's annual review of the financial statements, which was released yesterday, but the Office of the Chief Accountant warned there is a danger in "troubled times" that companies might stretch accounting rules to stabilize earnings.

"Accounting policies should not be used to manage earnings," it said. The report also criticized the "increasing trend towards the use of jargon, legalistic terms, and obscure language" in the annual report and the failure to give detailed financial breakdowns.

Required

Indicate how a company may manage its reported net income.

Answers to Objective
Review Questions

LO 1	(*d*)	LO 3	(*c*)	LO 5	(*e*)
LO 2	(*d*)	LO 4	(*d*)	LO 6	(*b*)

Accounting Systems

As businesses grow, the number of their transactions becomes very large. To handle this load, companies use special accounting methods and records. Today, most companies use the powerful capabilities of computers to achieve accurate and fast information processing.

*E*ven in a small business, a large amount of information must be processed through the accounting system. Thus, the accounting system should be designed to process the information efficiently. As you study this chapter, you will learn some general concepts to follow in designing an efficient accounting system. The chapter begins by explaining the basic components of an accounting system, whether it is a manual or computer-based system. After considering some of the special characteristics of computer-based systems, the chapter then explains some of the labour-saving procedures employed in manual systems. These include efficient ways of processing routine transactions such as credit sales, cash receipts, credit purchases, and cash disbursements.

Learning Objectives

After studying Chapter 6, you should be able to:

1. Describe the five basic components of an accounting system.
2. Describe the types of computers used in large and small accounting systems, the role of software in those systems, and the different approaches to inputting and processing data, including the use of networking.
3. Explain how special journals save labour and journalize and post transactions when special journals are used.
4. Explain how a controlling account and its subsidiary ledger are related and how a subsidiary ledger is used to maintain a separate account for each credit customer or each account payable.
5. Explain how to test the accuracy of the account balances in the Accounts Receivable and Accounts Payable subsidiary ledgers and prepare schedules of accounts in those subsidiary ledgers.
6. Explain how sales and goods and services taxes are recorded in special journals, how sales invoices can serve as a Sales Journal, and how sales returns and allowances are recorded.
7. Define or explain the words and phrases listed in the chapter glossary.

The Components of an Accounting System

LO 1 Describe the five basic components of an accounting system.

Accounting systems consist of people, forms, procedures, and equipment. These systems must be designed to capture data about the transactions of the entity and to generate from that data a variety of financial, managerial, and tax accounting reports. Because all accounting systems must accomplish these same objectives, both manual and computerized accounting systems include the same basic components. However, computer-based systems provide more accuracy, speed, efficiency, and convenience.

The five common components of manual and computerized accounting systems are:

- Source documents.
- Input devices.

- Data processor.
- Data storage.
- Output devices.

Illustration 6–1 shows the relationships between these five components.

Source Documents

Chapter 2 described some of the business papers that companies use in the process of completing transactions. These business papers are called *source documents* because they provide a basis for making accounting entries. In other words, they provide the data that are entered in and processed by the accounting system. From your personal experience, you are no doubt familiar with some kinds of source documents such as bank statements and cheques received from other parties. Other examples of source documents include invoices from suppliers, billings to customers, and employee earnings records.

In manual accounting systems, source documents always consist of paper documents. Paper documents are also very important for computerized systems, but newer technologies allow some source documents to take other forms. For example, some companies send invoices directly from their own computers to their customers' computers.

Accurate source documents are important for the proper functioning of an accounting system. If the information going into the system is faulty and incomplete, the information coming out of the system will also be faulty and incomplete. (In computer jargon, the results of defective input are sometimes described as "garbage in, garbage out.")

Input Devices

The second component of an accounting system is one or more input devices. As shown in Illustration 6–1, an input device transfers the information from source documents to the data processing component of the accounting system. In a computer-based system, this often involves converting the data on the source documents from a written form into electronic signals. In addition to transferring data from source documents to the data processor, input devices are used to tell the data processing component how to process the inputted data.

In prior chapters, you used an input device when you solved exercises and problems by recording the effects of transactions with journal entries. If you recorded transactions using the SPATS supplement that accompanies this text, you used the keyboard of a computer as the input device. When you recorded transactions using pencil and paper, you were using these items as the input device for a manual accounting system.

The most common input device for a computer-based accounting system is a keyboard. System operators use keyboards to transfer data from the source documents into the computer. Another input device is a *bar code reader* like those used in grocery and other retail stores. With a bar code reader, the clerk merely moves purchased items over the reader, which picks up their code numbers and sends the data to the computer. Other input devices

ILLUSTRATION 6–1

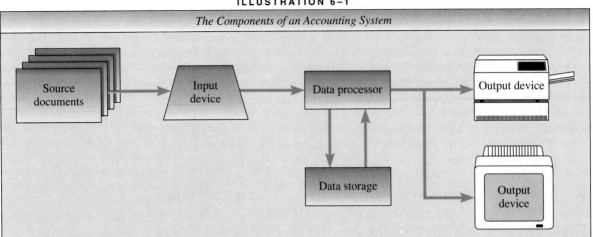

The Components of an Accounting System

include *scanners* that read words and numbers directly from source documents.

In both manual systems and computer systems, companies promote clerical accuracy by using routine procedures for inputting data. Also, controls should be in place to ensure that only authorized individuals can input data to the accounting system. Such controls help to protect the integrity of the system and also allow incorrect input to be traced back to its source.

Data Processor

The third component of an accounting system is the **data processor,** which interprets, manipulates, and summarizes recorded information so it can be used in analyses and reports. In manual systems, the primary data processor is the accountant's brain. However, the manual processing of data is not entirely a mental process. That is, the accountant uses the journal, the ledger, the working papers, and such procedures as posting to convert the journal entry data into more useful information. Of course, few, if any, accounting systems are completely manual. For example, calculators are considered essential equipment for manual systems.

As a result of technological developments over the last two decades, many manual accounting systems have been replaced by computer-based systems. The data processor in a computer-based system includes both hardware and software. Hardware is the machinery that performs the steps called for by the software. The software consists of computer programs that specify the operations to be performed on the data. Software actually controls the whole system, including input, file management, processing, and output.

Data Storage

Data storage is an essential component of both manual and computer-based systems. As data is inputted and processed, it must be saved so it can be used as output or processed further. This stockpile of data (database) stored in the accounting system should be readily accessible so periodic financial reports can be compiled quickly. In addition, data storage should support the preparation of special-purpose reports that managers may request. The accounting database also serves as the primary source of information auditors use when they audit the financial statements. Companies also maintain files of source documents for use by auditors and to clear up errors or disputes.

In manual systems, data storage consists of files of paper documents. You learned about several of these documents, such as journals and ledgers, in prior chapters.

With a computer-based system, some of the data is stored in the form of paper documents. However, most of the data is stored on floppy diskettes, hard disks, or magnetic tapes. As a result of recent improvements, these devices can store very large amounts of data. For example, floppy diskettes can hold up to two megabytes of information (one megabyte is roughly equivalent to 500 double-spaced typed pages). Small digital-audio-tape (DAT) cassettes can hold hundreds of megabytes of information. Some hard disks can hold thousands of megabytes (one thousand megabytes is a gigabyte). Because of the recent improvements in data storage, accounting systems now store much more detailed and extensive databases than was possible in the past. As a result, managers have much more information available to help them plan and control business activities.

In a computer-based system, data storage can be on-line (usually on a hard disk), which means that the data can be accessed whenever it is needed by the software. In contrast, when data is stored off-line, the data cannot be accessed until the computer operator inserts a disk or a magnetic tape into a drive.

Generally, we do not use the concepts of *on-line* and *off-line* storage in reference to manual accounting systems. However, one might argue that in a manual system only the data stored in the accountant's brain is on-line; everything else is off-line.

Output Devices

The fifth component of an accounting system is the **output devices.** These allow information to be taken out of the system and placed in the hands of users. Examples of output include bills to customers, cheques payable to suppliers and employees, financial statements, and a variety of other internal reports.

For computer-based systems, the most common output devices are video screens and printers. Other output devices include telephones or direct phone line connections to the computer system of a supplier or customer. When requests for output are entered, the data processor searches the database for the needed data, organizes it in the form of a report, and sends the information to an output device.

Depending on the output device, the information may be displayed on a screen, printed on paper, or expressed as a voice over the telephone. For example, a bank customer may call to find out the balance in his or her chequing account. If a touch-tone telephone serves as an input/output device, a recording may ask the customer to enter appropriate identifying information including the number of the account. With this input, the computer searches the database for the information and sends it back over the telephone. If the telephone is not used as an input/output device, the bank employee who answers the phone inputs the information request using a keyboard. The employee then reads the output on a video screen and relays it over the phone to the customer.

Another kind of output involves paying employees without writing paycheques. Instead, the company's computer system may send the payroll data directly to the computer system of the company's bank. Thus, the output of the company's system is an electronic fund transfer (EFT) from the company's bank account to the employees' bank accounts. The output device in this instance is the link, or interface, between the computer systems of the company and the bank. Large companies are increasingly using EFTs. In other situations, the company's computer outputs the payroll data on a magnetic tape or disk. The tape or disk is then used by the bank to transfer the funds to the employees' bank accounts.

In addition to the preceding forms of output, many situations require printed output that computer systems produce on laser, impact, or ink-jet printers.

For companies using manual accounting systems, production of output involves physically searching the records to find the needed data and then organizing it in a written report.

Small and Large Computer-Based Systems

LO 2 Describe the types of computers used in large and small accounting systems, the role of software in those systems, and the different approaches to inputting and processing data, including the use of networking.

The world has seen radical changes in the use of computers since the first Apple computer was sold in 1980. Everyone reading this book has at least seen and probably operated a small computer. In fact, many of you are already proficient users of personal computers (PCs) such as those produced by International Business Machines (IBM) or by Apple Computer Company. If not, you probably will be by the time you finish your formal education. These computers (often called *microcomputers*) are physically small, easy to operate, and increasingly inexpensive.

Although the use of microcomputers in business has greatly expanded in recent years, many companies also use larger computers called *mainframes*. These machines are able to process huge quantities of accounting data quickly. In addition, they help businesses perform other important tasks such as analyzing the results of market research, compiling shareholder information, and doing engineering design work for products and production lines. These computers include the AS series of machines produced by IBM and the VAX family manufactured by Digital Equipment Company (DEC).

Regardless of its size and speed, every computer does nothing more than execute instructions organized as programs. A program consists of a series of very specific instructions for obtaining data from input or storage, processing it, returning it to storage for later use, and sending it to an output device to produce a report.

Illustration 6–2 presents a flowchart of the steps that a computer program might use to process a stack of customer orders for merchandise. When this program is executed in a normal situation, the system creates a shipping order that identifies the products to be sent to customers. If a shipment causes the quantity on hand to fall below the minimum level, the system generates a purchase order to be approved by a manager. If the quantity on hand is less than the customer ordered, the system produces a partial shipping order, as well as a report to the customer that the remainder is on back order. Then, if replacements have not already been ordered, the system produces a purchase order. If no units of the desired product are on hand, the system notifies the customer of the back order and issues a purchase order, unless one already exists. The system follows this process for each item ordered by each customer until the stack of orders is exhausted.

Despite the apparent complexity of the instructions in Illustration 6–2, this routine is actually incomplete. For example, it does not update the accounting records for sales and accounts receivable. Nor does it deal with cash and trade discounts that might be offered to customers.

In the early days of computer systems, each program had to be custom designed using a programming language such as COBOL or FORTRAN. Since then, programmers have developed more flexible and easier-to-use languages. However, programming is a skill that only a limited number of people need to master. Instead, today's markets are rich with two kinds of off-the-shelf programs that are ready to be used.

Some off-the-shelf programs are general, multipurpose applications that accomplish a variety of different tasks. These programs include familiar word processor programs (such as Microsoft Word® and WordPerfect®), spreadsheet programs (such as Microsoft Excel® and Lotus® 1–2–3®), and database management programs (such as dBASE®).

Other off-the-shelf programs are designed to meet very specific needs of users. These programs include a large number of accounting programs such as AccPac®, DacEasy Accounting®, Peachtree Complete III®, and Great Plains Accounting Series®. Off-the-shelf programs are user-friendly programs that guide users through the input steps and then ask which reports are desired.

Many of the off-the-shelf accounting programs save time and minimize errors because they operate as *integrated* systems. In an integrated system, actions taken in one part of the system also produce results in related parts.

For example, when a credit sale is recorded in an integrated system, several parts of the system are updated with one or two simple commands. First, the system stores the transaction data (as in a journal) so that you can review the entire entry at a later time. Second, it updates the Cash and Accounts Receivable accounts. Third, it updates a detailed record of the amount owed by the customer. Fourth, it might update a detailed record of the products held for sale to show the number of units sold and the number that remain on hand.

Custom Designed and Off-the-Shelf Programs

ILLUSTRATION 6–2

Flowchart for an Order-Processing Program

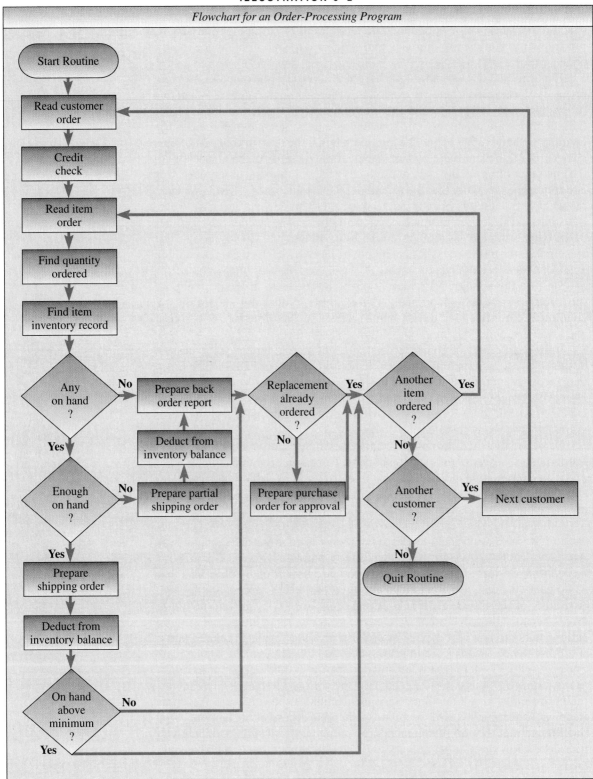

AS A MATTER OF
Opinion

Mr. Yu received his B.Sc. in mathematics from the University of Wisconsin and his M.Sc. degrees in education psychology and computing science from the University of Wisconsin and the University of Southern California. He also holds the CDP designation.

Mr. Yu has been in the computer industry since 1970, with a wide range of experience, including programming, systems analysis, management consulting, and senior management. He has written 10 microcomputer books, published in five countries. He presently heads a small computer consulting firm in Vancouver and is a columnist and editor for two national financial magazines.

Although accounting functions were the first to be computerized on mainframe computers for large organizations, smaller organizations did not obtain the benefits of computerization until the advent of microcomputers. Mainframe computers were too expensive, and accounting software was

John W. Yu, CGA

complicated and costly. Because of the large investments, organizations that use mainframe computers tend to have well-trained (and expensive) accounting and MIS staff.

For medium- to small-sized businesses, microcomputers are a godsend. Not only is hardware inexpensive, software is easy to use and affordable. Consequently, many businesses have taken advantage of computers, often without any in-house accounting expertise.

Technology is a two-edged sword. Inexpensive accounting software makes it possible for even the smallest business to keep its accounting records electronically and provide up-to-date information at the touch of a key. But if the user does not have sound accounting knowledge, accounting programs allow mistakes to be made much faster, with potentially disastrous results.

Not all accounting programs are created equal. Some have little to no internal controls, and some do not provide any audit trails. Even well-designed programs, if used improperly, do not prevent users from making basic accounting mistakes.

Accounting programs do not remove the need for users to have sound accounting knowledge. Indeed, more than ever, users must have a good grounding in accounting before computers can become an effective tool.

Computers and integrated software programs have dramatically reduced the bookkeeping tasks in accounting. However, do not think that computers have eliminated the need for accountants. Nor should you conclude that success in business no longer requires a knowledge of accounting. *The need for accountants and accounting knowledge is created by the need for information, not by the need for pencil and paper.* Accountants continue to be in demand because their expertise is necessary to determine what information ought to be produced and what data should be used to produce it. Accountants are also needed to analyze and explain the output. Furthermore, writing new, improved programs requires a knowledge of accounting.

In short, the value of accounting knowledge does not disappear just because mechanical steps are done with a computer. You still need to understand the effects of events on the company and how they are reflected in financial statements and management reports.

Batch and On-Line Systems

Accounting systems also differ in terms of how the input is entered and processed. With **batch processing,** the source documents are accumulated for a period of time and then processed all at the same time, such as once a day, week, or month. By comparison, with **on-line processing,** data is entered and processed as soon as source documents are available. As a result, the database is immediately updated.

The disadvantage of batch processing is that the database is not kept up to date during the times that source documents are being accumulated. In many situations, however, companies use batch processing because the database requires only periodic updating. For example, records used in sending bills to customers may require updating only once each month.

On-line processing has the advantage of keeping the database always up to date. However, it is more expensive because the software is more complicated and because it usually requires a much larger investment in hardware. On-line processing applications include airline reservations, credit card records, and rapid response mail-order processing.

Computer Networks

In many circumstances, firms derive advantages by linking their computer with those of others, thus becoming a part of a computer network. **Computer networks** allow different users to share access to the same data and the same programs. A relatively small computer network is called a *local area network (LAN)*. This type of network links the machines within an office by special *hard-wire* hookups. For example, many universities have networks in their computer labs. Larger computer networks that are spread over long distances communicate over telephone lines by using *modems*.

In some circumstances, the need for information requires very large networks. Examples include the system used by Federal Express for tracking its packages and billing its customers and the system used by The Bay Company for monitoring inventory levels in each of its stores. These networks involve many computers (desktops and mainframes) and satellite communications to gather information and to provide ready access to the database from all locations.

We now turn to a discussion of some of the labour-saving procedures used to process transactions in manual systems. However, remember that accounting systems have similar purposes whether they are computer-based or manual in operation. Thus, your understanding of computer-based systems will be improved when you understand manual procedures.

Special Journals

LO 3 Explain how special journals save labour and journalize and post transactions when special journals are used.

The General Journal is a flexible journal in which you can record any transaction. However, each debit and credit entered in a General Journal must be individually posted. As a result, a firm that uses a General Journal to record all the transactions of its business requires much time and labour to post the individual debits and credits.

One way to reduce the writing and the posting labour is to divide the transactions of a business into groups of similar transactions and to provide a separate **special journal** for recording the transactions in each group. For example,

AS A MATTER OF
Ethics

A public accountant has a client whose business has grown significantly over the last couple of years and has reached the point where its accounting system has become inadequate for handling both the volume of transactions and management's needs for financial information. The client asks the public accountant for advice on which software system would work best for the company.

The public accountant has been offered a 10% commission by a software company for each purchase of its system by one of the public accountant's clients. The price of one of these systems falls within the range specified by the client. Do you think that the public accountant's evaluation of the alternative systems could be affected by this commission arrangement? Should it be? Should the public accountant feel compelled to tell the client about the commission arrangement before making a recommendation?

most of the transactions of a merchandising business fall into four groups: sales on account, purchases on account, cash receipts, and cash disbursements. When a special journal is provided for each group, the journals are

1. A Sales Journal for recording credit sales.
2. A Purchases Journal for recording credit purchases.
3. A Cash Receipts Journal for recording cash receipts.
4. A Cash Disbursements Journal for recording cash payments.
5. A General Journal for all the miscellaneous transactions not recorded in the special journals and also for adjusting, closing, and correcting entries.

The following illustrations show how special journals save time in journalizing and posting transactions. They do this by providing special columns for accumulating the debits and credits of similar transactions. These journals allow you to post the amounts entered in the special columns as column totals rather than as individual amounts. For example, you can save posting labour if you record credit sales for a month in a Sales Journal like the one at the top of Illustration 6–3. As the illustration shows, you do not post the credit sales to the general ledger accounts until the end of the month. Then you calculate the total sales for the month and post the total as one debit to Accounts Receivable and as one credit to Sales. Only seven sales are recorded in the illustrated journal. However, if you assume the 7 sales represent 700 sales, you can better appreciate the posting labour saved by making only one debit to Accounts Receivable and one credit to Sales.

The special journal in Illustration 6–3 is also called a columnar journal because it has columns for recording the date, the customer's name, the invoice number, and the amount of each credit sale. Only credit sales are recorded in it, and they are recorded daily, with the information about each sale placed on a separate line. Normally, the information is taken from a copy of the sales ticket or invoice prepared at the time of the sale. However, before discussing the journal further, you need to understand the role played by subsidiary ledgers.

ILLUSTRATION 6–3

Sales Journal

Sales Journal					Page 3
Date	Account Debited	Invoice Number	PR		Amount
Feb. 2	James Henry	307	√		450.00
7	Albert Smith	308	√		500.00
13	Sam Moore.	309	√		350.00
15	Paul Roth.	310	√		200.00
22	James Henry	311	√		225.00
25	Frank Booth	312	√		175.00
28	Albert Smith	313	√		250.00
28	Total—Accounts Receivable, Dr.; Sales, Cr.				2,150.00
					(106/413)

Individual amounts are posted daily to the subsidiary ledger.

Total is posted at the end of the month to the general ledger accounts.

Accounts Receivable Ledger

Frank Booth

Date	PR	Debit	Credit	Balance
Feb. 25	S3	175.00		175.00

James Henry

Date	PR	Debit	Credit	Balance
Feb. 2	S3	450.00		450.00
22	S3	225.00		675.00

Sam Moore

Date	PR	Debit	Credit	Balance
Feb. 13	S3	350.00		350.00

Paul Roth

Date	PR	Debit	Credit	Balance
Feb. 15	S3	200.00		200.00

Albert Smith

Date	PR	Debit	Credit	Balance
Feb. 7	S3	500.00		500.00
28	S3	250.00		750.00

General Ledger

Accounts Receivable   No. 106

Date	PR	Debit	Credit	Balance
Feb. 28	S3	2,150.00		2,150.00

Sales   No. 413

Date	PR	Debit	Credit	Balance
Feb. 28	S3		2,150.00	2,150.00

Note that the customer accounts are in a subsidiary ledger and the financial statement accounts are in the General Ledger.

Explanation columns are omitted from the accounts due to a lack of space.

In previous chapters, when we recorded credit sales, we debited a single account called Accounts Receivable. However, when a business has more than one credit customer, the accounts must show how much each customer has purchased, how much each customer has paid, and how much remains to be collected from each customer. To provide this information, businesses with credit customers must maintain a separate Account Receivable for each customer.

One possible way of keeping a separate account for each customer would be to keep all of these accounts in the same ledger that contains the financial statement accounts. However, this usually is not done. Instead, the ledger that contains the financial statement accounts, now called the **General Ledger,** continues to hold a single Accounts Receivable account. Then a supplementary record is established in which a separate account is maintained for each customer. This supplementary record is called the **Accounts Receivable Subsidiary Ledger,** or simply *Accounts Receivable Ledger.* This subsidiary ledger may exist on tape or disk storage in a computerized system. In a manual system, the Accounts Receivable Ledger may take the form of a book or tray that contains the customer accounts. In either case, the customer accounts in the subsidiary ledger are kept separate from the Accounts Receivable account in the General Ledger.

Understand that when debits (or credits) to Accounts Receivable are posted twice (once to Accounts Receivable and once to the customer's account), this does not violate the requirement that debits equal credits. The equality of debits and credits is maintained in the General Ledger. The Accounts Receivable Ledger is simply a supplementary record that provides detailed information concerning each customer.

Illustration 6–4 shows the relationship between the Accounts Receivable controlling account and the accounts in the subsidiary ledger. Note that after all items are posted, the balance in the Accounts Receivable account should equal the sum of the balances in the customers' accounts. As a result, the Accounts Receivable account controls the Accounts Receivable Ledger and is called a **controlling account.** Since the Accounts Receivable Ledger is a supplementary record controlled by an account in the General Ledger, it is called a **subsidiary ledger.** After posting is completed, if the Accounts Receivable balance does not equal the sum of the customer account balances, you know an error has been made.

Keeping a Separate Account for Each Credit Customer

LO 4 Explain how a controlling account and its subsidiary ledger are related and how a subsidiary ledger is used to maintain a separate account for each credit customer or each account payable.

The Accounts Receivable account and the Accounts Receivable Ledger are not the only examples of controlling accounts and subsidiary ledgers. Most companies buy on account from several suppliers. As a result, a company must keep a separate account for each creditor. To accomplish this, the firm maintains an Accounts Payable controlling account in the General Ledger and a separate account for each creditor in a subsidiary **Accounts Payable Ledger.** The controlling account, subsidiary ledger, and columnar journal techniques demonstrated thus far with accounts receivable also apply to the creditor ac-

Maintaining a Separate Record for Each Account Payable

ILLUSTRATION 6–4

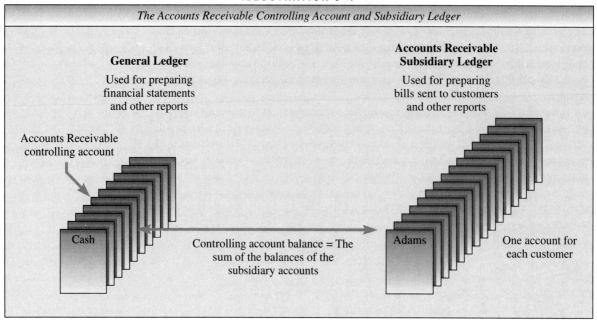

| The Accounts Receivable Controlling Account and Subsidiary Ledger |

General Ledger

Used for preparing
financial statements
and other reports

Accounts Receivable
controlling account

Cash

Controlling account balance = The
sum of the balances of the
subsidiary accounts

**Accounts Receivable
Subsidiary Ledger**

Used for preparing
bills sent to customers
and other reports

Adams

One account for
each customer

counts. The only difference is that a Purchases Journal and a Cash Disbursements Journal are used to record most of the transactions that affect these accounts. You will learn about these journals later in the chapter.

Another situation in which a subsidiary ledger often is used involves equipment. For example, a company with many items of office equipment might keep only one Office Equipment account in its General Ledger. This account would control a subsidiary ledger in which each item of equipment is recorded in a separate account.

Posting the Sales Journal

LO 3 Explain how special journals save labour and journalize and post transactions when special journals are used.

When customer accounts are maintained in a subsidiary ledger, a Sales Journal is posted as shown in Illustration 6–3. The individual sales recorded in the Sales Journal are posted each day to the proper customer accounts in the Accounts Receivable Ledger. These daily postings keep the customer accounts up-to-date. This is important in granting credit because the person responsible for granting credit should know the amount the credit-seeking customer currently owes. The source of this information is the customer's account, and if the account is not up-to-date, an incorrect decision may be made.

Note the check marks in the Sales Journal's Posting Reference column. They indicate that the sales recorded in the journal were individually posted to the customer accounts in the Accounts Receivable Ledger. Check marks rather than account numbers are used because customer accounts may not be numbered. When the accounts are not numbered, they are arranged alphabetically in the Accounts Receivable Ledger so they can be located easily.

In addition to the daily postings to customer accounts, the Sales Journal's Amount column is totaled at the end of the month. Then, the total is debited to

Accounts Receivable and credited to Sales. The credit records the month's revenue from charge sales. The debit records the resulting increase in accounts receivable.

When posting several journals to ledger accounts, you should indicate in the Posting Reference column to the left of each posted amount the journal and the page number of the journal from which the amount was posted. Indicate the journal by using its initial. Thus, items posted from the Cash Disbursements Journal carry the initial *D* before their journal page numbers in the Posting Reference columns. Likewise, items from the Cash Receipts Journal carry the letter *R*. Those from the Sales Journal carry the initial *S*. Items from the Purchases Journal carry the initial *P*, and from the General Journal, the letter *G*.

Identifying Posted Amounts

A Cash Receipts Journal that is designed to save labour through posting column totals must be a multicolumn journal. A multicolumn journal is necessary because different accounts are credited when cash is received from different sources. For example, the cash receipts of a store normally fall into three groups: (1) cash from credit customers in payment of their accounts, (2) cash from cash sales, and (3) cash from miscellaneous sources. Note in Illustration 6–5 that a special column is provided for the credits that result when cash is received from each of these sources.

Cash Receipts Journal

Cash from Credit Customers

When a Cash Receipts Journal similar to Illustration 6–5 is used to record cash received in payment of a customer's account, the customer's name is entered in the Journal's Account Credited column. The amount credited to the customer's account is entered in the Accounts Receivable Credit column, and the debits to Sales Discounts and Cash are entered in the journal's last two columns.

Look at the Accounts Receivable Credit column. First, observe that this column contains only credits to customer accounts. Second, the individual credits are posted daily to the customer accounts in the subsidiary Accounts Receivable Ledger. Third, the column total is posted at the end of the month as a credit to the Accounts Receivable controlling account. This is the normal recording and posting procedure when using special journals and controlling accounts with subsidiary ledgers. Transactions are normally entered in a special journal column and the individual amounts are then posted to the subsidiary ledger accounts and the column totals are posted to the general ledger accounts.

Cash Sales

After cash sales are entered on one or more cash registers and totaled at the end of each day, the daily total is recorded with a debit to Cash and a credit to Sales. When using a Cash Receipts Journal like Illustration 6–5, enter the

ILLUSTRATION 6-5

Cash Receipts Journal

	Account Credited	Explanation	PR	Other Accounts Credit	Accts. Rec. Credit	Sales Credit	Sales Discounts Debit	Cash Debit
Date								

Cash Receipts Journal — Page 2

Date	Account Credited	Explanation	PR	Other Accounts Credit	Accts. Rec. Credit	Sales Credit	Sales Discounts Debit	Cash Debit
Feb. 7	Sales	Cash sales	✓			4,450.00		4,450.00
12	James Henry	Invoice, 2/2	✓		450.00		9.00	441.00
14	Sales	Cash sales	✓			3,925.00		3,925.00
20	Notes Payable . . .	Note to bank	245	1,000.00				1,000.00
21	Sales	Cash sales	✓			4,700.00		4,700.00
23	Sam Moore.	Invoice, 13/2	✓		350.00		7.00	343.00
25	Paul Roth.	Invoice, 15/2	✓		200.00		4.00	196.00
27	Albert Smith	Invoice, 7/2	✓		500.00			500.00
28	Sales	Cash sales	✓			4,225.00		4,225.00
28	Totals			1,000.00	1,500.00	17,300.00	20.00	19,780.00
				(✓)	(106)	(413)	(415)	(101)

Individual amounts in the Other Accounts Credit and Accounts Receivable Credit columns are posted daily.

Total is not posted.

Totals posted at the end of the month.

Accounts Receivable Ledger

Frank Booth

Date	PR	Debit	Credit	Balance
Feb. 25	S3	175.00		175.00

James Henry

Date	PR	Debit	Credit	Balance
Feb. 2	S3	450.00		450.00
12	R2		450.00	–0–
22	S3	225.00		225.00

Sam Moore

Date	PR	Debit	Credit	Balance
Feb. 13	S3	350.00		350.00
23	R2		350.00	–0–

Paul Roth

Date	PR	Debit	Credit	Balance
Feb. 15	S3	200.00		200.00
25	R2		200.00	–0–

Albert Smith

Date	PR	Debit	Credit	Balance
Feb. 7	S3	500.00		500.00
27	R2		500.00	–0–
28	S3	250.00		250.00

General Ledger

Cash — No. 101

Date	PR	Debit	Credit	Balance
Feb. 28	R2	19,780.00		19,780.00

Accounts Receivable — No. 106

Date	PR	Debit	Credit	Balance
Feb. 28	S3	2,150.00		2,150.00
28	R2		1,500.00	650.00

Notes Payable — No. 245

Date	PR	Debit	Credit	Balance
Feb. 20	R2		1,000.00	1,000.00

Sales — No. 413

Date	PR	Debit	Credit	Balance
Feb. 28	S3		2,150.00	2,150.00
28	R2		17,300.00	19,450.00

Sales Discounts — No. 415

Date	PR	Debit	Credit	Balance
Feb. 28	R2	20.00		20.00

debits to Cash in the Cash Debit column, and the credits in a special column headed Sales Credit. By using a separate Sales Credit column, you can post the total cash sales for a month as a single amount, the column total. (Although cash sales are normally journalized daily based on the cash register reading, cash sales are journalized only once each week in Illustration 6–5 to shorten the illustration.)

At the time they record daily cash sales in the Cash Receipts Journal, some bookkeepers, as in Illustration 6–5, place a check mark in the Posting Reference (PR) column to indicate that no amount is individually posted from that line of the journal. Other bookkeepers use a double check ($\sqrt{}\sqrt{}$) to distinguish amounts that are not posted to customer accounts from amounts that are posted.

Miscellaneous Receipts of Cash

Most cash receipts are from collections of accounts receivable and from cash sales. However, other sources of cash include borrowing money from a bank or selling unneeded assets. The Other Accounts Credit column is for receipts that do not occur often enough to warrant a separate column. In most companies, the items entered in this column are few and are posted to a variety of general ledger accounts. As a result, postings are less apt to be omitted if these items are posted daily.

The Cash Receipts Journal's Posting Reference column is used only for daily postings from the Other Accounts and Accounts Receivable columns. The account numbers in the Posting Reference column indicate items that were posted to general ledger accounts. The check marks indicate either that an item (like a day's cash sales) was not posted or that an item was posted to the subsidiary Accounts Receivable Ledger.

Month-End Postings

At the end of the month, the amounts in the Accounts Receivable, Sales, Sales Discounts, and Cash columns of the Cash Receipts Journal are posted as column totals. However, the transactions recorded in any journal must result in equal debits and credits to general ledger accounts. Therefore, to be sure that the total debits and credits in a columnar journal are equal, you must *crossfoot* the column totals before posting them. To *foot* a column of numbers is to add it. To crossfoot, add the debit column totals and add the credit column totals; then compare the two sums for equality. For Illustration 6–5, the two sums appear as follows:

Debit Columns		Credit Columns	
Sales discounts debit	$ 30	Other accounts credit	$ 1,000
Cash debit.	19,770	Accounts receivable credit	1,500
		Sales credit	17,300
Total	$19,800	Total	$19,800

Because the sums are equal, you may assume that the debits in the journal equal the credits.

After crossfooting the journal to confirm that debits equal credits, post the totals of the last four columns as indicated in each column heading. As for the Other Accounts column, do not post the column total because the individual items in this column are posted daily. Note in Illustration 6–5 the check mark below the Other Accounts column. The check mark indicates that the column total was not posted. The account numbers of the accounts to which the remaining column totals were posted are in parentheses below each column.

Posting items daily from the Other Accounts column with a delayed posting of the offsetting items in the Cash column (total) causes the General Ledger to be out of balance during the month. However, this does not matter because posting the Cash column total causes the offsetting amounts to reach the General Ledger before the trial balance is prepared.

Posting Rule

Now that we have explained the procedures for posting from two different journals to a subsidiary ledger and its controlling account, the rule that governs all such postings should be clear. This is the rule for posting to a subsidiary ledger and its controlling account: *The controlling account must be debited periodically for an amount or amounts equal to the sum of the debits to the subsidiary ledger, and the controlling account must be credited periodically for an amount or amounts equal to the sum of the credits to the subsidiary ledger.*

Purchases Journal

You can use a Purchases Journal with one money column to record purchases of merchandise on account. However, a Purchases Journal usually is more useful if it is a multicolumn journal in which all credit purchases on account are recorded. Such a journal may have columns similar to those in Illustration 6–6. In the illustrated journal, the invoice date and terms together indicate the date on which payment for each purchase is due. The Accounts Payable Credit column is used to record the amounts credited to each creditor's account. These amounts are posted daily to the individual creditor accounts in a subsidiary Accounts Payable Ledger.

In Illustration 6–6, note that each line of the Account column shows the subsidiary ledger account that should be posted for the amount in the Accounts Payable Credit column. The Account column also shows the general ledger account to be debited when a purchase involves an amount recorded in the Other Accounts Debit column. If the Accounts Payable Credit column is limited to trade accounts, such purchases as equipment, buildings, and so on, would be recorded in the General Journal.

In this illustration, note the separate column for purchases of office supplies on account. A separate column such as this is useful whenever several transactions involve debits to a particular account. The Other Accounts Debit column in Illustration 6–6 allows the Purchases Journal to be used for all purchase transactions involving credits to Accounts Payable. The individual amounts in the Other Accounts Debit column typically are posted daily to the indicated General Ledger accounts.

ILLUSTRATION 6–6

Purchases Journal

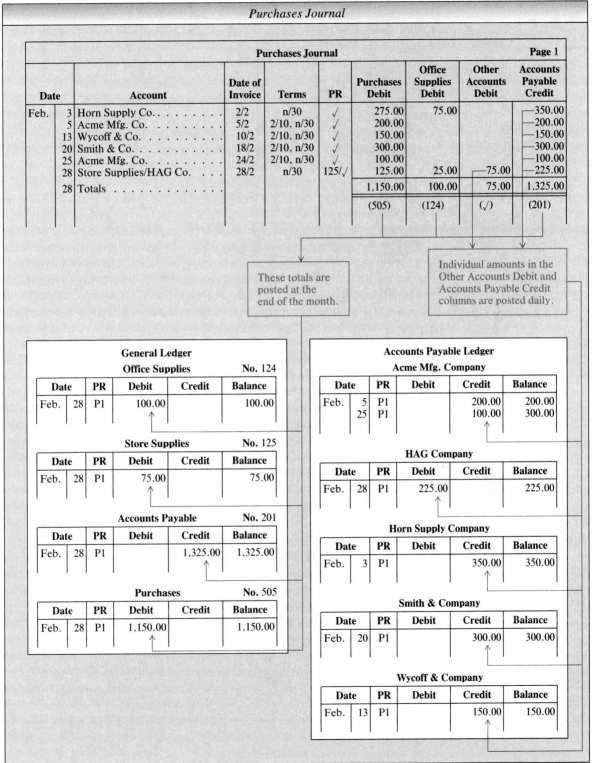

At the end of the month, all of the column totals except the Other Accounts Debit column are posted to the appropriate General Ledger accounts. After this is done, the balance in the Accounts Payable controlling account should equal the sum of the account balances in the subsidiary Accounts Payable Ledger.

The Cash Disbursements Journal or Cheque Register

The Cash Disbursements Journal, like the Cash Receipts Journal, has columns so that you can post repetitive debits and credits in column totals. The repetitive cash payments involve debits to the Accounts Payable controlling account and credits to both Purchases Discounts and Cash. Most companies usually purchase merchandise on account. Therefore, a Purchases column is not needed. Instead, the occasional cash purchase is recorded as shown on line 2 of Illustration 6–7.

Observe that the illustrated journal has a column headed Cheque Number (Ck. No.). To gain control over cash disbursements, all payments except for very small amounts should be made by cheque.[1] The cheques should be prenumbered by the printer and should be entered in the journal in numerical order with each cheque's number in the column headed Ck. No. This makes it possible to scan the numbers in the column for omitted cheques. When a Cash Disbursements Journal has a column for cheque numbers, it is often called a **Cheque Register.**

To post a Cash Disbursements Journal or Cheque Register similar to Illustration 6–7, do the following. Each day, post the individual amounts in the Other Accounts Debit column to the appropriate general ledger accounts. Also on a daily basis, post the individual amounts in the Accounts Payable Debit column to the named creditors' accounts in the subsidiary Accounts Payable Ledger. At the end of the month, after you crossfoot the column totals, post the Accounts Payable Debit column total to the Accounts Payable controlling account. Then post the Purchases Discounts Credit column total to the Purchases Discounts account and post the Cash Credit column total to the Cash account. Because the items in the Other Accounts column are posted individually, do not post the column total.

Testing the Accuracy of the Ledgers

Periodically, after all posting is completed, the account balances in the General Ledger and the subsidiary ledgers should be tested for accuracy. To do this, first prepare a trial balance of the General Ledger to confirm that debits equal credits. If the trial balance balances, that is, the total debits equal the total credits, the accounts in the General Ledger, including the controlling accounts, are assumed to be correct. Then test the subsidiary ledgers by preparing schedules of accounts receivable and accounts payable.

---

[1] In Chapter 7, we discuss a system that controls small payments made with currency and coins.

ILLUSTRATION 6–7

Cash Disbursements Journal

Date	Ch. No.	Payee	Account Debited	PR	Other Accounts Debit	Accounts Payable Debit	Purchases Discounts Credit	Cash Credit
Feb. 3	105	L. & N. Railroad . . .	Transportation-In . . .	508	15.00			15.00
12	106	East Sales Co.	Purchases	505	25.00			25.00
15	107	Acme Mfg. Co.	Acme Mfg. Co.	✓		200.00	4.00	196.00
15	108	Jerry Hale	Salaries Expense . . .	622	250.00			250.00
20	109	Wycoff & Co.	Wycoff & Co.	✓		150.00	3.00	147.00
28	110	Smith & Co.	Smith & Co.	✓		300.00	6.00	294.00
28		Totals			290.00	650.00	13.00	927.00
					(✓)	(201)	(507)	(101)

Page 2

Individual amounts in the Other Accounts Debit column and Accounts Payable Debit column are posted daily.

Totals posted at the end of the month.

Accounts Payable Ledger

Acme Mfg. Company

Date	PR	Debit	Credit	Balance
Feb. 5	P1		200.00	200.00
15	D2	200.00		–0–
25	P1		100.00	100.00

HAG Company

Date	PR	Debit	Credit	Balance
Feb. 28	P1		225.00	225.00

Horn Supply Company

Date	PR	Debit	Credit	Balance
Feb. 3	P1		350.00	350.00

Smith & Company

Date	PR	Debit	Credit	Balance
Feb. 20	P1		300.00	300.00
28	D2	300.00		–0–

Wycoff & Company

Date	PR	Debit	Credit	Balance
Feb. 13	P1		150.00	150.00
20	D2	150.00		–0–

General Ledger

Cash   No. 101

Date	PR	Debit	Credit	Balance
Feb. 28	R2	19,770.00		19,770.00
28	D2		927.00	18,843.00

Accounts Payable   No. 201

Date	PR	Debit	Credit	Balance
Feb. 28	P1		1,325.00	1,325.00
28	D2	650.00		675.00

Purchases   No. 505

Date	PR	Debit	Credit	Balance
Feb. 12	D2	25.00		25.00
28	P1	1,150.00		1,175.00

Purchases Discounts   No. 507

Date	PR	Debit	Credit	Balance
Feb. 28	D2		13.00	13.00

Transportation-In   No. 508

Date	PR	Debit	Credit	Balance
Feb. 3	D2	15.00		15.00

Salaries Expense   No. 622

Date	PR	Debit	Credit	Balance
Feb. 15	D2	250.00		250.00

ILLUSTRATION 6-8

Schedule of Accounts Payable, December 31, 19—

Acme Mfg. Company	$100
HAG Company	225
Horn Supply Company	350
Total accounts payable	$675

LO 5 Explain how to test the accuracy of the account balances in the Accounts Receivable and Accounts Payable subsidiary ledgers and prepare schedules of accounts in those subsidiary ledgers.

To prepare a **schedule of accounts payable,** for example, list the accounts in the Accounts Payable Ledger with their balances and calculate the sum of the balances. If the total is equal to the balance of the Accounts Payable controlling account, you can assume the accounts in the Accounts Payable Ledger are correct. Illustration 6–8 shows a schedule of accounts payable drawn from the Accounts Payable Ledger of Illustration 6–7.

You prepare a **schedule of accounts receivable** in the same way as a schedule of accounts payable. Also, if its total equals the balance of the Accounts Receivable controlling account, you can assume the accounts in the Accounts Receivable Ledger are correct.

Sales and Goods and Services Taxes

LO 6 Explain how sales and goods and services taxes are recorded in special journals, how sales invoices can serve as a Sales Journal, and how sales returns and allowances are recorded.

Provincial Sales Tax

All provinces except Alberta require retailers to collect a provincial sales tax (PST) from their customers and periodically to remit this tax to the appropriate provincial authority. When special journals are used, a column is provided for PST in the Sales Journal and the Cash Receipts Journal. A record of PST is obtained by recording in the PST column the appropriate amount of PST on cash sales (Cash Receipts Journal) and sales on account (Sales Journal). It should be noted that not all sales are subject to PST.

Goods and Services Tax

The goods and services tax (GST) is a 7% tax on almost all goods and services provided in Canada. It is a federal tax on the consumer. However, unlike the PST, businesses pay GST up front, but generally receive a full credit or refund for all GST paid. Ultimately, only the final consumer bears the burden of this tax. This is because businesses collect GST on sales, but since they receive full credit for GST paid on their purchases, they only remit the difference to the appropriate federal authority. To illustrate the collection and payment of GST consider the following example.

LM Company assembles riding mowers. It pays $200 for materials which are subject to GST of $14. LM pays the $14 to its suppliers who remit the $14 to Revenue Canada. LM now has a $14 GST credit, that is, prepaid GST.

LM sells the mower to KD Company, a dealer, for $500 and collects $35 in GST. LM remits the $35, minus the $14 input credit, that is, the GST paid to its suppliers. KD now has a $35 GST credit, that is, prepaid GST.

KD sells the mower to CC, the consumer, for $800 and collects $56 in GST. KD remits the $56, minus the $35 GST credit to Revenue Canada.

To summarize:

	GST Paid	GST Collected	GST Remitted
Materials supplier		$14	$14
LM Company	$14	35	21
KD Company	35	56	21
CC (the consumer)	56		$56

The total GST remitted is $56, the same amount that CC, the consumer, paid. The supplier and LM and KD companies act as collection agents, collecting the tax along each stage of the process.

To facilitate the recording of GST, special GST (credit) columns must be provided not only in the Sales Journal and the Cash Receipts Journal, as in the case of PST, but also debit GST columns in the Purchases Journal and Cash Disbursements Journal. To illustrate, assume that Berlasty Company uses specialized journals shown in Illustration 6–9. The following transactions were completed and recorded during December:

Dec. 1   Purchases on account, $1,000 from Jason Supply, terms n/30.
      3   Paid transportation on the Dec. 1 purchase, $30.
      9   Purchases for cash, $500.
    15   Cash sale, $1,200 (subject to PST and GST).
    28   Paid for the Dec. 1 purchase.
    30   Sales to S. Burns on account, $2,000 ($1,500 subject to PST and $2,000 subject to GST).

After the posting is completed, as described earlier in the chapter, the PST and GST T-accounts would appear as follows:

PST (530)			GST (531)		
SJ	120.00	PJ	70.00	SJ	140.00
CRJ	96.00	CDJ	37.10	CRS	84.00

On December 31, PST payable amounts to $216 and GST payable amounts to $116.90. The computation of GST is not uniform throughout the country. In some of the provinces, the computation is as illustrated above, that is, PST and GST are computed as a percentage of the selling price. In other provinces, PST is initially computed as a percentage of the selling price and GST is computed as a percentage of the total of the selling price plus the PST. It should also be noted that while GST is a 7% federal tax, thus uniform in each of the provinces, PST is a provincial tax and differs in percentage from province to province. The preceding discussion is based on Ontario's PST of 8%.

In Illustration 6–9, one account was used to record GST on purchases and on sales. Some accountants prefer to record GST on purchases in a Prepaid GST account and GST on sales in a GST Payable account. Thus, if two accounts are used in Illustration 6–9, the GST Payable Debit column in the Purchases Journal and the Cash Disbursements Journal would be changed to Pre-

ILLUSTRATION 6–9

Special Journals with PST and GST Columns as Applicable

Purchases Journal

Date		Account Credited	Terms	PR	Accounts Payable Credit	Purchases Debit	Office Supplies Debit	GST Payable Debit
Dec.	1	Jason Supply	n/30		1,070.00	1,000.00		70.00
								70.00
								(531)

Cash Disbursements Journal

Date	Ch. No.	Account Debited	PR	Other Accounts Debit	GST Payable Debit	Accts. Payable Debit	Purch. Disc. Credit	Cash Credit
Dec. 3	256	Transportation-in		30.00	2.10			32.10
9	257	Purchases		500.00	35.00			535.00
28	258	Accts. Pay/Jason Supply				1,070.00		1,070.00
				530.00	37.10	1,070.00		1,637.10
					(531)			

Sales Journal

Date		Account Debited	Invoice No.	PR	Acct. Rec. Debit	PST Payable Credit	GST Payable Credit	Sales Credit
Dec.	30	S. Burns	2734		2,260.00	120.00	140.00	2,000.00
						(530)	(531)	

Cash Receipts Journal

Date		Account Credited	Explanation	PR	Other Accounts Credit	Accts. Rec. Credit	PST Payable Credit	GST Payable Credit	Sales Credit	Cash Debit
Dec.	15						96.00	84.00	1,200.00	1,380.00
							(530)	(531)		

paid GST. The Sales Journal and the Cash Receipts Journal would remain as illustrated. The use of one or two accounts to account for GST is a matter of preference, the final result is the same.

Remittance of GST

The GST is administered by Revenue Canada Customs and Excise. Remittance is accompanied by a Goods and Services Tax Return shown in Illustration 6–10.

ILLUSTRATION 6–10

Goods and Services Tax Return

Revenue Canada | **Revenu Canada**
Customs and Excise | Douanes et Accise

PROTECTED WHEN COMPLETED
PROTÉGE UNE FOIS REMPLI

GOODS AND SERVICES TAX RETURN (Non-personalized)
DÉCLARATION DE LA TAXE SUR LES PRODUITS ET SERVICES (non personnalisée)

Prescribed by the Minister of National Revenue under subsection 238(4) of the Excise Tax Act / Prescrit par le ministre du Revenu national en vertu du paragraphe 238(4) de la Loi sur la taxe d'accise

This return is for use by a GST registrant, or by a person who is required to remit tax where a personalized return is not available for the reporting period.
Cette formule doit être utilisée par les inscrits ou par toute personne tenue de verser la taxe lorsqu'une déclaration personnalisée n'est pas disponible pour la période de déclaration.

● To complete this form, please refer to the Instructions on the back.
Pour remplir cette formule, voir les renseignements au verso de la déclaration.

GST Account Number / Numéro de compte TPS: A 1 2 3 4 9 7 3 4

Reporting Period / Période de déclaration
From/du: Y-A 9 2 1 M 0 0 D-J 0 1   To/au: Y-A 9 2 1 M 2 3 D-J 3 1

Due Date / Date d'échéance: Y-A 9 3 0 M 1 D-J 3 1

Name of Individual or Entity / Raison sociale ou nom: BERLASTY COMPANY

Trading Name if Different from Above / Nom commercial s'il diffère de la raison sociale ou du nom:

Mailing Address (No., Street and Apt. Number) / Adresse postale (n°, rue, app.): 125 SUNSET AVENUE

City / Ville: WINDSOR

Province: ONTARIO

Postal Code / Code postal: N9B 3P4

Name of the person we may contact concerning your return / Nom de la personne avec qui nous pouvons communiquer concernant votre déclaration: SANDRA BERLASTY

Telephone No. / N° de téléphone: (519) 253 - 4232

Personal information provided on this form is protected under the provisions of the Privacy Act and is maintained in Personal Information Bank RCC/P-PU-065.

Les renseignements personnels fournis dans cette formule sont protégés en vertu de la Loi sur la protection des renseignements personnels et sont conservés dans le Répertoire des renseignements personnels RND/P-PU-065.

SECTION TWO - TAX CALCULATIONS
PARTIE DEUX - CALCULS DE LA TAXE

GST Collectible / TPS percevable	**103**	2 2 4 0 0
GST Adjustments / Redressements de la TPS	**104**	Ø
Input Tax Credit (ITC) / Crédit de taxe sur les intrants (CTI)	**106**	-1 0 7 1 0
ITC Adjustments / Redressements du CTI	**107**	Ø

SECTION ONE - PERIOD SUMMARY
PARTIE UN - SOMMAIRE DE LA PÉRIODE

Total Taxable Supplies (sales and other revenue) / Total des fournitures taxables (ventes et autres recettes)	**101**	3 2 0 0 0 0
Total Purchases / Total des achats	**102**	1 5 3 0 0 0
Paid by instalments / Payée par acomptes provisionnels	**110**	Ø
Rebates / Remboursements	**111**	Ø

Add Lines 103 and 104 / Additionnez les montants des lignes 103 et 104	**105**	
Add Lines 106 and 107 / Additionnez les montants des lignes 106 et 107	**108**	
Subtract Line 108 from Line 105 (indicate if negative amount) / Soustrayez le montant de la ligne 108 de celui de la ligne 105 (indiquez s'il s'agit d'un montant négatif)	**109**	
Add Lines 110 and 111 / Additionnez les montants des lignes 110 et 111	**112**	
Subtract Line 112 from Line 109 (indicate if negative amount) / Soustrayez le montant de la ligne 112 de celui de la ligne 109 (indiquez s'il s'agit d'un montant négatif)	**113**	

Total GST and Adjustments for Period / Total de la TPS et des redressements pour cette période: 2 2 4 0 0

Total ITCs and Adjustments / Total du CTI et des redressements: -1 0 7 1 0

NET TAX - TAXE NETTE *: 1 1 6 9 0

Total Other Credits - Total des autres credits: Ø

BALANCE - SOLDE: 1 1 6 9 0

Refund Claimed / Remboursement demandé	**114**	
Payment Enclosed / Paiement inclus	**115**	1 1 6 9 0

OR / OU

If the balance is negative claim a refund, otherwise remit the amount owing. A balance of less than $1.00 will neither be charged nor refunded. All registrants must file a return regardless of the balance. Do not staple or paper clip.

Si le montant du solde est négatif, demandez un remboursement. S'il est positif, vous devez remettre le montant inscrit. Les soldes inférieurs à 1,00 $ ne sont ni exigés ni remboursés. Tous les inscrits doivent produire une déclaration, peu importe le montant du solde. N'utilisez ni agrafes ni trombones.

I hereby certify that the information given in this return and in any documents attached is true, correct and complete in every respect and that I am authorized to sign on behalf of the registrant.

J'atteste que les renseignements fournis dans cette déclaration et dans tout document qui y serait joint sont vrais, exacts et complets sous tous les rapports et que je suis autorisé à signer au nom de l'inscrit.

► IT IS A SERIOUS OFFENCE TO MAKE A FALSE RETURN.
LA PRODUCTION D'UNE DÉCLARATION FAUSSE EST UNE INFRACTION GRAVE.

Name / Nom: Sandra Berlasty

Title / Titre: Treasurer

Authorized Signature / Signature autorisée: Sandra Berlasty

Date: January 31, 1993

PART 1: DETACH AND FORWARD TO PROCESSING CENTRE
PARTIE 1: DÉTACHEZ ET FAITES PARVENIR AU CENTRE DE TRAITEMENT DES DONNÉES

GST 62 (90/11)

Frequency of filing returns is dependent on the size of the business. Large businesses (annual sales in excess of $6 million) are required to file GST returns monthly. Medium size businesses (annual sales of $500,000 to $6 million) are required to file quarterly. Small businesses (annual sales up to $500,000) have the option of filing annually but paying quarterly instalments. GST for a period must be remitted to Revenue Canada by the end of the month following the month (quarter) collected.

Sales Invoices as a Sales Journal

To save labour, some retailers avoid using Sales Journals for credit sales. Instead, they post each sales invoice total directly to the customer's account in a subsidiary Accounts Receivable Ledger. Then they place copies of the invoices in numerical order in a binder. At the end of the month, they total all the invoices of that month and make a General Journal entry to debit Accounts Receivable and credit Sales, PST, and GST for the appropriate totals. In effect, the bound invoice copies act as a Sales Journal. Such a procedure is known as *direct posting of sales invoices*.

Sales Returns

A business that has only a few sales returns may record them in a General Journal with an entry like the following:

Oct.	17	Sales Returns and Allowances.	414	17.50	
		Accounts Receivable—George Ball	106/√		17.50
		Customer returned merchandise.			

The debit of the entry is posted to the Sales Returns and Allowances account. The credit is posted to both the Accounts Receivable controlling account and the customer's account. Note the account number and the check mark, 106/√, in the PR column on the credit line. This indicates that both the Accounts Receivable controlling account in the General Ledger and the George Ball account in the Accounts Receivable Ledger were credited for $17.50. Both were credited because the balance of the controlling account in the General Ledger will not equal the sum of the customer account balances in the subsidiary ledger unless both are credited.

A company with a large number of sales returns can save posting labour by recording them in a special Sales Returns and Allowances Journal similar to Illustration 6–11. Note that this is in keeping with the idea that a company can design and use a special journal for any group of similar transactions if there are enough transactions to warrant the journal. When using a Sales Returns and Allowances Journal to record returns, the amounts in the journal are posted daily to the customers' accounts. Then, at the end of the month, the journal total is posted as a debit to Sales Returns and Allowances and as a credit to Accounts Receivable.

ILLUSTRATION 6-11

Sales Returns and Allowances Journal								
Date	Account Credited	Explanation	Credit Memo No.	PR	PST Payable Dr.	GST Payable Dr.	Sales Re- turn and Allow. Dr.	Acct. Rec. Cr.
Oct. 7	Robert Moore. .	Defective merchandise .	203	√	2.40	2.10	30.00	34.50
14	James Warren. .	Defective merchandise .	204	√	.80	.70	10.00	11.50
18	T. M. Jones . . .	Not ordered.	205	√	1.60	1.40	20.00	23.00
23	Sam Smith . . .	Defective merchandise .	206	√	3.20	2.80	40.00	46.00

General Journal Entries

When special journals are used, a General Journal is always necessary for adjusting, closing, and correcting entries and for a few transactions that cannot be recorded in the special journals. If a Sales Returns and Allowances Journal is not provided, some of these transactions are sales returns, purchases returns, and purchases of plant assets.

Summary of the Chapter in Terms of Learning Objectives

LO 1. The five components of accounting systems are source documents, input devices, the data processor, data storage, and output devices. Both manual and computerized systems must have all five components.

LO 2. There are many different ways to set up computer systems, including small and large systems, self-developed and off-the-shelf programming, batch and on-line processing, and computer networks.

LO 3. Columnar journals are designed so that repetitive debits to a specific account are entered in a separate column. The same is done for repetitive credits. As a result, the column totals can be posted as single amounts, thereby eliminating the need to post individually each debit and credit.

Companies that use special journals enter all credit sales in a Sales Journal. Purchases on account are entered in a Purchases Journal. All cash receipts are entered in the Cash Receipts Journal and all cash payments by cheque are entered in the Cash Disbursements Journal (or Cheque Register). Any transactions that cannot be entered in the special journals are entered in the General Journal.

When posting transactions from special journals to the accounts, post individual debits and credits to subsidiary Accounts Receivable and Accounts Payable Ledgers daily. Other amounts that must be posted individually also may be posted daily. Normally, the columns of each special journal are totaled and crossfooted at the end of each month. Then the column totals are posted to the appropriate General Ledger accounts.

LO 4. When many accounts of the same type are required, such as an account receivable for each credit customer, they usually are kept in a separate subsidiary ledger. Then a single controlling account is maintained in the General Ledger. After all transactions are posted to the accounts in the subsidiary ledger and to the controlling account, the controlling account balance should equal the sum of the account balances in the subsidiary ledger.

LO 5. To test the accuracy of a subsidiary ledger after all posting is completed, you should prepare a schedule of the accounts in the ledger and compare the total of the account balances with the balance in the related controlling account. If they are not equal, you know an error has been made. If they are equal, you assume the balances are correct.

LO 6. To record provincial sales taxes, the Sales Journal and the Cash Receipts Journal should include a separate Credit PST Payable column. To record the federal goods and services tax, all the special journals should include a separate GST Payable column (credit in the Sales Journal and the Cash Receipts Journal and debit in the Purchases Journal and the Cash Disbursements Journal). When sales invoices substitute for a Sales Journal, the customer accounts in the Accounts Receivable Ledger are posted directly from the sales invoices. Copies of the invoices for each month are then bound and totaled as a basis for recording the sales in the General Ledger. Sales returns and allowances may be recorded in the General Journal, or a special journal for sales returns and allowances may be used.

Glossary

LO 7 Define or explain the words and phrases listed in the chapter glossary.

Accounting system the people, forms, procedures, and equipment that are used to capture data about the transactions of an entity and to generate from that data a variety of financial, managerial, and tax accounting reports. pp. 302–306

Accounts Payable Ledger a subsidiary ledger that contains a separate account for each party that grants credit on account to the entity. pp. 313–14

Accounts Receivable Subsidiary Ledger a subsidiary ledger that contains an account for each credit customer. p. 313

Batch processing an approach to inputting data that accumulates source documents for a period of time such as a day, week, or month and inputs all of them at the same time. p. 310

Cheque Register a book of original entry for recording cash payments by cheque. p. 320

Columnar journal a book of original entry having columns, each of which is designated as the place for entering specific data about each transaction of a group of similar transactions. p. 311

Computer network a system in which computers are linked with each other so that different users on different computers can share access to the same data and the same programs. p. 310

Controlling account a General ledger account the balance of which (after posting) equals the sum of the balances of the accounts in a related subsidiary ledger. p. 313

Data processor the component of an accounting system that interprets, manipulates, and summarizes the recorded information so that it can be used in analyses and reports. p. 304

Data storage the component of an accounting system that keeps the inputted data in a readily accessible manner so that financial reports can be drawn from it efficiently. p. 305

General Ledger the ledger that contains the financial statement accounts of a business. p. 313

Input device a means of transferring information from source documents to the data processing component of an accounting system. pp. 303–304

On-line processing an approach to inputting data whereby the data on each source document is inputted as soon as the document is available. p. 310

Output devices the means by which information is taken out of the accounting system and made available for use. pp. 305–306

Schedule of accounts payable a list of the balances of all the accounts in the Accounts Payable Ledger that is summed to show the total amount of accounts payable outstanding. p. 322

Schedule of accounts receivable a list of the balances of all the accounts in the Accounts Receivable Ledger that is summed to show the total amount of accounts receivable outstanding. p. 322

Special journal a book of original entry that is designed and used for recording only a specified type of transaction. pp. 310–12

Subsidiary ledger a group of accounts that show the details underlying the balance of a controlling account in the General Ledger. p. 313

Objective Review

Answers to the following questions are listed at the end of this chapter. Be sure that you decide which is the one best answer to each question *before* you check the answers.

LO 1 In a computer-based accounting system, which basic component of the system is likely to include a hard disk located in the computer?

a. Source documents.
b. Input device.
c. Data processor.
d. Data storage.
e. Output devices.

LO 2 In a computer-based accounting system:

a. The accounting software is more efficient if it operates as an integrated system.
b. Bookkeeping tasks take somewhat more time than they do with a manual system.
c. Data about transactions must be entered with on-line processing.
d. The accountant must have the ability to program the computer.
e. None of the above is correct.

LO 3 When special journals are used:

a. A General Journal is not used.
b. All cash payments by cheque are recorded in the Cash Disbursements Journal.
c. All purchase transactions are recorded in the Purchases Journal.
d. All sales transactions are recorded in the Sales Journal.
e. All cash receipts except from cash sales of merchandise are recorded in the Cash Receipts Journal.

LO 4 If an accounting system includes an Accounts Receivable controlling account and an Accounts Receivable Ledger:

a. Two accounts are debited when posting sales on account.
b. The rule that debits must equal credits is not maintained.
c. Two accounts are debited when posting cash sales.
d. Two accounts are credited when posting cash receipts from credit customers.
e. Both (*a*) and (*d*) are correct.

LO 5 A schedule of accounts receivable:

a. Serves as the means of data storage with respect to the amounts customers owe to the entity.
b. May be prepared at any point during an accounting period for the purpose of testing the equality of the General Ledger Accounts Receivable account balance and the sum of the account balances in the subsidiary ledger.
c. Should, if all transactions have been correctly posted, disclose a total amount equal to the total amount of credit sales made during the period.
d. Should, if all transactions have been correctly posted, disclose a total amount equal to the balance of the General Ledger Accounts Receivable account.
e. None of the above is correct.

LO 6 If provincial sales taxes must be recorded and special journals are used:

a. The provincial sales taxes must be recorded in the General Journal.

b. A separate column for provincial sales taxes should be included in the Cash Disbursements Journal.

c. A separate column for provincial sales taxes should be included in the Purchases Journal.

d. A special PST and GST Journal should be used.

e. None of the above is correct.

---

1. What advantages do computer systems offer over manual systems?
2. What are the five basic components of an accounting system?
3. What are source documents? Give some examples.
4. What is the purpose of an input device? Give some examples of input devices for computer systems.
5. What does the data processor component of a system accomplish?
6. The data processor of a computer system consists of two subcomponents. What are they?
7. What uses are made of the data that is stockpiled in the data storage of an accounting system?
8. What is a computer program?
9. How does a columnar journal save posting labour?
10. When special journals are used, separate special journals normally are used to record each of four different types of transactions. What are these four types of transactions?
11. Why should sales to, and receipts of cash from, credit customers be recorded and posted daily?
12. Both credits to customer accounts and credits to miscellaneous accounts are individually posted from a Cash Receipts Journal similar to the one in Illustration 6–5. Why not put both kinds of credits in the same column and thus save journal space?
13. What procedures allow copies of a company's sales invoices to be used as a Sales Journal?
14. When a general journal entry is used to record a returned credit sale, the credit of the entry must be posted twice. Does this cause the trial balance to be out of balance? Why or why not?
15. How does one tell from which journal a particular amount in a ledger account was posted?

Questions for Class
Discussion

Mini Discussion Case

Case 6–1

Two students were discussing the similarities and dissimillarities of manual and computerized accounting systems. Their discussion focused on the following:

a. Recording of data—use of specialized journals, and so on.
b. Processing of data—posting, and so on.
c. Necessity and function of trial balance.
d. Problems of tracing entries in connection with verification and tracing of errors.

Required

Present your comparison of the two systems, focusing on the four areas given in the case.

Exercises

Exercise 6–1
Special journals
(LO 3)

A company uses a Sales Journal, a Purchases Journal, a Cash Receipts Journal, a Cash Disbursements Journal, and a General Journal like the ones described in the chapter. The company recently completed the following transactions. List the transactions by letter, and opposite each letter give the name of the journal in which the transaction would be recorded.

a. Purchased merchandise on account.
b. Gave a customer credit for merchandise purchased on account and returned.
c. Purchased office equipment and signed a promissory note for the purchase price.
d. Sold merchandise for cash.
e. A customer paid for merchandise previously purchased on credit.
f. Sold merchandise on account.
g. Recorded adjusting and closing entries.
h. Returned merchandise purchased on account.
i. Purchased office supplies on account.
j. Paid a creditor.
k. A customer returned merchandise sold for cash; a cheque was issued.

Exercise 6–2
The Sales Journal
(LO 3)

A company uses a Sales Journal, a Purchases Journal, a Cash Receipts Journal, a Cash Disbursements Journal, and a General Journal. The following transactions occurred during April:

Apr. 1 Purchased merchandise for $460 on account from Trader Company.
     3 Sold merchandise to O. Neville for $280 cash, Invoice No. 1511.
     6 Sold merchandise to R. Davis for $1,200; terms 2/10, n/60; Invoice No. 1512.
     7 Borrowed $2,500 from the bank by giving a note to the bank.

Apr. 9 Sold merchandise to G. Hoffman for $810, terms n/30, Invoice No. 1513.

15 Received $1,176 from R. Davis to pay for the purchase of April 6.

26 Sold used store equipment to Barker Company for $620.

29 Sold merchandise to M. Rogers for $280, terms n/30, Invoice No. 1514.

Required

On a sheet of notebook paper, draw a Sales Journal like the one that appears in Illustration 6–3. Journalize the April transactions that should be recorded in the Sales Journal.

A company uses a Sales Journal, a Purchases Journal, a Cash Receipts Journal, a Cash Disbursements Journal, and a General Journal. The following transactions occurred during October:

Exercise 6–3
The Cash Receipts Journal
(LO 3)

Oct. 2 F. Ray, the owner of the business, invested $7,000 in the business.

5 Purchased merchandise for $4,300 on account from TQ Company.

11 Sold merchandise on account to D. Parker for $3,750, subject to a $75 sales discount if paid by the end of the month.

14 Borrowed $1,500 from the bank by giving a note to the bank.

15 Sold merchandise to T. Sharpe for $240 cash.

19 Paid TQ Company $4,300 for the merchandise purchased on October 5.

28 Received $3,675 from D. Parker to pay for the purchase of October 11.

31 Paid salaries of $900.

Required

1. On a sheet of notebook paper, draw a multicolumn Cash Receipts Journal like the one that appears in Illustration 6–5.

2. Journalize the October transactions that should be recorded in the Cash Receipts Journal.

A company uses a Sales Journal, a Purchases Journal, a Cash Receipts Journal, a Cash Disbursements Journal, and a General Journal. The following transactions occurred during May:

Exercise 6–4
The Purchases Journal
(LO 3)

May 2 B. Wolfe, the owner of the business, invested $8,000 in the business.

4 Purchased merchandise for $4,400 on account from Isle Company, terms n/30.

7 Purchased store supplies from Best Company for $60 cash.

9 Sold merchandise on account to H. Sawyer for $900, subject to a $27 sales discount if paid by the end of the month.

12 Purchased on account from P Company office supplies for $90 and store supplies for $175, terms n/30.

19 Sold merchandise to Z. Bennett for $650 cash.

31 Paid Isle Company $4,400 for the merchandise purchased on May 4.

Required

1. On a sheet of notebook paper, draw a multicolumn Purchases Journal like the one that appears in Illustration 6–6.

2. Journalize the May transactions that should be recorded in the Purchases Journal.

334

Part II Processing Accounting Data

Exercise 6–5
The Cash Disbursements Journal
(LO 3)

A company uses a Sales Journal, a Purchases Journal, a Cash Receipts Journal, a Cash Disbursements Journal, and a General Journal. The following transactions occurred during August:

Aug. 2 Purchased merchandise for $1,100 on account from Zap Company; terms 2/10, n/30.

4 Purchased merchandise for $3,300 on account from B&B Company; terms 2/15, n/60.

7 Issued Cheque No. 57 to T Company to buy store supplies for $88.

17 Sold merchandise on account to F. Hoyt for $390, terms n/30.

18 Issued Cheque No. 58 for $270 to repay a note payable to State Bank.

19 Issued Cheque No. 59 to B&B Company to pay the amount due for the purchase of August 4, less the discount.

31 Issued Cheque No. 60 to Zap Company to pay the amount due for the purchase of August 2.

31 Paid salary of $1,000 to S. Capra by issuing Cheque No. 61.

Required

1. On a sheet of notebook paper, draw a multicolumn Cash Disbursements Journal like the one that appears in Illustration 6–7.
2. Journalize the August transactions that should be recorded in the Cash Disbursements Journal.

Exercise 6–6
General Journal transactions
(LO 3)

A company uses a Sales Journal, a Purchases Journal, a Cash Receipts Journal, a Cash Disbursements Journal, and a General Journal. The following transactions occurred during January:

Jan. 1 P. Lewis, the owner of the business, invested $12,000 in the business.

4 Purchased merchandise for $7,600 on account from Bay Company; terms 2/10, n/30.

9 P. Lewis, the owner of the business, contributed an automobile worth $16,000 to the business.

11 Issued Cheque No. 141 to V&J Company to buy store supplies for $157.

14 Sold merchandise on account to K. Whalem for $840, terms n/30.

16 Returned $250 of defective merchandise to Bay Company from the purchase on January 4.

22 Issued Cheque No. 142 to Madd Company to pay the $905 due for a purchase of December 20.

25 K. Whalem returned $85 of merchandise originally purchased on August 14.

31 Accrued salaries payable were $750.

Required

Journalize the January transactions that should be recorded in the General Journal.

Exercise 6–7
Special journal transactions
(LO 3)

A company uses the following journals: Sales Journal, Purchases Journal, Cash Receipts Journal, Cash Disbursements Journal, and General Journal. On February 10, the company purchased merchandise priced at $22,700, subject to credit terms of 2/10, n/30. On February 20, the company paid the net amount due. However, in journalizing the payment, the bookkeeper debited Accounts Payable for $22,700 and failed to record the cash discount. Cash was credited for the actual amount paid. In what journals would the February 10 and the February 20 transactions have been recorded? What procedure is likely to discover the error in journalizing the February 20 transaction?

As of the end of June, the Sales Journal of Abilene Company appeared as follows:

Exercise 6–8
Posting to subsidiary
ledger accounts
(LO 3, 4, 5)

Sales Journal

Date		Account Debited	Invoice Number	PR	Amount
June	3	Sheila Lee.	604		845.00
	12	Barbara Lyon	605		630.00
	18	Tomas Cantu.	606		1,280.00
	23	Tomas Cantu.	607		460.00
	30	Total.			3,215.00

The company had also recorded the return of merchandise with the following entry:

June	15	Sales Returns and Allowances	140.00	
		Accounts Receivable—Barbara Lyon		140.00
		Customer returned merchandise.		

Required

1. On a sheet of notebook paper, open a subsidiary Accounts Receivable Ledger that has a T-account for each customer listed in the Sales Journal. Post to the customer accounts the entries of the Sales Journal and also the portion of the general journal entry that affects a customer's account.

2. Open a General Ledger that has T-accounts for Accounts Receivable, Sales, and Sales Returns and Allowances. Post the Sales Journal and the portions of the General Journal entry that affect these accounts.

3. Prepare a list or schedule of the accounts in the subsidiary Accounts Receivable Ledger and add their balances to show that the total equals the balance in the Accounts Receivable controlling account.

Robon Company posts its sales invoices directly and then binds the invoices into a Sales Journal. Robon had the following sales during November:

Exercise 6–9
Accounts Receivable
Ledger
(LO 4, 5, 6)

Nov.	7	Teresa Katz.	$ 4,900
	9	Arnold Swartz	8,100
	13	Sam Smith	17,900
	21	Milton Gibbs	27,300
	26	Sam Smith	15,000
	30	Teresa Katz.	9,800
		Total	$83,000

Required

1. On a sheet of notebook paper, open a subsidiary Accounts Receivable Ledger having a T-account for each customer. Post the invoices to the subsidiary ledger.

2. Give the General Journal entry to record the end-of-month total of the Sales Journal.

3. Open an Accounts Receivable controlling account and a Sales account and post the General Journal entry.

4. Prepare a list or schedule of the accounts in the subsidiary Accounts Receivable Ledger and add their balances to show that the total equals the balance in the Accounts Receivable controlling account.

Exercise 6–10
Posting from special journals to T-accounts (LO 3)

Following are the condensed journals of a merchandising concern. The journal column headings are incomplete in that they do not indicate whether the columns are debit or credit columns.

Required

1. Prepare T-accounts on notebook paper for the following General Ledger and subsidiary ledger accounts. Separate the accounts of each ledger group as follows:

General Ledger Accounts	Accounts Receivable Ledger Accounts
Cash	Customer A
Accounts Receivable	Customer B
Prepaid Insurance	Customer C
Store Equipment	
Accounts Payable	
Notes Payable	
Sales	**Accounts Payable Ledger Accounts**
Sales Returns and Allowances	
Sales Discounts	Company One
Purchases	Company Two
Purchases Returns and Allowances	Company Three
Purchases Discounts	

2. Without referring to any of the illustrations in the chapter that show complete column headings for the journals, post the following journals to the proper T-accounts.

Sales Journal

Account	Amount
Customer A	7,650
Customer B	2,050
Customer C	11,200
Total	20,900

Purchases Journal

Account	Amount
Company One.	4,200
Company Two.	9,600
Company Three. . . .	3,990
Total	17,790

General Journal

. . . . . .	Sales Returns and Allowances	250.00	
. .	Accounts Receivable—Customer B		250.00
. .	Accounts Payable—Company Two	1,200.00	
. .	Purchases Returns and Allowances.		1,200.00

Cash Receipts Journal

Account	Other Accounts	Accounts Receivable	Sales	Sales Discounts	Cash
Customer B		1,800		36	1,764
Cash sales			8,080		8,080
Notes payable	8,000				8,000
Cash sales			9,475		9,475
Customer C		11,200		224	10,976
Store Equipment	990				990
Totals	8,990	13,000	17,555	260	39,285

Cash Disbursements Journal

Accounts	Other Accounts	Accounts Payable	Purchases Discounts	Cash
Prepaid insurance . . .	720			720
Company One		4,200	126	4,074
Company Two		8,400	168	8,232
Store equipment	3,850			3,850
Totals.	4,570	12,600	294	16,876

A company that records credit purchases in a Purchases Journal and records purchases returns in its General Journal made the following errors. List each error by letter, and opposite each letter tell when the error should be discovered:

Exercise 6–11
Errors related to the Purchases Journal
(LO 3, 4, 5)

a. Made an addition error in totaling the Accounts Payable column of the Purchases Journal.

b. Posted a purchases return to the Accounts Payable account and to the creditor's account but did not post to the Purchases Returns and Allowances account.

c. Posted a purchases return to the Purchases Returns and Allowances account and to the Accounts Payable account but did not post to the creditor's account.

d. Correctly recorded a $2,500 purchase in the Purchases Journal but posted it to the creditor's account as a $250 purchase.

e. Made an addition error in determining the balance of a creditor's account.

Problems

Semnar Company completed these transactions during November of the current year:

Problem 6–1
Special journals and subsidiary ledgers
(LO 3, 4, 5)

Nov. 1 Purchased merchandise on account from Fiore Company, invoice dated November 1; terms 2/10, n/60, $10,700.

2 Issued Cheque No. 237 to *The National Journal* for advertising expense, $650.

3 Sold merchandise on account to Frank Mendoza, Invoice No. 530, $1,600. (The terms of all credit sales are 2/10, n/30.)

3 Purchased on account from Weisman Company office supplies, $1,110. Invoice dated November 2, terms n/10 EOM.

5 Received a $680 credit memorandum from Weisman Company for unsatisfactory merchandise received on November 3 and returned for credit.

Nov. 5 Sold merchandise on account to Janet Dalton, Invoice No. 531, $4,850.

  7 Purchased store equipment on account from Century Company, invoice dated November 7, terms n/10 EOM, $8,900.

  11 Issued Cheque No. 238 to Fiore Company in payment of its November 1 invoice, less the discount.

  11 Sold merchandise on account to Cynthia Montgomery, Invoice No. 532, $7,600.

  13 Received payment from Frank Mendoza for the November 3 sale, less the discount.

  15 Sold merchandise on account to Frank Mendoza, Invoice No. 533, $3,250.

  15 Issued Cheque No. 239, payable to Payroll, in payment of the sales salaries for the first half of the month, $7,800. Cashed the cheque and paid the employees.

  15 Cash sales for the first half of the month were $40,670. (Cash sales are usually recorded daily from the cash register readings. However, they are recorded only twice in this problem to reduce the repetitive transactions.)

  15 Received payment from Janet Dalton for the November 5 sale, less the discount.

  17 Purchased merchandise on account from Kramer Company, invoice dated November 16; terms 2/10, n/30; $10,200.

  18 Borrowed $32,000 from First National Bank by giving a long-term note payable.

  21 Received payment from Cynthia Montgomery for the November 11 sale, less the discount.

  21 Purchased on account from Century Company store supplies, $585. Invoice dated November 20, terms n/10 EOM.

  25 Received payment from Frank Mendoza for the November 15 sale, less the discount.

  25 Purchased merchandise on account from Fiore Company, invoice dated November 24; terms 2/10, n/60; $8,300.

  25 Received a $350 credit memorandum from Kramer Company for defective merchandise received on November 17 and returned.

  26 Issued Cheque No. 240 to Kramer Company in payment of its November 16 invoice, less the return and the discount.

  27 Sold merchandise on account to Janet Dalton, Invoice No. 534, $2,460.

  28 Sold merchandise on account to Cynthia Montgomery, Invoice No. 535, $4,620.

  30 Issued Cheque No. 241, payable to Payroll, in payment of the sales salaries for the last half of the month, $7,800.

  30 Cash sales for the last half of the month were $56,780.

Required

1. Open the following General Ledger accounts: Cash, Accounts Receivable, Long-Term Notes Payable, Sales, and Sales Discounts. Also open subsidiary accounts receivable ledger accounts for Janet Dalton, Frank Mendoza, and Cynthia Montgomery.

2. Prepare a Sales Journal and a Cash Receipts Journal like the ones illustrated in this chapter.

3. Review the transactions of Semnar Company and enter those transactions that should be journalized in the Sales Journal and those that should be journalized in the Cash Receipts Journal. Ignore any transactions that should be journalized in a Purchases Journal, a Cash Disbursements Journal, or a General Journal.

4. Post the items that should be posted as individual amounts from the journals. (Normally, such items are posted daily; but since they are few in number in this problem you are asked to post them only once.)

5. Foot and crossfoot the journals and make the month-end postings.

6. Prepare a trial balance of the General Ledger and test the accuracy of the subsidiary ledger by preparing a schedule of accounts receivable.

On October 31, Semnar Company had a cash balance of $134,000 and a Long-Term Notes Payable balance of $134,000. The November transactions of Semnar Company included those listed in Problem 6–1.

Problem 6–2
Special journals, subsidiary ledgers, schedule of accounts payable
(LO 3, 4, 5)

Required

1. Open the following General Ledger accounts: Cash, Office Supplies, Store Supplies, Store Equipment, Accounts Payable, Long-Term Notes Payable, Purchases, Purchases Returns and Allowances, Purchases Discounts, Sales Salaries Expense, and Advertising Expense. Enter the October 31 balances of Cash and Long-Term Notes Payable ($134,000 each).

2. Open subsidiary accounts payable ledger accounts for Century Company, Fiore Company, Kramer Company, and Weisman Company.

3. Prepare a General Journal and a Cash Disbursements Journal like the ones illustrated in this chapter. Prepare a Purchases Journal with a debit column for purchases, a debit column for other accounts, and a credit column for accounts payable.

4. Review the November transactions of Semnar Company and enter those transactions that should be journalized in the General Journal, the Purchases Journal, or the Cash Disbursements Journal. Ignore any transactions that should be journalized in a Sales Journal or Cash Receipts Journal.

5. Post the items that should be posted as individual amounts from the journals. (Normally, such items are posted daily, but since they are few in number in this problem you are asked to post them only once.)

6. Foot and crossfoot the journals and make the month-end postings.

7. Prepare a trial balance and a schedule of accounts payable.

(If the working papers that accompany this text are not being used, omit this problem.)
It is December 16 and you have just taken over the accounting work of Custom Design Company, whose annual accounting periods end each December 31. The company's previous accountant journalized its transactions through December 15 and posted all items that required posting as individual amounts, as an examination of the journals and ledgers in the working papers will show.
The company completed these transactions beginning on December 16:

Problem 6–3
Special journals, subsidiary ledgers, and a trial balance
(LO 3, 4, 5)

Dec. 16   Purchased on account from Southwest Supply Company office supplies, $685. Invoice dated December 15, terms n/10 EOM.

17   Received a $1,135 credit memorandum from Walker Company for merchandise received on December 15 and returned for credit.

Dec. 18   Received a $45 credit memorandum from Southwest Supply Company for office supplies received on December 16 and returned for credit.

19   Sold merchandise on account to Katherine Hoffer, Invoice No. 306, $8,600. (Terms of all credit sales are 2/10, n/30.)

20   Issued a credit memorandum to Kevin Oliver for defective merchandise sold on December 15 and returned for credit, $545.

21   Purchased store equipment on account from Southwest Supply Company, invoice dated December 21, terms n/10 EOM, $7,500.

22   Issued Cheque No. 543 to Walker Company in payment of its December 15 invoice less the return and the discount.

22   Received payment from Katherine Hoffer for the December 12 sale less the discount.

23   Issued Cheque No. 544 to Starbrite Company in payment of its December 15 invoice less a 2% discount.

24   Sold merchandise on account to Maria Perez, Invoice No. 307, $1,400.

24   Sold a neighbouring merchant five boxes of file folders (office supplies) for cash at cost, $56.

25   Received payment from Kevin Oliver for the December 15 sale less the return and the discount.

26   Received merchandise and an invoice dated December 25, terms 2/10, n/60, from Starbrite Company, $8,900.

30   Carol Morgan, the owner of Custom Design Company, used Cheque No. 545 to withdraw $2,800 cash from the business for personal use.

31   Issued Cheque No. 546 to Mark Arlos, the company's only sales employee, in payment of his salary for the last half of December, $1,800.

31   Issued Cheque No. 547 to City Electric Company in payment of the December hydro bill, $565.

31   Cash sales for the last half of the month were $32,890. (Cash sales are usually recorded daily but are recorded only twice in this problem to reduce the repetitive transactions.)

Required

1. Record the transactions in the journals provided.

2. Post to the customer and creditor accounts and also post any amounts that should be posted as individual amounts to the general ledger accounts. (Normally, these amounts are posted daily, but they are posted only once by you in this problem because they are few in number.)

3. Foot and crossfoot the journals and make the month-end postings.

4. Prepare a December 31 trial balance and test the accuracy of the subsidiary ledgers by preparing schedules of accounts receivable and payable.

Problem 6–4
Special journals, preparing and proving the trial balance
(LO 3, 4, 5)

Xanox Company completed these transactions during July of the current year:

July 1   Received merchandise and an invoice dated June 30, terms 2/10, n/30, from Farnswood Company, $21,300.

2   Sold merchandise on account to John Nelson, Invoice No. 324, $7,900. (Terms of all credit sales are 2/10, n/30.)

3   Purchased on account from Corsair Company office supplies, $560. Invoice dated July 3, terms n/10 EOM.

July 3 Sold merchandise on account to Thomas Zak, Invoice No. 325, $4,600.

6 Borrowed $18,000 by giving National Bank a long-term promissory note payable.

9 Purchased office equipment on account from McKay Company, invoice dated July 9, terms n/10 EOM, $10,400.

10 Sent Farnswood Company Cheque No. 876 in payment of its June 30 invoice less the discount.

10 Sold merchandise on account to Margo Edwards, Invoice No. 326, $2,300.

12 Received payment from John Nelson for the July 2 sale less the discount.

13 Received payment from Thomas Zak for the July 3 sale less the discount.

14 Received merchandise and an invoice dated July 13, terms 2/10, n/30, from Wellsbranch Company, $15,825.

15 Issued Cheque No. 877, payable to Payroll, in payment of sales salaries for the first half of the month, $7,950. Cashed the cheque and paid the employees.

15 Cash sales for the first half of the month were $67,340. (Normally, cash sales are recorded daily; however, they are recorded only twice in this problem to reduce the repetitive entries.)

16 Purchased on account from Corsair Company store supplies, $840, invoice dated July 16, terms n/10 EOM.

17 Received a credit memorandum from Wellsbranch Company for unsatisfactory merchandise received on July 14 and returned for credit, $1,225.

19 Received a credit memorandum from McKay Company for office equipment received on July 9 and returned for credit, $300.

20 Received payment from Margo Edwards for the sale of July 10 less the discount.

23 Issued Cheque No. 878 to Wellsbranch Company in payment of its invoice of July 13 less the return and the discount.

27 Sold merchandise on account to Margo Edwards, Invoice No. 327, $6,540.

28 Sold merchandise on account to Thomas Zak, Invoice No. 328, $2,650.

31 Issued Cheque No. 879, payable to Payroll, in payment of sales salaries for the last half of the month, $7,950. Cashed the cheque and paid the employees.

31 Cash sales for the last half of the month were $72,345.

31 *Foot and crossfoot the journals and make the month-end postings.*

Required

1. Open the following General Ledger accounts: Cash, Accounts Receivable, Office Supplies, Store Supplies, Office Equipment, Accounts Payable, Long-Term Notes Payable, Sales, Sales Discounts, Purchases, Purchases Returns and Allowances, Purchases Discounts, and Sales Salaries Expense.

2. Open the following accounts receivable ledger accounts: Margo Edwards, John Nelson, and Thomas Zak.

3. Open the following accounts payable ledger accounts: Corsair Company, Farnswood Company, McKay Company, and Wellsbranch Company. Enter the transactions in a Sales Journal, a Purchases Journal, a Cash Receipts Journal, a Cash Disbursements Journal, and a General Journal similar to the ones illustrated in this chapter. Post when instructed to do so.

4. Prepare a trial balance and test the accuracy of the subsidiary ledgers by preparing schedules of accounts receivable and payable.

Problem 6–5
Special journals,
subsidiary ledgers, and
the trial balance
(LO 3, 4, 5)

Crawford Company completed these transactions during June of the current year:

June 1 Received merchandise and an invoice dated May 31, terms 2/10, n/60, from Hollingsworth Company, $47,800.

2 Purchased office equipment on account from Dunlap Company, invoice dated June 2, terms n/10 EOM, $14,625.

3 Sold merchandise on account to Tamara Smith, Invoice No. 902, $22,300. (Terms of all credit sales are 2/10, n/30.)

5 Sold merchandise on account to Dean Grammer, Invoice No. 903, $31,700.

8 Cash sales for the week ended June 8 were $38,950.

8 Issued Cheque No. 548 to *The Monthly News* for advertising, $275.

9 Sold merchandise on account to Mary Cortez, Invoice No. 904, $12,400.

10 Issued Cheque No. 549 to Hollingsworth Company in payment of its May 31 invoice less the discount.

10 Purchased on account from The Store Depot merchandise, $5,870, and office supplies, $570, invoice dated June 10, terms n/10 EOM.

11 Sold unneeded office equipment at cost for cash, $940.

13 Received payment from Tamara Smith for the sale of June 3 less the discount.

15 Cash sales for the week ended June 15 were $23,620.

15 Issued Cheque No. 550, payable to Payroll, in payment of the sales salaries for the first half of the month, $16,280. Cashed the cheque and paid the employees.

15 Received payment from Dean Grammer for the sale of June 5 less the discount.

16 Sold merchandise on account to Mary Cortez, Invoice No. 905, $9,735.

19 Sold merchandise on account to Tamara Smith, Invoice No. 906, $6,430.

19 Received payment from Mary Cortez for the sale of June 9 less the discount.

20 Received merchandise and an invoice dated June 18, terms 2/10, n/60, from Riteway Company, $17,500.

21 Issued a credit memorandum to Mary Cortez for defective merchandise sold on June 16 and returned for credit, $1,835.

22 Cash sales for the week ended June 22 were $28,150.

24 Received a $1,700 credit memorandum from Riteway Company for defective merchandise received on June 18 and returned for credit.

25 Purchased on account from The Store Depot merchandise, $22,390, and store supplies, $2,825, invoice dated June 25, terms n/10 EOM.

25 Received merchandise and an invoice dated June 24, terms 2/10, n/60, from Hollingsworth Company, $35,860.

26 Received payment from Mary Cortez for the June 16 sale less the return and the discount.

26 Sold merchandise on account to Dean Grammer, Invoice No. 907, $22,540.

28 Issued Cheque No. 551 to Riteway Company in payment of its June 18 invoice, less the return and the discount.

30 Issued Cheque No. 552, payable to Payroll, in payment of the sales salaries for the last half of the month, $16,280.

June 30 Cash sales for the week ended June 30 were $31,230.

30 *Foot and crossfoot the journals and make the month-end postings.*

Required

1. Open the following General Ledger accounts: Cash, Accounts Receivable, Office Supplies, Store Supplies, Office Equipment, Accounts Payable, Sales, Sales Returns and Allowances, Sales Discounts, Purchases, Purchases Returns and Allowances, Purchases Discounts, Sales Salaries Expense, and Advertising Expense.

2. Open the following subsidiary Accounts Receivable Ledger accounts: Mary Cortez, Dean Grammer, and Tamara Smith.

3. Open the following subsidiary Accounts Payable Ledger accounts: Dunlap Company, Hollingsworth Company, Riteway Company, and The Store Depot.

4. Prepare a Sales Journal, a Cash Receipts Journal, a Cash Disbursements Journal, and a General Journal like the ones illustrated in this chapter. Prepare a Purchases Journal with a debit column for purchases, a debit column for other accounts, and a credit column for accounts payable. Enter the transactions in the journals and post.

5. Prepare a trial balance and test the accuracy of the subsidiary ledgers with schedules of accounts receivable and payable.

Lynn's Products uses a Cash Receipts Journal similar to the one in Illustration 6–5. In the process of crossfooting the journal at the end of a month, the company's bookkeeper found that the sum of the debits did not equal the sum of the credits.

Problem 6–6
Analytical essay
(LO 3)

Required

Describe the procedures you would follow in an effort to discover the reason why the journal does not crossfoot correctly.

Tucker's Tidbits is a merchandising company that uses the special journals described in Chapter 6. At the end of the accounting period, the bookkeeper for the company prepared a trial balance and a schedule of accounts receivable. The trial balance is in balance, but the sum of the account balances on the schedule of accounts receivable does not equal the balance in the controlling account.

Problem 6–7
Analytical essay
(LO 5)

Required

Describe the procedures you would follow to discover the reason for the imbalance between the controlling account and the total shown on the schedule of accounts receivable.

Alternate Problems

Stanford Equipment Company completed these transactions during October of the current year:

Problem 6–1A
Special journals and
subsidiary ledgers
(LO 3, 4, 5)

Oct. 1 Issued Cheque No. 640 to *Pacific Monthly* for advertising expense, $980.

1 Purchased merchandise on account from Fiore Company, invoice dated September 30, terms 2/10, n/30, $3,500.

Oct. 5 Sold merchandise on account to Frank Mendoza, Invoice No. 768, $10,200. (The terms of all credit sales are 2/10, n/30.)

5 Purchased on account from Weisman Company store supplies, $750. Invoice dated October 5, terms n/10 EOM.

6 Sold merchandise on account to Janet Dalton, Invoice No. 769, $4,700.

8 Received an $80 credit memorandum from Weisman Company for unsatisfactory merchandise received on October 5 and returned for credit.

9 Purchased store equipment on account from Century Company, invoice dated October 8, terms n/10 EOM, $20,950.

10 Issued Cheque No. 641 to Fiore Company in payment of its September 30 invoice, less the discount.

13 Sold merchandise on account to Cynthia Montgomery, Invoice No. 770, $4,650.

15 Received payment from Frank Mendoza for the October 5 sale, less the discount.

15 Issued Cheque No. 642, payable to Payroll, in payment of the sales salaries for the first half of the month, $15,900. Cashed the cheque and paid the employees.

15 Sold merchandise on account to Frank Mendoza, Invoice No. 771, $2,300.

15 Cash sales for the first half of the month were $56,320. (Cash sales are usually recorded daily from the cash register readings. However, they are recorded only twice in this problem to reduce the repetitive transactions.)

16 Received payment from Janet Dalton for the October 6 sale, less the discount.

17 Purchased merchandise on account from Kramer Company, invoice dated October 17, terms 2/10, n/30, $4,600.

21 Borrowed $8,500 from Count Bank by giving a long-term note payable.

23 Received payment from Cynthia Montgomery for the October 13 sale, less the discount.

24 Received a $1,300 credit memorandum from Kramer Company for defective merchandise received on October 17 and returned.

25 Purchased on account from Century Company office supplies, $420, invoice dated October 24, terms n/10 EOM.

25 Received payment from Frank Mendoza for the October 15 sale, less the discount.

26 Purchased merchandise on account from Fiore Company, invoice dated October 26, terms 2/10, n/30, $5,430.

27 Issued Cheque No. 643 to Kramer Company in payment of its October 17 invoice, less the return and the discount.

29 Sold merchandise on account to Janet Dalton, Invoice No. 772, $15,600.

30 Sold merchandise on account to Cynthia Montgomery, Invoice No. 773, $8,750.

31 Issued Cheque No. 644, payable to Payroll, in payment of the sales salaries for the last half of the month, $15,900.

31 Cash sales for the last half of the month were $43,900.

Required

1. Open the following General Ledger accounts: Cash, Accounts Receivable, Long-Term Notes Payable, Sales, and Sales Discounts. Also open subsidiary Accounts Receivable Ledger accounts for Janet Dalton, Frank Mendoza, and Cynthia Montgomery.

2. Prepare a Sales Journal and a Cash Receipts Journal similar to the ones illustrated in this chapter.

3. Review the transactions of Stanford Equipment Company and enter those that should be journalized in the Sales Journal and those that should be journalized in the Cash Receipts Journal. Ignore any transactions that should be journalized in a Purchases Journal, a Cash Disbursements Journal, or a General Journal.

4. Post the items that should be posted as individual amounts from the journals. (Normally, such items are posted daily; but since they are few in number in this problem you are asked to post them only once.)

5. Foot and crossfoot the journals and make the month-end postings.

6. Prepare a trial balance of the General Ledger and test the accuracy of the subsidiary ledger by preparing a schedule of accounts receivable.

On September 30, Stanford Equipment Company had a cash balance of $92,000 and a Long-Term Notes Payable balance of $92,000. The October transactions of Stanford Equipment Company included those listed in Problem 6–1A.

Problem 6–2A
Special journals,
subsidiary ledgers,
schedule of accounts
payable
(LO 3, 4, 5)

Required

1. Open the following General Ledger accounts: Cash, Office Supplies, Store Supplies, Store Equipment, Accounts Payable, Long-Term Notes Payable, Purchases, Purchases Returns and Allowances, Purchases Discounts, Sales Salaries Expense, and Advertising Expense. Enter the September 30 balances of Cash and Long-Term Notes Payable ($92,000 each).

2. Open subsidiary Accounts Payable Ledger accounts for Century Company, Fiore Company, Kramer Company, and Weisman Company.

3. Prepare a General Journal and a Cash Disbursements Journal like the ones illustrated in this chapter. Prepare a Purchases Journal with a debit column for purchases, a debit column for other accounts, and a credit column for accounts payable.

4. Review the October transactions of Stanford Equipment Company and enter those transactions that should be journalized in the General Journal, the Purchases Journal, or the Cash Disbursements Journal. Ignore any transactions that should be journalized in a Sales Journal or Cash Receipts Journal.

5. Post the items that should be posted as individual amounts from the journals. (Normally, such items are posted daily; but since they are few in number in this problem you are asked to post them only once.)

6. Foot and crossfoot the journals and make the month-end postings.

7. Prepare a trial balance and a schedule of accounts payable.

(If the working papers that accompany this text are not being used, omit this problem.)
   It is December 16 and you have just taken over the accounting work of Sierra Company, whose annual accounting periods end each December 31. The company's previous accountant journalized its transactions through December 15 and posted all items that required posting as individual amounts, as an examination of the journals and ledgers in the booklet of working papers will show.
   The company completed these transactions beginning on December 16:

Problem 6–3A
Special journals,
subsidiary ledgers, and a
trial balance
(LO 3, 4, 5)

Dec. 16   Sold merchandise on account to Katherine Hoffer, Invoice No. 306, $3,500. (Terms of all credit sales are 2/10, n/30.)

   17   Received a $435 credit memorandum from Walker Company for merchandise received on December 15 and returned for credit.

Dec. 17   Purchased on account from Southwest Supply Company office supplies, $850. invoice dated December 17, terms n/10 EOM.

19   Issued a credit memorandum to Kevin Oliver for defective merchandise sold on December 15 and returned for credit, $145.

20   Received a $270 credit memorandum from Southwest Supply Company for office supplies received on December 17 and returned for credit.

20   Purchased store equipment on account from Southwest Supply Company, invoice dated December 19, terms n/10 EOM, $8,300.

21   Sold merchandise on account to Maria Perez, Invoice No. 307, $4,600.

22   Received payment from Katherine Hoffer for the December 12 sale less the discount.

24   Received payment from Kevin Oliver for the December 15 sale less the return and the discount.

25   Issued Cheque No. 543 to Walker Company in payment of its December 15 invoice less the return and the discount.

25   Issued Cheque No. 544 to Starbrite Company in payment of its December 15 invoice less a 2% discount.

28   Received merchandise and an invoice dated December 28, terms 2/10, n/60, from Starbrite Company, $6,700.

28   Sold a neighbouring merchant a carton of calculator tape (store supplies) for cash at cost, $60.

29   Carol Morgan, the owner of Sierra Company, used Cheque No. 545 to withdraw $6,900 cash from the business for personal use.

31   Issued Cheque No. 546 to City Power Company in payment of the December hydro bill, $980.

31   Issued Cheque No. 547 to Mark Arlos, the company's only sales employee, in payment of his salary for the last half of December, $1,800.

31   Cash sales for the last half of the month were $46,750. (Cash sales are usually recorded daily but are recorded only twice in this problem to reduce the repetitive entries.)

Required

1. Record the transactions in the journals provided.

2. Post to the customer and creditor accounts and also post any amounts that should be posted as individual amounts to the General Ledger accounts. (Normally, these amounts are posted daily, but they are posted only once by you in this problem because they are few in number.)

3. Foot and crossfoot the journals and make the month-end postings.

4. Prepare a December 31 trial balance and test the accuracy of the subsidiary ledgers by preparing schedules of accounts receivable and payable.

Problem 6–4A
Special journals, preparing and proving the trial balance
(LO 3, 4, 5)

Safelite Company completed these transactions during August of the current year:

Aug. 1   Borrowed $75,000 by giving National Bank a long-term promissory note payable.

4   Received merchandise and an invoice dated August 3, terms 2/10, n/30, from Farnswood Company, $15,200.

5   Purchased on account from Corsair Company store supplies, $1,360, invoice dated August 5, terms n/10 EOM.

6   Sold merchandise on account to John Nelson, Invoice No. 789, $8,500. (Terms of all credit sales are 2/10, n/30.)

Aug. 7 Purchased office equipment on account from McKay Company, invoice dated August 6, terms n/10 EOM, $6,750.

10 Sold merchandise on account to Thomas Zak, Invoice No. 790, $16,700.

13 Sent Farnswood Company Cheque No. 423 in payment of its August 3 invoice less the discount.

13 Received merchandise and an invoice dated August 13, terms 2/10, n/30, from Wellsbranch Company, $3,850.

15 Issued Cheque No. 424, payable to Payroll, in payment of sales salaries for the first half of the month, $11,250. Cashed the cheque and paid the employees.

15 Cash sales for the first half of the month were $22,760. (Normally, cash sales are recorded daily; however, they are recorded only twice in this problem to reduce the repetitive entries.)

15 *Post to the customer and creditor accounts and also post any amounts that should be posted as individual amounts to the General Ledger accounts. (Normally, such items are posted daily, but you are asked to post them on only two occasions in this problem because they are few in number.)*

15 Sold merchandise on account to Margo Edwards, Invoice No. 791, $5,700.

16 Received payment from John Nelson for the August 6 sale less the discount.

16 Purchased on account from Corsair Company office supplies, $745, invoice dated August 16, terms n/10 EOM.

20 Received payment from Thomas Zak for the August 10 sale less the discount.

20 Received a credit memorandum from Wellsbranch Company for unsatisfactory merchandise received on August 13 and returned for credit, $650.

23 Issued Cheque No. 425 to Wellsbranch Company in payment of its invoice of August 13 less the return and the discount.

24 Sold merchandise on account to Margo Edwards, Invoice No. 792, $4,330.

25 Received payment from Margo Edwards for the sale of August 15 less the discount.

26 Received a credit memorandum from McKay Company for office equipment received on August 7 and returned for credit, $1,230.

27 Sold merchandise on account to Thomas Zak, Invoice No. 793, $3,460.

31 Issued Cheque No. 426, payable to Payroll, in payment of sales salaries for the last half of the month, $11,250. Cashed the cheque and paid the employees.

31 Cash sales for the last half of the month were $34,270.

31 *Post to the customer and creditor accounts and post any amounts that should be posted as individual amounts to the General Ledger accounts.*

31 *Foot and crossfoot the journals and make the month-end postings.*

Required

1. Open the following General Ledger accounts: Cash, Accounts Receivable, Office Supplies, Store Supplies, Office Equipment, Accounts Payable, Long-Term Notes Payable, Sales, Sales Discounts, Purchases, Purchases Returns and Allowances, Purchases Discounts, and Sales Salaries Expense.

2. Open the following Accounts Receivable Ledger accounts: Margo Edwards, John Nelson, and Thomas Zak.

3. Open the following Accounts Payable Ledger accounts: Corsair Company, Farnswood Company, McKay Company, and Wellsbranch Company. Enter the transactions in a Sales Journal, a Purchases Journal, a Cash Receipts Journal, a Cash Disbursements Journal, and a General Journal similar to the ones illustrated in this chapter. Post when instructed to do so.

4. Prepare a trial balance and test the accuracy of the subsidiary ledgers by preparing schedules of accounts receivable and payable.

Problem 6–5A
Special journals,
subsidiary ledgers, and
the trial balance
(LO 3, 4, 5)

Wolfe Company completed these transactions during April of the current year:

Apr. 1   Received merchandise and an invoice dated April 1, terms 2/10, n/30, from Hollingsworth Company, $5,400.

1   Sold merchandise on account to Tamara Smith, Invoice No. 234, $1,600. (Terms of all credit sales are 2/10, n/30.)

3   Issued Cheque No. 722 to *Northern Living* for advertising, $545.

3   Purchased office equipment on account from Dunlap Company, invoice dated April 2, terms n/10 EOM, $3,790.

5   Sold merchandise on account to Dean Grammer, Invoice No. 235, $4,300.

8   Cash sales for the week ended April 8 were $15,870.

8   Sold merchandise on account to Mary Cortez, Invoice No. 236, $2,400.

9   Received a credit memorandum from Dunlap Company for the return of defective equipment originally purchased on April 3, $390.

11   Issued Cheque No. 723 to Hollingsworth Company in payment of its April 1 invoice less the discount.

11   Sold unneeded office equipment at cost for cash, $550.

11   Received payment from Tamara Smith for the sale of April 1 less the discount.

15   Cash sales for the week ended April 15 were $12,340.

15   Issued Cheque No. 724, payable to Payroll, for the sales salaries for the first half of the month, $3,860. Cashed the cheque and paid the employees.

15   Received payment from Dean Grammer for April 5 sale less the discount.

17   Purchased on account from The Store Depot merchandise, $6,820, and store supplies, $540. Invoice dated April 16, terms n/10 EOM.

18   Received merchandise and an invoice dated April 18, terms 2/10, n/60, from Riteway Company, $4,740.

18   Sold merchandise on account to Mary Cortez, Invoice No. 237, $3,630.

18   Sold merchandise on account to Tamara Smith, Invoice No. 238, $5,700.

18   Received payment from Mary Cortez for April 8 sale less the discount.

22   Issued a credit memorandum to Mary Cortez for defective merchandise sold on April 18 and returned for credit, $230.

22   Cash sales for the week ended April 22 were $17,220.

23   Received a $1,140 credit memorandum from Riteway Company for defective merchandise received on April 18 and returned for credit.

24   Purchased on account from The Store Depot merchandise, $9,780, and office supplies, $965, invoice dated April 23, terms n/10 EOM.

25   Received merchandise and an invoice dated April 25, terms 2/10, n/30, from Hollingsworth Company, $7,540.

Apr. 28 Received payment from Mary Cortez for the April 18 sale less the return and the discount.

28 Issued Cheque No. 725 to Riteway Company in payment of its April 18 invoice, less the return and the discount.

29 Sold merchandise on account to Dean Grammer, Invoice No. 239, $2,970.

Apr. 30 Issued Cheque No. 726, payable to Payroll, in payment of the sales salaries for the last half of the month, $3,860.

30 Cash sales for the week ended April 30 were $9,520.

30 *Foot and crossfoot the journals and make the month-end postings.*

Required

1. Open these general ledger accounts: Cash, Accounts Receivable, Office Supplies, Store Supplies, Office Equipment, Accounts Payable, Sales, Sales Returns and Allowances, Sales Discounts, Purchases, Purchases Returns and Allowances, Purchases Discounts, Sales Salaries Expense, and Advertising Expense.

2. Open the following subsidiary Accounts Receivable Ledger accounts: Mary Cortez, Dean Grammer, and Tamara Smith.

3. Open the following subsidiary Accounts Payable Ledger accounts: Dunlap Company, Hollingsworth Company, Riteway Company, and The Store Depot.

4. Prepare a Sales Journal, a Cash Receipts Journal, a Cash Disbursements Journal, and a General Journal like the ones illustrated in this chapter. Prepare a Purchases Journal with a debit column for purchases, a debit column for other accounts, and a credit column for accounts payable. Enter the transactions in the journals and post.

5. Prepare a trial balance and test the accuracy of the subsidiary ledgers with schedules of accounts receivable and payable.

Russell's Novelties uses a Cash Disbursements Journal similar to the one in Illustration 6–7. In the process of crossfooting the journal at the end of a month, the company's bookkeeper found that the sum of the debits did not equal the sum of the credits.

Problem 6–6A
Analytical essay
(LO 3)

Required

Describe the procedures you would follow in an effort to discover the reason why the journal does not crossfoot correctly.

Michael's Autoparts is a merchandising company that uses the special journals described in Chapter 6. At the end of the accounting period, the bookkeeper for the company prepared a trial balance and a schedule of accounts payable. The trial balance is in balance but the sum of the account balances on the schedule of accounts payable does not equal the balance in the controlling account.

Problem 6–7A
Analytical essay
(LO 5)

Required

Describe the procedures you would follow to discover the reason for the imbalance between the controlling account and the total on the schedule of accounts payable.

Provocative Problem

Review the "As a Matter of Ethics" case presented on page 311. Discuss the problem faced by the public accountant and the factors the public accountant should consider in deciding on a course of action.

Provocative Problem 6–1
As a Matter of Ethics:
Essay

Ethics

Analytical and Review Problem

A&R Problem 6–1
The following problem is designed to test your ability in the use of special journals and subsidiary ledgers. The special journals of James Bay Department Store are reproduced below, followed by a number of representative transactions which occurred during the period. The money columns in the journals are numbered to minimize clerical work in recording each transaction.

Accounts Receivable Debit	Sales Credit							PST Credit	GST Credit
	Men's Clothing	Women's Clothing	Appliances	Furniture	Bargain Basement	Other Departments			
1	2	3	4	5	6	7		8	9

Cash Debit	Sales Discounts Debit	Sales Credit						Accounts Receivable Credit	Other Accounts Credit	PST Credit	GST Credit
		Men's Clothing	Women's Clothing	Appli-ances	Furni-ture	Bargain Basement	Other Departments				
10	11	12	13	14	15	16	17	18	19	20	21

Purchases Debit						Prepaid GST Debit	Accounts Payable Credit
Men's Clothing	Women's Clothing	Appliances	Furniture	Bargain Basement	Other Departments		
22	23	24	25	26	27	28	29

Accounts Payable Debit	Supplies Expense Debit	Other Accounts Debit	Prepaid GST Debit	Cash Credit
30	31	32	33	34

Debit	Credit
35	36

Transactions (*Note:* All sales are subject to a provincial sales tax (PST) of 8% and the federal goods and services tax (GST) of 7%.)

	Debit	Credit
a. Purchases of $8,200 on account of Appliances from E. G. Inc.		
b. Sale on account $1,400 of Furniture to Gates Brown.		
c. Sale for cash $1,000 less 5% discount—Appliances.		
d. Collection of account receivable from Cec Oak, $600.		
e. Payment of account payable to J. T. Inglis, $4,200.		
f. Borrowed $25,000 from Great Northern Bank on note payable.		
g. Sale on account $300 to J.C. Snead—Men's Clothing.		
h. Sale for cash of baked goods—$10.		
i. Purchases of $7,500 on account of goods—Bargain Basement from C. L. Co.		
j. J. C. Snead returned for credit a shirt that had a flaw—$40.		

Required

1. Identify each of the journals.
2. Journalize by indicating the column number in the spaces provided after each transaction. For example: Purchase for cash of supplies (immediately expensed).

Debit	Credit
31, 33	34

3. Indicate how the data in the special journals are posted to various accounts by filling in the spaces provided with the following posting possibilities.
   a. Posted as a *debit* to some General Ledger account.
   b. Posted as a *debit* to some subsidiary ledger account.
   c. Posted as a *credit* to some General Ledger account.
   d. Posted as a *credit* to some subsidiary ledger account.
   e. Not posted.

Note: The numbers in parentheses are the identification numbers for the money columns of the special journals. For example: (31) money column.

	Posted as
(00) Total of column (34) Example	e
a. Total of column 1.	
b. Detail items of column 3.	
c. Detail items of column 8.	
d. Total of column 9.	
e. Detail items of column 17.	
f. Total of column 20.	
g. Total of column 26.	
h. Detail items of column 27.	
i. Detail items of column 32.	
j. Detail items of column 1.	
k. Total of column 19.	
l. Detail items of column 18.	
m. Total of column 29.	
n. Total of column 5.	
o. Detail items of column 10.	
p. Detail items of column 21.	

As a Matter of Record

Record Case 6–1

The following report, "Byte Nips Daily's Budget: Glitch Forces Cuts in Spending," appeared in *The Globe and Mail*, February 21, 1992, page B8:

> A misplaced computer byte has forced a daily newspaper in Kingston to chew a sizable hunk of its budget for 1992.
>
> The $300,000 glitch, discovered late last month, means *The Whig-Standard* will be hiring only two students to work as reporters or editors this summer instead of five, and also has forced it to reduce its spending for freelance stories, editor Neil Reynolds said.
>
> The computer in the newspaper's accounting department somehow managed to understate editorial costs by $300,000 when it spewed out editorial budget-planning numbers last fall, Mr. Reynolds said yesterday from Kingston.

Required

Do you agree with Mr. Reynolds that "the computer . . . somehow managed to understate editorial costs"? Support your answer.

Answers to Objective Review Questions

LO 1 (d)	LO 3 (b)	LO 5 (d)
LO 2 (a)	LO 4 (e)	LO 6 (e)

(If the working papers that accompany this text are not available, omit this comprehensive problem.)

Draper Company
(LO 3, 4, 5)

Assume it is Monday, May 1, the first business day of the month, and you have just been hired as the accountant for Draper Company, which operates with monthly accounting periods. All of the company's accounting work has been completed through the end of April and its ledgers show April 30 balances. During your first month on the job, you record the following transactions:

May 3   Purchased on account from Flintrock Suppliers merchandise, $19,650; store supplies, $340; and office supplies, $80; invoice dated May 3, terms n/10 EOM.

4   Sold merchandise on account to Arcam Company, Invoice No. 622, $6,500. (The terms of all credit sales are 2/10, n/30.)

5   Issued Cheque No. 817 to Ross Realty in payment of the May rent, $4,150. (Use two lines to record the transaction. Charge 80% of the rent to Rent Expense, Selling Space, and the balance to Rent Expense, Office Space.)

6   Received a $390 credit memorandum from Natural Products for merchandise received on April 28 and returned for credit.

6   Issued a $350 credit memorandum to Legacy Company for defective merchandise sold on April 30 and returned for credit. The total selling price (gross) was $2,750.

7   Purchased office equipment on account from Flintrock Suppliers, invoice dated May 5, terms n/10 EOM, $4,740.

8   Sold store supplies to the merchant next door at cost for cash, $30.

9   Issued Cheque No. 818 to Natural Products to pay for the $2,790 of merchandise received on April 28 less the return and a 2% discount.

10   Received payment from Legacy Company for the remaining balance from the sale of April 30 less the return and the discount.

13   Received merchandise and an invoice dated May 11, terms 2/10, n/30, from Carousel, Inc., $8,000.

13   Received a $180 credit memorandum from Flintrock Suppliers for defective office equipment received on May 7 and returned for credit.

14   Received payment from Arcam Company for the May 4 sale less the discount.

15   Issued Cheque No. 819, payable to Payroll, in payment of sales salaries, $2,200, and office salaries, $1,340. Cashed the cheque and paid the employees.

15   Cash sales for the first half of the month, $28,285. (Such sales are normally recorded daily. They are recorded only twice in this problem to reduce the repetitive entries.)

15   *Post to the customer and creditor accounts. Also, post individual items that are not included in column totals at the end of the month to the General Ledger accounts. (Such items are normally posted daily, but you are asked to post them only twice each month because they are few in number.)*

May 17   Received merchandise and an invoice dated May 16, terms 2/10, n/60, from Sante Fe Designs, $12,950.

    19   Sold merchandise on account to Seaside Clinic, Invoice No. 623, $7,400.

    20   Issued Cheque No. 820 to Carousel, Inc., in payment of its May 11 invoice less the discount.

    21   Sold merchandise on account to Legacy Company, Invoice No. 624, $1,900.

    22   Purchased on account from Flintrock Suppliers merchandise, $3,060; store supplies, $140; and office supplies, $100; invoice dated May 22, terms n/10 EOM.

    25   Sold merchandise on account to Applause Interiors, Invoice No. 625, $11,100.

    25   Issued Cheque No. 821 to Sante Fe Designs in payment of its May 16 invoice less the discount.

    27   Received merchandise and an invoice dated May 26, terms 2/10, n/30, from Carousel, Inc., $1,900.

    28   Received payment from Seaside Clinic for the May 19 sale less the discount.

    28   Frank Holcomb, the owner of Draper Company, used Cheque No. 822 to withdraw $3,000 from the business for personal use.

    30   Issued Cheque No. 823, payable to Payroll, in payment of sales salaries, $2,200, and office salaries, $1,340. Cashed the cheque and paid the employees.

    30   Issued Cheque No. 824 to City Utility in payment of the May hydro bill, $1,180.

    31   Cash sales for the last half of the month were $21,960.

    31   *Post to the customer and creditor accounts. Also, post individual items that are not included in column totals at the end of the month to the General Ledger accounts.*

    31   *Foot and crossfoot the journals and make the month-end postings.*

Required

1. Enter the transactions in the appropriate journals and post when instructed to do so.

2. Prepare a trial balance in the Trial Balance columns of the provided work sheet form and complete the work sheet using the following information:
   a.   Ending merchandise inventory, $189,430.
   b.   Expired insurance, $280.
   c.   Ending store supplies inventory, $730; and office supplies inventory, $270.
   d.   Estimated depreciation of store equipment, $550; and of office equipment, $170.

3. Prepare a multiple-step classified May income statement, a May statement of changes in owner's equity, and a May 31 classified balance sheet.

4. Prepare and post adjusting and closing entries.

5. Prepare a post-closing trial balance. Also prepare a list of the Accounts Receivable Ledger accounts and a list of the Accounts Payable Ledger accounts. Total the balances of each to confirm that the totals equal the balances in the controlling accounts.

Accounting for Assets

Businesses use many different kinds of assets in carrying on their operations. These include such things as cash, receivables, merchandise inventories, land, buildings, equipment, natural resources, and intangible assets. As you study the next five chapters, you will learn the basic principles of accounting for all these different assets. You will see how transactions that involve assets are recorded. You will also learn how the assets and events concerning them are reported in the financial statements. In addition, you will learn several accounting procedures that help management safeguard and control the assets of the business.

Part III consists of the following chapters:

Internal Control and Accounting for Cash

Because almost all business activities involve cash, it must be carefully controlled. Internal control systems are designed to make accounting information dependable and to help companies avoid misplacing or misusing their assets.

C ash is an asset that every business owns and uses. Cash includes such specific items as currency, coins, chequing accounts (also called *demand deposits*), and perhaps savings accounts (also called *time deposits*). Most organizations also own at least some assets known as *cash equivalents,* which are very similar to cash. In studying this chapter, you will learn the principles of internal control that guide businesses in managing and accounting for cash. The chapter shows how to establish and use a petty cash fund and how to reconcile a chequing account. Also, you will learn a method of accounting for purchases that helps management determine whether cash discounts on purchases are being lost and, if so, how much has been lost.

Learning Objectives

After studying Chapter 7, you should be able to:

1. Explain the concept of liquidity and the difference between cash and cash equivalents.
2. Explain why internal control procedures are needed in a large organization and state the broad principles of internal control.
3. Describe internal control procedures used to protect cash received from cash sales, cash received through the mail, and cash disbursements.
4. Explain the operation of a petty cash fund and be able to prepare journal entries to record petty cash fund transactions.
5. Explain why the bank balance and the book balance of cash should be reconciled and be able to prepare a reconciliation.
6. Tell how recording invoices at net amounts helps gain control over cash discounts taken and be able to account for invoices recorded at net amounts.
7. Define or explain the words and phrases listed in the chapter glossary.

After studying Appendix D at the end of Chapter 7, you should be able to:

8. Explain the use of a Voucher Register and Cheque Register and prepare entries to record and pay liabilities when these registers are used in a manual accounting system.

Cash, Cash Equivalents, and the Concept of Liquidity

LO 1 Explain the concept of liquidity and the difference between cash and cash equivalents.

In previous chapters, you have learned that a company can own many different kinds of assets, including accounts receivable, merchandise inventory, and various kinds of equipment. You have also learned that the value invested in these assets is not lost when they are acquired. For example, if cash of $10,000 is spent on equipment, the equipment is recorded at a cost of $10,000. The transaction does not involve an expense; owner's equity is not reduced.

Although value is not lost when equipment is purchased for cash, the equipment is not as easily used as cash to buy other assets, acquire services, or pay off liabilities. Another way to state this is to say that cash is more *liquid* than equipment. Thus, although value is not lost when equipment is purchased for cash, the investment in equipment is less liquid than was the investment in cash.

In more general terms, the **liquidity** of an asset refers to how easily the asset can be converted into other types of assets or be used to buy services or satisfy obligations. All assets can be evaluated in terms of their relative liquidity. Assets such as cash are said to be **liquid assets** because they can be easily converted into other types of assets or used to buy services or pay liabilities.

You should realize that a company needs more than valuable assets to stay in business. That is, the company must own some liquid assets so that bills will be paid on time and purchases can be made for cash when that is necessary.

For financial accounting, the asset *cash* includes not only currency and coins but also amounts on deposit in bank accounts, including chequing accounts (sometimes called *demand deposits*) and some savings accounts (also called *time deposits*). Cash also includes items that are acceptable for deposit in those accounts, especially customers' cheques made payable to the company.

To increase their return, many companies invest their idle cash balances in assets called **cash equivalents.** These assets are short-term, highly liquid investments that satisfy two criteria:

1. The investment must be readily convertible to a known amount of cash.
2. The investment must be sufficiently close to its maturity date so that its market value is relatively insensitive to interest rate changes.

Examples of cash equivalents include temporary investments in treasury bills, commercial paper (short-term corporate notes payable), and money market funds.

Because cash equivalents are so similar to cash, many companies combine them with cash on the balance sheet. Others show them separately. For example, IBM Corporation shows these items on its published balance sheet:

(in millions)	December 31	
	1990	**1989**
Cash	$1,189	$ 741
Cash equivalents	2,664	2,959

Note that IBM had two to four times as much invested in cash equivalents as it did in cash.

As you would expect, cash is an important asset for every business. Because cash is so important, companies need to be careful about keeping track of it. They also need to carefully control access to cash by employees and others who might want to take it for their own use. A good accounting system provides for both goals. It can keep track of how much cash is on hand, and it can control who has access to the cash. Because of the special importance of cash, this chapter describes the practices companies follow to account for and protect cash.

Internal Control

LO 2 Explain why internal control procedures are needed in a large organization and state the broad principles of internal control.

In a small business, the owner-manager often controls the entire operation through personal supervision and direct participation in all its activities. For example, he or she commonly buys all the assets and services used in the business. The manager also hires and supervises all employees, negotiates all contracts, and signs all cheques. As a result, the manager knows from personal contact and observation whether the business actually received the assets and services for which the cheques were written. However, as a business grows, it becomes increasingly difficult to maintain this close personal contact. Therefore, at some point the manager must delegate responsibilities and rely on formal procedures rather than personal contact in controlling the operations of the business.

The procedures that control the operations of a business make up its **internal control system.** A properly designed internal control system encourages adherence to prescribed managerial policies. In doing so, it also promotes operational efficiencies and protects the business assets from waste, fraud, and theft. The system also helps ensure that accurate and reliable accounting data are produced.

Specific internal control procedures vary from company to company and depend on such factors as the nature of the business and its size. However, the same broad principles of internal control apply to all companies. Some of these broad principles are:

1. Clearly establish responsibilities.
2. Maintain adequate records.
3. Insure assets and bond employees.
4. Separate record-keeping from custody over assets.
5. Divide responsibilities for related transactions.
6. Use mechanical devices whenever practicable.
7. Perform regular and independent reviews.

We discuss these seven principles in the following paragraphs. Throughout, we describe various internal control procedures in terms of their ability to prevent fraud and theft. Remember, however, that these procedures are needed to ensure that the accounting records are complete and accurate.

Clearly Establish Responsibilities

To have good internal control, responsibility for each task must be clearly established and one person made accountable for its fulfillment. When responsibility is not clearly spelled out, it is difficult to determine who is at fault when something goes wrong. For example, when two sales clerks share access to the same cash register and there is a shortage, it may not be possible to tell which clerk is at fault. Each tends to blame the other. Neither can prove that he or she did not cause the shortage. To prevent this problem, one clerk should be given responsibility for making all change. Alternatively, the business can use a register with separate cash drawers for each operator.

AS A MATTER OF

Fact

Cash; Once Trash, Now Treasure

Ex-billionaire Donald Trump knows a hot idea when he hears one. Several months ago, when he was trying to unload the Trump shuttle, he announced that cash was in, debt was out. Poor Donald—if only he had put his money where his mouth was, he wouldn't be in hock to banks and bondholders today.

In the decade of debt financing, cash was trash. It wasn't smart to sit with it when other assets were going to the moon. But in the past 12 months, everything except cash has come crashing down to earth. Mergers and acquisitions are off nearly 50% because few corporations can borrow the money to swing a deal. Reputable real estate developers are going bust, and heavily mortgaged homeowners cannot afford to sell at rock-bottom prices. Meanwhile, cash in the form of Treasury bills is returning a steady 7% to 8%.

The ascendancy of cash implies that credit will be tighter in the Nineties than in the Eighties. Lenders will discriminate against corporations with weak balance sheets, putting them at a competitive disadvantage. Compare Nordstrom, the well-financed Seattle-based department store chain that is steadily expanding, with R. H. Macy, which is selling equity and trying to shed assets to pay down debt.

For homeowners and commercial real estate developers, King Cash means that property prices will likely remain depressed. Why? Explains investment banker Lewis Ranieri, chairman of Ranieri Wilson & Co.: "In today's environment, where asset values are falling, tighter credit standards are being imposed." Take, for example, a $100 million office building. In the good old days of debt, you could finance its purchase by putting up only 5%

cash—$5 million. Today, not only has the value of the property fallen to, say, $60 million, but a potential buyer must also come up with 25% cash—$15 million. That's a high enough hurdle to forestall any rapid recovery in real estate.

The implications of cash as an appreciating asset may not be pretty. James Grant, for one, thinks that deflation—that rare bird not seen on the American continent since the 1930s—is a distinct possibility. Says he: "If people decide that cash is a better store of value, then prices for houses and companies can only decline further. Potential buyers will demand that sellers capitulate on price before they will exchange the safety of cash for the illiquidity of other assets."

Source: Brett D. Fromson, *Fortune,* January 14, 1991, pp. 54 and 58, © 1991 The Time Inc. Magazine Company. All rights reserved.

Maintain Adequate Records

A good record-keeping system helps protect assets and ensures that employees follow prescribed procedures. Reliable records are also a source of information that management uses to monitor the operations of the business. For example, if detailed records of manufacturing equipment and tools are maintained, items are unlikely to be lost or otherwise disappear without any discrepancy being noticed. As another example, expenses and other expenditures are less likely to be debited to the wrong accounts if a comprehensive chart of accounts is established and followed carefully. If the chart is not in place or is not used correctly, management may never discover that some expenses are excessive.

Numerous preprinted forms and internal business papers should be designed and properly used to maintain good internal control. For example, if sales slips are properly designed, sales personnel can record the needed information efficiently without errors or delays to customers. And if all sales slips are prenumbered and controlled, each salesperson can be held responsible for the sales slips issued to him or her. As a result, a salesperson is not able to pocket cash by making a sale and destroying the sales slip. Computerized point-of-sale systems can be designed to achieve the same control results.

Insure Assets and Bond Key Employees

Assets should be covered by adequate casualty insurance, and employees who handle cash and negotiable assets should be bonded. An employee is said to be *bonded* when the company purchases an insurance policy, or bond, against losses from theft by that employee. Bonding clearly reduces the loss suffered by a theft. It also tends to discourage theft because bonded employees know that an impersonal bonding company must be dealt with when a theft is discovered, and future bondability may be at stake.

Separate Record-Keeping and Custody over Assets

A fundamental principle of internal control is that the person who has access to or is otherwise responsible for an asset should not maintain the accounting record for that asset. When this principle is followed, the custodian of an asset, knowing that a record of the asset is being kept by another person, is not as likely to misplace, misappropriate, or waste the asset. And, the record-keeper, who does not have access to the asset, has no reason to falsify the record. As a result, two people would have to agree to commit a fraud (called *collusion*) if the asset were to be misappropriated and the theft concealed in the records. Because collusion is necessary to commit the fraud, it is far less likely to happen.

Divide Responsibility for Related Transactions

Responsibility for a transaction or a series of related transactions should be divided among individuals or departments so that the work of one acts as a check on the other. However, this principle does not call for duplication of work. Each employee or department should perform an unduplicated portion.

For example, responsibility for placing orders, receiving the merchandise, and paying the vendors should not be given to one individual or department. Doing so creates a situation in which mistakes and perhaps fraud are more likely to occur. Having a different person check incoming goods for quality and quantity may encourage more care and attention to detail than having it done by the person who placed the order. And designating a third person to approve the payment of the invoice offers additional protection against error and fraud. Finally, giving a fourth person the authority to actually write cheques adds another measure of protection.

Use Mechanical Devices Whenever Practicable

Cash registers, cheque protectors, time clocks, and mechanical counters are examples of control devices that should be used whenever practicable. A cash register with a locked-in tape makes a record of each cash sale. A cheque protector perforates the amount of a cheque into its face, and makes it difficult to change the amount. A time clock registers the exact time an employee arrives on the job and the exact time the employee departs. Using mechanical change and currency counters is faster and more accurate than counting by hand and reduces the possibility of loss.

Perform Regular and Independent Reviews

Even a well-designed internal control system has a tendency to deteriorate as time passes. Changes in personnel and computer equipment present opportunities for shortcuts and other omissions. The stress of time pressures tends to bring about the same results. Thus, regular reviews of internal control systems are needed to be sure that the standard procedures are being followed. Where possible, these reviews should be performed by internal auditors who are not directly involved in operations. From their independent perspective, internal auditors can evaluate the overall efficiency of operations as well as the effectiveness of the internal control system.

Many companies also have audits by independent auditors who are public accountants. After testing the company's financial records, the public accountants give an opinion as to whether the company's financial statements are presented fairly in accordance with generally accepted accounting principles. However, before public accountants decide on how much testing they must do, they first evaluate the effectiveness of the internal control system. When making their evaluation, they can find areas for improvement and offer suggestions.

Computers and Internal Control

The broad principles of internal control should be followed for both manual and computerized accounting systems. However, computers have several important effects on internal control. Perhaps the most obvious is that computers provide rapid access to large quantities of information. As a result, management's ability to monitor and control business operations can be greatly improved.

LO 2 Explain why internal control procedures are needed in a large organization and state the broad principles of internal control.

Computers Reduce Processing Errors

Computers reduce the number of errors in processing information. Once the data are entered correctly, the possibility of mechanical and mathematical errors is largely eliminated. On the other hand, data entry errors may occur because the process of entering data may be more complex in a computerized system. Also, the lack of human involvement in later processing may cause data entry errors to go undiscovered.

Computers Allow More Extensive Testing of Records

The regular review and audit of computerized records can include more extensive testing because information can be accessed so rapidly. When manual methods are used, managers may select only small samples of data to test in order to reduce costs. But, when computers are used, large samples or even complete data files can be reviewed and analyzed.

Computerized Systems May Limit Hard Evidence of Processing Steps

Because many data processing steps are performed by the computer, fewer items of documentary evidence may be available for review. However, computer systems can actually create additional evidence by recording more information about who made entries and even when they were made. And the computer can be programmed to require the use of passwords before making entries so that access to the system is limited. Therefore, internal control may depend more on reviews of the design and operation of the computerized processing system and less on reviews of the documents left behind by the system.

Separation of Duties Must Be Maintained

Because computerized systems are so efficient, it is common to find that fewer employees are needed. This savings carries the risk that the separation of critical responsibilities may not be maintained. In addition, companies that use computers need employees with special skills to program and operate them. The duties of such employees must be controlled to minimize undetected errors and the risk of fraud. For example, better control is maintained if the person who designs and programs the system does not also serve as the operator. Similarly, control over programs and files related to cash receipts and disbursements should be separated. To prevent fraud, cheque-writing activities should not be controlled by the computer operator. However, achieving a suitable separation of duties can be especially difficult in small companies that have only a few employees.

Internal Control for Cash

LO 3 Describe internal control procedures used to protect cash received from cash sales, cash received through the mail, and cash disbursements.

Now that we have covered the principles of good internal control in general, it will be helpful to see how they are applied to cash, the most liquid of all assets.

A good system of internal control for cash should provide adequate procedures for protecting both cash receipts and cash disbursements. In designing the procedures, three basic guidelines should always be observed:

1. Duties should be separated so that people responsible for actually handling cash are not also responsible for keeping the cash records.
2. All cash receipts should be deposited in the bank, intact, each day.
3. All cash payments should be made by cheque.

The reason for the first principle is that a division of duties helps avoid errors. It also requires two or more people to collude if cash is to be embezzled (stolen) and the theft concealed in the accounting records. One reason for the second guideline is that the daily deposit of all receipts produces a timely independent test of the accuracy of the count of the cash received and the deposit. It also helps prevent loss or theft and keeps an employee from personally using the money for a few days before depositing it.

Finally, if all payments are made by cheque, the bank records provide an independent description of cash disbursements. This arrangement also tends to prevent thefts of cash. (One exception to this principle allows small disbursements of currency and coins to be made from a petty cash fund. Petty cash funds are discussed later in this chapter.) Note especially that the daily intact depositing of receipts and making disbursements by cheque allow you to use the bank records as a separate and external record of essentially all cash transactions. Later in the chapter, you will learn how the bank records are used to confirm the accuracy of your own records.

The exact procedures used to achieve control over cash vary from company to company. They depend on such factors as company size, number of employees, the volume of cash transactions, and the sources of cash. Therefore, the procedures described in the following paragraphs illustrate many but not all situations.

Cash from Cash Sales

Cash sales should be recorded on a cash register at the time of each sale. To help ensure that correct amounts are entered, each register should be placed so that customers can read the amounts when they are displayed. Also, clerks should be required to ring up each sale before wrapping the merchandise and should give the customer a receipt. Finally, each cash register should be designed to provide a permanent, locked-in record of each transaction. In some systems, the register is directly connected to a computer. The computer is programmed to accept cash register transactions and enter them in the accounting records. In other cases, the register simply prints a record of each transaction on a paper tape that is locked inside the register.

We stated earlier that custody over cash should be separated from record-keeping for cash. For cash sales, this separation begins with the cash register. The salesclerk who has access to the cash in the register should not have access to its locked-in record. At the end of each day, the salesclerk should count the cash in the register, record the result, and turn the cash and this record of the count over to an employee in the cashier's office. The employee in the cashier's office, like the salesclerk, has access to the cash and should not have access to the computerized accounting records (or the register tape). A third employee, preferably from the accounting department, examines the computerized record of register transactions (or the register tape) and compares its total with the cash receipts reported by the cashier's office. The computer record (or register tape) becomes the basis for the journal entry to record cash sales. Note that the accounting department employee has access to the records for cash but does not have access to the actual cash. The salesclerk and the employee from the cashier's office have access to the cash but not to the accounting records. Thus, their accuracy is automatically checked, and none of them can make a mistake or divert any cash without the difference being revealed.

Cash Received through the Mail

Control of cash that comes in through the mail begins with the person who opens the mail. Preferably, two people should be present when the mail is opened. One should make a list (in triplicate) of the money received. The list should record each sender's name, the amount, and the purpose for which the money was sent. One copy is sent to the cashier with the money. The second copy goes to the accounting department. The third copy is kept by the clerk who opened the mail. The cashier deposits the money in the bank, and the bookkeeper records the amounts received in the accounting records. Then, when the bank balance is reconciled (this process is discussed later in the chapter) by a fourth person, errors or fraud by the clerk, the cashier, or the bookkeeper will be detected. They will be detected because the bank's record of the amount of cash deposited and the records of three people must agree. Note how this arrangement makes errors and fraud nearly impossible unless the employees enter into collusion. If the clerk does not report all receipts accurately, the customers will question their account balances. If the cashier does not deposit all receipts intact, the bank balance will not agree with the bookkeeper's cash balance. The bookkeeper and the fourth person who reconciles the bank balance do not have access to cash and, therefore, have no opportunity to divert any to themselves. Thus, undetected errors and fraud are made highly unlikely.

Cash Disbursements

The previous discussions clearly show the importance of gaining control over cash from sales and cash received through the mail. Most large embezzlements, however, are actually accomplished through payments of fictitious invoices. Therefore, controlling cash disbursements is perhaps even more critical than controlling cash receipts.

As described earlier, the key to controlling cash disbursements is to require all expenditures to be made by cheque, except very small payments from petty cash. And, if authority to sign cheques is assigned to some person other than the business owner, that person should not have access to the accounting records. This separation of duties helps prevent an employee from concealing fraudulent disbursements in the accounting records.

In a small business, the owner-manager usually signs cheques and normally knows from personal contact that the items being paid for were actually received. However, this arrangement is impossible in a medium-sized or large business. In these settings, internal control procedures must be substituted for personal contact. The procedures are designed to assure the cheque signer that the obligations to be paid were properly incurred and should be paid. Often these controls are achieved through a voucher system.

A **voucher system** is a set of procedures designed to control the incurrence of obligations and disbursements of cash. This kind of system:

1. Establishes procedures for incurring obligations that result in cash disbursements, such as permitting only authorized individuals to make purchase commitments.
2. Provides established procedures for verifying, approving, and recording these obligations.
3. Permits cheques to be issued only in payment of properly verified, approved, and recorded obligations.
4. Requires that every obligation be recorded at the time it is incurred and that every purchase be treated as an independent transaction, complete in itself.

A good voucher system produces these results for every transaction, even if several purchases are made from the same company during a month or other billing period.

When a voucher system is used, control over cash disbursements begins as soon as the company incurs an obligation that will result in cash being paid out. A key factor in making the system work is that only specified departments and individuals are authorized to incur such obligations. Managers should also limit the kind of obligations that each department or individual can incur. For example, in a large retail store, only a specially created purchasing department should be authorized to incur obligations through merchandise purchases. In addition, the procedures for purchasing, receiving, and paying for merchandise should be divided among several departments. These departments include the one that originally requested the purchase, the purchasing department, the receiving department, and the accounting department. To coordinate and control the responsibilities of these departments, several different business papers are used. Illustration 7–1 shows how these papers are accumulated in a **voucher**. A voucher is an internal business paper used to accumulate other papers and information needed to control the disbursement of cash and to ensure that the transaction is properly recorded. The following explanation of each paper going into the voucher shows how companies use this system to gain control over cash disbursements for merchandise purchases.

The Voucher System and Control

LO 3 Describe internal control procedures used to protect cash received from cash sales, cash received through the mail, and cash disbursements.

Purchase Requisition

In a large retail store, department managers generally are not allowed to place orders directly with suppliers. If each manager could deal directly with suppliers, the amount of merchandise purchased and the resulting liabilities would not be well controlled. Therefore, to gain control over purchases and the resulting liabilities, department managers are usually required to place all orders through the purchasing department. When merchandise is needed, the department managers inform the purchasing department of their needs. Each manager performs this function by preparing and signing a business paper called a **purchase requisition.** On the requisition, the manager lists the merchandise needed by the department and requests that it be purchased. The original and

ILLUSTRATION 7–1

The Accumulation of Documents in the Voucher

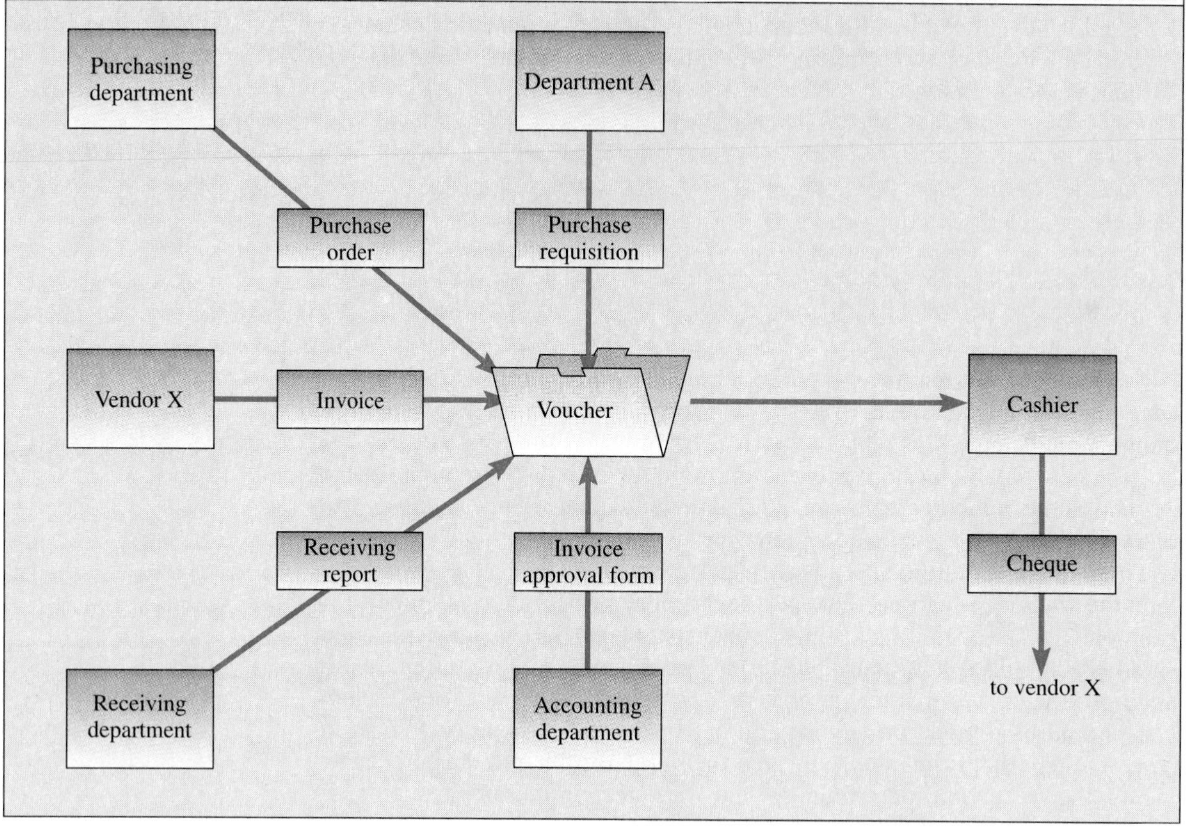

one copy of the purchase requisition are sent to the purchasing department. The manager of the requisitioning department (identified in Illustration 7–1 as department A) keeps the third copy as a back up. The purchasing department sends the second copy to the accounting department. When it is received, the accounting department creates a new voucher.

Purchase Order

A **purchase order** is a business paper used by the purchasing department to place an order with the seller, or **vendor,** which usually is a manufacturer or wholesaler. The purchase order (often abbreviated P.O.) authorizes the vendor to ship the ordered merchandise at the stated price and terms.

When a purchase requisition is received by the purchasing department, it prepares at least four copies of a purchase order. The copies are distributed as follows:

Copy 1, the original, is sent to the vendor as a request to purchase and as authority to ship the merchandise.

Copy 2, with a copy of the purchase requisition attached, is sent to the accounting department, where it is used in approving the payment of the invoice for the purchase; this copy is shown in Illustration 7–1.

Copy 3 is sent to the department originally issuing the requisition to inform its manager that the action has been taken.

Copy 4 is retained on file by the purchasing department.

Invoice

An **invoice** is an itemized statement prepared by the vendor that lists the customer's name, the items sold, the sales prices, and the terms of sale. In effect, the invoice is the bill sent to the buyer by the seller. (From the vendor's point of view, it is a *sales invoice*.) The vendor sends the invoice to the buyer, or **vendee,** who treats it as a *purchase invoice*. On receiving a purchase order, the vendor ships the ordered merchandise to the buyer and mails a copy of the invoice that covers the shipment. The goods are delivered to the buyer's receiving department, and the invoice is sent directly to the buyer's accounting department, where it is placed in the voucher. Illustration 7–1 also presents this document flow.

Receiving Report

Most large companies maintain a special department that receives all merchandise or other purchased assets. When each shipment arrives, this receiving department counts the goods and checks them for damage and agreement with the purchase order. Then it prepares four or more copies of a **receiving report.** This report is a form used within the business to notify the appropriate persons that ordered goods were received and to describe the quantities and condition of the goods. As shown in Illustration 7–1, one copy is sent to the accounting department and placed in the voucher. Copies are also sent to the original requisitioning department and the purchasing department to notify them that the goods have arrived. The receiving department retains a copy in its files.

Invoice Approval Form

After the receiving report arrives, the accounting department should have copies of these papers on file in the voucher:

1. The *purchase requisition* listing the items to be ordered.
2. The *purchase order* listing the merchandise that was actually ordered.
3. The *invoice* showing the quantity, description, price, and total cost of the goods shipped by the seller.
4. The *receiving report* listing the quantity and condition of the items actually received by the buyer.

With the information on these papers, the accounting department is in a position to make an entry recording the purchase and to approve its eventual

ILLUSTRATION 7–2

An Invoice Approval Form

	By	Date
Purchase order number	———	———
Requisition check	———	———
Purchase order check	———	———
Receiving report check	———	———
Invoice check:		
Price approval	———	———
Calculations	———	———
Terms	———	———
Approved for payment	———	———

payment before the end of the discount period. In approving the invoice for payment, the accounting department checks and compares the information on all the papers. To facilitate the checking procedure and to ensure that no step is omitted, the department commonly uses an **invoice approval form.** (See Illustration 7–2.) This form is a document on which the accounting department notes that it has performed each step in the process of checking an invoice and approving it for recording and payment. An invoice approval form may be a separate business paper that is filed in the voucher or it may be preprinted on the voucher. It may also be stamped on the invoice. For clarity, the flowchart in Illustration 7–1 shows the form as a separate document.

As each of the steps in the checking procedure is finished, the clerk initials the invoice approval form and records the current date. Initials in each space on the form indicate that the following administrative actions have been taken:

1. **Requisition check** . . . . The items on the invoice were actually requisitioned, as shown on the copy of the purchase requisition.

2. **Purchase order check** . . . . . The items on the invoice were actually ordered, as shown on the copy of the purchase order.

3. **Receiving report check** . . . . The items on the invoice were actually received, as shown on the copy of the receiving report.

4. **Invoice check:**
   Price approval . . . . The invoice prices are stated as agreed with the vendor.

   Calculations . . . . The invoice has no mathematical errors.

   Terms . . . . The terms are stated as agreed with the vendor.

ILLUSTRATION 7–3

Inside of a Voucher

VALLEY SUPPLY COMPANY   Voucher No.   93–767
Vancouver, B.C.

Date ____Oct. 1, 1993_____

Pay to ____A. B. Seay Wholesale Company_____

City____New Westminster_____   Province ____British Columbia_____

For the following: (attach all invoices and supporting papers)

Date of Invoice	Terms	Invoice Number and Other Details	Amount
Sept. 30, 1993	2/10, n/60	Invoice No. C-11756 Less discount Net amount payable	800.00 16.00 784.00

Payment approved

____*N. O. Neal*____
Auditor

The Voucher

After an invoice is checked and approved, the voucher is complete. At this point, the voucher is a record that summarizes the transaction. The voucher shows that the transaction has been certified as correct and authorizes its recording as an obligation of the buyer. The voucher also contains approval for paying the obligation on the appropriate date. Of course, the actual physical form used for vouchers varies substantially from company to company. In general, they are designed so that the invoice and other documents from which they are prepared are placed inside the voucher, which is often a folder. The information printed on the inside of a typical voucher is shown in Illustration 7–3, and the information on the outside is shown in Illustration 7–4.

The preparation of a voucher requires a clerk to enter the specified information in the proper blanks. The information is taken from the invoice and all the supporting documents and filed inside the voucher. Once the steps are completed, the voucher is sent to the appropriate authorized individual, who completes one final review of the information, approves the accounts and amounts to be debited (called the *accounting distribution*), and approves the voucher for recording.

After a voucher is approved and recorded, it is filed until its due date, when it is sent to the cashier's office for payment. Here, the person responsible for issuing cheques relies on the approved voucher and its signed support-

ILLUSTRATION 7–4

Outside of a Voucher	

ACCOUNTING DISTRIBUTION

Voucher No. _93–767_

Account Debited	Amount
Purchases	800.00
Transportation-In	
Store Supplies	
Office Supplies	
Sales Salaries	
Other	
Total Vouch. Pay. Cr.	800.00

Due date _____ *October 10, 1993*

Pay to _A. B. Seay Wholesale Company_
City_ *New Westminster*
Province ___ *British Columbia*

Summary of charges:
    Total charges _____ *800.00*
    Discount _____ *16.00*
    Net payment _____ *784.00*

Record of payment:
    Paid _____
    Cheque No _____

ing documents as proof that the obligation was properly incurred and should be paid. As described earlier, the purchase requisition and purchase order attached to the voucher confirm that the purchase was authorized. The receiving report shows that the items were received, and the invoice approval form verifies that the invoice was checked for errors. As a result, there is little chance for error. There is even less chance for fraud without collusion, unless all the documents and signatures are forged.

The Voucher System and Expenses

LO 3 Describe internal control procedures used to protect cash received from cash sales, cash received through the mail, and cash disbursements.

Under a voucher system, obligations should be approved for payment and recorded as liabilities as soon as possible after they are incurred. As shown in the example, this practice should be followed for all purchases. It should also be followed for all expenses. For example, when a company receives a monthly telephone bill, the charges (especially long-distance calls) should be examined for accuracy. A voucher should be prepared, and the telephone bill should be filed inside the voucher. The voucher is then recorded with a journal entry. If the amount is due at once, a cheque should be issued. Otherwise, the voucher should be filed for payment on the due date.

    The requirement that expenses be recorded in a voucher when they are incurred helps ensure that every expense payment is approved only when adequate information is available. However, invoices or bills for such things as equipment repairs are sometimes not received until weeks after the work is done. If no record of the repairs exists, it may be difficult to determine whether the invoice or bill correctly states the amount owed. Also, if no records exist, it may be possible for a dishonest employee to arrange with an outsider for more than one payment of an obligation, or for payment of excessive amounts, or for payment for goods and services not received. A properly functioning voucher system helps prevent all of these undesirable results.

Recording Vouchers

Normally, a company large enough to use a voucher system uses a computer in recording its transactions. For this reason and also because the primary purpose of this discussion is to describe the control techniques of a voucher system, we do not describe a manual system of recording vouchers here. However, Appendix D at the end of this chapter describes such a system.

The Petty Cash Fund

LO 4 Explain the operation of a petty cash fund and be able to prepare journal entries to record petty cash fund transactions.

A basic principle for controlling cash disbursements requires that all disbursements be made by cheque. However, an exception to this rule is made for *petty cash disbursements*. Every business must make many small payments for items such as postage, express charges, repairs, and small items of supplies. If firms made such payments by cheque, they would end up writing many cheques for small amounts. This arrangement would be both time consuming and expensive. Therefore, to avoid writing cheques for small amounts, a business establishes a petty cash fund and uses the money in this fund to make payments such as those listed above.

The first step in establishing a petty cash fund requires estimating the total amount of small payments likely to be made during a short period, such as a month. Then a cheque payable to the petty cash custodian (*petty cashier*) is drawn by the company cashier's office for an amount slightly in excess of this estimate. This cheque is recorded with a debit to the Petty Cash account (an asset) and a credit to Cash. The petty cashier is responsible for the safekeeping of the cash, for making payments from this fund, and for keeping accurate records.

The petty cashier should keep the petty cash in a locked box in a safe place. As each authorized disbursement is made, the person receiving payment signs a *petty cash receipt* (see Illustration 7–5). The receipt is then placed in the petty cashbox with the remaining money. Under this system, the cashbox should always contain petty cash receipts and cash equal to the amount of the fund. The total should remain constant. For example, a $100 petty cash fund could have (*a*) $100 in cash, (*b*) $80 in cash and $20 in receipts, or (*c*) $10 in cash and $90 in receipts. Notice that each disbursement reduces the cash and increases the sum of the receipts in the petty cashbox. When the cash is nearly gone, the fund should be reimbursed.

To reimburse the fund, the petty cashier presents the receipts to the company cashier. The company cashier stamps all receipts *paid* so that they cannot be reused, retains them, and gives the petty cashier a cheque for their sum. When this cheque is cashed and the proceeds returned to the cashbox, the money in the box is restored to its original amount, and the fund is ready to begin a new cycle of operations.

ILLUSTRATION 7–5

A Petty Cash Receipt

No. _- 1 -_ $ _$10.00_

RECEIVED OF PETTY CASH

Date _Nov. 2_ 19 _93_

For _Washing windows_

Charge to _Miscellaneous expenses_

Approved by
_C a B_

Received by
Bob Jone

TOPS-Form 3008

At the time a cheque is written to reimburse the petty cash fund, the petty cashier should sort the paid receipts according to the type of expense or other accounts to be debited in recording payments from the fund. Each group is then totaled and used in making the entry to record the reimbursement.

Illustration of a Petty Cash Fund

To avoid writing numerous cheques for small amounts, a company established a petty cash fund on November 1, designating one of its office clerks, Carl Burns, as petty cashier. A $75 cheque was drawn, cashed, and the proceeds turned over to Burns. The following entry recorded the cheque:

Nov.	1	Petty Cash.	75.00	
		Cash		75.00
		Established a petty cash fund.		

Notice that this entry transfers $75 from the regular Cash account to the Petty Cash account. After the petty cash fund is established, the Petty Cash account is not debited or credited again unless the size of the total fund is changed. For example, the fund should be increased if it is being exhausted and reimbursed too frequently. Another entry like the preceding one would be made to record an increase in the size of the fund. That is, there would be a debit to Petty Cash

ILLUSTRATION 7–6

Summary of Petty Cash Payments		
Miscellaneous expenses:		
Nov. 2, washing windows	$10.00	
Nov. 17, washing windows	10.00	
Nov. 27, computer repairs	26.50	$46.50
Transportation-in:		
Nov. 5, delivery of merchandise purchased	$ 6.75	
Nov. 20, delivery of merchandise purchased	8.30	15.05
Delivery expense:		
Nov. 18, customer's package delivered		5.00
Office supplies:		
Nov. 15, purchased office supplies		4.75
Total		$71.30

and credit to Cash for the amount of the increase. If the fund is too large, some of the money in the fund should be redeposited in the bank chequing account. Such a reduction in the fund is recorded with a debit to Cash and a credit to Petty Cash.

During November, Carl Burns, the petty cashier, made several payments from the cash fund. Each time, he asked the person who received payment to sign a receipt. On November 27, after making a $26.50 payment for repairs to an office computer, Burns decided there might not be enough cash in the fund for another payment. Therefore, he summarized and totaled the petty cash receipts as shown in Illustration 7–6. Then the summary and the petty cash receipts were given to the company cashier in exchange for a $71.30 cheque to reimburse the fund. Burns cashed the cheque, put the $71.30 proceeds in the petty cashbox, and was then ready to make additional payments from the fund.

The reimbursing cheque is recorded with the following journal entry:

Nov.	27	Miscellaneous Expenses	46.50	
		Transportation-In	15.05	
		Delivery Expense	5.00	
		Office Supplies	4.75	
		Cash		71.30
		Reimbursed petty cash.		

Information for this entry came from the petty cashier's summary of payments. Note that the debits in the entry record the petty cash payments. Even if the petty cash fund is not low on funds at the end of an accounting period, it may be reimbursed at that time to record the expenses in the proper period. Otherwise, the financial statements will show an overstated petty cash asset and understated expenses or assets that were paid for out of petty cash. (Of course, the amounts involved are seldom if ever significant to users of the financial statements.)

Cash Over and Short

Sometimes, a petty cashier fails to get a receipt for a payment. Then, when the fund is reimbursed, he or she may forget the purpose of the expenditure. This mistake causes the fund to be short. If, for whatever reason, the petty cash fund is short at reimbursement time, the shortage is recorded as an expense in the reimbursing entry with a debit to the **Cash Over and Short account.** This account is an income statement account that records the income effects of cash overages and cash shortages arising from omitted petty cash receipts and from errors in making change.

Errors in making change are discovered when there are differences between the cash in a cash register and the record of the amount of cash sales. Even though a cashier is careful, some customers may be given too much or too little change. As a result, at the end of a day, the actual cash from a cash register may not equal the cash sales rung up. For example, assume that a cash register shows cash sales of $550 but the actual count of cash in the register is $555. The entry to record the cash sales and the overage would be:

Nov.	23	Cash.	555.00	
		Cash Over and Short		5.00
		Sales		550.00
		Day's cash sales and overage.		

On the other hand, if there were a shortage of cash in the register on the next day, the entry to record cash sales and the shortage would look like the following:

Nov.	24	Cash.	621.00	
		Cash Over and Short	4.00	
		Sales		625.00
		Day's cash sales and shortage.		

Because customers are more likely to dispute being shortchanged, the Cash Over and Short account usually has a debit balance by the end of the accounting period. Because it is a debit, this balance represents an expense. This expense can be shown on the income statement as a separate item in the general and administrative expense section. Or, because the amount is usually small, you can combine it with other small expenses and report them as a single item called *miscellaneous expenses*. If Cash Over and Short has a credit balance at the end of the period, it usually is shown on the income statement as part of *miscellaneous revenues*.

Reconciling the Bank Balance

At least once every month, banks send depositors a bank statement that shows the activity in their accounts during the month. Different banks use a variety of formats for their bank statements. However, all of them include the following items of information in one place or another:

AS A MATTER OF
Ethics

Nancy Tucker is an internal auditor for a large corporation and is in the process of making surprise counts of three $200 petty cash funds in various offices in the headquarters building. She arrived at the office of one of the fund custodians shortly before lunch while he was on the telephone. Tucker explained the purpose of her visit, and the custodian asked politely that she come back after lunch so that he could finish the business he was conducting by long distance. She agreed and returned around 1:30. The custodian opened the petty cashbox and showed her nine new $20 bills with consecutive serial numbers plus receipts that totaled $20. Would you suggest that the auditor take any further action or comment on these events in her report to management?

1. The balance of the depositor's account at the beginning of the month.
2. Deposits and any other amounts added to the account during the month.
3. Cheques and any other amounts deducted from the account during the month.
4. The account balance at the end of the month.

LO 5 Explain why the bank balance and the book balance of cash should be reconciled and be able to prepare a reconciliation.

Of course, all this information is presented as it appears in the bank's records. Illustration 7–7 presents an example of a typical bank statement. Examine it now to find the four items just listed.

Enclosed with the monthly statement are the depositor's **canceled cheques** and any debit or credit memoranda that have affected the account. Canceled cheques are cheques that the bank has paid and deducted from the customer's account during the month. They are called *canceled cheques* because they have been stamped to show that they were paid. Other deductions that may appear on the bank statement for an individual include withdrawals through automatic teller machines and periodic payments arranged in advance by the depositor.[1] Other deductions from the depositor's account may include service charges and fees assessed by the bank (note that Valley Company's account was debited for a $1 service charge), customer cheques deposited that prove to be uncollectible, and corrections of previous errors. Except for the service charges, the bank notifies the depositor of the deduction in each case with a debit memorandum at the time that the bank reduces the balance. For completeness, a copy of each debit memorandum is usually sent with the monthly statement.[2]

---

[1] Because of the need to make all disbursements by cheque, it is unusual to find a business chequing account that allows withdrawals.

[2] As a matter of clarification, the depositor's account is a liability on the bank's records. Thus, a deposit increases the depositor's account balance, and the bank records it with a *credit* to the account—an increase in the bank's liability. The depositor, on the other hand, considers the deposit to be an increase in an asset, and records it with a *debit* to the Cash account. Cheques reduce the depositor's account balance, and the bank records them as a *debit* while the depositor records them with a *credit*. Debit memos from the bank produce *credits* on the depositor's books, and credit memos lead to *debits*.

ILLUSTRATION 7–7

A Typical Bank Statement				

LONDON BANK LB

VALLEY COMPANY   LONDON BANK
39 MAPLE STREET   NOV 30
LONDON, ONTARIO   DAILY INTEREST
K2M 4K6   ACCOUNT

BRANCH   ACCOUNT NUMBER | BALANCE FORWARD |
LONDON MAIN   007–500865 | 7,502.02 |

DATE	SYMBOL	WITHDRAWALS	DEPOSITS	BALANCE
OCT 31	756	1,102.31		6,399.71
OCT 31	757	179.00		6,220.71
NOV 02	NBD		20,000.00	26,220.71
NOV 02	755	835.17		25,385.54
NOV 03	PL	250.00		25,135.54
NOV 04	759	1,116.00		24,019.54
NOV 08	749	32.00		23,987.54
NOV 08	747	4,212.00		19,775.54
NOV 09	751	50.00		19,725.54
NOV 10	762	1,906.81		17,818.73
NOV 14	PL	250.00		17,568.73
NOV 14	764	940.43		16,628.30
NOV 14	750	113.78		16,514.52
NOV 15	CM		2,075.05	18,589.57
NOV 15	770	10,000.00		8,589.57
NOV 15	763	267.29		8,322.28
NOV 15	767	86.46		8,235.82
NOV 17	766	125.00		8,110.82
NOV 17	769	164.00		7,946.82
NOV 21	765	89.78		7,857.04
NOV 23	771	150.00		7,707.04
NOV 24	768	178.29		7,528.75
NOV 30	INT		78.89	7,607.64
NOV 30	S/C	1.00		7,606.64**

EXPLANATION OF SYMBOLS

Each transaction is identified by one of the following symbols.
Talk to your branch staff if you have any questions.

AID Investment Certificate Interest	INT Interest	OBC Other Bank Service Charge
CHQ Cheque	JCW Johnny Cash Withdrawal	PAY Payroll Deposit
CM Miscellaneous Credit	MCM Merchant MasterCard Credit	PL Loan Payment
COR Correction	MDM Merchant MasterCard Debit	PWR Powerline Payment
CSB Canada Savings Bond Transaction	MTC MasterTeller Service Charge	RTD Returned Item
DEP Deposit	MTG Mortgage Payment	SC Service Charge
DM Miscellaneous Debit	MTW MasterTeller Withdrawal	SDB Safe Deposit Box Payment
ECM Electronic Funds Credit	NBD No Book Deposit	WD Withdrawal
EDM Electronic Funds Debit	NBW No Book Withdrawal	
ICW Interac Withdrawal	NRT Non Resident Tax	

In addition to deposits made by the depositor, the bank may add amounts to the depositor's account. Examples of additions would be amounts the bank has collected on behalf of the depositor and corrections of previous errors. Credit memoranda notify the depositor of all additions when they are first recorded. For completeness, a copy of each credit memorandum may be sent with the monthly statement.

Another item commonly added to the bank balance on the statement is interest earned by the depositor. Some chequing accounts pay the depositor interest based on the average cash balance maintained in the account. The bank calculates the amount of interest earned and credits it to the depositor's account each month. In Illustration 7–7, note that the bank credited $78.89 of interest to the account of Valley Company. (The methods used to calculate interest are discussed in the next chapter.)

When the business deposits all receipts intact and when all payments (other than petty cash payments) are paid from the account, the bank statement is a device for proving the accuracy of the depositor's cash records. The test of the accuracy begins by preparing a **bank reconciliation**, which is an analysis that explains the difference between the balance of a chequing account shown in the depositor's records and the balance shown on the bank statement.

Need for Reconciling the Bank Balance

For virtually all chequing accounts, the balance shown on the bank statement does not agree with the balance in the depositor's accounting records. Therefore, to prove the accuracy of both the depositor's records and those of the bank, you must **reconcile** the two balances. In other words, you must explain or account for the differences between them.

Numerous factors cause the bank statement balance to differ from the depositor's book balance. Some are:

1. **Outstanding cheques.** These cheques were written (or drawn) by the depositor, deducted on the depositor's records, and sent to the payees. However, they are called **outstanding cheques** because they had not reached the bank for payment and deduction before the statement date.

2. **Unrecorded deposits.** Companies often make deposits at the end of each business day, after the bank is closed. These deposits are made in the bank's night depository and are not recorded by the bank until the next business day. Therefore, if a deposit is placed in the night depository on the last day of the month, it will not appear on the bank statement for that month. In addition, deposits mailed to the bank toward the end of the month may be in transit and unrecorded when the statement is prepared.

3. **Charges for uncollectible items and for service.** Occasionally, a company deposits a customer's cheque that bounces, or turns out to be uncollectible. Usually, the problem is nonsufficient funds in the customer's account to cover the cheque. In these cases, the cheque is called a *nonsufficient funds (NSF) cheque*. In other situations, the customer's account has been closed. In processing deposited cheques, the bank first credits

the depositor's account for the full amount. Later, when the bank learns that the cheque is uncollectible, it debits (reduces) the depositor's account for the amount of the cheque. Also, the bank may charge the depositor a fee for processing the uncollectible cheque. At the same time, the bank notifies the depositor of each deduction by mailing a debit memorandum. Although each deduction should be recorded by the depositor on the day the debit memorandum is received, sometimes an entry is not made until the bank reconciliation is prepared.

Other charges to a depositor's account that a bank might report on the bank statement include the printing of new cheques. Also, the bank may assess a monthly service charge for maintaining the account. Notification of these charges is not provided until the statement is mailed.

4. **Credits for collections and for interest.** Banks occasionally act as collection agents for their depositors by collecting promissory notes and other items. When the bank collects an item, it deducts a fee and adds the net proceeds to the depositor's account. At the same time, it sends a credit memorandum to notify the depositor of the transaction. As soon as the memorandum is received, it should be recorded by the depositor. However, these items may remain unrecorded until the time of the bank reconciliation.

    Many bank accounts earn interest on the average cash balance in the account during the month. If an account earns interest, the bank statement includes a credit for the amount earned during the past month. Notification of earned interest is provided only by the bank statement.

5. **Errors.** Regardless of care and systems of internal control for automatic error detection, both banks and depositors make errors. Errors by the bank may not be discovered until the depositor completes the bank reconciliation. Also, the depositor's errors often are not discovered until the balance is reconciled.

Steps in Reconciling the Bank Balance

To obtain the benefits of separated duties, an employee who does not handle cash receipts, process cheques, or maintain cash records should prepare the bank reconciliation. In preparing to reconcile the balance, this employee must gather information from the bank statement and from other sources in the records. The person who performs the reconciliation must do the following:

- Compare the deposits listed on the bank statement with the deposits shown in the accounting records. Identify any discrepancies and determine which is correct. Make a list of any errors or unrecorded deposits.

- Examine all other credits shown on the bank statement and determine whether each was recorded in the books. These items include collections by the bank, correction of previous bank statement errors, and interest earned by the depositor. List any unrecorded items.

- Compare the canceled cheques listed on the bank statement with the actual cheques returned with the statement. For each cheque, make sure that the correct amount was deducted by the bank and that the returned cheque was properly charged to the company's account. List any discrepancies or errors.

■ Compare the canceled cheques listed on the bank statement with the cheques recorded in the books. Prepare a list of any outstanding cheques.

Although an individual may occasionally issue a cheque and fail to record it in the books, companies with reasonable internal controls would rarely, if ever, write a cheque without recording it. Nevertheless, prepare a list of any canceled cheques unrecorded in the books.

■ Determine whether any outstanding cheques listed on the previous month's bank reconciliation are not included in the canceled cheques listed on the bank statement. Prepare a list of any of these cheques that remain outstanding at the end of the current month. Send this list to the cashier's office for follow-up with the payees to see if the cheques were actually received.

■ Examine all other debits to the account shown on the bank statement and determine whether each one was recorded in the books. These include bank charges for newly printed cheques, NSF cheques, and monthly service charges. List those not yet recorded.

When this information has been gathered, the employee can complete the reconciliation like the one in Illustration 7–8 by using these steps:

1. Start with the bank balance of the cash account.
2. Identify and list any unrecorded deposits and any bank errors that understated the bank balance. Add them to the bank balance.
3. Identify and list any outstanding cheques and any bank errors that overstated the bank balance. Subtract them from the bank balance.
4. Compute the adjusted balance. This amount is also called the *correct,* or *reconciled,* balance.
5. Start with the book balance of the cash account.
6. Identify and list any unrecorded credit memoranda from the bank (perhaps for the proceeds of a collected note), interest earned, and any errors that understated the book balance. Add them to the book balance.
7. Identify and list any unrecorded debit memoranda from the bank (perhaps for an NSF cheque from a customer), service charges, and any errors that overstated the book balance. Subtract them from the book balance.
8. Compute the reconciled balance. This is also the correct balance.
9. Verify that the two adjusted balances from steps 4 and 8 are equal. If so, they are reconciled. If not, check for mathematical accuracy and for any missing data.

When the reconciliation is complete, the employee should send a copy to the accounting department so that any needed journal entries can be recorded. For example, entries are needed to record any unrecorded debit and credit

ILLUSTRATION 7–8

A Typical Bank Reconciliation

MOUNTAIN COMPANY
Bank Reconciliation
October 31, 1993

① Bank statement balance . . . . $2,050.00   ⑤ Book balance $1,404.58
② Add: ⑥ Add:
    Deposit of 31/10 . . . . 145.00   Proceeds of note less
    Deposits in transit.   collection fee of $15 . . . . $ 485.00 → ⓐ
                                                            Interest earned . . . .   8.42 → ⓑ
                                                           Total . . . . $ 493.42
    Total . . . . $2,195.00   Total $1,898.00
③ Deduct: ⑦ Deduct:
    Outstanding cheques: NSF cheque plus service
        No. 124 . . . . $ 150.00   charge . . . . $ 30.00 → ⓒ
        No. 126 . . . .   200.00   Cheque printing charge. . . .   23.00 → ⓓ
    Total. . . . . $ 350.00   Total . . . . $ 53.00
③ Reconciled balance. . . . . . . $1,845.00   ⑧ Reconciled balance $1,845.00
                true cash balance

⑨ The two balances both equal $1,845.00

memoranda and any of the company's mistakes. Another copy should go to the cashier's office, especially if the bank has made an error that needs to be corrected.

Illustration of a Bank Reconciliation

We can illustrate a bank reconciliation by preparing one for Mountain Company as of October 31. In preparing to reconcile the bank account, the Mountain Company employee gathered the following facts:

- The bank balance shown on the bank statement was $2,050.
- The cash balance according to the accounting records was $1,404.58.
- A $145 deposit was placed in the bank's night depository on October 31 and was unrecorded by the bank when the bank statement was mailed.
- Enclosed with the bank statement was a copy of a credit memorandum showing that the bank had collected a note receivable for the company on October 23. The note's proceeds of $500 (less a $15 collection fee) were credited to the company's account. This credit memorandum had not been recorded by the company.
- The bank statement also showed a credit of $8.42 for interest earned on the average cash balance in the account. Because there had been no prior notification of this item, it had not been recorded on the company's books.
- A comparison of canceled cheques with the company's books showed that two cheques were outstanding—No. 124 for $150 and No. 126 for $200.
- Other debits on the bank statement that had not been previously re-

corded on the books included (*a*) a $23 charge for cheques printed by the bank, and (*b*) an NSF (nonsufficient funds) cheque for $20 plus the related processing fee of $10. The NSF cheque had been received from a customer, Frank Green, on October 16 and had been included in that day's deposit.

Illustration 7–8 shows the bank reconciliation that reflects these items. The numbers in the circles beside the various parts of the reconciliation correspond to the numbers of the steps listed earlier.

Preparing a bank reconciliation helps locate any errors made by either the bank or the depositor. It also identifies unrecorded items that should be recorded on the company's books. For example, in Mountain Company's reconciliation, the adjusted balance of $1,845.00 is the correct balance as of October 31, 1993. However, at that date, Mountain Company's accounting records show a $1,404.58 balance. Therefore, journal entries must be made to increase the book balance to the correct balance. This process requires four entries. The first is

Nov.	2	Cash.	485.00	
		Collection Expense	15.00	
		Notes Receivable.		500.00
		To record the collection fee and proceeds of a note collected by the bank.		

This entry records the net proceeds of Mountain Company's note receivable that had been collected by the bank, the expense of having the bank perform that service, and the reduction in the Notes Receivable account.

The second entry records the interest credited to Mountain Company's account by the bank:

Nov.	2	Cash.	8.42	
		Interest Earned.		8.42
		To record interest earned on the average cash balance maintained in the chequing account.		

Interest earned is a revenue, and the entry recognizes both the revenue and the related increase in Cash.

The third entry records the NSF cheque that was returned as uncollectible. The $20 cheque was received from Green in payment of his account and deposited. The bank charged $10 for handling the NSF cheque and deducted $30 from Mountain Company's account. Therefore, the company must reverse the entry made when the cheque was received and also record the $10 processing fee:

Nov.	2	Accounts Receivable—Frank Green	30.00	
		Cash		30.00
		To charge Frank Green's account for his NSF cheque and for the bank's fee.		

This entry reflects the fact that Mountain Company followed customary business practice and added the NSF $10 fee to Green's account. Thus, it will try to collect the entire $30 from Green.

The fourth entry debits Miscellaneous General Expenses for the cheque printing charge. The entry is

Nov.	2	Miscellaneous Expenses	23.00	
		Cash		23.00
		Cheque printing charge.		

After these entries are recorded, the balance of cash is increased to the correct amount of $1,845.00 ($1,404.58 + $485.00 + 8.42 − $30.00 − $23.00).

Other Internal Control Procedures

LO 6 Tell how recording invoices at net amounts helps gain control over cash discounts taken and be able to account for invoices recorded at net amounts.

Internal control principles apply to every phase of a company's operations, including merchandise purchases, sales, cash receipts, cash disbursements, and owning and operating plant assets. Many of these procedures are discussed in later chapters. At this point, we consider a way that a company can gain more control over *purchases discounts*.

Recall that entries such as the following have been used to record the receipt and payment of an invoice for a purchase of merchandise:

Oct.	2	Purchases	1,000.00	
		Accounts Payable		1,000.00
		Purchased merchandise, terms 2/10, n/60.		
	12	Accounts Payable	1,000.00	
		Purchases Discounts		20.00
		Cash		980.00
		Paid the invoice of October 2.		

These entries reflect the **gross method of recording purchases.** That is, the invoice was recorded at its gross amount of $1,000 before considering the cash discount. Many companies record invoices in this way. However, the **net method of recording purchases** records invoices at their *net* amounts (after cash discounts). This method is widely thought to provide more useful information to management.

To illustrate the net method, assume that a company purchases merchandise with a $1,000 invoice price and terms of 2/10, n/60. On receiving the goods, the purchasing company deducted the offered $20 discount from the gross amount and recorded the purchase at the $980 net amount:

Oct.	2	Purchases	980.00	
		Accounts Payable		980.00
		Purchased merchandise on account.		

If the invoice for this purchase is paid within the discount period, the entry to record the payment debits Accounts Payable and credits Cash for $980. How-

ILLUSTRATION 7–9

Reporting Discounts Lost When the Net Method of Recording Purchases Is Used

XYZ COMPANY
Income Statement
For Year Ended December 31, 1993

Sales	$100,000
Cost of goods sold	60,000
Gross profit from sales	$ 40,000
Operating expenses	28,000
Income from operations	$ 12,000
Other expenses:	
Discounts lost	(150)
Net income.	$ 11,850

ever, if payment is not made within the discount period and the discount is *lost*, an entry such as the following must be made either before or when the invoice is paid:

Dec.	1	Discounts Lost	20.00	
		Accounts Payable		20.00
		To record the discount lost.		

A cheque for the full $1,000 invoice amount is then written, recorded, and mailed to the creditor.[3]

Advantage of the Net Method

When invoices are recorded at *gross* amounts, the amount of discounts taken is deducted from the balance of the Purchases account on the income statement to arrive at the cost of merchandise purchased. However, the amount of any lost discounts does not appear in any account or on the income statement. Therefore, lost discounts may not come to the attention of management.

On the other hand, when purchases are recorded at *net* amounts, the amount of discounts taken does not appear on the income statement. Instead, an expense for **discounts lost** is brought to management's attention through its appearance on the income statement. This practice is shown in the condensed income statement of Illustration 7–9. Its balance equals the cost resulting from the failure to take advantage of cash discounts on purchases.

Recording invoices at their net amounts supplies management with useful information about the amount of discounts missed through oversight, carelessness, or some other reason. Thus, this practice gives management better control over the people responsible for paying bills on time so that cash

[3] Alternatively, the lost discount can be recorded with the late payment in a single entry.

discounts can be taken. When the accounts record the fact that discounts are missed, someone has to explain why. As a result, it is likely that fewer discounts are lost through carelessness.

Summary of the Chapter in Terms of Learning Objectives

LO 1. The liquidity of an asset refers to how easily the asset can be converted into other types of assets or used to buy services or satisfy obligations. Cash is the most liquid asset. To increase their return, companies may invest their idle cash balances in cash equivalents. These investments are readily convertible to a known amount of cash and are purchased so close to their maturity date that their market values are relatively insensitive to interest rate changes.

LO 2. Internal control systems are designed to encourage adherence to prescribed managerial policies. In doing so, they promote operational efficiencies, and protect assets against theft or misuse. They also help ensure that accurate and reliable accounting data are produced. Principles of good internal control include establishing clear responsibilities, maintaining adequate records, insuring assets and bonding employees, separating record-keeping and custody of assets, dividing responsibilities for related transactions, using mechanical devices whenever practicable, and performing regular independent reviews of internal control practices.

LO 3. To maintain control over cash, custody must be separated from record-keeping for cash. All cash receipts should be deposited intact in the bank on a daily basis, and all payments (except for minor petty cash payments) should be made by cheque. A voucher system helps maintain control over cash disbursements by ensuring that payments are made only after full documentation and approval.

LO 4. The petty cashier, who should be a responsible employee, makes small payments from the petty cash fund and obtains signed receipts for the payments. The Petty Cash account is debited when the fund is established or increased in size. Petty cash disbursements are recorded with a credit to cash whenever the fund is replenished.

LO 5. A bank reconciliation is produced to prove the accuracy of the depositor's and the bank's records. In completing the reconciliation, the bank statement balance is adjusted for such items as outstanding cheques and unrecorded deposits made on or before the bank statement date but received by the bank after that date. The depositor's cash account balance is adjusted to the correct balance. The difference also arises from such items as service charges, collections the bank has made for the depositor, and interest earned on the average chequing account balance.

LO 6. When the net method of recording invoices is used, missed cash discounts are reported as an expense. In contrast, when the gross method is used, discounts taken are reported as reductions in the cost of the purchased goods. Therefore, the net method directs management's attention to instances where the company failed to take advantage of discounts.

Complete the following table for a bank reconciliation as of September 30. Place an *x* in the appropriate columns to indicate whether the item should be added to or deducted from the book or bank balance, or whether it should not appear on the reconciliation. If the book balance is to be adjusted, place a *Dr.* or *Cr.* in the Must Adjust column to indicate whether the cash balance should be debited or credited.

Demonstration Problem

	Bank Balance		Book Balance			Not Shown on the Reconciliation
	Add	Deduct	Add	Deduct	Must Adjust	
1. Interest earned on the account.						
2. Deposit made on September 30 after the bank was closed.						
3. Cheques outstanding on August 31 that cleared the bank in September.						
4. NSF cheque from customer returned on September 15 but not recorded by the company.						
5. Cheques written and mailed to payees on September 30.						
6. Deposit made on September 5 that was processed on September 8.						
7. Unrecorded withdrawal by owner using Automatic Teller Machine.						
8. Bank service charge.						
9. Cheques written and mailed to payees on October 5.						
10. Cheque written by another depositor but charged against the company's account.						
11. Principal and interest collected by the bank but not recorded by the company.						
12. Special charge for collection of note in No. 11 on company's behalf.						
13. Cheque written against the account and cleared by the bank; erroneously omitted by the bookkeeper.						

Solution to Demonstration Problem

Planning the Solution

- Examine each item to determine whether it affects the book balance or the bank balance.
- If it acts to increase the balance, place an *x* in the Add column. If it acts to decrease the balance, place an *x* in the Deduct column.
- If the item increases or decreases the book balance, enter a *Dr.* or *Cr.* in the adjustment column.
- If the item does not affect either balance, place an *x* in the Not Shown on the Reconciliation column.

	Bank Balance		Book Balance			Not Shown on the Reconciliation
	Add	Deduct	Add	Deduct	Must Adjust	
1. Interest earned on the account.			x		Dr.	
2. Deposit made on September 30 after the bank was closed.	x					
3. Cheques outstanding on August 31 that cleared the bank in September.						x
4. NSF cheque from customer returned on September 15 but not recorded by the company.				x	Cr.	
5. Cheques written and mailed to payees on September 30.		x				
6. Deposit made on September 5 that was processed on September 8.						x
7. Unrecorded withdrawal by owner using Automatic Teller Machine.				x	Cr.	
8. Bank service charge.				x	Cr.	
9. Cheques written and mailed to payees on October 5.						x
10. Cheque written by another depositor but charged against the company's account.	x					
11. Principal and interest collected by the bank but not recorded by the company.			x		Dr.	
12. Special charge for collection of note in No. 11 on company's behalf.				x	Cr.	
13. Cheque written against the account and cleared by the bank; erroneously omitted by the bookkeeper.				x	Cr.	

D

Recording Vouchers: Manual System

When a voucher system is in use, an account called *Vouchers Payable* replaces the Accounts Payable account described in previous chapters. And for every transaction that will result in a cash disbursement, a voucher is prepared and credited to this account. For example, when merchandise is purchased, the voucher covering the transaction is recorded with a debit to Purchases and a credit to Vouchers Payable. Likewise, when a plant asset is purchased or an expense is incurred, the voucher of the transaction is recorded with a debit to the proper plant asset or expense account and a credit to Vouchers Payable.

In a manual system, vouchers are recorded in a **Voucher Register** similar to Illustration D–1. Such a register has a Vouchers Payable Credit column and a number of debit columns. The exact debit columns vary from company to company, but merchandising concerns always provide a Purchases Debit column. Also, as long as space is available, special debit columns are provided for transactions that occur frequently. In addition, an Other Accounts Debit column is provided for transactions that do not occur often.

In recording vouchers in a register like that of Illustration D–1, all information about each voucher, other than information about its payment, is entered as soon as the voucher is approved for recording. The information as to payment date and the number of the paying cheque is entered later as each voucher is paid.

In posting a Voucher Register like that in Illustration D–1, the columns are first totaled and crossfooted to prove their equality. The Vouchers Payable column total is then credited to the Vouchers Payable account. The totals of the Purchases, Transportation-In, Sales Salaries Expense, Advertising Expense, Delivery Expense, and Office Salaries Expense columns are debited to these accounts. None of the individual amounts in these columns are posted. However, the individual amounts in the Other Accounts column are posted as individual amounts, and the column total is not posted.

LO 8 Explain the use of a Voucher Register and Cheque Register and prepare entries to record and pay liabilities when these registers are used in a manual accounting system.

ILLUSTRATION D–1

A Voucher Register

Page 32   Voucher

Date 19—		Voucher No.	Payee	When and How Paid		Vouchers Payable Credit	Purchases Debit	Transpor- tation-In Debit	
				Date	Cheque No.				
Oct.	1	767	A. B. Seay Co.	6/10	733	800.00	800.00		1
	1	768	Daily Sentinel	9/10	744	53.00			2
	2	769	Seaboard Supply Co.	12/10	747	235.00	155.00	10.00	3
	6	770	George Smith	6/10	734	85.00			4
	6	771	Frank Jones	6/10	735	95.00			5
	6	772	George Roth	6/10	736	95.00			6
	30	998	First National Bank	30/10	972	505.00			33
									34
	30	999	Pacific Telephone Co.	30/10	973	18.00			35
	31	1000	Tarbell Wholesale Co.			235.00	235.00		36
	31	1001	Office Equipment Co.	31/10	974	195.00			37
	31		Totals			5,079.00	2,435.00	156.00	38
						(226)	(505)	(508)	39
									40
									41

The Unpaid Vouchers File

When a voucher system is in use, some vouchers are paid as soon as they are recorded. Others must be filed until payment is due. As an aid in taking cash discounts, vouchers for which payment is not due are generally filed in an unpaid vouchers file under the dates on which they are to be paid.

The file of unpaid vouchers takes the place of a subsidiary Accounts Payable Ledger. Actually, the file is a subsidiary ledger of amounts owed creditors. Likewise, the Vouchers Payable account is in effect a controlling account controlling the unpaid vouchers file. Therefore, after posting is completed at the end of a month, the balance of the Vouchers Payable account should equal the sum of the unpaid vouchers in the unpaid vouchers file. This is verified each month by preparing a schedule or an adding machine list of the unpaid vouchers in the file and comparing its total with the balance of the Vouchers Payable account. In addition, the unpaid vouchers in the file are compared with the unpaid vouchers shown in the Voucher Register's record of payments column. The number of each paying cheque and the payment date are entered in the Voucher Register's payments column as each voucher is paid. Therefore, the vouchers in the register without cheque numbers and payment dates should be the same as those in the unpaid vouchers file.

ILLUSTRATION D-1

(Continued)

Register						Page 32
	Sales Salaries Expense Debit	Adver-tising Expense Debit	Delivery Expense Debit	Office Salaries Expense Debit	**Other Accounts Debit**	
					Account Name	PR	Amount Debit

	Sales Salaries Expense Debit	Adver-tising Expense Debit	Delivery Expense Debit	Office Salaries Expense Debit	Account Name	PR	Amount Debit
1							
2		53.00					
3					Store Supplies	125	70.00
4				85.00			
5	95.00						
6	95.00						
33					Notes Payable	245	500.00
34					Interest Expense.	633	5.00
35					Telephone Expense	688	18.00
36							
37					Office Equipment	163	195.00
38	740.00	115.00	358.00	340.00			935.00
39	(621)	(655)	(663)	(620)			(√)
40							
41							

The Voucher System Cheque Register

In a voucher system, the Cash Disbursements Journal is replaced by a simpler *Cheque Register.* All cheques drawn in payment of vouchers are recorded in the Cheque Register. No obligation is paid until a voucher covering the payment is prepared and recorded in the Voucher Register. Likewise, no cheque is drawn except in payment of a specific voucher. Therefore, all cheques drawn result in debits to Vouchers Payable and credits to Cash, unless a discount must be recorded. Then there are credits to both Purchases Discounts and to Cash. A Cheque Register is shown in Illustration D–2. Note that it has columns for debits to Vouchers Payable and credits to Purchases Discounts and to Cash. In posting, all amounts entered in these columns are posted in the column totals.

Purchases Returns

Occasionally, an item must be returned after the voucher recording its purchase has been prepared and entered in the Voucher Register. In such cases, the return is recorded with a general journal entry like the one on the following page.

ILLUSTRATION D–2

A Cheque Register

Cheque Register						
Date 19—	Payee	Voucher No.	Cheque No.	Vouchers Payable Debit	Purchases Discounts Credit	Cash Credit
Oct. 1	C. B. & Y. RR Co.	765	728	14.00		14.00
3	Frank Mills	766	729	73.00		73.00
3	Ajax Wholesale Co.	753	730	250.00	5.00	245.00
4	Normal Supply Co.	747	731	100.00	2.00	98.00
5	Office Supply Co.	763	732	43.00		43.00
6	A. B. Seay Co.	767	733	800.00	16.00	784.00
6	George Smith	770	734	85.00		85.00
6	Frank Jones	771	735	95.00		95.00
30	First National Bank	998	972	505.00		505.00
30	Pacific Telephone Co.	999	973	18.00		18.00
31	Office Equipment Co.	1001	974	195.00		195.00
31	Totals			6,468.00	28.00	6,440.00
				(226)	(507)	(101)

Nov.	5	Vouchers Payable.	15.00	
		Purchases Returns and Allowances.		15.00
		Returned defective merchandise.		

In addition to the entry, the amount of the return is deducted on the voucher, and the credit memorandum and other documents verifying the return are attached to the voucher. Then, when the voucher is paid, a cheque is drawn for its corrected amount.

Summary of Appendix D in Terms of Learning Objective

LO 8. When a voucher system is used, all transactions that will require payments by cheque are recorded in a Voucher Register, which serves as a book of original entry. A Purchases Journal is not used. Cheques drawn in payment of vouchers are recorded in the Cheque Register, which replaces the Cash Disbursements Journal. The file of unpaid vouchers takes the place of a subsidiary Accounts Payable Ledger.

Glossary

LO 7 Define or explain the words and phrases listed in the chapter glossary.

Bank reconciliation an analysis that explains the difference between the balance of a chequing account shown in the depositor's records and the balance shown on the bank statement. p. 381

Canceled cheques cheques that the bank has paid and deducted from the customer's account during the month; they are called *canceled cheques* because they have been stamped to show that they were paid. p. 379

Cash equivalents temporary liquid investments that can be easily and quickly converted to cash. p. 361

Cash Over and Short account an income statement account used to record cash overages and cash shortages arising from omitted petty cash receipts and from errors in making change. p. 378

Discounts lost an expense resulting from failing to take advantage of cash discounts on purchases. p. 387

Gross method of recording purchases a method of recording purchases at the full invoice price without deducting any cash discounts. p. 386

Internal control system procedures adopted by a business to encourage adherence to prescribed managerial policies; in doing so, the system also promotes operational efficiencies and protects the business assets from waste, fraud, and theft, and helps ensure that accurate and reliable accounting data are produced. p. 362

Invoice an itemized statement prepared by the vendor that lists the customer's name, the items sold, the sales prices, and the terms of sale. p. 371

Invoice approval form a document on which the accounting department notes that it has performed each step in the process of checking an invoice and approving it for recording and payment. p. 372

Liquid asset an asset, such as cash, that is easily converted into other types of assets or used to buy services or pay liabilities. p. 361

Liquidity a characteristic of an asset that refers to how easily the asset can be converted into another type of asset or used to buy services or to satisfy obligations. p. 361

Net method of recording purchases a method of recording purchases at the full invoice price less any cash discounts. p. 386

Outstanding cheques cheques that were written (or drawn) by the depositor, deducted on the depositor's records, and sent to the payees; however, they had not reached the bank for payment and deduction before the statement date. p. 381

Purchase order a business paper used by the purchasing department to place an order with the vendor; authorizes the vendor to ship the ordered merchandise at the stated price and terms; often abbreviated P.O. pp. 370–71

Purchase requisition a business paper used to request that the purchasing department buy the needed merchandise or other items. pp. 369–70

Receiving report a form used within the business to notify the appropriate persons that ordered goods were received and to describe the quantities and condition of the goods. p. 371

Reconcile to explain or account for the difference between two amounts. p. 381

Vendee the buyer, or purchaser, of goods or services. p. 371

Vendor the seller of goods or services, usually a manufacturer or wholesaler. p. 370

Voucher an internal business paper used to accumulate other papers and information needed to control the disbursement of cash and to ensure that the transaction is properly recorded. p. 369

Voucher Register   a book of original entry in which approved vouchers are recorded. p. 391

Voucher system   a set of procedures designed to control the incurrence of obligations and disbursements of cash. p. 369

Synonymous Terms

Chequing account   demand deposit.

Invoice   bill.

Purchase order   P.O.

Savings account   time deposit.

Unrecorded deposits   deposits in transit.

Vendee   buyer.

Vendor   seller.

Write a cheque   draw a cheque.

Objective Review

Answers to the following questions are listed at the end of this chapter. Be sure that you decide which is the one best answer to each question *before* you check the answers.

LO 1   Which of the following assets should be classified as a cash equivalent?

a. Land purchased as an investment.

b. Accounts receivable.

c. Common shares purchased as a temporary investment.

d. A 90-day Treasury bill issued by the government of Canada.

e. None of the above.

LO 2   The broad principles of internal control require that:

a. Responsibility for a series of related transactions (such as placing orders for, receiving, and paying for merchandise) should be lodged in one person so that responsibility is clearly assigned.

b. An employee who has custody over an asset should also keep the accounting records for that asset to ensure that the records are kept current.

c. Responsibility for specific tasks should be shared by more than one employee so that one serves as a check on the other.

d. Employees who handle cash and negotiable assets should be bonded.

e. All of the above are correct.

LO 3   Regarding internal control procedures for cash receipts:

a. All cash disbursements, other than from petty cash, should be made by cheque.

b. At the end of each day, each salesclerk who receives cash should analyze and correct any errors in the cash register's record of receipts before the records are submitted to the accounting department.

c. An accounting department employee should count the cash received from sales and promptly deposit the cash receipts in the bank.

d. Mail containing cash receipts should be opened by an accounting department employee who is responsible for recording the amount of the receipts and for depositing the receipts in the bank.

e. All of the above are correct.

LO 4 When a petty cash fund is used:

a. The balance in the Petty Cash account should be reported in the balance sheet as a long-term investment since this amount is kept in the fund on a long-term basis.

b. The petty cashier's summary of petty cash payments serves as a journal entry that is posted to the appropriate General Ledger accounts.

c. At the time that they are made, payments from the petty cash fund should be recorded with entries that include a credit to the Cash account.

d. At the time that they are made, payments from the petty cash fund should be recorded with entries that include a credit to the Petty Cash account.

e. Reimbursements of the petty cash fund should be credited to the Cash account.

LO 5 In the process of preparing a bank reconciliation:

a. Outstanding cheques should be added to the bank balance of cash.

b. Outstanding cheques should be subtracted from the book balance of cash.

c. All of the reconciling items shown on a bank reconciliation must be entered in the accounting records after the reconciliation is completed.

d. Items that appear on the reconciliation as corrections to the book balance of cash should be entered in the accounting records.

e. Items that appear on the reconciliation as corrections to the bank statement balance should be entered in the accounting records.

LO 6 When invoices are recorded at net amounts:

a. The Purchases account is debited for the amount of any purchases discounts offered plus the amount to be paid if a purchase discount is taken.

b. The amount of purchases discounts lost is not recorded in a separate account.

c. The amount of purchases discounts taken is not recorded in a separate account.

d. Purchases discounts taken are recorded in a Purchases Discounts account.

e. The cash expenditures for purchases will always be less than if the invoices are recorded at gross amounts.

LO 7 A form used within a business to notify the appropriate persons that ordered goods were received and to describe the quantities and condition of the goods is called a (an):

a. Invoice.

b. Invoice approval form.

c. Purchase order.

d. Receiving report.

e. Voucher.

LO 8 When a voucher system is in use, a Voucher Register:

a. Is used in place of a Cash Disbursements Journal.

b. Is used in place of a Cash Receipts Journal.

c. Serves as the journal in which purchases returns and allowances are recorded.

d. Is used in place of a Cheque Register.

e. Is used in place of a Purchases Journal.

A letter ^D identifies the questions, exercises, and problems based on Appendix D at the end of the chapter.

Questions for Class Discussion

1. Why does a company need to own liquid assets?

2. List the seven broad principles of internal control.

3. Why should the person who keeps the record of an asset not be the person responsible for custody of the asset?

4. In a small business, it may be impossible to separate the functions of record-keeping and asset custody, and it is sometimes impossible to divide responsibilities for related transactions. What should be substituted for these control procedures?

5. Are the principles of internal control for computerized accounting systems different from the principles of internal control for manual accounting systems?

6. What is meant by the phrase *all receipts should be deposited intact?* Why should all receipts be deposited intact on the day of receipt?

7. Why should a company's bookkeeper not be given responsibility for receiving cash for the company or for signing cheques or making cash disbursements in any other way?

8. When merchandise is purchased for a large store, why are department managers not permitted to deal directly with suppliers?

9. When a disbursing officer issues a cheque for a large business, he or she usually cannot know from personal contact that the assets, goods, or services being paid for were received by the business or that the purchase was properly authorized. However, if the company has an internal control system, the officer can depend on it. Exactly which documents does the officer depend on to tell that the purchase was authorized and that the goods were actually received?

10. Why are some cash payments made from a petty cash fund?

11. Explain how a petty cash fund operates.

12. What are two results of reimbursing the petty cash fund?

13. Why should you reconcile the bank statement balance of cash and the depositor's book balance of cash?

14. What valuable information becomes readily available to management when invoices are recorded at net amounts? Is this information as readily available when invoices are recorded at gross amounts?

^D15. What kind of transactions are entered in a Voucher Register?

To add to Laliberte's problems (Mini Discussion Case 5–1), auditors hired by him (after the purchase was completed) discovered that the purchased accounts receivable were substantially overstated. Reconstruction of events prior to the purchase by Gerald Laliberte revealed that all cash sales made during the period January 1 to August 15 (date of purchase of the business) were recorded as sales on account; the cash was "pocketed" and fictitious accounts receivable created. Cash sales during the period recorded as credit sales totaled $40,000.

Case 7–1

Required

1. Discuss the effect on the financial statements of the manner in which cash sales were handled.
2. Discuss the safeguards or internal control that was lacking in the situation.

Refer to Case 7–1.

Case 7–2

Required

Discuss procedures that should have been followed prior to the purchase of the business to ensure the accuracy of accounts receivable.

Gladstone Company is a young business that has grown rapidly. The company's bookkeeper, who was hired two years ago, left town suddenly after the owner discovered that a great deal of money had disappeared over the past 18 months. An audit disclosed that the bookkeeper had written and signed cheques made payable to the bookkeeper's cousin, and then recorded the cheques as salaries expense. The cousin, who cashed the cheques but had never worked for the company, left town with the bookkeeper. As a result, the company incurred an uninsured loss of $81,000.

Evaluate Gladstone Company's internal control system and indicate which principles of internal control appear to have been ignored in this situation.

Exercise 7–1
Analyzing internal control
(LO 2, 3)

What internal control procedures would you recommend in each of the following situations?

a. Campus T's has one employee who sells T-shirts at a stand next to a college campus. Each day, the employee is given enough T-shirts to last through the day and enough cash to make change. The money is kept in a box at the stand.
b. A used goods variety store has one employee who is given cash and sent to garage sales each weekend. The employee pays cash for merchandise to be resold at the variety store.

Exercise 7–2
Recommending internal control procedures
(LO 2, 3)

Exercise 7–3
Petty cash fund
(LO 4)

A company established a $200 petty cash fund on October 1. Two weeks later, on October 15, there was $37.25 in cash in the fund and receipts for these expenditures: postage, $36.50; transportation-in, $19.00; miscellaneous expenses, $61; and office supplies, $46.25.

Prepare the journal entries (*a*) to establish the fund and (*b*) to reimburse it on October 15.

Now assume (*c*) that the fund was not only reimbursed on October 15 but also increased to $300 because it was exhausted so quickly. Give the entry to reimburse and increase the fund to $300.

Exercise 7–4
Petty cash fund
(LO 4)

A company established a $100 petty cash fund on February 5. On February 28, there was $30.80 in cash in the fund and receipts for these expenditures: transportation-in, $6.05; miscellaneous expenses, $18.70; and office supplies, $42.45. The petty cashier could not account for the $2 shortage in the fund. Prepare (*a*) the February 5 entry to establish the fund and (*b*) the February 28 entry to reimburse the fund and reduce it to $75.

Exercise 7–5
Internal control over cash receipts
(LO 2, 3)

Some of APL Company's cash receipts from customers are sent to the company in the mail. APL Company's bookkeeper opens the letters and deposits the cash received each day. What internal control problem is inherent in this arrangement? What changes would you recommend?

Exercise 7–6
Bank reconciliation
(LO 5)

Quantum Company deposits all receipts intact on the day received and makes all payments by cheque. On November 30, 1993, after all posting was completed, its Cash account showed a $3,180 debit balance. However, its November 30 bank statement showed only $2,627 on deposit in the bank on that day. Prepare a bank reconciliation for the store, using the following information:

a. Outstanding cheques, $482.

b. Included with the November canceled cheques returned by the bank was a $10 debit memorandum for bank services.

c. Cheque No. 977, returned with the canceled cheques, was correctly drawn for $124 in payment of the telephone bill and was paid by the bank on November 9. However, it had been recorded with a debit to Telephone Expense and a credit to Cash as though it were for $142.

d. The November 30 cash receipts, $1,043, were placed in the bank's night depository after banking hours on that date and were unrecorded by the bank at the time the November bank statement was prepared.

Exercise 7–7
Adjusting entries resulting from bank reconciliation
(LO 5)

Give the journal entries that Quantum Company should make as a result of having prepared the bank reconciliation in the previous exercise.

Exercise 7–8
Recording invoices at gross or net amounts
(LO 6)

Shoney, Inc., incurred $147,000 of operating expenses in April 1993, a month in which its sales were $302,000. The company began April with a $175,000 merchandise inventory and ended the month with a $306,200 inventory. During the month, it purchased merchandise having a $252,000 invoice price, all of which was subject to a 2% discount for prompt payment. The company took advantage of the discounts on $228,000 of the purchases. However, a filing error caused it to miss taking the discount on a $24,000 invoice paid on April 30.

Required

1. Prepare an April income statement for the company under the assumption that it records invoices at gross amounts.

2. Prepare an April income statement for the company under the assumption that it records invoices at net amounts.

Complete the following bank reconciliation by filling in the missing amounts:

Exercise 7–9
Completion of bank reconciliation
(LO 5)

CAMBRIDGE COMPANY
Bank Reconciliation
March 31, 1993

Bank statement balance	$6,420	Book balance of cash	$?
Add: Deposit of March 31	?	Add: Collection of note	5,000
Bank error	30	Interest earned	150
	$?		$7,880
Deduct: Outstanding cheques. . . .	1,635	Deduct: Service charge	?
		NSF cheque	200
Reconciled balance	$7,670	Reconciled balance	$?

Problems

A concern completed the following petty cash transactions during September of the current year:

Problem 7–1
Establishing and reimbursing petty cash fund
(LO 4)

Sept. 1 Drew a $100 cheque, cashed it, and gave the proceeds and the petty cash-box to Joy Reed, the petty cashier.

   5 Purchased computer paper, $14.80.

   7 Paid $7.55 COD delivery charges on merchandise purchased for resale.

   10 Paid $4.50 parcel post charges on merchandise sold to a customer and delivered by mail.

   12 Gave June Donners, wife of the business owner, $10 from petty cash for cab fare and other personal expenses.

   19 Paid $6.50 COD delivery charges on merchandise purchased for resale.

   23 Paid a service station attendant $7.50 for washing the personal car of Phil Donners, the business owner.

   24 Paid Zippy Delivery Service $15.00 from petty cash to deliver merchandise sold to a customer.

   26 Paid $32.00 for minor repairs to an office computer.

   29 Joy Reed sorted the petty cash receipts by accounts affected and exchanged them for a cheque to reimburse the fund for expenditures. However, there was only $1.15 in cash in the fund, and she could not account for the shortage.

Required

1. Prepare a General Journal entry to record establishing the petty cash fund.
2. Prepare a summary of petty cash payments that has these categories: Office supplies, Transportation-in, Delivery expense, Withdrawals, and Miscellaneous expenses. Sort the payments into the appropriate categories and total the expenses in each category.
3. Prepare the General Journal entry to record the reimbursement of the fund.

Problem 7–2
Establishing, reimbursing, and increasing petty cash fund
(LO 4)

A business completed these transactions:

Mar. 8 Drew a $150 cheque to establish a petty cash fund, cashed it, and delivered the proceeds and the petty cashbox to Jay Yi, an office secretary who was to act as petty cashier.

  12 Paid Town's Delivery Service $25 to deliver merchandise sold to a customer.

  21 Purchased office supplies with petty cash, $37.50.

  22 Paid $45 from petty cash to have the office windows washed.

  29 Rita Moore, the owner of the business, signed a petty cash receipt and took $10 from petty cash for lunch.

Apr. 3 Paid $11.25 COD delivery charges on merchandise purchased for resale.

  5 Jay Yi noted that there was only $21.25 cash remaining in the fund. Thus, he sorted the paid petty cash receipts by accounts affected and exchanged them for a cheque to reimburse the fund. Because the fund was so quickly used up, the cheque was made for an amount large enough to increase the size of the fund to $200.

  9 Paid Town's Delivery Service $15.00 to deliver merchandise to a customer.

  12 Paid the AmeriCan Cleaner's delivery person $40.80 on the delivery to the office of clothes Moore had dropped off for dry cleaning.

  13 Paid $35.50 COD delivery charges on merchandise purchased for resale.

  16 Gave Tom Moore, the husband of the business owner, $20 from petty cash for cab fare and other personal expenditures.

  20 Paid $30.85 for maintenance on an office copier.

  26 Purchased office supplies with petty cash, $23.90.

  27 Paid $9.45 COD delivery charges on merchandise purchased for resale.

  30 Since there was $21.20 in cash in the fund, Jay Yi sorted the petty cash receipts by accounts affected and exchanged them for a cheque to reimburse the fund. There was also a small shortage that he could not explain.

Required

1. Prepare a journal entry to record the cheque establishing the petty cash fund.
2. Prepare a summary of petty cash payments for March 8 to April 5 that has these categories: Office supplies, Transportation-in, Delivery expense, Withdrawals, and Miscellaneous expenses. Sort the payments into the appropriate categories and total each category. Prepare a similar summary of petty cash payments after April 5.
3. Prepare entries to reimburse the fund and increase its size on April 5 and to reimburse the fund on April 30.

The incomplete bank reconciliation statement of Luna Company appears below:

Problem 7–3
Completion of bank
reconciliation and
recording adjustments
(LO 5)

LUNA COMPANY
Bank Reconciliation
May 31, 1994

Book balance of cash	($2,450)	Bank statement balance	$?
Add:		Add:	
Collection of note	?	Deposit of May 31	800
Interest earned	80	Bank error	60
Deduct:	($ 970)	Deduct:	$?
Service charge	20	Outstanding cheques	2,600
NSF cheque of S. Allen	300		
Reconciled balance	$?		$?

Required

1. Complete Luna's bank reconciliation statement.
2. Prepare the General Journal entries necessary to bring the company's bank balance of cash into conformity with the reconciled balance.

The following information was available to reconcile Repcon Company's book cash balance with its bank statement balance as of December 31, 1993:

Problem 7–4
Preparation of bank
reconciliation and
recording adjustments
(LO 5)

a. The December 31 cash balance according to the accounting records was $8,263, and the bank statement balance for that date was $11,562.
b. Cheque No. 1976 for $278 and Cheque No. 1979 for $100, both written and entered in the accounting records in December, were not among the canceled cheques returned. Two cheques, No. 1843 for $587 and No. 1902 for $95, were outstanding on November 30 when the bank and book statement balances were last reconciled. Cheque No. 1902 was returned with the December canceled cheques, but Cheque No. 1843 was not.
c. When the December cheques were compared with entries in the accounting records, it was found that Cheque No. 1954 had been correctly drawn for $654 in payment for store supplies but was erroneously entered in the accounting records as though it were drawn for $645.
d. Two debit memoranda and a credit memorandum were included with the returned cheques and were unrecorded at the time of the reconciliation. The credit memorandum indicated that the bank had collected a $5,000 note receivable for the company, deducted a $25 collection fee, and credited the balance to the company's account. One of the debit memoranda was for $215 and dealt with an NSF cheque for $205 that had been received from a customer, Ralph Crumley, in payment of his account. It also assessed a $10 fee for processing. The second debit memorandum covered cheque printing and was for $72.
e. The December 31 cash receipts, $2,345, had been placed in the bank's night depository after banking hours on that date and did not appear on the bank statement.

Required

1. Prepare a bank reconciliation for the company as of December 31.
2. Prepare the General Journal entries necessary to bring the company's book balance of cash into conformity with the reconciled balance.

Problem 7–5
Preparation of bank
reconciliation and
recording adjustments
(LO 5)

Pneumo Company reconciled its bank and book statement balances of cash on March 31 and showed two cheques outstanding at that time, No. 3762 for $500 and No. 3776 for $1,240. The following information was available for the April 30, 1993, reconciliation:

Analysis of the April 30 bank statement:

BALANCE OF PREVIOUS STATEMENT ON 31/3/93	10,265.00
5 DEPOSITS AND OTHER CREDITS TOTALING	6,404.00
INTEREST AT 4.75%	30.00
9 CHEQUES AND OTHER DEBITS TOTALING	8,117.00
CURRENT BALANCE AS OF 30/4/93	8,582.00

CHEQUING ACCOUNT TRANSACTIONS°°°

DATE	AMOUNT . . .	TRANSACTION DESCRIPTION . . . .
6/4	1,980.00+	Deposit
13/4	852.00+	Deposit
20/4	1,113.00+	Deposit
27/4	857.00+	Deposit
28/4	85.00−	NSF cheque
30/4	30.00+	Interest
30/4	1,572.00+	Credit memorandum

DATE . . .	CHEQUE NO. . . .	AMOUNT . . .	DATE . . .	CHEQUE NO. . . .	AMOUNT
2/4	3776	1,240.00	14/4	3782	672.00
6/4	3779	95.00	19/4	3783	32.00
7/4	3780	5,078.00	22/4	3785	143.00
11/4	3781	271.00	28/4	3786	501.00

From Pneumo Company's accounting records:

Cash Receipts Deposited

Date			Cash Debit
Apr. 6			1,980.00
13			852.00
20			1,113.00
27			857.00
30			690.00
			5,492.00

Cash Disbursements

Cheque No.			Cash Credit
3779			95.00
3780			5,078.00
3781			271.00
3782			692.00
3783			32.00
3784			750.00
3785			143.00
3786			501.00
3787			76.00
			7,638.00

Cash   **Acct. No. 101**

Date	Explanation	PR	Debit	Credit	Balance
Mar. 31	Balance				8,555.00
Apr. 30	Total receipts	R8	5,492.00		14,047.00
30	Total disbursements	D9		7,638,00	6,409.00

Cheque No. 3782 was correctly drawn for $672 in payment for office equipment; however, the bookkeeper misread the amount and entered it in the accounting records with a debit to Office Equipment and a credit to Cash as though it were for $692.

The NSF cheque was originally received from a customer, Pat Carriker, in payment of her account. Its return was not recorded when the bank first notified the company. The credit memorandum resulted from the collection of a $1,600 note for Pneumo Company by the bank. The bank had deducted a $28 collection fee. The collection has not been recorded.

Required

1. Prepare an April 30 bank reconciliation for the company.
2. Prepare the General Journal entries needed to adjust the book balance of cash to the reconciled balance.

The July 31, 1993, credit balance in the Sales account of Cardina Company showed it had sold merchandise for $147,000 during the month. The concern began July with a $280,700 merchandise inventory and ended the month with a $237,000 inventory. It had incurred $34,300 of operating expenses during the month, and it had also recorded the following transactions:

Problem 7–6
Recording invoices at gross or net amounts
(LO 6)

  2 Received merchandise purchased at a $6,300 invoice price, invoice dated June 27, terms 2/10, n/30.

  5 Received a $1,300 credit memorandum (invoice price) for merchandise received on July 2 and returned for credit.

 10 Received merchandise purchased at a $14,000 invoice price, invoice dated July 8, terms 2/10, n/30.

 14 Received merchandise purchased at a $7,800 invoice price, invoice dated July 12, terms 2/10, n/30.

 17 Paid for the merchandise received on July 10, less the discount.

 21 Paid for the merchandise received on July 14, less the discount.

 27 Paid for the merchandise received on July 2. Payment was delayed because the invoice was mistakenly filed for payment today. This error caused the discount to be lost. The filing error occurred after the credit memorandum received on July 5 was attached to the invoice dated June 27.

Required

1. Assume that Cardina Company records invoices at gross amounts.
   a. Prepare General Journal entries to record the transactions.
   b. Prepare a July income statement.
2. Assume that Cardina Company records invoices at net amounts.
   a. Prepare General Journal entries to record the transactions.
   b. Prepare a July income statement.

In Problem 7–1, several of the transactions involved payments of cash from a petty cash fund. Nevertheless, the entry to record these payments does not include a credit to Petty Cash. Explain why this is true. Under what circumstances would the entry to record payments from the petty cash fund include a credit to Petty Cash?

Problem 7–7
Analytical essay
(LO 4)

The bank statement in Problem 7–5 discloses two places where the canceled cheques returned with the bank statement are not numbered sequentially. In other words, some of the prenumbered cheques in the sequence are missing. There are several possible situations that would explain why the canceled cheques returned with a bank statement might not be numbered sequentially. Describe three situations, each of which is a possible explanation of why the canceled cheques returned with a bank statement are not numbered sequentially.

Problem 7–8
Analytical essay
(LO 5)

^D**Problem 7–9**
Using a voucher system
(LO 8)

Coltrain Company completed these transactions involving vouchers payable:

July 3 Recorded Voucher No. 281 payable to Zachary Company for merchandise having a $1,600 invoice price, invoice dated June 30, terms FOB factory, 2/10, n/30. The vendor had prepaid the freight, $65, adding the amount to the invoice and bringing its total to $1,665.

5 Recorded Voucher No. 282 payable to *The Herald* for advertising expense, $175. Issued Cheque No. 424 in payment of the voucher.

6 Received a credit memorandum for merchandise having a $133 invoice price. The merchandise had been received from Zachary Company on July 3, recorded on Voucher No. 281, and later returned for credit.

7 Recorded Voucher No. 283 payable to Global Realty for one month's rent on the space occupied by the store, $1,100. Issued Cheque No. 425 in payment of the voucher.

10 Recorded Voucher No. 284 payable to Carroll Supply Company for store supplies, $147, terms n/10 EOM.

11 Recorded Voucher No. 285 payable to Penn Company for merchandise having a $3,800 invoice price, invoice dated July 9, terms FOB factory, 2/10, n/60. The vendor had prepaid the freight charges, $141, adding the amount to the invoice and bringing its total to $3,941.

14 Recorded Voucher No. 286 payable to Payroll for sales salaries, $1,500, and office salaries, $1,200. Issued Cheque No. 426 in payment of the voucher. Cashed the cheque and paid the employees.

17 Recorded Voucher No. 287 payable to Northwood Company for merchandise having a $798 invoice price, invoice dated July 14, terms 2/10, n/60, FOB factory. The vendor had prepaid the freight charges, $39, adding the amount to the invoice and bringing its total to $837.

19 Issued Cheque No. 427 in payment of Voucher No. 285.

21 Recorded Voucher No. 288 payable to Penn Company for merchandise having a $4,663 invoice price, invoice dated July 18, terms FOB factory, 2/10, n/60. The vendor had prepaid the freight charges, $186, adding the amount to the invoice and bringing its total to $4,849.

24 Discovered that Voucher No. 281 had been filed in error for payment on the last day of its credit period rather than on the last day of its discount period, causing the discount to be lost. Issued Cheque No. 428 in payment of the voucher, less the return.

28 Recorded Voucher No. 289 payable to Payroll for sales salaries, $1,500, and office salaries, $1,200. Issued Cheque No. 429 in payment of the voucher. Cashed the cheque and paid the employees.

Required

1. Assume that Coltrain Company records vouchers at gross amounts. Prepare a Voucher Register, a Cheque Register, and a General Journal, and record the transactions.

2. Prepare a Vouchers Payable account and post those entry portions that affect the account.

3. Prove the balance of the Vouchers Payable account by preparing a schedule of vouchers payable.

A concern completed the following petty cash transactions during May of the current year:

Problem 7–1A
Establishing and reimbursing petty cash fund
(LO 4)

May 1 Drew a $100 cheque, cashed it, and turned the proceeds and the petty cashbox over to Walter Cleaver, the petty cashier.

4 Paid $4.35 parcel post charges on merchandise sold to a customer and delivered by mail.

6 Purchased office supplies, $11.75.

10 Paid $21.20 for repairs to an office copier.

12 Paid $7 COD delivery charges on merchandise purchased for resale.

16 Paid Hatley Delivery Service $8.50 to deliver merchandise sold to a customer.

21 Gave Russell Johnson, the owner of the business, $10 from petty cash for personal use.

24 Paid $23.55 COD delivery charges on merchandise purchased for resale.

27 Russell Johnson, owner of the business, signed a petty cash receipt and took $10 from petty cash for lunch.

31 Walter Cleaver exchanged his paid petty cash receipts for a cheque reimbursing the fund for expenditures and a shortage of cash in the fund that he could not account for. He reported a cash balance of $2.55 in the fund.

Required

1. Prepare a General Journal entry to record establishing the petty cash fund.

2. Prepare a summary of petty cash payments that has these categories: Office supplies, Transportation-in, Delivery expense, Withdrawals, and Miscellaneous expenses. Sort the payments into the appropriate categories and total the expenses in each category.

3. Prepare the general journal entry to record the reimbursement of the fund.

A company completed these petty cash transactions:

Problem 7–2A
Establishing, reimbursing, and increasing petty cash fund
(LO 4)

July 6 Drew an $85 cheque to establish a petty cash fund, cashed it, and turned the proceeds and the petty cashbox over to Jean Fisher, the petty cashier.

8 Paid $6.30 parcel post charges on merchandise sold to a customer and delivered by mail.

9 Paid $35 to have the office windows washed.

13 Purchased office supplies with petty cash, $12.25.

15 Marilyn Morgan, owner of the business, signed a petty cash receipt and took $7 from petty cash for coffee money.

18 Paid $21.70 COD delivery charges on merchandise purchased for resale.

20 Jean Fisher noted that only $2.75 remained in the petty cashbox. Thus, she sorted the petty cash receipts into the accounts affected and exchanged the receipts for a cheque to reimburse the fund. Because the fund was so quickly used up, the cheque was made for an amount large enough to increase the size of the fund to $150.

22 Paid $41 from petty cash for minor repairs to an office machine.

July 25　Paid $18 COD delivery charges on merchandise purchased for resale.

　26　Paid Express Courier $10.85 to deliver merchandise sold to a customer.

　27　Purchased office supplies with petty cash, $16.30.

　29　Marilyn Morgan, owner of the business, signed a petty cash receipt and took $20 from petty cash for lunch.

Aug.　1　Paid $15 COD delivery charges on merchandise purchased for resale.

　4　Purchased paper clips and pencils with petty cash, $7.45.

　11　Paid $18.50 COD delivery charges on merchandise purchased for resale.

　15　Jean Fisher sorted the petty cash receipts by accounts affected and exchanged them for a cheque to reimburse the fund. There was also a small shortage that she could not explain. There was only $2.50 cash left in the fund.

Required

1. Prepare a journal entry to record the cheque establishing the petty cash fund.

2. Prepare a summary of petty cash payments for July 6 to July 20 that has these categories: Delivery expense, Office supplies, Miscellaneous expenses, Withdrawals, and Transportation-in. Sort the payments into the appropriate categories and total the expenses in each category. Prepare a similar summary of petty cash payments after July 20.

3. Prepare entries to reimburse the fund and increase its size on July 20 and to reimburse the fund on August 15.

Problem 7–3A
Completion of bank reconciliation and recording adjustments (LO 5)

The incomplete bank reconciliation statement of Lumax Company follows:

LUMAX COMPANY
Bank Reconciliation
May 31, 1994

Book balance of cash	$ 400	Bank statement balance	($1,200)
Add:		Add:	
Collection of note	600	Deposit of May 31	?
Interest earned	60	Bank error	120
	$1,060		
Deduct:		Deduct:	
Service charge	40	Outstanding cheques	300
NSF cheque of J. Kalen	?		
Error re Cheque No. 237— correct amount of cheque $292, entered on books as $229.	?		
Reconciled balance	$ 657	Reconciled balance	$ 657

Required

1. Complete Lumax's bank reconciliation statement.

2. Prepare the General Journal entries necessary to bring the company's book balance of cash into conformity with the reconciled balance.

Problem 7–4A
Preparation of bank reconciliation and recording adjustments (LO 5)

The following information was available to reconcile Advance Company's book balance of cash with its bank statement balance as of April 30, 1993:

a. After all posting was completed on April 30, the company's Cash account had a $1,699 debit balance, but its bank statement showed a $4,006 balance.

b. Cheques No. 617 for $78 and No. 622 for $457 were outstanding on the March 31 bank reconciliation. Cheque No. 622 was returned with the April canceled cheques, but Cheque No. 617 was not. It was also found that Cheque No. 631 for $383 and Cheque No. 633 for $17, both drawn in April, were not among the canceled cheques returned with the statement.

c. In comparing the canceled cheques returned with the bank statement with the entries in the accounting records, it was found that Cheque No. 697 for the purchase of office equipment was correctly drawn for $1,477 but was erroneously entered in the accounting records as though it were for $1,747.

d. A credit memorandum enclosed with the bank statement indicated that the bank had collected a $2,700 noninterest-bearing note for Advance Company, deducted a $27 collection fee, and had credited the remainder to the account. This event was not recorded by Advance Company before receiving the statement.

e. A debit memorandum for $315 listed a $300 NSF cheque plus a $15 NSF charge. The cheque had been received from a customer, Walter Bellows. Advance Company had not recorded this bounced cheque before receiving the statement.

f. Also enclosed with the statement was a $10 debit memorandum for bank services. It had not been recorded because no previous notification had been received.

g. The April 30 cash receipts, $789, were placed in the bank's night depository after banking hours on that date and this amount did not appear on the bank statement.

Required

1. Prepare a bank reconciliation for the company as of April 30, 1993.
2. Prepare the General Journal entries necessary to bring the company's book balance of cash into conformity with the reconciled balance.

Lange Company reconciled its bank balance on September 30 and showed two cheques outstanding at that time, No. 1408 for $67 and No. 1409 for $124. The following information is available for the October 31, 1993, reconciliation:

Problem 7–5A
Preparation of bank reconciliation and recording adjustments (LO 5)

Analysis of the October 31 bank statement:

BALANCE OF PREVIOUS STATEMENT ON 30/9/93.	1,256.00
5 DEPOSITS AND OTHER CREDITS TOTALING	2,443.00
8 CHEQUES AND OTHER DEBITS TOTALING	1,897.00
SERVICE CHARGE AMOUNT	7.00
CURRENT BALANCE AS OF THIS STATEMENT.	1,795.00

CHEQUING ACCOUNT TRANSACTIONS

DATE	AMOUNT	TRANSACTION DESCRIPTION
6/10	387.00+ ✓	Deposit
13/10	460.00+ ✓	Deposit
20/10	286.00+ ✓	Deposit
27/10	330.00+ ✓	Deposit
30/10	59.00−	NSF cheque
31/10	7.00−	Service charge
31/10	980.00+	Credit memorandum

DATE	CHEQUE NO.	AMOUNT	DATE	CHEQUE NO.	AMOUNT
26/10	1409 ✓	124.00	17/10	1413	✓ 25.00
4/10	1410 ✓	65.00	14/10	1414	✓ 1,275.00
2/10	1411 ✓	31.00	28/10	1416	88.00
7/10	1412 ✓	230.00			

From Lange Company's accounting records:

Cash Receipts Deposited			Cash Disbursements		
Date		**Cash Debit**	**Cheque No.**		**Cash Credit**
Oct. 6		387.00 ✓	1410		✓ 65.00
13		460.00 ✓	1411		✓ 31.00
20		286.00 ✓	1412		✓230.00
27		330.00 ✓	1413		✓25.00
31		401.00 o\s	1414		✓1,275.00
		1,864.00	1415		o\s 107.00
			1416		Error 80.00
			1417		o\s 194.00
					2,007.00

Cash   Acct. No. 101

Date	Explanation	PR	Debit	Credit	Balance
Sept. 30	Balance				1,065.00
Oct. 31	Total receipts	R8	1,864.00		2,929.00
31	Total disbursements	D9		2,007.00	922.00

Cheque No. 1416 was correctly drawn for $88 in payment for store supplies; however, the bookkeeper misread the amount and entered it in the accounting records with a debit to Store Supplies and a credit to Cash as though it were for $80. The bank paid and deducted the correct amount.

The NSF cheque was originally received from a customer, Wilma Stone, in payment of her account. Its return was unrecorded. The credit memorandum resulted from a $1,000 note that the bank had collected for the company. The bank had deducted a $20 collection fee and deposited the remainder in the company's account. The collection has not been recorded.

Required

1. Prepare a bank reconciliation for Lange Company.
2. Prepare the General Journal entries needed to adjust the book balance of cash to the reconciled balance.

Problem 7–6A
Recording invoices at gross or net amounts (LO 6)

The June 30, 1993, credit balance in the Sales account of Clipper Company showed it had sold merchandise for $288,000 during the month. The concern began June with a $227,000 merchandise inventory and ended the month with a $185,000 inventory. It had incurred $74,000 of operating expenses during the month, and it had also recorded the following transactions:

June 2 Received merchandise purchased at a $54,000 invoice price, invoice dated May 30, terms 2/10, n/30.

7 Received a $5,000 credit memorandum (invoice price) for merchandise received on June 2 and returned for credit.

12 Received merchandise purchased at a $42,000 invoice price, invoice dated June 11, terms 2/10, n/30.

15 Received merchandise purchased at a $137,750 invoice price, invoice dated June 13, terms 2/10, n/30.

20 Paid for the merchandise received on June 12, less the discount.

22 Paid for the merchandise received on June 15, less the discount.

June 29   Paid for the merchandise received on June 2. Payment was delayed because the invoice was mistakenly filed for payment today. This error caused the discount to be lost. The filing error occurred after the credit memorandum received on June 7 was attached to the invoice dated May 30.

Required

1. Assume that Clipper Company records invoices at gross amounts.
   a. Prepare General Journal entries to record the transactions.
   b. Prepare a June income statement.
2. Assume that Clipper Company records invoices at net amounts.
   a. Prepare General Journal entries to record the transactions.
   b. Prepare a June income statement.

In Problem 7–1A, several of the transactions involved payments of cash from a petty cash fund. Assume that when the petty cash fund was reimbursed, the company's bookkeeper made an entry of the following general form:

Problem 7–7A
Analytical essay
(LO 4)

Dec.	31	xxxxxxxxxxxx (Expense).	xxx	
		xxxxxxxxxxxx (Expense).	xxx	
		xxxxxxxxxxxx (Asset)	xxx	
		Petty Cash		xxx

Explain why this entry is not correct. Also explain the effects of the error on the General Ledger and on the balance sheet.

Review the facts about Advance Company presented in Problem 7–4A. Assume that an April 30, 1993, bank reconciliation for the company has already been prepared and some of the items were treated incorrectly in preparing the reconciliation. For each of the following errors, explain the effect of the error on (1) the final balance that was calculated by adjusting the bank statement balance, and (2) the final balance that was calculated by adjusting the Cash account balance.

Problem 7–8A
Analytical essay
(LO 5)

a. The company's Cash account balance of $1,699 was listed on the reconciliation as $1,996.
b. Cheque No. 622 for $457 was deducted from the bank statement balance as an outstanding cheque.
c. The correction for Cheque No. 697 was subtracted from the bank statement balance.
d. The bank's collection of a $2,700 note less the deduction of a $27 collection fee was added to the bank statement balance.

Garth Company completed these transactions involving vouchers payable:

^D**Problem 7–9A**
Using a voucher system
(LO 8)

Oct. 2   Recorded Voucher No. 827 payable to Blackmon Company for merchandise having a $4,300 invoice price, invoice dated September 29, terms FOB destination, 2/10, n/30.

    4   Recorded Voucher No. 828 payable to Swann Company for merchandise having a $2,400 invoice price, invoice dated October 2, terms FOB fac-

Oct.   tory, 2/10, n/60. The vendor had prepaid the freight charges, $110, adding
         the amount to the invoice and bringing its total to $2,510.

6   Received a credit memorandum for merchandise having a $550 invoice
         price. The merchandise was received on October 2, Voucher No. 827, and
         returned for credit.

11   Issued Cheque No. 630 in payment of Voucher No. 828.

15   Recorded Voucher No. 829 payable to Payroll for sales salaries, $2,100,
         and office salaries, $1,100. Issued Cheque No. 631 in payment of the
         voucher. Cashed the cheque and paid the employees.

17   Recorded Voucher No. 830 payable to Miaki Company for the purchase of
         office equipment having a $1,250 invoice price, terms n/10 EOM.

20   Recorded Voucher No. 831 payable to *The Daily Echo* for advertising ex-
         pense, $479. Issued Cheque No. 632 in payment of the voucher.

24   Recorded Voucher No. 832 payable to Plaza Industries for merchandise
         having a $1,730 invoice price, invoice dated October 22, terms FOB fac-
         tory, 2/10, n/60. The vendor had prepaid the freight charges, $86, adding
         the amount to the invoice and bringing its total to $1,816.

27   Discovered that Voucher No. 827 had been filed in error for payment on
         the last day of its credit period rather than on the last day of its discount
         period, causing the discount to be lost. Issued Cheque No. 633 in payment
         of the voucher, less the return.

31   Recorded Voucher No. 833 payable to Payroll for sales salaries, $2,100,
         and office salaries, $1,100. Issued Cheque No. 634 in payment of the
         voucher. Cashed the cheque and paid the employees.

Required

1. Assume that Garth Company records vouchers at gross amounts. Prepare a
    Voucher Register, a Cheque Register, and a General Journal and record the
    transactions.

2. Prepare a Vouchers Payable account and post those portions of the journal and
    register entries that affect the account.

3. Prove the balance of the Vouchers Payable account by preparing a schedule of
    unpaid vouchers.

Provocative Problems

Provocative Problem 7–1
Ridgefield Company
(LO 2, 3)

The bookkeeper at Ridgefield Company will retire next week. Originally hired more
than 30 years ago by the father of the store's present owner, he has always been very
dependable. As a result, the bookkeeper has been given more and more responsibilities
over the years. Actually, for the past 15 years, he has run the company's office, keeping
the books, verifying invoices, and issuing cheques in their payment. Whenever the
store's owner, L. F. Winfield, was not around, the bookkeeper even signed the
cheques. In addition, at the end of each day, the store's salesclerks turned over their
daily cash receipts to the bookkeeper. After counting the money and comparing the
amounts with the cash register tapes—which he was responsible for removing from the
cash registers—he made the journal entry to record cash sales and then deposited the
money in the bank. He also reconciled the bank balance with the book balance of cash
each month.

Winfield realizes he cannot expect a new bookkeeper to do as much as the old bookkeeper. And because the store is not large enough to warrant more than one office employee, he knows that he will probably have to take over some of the duties after the bookkeeper retires. Winfield already places all orders for merchandise and supplies and closely supervises all employees and does not want to add more to his duties than necessary.

Identify the internal control principle that has been violated and select the book-keeper's tasks that should be taken over by Winfield to improve the store's internal control over cash.

The Tom Mix Company has enjoyed rapid growth since it was created several years ago. Last year, for example, its sales exceeded $8 million. However, its purchasing procedures have not kept pace with its growth. When a plant supervisor or department head needs raw materials, plant assets, or supplies, he or she telephones a request to the purchasing department manager. The purchasing department manager then prepares a purchase order in duplicate, sends one copy to the company selling the goods, and keeps the other copy in the files. When the seller's invoice is received, it is sent directly to the purchasing department. When the goods arrive, receiving department personnel count and inspect the items and prepare only one copy of a receiving report, which is then sent to the purchasing department. The purchasing department manager attaches the receiving report and the file copy of the purchase order to the invoice. If all is in order, the invoice is stamped *approved for payment* and signed by the purchasing department manager. The invoice and its supporting documents are then sent to the accounting department to be recorded and filed until due. On its due date, the invoice and its supporting documents are sent to the office of the company treasurer, and a cheque is prepared and mailed. The number of the cheque is entered on the invoice, and the invoice is sent to the accounting department for an entry to record its payment.

Do the procedures of Tom Mix Company make it fairly easy for someone in the company to initiate the payment of fictitious invoices by the company? If so, who is most likely to commit the fraud and what would that person have to do to receive payment of a fictitious invoice? What changes should be made in the company's purchasing procedures, and why should each change be made?

Provocative Problem 7–2
Tom Mix Company
(LO 2, 3)

For this problem, turn to the financial statements of Bombardier Inc. in Appendix I. Use the information presented in the financial statements to answer these questions:

1. What items make up Bombardier's cash and cash equivalents?
2. Did Bombardier hold any temporary investments on January 31, 1992?
3. Is the split between cash and term deposits determinable?
4. For both 1992 and 1991, determine the total amount of cash and cash equivalents that Bombardier held at the end of the year. Determine the percentage that this amount represents of total current assets, total current liabilities, total share-holders' equity, and total assets.
5. For 1992, use the information in the statement of changes in financial position to determine the percentage change between the beginning of the year and end of the year holding of cash and cash equivalents.

Provocative Problem 7–3
Bombardier Inc.
(LO 1)

Provocative Problem 7–4
As a Matter of Ethics:
Essay

Review the "As a Matter of Ethics" case on page 379. Discuss the nature of the problem faced by Nancy Tucker and evaluate the alternative courses of action she should consider.

Analytical and Review Problems

A&R Problem 7–1

The bank statement for October arrived in Friday's mail. You were especially anxious to receive the statement as one of your assignments was to prepare a bank reconciliation for the Saturday meeting. You got around to preparing the reconciliation rather late in the afternoon and found all the necessary data with the exception of the bank balance. The bottom portion of the bank statement was smudged, and several figures, including the balance, were obliterated. A telephone call to the bank was answered by a recording with the information that the bank was closed until 10 A.M. Monday. Since the reconciliation had to be prepared you decided to plug-in the bank balance.

In preparation, you assembled the necessary material as follows:

a. Cash balance per books was $6,800.
b. From the canceled cheques returned by the bank you determined that six cheques remained outstanding. The total of these cheques was $2,700.
c. In checking the canceled cheques you noted that Cheque No. 274 was properly made for $418 but was recorded in the cash disbursement journal as $481. The cheque was in payment of an account.
d. Included with the bank statement were two memoranda; the credit memorandum was for collection of a note for $1,200 and $90 of interest thereon and the debit memorandum was for $12 of bank charges.
e. While you were sorting the canceled cheques, one of the cheques caught your attention. You were astounded by the similarity of name with that of your company and the similarity of the cheques. The cheque was for $620 and was obviously in error charged to your company's account.
f. From the deposit book you determined that a $2,500 deposit was made after hours on October 31.

Required

1. Prepare a bank reconciliation statement as of October 31 (plug in the indicated bank balance).
2. Prepare the necessary journal entries.

The newly hired junior account of McGuire Company prepared the November 30 bank   A&R Problem 7–2
reconciliation statement as follows:

MCGUIRE COMPANY
Bank Reconciliation
November 30, 1993

Balance per books.		$10,200
Add:		
Collection of note by bank . . .	$4,500	
Interest thereon.	468	
Error re MacGuire Company		
cheque	900	
Error re Cheque No. 282	54	5,922
		16,122
Deduct:		
Bank charges		45
True cash balance		$16,077
Balance per bank		$14,100
Add:		
Deposit in transit	5400	
NSF cheque.	975	6,375
		20,475
Deduct:		
Outstanding cheques		4,398
True cash balance		$16,077

    The controller took one glance at the reconciliation statement prepared by the
junior accountant and screamed, "Where did we get him?" Therefore, the task of
preparing a correct bank reconciliation fell upon you.
    You determined the following:

a. All amounts in the reconciliation prepared by the junior accountant were
correct.
b. The $900 MacGuire Company cheque was erroneously credited by the bank to
the McGuire Company account.
c. McGuire Company's Cheque No. 282 was properly drawn for $439 but was en-
tered in the cash disbursement journal as $493. The cheque was in payment of
an account.
d. The NSF cheque returned by the bank was from one of McGuire Company's
customers.

Required

1. Prepare a proper bank reconciliation statement indicating the true cash balance.
2. Prepare the required journal entries.

A&R Problem 7-3

Your assistant prepared the following bank reconciliation statement. Obviously the statement is unacceptable and the task of preparing a proper reconciliation falls upon you.

JACKSON COMPANY
Bank Reconciliation
October 31, 1993

Balance per books October 31.		$ 8,000
Add:		
Note collected	$1,000	
Interest on note	110	
Deposit in transit	2,455	3,565
		11,565
Deduct:		
Bank charges	10	
NSF cheque.	400	
Outstanding cheques	1,800	
Error in Cheque No. 78 issued for $872 and		
recorded in the books as $827.	45	2,255
Indicated bank balance		9,310
Balance per bank statement		8,000
Discrepancy		$1,310

Required

1. Prepare a proper bank reconciliation showing the true cash balance.

2. Prepare the necessary journal entries.

A&R Problem 7-4

George Gee acquired a sports equipment distribution business with a staff of six salespersons and two clerks. Because of the trust that George had in his employees—after all, they were all his friends and just like members of his family—he believed that an honour system was regard to the operation of the petty cash fund was adequate. Consequently, George placed $300 in a coffee jar, which, for convenience, was kept in a cupboard in the common room. All employees had access to the petty cash fund and withdrew amounts as required. No vouchers were required for withdrawals. As required, additional funds were placed in the coffee jar and the amount of the replenishment was charged to "miscellaneous selling expense."

Required

1. From the internal control point of view, discuss the weaknesses of the petty cash fund operation and suggest steps necessary for improvement.

2. Does the petty cash fund operation as described above violate any of the generally accepted accounting principles? If yes, which and how is the principle(s) violated?

Matter of Record

Record Case 7–1

Robert Chambers is national direct of the Forensic and Investigative Accounting Practice at Peat Marwick Thorne. He is based in Toronto. In his paper ''When Trusted Employees Turn to Fraud'' he lists the following warning signs to watch out for:

1. Variations between goods received and products sold, no matter how small.
2. Staff working unpaid or paid overtime without supervision, especially in unsecured areas.
3. Offers to assume extra duties or responsibilities without being asked.
4. A growing list of debtors. (Are some of these false inventions? If cash is received, where is it going?)
5. A dramatic increase in payroll cost.

6. Aging or delinquent debts, or outstanding lump sums.
7. An increasing number of creditors, amid more reports of goods not received.
8. Unaccounted-for units of sale or stock.
9. A higher-than-normal cost of materials or overheads.
10. Bank accounts that cannot be reconciled.

Chambers continues:

> Some companies call on forensic accountants as a preventive measure, to assess their vulnerability to fraud and possible penetration of their operations.
>
> Whatever your business, you have a responsibility to shareholders and creditors to defend against fraud. Monitor employee control procedures, protect cash from incidental access, reassess and update all costings and material waste levels—and keep a constant eye for the unexpected security foul-up.

Required

Discuss how fraud would be facilitated under 1, 2, 4, 5, 7, and 10.

Answers to Objective Review Questions

LO 1 (*d*)	LO 4 (*e*)	LO 7 (*d*)
LO 2 (*d*)	LO 5 (*d*)	LO 8 (*e*)
LO 3 (*a*)	LO 6 (*c*)	

Temporary Investments and Receivables

Companies rarely operate in today's economy without extending credit to customers. By being careful in granting credit, a business can increase sales without incurring high costs. Accounting information helps managers assess the risk and the success of their credit decisions.

*T*he focus of the prior chapter was on accounting for cash, which is the most liquid of all assets. This chapter continues the discussion of liquid assets by focusing on temporary investments, accounts receivable, and temporary notes receivable.

Learning Objectives

After studying Chapter 8, you should be able to:

1. Prepare journal entries to account for temporary investments and calculate, record, and report the lower of cost or market of temporary investments in marketable equity securities.

2. Prepare entries to account for credit card sales.

3. Prepare entries to account for transactions with credit customers, including accounting for bad debts under the allowance method and the direct write-off method.

4. Calculate the interest on promissory notes and prepare entries to record the receipt of promissory notes and their payment or dishonour.

5. Calculate the discount and proceeds on discounted notes receivable and prepare entries to record the discounting of notes receivable and their dishonouring, if necessary.

6. Define or explain the words and phrases listed in the chapter glossary.

After studying Appendix E at the end of Chapter 8, you should be able to:

7. Classify equity investments as current assets or as long-term investments and prepare entries to account for long-term equity investments according to the cost method and the equity method and to reflect lower of cost or market.

Because cash is used by companies to acquire assets and to pay expenses and obligations, good management generally requires that companies have an adequate amount available, including a surplus over the minimum amount that might be needed. Also, surplus cash may be available during some months of each year because of seasonal variations in sales volume. Rather than leave this unneeded cash in chequing accounts that pay low rates of interest at best, most concerns invest their surplus where it can earn higher returns.

Temporary Investments

Recall from Chapter 7 that cash equivalents are investments that are readily convertible into a known amount of cash; generally, they mature within a relatively short period of time. Some investments of idle cash balances do not meet these criteria of cash equivalents but, nevertheless, are classified as current assets. Although these **temporary investments,** or **short-term investments,** do not qualify as cash equivalents, they serve a similar purpose. Like cash equivalents, temporary investments can be converted into cash easily and are held as a source of cash to satisfy the needs of current operations. Management usually expects to convert them into cash within one year or the current operating cycle of the business, whichever is longer.

Temporary investments may be made in the form of government or corporate debt obligations (called *debt securities*) or in the form of shares (called *equity securities*). Some investments in debt securities are classified as current assets because they mature within one year or the current operating cycle of the business. Investments in other securities that do not mature in a short time can be classified as current assets only if they are marketable. In other words, such securities must be sellable without excessive delays. For example, shares that are actively traded on a stock exchange qualify as marketable.

When temporary investments are purchased, you should record them at cost. For example, assume that Alpha Company purchased Ford Motor Company's short-term notes payable for $40,000. Alpha's entry to record the transaction is:

Jan.	10	Temporary Investments.	40,000.00	
		Cash		40,000.00
		Bought $40,000 of Ford Motor Company notes due March 31.		

Assume that these notes mature, and that the cash proceeds are $40,000 plus $800 interest. When the receipt is recorded, you must credit the interest to a revenue account, as follows:

Mar.	31	Cash.	40,800.00	
		Temporary Investments		40,000.00
		Interest Earned.		800.00
		Received cash proceeds from matured notes.		

To determine the cost of an investment, you must include any commissions paid. For example, assume that on April 15, 1993, Bailey Company purchased 1,000 shares of Noranda Mines common shares as a temporary investment. The purchase price was 19⅛ ($19.125 per share) plus a $225 broker's commission. The entry to record the transaction is:[1]

Apr.	15	Temporary Investments.	19,350.00	
		Cash		19,350.00
		Bought 1,000 of Noranda common shares at 19⅛ plus $225 broker's commission ($19,125 + $225 = $19,350).		

LO 1 Prepare journal entries to account for temporary investments and calculate, record, and report the lower of cost or market of temporary investments in marketable equity securities.

---

[1] Share prices are quoted on stock exchanges on the basis of dollars and ⅛ dollars per share. For example, shares quoted at 23⅛ sold for $23.125 per share and those quoted at 36½ sold for $36.50 per share.

Notice that the commission is not recorded in a separate account.

When cash dividends are received on shares held as a temporary investment, they are credited to a revenue account as follows:

Dec.	12	Cash.	250.00	
		Dividends Earned		250.00
		Received dividend of 25 cents per share on 1,000		
		Noranda shares.		

When a company sells a temporary investment, it records the difference between its cost and the cash proceeds from the sale as a gain or loss. For example, assume that on December 20, 1993, Bailey Company sells 500 shares of Noranda for 18¼ per share less a $120 commission. Bailey receives cash proceeds from the sale of $9,005, or [(500 × $18.25) − $120]. Bailey's cost of the sold shares is $9,675, or one half of the $19,350 original cost of the 1,000 shares. The following entry records the sale:

Dec.	20	Cash.	9,005.00	
		Loss on Sale of Temporary Investments	670.00	
		Temporary Investments		9,675.00
		Sold 500 Noranda shares at 18¼ less $120		
		broker's commission.		

Temporary investments in marketable securities should be reported on the balance sheet at the **lower of cost or market (LCM).** To calculate the lower of cost or market, the *total* cost of all marketable securities held as temporary investments (called the *portfolio*) is compared with the *total* market value of the portfolio. Comparison on an item-by-item basis is normally not done.

For example, assume that Bailey Company did not have any temporary investments prior to its purchase of the Noranda shares on April 15, 1993. Later during 1993, Bailey Company purchased two other temporary investments in marketable securities. On December 31, 1993, the lower of cost or market is determined by comparing the total cost and total market value of the entire portfolio, as follows:

Temporary Investments	Cost	Market	LCM
Alcan Aluminum common shares. .	$42,600	$43,500	
Imperial Oil common shares	30,500	28,200	
Noranda Mines common shares . .	9,675	9,000	
Total	$82,775	$80,700	$80,700

The difference between the $82,775 cost and the $80,700 market value amounts to a $2,075 loss of market value.

Since all of the temporary investments were purchased during 1993, this $2,075 market value decline occurred entirely during 1993. The following adjusting entry on December 31, 1993, records the loss:

1993				
Dec.	31	Loss on Market Decline of Temporary Investments.	2,075.00	
		Allowance to Reduce Temporary Investments		
		to Market.		2,075.00
		To record the decline in value of the investments below		
		their original cost.		

The Loss on Market Decline of Temporary Investments account is closed to Income Summary and is reported on the income statement. The Allowance to Reduce Temporary Investments to Market account is a contra asset account. Its balance is subtracted from the total cost of the temporary investments so that on the balance sheet they are reported at the lower of cost or market. For example, the Bailey Company would report its temporary investments as follows:

Current assets:	
Cash and cash equivalents	$ xx,xxx
Temporary investments, at lower of	
cost or market (cost is $82,775) . .	80,700

In this example, notice that the $2,075 loss recorded during 1993 is equal to the December 31, 1993, balance in the allowance account. This occurs because we have assumed that no investments were owned prior to 1993. Therefore, the allowance account had a zero balance on December 31, 1992.

If an additional loss occurs in a future year, the allowance account balance after recording that loss probably will not equal the amount of that loss. To see why this is true, assume that on December 31, 1994, the total cost of Bailey Company's temporary investments portfolio is $108,475 and the total market value is $104,700 (assume additions to the investment portfolio during 1994). In other words, market value is $3,775 less than cost. Because the allowance account already has a credit balance of $2,075 as a result of the adjusting entry made on December 31, 1993, the adjusting entry to record the 1994 loss is:

1994				
Dec.	31	Loss on Market Decline of Temporary Investments*	1,700.00	
		Allowance to Reduce Temporary Investments		
		to Market.		1,700.00
		To record the market value decline during 1994.		

* Current Canadian GAAP do not allow a reversal of a writedown.

Thus, the loss recorded in 1994 is $1,700 and the December 31, 1994, balance in the allowance account is $3,775.

Because temporary investments in marketable equity securities must be reported at the *lower* of cost or market, market value increases above cost are not recorded as gains until the investments are sold. However, if a portfolio of temporary investments has been written down to a market value below cost, later increases in market value up to the original cost are reported on the income statement.

For example, assume that on December 31, 1995, the market value of Bailey Company's temporary investments is $500 less than cost. Since the allowance account had a credit balance of $3,775 at the end of 1994, the December 31, 1995, adjusting entry is:

1995				
Dec.	31	Allowance to Reduce Temporary Investments to Market . .	3,275.00	
		Recovery of Market Value Decline, Temporary		
		Investments		3,275.00
		To adjust the allowance account from $3,775 to $500.		

Notice that the only entries that change the allowance (contra asset) account balance are the end-of-period adjusting entries. The entries to record purchases and sales of investments during a period do not affect the allowance account.

If cost and market are about the same, a company can just report the investments at cost. For example, the 1991 balance sheet for Northern Telecom Limited shows this information:

Current assets:
   Cash and short-term investments at
     cost (approximates market value) $182,600,000

Some people criticize the lower of cost or market method because it is a departure from the *cost principle*. In recent years, however, an increasing number of people have criticized LCM because it does not record all changes in value, including increases above the original cost. In fact, accounting principles may in the future require reporting all investments at market value, whether higher or lower than cost. (See the "As a Matter of Fact" excerpts from recent articles on page 425.)

In addition to cash, cash equivalents, and temporary investments, the liquid assets of a business include receivables that result from credit sales to customers. In the following sections, we first discuss the procedures to account for sales when customers use credit cards issued by banks or credit card companies. Then we focus on accounting for credit sales when a business grants credit directly to its customers. This situation requires the company (1) to maintain a separate account receivable for each customer and (2) to account for bad debts that result from credit sales. In addition, we discuss how to account for notes receivable, many of which arise from extending credit to customers.

Credit Card Sales

Many customers use credit cards such as VISA, MasterCard, or American Express to charge purchases from various businesses. This practice gives the customers the ability to make purchases without carrying cash or writing cheques. It also allows them to defer their payments to the credit card com-

AS A MATTER OF
Fact

To encourage companies to take writeoffs earlier, the OSC said the CICA should consider allowing companies to reverse writeoffs if economic conditions then improve. "Current accounting standards do not allow issuers to reverse a writedown previously taken."

The OSC said the International Accounting Standards Committee permits the reversal of writedowns. The CICA is currently reviewing its policy.

*   *   *

While Mr. Schuetze, a longtime KPMG Peat Marwick partner, has in the past argued in favor of market-value accounting, his statements added a sense of urgency to the debate by showing the agency's impatience with the rule-making process. This pressure to change is causing banks to worry about the impact on their balance sheets.

*   *   *

The SEC's push on the subject is spooking banks, which have complained that the move would be too costly, too time-consuming and too confusing to investors. Bankers also have said they can't get an accurate reading of the loans that make up about 60% of their balance sheet assets. The FASB received 204 comment letters on the issue, about three quarters of which opposed market-value accounting.

*   *   *

Current-value accounting "is woefully bad because of the inexactness of the presented numbers," said Bob Muth, president and chief executive officer of Andover Bank in Andover, Ohio, and chairman of the Independent Bankers Association of America's Bank Operations Committee.

Source: Allan Robinson, "OSC Issues Warning," *The Globe and Mail*, January 15, 1992. Reprinted by permission. Kevin G. Salven, "SEC Renews Call for Pressure on Banks and S&Ls to Update Accounting Rules," *The Wall Street Journal*, January 8, 1992, p. A3. Reprinted by permission of *The Wall Street Journal*, © Dow Jones & Company, Inc. 1992. All rights reserved.

pany. Furthermore, once credit is established with the credit card company, the customer does not have to open an account with each store. Finally, customers who use credit cards can make single monthly payments instead of several to different creditors.

LO 2 Prepare entries to account for credit card sales.

There are good reasons why businesses allow customers to use credit cards instead of maintaining their own accounts receivable. First, the business does not have to evaluate the credit standing of each customer or make decisions about who should get credit and how much. Second, the business avoids the risk of extending credit to customers who cannot or do not pay. Instead, this risk is faced by the credit card company. Third, the business typically receives cash from the credit card company sooner than it would if it granted credit directly to its customers.

In dealing with some credit cards, usually those issued by banks, the business deposits a copy of each credit card sales receipt in its bank account just like it deposits a customer's cheque. Thus, the business receives a credit to its chequing account immediately on deposit. With other credit cards, the business sends the appropriate copy of each receipt to the credit card company and is paid shortly thereafter. Until payment is received, the business has an account receivable from the credit card company. In return for the services provided by the credit card company, a business will pay a fee ranging from 2% to 5% of credit card sales. This charge is deducted from the credit to the chequing account or the cash payment to the business.

The procedures used in accounting for credit card sales depend on whether cash is received immediately on deposit or is delayed until paid by the credit card company. If cash is received immediately, the entry to record $100 of credit card sales with a 4% fee would be:

Jan.	25	Cash.	96.00	
		Credit Card Expense	4.00	
		Sales		100.00
		To record credit card sales less a 4% credit card		
		expense.		

If the business must send the receipts to the credit card company and wait for payment, this entry on the date of the sale records them:

Jan.	25	Accounts Receivable, Credit Card Company	100.00	
		Sales		100.00
		To record credit card sales.		

When cash is received from the credit card company, the entry to record the receipt and the deduction of the fee is:

Feb.	10	Cash.	96.00	
		Credit Card Expense	4.00	
		Accounts Receivable, Credit Card Company.		100.00
		To record cash receipt less 4% credit card expense.		

In the last two entries, notice that the credit card expense was not recorded until cash was received from the credit card company. This practice is used merely as a matter of convenience. By following this procedure, the business avoids having to calculate and record the credit card expense each time sales are recorded. Instead, the expense related to many sales can be calculated once and recorded when cash is received. However, the *matching principle* requires reporting credit card expense in the same period as the sale. Therefore, if the sale and the cash receipt occur in different periods, you must accrue and report the credit card expense in the period of the sale by using an adjusting entry at the end of the year. For example, this year-end adjustment accrues $24 of credit card expense on a $600 receivable that the Credit Card Company has not yet paid.

Dec.	31	Credit Card Expense	24.00	
		Accounts Receivable, Credit Card Company.		24.00
		To accrue credit card expense that is unrecorded at		
		the end of the year.		

Then, when the account is collected in January, the following entry is made:

Jan.	5	Cash.	576.00	
		Accounts Receivable, Credit Card Company.		576.00
		To record collection of the amount due from Credit Card		
		Company.		

Some firms report credit card expense in the income statement as a type of discount that is deducted from sales to get net sales. Other companies classify it as a selling expense or even as an administrative expense. Arguments can be made for all three alternatives but there is little practical difference in the result.

Maintaining a Separate Account for Each Customer

In previous chapters, we introduced the use of an Accounts Receivable control account and a subsidiary Accounts Receivable Ledger. In this section, we review and expand upon this subject matter. A business with more than one credit customer must design its accounting system to show how much each customer has purchased, how much each customer has paid, and how much remains to be collected from each customer. This information provides the basis for sending bills to the customers. To have this information on hand, businesses that extend credit directly to their customers must maintain a separate account receivable for each of them.

LO 3 Prepare entries to account for transactions with credit customers, including accounting for bad debts under the allowance method and the direct write-off method.

One possible way of keeping a separate account for each customer would be to include all of these accounts in the same ledger that contains the financial statement accounts. However, this approach is usually not used because there are too many customers. Instead, as discussed in Chapter 6, the **General Ledger**, which is the ledger that contains the financial statement accounts, has only a single Accounts Receivable account. In addition, a supplementary record is established in which a separate account is maintained for each customer. This supplementary record is the **Accounts Receivable Ledger.**

Illustration 8–1 reviews the relationship between the Accounts Receivable account in the General Ledger and the individual customer accounts in the Accounts Receivable Ledger. In Part A of Illustration 8–1, notice that the $3,000 sum of the three balances in the Accounts Receivable Ledger is equal to the balance of the Accounts Receivable account in the General Ledger as of February 1. To maintain this relationship, each time that credit sales are posted with a debit to the Accounts Receivable account in the General Ledger, they are also posted with debits to the appropriate customer accounts in the Accounts Receivable Ledger. Also, cash receipts from credit customers must be posted with credits to both the Accounts Receivable account in the General Ledger and the appropriate customer accounts.

Part B shows the General Journal entry that would be made to record two credit sales on February 5 and February 14 to customers V. F. Zeller and Karen Johnson. It also shows the entry to record the collection of $720 from James Harrison.

ILLUSTRATION 8–1

The Accounts Receivable Account and the Accounts Receivable Ledger

Part A—Beginning situation: February 1

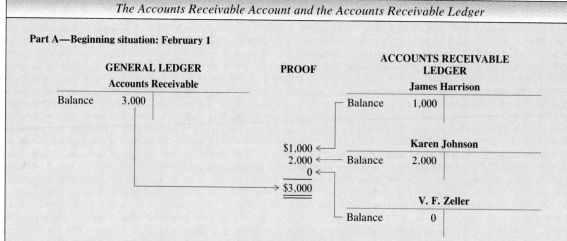

GENERAL LEDGER

Accounts Receivable

Balance   3,000

PROOF

$1,000 ←
2,000 ←
0 ←
$3,000 →

ACCOUNTS RECEIVABLE LEDGER

James Harrison

Balance   1,000

Karen Johnson

Balance   2,000

V. F. Zeller

Balance   0

Part B—Entries to record $1,800 sale to V. F. Zeller and $950 sale to Karen Johnson, and $720 collection from James Harrison

GENERAL JOURNAL

Feb.	5	Accounts Receivable—V. F. Zeller	1,800.00	
		Sales		1,800.00
	14	Accounts Receivable—Karen Johnson	950.00	
		Sales		950.00
	23	Cash	720.00	
		Accounts Receivable—James Harrison		720.00

Part C—Ending situation: February 28

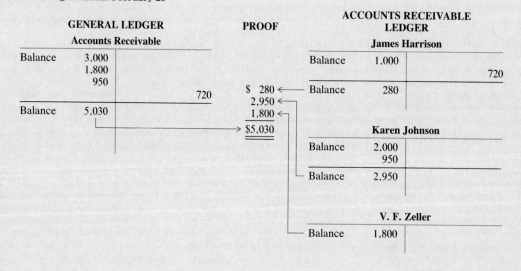

GENERAL LEDGER

Accounts Receivable

Balance	3,000	
	1,800	
	950	
		720
Balance	5,030	

PROOF

$ 280 ←
2,950 ←
1,800 ←
$5,030 →

ACCOUNTS RECEIVABLE LEDGER

James Harrison

Balance	1,000	
		720
Balance	280	

Karen Johnson

Balance	2,000	
	950	
Balance	2,950	

V. F. Zeller

Balance   1,800

Part C presents the General Ledger account and the Accounts Receivable Ledger as of February 28. Notice how the General Ledger account shows the effects of the sales and the collection, and that it has a $5,030 balance. The same events are reflected in the accounts for the three customers: Harrison now has a balance of only $280, Johnson owes $2,950, and Zeller has a balance of $1,800. The $5,030 sum of their accounts equals the debit balance of the General Ledger account.

Note that posting debits or credits to Accounts Receivable twice does not violate the requirement that debits equal credits. The equality of debits and credits is maintained *in the General Ledger*. The Accounts Receivable Ledger is simply a supplementary record that provides detailed information concerning each customer.

Because the balance in the Accounts Receivable account is always equal to the sum of the balances in the customers' accounts, the Accounts Receivable account is said to control the Accounts Receivable Ledger and is an example of a **controlling account.** Also, the Accounts Receivable Ledger is an example of a supplementary record that is controlled by an account in the General Ledger; this kind of supplementary record is called a **subsidiary ledger.**

The Accounts Receivable account and the Accounts Receivable Ledger are not the only examples of controlling accounts and subsidiary ledgers. Most companies buy on credit from several suppliers and must use a controlling account and subsidiary ledger for accounts payable. Another example might be an Office Equipment account that would control a subsidiary ledger in which the cost of each item of equipment is recorded in a separate account.

Bad Debts

When a company grants credit to its customers, there usually are a few who do not pay what they promised. The accounts of such customers are called **bad debts.** These bad debt amounts that cannot be collected are an expense of selling on credit.

You might ask why merchants sell on credit if it is likely that some of the accounts will prove to be uncollectible. The answer is that they believe granting credit increases revenues and profits. They are willing to take a reasonable loss from bad debts if the results are greater sales and profits than would have been achieved if all customers had to pay cash. Therefore, bad debt losses are an expense of selling on credit that is incurred to increase sales.

The reporting of bad debts expense on the income statement is governed by the *matching principle*. This principle requires that the expense from bad debts be reported in the same accounting period as the revenues they helped produce.

Matching Bad Debt Expenses with Sales

When credit sales are made, management usually realizes that some portion of those sales will result in bad debts. However, the fact that a specific credit sale will not be collected does not become apparent until later. If a customer fails to pay within the credit period, most businesses send out several repeat billings and make other efforts to collect. Usually, they do not accept the fact that a customer is not going to pay until every reasonable means of collection has been exhausted. In many cases, this point may not be reached until one or more accounting periods after the period in which the sale was made. Thus, matching this expense with the revenue it produced requires the company to estimate its unknown amount at the end of the year. The **allowance method of accounting for bad debts** is used to accomplish this matching of bad debts expense with revenues.

Allowance Method of Accounting for Bad Debts

At the end of each accounting period, the allowance method of accounting for bad debts requires estimating the total bad debts expected to result from the period's sales. An allowance is then provided for the loss. This method has two advantages: (1) the estimated expense is charged to the period in which the revenue is recognized, and (2) the accounts receivable are reported on the balance sheet at the amount of cash proceeds that is expected from their collection.

Recording the Estimated Bad Debts Expense

Under the allowance method of accounting for bad debts, the estimated bad debts expense is calculated at the end of each accounting period. Then, the amount is entered as an adjustment on the work sheet and recorded with an adjusting journal entry. For example, assume that Fritz Company had credit sales of $300,000 during the first year of its operations. At the end of the year, $20,000 remains uncollected in accounts receivable. Based on the experience of similar businesses, Fritz Company estimates that $1,500 of accounts receivable will be uncollectible. This estimated expense is recorded with the following adjusting entry:

Dec.	31	Bad Debts Expense	1,500.00	
		Allowance for Doubtful Accounts		1,500.00
		To record the estimated bad debts.		

The debit part of this entry causes the estimated bad debts expense to appear on the income statement of the year in which the sales were made. As a result, the estimated $1,500 expense of selling on credit is matched with the $300,000 of revenue it helped produce.

Note that the credit of the entry is to a contra account called the **Allowance for Doubtful Accounts.** A contra account must be used because at the time of the adjusting entry, you do not know for certain which customers will not pay. In fact, you will not know exactly which customers will not pay until every means of collection is exhausted. Therefore, because specific bad accounts are not identifiable at the time of the adjusting entry, they cannot be removed from the subsidiary Accounts Receivable Ledger. Because the customer accounts are left in the subsidiary ledger, the controlling account for Accounts

Receivable cannot be reduced. Instead, the Allowance for Doubtful Accounts account *must* be credited.

Observe that if the controlling account had been credited directly, its balance would be less than the sum of the balances in the subsidiary ledger. This result would not be consistent with the purpose served by the subsidiary ledger system.

Bad Debts in the Accounts and in the Financial Statements

The process of evaluating customers and approving them for credit usually is not assigned to the selling department of a business. Otherwise, given the primary objective of increasing sales, the selling department might not use good judgment in approving customers for credit. Because the sales department is not responsible for granting credit, it should not be held responsible for bad debts expense. Therefore, bad debts expense normally appears on the income statement as an administrative expense rather than a selling expense.

Recall from the previous example that Fritz Company has $20,000 of outstanding accounts receivable at the end of its first year of operations. Thus, after the bad debts adjusting entry is posted, the company's Accounts Receivable and Allowance for Doubtful Accounts accounts show these balances:

Accounts Receivable		Allowance for Doubtful Accounts	
Dec. 31 20,000		Dec. 31 1,500	

The Allowance for Doubtful Accounts credit balance of $1,500 has the effect of reducing accounts receivable (net of the allowance) to their estimated **realizable value.** This term *realizable value* means the expected proceeds from converting the assets into cash. Although $20,000 is legally owed to Fritz Company by all of its customers, only $18,500 is likely to be realized in cash collections from customers.

When the balance sheet is prepared, the allowance for doubtful accounts is subtracted from the accounts receivable to show the amount that is expected to be realized from the accounts. For example, this information could be reported as follows:

Current assets:		
Cash and cash equivalents		$11,300
Temporary investments, at lower of cost or market (cost is $16,200).		14,500
Accounts receivable	$20,000	
Less allowance for doubtful accounts	(1,500)	18,500
Merchandise inventory		52,700
Prepaid expenses		1,100
Total current assets		$98,100

In this example, compare the presentations of temporary investments and accounts receivable, and note that contra accounts are subtracted in both cases. Even though the contra account to the Temporary Investments account is not shown on the statement, you can easily determine that its balance is $1,700 by comparing the $16,200 cost with the $14,500 net amount. Sometimes, the contra account to Accounts Receivable is presented in a similar fashion, as follows:

Accounts receivable (net of $1,500 estimated
   uncollectible accounts) $18,500

Writing Off a Bad Debt

When specific accounts are identified as uncollectible, they are written off against the Allowance for Doubtful Accounts. For example, after spending a year trying to collect from Jack Vale, the Fritz Company finally decided that his $100 account was uncollectible and made the following entry to write it off:

Jan.	23	Allowance for Doubtful Accounts.	100.00	
		Accounts Receivable—Jack Vale.		100.00
		To write off an uncollectible account.		

Posting the credit of the entry to the Accounts Receivable account removes the amount of the bad debt from the controlling account. Posting it to the Jack Vale account removes the amount of the bad debt from the subsidiary ledger. And, removing it from the subsidiary ledger ensures that Fritz Company will no longer send bills to Vale. After the entry is posted, the general ledger accounts appear as follows:

Accounts Receivable			Allowance for Doubtful Accounts	
Dec. 31 20,000				Dec. 31 1,500
	Jan. 23 100	Jan. 23 100		

   Notice two aspects of the entry and the accounts. First, although bad debts are an expense of selling on credit, the allowance account is debited in the write-off. The expense account is *not* debited. The expense account is not debited because the estimated expense was previously recorded at the end of the period in which the sale occurred. At that time, the expense was estimated and recorded with an adjusting entry.
   Second, although the write-off removed the amount of the account receivable from the ledgers, it did not affect the estimated realizable value of Fritz Company's net accounts receivable, as the following tabulation shows:

	Before	After
Accounts receivable	$20,000	$19,900
Less allowance for doubtful accounts . . .	1,500	1,400
Estimated realizable accounts receivable . .	$18,500	$18,500

Thus, neither total assets nor net income are affected by the decision to write off a specific account. However, both total assets and net income are affected by the recognition of the year's bad debts expense in the adjusting entry. Again, a primary purpose of writing off a specific account is to avoid the cost of additional collection efforts.

When a customer fails to pay and the account is written off, his or her credit standing is jeopardized. Therefore, the customer may choose to voluntarily pay all or part of the amount owed after the account is written off as uncollectible. This payment helps restore the credit standing. Thus, when this event happens, it should be recorded in the customer's subsidiary account where the information will be retained for use in future credit evaluations.

Bad Debt Recoveries

When a company collects an account that was previously written off, it makes two journal entries. The first reverses the original write-off and has the effect of reinstating the customer's account. The second entry merely records the collection of the reinstated account. For example, assume that on August 15 Jack Vale pays in full the account that Fritz Company had previously written off. The entries to record the bad debt recovery are

Aug.	15	Accounts Receivable—Jack Vale	100.00	
		Allowance for Doubtful Accounts		100.00
		To reinstate the account of Jack Vale written off on January 23.		
	15	Cash.	100.00	
		Accounts Receivable—Jack Vale.		100.00
		Received full payment of account.		

In this case, Jack Vale paid the entire amount previously written off. In other situations, the customer may pay only a portion of the amount owed. The question then arises of whether the entire balance of the account should be returned to accounts receivable or just the amount paid. The answer is a matter of judgment. If you believe the customer will later pay in full, the entire amount owed should be returned. However, only the amount paid should be returned if you believe that no more will be collected.

Estimating the Amount of Bad Debts Expense

As you already learned, the allowance method of accounting for bad debts requires an adjusting entry at the end of each accounting period to record management's estimate of the bad debts expense for the period. That entry takes the following form:

Dec.	31	Bad Debts Expense	????	
		Allowance for Doubtful Accounts		????
		To record the estimated bad debts.		

What process does a business use to predict the amount to record in this entry? There are actually two broad alternatives. One focuses on the income statement relationship between bad debts expense and sales. The other focuses on the balance sheet relationship between accounts receivable and the allowance for doubtful accounts. Both alternatives require a careful analysis of past experience.

Estimating Bad Debts by Focusing on the Income Statement

The income statement approach to estimating bad debts is based on the idea that some particular percentage of a company's credit sales for the period will become uncollectible.[2] Hence, in the income statement, the amount of bad debts expense should equal that amount.

For example, suppose that Baker Company had credit sales of $400,000 in 1993. Based on past experience and the experience of similar companies, Baker Company estimates that 0.6% of credit sales will be uncollectible. Using this prediction, Baker Company can expect $2,400 of bad debts expense to result from the year's sales ($400,000 × 0.006 = $2,400). The adjusting entry to record this estimated expense is:

Dec.	31	Bad Debts Expense	2,400.00	
		Allowance for Doubtful Accounts		2,400.00
		To record the estimated bad debts.		

This entry does *not* mean the December 31, 1993, balance in Allowance for Doubtful Accounts will be $2,400. A $2,400 balance would occur only if the account had a zero balance immediately prior to posting the adjusting entry. For several reasons, however, the unadjusted balance of Allowance for Doubtful Accounts is not likely to be zero.

First, unless the Baker Company was created during the current year, the Allowance for Doubtful Accounts would have had a credit balance at the beginning of the year. The beginning-of-year credit balance would have resulted from entries made in past years to record estimated bad debts expense and to write off uncollectible accounts. The cumulative effect of these entries would show up as a credit balance at the beginning of the current year.

Second, because bad debts expense must be estimated each year, the total amount of expense recorded in past years is not likely to equal the amounts that were written off as uncollectible. Although annual expense estimates are based on past experience, some residual difference between recorded expenses and amounts written off should be expected to show up in the unadjusted Allowance for Doubtful Accounts balance.

---

[2] Note that the factor to be considered is *credit* sales. Naturally, cash sales do not normally produce bad debts, and they generally should not be used in the calculation. However, if cash sales are relatively small compared to credit sales, there will be no practical difference in the result.

Third, some of the amounts written off as uncollectible during the current year probably relate to credit sales made during the current year. These debits affect the unadjusted Allowance for Doubtful Accounts balance. In fact, they may cause the account to have a debit balance prior to posting the adjusting entry for bad debts expense.

For these reasons, you should not expect the Allowance for Doubtful Accounts to have an unadjusted balance of zero at the end of the year. As we stated earlier, this means that the adjusted balance reported on the balance sheet normally will not equal the amount of expense reported on the income statement.

Remember that expressing bad debts expense as a percentage of sales is an estimate based on past experience. As new experience is gained over time, the percentage used may appear to have been too large or too small. When this happens, a different rate should be used in future periods.

Estimating Bad Debts by Focusing on the Balance Sheet

The balance sheet approach to estimating bad debts is based on the idea that information about the realizable value of accounts receivable is useful to investors, creditors, and managers. From this point of view, the goal of the bad debts adjusting entry is to make the Allowance for Doubtful Accounts balance equal to the portion of outstanding accounts receivable estimated to be uncollectible. To obtain this required balance in the Allowance for Doubtful Accounts account, simply compare its balance before the adjustment with the required balance. The difference between the two is debited to Bad Debts Expense and credited to Allowance for Doubtful Accounts. Estimating the required balance of the Allowance account can be done in two ways: (1) by the simplified approach and (2) by aging the accounts receivable.

The Simplified Balance Sheet Approach. Using the simplified balance sheet approach, a company estimates that a certain percentage of its outstanding receivables will prove to be uncollectible. This estimated percentage is based on past experience and the experience of similar companies. It also may include taking into consideration current conditions such as recent prosperity or economic difficulties faced by the firm's customers. The total dollar amount of all outstanding receivables is multiplied by the estimated percentage to determine the estimated dollar amount of uncollectible accounts. This amount must appear in the balance sheet as the balance of the Allowance for Doubtful Accounts. To put this balance in the account, you must prepare an adjusting entry that debits Bad Debts Expense and credits Allowance for Doubtful Accounts. The amount of the adjustment is the amount necessary to provide the required balance in Allowance for Doubtful Accounts.

For example, assume that Baker Company (of the previous illustration) has $50,000 of outstanding accounts receivable on December 31, 1993. Past experience suggests that 5% of the outstanding receivables are uncollectible. Thus, after the adjusting entry is posted, the Allowance for Doubtful Accounts should have a $2,500 credit balance (5% of $50,000). Assume that the account appears as follows before any adjustment:

Allowance for Doubtful Accounts

			Dec. 31, 1992, balance	2,000
Feb. 6	800			
July 10	600			
Nov. 20	400			
			Unadjusted balance	200

The $2,000 beginning balance appeared on the December 31, 1992, balance sheet. During 1993, accounts of specific customers were written off on February 6, July 10, and November 20. As a result, the account has a $200 credit balance prior to the December 31, 1993, adjustment. The adjusting entry to give the Allowance the required $2,500 balance is

Dec.	31	Bad Debts Expense	2,300.00	
		Allowance for Doubtful Accounts		2,300.00
		To record the estimated bad debts.		

After this entry is posted, the Allowance has a $2,500 credit balance, as shown here:

Allowance for Doubtful Accounts

			Dec. 31, 1992, balance	2,000
Feb. 6	800			
July 10	600			
Nov. 20	400			
			Unadjusted balance	200
			Dec. 31	2,300
			Dec. 31, 1993, balance	2,500

Aging Accounts Receivable.   Both the income statement approach and the simplified balance sheet approach use knowledge gained from past experience to estimate the amount of bad debts expense. Another balance sheet–centered method produces a more refined estimate based on information about current conditions.

This method involves **aging of accounts receivable.** Under this method, each account receivable is examined in the process of estimating the amount that is uncollectible. Specifically, the receivables are classified in terms of how long they have been outstanding. Then estimates of uncollectible amounts are made under the assumption that the longer an amount is outstanding, the more likely it will be uncollectible.

To age the accounts receivable outstanding at the end of the period, you must examine each account and classify the outstanding amounts in terms of how much time has passed since they were created. The selection of the classes to be used depends on the judgment of each company's management. It is typical, however, for them to be based on 30-day (or one month) periods. After the outstanding amounts have been classified (or aged), past experience is used to estimate a percentage of each class that will become uncollectible.

ILLUSTRATION 8–2

Estimating Bad Debts by Aging the Accounts

BAKER COMPANY Schedule of Accounts Receivable by Age December 31, 1993						
Customer's Name	Total	Not Due	1 to 30 Days Past Due	31 to 60 Days Past Due	61 to 90 Days Past Due	Over 90 Days Past Due
Charles Abbot	$ 450.00	$ 450.00				
Frank Allen	710.00			$ 710.00		
George Arden	500.00	300.00	$ 200.00			
Paul Baum	740.00				$ 100.00	$ 640.00
ZZ Services	1,000.00	810.00	190.00			
Totals.	$49,900.00	$37,000.00	$6,500.00	$3,500.00	$1,900.00	$1,000.00
Rate		×2%	×5%	×10%	×25%	×40%
Estimated uncol- lectible accounts	$ 2,290.00	$ 740.00	$ 325.00	$ 350.00	$ 475.00	$ 400.00

These percentages are applied to the amounts in the classes to determine the required balance of the Allowance for Doubtful Accounts. The calculation is completed by setting up a schedule like the one in Illustration 8–2 for Baker Company.

In Illustration 8–2, notice that each customer's account is listed with its total balance. Then each balance is allocated to five categories based on the age of the unpaid charges that make up the balance. (In computerized systems, this allocation is done automatically.) When all accounts have been aged, the amounts in each category are totaled and multiplied by the estimated percentage of uncollectible accounts for each category.

For example, Illustration 8–2 shows that Baker Company is owed $3,500 that is 31 to 60 days past due. Baker's management estimates that 10% of the amounts in this age category will not be collected. Thus, the dollar amount of uncollectible accounts in this category is $350 ($3,500 × 10%). The total in the first column tells us that the adjusted balance in Baker Company's Allowance for Doubtful Accounts should be $2,290 ($740 + $325 + $350 + $475 + $400). Because the Allowance has an unadjusted credit balance of $200, the aging of accounts receivable approach requires the following change in its balance:

Unadjusted balance.	$ 200 credit
Required balance	2,290 credit
Required adjustment	$2,090 credit

As a result, Baker should record the following adjusting entry:

Dec.	31	Bad Debts Expense	2,090.00	
		Allowance for Doubtful Accounts		2,090.00
		To record the estimated bad debts.		

Alternatively, suppose that Baker's Allowance had an unadjusted *debit* balance of $500. In this case, the calculation of the adjustment amount and the entry would be:

Unadjusted balance.	$ 500 debit
Required balance	2,290 credit
Required adjustment	$2,790 credit

Dec.	31	Bad Debts Expense	2,790.00	
		Allowance for Doubtful Accounts		2,790.00
		To record the estimated bad debts.		

Recall from page 432 that when the income statement approach was used, Baker's bad debts expense for 1993 was estimated to be $2,400. When the simplified balance sheet approach was used (see page 435), the estimate was $2,300. And when aging of accounts receivable was used the first time, the estimate was $2,090. Do not be surprised that the amounts are different; after all, each approach is only an estimate of what will prove to be true. However, the aging of accounts receivable is based on a more detailed examination of specific outstanding accounts and is usually the most reliable.[3]

Direct Write-Off Method of Accounting for Bad Debts

The allowance method of accounting for bad debts is designed to satisfy the requirements of the *matching principle*. Therefore, it is the method that should be used in most cases. However, another method may be suitable under certain limited circumstances. Under this method, the direct write-off method of accounting for bad debts, no attempt is made to estimate uncollectible accounts or bad debts expense at the end of each period. In fact, no adjusting entry is made. Instead, when you decide an account is uncollectible, you write it off directly to Bad Debts Expense with an entry such as this one, which removes a receivable with a $52 balance:

---

[3] In many cases, the aging analysis is supplemented with information about specific customers that allows management to decide whether those accounts should be classified as uncollectible. This information often is supplied by the sales and credit department managers.

Nov.	23	Bad Debts Expense	52.00	
		Accounts Receivable—Dale Hall.		52.00
		To write off the uncollectible account under the direct		
		write-off method.		

The debit of the entry charges the uncollectible amount directly to the current year's Bad Debts Expense account. The credit removes the balance of the account from the subsidiary ledger and from the controlling account.

If an account previously written off directly to Bad Debts Expense is later collected in full, the following entries record the recovery:

Mar.	11	Accounts Receivable—Dale Hall	52.00	
		Bad Debts Expense.		52.00
		To reinstate the account of Dale Hall previously		
		written off.		
	11	Cash.	52.00	
		Accounts Receivable—Dale Hall.		52.00
		In full payment of account.		

Sometimes an amount previously written off directly to Bad Debts Expense is recovered in the year following the write-off. If there is no balance in the Bad Debts Expense account from previous write-offs and no other write-offs are expected, the credit portion of the entry recording the recovery can be made to a Bad Debt Recoveries revenue account.

As discussed next, the direct write-off method should be used only in limited situations.

Direct Write-Off Mismatches Revenues and Expenses

The direct write-off method usually mismatches revenues and expenses. The mismatch occurs because bad debts expense is not recorded until an account becomes uncollectible, which often does not occur during the same period as the credit sale. Despite this weakness, the direct write-off method may be used when a company's bad debts expenses are very small in relation to other financial statement items such as total sales and net income. In such cases, the direct write-off method is justified by the materiality principle, which is explained next.

The basic idea of the **materiality principle** is that the requirements of accounting principles may be ignored if the effect on the financial statements is unimportant to their users. In other words, failure to follow the requirements of an accounting principle is acceptable when the failure does not produce an error or misstatement large enough to influence a financial statement reader's judgment of a given situation.

The Materiality Principle

Installment Accounts and Notes Receivable

Many companies allow their credit customers to make periodic payments over several months. When this is done, the selling company's assets may be in the form of **installment accounts receivable** or notes receivable. As is true for other accounts receivable, the evidence behind installment accounts receivable includes sales slips or invoices that describe the sales transactions. A note receivable, on the other hand, is a written document that promises payment and is signed by the customer. In either case, when payments will be made over several months or if the credit period is long, the customer is usually charged interest. Although the credit period of installment accounts and notes receivable is often more than one year, they should be classified as current assets if the company regularly offers customers such terms.

Generally, creditors prefer notes receivable over accounts receivable when the credit period is long and the receivable relates to a single sale for a fairly large amount. Notes are also used to replace accounts receivable when customers ask for additional time to pay their past-due accounts. In these situations, creditors prefer notes to accounts receivable because the notes can be more easily converted into cash before becoming due by discounting (or selling) them to a bank. (However, accounts receivable also may be sold at a discount.) Notes are also preferred for legal reasons. If a lawsuit is needed to collect from a customer, a note represents a clear written acknowledgment by the debtor of the debt, its amount, and its terms.

Promissory Notes

LO 4 Calculate the interest on promissory notes and prepare entries to record the receipt of promissory notes and their payment or dishonour.

A **promissory note** is an unconditional written promise to pay a definite sum of money on demand or at a fixed or determinable future date. In the promissory note shown in Illustration 8–3, Hugo Brown promises to pay Frank Tomlinson or to his order (i.e., according to Tomlinson's instructions) a definite sum of money ($1,000), called the **principal of the note**, at a fixed future date (April 8, 1993). As the one who signed the note and promised to pay it at maturity, Hugo Brown is the **maker of the note**. As the person to whom the note is payable, Frank Tomlinson is the **payee of the note**. To Hugo Brown, the illustrated note is a liability called a *note payable*. To Frank Tomlinson, the same note is an asset called a *note receivable*.

The Hugo Brown note bears **interest** at 12%. Interest is the charge assessed for the use of money. To a borrower, interest is an expense. To a lender, it is a revenue. The rate of interest that a note bears is stated on the note. (In Chapter 12, we discuss notes having no stated interest rate, called *noninterest-bearing notes*.)

Calculating Interest

Unless otherwise stated, the rate of interest on a note is the rate charged for the use of the principal for one year. The formula for calculating interest is

$$\begin{array}{ccccc} \text{Principal} & & \text{Annual} & & \text{Time of the} \\ \text{of the} & \times & \text{rate of} & \times & \text{note expressed} = \text{Interest} \\ \text{note} & & \text{interest} & & \text{in years} \end{array}$$

For example, interest on a $1,000, 12%, six-month note is calculated as:

$$\$1,000 \times 12\% \times \frac{6}{12} = \$60$$

ILLUSTRATION 8–3

A Promissory Note

$1,000.00	Winnipeg, Manitoba	March 9, 1993

Thirty days after date _____ I _____ promise to pay to

the order of _____ Frank Tomlinson _____

One thousand and no / 100 - dollars

for value received with interest at _____ 12% _____

payable at _____ Royal Bank, Winnipeg _____

Hugo Brown

The **maturity date of a note** is the day on which the note (principal and interest) must be repaid. Many notes mature in less than a full year, and the period covered by them is often expressed in days. When the time of a note is expressed in days, the maturity date is the specified number of days after the day the note is dated. As a simple example, a one-day note dated June 15 matures and is due on June 16. Also, a 90-day note dated July 10 matures on October 8. This October 8 due date is calculated as follows:[4]

Number of days in July	31
Minus the date of the note.	10
Gives the number of days the note runs in July	21
Add the number of days in August	31
Add the number of days in September	30
Total through September 30.	82
Days in October needed to equal the 90-day time of the note, also the maturity date of the note—October	8
Total time the note runs in days.	90

In other situations, the period of a note is expressed in months. In these cases, the note matures and is payable in the month of its maturity on the same day of the month as its original date. For example, a three-month note dated July 10 is payable on October 10.

---

[4] Specific types of note may legally allow for three days of grace. For example, a 90-day note becomes due and payable on the 93rd day, and interest is calculated for 93 days. Because it is common practice that notes are due and payable on a specified date, illustrations are based on the time period specified on the face of the note. Unless otherwise instructed, you are to solve problems using the specified number of days and a 365-day year.

The formula for calculating interest for notes stated in days is as follows:

$$\text{Principal of the Note} \times \text{Rate of interest} \times \frac{\text{Time of the note expressed in days}}{365} = \text{Interest}$$

For example, interest on a $1,000, 12%, 90-day note is calculated as:

$$\$1,000 \times 12\% \times \frac{90}{365} = \$29.59$$

Recording the Receipt of a Note

To simplify record-keeping, notes receivable are usually recorded in a single Notes Receivable account. When a balance column account is used, each note may be identified by writing the name of the maker in the Explanation column on the line of the entry to record its receipt or payment. Only one account is needed because the individual original notes are on hand. Therefore, the maker, rate of interest, due date, and other information may be learned by examining each note.[5]

When a company receives a note at the time of a sale, an entry such as this one is recorded:

Dec.	5	Notes Receivable	650.00	
		Sales		650.00
		Sold merchandise, terms six-month, 9% note.		

A business also may accept a note from an overdue customer as a way of granting a time extension on the past-due account receivable. When this happens, the business usually collects part of the past-due balance in cash. This partial payment forces a concession from the customer, reduces the customer's debt (and the seller's risk), and produces a note for a smaller amount. For example, Symplex Company agrees to accept $232 in cash and a $600, 60-day, 15% note from Joseph Cook to settle his $832 past-due account. When Symplex receives the cash and note, the following entry is made:

Oct.	5	Cash.	232.00	
		Notes Receivable	600.00	
		Accounts Receivable—Joseph Cook		832.00
		Received cash and a note in settlement of an account.		

---

[5] If the company holds a large number of notes, it may be more efficient to set up a controlling account and a subsidiary ledger.

When Cook pays the note on the due date, this entry records the receipt:

Dec.	4	Cash.	614.79	
		Notes Receivable.		600.00
		Interest Earned.		14.79
		Collected the Joseph Cook note.		

The $14.79 of interest is computed as $600 \times 15\% \times {}^{60}\!/_{365}$.

Dishonoured Notes Receivable

Occasionally, the maker of a note either cannot or will not pay the note at maturity. When a note's maker is unable or refuses to pay at maturity, the note is said to be dishonoured. This act of **dishonouring a note** does not relieve the maker of the obligation to pay. Furthermore, the payee should use every legitimate means to collect. However, collection may require lengthy legal proceedings.

LO 5 Calculate the discount and proceeds on discounted notes receivable and prepare entries to record the discounting of notes receivable and their dishonouring, if necessary.

The usual practice is to have the balance of the Notes Receivable account show only the amount of notes that have not matured. Therefore, when a note is dishonoured, you should remove the amount of the note from the Notes Receivable account and charge it back to an account receivable from its maker. To illustrate, Symplex Company holds an $800, 12%, 60-day note of George Hart. At maturity, Hart dishonours the note. To remove the dishonoured note from the Notes Receivable account, the company makes the following entry:

Oct.	14	Accounts Receivable—George Hart	815.78	
		Interest Earned.		15.78
		Notes Receivable.		800.00
		To charge the account of George Hart for his		
		dishonoured note.		

The $15.78 of interest is computed as $800 \times 12\% \times {}^{60}\!/_{365}$.

Charging a dishonoured note back to the account of its maker serves two purposes. First, it removes the amount of the note from the Notes Receivable account, leaving in the account only notes that have not matured. It also records the dishonoured note in the maker's account. The second purpose is important. If the maker of the dishonoured note again applies for credit in the future, his or her account will show all past dealings, including the dishonoured note. Restoring the account also reminds the business to continue collection efforts.

Note that Hart owes both the principal and the interest. Therefore, the entry records the full amount owed in Hart's account and credits the interest to Interest Earned. This procedure assures that the interest will be included in future efforts to collect from Hart.

Discounting Notes Receivable

As previously stated, a note receivable often is preferred to an account receivable. One reason is that a note may be more easily converted into cash before the due date. This conversion might be done for a number of reasons; perhaps the most common is to allow the holder to avoid having to borrow money by signing its own note. One frequently used way of obtaining cash early is by **discounting the note receivable.** In essence, this step involves selling the note to a bank or to some other buyer. When a note receivable is discounted, the owner endorses and delivers the note to the bank in exchange for cash. The bank holds the note to maturity and then collects its maturity value from the original maker.

To illustrate, assume that on May 28, Symplex Company received a $1,200, 60-day, 12% note dated May 27 from John Owen. It held the note until June 2 and then discounted it at the bank at 14%. Since the maturity date of this note is July 26, the bank must wait 54 days after discounting the note to collect from Owen. These 54 days are called the **discount period,** which is the number of days between the date on which a note is discounted at the bank and its maturity date. The discount period is calculated for this note as follows:

Original period of the note in days		60
Less time held by Symplex Company:		
Number of days in May	31	
Less the date of the note.	27	
Days held in May	4	
Days held in June	2	
Total days held by Symplex		6
Discount period in days		54

At the end of the discount period, the bank expects to collect the maturity value of this note from Owen. The **maturity value of a note** is its principal plus any interest due on its maturity date. The maturity value of the Owen note is

Principal of the note.	$1,200.00
Interest on $1,200 for 60 days at 12%	23.67
Maturity value.	$1,223.67

In calculating the interest or discount to be charged, banks traditionally base their discount on the maturity value of the note. In this case, we assume the bank has a 14% **discount rate,** which is the rate of interest it charges for lending money by discounting a note. Therefore, in discounting this note, the bank deducts 54 days' interest at 14% from the note's maturity value and gives Symplex Company the remainder. The amount of interest deducted in advance is called the **bank discount,** and the remainder is called the **proceeds of the discounted note.** The bank discount and the proceeds are calculated as follows:

Maturity value of the note.		$1,223.67
Less discount on $1,223.67 for 54 days at 14% . .		25.35*
Proceeds		$1,198.32

* $1,223.67 × .14 × ($^{54}/_{365}$) = $25.35

In this case, the proceeds, $1,198.32, are $1.68 less than the $1,200 principal amount of the note. Therefore, Symplex makes this entry to record the discount transaction:

June	2	Cash.	1,198.32	
		Interest Expense	1.68	
		Notes Receivable.		1,200.00
		Discounted the John Owen note for 54 days at 14%.		

In this entry, note that the $23.67 of interest Symplex would have earned by holding the note to maturity is offset against the $25.35 discount charged by the bank. The $1.68 difference is debited to Interest Expense.

In the situation just described, the principal of the discounted note exceeded the proceeds. However, in other cases, the proceeds can exceed the principal. When this happens, the difference is credited to Interest Earned. For example, suppose that instead of discounting the John Owen note on June 2, Symplex discounted it on June 26 at 14%. Therefore, the discount period is 30 days, the discount is $14.08, and the proceeds of the note are $1,209.59, calculated as follows:

Maturity value of the note.		$1,223.67
Less discount on $1,223.67 for 30 days at 14% . .		14.08*
Proceeds		$1,209.59

* $1,223.67 × .14 × ($^{30}/_{365}$) = $14.08

Because the proceeds exceed the principal, the transaction is recorded as follows:

June	26	Cash.	1,209.59	
		Interest Earned.		9.59
		Notes Receivable.		1,200.00
		Discounted the John Owen note for 30 days at 14%.		

Contingent Liability

A person or company that discounts a note receivable is ordinarily required to endorse the note. This endorsement, unless it is qualified, makes the endorser contingently liable for payment of the note.[6] This endorsement creates a **contingent liability,** which is a potential liability that will become an actual liability only if certain events occur. The event that would turn a discounted note from a contingent liability to an actual liability would be the dishonouring of the note by its maker. If the maker pays as agreed, the endorser has no liability. However, if the maker defaults, the endorser's contingent liability becomes an *actual* liability, and the endorser must pay the maturity value of the note to the bank. The endorser then has the legal right to collect that amount from the maker.

Because a contingent liability can become an actual liability, it may affect the credit standing of the person who is contingently liable. Therefore, the existence of a material contingent liability should be disclosed in the financial statements. To help the accountant know that the contingency exists, a discounted note should be identified in the Explanation column of the Notes Receivable account. For example, assume that Symplex Company holds $500 of notes receivable in addition to the John Owen note. After the entry to record the discounting of John Owen's note is posted, the Notes Receivable account appears as follows:

Notes Receivable					Account No. 111	
Date		Explanation	PR	Debit	Credit	Balance
May	28	John Owen note	G6	1,200.00		1,200.00
June	7	Earl Hill note	G6	500.00		1,700.00
	26	Discounted the John Owen note	G7		1,200.00	500.00

Alternatively, it is possible to reflect the contingent liability by crediting a contra account for Notes Receivable Discounted instead of crediting the Notes Receivable account.

Contingent liabilities resulting from discounting notes receivable are commonly disclosed in a footnote to the balance sheet. If Symplex Company follows this practice, the company's June 30 balance sheet will show the $500 of notes it has not discounted and the contingent liability that resulted from discounting the John Owen note as follows:

```
Current assets:
    Cash . . . . . . . . . . . . . . . . .    $ 5,315
    Accounts receivable . . . . . . . . . .    21,275
    Notes receivable (See note 2.) . . . .       500
```

```
Note 2: Symplex Company is contingently liable for
$1,200 of discounted notes receivable.
```

---

[6] A qualified endorsement is one in which the endorser states in writing that he or she will not be liable for payment. Such an endorsement is also said to be "without recourse."

The balance sheet disclosure of contingent liabilities is required by the **full-disclosure principle.** This principle requires a concern's financial statements (including the footnotes) to contain all relevant information about the operations and financial position of the entity. Any data that are important enough to affect a statement reader's evaluation of the concern's operations and financial position should be reported. This principle does not mean that the concern should report excessive amounts of detail. It simply means that no significant information should be withheld and that enough information should be provided to make the reports understandable. Examples of items that need to be reported to satisfy the full-disclosure principle include the following:

Full-Disclosure Principle

Contingent Liabilities. In addition to discounted notes, a company should disclose in its financial reports any items for which the company is contingently liable. Examples of such items are possible additional tax assessments, debts of other parties that the company has guaranteed, and pending lawsuits against the company.

Long-Term Commitments under Contracts. A company should disclose that it has signed a long-term lease requiring material annual payments, even though the obligation does not appear in the accounts. Also, the company should reveal that it has pledged certain of its assets as security for a loan.

Accounting Methods Used. Whenever several acceptable accounting methods may be followed, a company should report the method it uses, especially when the choice of methods can materially affect reported net income. For example, a company should report by means of financial statement footnotes such items as the inventory method or methods used, amortization methods used, and the method of recognizing revenue under long-term construction contracts. (These methods are all described in future chapters.)

A bank always tries to collect a discounted note directly from the maker. If it is able to do so, the endorser (the one who discounted the note) does not hear from the bank and needs to do nothing more in regard to the note. However, if a discounted note is dishonoured, the bank promptly notifies the endorser of the note in order to hold that person liable for its payment. (In fact, there may be more than one endorser if the note is discounted more than once.) The process of notifying an endorser that a note has been dishonoured is called *protesting the note.* To protest a note, the bank prepares and mails a **notice of protest** to each endorser. A notice of protest is a statement, usually witnessed by a notary public, that says the note was duly presented to the maker for payment and that payment was refused. The fee charged for preparing and issuing a notice of protest is called a **protest fee.** The bank tries to collect both the note's maturity value and the protest fee from the one who discounted the note.

Dishonour of a Discounted Note

For example, suppose that John Owen dishonoured the $1,200 note previously discussed. In this case, the bank would immediately notify Symplex Company of the dishonouring by mailing a notice of protest and a letter asking payment for the note's maturity value plus the protest fee. If the protest fee is $25, Symplex must pay the bank $1,248.67. To record the payment, Symplex charges the $1,248.67 to the account of John Owen, as follows:

July	27	Accounts Receivable—John Owen	1,248.67	
		Cash		1,248.67
		To charge the account of Owen for the maturity value of his dishonoured note ($1,200 + $23.67) plus the protest fee ($25).		

On receipt of the $1,248.67, the bank delivers the dishonoured note to Symplex Company. Symplex then makes every reasonable effort to make Owen pay not only the maturity value of the note and the protest fee but also additional interest on the total of those two amounts from the maturity date (the date of dishonour) until the date of final settlement. However, after exhausting every reasonable means to collect, it may have to write off the account as a bad debt. For example, if Symplex Company concludes on August 24 that John Owen will not be able to pay, the account should be written off as follows:

Aug.	24	Allowance for Doubtful Accounts.	1,248.67	
		Accounts Receivable—John Owen.		1,248.67
		To write off uncollectible account.		

On the other hand, some dishonoured notes are eventually paid by their makers. For example, assume that the entry on August 24 was not made. Instead, assume that 30 days beyond maturity, John Owen pays the maturity value of his dishonoured note, plus the protest fee, plus interest at 12% on both for 30 days. The total amount is:

Maturity value	$1,223.67
Protest fee	25.00
Total paid to the bank.	$1,248.67
Interest on $1,248.67 at 12% for 30 days	12.32
Total	$1,260.99

Symplex records the payment by Owen as follows:

Aug.	25	Cash.	1,260.99	
		Interest Earned.		12.32
		Accounts Receivable—John Owen.		1,248.67
		Dishonoured note and protest fee collected with interest.		

When notes receivable are outstanding at the end of an accounting period, the accrued interest should be calculated and recorded. This procedure recognizes the interest revenue when it is earned and recognizes the additional asset owned by the note's holder. For example, on December 16, Perry Company accepted a $3,000, 60-day, 12% note from a customer in granting an extension on a past-due account. When the company's accounting period ends on December 31, $14.79 of interest will have accrued on this note ($3,000 × 12% × $^{15}/_{365}$). The following adjusting entry records this revenue:

End-of-Period
Adjustments

Dec.	31	Interest Receivable	14.79	
		Interest Earned.		14.79
		To record accrued interest.		

The adjusting entry causes the interest earned to appear on the income statement of the period in which it was earned. It also causes the interest receivable to appear on the balance sheet as a current asset.

Collecting Interest Previously Accrued

When the note is collected, Perry Company's entry to record the cash receipt is

Feb.	14	Cash.	3,059.18	
		Interest Earned.		44.39
		Interest Receivable.		14.79
		Notes Receivable.		3,000.00
		Received payment of a note and its interest.		

Observe that the entry's credit to Interest Receivable records collection of the interest accrued at the end of the previous period. Only the $44.39 of interest earned between January 1 and February 14 is recorded as revenue.

Recording the Collection When Reversing Entries Are Used

In Appendix B at the end of Chapter 4, we explained how some companies make *reversing entries* on the first day of a new accounting period. These entries are not necessary but are often used as a bookkeeping convenience. In the previous example, if Perry Company had used reversing entries, the December 31 accrual of interest would have been reversed on January 1, as follows:

Jan.	1	Interest Earned	14.79	
		Interest Receivable.		14.79
		To reverse the accrual of interest.		

Because the Interest Earned account was closed to Income Summary on December 31, the preceding entry would give the Interest Earned account an initial debit balance of $14.79. Also, the Interest Receivable debit balance would be reduced from $14.79 to $0. The entry recording the cash receipt on February 14 would be as follows:

Feb.	14	Cash.	3,059.18	
		Interest Earned.		59.18
		Notes Receivable.		3,000.00
		Received payment of a note and its interest.		

Observe that the result of these two entries is a $44.39 credit balance in the Interest Earned account ($59.18 credit − $14.79 debit). This balance is exactly the same as when the receipt was recorded without using reversing entries (see the February 14 entry on page 449).

Alternative Method of Interest Calculation

In calculating interest in the foregoing examples, the "exact," or proper, method was used. For classroom purposes, however, instructors may prefer to use a less accurate simplified method of interest calculation in order to focus on comprehension rather than on lengthy procedural calculation. To simplify interest calculations, the following assumptions are made:

1. Treat a year as having 360 days divided into 12 months of 30 days each.
2. Use the exact days of the note; that is, do not give consideration to the days of grace.

Thus, interest on a 90-day, 12%, $1,500 note is calculated as:

$$\$1,500 \times \frac{12}{100} \times \frac{90}{360} = \$45$$

To facilitate the use of the alternative method of interest calculation, certain exercises and problems may be designated for use of this method.

Summary of the Chapter in Terms of Learning Objectives

LO 1. Temporary investments are recorded at cost; dividends, interest, gains, and losses on the investments are recorded in appropriate income statement accounts. The total cost of the entire portfolio of temporary investments in marketable equity securities is compared with its market value to determine the lower of cost or market. Write-downs to market are credited to a contra account, the Allowance to Reduce Temporary Investments to Market.

LO 2. When credit card receipts are deposited in a bank account, the credit card expense is recorded at the time of the deposit. When credit card receipts must be submitted to the credit card company for payment, Accounts Receivable is debited for the sales amount. Credit card expense is recorded when cash is received from the credit card company. However, any unrecorded credit card expense should be accrued at the end of each accounting period.

LO 3. Under the allowance method, bad debts expense is recorded with an adjustment at the end of each accounting period that debits the expense and credits the Allowance for Doubtful Accounts. The amount of the adjustment is determined by either (*a*) focusing on the income statement relationship between bad debts expense and credit sales or (*b*) focusing on the balance sheet relationship between accounts receivable and the Allowance for Doubtful Accounts. The latter approach may involve using a simple percentage relationship or aging the accounts. Uncollectible accounts are written off with a debit to the Allowance for Doubtful Accounts. The direct write-off method charges Bad Debts Expense when accounts are written off as uncollectible. This method is suitable only when the amount of bad debts expense is immaterial.

LO 4. Interest rates are typically stated in annual terms. When a note's time to maturity is more or less than one year, the amount of interest on the note must be determined by expressing the time as a fraction of one year and multiplying the note's principal by that fraction and the annual interest rate. Dishonoured notes are credited to Notes Receivable and debited to Accounts Receivable and to the account of the maker.

LO 5. The holder of a note may discount it at a bank to get cash before the scheduled maturity date. The bank's discount rate is applied to the maturity value of a note to determine the discount, which is subtracted from the maturity value to determine the proceeds. Until the note matures, the original holder has a contingent liability to the bank. If a discounted note receivable is dishonoured, the original payee must pay the note's maturity value plus any protest fee.

Garden Company had the following transactions during 1993:

Demonstration Problem

May   8   Purchased 300 common shares of Bank of Montreal as a temporary investment. The cost of $40 per share plus $975 in broker's commissions was paid in cash.

July   3   Received $800 in dividends from the Bank of Montreal shares.

     14   Wrote off a $750 account receivable from 1992. (Garden Company uses the allowance method.)

     26   Bank credit card sales amounted to $15,000. Deposited the sales slips in the local bank, which deducts 5% as its fee.

     30   Received $400 in partial settlement of a $2,000 account receivable. The remaining balance was converted to a $1,600, one-year, 12% note receivable.

Aug.   4   Wrote off a $1,100 account receivable arising from a sale earlier in 1993.

     15   Accepted a $2,000 down payment and a $10,000 note receivable from a customer in exchange for an inventory item that normally sells for $12,000. The note was dated August 15, bears 12% interest, and matures in six months.

Sept. 2   Sold 100 Bank of Montreal shares at $47 per share, and continued to hold the other 200 shares. The broker's commission on the sale was $225.

Nov. 15   Discounted the $10,000 note (dated August 15) at the local bank at a rate of 16%.

Dec. 2   Purchased 1,600 Telus Corp. shares at $15 per share plus $1,600 in commissions. The shares are to be held as a temporary investment.

Required

1. Prepare journal entries to record these transactions on the books of Garden Company.

2. Prepare adjusting journal entries as of December 31, 1993, for the following items:

   a. The market prices of the equity securities held by Garden Company are $48 per share for the Bank of Montreal, and $13.75 per share for the Telus Corporation.

   b. Bad debts expense is estimated by an aging of accounts receivable. The unadjusted balance of the Allowance for Doubtful Accounts account is a $1,000 debit, while the required balance is estimated to be a $20,400 credit.

   c. Interest is accrued on the note dated July 30, 1993.

Solution to Demonstration Problem

Planning the Solution

- Examine each item to determine which accounts are affected and produce the needed journal entries.

- With respect to the year-end adjustments, apply the lower of cost or market method to the temporary investments, record the bad debts expense, and compute the amount of interest on the note receivable.

1.

May	8	Temporary Investments	12,975.00	
		Cash		12,975.00
		Purchased 300 shares of Bank of Montreal.		
		Cost is (300 × $40) + $975.		
July	3	Cash.	800.00	
		Dividends Earned		800.00
		Received dividends on Bank of Montreal shares.		
	14	Allowance for Doubtful Accounts.	750.00	
		Accounts Receivable		750.00
		Wrote off an uncollectible account.		
	26	Cash.	14,250.00	
		Credit Card Expense	750.00	
		Sales		15,000.00
		Deposited credit receipts in bank. The fee is		
		($15,000 × 0.05).		
	30	Notes Receivable	1,600.00	
		Cash.	400.00	
		Accounts Receivable		2,000.00
		Accepted a $1,600, one-year, 12% note receivable and		
		$400 in cash in settlement of a customer's account.		
Aug.	4	Allowance for Doubtful Accounts.	1,100.00	
		Accounts Receivable		1,100.00
		Wrote off an uncollectible account.		
	15	Cash.	2,000.00	
		Notes Receivable	10,000.00	
		Sales		12,000.00
		Sold merchandise to customer for $2,000 cash and		
		$10,000 note receivable.		
Sept.	2	Cash.	4,475.00	
		Gain on Sale of Investment.		150.00
		Temporary Investments		4,325.00
		Sold 100 shares of Bank of Montreal for $47 per share		
		less a $225 commission. The original cost is		
		($12,975 × $^{100}/_{300}$).		
Nov.	15	Cash.	10,176.00	
		Interest Earned.		176.00
		Notes Receivable.		10,000.00
		Discounted a note receivable at 16% for three months.		

Principal	$10,000
Interest earned ($10,000 × 12% × $^6/_{12}$)	600
Maturity value	$10,600
Less discount ($10,600 × 16% × $^3/_{12}$)	424
Proceeds	$10,176

Note: Months are used in the calculation because the time period of the note was expressed in months.

Dec.	2	Temporary Investments.	25,600.00	
		Cash		25,600.00
		Purchased 1,600 shares of Telus Corp. for $15 per share plus $1,600 in commissions.		
	31	Loss on Market Decline of Temporary Investments.	2,650.00	
		Allowance to Reduce Temporary Investments to Market		2,650.00
		To record the decline in market value of temporary investments.		

Temporary Investments	Shares	Cost per Share	Total Cost	Value per Share	Total Market	Differ- ence
Bank of Montreal . .	200	$43.25	$ 8,650	$48.00	$ 9,600	
Telus Corp.	1,600	16.00	25,600	13.75	22,000	
Total.			$34,250		$31,600	$2,650

	31	Bad Debts Expense	21,400.00	
		Allownce for Doubtful Accounts		21,400.00
		To adjust the allowance account from $1,000 debit balance to $20,400 credit balance.		
	31	Interest Receivable	80.00	
		Interest Earned.		80.00
		To accrue interest on July 30 note receivable ($1,600 × 12% × 5/12).		

APPENDIX

E

Investments in Equity Securities

Most large corporations invest in the shares of other corporations. The financial statement effects of such investments often are very important. As a result, your study of this topic in this appendix will enrich your ability to understand and interpret the accounting for long-term equity securities.

Shares as Investments

In Chapter 8 you learned that companies often invest idle cash in temporary investments. However, companies also purchase equity securities as long-term investments. These purchase and sale transactions between investors are usually arranged through agents, called *brokers,* who charge a commission for their services.

In acting as agents for their customers, brokers buy and sell many shares and bonds on exchanges, such as the Toronto Stock Exchange. Other shares and bonds are not listed or traded on an organized stock exchange. Instead, they are bought and sold in the *over-the-counter market*. Each security in this market is handled by brokers who receive offers to buy or sell the security at specific *bid* or *asked* prices through a network of other brokers.

Recall that per share prices are quoted on the basis of dollars and one-eighth fractions of dollars. A share quoted at 29¼ will sell for $29.25 per share, and one quoted at 28⅞ will sell for $28.875 per share. For example, the purchases and sales of Alcan Aluminum Limited's common shares and Cineplex Odeon Corporation's common shares were reported in many newspapers on Wednesday, September 2, 1992, as follows:

Shares	High	Low	Close	Net Change
Alcan	22½	22¼	22¼	−¼
Cineplex	2.69	2.60	2.69	+0.14

455

These reported prices are the highest and lowest prices at which the shares traded during Tuesday, September 1, and the price of the last transaction that occurred at the end of the day. The net change is the difference between the closing price on Tuesday and the closing price for Monday, August 31.

Classifying Investments

LO 8 Classify equity investments as current assets or as long-term investments and prepare entries to account for long-term equity investments according to the cost method and the equity method and to reflect lower of cost or market.

Equity securities include common and preferred shares. Temporary investments are identified by the CICA Handbook as those that are "capable of reasonably prompt liquidation."[1]

If an investment in marketable equity securities is held as to "obtain a return on a temporary basis," it is classified as a current asset.[2] (You learned how to account for temporary investments in marketable equity securities in Chapter 8.)

Investments that are not held as a ready source of cash are called long-term investments. They include funds earmarked for a special purpose, such as bond sinking funds, as well as land or other assets that are owned but not used in the regular operations of the business. Long-term investments also include investments in bonds and shares that are not marketable or that, although marketable, are not intended to serve as a ready source of cash. These assets are reported on the balance sheet in a separate category called *Long-term investments*.

Accounting for Long-Term Investments in Shares

The method used to account for a long-term investment in shares or equity investments depends on the relationship between the investor and the investee. This relationship takes one of three forms:

1. The investor is not able to significantly influence the operations of the investee.
2. The investor has a significant influence but does not control the investee.
3. The investor controls the investee.

When a company invests in another company's shares, the shares owned by the investor may represent only a small percentage of the total amount of shares outstanding. In this case, the investor usually does not have the ability to influence the operations of the investee corporation. Normally, an investor does not have a significant influence if it owns less than 20% of the investee's voting shares.[3]

Sometimes, an investor buys a large block of a corporation's voting shares and is able to exercise a significant influence over the investee corporation. An investor who owns 20% or more of a corporation's voting shares is normally presumed to have a significant influence over the investee. There may be cases, however, where the ac-

---

[1] *CICA Handbook* (Toronto: The Canadian Institute of Chartered Accountants), par.3010.02.

[2] Ibid., par. 3050.21.

[3] Ibid., par. 3050.21.

countant concludes that the 20% test of significant influence should be overruled by other, more persuasive, evidence.[4]

If an investor owns more than 50% of a corporation's voting shares, the investor can dominate all of the other shareholders in electing the corporation's board of directors. Thus, the investor has control over the investee corporation's management.[5]

As we stated earlier, the method of accounting for an equity investment depends on the relationship between the investor and the investee. Illustration E–1 shows each type of investor/investee relationship and the corresponding accounting methods used. In studying this illustration, note that if the investor does not have a significant influence, the accounting method used is the cost method. If the investor has a significant influence, the accounting method used is the equity method. Finally, if the investor controls the investee, the investor reports consolidated financial statements to the public. As shown in Illustration E–1, an investor that controls an investee presents consolidated financial statements but uses the equity method in its records. Also note that the marketability of the shares does not affect the choice between the equity method and consolidation. We explain the first two of these accounting methods in the following sections.

The Cost Method of Accounting for Equity Investments

When shares are purchased as an investment, the asset is recorded at its total cost, which includes any commission paid to the broker. For example, Gordon Company purchased 1,000 (1%) of Dot Corporation's 100,000 outstanding common shares as a long-term investment at 23¼ plus a $300 broker's commission. Gordon's entry to record the transaction is:

Sept.	10	Investment in Dot Corporation Shares	23,550.00	
		Cash		23,550.00
		Purchased 1,000 shares for $23,250 plus a		
		$300 broker's commission.		

When the cost method is used and a cash dividend is received on the shares, Gordon records the dividend as follows:

Oct.	5	Cash.	1,000.00	
		Dividends Earned		1,000.00
		Received a $1 per share dividend on the Dot Corporation		
		shares.		

---

[4] Ibid., par. 3050.21.

[5] Ibid., par. 3050.03.

ILLUSTRATION E-1

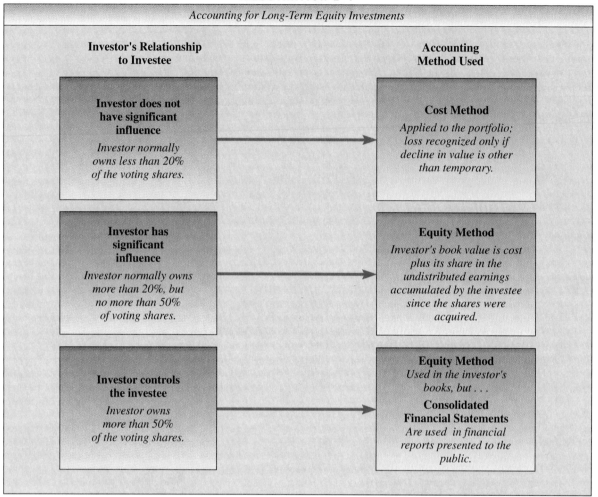

Accounting for Long-Term Equity Investments

Investor's Relationship to Investee

Accounting Method Used

Investor does not have significant influence
Investor normally owns less than 20% of the voting shares.

Cost Method
Applied to the portfolio; loss recognized only if decline in value is other than temporary.

Investor has significant influence
Investor normally owns more than 20%, but no more than 50% of voting shares.

Equity Method
Investor's book value is cost plus its share in the undistributed earnings accumulated by the investee since the shares were acquired.

Investor controls the investee
Investor owns more than 50% of the voting shares.

Equity Method
Used in the investor's books, but . . .
Consolidated Financial Statements
Are used in financial reports presented to the public.

Unlike interest on bonds and notes, dividends are not earned merely as time passes. Therefore, you never make an end-of-period entry to accrue dividends that have not been declared. However, if the investor's balance sheet is prepared after a cash dividend is declared but before it is received, record the effects of the declaration with a debit to Dividends Receivable and a credit to Dividends Earned.

Under the cost method, a gain or loss must be recorded when an equity is sold and the proceeds (net of any sales commission paid) differ from cost. For example, consider the 1,000 common shares of Dot Corporation purchased at a cost of $23,550. If Gordon Company sells these shares on some later date at 25¾ less a sales commission of $315, the sale results in a $1,885 gain that is recorded as follows:

Jan.	7	Cash.	25,435.00	
		Investment in Dot Corporation Shares		23,550.00
		Gain on Sale of Investments		1,885.00
		Sold 1,000 shares for $25,750 less a $315 commission.		

If the net amount received for these shares had been less than their $23,550 cost, there would have been a loss on the transaction.

Lower of Cost or Market

When using the cost method to account for an equity investment, report the asset on the balance sheet at cost. However, as you learned in Chapter 8, investments in marketable equity securities are divided into (1) a temporary portfolio and (2) a long-term portfolio. Then, the total market value of each portfolio is calculated and compared to the total cost of each portfolio. Portfolios of temporary investments are reported at the lower of cost or market.[6]

Long-term investments are shown at cost with market value disclosed even if market value is below cost as long as the decline in value is temporary. However, when there has been a loss in value that is other than temporary, the investment is written down to recognize the loss.[7] The writedown (loss) would be included in determining net income. When the investment has been written down to recognize the loss, the new carrying value is deemed to be the new cost basis for subsequent accounting purposes. A subsequent increase in value would be recognized only when realized (i.e., when the shares are sold). For purposes of calculating a gain or loss on sale of the investment, the cost of the investments sold should be calculated on the basis of the average carrying value (total cost of the shares ÷ number of shares held).[8]

The Equity Method of Accounting for Equity Investments

If an investor in common shares has significant influence over the investee, the *equity method* of accounting for the investment must be used. When the shares are acquired, the investor records the purchase at cost, just as under the cost method. For example, on January 1, 1993, Gordon Company purchased 3,000 common shares (30%) of JWM, Inc., for a total cost of $70,650. This entry would be made to record the purchase on Gordon's books:

Jan.	1	Investment in JWM, Inc.	70,650.00	
		Cash		70,650.00
		Purchased 3,000 common shares.		

---

[6] Ibid., par. 3010.06.

[7] Ibid., par. 3050.20.

[8] Ibid., par. 3050.27.

Under the equity method, the earnings of the investee corporation not only increase the investee's net assets but also increase the investor's equity claims against the investee's assets. Therefore, when the investee closes its books and reports the amount of its earnings, the investor takes up its share of those earnings in its investment account. For example, assume that JWM, Inc., reported net income of $20,000 for 1993. Gordon's entry to record its 30% share of these earnings is:

Dec.	31	Investment in JWM, Inc.	6,000.00	
		Earnings from Investment in JWM, Inc.		6,000.00
		To record 30% equity in investee's earnings of $20,000.		

The debit records the increase in Gordon Company's equity in JWM, Inc. The credit causes 30% of JWM, Inc.'s net income to appear on Gordon's income statement as earnings from the investment. As with any other revenue, Gordon closes the equity method Earnings from Investment in JWM, Inc. to Income Summary and then to Retained Earnings.

If the investee corporation incurs a net loss instead of a net income, the investor debits its share of the loss to an account called Loss from Investment and reduces (credits) its Investment in JWM, Inc. account. Then, the investor closes the loss to Income Summary and finally to Retained Earnings.

Dividends paid by the investee corporation decrease its assets and retained earnings. Dividends also decrease the investor's equity in the investee. Under the equity method, the receipt of cash dividends is not recorded as revenue because the investor has already recorded its share of the earnings reported by the investee. Instead, dividends received from the investee are nothing more than a conversion of the form of the investor's asset from an equity investment to cash. In effect, part of the investor's equity claim against the investee is settled by the dividend. Thus, the equity method records dividends as a reduction in the balance of the investment account.

For example, assume that JWM, Inc., declared and paid $10,000 in cash dividends on its common shares. Gordon's entry to record its 30% share of these dividends, which it received on January 9, 1994, is:

Jan.	9	Cash.	3,000.00	
		Investment in JWM, Inc.		3,000.00
		To record receipt of 30% of the $10,000 dividend paid by JWM, Inc.		

Thus, when the equity method is used, the carrying value of an investment in common shares equals the cost of the investment plus the investor's equity in the *undistributed* earnings of the investee. For example, after the preceding transactions are recorded on the books of Gordon Company, the investment account appears as follows:

Investment in JWM, Inc.

Date		Explanation	Debit	Credit	Balance
1993					
Jan.	1	Investment	70,650		70,650
Dec.	31	Share of earnings	6,000		76,650
1994					
Jan.	9	Share of dividend		3,000	73,650

When an equity method share investment is sold, the gain or loss on the sale is determined by comparing the proceeds from the sale with the carrying value (book value) of the investment on the date of sale. For example, suppose that Gordon Company sold its JWM, Inc., shares for $80,000 on January 10, 1994. The entry to record the sale is:

Jan.	10	Cash.	80,000.00	
		Investment in JWM, Inc..		73,650.00
		Gain on Sale of Investments		6,350.00
		Sold 3,000 shares for $80,000.		

Corporations frequently own shares in and may even control other corporations. For example, if Par Company owns more than 50% of the voting shares of Sub Company, Par Company can elect Sub Company's board of directors and thus control its activities and resources. In this case, the controlling corporation, Par Company, is known as the parent company and Sub Company is called a subsidiary.

When a corporation owns all the outstanding shares of a subsidiary, it can take over the subsidiary's assets, cancel the subsidiary's shares, and merge the subsidiary into the parent company. However, there often are financial, legal, and tax advantages if a large business is operated as a parent corporation that controls one or more subsidiary corporations. In fact, most large companies are parent corporations that own one or more subsidiaries.

Some parent corporations are organized solely for the purpose of holding the shares of their subsidiaries. In such cases, the parent corporations have no operating activities of their own and are called *holding companies.*

When a business operates as a parent company with subsidiaries, separate accounting records are maintained by each corporation. From a legal viewpoint, the parent and each subsidiary are still separate entities with all the rights, duties, and responsibilities of individual corporations. However, investors in the parent company indirectly are investors in the subsidiaries. To evaluate their investments, parent company investors must consider the financial status and operations of the subsidiaries as well as the parent. This information is provided in *consolidated financial statements.*

Consolidated statements show the financial position, the results of operations, and the cash flows of all corporations under the parent shareholders' control, including the subsidiaries. These statements are prepared as if the business is organized as a single company. In other words, the assets and liabilities of all affiliated companies are combined on a single balance sheet. Also, their revenues and expenses are combined on a single income statement and their cash flows are combined on a single statement of

Parent and Subsidiary Corporations

ILLUSTRATION E–2

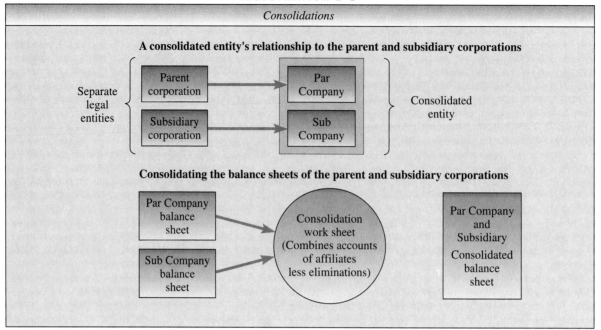

changes in financial position. The relationship between the consolidated entity and the separate parent and subsidiary corporations is represented in the top section of Illustration E–2.

Summary of
Appendix E in Terms
of Learning Objective

LO 7. Equity investments are classified as current assets if they are marketable and are held as a source of cash to be used in current operations. All other equity investments are classified as long-term investments. The cost method is used to account for the long-term investment if the investor does not have a significant influence over the investee corporation. The equity method is used if the investor has a significant influence over the investee. Under the cost method, the investment account is maintained at cost and dividends received are credited to a revenue account. Under the equity method, the investor records its share of the investee's earnings with a debit to the investment account and a credit to a revenue account. Dividends received satisfy the investor's equity claims and reduce the investment account balance.

Glossary

LO 6 Define or explain the words and phrases listed in the chapter glossary.

Accounts Receivable Ledger   a supplementary record (also called a *subsidiary ledger*) having an account for each customer. p. 427

Aging of accounts receivable   a process of classifying accounts receivable in terms of how long they have been outstanding for the purpose of estimating the amount of uncollectible accounts. pp. 436–38

Allowance for Doubtful Accounts   a contra asset account with a balance equal to the estimated amount of accounts receivable that will be uncollectible. p. 430

Allowance method of accounting for bad debts   an accounting procedure that (1) estimates and reports bad debts expense from credit sales during the period of the sales, and (2) reports accounts receivable at the amount of cash proceeds that is expected from their collection (their estimated realizable value). pp. 430–38

Bad debts   accounts receivable from customers that are not collected; the amount is an expense of selling on credit. pp. 429–39

Bank discount   the amount of interest charged by a bank when the bank accepts a discounted note from a customer. Also, the interest a bank deducts in advance when making a loan. p. 444

Contingent liability   a potential liability that will become an actual liability only if certain events occur. pp. 445–47

Controlling account   a general ledger account with a balance that is always equal to the sum of the balances in a related subsidiary ledger. p. 429

Cost method of accounting for equity investments   an accounting method whereby the investment is recorded at total cost and maintained at that amount; any earnings subsequently reported and dividends paid by the investee do not normally affect the investment account balance. pp. 457–59

Direct write-off method of accounting for bad debts   a method that makes no attempt to estimate uncollectible accounts or bad debts expense at the end of each period; instead, when an account is found to be uncollectible, it is written off directly to Bad Debts Expense; this method is generally considered to be inferior to the allowance method. pp. 438–39

Discount period   the number of days between the date on which a note is discounted at the bank and its maturity date. p. 444

Discount rate   the rate of interest a bank charges for lending money by discounting a note. p. 444

Discounting a note receivable   selling a note receivable to a bank or other buyer, usually with the provision that the seller assumes a contingent liability to pay the note if it is dishonoured. pp. 444–46

Dishonouring a note   failure by a promissory note's maker to pay the amount due at maturity. p. 443

Equity method of accounting for equity investments   an accounting method used when the investor has influence or control over the investee. Under this method, the investment is initially recorded at its total cost, and the investment account balance is subsequently increased to reflect the investor's share of the investee's earnings and decreased to reflect the investor's share of the investee's earnings and decreased to reflect the investor's receipt of dividends paid by the investee. pp. 457, 459–61

Full-disclosure principle   the accounting principle that requires financial statements (including the footnotes) to contain all relevant information about the operations and financial position of the entity; it also requires that the information be presented in an understandable manner. p. 447

General Ledger the ledger that contains all the financial statement accounts of an organization. p. 427

Installment accounts receivable accounts receivable that allow the customer to make periodic payments over several months and that typically earn interest for the seller. p. 440

Interest the charge assessed for the use of money. pp. 440–42

Long-term investments investments that are not intended to be a ready source of cash in case of need. They also include items such as bond sinking funds, land, bonds, and shares that are not marketable, or, if they are marketable, it is not management's intent to dispose of them within the next year or operating cycle, whichever is longer. p. 456

Lower of cost or market (LCM) the required method of reporting temporary investments in marketable equity securities in the balance sheet at the lower of the total cost of all the securities (called the *portfolio*) or their total market value on the date of the balance sheet. pp. 422–24

Maker of a note one who signs a note and promises to pay it at maturity. p. 440

Materiality principle the idea that the requirements of an accounting principle may be ignored if the effect on the financial statements is unimportant to their users. p. 439

Maturity date of a note the date on which a note and any interest are due and payable. p. 441

Maturity value principal of a note plus any interest due on its maturity date. p. 444

Notice of protest a written statement, usually witnessed by a notary public, that says a note was duly presented to the maker for payment and that payment was refused. p. 447

Payee of a note the one to whom a promissory note is made payable. p. 440

Principal of a note the amount that the signer of a promissory note agrees to pay back when it matures, not including the interest. p. 440

Proceeds of a discounted note the maturity value of a note minus any interest deducted when it is discounted before maturity. pp. 444–45

Promissory note an unconditional written promise to pay a definite sum of money on demand or at a fixed or determinable future date. p. 440

Protest fee the fee charged for preparing and issuing a notice of protest. p. 447

Realizable value the expected proceeds from converting assets into cash. p. 431

Short-term investments another name for *temporary investments*. p. 420

Subsidiary ledger a collection of accounts (other than general ledger accounts) that contains the details underlying the balance of a controlling account in the General Ledger. p. 429

Temporary investments common and preferred shares and fixed income securities that are actively traded, such that sales prices or bid and ask prices are currently available on national securities exchanges or in the over-the-counter market, and that management intends to sell as a source of cash to satisfy the needs of current operations. pp. 420, 456

Synonymous Terms

Allowance for doubtful accounts allowance for bad debts.

Common shares common stock

Credit sales charge sales.

Debt obligations debt securities.

Equity investment share or stock investment

Maker of a note borrower.

Payee of a note lender.

Preferred shares preferred stock

Shareholders' equity stockholders' equity

Stocks equity securities.

Temporary investments short-term investments.

Answers to the following questions are listed at the end of this chapter. Be sure that you decide which is the one best answer to each question *before* you check the answers.

Objective Review

LO 1 In accounting for a portfolio of temporary investments in marketable securities:

a. Any cash received as dividends from temporary investments is debited to Dividends Earned.

b. The lower of cost or market of each investment is calculated; then, the lower of cost or market amounts are summed to determine the lower of cost or market for the whole portfolio.

c. The total cost of the investment portfolio is calculated and compared to the total market value of the investment portfolio to determine the lower of cost or market of the portfolio.

d. Increases in the market value above the cost of the temporary portfolio are credited to Gain from Temporary Investments.

e. A loss on the market decline of temporary investments is debited to Allowance to Reduce Temporary Investments to Market.

LO 2 In accounting for credit card sales:

a. The seller does not incur any credit card expense when the seller must submit accumulated sales receipts to the credit card company and then time passes before cash is received from the company.

b. The entry to record credit card sales always includes a debit to Accounts Receivable.

c. The seller does not incur any credit card expense when the bank credits the seller's chequing account immediately on the seller's deposit of sales receipts.

d. The seller records credit card sales with a debit to Cash when the bank credits the seller's chequing account immediately on the seller's deposit of sales receipts.

e. Credit card expense that results from credit sales made in Period One should be reported as expense in Period Two if the cash from the sale is received in Period Two.

LO 3 Just before adjusting entries are made at year-end, Clayton Company's Accounts Receivable balance is $440,000 and the Allowance for Doubtful Accounts has a debit balance of $1,400. Credit sales for the year were $1,050,000, and the experience of past years suggests that 2% of credit sales prove to be uncollectible. However, an aging of accounts receivable results in a $31,500 estimate of uncollectible accounts at the end of the year. Using the aging of accounts receivable method, the Bad Debts Expense for the year is

a. $32,900.

b. $31,500.

c. $30,100.

d. $21,000.

e. None of the above is correct.

LO 4 White Corporation purchased $7,000 of merchandise from Stamford Company on December 16, 1993. Stamford accepted White's $7,000, 90-day, 12% note as payment. Assuming Stamford's annual accounting period ends on December 31, and Stamford does not make reversing entries, which entry should Stamford make on March 16, 1994, when the note is paid? (Assume a 360-day year.)

a.	Cash	7,210.00	
	Interest Earned		210.00
	Notes Receivable		7,000.00
b.	Cash	7,210.00	
	Interest Earned		175.00
	Interest Receivable		35.00
	Notes Receivable		7,000.00
c.	Cash	7,175.00	
	Interest Earned		175.00
	Notes Receivable		7,000.00
d.	Cash	7,210.00	
	Notes Receivable		7,210.00
e.	None of the above.		

LO 5 Assuming a 360-day year, the proceeds from a $6,000, 10%, 90-day note discounted 60 days before maturity at 12% are:

a. $6,100.

b. $6,123.

c. $6,027.

d. $6,150.

e. None of the above.

LO 6 A temporary investment is:

a. An uncollectible receivable.

b. A potential liability that will become an actual liability if and only if certain events occur.

c. An account receivable that allows the customer to make periodic payments over several months and which typically earns interest.

d. A short-term investment called by another name.

e. A promissory note.

LO 7 On January 1, 1993, Brenner Wholesale Corporation purchased 7,000 shares (35%) of Outback Cargo Company's common shares at a total cost of $140,000. Outback Cargo's net income over the next three years totaled $450,000, and the company declared and paid $200,000 in dividends on its outstanding common shares. Brenner Wholesale sold its Outback Cargo Company shares on January 3, 1996, for $34.50 per share. The entry to record the sale is as follows:

a.	Cash	241,500.00	
	Investment in Outback Cargo Company.		70,000.00
	Gain on Sale of Investments.		171,500.00
b.	Cash	241,500.00	
	Investment in Outback Cargo Company.		140,000.00
	Gain on Sale of Investments.		101,500.00
c.	Cash	241,500.00	
	Loss on Sale of Investments	56,000.00	
	Investment in Outback Cargo Company.		297,500.00
d.	Cash	241,500.00	
	Investment in Outback Cargo Company.		227,500.00
	Gain on Sale of Investments.		14,000.00
e.	Cash	241,500.00	
	Investment in Outback Cargo Company.		241,500.00

A letter ^{E} identifies the questions, exercises, and problems that are based on Appendix E at the end of the chapter.

1. Under what conditions should investments be classified as current assets?

2. If a temporary investment that cost $6,780 was sold for $7,500, how should the difference between the two amounts be recorded?

3. What is the relationship between the Accounts Receivable controlling account and the Accounts Receivable Subsidiary Ledger?

4. In meeting the requirements of the matching principle, why must bad debts expenses be matched with sales on an estimated basis?

5. What term describes the balance sheet valuation of accounts receivable less the allowance for doubtful accounts?

6. What is a contra account? Why is estimated bad debts expense credited to a contra account rather than to the Accounts Receivable controlling account?

7. When bad debts are estimated by the income statement approach, what relationship is the focus of attention?

8. Explain why writing off a bad debt against the allowance account does not reduce the estimated realizable value of a company's accounts receivable.

9. Why does the Bad Debts Expense account usually not have the same adjusted balance as the Allowance for Doubtful Accounts?

10. When bad debts are estimated by the simplified balance sheet approach, what relationship is the focus of attention?

11. Why does the direct write-off method of accounting for bad debts commonly fail to match revenues and expenses?

12. What is the essence of the accounting principle of materiality?

13. What does the full-disclosure principle require in a company's financial statements?

^{E}14. In accounting for common share investments, when should the cost method be used? When should the equity method be used?

^{E}15. Refer to the financial statements of Bombardier, Inc. presented in Appendix I. Does Bombardier own any shares issued by other corporations? How did you determine your answer?

Questions for Class Discussion

Mini Discussion Cases

Case 8–1

In addition to recording cash sales as indicated in Mini Discussion Case 7–1, there also were a number of fictitious sales recorded as receivables. Inventory represented by the fictitious sales was removed by the seller to another location. Interviews with employees in the stockroom also indicated that there was some substitution of inventory by the previous onwer. That is, he removed the newest lines in inventory to his other place of business and brought in older and slow-moving items.

The auditor's report indicated $90,000 of fictitious sales and the corresponding cost of goods sold of $60,000.

The auditors were not able to fully document the amount of inventory substitution.

Required

1. Discuss the effect on the financial statements of the fictitious sales.
2. Discuss the safeguards or internal control that was lacking in the situation.

Case 8–2

John Crowe could not understand the discounting procedure followed with regard to customers' notes receivable. Specifically, he could not understand why the discount was based on the maturity value of the note and not on the face value or the face value plus accrued interest to the discount date.

Required

Explain to John Crowe why the maturity value of the note receivable is discounted.

Exercises

Exercise 8–1
Transactions involving temporary investments
(LO 1)

Prepare General Journal entries to record the following transactions involving Jennings Company's temporary investments, all of which occurred during 1993:

a. On March 21, paid $60,000 to purchase $60,000 of Kendan Corporation's temporary (90-day) notes payable, which are dated March 21, and pay interest at a 10% rate.

b. On April 16, bought 2,000 United Motors common shares at 25½ plus a $750 brokerage fee.

c. On May 2, paid $40,000 to purchase Eastman Corporation's 9% notes payable, $40,000 principal value, due May 2, 1994.

d. On June 20, received a cheque from Kendan Corporation in payment of the principal and 90 days' interest on the notes purchased in (*a*).

e. On September 21, received a $1 per share cash dividend on the United Motors common shares purchased in (*b*).

f. On October 6, sold 1,000 United Motors common shares for $28 per share, less a $450 brokerage fee.

g. On November 2, received a cheque from Eastman Corporation for six months' interest on the notes purchased in (*c*).

On December 31, 1993, Edgeware Corporation owned the following temporary investments in marketable equity securities:

	Cost	Market Value
Magna International Inc. common shares . .	$18,600	$20,550
Imperial Oil Limited common shares.	25,200	24,250
Inco Limited common shares	34,800	31,950
Northern Electric common shares	42,750	42,050

Edgeware Corporation had no temporary investments prior to 1993. Calculate the
lower of cost or market of Edgeware Corporation's temporary investments and, if
necessary, prepare a General Journal entry to record the decline in market value of the
investments.

Exercise 8–2
Reducing temporary
investments to lower of
cost or market
(LO 1)

Ishtar Company's annual accounting period ends on December 31. The cost and market values of the company's temporary investments in marketable equity securities
were as follows on the given balance sheet dates:

	Cost	Market Value
Temporary investments in marketable equity securities:		
On December 31, 1992	$22,500	$21,000
On December 31, 1993	25,500	23,250

Prepare a General Journal entry on December 31, 1993, to adjust the balance in the
allowance account that is contra to Temporary Investments.

Exercise 8–3
Adjusting the Allowance
for Market Decline of
Temporary Investments
Account
(LO 1)

Detweiler Company allows customers to use two alternative credit cards in charging
purchases. With the First National Bank Card, Detweiler receives an immediate credit
on depositing sales receipts in its chequing account. First National Bank assesses a
3.5% service charge for credit card sales. The second credit card that Detweiler accepts
is NAC Card. Detweiler sends the accumulated NAC Card receipts to the NAC Company on a weekly basis and is paid by NAC Company approximately 10 days later.
NAC charges 3% of sales for using its card. Prepare entries in General Journal form to
record the following credit card transactions of Detweiler Company:

Exercise 8–4
Credit card transactions
(LO 2)

Nov. 2 Sold merchandise for $4,200 on this day, accepting the customer's First
National Bank Card. At the end of the day, the First National Bank Card
receipts were deposited in the company's account at the bank.

3 Sold merchandise for $270, accepting the customer's NAC Card.

8 Mailed $7,200 of credit card receipts to NAC Company, requesting
payment.

20 Received NAC Company's cheque for the November 8 billing, less the
normal service charge.

Exercise 8–5
Subsidiary ledger accounts
(LO 3)

Conrack Company recorded the following transactions during June 1993:

June	5	Accounts Receivable—Dave Ganges	1,000.00	
		Sales		1,000.00
	9	Accounts Receivable—Betty Akin	900.00	
		Sales		900.00
	20	Accounts Receivable—Marty Fagin	720.00	
		Sales		720.00
	21	Sales Returns and Allowances	225.00	
		Accounts Receivable—Marty Fagin		225.00
	27	Accounts Receivable—Dave Ganges	450.00	
		Sales		450.00

Required

1. Open a General Ledger having T-accounts for Accounts Receivable, Sales, and Sales Returns and Allowances. Also, open a subsidiary Accounts Receivable Ledger having a T-account for each customer. Post the preceding entries to the General Ledger accounts and the customer accounts.
2. List the balances of the accounts in the subsidiary ledger, total the balances, and compare the total with the balance of the Accounts Receivable controlling account.

Exercise 8–6
Allowance for doubtful accounts
(LO 3)

On December 31, at the end of its annual accounting period, a company estimated its bad debts as one half of 1% of its $650,000 of credit sales made during the year, and made an addition to its Allowance for Doubtful Accounts equal to that amount. On the following April 10, management decided the $500 account of Sam Baker was uncollectible and wrote it off as a bad debt. Two months later, on June 9, Baker unexpectedly paid the amount previously written off. Give the General Journal entries required to record these events.

Exercise 8–7
Bad debts expense
(LO 3)

At the end of each year, a company uses the simplified balance sheet approach to estimate bad debts. On December 31, 1993, it has outstanding accounts receivable of $68,000 and estimates that 4% will be uncollectible: (*a*) give the entry to record bad debts expense for 1993 under the assumption that the Allowance for Doubtful Accounts had a $420 credit balance before the adjustment; (*b*) give the entry under the assumption that the Allowance for Doubtful Accounts has a $500 debit balance before the adjustment.

Exercise 8–8
Dishonour of a note
(LO 3)

Prepare General Journal entries to record these transactions:

Mar. 7   Accepted a $2,000, two-month, 12% note dated today from Greta Arbo in granting a time extension on her past-due account.

May 7   Greta Arbo dishonoured her note when presented for payment.

Dec. 31   After exhausting all legal means of collecting, wrote off the account of Greta Arbo against the Allowance for Doubtful Accounts.

Prepare General Journal entries to record these transactions:

Apr. 12 Sold merchandise to Vern Jacks, $3,000, terms 2/10, n/60.

June 12 Received $400 in cash and a $2,600, 90-day, 10% note dated June 12 in granting a time extension on the amount due from Vern Jacks.

July 12 Discounted the Vern Jacks note at the bank at 12%.

Sept. 10 Because no notice protesting the Vern Jacks note had been received, assumed that it had been paid.

Exercise 8–9
Discounting a note receivable
(LO 4)

Prepare General Journal entries to record these transactions:

Apr. 7 Accepted a $5,400, 60-day, 12% note dated April 5 from Bob Rocker granting a time extension on his past-due account.

    12 Discounted the Bob Rocker note at the bank at 14%.

June 6 Received notice protesting the Bob Rocker note. Paid the bank the maturity value of the note plus a $25 protest fee.

    18 Received payment from Bob Rocker of the maturity value of his dishonoured note, the protest fee, and interest at 12% on both for 15 days beyond maturity.

Exercise 8–10
Dishonour of a discounted note
(LO 4)

On September 8, Collier Sales sold Greg Limon merchandise having a $7,500 catalogue list price, less a 20% trade discount, terms 2/10, n/60. (Trade discounts were explained on page 262.) Limon was unable to pay and was granted a time extension when he signed his 60-day, 15% note for the amount of the debt, dated November 7. Collier Sales held the note until November 22, when it was discounted at the bank at 16%. The note was not protested. Answer these questions:

Exercise 8–11
Analysis of sales terms and discounted note
(LO 5)

a. How many dollars of trade discount were granted on the sale?

b. How many dollars of cash discount could Limon have earned?

c. What was the maturity date of the note?

d. How many days were in the note's discount period?

e. How much bank discount was deducted by the bank?

f. What were the proceeds of the discounted note?

Prepare General Journal entries to record the following events on the books of The Shoe Depot, Inc.:

ᴱExercise 8–12
Equity investment transactions
(LO 7)

1993

Jan. 4 Purchased 23,000 common shares of Crestway Company for $72,500 plus broker's fee of $3,400. Crestway Company has 287,500 common shares outstanding, and The Shoe Depot does not have a significant influence on Crestway Company policies.

June 3 Crestway Company declared and paid a cash dividend of $0.20 per share.

Dec. 31 Crestway Company announced that new income for the year amounted to $338,900.

1994

Feb. 14   Crestway Company declared and paid a cash dividend of $0.75 per share.

Dec. 30   The Shoe Depot sold 6,400 shares of Crestway Company for $29,600.

  31   Crestway Company announced that new income for the year amounted to $526,250.

^EExercise 8–13
Share investment
transactions
(LO 7)

Prepare General Journal entries to record the following events on the books of Quorum Company:

1993

Jan. 5   Purchased 13,500 shares of Maxey Corporation for $172,800 plus broker's fee of $5,000. Maxey Corporation has 67,500 common shares outstanding and has acknowledged the fact that its policies will be significantly influenced by Quorum Company.

Aug. 24   Maxey Corporation declared and paid a cash dividend of $1.20 per share.

Dec. 31   Maxey Corporation announced that net income for the year amounted to $232,800.

1994

Feb. 22   Maxey Corporation declared and paid a cash dividend of $1.50 per share.

Dec. 31   Maxey Corporation announced that net income for the year amounted to $332,950.

  31   Quorum Company sold 4,500 shares of Maxey Corporation for $91,000.

Problems

Problem 8–1
Accounting for temporary
investments
(LO 1)

Roland Company had no temporary investments on December 31, 1992, but had the following transactions involving temporary investments during 1993:

Jan. 15   Paid $100,000 to buy six-month, Treasury bills, $100,000 principal amount, 8%, dated January 15.

Feb. 7   Purchased 2,000 Royal Bank common shares at 26⅛ plus a $500 brokerage fee.

  19   Purchased 1,200 Imperial Oil common shares at 51¾ plus a $600 brokerage fee.

Mar. 1   Paid $50,000 for Treasury notes, $50,000 principal amount, 9%, dated March 1, 1993, due March 1, 1994.

  26   Purchased 2,000 Abitibi Price common shares at 13⅜ plus a $250 brokerage fee.

June 1   Received a $0.25 per share cash dividend on the Royal Bank common shares.

  17   Sold 1,200 Royal Bank common shares at 27 less a $300 brokerage fee.

July 17   Received a cheque for the principal and accrued interest on the Treasury bills that matured on July 15.

Aug. 5 Received a $0.50 per share cash dividend on the Imperial Oil common shares.

Sept. 1 Received a cheque for six months' interest on the Treasury notes purchased on March 1.

      1 Received a $0.275 per share cash dividend on the remaining Royal Bank common shares owned.

Nov. 5 Received a $0.45 per share cash dividend on the Imperial Oil common shares.

On December 31, 1993, the market prices of the equity securities held by Roland Company were Royal Bank, 27½; Imperial Oil, 50⅝; and Abitibi Price, 13½.

Required

1. Prepare General Journal entries to record the preceding transactions.

2. Prepare a schedule to calculate the lower of cost or market of Roland's temporary investments in marketable equity securities.

3. Prepare adjusting entries, if necessary, to record accrued interest on Roland Company's investments in debt obligations and to reduce the marketable equity securities to the lower of cost or market.

Baron Company allows a few customers to make purchases on credit. Other customers may use either of two credit cards. The First Bank deducts a 3% service charge for sales on its credit card but immediately credits the chequing account of its commercial customers when credit card receipts are deposited. Baron deposits the First Bank credit card receipts at the close of each business day.

Problem 8–2
Credit sales and credit card sales
(LO 2)

When customers use the National Credit card, Baron Company accumulates the receipts for several days and then submits them to the National Credit Company for payment. National deducts a 2% service charge and usually pays within one week of being billed.

Baron Company completed the following transactions:

Aug. 2 Sold merchandise on credit to L. L. Terry for $1,360. (Terms of all credit sales are 2/15, n/60; all sales are recorded at the gross price.)

      3 Sold merchandise for $1,940 to customers who used their First Bank credit cards. Sold merchandise for $2,750 to customers who used their National Credit cards.

      5 Sold merchandise for $1,400 to customers who used their National Credit cards.

      7 Wrote off the account of R. Brown against Allowance for Doubtful Accounts. The $340 balance in Brown's account stemmed from a credit sale in December of last year.

      8 The National Credit card receipts accumulated since August 3 were submitted to the credit card company for payment.

      17 Received L. L. Terry's cheque paying for the purchase of August 2.

      19 Received the amount due from National Credit Company.

Required

Prepare General Journal entries to record the preceding transactions and events.

Problem 8–3
Estimating bad debts expense
(LO 3)

On December 31, 1993, Pitts Company's records showed the following results for the year:

Cash sales.	$240,500
Credit sales	471,200

In addition, the unadjusted trial balance included the following items:

Accounts receivable.	$142,700 debit
Allowance for doubtful accounts	2,100 debit

Required

1. Prepare the adjusting entry needed on the books of Pitts Company to recognize bad debts under each of the following independent assumptions:
   a. Bad debts are estimated to be 1.5% of total sales.
   b. Bad debts are estimated to be 3% of credit sales.
   c. An analysis suggests that 7% of outstanding accounts receivable on December 31, 1993, will become uncollectible.

2. Show how Accounts Receivable and the Allowance for Doubtful Accounts would appear on the December 31, 1993, balance sheet given the facts in requirement 1b.

3. Show how Accounts Receivable and the Allowance for Doubtful Accounts would appear on the December 31, 1993, balance sheet given the facts in requirement 1c.

Problem 8–4
Aging accounts receivable
(LO 3)

Sydney Corporation had credit sales of $2.7 million in 1993. On December 31, 1993, the company's Allowance for Doubtful Accounts had a credit balance of $3,000. The accountant for Sydney Corporation has prepared a schedule of the December 31, 1993, accounts receivable by age, and on the basis of past experience has estimated the percentage of the receivables in each age category that will become uncollectible. This information is summarized as follows:

December 31, 1993, Accounts Receivable	Age of Accounts Receivable	Expected Percentage Uncollectible
$730,000	Not due (under 30 days)	1.50%
354,000	1 to 30 days past due	3.75
82,000	31 to 60 days past due	10.50
39,000	61 to 90 days past due	40.00
17,000	over 90 days past due	75.00

Required

1. Calculate the amount that should appear in the December 31, 1993, balance sheet as the Allowance for Doubtful Accounts.

2. Prepare the General Journal entry to record bad debts expense for 1993.

3. On May 2, 1994, Sydney Corporation concluded that a customer's $3,200 receivable (created in 1993) was uncollectible and that the account should be written off. What effect will this action have on Sydney Corporation's 1994 net income? Explain your answer.

Problem 8–5
Recording accounts receivable transactions and bad debts adjustments
(LO 3)

Botello Company began operations on January 1, 1992. During the next two years, the company completed a number of transactions involving credit sales, accounts receivable collections, and bad debts. These transactions are summarized as follows:

1992

a. Sold merchandise on credit for $54,500, terms n/60.

b. Wrote off uncollectible accounts receivable in the amount of $850.

c. Received cash of $45,100 in payment of outstanding accounts receivable.

d. In adjusting the accounts on December 31, concluded that 2% of the outstanding accounts receivable would become uncollectible.

1993

e. Sold merchandise on credit for $67,800, terms n/60.

f. Wrote off uncollectible accounts receivable in the amount of $1,280.

g. Received cash of $65,900 in payment of outstanding accounts receivable.

h. In adjusting the accounts on December 31, concluded that 2% of the outstanding accounts receivable would become uncollectible.

Required

Prepare General Journal entries to record the 1992 and 1993 summarized transactions of Botello Company and the adjusting entries to record bad debts expense at the end of each year.

Prepare General Journal entries to record these transactions and events experienced by Petrol Company:

Problem 8–6
Journalizing notes receivable and bad debts transactions
(LO 4)

Jan. 8 Accepted a $2,850, 60-day, 10% note dated this day in granting a time extension on the past-due account of Pat Wilkins.

Mar. 9 Pat Wilkins paid the maturity value of his $2,850 note.

11 Accepted a $3,300, 60-day, 11% note dated this day in granting a time extension on the past-due account of Paula Mathers.

May 10 Paula Mathers dishonoured her note when presented for payment.

17 Accepted a $2,000, 90-day, 13% note dated May 15 in granting a time extension on the past-due account of Elmer Mayes.

25 Discounted the Elmer Mayes note at the bank at 15%.

Aug. 16 Because the company had not received a notice protesting the Elmer Mayes note, assumed that it had been paid.

17 Accepted a $1,500, 60-day, 11% note dated August 15 in granting a time extension on the past-due account of Steve Rollins.

Sept. 8 Discounted the Steve Rollins note at the bank at 13%.

Oct. 15 Received notice protesting the Steve Rollins note. Paid the bank the maturity value of the note plus a $20 protest fee.

16 Received a $4,100, 60-day, 12% note dated this day from Martha Watson in granting a time extension on her past-due account.

Nov. 15 Discounted the Martha Watson note at the bank at 15%.

Dec. 16 Received notice protesting the Martha Watson note. Paid the bank the maturity value of the note plus a $20 protest fee.

27 Received payment from Martha Watson of the maturity value of her dishonoured note, the protest fee, and interest on both for 12 days beyond maturity at 12%.

31 Wrote off the accounts of Paula Mathers and Steve Rollins against Allowance for Doubtful Accounts.

Problem 8–7
Analysis and journalizing
of notes receivable
transactions
(LO 5)

Prepare General Journal entries to record the following transactions of Ute City Company:

1992

Dec. 11   Accepted a $5,000, 60-day, 12% note dated this day in granting Fred Calhoun a time extension on his past-due account.

      31   Made an adjusting entry to record the accrued interest on the Fred Calhoun note.

      31   Closed the Interest Earned account.

1993

Jan. 10   Discounted the Fred Calhoun note at the bank at 14%.

Feb. 10   Received notice protesting the Fred Calhoun note. Paid the bank the maturity value of the note plus a $20 protest fee.

Mar.   5   Accepted a $1,500, 11%, 60-day note dated this day in granting a time extension on the past-due account of Donna Reed.

      29   Discounted the Donna Reed note at the bank at 15%.

May   7   Because no notice protesting the Donna Reed note had been received, assumed that it had been paid.

June   9   Accepted a $2,250, 60-day, 10% note dated this day in granting a time extension on the past-due account of Jack Miller.

Aug.   8   Received payment of the maturity value of the Jack Miller note.

      11   Accepted a $2,700, 60-day, 10% note dated this day in granting Roger Addison a time extension on his past-due account.

      31   Discounted the Roger Addison note at the bank at 13%.

Oct. 12   Received notice protesting the Roger Addison note. Paid the bank the maturity value of the note plus a $20 protest fee.

Nov. 19   Received payment from Roger Addison of the maturity value of his dishonoured note, the protest fee, and interest on both for 40 days beyond maturity at 10%.

Dec. 23   Wrote off the Fred Calhoun account against Allowance for Doubtful Accounts.

Problem 8–8
Entries and LCM
application for temporary
investments
(LO 1)

The David Gregory Company had some surplus cash balances on hand and projected that excess cash would continue to be available over the next few years. Gregory decided to invest company funds in the stock market, and obtained professional advice in putting together the company's portfolio.

     Following is a series of events and other facts relevant to the temporary investment activity of the company:

1993

May   8   Purchased 1,000 shares of BCE at $50.50 plus $1,515 commission.

July 14   Purchased 2,000 shares of Dupont A at $40.50 plus $2,430 commission.

Sept. 29   Purchased 3,000 shares of Molson A at $24.00 plus $2,160 commission.

Dec. 31   These per share market values were known for the shares in the portfolio: BCE, $62.50; Dupont A, $36.25; Molson A, $18.00.

1994

Feb.   4   Sold 2,000 shares of Dupont A at $25.25 less $1,515 commission.

July 12   Sold 3,000 shares of Molson A, at $21.50 less $1,935 commission.

Aug. 17   Purchased 4,000 shares of Oshawa A at $17.00 plus $2,040 commission.

Dec. 15 Purchased 2,400 shares of Imperial Oil at $50.75 plus $3,654 commission.

  31 These per share market values were known for the shares in the portfolio: BCE, $75.75; Oshawa A, $10.25; Imperial Oil, $43.50.

1995

Jan. 2 Purchased 4,000 shares of Petro Canada at $9.00 plus $1,080 commission.

Feb. 5 Sold 4,000 shares of Oshawa A at $24.75 less $2,970 commission.

May 18 Sold 1,000 shares of BCE at $90.50 less $2,715 commission.

Nov. 28 Purchased 1,000 shares of The Bay at $32.00 plus $960 commission.

  30 Sold 2,400 shares of Imperial Oil at $38.00 less $2,736 commission.

Dec. 31 These per share market values were known for the shares in the portfolio: Petro Canada, $14.25; The Bay, $22.50.

Required

1. Prepare journal entries to record the events and any year-end adjustments needed to record the application of the lower of cost or market method of accounting for temporary investments.

2. Prepare a schedule that shows how the temporary investment portfolio would be described on the balance sheet at the end of each of the three years.

3. Prepare a schedule that shows the components of income (gains and losses, including LCM effects) from these investment activities, and their total effect, for each of the three years. Ignore dividends.

Holden Enterprises, Inc., was organized on January 3, 1993, for the purpose of investing in the shares of other companies. Holden Enterprises immediately issued 150,000 common shares for which it received $150,000 cash. On January 6, 1993, Holden Enterprises purchased 30,000 shares (20%) of Compusystem Company's outstanding common shares at a cost of $150,000. The following transactions and events subsequently occurred:

^EProblem 8–9
Share investments—cost and equity methods
(LO 7)

1993

June 5 Compusystem Company declared and paid a cash dividend of $.60 per share.

Dec. 31 Compusystem Company announced that its net income for 1993 was $160,000.

1994

July 25 Compusystem Company declared and paid a cash dividend of $0.55 per share.

Dec. 31 Compusystem Corporation announced that its net income for 1994 was $120,000.

1995

Jan. 3 Holden Enterprises, Inc. sold all of its investment in Compusystem Company for $168,000 cash.

Part 1. Holden Enterprises is presumed to have a significant influence over Compusystem Company because it owns 20% of the shares.

Required

1. Give the entries on the books of Holden Enterprises, Inc. to record the preceding events regarding its investment in Compusystem Company.

2. Calculate Holden Enterprises, Inc.'s retained earnings balance on January 4, 1995, including any gain or loss from the sale of the Compusystem shares.

Part 2. Although Holden Enterprises, Inc., owns 20% of Compusystem Company's outstanding shares, a thorough investigation of the surrounding circumstances indicates that it does not have a significant influence over the investee. Therefore, the cost method is the appropriate procedure to use in accounting for the investment.

Required

1. Give the entries on the books of Holden Enterprises, Inc. to record the preceding events regarding its investment in Compusystem Company.
2. Calculate Holden Enterprises, Inc.'s retained earnings balance on January 4, 1995, including any gain or loss from the sale of the Compusystem shares.

^EProblem 8–10
Analytical essay
(LO 7)

Apex Corporation began operations in January 1993. During the year, Apex invested in several companies by purchasing common shares. The following information pertains to the investment portfolio of Apex at December 31, 1993:

Investment	Cost	Market
A	$20,000	$21,000
B	3,100	3,000
C	56,900	49,000
	$80,000	$73,000

Assume that all the investments are marketable and that Apex's ownership in each investee is less than 20%.

Required

Consider the two alternatives of classifying the portfolio as temporary investments or long-term investments. For these two alternatives, briefly discuss the similarities and the differences in accounting for the investment portfolio during 1993, including the effects of the investments on the 1993 financial statements.

Problem 8–11
Analytical essay
(LO 1)

Blalock Company did not own any temporary investments prior to 1993. After purchasing some temporary investments in 1993, the company's accountant made the following December 31, 1993, adjusting entry:

Dec.	31	Loss on Market Decline of Temporary Investments.	1,100.00	
		Allowance to Reduce Temporary Investments		
		to Market.		1,100.00
		To adjust temporary investments portfolio to the		
		LCM amount.		

When Blalock Company's accountant reviewed the year-end adjustments with an office manager of the company, the accountant commented that the previous adjustment might have been different if the company had owned temporary investments on December 31, 1992. The office manager thought the accountant must be confused. The manager said that since the December 31, 1993, adjustment was supposed to record a loss that occurred during 1993, it should not be affected by any events that occurred during 1992.

Required

Explain why the accountant's comment is correct.

Review the facts about Pitts Company presented in Problem 8–3.

Required

1. Recall that Allowance for Doubtful Accounts is a contra asset account. Nevertheless, Pitts Company's unadjusted trial balance shows that this account has a $2,100 debit balance. Explain how this contra asset account could have a debit balance.
2. In Problem 8–3, requirement 1*c* indicates that 7% of the outstanding accounts receivable ($142,700 × 7% = $9,989) will become uncollectible. Given this conclusion, explain why the adjusting entry should not include a $9,989 credit to Accounts Receivable.

Alternate Problems

Columbia Company had no temporary investments on December 31, 1992, but had these transactions involving temporary investments during 1993:

Jan. 11 Paid $20,000 to buy six-month, Treasury bills, $20,000 principal amount, 8%, dated January 11.

Feb. 2 Purchased 600 Shell Canada common shares at 38½ plus a $230 brokerage fee.

15 Purchased 2,000 Air Canada common shares at 9¾ plus a $200 brokerage fee.

Mar. 5 Paid $25,000 for Treasury notes, $25,000 principal amount, 9%, dated March 2, 1993, due March 2, 1994.

16 Purchased 1,200 Imasco common shares at 34⅝ plus a $350 brokerage fee.

June 8 Received a $0.35 per share cash dividend on the Shell Canada common shares.

16 Sold 400 Shell Canada common shares at 40 less a $160 brokerage fee.

July 13 Received a cheque for the principal and accrued interest on the Treasury bills that matured on July 11.

Aug. 15 Received a $0.10 per share cash dividend on the Air Canada common shares.

Sept. 5 Received a cheque for six-months' interest on the Treasury notes purchased on March 5.

8 Received a $0.35 per share cash dividend on the remaining Shell Canada common shares owned by Columbia Company.

Nov. 15 Received a $0.10 per share cash dividend on the Air Canada common shares.

On December 31, 1993, the market prices of the equity securities held by Columbia Company were: Shell Canada, 40⅛; Air Canada, 8½; and Imasco, 34.

Required

1. Prepare General Journal entries to record the preceding transactions.
2. Prepare a schedule to calculate the lower of cost or market of Columbia's temporary investments in marketable equity securities.

3. Prepare adjusting entries, if necessary, to record accrued interest on Columbia Company's investments in debt obligations and to reduce the marketable equity securities to the lower of cost or market.

Problem 8–2A
Credit sales and credit card sales
(LO 2)

Carr Company allows a few customers to make purchases on credit. Other customers may use either of two credit cards. The Tower Bank deducts a 2% service charge for sales on its credit card but immediately credits the chequing account of its commercial customers when credit card receipts are deposited. Carr deposits the Tower Bank credit card receipts at the close of each business day.

When customers use the Pacific credit card, Carr Company accumulates the receipts for several days and then submits them to the Pacific Credit Company for payment. Pacific deducts a 3% service charge and usually pays within one week of being billed.

Carr Company completed the following transactions:

June 3   Sold merchandise on credit to Jan Burr for $980. (Terms of all credit sales are 2/15, n/60; all sales are recorded at the gross price.)

4   Sold merchandise for $4,990 to customers who used their Tower Bank credit cards. Sold merchandise for $7,230 to customers who used their Pacific credit cards.

7   Sold merchandise for $1,700 to customers who used their Pacific credit cards.

9   Wrote off the account of R. Carne against Allowance for Doubtful Accounts. The $650 balance in Carne's account stemmed from a credit sale in August of last year.

14   The Pacific credit card receipts accumulated since June 2 were submitted to the credit card company for payment.

17   Received Jan Burr's cheque paying for the purchase of June 3.

20   Received the amount due from Pacific Credit Company.

Required
Prepare General Journal entries to record the preceding transactions.

Problem 8–3A
Estimating bad debts expense
(LO 3)

On December 31, 1993, Eagle Corporation's records showed the following results for the year:

Cash sales.	$537,000
Credit sales	731,000

In addition, the unadjusted trial balance included the following items:

Accounts receivable.	$345,000 debit
Allowance for doubtful accounts	1,300 credit

Required

1. Prepare the adjusting entry on the books of Eagle Corporation to estimate bad debts under each of the following independent assumptions:

   a. Bad debts are estimated to be 2% of total sales.
   b. Bad debts are estimated to be 3.5% of credit sales.
   c. An analysis suggests that 7.5% of outstanding accounts receivable on December 31, 1993, will become uncollectible.

2. Show how Accounts Receivable and the Allowance for Doubtful Accounts would appear on the December 31, 1993, balance sheet given the facts in requirement 1*b*.

3. Show how Accounts Receivable and the Allowance for Doubtful Accounts would appear on the December 31, 1993, balance sheet given the facts in requirement 1*c*.

Cosmic Corporation had credit sales of $3.4 million in 1993. On December 31, 1993, the company's Allowance for Doubtful Accounts had a debit balance of $2,800. The accountant for Cosmic Corporation has prepared a schedule of the December 31, 1993, accounts receivable by age, and on the basis of past experience has estimated the percentage of the receivables in each age category that will become uncollectible. This information is summarized as follows:

Problem 8–4A
Aging accounts receivable
(LO 3)

December 31, 1993, Accounts Receivable	Age of Accounts Receivable	Expected Percentage Uncollectible
$470,000	Not due (under 30 days)	2%
265,000	1 to 30 days past due	3
30,000	31 to 60 days past due	15
18,000	61 to 90 days past due	40
9,000	over 90 days past due	75

Required

1. Calculate the amount that should appear in the December 31, 1993, balance sheet as the Allowance for Doubtful Accounts.

2. Prepare the General Journal entry to record bad debts expense for 1993.

3. On July 31, 1994, Cosmic Corporation concluded that a customer's $3,900 receivable (created in 1993) was uncollectible and that the account should be written off. What effect will this action have on Cosmic Corporation's 1994 net income? Explain your answer.

After beginning operations on January 1, 1992, Cyborg Corporation completed a number of transactions during 1992 and 1993 that involved credit sales, accounts receivable collections, and bad debts. These transactions are summarized as follows:

Problem 8–5A
Recording accounts receivable transactions and bad debts adjustments
(LO 3)

1992

a. Sold merchandise on credit for $277,400, terms n/30.

b. Received cash of $228,000 in payment of outstanding accounts receivable.

c. Wrote off uncollectible accounts receivable in the amount of $800.

d. In adjusting the accounts on December 31, concluded that 1.5% of the outstanding accounts receivable would become uncollectible.

1993

e. Sold merchandise on credit for $375,300, terms n/30.

f. Received cash of $390,600 in payment of outstanding accounts receivable.

g. Wrote off uncollectible accounts receivable in the amount of $1,200.

h. In adjusting the accounts on December 31, concluded that 1.5% of the outstanding accounts receivable would become uncollectible.

Required

Prepare General Journal entries to record the 1992 and 1993 summarized transactions of Cyborg Corporation and the adjusting entries to record bad debts expense at the end of each year.

Problem 8–6A
Journalizing notes receivable and bad debts transactions
(LO 4)

Prepare General Journal entries to record these transactions by Tom Mix Company:

Jan.   9   Accepted a $1,000, 30-day, 10% note dated this day in granting a time extension on the past-due account of Daniel Ford.

Feb.   8   Daniel Ford dishonoured his note when presented for payment.

Mar. 14   Accepted a $3,600, 90-day, 12% note dated this day in granting a time extension on the past-due account of Rhonda Jackson.

        20   Discounted the Rhonda Jackson note at the bank at 16%.

June 20   Because the company had not received a notice protesting the Rhonda Jackson note, assumed the note had been paid.

        26   Accepted $500 in cash and a $1,500, 60-day, 11% note dated this day in granting a time extension on the past-due account of Paula Walker.

July   20   Discounted the Paula Walker note at the bank at 14%.

Aug. 27   Received notice protesting the Paula Walker note. Paid the bank the maturity value of the note plus a $20 protest fee.

Sept.   4   Accepted a $1,800, 60-day, 11% note dated this day in granting a time extension on the past-due account of Jean Tyne.

Oct. 10   Discounted the Jean Tyne note at the bank at 15%.

Nov.   6   Received notice protesting the Jean Tyne note. Paid the bank the maturity value of the note plus a $20 protest fee.

Dec.   3   Received payment from Jean Tyne of the maturity value of her dishonoured note, the protest fee, and interest at 11% on both for 30 days beyond maturity.

        28   Decided the accounts of Daniel Ford and Paula Walker were uncollectible and wrote them off against Allowance for Doubtful Accounts.

Problem 8–7A
Analysis and journalizing of notes receivable transactions
(LO 5)

Prepare General Journal entries to record the following transactions of Global Company:

1992

Dec.   6   Accepted a $4,500, 60-day, 12% note dated this day in granting a time extension on the past-due account of Joe Garza.

        31   Made an adjusting entry to record the accrued interest on the Joe Garza note.

        31   Closed the Interest Earned account.

1993

Jan.   5   Discounted the Joe Garza note at the bank at 14%.

Feb.   8   Because no notice protesting the Joe Garza note had been received, assumed that it had been paid.

Mar.   1   Accepted a $3,000, 90-day, 13% note dated this day in granting a time extension on the past-due account of David Pittard.

        11   Discounted the David Pittard note at the bank at 15%.

June   1   Received notice protesting the David Pittard note. Paid the bank the maturity value of the note plus a $30 protest fee.

June 30 Received payment from David Pittard of the maturity value of his dishonoured note, the protest fee, and interest on both for 30 days beyond maturity at 13%.

July   2 Accepted a $1,500, 60-day, 10% note dated July 1 in granting a time extension on the past-due account of Janet Evans.

Aug. 30 Janet Evans dishonoured her note when presented for payment.

Sept. 5 Accepted $1,200 in cash and a $2,400, 60-day, 12% note dated this day in granting a time extension on the past-due account of T. J. Fields.

Oct. 10 Discounted the T. J. Fields note at the bank at 14%.

Nov.   5 Received notice protesting the T. J. Fields note. Paid the bank its maturity value plus a $25 protest fee.

Dec. 29 Decided the Janet Evans and T. J. Fields accounts were uncollectible and wrote them off against Allowance for Doubtful Accounts.

The Laser Printer Company had some surplus cash balances on hand and projected that excess cash would continue to be available over the next few years. Sandy Thomas, the president, decided to invest company funds in the stock market, and obtained professional advice in putting together the company's portfolio.

    Following is a series of events and other facts relevant to the temporary investment activity of the company:

Problem 8–8A
Entries and LCM
application for temporary
investments
(LO 1)

1993

Jan.   2 Purchased 2,000 shares of Southam at $22.50 plus $1,350 commission.

Aug. 17 Purchased 3,000 shares of TD Bank at $15.25 plus $1,373 commission.

Dec. 15 Purchased 1,000 shares of Magna at $30.00 plus $900 commission.

    31 These per share market values were known for the stocks in the portfolio: Southam, $27.50; TD Bank, $12.50; Magna, $18.00.

1994

Feb.   9 Sold 3,000 shares of TD Bank at $11.75 less $1,058 commission.

June 12 Sold 1,000 shares of Magna at $36.00 less $1,080 commission.

July 14 Purchased 3,500 shares of Logitech at $11.75 plus $1,234 commission.

Sept. 29 Purchased 4,000 shares of MCI at $33.25 plus $3,990 commission.

Dec. 31 These per share market values were known for the stocks in the portfolio: Southam, $35.00; Logitech, $15.50; MCI, $19.00.

1995

Feb.   5 Purchased 5,000 shares of Novell at $16.50 plus $2,475 commission.

May   8 Sold 3,500 shares of Logitech at $24.00 less $2,520 commission.

June 18 Sold 2,000 shares of Southam at $45.50 less $2,730 commission.

Nov. 29 Purchased 1,500 shares of BCE at $60.50 plus $2,723 commission.

Dec.   1 Sold 4,000 shares of MCI at $21.50 less $2,580 commission.

    31 These per share market values were known for the shares in the portfolio: Novell, $25.00; BCE, $54.00.

Required

1. Prepare journal entries to record the events and any year-end adjustments needed to record the application of the lower of cost or market method of accounting for temporary investments.

2. Prepare a schedule that shows how the temporary investment portfolio would be described on the balance sheet at the end of each of the three years.

3. Prepare a schedule that shows the components of income (gains and losses, including LCM effects) from these investment activities, and their total effect, for each of the three years. Ignore dividends.

^E**Problem 8–9A**
Share investments—cost and equity methods
(LO 7)

Global Securities Company was organized on January 3, 1993, for the purpose of investing in the shares of other companies. Global Securities immediately issued 200,000 common shares for which it received $600,000 cash. On January 8, 1993, Global Securities Company purchased 50,000 shares (25%) of Syntex Company's outstanding shares at a cost of $600,000. The following transactions and events subsequently occurred:

1993

July   7   Syntex Company declared and paid a cash dividend of $1.10 per share.

Dec. 31   Syntex Company announced that its net income for 1993 was $490,000.

1994

Aug.   2   Syntex Company declared and paid a cash dividend of $0.96 per share.

Dec. 31   Syntex Company announced that its net income for 1994 was $380,000.

1995

Jan.   5   Global Securities Company sold all of its investment in Syntex Company for $716,000 cash.

Part 1.   Global Securities Company is presumed to have a significant influence over Syntex Company because it owns 25% of the common shares.

Required

1. Give the entries on the books of Global Securities Company to record the events regarding its investment in Syntex Company.
2. Calculate Global Securities Company's retained earnings balance on January 6, 1995, including any gain or loss from the sale of the Syntex shares.

Part 2.   Although Global Securities Company owns 25% of Syntex Company's outstanding shares, a thorough investigation of the surrounding circumstances indicates that Global Securities Company does not have a significant influence over Syntex Company, and the cost method is the appropriate method of accounting for the investment.

Required

1. Give the entries on the books of Global Securities Company to record the preceding events regarding its investment in Syntex Company.
2. Calculate Global Securities Company's retained earnings balance on January 6, 1995, including any gain or loss from the sale of the Syntex shares.

^E**Problem 8–10A**
Analytical essay
(LO 7)

Juarez Corporation began operations in January 1992. Since Juarez's inception, it has invested in several companies by purchasing common shares. The following information pertains to the investment portfolio of Juarez at December 31, 1993:

Investment	Cost	Market
A	$45,200	$46,500
B	15,000	18,200
C	10,600	9,100
	$70,800	$73,800

Prior to December 31 adjusting entries, the balance in the allowance account reducing the investments to market is $2,000. Assume that all the investments are marketable and that Juarez's ownership in each investee is less than 20%.

Required

Consider the two alternatives of classifying the portfolio as temporary investments or as long-term investments. For these two alternatives, briefly discuss the similarities and the differences in accounting for the investment portfolio during 1993, including the effects of the investments on the 1993 financial statements.

On December 31, 1992, Jones-Meyer Company's balance sheet included the following:

Problem 8–11A
Analytical essay
(LO 1)

Temporary investments	$50,000	
Allowance to reduce temporary investments to market	4,500	$45,500

On December 31, 1993, an analysis of the temporary investments portfolio showed a total cost of $75,000 and a total market value of $67,000. As a result of this analysis, the company recorded the following adjusting entry:

Dec.	31	Loss on Market Decline of Temporary Investments.	8,000.00	
		Temporary Investments		8,000.00
		To adjust temporary investments portfolio to the LCM amount.		

Required

Explain why the 1993 adjusting entry is not correct.

Review the facts about Eagle Corporation presented in Problem 8–3A.

Problem 8–12A
Analytical essay
(LO 1)

Required

1. Prior to making the December 31, 1993, adjustments, Eagle Corporation's Allowance for Doubtful Accounts has a $1,300 credit balance. Explain how this account balance affects the bad debts expense adjusting entry, assuming the company estimates bad debts by aging its accounts receivable.
2. Requirement 1c of Problem 8–3A indicates that 7.5% of the outstanding accounts receivable ($345,000 × 7.5% = $25,875) will become uncollectible. Given this conclusion, explain why the adjusting entry should not include a $25,875 credit to Accounts Receivable.

Provocative Problems

When the auditor arrived early in January to begin the annual audit, Sandra Grey, the owner of Prism Place, asked that careful attention be given to accounts receivable. Two things caused this request. First, during the previous week, Grey had met Greg Box, a former customer, and had asked him about his account that had recently been written off as uncollectible. Box was surprised, and explained that he had returned $90 of merchandise and paid the remaining $580 account balance. Later, he provided copies of his canceled cheque endorsed by Prism Place to prove that the balance had been

Provocative Problem 8–1
Prism Place
(Review problem)

paid. Second, the income statement prepared for the quarter ended the previous July 31 showed an unusually large volume of sales returns. The bookkeeper who had prepared the statement was new, having begun work on May 1, after being hired on the basis of out-of-town letters of reference. In addition to doing all the record-keeping, the book-keeper also acted as the cashier, depositing the cash from sales and from mail receipts.

In performing the audit, the auditor used the company's records to prepare the following analysis of all the accounts receivable activity for May 1 through July 31:

	Able	Box	Cole	Dunn	Ellis	Friar	Gold	Total
Balance, May 1. . .	$ 390	$ 100	$ 210	$ 400	$ 860	$1,850	$ 370	$ 4,180
Sales	2,440	570	1,455		6,300	420	1,450	12,635
Total	$2,830	$ 670	$1,665	$ 400	$7,160	$2,270	$1,820	$16,815
Collections	(2,080)		(985)		(6,040)	(1,475)	(1,300)	(11,880)
Returns.	(450)	(90)	(130)		(290)	(250)	(70)	(1,280)
Bad debts written off		(580)		(400)				(980)
Balance, July 31 . .	$ 300	$-0-	$ 550	$-0-	$ 830	$ 545	$ 450	$ 2,675

The auditor contacted all charge customers and learned that although their account balances as of July 31 agreed with the amounts shown in the company's records, the individual transactions did not. The customers provided information that allowed the auditor to determine that credit sales actually totaled $14,050 during the three-month period. Also, there were actual sales returns of $395 on credit sales to these customers. Correspondence with Perry Dunn, a customer whose $400 account had been written off, revealed that he had become bankrupt and his creditor's claims had been settled by his receiver in bankruptcy at $0.25 on the dollar. The cheques had been mailed by his receiver on May 30, and all had been paid and returned by the bank, properly endorsed by the recipients.

Under the assumption that the bookkeeper has embezzled cash from the company, determine the total amount he has taken and attempted to conceal with false entries to Accounts Receivable. Explain the deficiency by listing the concealment methods used and the amount he attempted to conceal with each method. Also, outline an internal control system that would help protect the company's cash from future embezzlements. Assume the company will hire a new bookkeeper, but will continue to have only one office employee who must do all the bookkeeping.

Provocative Problem 8–2
FootGear
(LO 3)

John Holcomb has operated FootGear for five years. Three years ago, he liberalized the store's credit policy in an effort to increase credit sales. Credit sales have increased, but now Holcomb is concerned with the effects of the more liberalized credit policy. Bad debts written off (the store uses the direct write-off method) have increased materially in the last three years, and now Holcomb wonders if the increase justifies the substantial bad debt losses that he is certain have resulted from the new credit policy.

An examination of the store's credit sales records, bad debt losses, and accounts receivable for the five years' operations reveal:

	1st Year	2nd Year	3rd Year	4th Year	5th Year
Credit sales	$84,000	$92,400	$126,000	$151,200	$167,500
Cost of goods sold.	50,400	55,440	75,600	90,720	100,500
Gross profit from credit sales . . .	$33,600	$36,960	$ 50,400	$ 60,480	$ 67,000
Expenses other than bad debts . .	25,200	27,680	37,700	45,170	49,980
Income before bad debts	$ 8,400	$ 9,280	$ 12,700	$ 15,310	$ 17,020
Bad debts written off	85	370	630	1,980	2,020
Income from credit sales	$ 8,315	$ 8,910	$ 12,070	$ 13,330	$ 15,000
Bad debts by year of sale	$ 335	$ 280	$ 1,640	$ 1,820	$ 2,340

The last line in the tabulation results from reclassifying bad debt losses so that the losses appear in the same years as the sales that produced them. Because some of the fifth-year sales had not been collected at year-end, the $2,340 of fifth-year losses includes $1,320 of estimated bad debts that are still in the accounts receivable.

Prepare a schedule showing the following by years: income from credit sales before bad debt losses, bad debts incurred, and the resulting income from credit sales. Then, below the income figures, show for each year bad debts written off as a percentage of sales, followed on the next line by estimated bad debts expense incurred as a percentage of sales. Also prepare a report for Holcomb in which you answer his concern about the new credit policy and recommend any changes you consider desirable in his accounting for bad debts.

When corporations have their annual meetings with shareholders, the managements often have to deal with difficult questions from shareholders. For example, at a recent shareholders' meeting of Omega Corporation, one of the shareholders said:

[E]Provocative Problem 8–3
Omega Corporation
(LO 7)

I have owned shares of Omega for several years, but I am now questioning whether management is telling the truth in the annual financial statements. At the end of 1992, you announced that Omega had just acquired a 35% interest in the outstanding shares of Intex Corporation. You also stated that the 250,000 shares had cost Omega about $4.25 million. In the financial statements for 1993, you told us that the investments of Omega were proving to be very profitable and reported that earnings from all investments had amounted to more than $3.75 million. In the financial statements for 1994, you explained that Omega had sold the Intex shares during the first week of the year, receiving $5,025,000 cash proceeds from the sale. Nevertheless, the income statement for 1994 reports a $12,500 loss on the sale before taxes. I realize that Intex Corporation did not pay any dividends during 1993, but it was very profitable. As I recall, it reported net income of $2.25 million for 1993. Personally, I do not think you should have sold the shares. But, much more importantly, you reported to us that our company had a loss of $12,500 from the sale. How can that be true if the shares were purchased for $4,250,000 and were sold for $5,025,000?

Explain to this shareholder why the $12,500 loss is correctly reported.

Analytical and Review Problems

Hard Pressed Company required a loan of $10,000 and was offered two alternatives by the Security Bank. The alternatives are:

A&R Problem 8–1*

a. Hard Pressed would give the bank a one-year $10,000 note payable, dated November 1, 1993, with interest at 12%.

b. Hard Pressed would give the bank a one-year $11,200 noninterest-bearing note payable dated November 1, 1993. The bank would precalculate and deduct $1,200 of interest from the face amount of the note.

Required

1. Prepare *all* the necessary entries (including repayment on October 31, 1994) with regard to alternative *a*. Assume that Hard Pressed Company's fiscal year ends December 31.
2. Repeat the journal entries for alternative *b*.

_____
* Interest to be calculated on a monthly basis.

A&R Problem 8-2

The Tor-Mont Company has been in business three years and has applied for a significant bank loan. Prior to considering the applications, the bank asks you to conduct an audit for the last three years. Concerning accounts receivable, you find that the company has been charging off receivables as they finally proved uncollectible and treating them as expenses at the time of write-off.

Your investigation indicates that receivable losses have approximated (and can be expected to approximate) 2% of net sales. Until this first audit, the company's sales and direct receivable write-off experience was:

		Accounts Written Off In		
Year of Sales	Amount of Sales	19X1	19X2	19X3
19X1	$300,000	$1,000	$4,000	$1,200
19X2	400,000	—	2,000	4,800
19X3	500,000	—	—	3,000

Required

1. Indicate the amount by which net income was understated or overstated each year because the company used the direct write-off method rather than the generally acceptable allowance method.

2. Prepare all the entries for each of the three years that would have been made if Tor-Mont had used the allowance method from the start of the business.

3. Which of the entries in (2) are year-end adjusting entries?

As a Matter of Record

Record Case 8-1

Refer to Case 7-1 page 416.

Required

Discuss the usefulness of warning signs 6 and 8 to the business entity.

Answers to Objective Review Questions

LO 1 (c)	LO 4 (b)	LO 6 (d)
LO 2 (d)	LO 5 (c)	LO 7 (d)
LO 3 (a)		

Inventories and Cost of Goods Sold

Merchandising companies buy and sell large quantities and varieties of goods. These activities lead to complex accounting problems in measuring profits. Companies use several different methods to develop information about their inventories and cost of goods sold.

*T*he operations of merchandising businesses involve the purchase and resale of tangible commodities. In Chapter 5, when we first introduced the topic of accounting for merchandising businesses, we left several important matters for later consideration. In this chapter, we return to the topic and examine the methods businesses use at the end of each period to assign dollar amounts to merchandise inventory and to cost of goods sold. The principles and procedures that we explain in this chapter are used in department stores, grocery stores, automobile dealerships, and any other businesses that purchase goods for resale.

Learning Objectives

After studying Chapter 9, you should be able to:

1. Describe (*a*) how the matching principle relates to accounting for merchandise, (*b*) the types of items that should be included in merchandise inventory, and (*c*) the elements that make up the cost of merchandise.
2. Calculate the cost of an inventory and cost of goods sold based on (*a*) specific invoice prices, (*b*) weighted-average cost, (*c*) FIFO, and (*d*) LIFO, and explain the financial statement effects of choosing one method over the others.
3. Calculate the lower-of-cost-or-market amount of an inventory.
4. Explain the effect of an inventory error on the income statements of the current and succeeding years.
5. Describe perpetual inventory systems and prepare entries to record merchandise transactions and maintain subsidiary inventory records under a perpetual inventory system.
6. Estimate an inventory by the retail method and by the gross profit method.
7. Define or explain the words and phrases listed in the chapter glossary.

The assets that a business buys and holds for resale are called *merchandise inventory*. As a rule, the items held as merchandise inventory are sold within one year or one operating cycle. Therefore, merchandise inventory is a current asset, usually the largest current asset on the balance sheet of a merchandiser.

Matching Merchandise Costs with Revenues

Accounting for inventories affects both the balance sheet and the income statement. However, "the method of determining cost should be one which results in the fairest matching of costs against revenues regardless of whether or not the method corresponds to the [order in which the goods leave the firm]."[1] The matching process is already a familiar topic. For inventories, it

---

[1] *CICA Handbook* (Toronto: The Canadian Institute of Chartered Accountants), par. 3030.09.

consists of deciding how much of the cost of the goods available for sale during a period should be deducted from the period's revenue and how much should be carried forward as inventory to be matched against a future period's revenue.

In a periodic inventory system, when the cost of goods available for sale is allocated between cost of goods sold and ending inventory, the key problem is assigning a cost to the ending inventory. Remember, however, that by assigning a cost to the ending inventory, you are also determining cost of goods sold. This is true because the ending inventory is subtracted from the cost of goods available for sale to determine cost of goods sold.

LO 1 Describe (*a*) how the matching principle relates to accounting for merchandise, (*b*) the types of items that should be included in merchandise inventory, and (*c*) the elements that make up the cost of merchandise.

Items to Include in Merchandise Inventory

The merchandise inventory of a business includes all goods owned by the business and held for sale, regardless of where the goods may be located at the time inventory is counted. In applying this rule, most items present no problem. All that is required is to see that all items are counted, that nothing is omitted, and that nothing is counted more than once. However, goods in transit, goods sold but not delivered, goods on consignment, and obsolete and damaged goods require special attention.

Should merchandise be included in the inventory of a business if the goods are in transit from a supplier to a business on the date the business takes an inventory? The answer to this question depends on whether the rights and risks of ownership have passed from the supplier to the purchasing business. If ownership has passed to the purchaser, they should be included in the purchaser's inventory. Usually, if the buyer is responsible for paying the freight charges, ownership passes as soon as the goods are loaded on the means of transportation. (As mentioned in Chapter 5, the terms would be FOB the seller's factory or warehouse.) On the other hand, if the seller is to pay the freight charges, ownership passes when the goods arrive at their destination (FOB destination).

Goods on consignment are goods shipped by their owner (known as the **consignor**) to another person or firm (called the **consignee**) who is to sell the goods for the owner. Consigned goods belong to the consignor and should appear on the consignor's inventory.

Damaged goods and deteriorated or obsolete goods should not be counted in the inventory if they are not salable. If such goods are salable at a reduced price, they should be included in the inventory at a conservative estimate of their **net realizable value** (sales price less the cost of making the sale). Thus, the accounting period in which the goods deteriorated, were damaged, or became obsolete suffers the resultant loss.

Elements of Merchandise Cost

As applied to merchandise, cost means the sum of the expenditures and charges directly or indirectly incurred in bringing an article to its existing condition and location.[2] Therefore, the cost of an inventory item includes the invoice price, less the discount, plus any additional or incidental costs necessary to put the item into place and condition for sale. The incidental costs may

---

[2] Ibid., see paragraphs 3030.02 to 3030.06.

include import duties, transportation-in, storage, insurance, and any other related costs such as those incurred during an aging process (e.g., the aging of wine).

All of these costs should be included in the cost of merchandise. When calculating the cost of a merchandise inventory on hand at the end of the fiscal year, however, some concerns do not include the incidental costs of acquiring merchandise. They price the inventory on the basis of invoice prices only. As a result, the incidental costs are allocated to cost of goods sold during the period in which they are incurred.

In theory, a share of each incidental cost should be assigned to every unit purchased. This causes a portion of each to be carried forward in the inventory to be matched against the revenue of the period in which the inventory is sold. However, the effort of computing costs on such a precise basis may outweigh the benefit from the extra accuracy. Therefore, many businesses take advantage of the *materiality principle* and charge such costs to cost of goods sold.

Taking an Ending Inventory

As you learned in Chapter 5, when a *periodic inventory system* is used, the dollar amount of the ending inventory is determined as follows: count the units of each product on hand, multiply the count for each product by its cost, and add the costs for all products. In making the count, items are less likely to be counted twice or omitted from the count if you use prenumbered **inventory tickets** like the one in Illustration 9–1.

Before beginning the inventory count, a sufficient number of the tickets, at least one for each product on hand, is issued to each department in the store. Next, a clerk counts the quantity of each product. From the count and the price tag attached to the merchandise, the clerk fills in the information on the inventory ticket and attaches it to the counted items. After the count is completed, clerks check each department for uncounted items. At this stage, because inventory tickets should be attached to all counted items, any products without tickets attached are uncounted. After all the items are counted, the tickets are removed and sent to the accounting department for completion of the inventory. To ensure that no ticket is lost or left attached to merchandise, the accounting department verifies that all the prenumbered tickets issued have been returned.

In the accounting department, the unit and cost data on the tickets are aggregated by multiplying the number of units of each product by its unit cost. This gives the dollar amount of each product in the inventory and the total for all the products is the dollar total of the inventory.

Assigning Costs to Inventory Items and to Cost of Goods Sold

One of the major issues in accounting for merchandise involves determining the unit cost amounts that will be assigned to items in the inventory. When all units are purchased at the same unit cost, this process is easy. However, when identical items were purchased at different costs, a problem arises as to which costs apply to the ending inventory and which apply to the goods sold. There are four commonly used methods of assigning costs to goods in the ending inventory and to goods sold. They are (1) specific invoice prices; (2) weighted-

ILLUSTRATION 9-1

Inventory Tickets Used to Tag Inventory Items as They Are Counted

```
INVENTORY
TICKET          No.     786

Item
            _____




Quantity counted  _____

Sales price       $_____

Cost price        $_____

Purchase date     _____


Counted by _____
Checked by _____
```

average cost; (3) first-in, first-out; and (4) last-in, first-out. All four methods fall within generally accepted accounting principles.

The units in ending inventory plus the units sold equal the units available for sale. Therefore, calculating the value of the ending inventory also determines the cost of goods sold. Similarly, calculating the cost of goods sold also determines the value of the ending inventory. In the illustrations which follow, the closing inventory is deducted from the goods available to arrive at the cost of goods sold.

To illustrate the four methods, assume that a company has 12 units of Product X on hand at the end of its annual accounting period. Also, assume that the inventory at the beginning of the year and the purchases during the year were as follows:

LO 2 Calculate the cost of an inventory and cost of goods sold based on (*a*) specific invoice prices, (*b*) weighted-average cost, (*c*) FIFO, and (*d*) LIFO, and explain the financial statement effects of choosing one method over the others.

Jan. 1	Beginning inventory	10 units @ $100 = $1,000
Mar. 13	Purchased	15 units @ $108 = 1,620
Aug. 17	Purchased	20 units @ $120 = 2,400
Nov. 10	Purchased	10 units @ $125 = 1,250
Total		55 units $6,270

Specific Invoice Prices

When each item in an inventory can be clearly related to a specific purchase and its invoice, **specific invoice inventory pricing** may be used to assign costs. For example, assume that 6 of the 12 unsold units of Product X were from the

November purchase and 6 were from the August purchase. With this information, specific invoice prices can be used to assign cost to the ending inventory and to the goods sold as follows:

Total cost of 55 units available for sale.		$6,270
Less ending inventory priced by means of specific invoices:		
6 units from the November purchase at $125 each.	$750	
6 units from the August purchase at $120 each.	720	
Ending inventory (12 units)		1,470
Cost of goods sold		$4,800

Weighted Average

When using **weighted-average inventory pricing,** multiply the per unit costs of the beginning inventory and of each purchase by the number of units in the beginning inventory and in each purchase. Then divide the total of these amounts by the total number of units available for sale to find the weighted-average cost per unit as follows:[3]

Jan. 1 Beginning inventory	10 units @ $100 =	$1,000
Mar. 13 Purchased	15 units @ $108 =	1,620
Aug. 17 Purchased	20 units @ $120 =	2,400
Nov. 10 Purchased	10 units @ $125 =	1,250
Total	55	$6,270

$6,270/55 = $114 weighted-average cost per unit

After determining the weighted-average cost per unit, use this average to assign costs to the inventory and to the units sold as follows:

Total cost of 55 units available for sale	$6,270
Ending inventory priced on a weighted-average	
cost basis: 12 units at $114 each.	1,368
Cost of goods sold.	$4,902

First-In, First-Out

When using **first-in, first-out (FIFO) inventory pricing,** assume the items in the beginning inventory are to be sold first. Additional sales are assumed to come in the order in which they were purchased. Thus, the costs of the last items received are assigned to the ending inventory, and the remaining costs are assigned to goods sold. For example, when first-in, first-out is used, the costs of Product X are assigned to the inventory and goods sold as follows:

---

[3] Often the weighted-average cost per unit will not calculate evenly. In such cases, rounding is necessary. Any differences are seldom material.

Total cost of 55 units available for sale.		$6,270
Less ending inventory priced on a basis of FIFO:		
10 units from the November purchase at $125 each . .	$1,250	
2 units from the August purchase at $120 each	240	
Ending inventory (12 units)		1,490
Cost of goods sold		$4,780

You need to understand that the use of FIFO is acceptable whether or not the physical flow of goods actually follows a first-in, first-out pattern. The physical flow of products depends on the nature of the product and the way the products are stored. If a product is perishable (e.g., fresh tomatoes), the business attempts to sell it in a first-in, first-out pattern. Other products, for example, bolts or screws kept in a large bin, may tend to be sold on a last-in, first-out basis. In either case, the FIFO method of allocating cost may be used.

Last-In, First-Out

Under the **last-in, first-out (LIFO) inventory pricing** method, the cost of the last goods received are charged to cost of goods sold and matched with revenue from sales. Again, this method is acceptable even though the physical flow of goods may not be on a last-in, first-out basis.

One argument for the use of LIFO is based on the fact that a going concern must replace the inventory items it sells. When goods are sold, replacements are purchased. Thus, a sale causes the replacement of goods. According to this point of view, a correct matching of costs with revenues requires matching replacement costs with the sales that made replacements necessary. Although the costs of the most recent purchases are not quite the same as replacement costs, they usually are close approximations of replacement costs. Because LIFO assigns the most recent purchase costs to the income statement, LIFO (compared to FIFO or weighted average) comes closest to matching replacement costs with revenues.

Under LIFO, costs are assigned to the 12 remaining units of Product X and to the goods sold as follows:

Total cost of 55 units available for sale.		$6,270
Less ending inventory priced on a basis of LIFO:		
10 units in the beginning inventory at $100 each. .	$1,000	
2 units from the March purchase at $108 each . .	216	
Ending inventory (12 units)		1,216
Cost of goods sold		$5,054

Notice that when LIFO is used to match costs and revenues, the ending inventory cost is the cost of the oldest 12 units.

Comparison of Methods

In a stable market where prices remain unchanged, the choice of an inventory pricing method has little importance. When prices are unchanged over a period of time, all methods give the same cost figures. However, in a changing

ILLUSTRATION 9-2

The Income Statement Effects of Alternative Inventory Pricing Methods

	Specific Invoice Prices	Weighted Average	FIFO	LIFO
Sales	$6,000	$6,000	$6,000	$6,000
Cost of goods sold:				
Merchandise inventory, January 1	$1,000	$1,000	$1,000	$1,000
Purchases	5,270	5,270	5,270	5,270
Cost of goods available for sale	$6,270	$6,270	$6,270	$6,270
Merchandise inventory, December 31	1,470	1,368	1,490	1,216
Cost of goods sold	$4,800	$4,902	$4,780	$5,054
Gross profit	$1,200	$1,098	$1,220	$ 946
Operating expenses	500	500	500	500
Income	$ 700	$ 598	$ 720	$ 446

market where prices are rising or falling, each method may give a different result. These differences are shown in Illustration 9–2, where we assume that Product X sales were $6,000 and operating expenses were $500. In Illustration 9–2, note the differences that resulted from the choice of an inventory pricing method.

Because purchase prices were rising throughout the period, FIFO resulted in the lowest cost of goods sold, the highest gross profit, and the highest net income. On the other hand, LIFO resulted in the highest cost of goods sold, the lowest gross profit, and the lowest net income. As you would expect, the results of using the weighted-average method fall between FIFO and LIFO. The results of using specific invoice prices depend entirely on which units were actually sold.

Each of the four pricing methods is generally accepted, and arguments can be made for using each. In one sense, one might argue that specific invoice prices exactly match costs and revenues. However, this method is practical only for relatively high-priced items when just a few units are kept in stock and sold. Weighted-average costs tend to smooth out price fluctuations. FIFO provides an inventory valuation on the balance sheet that most closely approximates current replacement cost. LIFO causes the last costs incurred to be assigned to cost of goods sold; therefore, it results in a better matching of current costs with revenues on the income statement.

Because the choice of an inventory pricing method often has material effects on the financial statements, the choice of a method should be disclosed in the notes to the statements. This information is important to an understanding of the statements and is required by the *full-disclosure principle*.[4]

---

[4] *CICA Handbook*, par. 3030.10.

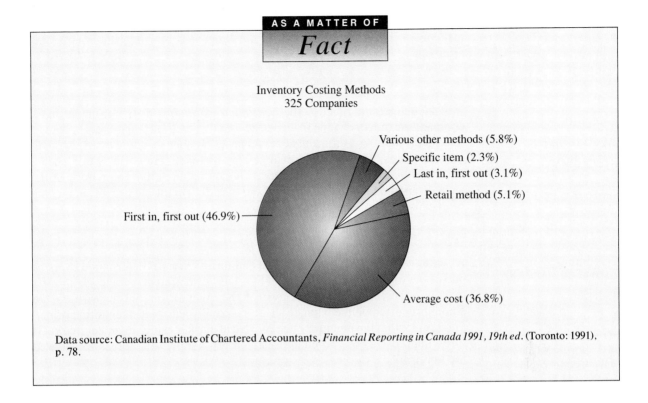

AS A MATTER OF

Fact

Inventory Costing Methods
325 Companies

Various other methods (5.8%)

Specific item (2.3%)

Last in, first out (3.1%)

Retail method (5.1%)

First in, first out (46.9%)

Average cost (36.8%)

Data source: Canadian Institute of Chartered Accountants, *Financial Reporting in Canada 1991, 19th ed.* (Toronto: 1991), p. 78.

The Consistency Principle

Because the choice of an inventory pricing method can have a material effect on the financial statements, some companies might be inclined to make a new choice each year. Their objective would be to select whichever method would result in the most favourable financial statements. If this were allowed, however, readers of financial statements would find it extremely difficult to compare the company's financial statements from one year to the next. If income increased, the reader would have difficulty deciding whether the increase resulted from more successful operations or from the change in the accounting method. The **consistency principle** is used to avoid this problem.

The *consistency principle* requires that a company use the same accounting methods period after period, so that the financial statements of succeeding periods will be comparable.[5] The *consistency principle* is not limited just to inventory pricing methods. Whenever a company must choose between alternative generally accepted accounting methods, consistency requires that the company continue to use the selected method period after period. As a result, a reader of a company's financial statements may assume that in keeping its records and in preparing its statements, the company used the same proce-

---

[5] Ibid., par. 1000.23.

dures employed in previous years. Only on the basis of this assumption can meaningful comparisons be made of the data in a company's statements year after year.

Changing Accounting Procedures

In achieving comparability, the *consistency principle* does not mean that a company can never change from one accounting method to another. Rather, if a company justifies a different acceptable method or procedure as an improvement in financial reporting, a change may be made. However, when such a change is made, the *full-disclosure principle* requires that the nature of the change, justification for the change, and the effect of the change on net income be disclosed in notes to the statements.[6]

Lower of Cost or Market

LO 3 Calculate the lower-of-cost-or-market amount of an inventory.

As we have discussed, the cost of the ending inventory is determined by using one of the four pricing methods (FIFO, LIFO, weighted average, or specific invoice prices). However, the cost of the inventory is not necessarily the amount reported on the balance sheet. Generally accepted accounting principles require that the inventory be reported at market value whenever market is lower than cost. Thus, merchandise inventory is shown on the balance sheet at the *lower of cost or market*.

Determination of Market

In applying lower of cost or market to merchandise inventories, what do accountants mean by the term *market*? For the purpose of assigning a value to merchandise inventory, market can be either *net realizable value* or *replacement cost*. Replacement cost means the price a company would pay if it bought new items to replace those in its inventory. When the cost to replace merchandise drops below original cost, the sales price of the merchandise is also likely to fall. Therefore, the merchandise is worth less to the company and should be written down to replacement cost (or market). Net realizable value means the amount the company expects to receive when it sells the merchandise less any costs of preparing the merchandise for sale, such as repairs, or selling costs, such as commissions. If the net realizable value (NRV) is less than original cost, then the merchandise should be written down to NRV (or market).

The choice of either NRV or replacement cost as the market value depends on which amount is more reliable. Most Canadian companies tend to use NRV as their definition of market value.[7]

Lower of cost or market may be applied to merchandise inventory in either of two ways. First, it may be applied to the inventory as a whole. Alternatively, it may be applied separately to each product in the inventory. To illustrate, assume that a company's year-end inventory contains three products (X, Y, and Z) with the following costs and market values:

---

[6] Ibid., par. 1506.16.

[7] CICA, *Financial Reporting in Canada 1991*, (Toronto: 1991), p. 79.

Product	Units on Hand	Per Unit Cost	Per Unit Market	Total Cost	Total Market	Lower of Cost or Market (by Product)
X	20	$8	$7	$160	$140	$140
Y	10	5	6	50	60	50
Z	5	9	7	45	35	35
				$255	$235	$225

Note that when the whole inventory is priced at market, the total is $235, which is $20 lower than the $255 cost. Alternatively, when the lower of cost or market is applied separately to each product, the sum is only $225. A company may use either approach to calculate the lower of cost or market of merchandise inventory.

Recall from Chapter 8 that lower of cost or market is also used to value a company's temporary investments in marketable equity securities. However, in that case, only one approach is allowed. The total cost and total market value of the entire portfolio of investments is compared to determine the lower of cost or market. Thus, while the lower-of-cost-or-market calculation for merchandise inventory may be done two different ways, the calculation for temporary investments is restricted to one way.

Inventory Should Never Be Valued at More than Its Net Realizable Value

The idea that *market* is defined as replacement cost is subject to two important exceptions. One exception is that inventory should never be valued at more than its net realizable value, which is the expected sales price less additional costs to sell. Understand that merchandise is written down to market because the value of the merchandise to the company has declined. Sometimes, the net realizable value is even less than replacement cost. In that case, the merchandise is worth no more than net realizable value and should be written down to that amount.

For example, assume that merchandise was purchased for $100 and was originally priced to sell for $125. By year-end, a general decline in prices resulted in a replacement cost of $90. However, assume that the merchandise in question has been damaged. Management expects that the merchandise can be sold for $95 if it is first cleaned at a cost of $10. Therefore, net realizable value is $95 − $10, or $85. Since net realizable value ($85) is less than replacement cost ($90), the merchandise should be written down to net realizable value.

Inventory Should Never Be Valued at Less than Net Realizable Value minus a Normal Profit Margin

A second exception to defining market as replacement cost, according to some accountants, is that merchandise should never be written down to an amount that is less than net realizable value minus a normal profit margin. To illustrate, suppose that a company normally buys merchandise for $80 and sells it for $100. The gross profit of $20 is 20% of the selling price. Now suppose the selling price falls from $100 to $90. A normal gross profit margin would be $90 × 20% = $18. Therefore, the inventory should not be written down below $90 − $18 = $72, even if replacement cost is less than $72. If the inventory were written down below $72, the income statement of the current period would show an abnormally low gross profit margin. And when the merchandise is sold for $90 the next period, the income statement of that period would show an abnormally high gross profit margin.

The Conservatism Principle

Generally accepted accounting principles require writing inventory down to market when market is less than cost. On the other hand, inventory generally cannot be written up to market when market exceeds cost. If writing inventory down to market is justified, why not also write inventory up to market? What is the reason for this apparent inconsistency?

The reason inventory is not written up above cost to a higher market value is that the gain from a market value increase is not realized until a sales transaction provides verifiable evidence of the amount of the gain. But why, then, are inventories written down when market is below cost?

Accountants often justify the lower of cost or market rule by citing the **conservatism principle.** The principle of conservatism attempts to guide the accountant in uncertain situations where amounts must be estimated. In general terms, it implies that when ''uncertainty exists, estimates of a conservative nature attempt to ensure net assets or net income are not overstated.''[8] Because the value of inventory is uncertain, writing the inventory down when its market value falls is clearly the less optimistic estimate of the inventory's value to the company.

Inventory Errors—Periodic System

LO 4 Explain the effect of an inventory error on the income statements of the current and succeeding years.

When the *periodic inventory system* is used, you must be especially careful in taking the end-of-period inventory. If an error is made, it will cause misstatements in cost of goods sold, gross profit, net income, current assets, and owner's equity. Also, the ending inventory of one period is the beginning inventory of the next. Therefore, the error will carry forward and cause misstatements in the succeeding period's cost of goods sold, gross profit, and net income. Furthermore, since the amount involved in an inventory often is large, the misstatements can materially reduce the usefulness of the financial statements.

To illustrate the effects of an inventory error, assume that in each of the years 1993, 1994, and 1995, a company had $100,000 in sales. If the company maintained a $20,000 inventory throughout the period and made $60,000 in purchases in each of the years, its cost of goods sold each year was $60,000 and its annual gross profit was $40,000. However, assume the company incorrectly calculated its December 31, 1993, inventory at $18,000 rather than $20,000. Illustration 9–3 shows the effects of the error compared to the correct results.

---

[8] *CICA Handbook,* par. 1000.20.

ILLUSTRATION 9–3

Effects of Inventory Errors—Periodic Inventory System

With Incorrect Inventory	1993		1994		1995	
Sales		$100,000		$100,000		$100,000
Cost of goods sold:						
Beginning inventory	$20,000		$18,000		$20,000	
Purchases	60,000		60,000		60,000	
Goods for sale	$80,000		$78,000		$80,000	
Ending inventory.	18,000		20,000		20,000	
Cost of goods sold		62,000		58,000		60,000
Gross profit.		$ 38,000		$ 42,000		$ 40,000

With Correct Inventory	1993		1994		1995	
Sales		$100,000		$100,000		$100,000
Cost of goods sold:						
Beginning inventory	$20,000		$20,000		$20,000	
Purchases	60,000		60,000		60,000	
Goods for sale	$80,000		$80,000		$80,000	
Ending inventory.	20,000		20,000		20,000	
Cost of goods sold		60,000		60,000		60,000
Gross profit.		$40,000		$ 40,000		$ 40,000

Observe in Illustration 9–3 that the $2,000 understatement of the December 31, 1993, inventory caused a $2,000 overstatement in 1993 cost of goods sold and a $2,000 understatement in gross profit and net income. Also, because the ending inventory of 1993 became the beginning inventory of 1994, the error caused an understatement in the 1994 cost of goods sold and a $2,000 overstatement in gross profit and net income. However, by 1995 the error had no effect on the operating results for that year.

In Illustration 9–3, the December 31, 1993, inventory is understated. Had it been overstated, it would have caused opposite results—the 1993 net income would have been overstated and the 1994 income understated.

Because inventory errors correct themselves by causing offsetting errors in the next period, you might be inclined to think that they are not serious. Do not make this mistake. Management, creditors, and owners base many important decisions on fluctuations in reported net income. Therefore, inventory errors must be avoided.

Perpetual Inventory Systems

The previous discussion of inventories focused on the periodic inventory system. Under the periodic system, the Merchandise Inventory account is updated only once each accounting period, at the end of the period. The Merchandise Inventory account then reflects the current balance of inventory, but only until the first purchase or sale in the following period. Thereafter, the Merchandise Inventory account no longer reflects the current balance.

Grant O'Neill, CA

Mr. O'Neill is corporate controller for Custom Trim Ltd., an automotive supplier of leather interior trim products. Custom Trim Ltd. has manufacturing locations in Waterloo, Canada, and Matamoros, Mexico, as well as sales/administrative offices in Brownsville, Texas, and Detroit, Michigan. The company employs over 1,000 people.

Mr. O'Neill started his career with Deloitte, Haskins & Sells and was controller for Electrohome, Motor Division, before joining Custom Trim Ltd. He is a chartered accountant and a graduate of McMaster University with a Bachelor of Commerce degree. Mr. O'Neill has taught numerous accounting courses at Wilfrid Laurier University over the past 10 years.

To be supplier of choice to the automotive industry, profitably, with the highest quality at the lowest possible cost requires total management commitment and interaction. Success depends on the qualitative as well as the quantitative information provided by the accounting personnel. Their role must expand from information gatherers to information interpreters and prognosticators. This expertise is needed by today's production and marketing managers to enact strategic plans as well as to make day-to-day decisions.

Today's accountant has many tools available to practice this sophisticated accounting. Our perpetual inventory system also provides the basis for Electronic Data Interchange (EDI). This automates the replenishment of inventories and reduces the cycle time from ordering to use in manufacturing. In addition to providing financial information, the perpetual system automates invoice matching with payments to suppliers and allows us to integrate techniques such as activity-based costing.

Accounting truly becomes the language of business when the accounting system is integrated into an active, day-to-day, management decision-making process. Perpetual inventory systems are an important example of this integration.

LO 5 Describe perpetual inventory systems and prepare entries to record merchandise transactions and maintain subsidiary inventory records under a perpetual inventory system.

By contrast, a *perpetual inventory system* updates the Merchandise Inventory account after each purchase and after each sale. As long as all entries have been posted, the account shows the current amount of inventory on hand. The system takes its name from the fact that the Merchandise Inventory account is perpetually up to date. When a perpetual inventory system is used, management is able to monitor the inventory on hand on a regular basis. This aids in planning future purchases.

Before the widespread use of computers in accounting, only companies that sold a limited number of products of relatively high value used perpetual inventory systems. The cost and effort of maintaining perpetual inventory records were simply too great for other types of companies. However, since computers have made the record-keeping chore much easier, an increasing number of firms are switching from periodic to perpetual systems.

ILLUSTRATION 9–4

A Comparison of Entries under Periodic and Perpetual Inventory Systems

X Company purchases merchandise for $15 per unit and sells it for $25. The company begins the current period with five units of product on hand, which cost a total of $75.

Periodic		Perpetual	

1. *Purchased on credit 10 units of merchandise for $15 per unit.*

Purchases 150		Merchandise Inventory. 150	
Accounts Payable	150	Accounts Payable	150

2. *Returned three units of merchandise purchased in (1).*

Accounts Payable 45		Accounts Payable 45	
Purchases Ret. and Allow..	45	Merchandise Inventory	45

3. *Sold eight units for $200 cash.*

Cash 200		Cash 200	
Sales.	200	Sales	200
		Cost of Goods Sold. 120	
		Merchandise Inventory	120

4. *Closing entries:*

Merchandise Inventory (Ending). . . . 60		Income Summary. 120	
Sales 200		Cost of Goods Sold.	120
Purchases Ret. and Allow.. 45			
Income Summary	305	Sales 200	
		Income Summary	200
Income Summary 225			
Merchandise Inv. (Beginning)	75		
Purchases	150		

	Units	Cost
Beginning inventory	5	$ 75
Purchases	10	150
Purchase returns	(3)	(45)
Goods available	12	$180
Goods sold	(8)	(120)
Ending inventory.	4	$ 60

Using parallel columns, Illustration 9–4 shows the typical journal entries made under periodic and perpetual inventory systems. In Illustration 9–4, observe the entries for the purchase of transaction 1. The perpetual system does not use a Purchases account. Instead, the cost of the items purchased is debited directly to Merchandise Inventory. Also, in transaction 2, the perpetual system credits the cost of purchase returns directly to the Merchandise Inventory account instead of using a Purchases Returns and Allowances account.

Transaction 3 involves the sale of merchandise. Note that the perpetual system requires two entries to record the sale, one to record the revenue and

Comparing Journal Entries under Perpetual and Periodic Inventory Systems

ILLUSTRATION 9–5

First-In, First-Out Cost Flow									

Item **_Product Z_**   Location in stockroom **_Bin 8_**

Maximum **_25_**   Minimum **_5_**

	Purchased			Sold			Balance		
Date	Units	Cost	Total	Units	Cost	Total	Units	Cost	Total
Jan. 1							10	10.00	100.00
Jan. 5				5	10.00	50.00	5	10.00	50.00
Jan. 8	20	10.50	210.00				5	10.00	
							20	10.50	260.00
Jan. 10				3	10.00	30.00	2	10.00	
							20	10.50	230.00

another to record cost of goods sold. Thus, the perpetual system uses a Cost of Goods Sold account. In the periodic system the elements of cost of goods sold are not transferred to such an account. Instead, they are transferred to Income Summary in the process of recording the closing entries.

The closing entries under the two systems are shown as item 4 in Illustration 9–4. Under the perpetual system, the cost elements were already recorded in a Cost of Goods Sold account. Thus, the closing entries simply transfer the balance in the Cost of Goods Sold account to Income Summary. By comparison, under the periodic system, all of the cost elements related to inventories are transferred to Income Summary. Of course, Sales must be closed under both inventory systems. In Illustration 9–4, both inventory systems result in the same amounts of sales, cost of goods sold, and end-of-period merchandise inventory.

Subsidiary Inventory Records—Perpetual System

When a company sells more than one product and uses the perpetual inventory system, the Merchandise Inventory account serves as a controlling account to a subsidiary Merchandise Inventory Ledger. This ledger contains a separate record for each product in stock. This ledger may be computerized or kept on a manual basis. In either case, the record for each product shows the number of units and cost of each purchase, the number of units and cost of each sale, and the resulting balance of product on hand.

Illustration 9–5 shows an example of a subsidiary merchandise inventory record. This particular record is for Product Z, which is stored in Bin 8 of the stockroom. In this case, the record also shows the company's policy of maintaining no more than 25 or no less than 5 units of Product Z on hand.

ILLUSTRATION 9–6

Weighted Average										

Item ____*Product Z*____   Location in stockroom ____*Bin 8*____

Maximum ____*25*____   Minimum ____*5*____

	Received			Sold			Balance		
Date	Units	Cost	Total	Units	Cost	Total	Units	Cost	Total
Jan.1							*10*	*10.00*	*100.00*
Jan. 5				*5*	*10.00*	*50.00*	*5*	*10.00*	*50.00*
Jan. 8	*20*	*10.50*	*210.00*				*25*	*10.40*	*260.00*
Jan. 10				*3*	*10.40*	*31.20*	*22*	*10.40*	*228.80*

In Illustration 9–5, note that the beginning inventory consisted of 10 units that cost $10 each. The first transaction occurred on January 5 and was a sale of 5 units at $17. Next, 20 units were purchased on January 8 at a cost of $10.50 per unit. And on January 10, 3 units were sold. Observe that these 3 units were costed out at $10 per unit. This indicates that a first-in, first-out basis is being assumed for this product.

First-In, First-Out— Perpetual Inventory System

The entries to record the sale in the General Journal, assuming a selling price of $15 per unit, are the following:

Jan.	10	Cash (or Accounts Receivable)	45.00	
		Sales		45.00
	10	Cost of Goods Sold	30.00	
		Merchandise Inventory.		30.00
		3 × $10.00 = $30.00		

Perpetual inventories also may be kept on a weighted-average basis. When this is done, each purchase creates a new weighted-average cost. Each sale is costed at the latest weighted-average cost. For example, if weighted average was used for Product Z, the subsidiary merchandise inventory record would appear as in Illustration 9–6.

Weighted Average— Perpetual Inventory System

Compare Illustration 9–6 (weighted average) with Illustration 9–5 (FIFO). Observe that in both illustrations, the sale of five units on January 5 is recorded the same way. The cost of these units came from the 10 units in the beginning inventory. However, the sale of three units on January 10 is recorded differently under the two methods. Assuming weighted average, as in Illustration 9–6, the January 10 sale is "costed out" at the new average cost of $10.40 per unit. This results in an inventory cost of $228.80, for the 22 units remaining.

The General Journal entries to record the January 10 sale, assuming weighted average, are as follows:

Jan.	10	Cash (or Accounts Receivable)	45.00	
		Sales		45.00
	10	Cost of Goods Sold	31.20	
		Merchandise Inventory.		31.20
		3 × $10.40 = $31.20		

The Difference between Weighted Average (Perpetual) and Weighted Average (Periodic)

Under the weighted-average (periodic) system, the cost amount is calculated as the average cost of all the units on hand or purchased during the period. Thus, the cost per unit used is the same for the sales on January 3 and January 10. Under the weighted-average (perpetual) system, a purchase was made on January 8 which necessitated the calculation of a revised average cost. It is this revised cost which was used for the sale on January 10.

A comparison of weighted average (perpetual) and weighted average (periodic) is summarized as follows:

	Wtd. Avg. (Perpetual)	Wtd. Avg. (Periodic)
Cost of goods sold:		
January 5 sale	5 × $10.00 = $ 50.00	
January 10 sale	3 × $10.40 = 31.20	
Total	$ 81.20	8 × $10.33* = $ 82.67
Ending inventory:		
Total	22 × $10.40 = $228.80	22 × $10.33 = $227.33
Total goods available	$310.00	$310.00

* ($100.00 + $210.00) ÷ (10 + 20) = $10.3333

In addition to FIFO and weighted average, perpetual inventory systems can be designed to accomodate a LIFO cost flow assumption. However, illustration of this alternative is deferred to a later course.

The Retail Method of Estimating Inventories

Good management requires that income statements be prepared more often than once each year, and inventory information is necessary each time an income statement is prepared. However, taking a physical inventory in a retail store is both time-consuming and expensive. Therefore, some retailers use the so-called **retail inventory method** to estimate inventories without stopping to take a physical count of inventory. Many companies use the retail inventory method to estimate inventory for their monthly or quarterly statements; then they take a physical inventory at the end of each year. The monthly or quarterly statements are called **interim statements** because they are prepared between the regular year-end statements. Other companies also use the retail inventory method to prepare the year-end statements. However, all companies must take a physical inventory at least once each year to correct any errors or shortages.

LO 6 Estimate an inventory by the retail method and by the gross profit method.

Estimating an Ending Inventory by the Retail Method

When the retail method is used to estimate an inventory, the company's records must show the amount of inventory it had at the beginning of the period both at *cost* and at *retail*. You already know what is meant by the cost of an inventory. The retail amount of an inventory simply means the dollar amount of the inventory at the marked selling prices of the inventory items.

In addition to the beginning inventory, the accounting records must also show the amount of goods purchased during the period both at cost and at retail. Also, the records must show the amount of net sales at retail. This is the balance of the Sales account less returns and discounts. With this information, you estimate the ending inventory as follows:

Step 1: Compute the amount of goods available for sale during the period both at cost and at retail.

Step 2: Divide the goods available at cost by the goods available at retail to obtain a **retail method cost ratio.**

Step 3: Deduct sales (at retail) from goods available for sale (at retail) to determine the ending inventory at retail.

Step 4: Multiply the ending inventory at retail by the cost ratio to reduce the inventory to a cost basis.

Illustration 9–7 shows these calculations.

This is the essence of Illustration 9–7: (1) The company had $100,000 of goods (at marked selling prices) for sale during the period; (2) these goods cost 60% of the $100,000 total amount at which they were marked for sale; (3) the company's records (its Sales account) showed that $70,000 of these goods were sold, leaving $30,000 (retail value) of merchandise unsold and presumably in the ending inventory; (4) since cost in this store is 60% of retail, the estimated cost of this ending inventory is $18,000.

An ending inventory calculated as in Illustration 9–7 is an estimate arrived at by deducting sales (goods sold) from goods available for sale. As we said before, this method may be used for interim statements or even for year-end statements. Nonetheless, a store must take a physical count of the inventory at least once each year to correct any errors or shortages.

Using the Retail Method to Reduce a Physical Inventory to Cost

In retail stores, items for sale normally have price tags that show selling prices. So, when a store takes a physical inventory, it commonly takes the inventory at the marked selling prices of the items on hand. It then reduces the dollar total of this inventory to a cost basis by applying its cost ratio. It does this

ILLUSTRATION 9–7

Calculating the Ending Inventory Cost by the Retail Method		
	At Cost	At Retail
(Step 1) Goods available for sale:		
Beginning inventory	$20,500	$ 34,500
Net purchases	39,500	65,500
Goods available for sale	$60,000	$100,000
(Step 2) Cost ratio: ($60,000/$100,000) × 100 = 60%		
(Step 3) Deduct sales at retail		70,000
Ending inventory at retail		$ 30,000
(Step 4) Ending inventory at cost ($30,000 × 60%) . .	$18,000	

because the selling prices are readily available and the application of the cost ratio eliminates the need to look up the invoice price of each item on hand.

For example, assume that the company in Illustration 9–7 estimates its inventory by the retail method and takes a physical inventory at the marked selling prices of the inventoried goods. Assume further that the total retail amount of this physical inventory is $29,600. Under these assumptions, the company may calculate the cost for this inventory, without having to look up the cost of each item on hand, simply by applying its cost ratio to the $29,600 inventory total as follows:

$$\$29,600 \times 60\% = \$17,760$$

The $17,760 cost figure for this company's ending physical inventory is a satisfactory figure for year-end statement purposes. It is also acceptable for income tax purposes.

Inventory Shortage

An inventory determined as in Illustration 9–7 is an estimate of the amount of goods on hand. Since it is arrived at by deducting sales from goods for sale, it does not reveal any shortages due to breakage, loss, or theft. However, you can estimate the amount of such shortages by comparing the inventory as calculated in Illustration 9–7 with the amount that results from taking a physical inventory.

For example, in Illustration 9–7, we estimated that the ending inventory at retail was $30,000. We then assumed that this same company took a physical inventory and counted only $29,600 of merchandise on hand (at retail). Therefore, the company must have had an inventory shortage at retail of $30,000 − $29,600 = $400. Stated in terms of cost, the shortage is $400 × 60% = $240.

Markups and Markdowns

The calculation of a cost ratio is often not as simple as that shown in Illustration 9–7. It is not simple because, after merchandise is purchased and marked at retail prices, a store may decide to change the retail prices by marking the

ILLUSTRATION 9–8

The Effect of Markups and Markdowns on the Retail Method		
	At Cost	**At Retail**
Goods available for sale:		
Beginning inventory	$18,000	$27,800
Net purchases	34,000	50,700
Additional markups.	———	1,500
Goods available for sale	$52,000	$80,000
Cost ratio: ($52,000/$80,000) × 100 = 65%		
Sales at retail		$54,000
Markdowns.		2,000
Total sales and markdowns		$56,000
Ending inventory at retail ($80,000 less $56,000) . .		$24,000
Ending inventory at cost ($24,000 × 65%)	$15,600	

goods up or down. When goods are first purchased and marked at selling price, the amount or percentage by which the marked selling prices exceed cost is called a **normal markup**. It is also called a **markon**. For example, if a store's normal markup is 50% on cost and it applies this markup to an item that cost $10, it will mark the item for sale at $15. Normal markups appear in the calculation of a store's cost ratio as the difference between net purchases at cost and at retail.

After goods are first priced to sell at the normal markup, if the prices are increased, the amount of the additional price increases are called **markups**. And if selling prices are decreased, the amounts of the decreases are called **markdowns**. Stores may add markups to the price of goods because the quality or style of the goods make them especially attractive to customers. Goods often are marked down for a clearance sale or whenever the goods are moving slowly.

When using the retail inventory method, the store must keep a record of additional markups and markdowns. This information is used to calculate the ending inventory as shown in Illustration 9–8.

In Illustration 9–8, notice that the store's $80,000 of goods available for sale at retail were reduced $54,000 by sales and $2,000 by markdowns, a total of $56,000. To understand the markdowns, visualize this effect of a markdown. The store had an item for sale during the period at $25. The item did not sell, so the manager marked its price down from $25 to $20. By this act, the retail amount of goods for sale in the store was reduced by $5. The total of such markdowns during the year amounted to $2,000.

In the calculations of Illustration 9–8, note that the estimated ending inventory at retail is $24,000. Therefore, since cost is 65% of retail, the ending inventory at cost is $15,600.

Observe in Illustration 9–8 that markups enter into the calculation of the cost ratio but markdowns do not. Why are markdowns excluded from the cost ratio calculation? The reason for this is that a more conservative figure for the ending inventory results, a figure that approaches "the lower of cost or market." Further discussion of this version of the retail inventory method is reserved for a more advanced accounting course.

Gross Profit Method of Estimating Inventories

Sometimes, a business that does not use a perpetual inventory system or the retail method may need to estimate the cost of its inventory. For example, if a fire destroys the inventory or a burglary results in the theft of the inventory, the business must estimate the inventory so that it can file a claim with its insurance company. In cases such as this, the cost of the inventory can be estimated by the **gross profit method.** With this method, a business's historical relationship between cost of goods sold and sales is applied to sales of the current period as a way of estimating cost of goods sold during the current period. Then cost of goods sold is subtracted from the cost of goods available for sale to get the estimated cost of the ending inventory.

To use the gross profit method, several items of accounting information must be available. This includes information about the normal gross profit margin or rate, the cost of the beginning inventory, the cost of net purchases, transportation-in, and the amount of sales and sales returns.

For example, assume that the inventory of a company was totally destroyed by a fire on March 27, 1993. The company's average gross profit rate during the past five years has been 30% of net sales. On the date of the fire, the company's accounts showed the following balances:

Sales	$31,500
Sales returns	1,500
Inventory, January 1, 1993	12,000
Net purchases.	20,000
Transportation-in	500

With this information, the gross profit method may be used to estimate the company's inventory loss. To apply the gross profit method, the first step is to recognize that whatever portion of each dollar of net sales was gross profit, the remaining portion was cost of goods sold. Thus, if the company's gross profit rate averages 30%, then 30% of each net sales dollar was gross profit, and 70% was cost of goods sold. Illustration 9–9 shows how the 70% is used to estimate the inventory that was lost.

To understand Illustration 9–9, recall that an ending inventory is normally subtracted from goods available for sale to determine the cost of goods sold. Then observe in Illustration 9–9 that the opposite subtraction is made. Estimated cost of goods sold is subtracted from goods available for sale to determine the estimated ending inventory.

As we mentioned, the gross profit method is often used to estimate the amount of an insurance claim. The method is also used by accountants to see if an inventory amount determined by management's physical count of the items on hand is reasonable. In addition, the method can be used to estimate the inventory value for interim financial statements when the retail inventory method is not being used.

ILLUSTRATION 9–9

The Gross Profit Method of Estimating Inventory		
Goods available for sale:		
Inventory, January 1, 1993.		$ 12,000
Net purchases	$20,000	
Add transportation-in	500	20,500
Goods available for sale		$ 32,500
Less estimated cost of goods sold:		
Sales	$31,500	
Less sales returns	(1,500)	
Net sales	$30,000	
Estimated cost of goods sold (70% × $30,000) . . .		(21,000)
Estimated March 27 inventory and inventory loss . .		$ 11,500

LO 1. The allocation of the cost of goods available for sale between cost of goods sold and ending inventory is an accounting application of the *matching principle*. Merchandise inventory should include all goods that are owned by the business and held for resale. This includes items the business has placed on consignment with other parties but excludes items that the business has taken on consignment from other parties. The cost of merchandise includes not only the invoice price less any discounts but also any additional or incidental costs that were incurred to put the merchandise into place and condition for sale.

LO 2. When specific invoice prices are used to price an inventory, each item in the inventory is identified and the cost of the item is determined by referring to the item's purchase invoice. With weighted-average cost, the total cost of the beginning inventory and of purchases is divided by the total number of units available to determine the weighted-average cost per unit. Multiplying this cost by the number of units in the ending inventory yields the cost of the inventory. FIFO prices the ending inventory based on the assumption that the first units purchased are the first units sold. LIFO is based on the assumption that the last units purchased are the first units sold. All of these methods are acceptable.

LO 3. When lower of cost or market is applied to merchandise inventory, market may mean either net realizable value or replacement cost. But market is never higher than net realizable value and never lower than net realizable value minus a normal profit. Lower of cost or market may be applied separately to each product or to the merchandise inventory as a whole.

LO 4. When the periodic inventory system is used, an error in counting the ending inventory affects assets (inventory), net income (cost of goods sold), and owner's equity. Since the ending inventory is the beginning inventory of the next period, an error at the end of one period affects the cost of goods sold and the net income of the next period. These next period effects offset the financial statement effects in the previous period.

Summary of the Chapter in Terms of Learning Objectives

LO 5. Under a perpetual inventory system, purchases and purchases returns are recorded in the Merchandise Inventory account. At the time sales are recorded, the cost of goods sold is credited to Merchandise Inventory. As a result, the Merchandise Inventory is kept up to date throughout the accounting period.

LO 6. When the retail method is used, sales are subtracted from the retail amount of goods available for sale to determine the ending inventory at retail. This is multiplied by the cost ratio to reduce the inventory amount to cost. To calculate the cost ratio, divide the cost of goods available by the retail value of goods available (including markups but excluding markdowns).

With the gross profit method, multiply sales by (1 − the gross profit rate) to estimate cost of goods sold. Then subtract the answer from the cost of goods available for sale to estimate the cost of the ending inventory.

Demonstration Problem

Tale Company uses a periodic inventory system and had the following beginning inventory and purchases during 1993:

Date		Item X Units	Item X Unit Cost	Item Y Units	Item Y Unit Cost
Jan. 1	Inventory	400	$14	200	$11
Mar. 10	Purchase	200	15	300	12
May 9	Purchase	300	16		
June 17	Purchase			450	18
Sept. 22	Purchase	250	20		
Nov. 28	Purchase	100	21	110	17

At December 31, 1993, there were 550 units of X and 320 units of Y on hand.

Required

1. Using the preceding information, apply FIFO inventory pricing and calculate the cost of goods available for sale in 1993, the ending inventory, and the cost of goods sold for each item and for both items combined.

2. In preparing the financial statements for 1993, the bookkeeper was instructed to use FIFO but failed to do so and computed the cost of goods sold according to LIFO. Determine the size of the misstatement of 1993's income from this error. Also determine the effect of the error on the 1994 income. Assume no income taxes.

3. Assume the following additional facts, and use the retail method to estimate the lower of cost or market of the ending inventory:

Retail value of the beginning inventory . .	$13,051
Retail value of purchases	41,381
Additional markups (at retail)	3,600
Sales	33,600
Markdowns	4,432

Planning the Solution

▪ For each product, multiply the units of each purchase and the beginning inventory by the appropriate unit costs to determine the total costs. Then calculate the cost of goods available for sale.

▪ For FIFO, calculate the ending inventory by multiplying the units on hand by the unit costs of the latest purchases. Then subtract the total ending inventory from the cost of goods available for sale.

▪ For LIFO, calculate the ending inventory by multiplying the units on hand by the unit costs of the beginning inventory and the earliest purchases. Then subtract the total ending inventory from the cost of goods available for sale.

▪ Compare the ending 1993 inventory amounts under FIFO and LIFO to determine the misstatement of 1993 income that resulted from using LIFO. The 1994 and 1993 errors are equal in amount but have opposite effects.

▪ Calculate the retail amount of goods available for sale including markups but excluding markdowns. Then compare the cost of goods available with the retail amount to determine the cost ratio.

▪ Subtract sales and markdowns from the retail amount of goods available for sale to determine the ending inventory at retail. Then determine the lower of cost or market of ending inventory by applying the cost ratio to the ending inventory at retail.

1. **FIFO basis:**

Item X

Jan. 1 inventory (400 @ $14)		$ 5,600
Purchases:		
Mar. 10 purchase (200 @ $15)	$3,000	
May 9 purchase (300 @ $16)	4,800	
Sept. 22 purchase (250 @ $20)	5,000	
Nov. 28 purchase (100 @ $21)	2,100	14,900
Cost of goods available for sale.		$20,500
Ending inventory at FIFO cost:		
Nov. 28 purchase (100 @ $21)	$2,100	
Sept. 22 purchase (250 @ $20)	5,000	
May 9 purchase (200 @ $16)	3,200	
Ending inventory.		10,300
Cost of goods sold		$10,200

Item Y

Jan. 1 inventory (200 @ $11)		$ 2,200
Purchases:		
Mar. 10 purchase (300 @ $12)	$3,600	
June 17 purchase (450 @ $18)	8,100	
Nov. 28 purchase (110 @ $17)	1,870	13,570
Cost of goods available for sale.		$15,770
Ending inventory at FIFO cost:		
Nov. 28 purchase (110 @ $17)	$1,870	
June 17 purchase (210 @ $18)	3,780	
Ending inventory.		5,650
Cost of goods sold		$10,120

Combined

Cost of goods available ($20,500 + $15,770) . .	$36,270
Cost of ending inventory ($10,300 + $5,650) . .	15,950
Cost of goods sold ($10,200 + $10,120).	$20,320

2. LIFO basis:

Item X

Cost of goods available for sale.		$20,500
Ending inventory at LIFO cost:		
Jan. 1 inventory (400 @ $14)	$5,600	
Mar. 10 purchase (150 @ $15)	2,250	
LIFO cost of ending inventory		7,850
Cost of goods sold		$12,650

Item Y

Cost of goods available for sale.		$15,770
Ending inventory at LIFO cost:		
Jan. 1 inventory (200 @ $11)	$2,200	
Mar. 10 purchase (120 @ $12)	1,440	
LIFO cost of ending inventory		3,640
Cost of goods sold		$12,130

Combined

Cost of goods available ($20,500 + $15,770) . .	$36,270
Cost of ending inventory ($7,850 + $3,640). . .	11,490
Cost of goods sold	$24,780

If LIFO is mistakenly used when FIFO should have been used, cost of goods sold in 1993 would be overstated by $4,460, which is the difference between the FIFO and LIFO amounts of ending inventory. Income would be understated in 1993 by $4,460. In 1994, income would be overstated by $4,460 because of the understatement of the beginning inventory.

3. Retail method of estimating inventory:

	At Cost	At Retail
Goods available for sale:		
Beginning inventory ($5,600 + $2,200 = $7,800) . .	$ 7,800	$13,051
Purchases ($14,900 + $13,570 = $28,470).	28,470	41,381
Markups		3,600
Goods available for sale.	$36,270	$58,032
Cost ratio: ($36,270/$58,032) × 100 = 62.5%		
Sales at retail		$33,600
Markdowns		4,432
Total sales and markdowns		$38,032
Ending inventory at retail ($58,032 − $38,032)		$20,000
Ending inventory at cost ($20,000 × 62.5%).	$12,500	

Glossary

LO 7 Define or explain the words and phrases listed in the chapter glossary.

Conservatism principle the accounting principle that guides accountants to select the less optimistic estimate when two estimates of amounts to be received or paid are about equally likely. p. 500

Consignee one who receives and holds goods owned by another party for the purpose of selling the goods for the owner. p. 491

Consignor an owner of goods who ships them to another party who will then sell the goods for the owner. p. 491

Consistency principle the accounting requirement that a company use the same accounting methods period after period so that the financial statements of succeeding periods will be comparable. p. 497

First-in, first-out (FIFO) inventory pricing the pricing of an inventory and cost of goods sold under the assumption that the first items received were the first items sold. p. 494

Gross profit inventory method a procedure for estimating an ending inventory in which the past gross profit rate is used to estimate cost of goods sold, which is then subtracted from the cost of goods available for sale to determine the estimated ending inventory. p. 510

Interim statements monthly or quarterly financial statements prepared in between the regular year-end statements. p. 507

Inventory ticket a form attached to the counted items in the process of taking a physical inventory. p. 492

Last-in, first-out (LIFO) inventory pricing the pricing of an inventory and cost of goods sold under the assumption that the last items received were the first items sold. p. 495

Markdown a reduction in the marked selling price of merchandise. p. 509

Markon the normal amount or percentage of cost that is added to the cost of merchandise to arrive at its selling price. p. 509

Markup an increase in the sales price of merchandise above the normal markon given to the goods. p. 509

Net realizable value the expected sales price of an item less any additional costs to sell. p. 491

Normal markup another name for *markon*. p. 509

Retail inventory method a method for estimating an ending inventory based on the ratio of the amount of goods for sale at cost to the amount of goods for sale at marked selling prices. p. 506

Retail method cost ratio the ratio of goods available for sale at cost to goods available for sale at retail prices. p. 507

Specific invoice inventory pricing the pricing of an inventory where the purchase invoice of each item in the ending inventory is identified and used to determine the cost assigned to the inventory. p. 493

Weighted-average inventory pricing an inventory pricing system in which the unit prices of the beginning inventory and of each purchase are weighted by the number of units in the beginning inventory and each purchase. The total of these amounts is then divided by the total number of units available for sale to find the unit cost of the ending inventory and of the units that were sold. p. 494

Synonymous Terms

Markon normal markup.

Specific invoice inventory pricing specific identification method.

Objective Review

Answers to the following questions are listed at the end of this chapter. Be sure that you decide which is the one best answer to each question *before* you check the answers.

LO 1 Kramer Gallery purchased an original painting for $11,400. Additional costs incurred in obtaining and selling the artwork included $130 for transportation-in, $150 for import duties, $100 for insurance during shipment, $180 for advertising costs, $400 for framing, and $800 for sales commissions. In calculating the cost of inventory, what total cost should be assigned to the painting?

a. $11,400.

b. $11,530.

c. $11,780.

d. $12,180.

e. $13,160.

LO 2 The following data relate to a single inventory item for Montgomery Company:

Date		Units	Unit Cost
May 1	Beginning inventory	110	$5
2	Purchase	30	6
17	Sale.	40	
19	Purchase	25	4
26	Sale.	20	

Using a perpetual inventory system and costing inventory by FIFO, the ending inventory is

a. $260.

b. $520.

c. $525.

d. $530.

e. $830.

LO 3 A company's ending inventory includes the following items:

Product	Units on Hand	Unit Cost	Market Value per Unit
A	20	$ 6	$ 5
B	40	9	8
C	10	12	15

Applied separately to each product, the inventory's lower of cost or market amount is

a. $520.

b. $540.

c. $570.

d. $600.

e. None of the above.

LO 4 Falk Company maintains its inventory records on a periodic basis. In making the physical count of inventory at 1992 year-end, an error was made that overstated the 1992 ending inventory by $10,000. What impact, if any, will this error have on cost of goods sold in 1992 and 1993?

a. 1992 overstated by $10,000; 1993 understated by $10,000.

b. 1992 understated by $10,000; 1993 overstated by $10,000.

c. 1992 overstated by $10,000; no impact on 1993.

d. 1992 understated by $10,000; no impact on 1993.

e. 1992 understated by $10,000; no impact on 1993 cost of goods sold, but 1993 ending inventory will be overstated by $10,000.

LO 5 With a perpetual inventory system:

a. The Merchandise Inventory account balance shows the amount of merchandise on hand.

b. Subsidiary inventory records are maintained for each type of product.

c. A sale of merchandise requires two entries, one to record the revenue and one to record the cost of goods sold.

d. A separate Cost of Goods Sold account is used.

e. All of the above are correct.

LO 6 The following data relate to Taylor Company's inventory during the year:

	Cost	Retail
Beginning inventory	$324,000	$530,000
Purchases	204,000	343,000
Purchases returns	3,600	8,000
Markups		9,000
Markdowns.		75,000
Sales		320,000

Using the retail method, the estimated cost of the ending inventory is

a. $129,400.

b. $287,400.

c. $290,370.

d. $314,368.

e. $479,000.

LO 7 The normal amount or percentage of cost that is added to the cost of merchandise to arrive at its selling price is a:

a. Markdown.

b. Profit.

c. Markup.

d. Markon.

e. Net markup.

Questions for Class Discussion

1. With respect to periodic inventory systems, it has been said that cost of goods sold and ending inventory are opposite sides of the same coin. What is meant by this?

2. If Fanshawe Company is the consignee and Johnson Company is the consignor with respect to goods being offered for sale, the goods should be included in the inventory of which company?

3. Why are incidental costs often ignored in pricing an inventory? Under what accounting principle is this permitted?

4. Give the meanings of the following when applied to inventory: (*a*) FIFO, (*b*) LIFO, (*c*) cost, and (*d*) perpetual inventory.

5. If prices are rising, will the LIFO or the FIFO method of inventory valuation result in the higher gross profit?

6. If prices are falling, will the LIFO or the FIFO method of inventory valuation result in the lower cost of goods sold?

7. Does the accounting principle of consistency preclude any changes from one accounting method to another?

8. What effect does the full-disclosure principle have if a company changes from one acceptable accounting method to another?

9. If inventory errors under a periodic inventory system correct themselves, why be concerned when such errors are made?

10. What guidance for accountants is provided by the principle of conservatism?

11. What accounts are used in a periodic inventory system but not in a perpetual inventory system?

12. Assuming a last-in, first-out cost flow, why do perpetual inventory systems and periodic inventory systems result in different amounts of cost of goods sold and ending inventory?

13. In deciding whether to reduce an item of merchandise to the lower of cost or market, what is the importance of the item's net realizable value?

14. Give the meanings of the following when applied in the retail method of estimating an inventory: (*a*) pricing inventory at retail, (*b*) cost ratio, (*c*) normal markup, (*d*) markon, (*e*) additional markup, and (*f*) markdown.

15. Refer to the financial statements of Bombardier Inc. in Appendix I. What method was used to determine the value of inventories?

Mini Discussion Cases

Case 9–1

Your friend is the controller of Elmira Manufacturing Company and has come to you for some advice about the valuation of the finished goods inventory. The inventory is currently listed on the books of the company at its cost of $105,000. The controller has recently learned that the goods could have been purchased from an overseas supplier for $88,700. The controller is unsure as to whether she should price the inventory on the year-end financial statements, which are to be prepared in two weeks, at the higher or lower value. She says that if she prices them at the lower value, she will violate both the cost and the consistency principles.

Required

Advise your friend and give the reasons behind your advice.

Case 9–2

In November of 1993 the accountant for Burlington Company discovered that the December 31, 1992, inventory had been misstated in the 1992 financial statements. The inventory should have been $68,000 but had been entered on the statements as $86,000.

His assistant indicated that the company would have to correct and restate the 1992 statements when preparing the statements for the 1993 year-end. The accountant said that no corrections will be necessary since the error will have corrected itself by the end of 1993 and that the Retained Earnings figure will be correct as of December 31, 1993.

Required

Comment on the positions taken by the accountant and his assistant. What do you propose should be done in preparing the financial statements for 1993? Why?

Exercises

Barnes Company began a year and purchased merchandise as follows:

Jan. 1	Beginning inventory	40 units @ $30.00 =	$ 1,200
Mar. 5	Purchased	200 units @ $28.00 =	5,600
July 10	Purchased	80 units @ $25.00 =	2,000
Oct. 2	Purchased	160 units @ $23.00 =	3,680
Dec. 22	Purchased	120 units @ $20.00 =	2,400
	Total	600 units	$14,880

Exercise 9–1
Alternative cost flow assumptions, periodic inventory system
(LO 2)

Required

The company uses a periodic inventory system, and the ending inventory consists of 150 units, 50 from each of the last three purchases. Determine the share of the $14,880 cost of the units for sale that should be assigned to the ending inventory and to goods sold under each of the following: (*a*) costs are assigned on the basis of specific invoice prices, (*b*) costs are assigned on a weighted-average cost basis, (*c*) costs are assigned on the basis of FIFO, and (*d*) costs are assigned on the basis of LIFO. Which method provides the highest and lowest net income?

Holt Company began a year and purchased merchandise as follows:

Jan. 1	Beginning inventory	40 units @ $20.00 =	$ 800
Mar. 5	Purchased	200 units @ $23.00 =	4,600
July 10	Purchased	80 units @ $25.00 =	2,000
Oct. 2	Purchased	160 units @ $28.00 =	4,480
Dec. 22	Purchased	120 units @ $30.00 =	3,600
	Total	600 units	$15,480

Exercise 9–2
Alternative cost flow assumptions, periodic inventory system
(LO 2)

Required

The company uses a periodic inventory system, and the ending inventory consists of 150 units, 50 from each of the last three purchases. Determine the share of the $15,480 cost of the units for sale that should be assigned to the ending inventory and to goods sold under each of the following: (*a*) costs are assigned on the basis of specific invoice prices, (*b*) costs are assigned on a weighted-average cost basis, (*c*) costs are assigned on the basis of FIFO, and (*d*) costs are assigned on the basis of LIFO. Which method provides the highest and lowest net income?

Exercise 9–3
Lower of cost or market
(LO 3)

Tucker Company's ending inventory includes the following items:

Product	Units on Hand	Unit Cost	Replacement Cost per Unit
A	20	$15	$17
B	25	24	20
C	30	13	12
D	22	10	10

After evaluating each product's selling price and normal profit margin, replacement cost is found to be the best measure of market. Calculate lower of cost or market for the inventory (*a*) as a whole, and (*b*) applied separately to each product.

Exercise 9–4
Lower of cost or market
(LO 3)

Calculate the lower of cost or market for the inventory in each of the following independent cases:

1. Horn Company's inventory consists of 50 units of Product Y, all of which have been damaged. The company bought the inventory for $19 per unit. Replacement cost is $18 per unit. Expected sales price is $22 per unit, but this can be realized only if $5 additional cost per unit is paid.

2. Post Company's inventory consists of 100 units of Product Z which were purchased for $35 per unit. Replacement cost is $22 per unit. Expected sales price is $39 per unit, and a normal profit margin based on this price is $12.

Exercise 9–5
Analysis of inventory
errors
(LO 4)

Reynolds Company had $145,000 of sales during each of three consecutive years, and it purchased merchandise costing $100,000 during each of the years. It also maintained a $35,000 inventory from the beginning to the end of the three-year period. However, in accounting under a periodic inventory system, it made an error at the end of year 1 that caused its ending year 1 inventory to appear on its statements at $30,000, rather than the correct $35,000.

Required

1. State the actual amount of the company's gross profit in each of the years.

2. Prepare a comparative income statement like Illustration 9–3 to show the effect of this error on the company's cost of goods sold and gross profit in year 1, year 2, and year 3.

Exercise 9–6
Perpetual inventory
system—FIFO cost flow
(LO 5)

In its beginning inventory on January 1, 1993, Zebra Company had 40 units of merchandise that had cost $4 per unit. Prepare General Journal entries for Zebra Company to record the following transactions during 1993, assuming a perpetual inventory system and a first-in, first-out cost flow.

June 5   Purchased on credit 150 units of merchandise at $5.00 per unit.

      12   Returned 30 defective units from the June 5 purchase to the supplier.

Oct. 2   Purchased for cash 90 units of merchandise at $4.25 per unit.

Nov. 10   Sold 100 units of merchandise for cash at a price of $6.25 per unit.

Dec. 31   Prepare entries to close the revenue and expense accounts to Income Summary.

Exercise 9–7
Perpetual inventory
system—LIFO cost flow
(LO 5)

In its January 1, 1993, inventory, Softy Company had 45 units of merchandise that had cost $3 per unit. Prepare General Journal entries for Softy Company to record the following transactions during 1993, assuming a perpetual inventory system and a last-in, first-out cost flow.

Feb. 15 Purchased on credit 70 units of merchandise at $3.50 per unit.

Apr. 4 Sold 55 units of merchandise for cash at $6.00 per unit.

July 12 Purchased for cash 50 units of merchandise at $4.00 per unit.

Oct. 23 Sold 60 units of merchandise for cash at a price of $6.25 per unit.

Dec. 31 Prepare entries to close the revenue and expense accounts to Income Summary.

During an accounting period, Baker sold $340,000 of merchandise at marked retail prices. At the period end, the following information was available from its records:

	At Cost	At Retail
Beginning inventory	$ 70,000	$125,000
Net purchases	195,100	345,000
Additional markups		12,000
Markdowns.		9,800

Use the retail method to estimate the store's ending inventory at cost.

Exercise 9–8
Estimating ending inventory—retail inventory method
(LO 6)

Assume that in addition to estimating its ending inventory by the retail method, Baker Company of Exercise 9–8 also took a physical inventory at the marked selling prices of the inventory items. Assume further that the total of this physical inventory at marked selling prices was $127,600. Then (*a*) determine the amount of this inventory at cost and (*b*) determine the store's inventory shrinkage from breakage, theft, or other cause at retail and at cost.

Exercise 9–9
Reducing physical inventory to cost— retail method
(LO 6)

On January 1, a store had a $72,000 inventory at cost. During the first quarter of the year, it purchased $245,000 of merchandise, returned $3,500, and paid freight charges on purchased merchandise totaling $8,500. During the past several years, the store's gross profit on sales has averaged 30%. Under the assumption the company had $305,000 of sales during the first quarter of the year, use the gross profit method to estimate its inventory at the end of the first quarter.

Exercise 9–10
Estimating ending inventory—gross profit method
(LO 6)

Problems

Smith Company began a year with 1,000 units of Product X in its inventory that cost $60 each, and it made successive purchases of the product as follows:

Feb. 11	1,750 units @ $65 each
May 25	2,000 units @ $70 each
Oct. 4	1,500 units @ $75 each
Dec. 9	1,750 units @ $70 each

Problem 9–1
Alternative cost flows— periodic system
(LO 2)

The company uses a periodic inventory system. On December 31, a physical count disclosed that 2,500 units of Product X remained in inventory.

Required

1. Prepare a calculation showing the number and total cost of the units available for sale during the year.

2. Prepare calculations showing the amounts that should be assigned to the ending inventory and to cost of goods sold assuming (*a*) a FIFO basis, (*b*) a LIFO basis, and (*c*) a weighted-average cost basis. Round your calculation of the weighted-average cost per unit to three decimal places.

Problem 9–2
Income statement comparisons and cost flow assumptions
(LO 2)

Tyler Company sold 3,000 units of its product at $75 per unit during 1993. Incurring operating expenses of $12 per unit in selling the units, it began the year and made successive purchases of the product as follows:

January 1 beginning inventory	300 units costing $45.00 per unit
Purchases:	
February 20	500 units costing $48.00 per unit
May 14	900 units costing $48.50 per unit
August 29.	1,500 units costing $50.50 per unit
November 20.	250 units costing $52.00 per unit

Required

Prepare a comparative income statement for the company showing in adjacent columns the net incomes earned from the sale of the product assuming the company uses a periodic inventory system and prices its ending inventory on the basis of (*a*) FIFO, (*b*) LIFO, and (*c*) weighted-average cost. Round your calculation of the weighted-average cost per unit to three decimal places.

Problem 9–3
Lower of cost or market
(LO 3)

Case 1: In this case, an evaluation of the expected selling price and normal profit margin for each product shows that replacement cost is the best measure of market. The inventory includes:

Product	Units on Hand	Cost	Replacement Cost
A	550	$12	$10
B	900	20	17
C	975	25	30

Case 2: In this case, the inventories of Products D and E have been damaged. If $7 additional cost per unit is paid to repackage the Product D units, they can be sold for $75 per unit. The Product E units can be sold for $60 per unit after paying additional cleaning costs of $6 per unit. The inventory includes:

Product	Units on Hand	Cost	Replacement Cost
D	150	$72	$70
E	400	58	64

Case 3: In this case, Product F normally is sold for $30 per unit and has a profit margin of 30%. However, the expected selling price has fallen to $20 per unit. Product G normally is sold for $65 per unit and has a profit margin of 25%. However, the expected selling price of Product G has fallen to $60 per unit. The inventory includes:

Product	Units on Hand	Cost	Replacement Cost
F	300	$19	$17
G	150	48	41

Required

In each of these independent cases, calculate the lower of cost or market (*a*) for the inventory as a whole and (*b*) for the inventory applied separately to each product.

Mitchell Company keeps its inventory records on a periodic basis. The company's financial statements reported the following amounts:

Problem 9–4
Analysis of inventory errors
(LO 4)

Financial Statements for Year Ended December 31,

	1992	1993	1994
(a) Cost of goods sold	$ 65,000	$ 77,000	$ 70,000
(b) Net income	20,000	25,000	21,000
(c) Total current assets	105,000	115,000	100,000
(d) Owners' equity	117,000	130,000	112,000

In making the physical counts of inventory the following errors were made:

Inventory on December 31, 1992 . . . . Understated $6,000
Inventory on December 31, 1993 . . . . Overstated   3,000

Required

1. For each of the preceding financial statement items—(a), (b), (c), and (d)—prepare a schedule similar to the following and show the adjustments that would have been necessary to correct the reported amounts.

	1992	1993	1994
Cost of goods sold:			
Reported.	———	———	———
Adjustments: Dec. 31, 1992 error	———	———	———
Dec. 31, 1993 error	———	———	———
Corrected	———	———	———

2. What is the error in the aggregate net income for the three-year period that resulted from the inventory errors?

The Kramer Company sells a product called Speedcleaner and uses a perpetual inventory system to account for its merchandise. The beginning balance of Speedcleaner and transactions during April of this year were as follows:

Problem 9–5
Inventory records under FIFO and weighted-average—perpetual systems
(LO 5)

Apr. 1 Balance: 35 units costing $4 each.
3 Purchased 60 units costing $5 each.
9 Sold 27 units.
15 Sold 32 units.
18 Purchased 55 units costing $6 each.
22 Sold 19 units.
30 Sold 37 units.

Required

1. Under the assumption the business keeps its records on a FIFO basis, enter the beginning balance and the transactions on a subsidiary inventory record like the one in Illustration 9–5.
2. Under the assumption the business keeps its inventory records on a weighted-average basis, enter the beginning inventory and the transactions on a second subsidiary inventory record like the one in Illustration 9–6.
3. Assume the 37 units sold on April 30 were sold on credit to Russell Sayer at $11 each and prepare General Journal entries to record the sale on a FIFO basis.

Problem 9–6
Retail inventory method
(LO 6)

Hammond Company takes a year-end physical inventory at marked selling prices and uses the retail method to reduce the inventory total to a cost basis for statement purposes. It also uses the retail method to estimate the amount of inventory it should have at the end of a year, and by comparison, estimates any inventory shortage due to shoplifting or other causes. At the end of the year, its physical inventory at marked selling prices totaled $80,600, and the following information was available from its records:

	At Cost	At Retail
Beginning inventory	$ 40,400	$ 60,400
Purchases	287,560	435,700
Purchases returns	2,700	4,300
Additional markups		8,600
Markdowns.		3,700
Sales		416,570
Sales returns		3,980

Required

1. Use the retail method to estimate the store's year-end inventory at cost.

2. Use the retail method to reduce the store's year-end physical inventory to a cost basis.

3. Prepare a schedule showing the inventory shortage at cost and at retail.

Problem 9–7
Retail inventory method
(LO 6)

The records of Westwood Company provided the following information for the year ended December 31:

	At Cost	At Retail
January 1 beginning inventory	$ 52,150	$ 88,300
Purchases.	369,740	609,400
Purchases returns.	6,200	11,320
Additional markups.		6,420
Markdowns.		3,400
Sales		523,400
Sales returns		5,200

Required

1. Prepare an estimate of the company's year-end inventory by the retail method.

2. Under the assumption the company took a year-end physical inventory at marked selling prices that totaled $159,600, prepare a schedule showing the store's loss from theft or other cause at cost and at retail.

Problem 9–8
Gross profit method
(LO 6)

While opening the Stereo Store for business on the morning of June 15, the owner discovered that thieves had broken in and stolen the store's entire inventory. The following information for the period January 1 through June 14 was available:

January 1 merchandise inventory at cost	$210,500
Purchases	454,725
Purchases returns	3,775
Transportation-in	3,940
Sales	700,500
Sales returns	5,450

Required

Under the assumption the store had earned an average 28% gross profit on sales during the past five years, prepare a statement showing the estimated loss.

Brown Supply wants to prepare interim financial statements for the first quarter of 1993. The company uses a periodic inventory system but would like to avoid making a physical count of inventory. During the last five years, the company's gross profit rate has averaged 30%; the following information for the year's first quarter is available from its records:

January 1 beginning inventory	$225,500
Purchases.	435,800
Purchases returns.	5,750
Transportation-in	6,800
Sales	710,500
Sales returns	9,600

Required

Use the gross profit method to prepare an estimate of the company's March 31 inventory.

Part 1. Draton Company's inventory includes a product that cost $9 per unit. Replacement cost is $8, expected sales price is $12, additional costs to sell are $0, and the normal profit margin is 30%. Explain the reason why the inventory should not be reported on the balance sheet at less than $8.40 per unit.

Part 2. Flavour Company's inventory includes a damaged product that cost $16 per unit. Replacement cost is $15, expected sales price is $17, additional costs that must be incurred to sell the product are $3, and the normal profit margin is 20%. Explain the reason why the inventory should not be reported on the balance sheet at more than $14.

Review the facts about Smith Company presented in Problem 9–1 and notice that Smith uses a periodic inventory system. The facts of Problem 9–1 indicate that Smith Company had 8,000 units of product available for sale, had 2,500 units on hand at the end of the period, and, therefore, had sales of 5,500 units during the period. Now assume that the sale occurred as follows:

March 1	1,500 units
June 1	1,000 units
November 1	2,000 units
December 20	1,000 units

Required

1. Explain what effect, if any, these additional facts would have on the solution to requirement 2*a* and 2*b* of Problem 9–1.
2. Given the preceding information about the timing of sales, explain whether the Problem 9–1 solution to requirement 2*a* and 2*b* would provide the same answers under a perpetual inventory system as it does under a periodic inventory system.

Alternate Problems

Problem 9–1A
Alternative cost flows—
periodic system
(LO 2)

Northwood Company began a year with 550 units of Product A in its inventory that cost $80 each, and it made successive purchases of the product as follows:

Feb. 10	750 units @ $ 85 each
May 4	850 units @ $ 95 each
July 6	900 units @ $110 each
Oct. 30	950 units @ $120 each

The company uses a periodic inventory system. On December 31, a physical count disclosed that 1,000 units of Product A remained in inventory.

Required

1. Prepare a calculation showing the number and total cost of the units available for sale during the year.

2. Prepare calculations showing the amounts that should be assigned to the ending inventory and to cost of goods sold assuming (*a*) a FIFO basis, (*b*) a LIFO basis, and (*c*) a weighted-average cost basis. Round your calculation of the weighted-average cost per unit to three decimal places.

Problem 9–2A
Income statement
comparisons and cost
flow assumptions
(LO 2)

Fairfield Company sold 3,800 units of its product at $75 per unit during 1993. Incurring operating expenses of $20 per unit in selling the units, it began the year and made successive purchases of the product as follows:

January 1 beginning inventory	950 units costing $30.00 per unit
Purchases:	
February 10	700 units costing $33.00 per unit
May 15	1,100 units costing $35.00 per unit
August 4	1,600 units costing $40.00 per unit
October 23	850 units costing $42.00 per unit

Required

Prepare a comparative income statement for the company showing in adjacent columns the net incomes earned from the sale of the product assuming the company uses a periodic inventory system and prices its ending inventory on the basis of (*a*) FIFO, (*b*) LIFO, and (*c*) weighted-average cost. Round your calculation of the weighted-average cost per unit to three decimal places.

Problem 9–3A
Lower of cost or market
(LO 3)

Case 1: In this case, an evaluation of the expected selling price and normal profit margin for each product shows that replacement cost is the best measure of market. The inventory includes:

Product	Units on Hand	Cost	Replacement Cost
X	550	$70	$75
Y	420	65	60
Z	300	43	41

Case 2: In this case, the inventories of Products V and W have been damaged. If $10 additional cost per unit is paid to repackage the Product V units, they can be sold for $28 per unit. The Product W units can be sold for $45 per unit after paying additional cleaning costs of $7 per unit. The inventory includes:

Product	Units on Hand	Cost	Replacement Cost
V	620	$19	$20
W	1,100	47	40

Case 3: In this case, Product T normally is sold for $75 per unit and has a profit margin of 15%. However, the expected selling price has fallen to $60 per unit. Product U normally is sold for $25 per unit and has a profit margin of 20%. However, the expected selling price of Product T has fallen to $18 per unit. The inventory includes:

Product	Units on Hand	Cost	Replacement Cost
T	650	$52	$45
U	400	15	16

Required

In each of these independent cases, calculate the lower of cost or market (*a*) for the inventory as a whole and (*b*) for the inventory applied separately to each product.

Kerwood Company keeps its inventory records on a periodic basis. The following amounts were reported in the company's financial statements:

Problem 9–4A
Analysis of inventory errors
(LO 4)

	Financial Statements for Year Ended December 31,		
	1992	**1993**	**1994**
Cost of goods sold	$135,000	$140,000	$129,000
Net income........	115,000	139,000	121,000
Total current assets....	175,000	182,000	173,000
Owners' equity......	200,000	208,000	221,000

In making the physical counts of inventory, the following errors were made:

Inventory on December 31, 1992	Overstated $14,000
Inventory on December 31, 1993	Understated 17,000

Required

1. For each of the preceding financial statement items, prepare a schedule similar to the following and show the adjustments that would have been necessary to correct the reported amounts.

	1992	1993	1994
Cost of goods sold:			
Reported..............	———	———	———
Adjustments: Dec. 31, 1992 error	———	———	———
Dec. 31, 1993 error	———	———	———
Corrected	═══	═══	═══

2. What is the error in the aggregate net income for the three-year period that resulted from the inventory errors?

The Romero Company sells a product called GlueIt and uses a perpetual inventory system to account for its merchandise. The beginning balance of GlueIt and transactions during March of this year were as follows:

Problem 9–5A
Inventory records under FIFO and weighted-average—perpetual systems
(LO 5)

Mar. 1 Balance: 65 units costing $15 each.
    5 Purchased 120 units costing $18 each.

Mar. 11 Sold 55 units.
    19 Sold 45 units.
    23 Purchased 75 units costing $20 each.
    25 Sold 45 units.
    31 Sold 58 units.

Required

1. Under the assumption the concern keeps its records on a FIFO basis, enter the beginning balance and the transactions on a subsidiary inventory record like the one in Illustration 9–5.

2. Under the assumption the concern keeps its inventory records on a weighted-average basis, enter the beginning inventory and the transactions on a second subsidiary inventory record like the one in Illustration 9–6.

3. Assume the 58 units sold on March 31 were sold on credit to Mark Gibson at $40 each and prepare General Journal entries to record the sale on a FIFO basis.

Problem 9–6A
Retail inventory method
(LO 6)

Worldwide Products takes a year-end physical inventory at marked selling prices and uses the retail method to reduce the inventory total to a cost basis for statement purposes. It uses the retail method to estimate the amount of inventory it should have at the end of a year, and by comparison, determines any inventory shortage due to shoplifting or other causes. At the end of the year, its physical inventory at marked selling prices totaled $192,400, and the following information was available from its records:

	At Cost	At Retail
Beginning inventory	$105,250	$153,570
Purchases	519,270	769,800
Purchases returns	2,760	4,200
Additional markups		8,830
Markdowns.		10,500
Sales		725,000
Sales returns		8,600

Required

1. Use the retail method to estimate the store's year-end inventory at cost.

2. Use the retail method to reduce the company's year-end physical inventory to a cost basis.

3. Prepare a schedule showing the inventory shortage at cost and at retail.

Problem 9–7A
Retail inventory method
(LO 6)

The records of McCoy Company provided the following information for the year ended December 31:

	At Cost	At Retail
January 1 beginning inventory	$ 60,200	$100,660
Purchases.	318,560	524,200
Purchases returns.	2,470	4,200
Additional markups.		6,490
Markdowns.		4,700
Sales		376,290
Sales returns		3,800

Required

1. Prepare an estimate of the company's year-end inventory by the retail method.
2. Under the assumption the company took a year-end physical inventory at marked selling prices that totaled $227,300, prepare a schedule showing the store's loss from theft or other cause at cost and at retail.

While opening the Appliance Store for business on the morning of August 5, the manager discovered that thieves had broken in and stolen the store's entire inventory. The following information for the period January 1 through August 4 was available:

Problem 9–8A
Gross profit method
(LO 6)

January 1 merchandise inventory at cost	$276,500
Purchases	824,000
Purchases returns	15,350
Transportation-in	27,450
Sales	945,600
Sales returns	19,700

Required

Under the assumption the store had earned an average 33% gross profit on sales during the past five years, prepare a statement showing the estimated loss.

The Sanford Company wants to prepare interim financial statements for the first quarter of 1993. The company uses a periodic inventory system but would like to avoid making a physical count of inventory. During the last five years, the company's gross profit rate has averaged 35%; the following information for the year's first quarter is available from its records:

Problem 9–9A
Gross profit method
(LO 6)

January 1 beginning inventory	$135,480
Purchases.	345,350
Purchases returns.	5,800
Transportation-in	11,100
Sales	624,500
Sales returns	10,200

Required

Use the gross profit method to prepare an estimate of the company's March 31 inventory.

Part 1. Graftex Company's inventory includes a damaged product that cost $35 per unit. Replacement cost is $32, expected sales price is $40, additional costs that must be incurred to sell the product are $12, and the normal profit margin is 15%. Explain the reason why the inventory should not be reported on the balance sheet at more than $28. **Part 2.** Monton Company's inventory includes a product that cost $32 per unit. Replacement cost is $28, expected sales price is $40, additional costs to sell are $0, and the normal profit margin is 25%. Explain the reason why the inventory should not be reported on the balance sheet at less than $30 per unit.

Problem 9–10A
Analytical essay
(LO 3)

Review the facts about Northwood Company presented in Problem 9–1A and notice that Northwood uses a periodic inventory system. The facts of Problem 9–1A indicate that Northwood Company had 4,000 units of product available for sale, had 1,000 units

Problem 9–11A
Analytical essay
(LO 2, 5)

on hand at the end of the period, and, therefore, had sales of 3,000 units during the period. Now assume that the sales occurred as follows:

April 7	1,000 units
June 14	400 units
September 17	700 units
December 3	900 units

Required

1. Explain what effect, if any, these additional facts would have on the solution to requirement 2a and 2b of Problem 9–1A.

2. Given the preceding information about the timing of sales, explain whether the Problem 9–1A solution to requirement 2a and 2b would provide the same answers under a perpetual inventory system as it does under a periodic inventory system.

Provocative Problems

Provocative Problem 9–1
Samson's Sporting Goods
(LO 6)

The retail outlet of Samson's Sporting Goods suffered extensive smoke and water damage and a small amount of fire damage on October 5. The company carried adequate insurance, and the insurance company's claims adjuster appeared the same day to inspect the damage. After completing his survey, the adjuster agreed with Sam Corbin, the store's owner, that the inventory could be sold to a company specializing in fire sales for about one third of its cost. The adjuster offered Corbin $235,400 in full settlement for the damage to the inventory. He suggested that the offer be accepted and said he had authority to deliver at once a cheque for that amount. He also pointed out that a prompt settlement would provide funds to replace the inventory in time for the store to participate in the Christmas shopping season.

Corbin felt the loss might exceed $235,400, but he recognized that a time-consuming count and inspection of each item in the inventory would be required to establish the loss more precisely. He was anxious to get back into business before the Christmas rush, the season making the largest contribution to annual net income, and was reluctant to take the time for the inventory count. Yet, he was also unwilling to take a substantial loss on the insurance settlement.

Corbin asked for and received one day in which to consider the insurance company's offer and immediately went to his records for the following information:

		At Cost	At Retail
a.	January 1 inventory	$ 387,700	$ 640,315
	Purchases, Jan. 1 through Oct. 5	1,347,200	2,250,450
	Net sales, Jan. 1 through Oct. 5		2,261,400

b. On March 1, the remaining inventory of winter sportswear and equipment was marked down from $110,400 to $87,000 and placed on sale in the annual end-of-the-winter-season sale. Two thirds of the merchandise was sold. The markdown on the remainder was canceled, thereby returning the prices to regular retail amounts. (A markdown cancellation is subtracted from a markdown, and a markup cancellation is subtracted from a markup.)

c. In May, a special line of swimwear proved popular, and 110 suits were marked up from their normal $42.00 retail price to $52.50 per suit. Seventy suits were sold at the higher price; and on August 5, the markup on the remaining 40 suits was canceled and they were returned to their regular $42.00 price.

d. Between January 1 and October 5, markdowns totaling $11,300 were taken on several odd lots of sportswear. Recommend whether or not you think Corbin should accept the insurance company's offer. Back your recommendation with figures.

Modern Furniture Store has been in operation for six years, during which it has earned a 32% average gross profit on sales. However, the night before last, June 2, it suffered a disastrous fire that destroyed its entire inventory, and Marie Lauzon, the store's owner, has filed a $119,040 inventory loss claim with the insurance company. When asked on what she based her claim, she replied that during the day before the fire, she had marked every item in the store down 20% in preparation for the annual summer clearance sale, and during the marking-down process, she had taken an inventory of the merchandise in the store. "Furthermore," she said, "it's a big loss, but every cloud has a silver lining, because I am giving you fellows [the insurance company] the benefit of the 20% markdown in filing this claim."

Provocative Problem 9–2
Modern Furniture Store
(LO 5)

When it was explained to Madame Lauzon that she had to back her loss claim with more than her word as to the amount of the loss, she produced the following information from her presale inventory and accounting records, which fortunately were in a fireproof vault and were not destroyed in the fire.

1. The store's accounts were closed on Dec. 31 of last year.
2. After posting was completed, the accounts showed the following June 2 balances:

Merchandise inventory, Jan. 1 balance	$103,800
Purchases	279,400
Purchases returns	2,950
Freight-in	7,050
Sales.	448,100
Sales returns.	10,100

3. Madame Lauzon's prefire inventory totaled $148,800 at premarkdown prices.

From the information given, present figures to show the amount of loss suffered by Madame Lauzon. Also, show how she arrived at the amount of her loss claim. Can her presale inventory figure be used to substantiate the actual amount of her loss. If so, use the presale inventory figure to substantiate the actual loss.

The financial statements and related disclosures from Bombardier's 1992 annual report are presented in Appendix I. Based on your examination of this information, answer the following:

Provocative Problem 9–3
Bombardier Inc.
(Analysis and review problem)

1. What was the total amount of inventories held as current assets by Bombardier at the end of 1992? At the end of 1991?
2. Inventories represented what percentage of total assets at the end of 1992? At the end of 1991?
3. Inventories at the end of 1992 represented what percentage of total revenue for the year? Calculate a similar percentage for 1991.
4. Based on your answers to questions 2 and 3, would you say that Bombardier was more or less efficient in its use of inventories during 1992 compared to 1991?
5. What method did Bombardier use to determine the inventory amounts reported on its balance sheet?

Analytical and Review Problems

A&R Problem 9–1

The following information is taken from the records of Bradford Company for four consecutive operating periods:

	Periods			
	1	**2**	**3**	**4**
Beginning inventory	$29,000	$41,000	$31,000	$37,000
Ending inventory.	41,000	31,000	37,000	19,000
Net income.	25,000	29,000	33,000	41,000

Assume that the company made the errors below:

Period	Error in Ending Inventory	
1	Overstated	$9,000
2	Understated	7,000
3	Overstated	8,000

Required

1. Compute the revised net income for each of the four periods.

2. Assuming that the company's ending inventory for period 4 is correct, how would these errors affect the total net income for the four periods combined? Explain.

A&R Problem 9–2

The records of Walker Company as of December 31, 1993, show the following:

	Net Purchases	Net Income	Accounts Payable	Inventory
Balance per company's books	$235,000	$22,100	$29,200	$20,500
(a)				
(b)				
(c)				
(d)				
(e)				
Correct balances				

The accountant of Walker Company discovers in the first week of January 1994 that the following errors were made by his staff.

a. Goods costing $4,500 were in transit (FOB shipping point) and were not included in the ending inventory. The invoice had been received and the purchase recorded.

b. Damaged goods (cost $3,900) which were being held for return to the supplier were included in inventory. The goods had been recorded as a purchase and the entry for the return of these goods had also been made.

c. Inventory items costing $2,600 were incorrectly excluded from the final inventory. These goods had not been recorded as a purchase and had not been paid for by the company.

d. Goods which were shipped FOB destination had not yet arrived and were not included in inventory. However, the invoice had arrived on December 30, 1993, and the purchase for $2,100 was recorded.

e. Goods which cost $2,700 were segregated and not included in inventory because a customer expressed an intention to buy the goods. The sale of the goods for $4,200 had been recorded in December 1993.

Required

Using the format provided above, show the correct amount for net purchases, net income, accounts payable, and inventory for Walker Company as at December 31, 1993.

For each of the statements enter *agree* or *disagree* and state why you agree or disagree.   **A&R Problem 9–3**

a. An improper valuation of inventory affects the income statement but does not affect the balance sheet.

b. Under the perpetual inventory system, an income statement may be prepared without taking a physical inventory.

c. In general, the inventory policy should be to select an assumed flow of goods that matches the physical flow of the goods.

d. The cost principle is the justification for the lower of cost or replacement rule.

e. Under the perpetual inventory method, cost of goods sold is computed as a residual.

f. Under the perpetual inventory method, a physical inventory count is never taken.

g. Damaged or obsolete inventory is valued at cost for balance sheet purposes until such time as sold.

h. The LIFO inventory costing method lends itself most to manipulation of reported net incomes between periods.

i. The specific inventory cost method of inventory flow is more likely to be employed by a jewelry store than a groceteria.

j. The LIFO inventory costing method emphasizes the income statement rather than the balance sheet.

As a Matter of Record

Record Case 9–1

Mr. Haynes said Imperial plans to switch to last-in, first-out (LIFO) accounting for its refining and marketing operations later this year.

The current accounting on a first-in, first-out (FIFO) basis hurts the company's financial performance during periods of wide swings in the price of crude oil.

When crude prices dip, Canadian refiners like Imperial are pressured to drop gasoline prices quickly because of competition from gasoline shipped in from the United States, where refiners use LIFO accounting.

On the other hand, when crude prices rise sharply, FIFO accounting forces Canadian refiners to wait at least 60 days before increasing their gasoline prices.

Mr. Haynes said that Imperial lost about $80 million last year as a result of the different accounting methods between U.S. and Canadian refiners.

From: "Imperial Mulls Heavy Oil Upgrades," *The Globe and Mail*, October 3, 1991. © 1991 *The Globe and Mail*.

Required

Did Imperial Oil really lose $80 million because they used FIFO instead of LIFO? Explain.

Answers to Objective Review Questions

LO 1 (*d*)	LO 4 (*b*)	LO 6 (*b*)
LO 2 (*d*)	LO 5 (*e*)	LO 7 (*d*)
LO 3 (*b*)		

Capital Assets: Plant and Equipment

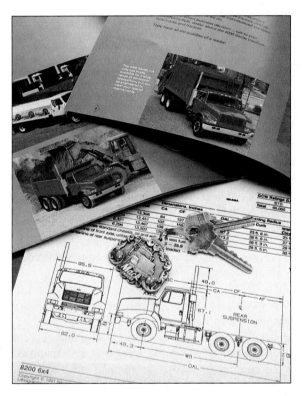

Companies invest large amounts in plant assets, such as trucks and equipment, that are used to produce and distribute goods and provides services to customers. Accounting provides information about the costs of obtaining, maintaining, and using these assets.

*T*he focus of this chapter is long-term, *tangible capital assets* used in the operations of a business. In studying the chapter, you will learn what distinguishes them from other types of assets, how to determine their cost, and how companies allocate their cost to the periods that benefit from their use.

Learning Objectives

After studying Chapter 10, you should be able to:

1. Describe the differences between tangible capital (plant) assets and other kinds of assets, calculate the cost of a plant asset, and prepare entries to record plant asset purchases.

2. Explain amortization accounting (including the reasons for amortization), calculate amortization by the straight-line and units-of-production methods, and calculate amortization after revising the estimated useful life of an asset.

3. Describe the use of accelerated amortization for financial accounting purposes and calculate accelerated amortization under the declining-balance method.

4. Define or explain the words and phrases listed in the chapter glossary.

Tangible Capital (Plant) Assets Compared to Other Types of Assets

LO 1 Describe the differences between tangible capital (plant) assets and other kinds of assets, calculate the cost of a plant asset, and prepare entries to record plant asset purchases.

Capital assets include all long-lived assets whether tangible or intangible. Tangible assets that are used in the production or sale of other assets or services and that have a useful life longer than one accounting period are called *plant assets*. In the past, such assets were often described as *fixed assets*. However, more descriptive terms such as *plant and equipment* or perhaps *property, plant, and equipment* are now used more frequently.

The main difference between plant assets and merchandise is that plant assets are held for *use* while merchandise is held for *sale*. For example, a computer is merchandise to an office equipment retailing business that purchases it with the intent to sell it. If the same retailer owns another computer that is used in business operations to account for the business and to prepare reports, it is classified as plant and equipment.

The characteristic that distinguishes capital assets from tangible current assets is the length of their useful lives. For example, supplies are consumed within a very short time after the company starts to use them. Thus, their cost is assigned to the single period in which they are used. By comparison, capital assets have longer useful lives that often extend over many accounting periods. As the usefulness of capital assets expires over these periods, their cost must be allocated among them. This allocation should be accomplished in a systematic and rational manner.[1]

---

[1] *CICA Handbook* (Toronto: The Canadian Institute of Chartered Accountants), par. 3060.31.

Capital assets are not the same as long-term investments. Although both are held for more than one accounting period, investments are not used in the primary operations of the business. For example, land that is held for future expansion is classified as a long-term investment. On the other hand, land on which the company's factory is located is a capital asset. In addition, standby equipment held for use in case of a breakdown or during peak periods of production is a capital asset. However, when equipment is removed from service and held for sale, it is no longer considered a capital asset.

The purchase of a capital asset should be recorded at cost. This cost includes all normal and reasonable expenditures necessary to get the asset in place and ready to use. For example, the cost of a factory machine includes its invoice price, less any cash discount for early payment, plus freight, unpacking, and assembling costs. The cost of an asset also includes the costs of installing a machine before placing it in service. Examples are the costs to build a concrete base or foundation for a machine, to provide electrical connections, and to adjust the machine before using it in operations.

Cost of a Capital Asset

A cost must be normal and reasonable as well as necessary if it is to be properly included in the cost of a plant asset. For example, if a machine is damaged by being dropped during unpacking, the repairs should not be added to its cost. Instead, they should be charged to an expense account. Also, a fine paid for moving a heavy machine on city streets without proper permits is not part of the cost of the machine. However, if proper permits are obtained, their cost is included in the cost of the asset. Sometimes, additional costs to modify or customize a new plant asset must be incurred before the asset meets the purchaser's needs. In this case, the expenditures should be charged to the asset's cost.

When a capital asset is constructed by a business for its own use, cost includes material and labour costs plus a reasonable amount of indirect overhead costs such as heat, light, power, and amortization on the machinery used to construct the asset. Cost also includes design fees, building permits, and insurance during construction. However, insurance costs for coverage after the asset has been placed in service are an operating expense.

When land is purchased for a building site, its cost includes the total amount paid for the land, including any real estate commissions. It also includes legal fees and any accrued property taxes paid by the purchaser until the plant asset is substantially complete and ready for use. Payments for surveying, clearing, grading, draining, and landscaping also are included in the cost of land. Furthermore, any assessments by the local government, whether incurred at the time of purchase or later, for such things as installing streets, sewers, and sidewalks should be debited to the Land account because they add a more or less permanent value to the land.

Land purchased as a building site may have an old building that must be removed. In such cases, the entire purchase price, including the amount paid for the building, should be charged to the Land account. Also, the cost of removing the old building, less any amounts recovered through the sale of salvaged materials, should be charged to the Land account.

Because land has an unlimited life and is not consumed when it is used, it is not subject to amortization. However, **land improvements,** such as parking lot surfaces, fences, and lighting systems, have limited useful lives. Although these costs increase the usefulness of the land, they must be first charged to separate Land Improvement accounts so that they can be amortized. Of course, a separate Building account must be charged for the costs of purchasing or constructing a building that will be used as a plant asset.

Land, land improvements, and buildings often are purchased in a single transaction for a lump-sum price. When this occurs, you must allocate the cost of the purchase among the different types of assets based on their relative market values. These market values may be estimated by appraisal or by using the tax-assessed valuations of the assets.

For example, assume that a company pays $90,000 cash to acquire land appraised at $30,000, land improvements appraised at $10,000, and a building appraised at $60,000. The $90,000 cost is allocated on the basis of appraised values as follows:

	Appraised Value	Percentage of Total	Apportioned Cost
Land	$ 30,000	30%	$27,000
Land improvements	10,000	10	9,000
Building	60,000	60	54,000
Totals.	$100,000	100%	$90,000

This allocation is necessary for the proper determination of amortization expense in the future.

Nature of Amortization of Capital Assets

LO 2 Explain amortization accounting (including the reasons for amortization), calculate amortization by the straight-line and units-of-production methods, and calculate amortization after revising the estimated useful life of an asset.

Because capital assets are purchased for use, you can think of a capital asset as a quantity of usefulness that will contribute to the operations of the business throughout the service life of the asset. And, because the life of any capital asset (other than land) is limited, this quantity of usefulness expires as the asset is used. This expiration of a capital asset's quantity of usefulness is generally described as **amortization.** In accounting, this term describes the process of allocating and charging the cost of the usefulness to the accounting periods that benefit from the asset's use.

The term *amortization* is the general term used for many situations where amounts are allocated to different accounts over varying lengths of time. When the Accounting Standards Board revised and reissued the standard on capital assets (section 3060), they said that the cost of capital assets should be amortized over their useful lives in a rational and systematic manner. In practice, the term *depreciation* still tends to be used for plant assets such as machinery and buildings, and the term *depletion* still tends to be used for natural resources. Amortization continues to be used for intangible assets and other items such as premium or discount on long-term debt. We may use the terms depreciation and depletion from time to time. Remember that they are terms which are specialized names for amortization.

For example, when a company buys an automobile for use as a plant asset, it acquires a quantity of usefulness in the sense that it obtains a quantity of transportation. The cost of that transportation will expire during the useful life of the car. The total cost of the transportation is the cost of the car less the proceeds that will be received when the car is sold or traded in at the end of its service life. This net cost that will expire over the useful life of the car must be allocated to the accounting periods that benefit from the car's use. In other words, the asset's cost must be amortized. Note that the amortization process does not measure the decline in the car's market value each period. Furthermore, amortization does not measure the physical deterioration of the car each period. Under generally accepted accounting principles, amortization is a process of allocating a plant asset's cost to income statements of the years in which it is used.

Because amortization represents the cost of using a plant asset, you should not begin recording amortization charges until the asset is actually put to use providing services or producing products.

Service (Useful) Life of a Plant Asset

The **service life** of a plant asset is the length of time it will be used in the operations of the business. This service life (or useful life) may not be as long as the asset's potential life. For example, although computers have a potential life of six to eight years, a company may plan to trade in its old computers for new ones every three years. In this case, the computers have a three-year service life. Therefore, this company should charge the cost of the computers (less their expected trade-in value) to amortization expense over this three-year period.

The service life of a plant asset often is difficult to predict because of several factors. Wear and tear from use determine the service life of many assets. However, two additional factors, **inadequacy** and **obsolescence**, often need to be considered. Usually, when a business acquires capital assets, it attempts to anticipate how much the business will grow and then acquires assets of a size and capacity to take care of its foreseeable needs. However, if a business grows more rapidly than anticipated, the capacity of the assets may become too small for the productive demands of the business. When this happens, the assets become inadequate. Obsolescence, like inadequacy, is difficult to anticipate because the exact occurrence of new inventions and improvements normally cannot be predicted. Yet, new inventions and improvements often cause an asset to become obsolete and the company may simply discard it long before it wears out.

Many times, a company is able to predict the service life of a new asset based on past experience with similar assets. In other cases, lacking experience with a particular type of asset, a company must depend on the experience of others or on engineering studies and judgment.

Salvage Value

The total amount of amortization that should be taken over an asset's service life is the asset's cost minus its estimated **salvage value.** The salvage value of a plant asset is the amount you expect to receive from selling the asset at the end of its life. If you expect an asset to be traded in on a new asset, the salvage value is the expected trade-in value.

When the disposal of a plant asset involves additional costs, as in the wrecking of a building, the salvage value is the *net* amount you expect to realize from the sale of the asset at the end of its service life. This net amount is the amount you expect to receive for the asset less the disposal costs.

Allocating Amortization

Many amortization methods for allocating a plant asset's total cost among the several accounting periods in its service life have been suggested and used in the past. However, at present, most companies use the *straight-line method* of amortization in their financial accounting records for presentation in their financial statements. Also, some types of assets are amortized according to the *units-of-production method*. After explaining these two methods next, we discuss some other methods, called *accelerated amortization*.

Straight-Line Method

When **straight-line amortization** (or depreciation) is used, each year in the asset's life receives the same amount of expense. The amount of amortization to be taken each period is calculated by first finding the cost of the asset minus its estimated salvage value. Then this amount, which is often called the **amortizable** (or depreciable) **cost,** is divided by the estimated number of accounting periods in the asset's service life.

For example, if a machine costs $26,000, has an estimated service life of five years, and has an estimated $1,000 salvage value, its amortization per year by the straight-line method is $5,000. This amount is calculated as follows:

$$\frac{\text{Cost} - \text{Salvage}}{\text{Service life in years}} = \frac{\$26,000 - \$1,000}{5 \text{ years}} = \$5,000 \text{ per year}$$

If this asset is purchased on December 31, 1992, and used throughout its predicted service life of five years, the straight-line method will allocate an equal amount of amortization to each of those years (1993 through 1997). The left graph in Illustration 10–1 shows that this $5,000 per year amount will be reported each year as an expense. The right graph shows the amount that will be reported on the six balance sheets that will be produced while the company actually owns the asset. This **book value** of the asset is its original cost less accumulated depreciation. The book value goes down by $5,000 each year. Both graphs show why this method is called *straight line*.

Units-of-Production Method

The purpose of recording amortization, or depreciation, is to provide relevant information about the cost of consuming an asset's usefulness. Basically, amortization accounting charges each accounting period in which an asset is used with a fair share of its cost. The straight-line method charges an equal share to each period. If capital assets are used about the same amount in each accounting period, this method produces a reasonable result. However, in some lines of business, the use of certain capital assets varies greatly from one accounting period to another. For example, a machine shop may use a particular piece of equipment for a month and then not use it again for many months.

ILLUSTRATION 10–1

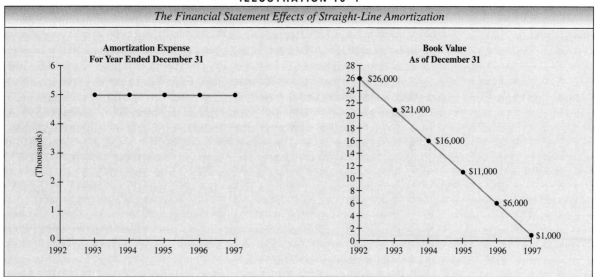

The Financial Statement Effects of Straight-Line Amortization

Because the use of such equipment changes from period to period, **units-of-production amortization** may provide a better matching of expenses with revenues than straight-line amortization. The units-of-production method allocates amortization for a plant asset based on the relationship between the units of product produced by the asset during a given period to the total units the asset is expected to produce during its entire life. In effect, this method computes the amount of amortization per unit of service provided by the asset. The amount of amortization taken in an accounting period is then determined by multiplying the units produced in that period by the amortization per unit.

When the units-of-production method is used, the cost of an asset minus its estimated salvage value is divided by the units that management predicts it will produce during its entire service life. Units of production may be expressed as units of product or in any other unit of measure such as hours of use or distance driven.

For example, a truck that cost $26,000 has a predicted salvage value of $1,000. Also, the truck's service life in kilometres is estimated to be 200,000 kilometres. The amortization per kilometre, or the amortization per unit of production, is $0.125, which is calculated as follows:

$$\text{Amortization per unit of production} = \frac{\text{Cost} - \text{Salvage value}}{\text{Predicted units of production}}$$

$$= \frac{\$26,000 - \$1,000}{200,000 \text{ km}}$$

$$= \$0.125 \text{ per km}$$

If these estimates are used and the truck is driven 30,000 km during its first year, amortization for the first year is $3,750 (30,000 km at $0.125 per km). If the truck is driven 24,000 km in the second year, amortization for the second year is 24,000 km times $0.125 per km, or $3,000.

Amortization for Partial Years

Of course, plant assets may be purchased or disposed of at any time during the year. When an asset is purchased (or disposed of) at some time other than the beginning or end of an accounting period, amortization must be recorded for part of a year. Otherwise, the year of purchase or the year of disposal is not charged with its share of the asset's amortization.

For example, assume that a machine was purchased and placed in service on October 8, 1993, and the annual accounting period ends on December 31. The machine cost $26,000, and has an estimated service life of five years and an estimated salvage value of $1,000. Because the machine was purchased and used nearly three months during 1993, the annual income statement should reflect amortization expense on the machine for that part of the year. The amount of amortization to be reported is often based on the assumption that the machine was purchased on the first of the month nearest the actual date of purchase. Therefore, since the purchase occurred on October 8, three months' amortization must be recorded on December 31. If the purchase had been on October 16 or later during October, amortization would be calculated as if the purchase had been on November 1.

Three months are $3/12$ of a year. Therefore, if straight-line amortization is used, the three months' amortization of $1,250 is calculated as follows:

$$\frac{\$26,000 - \$1,000}{5} \times \frac{3}{12} = \$1,250$$

This entry records amortization for 1993 on the machine purchased on October 8, 1993:

Dec.	31	Amortization Expense, Machinery	1,250.00	
		Accumulated Amortization, Machinery		1,250.00
		To record amortization for three months.		

On December 31, 1994, and at the end of each of the following three years, the following journal entry records a full year's amortization on this machine:

Dec.	31	Amortization Expense, Machinery	5,000.00	
		Accumulated Amortization, Machinery		5,000.00
		To record amortization for one year.		

After the December 31, 1997, amortization entry is recorded, the accounts show the history of this machine as follows:

Machinery		Accumulated Amortization, Machinery	
Oct. 8, 1993 26,000		Dec. 31, 1993	1,250
		Dec. 31, 1994	5,000
		Dec. 31, 1995	5,000
		Dec. 31, 1996	5,000
		Dec. 31, 1997	5,000

The disposal of an asset during a year also requires that amortization be recognized for the portion of the year it was actually used. For example, suppose that the preceding asset is sold for $2,250 on June 24, 1998. To record the disposal, amortization for six months (amortization to the nearest full month) must first be recorded. The entry for this is:

June	24	Amortization Expense, Machinery	2,500.00	
		Accumulated Amortization, Machinery		2,500.00
		To record amortization for one-half year.		

After making the entry to record amortization to the date of sale, a second entry to record the actual sale is needed:

June	24	Cash.	2,250.00	
		Accumulated Amortization, Machinery.	23,750.00	
		Machinery		26,000.00
		To record sale of machine at book value.		

The company sold the machine in this example for its book value. In the next chapter, we discuss more typical situations in which capital assets are sold for more or less than book value.

When amortization must be recorded for part of a year, it is often calculated to the nearest whole month, as in the preceding example. However, other conventions are sometimes used. For example, some companies take one half of a year's amortization in the year of purchase and one half in the year of disposal, regardless of the dates on which the asset was purchased or sold. Other companies take a full year's amortization in the year of acquisition and no amortization in the year of disposal. All of these policies are acceptable provided they are applied consistently.

Amortization on the Balance Sheet

In presenting information about the capital assets of a business, both the cost and accumulated amortization of plant assets should be reported. For example, DuPont Canada's balance sheet at the close of its 1990 fiscal year included the following:

(*Dollars in thousands*)	1990	1989
Property, plant, and equipment:		
Buildings and equipment	$ 948,437	$831,674
Construction in progress	150,672	92,486
Land	9,457	9,439
	1,108,566	933,599
Less: Accumulated depreciation and amortization . .	553,035	502,810
	$ 555,531	$430,789

Notice that DuPont reported only the total amount of accumulated depreciation and amortization. This is the usual practice in published financial statements. In fact, the balance sheets of many companies show plant and equipment on one line with the net amount of cost less accumulated depreciation. When this is done, however, the amount of accumulated depreciation is disclosed in a footnote. To satisfy the *full-disclosure principle,* companies also must provide a general description of the amortization method or methods used.[2] Usually, they present this in a note.

Reporting both the cost and the accumulated amortization of capital assets may help balance sheet readers compare the status of different companies. For example, a company that holds assets with $50,000 original cost and $40,000 of accumulated amortization may be in quite a different situation from that of a company with new assets that cost $10,000. Although the net unamortized cost is the same in both cases, the first company may have more productive capacity available but probably is facing the need to replace its older assets. These differences are not conveyed if the balance sheets report only the $10,000 book values.

From the discussion so far, you should recognize that amortization is a process of cost allocation rather than valuation. Capital assets are reported on balance sheets at their remaining undepreciated costs (book value), not at market values.

Some people involved in accounting have suggested that additional useful information would be provided if financial statements reported the market value of plant assets. However, this practice has not gained general acceptance. Instead, most accountants believe that financial statements should be based on the *continuing-concern,* or *going-concern, principle* described in Chapter 1. This principle dictates that, unless there is adequate evidence to the contrary, the accountant should assume the company will continue in business. As applied to amortization, this principle leads to the assumption that plant assets will not be sold but will be held and used long enough to recover their original costs through the sale of products and services. Therefore, plant assets are carried on the balance sheet at cost less accumulated amortization. This is the remaining portion of the original cost that is expected to be recovered in future periods. The ultimate outcome is that the book values of assets reported on the balance sheet rarely equal their market values.

Recovering the Cost of Plant Assets

Inexperienced financial statement readers may make the mistake of thinking that the accumulated amortization shown on a balance sheet represents funds accumulated to buy new assets when the presently owned assets must be replaced. However, you know that accumulated amortization is a contra account with a credit balance that cannot be used to buy anything. If a business has funds available to buy assets, the funds are shown on the balance sheet as liquid assets such as *cash,* not as accumulated amortization.

---

[2] Ibid., par. 3060.58.

ILLUSTRATION 10–2

Recovering the Cost of Plant Assets while Breaking Even

EVEN STEVEN COMPANY
Income Statement
For Year Ended December 31, 1993

Sales		$100,000
Cost of goods sold	$60,000	
Rent expense.	10,000	
Salaries expense	25,000	
Amortization expense	5,000	
Total		100,000
Net income.		$ –0–

A company that earns a profit or *breaks even* (a term that means the company neither earns a profit nor suffers a loss) recovers the original cost of its capital assets through the sale of its products and services. This result is demonstrated with a condensed income statement in Illustration 10–2, which shows that Even Steven Company broke even during 1993.

In Illustration 10–2, notice that the company broke even only after deducting $5,000 of the cost of its plant assets from its sales. As a result, we can say that the company recovered $5,000 of the cost of plant assets. This happened because $100,000 of cash and receivables flowed into the company from sales and only $95,000 of liability increases and cash and inventory outflows occurred for sold goods, rent, and salaries. No funds flowed out for amortization expense. In this sense, the company recovered this $5,000 portion of the cost of its plant assets through the sale of its products. If the company remains in business for the life of its plant assets, it will recover the entire cost of the assets as long as it breaks even or earns a profit. In other words, amortization is an expense like any other expense, except that it does not require cash to be paid out each year.

Revising Amortization Rates

Because the calculation of amortization or depreciation must be based on an asset's *predicted* useful life, depreciation expense is an estimate. Therefore, you should be alert to the possibility that during the life of an asset, new information may show that the original prediction of useful life was inaccurate. Thus, if your estimate of an asset's useful life changes, what should be done? The answer is to use a new estimate of the remaining useful life to calculate amortization in the future. In other words, revise the estimate of annual amortization expense in the future by spreading the residual cost to be amortized over the revised remaining useful life.

For example, assume that a machine was purchased seven years ago at a cost of $10,500. At that time, the machine was predicted to have a 10-year life with a $500 salvage value. Therefore, it was amortized by the straight-line method at the rate of $1,000 per year [($10,500 − $500)/10 = $1,000]. At the beginning of the asset's eighth year, its book value is $3,500, calculated as follows:

Cost	$10,500
Less seven years' accumulated amortization	7,000
Book value.	$ 3,500

At the beginning of its eighth year, the prediction of the number of years remaining in the useful life is changed from three years to five years. The salvage value is also changed to be $300. Amortization for each of the machine's five remaining years should be calculated as follows:

$$\frac{\text{Book value} - \text{Revised salvage value}}{\text{Revised remaining useful life}} = \frac{\$3,500 - \$300}{5 \text{ years}} = \$640 \text{ per year}$$

Thus, $640 of amortization should be recorded for the machine at the end of the eighth and each succeeding year in its life.

Because this asset was amortized at the rate of $1,000 per year for the first seven years, you might contend that amortization expense was overstated during the first seven years. While that view may have merit, accountants have concluded that amortization is an estimate based on the best information available at the time it is recorded. They have also concluded that past years' financial statements generally should not be restated to reflect facts that were *not* known when the statements were originally prepared.

A revision of the predicted useful life of a plant asset is an example of a **change in an accounting estimate.** Such changes result "from new information or subsequent developments and accordingly from better insight or improved judgment." Generally accepted accounting principles require that changes in accounting estimates, such as a change in estimated useful life or salvage value, be reflected only in future financial statements, not by modifying past statements.[3]

Accelerated Amortization Methods

LO 3 Describe the use of accelerated amortization for financial accounting purposes and calculate accelerated amortization under the declining-balance method.

In contrast to straight line, other amortization methods produce larger amortization charges during the early years of an asset's life and smaller charges in the later years. These techniques are called **accelerated amortization** methods. They are considered acceptable when more of the asset's usefulness is consumed in the early years of its life than in later years. A common method is *declining-balance amortization.* Some accountants reason that accelerated amortization methods provide better annual expenses associated with plant and equipment. Repair and maintenance costs are usually lower in the earlier years of an asset's life and greater in the later years. The higher amortization expense is recorded in the early years with lower repair costs. The lower amortization expense is recorded in the later years with the higher repair costs. Thus, the total annual costs (amortization plus repairs) are approximately the

---

[3] Ibid., par. 1506.25.

AS A MATTER OF

Ethics

Fascar Company has struggled financially for more than two years. The economic situation surrounding the company has been depressed and there are no signs of improvement for at least two more years. As a result, net income has been almost zero, and the future seems bleak.

The operations of Fascar require major investments in equipment. As a result, depreciation is a large factor in the calculation of income. Because competition in

Fascar's industry normally has required frequent replacements of equipment, the equipment has been depreciated over only three years. However, Fascar's president has recently instructed Sue Ann Meyer, the company's accountant, to revise the estimated useful lives of existing equipment to six years and to use a six-year life on new equipment.

Meyer suspects that the president's instruction is motivated by

a desire to improve the reported income of the company. In trying to determine whether to follow the president's instructions, Meyer is torn between her loyalty to her employer and her responsibility to the public, the shareholders, and others who use the company's financial statements. Meyer also wonders what the independent accountant who audits the financial statements will think about the change.

same from year to year over the life of the asset. This argument, however, does not appear to have gained a great deal of support since most companies still use straight-line amortization for accounting purposes.

The **Income Tax Act** requires that companies use a declining-balance method for calculating the maximum capital cost allowance (amortization or depreciation for tax purposes) that may be claimed in any period. The act specifies the rates for various classes of assets. For example, a rate of 20% would be used for general machinery and equipment, and a rate of 4% for most buildings. Further discussion of the details of tax accounting for capital assets is deferred to a more advanced course.

Declining-Balance Method

Under the **declining-balance amortization** method, an amortization rate of up to twice the straight-line rate is applied each year to the book value of the asset at the beginning of the year. Because the book value *declines* each year, the amount of amortization gets smaller each year.

When the amortization rate used is twice the straight-line rate, the method is called the *double-declining-balance method*. To use the double-declining-balance method: (1) calculate the straight-line amortization rate for the asset; (2) double it; and (3) at the end of each year in the asset's life, apply this rate to the asset's book value at the beginning of the year. Note that the salvage value is *not* used in the annual calculation.

For example, assume that the double-declining-balance method is used to calculate amortization on a new $26,000 asset for which you have predicted a five-year life and a salvage value of $1,000. The steps to follow are:

1. Divide 100% by five years to determine the straight-line annual amortization rate of 20% per year.
2. Double this 20% rate to get a declining-balance rate of 40% per year.
3. Calculate the annual amortization charges as shown in the following table:

Year	Beginning Book Value	Annual Amortization (40% of Book Value)	Accumulated Amortization at Year-end	Ending Book Value ($26,000 Cost less Accumulated Amortization)
First	$26,000.00	$10,400.00	$10,400.00	$15,600.00
Second	15,600.00	6,240.00	16,640.00	9,360.00
Third	9,360.00	3,744.00	20,384.00	5,616.00
Fourth	5,616.00	2,246.40	22,630.40	3,369.60
Fifth	3,369.60	1,347.84	23,978.24	2,021.76
Total		$23,978.24		

Notice that the book value of a plant asset would never quite reach zero no matter how many years of declining-balance amortization were taken. However, generally accepted accounting principles do not allow an asset to be amortized below its salvage value. Thus, if the asset in the previous example had an estimated salvage value of $2,500 instead of $1,000, amortization for its fifth year would be limited to $869.60. This would reduce the asset's book value to the $2,500 salvage value at the end of the fifth year, as follows:

Year	Beginning Book Value	Annual Amortization (40% of Book Value)	Accumulated Amortization at Year-end	Ending Book Value ($26,000 Cost less Accumulated Amortization)
First	$26,000.00	$10,400.00	$10,400.00	$15,600.00
Second	15,600.00	6,240.00	16,640.00	9,360.00
Third	9,360.00	3,744.00	20,384.00	5,616.00
Fourth	5,616.00	2,246.40	22,630.40	3,369.60
Fifth	3,369.60	869.60	23,500.00	2,500.00
Total		$23,500.00		

Apportioning Accelerated Amortization between Accounting Periods

When accelerated amortization methods are used and accounting periods do not coincide with the years in an asset's life, amortization must be apportioned between accounting periods. For example, consider the previous case where we used the declining-balance method to calculate amortization on a machine. Annual amortization on the machine is $10,400 during its first year of service, $6,240 during its second year, and so on for its five-year life. Assume that this machine is placed in service on April 1, 1993, and the annual accounting period ends on December 31. As a result, the machine will be in use for three fourths of a year during 1993. Therefore, this period should be charged with $7,800 depreciation ($10,400 × ¾ = $7,800). Then, 1994 should be charged with $7,280 depreciation [(¼ × $10,400) + (¾ × $6,240) = $7,280]. Similar calculations should be used for the remaining periods in the asset's life. The following table illustrates the apportioning process for the first three years:

Part of Year	Calculation	Total
Jan. 1, 1993–Mar. 31, 1993	none	$ –0–
Apr. 1, 1993–Dec. 31, 1993	¾ × $10,400	7,800
		$7,800
Jan. 1, 1994–Mar. 31, 1994	¼ × $10,400	$2,600
Apr. 1, 1994–Dec. 31, 1994	¾ × $ 6,240	4,680
		$7,280
Jan. 1, 1995–Mar. 31, 1995	¼ × $ 6,240	$1,560
Apr. 1, 1995–Dec. 31, 1995	¾ × $ 3,744	2,808
		$4,368

The table which follows presents the amortization expense for the first two years for the three methods described in the chapter.

Comparison of Amortization Methods

Year	Straight Line	Units of Production	Declining Balance
First	$5,000	$3,750	$10,400
Second	5,000	3,000	6,240

As you will notice the amounts of amortization vary considerably. However, each method is correct under GAAP provided it is applied consistently. As well, provided that the estimated salvage value of the asset does not change, each method will allocate a total of $25,000 of the asset's cost as amortization expense during the asset's useful life. You may wish to complete the schedule for the next three years (assume that the truck is driven a total of 200,000 km over the five years).

Summary of the Chapter in Terms of Learning Objectives

LO 1. Capital assets are tangible items that have a useful life longer than one accounting period. Capital assets are not held for sale but are used in the production or sale of other assets or services. The cost of capital assets includes all normal and reasonable expenditures necessary to get the assets in place and ready to use. The cost of a lump-sum purchase should be allocated among the individual assets based on their relative market values.

LO 2. The cost of capital assets that have limited service lives must be allocated to the accounting periods that benefit from their use. When this amortization is accomplished according to the straight-line method, divide the cost minus salvage value by the number of periods in the service life of the asset to determine the amortization expense of each period. Under the units-of-production method, divide the cost minus salvage value by the estimated number of units the asset will produce to determine the amortization per unit. If the estimated useful life of a plant asset is changed, the remaining cost to be amortized is spread over the remaining (revised) useful life of the asset.

LO 3. Accelerated amortization methods such as declining balance are acceptable for financial accounting purposes if they are based on realistic estimates of useful life.

Demonstration Problem

On July 14, 1993, Lachine Company paid $600,000 to acquire a fully equipped factory. The purchase included the following:

Asset	Appraised Value	Estimated Salvage Value	Estimated Service Life	Amortization Method
Land	$160,000			Not amortized
Land improvements . .	80,000	$ –0–	10 years	Straight-line
Building	320,000	100,000	10 years	Straight-line
Machinery	176,000	16,000	10,000 units	Units of production*
Computers	64,000	4,000	4 years	Declining balance (at twice the straight-line rate)
Total	$800,000			

* The machinery was used to produce 700 units in 1993 and 1,800 units in 1994.

Required

1. Allocate the total $600,000 cost among the five separate assets.
2. Calculate the 1993 (half year) and 1994 amortization expense for each type of asset and calculate the total each year for all assets.

Solution to Demonstration Problem

Planning the Solution

- Complete a three-column work sheet showing these amounts for each asset: appraised value, percent of total value, and allocated cost.
- Using the allocated costs, compute the amount of amortization for 1993 (only one-half year) and 1994 for each asset. Then summarize those calculations in a table showing the total amortization for each year.

1. Allocation of total cost among the assets:

Asset	Appraised Value	Percent of Total Value	Allocated Cost
Land	$160,000	20%	$120,000
Land improvements	80,000	10	60,000
Building	320,000	40	240,000
Machinery	176,000	22	132,000
Computers	64,000	8	48,000
Total	$800,000	100%	$600,000

2. Amortization for each asset:

Land Improvements:

Cost	$60,000
Salvage value.	–0–
Net cost	$60,000

Service life	10 years
Annual expense	$60,000/10 = $6,000
1993 amortization	$6,000 × (½) = $3,000
1994 amortization	$6,000

Building:

Cost	$240,000
Salvage value.	100,000
Net cost	$140,000

Service life	10 years
Annual expense.	$140,000/10 = $14,000
1993 amortization	$14,000 × (½) = $7,000
1994 amortization	$14,000

Machinery:

Cost	$132,000
Salvage value.	16,000
Net cost	$116,000
Total expected units	10,000
Expected cost per unit ($116,000/10,000) .	$ 11.60

Year	Units × Unit Cost	Amortization
1993	700 × $11.60	$ 8,120
1994	1,800 × $11.60	20,880

Computers:

Cost	$ 48,000
Salvage value.	4,000
Straight-line rate (100%/4 years)	25%
Twice the straight-line rate (25% × 2) . .	50%

Year	Rate	Beginning Book Value	Amortization Expense	Accumulated Amortization	Ending Book Value
1993	25%	$48,000	$12,000	$12,000	$36,000
1994	50	36,000	18,000	30,000	18,000

Note: The 25% rate for 1993 is one half of 50%; it is applied because the computers were used for only one-half year.

Total amortization expense:

	1993	1994
Land improvements	$ 3,000	$ 6,000
Building	7,000	14,000
Machinery	8,120	20,880
Computers	12,000	18,000
Total	$30,120	$58,880

Glossary

Accelerated amortization   amortization methods that produce larger amortization charges during the early years of an asset's life and smaller charges in the later years. p. 546

Amortizable cost   the amount that will be charged to expense over the useful life of a capital asset. It is the total cost of the asset less the estimated salvage value. p. 540

Amortization   the process of allocating the cost of capital assets to expense over their useful lives in a rational, systematic manner. p. 538

Book value   the amount assigned to an item in the accounting records and in the financial statements; for a plant asset, book value is its original cost less accumulated amortization. p. 540

Capital assets   all long-lived assets, tangible and intangible. p. 536

Change in an accounting estimate   a change in a calculated amount used in the financial statements that results from new information or subsequent developments and from better insight or improved judgment. p. 546

Declining-balance amortization   an amortization method in which a plant asset's amortization charge for the period is determined by applying a constant amortization rate (up to twice the straight-line rate) each year to the asset's beginning book value. p. 547

Inadequacy   a condition in which the capacity of plant assets becomes too small for the productive demands of the business. p. 539

Income Tax Act   the codification of the Canadian federal tax laws. p. 547

Land improvements   assets that increase the usefulness of land but that have a limited useful life and are subject to amortization. p. 538

Obsolescence   a condition in which, because of new inventions and improvements, a plant asset can no longer be used to produce goods or services with a competitive advantage. p. 539

Salvage value   the amount that management predicts will be recovered at the end of a plant asset's service life through a sale or as a trade-in allowance on the purchase of a new asset. p. 539

Service life   the length of time in which a plant asset will be used in the operations of the business. p. 539

Straight-line amortization   a method that allocates an equal portion of the total amortization for a plant asset (cost minus salvage) to each accounting period in its service life. p. 540

Units-of-production amortization   a method that allocates an equal portion of the total amortization for a plant asset (cost minus salvage) to each unit of product or service that it produces, or on a similar basis, such as hours of use or kilometres driven. p. 541

Synonymous Terms

Amortizable cost   depreciable cost.

Capital assets   plant assets; property, plant, and equipment; fixed assets.

Depletion   amortization.

Depreciation   amortization.

Service life   useful life.

Answers to the following questions are listed at the end of this chapter. Be sure that you decide which is the one best answer to each question *before* you check the answers.

Objective Review

LO 1 The recent purchase of a new production machine by the Wallace Company involved the following dollar amounts:

Gross purchase price	$700,000
Sales tax	49,000
Freight to move machine to plant	3,500
Assembly costs	3,000
Cost of foundation for machine	2,500
Cost of spare parts to be used in	
maintaining the machine.	4,200
Purchase discount taken.	21,000

The amount to be recorded as the cost of the machine is:

a. $737,000.

b. $733,500.

c. $728,000.

d. $679,000.

e. $741,200.

LO 2 Clandestine, Inc., purchased a new machine for $96,000 on January 1, 1993. Its predicted useful life is five years or 100,000 units of product, and salvage value is $8,000. During 1993, 10,000 units of product were produced. Assuming (1) straight-line depreciation and (2) units-of-production depreciation, respectively, the book value of the machine on December 31, 1993, would be:

	Straight Line	Units of Production
a.	$76,800	$86,400.
b.	$78,400	$79,200.
c.	$76,800	$86,400.
d.	$70,400	$78,400.
e.	$78,400	$87,200.

LO 3 Temperware Industries purchased a new machine for $108,000 on January 1, 1993. Its predicted useful life is five years, and salvage value is estimated to be $9,000. Depreciation expense for 1994 using double-declining balance is:

	Double Declining
a.	$17,280
b.	$25,920
c.	$43,200
d.	$25,920
e.	$23,760

LO 4 A condition in which the capacity of plant assets has become too small for the productive demands of the business is called:

a. Obsolescence.

b. Depreciation.

      c. Useful life.
      d. Service life.
      e. Inadequacy.

Questions for Class Discussion

1. What are the characteristics of a capital asset that make it different from other assets?

2. What is the balance sheet classification of land held for future expansion? Why is the land not classified as a capital asset?

3. In general, what is included in the cost of a capital asset?

4. Tack Company asked for bids from several machine manufacturers for the construction of a special machine. The lowest bid was $37,500. The company decided to build the machine itself and did so at a total cash outlay of $30,000. It then recorded the machine's construction with a debit to Machinery for $37,500, a credit to Cash for $30,000, and a credit to Gain on the Construction of Machinery for $7,500. Was this a proper entry? Discuss.

5. As used in accounting, what is the meaning of the term *amortization? depreciation?*

6. Is it possible to keep a plant asset in such an excellent state of repair that recording amortization is unnecessary?

7. A company purchases a machine that normally has a service life of 12 years. However, the company's management believes that the development of a more efficient machine will make it necessary to replace the machine in eight years. What useful life should be used in calculating amortization on this machine, and why?

8. A building estimated to have a useful life of 30 years was completed at a cost of $120,000. It was estimated that it would be demolished at the end of its life at a cost of $13,000 and that materials salvaged from the demolition would be sold for $25,000. How much straight-line amortization should be charged on the building each year?

9. Define the following terms used in accounting for plant assets:
    a. Trade-in value.   *c.* Book value.   *e.* Inadequacy.
    b. Market value.   *d.* Salvage value. *f.* Obsolescence.

10. Does the recording of amortization cause a plant asset to appear on the balance sheet at market value? What is accomplished by recording amortization?

11. Does the balance of the account, Accumulated Amortization, Machinery, represent funds accumulated to replace the machinery when it wears out? Describe what the balance of Accumulated Amortization represents.

12. It is discovered at the end of five years that a machine expected to have a six-year life will actually have an eight-year life. How is this new information reflected in the accounts?

13. Explain how a business that breaks even recovers the cost of its plant assets through the sale of its products. In what manner are the funds thus recovered?

BBD 14. In Bombardier Inc.'s consolidated balance sheet, which appears in Appendix I, what phrase does Bombardier use to describe its capital assets? On December 31, 1991, what percentage of total capital asset cost was represented by accumulated amortization?

Case 10–1

The Hull Company and the Ottawa Company have each purchased similar properties consisting of land and a small commercial building. The two properties each cost approximately $850,000 and are used for rental purposes.

Management of the Hull Company wishes to allocate a large portion of the purchase price to the building because of the company's excellent overall profitability. They argue that a large amortization expense will reduce income taxes, alleviate shareholders' demands for dividends, and allow the company to retain cash for future investment. In contrast, the Ottawa Company, which has been much less profitable, wishes to allocate a large portion of the purchase price to the land in order to show lower amortization expense and thus enhance their profits.

Required

a. Evaluate the approaches taken by each of the companies.
b. Indicate, with reasons, how the allocation of the purchase price between the land and building should be conducted for each company.

Case 10–2

Your friend, who has had no experience with accounting, says that there are a couple of items on the balance sheet that he does not understand. For example, he knows that the building, shown at $175,000, could be sold for almost twice that amount. He also wonders where all the cash has gone; accumulated depreciation is $67,650 but the cash account only shows $19,825.

Required

Explain what is wrong with your friend's reasoning about accounting.

Exercises

Exercise 10–1
Cost of a capital asset
(LO 1)

Isaacs Corporation purchased a machine for $57,000, terms 2/10, n/60, FOB shipping point. The seller prepaid the freight charges, $1,350, adding the amount to the invoice and bringing its total to $58,350. The machine required a special steel mounting and power connections costing $3,480, and another $1,225 was paid to assemble the machine and get it into operation. In moving the machine onto its steel mounting, it was dropped and damaged. The repairs cost $530. Later, $200 of raw materials were consumed in adjusting the machine so that it would produce a satisfactory product. The adjustments were normal for this type of machine and were not the result of the damage. However, the items produced while the adjustments were being made were not sellable. Prepare a calculation to show the cost of this machine for accounting purposes.

Exercise 10–2
Allocating cost between
land, land improvements,
and buildings
(LO 1)

RTF Company paid $245,500 for real estate plus $18,500 in closing costs. The real estate included the following: land appraised at $148,200, land improvements appraised at $22,800, and a building appraised at $114,000. The plan calls for using the building as a factory. Prepare a calculation showing the allocation of the total cost among the three purchased assets and present the journal entry that would be made to record the purchase.

Exercise 10–3
Lump-sum purchase of
capital assets
(LO 1)

Atlantis Company bought two pickup trucks and a forklift from a financially distressed supplier and had them shipped to the company's plant. The purchase price was $32,000. Another $1,500 was paid for shipping. The shipping charge was based on the weights of the vehicles. Each truck weighed 1,600 kilos, and the forklift weighed 800 kilos. The appraised values of the trucks and forklift follow with the other costs of repairs incurred to get them ready for service. Determine the cost of each asset for accounting purposes.

	Truck 1	Truck 2	Forklift
Appraised values	$18,000	$6,750	$20,250
Repair costs.	850	700	250

Exercise 10–4
Recording the costs of
real estate
(LO 1)

After planning to build a new manufacturing plant, Stage One Company purchased a large lot on which a small building was located. The negotiated purchase price for this real estate was $430,000 for the lot plus $120,000 for the building. The company paid $40,000 to have the old building torn down and $38,000 for landscaping the lot. Finally, it paid $2.9 million construction costs for a new building, which included $90,000 for lighting and paving a parking lot next to the building. Present a General Journal entry to record the costs incurred by the company, all of which were paid in cash.

Exercise 10–5
Calculating amortization;
three alternative methods
(LO 2, 3)

Apex Company installed a machine in its factory at a cost of $104,000. The machine's useful life was estimated at five years or 65,000 units of product, with a $6,500 trade-in value. During its second year, the machine produced 8,600 units of product. Determine the machine's second-year amortization calculated in each of the following ways: (a) straight line, (b) units of production, and (c) declining balance at twice the straight-line rate.

Exercise 10–6
Calculating amortization;
two alternative methods;
partial year
(LO 2, 3)

On October 1, 1993, Tandem Company purchased a machine for $290,000. The machine was expected to last four years and have a salvage value of $15,000. Calculate amortization expense for 1994, using (a) straight-line and (b) declining balance at twice the straight-line rate. Tandem calculates amortization for partial years to the nearest whole month of the date of purchase or disposal.

Exercise 10–7
Partial year's
amortization; disposal of
plant asset
(LO 2)

Winston Company purchased and installed a machine on January 2, 1990, at a total cost of $105,600. Straight-line amortization was taken each year for four years, based on the assumption of an eight-year life and no salvage value. The machine is disposed of on May 20, 1994, during its fifth year of service. Present the entries that would be made to record the partial year's amortization on May 20 and to record the disposal assuming the cash proceeds from the disposal equal the book value of the machine. Winston calculates amortization for partial years to the nearest whole month of the date of purchase or disposal.

Shipman Company used straight-line amortization for a machine that cost $29,000, under the assumption it would have a five-year life and a $3,000 trade-in value. After three years, Shipman determined that the machine still had four more years of remaining useful life, after which it would have an estimated $2,000 trade-in value. Calculate (*a*) the machine's book value at the end of its third year, and (*b*) the amount of amortization to be charged during each of the remaining years in the machine's revised useful life.

Exercise 10–8
Revising amortization
rates (LO 2)

Octet Company purchased and installed a plant asset that cost $55,000 and was estimated to have a five-year life and a $5,000 trade-in value. Use declining-balance amortization at twice the straight-line rate to determine the amount of amortization to be charged against the machine in each of the five years of its life.

Exercise 10–9
Declining-balance
amortization
(LO 3)

Throckmorton Company recently paid $112,000 for equipment that will last four years and have a salvage value of $25,000. By using the machine in its operations for four years, the company expects to earn $35,000 annually, after deducting all expenses except amortization. Present a schedule showing income before amortization, amortization expense, and net income for each year and the total amounts for the four-year period assuming (*a*) straight-line amortization and (*b*) declining-balance amortization at twice the straight-line rate.

Exercise 10–10
Income statement effects
of alternative amortization
methods
(LO 2, 3)

Problems

Part 1. A machine that cost $72,000 with a five-year life and an estimated $7,200 salvage value was installed in Lynch Company's factory. The factory manager estimated that the machine would produce 180,000 units of product during its life. It actually produced the following numbers of units: year 1, 30,000; year 2, 33,000; year 3, 36,000; year 4, 31,500; and year 5, 39,500.

Problem 10–1
Alternative amortization
methods; disposal of plant
assets
(LO 2, 3)

Required

1. Prepare a calculation showing the number of dollars of this machine's cost that should be amortized over its five-year life.
2. Prepare a form with the following column headings:

Year	Straight-Line	Units of Production	Declining Balance

Then show the amortization for each year and the total amortization for the machine under each amortization method. Use twice the straight-line rate for the declining-balance method.

Part 2. Canyon Company purchased a used machine for $52,700 on January 3. It was repaired the next day at a cost of $3,200 and installed on a new platform that cost $1,100. The company predicted that the machine would be used for four years and would then have a $6,000 salvage value. Amortization was to be charged on a straight-line basis. A full year's amortization was charged on December 31, at the end of the first year of the machine's use. On May 1 of its fourth year in service, it was retired from service.

Required

1. Prepare General Journal entries to record the purchase of the machine, the cost of repairing it, and the installation. Assume that cash was paid.

2. Prepare entries to record amortization on the machine on December 31 of its first year and on May 1 in the year of its disposal. Also record the disposal of the machine assuming it was sold for its book value.

Problem 10–2
Real estate costs and partial year's amortization
(LO 1, 2, 3)

In 1993, Barcelona Company paid $2.7 million for a tract of land on which two buildings were located. The plan was to demolish Building One and build a new store in its place. Building Two was to be used as a company office and was appraised at a value of $862,500, with a useful life of 15 years and a $120,000 salvage value. A lighted parking lot near Building Two had improvements valued at $287,500 that were expected to last another 10 years and have no salvage value. Without considering the buildings or improvements, the tract of land was estimated to have a value of $1,725,000.

Barcelona Company incurred the following additional costs:

Cost to demolish Building One.	$ 157,500
Cost of additional landscaping.	53,000
Cost to construct new building (Building Three), having a useful life of 25 years and a $257,000 salvage value	1,754,000
Cost of new land improvements near Building Three, which have a 20-year useful life and no salvage value.	243,000

Required

1. Prepare a form having the following column headings: Land, Building Two, Building Three, Land Improvements Two, and Land Improvements Three. Allocate the costs incurred by Barcelona Company to the appropriate columns and total each column.

2. Prepare a single journal entry dated June 1 to record all the incurred costs, assuming they were paid in cash on that date.

3. Prepare December 31 adjusting entries to record amortization for the seven months of 1993 during which the assets were in use. Use double-declining-balance amortization for the newly constructed Building Three and Land Improvements Three and straight-line amortization for Building Two and Land Improvements Two.

Problem 10–3
Plant asset costs and amortization
(LO 1, 2, 3)

Tabu Company recently negotiated a lump-sum purchase of several assets from a limousine company that was going out of business. The purchase was completed on August 31, 1993, at a total cash price of $930,000, and included a building, land, certain land improvements, and 14 vehicles. The estimated market value of each asset was as follows: building, $345,600; land, $268,800; land improvements, $57,600; and vehicles, $288,000.

Required

1. Prepare a schedule to allocate the lump-sum purchase price to the separate assets that were purchased. Also present the General Journal entry to record the purchase.

2. Calculate the 1994 amortization expense on the building using the straight-line method and assuming a 12-year life and a $35,000 salvage value.

3. Calculate the 1993 amortization expense on the land improvements assuming a 10-year life and declining-balance amortization at twice the straight-line rate.

On July 29, 1992, Phoenix Corporation made a lump-sum purchase of two machines from a company that was going out of business. The machines cost $525,600 and were placed in use on August 2, 1992. This additional information about the machines is available:

Problem 10–4
Plant asset costs and revising amortization rates
(LO 1, 2)

Machine Number	Appraised Value	Salvage Value	Estimated Life	Installation Cost
One	$367,500	$13,500	5 years	$ 600
Two	122,500	10,000	5 years	1,600

Phoenix Corporation uses the straight-line method of amortization and calculates amortization to the nearest whole month of the date of purchase. Shortly before recording 1993's amortization, Phoenix concluded that machine one's remaining useful life would be two and one-half years. Before recording 1995's amortization, Phoenix decided that machine two would have a zero salvage value and that the remaining useful life would be two years.

Required

Prepare a form that has the following column headings:

Machine Number	Amortization				
	1992	1993	1994	1995	1996

Calculate the amount of amortization to be charged during each year of the useful lives of machines one and two.

Frite Company's operations require the use of several items of equipment, which have estimated useful lives that range from 6 to 10 years. None of the assets has any salvage value. The senior managers of the company have decided that the company should use the method of amortization that generates the most amortization expense in the first year.

Problem 10–5
Analytical essay
(LO 3)

Required

Prepare a table that shows the first year's amortization assuming (*a*) the double-declining-balance method and (*b*) the straight-line method. Separate rows of the table should show the first year's amortization for assets with estimated lives of 6, 7, 8, 9, and 10 years. For each estimated useful life, assume the company owns one asset that cost $10,000.

Describe what the table reveals about the two alternative methods and state whether the company should use the double-declining-balance method or the straight-line method. Also, discuss how the comparison of the two amortization methods would change if each asset had an estimated salvage value.

Alternate Problems

Problem 10–1A
Alternative amortization
methods; disposal of plant
assets
(LO 2, 3)

Part 1. Ironworks Company purchased and installed a new machine that cost $75,000; it had a four-year life and an estimated $15,000 salvage value. Management estimated that the machine would produce 80,000 units of product during its life. Actual production of units of product was as follows: year 1, 8,000; year 2, 21,600; year 3, 27,000; and year 4, 23,200.

Required

1. Prepare a calculation showing the number of dollars of this machine's cost that should be amortized over its four-year life.
2. Prepare a form with the following column headings:

Year	Straight-Line	Units of Production	Declining Balance

Then show the amortization for each year and the total amortization for the machine under each amortization method. Use twice the straight-line rate for the declining-balance method.

Part 2. On January 4, Culby Company purchased a used machine for $159,000. The next day, it was repaired at a cost of $6,100 and was mounted on a new cradle that cost $4,900. Management estimated that the machine would be used for five years and would then have a $26,000 salvage value. Amortization was to be charged on a straight-line basis. A full year's amortization was charged on December 31 of the first and the second years of the machine's use; and on May 30 of its third year of use, the machine was retired from service.

Required

1. Prepare General Journal entries to record the purchase of the machine, the cost of repairing it, and the installation. Assume that cash was paid.
2. Prepare entries to record amortization on the machine on December 31 of its first year and on May 30 in the year of its disposal. Also record the disposal of the machine assuming it was sold for its book value.

Problem 10–2A
Real estate costs and
partial year's
amortization
(LO 1, 2, 3)

In 1993, Marathon Company paid $657,000 for a tract of land on which two buildings were located. The plan was to demolish Building A and build a new store in its place. Building B was to be used as a company office and was appraised at a value of $375,000, with a useful life of 20 years and a $59,700 salvage value. A lighted parking lot near Building B had improvements valued at $75,000 that were expected to last another five years and have no salvage value. Without considering the buildings or improvements, the tract of land was estimated to have a value of $300,000.

Marathon Company incurred the following additional costs:

Cost to demolish Building A.	$ 64,500
Cost of additional landscaping.	57,000
Cost to construct new building (Building C), having a useful life of 25 years and a $121,500 salvage value	1,350,000
Cost of new land improvements near Building C, which have an eight-year useful life and no salvage value	120,960

Required

1. Prepare a form having the following column headings: Land, Building B, Building C, Land Improvements B, and Land Improvements C. Allocate the costs incurred by Marathon Company to the appropriate columns and total each column.
2. Prepare a single journal entry dated June 1 to record all the incurred costs, assuming they were paid in cash on that date.
3. Prepare December 31 adjusting entries to record amortization for the seven months of 1993 during which the assets were in use. Use double-declining-balance amortization for the newly constructed Building C and Land Improvements C and straight-line amortization for Building B and Land Improvements B.

Segal Company recently negotiated a lump-sum purchase of several assets from a boat dealer who was planning to change locations. The purchase was completed on July 31, 1993, at a total cash price of $445,000, and included a building, land, certain land improvements, and a new general-purpose heavy truck. The estimated market value of each asset was: building, $252,450; land, $123,750; land improvements, $89,100; and truck, $29,700.

Problem 10–3A
Plant asset costs and amortization
(LO 1, 2, 3)

Required

1. Prepare a schedule to allocate the lump-sum purchase price to the separate assets that were purchased. Also present the General Journal entry to record the purchase.
2. Calculate the 1994 amortization expense on the building using the straight-line method and assuming a 15-year life and a $45,510 salvage value.
3. Calculate the 1993 amortization expense on the land improvements assuming a 10-year life and declining-balance amortization at twice the straight-line rate.

On April 25, 1992, McNair Company made a lump-sum purchase of two machines. The machines cost $168,500 and were placed in use on May 2, 1992. This additional information about the machines is available:

Problem 10–4A
Plant asset costs and revising amortization rates
(LO 1, 2)

Machine Number	Appraised Value	Salvage Value	Estimated Life	Installation Cost
One	$129,450	$23,000	5 years	$2,000
Two	86,300	2,100	5 years	3,400

McNair Company uses the straight-line method of amortization and calculates amortization to the nearest whole month of the date of purchase. Early in 1993, McNair decided that machine one's remaining useful life would be two years. In January 1994, McNair concluded that machine two would have a $200 salvage value and that the remaining useful life would be one and a half years.

Required

Prepare a form with the following column headings:

Machine Number	Amortization				
	1992	1993	1994	1995	1996

Calculate the amount of amortization to be charged during each year of the useful lives of machines one and two.

Problem 10–5A
Analytical essay
(LO 3)

The operations of J-Mark Company require the use of several different items of equipment that have estimated useful lives ranging from 8 to 12 years. None of the assets has any salvage value. Renee Glover, the president of J-Mark, has decided that the company should use either double-declining-balance or straight-line amortization. However, to keep the reported net income from appearing too conservative, Glover has asked you to select from these, the method that generates the least amount of amortization in the first year.

Required

Prepare a table that shows the first year's amortization assuming (*a*) the double-declining-balance method and (*b*) the straight-line method. Separate rows of the table should show the first year's amortization for assets with estimated lives of 8, 9, 10, 11, and 12 years. For each estimated useful life, assume that the company owns one asset that cost $20,000.

Describe what the table reveals about the two alternative methods and state whether the company should use the double-declining-balance method or the straight-line method. Also, discuss how the comparison of the two amortization methods would change if each asset had an estimated salvage value.

Provocative Problems

Provocative Problem 10–1
Cableshare Inc.
(LO 2, 3)

A recent Cableshare Inc.* annual report to its shareholders for the year ended December 31, included the following in the notes to the financial statements:

> **1. Accounting Principles.**
> (*c*) Fixed assets are stated at cost. Depreciation is provided on the straight-line basis for data processing equipment, test equipment, research equipment, and leasehold improvements and on the declining-balance basis for office equipment and automobiles, using the following annual rates:
>
> | | |
> |---|---|
> | Data processing equipment . . . . . | 15% |
> | Test and research equipment . . . . | 15% |
> | Leasehold improvements . . . . . . | Term of lease |
> | Office equipment . . . . | 20% |
> | Automobiles. . . . . | 30% |

What might have caused Cableshare Inc. to use straight-line basis of depreciation for some of its capital assets and the declining-balance basis for others?

* Source: CICA, *Financial Reporting in Canada, 1989* (Toronto, 1989), p. 126

Provocative Problem 10–2
Aerodyne Company
(LO 1, 2)

Aerodyne Company temporarily recorded the costs of a new plant in a single account called Land and Buildings. Management has now asked you to examine this account and prepare any necessary entries to correct the account balance. In doing so, you find the following debits and credits to the account:

Debits

Jan.	3	Cost of land and building acquired for new plant site . . . . , ...	$201,500
	11	Attorney's fee for title search.	930
	24	Cost of demolishing old building on plant site.	23,400
Feb.	2	Six months' liability and fire insurance during construction.	3,570
June	29	Payment to building contractor on completion	486,000
July	2	Architect's fee for new building.	31,025
	6	City assessment for street improvements	12,850
	14	Cost of landscaping new plant site	8,900
			$768,175

Credits

Jan.	26	Proceeds from sale of salvaged materials from building.	$2,650
July	2	Refund of one month's liability and fire insurance premium	595
Dec.	31	Depreciation at 2½% per year	15,000
			$ 18,245
Dec.	31	Debit balance	$749,930

An account called *Depreciation Expense, Land and Buildings* was debited in recording the $15,000 of depreciation. Your investigation suggests that 40 years is a reasonable life expectancy for a building of the type involved and that an assumption of zero salvage value is reasonable.

To summarize your analysis, set up a schedule with columns headed Date, Description, Total Amount, Land, Buildings, and Other Accounts. Next, enter the items found in the Land and Buildings account on the schedule, distributing the amounts to the proper columns. Show credits on the schedule by enclosing the amounts in parentheses. Also, draft any required correcting entry or entries, under the assumption that the accounts have not been closed.

Cantu Company and Havner Company are almost identical. Each began operations on January 1 of this year with $324,000 of equipment with a six-year life and a $51,000 salvage value. Each purchased merchandise during the year as follows:

Provocative Problem 10–3
Cantu and Havner
Companies
(A review problem)

Jan. 4	650 units @ $500 per unit =	$ 325,000
Mar. 22	730 units @ $525 per unit =	383,250
July 6	460 units @ $550 per unit =	253,000
Dec. 10	500 units @ $600 per unit =	300,000
		$1,261,250

Now, on December 31 at the end of the first year, each has 950 units of merchandise in its ending inventory. However, Cantu Company will use straight-line amortization in arriving at its net income for the year, while Havner Company will use double-declining-balance amortization. Also, Cantu Company will use FIFO in costing its ending inventory, and Havner Company will use LIFO. The December 31 trial balances of the two concerns carried these amounts:

	Cantu Company		Havner Company	
Cash	$ 37,600		$ 37,600	
Accounts receivable	58,900		58,900	
Equipment	324,000		324,000	
Accounts payable.		$ 72,300		$ 72,300
A. Cantu, capital		663,500		
S. Havner, capital				663,500
Sales		1,200,700		1,200,700
Purchases.	1,261,250		1,261,250	
Salaries expense	123,400		123,400	
Rent expense	32,750		32,750	
Other cash expenses	98,600		98,600	
Totals	$1,936,500	$1,936,500	$1,936,500	$1,936,500

Required

Prepare an income statement for each company and a schedule that explains the difference in their reported net incomes. Write a short answer to this question: Which, if either, of the companies is the more profitable and why?

Provocative Problem 10-4
As a matter of ethics:
Essay

Ethics

Review the "As a Matter of Ethics" case on page 547 and write a short essay discussing the situation faced by Sue Ann Meyer. Include a discussion of the alternative courses of action available to Meyer and indicate how you think she should deal with the situation.

Provocative Problem 10-5
Bombardier Inc.
(LO 2)

Refer to the annual report for Bombardier Inc. in Appendix I, particularly the balance sheet, the management discussion, and the notes to answer the following questions:

1. What percentage of the original cost of Bombardier fixed assets remains to be depreciated at the end of 1992 and 1991? (Assume the assets have no salvage value.)
2. What method of depreciation does Bombardier use for its fixed assets?

Analytical and Review Problems

A&R Problem 10-1

At the last meeting of the executive committee of Kearins, Ltd., Milton Vacon, controller, was severely criticized by both President Kearins and Kate Ryan, vice president of production. The subject of criticism was in the recognition of periodic amortization. President Kearins was unhappy with the fact that what he referred to as "a fictitious item" was deducted, resulting in depressed net income. In his words, "Depreciation is a fiction when the assets being depreciated are worth far more than we paid for them. What the controller is doing is unduly understating our net income. This in turn is detrimental to our shareholders because it results in the undervaluation of our shares on the market."

Vice President Ryan was equally adamant about the periodic amortization charges; however, she came on from another side. She said, "Our maintenance people tell me that the level of maintenance is such that our plant and equipment will last virtually forever." She further stated that charging depreciation on top of maintenance expenses is double-counting—it seems reasonable to charge either maintenance or depreciation but not both.

The time taken by other pressing matters did not permit Vacon to answer; instead, the controller was asked to prepare a report to the executive committee to deal with the issues raised by the president and vice president.

Required

The controller asks you, his assistant, to prepare the required report.

The Shape Company purchased a large earth-mover four years ago at a cost of $350,000. At that time it was estimated that the economic life of the equipment would be 12 years and that its ultimate salvage value would be $14,000.

A&R Problem 10–2

Assuming the company uses straight-line amortization, state whether each of the following events requires a revision of the original amortization rate, with reasons for your answer:

a. Due to the persistent inflation, the present replacement cost of the same type of equipment is $410,000.

b. Because of the higher replacement cost, as described in (a) above, the ultimate salvage value is now estimated at $25,000.

c. The company, in connection with having its line of credit increased, was required by the bank to have the assets appraised. The earth-mover was estimated to have a current value of $315,000.

d. At the time the appraisal was made in (c) above, it was determined that technological change was progressing more slowly than originally estimated and that the earth-mover would probably remain in service for 15 years with the ultimate salvage value as originally estimated at the end of 12 years.

LO 1 (a)   LO 3 (b)   LO 4 (e)

LO 2 (e)

Answers to Objective
Review Questions

CHAPTER

11

Capital Assets: Plant and Equipment, Natural Resources, and Intangible Assets

A company's assets include many things in addition to tangible equipment and buildings. Patents, natural resources, and outstanding employees all contribute to profits. However, they create unique accounting problems that must be solved.

*I*n this chapter, we continue to examine the accounting issues related to capital assets. In studying the chapter, you will learn how accounting records are used to maintain control over capital assets, how to account for the costs of maintaining or improving capital assets, and how to account for disposals of capital assets. The chapter also introduces you to the issues of accounting for natural resources and intangible assets.

Learning Objectives

After studying Chapter 11, you should be able to:

1. Explain how subsidiary ledgers and related controlling accounts are used to maintain control over capital assets.
2. Describe the difference between revenue and capital expenditures and account properly for costs such as repairs and betterments incurred after the original purchase of capital assets.
3. Prepare entries to record the disposal of capital assets and the exchange of capital assets under accounting principles and the recognition of gains and losses.
4. Prepare entries to account for natural resources and intangible assets, including entries to record depletion and amortization.
5. Define or explain the words and phrases listed in the chapter glossary.

Controlling Plant Assets

LO 1 Explain how subsidiary ledgers and related controlling accounts are used to maintain control over capital assets.

Good internal control requires that each capital asset[1] be separately identified, usually with a unique identification number that is either engraved on the asset or attached with a permanent sticker or tag such as the following:

> Avondale Company
> 163–002

Periodically, an inventory of capital assets should be taken to verify the existence, location, condition, and continued use of each asset. This count should be compared to the formal records of capital assets that every company should maintain. For good internal control, the custodians of the assets must not have access to the records.

---

[1] As in Chapter 10, we will use the term *capital asset* as the generic term for all long-lived tangible and intangible productive assets. However, in practice these assets are often referred to as *plant assets, natural resources,* and *intangible assets.* As well, the cost of all of these assets is amortized to expense over their useful lives. In practice this is still often referred to as *depreciation, depletion,* and *amortization.*

In keeping these records, companies usually divide their capital assets into functional groups and provide each group with a separate asset account and accumulated amortization account in the General Ledger. The asset account and the related accumulated amortization account for each group serve as controlling accounts for detailed subsidiary records. In many cases the term *depreciation* will still be used in reference to the amortization of tangible assets. For example, a store will create a Store Equipment account and a related Accumulated Depreciation, Store Equipment account. Together, they control the **Store Equipment Ledger,** which is a subsidiary ledger that contains a separate record for each item of store equipment. Similarly, the accountant creates accounts for Office Equipment and Accumulated Depreciation, Office Equipment, which control the **Office Equipment Ledger.**

Capital asset records provide the same basic information whether they are computerized or handwritten. To illustrate a capital plant asset record system, assume that a concern's collection of office equipment consists of only one desk and a chair. The general ledger accounts for these assets are Office Equipment and Accumulated Depreciation, Office Equipment. Both are controlling accounts that control the subsidiary record for the desk and chair. The general ledger and subsidiary ledger records for these assets are shown in Illustration 11–1.

At the top of each subsidiary record, observe the plant asset numbers assigned to these two items of office equipment (163–001 and 163–002). In each case, the assigned number consists of the number of the Office Equipment general ledger account, 163, followed by the asset's unique identification number. The remaining information on the subsidiary records is more or less self-evident. Notice how the $940 balance of the General Ledger account, Office Equipment, is equal to the sum of the $190 and $750 balances in the asset record section of the two subsidiary records. The General Ledger account controls this section of the subsidiary ledger.

Also observe how the Accumulated Depreciation, Office Equipment, account controls the amortization or depreciation record section of the subsidiary records. Specifically, the $375 balance at December 31, 1993, equals the sum of the $75 accumulated on the chair and the $300 accumulated on the desk.

The disposition section at the bottom of the subsidiary records is used to record facts about the final disposal of the asset. When the asset is discarded, sold, or exchanged, a notation describing this action is entered here. The record is then removed from the subsidiary ledger and filed for future reference. Again, good internal control requires that the records of the assets should not be kept by the person who is responsible for their safekeeping. Otherwise, the custodian of the assets can use the records to cover up an accident or a theft. Many larger companies require that all assets be turned over to a special salvage department for final disposal.

Revenue and Capital Expenditures

By this time, you have learned that a company's expenditures can be recorded as expenses right away or as assets, whose cost is allocated to expense over their useful lives. After a plant asset is acquired and put into service, additional

ILLUSTRATION 11–1

Subsidiary Records and Controlling Accounts for Plant Assets

Plant Asset
No. *163–001*

SUBSIDIARY PLANT ASSET AND DEPRECIATION RECORD

Item ___*Office chair*___   Account ___*Office Equipment*___
Description ___*Padded, straight-back, wood*___

Mfg. serial no. ___*4G81545*___   Purchased from ___*Chairco*___
Where located ___*Office*___
Person responsible for the asset ___*Office Manager*___
Estimated life ___*6 years*___   Estimated salvage value ___*$10.00*___
Depreciation per year ___*$30.00*___   per month ___*$2.50*___

Date	Explanation	PR	Asset Record Dr.	Asset Record Cr.	Asset Record Bal.	Depreciation Record Dr.	Depreciation Record Cr.	Depreciation Record Bal.
July 2, 1991		*G1*	*190.00*		*190.00*			
Dec. 31, 1991		*G23*					*15.00*	*15.00*
Dec. 31, 1992		*G42*					*30.00*	*45.00*
Dec. 31, 1993		*G65*					*30.00*	*75.00*

Final disposition of the asset _____

Plant Asset
No. *163–002*

SUBSIDIARY PLANT ASSET AND DEPRECIATION RECORD

Item ___*Desk*___   Account ___*Office Equipment*___
Description ___*Wood, left hand return*___

Mfg. serial no. ___*4527439*___   Purchased from ___*Office Equipment Co.*___
Where located ___*Office*___
Person responsible for the asset ___*Office Manager*___
Estimated life ___*6 years*___   Estimated salvage value ___*$30.00*___
Depreciation per year ___*$120.00*___   per month ___*$10.00*___

Date	Explanation	PR	Asset Record Dr.	Asset Record Cr.	Asset Record Bal.	Depreciation Record Dr.	Depreciation Record Cr.	Depreciation Record Bal.
July 2, 1991		*G1*	*750.00*		*750.00*			
Dec. 31, 1991		*G23*					*60.00*	*60.00*
Dec. 31, 1992		*G42*					*120.00*	*180.00*
Dec. 31, 1993		*G65*					*120.00*	*300.00*

Final disposition of the asset _____

ILLUSTRATION 11–1

(concluded)

Account No. *163*

Office Equipment

Date		Explanation	PR	Debit		Credit		Balance	
1991 *July*	*2*	*Desk and chair*	*G1*	*940*	*00*			*940*	*00*

Account No. *164*

Accumulated Depreciation, Office Equipment

Date		Explanation	PR	Debit		Credit		Balance	
1991 *Dec.*	*31*		*G23*			*75*	*00*	*75*	*00*
1992 *Dec.*	*31*		*G42*			*150*	*00*	*225*	*00*
1993 *Dec.*	*31*		*G65*			*150*	*00*	*375*	*00*

expenditures are incurred to operate, maintain, repair, and perhaps improve it. In recording these additional expenditures, the accountant must decide whether they should be debited to expense accounts or asset accounts. The issue faced by the accountant is whether more useful information is provided in the financial statements if these expenditures are reported as expenses on the income statement in the current year or if they are added to the plant asset's cost and amortized over future years.

LO 2 Describe the difference between revenue and capital expenditures and account properly for costs such as repairs and betterments incurred after the original purchase of capital assets.

In traditional terms, a **revenue expenditure** should be recorded as an expense and deducted from revenues on the current period's income statement. Revenue expenditures are reported on the income statement because they do not provide material benefits in future periods. Examples of revenue expenditures that relate to plant assets are wages, supplies, fuel, lubricants, and electrical power.

On the other hand, expenditures producing economic benefits that do not fully expire before the end of the current period are called **capital expenditures.** Because they are debited to asset accounts and reported on the balance sheet, they are also called **balance sheet expenditures.** Capital expenditures significantly modify or improve the kind or amount of service that an asset provides.

Because the information in the financial statements is affected for several years by the choice between recording a cost as a revenue or capital expenditure, you must be careful in deciding how to classify it. Although judgment is always involved, accountants have developed several guidelines that help you know what to do. The following sections describe these practices for repairs, betterments, and assets with low costs.

Repairs

Repairs are made to keep an asset in normal good operating condition. For example, keeping a wood-frame building in good condition requires that you periodically repaint it and maintain its roof. Similarly, machines must be cleaned, lubricated, and adjusted, and small parts must be replaced when they wear out. Such repairs and maintenance typically are made every year, and accountants treat them as *revenue expenditures*. Thus, these costs appear on the current income statement as expenses.

Betterments

A **betterment** (or improvement) occurs when a plant asset is modified to make it more efficient, usually by replacing one of its old components with an improved or superior component. The result of a betterment is more efficiency or more productivity, which may or may not increase the asset's useful life. For example, if the manual controls on a machine are replaced with automatic controls, future labour costs will be reduced. But the machine still wears out just as fast as it would have with the manual controls.

When a betterment occurs, accountants agree that its cost should be debited to the improved asset's account. Then the cost and accumulated amortization attributable to the replaced asset component should be removed from the accounts. Finally, the new book value (less salvage) should be amortized over the remaining service life of the asset.

For example, suppose that a company paid $80,000 for a machine with an eight-year service life and no salvage value. On January 6, after three years and $30,000 of amortization, the owner removes the manual control system and replaces it with an automatic system at a cost of $18,000. This betterment does not increase the service life beyond the remaining five years of the original prediction. The owner estimates that the cost of the manual control system represented approximately 10% of the total cost, or $8,000. The same proportion (10%) would also apply to the accumulated amortization, so that $3,000 would be attributed to the manual system. The old component was sold to another company for $2,700 cash. The entry to record the removal and sale of the manual system would be as follows:

Jan.	6	Cash.	2,700.00	
		Accumulated Amortization, Machinery.	3,000.00	
		Loss on Sale of Machinery	2,300.00	
		Machinery		8,000.00
		To record the removal and sale of the manual control system.		

The cost of the betterment would then be added to the Machinery account with this entry:

Jan.	6	Machinery.	18,000.00	
		Cash		18,000.00
		To record the installation of the automatic control system.		

At this point, the new cost of the machine is $90,000 ($80,000 − $8,000 + $18,000), the accumulated amortization is $27,000 ($30,000 − $3,000), and the book value is $63,000 ($90,000 − $27,000). Because five years remain in the useful life, the annual amortization expense hereafter will be $12,600 per year ($63,000/5 years).

In the case where a betterment increases the asset's useful life, the cost of the betterment is debited to the asset's account and the new book value (less salvage) is amortized over the revised service life of the asset.

For example, suppose that an electric motor is nearing the end of its service life, but that if the copper winding is replaced, the motor will last an additional 75,000 hours. The motor originally cost $40,000 and now has a net book value of $6,000. The cost of rewinding the motor is $15,000 and the motor's new salvage value is $3,000. The entry to record the betterment on January 4 is:

Jan.	4	Machinery.	15,000	
		Cash		15,000

To calculate the revised hourly amortization rate, we add the cost of the betterment to the net book value of $6,000, deduct the revised salvage value, and divide by the revised useful life as follows:

Jan. 4	Original cost	$40,000	
	Accumulated amortization	34,000	
	Book value		$ 6,000
	Betterment		15,000
	Total		21,000
	Less new salvage value		3,000
	Revised amortizable cost		$18,000

Hourly amortization rate: $18,000 ÷ 75,000 hours = $0.24 per hour.

Plant Assets with Low Costs

Even with the help of computers, keeping individual plant asset records can be expensive. Therefore, many companies do not keep detailed records for assets that cost less than some minimum amount such as $50 or $100. Instead, they treat the acquisition as a revenue expenditure, and charge the cost directly to an expense account at the time of purchase. As long as the amounts are small, this practice is acceptable under the *materiality principle*. That is, treating these capital expenditures as revenue expenditures is unlikely to mislead a user of the financial statements.

Capital Asset Disposals

LO 3 Prepare entries to record the disposal of capital assets and the exchange of capital assets under accounting principles and the recognition of gains and losses.

Sooner or later, plant assets wear out. They also may become obsolete or inadequate because of changes in the business. When these conditions arise, the assets are discarded, sold, or traded in on new assets. The journal entry to record the disposal of a plant asset depends on which action is taken.

Discarding a Capital Asset

When an asset's accumulated amortization is equal to its cost, the asset is said to be fully amortized. If a fully amortized asset with a cost of $1,500 is discarded on January 7, this entry would be made to record the disposal:

Jan.	7	Accumulated Amortization, Machinery.	1,500.00	
		Machinery		1,500.00
		Discarded a fully amortized machine.		

It is not unusual to find a fully amortized asset remaining in use beyond the end of its predicted service life. In these situations, the asset's cost and accumulated amortization should remain on the books until the asset is discarded, sold, or traded. Otherwise, the accounts and the financial statements do not show its continued existence. However, no additional amortization expense can be recorded since there is no more cost to be charged. In other words, the total amount of amortization expense for an asset cannot exceed its cost.

In other situations, an asset may be discarded before it is fully amortized. For example, suppose that an asset does not last as long as predicted, and becomes worthless, even though only $800 of its $1,000 cost has been amortized. If it is discarded, there is a loss equal to its book value, and the entry to record the disposal is:

Jan.	10	Loss on Disposal of Machinery	200.00	
		Accumulated Amortization, Machinery.	800.00	
		Machinery		1,000.00
		Discarded a worthless machine.		

Remember from the earlier discussion of partial year's amortization that it may be necessary to allocate depreciation to the part of the year in which the discarded asset is actually used. Because this particular asset was discarded early in January, nothing was recorded.

Discarding a Damaged Capital Asset

Occasionally, a plant asset may be wrecked or destroyed in an accident before the end of its service life. For example, a machine that had a cost of $900 and accumulated amortization of $400 was totally destroyed in a fire. If the machine was uninsured, a loss equal to the machine's $500 book value would be recorded as follows:

Jan.	12	Loss on Fire.	500.00	
		Accumulated Amortization, Machinery.	400.00	
		Machinery		900.00
		To record the destruction of machinery not covered by insurance.		

Or if the loss was partially covered by insurance and the insurance company paid $350 to settle the loss claim, the entry to record the machine's destruction would be:

Jan.	12	Cash.	350.00	
		Loss on Fire[2]	150.00	
		Accumulated Amortization, Machinery.	400.00	
		Machinery		900.00
		To record the destruction of machinery and the receipt of insurance compensation.		

Selling a Capital Asset

If a plant asset is sold and the selling price exceeds the asset's book value, a gain is recorded in the accounts and reported on the income statement. And if the price is less than book value, there is a loss. For example, assume a machine that cost $5,000 and has a book value of $1,000 is sold for $1,200. This sale results in a $200 gain and is recorded as follows:

Jan.	4	Cash.	1,200.00	
		Accumulated Amortization, Machinery.	4,000.00	
		Machinery		5,000.00
		Gain on Sale of Machinery		200.00
		Sold a machine at a price in excess of book value.		

---

[2] Note that the economic loss from the fire depends on the difference between the cost of replacing the asset and any insurance settlement. A difference between this economic loss and the reported loss arises from the fact that the accounting records do not attempt to reflect the value of plant assets.

However, if the machine is sold for only $750, there is a $250 loss and the entry to record the sale is:

Jan.	4	Cash.	750.00	
		Loss on Sale of Machinery	250.00	
		Accumulated Amortization, Machinery.	4,000.00	
		Machinery		5,000.00
		Sold a machine at a price below book value.		

Exchanging Capital Assets

LO 3 Prepare entries to record the disposal of capital assets and the exchange of capital assets under accounting principles and the recognition of gains and losses.

Many capital assets retired from use are sold for cash. Others, such as machinery, automobiles, and office equipment, are commonly exchanged for new assets that are similar in purpose. In a typical exchange, a trade-in allowance is received on the old asset, and any balance is paid in cash.

When a plant asset is exchanged for a new asset that is similar in purpose, the exchange may involve a loss or a gain. A loss occurs when the trade-in allowance is less than the book value of the old asset. A gain occurs when the trade-in allowance is more than the book value of the old asset. However, according to generally accepted accounting principles, a gain or loss on an exchange of similar assets is not recognized if the cash involved is less than 10% of the total consideration given up or received.

Recognizing a Loss

To illustrate recognition of a loss on an exchange of plant assets, assume that a machine that cost $18,000 and has been depreciated $15,000 is traded in on a new machine that has a $21,000 cash price. A $1,000 trade-in allowance is received, and the $20,000 balance is paid in cash. Under these assumptions, the book value of the old machine is $3,000, calculated as follows:

Cost of old machine	$18,000
Less accumulated amortization	15,000
Book value.	$ 3,000

Since the $1,000 trade-in allowance results in a $2,000 loss on the exchange, the transaction should be recorded as follows:

Jan.	5	Machinery.	21,000.00	
		Loss on Exchange of Machinery	2,000.00	
		Accumulated Amortization, Machinery.	15,000.00	
		Machinery		18,000.00
		Cash		20,000.00
		Exchanged old machine and cash for a similar machine.		

The $21,000 debit to Machinery puts the new machine in the accounts at its cash price. The debit to Loss on Exchange of Machinery records the loss. The old machine is removed from the accounts with the $15,000 debit to Accumulated Amortization and the $18,000 credit to Machinery.

Recognizing a Gain

To illustrate recognition of a gain on an exchange of plant assets, assume that in acquiring the $21,000 machine of the previous section, a $4,500 trade-in allowance, rather than a $1,000 trade-in allowance, was received, and a $16,500 balance was paid in cash. The transaction is recorded as follows:

Jan.	5	Machinery.	21,000.00	
		Accumulated Amortization, Machinery.	15,000.00	
		Machinery		18,000.00
		Cash		16,500.00
		Gain on Exchange of Machinery		1,500.00

Notice that the new machine is recorded in the books at its equivalent cash price. When assets are exchanged for newer or more efficient assets, the accountant may need to apply judgment in determining how much of the trade-in amount is, in fact, a discount on the new asset and how much is a reflection of the old asset's true value. The determination of the equivalent cash price of the asset acquired will provide guidance in calculating the proper gain or loss on the exchange.

Nonrecognition of a Loss or Gain

In the previous two sections, recognition of a loss and gain was discussed and illustrated. Such accounting procedure is dictated by adherence to the cost principle; that is, recording the new plant asset at the cash equivalent amount, the price that would be paid without a trade-in. In the illustrations above, $21,000 was given as the new machine's cash price. There are times when the cash price of the new machine may not be readily available; however, the old machine may have a ready market at an easily determinable amount. In such cases the cash equivalent amount of the new machine would be the sum of cash paid and the fair value of the trade-in. Once the cash equivalent amount of the new machine is determined, the recording of the trade-in transaction is the same as illustrated in the previous sections.

Notwithstanding the above discussion, departure from the outlined procedure is permitted under the *principle of materiality*. Under this principle, the loss or gain is not recognized if considered immaterial in amount. The new asset is then recorded at an amount equal to the sum of the book value of the trade-in plus the cash paid. For example, an old typewriter that cost $500 was traded in at $50 on a new $600 typewriter, with the $550 difference being paid in cash. Depreciation on the old typewriter in the amount of $420 had been taken.

In this case the old typewriter's book value is $80, and with the trade-in of $50, there was a $30 book loss on the exchange. However, the $30 loss may be regarded as an immaterial amount, and the following method may be used in recording the exchange.

Jan.	7	Office Equipment	630.00	
		Accumulated Amortization, Office Equipment	420.00	
		Office Equipment.		500.00
		Cash		550.00
		Traded an old typewriter and cash for a new typewriter.		

The $630 at which the new typewriter is taken into the accounts is calculated as follows:

Book value of old typewriter ($500 less $420). . . .	$ 80
Cash paid ($600 less the $50 trade-in allowance) . .	550
Cost basis of the new typewriter	$630

When there is an immaterial loss on an exchange, as in this case, the violation of the cost principle is permissible under the *principle of materiality*. Under this principle an adherence to any accounting principle is not required when the cost to adhere is proportionally great and the lack of adherence does not materially affect reported periodic net income. In this case, failing to record the $30 loss on the exchange would not materially affect the average company's statements.

Exchanges of Dissimilar Assets

If a company exchanges a plant asset for another asset that is *dissimilar* in use or purpose, the accounting treatment for a loss is exactly the same as already described for exchanges of similar assets. That is, the company will recognize a gain or loss on an exchange of dissimilar assets. Suppose that the previous transaction involved an exchange of machinery for merchandise inventory worth $21,000. This entry would record the exchange:

Jan.	5	Merchandise Inventory (or Purchases)	21,000.00	
		Accumulated Amortization, Machinery.	15,000.00	
		Machinery		18,000.00
		Cash		16,500.00
		Gain on Exchange of Machinery		1,500.00
		Exchanged old machine and cash for merchandise inventory.		

Natural Resources

Natural resources include such things as standing timber, mineral deposits, and oil reserves. Because they are physically consumed when they are used, they are known as *wasting assets*. In their natural state, they represent inventories of raw materials that will be converted into a product by cutting, mining, or pumping. However, until the conversion takes place, they are noncurrent assets and appear on a balance sheet under captions such as "Timberlands," "Mineral deposits," or "Oil reserves." Sometimes, this caption appears under the property, plant, and equipment category of assets and sometimes it is shown as a separate category.

LO 4 Prepare entries to account for natural resources and intangible assets, including entries to record depletion and amortization.

Natural resources are accounted for at their original cost. Like the cost of all capital assets, the cost of natural resources is allocated, or amortized, to the periods in which they are consumed. The cost created by consuming the usefulness of natural resources is called depletion. On the balance sheet, natural resources are shown at cost less *accumulated depletion*. The amount such assets are depleted each year by cutting, mining, or pumping is usually calculated on a units-of-production basis.

For example, if a mineral deposit has an estimated 500,000 tonnes of available ore and is purchased for $500,000, the depletion charge per tonne of ore mined is $1. Thus, if 85,000 tonnes are mined during the first year, the depletion charge for the year is $85,000 and is recorded as follows:

Dec.	31	Depletion of Mineral Deposit	85,000.00	
		Accumulated Depletion, Mineral Deposit		85,000.00
		To record depletion of the mineral deposit.		

On the balance sheet prepared at the end of the first year, the mineral deposit should appear at its $500,000 cost less accumulated depletion of $85,000. If the 85,000 tonnes of ore are sold by the end of the first year, the entire $85,000 depletion charge reaches the income statement as the depletion cost of the ore mined and sold. However, if a portion remains unsold at year-end, the depletion cost of the unsold ore is carried forward on the balance sheet as part of the cost of the unsold ore inventory, which is a current asset.

The conversion of natural resources through mining, cutting, or pumping often requires the use of machinery and buildings. Because the usefulness of these assets is related to the depletion of the natural resource, their costs should be amortized over the life of the natural resource in proportion to the annual depletion charges. For example, if a machine is installed in a mine and one eighth of the mine's ore is removed during a year, one eighth of the machine's cost (less salvage value) should be amortized. Furthermore, because the amortization is necessary for the mining operation, it should be recognized as an additional cost of the mined ore.

Intangible Assets

Some assets represent certain legal rights and economic relationships beneficial to the owner. Because they have no physical existence, they are called intangible assets. Patents, copyrights, leaseholds, leasehold improvements, goodwill, and trademarks are intangible assets. We discuss each of these items in more detail in following sections. Although notes and accounts receivable are also intangible in nature, they are not used to produce products or provide services. Therefore, they are not listed on the balance sheet as intangible assets; instead, they are classified as current assets or investments.

When an intangible asset is purchased, it is recorded at cost. Thereafter, its cost must be systematically written off to expense over its estimated useful life through the process of **amortization.** Generally accepted accounting principles require that the amortization period for an intangible asset be 40 years or less.[3]

Amortization of intangible assets is similar to depreciation of plant assets and depletion of natural resources in that all three are processes of cost allocation. However, only the straight-line method can be used for amortizing intangibles unless you can demonstrate that another method is more appropriate. Also, while the effects of depreciation and depletion on tangible assets are recorded in a contra account (Accumulated Amortization, Accumulated Depreciation, or Accumulated Depletion), amortization of intangibles has traditionally been credited directly to the intangible asset account. As a result, intangible assets are reported in the balance sheet at that portion of cost not previously written off without reporting the full original cost. Normally, intangible assets are shown in a separate balance sheet section that follows immediately after the plant and equipment section.

However, all companies do not follow these traditions. For example, Bombardier Inc. balance sheet in Appendix I does not identify any intangible assets. But in a note labeled Other Assets, the company reported $26.9 million in industrial designs and other assets and $6.2 million of goodwill at the end of 1992.

The following sections describe several specific types of intangible assets.

Patents

The federal government grants **patents** to encourage the invention of new machines, mechanical devices, and production processes. A patent gives its owner the exclusive right to manufacture and sell a patented machine or device or to use a process for 17 years. When patent rights are purchased, the cost of acquiring the rights is debited to an account called Patents. Also, if the owner engages in lawsuits to defend a patent, the cost of the lawsuits should be debited to the Patents account. However, the costs of research and development leading to a new patent are *not* debited to an asset account. Instead, research and development costs must be expensed as incurred because of the uncertainty, in many cases, of their future benefits to the entity.[4]

Although a patent gives its owner exclusive rights to the patented device or process for 17 years, the cost of the patent should be amortized over its predicted useful life, which might be less than the full 17 years. For example, if a patent that cost $25,000 has an estimated useful life of 10 years, the following adjusting entry is made at the end of each of those years to write off one tenth of its cost:

Dec.	31	Amortization expense, patents	2,500.00	
		Patents		2,500.00
		To write off patent costs over the expected 10-year life.		

---

[3] *CICA Handbook,* par. 3060.32.

[4] Ibid., section 3450.

The entry's debit causes $2,500 of patent costs to appear on the annual income statement as one of the costs of the product manufactured under the protection of the patent. Note that we have followed the convention of crediting the amortization directly to the Patents account.

Copyrights

A **copyright** is granted by the federal government or by international agreement. In most cases, a copyright gives its owner the exclusive right to publish and sell a musical, literary, or artistic work during the life of the composer, author, or artist and for 50 years thereafter. Most copyrights have value for a much shorter time, and their costs should be amortized over the shorter period. Often, the only identifiable cost of a copyright is the fee paid to the Copyright Office. If this fee is not material, it may be debited directly to an expense account. Otherwise, the copyright costs should be capitalized (recorded as a capital expenditure), and the periodic amortization of a copyright should be debited to an account called Amortization Expense, Copyrights.

Leaseholds

Property is rented under a contract called a **lease.** The person or company that owns the property and grants the lease is called the **lessor.** The person or company that secures the right to possess and use the property is called the **lessee.** The rights granted to the lessee by the lessor under the lease are called a **leasehold.** A leasehold is an intangible asset for the lessee.

Some leases require no advance payment from the lessee but do require monthly rent payments. In such cases, a Leasehold account is not needed and the monthly payments are debited to a Rent Expense account. Sometimes, a long-term lease requires the lessee to pay the final year's rent in advance when the lease is signed. If so, the lessee records the advance payment with a debit to its Leasehold asset account. Because the usefulness of the advance payment is not consumed until the final year is reached, the Leasehold account balance remains intact until that year. At that time, the balance is transferred to Rent Expense.

Leasehold Improvements

Long-term leases often require the lessee to pay for any alterations or improvements to the leased property, such as new partitions and storefronts. Normally, the costs of these **leasehold improvements** are debited to a Leasehold Improvements account. Also, since the improvements become part of the property and revert to the lessor at the end of the lease, the lessee must amortize the cost of the improvements over the life of the lease or the life of the improvements, whichever is shorter. The amortization entry commonly debits Rent Expense and credits Leasehold Improvements.

Goodwill

The term **goodwill** has a special meaning in accounting. In theory, a business has an intangible asset, called *goodwill,* when its rate of expected future earnings is greater than the rate of earnings normally realized in its industry. Above-average earnings and the existence of theoretical goodwill may be demonstrated with the following information about Companies A and B, both of which are in the same industry:

	Company A	Company B
Net assets (other than goodwill)	$100,000	$100,000
Normal rate of return in this industry	10%	10%
Normal return on net assets	$ 10,000	$ 10,000
Expected net income	10,000	15,000
Expected earnings above average	$ –0–	$ 5,000

Company B is expected to have an above-average earnings rate compared to its industry and, therefore, is said to have goodwill. This goodwill may be the result of excellent customer relations, the location of the business, the quality and uniqueness of its products, monopolistic market advantages, a superior management and work force, or a combination of these and other factors.[5] Consequently, a potential investor would be willing to pay more for Company B than for Company A. Thus, goodwill is theoretically an asset that has value.

To keep financial statement information from being too subjective, accountants have agreed that goodwill should not be recorded unless it is purchased. Normally, goodwill is purchased only when a business is acquired in its entirety.

When a business is to be purchased, the buyer and seller may estimate the amount of goodwill in several different ways. If the business is expected to have $5,000 each year in above-average earnings, its goodwill may be valued at, say, four times its above-average earnings, or $20,000. Or if the $5,000 is expected to continue indefinitely, they may think of it as a return on an investment at a given rate of return, say, 10%. In this case, the estimated amount of goodwill is $5,000/10% = $50,000. However, in the final analysis, the value of goodwill is confirmed only by the price the seller is willing to accept and the buyer is willing to pay.

Trademarks and Trade Names

Companies often adopt unique symbols or select unique names that they use in marketing their products. Sometimes, the ownership and exclusive right to use such a **trademark** or **trade name** can be established simply by demonstrating that one company has used the trademark or trade name before other businesses. However, ownership generally can be established more definitely by registering the trademark or trade name at the Patent Office. The cost of developing, maintaining, or enhancing the value of a trademark or trade name, perhaps through advertising, should be charged to expense in the period or periods incurred. However, if a trademark or trade name is purchased, the purchase cost should be debited to an asset account and amortized over time.

---

[5] Of course, the value of the location may be reflected in a higher cost for the land owned and used by the company.

AS A MATTER OF
Fact

Common Types of Intangible Assets

	Number of Companies			
	1990	**1989**	**1988**	**1987**
Goodwill	148	144	134	129
Licences/broadcast licenses	20	20	19	14
Customer lists	10	11	9	7
Trademarks.	13	12	11	11
Patents or patent rights	11	12	10	11
Franchises	5	5	6	6
Technology/know-how	5	4	4	4
Noncompetition agreements	4	3	3	1
Publishing rights	3	3	1	1

Source: Adapted from *CICA*, "Financial Reporting in Canada, 1991," (Toronto: 1991), p. 115.

Amortization of Intangibles

Some intangibles, such as patents, copyrights, and leaseholds, have limited useful lives that are determined by law, contract, or the nature of the asset. Other intangibles, such as goodwill, trademarks, and trade names, have indeterminable lives. In general, the cost of intangible assets should be amortized over the periods expected to be benefited by their use, which in no case is longer than their legal existence. However, as we stated earlier, generally accepted accounting principles require that the amortization period of intangible assets never be longer than 40 years. This limitation applies even if the life of the asset (e.g., goodwill) may continue indefinitely into the future.

Summary of the Chapter in Terms of Learning Objectives

LO 1. To maintain control over capital assets, detailed records should be kept. These records usually require the use of subsidiary ledgers that are controlled by asset and accumulated amortization accounts.

LO 2. All expenditures can be classified as revenue or capital expenditures. Revenue expenditures are debited to expense accounts and matched with current revenues. Capital expenditures are debited to asset accounts, and then charged to amortization expense in later years. Examples of revenue expenditures related to capital assets are wages, supplies, fuel, lubricants, power, and repairs. An example of a capital expenditure for capital assets subsequent to their acquisition is betterments. Technically, amounts paid for assets with low costs are capital expenditures, but they can be treated as revenue expenditures if they are not material.

LO 3. When a capital asset is discarded or sold, the cost and accumulated amortization are removed from the accounts. Any cash proceeds are recorded and compared to the asset's book value to determine gain or loss. When an old asset is exchanged for a new asset that is similar in purpose and the cash involved is less than 10%, a gain or loss is normally not recognized. Instead, the new asset account is debited for the book value of the old asset plus any cash paid. If the two assets are not similar, the new asset is recorded at its fair value, and either a gain or a loss on disposal is recognized. Accounting is the same for similar assets when the cash involved is more than 10% of the consideration.

LO 4.   The cost of a natural resource is recorded in an asset account. Then depletion of the natural resource is recorded by allocating the cost to expense according to a units-of-production basis. The depletion is credited to an accumulated depletion account. Intangible assets are recorded at the cost incurred to purchase the assets. The allocation of intangible asset cost to expense is done on a straight-line basis and is called *amortization*. Normally, amortization is recorded with credits made directly to the asset account instead of to a contra account.

Demonstration Problem	On January 13, 1990, the Morgan Company purchased seven identical machines and paid a total of $147,000 cash to the seller. The service life of each machine was predicted to be five years, and the salvage value of each was estimated at $1,000. All seven machines were placed in service at once. Amortization is based on the assumption that machines are purchased and sold on the first of the month nearest the actual dates of purchase and sale. The straight-line method is used, and the company has a December 31 year-end. Prepare entries to record each of the following transactions:

a.   Machine No. 1 was used until July 7, 1995, when it was retired from service and sold for $1,000 cash. Record amortization on Machine No. 1 for 1995 and record the sale of the machine.

b.   Machine No. 2 was used until December 20, 1992, when it was stolen. On December 24, the insurance company paid Maxwell $4,800 cash, which equalled the estimate of the asset's fair value. Record amortization on Machine No. 2 for 1992 and record the settlement with the insurance company.

c.   Machine No. 3 was used until January 4, 1993, at which time it was sold for $13,000 cash. Record the sale of Machine No. 3.

d.   Machine No. 4 was used until December 21, 1993, at which time it was traded in on Machine No. 8, with a cash payment of $20,000. Machine No. 8 had a cash price of $22,000. Record amortization on Machine No. 4 for 1993 and record the exchange for Machine No. 8.

e.   Machine No. 5 was used until December 23, 1993, when it was traded in on Machine No. 9, with a cash payment of $18,000. Machine No. 9 had a cash price of $25,500. Record amortization on Machine No. 5 for 1993 and record the exchange for Machine No. 9.

f.   Machine No. 6 was used until January 9, 1994, at which time it received a major overhaul and parts that extended its useful life until the end of 1998 and left its expected salvage value at $1,000. The cost of the overhaul was $7,100, which was paid in cash. Record the overhaul, compute the machine's book value after the overhaul, and record amortization for 1994.

g. Machine No. 7 was used only as a backup for the other six machines. Because the machines were more dependable than expected, Machine No. 7 did not deteriorate as quickly as the other machines. Therefore, during 1993, the company manager predicted that its useful life would probably extend until the end of 1997. The estimated salvage value was unchanged. Record amortization expense on Machine No. 7 for 1993.

Planning the Solution

■ Calculate amortization of each asset to the nearest whole month of the date of purchase or disposal, applying the straight-line method to cost less salvage value.

■ Record any gain or loss on disposals of machines for cash, after bringing amortization up to date.

■ On trading an asset (plus cash) for a similar asset, compare the book value of the old asset with its trade-in value. If book value exceeds trade-in value, record a loss. If trade-in value exceeds book value, record a gain.

■ Record the cost of the Machine No. 6 overhaul as a capital expenditure.

■ When the estimated useful life of a machine changes, amortize the remaining cost to be amortized over the remaining life as revised.

Solution to Demonstration Problem

For Machines No. 1 through 7, the initial cost of each is $147,000/7 = $21,000. Annual amortization for each machine is ($21,000 − $1,000)/5 = $4,000.

a.	1995				
	July	7	Cash	1,000.00	
			Accumulated Amortization, Machine No. 1	20,000.00	
			Machine No. 1		21,000.00
			($21,000 − $20,000 = $1,000)		

Machine No. 1 was fully amortized at the end of 1994, so amortization is not recorded in 1995. The machine was sold for its salvage value, so there was no gain or loss on the disposal.

b.

	1992				
	Dec.	20	Amortization Expense	4,000.00	
			Accumulated Amortization, Machine No. 2		4,000.00
		24	Cash	4,800.00	
			Accumulated Amortization, Machine No. 2	12,000.00	
			Loss on Theft	4,200.00	
			Machine No. 2		21,000.00
			$21,000 − $12,000 = $9,000		
			$9,000 − $4,800 = $4,200		

c.

	1993				
	Jan.	4	Cash	13,000.00	
			Accumulated Amortization, Machine No. 3	12,000.00	
			Gain on Disposal		4,000.00
			Machine No. 3		21,000.00
			$21,000 − $12,000 = $9,000		
			$13,000 − $9,000 = $4,000		

d.

	1993				
	Dec.	21	Amortization Expense	4,000.00	
			Accumulated Amortization, Machine No. 4		4,000.00
		21	Machine No. 8	22,000.00	
			Accumulated Amortization, Machine No. 4	16,000.00	
			Loss on Trade	3,000.00	
			Cash		20,000.00
			Machine No. 4		21,000.00
			$4,000 × 4 = $16,000		

Record the loss because the cash paid is more than 10% of the value of the machines in the transaction.

e.

	1993				
	Dec.	23	Amortization Expense	4,000.00	
			Accumulated Amortization, Machine No. 5		4,000.00
		23	Machine No. 9	25,500.00	
			Accumulated Amortization, Machine No. 5	16,000.00	
			Cash		18,000.00
			Machine No. 5		21,000.00
			Gain on Trade		2,500.00

f.

	1994				
	Jan.	9	Machine No. 6	7,100.00	
			Cash		7,100.00

Book value before the overhaul: $21,000 − $16,000 = $5,000.
Book value after the overhaul: $5,000 + $7,100 = $12,100.

Dec.	31	Amortization Expense	2,220.00	
		Accumulated Amortization, Machine No. 6		2,220.00
		($12,100 − $1,000)/5 = $2,220		

g. Book value at Dec. 31, 1992: $21,000 − $12,000 = $9,000. Revised remaining useful life is from Jan. 1, 1990 to Dec. 31, 1994, or 5 years, and the revised annual amortization charge is ($9,000 − $1,000)/5 = $1,600.

1993				
Dec.	31	Amortization Expense	1,600.00	
		Accumulated Amortization, Machine No. 7		1,600.00

Glossary

Amortization   the process of systematically writing off the cost of a capital asset, in particular, of an intangible asset, to expense over its estimated useful life. p. 580

Balance sheet expenditure   another name for *capital expenditure*. p. 571

Betterment   a modification to an asset to make it more efficient or to extend its life, usually by replacing one of its components with an improved or superior component. p. 572

Capital expenditure   an expenditure that produces economic benefits that do not fully expire before the end of the current period; because it creates or adds to existing assets, it should appear on the balance sheet as the cost of an asset. Also called a *balance sheet expenditure*. p. 571

Copyright   an exclusive right granted by the federal government or by international agreement to publish and sell a musical, literary, or artistic work for a period of years. p. 581

Depletion   the cost created by consuming the usefulness of natural resources. p. 579

Goodwill   an intangible capital asset of a business that creates future earnings greater than the average in its industry; recognized in the financial statements only when an entire business is acquired at a price in excess of the combined market values of its other assets. p. 581

Intangible asset   a capital asset representing certain legal rights and economic relationships; it has no physical existence but is beneficial to the owner. p. 579

Lease   a contract under which the owner of property (the lessor) grants the right to the lessee to use the property. p. 581

Leasehold   the rights granted to a lessee by the lessor under the terms of a lease contract. p. 581

Leasehold improvements   improvements to leased property made and paid for by the lessee. p. 581

Lessee   the individual or company that acquires the right to use property under the terms of a lease. p. 581

Lessor   the individual or company that owns property to be used by a lessee under the terms of a lease. p. 581

Office Equipment Ledger   a subsidiary ledger that contains a separate record for each individual item of office equipment. p. 569

Patent   exclusive right granted by the federal government for 17 years to manufacture and sell a patented machine or device or to use a process. p. 580

Repairs   actvities that keep a plant asset in normal operating condition; treated as a revenue expenditure. p. 572

Revenue expenditure   an expenditure that should appear on the current income statement as an expense and be deducted from the period's revenues because it does not provide a material benefit in future periods. p. 571

Store Equipment Ledger   a subsidiary ledger that contains a separate record for each individual item of store equipment. p. 569

Trademark   a unique symbol used by a company in marketing its products or services. p. 582

Trade name   a unique name used by a company in marketing its products or services. p. 582

Amortization depreciation, depletion.

Betterment improvement.

Capital expenditure balance sheet expenditure.

Natural resources wasting assets.

Assuming the company uses straight-line amortization, state whether each of the following events requires a revision of the original amortization rate, with reasons for your answer:

LO 1 In keeping capital asset records:

a. Computerized records always provide more information than handwritten records.

b. To record a purchase of an office desk, separate General Journal entries are made to Office Equipment and to the subsidiary account Office Desk.

c. The Office Equipment Ledger controls the Office Equipment account and the Accumulated Amortization, Office Equipment account.

d. Detailed subsidiary records serve as controlling accounts for the related General Ledger account.

e. The asset account and related accumulated amortization account for each group of assets serve as controlling accounts for detailed subsidiary records.

LO 2 At the beginning of the fifth year of a machine's estimated six-year useful life, the machine was completely overhauled and its estimated useful life was extended to nine years in total. The machine originally cost $110,000, and the overhaul cost was $12,000. The cost of the overhaul should be recorded as follows:

a.	Amortization Expense.	12,000.00	
	Cash		12,000.00
b.	Machinery.	12,000.00	
	Accumulated Amortization, Machinery		12,000.00
c.	Repairs Expense	12,000.00	
	Cash		12,000.00
d.	Machinery.	12,000.00	
	Cash		12,000.00
e.	Accumulated Amortization, Machinery	12,000.00	
	Cash		12,000.00

LO 3 Standard Company traded an old truck for a new one. The original cost of the old truck was $30,000, and its accumulated amortization at the time of the trade was $23,400. The new truck had a cash price of $45,000. However, Standard received a $3,000 trade-in allowance. Standard should record the new truck at the cost of:

a. $48,600.

b. $45,000.

c. $42,000.

d. $41,400.

e. $ 6,600.

LO 4 Prospect Mining Company paid $650,000 for an ore deposit. The deposit had an estimated 325,000 tons of ore that would be fully mined during the next 10 years. During the current year, 91,000 tons were mined, processed, and sold. The amount of depletion for the year is:

a. $ 65,000.
b. $ 91,000.
c. $182,000.
d. $156,000.
e. $ –0–.

LO 5 An expenditure that affects future periods because the economic benefits obtained do not fully expire by the end of the current period is called a(n):

a. Betterment.
b. Extraordinary repair.
c. Intangible asset.
d. Capital expenditure.
e. Revenue expenditure.

Questions for Class Discussion

1. What is the purpose of periodically taking an inventory of capital assets?
2. Distinguish between revenue expenditures and capital expenditures and describe how they should be recorded.
3. Distinguish between repairs and betterments.
4. What is a betterment? How should a betterment to a machine be recorded?
5. What accounting principle justifies charging the $75 cost of a plant asset immediately to an expense account?
6. When should a loss on the exchange of a plant asset be recorded? When is it permissible to absorb a loss into the cost basis of the new plant asset? Should a gain on a plant asset exchange be recorded?
7. If an asset that has been amortized is sold for cash and the remaining book value of the asset is more than the cash proceeds from the sale, should the difference be debited to amortization expense? How should the difference be recorded?
8. When cash and a plant asset are exchanged for a similar asset, what is the cost basis of the newly acquired asset?
9. What is the name for the process of allocating the cost of natural resources to expense as the natural resources are used?
10. What are the characteristics of an intangible asset?
11. Is the declining-balance method an acceptable means of calculating depletion of natural resources?
12. Define (a) lease, (b) lessor, (c) lessee, (d) leasehold, and (e) leasehold improvement.
13. When does a business have goodwill? Under what conditions can goodwill appear in a company's balance sheet?

14. X Company bought an established business and paid for goodwill. If X Company plans to incur substantial advertising and promotional costs each year to maintain the value of the goodwill, must the company also amortize the goodwill?

15. In the Bombardier Inc.'s consolidated balance sheet that appears in Appendix I, what was the net change in intangible assets from 1991 to 1992?

Mini Discussion Cases

You have just been appointed auditor of the Brandon Company. During your first examination of the records you discover that the company charges all of its repairs and maintenance costs to their respective asset accounts. Management indicates that regular maintenance increases the life of an asset; therefore, the maintenance costs, instead of being charged to expense as incurred, will be reflected in the increased amortization charges as the asset is being used.

Required

Evaluate Brandon's policy with respect to GAAP. Explain why their policy is correct or incorrect.

Case 11–1

Two of your classmates are having a discussion about accounting for intangible assets. Classmate 1 says that all intangible assets should be written off immediately since they have no physical substance. Classmate 2 argues that intangible assets should be written off over their lifetime, as provided by law.

Required

Mediate between your classmates explaining, with reasons, the proper accounting treatment for intangible assets.

Case 11–2

Exercises

Baytown Company paid $49,500 for a machine that was expected to last five years and have a salvage value of $7,500. Present General Journal entries to record the following costs related to the machine:

Exercise 11–1
Repairs and betterments
(LO 2)

a. During the second year of the machine's life, $1,300 was paid for repairs necessary to keep the machine in good working order.

b. During the third year of the machine's life, $4,500 was paid for a new component that was expected to increase the machine's productivity by 15% each year. The new component was added to the machine without removing any old component.

c. During the fourth year of the machine's life, $6,400 was paid for repairs that were expected to increase the service life of the machine from five to seven years.

Exercise 11–2
Betterments
(LO 2)

Topek Company owns a building that appeared on its balance sheet at the end of last year at its original $947,000 cost less $719,720 accumulated amortization. The building has been amortized on a straight-line basis under the assumption that it would have a 25-year life and no salvage value. During the first week in January of the current year, major structural repairs were completed on the building at a cost of $178,000. The repairs did not increase the building's capacity but they did extend its expected life for 10 years beyond the 25 years originally estimated.

a. Determine the building's age as of the end of last year.
b. Give the entry to record the repairs, which were paid with cash.
c. Determine the book value of the building after its repairs were recorded.
d. Give the entry to record the current year's amortization.

Exercise 11–3
Recording sales of plant assets
(LO 3)

A machine with an expected service life of seven years and salvage value of $7,000 was purchased by Bedrock Company for $63,000. After taking straight-line amortization for four years, the machine was sold. Present General Journal entries dated December 31 to record the sale assuming the cash proceeds from the sale were (a) $31,000, (b) $40,250, (c) $21,400.

Exercise 11–4
Recording plant asset disposal or trade-in
(LO 3)

On January 2, 1993, Revere Company disposed of a machine that cost $163,000 and that had been amortized $91,500. Present the General Journal entries to record the disposal under each of the following unrelated assumptions:

a. The machine was sold for $58,500 cash.
b. The machine was traded in on a new machine of like purpose having a $205,000 cash price. A $75,000 trade-in allowance was received, and the balance was paid in cash.
c. A $65,000 trade-in allowance was received for the machine on a new machine of like purpose having a $205,000 cash price. The balance was paid in cash.
d. The machine was traded for a used machine of like purpose and $1,500 cash was paid.
e. The machine was traded for vacant land adjacent to the company to be used as a parking lot. The land had a fair value of $150,000, and Revere paid $70,000 cash in addition to giving the seller the machine.

Exercise 11–5
Exchanging plant assets
(LO 3)

Anneal Company traded in its old truck on a new truck, receiving a $21,400 trade-in allowance and paying the remaining $53,400 in cash. The old truck cost $62,000, and straight-line amortization of $36,000 had been recorded under the assumption that it would last six years and have an $8,000 salvage value. Answer the following questions:

a. What was the book value of the old truck?
b. What is the loss on the exchange?
c. What amount should be debited to the new Truck account?

Travis Company purchased and installed a machine on January 3, 1993, at a total cost of $120,000. Straight-line amortization was taken each year for three years, based on the assumption of a five-year life and no salvage value. Travis disposed of the asset on April 30, 1996. Present the entries to record the partial year's amortization on April 30 and to record the disposal under each of the following unrelated assumptions: (*a*) the machine was sold for $56,500, (*b*) it was sold for $34,600, and (*c*) the machine was totally destroyed in a fire and the insurance company settled the insurance claim for $29,000.

Exercise 11–6
Mid-year disposal of asset
(LO 3)

On January 1, 1993, Redstone Company paid $812,000 for an ore deposit containing 2,030,000 tonnes of ore. The company also installed machinery in the mine that cost $91,350, had an estimated 12-year life and no salvage value, and was capable of removing all the ore in 6 years. The machine will be abandoned when the ore is completely mined. Redstone began operations on April 1, 1993, and mined 304,500 tonnes of ore during the remaining nine months of the year. Give the December 31, 1993, entries to record the depletion of the ore deposit and the amortization of the mining machinery.

Exercise 11–7
Depletion of natural resources
(LO 4)

Espy Company purchased the copyright to a trade manual for $72,500 on January 1, 1993. The copyright legally protects its owner for 25 more years. However, management believes the trade manual can be successfully published and sold for only five more years. Prepare journal entries to record (*a*) the purchase of the copyright and (*b*) the annual amortization of the copyright on December 31, 1993.

Exercise 11–8
Amortization of intangible assets
(LO 4)

R. Donovan has devoted years to developing a profitable business that earns an attractive return. Donovan is now considering the possibility of selling the business and is attempting to estimate the value of the goodwill in the business. The fair value of the net assets of the business (excluding goodwill) is $400,000, and in a typical year, net income is about $72,000. Most businesses of this type are expected to earn a return of about 15% on net assets. Estimate the value of the goodwill assuming (*a*) the value is equal to six times the excess earnings above average, and (*b*) the value can be found by capitalizing the excess earnings above average at a rate of 12%.

Exercise 11–9
Estimating goodwill
(LO 4)

Problems

Barker Ready Mix Company completed the following transactions involving plant assets:

1992

Jan.　3　Purchased on credit an electronic scale priced at $18,875 from Weigh Systems, Inc. The serial number of the scale was W–66557, its service life was estimated at five years with a trade-in value of $4,000, and the assigned plant asset number was 167–2.

Mar.　1　Purchased on credit a Bulldog mixer priced at $12,200 from Cement Systems, Inc. The serial number of the mixer was M–10102, its service life

Problem 11–1
Plant asset records
(LO 1)

was estimated at four years with a trade-in value of $2,000, and the assigned plant asset number was 167–3.

Dec. 31 Recorded straight-line amortization on the plant equipment for 1992.

1993

Oct. 2 Sold the Bulldog mixer to Crider Cement for $7,300 cash.

    4 Purchased on credit a new TopJob mixer from Stamford Equipment for $15,400. The serial number of the mixer was TJ–87651, its service life was estimated at six years with a trade-in value of $2,800, and the assigned plant asset number was 167–4.

Dec. 31 Recorded straight-line amortization on the plant equipment for 1993.

Required

1. Open General Ledger accounts for Plant Equipment and for Accumulated Amortization, Plant Equipment. Prepare a subsidiary plant asset record card for each item of equipment purchased.

2. Prepare General Journal entries to record the transactions and adjustments, and post them to the proper General Ledger and subsidiary ledger accounts.

3. Prove that the December 31, 1993, balances of the Plant Equipment and Accumulated Amortization, Plant Equipment accounts equal the totals of the balances shown on the subsidiary plant asset records. You should accomplish this step by preparing a list showing the cost and accumulated amortization on each item of plant equipment owned by Barker Ready Mix Company on that date.

Problem 11–2
Purchases, betterments, sales of plant assets, partial year's amortization
(LO 2, 3)

The Blackhawk Company completed these transactions involving the purchase and operation of delivery trucks:

1992

Mar. 29 Paid cash for a new truck, $26,600 plus $1,600 sales taxes. The truck was estimated to have a five-year life and a $4,300 salvage value.

Apr. 2 Paid $1,400 for special racks and cleats installed in the truck. The racks and cleats did not increase the truck's estimated trade-in value.

Dec. 31 Recorded straight-line amortization on the truck.

1993

July 7 Paid $1,825 to install an air-conditioning unit in the truck. The unit increased the truck's estimated trade-in value by $700.

Dec. 31 Recorded straight-line amortization on the truck.

1994

Aug. 13 Paid $280 for repairs to the truck's fender, which was damaged when the driver backed into a loading dock.

Dec. 31 Recorded straight-line amortization on the truck.

1995

July 2 Traded the old truck and paid $21,400 in cash for a new truck. The new truck was estimated to have a four-year life and an $8,000 trade-in value, and the invoice for the exchange showed these items:

Price of the new truck	$31,900
Trade-in allowance granted on the old truck	(12,500)
Balance of purchase price	$19,400
Sales taxes	2,000
Total paid in cash	$21,400

July 5 Paid $2,100 for special cleats and racks installed in the truck.

Dec. 31 Recorded straight-line amortization on the new truck.

Required

Prepare General Journal entries to record the transactions.

A company completed the following transactions involving machinery:

Problem 11-3
Amortizing and
exchanging plant assets
(LO 3)

Machine No. 106-12 was purchased for cash on February 1, 1989, at an installed cost of $29,400. Its useful life was estimated to be four years with a $3,000 trade-in value. Straight-line amortization was recorded for the machine at the end of 1989 and 1990, and on October 3, 1991, it was traded for Machine No. 106-13. A trade-in allowance of $12,800 was actually received, and the balance was paid in cash.

Machine No. 106-13 was purchased on October 3, 1991, at an installed cash price of $33,000, less the trade-in allowance received on Machine No. 106-12. The new machine's life was predicted to be five years with a $3,200 trade-in value. Straight-line amortization was recorded on each December 31 of its life, and on January 4, 1996, it was sold for $5,200.

Machine No. 107-24 was purchased for cash on January 6, 1991, at an installed cost of $63,000. Its useful life was estimated to be five years, after which it would have an $8,400 trade-in value. Declining-balance amortization at twice the straight-line rate was recorded for the machine at the end of 1991, 1992, and 1993; and, on January 3, 1994, it was traded in as part of the purchase of Machine No. 107-25. A $13,500 trade-in allowance was received, and the balance was paid in cash.

Machine No. 107-25 was purchased on January 3, 1994, at an installed cash price of $75,900, less the trade-in allowance received on Machine No. 107-24. It was estimated that the new machine would produce 70,000 units of product during its useful life, after which it would have a $3,800 trade-in value. Units-of-production amortization was recorded for the machine for 1994, a period in which it produced 7,000 units of product. Between January 1 and October 3, 1995, the machine produced 10,500 more units. On the latter date, it was sold for $50,000.

Required

Prepare general journal entries to record: (*a*) the purchase of each machine, (*b*) the amortization recorded on the first December 31 of each machine's life, and (*c*) the disposal of each machine. (Only one entry is needed to record the exchange of one machine for another.)

Part 1. Ten years ago, Aqua Products Company leased space in a building for 20 years. The lease contract calls for annual rental payments of $51,000 to be made on each January 1 throughout the life of the lease and also provides that the lessee must pay for all additions and improvements to the leased property. Because recent nearby construction has made the location more valuable, Aqua Products Company subleased the space to Oberon, Inc., on December 27 for the remaining 10 years of the lease, beginning the next January 1. Oberon paid $90,000 to Aqua Products for the right to sublease the property and agreed to assume the obligation to pay the $51,000 annual rental charges to the building owner. After taking possession of the leased space, Oberon, Inc., paid for improving the office portion of the leased space at a cost of $174,000. The improvement was paid for on January 7 and is estimated to have a life equal to the 20 years in the remaining life of the building.

Problem 11-4
Intangible assets and
natural resources
(LO 4)

Required

Prepare entries for Oberon, Inc., to record (*a*) its payment to sublease the building space, (*b*) its payment of the next annual rental charge to the building owner, and (*c*) payment for the improvements. Also, prepare the adjusting entries required at the end of the first year of the sublease to amortize (d) a proper share of the $90,000 cost of the sublease and (e) a proper share of the office improvement.

Part 2. On May 4 of the current year, Seacort Company paid $3,990,000 for land estimated to contain 9.5 million tonnes of recoverable ore of a valuable mineral. It installed machinery costing $855,000, which had an 18-year life and no salvage value, and was capable of exhausting the ore deposit in 15 years. The machinery was paid for on July 28, three days before mining operations began. The company removed 356,250 tonnes of ore during the first five months' operations.

Required

Prepare entries to record (a) the purchase of the land, (b) the installation of the machinery, (c) the first five months' depletion under the assumption that the land will be valueless after the ore is mined, and (d) the first five months' amortization on the machinery to be abandoned after the ore is fully mined.

Problem 11–5
Goodwill
(LO 4)

Lancelot Company's balance sheet on December 31, 1993, is as follows:

Cash	$ 81,750
Merchandise inventory	235,500
Buildings	422,000
Accumulated amortization	(253,200)
Land	178,500
Total assets	$664,550
Accounts payable.	$ 26,300
Long-term note payable.	187,750
Common shares.	304,600
Retained earnings.	145,900
Total liabilities and shareholders' equity	$664,550

In this industry, earnings average 12% of common shareholders' equity. Lancelot Company, however, is expected to earn $66,000 annually. The owners believe that the balance sheet amounts are reasonable estimates of fair market values for all assets except goodwill, which does not appear on the financial statement. In discussing a plan to sell the company, they have suggested to the potential buyer that goodwill can be measured by capitalizing the amount of above-average earnings at a rate of 15%. On the other hand, the potential buyer thinks that goodwill should be valued at five times the amount of excess earnings above the average for the industry.

Required

1. Calculate the amount of goodwill claimed by Lancelot Company's owners.
2. Calculate the amount of goodwill according to the potential buyer.
3. Suppose that the buyer finally agrees to pay the full price requested by Lancelot Company's owners. If the amount of expected earnings (before amortization of goodwill) is obtained and the goodwill is amortized over the longest permissible time period, what amount of net income will be reported for the first year after the company is purchased?
4. If the buyer pays the full price requested by Lancelot Company's owners, what rate of return on the purchaser's investment will be earned as net income the first year?

Part 1. On January 4, 1987, Meyer Company purchased for cash and placed in operation a machine estimated to have an eight-year life and no salvage value. The machine cost $288,000 and was amortized on a straight-line basis. On January 5, 1990, a $24,500 device was added to the machine that increased its output by one third. The device did not change the machine's estimated life or its zero salvage value. During the first week of January 1992, the machine was completely overhauled at a $90,380 cost (paid for on January 7). The overhaul added four additional years to the machine's estimated life but did not change its zero salvage value. On June 30, 1994, the machine was destroyed in a fire and the insurance company settled the loss claim for $122,400.

Required

Prepare General Journal entries to record (*a*) the purchase of the machine, (*b*) the 1987 amortization, (*c*) the addition of the new device, (*d*) the 1990 amortization, (*e*) the machine's overhaul, (*f*) the 1992 amortization, and (*g*) 1994 amortization and the insurance settlement.

Part 2. On January 4, 1989, Weishaar Company paid $124,900 cash for Machine No. 1. It was amortized on a straight-line basis at the end of 1989, 1990, 1991, and 1992 under the assumption it would have an eight-year life and a $19,300 salvage value. Before recording 1993 amortization, the company revised its estimate of the machine's remaining years downward from four years to three and revised the estimate of its salvage value downward to $6,100. On July 1, 1995, after recording 1993, 1994, and part of a year's amortization for 1995, the company traded in Machine No. 1 on Machine No. 2, receiving a $24,600 trade-in allowance. A discount of about 5% is quite common on these machines. The cash paid for Machine No. 2 was $138,800 less the trade-in allowance. On December 31, 1995, Machine No. 2 was amortized on a straight-line basis under the assumption it would have a five-year life and a $31,300 salvage value.

Required

Prepare entries to record (*a*) the purchase of Machine No. 1, (*b*) its 1989 amortization, (*c*) its 1993 amortization, (*d*) the exchange of the machines, and (*e*) the 1995 amortization on Machine No. 2.

It is January 15, 1994, and you have just been hired as an accountant for PetroServ Inc., an oil field service company. The previous accountant brought the accounting records up to date through December 31, the end of the fiscal year, including the year-end adjusting entries. In reviewing the entries made last year, you discover the following three items:

1. An expenditure for changing the oil on a truck was recorded as a debit to Accumulated Depreciation, Trucks.
2. An expenditure for upgrading the memory of the computer system was debited to Computer Equipment.
3. An expenditure to install a new engine in a fork lift was recorded as a debit to Repairs Expense, Machinery. As a result of the replacement, the fork lift is expected to last three years longer than originally estimated.

Required

For each of the three items, indicate whether it was classified by the previous accountant as a revenue expenditure or a capital expenditure. Then state whether or not you agree with this classification and explain why. If you disagree, indicate what the proper classification should be.

Problem 11–6
Amortization, repairs, and exchanges of plant assets
(LO 2, 4)

Problem 11–7
Analytical essay
(LO 2)

Problem 11–8
Analytical essay
(LO 2)

Refer to the transactions of PetroServ Inc. discussed in Problem 11–7. Assume that you prepare the 1993 financial statements for PetroServ Inc. without correcting any errors that may have been made in recording the transactions. Explain the effects of any recording errors on the 1993 income statement and the December 31, 1993, balance sheet.

Alternate Problems

Problem 11–1A
Plant asset records
(LO 1)

Avalon Gravel Company completed the following transactions involving plant assets:

1992

Jan. 3   Purchased on credit an electric grinder priced at $19,140 from AAA Equipment. The serial number of the grinder was 0–9470–2, its service life was estimated at six years with a trade-in value of $1,500, and the assigned plant asset number was 167–1.

Apr. 30   Purchased on credit a Halburn conveyor priced at $40,000 from AAA Equipment. The serial number of the conveyor was 7–8496–8, its service life was estimated at five years with a trade-in value of $4,000, and the assigned plant asset number was 167–2.

Dec. 31   Recorded straight-line amortization on the plant equipment for 1992.

1993

Nov. 2   Sold the Halburn conveyor to Colville Aggregate Products for $24,500 cash.

       7   Purchased on credit a new Weston conveyor from Jones Construction Equipment for $47,200. The serial number of the conveyor was JC–45736, its service life was estimated at seven years with a trade-in value of $5,200, and the assigned plant asset number was 167–3.

Dec. 31   Recorded straight-line amortization on the plant equipment for 1993.

Required

1. Open General Ledger accounts for Plant Equipment and for Accumulated Amortization, Plant Equipment. Prepare a subsidiary plant asset record card for each item of equipment purchased.

2. Prepare General Journal entries to record the transactions and adjustments, and post them to the proper general ledger and subsidiary ledger accounts.

3. Prove that the December 31, 1993, balances of the Plant Equipment and Accumulated Amortization, Plant Equipment accounts equal the totals of the balances shown on the subsidiary plant asset records. You should accomplish this step by preparing a list showing the cost and accumulated amortization on each item of plant equipment owned by Avalon Gravel Company on that date.

Problem 11–2A
Purchases, betterments,
and sales of plant assets
(LO 2, 3)

The Twins Company completed these transactions involving the purchase and operation of delivery trucks.

1992

July 2   Paid cash for a new delivery van, $42,450 plus $2,650 sales taxes. The van was estimated to have a four-year life and a $7,100 salvage value.

July   6   Paid $2,400 for special racks and bins installed in the van. The racks and bins did not increase the van's estimated trade-in value.

Dec.   31   Recorded straight-line amortization on the van.

1993

June   29   Paid $1,980 to install an air-conditioning unit in the van. The unit increased the van's estimated trade-in value by $240.

Dec.   31   Recorded straight-line amortization on the van.

1994

Mar.   15   Paid $410 for repairs to the van's fender damaged when the driver backed into a tree.

Dec.   31   Recorded straight-line amortization on the van.

1995

Sept. 29   Traded the old van and paid $30,590 in cash for a new van. The new van was estimated to have a four-year life and an $8,500 trade-in value, and the invoice for the exchange showed these items:

Price of the new van	$40,260
Trade-in allowance granted on the old van	(12,700)
Balance of purchase price.	$27,560
Sales taxes	3,030
Total paid in cash	$30,590

Oct.   4   Paid $3,210 for special racks and bins installed in the new van.

Dec.   31   Recorded straight-line amortization on the new van.

Required

Prepare General Journal entries to record the transactions.

Bart Company completed the following transactions involving machinery:

Problem 11–3A
Amortization and exchanges of plant assets (LO 3)

Machine No. 10–232 was purchased for cash on July 2, 1989, at an installed cost of $99,120. Its useful life was predicted to be five years with a $12,000 trade-in value. Straight-line amortization was recorded for the machine at the end of 1989 and 1990, and on October 4, 1991, it was traded for Machine No. 10–233. A trade-in allowance of $61,416 was actually received, and the balance was paid in cash.

Machine No. 10–233 was purchased on October 4, 1991, at an installed cash price of $110,800, less the trade-in allowance received on Machine No. 10–232. The new machine's life was estimated to be six years with a $19,000 trade-in value. Straight-line amortization was recorded on each December 31 of its life, and on February 5, 1996, it was sold for $34,400.

Machine No. 11–008 was purchased for cash on January 10, 1991, at an installed cost of $36,000. Its useful life was estimated to be five years, after which it would have a $5,400 trade-in value. Declining-balance amortization at twice the straight-line rate was recorded for the machine at the end of 1991, 1992, and 1993; and, on January 2, 1994, it was traded in as part of the purchase of Machine No. 11–009. A $7,590 trade-in allowance was received, and the balance was paid in cash.

Machine No. 11–009 was purchased on January 2, 1994, at an installed cash price of $50,310, less the trade-in allowance received on Machine No. 11–008. It was estimated that the new machine would produce 65,000 units of product during its useful life, after which it would have a $9,000 trade-in value. Units-of-production amortization was recorded for the machine for 1994, a period in which it produced 9,750 units of product. Between January 1 and October 2, 1995, the machine produced 13,000 more units. On the latter date, it was sold for $39,900.

Required

Prepare General Journal entries to record (*a*) the purchase of each machine, (*b*) the amortization recorded on the first December 31 of each machine's life, and (*c*) the disposal of each machine. (Only one entry is needed to record the exchange of one machine for another.)

Problem 11–4A
Intangible assets and
natural resources
(LO 4)

Part 1. Five years ago, Alba Corporation leased space in a building for 20 years. The lease contract calls for annual rental payments of $69,600 to be made on each January 1 throughout the life of the lease and also provides that the lessee must pay for all additions and improvements to the leased property. Because recent nearby construction has made the location more valuable, Alba Corporation subleased the space to Anson Company on December 30 for the remaining 15 years of the lease, beginning the next January 1. Anson paid $252,000 to Alba for the right to sublease the space and agreed to assume the obligation to pay the $69,600 annual rental charges to the building owner. After taking possession of the leased space, Anson Company paid for improving the office portion of the leased space at a cost of $189,000. The improvement was paid for on January 8 and is estimated to have a life equal to the 25 years in the remaining life of the building.

Required

Prepare entries for Anson Company to record (*a*) its payment to sublease the building space, (*b*) its payment of the next annual rental charge to the building owner, and (*c*) payment for the improvements. Also, prepare the adjusting entries required at the end of the first year of the sublease to amortize (*d*) a proper share of the $252,000 cost of the sublease and (*e*) a proper share of the office improvement.

Part 2. On June 4 of the current year, Standish Company paid $1,890,000 for land estimated to contain 7 million tonnes of recoverable ore of a valuable mineral. It installed machinery costing $231,000, which had an eight-year life and no salvage value, and was capable of exhausting the ore deposit in five years. The machinery was paid for on August 28, four days before mining operations began. The company removed 560,000 tonnes of ore during the first five months' operations.

Required

Prepare entries to record (*a*) the purchase of the land, (*b*) the installation of the machinery, (*c*) the first four months' depletion under the assumption that the land will be valueless after the ore is mined, and (*d*) the first four months' depreciation on the machinery to be abandoned after the ore is fully mined.

Problem 11–5A
Goodwill
(LO 4)

Trinity Company's balance sheet on December 31, 1993, is as follows:

Cash	$ 39,600
Merchandise inventory	198,300
Buildings	346,000
Accumulated amortization	(216,250)
Land	125,850
Total assets	$493,500
Accounts payable	$ 49,900
Long-term note payable	153,800
Common shares	225,000
Retained earnings	64,800
Total liabilities and shareholders' equity	$493,500

In this industry, earnings average 10% of common shareholders' equity. Trinity Company, however, is expected to earn $36,000 annually. The owners believe that the balance sheet amounts are reasonable estimates of fair market values for all assets except goodwill, which does not appear on the financial statement. In discussing a plan to sell the company, they have suggested to the potential buyer that goodwill can be measured by capitalizing the amount of above-average earnings at a rate of 15%. On the other hand, the potential buyer thinks that goodwill should be valued at four times the amount of excess earnings above the average for the industry.

Required

1. Calculate the amount of goodwill claimed by Trinity Company's owners.
2. Calculate the amount of goodwill according to the potential buyer.
3. Suppose that the buyer finally agrees to pay the full price requested by Trinity Company's owners. If the amount of expected earnings (before amortization of goodwill) is obtained and the goodwill is amortized over the longest permissible time period, what amount of net income will be reported for the first year after the company is purchased?
4. If the buyer pays the full price requested by Trinity Company's owners, what rate of return on the purchaser's investment will be earned as net income the first year?

Part 1. On January 2, 1987, Baylor Company purchased for cash a machine estimated to have a 12-year life and no salvage value. The machine cost $98,520 and was amortized on a straight-line basis. On January 6, 1992, a $14,280 improvement was added to the machine which had the effect of increasing its output by one third. The improvement did not change the machine's estimated life or its zero salvage value. During the first week of January 1994, the machine was completely overhauled at a $46,050 cost (paid for on January 4). The overhaul added two additional years to the machine's estimated life but did not change its zero salvage value. On October 1, 1996, the machine was destroyed in a fire and the insurance company settled the loss claim for $39,775.

Required

Prepare General Journal entries to record (*a*) the purchase of the machine, (*b*) the 1987 amortization, (*c*) the addition of the new improvement, (*d*) the 1992 amortization, (*e*) the machine's overhaul, (*f*) the 1994 amortization, and (*g*) the 1996 amortization and the insurance settlement.

Part 2. On January 9, 1990, Sierra Company purchased Machine No. 1 for a cash price of $267,000. It was amortized on a straight-line basis at the end of 1990 and 1991 under the assumption it would have a six-year life and a $63,000 salvage value. Before recording 1992 amortization, the company revised its estimate of the machine's remaining years downward from four years to three and revised the estimate of its salvage value downward to $43,000. On July 5, 1994, after recording 1992, 1993, and part of a year's amortization for 1994, the company traded in Machine No. 1 on Machine No. 2, receiving a $42,500 trade-in allowance. The cash paid for Machine No. 2 was $298,800 less the trade-in allowance. A discount of about 5% is quite common on these machines. Machine No. 2 was amortized on a straight-line basis under the assumption it would have a nine-year life and a $76,800 salvage value.

Required

Prepare entries to record (*a*) the purchase of Machine No. 1, (*b*) its 1990 amortization, (*c*) its 1992 amortization, (*d*) the exchange of the machines, and (*e*) the 1994 amortization on Machine No. 2.

Problem 11–6A
Amortization, repairs, and exchanges of plant assets
(LO 2, 4)

Problem 11–7A
Analytical essay
(LO 2)

Early in 1994, Phonic Company hired a public accountant to prepare its financial statements for the year ended December 31, 1993. The owner of the company had brought the accounting records up to date through December 31, except for the year-end adjusting entries. Prior to preparing the adjusting entries, the accountant becomes concerned that some expenditures may have been recorded incorrectly. For each of the following transactions, describe the correcting entry, if any, the accountant should make. Also, explain why you think a correction is or is not necessary.

1. An expenditure to have a factory machine reconditioned by the manufacturer so it would last three years longer than originally estimated was recorded as a debit to Repairs Expense, Machinery.
2. The lubrication of factory machinery was recorded as a debit to Machinery.
3. The installation of a security system for the building was recorded as a debit to Building Improvements. The new system allowed the company to reduce the number of security guards.

Problem 11–8A
Analytical essay
(LO 2)

Refer to the transactions of Phonic Company discussed in Problem 11–7A. Assume that the accountant prepares the financial statements for Phonic Company without making correcting entries for any errors made in recording the transactions. Explain the effects of any recording errors on the 1993 income statement and the December 31, 1993, balance sheet.

Provocative Problems

Provocative Problem 11–1
Distress Company
(LO 2, 3)

While examining the accounting records of Distress Company, you discover two 1993 entries that appear questionable. The first entry recorded the cash proceeds from an insurance settlement as follows:

Oct.	18	Cash.	34,000.00	
		Loss on Fire.	9,000.00	
		Accumulated Amortization, Machinery.	37,000.00	
		Machinery		80,000.00
		Received payment of fire loss claim.		

Your investigation shows that this entry was made to record the receipt of an insurance company's $34,000 cheque to settle a claim resulting from the destruction of a machine in a small fire on September 29, 1993. The machine originally cost $74,000 and was put in operation on January 4, 1990. It was amortized on a straight-line basis for three years, under the assumptions that it would have a six-year life and no salvage value. During the first week of January 1993, the machine had been overhauled at a cost of $6,000. The overhaul did not increase the machine's capacity or its salvage value. However, it was expected that the overhaul would lengthen the machine's service life two years beyond the six originally expected.

The second entry that appears questionable was made to record the receipt of a cheque from selling a portion of a tract of land. The land was adjacent to the company's plant and had been purchased the year before. It cost $88,000, and another $11,000 was paid for clearing and grading it. Both amounts had been debited to the Land account.

The land was to be used for storing finished product, but sometime after the grading was completed, it became obvious the company did not need the entire tract. Distress Company received an offer from a purchaser to buy the east half for $54,000 or the west half for $66,000. The company decided to sell the west half, and recorded the receipt of the purchaser's cheque with the following entry:

Dec.	10	Cash.	66,000.00	
		Land		66,000.00
		Sold unneeded land.		

   Were any errors made in recording these transactions? If so, describe them and, in each case, provide an entry or entries to correct the account balances under the assumption that the 1993 gain and loss accounts have not been closed.

Nickel Company and Dime Company are similar businesses that sell competing products. Both companies acquired their equipment and began operating five years ago. Now both of them are up for sale. The Dollar Company is considering the possibility of buying either Nickel or Dime.

Provocative Problem 11–2
Nickel and Dime Companies
(A review problem)

   In evaluating the two companies, the management of Dollar has observed that Nickel Company has reported an average annual net income of $98,920. Dime Company, on the other hand, has reported an average of $127,095. However, the companies have not used the same accounting procedures, and Dollar Company management is concerned that the numbers are not comparable. The current balance sheets of the two companies show these items:

	Nickel Company	Dime Company
Cash	$ 65,750	$ 72,200
Accounts receivable	486,200	538,500
Allowance for doubtful accounts	(28,500)	–0–
Merchandise inventory	634,100	833,000
Store equipment	248,400	210,400
Accumulated amortization, store equipment . . .	(207,000)	(131,500)
Total assets	$1,198,950	$1,522,600
Current liabilities	$ 588,400	$ 704,300
Owners' equity	610,550	818,300
Total liabilities and owners' equity	$1,198,950	$1,522,600

   Nickel Company has used the allowance method of accounting for bad debts and has added to its allowance each year an amount equal to 1% of sales. However, this amount is revealed to be excessive by an audit that shows that only $15,000 of its accounts are probably uncollectible. Dime Company has used the direct write-off method but has been slow to write off bad debts. An examination of its accounts shows $27,000 of accounts that are probably uncollectible.

   During the past five years, Nickel Company has priced its inventories on a LIFO basis, with the result that its current inventory appears on its balance sheet at an amount that is $88,000 below replacement cost. Dime Company has used FIFO, and its ending inventory appears at its approximate replacement cost. Dollar Company management believes that FIFO produces the most useful measure of inventory and cost of goods sold.

   Both companies have assumed eight-year lives and no salvage value in amortizing equipment. However, Nickel Company has used double-declining-balance amortization, while Dime Company has used straight-line. The management of Dollar Company believes that straight-line amortization has resulted in reporting Dime Company's equipment on the balance sheet at its approximate fair market value. They believe that straight-line would have had the same result for Nickel Company.

Dollar Company is willing to pay what its management considers fair market value for the assets of either business. The management of Dollar believes that each company has goodwill equal to four times the average annual earnings in excess of 15% of the fair market value of the net tangible assets. Dollar Company's management defines net tangible assets as all assets (including accounts receivable) other than goodwill, minus liabilities. Dollar Company will also assume the liabilities of the purchased business, paying its owner the difference between total assets purchased (excluding cash) and the liabilities assumed.

Required

Prepare the following schedules: (*a*) the net tangible assets of each company at fair market values assessed by Dollar Company management; (*b*) the revised net incomes of the companies based on adjusted amounts of bad debts expense, FIFO inventories, and straight-line amortization; (*c*) the calculation of each company's goodwill; and (*d*) the maximum amount Dollar Company would offer to pay for each business and the net cash cost for each one, after deducting the cash that it owns.

Provocative Problem 11–3
Bombardier Inc.
(LO 4)

Refer to the annual report for Bombardier Inc. in Appendix I. Based on the information presented in the consolidated balance sheet and in the accompanying notes, answer the following:

1. How is goodwill reported on Bombardier's consolidated balance sheet?
2. What percentage of Bombardier's total assets consists of goodwill as of January 31, 1992?
3. What method does Bombardier's use to amortize goodwill? What is the period of time over which goodwill is amortized?

Analytical and Review Problems

A&R Problem 11–1

Rita's Rockers traded in an old planing machine for a new heavy-duty automated model. The following data are available:

Old machine—cost	$10,500*
Accumulated amortization.	7,000
List price of new model	19,750
Amount paid with trade-in.	17,250
Expected life of 10 years with a $1,500 residual value.	
Rita's uses straight-line amortization.	

*Market value at time of trade-in is $2,000.

Required

1. Prepare the journal entry to record the purchase of the new machine.
2. Using the data above, explain why it is important to current and future periods to determine the proper "cost" for assets subject to amortization, particularly when trade-ins are involved.

Part 1. Taylor has been amortizing equipment over a 20-year life on a straight-line basis. The equipment cost $153,000 and has an estimated residual value of $18,000. On the basis of experience, since acquisition on January 2 five years ago, management has decided that a total life of 14 years instead of 20 years is more appropriate, with no change in residual value. The change is to be effective January 1 of the fifth year.

A&R Problem 11–2

Required

Prepare the December 31 adjusting entry to recognize amortization expense for the fifth year. Show calculations.

Part 2. Taylor discovered during the year that the cost of an operational asset purchased on January 3, three years before January of the current year, was debited to operating expenses. The asset cost $60,000 and was estimated to have a five-year service life with no residual value. The company uses the declining-balance method of amortization at twice the straight-line rate for assets of this nature.

Required

Compute the understatement/overstatement of net income for each of the three years as a result of the error.

As a Matter of Record

The following article, ''Imperial Mulls Heavy Oil Upgrader: Possible $3-billion Project Part of Plans for Improving Cold Lake Production,'' by Dennis Slocum, appeared in *The Globe and Mail,* October 3, 1991, p. B5:

Record Case 11–1

> Imperial Oil Ltd. is considering building a heavy oil upgrading plant at Cold Lake, Alta., at a cost of as much as $3-billion.
>
> The plant would take heavy oil—used largely in making asphalt—and process it into a lighter grade of oil that can be refined into gasoline products. Much of Canada's heavy oil output is currently exported to the United States.
>
> Following an address to analysts, Arden Haynes, Imperial's chairman and chief executive, said the company would need assurances of favourable fiscal terms from the Alberta and Canadian governments to make the project attractive.
>
> Mr. Haynes said that oil sands and heavy oil deposits in Western Canada offer the potential for large amounts of recoverable oil.
>
> Citing new U.S. refinery capacity that will increase demand for Canadian heavy oils by more than 100,000 barrels a day over the next couple of years, he said Imperial is working to improve its heavy oil output. It is spending $100-million a year on exploration at Cold Lake, where it has been producing heavy oil since 1985.
>
> He told analysts attending a conference sponsored by the American Stock Exchange that the company may start production next year from two new facilities at Cold Lake.
>
> In full operation, they would add about 20,000 barrels a day of heavy oil production to Imperial's current output of about 80,000 barrels a day.
>
> In 1988, Toronto-based Imperial spent $220-million to develop the facilities, but mothballed them late in the year due to market conditions. Last fall, the company spent a further $25-million to ready the two facilities for startup, pending a final go-ahead.
>
> Mr. Haynes said market conditions currently appear favourable to expand production from Cold Lake. He said the spread between the prices of light and heavy-

grade crude has narrowed to about $8.50 a barrel from a high of $11 earlier this year. In March, Imperial said it would delay the new Cold Lake production due to those widening spreads.

      Mr. Haynes said a final decision on increasing production will be made by year-end.

Required

1. At what point would you begin to amortize the cost of the production facilities at Cold Lake?

2. On what basis should the costs be amortized?

Answers to Objective Review Questions

LO 1 (*e*)	LO 3 (*b*)	LO 5 (*d*)
LO 2 (*d*)	LO 4 (*c*)	

PART

IV

Accounting for Liabilities and Partnerships

In this part of the book, you will learn about some of the liabilities incurred by businesses and about the special accounting issues that relate to partnerships. Businesses incur many different kinds of liabilities in the process of conducting their operations. Some of these liabilities are short-term obligations such as accounts payable, notes payable, unearned revenues, property taxes payable, product warranties, and payroll liabilities. Business liabilities also include long-term obligations such as capital leases and notes payable.

Many small businesses and some large businesses are organized as partnerships. Accounting issues that are unique to partnerships include the allocation of net incomes and losses among the partners, the admission of a new partner to the business, the withdrawal of a partner from the business, and the liquidation of the business.

CHAPTER

12

Current and Long-Term Liabilities

Despite the risks of being in debt, companies with liabilities enjoy many advantages. For example, sales can be increased if a company agrees to repair or replace defective products under a warranty obligation. Careful borrowing also allows companies to increase their income and assets.

Topical Coverage

*A*s you already know, liabilities are one of the three elements in the accounting equation. Some of the liabilities we discussed in previous chapters include accounts payable, notes payable, wages payable, and unearned revenues. In this chapter, we examine liabilities such as property taxes payable, product warranty liabilities, single-payment notes payable, and lease liabilities. We also introduce the important concept of present values and reconsider the topic of contingent liabilities. As you study this chapter, you will learn how to define, classify, and measure liabilities.

Learning Objectives

After studying Chapter 12, you should be able to:

1. Explain the difference between current and long-term liabilities.
2. Explain the difference between definite and estimated liabilities.
3. Record transactions that involve such liabilities as property taxes payable, sales taxes payable, product warranty liabilities, and short-term notes payable.
4. Explain the difference between liabilities and contingent liabilities.
5. Calculate the present value of a sum of money that will be received a number of periods in the future or that will be received periodically.
6. Prepare entries to account for long-term noninterest-bearing notes payable and for capital and operating leases.
7. Define or explain the words and phrases listed in the chapter glossary.

The Definition and Classification of Liabilities

LO 1 Explain the difference between current and long-term liabilities.

Liabilities are present obligations that require the future payment of assets or performance of services. Not every expected future payment is a liability. To qualify as a liability, the future payment must be a present obligation of the debtor that resulted from a past transaction. Because liabilities result from past transactions, they normally are enforceable as legal claims against the enterprise. However, in some circumstances, an obligation should be recognized as a liability on the debtor's balance sheet, even if it is not legally enforceable as of that date. These important characteristics of liabilities were summarized by the AcSB when it defined liabilities as "obligations of an entity arising from past transactions or events, the settlement of which may result in the transfer or use of assets, provision of services or other yielding of economic benefits in the future."[1]

Current and Long-Term Liabilities

A business typically classifies its liabilities as either current or long-term liabilities. *Current liabilities* are debts or other obligations that are expected to be

---

[1] *CICA Handbook*, par. 1000.32.

liquidated (paid) by using existing current assets or creating other current liabilities. Current liabilities are due within one year of the balance sheet date or within the operating cycle of the business, whichever is longer.[2] Examples of current liabilities are accounts payable, short-term notes payable, wages payable, dividends payable, product warranty liabilities, payroll and other taxes payable, and unearned revenues.

Obligations that do not mature within one year (or one operating cycle, whichever is longer) are classified as *long-term liabilities*. Examples of long-term liabilities include lease liabilities, long-term notes payable, product warranty liabilities, and bonds payable. However, any given liability—such as a note payable—may be either current or long-term. The critical difference is the question of whether or not payment will be made within one year or the current operating cycle of the business, whichever is longer.

Some liabilities will be settled with installment payments occurring in the current year and future years. Such liabilities are classified on the balance sheet in part as current liabilities and in part as long-term liabilities. Other liabilities do not have a fixed due date but are payable on the creditor's demand. Since the creditor can demand payment at any time, such liabilities are classified as current liabilities.

Definite versus Estimated Liabilities

Three important questions concerning liabilities are: Who must be paid? When is payment due? How much is to be paid? In many situations, the answers to these three questions are determined at the time the liability is incurred. For example, assume that a company has an account payable for precisely $100, payable to R. L. Tucker, and due on August 15, 1994. This liability is definite with respect to all three points. Other types of liabilities may be indefinite with respect to one or more of the three questions.

LO 2 Explain the difference between definite and estimated liabilities.

When the Identity of the Creditor Is Uncertain. In some cases, financial statements are prepared when the debtor knows a future payment will be required but does not know who will be paid. For example, in the case of dividends payable, the amount that will be paid and the due date are definite. The question of who will be paid, however, is not answerable until after the *date of record*. Even though the identity of the creditor may be uncertain, there is no doubt that the debtor is obligated to pay and the liability should be recognized.

When the Due Date Is Uncertain. An example of a liability with an uncertain due date is unearned legal fees revenue that a lawyer accepts in return for the obligation to provide services to a client on call. In this situation, the amount of the liability is known. The client for whom services will be provided is also known. However, the question of *when* the services will be performed is not definite. Usually, such arrangements are settled in the short term and are classified as current liabilities on the debtor's balance sheet.

---

[2] *CICA Handbook*, par. 1510.03.

When the Amount to Be Paid Is Uncertain. When an obligation definitely exists but the amount that will be paid is uncertain, the obligation is called an **estimated liability.** Two important examples of estimated liabilities involve property taxes and product warranties.

Property Taxes Payable

LO 3 Record transactions that involve such liabilities as property taxes payable, sales taxes payable, product warranty liabilities, and short-term notes payable.

Property taxes are levied annually by a variety of governmental authorities, such as counties, cities, and school districts. In many cases, the exact amount of tax to be paid is not known until the tax year is partially over. For example, suppose that the amount of property tax that will be paid for calendar year 1993 will not be fixed in amount until September 1993. Also assume that the tax payment is not due until October 1993. Thus, if monthly financial statements are prepared during 1993, the amount of property tax expense must be estimated when statements are prepared for January through August.

To illustrate, assume that a company owns property throughout 1993. The tax on the property for 1992 was $11,400. In preparing monthly financial statements during the first part of 1993, before the actual amount of tax is known, the company estimates that it has a monthly tax expense of $950 ($11,400/12). Until the amount of the 1993 tax becomes definite, the company will make monthly entries like this one:

1993				
Jan.	31	Property Taxes Expense	950.00	
		Estimated Property Taxes Payable		950.00
		To accrue property taxes for the month.		

In September 1993, the city announces that the tax levy for 1993 will be $3 per $100 of assessed value. The city also notifies the taxpayer that this property has an assessed valuation of $400,000 for property tax purposes. Now, the company can calculate the actual amount of property tax for 1993 as $12,000 [$400,000 × ($3/$100)], which is $1,000 per month. For the first eight months (January through August), the accumulated estimated tax expense was only $7,600 (8 × $950), which is $400 less than the actual tax. This entry should be recorded at the end of September to accrue September's $1,000 expense and to catch up for the $400 understatement of the expense and the liability:

Sept.	30	Property Taxes Expense	1,400.00	
		Estimated Property Taxes Payable		1,400.00
		To record property taxes for September and to correct		
		the $400 estimated shortfall in prior months.		

When the annual tax is paid at the end of October 1993, the entry to record the payment is:

Oct.	31	Property Taxes Expense	1,000.00	
		Prepaid Property Taxes	2,000.00	
		Estimated Property Taxes Payable	9,000.00	
		Cash		12,000.00
		To pay property tax for 1993.		

At the end of November and December, two entries like the following one will be made to record the monthly expense. They also remove the Prepaid Property Taxes account balance from the books:

Nov.	30	Property Taxes Expense	1,000.00	
		Prepaid Property Taxes.		1,000.00
		To record property tax expense for November.		

Note that the total expense recorded for 1993 is $12,000, which has been accumulated in the account as follows:

January–August	$ 7,600
September	1,400
October.	1,000
November	1,000
December	1,000
Total	$12,000

Sales tax liabilities arise because the federal government and most provincial governments require businesses to act as collection agencies for the Goods and Services Tax (GST) and provincial sales taxes (PSTs). When a business makes a sale, the customer is charged for the sales tax on top of the selling price, in most cases, and the tax is later paid to the government(s).

Chapter 6 illustrated how the sales taxes would be accumulated in the sales journal. Assume that Superior Clothing Store collected $8,750 of GST and $7,500 of PST during September. At the end of September these amounts would appear on the balance sheet as current liabilities. The entry to pay these taxes during October would be as follows:

Sales Taxes Payable

LO 3 Record transactions that involve such liabilities as property taxes payable, sales taxes payable, product warranty liabilities, and short-term notes payable.

Oct.	25	GST Payable	8,750	
		Cash		8,750
		To pay GST for September.		
		PST Payable.	7,500	
		Cash		7,500
		To pay PST for September.		

Note that the sales taxes are neither a revenue nor an expense for the enterprise. However, when a business purchases goods and services for its own use, the sales taxes paid become part of the cost of these items. In the case of goods purchased for resale, either the business would be exempt from paying the sales taxes on the purchase or the sales taxes paid could be deducted from the sales taxes collected when determining the amount to be remitted to the government(s).

Product Warranty Liabilities

LO 3 Record transactions that involve such liabilities as property taxes payable, sales taxes payable, product warranty liabilities, and short-term notes payable.

A product warranty liability is another estimated liability. Most companies incur this kind of liability because they provide warranties (or guarantees) for their products. A **product warranty** is a promise to the customer that obligates the seller or manufacturer for a limited time to pay for such things as replacement parts or other repair costs if the product breaks or otherwise fails to perform. For example, an automobile may be sold with a warranty that covers the mechanical parts for a period of one year or 20,000 kilometres, whichever comes first. The warranty also may include the cost of labour to install replacement parts.

The *matching principle* requires recording all expenses that help produce the sale in the same period as the sale. Therefore, when a product is sold with a warranty, the expense of fulfilling the warranty must be recognized at the time of the sale. Because the exact amount of expense is not known at the time of the sale, the expense and the related liability must be estimated based on past experience.

For example, assume that a used car is sold on September 1, 1993, with a one-year or 20,000-kilometre warranty. The warranty covers mechanical parts, but the customer must pay any labour charges. Also suppose that the car was sold at a price of $16,000. Past experience shows that warranty expense is about 2% of the sales price. In this case, the expense is $320 ($16,000 × 0.02). The entry to record the expense and liability would be:

1993				
Sept.	1	Warranty Expense	320.00	
		Estimated Warranty Liability.		320.00
		To record warranty expense and liability at 2% of the		
		selling price.		

Now suppose that the customer has a problem with the car and returns it for warranty repairs on January 9, 1994. The auto dealer performs the warranty work by replacing parts that cost $90 and charges the customer $110 for labour. The entry to record the warranty work and the customer's payment is as follows:

1994					
Jan.	9	Cash	110.00		
		Estimated Warranty Liability	90.00		
		Auto Parts Inventory		90.00	
		Service Revenue		110.00	
		To record warranty work and service revenue.			

Observe that no expense is recorded in 1994 for the cost of the parts. Instead, the warranty liability is reduced. This process includes the warranty expense in the income for 1993, when the car was sold.

What happens if the total warranty costs actually turn out to be different from the estimated $320 amount? In fact, some difference is likely on any particular sale. Over the longer term, management must monitor warranty costs to be sure that 2% is the best estimate. When continued experience shows that the rate of warranty costs has changed, the percentage should be modified.

Contingent Liabilities

LO 4 Explain the difference between liabilities and contingent liabilities.

We first discussed contingent liabilities in Chapter 8, where we presented discounted notes receivable as an example of contingent liabilities. Contingent liabilities are not existing obligations and, therefore, are not recorded in the books as liabilities. However, the *full-disclosure principle* requires disclosure of contingent liabilities in the financial statements or in the notes.

What Distinguishes Liabilities from Contingent Liabilities?

Contingent liabilities become definite obligations only if some previously uncertain event actually takes place. For example, a discounted note receivable is a contingent liability that becomes a definite obligation only if the original signer of the note fails to pay it at maturity.

Does a product warranty create a liability or a contingent liability? A product warranty requires service or payment only if the product fails and the customer returns it for service. These conditions make it appear to be like a contingent liability. However, the AcSB ruled that *a contingent loss should be recorded in the books as a liability if the occurrence of the future contingency is likely and if the amount of the liability can be reasonably estimated.*[3] Therefore, product warranties are usually recorded as liabilities because (1) the failure of some percentage of the sold products is likely, and (2) past experience allows the seller to develop a reasonable estimate of the amount to be paid.

Other Examples of Contingent Liabilities

Potential Legal Claims. In today's legal environment, many companies find themselves being sued for damages for a variety of reasons. The accounting question to be asked is whether the defendant should recognize a liability on

---

[3] *CICA Handbook,* par. 3290.12.

the balance sheet or disclose a contingent liability in the notes to the financial statements while a lawsuit is outstanding and not yet settled. The answer is that the potential claim should be recorded as a liability only if a payment for damages is likely and the amount can be reasonably estimated. Otherwise, the potential claim is a contingent liability.

Debt Guarantees. Sometimes a company will guarantee the payment of a debt owed by a supplier, customer, or other company. This arrangement is usually created by cosigning a note payable of the other party. When this is done, the guarantor is contingently liable for the debt of the other company. The guarantor will not recognize the liability unless it is likely that the original debtor will default.

Short-Term Notes Payable

LO 3 Record transactions that involve such liabilities as property taxes payable, sales taxes payable, product warranty liabilities, and short-term notes payable.

Another category of current liabilities that requires careful study is short-term notes payable. When a business purchases merchandise on credit and then needs to gain an extension of the credit period, a short-term note payable may be substituted for the account payable. Also, short-term notes payable frequently arise when borrowing from a bank.

Note Given to Secure a Time Extension on an Account

A note payable may be given to secure an extension of time for paying an account payable. For example, assume that Brock Company cannot pay its past-due $600 account with Ajax Company. As an accommodation, Ajax Company agrees to accept Brock Company's 60-day, 12%, $600 note in granting an extension on the due date of the debt. Brock Company records the issuance of the note as follows:

Aug.	23	Accounts Payable—Ajax Company.	600.00	
		Notes Payable		600.00
		Gave a 60-day, 12% note to extend the due date on the amount owed.		

Observe that the note does not pay off the debt. Rather, the form of the debt is merely changed from an account payable to a note payable. Ajax Company should prefer holding the note to the account because, in case of default, the note is very good written evidence of the debt's existence and its amount.

When the note becomes due, Brock Company will give Ajax Company a cheque for $611.84 and record the payment of the note and its interest with this entry:

Oct.	22	Notes Payable.	600.00	
		Interest Expense	11.84	
		Cash		611.84
		Paid our note with interest.		

Ms. Yeh is a graduate of Wilfrid Laurier University's Business Administration/CO-OP program. She worked with Canron Inc. of Toronto as an internal auditor and then joined F. W. Woolworth Company of Toronto as retail accounting manager. In 1987 she joined Minicom Data Corporation as an education consultant. Minicom is a software developer for the real estate management and development industry. In 1989 she advanced to the position of client manager and more recently advanced to the position of executive client manager, where she now manages a vast portfolio of clients in North America and Bermuda to ensure that they are continually using Minicom's systems to meet their evolving processing and reporting objectives. She also examines and recommends further automated solutions to increase productivity in clients' operations.

If the 80s is the "excess" decade, then the 90s is the "green" decade. Following the overindulgence in the mid-80s, the slowdown in the late 80s and into the 90s has made people consider what is important to them in the long run. As a result, in recent years, there have been more and more stringent regulations on environmental concerns.

Linda L. M. Yeh, CMA

There is definitely increased awareness by all business entities of the impact of their activities on the environment. Corporations generally have vast financial and people resources available to them and thus can project a greater and more widespread influence. They should, therefore, take the lead in developing and implementing solutions to protect the environment for the long term.

The accounting profession has always served as advisors to management and decision makers and thus should be supportive in developing accounting rules and standards to be used as benchmarks for the implementation of control systems to manage environmental issues and systems for evaluating their effectiveness. To be able to track this accountability, there must be certain expectations of entities to report on what role they play in environmental issues and how they have managed their environmental responsibilities.

Accountants can also serve as advisors to businesses and governments to ensure that they are not faced with future liabilities and entanglements from their current activities. If environmental regulations are becoming more stringent, then it will be even more difficult to determine an entity's future liability. The entities, therefore, need assistance to clearly understand these regulations and their implications—now and in the future.

The bottom line is that corporations realize that implementing environmental management and control systems can only mean a stronger competitive edge in ensuring them the key success factor of leadership in the ever-evolving market place. Corporations are beginning to recognize that short-run profitability is not the only factor in being successful.

Chapter 8 illustrated how to calculate the amount of interest on a note for a specified period by using the following formula:

$$\frac{\text{Principal of}}{\text{the note}} \times \frac{\text{Rate of}}{\text{interest}} \times \frac{\text{Term of the note expressed in days}}{365} = \text{Interest}$$

Borrowing from a Bank

When lending money, banks typically require that the borrower sign a promissory note. Sometimes, the note states that the signer of the note promises to pay the principal (the amount borrowed) plus interest. If the note is written in this way, the *face value* of the note is the principal and the lending transaction is called a *loan*. Alternatively, a note may say nothing about interest and simply state that the signer promises to pay a given amount. In this case, the face value of the note includes the amount borrowed plus the interest to be charged and the lending transaction involves discounting the note. The *discount* is the difference between the face value of the note and the amount of cash advanced by the bank to the borrower. In other words, the discount equals the amount of interest to be paid. To illustrate loans and discounts, assume that H. A. Green wishes to borrow approximately $2,000 for 60 days at the prevailing 15% rate of interest.

A Loan.   In a loan transaction, the bank lends Green $2,000 in exchange for a signed promissory note that reads: "Sixty days after September 10, I promise to pay $2,000 plus interest at 15%." Thus, the face value of the note is $2,000, which is the amount borrowed by Green. This loan transaction is recorded by Green as follows:

Sept.	10	Cash	2,000.00	
		Notes Payable		2,000.00
		Gave the bank a 60-day, 15% note.		

When the note and interest are paid, Green makes this entry:

Nov.	9	Notes Payable.	2,000.00	
		Interest Expense	49.32	
		Cash		2,049.32
		Paid our 60-day, 15% note.		

Observe that in this loan transaction, the interest was paid at maturity in addition to the principal amount of the debt.

A Discount.   If Green's bank deducts interest at the time a loan is made, the bank is said to have *discounted* Green's note. If it discounts the $2,000 note at 15% for 60 days, it will loan Green only $1,950.68. This amount equals the face amount of the note less 60 days' interest at 15%, which is $49.32 [$2,000 × 15% × ($60/365$)]. The $49.32 of deducted interest is called the **bank discount.** The net amount received by Green, $1,950.68, is called the *proceeds* of the discounted note. Green records the transaction as follows:

Sept.	10	Cash	1,950.68	
		Interest Expense	49.32	
		Notes Payable		2,000.00
		Discounted our $2,000 note payable at 15%.		

Because the interest is deducted from the principal at the time a debt is created in a discount transaction, the note states that only the principal amount is to be repaid at maturity. That is, the note does not call for any additional interest to be paid at maturity. For example, Green's note would read: "Sixty days after September 10, I promise to pay $2,000, with no interest." As a result, this type of note is commonly called a *noninterest-bearing note*. However, we all know that banks are not in business to lend money interest free. In a discount transaction, the interest is simply deducted in advance. Because the amount of the interest is not loaned when the debt is created, the note simply states that no additional interest will be collected at maturity beyond the face amount. In fact, the rate of interest in a discount situation is actually higher than in a loan situation at the same stated interest rate. For example, Green paid $49.32 for the use of $1,950.68 for 60 days, so the effective interest rate was a little in excess of 15% on the $1,950.68 received.[4]

Discount on Notes Payable

When a note payable is discounted at a bank, and the note will not become due until the next accounting period, the interest deducted in advance should be debited to a *contra liability* account, Discount on Notes Payable. In the same entry, Notes Payable is credited for the face amount of the note. As a result, the net liability equals the amount of cash borrowed. Then, at the end of the period, an adjusting entry records the accrued interest expense. This adjustment reduces the balance of the discount account and thereby increases the size of the net liability by the amount of accrued interest.

For example, suppose that on December 11, 1993, a company discounts at 15% its own $6,000, 60-day, noninterest-bearing note payable. The amount of the discount is $147.95 [$6,000 \times 15\% \times (^{60}/_{365})$], and the company records the transaction as follows:

Dec.	11	Cash	5,852.05	
		Discount on Notes Payable	147.95	
		Notes Payable		6,000.00
		Discounted our noninterest-bearing, 60-day note at 15%.		

End-of-Period
Adjustments

---

[4] Green pays $49.32 interest for the use of $1,950.68 for 60 days. This amount represents 2.528% for the 60 days, which is equivalent to 15.38% per year [($49.32/$1,950.68) \times (^{365}/_{60})$].

Thus, the net liability equals the $5,852.05 of cash borrowed [$6,000 − $147.95].

If this company's accounting period ends on December 31, it needs to recognize 20 days' interest on this note as an expense of the 1993 accounting period. This amount is $49.32 [$147.95 × ($20/60$)]. Therefore, the company must make the following adjusting entry on December 31, 1993:

Dec.	31	Interest Expense	49.32	
		Discount on Notes Payable.		49.32
		To record 1993 interest expense.		

This adjusting entry records interest expense of $49.32 in 1993 and removes the same amount from the Discount on Notes Payable account. The $49.32 then appears on the 1993 income statement as an expense. The entry also leaves $98.63 in the discount account until it is reported as an expense of 1994.

On the December 31, 1993, balance sheet, the $98.63 is deducted from the $6,000 nominal balance of the note payable, so that the net liability is shown at the proper amount of $5,901.37. If this note is the only one the company has outstanding, the December 31, 1993, balance sheet is as follows:

Current liabilities:		
Notes payable	$6,000.00	
Less discount on notes payable	98.63	
Net liability.		$5,901.37

Alternatively, the note may be presented this way:

Current liabilities:	
Notes payable (less discount of $98.63)	$5,901.37

Or the note can be reported on the balance sheet at $5,901.37 with the amount of the discount mentioned in the notes to the financial statements.

Accrued Interest Expense

The preceding section showed how interest is accrued on a noninterest-bearing note created in a discount transaction. Interest on an interest-bearing note also accrues as time passes, and must be recorded to produce a complete income statement and balance sheet. Therefore, if any interest-bearing notes payable are outstanding at the end of an accounting period, the accrued interest should be recorded.

For example, suppose that a company borrowed $4,000 on December 16, 1993, and gave its bank a $4,000, 60-day, 12% note. When the company's accounting period ends 15 days later on December 31, $19.73 of interest has accrued [$4,000 × 12% × ($15/365$)]. This adjusting entry records the interest:

1993				
Dec.	31	Interest Expense	19.73	
		Interest Payable		19.73
		To record accrued interest on a note payable.		

This adjusting entry causes the $19.73 accrued interest to appear on the income statement as an expense of the period that benefits from 15 days' use of the money. It also causes the interest payable to appear on the balance sheet, thereby causing the total debt of $4,019.73 to be reported as a current liability.

When the note matures in the next accounting period, its payment is recorded as follows:

1994				
Feb.	14	Notes Payable.	4,000.00	
		Interest Payable.	19.73	
		Interest Expense	59.17	
		Cash		4,078.90
		Paid a $4,000 note and its interest.		

Interest expense on this note for the 45 days during 1994 is $59.17 [$4,000 × 12% × ($^{45}/_{365}$)]. The two entries show that the total interest expense of $78.90 is allocated between the two accounting periods, with $19.73 assigned to 1993 and $59.17 assigned to 1994.

The Concept of Present Value

Information based on the concept of *present value* enters into many financing and investing decisions. It also enters into accounting for liabilities resulting from those decisions. Therefore, an understanding of present value is important for all business students. The concept is based on the idea that the right to receive, say, $1 one year from today (or at any other point in the future) is worth less than $1 today because the $1 received today may be invested to earn income. That is, $1 to be received one year from now has a **present value** of less than $1. How much less depends on how much can be earned with invested funds. In general terms, present value is the amount of money that can be currently invested at a given interest rate to accumulate a total value equal to a given amount to be received (or paid) at some future date. This amount to be invested is the *value* in the *present* of the future amount.

For example, if an 8% annual return can be earned, the expectation of receiving $1 one year from now has a present value of $0.9259. This can be verified as follows: $0.9259 invested today to earn 8% annually will earn $0.0741 in one year. When the $0.0741 earned is added to the $0.9259 invested, the original investment plus the earnings equals $1.0000, as shown here:

LO 5 Calculate the present value of a sum of money that will be received a number of periods in the future or that will be received periodically.

Investment.	$0.9259
Earnings	0.0741
Total	$1.0000

Likewise, the present value of $1 to be received two years from now is $0.8573 if an 8% compound annual return is expected. This amount can be verified as follows: $0.8573 invested to earn 8% compounded annually will earn $0.0686 the first year it is invested. When the original investment of $0.8573 is added to the return of $0.0686, the result is:

Investment.	$0.8573
First year earnings	0.0686
End-of-year-1 amount	$0.9259

When this $0.9259 remains invested another year at 8%, it earns $0.0741, and the accumulated amount equals $1.0000:

End-of-year-1 amount	$0.9259
Second year earnings.	0.0741
End-of-year-2 amount	$1.0000

Thus, you can see how the present value of $0.8573 accumulates to a future amount of $1.0000 in two years if it can be invested to return 8% compounded, which means that the income can also be invested to earn 8%.

Present Value Tables

The present value of $1 to be received any number of years in the future can be calculated by using the formula $1/(1 + i)^n$. The i is the interest rate, and n is the number of years to the expected receipt. Fortunately, you do not need to use the formula because inexpensive electronic calculators are preprogrammed to find present values. As an alternative, you can use a **present value table** that shows present values computed with the formula at various interest rates for various time periods. In fact, you may find it to your advantage in learning this material to use the tables until you become comfortable with present value concepts.

The present value table presented in Table 12–1 shows the present value amounts rounded to four decimal places.[5] Notice that the first amount in the 8% column in Table 12–1 is the value of 0.9259 used in the previous section to introduce the concept of present value. The value of 0.9259 in the 8% column means that the expectation of receiving $1 one period from now has a present value of $0.9259 when discounted at 8%. Also note that the amount in the second row of the 8% column is the 0.8573 previously used. This number means that the expectation of receiving $1 two periods from now, discounted at 8%, has a present value of $0.8573.

---

[5] Four decimal places may not be sufficiently precise for some uses but they are certainly sufficient for the applications described in this book.

TABLE 12-1

Present Value of $1 at Compound Interest

Periods Hence	4½%	5%	6%	7%	8%	9%	10%	12%	14%	16%
1	0.9569	0.9524	0.9434	0.9346	0.9259	0.9174	0.9091	0.8929	0.8772	0.8621
2	0.9157	0.9070	0.8900	0.8734	0.8573	0.8417	0.8264	0.7972	0.7695	0.7432
3	0.8763	0.8638	0.8396	0.8163	0.7938	0.7722	0.7513	0.7118	0.6750	0.6407
4	0.8386	0.8227	0.7921	0.7629	0.7350	0.7084	0.6830	0.6355	0.5921	0.5523
5	0.8025	0.7835	0.7473	0.7130	0.6806	0.6499	0.6209	0.5674	0.5194	0.4761
6	0.7679	0.7462	0.7050	0.6663	0.6302	0.5963	0.5645	0.5066	0.4556	0.4104
7	0.7348	0.7107	0.6651	0.6228	0.5835	0.5470	0.5132	0.4523	0.3996	0.3538
8	0.7032	0.6768	0.6274	0.5820	0.5403	0.5019	0.4665	0.4039	0.3506	0.3050
9	0.6729	0.6446	0.5919	0.5439	0.5003	0.4604	0.4241	0.3606	0.3075	0.2630
10	0.6439	0.6139	0.5584	0.5084	0.4632	0.4224	0.3855	0.3220	0.2697	0.2267
11	0.6162	0.5847	0.5268	0.4751	0.4289	0.3875	0.3505	0.2875	0.2366	0.1954
12	0.5897	0.5568	0.4970	0.4440	0.3971	0.3555	0.3186	0.2567	0.2076	0.1685
13	0.5643	0.5303	0.4688	0.4150	0.3677	0.3262	0.2897	0.2292	0.1821	0.1452
14	0.5400	0.5051	0.4423	0.3878	0.3405	0.2993	0.2633	0.2046	0.1597	0.1252
15	0.5167	0.4810	0.4173	0.3625	0.3152	0.2745	0.2394	0.1827	0.1401	0.1079
16	0.4945	0.4581	0.3937	0.3387	0.2919	0.2519	0.2176	0.1631	0.1229	0.0930
17	0.4732	0.4363	0.3714	0.3166	0.2703	0.2311	0.1978	0.1456	0.1078	0.0802
18	0.4528	0.4155	0.3503	0.2959	0.2503	0.2120	0.1799	0.1300	0.0946	0.0691
19	0.4333	0.3957	0.3305	0.2765	0.2317	0.1945	0.1635	0.1161	0.0830	0.0596
20	0.4146	0.3769	0.3118	0.2584	0.2146	0.1784	0.1486	0.1037	0.0728	0.0514

Using a Present Value Table

To demonstrate the use of a present value table like Table 12–1, assume that a company has an opportunity to invest $55,000 in a project. The investment will return $20,000 at the end of the first year, $25,000 at the end of the second year, $30,000 at the end of the third year, and nothing thereafter. Also assume that the company believes the risks of the project justify a 12% return, compounded annually.

Will the project return the original investment plus the 12% demanded? The calculations shown in Illustration 12–1 indicate that it will do so, with an excess. Illustration 12–1 shows the expected returns in the second column, and then multiplies them by the present value table amounts in the third column to determine their present values in the fourth column. Note that the total of the present values exceeds the required investment. Thus, we can conclude that the project will return the $55,000 investment, plus a 12% return on the investment, plus an additional amount that has a present value of $4,142.

In Illustration 12–1, the present value of each year's return was calculated separately. Then the present values of each expected return were totaled. When the periodic inflows of cash (called *returns*) are unequal, as in this example, you must separately calculate the present value of each one. However, when the periodic returns are equal, there is a simpler way to calculate the sum of their present values.

ILLUSTRATION 12–1

Present Value of a Series of Unequal Amounts

Years from Now	Expected Returns	Present Value of $1 at 12%	Present Value of Expected Returns
1	$20,000	0.8929	$17,858
2	25,000	0.7972	19,930
3	30,000	0.7118	21,354
Total present value of the returns.			$59,142
Less investment required.			(55,000)
Excess present value over 12% demanded . .			$ 4,142

ILLUSTRATION 12–2

Present Value of a Series of Equal Amounts

Years from Now	Expected Returns	Present Value of $1 at 12%	Present Value of Expected Returns
1	$5,000	0.8929	$ 4,465
2	5,000	0.7972	3,986
3	5,000	0.7118	3,559
4	5,000	0.6355	3,177
5	5,000	0.5674	2,837
		3.6048	
Total present value of the returns . . .			$18,024

For instance, suppose that a $17,500 investment will return $5,000 at the end of each year in its five-year life and that an investor wants to know the present value of these returns, discounted at 12%. In this case, the present value can be calculated as shown in Illustration 12–2. But, because the periodic returns are equal, there is a shorter way to determine their total present value at 12%. To do so, add the present values of $1 at 12% for periods 1 through 5 (from Table 12–1) as shown in the third column of Illustration 12–2. Then multiply the 3.6048 total by the $5,000 annual return to get the present value of $18,024. Although the result is the same either way, the method demonstrated in Illustration 12–2 requires four fewer multiplications.

Present Value of $1 Received Periodically for a Number of Periods

Table 12–2 is designed to help you work with situations like the one discussed in the preceding paragraphs. That is, the present value of a series of equal returns to be received at periodic intervals can be calculated by taking the sum of the present values of the individual returns.[6] Note the amount on the table's fifth line in the 12% column. This 3.6048 is the same amount that is calculated

---

[6] A common term used to describe a stream of equal returns occurring at equal time intervals is *annuity*. Notice the similarity between the words *annuity* and *annual*.

TABLE 12–2

Present Value of $1 Received Periodically for a Number of Periods										
Payments	**4½%**	**5%**	**6%**	**7%**	**8%**	**9%**	**10%**	**12%**	**14%**	**16%**
1	0.9569	0.9524	0.9434	0.9346	0.9259	0.9174	0.9091	0.8929	0.8772	0.8621
2	1.8727	1.8594	1.8334	1.8080	1.7833	1.7591	1.7355	1.6901	1.6467	1.6052
3	2.7490	2.7232	2.6730	2.6243	2.5771	2.5313	2.4869	2.4018	2.3216	2.2459
4	3.5875	3.5460	3.4651	3.3872	3.3121	3.2397	3.1699	3.0373	2.9137	2.7982
5	4.3900	4.3295	4.2124	4.1002	3.9927	3.8897	3.7908	3.6048	3.4331	3.2743
6	5.1579	5.0757	4.9173	4.7665	4.6229	4.4859	4.3553	4.1114	3.8887	3.6847
7	5.8927	5.7864	5.5824	5.3893	5.2064	5.0330	4.8684	4.5638	4.2883	4.0386
8	6.5959	6.4632	6.2098	5.9713	5.7466	5.5348	5.3349	4.9676	4.6389	4.3436
9	7.2688	7.1078	6.8017	6.5152	6.2469	5.9953	5.7590	5.3282	4.9464	4.6065
10	7.9127	7.7217	7.3601	7.0236	6.7101	6.4177	6.1446	5.6502	5.2161	4.8332
11	8.5289	8.3064	7.8869	7.4987	7.1390	6.8052	6.4951	5.9377	5.4527	5.0286
12	9.1186	8.8633	8.3838	7.9427	7.5361	7.1607	6.8137	6.1944	5.6603	5.1971
13	9.6829	9.3936	8.8527	8.3577	7.9038	7.4869	7.1034	6.4235	5.8424	5.3423
14	10.2228	9.8986	9.2950	8.7455	8.2442	7.7862	7.3667	6.6282	6.0021	5.4675
15	10.7395	10.3797	9.7123	9.1079	8.5595	8.0607	7.6061	6.8109	6.1422	5.5755
16	11.2340	10.8378	10.1059	9.4467	8.8514	8.3126	7.8237	6.9740	6.2651	5.6685
17	11.7072	11.2741	10.4773	9.7632	9.1216	8.5436	8.0216	7.1196	6.3729	5.7487
18	12.1600	11.6896	10.8276	10.0591	9.3719	8.7556	8.2014	7.2497	6.4674	5.8179
19	12.5933	12.0853	11.1581	10.3356	9.6036	8.9501	8.3649	7.3658	6.5504	5.8775
20	13.0079	12.4622	11.4699	10.5940	9.8182	9.1286	8.5136	7.4694	6.6231	5.9288

in Illustration 12–2 by adding the first five present values of $1 at 12% from Table 12–1. All the amounts shown in Table 12–2 can be determined by adding amounts found in Table 12–1. However, there might be some slight variations due to rounding.[7]

Table 12–2 can be used to determine the present value of a series of equal amounts to be received at periodic intervals. For example, what is the present value of a series of 10 amounts of $1,000 to be received at the end of each of 10 successive years, discounted at 8%? To determine the answer, look down the 8% column to the amount on the row for 10 periods (in this case, years). The table value is 6.7101, and $6.7101 is the present value of $1 to be received annually at the end of each of 10 years, discounted at 8%. Therefore, the present value of the 10 amounts of $1,000 is $6,710.10 ($1,000 × 6.7101).

In the examples presented so far, the interest rates have been applied to time periods that were one year in length. However, interest is often applied to time periods shorter than one year. For instance, the interest on corporate bonds is normally paid semiannually, although interest rates on such bonds are usually quoted on an annual basis. As a result, the present value of the interest payments to be received from these bonds must be based on interest periods that are six months long.

Interest Periods Less than One Year in Length

[7] The formula for finding these values: $\dfrac{1 - \dfrac{1}{(1 + i)^n}}{i}$.

To illustrate a calculation based on six-month interest periods, assume an investor wants to know the present value of the interest that will be received over five years on some corporate bonds. The bonds have a $10,000 par value, and interest is paid on them every six months at a 14% annual rate. Although the interest rate is described as an annual rate of 14%, it is actually a rate of 7% per six-month interest period. Therefore, the investor receives $700 interest on these bonds at the end of each six-month interest period ($10,000 × 7%). In five years, there are 10 six-month periods. Therefore, to determine the present value of these 10 receipts of $700 each, discounted at the 7% interest rate of the bonds, look down the 7% column of Table 12–2 to the amount on the row for 10 periods. The table value is 7.0236, and the present value of the 10 semiannual receipts of $700 is $4,916.52 (7.0236 × $700).

For a more complete discussion of discounting, turn to Appendix G at the end of the book. Appendix G expands the discussion of how present value tables are developed and explains the development of future value tables. More complete present value and future value tables are included in the appendix, which also has numerous exercises related to discounting.

Exchanging a Note for a Plant Asset

When purchasing a high-cost asset on credit, particularly if the credit period is long, the buyer often gives a note in exchange for the asset. For example, if the cash price of an asset is $4,500 and the stated interest rate on the note corresponds to the prevailing market rate, the amount of the note will probably be $4,500. The entry to record the transaction would be as follows:

Feb.	12	Store Equipment	4,500.00	
		Notes Payable		4,500.00
		Exchanged a $4,500, three-year, 12% note payable for a refrigerated display case.		

A note given in exchange for a plant asset has two elements, which may or may not be stated in the note. They are (1) a dollar amount equal to the bargained cash price of the asset, and (2) an interest factor to compensate the supplier for the use of the funds that would have been received in a cash sale. Therefore, when a note is exchanged for a plant asset, if the face amount of the note approximates the cash price of the asset and the note's interest rate approximates the prevailing market rate, the asset is recorded at the face amount of the note.

Notes that Have an Unreasonable or No Stated Interest Rate

In some cases, notes exchanged for assets do not have a stated interest rate. In others, the stated interest rate does not approximate the prevailing market rate. In both situations, the face amount of the note does *not* equal the cash price of the asset obtained in exchange for the note. Because the face amount of the note does not equal the asset's value in these cases, recording the asset at the note's face amount would initially misstate the asset and liability. Subsequently, these misstatements would lead to other misstatements of amortization and interest expense. These misstatements may be material, especially for a long-term note of a large amount, so you must record the acquisition using the best information available. Therefore, the asset must be recorded at its cash price or at the fair value (present value) of the note, whichever is more clearly determinable.[8]

LO 6 Prepare entries to account for long-term noninterest-bearing notes payable and for capital and operating leases.

To illustrate a situation in which a note with no stated interest rate is exchanged for a plant asset, assume that a noninterest-bearing, five-year, $10,000 note payable is exchanged for a factory machine on January 2, 1993. Also assume that you cannot readily determine the cash price of the asset. If the prevailing market rate of interest on the day of the exchange is 14%, the present value of the note on that day is $5,194. This amount was calculated by multiplying the face amount of the note by the value on the fifth row in the 14% column of Table 12–1 ($10,000 × 0.5194 = $5,194). Thus, the purchase should be recorded as follows:

1993				
Jan.	2	Machinery	5,194.00	
		Discount on Notes Payable	4,806.00	
		Long-Term Notes Payable		10,000.00
		Exchanged a five-year, noninterest-bearing note for a machine.		

The $5,194 amount debited to the Machinery account is the present value of the note on the day of the exchange. Since the buyer and seller have agreed to the terms of the transaction, the present value must approximate the cash price of the machinery. Therefore, the present value of the note is established as the cost of the machine and is the amount you must use to calculate depreciation.

The debit to Discount on Notes Payable and credit to Long-Term Notes Payable together measure the liability that resulted from the transaction. They would appear as follows on a balance sheet prepared immediately after the exchange:

Long-term liabilities:		
Long-term notes payable	$10,000	
Less unamortized discount based on the 14% interest		
rate prevailing on the date of issue	4,806	$5,194

As described before, alternative forms of presentation can be used. The main point to observe is that the net liability is reported at the present value of the note's future cash flows.

---

[8] FASB, *Accounting Standards—Current Text* (Norwalk, Conn., 1990), sec. I69.105. First published as *APB Opinion No. 21*, par. 12. The AcSB has begun work on a similar standard.

ILLUSTRATION 12–3

Allocation of Interest for a Five-Year, $10,000 Note Payable, with an Initial Net Balance of $5,194

Year	(a) Beginning Net Liability	(b) 14% Interest Expense	(c) Ending Net Liability (a) + (b)
1993	$5,194	$ 727	$ 5,921
1994	5,921	829	6,750
1995	6,750	945	7,695
1996	7,695	1,077	8,772
1997	8,772	1,228	10,000
Total expense		$4,806	

Amortizing the Discount on a Note Payable

As you have learned, the $4,806 discount on the preceding note is contra to the gross liability of $10,000. This amount is also the interest component of the purchase transaction in the sense that it is the difference between the value that the buyer received and the cash that the buyer will pay later. That is, the buyer essentially borrowed $5,194 and will have to pay back $10,000 in five years. The $4,806 difference is interest expense for the buyer.

In this discount situation, an important task faced by the accountant is to allocate the total interest among the five reporting years covered by the note. Illustration 12–3 shows one method of calculating the annual interest expense. This illustration presents the beginning net liability for each year in the second column, labeled (a). The next column, labeled (b), computes the interest expense for each year as 14% of the beginning balance. (Recall that 14% is the prevailing rate of interest at the date the note is signed.) This amount should appear on the buyer's income statement as an expense. The last column, labeled (c), shows the ending balance of the net liability, which equals the beginning balance plus the unpaid interest expense accrued for the year. The ending balance is also equal to the present value of the future payment, discounted at the original interest rate.[9]

Note several points from the illustration: First, observe that the total interest expense for the five years equals the initial discount of $4,806. Second, notice that the ending net liability increases each year until it reaches the maturity amount of $10,000. Third, the amount of interest allocated to each year increases because the balance of the liability is increasing.

This process of allocating interest can also be described as a process of amortizing the discount on the note. In Illustration 12–4, an amortization schedule shows how the balance of the discount is reduced by amortization over the life of the note.

---

[9] For example, the present value of the $10,000 maturity amount at December 31, 1995, is $7,695 ($10,000 × 0.7695).

ILLUSTRATION 12-4

Amortization Schedule for a Five-Year, $10,000 Note Payable, Discounted at 14%

Year	(a) Face Amount of Note	(b) Unamortized Discount at Beginning of Year	(c) Beginning Net Liability (a) − (b)	(d) Discount to Be Amortized (c) × 14%	(e) Unamortized Discount at Year-End (b) − (d)	(f) Ending Net Liability (a) − (e)
1993	$10,000	$4,806	$5,194	$ 727	$4,079	$ 5,921
1994	10,000	4,079	5,921	829	3,250	6,750
1995	10,000	3,250	6,750	945	2,305	7,695
1996	10,000	2,305	7,695	1,077	1,228	8,772
1997	10,000	1,228	8,772	1,228	–0–	10,000
Total				$4,806		

Look carefully at Illustration 12–4. Column (*a*) shows the $10,000 *gross* liability equal to the face amount of the note. Column (*b*) shows the remaining balance of the unamortized discount, which is deducted from the value in column (*a*) to show the *net* liability at the beginning of the year in column (*c*). For example, the $5,194 amount in column (*c*) for 1993 is the difference between the $10,000 face value of the note and the $4,806 discount. (This column is identical to column (*a*) of Illustration 12–3.) Column (*d*) shows the amount of interest expense allocated to each year, which is also the amount of discount to be amortized for the year. In each year, it equals 14% of the net liability in column (*c*). The amounts in this column are the same as those in column (*b*) of Illustration 12–3.

Using this information, the first year's amortization entry should be:

1993 Dec.	31	Interest Expense	727.00	
		Discount on Notes Payable.		727.00
		To recognize interest expense on our long-term note.		

This entry accrues the expense that will appear on the income statement. It also reduces the balance of the discount account, which has the effect of increasing the net liability. Notice that the total amortization over the five years equals the initial $4,806 discount, and equals the total interest expense over those five years.

Column (*e*) of Illustration 12–4 shows the new balance of the discount account after the year-end adjusting entry. Notice that it grows smaller each year until it is eliminated completely at the end of 1997, when the note matures. Finally, column (*f*) shows the ending net liability, which is the difference between the note's face value in column (*a*) and the ending balance of the discount in column (*e*). For example, the $5,921 ending net liability for 1993 is the difference between the $10,000 face value and the remaining unamortized discount of $4,079. Also notice that the amounts presented in columns (*e*) and (*f*) become the amounts presented on the next year's columns (*b*) and (*c*).

Posting the December 31, 1993, amortization entry to the Discount on Notes Payable account causes the note to be presented on the buyer's balance sheet as follows:

Long-term liabilities:		
Long-term notes payable	$10,000	
Less unamortized discount based on the 14% interest rate prevailing on the date of issue	4,079	$5,921

Compare this $5,921 net amount at which the note is carried on the December 31, 1993, balance sheet with the $5,194 net amount presented for the note on the balance sheet prepared on its date of issue. Observe that the net liability, also called the **carrying amount of the note,** increased by $727 between the two dates. The $727 is the amount of discount amortized and charged to Interest Expense at the end of 1993.

At the end of 1993 and each succeeding year, the remaining amounts of discount shown in column (*d*) of Illustration 12–4 should be amortized and charged to Interest Expense. This process causes the carrying amount of the note to increase each year by the amount of discount amortized that year and to reach $10,000, the note's maturity value, at the end of the fifth year. Payment of the note will be recorded as follows:

1998					
Jan.	2	Long-Term Notes Payable		10,000.00	
		Cash			10,000.00
		Paid our long-term noninterest-bearing note.			

In this example, the note payable will be shown on each year-end balance sheet as a long-term liability until the balance sheet of December 31, 1997, where it will appear as a current liability. Other notes call for a series of installment payments, so that part of the principal is due within one year (or the current operating cycle, whichever is longer). In these cases, generally accepted accounting principles require the carrying amount of a note payable to be divided into two parts for presentation on the balance sheet. The portion of the note to be paid during the next year (or operating cycle) must be shown as a current liability, with the remaining portion shown as a long-term liability.

Liabilities from Leasing

For a number of reasons, many businesses choose to lease plant assets instead of purchasing them. In most cases, the lease contract requires a series of payments to be made by the lessee, the user of the lease asset, to the lessor, the owner of the lease asset, over the life of the lease. As a result, by leasing instead of purchasing, a business avoids the immediate cash outflow of the full purchase price that must be paid for the asset.

Although leases are contracts that require a series of future payments, all leases do not produce the same economic effect on the firm. Consequently, all leases are not accounted for the same way.

LO 6 Prepare entries to account for long-term noninterest-bearing notes payable and for capital and operating leases.

Categories of Leases

Some leases, called **capital leases** or **financing leases**, have essentially the same effect on the lessee and lessor as a purchase-sale transaction. That is, the outcome is just as if the lessee obtained a loan from the lessor and used the proceeds to purchase the leased asset. When an asset is leased under a capital lease, the lessee records the asset as if it has been purchased and also records a liability equal to the present value of the future lease payments. In most cases, this amount approximates the fair value of the leased asset.

In contrast to capital leases, other leases do not have the characteristics of a purchase-sale transaction. These **operating leases** merely give the lessee the right to use the leased asset for the time period covered by the contract. That is, the lessee does *not* acquire an ownership interest in the leased property, and the risks of ownership remain with the lessor.

When a lease is identified as an operating lease, the lessee's obligation to make payments is *not* recorded as a liability. Because these operating leases are not recorded as liabilities, they do not appear on the balance sheet. This kind of leasing activity is sometimes called *off-balance sheet financing*.

Whether a lease is classified as an operating lease or as a capital lease can have a significant effect on the financial statements. As a result, the financial statements of different lessees will not be comparable unless the companies use the same criteria to classify their leases. To make financial statements more comparable, the AcSB has established rules or criteria that accountants use to decide how leases should be classified. According to the AcSB's decision, a lease that meets any of the following criteria is a capital lease.

1. Ownership of the leased asset is automatically transferred to the lessee at the end of the lease period.
2. The lessee has the option to purchase the leased asset either during or at the end of the lease period at a bargain price. The price must be sufficiently less than the asset's expected fair value so that the option is likely to be exercised. (This arrangement is called a **bargain purchase option.**)
3. The period covered by the lease is 75% or more of the estimated service life of the leased asset.
4. The present value of the minimum payments under the lease is 90% or more of the fair value of the leased asset.[10]

---

[10] *CICA Handbook*, par. 3065.06.

A lease that does not meet any of these four criteria is classified by the lessee as an operating lease.

To illustrate accounting for leases, assume that Alpha Company plans to produce a product with a new machine that has a cash price of approximately $32,800 and an estimated 10-year life with no salvage value. Alpha Company does not have that much cash available and plans to lease the machine starting on December 31, 1993. Alpha Company will lease the machine under one of the following contracts, both of which require it to pay for maintenance, taxes, and insurance on the machine:

(a) Lease the machine for five years, with annual payments of $7,500 payable at the end of each of the five years. The machine will be returned to the lessor at the end of the lease period.

(b) Lease the machine for five years, with annual payments of $10,000 payable at the end of each of the five years. The machine will become the property of Alpha Company at the end of the lease period.

If Alpha had chosen to borrow sufficient cash to purchase the machine, it would have paid interest at an annual rate of 16%.

Accounting for an Operating Lease

The first lease contract does not pass ownership to the lessee, does not have a bargain purchase option, and covers only half of the asset's 10-year useful life. Therefore, it does not meet any of the first three criteria of a capital lease. Also, the present value of the lease payments, discounted at the 16% interest rate, is $24,557 ($7,500 × 3.2743). This amount is less than 90% of $32,800, so the lease also does not meet the fourth criterion of a capital lease. Therefore, the lease must be classified as an *operating lease*.

If Alpha Company chooses contract *a*, no entry is made at the time the lease contract is signed. Later, each annual rental payment is recorded with an entry like the following one, which records the first payment at the end of 1994:

1994				
Dec.	31	Machinery Rental Expense	7,500.00	
		Cash		7,500.00
		Paid the annual rent on a leased machine.		

Alpha Company also must record any expenses it incurs for maintenance, taxes, and insurance on the machine. In addition, Alpha should add a note to its financial statements that gives a general description of the leasing arrangements. However, because the leased machine was not recorded as an asset, no entries are made for depreciation expense.

Accounting for a Capital Lease

The second lease contract, (b), meets the first capital lease criterion in that title to the asset is transferred to Alpha at the end of the lease. The contract also meets the fourth criterion because the present value of the five $10,000 payments is $32,743 ($10,000 × 3.2743), which is greater than 90% of the $32,800 cash price of the asset. Thus, it is a *capital lease*. In effect, this lease is a credit purchase transaction with the lessor providing financing to the lessee for acquiring the machine.

Recording the Lease Liability. If Alpha Company chooses the second lease contract, it should record the asset and the liability at the $32,743 present value of the five lease payments. Alpha makes this entry on the day the lease is signed:

1993				
Dec.	31	Machinery.	32,743.00	
		Discount on Lease Financing	17,257.00	
		Long-Term Lease Liability.		50,000.00
		Purchased a machine through a long-term lease		
		contract.		

In effect, the cost of the leased machine is $32,743. Like the cost of any other asset, this amount should be charged to depreciation expense over the machine's expected service life of 10 years. Sometimes, however, the terms of a lease are such that the expected service life of the leased asset is limited to the term of the lease. This condition exists if the lessee does not obtain ownership at the end of the lease and the lease period is shorter than the asset's expected life.

Reporting Long-Term Lease Liability on the Balance Sheet. As we showed for a noninterest-bearing note, the $17,257 discount on the lease liability is the interest component of the transaction. The net liability that results from the lease is the gross long-term lease liability less the amount of the discount. The two items should appear as follows on Alpha Company's December 31, 1993, balance sheet:

Long-term liabilities:
Long-term lease liability[11] $50,000
Less unamortized discount based on the 16% interest
rate available on the date of the contract 17,257 $32,743

Entries to Record Amortization, Lease Payments, and Interest. If Alpha Company amortizes the machine on a straight-line basis over its 10-year life, it will make the following entries at the end of the first year in the life of the lease:

[11] To simplify the illustration, we have disregarded the requirement that the lease liability be divided into its current and noncurrent portions. You should do the same thing when you work the exercises and problems at the end of the chapter.

1994				
Dec.	31	Amortization Expense, Machinery	3,274.30	
		Accumulated Amortization, Machinery		3,274.30
		To record amortization on the machine.		
		$32,743/10 years = $3,274.30		
	31	Long-Term Lease Liability	10,000.00	
		Cash		10,000.00
		Made the annual payment on the lease.		
	31	Interest Expense	5,239.00	
		Discount on Lease Financing.		5,239.00
		Amortized a portion of the discount on the lease		
		financing.		

The first entry records straight-line depreciation equal to the asset's cost of $32,743 divided by 10 years (there is no salvage value). The second entry records the first of the five $10,000 lease payments as a reduction in the gross lease liability. The third entry records $5,239 as interest expense on the net lease liability. To calculate this amount, apply the 16% interest rate to the $32,743 beginning carrying amount of the lease liability [$32,743 × 16% = $5,239].

Illustration 12–5 contains two schedules: The first is like Illustration 12–3, and shows the allocation of the total interest expense of $17,257 over the five years of the lease. This schedule differs from Illustration 12–3 by including an extra column that shows the decrease in the gross liability from the annual $10,000 payment.

The second schedule in Illustration 12–5 shows the amortization of the discount on the lease liability. To determine the amount of discount to be amortized each year, the net lease liability at the beginning of each year is multiplied by 16%. For example, the amount of discount to be amortized in 1995 is $4,477 ($27,982 × 16%). Each ending net liability amount is found by subtracting the ending unamortized discount in column (*e*) from the ending gross liability in column (*f*). For example, the December 31, 1995, carrying amount is $22,459 ($30,000 − $7,541). Notice that the gross liability in column (*f*) gets smaller by $10,000 for each annual payment made on December 31. This process eventually reduces the gross and net liability measures to zero.

The **carrying amount of the lease** is the difference between the sum of the remaining rental payments less the unamortized discount. After posting the December 31, 1994, entries to record the $10,000 payment and the amortization of the discount, the carrying amount of the lease appears on the December 31, 1994, balance sheet as follows:

Long-term liabilities:		
Long-term lease liability.	$40,000	
Less unamortized discount based on the 16% interest		
rate available on the date of the contract	12,018	$27,982

ILLUSTRATION 12-5

Allocation of Interest for a Five-Year Lease Liability, $10,000 Payable per Year, with an Initial Net Balance of $32,743				
	(a)	(b)	(c)	(d)
		Interest	Less	Ending
	Beginning	Expense	Annual	Net Liability
Year	Net Liability	(a) × 16%	Payment	(a) + (b) − (c)
1994	$32,743	$ 5,239	$10,000	$27,982
1995	27,982	4,477	10,000	22,459
1996	22,459	3,593	10,000	16,052
1997	16,052	2,568	10,000	8,620
1998	8,620	1,380*	10,000	–0–
Total expense		$17,257		

Amortization Schedule for a Five-Year Lease Liability, $10,000 Payable per Year, Discounted at 16%

	(a)	(b)	(c)	(d)	(e)	(f)	(g)
	Beginning	Unamortized	Beginning	Discount	Unamortized Discount at	Ending Gross	Ending
	Gross	Discount at	Net	to Be	the End	Lease	Net
	Lease	Beginning	Liability	Amortized	of Year	Liability	Liability
Year	Liability	of Year	(a) − (b)	(c) × 16%	(b) − (d)	(a) − $10,000	(f) − (e)
1994	$50,000	$17,257	$32,743	$ 5,239	$12,018	$40,000	$27,982
1995	40,000	12,018	27,982	4,477	7,541	30,000	22,459
1996	30,000	7,541	22,459	3,593	3,948	20,000	16,052
1997	20,000	3,948	16,052	2,568	1,380	10,000	8,620
1998	10,000	1,380	8,620	1,380*	–0–	–0–	–0–
Total				$17,257			

* Adjusted to compensate for rounding.

Summary of Chapter in Terms of Learning Objectives

LO 1. Current liabilities are due within one year of the balance sheet date or within one operating cycle, whichever is longer. The liquidation (payment) of current liabilities requires the use of existing current assets or the creation of other current liabilities. Long-term liabilities do not have to be paid within one year or one operating cycle.

LO 2. A liability is definite when you know the answer to all three of these questions: (a) Who will be paid? (b) When is payment due? (c) How much will be paid? When the amount to be paid is not precisely known, the obligation is called an estimated liability.

LO 3. Expenses for property taxes and product warranties often must be recorded before the amounts to be paid are known. Therefore, you must estimate the amounts of the liabilities based on the best information currently available. After more information becomes known, the liabilities should be corrected with corresponding adjustments to expense. Short-term notes payable are recorded at their face amounts when the stated interest rates of the notes are reasonable approximations of current market rates of interest. When the notes are not interest-bearing or the stated rates of interest do not reflect the current market rate, the notes are recorded at their present values or at the value of the assets received in exchange, whichever is more reliably known.

LO 4. Many obligations that qualify as liabilities do not depend on uncertain future events. In contrast, when an economic entity is obligated to make a future payment only if some future event takes place, the potential obligation is a contingent liability. However, if the future event that will confirm the existence of a present obligation is probable and the amount of the future payment can be reasonably estimated, the obligation is reported as a liability.

LO 5. The present value of an amount to be received or paid in the future is the amount that could be invested now at the given rate of interest to accumulate a total value equal to the amount to be received or paid. The present value of a series of equal payments is the sum of the present values of each payment.

LO 6. A long-term, noninterest-bearing note must be recorded at its present value calculated with the market interest rate. This amount should approximate the fair value of the assets received in exchange for the note. Each period during the life of the note, interest expense is calculated by multiplying the carrying value of the note at the beginning of the period by the interest rate that was used to discount the note. When an asset is acquired with a capital lease, the lessee records the leased asset and the lease liability at the present value of the lease payments calculated with the market interest rate. This amount should approximate the fair value of the asset. On the other hand, the periodic payments under an operating lease are debited to rent expense as they are incurred.

Demonstration Problem

Prepare journal entries for the following 1993 transactions of Kearns Company:

a. Kearns accrued estimated property taxes during the first eight months of 1993 at the rate of $2,000 per month. On September 10, Kearns learned that the 1993 tax bill would be $21,720. The due date for these taxes is December 31. Show the property tax entries on September 30 and October 31.

b. During September, Kearns sold $140,000 of merchandise under a 180-day warranty. Prior experience shows that the costs of fulfilling the warranty will equal 5% of the selling price. Record the month's warranty expense and increase in the warranty liability as a September 30 adjusting entry. Also record an October 8 expenditure of $300 cash to service an item sold in September.

c. On October 10, Kearns arranged with a supplier to pay 25% of an overdue $10,000 account payable by Kearns to the supplier. The remaining balance was converted to a $7,500, 90-day note bearing 12% interest.

d. On October 15, Kearns borrowed $98,000 by discounting its $100,000, 60-day note to the bank. The discount rate charged by the bank was 12% per year.

e. On December 1, Kearns acquired a machine by giving a $60,000, noninterest-bearing note due in one year. The rate of interest available to Kearns for this type of debt was 12%.

f. On December 14, Kearns paid the note described in (*d*).

g. On December 31, Kearns accrued the interest on the notes described in (*c*) and (*e*). Show separate adjusting entries.

In addition to the preceding transactions, Kearns entered into a three-year lease of machinery on January 1, 1993, and agreed to make three payments of $30,158 on December 31, 1993, 1994, and 1995. The appropriate interest rate for this lease is 10%. Title to the machinery will pass to Kearns at the end of the lease, and the lease should be recorded as a capital lease.

h. Show the entry to record entering into the lease.

i. Prepare a table that shows the amount of interest expense to allocate to each year of the lease.

j. Show the entries to record the first payment on December 31, 1993; the interest expense for 1993; and the depreciation expense for 1993. The machine's useful life is predicted to be five years, with no salvage value, and straight-line depreciation is used.

k. Show how the leased asset and lease liability would appear on the balance sheet as of December 31, 1993.

Planning the Solution

- Examine each situation to determine the required calculation and entry.
- For (*a*), determine the amount of liability that has been recorded and the balance that ought to be recorded as of September 30, and make an entry for the difference. Then accrue the expense for October.
- For (*b*), compute and record the warranty expense for the month, and then show the expenditure in October as a reduction of the liability.
- For (*c*), eliminate the balance of the account payable, and create the note payable.
- For (*d*), record the discount deducted by the bank from the $100,000 face value of the note. Observe that the note will mature and be paid before the end of the year.
- For (*e*), estimate the cost of the asset by finding the present value of the cash that will be paid when the note payable matures.
- For (*f*), record the cash expenditure.
- For (*g*), calculate the interest expense on the note from (*c*) for 82 days, and on the note from (*e*) for 30 days, and record them. Pay close attention to the original entries to determine whether a discount should be involved in the adjusting entries.
- For (*h*), determine the present value of the lease payments, and record the effects of entering into the lease.
- For (*i*), prepare a table showing the calculation of interest expense by applying the rate to the net lease liability. (Two formats are possible.)
- For (*j*), prepare three entries to record the lease payment, the accrual of interest on the lease liability, and the depreciation on the asset, using its useful life.

Solution to Demonstration Problem

- For (*k*), determine the gross liability, the unamortized discount, and the net liability for the lease as of the end of 1993.

a.	Sept.	30	Property Tax Expense	290.00	
			Estimated Property Taxes Payable		290.00

Actual liability on Sept. 30 ($21,720 × ⁹/₁₂) . . . $16,290
Recorded liability as of Aug. 31 ($2,000 × 8) . . 16,000
Additional liability to record on Sept. 30 . . . . $ 290

	Oct.	31	Property Tax Expense	1,810.00	
			Estimated Property Taxes Payable		1,810.00
			$21,720/12 = $1,810 per month		
b.	Sept.	30	Warranty Expense	7,000.00	
			Estimated Warranty Liability		7,000.00
			$140,000 × 5% = $7,000		
	Oct.	8	Estimated Warranty Liability.	300.00	
			Cash		300.00
c.	Oct.	10	Accounts Payable	10,000.00	
			Cash		2,500.00
			Notes Payable		7,500.00
d.	Oct.	15	Cash	98,027.40	
			Interest Expense	1,972.60	
			Notes Payable		100,000.00
			$100,000 × 12% × (⁶⁰/₃₆₅) = $1,972.60		
e.	Dec.	1	Machinery	53,574.00	
			Discount on Notes Payable.	6,426.00	
			Notes Payable		60,000.00
			$60,000 × 0.8929 = $53,574		
f.	Dec.	14	Notes Payable	100,000.00	
			Cash		100,000.00

g.

For the note in (c):

	Dec.	31	Interest Expense	202.19	
			Interest Payable		202.19
			Oct. 10 to Dec. 31 = 82 days		
			$7,500 × 12% × ⁸²/₃₆₅ = $202.19		

For the note in (e):

	Dec.	31	Interest Expense	528.40	
			Discount on Notes Payable		528.40
			Dec. 1 to Dec. 31 = 30 days		
			$53,574 × 12% × ³⁰/₃₆₅ = $528.40		
h.	Jan.	1	Machinery	75,000.00	
			Discount on Lease Financing.	15,474.00	
			Long-Term Lease Liability		90,474.00
			$30,158 × 2.4869 = $75,000		
			$30,158 × 3 = $90,474		

i. Allocation of interest for a 3-year, $15,474 per year lease liability payable, with an initial balance of $75,000:

Year	(a) Beginning Net Liability	(b) 10% Interest Expense	(c) Less Annual Payment	(d) Ending Net Liability (a) + (b) − (c)
1993.	$75,000	$ 7,500	$30,158	$52,342
1994.	52,342	5,234	30,158	27,418
1995.	27,418	2,740*	30,158	–0–
Total		$15,474		

* Adjusted for rounding.

Amortization schedule for a 3-year, $75,000 lease liability, discounted at 10%:

Year	(a) Beginning Gross Lease Liability	(b) Unamortized Discount at Beginning of Year	(c) Beginning Net Liability (a) − (b)	(d) Discount to Be Amortized (c) × 10%	(e) Unamortized Discount at Year-End (b) − (d)	(f) Ending Gross Lease Liability (a) − $30,158	(g) Ending Net Liability (a) − (e)
1993.	$90,474	$15,474	$75,000	$ 7,500	$7,974	$60,316	$52,342
1994.	60,316	7,974	52,342	5,234	2,740	30,158	27,418
1995.	30,158	2,740	27,418	2,740*	–0–	–0–	–0–
Total				$15,474			

* Adjusted for rounding.

j.

Dec.	31	Long-Term Lease Liability.	30,158.00	
		Cash		30,158.00
	31	Interest Expense	7,500.00	
		Discount on Lease Financing		7,500.00
	31	Amortization Expense, Machinery.	15,000.00	
		Accumulated Amortization, Machinery		15,000.00
		$75,000/5 = $15,000		

k. Long-term liabilities:

Long-term lease liability	$60,316	
Less unamortized discount based on the 10% interest rate available on the date of the contract.	7,974	$52,342

Glossary

LO 7 Define or explain the words and phrases listed in the chapter glossary.

Bank discount   interest deducted by a bank from the principal of the note when a debt is created. pp. 620–21

Bargain purchase option   an option that allows the lessee to purchase the leased asset at the end of the lease period at a price sufficiently less than its expected fair value to make it likely that the option will be exercised. p. 633

Capital lease   a lease that has essentially the same effect on the lessee and lessor as a purchase transaction in that the outcome is just as if the lessee obtained a loan and used the proceeds to purchase the leased asset; a lease is accounted for as a capital lease if it meets any of four criteria established by the AcSB. pp. 633–36

Carrying amount of a lease   the difference between the sum of the remaining rental payments less the unamortized discount. p. 636

Carrying amount of a note   the face amount of a note minus the unamortized discount on the note. p. 632

Estimated liability   an obligation that definitely exists but that has uncertainty about the amount that is to be paid. p. 614

Financing lease   another name for a capital lease. pp. 633–36

Operating lease   a lease that merely gives the lessee the right to use the leased asset for the time period covered by the contract; an operating lease does not meet any of the criteria established by the AcSB that would make it a capital lease. pp. 633–34

Present value   the amount of money that can be invested today at a given interest rate to accumulate a total value equal to a given amount to be received or paid at some future date or dates. pp. 623–27

Present value table   a table that shows the present values of an amount to be received when discounted at various interest rates for various numbers of time periods, or that shows the present values of a series of equal payments to be received for a varying number of periods when discounted at various interest rates. pp. 624–25, 627

Product warranty   a promise to a customer that obligates the seller or manufacturer for a limited period of time to pay for items such as replacement parts or repair costs if the product breaks or otherwise fails to perform. pp. 616–17

Synonymous Terms

Capital lease   financing lease.

Carrying value of a note   book value of a note.

Warranty   guarantee.

Objective Review

Answers to the following questions are listed at the end of this chapter. Be sure that you decide which is the one best answer to each question *before* you check the answers.

LO 1   Which of the following items would normally be classified as a current liability of a company that has a 14-month current operating cycle?

a. The portion of a long-term lease liability that is due within 14 months.

b. Salaries payable.

c. A note payable due in 10 months.

d. Accounts payable due in 12 months.

e. All of the above.

LO 2 Estimated liabilities include:

a. Obligations to pay an amount to an outside party if some uncertain future event occurs.

b. Obligations to pay a specific person on a specific date when the amount to be paid is uncertain but can be reasonably estimated.

c. Obligations to pay a specific amount to a specific person when the due date is not known.

d. Obligations to pay a specific amount on a specific date when the party to be paid is not known.

e. All of the above.

LO 3 An automobile was sold for $15,000 on June 1, 1993, with a one-year or 10,000-kilometre warranty. The warranty covers parts only. Based on past experience, warranty expense is estimated at 1.5% of the sales price. On March 1, 1994, the customer returned the car for warranty repairs. Replacement parts amounted to $75 and total labour charges were $60. The amount that should be recorded as warranty expense for the March 1 repair work performed is:

a. $ 0.

b. $ 60.

c. $ 75.

d. $135.

e. $225.

LO 4 A future payment should be reported on the balance sheet as a liability if:

a. The payment is contingent on a future event that is likely but the amount of the payment cannot reasonably be estimated.

b. The payment is contingent on a future event that is likely and the amount of the payment can reasonably be estimated.

c. The payment is contingent on a future event that is likely and the amount of the payment is certain.

d. The payment is contingent on a future event that is not likely but the amount of the payment can reasonably be estimated.

e. Both (*b*) and (*c*) are correct.

LO 5 A company enters into an agreement whereby it will make five semiannual payments of $1,000 each, the first to be made in six months, plus an additional $15,000 payment to be made 30 months from now. If the annual rate of interest is 10%, the present value of these payments is

a. $ 9,934.40.

b. $12,536.00.

c. $13,104.30.

d. $13,643.00.

e. $16,082.00.

LO 6 On December 31, 1993, Fairview Paint Supply leased a building for 20 years. The building had a fair value of $400,000 and an estimated useful life of 30 years. Annual lease payments of $59,639.75 begin on December 31, 1994, and the prevailing interest rate available to Fairview Paint Supply was 14%. Which of the following expenses will be recognized on this lease during 1994?

a. Rental expense, $59,639.75.

b. Interest expense, $55,300.00.

c. Interest expense, $46,666.67.

d. Rental expense, $29,819.88.

e. Interest expense, $8,349.57.

LO 7 The interest deducted by a bank from the principal when a debt is created is called:

a. A bank discount.

b. A cash discount.

c. A debt guarantee.

d. A liability discount.

e. An interest deduction.

Questions for Class Discussion

1. What is a liability?
2. Are all expected future payments liabilities?
3. Define (*a*) a current liability and (*b*) a long-term liability.
4. Three important factors about a liability may or may not be definite. What are those factors?
5. If a company has a definite obligation to pay a given amount of money to an outside party but the date the obligation must be paid is indefinite, should the obligation be reported as a liability on the balance sheet or disclosed as a contingent liability?
6. If a property tax liability is estimated at the end of year 1 and the actual payment of the liability in year 2 turns out to be more than the amount that was estimated, how is the excess accounted for in year 2?
7. Why are product warranties often recorded as liabilities instead of being disclosed as contingent liabilities?
8. What is the difference between a *loan* and a *discount* as those terms relate to borrowing money from a bank?
9. Which arrangement is more advantageous to a bank: (*a*) making a loan to a customer in exchange for the customer's $2,000, 90-day, 12% note or (*b*) making a loan to the customer by discounting the customer's $2,000 noninterest-bearing note for 90 days at 12%? Why?
10. Distinguish between bank discount and cash discount.
11. Is $2,000 to be received in one year always worth less than a series of two $1,000 payments to be received semiannually for the next year?
12. If a $10,000 noninterest-bearing, five-year note is exchanged for a machine, the face amount of the note equals the sum of two different economic costs. What are these two costs?
13. Distinguish between an operating lease and a capital lease. Which causes an asset and a liability to appear on the balance sheet?

14. When a capital lease is to be recorded, how do you determine the amount to be debited to the asset account?

15. In Bombardier Inc.'s January 31, 1992, balance sheet that appears in Appendix I, what amount of the long-term debt was payable during the next year?

BBD

Mini Discussion Cases

Your friend has indicated that according to GAAP, all possible liabilities should be recorded in the financial statements. Therefore, he continues, even those items called *contingent liabilities* must be accrued in accordance with the conservatism principle. Otherwise, the financial statements would be misleading.

Case 12–1

Required

Is your friend correct? Why (not)?

Jamie Keyes, ace lefthander with the York Bluebirds, is negotiating for renewal of his contract. Prior to making an offer to Keyes, George Megabucks—owner of the team—asks you to check out three alternatives he intends to present to the pitcher. George is only willing to offer a three-year contract but is offering three different payment schemes as follows:

Case 12–2

a. $300,000 payable at the end of each year for 10 years.

b. $750,000 payable at the end of each year for 3 years.

c. $1,800,000 payable on signing the three-year contract.

Required

1. Identify the accounting issues raised in the case.
2. Discuss how the issues should be resolved in light of GAAP.

Exercises

Throughout 1994, Rockland Supply Company owned property subject to civic property taxes. The property's assessed valuation for tax purposes was $600,000. The 1993 tax levy was $1.10 per $100 of assessed valuation, and the company expected the 1994 rate to remain unchanged. In early August, the city announced that the 1994 tax levy would be $1.25 per $100 and that taxes would be due September 30, 1994. The annual taxes were paid on the due date. Prepare entries to record property tax expense for the months of July, August, and September.

Exercise 12–1
Property tax expense
(LO 3)

Twin Oaks Electronics manufactures a product for $35 per unit and sells it for $52 per unit. In May, the company sold 60,000 units subject to a one-year warranty. According to the warranty, customers must pay a $5.75 service charge to return a defective unit and have it replaced by a new one. When a unit under warranty fails, the company simply discards the broken one and replaces it with a new unit. Past experience suggests a 1.5% failure rate of new products sold. In May, customers actually returned 750

Exercise 12–2
Product warranty expense
(LO 3)

defective units. Prepare summary entries as of the end of May to record product warranty expense and to record the replacement of the 750 units.

Exercise 12–3
Short-term notes payable
(LO 3)

On December 1, 1993, Rizutto Furniture Company borrowed $75,000 by giving a 60-day, 10% note payable. The company has a calendar-year accounting period and does not make reversing entries. Prepare General Journal entries to record (*a*) the issuance of the note, (*b*) the required year-end adjusting entry, and (*c*) the entry to pay the note on its due date.

Exercise 12–4
Discounted notes payable
(LO 3)

On December 1, 1993, Westwood Apparel discounted its own $75,000, 60-day note payable at the bank. The discount rate was 10%. Prepare General Journal entries to record (*a*) the issuance of the note; (*b*) the required December 31, 1993, adjusting entry; (*c*) the payment of the note on its due date; and (*d*) the interest expense on the note during 1994.

Exercise 12–5
Present value calculations
(LO 5)

Show calculations to produce the following:

(*a*) The present value of $50,000 to be received six years from now, discounted at 12%.

(*b*) The total present value of three payments consisting of $15,000 to be received two years from now, $20,000 to be received three years from now, and $45,000 to be received four years from now, all discounted at 8%.

(*c*) The present value of nine payments of $22,000 each, with a payment to be received at the end of each of the next nine years, discounted at 16%.

Exercise 12–6
Present value of
investment
(LO 5)

AAA Service Company is offered an investment contract whereby it will be paid $6,000 every six months for the next five years. The first payment would be received six months from today. What will the company be willing to pay for this contract if it expects a 12% annual return on the investment? What if it expects an annual return of only 9%?

Exercise 12–7
Present value of
investment
(LO 5)

Oakwood Corporation is offered an investment contract whereby it will be paid $8,000 annually for the next six years. The first payment would be received one year from today. What will the company be willing to pay for this contract if it expects a 16% annual return on the investment? What if it expects an annual return of only 12%?

Exercise 12–8
Choosing between
payment patterns
based on present values
(LO 5)

An individual has offered to sell equipment for $18,000. A potential buyer has agreed to purchase the equipment for the stated price but, as an alternative, has given the seller the option of receiving eight annual payments of $3,200 each, the first payment to be one year from now. Assuming the seller expects an annual return of at least 10%, which of the two alternatives should the seller accept?

Montvale Manufacturing Company purchased a machine on December 31, 1993. The terms of purchase included $8,000 cash plus a $20,000, noninterest-bearing, four-year note. The available interest rate on this date was 14%. You should (*a*) prepare the entry to record the purchase of the machine, (*b*) show how the liability will appear on a balance sheet prepared on the day of the purchase, and (*c*) prepare the entry to recognize interest expense and amortize a portion of the discount on the note at the end of 1994.

Exercise 12–9
Exchanging a noninterest-bearing note for a plant asset
(LO 6)

On December 31, 1993, a day when the available interest rate was 10%, North Point Printing Company leased equipment with an eight-year life under a contract calling for a $6,000 annual lease payment at the end of each of the next five years, with the equipment becoming the property of the lessee at the end of that period. Prepare entries to record (*a*) the leasing of the equipment; (*b*) the recognition of interest expense on the lease liability at December 31, 1994; (*c*) depreciation expense for 1994; and (*d*) the December 31, 1994, payment under the lease.

Exercise 12–10
Liabilities from leasing
(LO 6)

Problems

Part 1. Faulkner Company buys and sells a single product subject to a six-month warranty that covers replacement parts but not labour. Prepare journal entries to record the following transactions completed by the company during the month of July. Cash was received or paid in each transaction.

Problem 12–1
Product warranty expense and property tax expense
(LO 2, 4)

July 6 Purchased 750 units of product for $40 per unit.

     10 Purchased $2,300 of spare parts to be used in repairs to products that are expected to be returned for warranty work.

     12 Sold 200 units of product for $75 per unit, receiving cash.

     16 Repaired 12 units of product that customers returned under the warranty. Replacement parts cost $220, and the customers paid $180 for labour.

     20 Sold 300 units of product for $80 per unit.

     24 Repaired 18 units of product under the warranty. Replacement parts cost $310, and the customers paid $245 for labour.

     31 Recorded warranty expense for July. Past experience shows that 3% of the units sold require warranty work, and the average cost of replacement parts is $17 per unit returned. Average labour charges are $13.95 per unit.

Part 2. Midland Flooring Company expects to accrue 1994 property taxes at the end of each month using the experience of 1993 to estimate the 1994 tax. In March 1993, Midland Flooring's property was assessed at $650,000. The 1993 tax levy was $1.50 per $100. In March 1994, Midland Flooring's property was reassessed at $720,000. (The reassessment was not expected to affect the tax levy of $1.50 per $100.) Early in August 1994, the annual tax levy was set at $1.80 per $100. On October 31, 1994, Midland Flooring paid the 1994 tax. Complete financial statements are prepared by the company every month.

Required

Prepare entries to be recorded at the end of January, March, August, October, and November 1994, to accrue property tax expense for each of those months and to record the annual tax payment.

Problem 12–2
Journalizing notes payable transactions
(LO 3)

Prepare general journal entries to record these transactions of Midtown Glass Company.

1993

Mar. 14   Purchased merchandise on credit from Precision Windows, invoice dated March 13, terms 2/10, n/30, $8,400.

Apr. 2   Borrowed money at National Bank by discounting Midtown's own $16,000 note payable for 90 days at 14%. (Because the note matures before the end of the year, the discount should be charged to Interest Expense.)

     12   Gave Precision Windows $1,600 cash and a $6,800, 90-day, 14% note to secure an extension on Midtown's account that was due.

July 1   Paid the note discounted at National Bank on April 2.

     11   Paid the note given Precision Windows on April 12.

Nov. 16   Borrowed money at National Bank by discounting Midtown's own $15,000 note payable for 60 days at 12%.

Dec. 16   Borrowed money at Royal Bank by giving an $18,500, 90-day, 12% note payable.

     31   Made an adjusting entry to record interest on the November 16 note to National Bank.

     31   Made an adjusting entry to record the accrued interest on the December 16 note to Royal Bank.

1994

Jan. 15   Paid the November 16 note to National Bank. Also recorded interest expense related to the note.

Mar. 16   Paid the principal and interest on the note given to Royal Bank on December 16.

Problem 12–3
Present values of alternative payment patterns
(LO 5)

Slawson Enterprises is negotiating with a contractor for the construction of a new office complex. The complex will be completed and ready for occupation two years from now. If Slawson pays for the complex immediately (Payment Plan A), it will cost $5,551,200. However, two alternative payment plans are available. Plan B would require a payment of $6,900,000 on completion. Plan C would require two annual payments of $3,600,000, the first of which would be made one year from now. In evaluating the three alternatives, the management of Slawson has decided to assume an interest rate of 14%.

Required

Calculate the present value of each payment plan and use the results to indicate which one Slawson Enterprises should choose.

Problem 12–4
Exchanging a noninterest-bearing note for a plant asset
(LO 6)

On January 1, 1993, Bertolet Company acquired an item of equipment by issuing a $500,000, noninterest-bearing, six-year note payable on December 31, 1998. A reliable cash price for the equipment was not readily available. The market rate of interest for notes like this one was 12% (annual) on the day of the exchange.

Required

(Round all amounts in your answers to the nearest whole dollar.)

1. Determine the initial net liability created by the issuance of this note.
2. Prepare a table showing the calculation of the amount of interest expense allocated to each year the note is outstanding and the carrying amount of the net liability at the end of each of those years.
3. Prepare General Journal entries to record (*a*) the acquisition of the equipment; (*b*) the amortization of the discount at the end of 1993, 1994, and 1995; and (*c*) the amortization of the discount and the payment of the note on December 31, 1998.
4. Show how the note should be presented on the December 31, 1995, balance sheet.

Wesson Engineering Company leased a machine on January 1, 1993, under a contract calling for four annual payments of $15,000 on December 31 of 1993 through 1996, with the machine becoming the property of the lessee after the fourth payment. The machine was predicted to have a service life of six years and no salvage value, and the interest rate available to Wesson Engineering for equipment loans was 12% on the day the lease was signed. The machine was delivered on January 10, 1993, and was immediately placed in service. On January 4, 1998, it was overhauled at a total cost of $2,500. The overhaul did not increase the machine's efficiency but it did add two additional years to its expected service life. On June 30, 2000, the machine was traded in on a similar new machine having a $42,000 cash price. A $3,000 trade-in allowance was received, and the balance was paid in cash. Assume any gain or loss on the exchange is immaterial.

Problem 12–5
Capital leases and exchanges of plant assets
(LO 6)

Required

(Round all amounts in your answers to the nearest whole dollar.)

1. Determine the initial net liability created by this lease and the cost of the leased asset.
2. Prepare a table showing the calculation of the amount of interest expense allocated to each year the lease is in effect and the carrying amount of the liability at the end of each of those years.
3. Prepare the entry to record the leasing of the machine.
4. Prepare entries that would be made on December 31, 1994, to record the annual amortization on a straight-line basis, to record the lease payment, and to amortize the discount. Also show how the machine and the lease liability should appear on the December 31, 1994, balance sheet.
5. Prepare the entries to record the machine's overhaul in 1998 and amortization at the end of that year.
6. Prepare the entries that would be needed to record the exchange of the machines on June 30, 2000.

The Clearview Drilling Company needs two new trailers, each of which has an estimated service life of 12 years. The trailers could be purchased for $50,000 each, but Clearview does not have enough cash to pay for them. Instead, Clearview agrees to lease Trailer 1 for four years, after which the trailer remains the property of the lessor. In addition, Clearview agrees to lease Trailer 2 for six years, after which the trailer remains the property of the lessor. According to the lease contracts, Clearview must pay $13,000 annually for each trailer, with the payments to be made at the end of each lease year. Both leases were signed on December 31, 1993, at which time the prevailing interest rate available to Clearview for equipment loans was 14%.

Problem 12–6
Accounting for capital and operating leases
(LO 6)

Required

(Round all amounts in your answers to the nearest whole dollar.)

1. Determine whether each of these two leases is an operating or capital lease.
2. Prepare any required entries to record entering into the lease of (*a*) Trailer 1 and (*b*) Trailer 2.
3. Prepare the entries required on December 31, 1994, for (*a*) Trailer 1 and (*b*) Trailer 2. Use straight-line amortization for any capital leases. (Remember, if the asset remains the property of the lessor, the lessee must take amortization over the period of the capital lease.)
4. Trailer 1 was returned to the lessor on December 31, 1997, the end of the fourth and final year of the lease. Prepare the required entries as of December 31, 1997, for (*a*) Trailer 1 and (*b*) Trailer 2.
5. Show how Trailer 2 and the lease liability for the trailer should appear on the balance sheet as of December 31, 1997 (after the year-end lease payment).

Problem 12–7
Analytical essay
(LO 6)

On January 1, 1993, Compton Company made an entry like the following to record the receipt of cash in exchange for a six-year, noninterest-bearing note payable:

1993					
Jan.	1	Cash	xx,xxx.xx		
		Discount on Notes Payable	x,xxx.xx		
		Long-Term Notes Payable		xx,xxx.xx	

Concerning the note, assume that the only dollar amounts you have knowledge of are the following:

a. The amount of the liability (net of discount) reported on the December 31, 1993, balance sheet.

b. The amount credited to the Discount on Notes Payable account on December 31, 1993.

Required

Explain how you would determine the following items, assuming you know only the preceding information. (*Hint:* You may find it helpful to review Illustration 12–4.)

1. The amount of the liability (net of discount) on the date the note was issued.
2. The market rate of interest on the date the note was issued.
3. The amount of the December 31, 1994, adjusting entry to amortize the discount for the note payable. (Adjustments are made annually on December 31.)
4. The face amount of the note. (Assume that you also have access to present value tables.)

Problem 12–8
Analytical essay
(LO 6)

On January 2, 1993, Hasting Company has decided to lease a delivery truck for four years. Lease payments are to be made on December 31, the end of Hasting's fiscal year. The truck has an estimated service life of eight years. The terms of the lease agreement are such that Hasting would account for the lease as an operating lease. At the last minute, Hasting and the lessor agree to change the period covered by the lease to six years. Describe the entries Hasting Company should make in 1993 to account for the lease.

Part 1. Harris & Sons buys and sells a single product subject to a one-year warranty that covers replacement parts but not labour. Prepare journal entries to record the following transactions completed by the company during the month of March. Cash was received or paid in each transaction.

Mar.　4　Purchased 7,200 units of product for $30 per unit.

　　　8　Purchased $18,500 of spare parts to be used in repairs to products that are expected to be returned for warranty work.

　　11　Sold 3,900 units of product for $80 per unit, receiving cash.

　　17　Repaired 150 units of product that customers returned under the warranty. Replacement parts cost $980 and the customers paid $1,250 for labour.

　　20　Sold 4,100 units of product for $95 per unit.

　　26　Repaired 176 units of product under the warranty. Replacement parts cost $1,125 and the customers paid $1,575 for labour.

　　31　Recorded warranty expense for March. Past experience shows that 3% of the units sold require warranty work, and the average cost of replacement parts is $6.50 per unit returned. Average labour charges are $8.60 per unit.

Part 2. Odessa Paint Supply expects to accrue 1994 property taxes at the end of each month using the experience of 1993 to estimate the 1994 tax. In early 1993, Odessa's property was assessed at $300,000. The 1993 tax levy was $2.20 per $100. In April 1994, Odessa's property was reassessed at $330,000. (The reassessment was not expected to affect the tax levy of $2.20 per $100.) Early in June 1994, the annual tax levy was set at $2.40 per $100. On September 30, 1994, Odessa paid the 1994 tax. Complete financial statements are prepared by the company every month.

Required

Prepare entries to be recorded at the end of January, April, June, September, and October 1994 to accrue property tax expense for each of those months and to record the annual tax payment.

Prepare General Journal entries to record these transactions of Pine Company:

1993

Feb.　4　Purchased merchandise on credit from Ridgewood Supply Company, invoice dated February 3, terms 2/10, n/60, $35,200.

Mar.　2　Borrowed money at First Bank by discounting Pine's own $120,000 note payable for 30 days at 14%. (Because the note matures before the end of the year, the discount should be charged to Interest Expense.)

Apr.　1　Paid the note discounted at First Bank on March 2.

　　　5　Gave Ridgewood Supply Company $11,200 cash and a $24,000, 30-day, 12% note to secure an extension on Pine's past-due account.

May　5　Paid the note given Ridgewood Supply Company on April 5.

Nov. 16　Borrowed money at First Bank by discounting Pine's own $108,000 note payable for 60 days at 10%.

Problem 12–1A
Product warranty expense and property tax expense
(LO 2, 4)

Problem 12–2A
Journalizing notes payable transactions
(LO 4)

Dec.   1   Borrowed money at Second Bank by giving a $150,000, 90-day, 15% note payable.

     31   Made an adjusting entry to record interest on the November 16 note to First Bank.

     31   Made an adjusting entry to record the accrued interest on the December 1 note to Second Bank.

1994

Jan.   15   Paid the November 16 note to First Bank and recorded interest expense on the note.

Mar.   1   Paid the principal and interest on the December 1 note given to Second Bank.

Problem 12–3A
Present values of
alternative payment
patterns
(LO 5)

Lakeside Amusement Park is negotiating with an engineering firm in planning the design and construction of a new roller coaster. The ride will be completed and ready for service five years from now. If Lakeside pays for the roller coaster immediately (Payment Plan A), it will cost $950,000. However, two alternative payment plans are available. Plan B would require a payment of $1,325,000 on completion. Plan C would require five annual payments of $230,000, the first of which would be made one year from now. In evaluating the three alternatives, the management of Lakeside has decided to assume an interest rate of 8%.

Required

Calculate the present value of each payment plan and use the results to indicate which one Lakeside's management should choose.

Problem 12–4A
Exchanging a
noninterest-bearing note
for a plant asset
(LO 6)

On January 1, 1993, Fairview Manufacturing acquired an item of equipment by issuing a $390,000, noninterest-bearing, five-year note payable on December 31, 1997. A reliable cash price for the equipment was not readily available. The market rate of interest for notes like this one was 10% (annual) on the day of the exchange.

Required

(Round all amounts in your answers to the nearest whole dollar.)

1. Determine the initial net liability created by the issuance of this note.
2. Prepare a table showing the calculation of the amount of interest expense allocated to each year the note is outstanding and the carrying amount of the net liability at the end of each of those years.
3. Prepare General Journal entries to record (*a*) the acquisition of the equipment; (*b*) the amortization of the discount at the end of 1993, 1994, and 1995; and (*c*) the amortization of the discount and the payment of the note on December 31, 1997.
4. Show how the note should be presented on the December 31, 1996, balance sheet.

Problem 12–5A
Capital leases and
exchanges of plant
assets
(LO 6)

Stony Point Service Company leased a machine on January 1, 1993, under a contract calling for six annual payments of $130,000 on December 31 of 1993 through 1998, with the machine becoming the property of the lessee after the sixth payment. The machine was predicted to have a service life of seven years and no salvage value, and the interest rate available to Stony Point for equipment loans was 9% on the day the lease was signed. The machine was delivered on January 8, 1993, and was immediately placed in service. On January 2, 1996, it was overhauled at a total cost of $29,200. The overhaul did not increase the machine's efficiency, but it did add an additional three years to its expected service life. On September 30, 1999, it was traded in on a similar new machine having a $330,000 cash price. A $65,000 trade-in allowance was received, and the balance was paid in cash. Assume any gain or loss on the exchange is material.

Required

(Round all amounts in your answers to the nearest whole dollar.)

1. Determine the initial net liability created by this lease and the cost of the leased asset.
2. Prepare a table that shows the calculation of the amount of interest expense allocated to each year the lease is in effect and the carrying amount of the liability at the end of each of those years.
3. Prepare the entry to record the leasing of the machine.
4. Prepare entries that would be made on December 31, 1994, to record the annual amortization on a straight-line basis, to record the lease payment, and to amortize the discount. Also show how the machine and the lease liability should appear on the December 31, 1994, balance sheet.
5. Prepare the entries to record the machine's overhaul in 1996 and amortization at the end of that year.
6. Prepare the entries that would be needed to record the exchange of the machines on September 30, 1999.

The Security Moving Company leased two new trucks. Each of the trucks has an estimated service life of six years. Truck 1 was leased for two years. Truck 2 was leased for three years. Each lease agreement calls for $75,000 annual lease payments at the end of the year. At the end of each lease, the truck will be returned to the lessor. Both leases were signed on December 31, 1993, at which time the prevailing interest rate available to Security Moving for equipment loans was 12%. Each of the trucks could have been purchased for $190,000 cash.

Problem 12–6A
Accounting for capital and operating leases
(LO 6)

Required

(Round all amounts in your answers to the nearest whole dollar.)

1. Determine whether each of these two leases is an operating or capital lease.
2. Prepare any required entries to record entering into the lease of (*a*) Truck 1 and (*b*) Truck 2.
3. Prepare the entries required on December 31, 1994, for (*a*) Truck 1 and (*b*) Truck 2. Use straight-line amortization for any capital leases. (Remember, if the asset remains the property of the lessor, the lessee must take amortization over the period of the capital lease.)
4. Truck 1 was returned to the lessor on December 31, 1995, the end of the second and final year of the lease. Prepare the required entries as of December 31, 1995, for (*a*) Truck 1 and (*b*) Truck 2.
5. Show how Truck 2 and the lease liability for the truck should appear on the balance sheet as of December 31, 1995 (after the year-end lease payment).

On January 1, 1993, Steck Corporation made an entry like the following to record the receipt of cash in exchange for a five-year, noninterest-bearing note payable:

Problem 12–7A
Analytical essay
(LO 6)

1993					
Jan.	1	Cash		xx,xxx.xx	
		Discount on Notes Payable		x,xxx.xx	
		Long-Term Notes Payable			xx,xxx.xx

Concerning the note, assume that the only dollar amounts you have knowledge of are the following:

a. The amount of the liability (net of discount) reported on the December 31, 1994, balance sheet.

b. The amount of the liability (net of discount) reported on the December 31, 1993, balance sheet.

Required

Explain how you would determine the following items, assuming you know only the preceding information. (*Hint:* You may find it helpful to review Illustration 12–4.)

1. The amount of the December 31, 1994, adjusting entry to amortize the discount on the note payable.

2. The market rate of interest on the date the note was issued.

3. The face amount of the note.

Problem 12–8A
Analytical essay
(LO 6)

On January 1, 1994, Jester Corporation is negotiating the lease of equipment for 10 years. The equipment has an estimated service life of 12 years. Tentatively, the lease agreement stipulates that lease payments are to be made on December 31, the end of Jester's fiscal year. Ownership does not transfer to Jester at the end of the 10 years. The lease agreement does not contain a bargain purchase option, and the present value of the lease payments is 88% of the fair value of the equipment. Jester wants to account for the lease as an operating lease.

Required

Suggest a revision to the lease contract that would accommodate Jester. Describe the entries Jester Corporation would make in 1994 to account for the lease under the revised lease agreement. How should Jester report the lease on the 1994 financial statements?

Provocative Problems

Provocative Problem 12–1
Wiggins Supply Company
(LO 6)

Wiggins Supply Company is planning to acquire some new equipment from Clarksville Corporation and has asked you to assist in analyzing the situation. The equipment may be purchased for $750,000 and then leased by Wiggins under a six-year lease contract to a customer for $160,000 payable at the end of each year. After the lease expires, Wiggins expects to sell the equipment for $260,000.

1. Suppose Wiggins has $750,000 cash available to buy the equipment and requires a 12% rate of return on its investments. Should the company buy the equipment and lease it to the customer?

2. As an alternative to paying cash, Wiggins can invest the $750,000 in other operations for four years and earn 12% annually on its investment. If this is done, the

equipment may be purchased by signing a $1,150,000, four-year, noninterest-bearing note payable to Clarksville Corporation. Should Wiggins pay $750,000 now or sign the $1,150,000 note?

3. Now suppose Wiggins does not have the option of signing a $1,150,000, four-year, noninterest-bearing note. Instead, the company may either pay $750,000 cash or lease the equipment from Clarksville Corporation for four years, after which the equipment would become the property of Wiggins. The lease contract would require $250,000 payments at the end of each year. If Wiggins leases the equipment, it will invest the $750,000 available cash in other operations and earn 12% on the investment. Should Wiggins pay cash or lease the equipment from Clarksville Corporation?

Look in Appendix I at the financial statements for Bombardier Inc. and the accompanying notes to the financial statements, and answer the following questions:

1. Examine the note on long-term debt. What type of long-term debt does Bombardier have? What proportion is due within the next fiscal year?

2. Is Bombardier a party to any lease contracts as a lessee? If so, are they capital leases or operating leases? How much expense was reported for 1992 from these leases? What kind of property is being leased?

Provocative Problem 12–2
Bombardier Inc.
(LO 1, 6)

BBD

Analytical and Review Problems

Refer to Mini Discussion Case 12–2 and prepare journal entries for each of the alternatives as of the date of signing the contract and at the end of the first year. Also indicate balance sheet presentation as of the end of the first year. Assume:

1. The going rate of interest is 12%.
2. The company amortizes assets on a straight-line basis.
3. Use interest method to recognize interest expense.

A&R Problem 12–1

On September 1, 1993, Chang Company acquired a machine by paying $15,000 cash and signing a two-year note that carried a face amount of $90,000 due at the end of the two-year period; the note did not specify interest. Assume the going rate of interest for this company for this type of loan is 12%. The accounting period ends December 31.

A&R Problem 12–2

Required
Give the entry to record the purchase of the machine and complete a tabulation as follows (round amounts to nearest dollar):

	Straight-Line Method	Interest Method
1. Cash to be paid at maturity	$_____	$_____
2. Total interest expense	$_____	$_____
3. Interest expense on income statement for 1993	$_____	$_____
4. Amount of the liability reported on balance sheet at end of 1993	$_____	$_____
5. Amortization expense for 1993 (assume straight-line, partial year, no residual value, and useful life of five years)	$_____	$_____

As a Matter of Record

Record Case 12–1

The following item, "Ottawa to Launch Real Return Bonds," appeared in the *Globe and Mail,* October 17, 1991, p. B10:

> The federal government is planning to launch a new program of "real return" bonds that will offer investors a return adjusted for movements in the consumer price index, Finance Minister Donald Mazankowski says.
>
> As an example of how such bonds would work, the department said that, if the CPI rose 1.5 per cent in the first six-month period, the value of a $1,000 real return bond would be calculated as $1,015. The coupon interest rate covering that half year would be based on $1,015 rather than on the original $1,000 value.
>
> The same sort of calculation would be made—multiplying the original face value of the bond by the total amount of inflation since it was issued—when the bonds were redeemed at maturity.

Required

If a company were to issue "real return" bonds, explain how interest expense would be calculated on an annual basis. What effect would this have on the balance sheet?

Answers to Objective Review Questions

LO 1 (*e*)	LO 4 (*e*)	LO 6 (*b*)
LO 2 (*b*)	LO 5 (*e*)	LO 7 (*a*)
LO 3 (*a*)		

The following December 31, 1993, unadjusted trial balance is for the Corley Owney Exterminator Company, which provides both interior and exterior pest control services. In addition, the company sells extermination products manufactured by other companies.

Corley Owney
Exterminator Company
(Review of Chapters 1–12)

CORLEY OWNEY EXTERMINATOR COMPANY
Unadjusted Trial Balance
December 31, 1993

Cash	$ 62,700	
Accounts receivable	56,250	
Allowance for doubtful accounts		$ 750
Merchandise inventory	42,100	
Trucks	25,000	
Accumulated amortization, trucks		–0–
Equipment	192,500	
Accumulated amortization, equipment		94,500
Leasehold improvements	–0–	
Accounts payable		12,900
Estimated warranty liability		4,680
Unearned extermination services revenue		–0–
Long-term notes payable		75,000
Discount on notes payable	27,338	
Corley Owney, capital (December 31, 1992, balance)		98,278
Corley Owney, withdrawals	55,000	
Extermination services revenue		284,200
Interest earned		1,400
Sales		177,400
Purchases	119,900	
Amortization expense, trucks	–0–	
Amortization expense, equipment	–0–	
Wages expense	45,500	
Interest expense	–0–	
Rent expense	82,620	
Bad debts expense	–0–	
Miscellaneous expenses	9,800	
Repairs expense	16,800	
Utilities expense	13,600	
Warranty expense	–0–	
Totals	$749,108	$749,108

The following additional information is available:

a. The bank statement reconciliation on December 31, 1993, showed these items:

Balance per bank	$58,105
Balance per books	62,700
Outstanding cheques	8,430
Deposit in transit	12,000
Interest earned	125
Service charges (miscellaneous expenses)	40
Included with the bank statement was a canceled cheque the company had failed to record (the amount of the cheque, which was a payment of an account payable, can be determined from the preceding information).	?

b. An examination of customers' accounts shows that accounts totaling $365 should be written off as uncollectible. In addition, the ending balance of the allowance account should be $840.

c. A truck was purchased and placed in service on July 1, 1993, and is being amortized under the declining-balance method at twice the straight-line rate. These facts are also known:

Original cost.	$25,000
Expected salvage value	3,000
Useful life	4 years

d. Two items of equipment (No. 7 and No. 9) were purchased in January 1990 and are being amortized by the straight-line method. These facts are known about these assets:

	No. 7	No. 9
Original cost.	$124,500	$68,000
Expected salvage value	19,500	5,000
Useful life	5 years	6 years

e. On October 1, 1993, Owney was paid $10,500 in advance to provide extermination services each month for an apartment complex for one year. Services began in October and the amount received was recorded in the Extermination Services Revenue account.

f. The expected cost of servicing items sold this year under warranty is estimated to be 3% of sales. No warranty expense has been recorded for 1993.

g. The $75,000 long-term note is a five-year, noninterest-bearing note obtained from City Bank on December 31, 1991. The interest rate available to Corley Owney on the date of the loan was 12%.

h. In January 1993, Owney put a new storefront on the building she was leasing. These improvements totaled $16,800 and were recorded in the Repairs Expense account. The expected life of the improvements is six years but the remaining life of the lease is only four years. Owney is planning to move to a new location at the end of the four years.

i. In drafting the income statement and preparing the closing entries, a measure of the ending inventory is needed. It is measured with the retail method, and this information is known for 1993:

	Cost	Retail
Beginning inventory	$ 42,100	$ 64,600
Purchases	119,900	192,400
Additional markups		13,000
Markdowns.		7,250
Sales		177,400

Required

1. Prepare a work sheet for the company using the preceding information.
2. Journalize entries resulting from the bank reconciliation and journalize the adjusting entries. Also present all calculations that support the entries.
3. Journalize closing entries for the company.
4. Prepare a single-step income statement with a supporting calculation of cost of goods sold, a statement of changes in owner's equity, and a classified balance sheet.

Payroll Liabilities

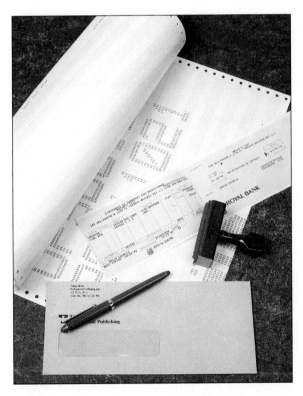

Accounting for employees' wages and salaries is one task that is shared by almost every business entity. Payroll accounting provides the means to comply with governmental regulations and provides valuable information regarding labour costs.

W ages or salaries generally amount to one of the largest expenses incurred by a business. Accounting for these items involves much more than simply recording liabilities and cash payments to employees. It also includes accounting for (1) amounts withheld from employees' wages, (2) payroll costs levied on the employer, and (3) employee (fringe) benefits paid by the employer. As you study this chapter, you will learn the general processes all businesses follow to account for these items.

Learning Objectives

After studying Chapter 13, you should be able to:

1. List the taxes and other items frequently withheld from employees' wages.
2. Make the calculations necessary to prepare a Payroll Register, and prepare the entry to record payroll liabilities.
3. Prepare journal entries to record the payments to employees and explain the operation of a payroll bank account.
4. Calculate the payroll costs levied on employers and prepare the entries to record the accrual and payment of these amounts.
5. Calculate and record employee fringe benefit costs and show the effect of these items on the total cost of employing labour.
6. Define or explain the words and phrases listed in the chapter glossary.

Items Withheld from Employees' Wages

LO 1 List the taxes and other items frequently withheld from employees' wages.

An understanding of payroll accounting and the design and use of payroll records require some knowledge of the laws and programs that affect payrolls. Many of these require that amounts be withheld from the wages of employees. Consequently, the more pertinent of these are discussed in the first portion of this chapter before the subject of payroll records is introduced.

Unemployment Insurance (UI)

To alleviate hardships caused by interruptions in earnings through unemployment, the federal government, with the concurrence of all provincial governments, implemented an employee-employer financed unemployment insurance plan in 1940. In 1971 the then existing legislation was rescinded, and the Unemployment Insurance Act, 1971, was passed. Under this act, compulsory **unemployment insurance** coverage was extended to all Canadian workers who are not self-employed. As of January 1, 1992, over 12 million employees, including teachers, hospital workers, and top-level executives, were covered by the insurance plan.

The purpose of an unemployment insurance program is usually twofold:

1. To pay unemployment compensation for limited periods to unemployed individuals eligible for benefits.

2. To establish and operate employment facilities that assist unemployed individuals in finding suitable employment and assist employers in finding employees.

Such was the purpose of the original Unemployment Insurance Act from its passage to April 1, 1966. On that date the employment function was transferred to Employment and Immigration Canada. The Unemployment Commission continued the compensation function with responsibility for (1) revenue collection and control and (2) administration of claims and benefits. On July 1, 1971, the collection function was assumed by Revenue Canada, Taxation Division.

The unemployment insurance fund from which benefits are paid is jointly financed by employees and their employers. Under the current act, in 1992 employers are required to deduct from their employees' wages 3% of insured earnings, to add a contribution of 1.4 times the amount deducted from employees' wages, and to remit both amounts to the Receiver General of Canada. Insured earnings refer to average weekly *gross pay* in the range of $142 to $710. Employees paid in whole or in part on a time-worked or fixed-salary basis must be employed at least 15 hours in a weekly pay period or earn 20% of the maximum weekly insurable earnings ($710 in 1992) in order to be insurable. The maximum amount deductible per year is $1,107.60 (in 1992). This amount is adjusted for weekly or monthly pay periods by dividing by the appropriate number; that is, 52, 12, and so on.

The Unemployment Insurance Act, in addition to setting rates, requires that an employer:

1. Withhold from the wages of each employee each payday an amount of unemployment insurance tax calculated at the current rate.

2. Pay an unemployment insurance tax equal to 1.4 times the amount withheld from the wages of all employees.

3. Periodically remit both the amounts withheld from employees' wages and the employer's tax to the Receiver General of Canada. (Remittance is discussed later in this chapter.)

4. Complete a "Record of Employment" form for employees who experience an "interruption of earnings" because of termination of employment, illness, injury, or pregnancy.

5. Keep a record for each employee that shows among other things wages subject to unemployment insurance and taxes withheld. (The law does not specify the exact form of the record, but most employers keep individual employees earnings records similar to the one shown later in this chapter.)

Weekly Unemployment Benefits. The amount of weekly benefits received by an unemployed individual who qualifies is based on his or her average insurable weekly earnings. The federal government has varied the benefit period from region to region on the basis of percentage and duration of unemployment in the region.

Withholding Employees' Income Tax

With few exceptions, employers are required to calculate, collect, and remit to the Receiver General of Canada the income taxes of their employees. Historically, when the first federal income tax law became effective in 1917, it applied to only a few individuals having high earnings, and it was not until World War II that income taxes were levied on substantially all wage earners. At that time Parliament recognized that many individual wage earners could not be expected to save sufficient money with which to pay their income taxes once each year. Consequently, Parliament instituted a system of pay-as-you-go withholding of taxes each payday at their source. This pay-as-you-go withholding of employee income taxes requires an employer to act as a tax collecting agent of the federal government.

The amount of income taxes to be withheld from an employee's wages is determined by his or her wages and the amount of the personal tax credits. Each individual is entitled, in 1992, to some or all of the following amounts which are subject to tax credits (as applicable):

1. Basic personal amount	$6,456
2. Married or equivalent	5,380
3. Dependants under 19 years old:	
First and second dependant (each) . .	417
Third and each additional (each)	834

with maximum earnings stipulated

The amount subject to personal tax credit total for each taxpayer determines the level of income tax deductions from the individual's gross pay. For example, an individual with a gross weekly salary of $500 and personal tax credits of $6,456 (1992 net claim code 1 on the TD1 form) would have $94.35 of income taxes withheld. Another individual with the same gross salary but with personal tax credits of $11,202 (claim code 5) would have $65.75 withheld.

Employers are responsible for determining and withholding each payday the required amount from each of their employees' pay for income taxes. However, to do so an employer must know the exemptions claimed by each employee. Consequently, every employee is required to file with the employer an Employee's Tax Deduction Return, Form TD1, on which he or she claims the credit entitled. The taxpayer must file a revised Form TD1 each time the exemptions change during a year.

In determining the amounts of income taxes to be withheld from the wages of employees, employers normally use tax withholding tables provided by Revenue Canada, Taxation. The tables indicate the tax to be withheld from any amount of wages and with any number of credits. The to-be-withheld amounts include both federal and provincial income taxes except for the province of Quebec. The province of Quebec levies and collects its own income tax and its own pension plan contributions. Employers in that province remit separately, to the respective authority, federal and provincial tax deductions.

In addition to determining and withholding income taxes from each employee's wages every payday, employers are required to:

1. Remit the withheld taxes to the Receiver General of Canada.
2. On or before the last day of February following each year give each

employee a T-4 summary, a statement that tells the employee:
   a. Total wages for the preceding year.
   b. Taxable benefits received from the employer.
   c. Income taxes withheld.
   d. Deductions for registered pension plan.
   e. Canada Pension Plan contributions.
   f. Unemployment insurance deductions.
3. On or before the last day of February following each year forward to the district Taxation office copies of the employees' T-4 statements plus a T-4 which summarizes the information contained on the employees' T-4 statements.

The **Canada Pension Plan** applies, with few exceptions, to everyone who is working. Every employee and the self-employed between the ages of 18 and 70 must make contributions in required amounts to the Canada Pension Plan (CPP). Self-employed individuals are required to remit periodically appropriate amounts to the Receiver General of Canada. Employee contributions are deducted by the employer from salary, wages, or other remuneration paid to the employee. Furthermore, each employer is required to contribute an amount equal to that deducted from the employees' earnings.

Canada Pension Plan (CPP)

Contributions are based on earnings, with the first $3,200 of each employee's annual income being exempt. On earnings above that amount and up to the 1992 ceiling of $32,200 a year, the employee contributes at a rate of 2.4%. The total contribution from both employee and employer is 4.8% on the $29,000 of annual earnings between $3,200 and $32,200. Thus, the maximum contribution to the Canada Pension Plan is $696 each from the employee and the employer. The $3,200 exemption is adjusted for weekly or monthly pay periods by dividing by the appropriate number; that is, 52, 12, and so on.

Employers are responsible for making the proper deductions from their employees' earnings. They remit these deductions each month, together with their own contributions, to the Receiver General of Canada.

Self-employed individuals pay the combined rate for employees and employers, or 4.8% on annual earnings between $3,200 and the tax-exempt ceiling of $32,200.

Most employers use **wage bracket withholding tables** similar to the one for 1992 shown in Illustration 13–1 in determining Canada Pension Plan and unemployment insurance to be withheld from employee's gross earnings. The illustrated table is for a weekly pay period; different tables are provided for different pay periods. Somewhat similar tables are available for determining income tax withholdings.

Determining the amount of withholdings from an employee's gross wages is quite easy when withholding tables are used. First, the employee's wage bracket is located in the first two columns. Then the amounts to be withheld for Canada Pension Plan and unemployment insurance are found on the line of the wage bracket in the appropriate columns.

ILLUSTRATION 13–1

Wage Bracket Withholding Tables

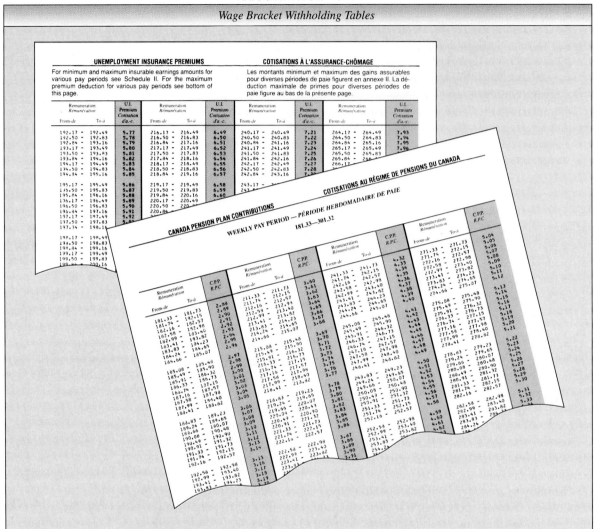

Workers' Compensation

Legislation is in effect in all provinces for payments to employees for an injury or disability arising out of or in the course of their employment. Under the provincial workers' compensation acts, employers are, in effect, required to insure their employees against injury or disability that may arise as a result of employment. Premiums are normally based on (1) accident experience of the industrial classification to which each business is assigned and (2) the total payroll.

   Procedures for payment are as follows:

1. At the beginning of each year, every covered employer is required to submit to the Workers' Compensation Board an estimate of his or her expected payroll for the ensuing year.

2. Provisional premiums are then established by the board by relating estimated requirements for disability payments to estimated payroll. Provisional premium notices are then sent to all employers.
3. Provisional premiums are normally payable in from three to six installments during the year.
4. At the end of each year, actual payrolls are submitted to the board, and final assessments are made based on actual payrolls and actual payments. Premiums are normally between 1% and 3% of gross payroll and are borne by the employer.

Wages, Hours, and Union Contracts

All provinces have laws establishing maximum hours of work and minimum pay rates. And while the details vary with each province, generally, employers are required to pay an employee for hours worked in excess of 40 in any one week at the employee's regular pay rate plus an overtime premium of at least one half of his or her regular rate. This gives an employee an overtime rate of at least 1½ times his or her regular hourly rate for hours in excess of 40 in any one week. In addition, employers commonly operate under contracts with their employees' union that provide even better terms. For example, union contracts often provide for time and a half for work on Saturdays, and double time for Sundays and holidays. When an employer is under such a union contract, since the contract terms are better than those provided for by law, the contract terms take precedence over the law.

In addition to specifying working hours and wage rates, union contracts often provide for the collection of employees' union dues by the employer. Such a requirement commonly provides that the employer shall deduct dues from the wages of each employee and remit the amounts deducted to the union. The employer is usually required to remit once each month and to report the name and amount deducted from each employee's pay.

Other Payroll Deductions

In addition to the payroll deductions discussed thus far, employees may individually authorize additional deductions. Some examples of these might be:

1. Deductions to accumulate funds for the purchase of Canada Savings Bonds.
2. Deductions to pay health, accident, hospital, or life insurance premiums.
3. Deductions to repay loans from the employer or the employees' credit union.
4. Deductions to pay for merchandise purchased from the company.
5. Deductions for donations to charitable organizations such as the United Way.

Timekeeping

Compiling a record of the time worked by each employee is called **timekeeping.** The method used to compile such a record depends on the nature of the company's business and the number of its employees. In a very small business, timekeeping may consist of no more than notations of each employee's working time made in a memorandum book by the manager or owner. In many companies, however, time clocks are used to record on **clock cards** each employee's time of arrival and departure. The time clocks are usually placed near entrances to the office, store, or factory. At the beginning of each payroll period, a clock card for each employee (see Illustration 13–2) is placed in a rack for use by the employee. Upon arriving at work, each employee takes his or her card from the rack and places it in a slot in the time clock. This actuates the clock to stamp the date and arrival time on the card. The employee then returns the card to the rack. Upon leaving the plant, store, or office for lunch or at the end of the day, the procedure is repeated. The employee takes the card from the rack, places it in the clock, and the time of departure is automatically stamped. As a result, at the end of each pay period, the card shows the hours the employee was at work.

The Payroll Register

LO 2 Make the calculations necessary to prepare a Payroll Register, and prepare the entry to record payroll liabilities.

Each pay period the total hours worked as compiled on clock cards or otherwise is summarized in a Payroll Register, an example of which is shown in Illustration 13–3. The illustrated register is for a weekly pay period and shows the payroll data for each employee on a separate line.

In Illustration 13–3, the columns under the heading Daily Time show the hours worked each day by each employee. The total of each employee's hours is entered in the column headed Total Hours. If hours worked include overtime hours, these are entered in the column headed O.T. Hours.

The Regular Pay Rate column shows the hourly pay rate of each employee. Total hours worked multiplied by the regular pay rate equals regular pay. Overtime hours multiplied by the overtime premium rate (50% in this case) equals overtime premium pay. And, regular pay plus overtime premium pay is the **employee's gross pay.**

The amounts withheld from each employee's gross pay are recorded in the Deductions columns of the payroll register. For example, you determine the income tax deductions by matching the gross pay of each employee to the tax deduction tables and then enter the results in the tax deduction column. Income tax deductions are based on the gross pay less the amounts deducted for unemployment insurance and Canada Pension Plan. The tax tables allow for these adjustments and separate books are available for each province. However, for simplicity, assume that income tax deductions are 20% of the employee's gross pay.

As previously stated, the income tax withheld depends on each employee's gross pay and personal tax credits. You can determine these amounts by referring to the appropriate wage bracket withholding tables. You then enter them in the column headed Income Taxes.

The column headed Hosp. Ins. shows the amounts withheld to pay for hospital insurance for the employees and their families. The total withheld from all employees is a current liability of the employer until paid to the insurance company. Likewise, the total withheld for employees' union dues is a current liability until paid to the union.

ILLUSTRATION 13–2

An Employee's Clock Card

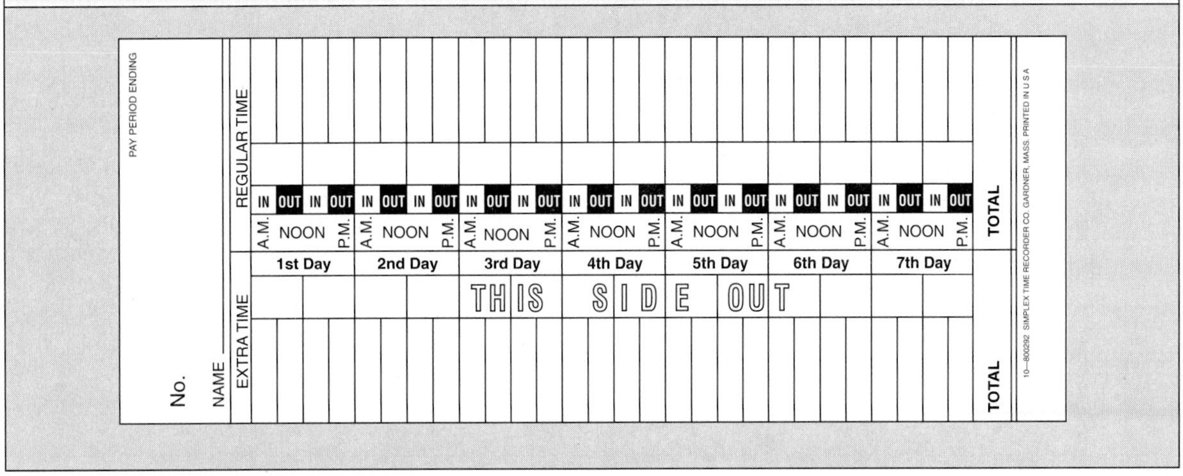

Courtesy Simplex Time Recorder Co.

Additional columns may be added to the Payroll Register for any other deductions that occur sufficiently often to warrant special columns. For example, a company that regularly deducts amounts from its employees' pay for Canada Savings Bonds may add a special column for this deduction.

An employee's gross pay less total deductions is the **employee's net pay** and is entered in the Net Pay column. The total of this column is the amount the employees are to be paid. The numbers of the cheques used to pay the employees are entered in the column headed Cheque No.

The Distribution columns are used to classify the various salaries in terms of different kinds of expense. Here you enter each employee's gross salary in the proper column according to the type of work performed. The column totals then indicate the amounts to be debited to the salary expense accounts.

Recording the Payroll

Generally, a Payroll Register such as the one shown is a supplementary memorandum record. As such, you do not post its information directly to the accounts. Instead, you must first record the payroll with a General Journal entry, which is then posted to the accounts. The entry to record the payroll shown in Illustration 13–3 is:

Mar.	23	Sales Salaries Expense	2,444.00	
		Office Salaries Expense	1,520.00	
		Unemployment Insurance Payable		115.38
		Employees' Income Taxes Payable		792.80
		Employees' Hospital Insurance Payable		300.00
		Canada Pension Plan Payable		86.27
		Accrued Salaries Payable		2,669.55
		To record the March 23 payroll		

ILLUSTRATION 13–3

Payroll Register

											Payroll Week Ended			
												Earnings		
Employees	Clock Card No.	Daily Time							Total Hours	O.T. Hours	Reg. Pay Rate	Regular Pay	O.T. Premium Pay	Gross Pay
		M	T	W	T	F	S	S						
Austin, Robert	114	8	8	8	8	8			40		14.00	560.00		560.00
Cheung, Joe	102	8	8	8	8	8			40		20.00	800.00		800.00
Cross, Judith	108		8	8	8	8	8		40		18.00	720.00		720.00
Curzon, Jean	109	8	8	8	8	8	8		48	8	14.00	672.00	56.00	728.00
Keife, Kay	112	8	8	8	8				32		16.00	512.00		512.00
Prasad, Sunil	103	8	8	8	8	8	4		44	4	14.00	616.00	28.00	644.00
Totals												3,880.00	84.00	3,964.00

ILLUSTRATION 13–4

Cash Disbursements Journal

			Cash Disbursements Journal							
Date	Cheque No.	Payee	Account Debited	PR	Other Accts. Debit	Accts. Pay. Debit	Sal. Pay. Debit	Pur. Dis. Credit	Cash Credit	
Feb. 16	893	Austin, Robert	Salaries Payable				369.24		369.24	
Feb. 16	894	Cheung, Joe	"				550.98		550.98	
Feb. 16	895	Cross, Judith	"				488.90		488.90	
Feb. 16	896	Curzon, Jean	"				495.10		495.10	
Feb. 16	897	Keife, Kay	"				333.43		333.43	
Feb. 16	898	Prasad, Sunil	"				431.90		431.90	

The debits of the entry were taken from the Payroll Register's distribution column totals. They charge the employees' gross earnings to the proper salary expense accounts. The credits to UI Payable, Employees' Income Taxes Payable, Employees' Hospital Insurance Payable, and CPP Payable record these amounts as current liabilities. The credit to Salaries Payable records as a liability the net amount to be paid to the employees.

Paying the Employees

LO 3 Prepare journal entries to record the payments to employees and explain the operation of a payroll bank account.

Almost every business pays its employees with cheques. In a company that has few employees, these cheques often are drawn on the regular bank account and entered in a Cash Disbursements Journal (or Cheque Register) like the one described in Chapter 6. Since each cheque is debited to the Salaries Payable account, posting labour can be saved by adding a Salaries Payable column in the journal. If such a column is added, entries to pay the employees of the Illustration 13–3 payroll will appear as in Illustration 13–4.

Most employers furnish each employee an earnings statement each payday. The statement gives the employee a record of hours worked, gross pay,

Register February 16, 1992								
Deductions					**Payments**		**Distribution**	
Unem- ployment Ins.	Canada Pension Plan	Income Tax	Hosp. Ins.	Total Deductions	Net Pay	Ch. No.	Office Salaries Expense	Sales Salaries Expense
16.80	11.96	112.00	50.00	190.76	369.24	893		560.00
21.30	17.72	160.00	50.00	249.02	550.98	894	800.00	
21.30	15.80	144.00	50.00	231.10	488.90	895	720.00	
21.30	16.00	145.60	50.00	232.90	495.10	896		728.00
15.36	10.81	102.40	50.00	178.57	333.43	897		512.00
19.32	13.98	128.80	50.00	212.10	431.90	898		644.00
115.38	86.27	792.80	300.00	1,294.45	2,669.55		1,520.00	2,444.00

ILLUSTRATION 13–5

A Payroll Cheque

Robert Austin	40		14.00	560.00		560.00	16.80	112.00	11.96	50.00	190.76	369.24
Employee	Total Hours	O.T. Hours	Reg. Pay Rate	Reg- ular Pay	O.T. Prem. Pay	Gross Pay	U.I. Pre- mium	Income Taxes	C.P. Plan	Hosp. Ins.	Total Deduc- tions	Net Pay

STATEMENT OF EARNINGS AND DEDUCTIONS FOR EMPLOYEE'S RECORDS—DETACH BEFORE CASHING CHEQUE

- -

VALLEY SALES COMPANY

2590 Dixon Road • Cambridge, Ontario   **No. 893**

PAY TO THE
ORDER OF   *Robert Austin*   Date *Feb. 16, 1992* $ *369.24*

Three hundred sixty-nine dollars and twenty-four cents - - - - - - - - - - - - - - - - - -

Merchants National Bank
Cambridge, Ontario

VALLEY SALES COMPANY

Jane R. Morris

deductions, and net pay. The statement often takes the form of a detachable
paycheque portion that is removed before the cheque is cashed. A paycheque
with a detachable earnings statement is reproduced in Illustration 13–5.

A business with many employees normally uses a special **payroll bank account**
to pay its employees. When such an account is used, one cheque for the total
payroll is drawn on the regular bank account and deposited in the special

Payroll Bank Account

payroll bank account. Then individual payroll cheques are drawn on this special account. Because only one cheque for the payroll total is drawn on the regular bank account each payday, use of a special payroll bank account simplifies internal control, especially the reconciliation of the regular bank account. It may be reconciled without considering the payroll cheques outstanding, and there may be many of these.

When a company uses a special payroll bank account, you must complete the following steps to pay the employees:

1. Record the information shown on the Payroll Register in the usual manner with a General Journal entry similar to the one previously illustrated. This entry causes the sum of the employees' net pay to be credited to the liability account (Salaries Payable).
2. Have a single cheque written that is payable to Payroll Bank Account for the total amount of the payroll and enter the payment in the Cheque Register. This requires a debit to Salaries Payable and a credit to Cash.
3. Have the cheque deposited in the payroll bank account. This transfers an amount of money equal to the payroll total from the regular bank account to the special payroll bank account.
4. Have individual payroll cheques drawn on the special payroll bank account and delivered to the employees. As soon as all employees cash their cheques, the funds in the special account will be exhausted. Typically, companies will arrange for the bank to charge all service costs to the regular bank account.

A special Payroll Cheque Register may be used in connection with a payroll bank account. However, most companies do not use such a register. Instead, the payroll cheque numbers are entered in the Payroll Register so that it serves as a Cheque Register.

Employee's Individual Earnings Record

An **Employee's Individual Earnings Record**, as shown in Illustration 13–6, provides for each employee in one record a full year's summary of the employee's working time, gross earnings, deductions, and net pay. In addition, it accumulates information that:

1. Serves as a basis for the employer's payroll tax returns.
2. Indicates when an employee's earnings have reached the maximum amounts for CPP and UI deductions.
3. Supplies data for the T4 slip, which must be given to the employee at the end of the year.

The payroll information on an Employee's Individual Earnings Record is taken from the Payroll Register. The information as to earnings, deductions, and net pay is first recorded on a single line in the Payroll Register. Then, each pay period, the information is posted from the Payroll Register to the earnings record. Note the last column of the record. It shows an employee's cumulative earnings and is used to determine when the earnings reach the maximum amounts taxed and are no longer subject to the various payroll taxes.

ILLUSTRATION 13-6

	Employee's Individual Earnings Record

Employee's Name _____ Robert Austin _____ SIN. No. _____ 123-456-789 _____ Employee No. _____ 114 _____

Home Address _____ 111 South Greenwood _____ Notify in Case of Emergency _____ Margaret Austin _____ Phone No. _____ 964-9834 _____

Employed _____ June 7, 1980 _____ Date of Termination _____ Reason _____

Date of Birth _____ June 6, 1962 _____ Date Becomes 65 _____ June 6, 2027 _____ Male (X) Married (X) Number of Female ( ) Single ( ) Exemptions 1 Pay Rate _____ $14.00

Occupation _____ Clerk _____ Place _____ Office _____

Date				Time Lost		Time Worked											
Per. Ends	Paid	Hrs.	Rea-son	Total	O.T. Hours	Reg. Pay	O.T. Prem. Pay	Gross Pay	U.I. Prem.	Income Taxes	Hosp. Ins.	CPP	Total Deduc-tions	Net Pay	Cheque No.	Cumu-lative Pay
Ja 5	Ja 5			40		560.00		560.00	16.80	112.00	50.00	11.96	190.76	369.24	673	560.00
Ja 12	Ja 12			40		560.00		560.00	16.80	112.00	50.00	11.96	190.76	369.24	701	1,120.00
Ja 19	Ja 19			40		560.00		560.00	16.80	112.00	50.00	11.96	190.76	369.24	743	1,680.00
Ja 26	Ja 26	4	Sick	36		504.00		504.00	15.12	100.80	50.00	10.62	176.54	327.46	795	2,184.00
Fe 2	Fe 2			40		560.00		560.00	16.80	112.00	50.00	11.96	190.76	369.24	839	2,744.00
Fe 9	Fe 9			40		560.00		560.00	16.80	112.00	50.00	11.96	190.76	369.24	854	3,304.00
Fe 16	Fe 16			40		560.00		560.00	16.80	112.00	50.00	11.96	190.76	369.24	893	3,864.00

Payroll Deductions Required by the Employer

Under the previous discussion of the Canada Pension Plan, it was pointed out that pension deductions are required in like amounts on both employed workers and their employers. A covered employer is required by law to deduct from the employees' pay the amounts of their Canada Pension Plan, but in addition, the employer must pay an amount equal to the sum of the employees' Canada pension. Commonly, the amount deducted by the employer is recorded at the same time the payroll to which it relates is recorded. Also, since both the employees' and employer's shares are reported on the same form and are paid in one amount, the liability for both is normally recorded in the same liability account, the Canada Pension Plan Payable account.

In addition to the Canada Pension Plan, an employer is required to pay unemployment insurance that is 1.4 times the sum of the employees' unemployment insurance deductions. Most employers record both of these **payroll deductions** with a General Journal entry that is made at the time the payroll to which they relate is recorded. For example, the entry to record the employer's amounts on the payroll of Illustration 13–3 is:

LO 4 Calculate the payroll costs levied on employers and prepare the entries to record the accrual and payment of these amounts.

Mar.	23	Benefits Expense	247.80	
		Unemployment Insurance Payable		161.53
		Canada Pension Plan Payable.		86.27
		To record the employer's payroll taxes.		

The debit of the entry records as an expense the payroll taxes levied on the employer, and the credits record the liabilities for the taxes. The $161.53 credit to Unemployment Insurance Payable is 1.4 times the sum of the amounts deducted from the pay of the employees whose wages are recorded in the Payroll Register of Illustration 13–3, and the credit to Canada Pension Plan Payable is equal to the total of the employees' pension plan deductions.

Paying the Payroll Deductions

Income tax, Unemployment Insurance, and Canada Pension Plan amounts withheld each payday from the employees' pay plus the employer's portion of unemployment insurance and Canada Pension Plan are current liabilities until paid to the Receiver General of Canada. The normal method of payment is to pay the amounts due at any chartered bank or remit directly to the Receiver General of Canada. Payment of these amounts is usually required to be made before the 15th of the month following the month that deductions were made from the earnings of the employees. Large employers are required to remit on the 10th and 25th of each month. Payment of these liabilities is recorded in the same manner as payment of any other liabilities.

Accruing Taxes on Wages

Mandatory payroll deductions are levied on wages actually paid. In other words, accrued wages are not subject to payroll deductions until they are paid. Nevertheless, if the requirements of the *matching principle* are to be met, both accrued wages and the accrued deductions on the wages should be recorded at the end of an accounting period. However, since the amounts of such deductions vary little from one accounting period to the next and often are small in amount, many employers apply the *materiality principle* and do not accrue payroll deductions.

Employee (Fringe) Benefit Costs

LO 5 Calculate and record employee fringe benefit costs and show the effect of these items on the total cost of employing labour.

In addition to the wages earned by employees and the related payroll amounts paid by the employer, many companies provide their employees a variety of benefits. Since the costs of these benefits are paid by the employer and the benefits are in addition to the amount of wages earned, they are often called **employee fringe benefits.** For example, an employer may pay for part (or all) of the employees' medical insurance, life insurance, and disability insurance. Another typical employee benefit involves employer contributions to a retirement income plan. Perhaps the most typical employee benefit is vacation pay.

Employer Contributions to Employee Insurance and Retirement Plans

The entries to record employee benefit costs depend on the nature of the benefit. Some employee retirement plans are quite complicated and involve accounting procedures that are too complex for discussion in this introductory course. In other cases, however, the employer simply makes periodic cash contributions to a retirement fund for each employee and records the amounts contributed as expense. Other employee benefits that require periodic cash payments by the employer include employer payments of insurance premiums for employees.

In the case of employee benefits that simply require the employer to make periodic cash payments, the entries to record the employer's obligations are similar to those used for payroll deductions.[1] For example, assume an employer with five employees has agreed to pay medical insurance premiums of $40 per month for each employee. The employer also will contribute 10% of each employee's salary to a retirement program. If each employee earns $1,500 per month, the entry to record these employee benefits for the month of March is:

Mar.	31	Benefits Expense	950.00	
		Employees' Medical Insurance Payable		200.00
		Employees' Retirement Program Payable		750.00
		($1,500 × 5) × 10% = $750.		

Vacation Pay

Nearly all employers are required to allow their employees paid vacation time as a benefit of employment. For example, many employees receive 2 weeks' vacation in return for working 50 weeks each year. The effect of a 2-week vacation is to increase the employer's payroll expenses by 4% (2/50 = .04). However, new employees often do not begin to accrue vacation time until after they've worked for a period of time, perhaps as much as a year. The employment contract may say that no vacation is granted until the employee works one year; but if the first year is completed, the employee receives the full 2 weeks.

To account for vacation pay, an employer should estimate and record the additional expense during the weeks the employees are working and earning the vacation time. For example, assume that a company with a weekly payroll of $20,000 grants two weeks' vacation after one year's employment. The entry to record the estimated vacation pay is:

Date	Benefits Expense	800.00	
	Estimated Vacation Pay Liability.		800.00
	$20,000 × .04 = $800.		

As employees take their vacations and receive their vacation pay, the entries to record the vacation payroll take the following general form:

---

[1] Some payments of employee benefits must be added to the gross salary of the employee for the purpose of calculating income tax, CPP, and UI payroll deductions. However, in this chapter and in the problems at the end of the chapter, the possible effect of employee benefit costs on payroll taxes is ignored to avoid undue complexity in the introductory course.

Date	Estimated Vacation Pay Liability	xxx	
	Employees' UI and CPP Payable.		xxx
	Employees' Income Taxes Payable.		xxx
	Other withholding liability accounts such as Employees'		
	Hospital Insurance Payable		xxx
	Accrued Salaries Payable.		xxx

Mandatory payroll deductions and employee benefits costs are often a major category of expense incurred by a company. They may amount to well over 25% of the salaries earned by employees.

Computerized Payroll Systems

Manually prepared records like the ones described in this chapter are used in many small companies. However, an increasing number of companies use computers to process their payroll. The computer programs are designed to take advantage of the fact that the same calculations are performed each pay period. Also, much of the same information must be entered for each employee in the Payroll Register, on the employee's earnings record, and on the employee's paycheque. The computers simultaneously store or print the information in all three places.

Summary of the Chapter in Terms of Learning Objectives

LO 1. Amounts withheld from employees' wages include federal income taxes, unemployment insurance, and Canada Pension Plan. Payroll costs levied on employers include unemployment insurance, Canada Pension, and workers' compensation.

An employee's gross pay may be the employee's specified wage rate multiplied by the total hours worked plus an overtime premium rate multiplied by the number of overtime hours worked. Alternatively, it may be the given periodic salary of the employee. Taxes withheld and other deductions for items such as union dues, insurance premiums, and charitable contributions are subtracted from gross pay to determine the net pay.

LO 2. A Payroll Register is used to summarize all employees' hours worked, regular and overtime pay, payroll deductions, net pay, and distribution of gross pay to expense accounts during each pay period. It provides the necessary information for journal entries to record the accrued payroll and to pay the employees.

LO 3. A payroll bank account is a separate account that is used solely for the purpose of paying employees. Each pay period, an amount equal to the total net pay of all employees is transferred from the regular bank account to the payroll bank account. Then cheques are drawn against the payroll bank account for the net pay of the employees.

LO 4. When a payroll is accrued at the end of each pay period, payroll deductions and levies also should be accrued with a debit to Benefits Expense and credits to appropriate liability accounts.

LO 5. Fringe benefit costs that involve simple cash payments by the employee should be accrued with an entry similar to the one used to accrue payroll levies. To account for the expense associated with vacation pay, you should estimate the expense and allocate the estimated amount to the pay periods during the year. These allocations are recorded with a debit to Employees' Benefits Expense and a credit to Estimated Vacation Pay Liability. Then payments to employees on vacation are charged to the estimated liability.

Presented below are various items of information about three employees of the Jasmine Company for the week ending October 25, 1992.

Demonstration Problem

	Babcock	**Dawson**	**Sanders**
Wage rate (per hour)	$10	$30	$16
Overtime premium	50%	50%	50%
Annual vacation	2 weeks	4 weeks	2 weeks
Cumulative wages as of October 18, 1992 . .	$17,500	$49,200	$5,200
For the week (pay period) ended October 25, 1992:			
Hours worked	46	40	50
Medical insurance:			
Jasmine's contribution	$25	$ 25	$ 25
Withheld from employee	15	15	15
Union dues withheld	40	60	40
Income tax withheld	98	480	176
Unemployment insurance withheld	15	21	21
Canada Pension withheld	10	—	20
Payroll deduction rates:			
Income taxes	assume 20% of gross wages		
Unemployment insurance	3.0% to a maximum of $21 per week		
Canada Pension Plan	2.4% less annual exemption of $3,200; maximum per year is $696.		

Required

In solving the following requirements, round all amounts to the nearest whole dollar. Prepare schedules that determine, for each employee and for all employees combined, the following information:

1. Wages earned for the regular 40-hour week, total overtime pay, and gross wages.
2. Vacation pay accrued for the week.
3. Deductions withheld from the employees' wages.
4. Costs imposed on the employer.
5. Employees' net pay for the week.
6. Employer's total payroll-related cost (wages, mandatory deductions, and fringe benefits).

Present journal entries to record the following:

7. Payroll expense.
8. Payroll deductions and employees' benefits expense.

Solution to
Demonstration
Problem

1. The gross wages (including overtime) for the week.

	Babcock	Dawson	Sanders	Total
Regular wage rate	$ 10	$ 30	$ 16	
Regular hours	×46	×40	×50	
Regular pay	$460	$1,200	$800	$2,460
Overtime premium	$ 5	$ 15	$ 8	
Overtime hours	×6	×–0–	×10	
Total overtime pay	$ 30	$ –0–	$ 80	110
Gross wages	$490	$1,200	$880	$2,570

2. The vacation pay accrued for the week.

	Babcock	Dawson	Sanders	Total
Annual vacation	2 weeks	4 weeks	2 weeks	
Weeks worked in year	50 weeks	48 weeks	50 weeks	
Vacation pay as a percentage of regular pay	4.00%	8.33%	4.00%	
Regular pay this week	×$ 400	×$1,200	×$ 640	
Vacation pay this week	$ 16	$ 100	$ 26	$142

The information in the following table is needed for parts 3 and 4:

			Earnings Subject To	
Employees	Earnings through October 13	Earnings This Week	CPP	Unemployment Ins.
Babcock	$17,500	$ 490	$ 428	$ 490
Dawson	49,200	1,200	—	710
Sanders	5,200	880	818	710
Totals		$2,570	$1,246	$1,910

3. Amounts withheld from the employees.

	Babcock	Dawson	Sanders	Total
Income tax withheld	$ 98	$480	$176	$754
CPP withheld	10	—	20	30
UI withheld	15	21	21	57
Totals	$123	$501	$217	$841

4. The costs imposed on the employer.

	Babcock	Dawson	Sanders	Total
CPP (1.0)	$10	—	$20	$ 30
Unemployment insurance (1.4)	21	$29	29	79
Totals	$31	$29	$49	$109

5. The net amount paid to the employees.

	Babcock	Dawson	Sanders	Total
Regular pay	$460	$1,200	$800	$2,460
Overtime pay	30	–0–	80	110
Gross pay	$490	$1,200	$880	$2,570
Withholdings:				
Income tax withholding	$ 98	$480	$176	$ 754
CPP withholding	10	—	20	30
UI withholding	15	21	21	57
Medical insurance.	15	15	15	45
Union dues	40	60	40	140
Total withholdings.	$178	$576	$272	$1,026
Net pay to employees	$312	$624	$608	$1,544

6. The total payroll-related cost to the employer.

	Babcock	Dawson	Sanders	Total
Regular pay	$460	$1,200	$800	$2,460
Overtime pay	30	–0–	80	110
Gross pay	$490	$1,200	$880	$2,570
Deductions and fringe benefits:				
CPP.	$ 10	$ —	$ 20	$ 30
UI.	21	29	29	79
Vacation Pay	16	100	26	142
Medical insurance.	25	25	25	75
Total deductions and fringe benefits.	$ 72	$ 154	$100	$ 326
Total payroll related cost	$562	$1,354	$980	$2,896

7. Journal entry for salary expense.

1992				
Oct.	25	Salary Expense	2,570.00	
		Employees' Income Taxes Payable.		754.00
		Employees' CPP Payable.		30.00
		Employees' UI Payable.		57.00
		Employees' Medical Insurance Payable		45.00
		Employees' Union Dues Payable.		140.00
		Accrued Payroll Payable		1,544.00
		To record payroll expense.		

8. Journal entries to record payroll tax and fringe benefit expense.

1992				
Oct.	25	Benefits Expense	109.00	
		CPP Payable		30.00
		UI Payable		79.00
		To record payroll expense.		
	25	Benefits Expense	217.00	
		Accrued Vacation Pay		142.00
		Medical Insurance Payable.		75.00
		To record fringe benefits expense.		

Glossary

LO 6 Define or explain
the words and phrases
listed in the chapter
glossary.

Canada Pension Plan A national contributory retirement pension scheme. p. 663

Clock card a card issued to each employee that the employee inserts in a time clock to record the time of arrival and departure to and from work. p. 666

Employee fringe benefits payments by an employer, in addition to wages and salaries, that are made to acquire employee benefits such as insurance coverage and retirement income. p. 672

Employee's gross pay the amount an employee earns before any deductions for taxes withheld or other items such as union dues or insurance premiums. p. 666

Employee's Individual Earnings Record a record of an employee's hours worked, gross pay, deductions, net pay, and certain personal information about the employee. p. 670

Employee's net pay the amount an employee is paid, determined by subtracting from gross pay all deductions for taxes and other items that are withheld from the employee's earnings. p. 667

Payroll bank account a special bank account a company uses solely for the purpose of paying employees by depositing in the account each pay period an amount equal to the total employees' net pay and drawing the employees' payroll cheques on that account. p. 669

Payroll deduction an amount deducted usually based on the amount of an employee's gross pay. p. 671

Personal tax credits amounts which may be deducted from an individual's income taxes and which determine the amount of income taxes to be withheld. p. 662

Timekeeping the process of recording the time each employee is on the job. p. 665

Unemployment insurance an employee-employer financed unemployment insurance plan. p. 660

Wage bracket withholding table a table showing the amounts to be withheld from employees' wages at various levels of earnings. p. 663

Objective Review

Answers to the following questions are listed at the end of this chapter. Be sure that you decide which is the one best answer to each question *before* you check the answers.

LO 1 Which item is *not* an amount withheld from employees' wages?

a. Income tax.
b. Workers' compensation.
c. Unemployment insurance.
d. Canada Pension Plan.
e. Life insurance premium.

LO 2 The weekly payroll register shows:

a. The number of hours worked by each employee for the week.
b. The regular pay rate for each employee.
c. The earnings of each employee.
d. The deductions of each employee to determine the net pay.
e. All of the above.

LO 3 Which of the following steps must be completed when a company uses a special bank account?

a. Record the information shown on the Payroll Register with a General Journal entry.

b. Write a single cheque that is payable to Payroll Bank Account for the total amount of the payroll and enter the amount in the Cheque Register.

c. Deposit a cheque for the total amount of the payroll in the payroll bank account.

d. Write individual payroll cheques to be drawn on the payroll bank account.

e. All of the above.

LO 4 A company deducts $230 in unemployment insurance and $195 in Canada pension from the weekly payroll of its employees. How much is the company's expense for these items for the week?

a. $ 425

b. $ 195

c. $ 850

d. $ 517

e. $1,034

LO 5 Datatel employs two people at $2,310 per month and two people at $4,180 per month. Every employee receives one month's vacation annually. Although no employees took vacation in May, all are expected to take their vacation later this year. In addition, Datatel pays medical insurance premiums of $155 per month per employee and contributes 6% of total salaries to a retirement program. The entry to record these benefits for Datatel employees for the month of May is:

a.	Benefits Expense	2,579	
	Estimated Vacation Pay Liability		1,180
	Employees' Medical Insurance Payable.		620
	Employees' Retirement Payable.		779
b.	Salaries Expense.	12,980	
	Estimated Vacation Pay Liability		1,180
	Employees' Medical Insurance Payable.		620
	Employees' Retirement Payable.		779
	Salaries Payable.		10,401
c.	Benefits Expense	2,481	
	Estimated Vacation Pay Liability		1,082
	Employees' Medical Insurance Payable.		620
	Employees' Retirement Payable.		779
d.	Benefits Expense	2,579	
	Cash.		2,579
e.	None of the above.		

1. Who pays under the Canada Pension Plan?

2. Who pays premiums under the workers' compensation laws?

Questions for Class Discussion

3. What benefits are paid to unemployed workers for funds raised by the Federal Unemployment Insurance Act?

4. Who pays federal unemployment insurance? What is the rate?

5. What are the objectives of unemployment insurance laws?

6. To whom and when are payroll deductions remitted?

7. What determines the amount that must be deducted from an employee's wages for income taxes?

8. What is a tax withholding table?

9. What is the Canada Pension Plan deduction rate for self-employed individuals?

10. How is a clock card used in recording the time an employee is on the job?

11. How is a special payroll bank account used in paying the wages of employees?

12. At the end of an accounting period a firm's special payroll bank account has a $562.35 balance because the payroll cheques of two employees have not cleared the bank. Should this $562.35 appear on the firm's balance sheet? If so, where?

13. What information is accumulated on an employee's individual earnings record? Why must this information be accumulated? For what purposes is the information used?

14. What payroll charges are levied on the employer? What amounts are deducted from the wages of an employee?

15. What are employee fringe benefits? Name some examples.

Mini Discussion Case

Case 13–1

You are the accountant for a high-tech company most of whose employees have an annual salary in excess of $36,000 per year. In discussing the cost of salary increases for the coming year, senior management has asked you to outline what additional costs are involved. After all, they reason, there are caps on the amounts deducted for both unemployment insurance and Canada Pension Plan. Therefore, these would not add to the company's cost since the employees are already over the maximum amounts.

Required

Respond to senior management.

Exercises

Exercise 13–1
Calculating gross and net pay
(LO 1)

Millie Vacon, an employee of the Deer Company Limited, worked 46 hours during the week ended January 5. Her pay rate is $18 per hour, and her wages are subject to no deductions other than income taxes, unemployment insurance, and Canada Pension Plan. The overtime premium is 50% and is applicable to any time greater than 40 hours per week. Calculate her regular pay, overtime premium pay, gross pay, UI, CPP, income tax deductions (assume a tax deduction rate of 20%), total deductions, and net pay.

On January 5, at the end of its first weekly pay period in the year, Claud Company's payroll record showed that its sales employees had earned $3,680 and its office employees had earned $2,100. The employees were to have $160 of UI and $140 of CPP withheld plus $950 of income taxes, $150 of union dues, and $540 of hospital insurance premiums. Give the General Journal entry to record the payroll.

Exercise 13–2
Journalizing payroll information
(LO 3)

The following information as to earnings and deductions for the pay period ended May 17 was taken from a company's payroll records:

Exercise 13–3
Calculating payroll deductions and recording the payroll
(LO 1)

Employees' Names	Weekly Gross Pay	Earnings to End of Previous Week	Income Taxes	Health Insurance Deductions
Hellen Barnes	$ 680	$ 6,785	$106.00	$ 82.00
Joseph Chia	610	6,320	81.00	82.00
Dipak Patel	520	5,500	52.00	56.50
Anne Lauzon	1,600	18,200	465.00	42.50
	$3,410		$704.00	$263.00

Calculate the employees' UI and CPP withholdings, the amounts paid to each employee, and prepare a General Journal entry to record the payroll. Assume all employees work in the office.

Use the information provided in Exercise 13–3 to complete the following requirements:

Exercise 13–4
Calculating and recording payroll taxes
(LO 4)

1. Prepare a General Journal entry to record the employer's payroll costs resulting from the payroll.
2. Prepare a General Journal entry to record the following employee benefits incurred by the company: (1) health insurance costs equal to the amounts contributed by each employee and (2) contributions equal to 10% of gross pay for each employee's retirement income program.

Mancini Company's employees earn a gross pay of $18 per hour and work 40 hours each week. Mancini Company contributes 10% of gross pay to a retirement program for employees and pays medical insurance premiums of $40 per week per employee. What is Mancini Company's total cost of employing a person for one hour? (Assume that individual wages are less than the $32,200 Canada Pension Plan limit.)

Exercise 13–5
Analyzing total labour costs
(LO 5)

Lawson Corporation grants those employees who have worked for the company one complete year vacation time of two weeks. After 10 years of service, employees receive four weeks of vacation. Lawson estimates that 96% of its employees with less than 10 years' service will be granted two weeks of vacation this year, and 99% of those who will have completed 10 or more years of service during the year will be granted four weeks' vacation (1% are expected to resign during their 10th year). The monthly payroll for January includes $190,000 to persons who will not complete 10 years of service this year and $84,000 to persons who, if they do not resign, will have completed 10 years of service by year-end. On January 31, record the January expense arising from the vacation policy of the company.

Exercise 13–6
Calculating fringe benefit costs
(LO 5)

Exercise 13–7
Analyzing the cost of
payroll taxes and fringe
benefits
(LO 4, 5)

Ridley Company's payroll costs and fringe benefit expenses include the normal CPP and UI contributions, retirement fund contributions of 10% of total earnings, and health insurance premiums of $160 per employee per month. Given the following list of employee annual salaries, payroll costs and fringe benefits constitute what percentage of salaries?

Doran	$34,000
Foon.	58,000
Klynn	62,000
Marin	39,000
Pande	46,000

Exercise 13–8
Other payroll deductions
(LO 1)

Shane Vanen is single and earns a weekly salary of $885. In response to a citywide effort to obtain charitable contributions to the local United Way programs, Vanen has requested that his employer withhold 1% of his salary (net of CPP, UI, and income taxes—assume a tax deduction rate of 20%). Under this program, what will be Vanen's annual contribution to the United Way?

Problems

Problem 13–1
The Payroll Register and
the payroll bank account
(LO 1, 3)

On January 6, at the end of the first weekly pay period of the year, a company's Payroll Register showed that its employees had earned $18,250 of sales salaries and $4,650 of office salaries. Withholdings from the employees' salaries were to include $610 of UI, $520 of CPP, $2,965 of income taxes, $840 of hospital insurance, and $275 of union dues.

Required

1. Prepare the General Journal entry to record the January 6 payroll.
2. Prepare a General Journal entry to record the employer's payroll expenses resulting from the January 6 payroll.
3. Under the assumption the company uses a payroll bank account and special payroll cheques in paying its employees, give the Cheque Register entry (Cheque No. 542) to transfer funds equal to the payroll from the regular bank account to the payroll bank account.
4. Answer this question: After the Cheque Register entry is made and posted, are additional debit and credit entries required to record the payroll cheques and pay the employees?

Problem 13–2
The Payroll Register, the
payroll bank account, and
payroll deductions
(LO 1, 3, 4)

The payroll records of Broulee Corporation provided the following information for the weekly pay period ended December 21:

Employees	Clock Card No.	M	T	W	T	F	S	S	Pay Rate	Hospital Insurance	Union Dues	Earnings to End of Previous Week
Ralph Lapin	11	8	8	7	7	8	1	0	$21.00	$ 50.00	$15.50	$40,000
Helen Moule	12	8	7	8	8	8	4	0	17.00	50.00		48,000
Gary Simms	13	8	8	8	8	8	0	0	18.00	50.00	15.50	5,300
Nicole Paxton	14	8	8	8	8	8	2	0	22.00	50.00	15.50	35,600
Debra Wood	15	8	7	8	8	7	3	0	29.00	50.00	15.50	52,800
										$250.00	$62.00	

Required

1. Enter the relevant information in the proper columns of a Payroll Register and complete the register for CPP and UI deductions. Charge the wages of Debra Wood to Office Salaries Expense and the wages of the remaining employees to Service Wages Expense. Calculate income tax deductions at 20% of gross pay.

2. Prepare a General Journal entry to record the Payroll Register information.

3. Make the Cheque Register entry (Cheque No. 399) to transfer funds equal to the payroll from the regular bank account to the payroll bank account under the assumption the company uses special payroll cheques and a payroll bank account in paying its employees. Assume the first payroll cheque is numbered 530 and enter the payroll cheque numbers in the Payroll Register.

4. Prepare a General Journal entry to record the employer's payroll costs resulting from the payroll.

A company accumulated the following payroll information for the weekly pay period ended December 22:

Problem 13–3
The Payroll Register, payroll taxes, and employee fringe benefits
(LO 1, 4, 5)

Employees	Clock Card No.	Daily Time							Pay Rate	Medical Insurance	Union Dues	Earnings to End of Previous Week
		M	T	W	T	F	S	S				
David Foon	31	7	8	8	8	8	3	0	$14.00	$30.00	$15.00	$20,000
Vicki Frank	32	8	6	8	8	8	4	0	17.00	35.00	15.00	6,200
Lisa Gibson	33	8	8	8	8	8	0	0	15.00	45.00	15.00	32,200
Babs Klyn	34	8	9	8	8	9	1	0	16.00	45.00		5,400

Required

1. Enter the relevant information in the proper columns of a Payroll Register and complete the register for CPP and UI deductions. Assume the first employee is a salesperson, the second two work in the shop, and the last one works in the office. Calculate income tax deductions at 20% of gross pay.

2. Prepare a General Journal entry to record the Payroll Register information.

3. Make the Cheque Register entry to transfer funds equal to the payroll from the regular bank account to the payroll bank account (Cheque No. 522) under the assumption the company uses special payroll cheques and a payroll bank account in paying its employees. Assume the first payroll cheque is numbered 230 and enter the payroll cheque numbers in the Payroll Register.

4. Prepare a General Journal entry to record the employer's payroll deductions resulting from the payroll.

5. Prepare General Journal entries to accrue employee fringe benefit costs for the week. Assume the company matches the employees' payments for medical insurance and contributes an amount equal to 10% of each employees' gross pay to a retirement program. Also, each employee accrues vacation pay at the rate of 5% of the wages and salaries earned. The company estimates that all employees eventually will be paid their vacation pay.

A company has three employees, each of whom has been employed since January 1, earns $2,400 per month, and is paid on the last day of each month. On March 1, the following accounts and balances appeared in its ledger:

Problem 13–4
General Journal entries for payroll transactions
(LO 3)

a. Employees Income Taxes Payable, $1,320 (liability for February only).

b. Unemployment Insurance Payable, $468 (liability for February).

c. Canada Pension Plan Payable, $365 (liability for February).

d. Employees' Medical Insurance Payable, $940 (liability for January and February).

During March and April, the company completed the following transactions related to payroll:

Mar. 11   Issued Cheque No. 320 payable to Receiver General of Canada. The cheque was in payment of the February employee income taxes, UI, and CPP amounts due.

31   Prepared a General Journal entry to record the March Payroll Record which had the following column totals:

Income Taxes	UI	CPP	Medical Insurance	Total Deductions	Net Pay	Office Salaries	Shop Wages
$1,320	$201	$180	$235	$1,936	$5,264	$2,400	$4,800

31   Recorded the employer's $235 liability for its 50% contribution to the medical insurance plan of employees.

31   Issued Cheque No. 351 payable to Payroll Bank Account in payment of the March payroll. Endorsed the cheque, deposited it in the payroll bank account, and issued payroll cheques to the employees.

31   Recorded the employer's $235 liability for its 50% contribution to the medical insurance plan of employees.

Apr. 15   Issued Cheque No. 375 payable to the Receiver General in payment of the March mandatory deductions.

15   Issued Cheque No. 376 payable to All Canadian Insurance Company in payment of the employee medical insurance premiums for the first quarter.

Required

Prepare the necessary Cheque Register and General Journal entries to record the transactions.

Alternate Problems

Problem 13–1A
The Payroll Register and the payroll bank account
(LO 1, 3)

Checker Company's first weekly pay period of the year ended on January 8. On that date the column totals of the company's Payroll Register indicated its sales employees had earned $21,500, its office employees had earned $9,700, and its delivery employees had earned $2,800. Withholdings from the employees' salaries included $980 of UI, $830 of CPP, $4,700 federal income taxes, $1,425 medical insurance deductions, and $340 of union dues.

Required

1. Prepare the General Journal entry to record the January 8 payroll.

2. Prepare a General Journal entry to record the employer's payroll deductions resulting from the January 8 payroll.

3. Under the assumption the company uses special payroll cheques and a payroll bank account in paying its employees, give the Cheque Register entry (Cheque No. 378) to transfer funds equal to the payroll from the regular bank account to the payroll bank account.

4. Answer this question: After the Cheque Register entry is made and posted, are additional debit and credit entries required to record the payroll cheques and pay the employees?

The following information was taken from the payroll records of Specialty Software Company for the weekly pay period ending December 20:

Problem 13–2A
The Payroll Register, the payroll bank account, and payroll deductions
(LO 1, 3, 4)

Employees	Clock Card No.	Daily Time							Pay Rate	Medical Insurance	Union Dues	Earnings to End of Previous Week
		M	T	W	T	F	S	S				
Kim Fraser	41	8	9	8	8	8	4	0	$19.00	$ 35.00		$42,500
Shaun Giddy	42	7	7	6	8	8	0	0	20.00	23.00	$20.00	55,800
Charles Lam	43	8	8	8	8	8	2	0	22.00	46.00	20.00	6,075
Hitesh Patel	44	6	7	8	8	7	2	0	18.00	56.00	20.00	35,600
Greg Yovich	45	8	8	8	9	8	0	0	21.00	30.00		49,000
										$190.00	$60.00	

Required

1. Enter the relevant information in the proper columns of a Payroll Register and complete the register for CPP and UI deductions. The company pays time and one half for hours in excess of 40 each week. Also, work on Saturdays is paid at time and one half whether the total for the week is over 40 or not. Charge the wages of Kim Fraser to Office Salaries Expense and the wages of the remaining employees to Plant Salaries Expense. Calculate income tax deductions at 20% of gross pay.

2. Prepare a General Journal entry to record the Payroll Register information.

3. Assume the company uses special payroll cheques drawn on a payroll bank account in paying its employees and make the Cheque Register entry (Cheque No. 484) to transfer funds equal to the payroll from the regular bank account to the payroll bank account. Also, assume the first payroll cheque is No. 632 and enter the payroll cheque numbers in the Payroll Register.

4. Prepare a General Journal entry to record the employer's payroll deductions resulting from the payroll.

The following information for the weekly pay period ended December 10 was taken from the records of a company:

Problem 13–3A
The Payroll Register, payroll taxes, and employee fringe benefits
(LO 1, 3, 5)

Employees	Clock Card No.	Daily Time							Pay Rate	Medical Insurance	Union Dues	Earnings to End of Previous Week
		M	T	W	T	F	S	S				
Pavel Berka	34	7	8	8	7	8	5	0	$18.00	$25.50		$25,600
David Coy	35	8	8	7	8	8	3	0	15.00	18.00	$15.00	6,100
Sarah Hagan	36	8	8	8	8	7	1	0	19.00	30.50		28,200
Anjum Raman	37	8	7	9	9	7	4	0	17.00	22.00	15.00	6,700

Required

1. Enter the relevant information in the proper columns of a Payroll Register and complete the register for CPP and UI deductions. Assume that the first employee works in the office, the second is a salesperson, and the last two work in the shop. Calculate tax deductions at 20% of gross pay.

2. Prepare a General Journal entry to record the Payroll Register information.

3. Make the Cheque Register entry (Cheque No. 389) to transfer funds equal to the payroll from the regular bank account to the payroll bank account. Assume the first payroll cheque is numbered 632 and enter the payroll cheque numbers in the Payroll Register.

4. Prepare a General Journal entry to record the employer's payroll deductions resulting from the payroll.

5. Prepare a General Journal entry to accrue employee fringe benefit costs for the week. Assume the company matches the employees' payments for medical insurance and contributes an amount equal to 10% of each employees' gross pay to a retirement program. Also, each employee accrues vacation pay at the rate of 7% of the wages and salaries earned. The company estimates that all employees eventually will be paid their vacation pay.

Problem 13–4A
General Journal entries for payroll transactions
(LO 3)

A company has five employees, each of whom has been employed since January 1, earns $1,800 per month, and is paid on the last day of each month. On June 1 the following accounts and balances appeared on its ledger:

a. Employees' Income Taxes Payable, $1,550. (The balance of this account represents the liability for the May 31 payroll only.)

b. Unemployment Insurance Payable, $780 (liability for May only).

c. Canada Pension Payable, $475 (liability for May).

d. Employees' Medical Insurance Payable, $1,620 (liability for April and May).

During June and July, the company completed the following payroll-related transactions:

June 10 Issued Cheque No. 726 payable to the Receiver General for Canada. The cheque was in payment of the May employee income taxes, CPP, and UI amounts due.

    30 Prepared a General Journal entry to record the June Payroll Record which had the following column totals:

Federal Income Taxes	CPP	UI	Medical Insurance	Total Deductions	Net Pay	Office Salaries	Shop Wages
$1,800	$245	$331	$405	$2,781	$6,219	$3,600	$5,400

    30 Recorded the employer's $405 liability for its 50% contribution to the medical insurance plan of employees.

    30 Issued Cheque No. 766 payable to Payroll Bank Account in payment of the June payroll. Endorsed the check, deposited it in the payroll bank account, and issued payroll cheques to the employees.

    30 Prepared a General Journal entry to record the employer's payroll costs resulting from the June payroll.

July   15   Issued Cheque No. 790 payable to Receiver General in payment of the
            June mandatory deductions.

        15   Issued Cheque No. 791 payable to Blacke Insurance Company. The
            cheque was in payment of the April, May, and June employee health in-
            surance premiums.

Required

Prepare the necessary Cheque Register and General Journal entries to record the transactions.

Provocative Problems

Target Limited, which has 80 regular employees, has recently received an order for a
line of archery equipment from a chain of department stores. The order should be very
profitable and will probably be repeated each year. In filling the order, Target can
manufacture the various bows and other supplies with present machines and employees. However, it will have to add 20 persons to its work force for 40 hours per week for
10 weeks to finish the crossbows and pack them for shipment.

   The company can hire these workers and add them to its own payroll, or it can
secure the services of 20 people through Personnel, Inc. Target will pay Personnel,
Inc., $12.50 per hour for each hour worked by each person supplied. The people will be
employees of Personnel, Inc., and it will pay their wages and all taxes on the wages. On
the other hand, if Target Limited employs the workers and places them on its payroll, it
will pay them $11 per hour and will also pay the following payroll costs on their wages:
Canada Pension Plan and unemployment insurance. The company will also have to pay
medical insurance costs of $10 per employee per week.

   Should Target Limited place the temporary help on its own payroll, or should it
secure their services through Personnel, Inc.? Justify your answer.

Provocative Problem 13–1
Target Limited
(LO 1, 4)

PromCom Company employs a systems specialist at an annual salary of $74,400. The
company pays the usual portion of mandatory unemployment insurance and Canada
Pension. Promcom also pays $85 per month for the employee's medical insurance.
Effective June 1, the company agreed to contribute 8% of the specialist's gross pay to a
retirement program.

   What was the total monthly cost of employing the specialist in January, March,
July, and December? Assuming the employee works 180 hours each month, what is the
cost per hour in January? If the annual gross salary is increased by $4,000, what will be
the increase in the total annual costs of employing the specialist?

Provocative Problem 13–2
PromCom Company
(LO 4, 5)

Analytical and
Review Problems

Using current year's withholding tables for Canada Pension Plan, unemployment insurance, and income tax, update the Payroll Register of Illustration 13–3. In computing
income tax withholdings, state *your* assumption as to each employee's personal deductions. Assume that hospital insurance deductions continue at the same amounts as in
Illustration 13–3.

A&R Problem 13–1

A&R Problem 13–2   The following data were taken from the Payroll Register of Haliburton Company:

Gross salary	xxx
Employees' income tax deductions	xxx
UI deductions	xxx
CPP deductions	xxx
Hospital insurance deductions.	xxx
Union dues deductions	xxx

Haliburton contributes an equal amount to the hospital insurance plan, in addition to the statutory payroll taxes, and 6% of gross salaries to a pension program.

Required

Record in General Journal form the payroll, payment of the employees, and remittance to the appropriate authority amounts owing in connection with the payroll. (Note: All amounts are to be indicated as xxx.)

Answers to Objective   LO 1 (*b*)   LO 3 (*e*)   LO 5 (*a*)
Review Questions   LO 2 (*e*)   LO 4 (*d*)

Partnership Accounting

As a business enterprise becomes more complex, it needs more human and financial resources. A partnership allows the owners to pool their talents and funds to achieve more than they could individually. A partnership also creates needs for special accounting information.

*T*he early chapters of this book introduced the three common types of business organizations: single proprietorships, partnerships, and corporations. In this chapter, we examine the partnership form of business in greater detail. The partnership form is widely used, especially in businesses where the owners know each other well. Many professional businesses, including public accounting firms, are organized as partnerships.

Learning Objectives

After studying Chapter 14, you should be able to:

1. List the characteristics of a partnership and explain the concepts of mutual agency and unlimited liability in a partnership.
2. Allocate partnership earnings to partners (*a*) on a stated fractional basis, (*b*) in the partners' capital ratio, and (*c*) through the use of salary and interest allowances.
3. Prepare entries for (*a*) the sale of a partnership interest, (*b*) the admission of a new partner by investment, and (*c*) the retirement of a partner by the withdrawal of partnership assets.
4. Prepare entries required in the liquidation of a partnership.
5. Define or explain the words and phrases listed in the chapter glossary.

Characteristics of Partnerships

LO 1 List the characteristics of a partnership and explain the concepts of mutual agency and unlimited liability in a partnership.

Many businesses, such as small retail and service businesses, are organized as partnerships. Also, many professional practitioners—physicians, lawyers, and public accountants—have traditionally organized their practices as partnerships. The provincial Partnership Acts and the Civil Code, with minor variations, define a **partnership** as "the relation which subsists between persons carrying on a business in common with a view of profit." Another definition of a partnership is "an association of two or more competent persons under a contract to combine some or all of their property, labour, and skills in the operation of a business." Both of these definitions say something about the legal nature of a partnership. However, the nature of the partnership form of business becomes clearer when you understand some of the specific features that characterize partnerships.

A Voluntary Association

A partnership is a voluntary association between the partners. This voluntary nature of a partnership is important because a person assumes some risk by entering a partnership. For example, each partner is responsible for the business acts of his or her partners when the acts are within the scope of the partnership. Also, a partner is personally liable for all of the debts of his or her partnership. As a result, you never have to join a partnership without agreeing who will be the partners. Normally, you should select only financially responsible people who have good judgment.

Based on a Contract

One advantage of a partnership as a form of business organization is that it is easy to organize. All that is necessary is for two or more legally competent people to agree to become partners. Their agreement becomes a **partnership contract.** This contract should be carefully written so that all anticipated points of future disagreement are covered. However, even if the partners make their agreement orally and fail to put it in writing, the partnership contract is binding.

Limited Life

The life of a partnership is always limited. Death, bankruptcy, or anything that takes away the ability of one of the partners to contract automatically ends a partnership. In addition, because a partnership is based on a contract, the contract may stipulate a period of time after which the partnership ends. If the contract does not specify a time period, the partnership ends when the business for which it was created is completed. Or if no time is stated because the business is expected to go on indefinitely, the partnership may be terminated at will by any one of the partners.

Mutual Agency

In many partnerships, the relationship between the partners involves **mutual agency.** This means that every partner is an agent of the partnership. As its agent, a partner can commit or bind the partnership to any contract that is within the apparent scope of the partnership's business. For example, a partner in a merchandising business can sign contracts that bind the partnership to buy merchandise, lease a store building, borrow money, or hire employees. These activities are all within the scope of the business of a merchandising firm. On the other hand, a partner in a law firm, acting alone, cannot bind his or her partners to a contract to buy merchandise for resale or rent a retail store building. These actions are not within the normal scope of a law firm's business.

Partners may agree to limit the power of any one or more of the partners to negotiate certain contracts for the partnership. Such an agreement is binding on the partners and on outsiders who know that it exists. However, it is not binding on outsiders who do not know that it exists. Outsiders who are not aware of the agreement have the right to assume that each partner has the right to act as an agent for the partnership.

Because mutual agency exposes all partners to the risk of unwise actions by any one partner, carefully evaluate your potential partners before agreeing to join a partnership. The importance of this advice is underscored by the fact that most partnerships are also characterized by unlimited liability. Mutual agency and unlimited liability are the main reasons why most partnerships have only a few members.

Unlimited Liability

When a partnership cannot pay its debts, the creditors normally can satisfy their claims from the *personal* assets of the partners. Also, if the property of one partner is insufficient to meet his or her share of the partnership's debts, the creditors can turn to the assets of the remaining partners who are able to pay. Thus, a partner may be called on to pay all the debts of the partnership. This **unlimited liability of partners** is a very important characteristic of partnerships.

   To illustrate the concept of unlimited liability, suppose that Tom Anderson and Carol Brown each invested $5,000 in a store to be operated as a partnership. They also agreed to share incomes and losses equally. Anderson has no property other than his $5,000 investment. However, Brown has sizable savings in addition to her investment. The partners rented a store and bought merchandise for $32,000. They paid $10,000 in cash and promised to pay the $22,000 balance later. However, before the business opened, the store burned and the merchandise was totally destroyed. There was no insurance and all the partnership assets were lost. Unlimited liability means that the partnership creditors can try to collect the full $22,000 of their claims from Brown because Anderson has no other assets. However, Brown can later try to collect $11,000 from Anderson, if he is ever able to save that much money. Partnerships in which all of the partners have unlimited liability are called **general partnerships.**

Limited Partnerships

So far, we have said that all partners normally have unlimited liability. Sometimes, however, individuals who want to invest in a partnership are not willing to accept the risk of unlimited liability. Their needs can be met by using a **limited partnership.** A limited partnership has two classes of partners, general and limited. At least one partner has to be a **general partner** who must assume unlimited liability for the debts of the partnership. The remaining **limited partners** have no personal liability beyond the amounts that they invest in the business. Usually, a limited partnership is managed by the general partner or partners. The limited partners have no active role except for major decisions specified in the partnership agreement.

Advantages and Disadvantages of a Partnership

Limited life, mutual agency, and unlimited liability are disadvantages of a partnership. Yet, there are other reasons why a partnership may be a preferred form of business organization. A partnership has the advantage of being able to bring together more money and skills than a single proprietorship. A partnership is easier to organize than a corporation. Also, a partnership may escape some of the regulations and taxes imposed on corporations. Finally, partners may act without having to hold shareholders' or directors' meetings, which are required of a corporation.

Partnership Accounting

Accounting for a partnership does not differ from accounting for a single proprietorship except for transactions directly affecting the partners' equities. Because ownership rights in a partnership are divided among two or more partners, partnership accounting requires the use of:

- A capital account for each partner.
- A withdrawals account for each partner.
- An accurate measurement and division of earnings.

When a partner invests in a partnership, his or her capital account is credited for the amount invested. Withdrawals of assets by a partner are debited to his or her withdrawals account. And in the end-of-period closing procedure, each partner's capital account is credited or debited for a share of the net income or loss. Finally, the withdrawals account of each partner is closed to that partner's capital account. These closing procedures are like those used for a single proprietorship. The only difference is that separate capital and withdrawals accounts are maintained for each partner. Thus, the closing procedures for a partnership require no further consideration. However, the matter of dividing the partnership's earnings among the partners requires additional discussion.

Nature of Partnership Earnings

Because they are its owners, partners cannot enter into an employer-employee contractual relationship with the partnership. They cannot legally hire themselves or pay themselves salaries. If partners devote their time and services to the affairs of their partnership, they are understood to do so for profit, not for salary. Therefore, when you calculate the net income of a partnership, salaries to partners are not deducted as expenses on the income statement. However, when the net income or loss of the partnership is allocated among the partners, the partners may agree to base part of the allocation on salary allowances that reflect the relative amounts of service provided by the partners. Likewise, if the services of one partner are much more valuable than those of another, salary allowances provide for the unequal service contributions.

Partners are also understood to have invested in a partnership for profit, not for interest. Nevertheless, partners may agree that the division of partnership earnings should include a return based on their invested capital. For example, if one partner contributes five times as much capital as another, it is only fair that this fact be taken into consideration when earnings are allocated among the partners. Thus, a partnership agreement may provide for interest allowances based on the partners' capital balances. Like salary allowances, interest allowances are not expenses to be reported on the income statement.

Division of Earnings

In the absence of a contrary agreement, the law states that the incomes and losses of a partnership are shared equally by the partners. However, partners may agree to any method of sharing. If they agree on how they will share incomes but say nothing about losses, then losses are shared in the same way as income.

Several methods of sharing partnership earnings can be used. Three frequently used methods divide earnings (1) on a stated fractional basis, (2) on the ratio of capital investments, or (3) partially on salary and interest allowances with any remainder in a fixed ratio.

Earnings Allocated on a Stated Fractional Basis

The easiest way to divide partnership earnings is to give each partner a fraction of the total. When this basis is used, the partners may receive equal fractions if their service and capital contributions are equal. Or if their service and capital contributions are not equal, the agreement may provide for an unequal sharing. All that is necessary is for the partners to agree on the fractional share that each will receive.

For example, assume that the partnership agreement of Morse and North states that Morse will receive two thirds and North will receive one third of the partnership earnings. In accounting for the partnership, this agreement shapes the entry to close the Income Summary account. If the partnership's net income is $30,000, the following entry closes the Income Summary account and allocates the earnings to the partners.

Dec.	31	Income Summary	30,000.00	
		A. P. Morse, Capital		20,000.00
		R. G. North, Capital		10,000.00
		To close the Income Summary account and allocate		
		the earnings.		

Division of Earnings Based on the Ratio of Capital Investments

If the nature of a partnership's business is such that earnings are closely related to money invested, a division of earnings based on the ratio of partners' investments offers a fair sharing method. To illustrate this method, assume that Chase, Davis, and Fall have agreed to share earnings in the ratio of their investments. These are: Chase, $50,000; Davis, $30,000; and Fall, $40,000. If net income for the year is $48,000, the following calculation indicates the respective shares of the partners:

Step 1: Chase, capital . . . . $ 50,000
Davis, capital 30,000
Fall, capital 40,000
Total invested $120,000

Step 2: Share of earnings to Chase: $\dfrac{\$50,000}{\$120,000} \times \$48,000 = \$20,000$

Share of earnings to Davis: $\dfrac{\$30,000}{\$120,000} \times \$48,000 = \$12,000$

Share of earnings to Fall: $\dfrac{\$40,000}{\$120,000} \times \$48,000 = \$16,000$

This entry allocates the earnings to the partners:

Dec.	31	Income Summary	48,000.00	
		T. S. Chase, Capital		20,000.00
		S. A. Davis, Capital		12,000.00
		R. R. Fall, Capital		16,000.00
		To close the Income Summary account and allocate the earnings.		

Salaries and Interest as Aids in Sharing

As we have mentioned, partners' service contributions are not always equal. Also, the capital contributions of the partners often are not equal. If the service contributions are not equal, the partners may use salary allowances to compensate for the differences. Or when capital contributions are not equal, they may allocate part of the earnings with interest allowances that compensate for the unequal investments. When investment and service contributions are both unequal, the allocation of net incomes and losses may include both interest and salary allowances.

For example, in Hill and Dale's new partnership, Hill is to provide annual services that they agree are worth an annual salary of $36,000. Dale is less experienced in the business, so his service contribution to the business is worth only $24,000. Also, Hill will invest $30,000 in the business and Dale will invest $10,000. So that they are compensated fairly in light of the differences in their service and capital contributions, Hill and Dale agree to share incomes or losses as follows:

1. The partners grant annual salary allowances of $36,000 to Hill and $24,000 to Dale.
2. The partners grant an interest allowance equal to 10% of each partner's beginning-of-year capital balance.
3. The partners are to share equally the remaining balance of income or loss.

ILLUSTRATION 14–1

	Share to Hill	Share to Dale	Income to be Allocated
Total net income.			$70,000
Allocated as salary allowances:			
Hill	$36,000		
Dale.		$24,000	
Total allocated as salary allowances.			60,000
Balance of income after salary allowances.			$10,000
Allocated as interest:			
Hill (10% on $30,000)	3,000		
Dale (10% on $10,000).		1,000	
Total allocated as interest			4,000
Balance of income after salary and interest allowances .			$ 6,000
Balance allocated equally:			
Hill	3,000		
Dale.		3,000	
Total allocated equally.			6,000
Balance of income			$ –0–
Shares of the partners	$42,000	$28,000	
Percentages of total net income	60%	40%	

Sharing Income When Income Exceeds Interest and Salary Allowances

Note that the provisions for salaries and interest in this partnership agreement are called *allowances*. Also remember that, in the legal sense, partners do not work for salaries and do not invest in a partnership to earn interest. Rather, they work and invest for profits. Therefore, when a partnership agreement provides for salary and interest allowances to the partners, these allowances are not reported on the income statement as salaries and interest expense. They are only a means of splitting up the net income or net loss of the partnership.

Under the partnership agreement, Hill and Dale share the first year's net income of $70,000, as shown in Illustration 14–1. Notice that Hill is allocated $42,000, or 60% of the income, while Dale is allocated $28,000, or 40%.

In Illustration 14–1, notice that the $70,000 net income exceeds the salary and interest allowances of the partners. However, the method of sharing agreed to by Hill and Dale must be followed even if the net income is smaller than the salary and interest allowances. For example, if the first year's net income were $50,000, it would be allocated to the partners as shown in Illustration 14–2. Notice that this circumstance provides Hill with 64% of the total income, while Dale gets only 36%.

Hill and Dale would share a net loss in the same manner as the $50,000 net income. The only difference is that the income-and-loss-sharing procedure would begin with a negative amount of income because of the net loss. After the salary and interest allowances, the remaining balance to be allocated equally would then be a larger negative amount.

ILLUSTRATION 14–2

Sharing Income When Interest and Salary Allowances Exceed Income

	Share to Hill	Share to Dale	Income to be Allocated
Total net income.			$ 50,000
Allocated as salary allowances:			
Hill	$36,000		
Dale.		$24,000	
Total allocated as salary allowances.			60,000
Balance of income after salary allowances.			$(10,000)
Allocated as interest:			
Hill (10% on $30,000)	3,000		
Dale (10% on $10,000).		1,000	
Total allocated as interest			4,000
Balance of income after salary and interest allowances .			$(14,000)
Balance allocated equally:			
Hill	(7,000)		
Dale.		(7,000)	
Total allocated equally			(14,000)
Balance of income			$ -0-
Shares of the partners	$32,000	$18,000	
Percentages of total net income	64%	36%	

In most respects, partnership financial statements are like those of a single proprietorship. On the balance sheet of a partnership, the owner's equity section often shows the separate capital account balance of each partner. The **statement of changes in partners' equity** shows the total capital balances at the beginning of the period, any additional investments made by the partners, the net income or loss of the partnership, withdrawals by the partners, and the ending capital balances. Usually, this statement shows these changes for each partner's capital account and includes the allocation of income among the partners.

For example, recall that Hill and Dale began their partnership by making investments of $30,000 and $10,000, respectively. During the first year of operations, in which the partnership earned $50,000, assume that Hill withdrew $20,000 and Dale withdrew $12,000. The statement of changes in partners' equity appears in Illustration 14–3. The inclusion of salary and interest allowances and the allocation of the balances are generally not reported in such a statement. However, the detail in Illustration 14–3 is shown to demonstrate how the division of net income is attained.

A partnership is based on a contract between specific individuals. Therefore, when a partner withdraws from a partnership, the old partnership ceases to exist. Nevertheless, the business may continue to operate as a new partnership among the remaining partners.

Partnership Financial Statements

Withdrawal or Addition of a Partner

ILLUSTRATION 14–3

A Statement of Changes in Partners' Equity

HILL AND DALE
Statement of Changes in Partners' Equity
For Year Ended December 31, 19—

	Hill	Dale	Total
Beginning capital balances.	$ –0–	$ –0–	$ –0–
Plus:			
Investments by owners	30,000	10,000	40,000
Net income:			
Salary allowances.	$36,000	$24,000	
Interest allowances	3,000	1,000	
Balance	(7,000)	(7,000)	
Total net income	32,000	18,000	50,000
Total.	$62,000	$28,000	$90,000
Less partners' withdrawals	(20,000)	(12,000)	(32,000)
Ending capital balances	$42,000	$16,000	$58,000

LO 3 Prepare entries for (*a*) the sale of a partnership interest, (*b*) the admission of a new partner by investment, and (*c*) the retirement of a partner by the withdrawal of partnership assets.

The withdrawal of a partner from a partnership may take place in two ways. First, the withdrawing partner may sell his or her interest to another person who pays for the interest by transferring cash or other assets to the withdrawing partner. Second, cash or other assets of the partnership may be distributed to the withdrawing partner in settlement of his or her interest in the partnership.

When a new partner is admitted to a partnership, the old partnership technically ends and is replaced by a new partnership. Similar to the withdrawal of a partner, there are two ways a new partner may be admitted to an existing partnership: First, the new partner may purchase an interest directly from one or more of its partners. In other words, the new partner may pay cash to one or more of the existing partners in exchange for an interest in the partnership. Second, a new partner may join an existing partnership by investing cash or other assets in the business.

Sale of a Partnership Interest

Assume that the Abbott, Burns, and Camp partnership owes no liabilities and has the following assets and owners' equity:

Assets		Owners' Equity	
Cash.	$ 3,000	Abbott, capital	$ 5,000
Other assets	12,000	Burns, capital	5,000
		Camp, capital	5,000
Total assets	$15,000	Total owners' equity.	$15,000

Camp's equity in this partnership is $5,000. If Camp sells this equity to Davis for $7,000, Camp is selling a $5,000 recorded interest in the partnership assets. The entry on the partnership books to transfer the equity is:

Feb.	4	Camp, Capital.	5,000.00	
		Davis, Capital		5,000.00
		To transfer Camp's equity in the partnership to Davis.		

After this entry is posted, the assets and owners' equity of the new partnership are:

Assets		Owners' Equity	
Cash.	$ 3,000	Abbott, capital	$ 5,000
Other assets	12,000	Burns, capital	5,000
		Davis, capital	5,000
Total assets	$15,000	Total owners' equity.	$15,000

Two aspects of this transaction are especially important. First, the $7,000 Davis paid to Camp is not recorded in the partnership books. Camp sold and transferred a $5,000 recorded equity in the partnership assets to Davis. The entry that records the transfer is a debit to Camp, Capital, and a credit to Davis, Capital, for $5,000. Furthermore, the entry is the same whether Davis pays Camp $7,000, or $70,000. The amount is paid directly to Camp. Because the partnership is not a party to the transaction, its assets and total equity are not affected by the transaction.

The second important aspect of this transaction is the question of whether Davis's purchase of Camp's interest qualifies Davis as a new partner. In fact, Abbott and Burns must agree if Davis is to become a partner. Abbott and Burns cannot prevent Camp from selling the interest to Davis. But Abbott and Burns do not have to accept Davis as a partner. If Abbott and Burns agree to accept Davis, a new partnership is formed and a new contract with a new income-and-loss-sharing ratio must be drawn.

What if either Abbott or Burns refuses to accept Davis as a partner? Under the partnership acts, Davis gets Camp's share of partnership income and losses. And if the partnership is liquidated, Davis gets Camp's share of partnership assets. However, Davis gets no voice in the management of the firm until being admitted as a partner.

Investing Assets in an Existing Partnership

Instead of purchasing the equity of an existing partner, an individual may gain an equity by investing assets in the business. The invested assets then become the property of the partnership. For example, assume that the partnership of Evans and Gage has assets and owners' equity as follows:

Assets		Owners' Equity	
Cash.	$ 3,000	Evans, capital	$20,000
Other assets	37,000	Gage, capital	20,000
Total assets	$40,000	Total owners' equity.	$40,000

Also, assume that Evans and Gage have agreed to accept Hart as a partner with a one-half interest in the business on his investment of $40,000. This entry records Hart's investment:

Mar.	2	Cash.	40,000.00	
		Hart, Capital		40,000.00
		To record the investment of Hart.		

After the entry is posted, the assets and owners' equity of the new partnership appear as follows:

Assets		Owners' Equity	
Cash.	$43,000	Evans, capital	$20,000
Other assets	37,000	Gage, capital	20,000
		Hart, capital.	40,000
Total assets	$80,000	Total owners' equity.	$80,000

In this case, Hart has a 50% equity in the assets of the business. However, he does not necessarily have a right to one half of its net income. The sharing of incomes and losses is a separate matter on which the partners must agree. As you learned earlier in the chapter, the sharing of profits and losses may be in the ratio of the partners' relative capital contributions. However, the method of sharing also may depend on other factors.

A Bonus to the Old Partners

Sometimes, when the current value of a partnership is greater than the recorded amounts of equity, the partners may require an incoming partner to give a bonus for the privilege of joining the firm. For example, Judd and Kirk operate a partnership business, sharing its earnings equally. The partnership's accounting records show that Judd's recorded equity in the business is $38,000 and Kirk's recorded equity is $32,000. Judd and Kirk agree to accept Lee's $50,000 investment in the business in return for a one-third share of the partnership's earnings and a one-third equity in net assets. Lee's equity is determined with a calculation as follows:

Equities of the existing partners ($38,000 + $32,000) . .	$ 70,000
Investment of the new partner.	50,000
Total partnership equity	$120,000
Equity of Lee ($\frac{1}{3}$ of total)	$ 40,000

Notice that although Lee invested $50,000 in the partnership, his equity in the recorded net assets of the partnership is only $40,000. The $10,000 difference usually is described as a bonus allocated to the existing partners (Judd and Kirk). Therefore, this entry records Lee's investment:

May	15	Cash.	50,000.00	
		Lee, Capital		40,000.00
		Judd, Capital		5,000.00
		Kirk, Capital		5,000.00
		To record the investment of Lee.		

Notice that the $10,000 difference between the $50,000 invested by Lee and the $40,000 credited to his capital account is shared by Judd and Kirk according to their income-and-loss-sharing ratio. Such a bonus is always shared by the old partners in their income-and-loss-sharing ratio. This ratio is used because the bonus compensates the old partners for increases in the worth of the partnership that have not yet been recorded as income.

Recording Goodwill

As discussed previously, when a new partner's investment exceeds his or her equity in the partnership's net assets, the entry to record the new partner's admission normally allocates a bonus to the existing partners. Occasionally, however, firms use an alternative method to record the admission of a new partner. The alternative method involves recording goodwill on the books of the partnership. The debit to Goodwill is matched with credits that increase the equities of the existing partners.

The goodwill method of recording a new partner's admission would be used only if the evidence indicates that future earnings of the partnership are large enough to justify the increased partnership equity. Evidence of such future earnings might be provided by a historical record of earnings that are consistently in excess of the average for the industry.

In practice, goodwill is seldom recognized upon the admission of a new partner. Instead, the bonus method usually is used.

Bonus to the New Partner

Sometimes, the members of an existing partnership may be very eager to bring a new partner into their firm. The business may need additional cash or the new partner may have exceptional abilities or business contacts that will increase profits. Thus, the old partners may be willing to give the new partner a larger equity in the business than the amount of his or her investment. In this case, the old partners give a bonus to the new partner.

For example, Jay Moss and Mike Owen are partners with capital account balances of $30,000 and $18,000, respectively. They share incomes and losses in a 2:1 ratio. Anxious to have Kay Pitt join their partnership, the partners will grant her a one-fourth equity in the firm if she invests $12,000. If Pitt accepts, her equity in the new firm is calculated as follows:

Equity of the existing partners ($30,000 + $18,000) . .	$48,000
Investment of the new partner	12,000
Total equity in the new partnership	$60,000
Equity of Pitt (¼ of total)	$15,000

This entry records Pitt's investment:

June	1	Cash.	12,000.00	
		Moss, Capital ($3,000 × ⅔)	2,000.00	
		Owen, Capital ($3,000 × ⅓).	1,000.00	
		Pitt, Capital.		15,000.00
		To record the investment of Pitt.		

Note that Pitt's bonus is contributed by the old partners in their income-and-loss-sharing ratio. Also remember that Pitt's one-fourth equity does not necessarily entitle her to one fourth of the earnings of the business. The sharing of income and losses is a separate matter for agreement by the partners.

Withdrawal of a Partner

When a new partnership is formed, the contract should include the procedures to follow when a partner retires from the partnership. These procedures often state that a withdrawing partner shall withdraw assets equal to the current value of the partner's equity. To accomplish this, the procedures may require an audit of the accounting records and a revaluation of the partnership assets. The revaluation places the assets on the books at current values. It also causes the partners' capital accounts to reflect the current value of their equity.

For example, assume that Blue is retiring from the partnership of Smith, Blue, and Short. The partners have always shared incomes and losses in the ratio of one half to Smith, one fourth to Blue, and one fourth to Short. Their partnership agreement provides for an audit and asset revaluation on the retirement of a partner. Just prior to the audit and revaluation, their balance sheet shows the following assets and owners' equity:

Assets			Owners' Equity	
Cash		$11,000	Smith, capital.	$22,000
Merchandise inventory. .		16,000	Blue, capital	10,000
Equipment	$20,000		Short, capital	10,000
Less accum. amort. . .	5,000	15,000		
Total assets.		$42,000	Total owners' equity	$42,000

The audit and appraisal indicate that the merchandise inventory is overvalued by $4,000. Also, due to market changes, the partnership's equipment should be valued at $25,000, less accumulated depreciation of $8,000. The entries to record these revaluations are:

Oct.	31	Smith, Capital.	2,000.00	
		Blue, Capital	1,000.00	
		Short, Capital	1,000.00	
		Merchandise Inventory.		4,000.00
		To revalue the inventory.		
	31	Equipment	5,000.00	
		Accumulated Depreciation, Equipment		3,000.00
		Smith, Capital		1,000.00
		Blue, Capital		500.00
		Short, Capital.		500.00
		To revalue the equipment.		

Note in these entries that the partners share the amount of the revaluations in their income-and-loss-sharing ratio. This is fair because revaluations of assets are actually gains and losses. If the partnership were not terminated, these gains and losses would sooner or later show up on the income statement as increases and decreases in net income. The revaluation simply records the effect of the gains and losses earlier than would have occurred.

After the entries revaluing the partnership assets are recorded, the balance sheet for the Smith, Blue, and Short partnership is as follows:

Assets			**Owners' Equity**	
Cash		$11,000	Smith, capital.	$21,000
Merchandise inventory. .		12,000	Blue, capital	9,500
Equipment	$25,000		Short, capital	9,500
Less accum. depr. . . .	8,000	17,000		
Total assets.		$40,000	Total owners' equity	$40,000

After the revaluation, if Blue retires and takes cash equal to his revalued equity, this entry records the withdrawal:

Oct.	31	Blue, Capital	9,500.00	
		Cash		9,500.00
		To record the withdrawal of Blue.		

In withdrawing, Blue does not have to take cash in settlement of his equity. He may take any combination of assets to which the partners agree, or he may take the new partnership's promissory note. Also, the withdrawal of Blue generally creates a new partnership between the remaining partners. Therefore, a new partnership contract and a new income-and-loss-sharing agreement may be required.

Withdrawing Partner Takes Fewer Assets than Recorded Equity

Sometimes, when a partner retires, the remaining partners may not wish to revalue the assets on the books of the partnership. Nevertheless, they must determine the current values of the partnership assets to establish the amount of assets to be taken by the retiring partner. For example, the partners may agree that the assets are overvalued. As a result, the retiring partner should receive assets of less value than the book value of his or her equity. Also, even if the assets are not overvalued, a retiring partner may be willing to take less than the current value of his or her equity just to get out of the partnership.

When a partner retires and takes assets of less value than his or her recorded equity, the partner in effect leaves a portion of the equity in the business. The remaining partners share the unwithdrawn equity portion in their income-and-loss-sharing ratio. For example, assume that partners Black, Brown, and Green share incomes and losses in a 2:2:1 ratio. Their assets and equities are as follows:

Assets		Owners' Equity	
Cash.	$ 5,000	Black, capital	$ 6,000
Merchandise inventory	9,000	Brown, capital.	6,000
Store equipment.	4,000	Green, capital	6,000
Total assets	$18,000	Total owners' equity.	$18,000

Brown is anxious to withdraw from the partnership and offers to take $4,500 in cash in settlement for his equity. Black and Green agree to the $4,500 withdrawal, and Brown retires. This entry records the retirement:

Mar.	4	Brown, Capital	6,000.00	
		Cash		4,500.00
		Black, Capital		1,000.00
		Green, Capital		500.00
		To record the withdrawal of Brown.		

In retiring, Brown withdrew $1,500 less than his recorded equity. This is divided between Black and Green in their income-and-loss-sharing ratio. The income-and-loss-sharing ratio of the original partnership was Black, 2; Brown, 2; and Green, 1. Therefore, the ratio for sharing between Black and Green was 2:1, and the unwithdrawn book equity of Brown is shared by Black and Green in this ratio.

Withdrawing Partner Takes More Assets than Recorded Equity

There are two common reasons why a retiring partner might withdraw more assets than his or her recorded equity: First, the partnership assets may be undervalued on the books. Second, the continuing partners may want to encourage the retiring partner to withdraw by giving up assets of greater value than the retiring partner's recorded equity.

When assets are undervalued, the partners may not wish to change the recorded values. A retiring partner allowed to withdraw assets of greater value than that partner's recorded equity is, in effect, withdrawing his or her own equity plus a portion of the continuing partners' equities.

For example, assume that partners Jones, Thomas, and Finch share incomes and losses in a 3:2:1 ratio. The assets and owners' equity of the partnership are as follows:

Assets		Owners' Equity	
Cash	$ 5,000	Jones, capital	$ 9,000
Merchandise inventory	10,000	Thomas, capital	6,000
Equipment	3,000	Finch, capital	3,000
Total assets	$18,000	Total owners' equity	$18,000

Finch wishes to withdraw from the partnership. Jones and Thomas plan to continue the business. The partners agree that some of the partnership's assets are undervalued, but they do not wish to increase the recorded values. They further agree that if current values were recorded, the asset total would be increased by $6,000 and the equity of Finch would be increased by $1,000. Therefore, the partners agree that $4,000 is the proper value for Finch's equity and that amount of cash may be withdrawn. This entry records the withdrawal:

May	7	Finch, Capital	3,000.00	
		Jones, Capital	600.00	
		Thomas, Capital	400.00	
		Cash		4,000.00
		To record the withdrawal of Finch.		

Death of a Partner

A partner's death automatically dissolves a partnership. As a result, the deceased partner's estate is entitled to receive the amount of his or her equity. The partnership contract should contain provisions for settlement in case a partner dies. Included should be provisions for (*a*) an immediate closing of the books to determine earnings since the end of the previous accounting period and (*b*) a method for determining and recording current values for the assets and liabilities. After these steps are taken, the remaining partners and the deceased partner's estate must agree to a disposition of the deceased partner's equity. This may involve selling the equity to the remaining partners or to an outsider, or it may involve the withdrawal of assets in settlement. We explained the appropriate entries for both cases in the previous paragraphs.

Liquidations

When a partnership is liquidated, its business is ended. The assets are converted into cash, and the creditors are paid. The remaining cash is then distributed to the partners, and the partnership is dissolved. **Partnership liquidations** may follow a variety of different steps. However, we limit the following discussion to three typical situations.

LO 4 Prepare entries required in the liquidation of a partnership.

AS A MATTER OF

Ethics

Janis Carpenter is an accountant who has been engaged by Ed Hansen and Howard French, the remaining partners of the Hansen, Baker, French Partnership. Following the recent accidental death of the third partner, Renee Baker, Hansen and French have been negotiating with the executor of Baker's estate to settle the estate's claim against the partnership. The three partners had shared incomes and losses in the ratio of their capital balances, which were equal. Hansen and French have asked Carpenter to advise them in trying to reach a fair settlement.

Among the records is the partnership agreement, which has only a brief section dealing with settlements in the event of a partner's death. It says that a deceased partner's estate is entitled to the "deceased partner's percentage share of the partnership assets."

The executor of the estate has suggested that the estate is entitled to one third of the current value of the partnership's total assets. Hansen, on the other hand, has suggested that the distribution should be based on the book value of the assets, which is only 75% of the current value.

French has pointed out that the others seem to ignore the liabilities of the partnership, which equal 40% of the assets' book value, and 30% of current value. French thinks the estate is entitled to only one third of the recorded equity. Given the close friendship of the three partners and the tragedy of Baker's death, both the executor and the remaining partners want a fair settlement for all parties. None of them are willing to file a lawsuit to resolve the difference. What would you suggest?

All Assets Are Sold at a Net Gain

One typical partnership liquidation is the situation in which all of the partnership assets are converted into cash at a net gain. Then the cash is distributed and the partnership is dissolved. The following example shows the necessary accounting entries to be made under these conditions.

Ottis, Skinner, and Parr have operated a partnership for a number of years, sharing incomes and losses in a 3:2:1 ratio. Due to several unsatisfactory conditions, the partners decide to liquidate as of December 31. On that date, the books are closed, and the income from operations is transferred to the partners' capital accounts. Thereafter, the partnership's balance sheet appears as follows:

Assets		Liabilities and Owners' Equity	
Cash.	$10,000	Accounts payable	$ 5,000
Merchandise inventory	15,000	Ottis, capital.	15,000
Other assets	25,000	Skinner, capital	15,000
		Parr, capital	15,000
		Total liabilities and	
Total assets	$50,000	owners' equity	$50,000

In a liquidation, some gains or losses normally result from the sale of non-cash assets. These losses and gains are called *losses and gains from liquidation*. Just like any other net incomes or losses, the partners share the losses and gains from liquidation in their income-and-loss-sharing ratio. Assume, for example, Ottis, Skinner, and Parr sell their inventory for $12,000 and their other assets for $34,000. This entry records the sales and the net gain allocation:

Jan.	12	Cash.	12,000.00	
		Loss or Gain from Liquidation	3,000.00	
		Merchandise Inventory.		15,000.00
		Sold the inventory at a loss.		
	15	Cash.	34,000.00	
		Other Assets		25,000.00
		Loss or Gain from Liquidation		9,000.00
		Sold the other assets at a profit.		
	15	Loss or Gain from Liquidation	6,000.00	
		Ottis, Capital		3,000.00
		Skinner, Capital		2,000.00
		Parr, Capital		1,000.00
		To allocate the net gain from sale of assets to the		
		partners in their 3:2:1 income-and-loss-sharing ratio.		

Notice in the last entry that the losses and gains from liquidation were shared in the partner's income-and-loss-sharing ratio. In solving liquidation problems, do not make the mistake of allocating the losses and gains in the ratio of the partners' capital balance.

After the merchandise inventory and other assets of Ottis, Skinner, and Parr are sold and the net gain is allocated, a new balance sheet shows the following:

Assets		Liabilities and Owners' Equity	
Cash.	$56,000	Accounts payable	$ 5,000
		Ottis, capital.	18,000
		Skinner, capital	17,000
		Parr, capital	16,000
		Total liabilities and	
Total assets	$56,000	owners' equity	$56,000

Observe that the one asset, cash of $56,000, exactly equals the sum of the liabilities and the equities of the partners.

After partnership assets are sold and the gain or loss shared, the realized cash is distributed to the proper parties. Because creditors have first claim, they are paid first. After the creditors are paid, the remaining cash is divided among the partners. Each partner has the right to cash equal to his or her equity or, in other words, cash equal to the balance of his or her capital account. These entries record the final cash payments and distribution to Ottis, Skinner, and Parr:

Jan.	15	Accounts Payable	5,000.00	
		Cash		5,000.00
		To pay the claims of the creditors.		
	15	Ottis, Capital	18,000.00	
		Skinner, Capital	17,000.00	
		Parr, Capital	16,000.00	
		Cash		51,000.00
		To distribute the remaining cash to the partners according to their capital account balances.		

Notice that after gains and losses are shared and the creditors are paid, each partner receives cash equal to the balance remaining in his or her capital account. The partners receive these amounts because cash is the only remaining partnership asset and a partner's capital account balance represents the partner's equity in that asset. In making the entry to distribute cash to the partners, be sure that you do not make the mistake of distributing it in the partners' income-and-loss-sharing ratio. Gains and losses from liquidation are allocated according to the income-and-loss-sharing ratio; but cash must be distributed to the partners in relation to their capital account balances.

All Assets Are Sold at a Net Loss: Each Partner's Capital Account Is Sufficient to Absorb His or Her Share of the Loss

In a liquidation, the partnership sometimes sells its assets at a net loss. For example, assume that the Ottis, Skinner, and Parr partnership does not sell its assets at a profit. Instead, assume that they sell the inventory for $10,000 and the other assets for $12,000. These entries record the sales and loss allocation:

Jan.	12	Cash	10,000.00	
		Loss or Gain on Liquidation	5,000.00	
		Merchandise Inventory		15,000.00
		Sold the inventory at a loss.		
	15	Cash	12,000.00	
		Loss or Gain on Liquidation	13,000.00	
		Other Assets		25,000.00
		Sold the other assets at a loss.		
	15	Ottis, Capital	9,000.00	
		Skinner, Capital	6,000.00	
		Parr, Capital	3,000.00	
		Loss or Gain on Liquidation		18,000.00
		To allocate the loss from sale of assets to the partners in their income-and-loss-sharing ratio.		

After the entries are posted, a balance sheet shows that the partnership cash exactly equals the liabilities and the equities of the partners, as follows:

Assets		Liabilities and Owners' Equity	
Cash.	$32,000	Accounts payable	$ 5,000
		Ottis, capital.	6,000
		Skinner, capital	9,000
		Parr, capital	12,000
		Total liabilities and	
Total assets	$32,000	owners' equity	$32,000

The following entries record the distribution of the cash to the proper parties:

Jan.	15	Accounts Payable	5,000.00	
		Cash		5,000.00
		To pay the partnership creditors.		
	15	Ottis, Capital	6,000.00	
		Skinner, Capital	9,000.00	
		Parr, Capital.	12,000.00	
		Cash		27,000.00
		To distribute the remaining cash to the partners		
		according to the balances of their capital accounts.		

Notice again that after losses are shared and creditors are paid, the partners receive the remaining cash in the ratio of their capital account balances.

All Assets Are Sold at a Net Loss: A Partner's Capital Account Is Not Sufficient to Cover His or Her Share of the Loss

Sometimes the liquidation losses allocated to a partner exceed that partner's capital account balance. In such cases, the partner must, if possible, cover the deficit by paying cash into the partnership. For example, contrary to the situations described in the previous illustrations, assume that the Ottis, Skinner, and Parr partnership sells its merchandise for $3,000 and sells its other assets for $4,000. These entries record the sales and the loss allocation:

Jan.	12	Cash.	3,000.00	
		Loss or Gain on Liquidation	12,000.00	
		Merchandise Inventory.		15,000.00
		Sold the inventory at a loss.		
	15	Cash.	4,000.00	
		Loss or Gain on Liquidation	21,000.00	
		Other Assets		25,000.00
		Sold the other assets at a loss.		
	15	Ottis, Capital	16,500.00	
		Skinner, Capital.	11,000.00	
		Parr, Capital.	5,500.00	
		Loss or Gain on Liquidation		33,000.00
		To allocate the loss from sale of assets to the partners in *their income-and-loss-sharing ratio.*		

After posting the entry to allocate the loss, the capital account of Ottis has a $1,500 debit balance and appears as follows:

Ottis, Capital

Date		Explanation	Debit	Credit	Balance
Dec.	31	Balance			15,000.00
Jan.	15	Share of loss on sale	16,500.00		1,500.00 dr.

The partnership agreement states that one half of all losses or gains should be allocated to Ottis. Therefore, since Ottis's capital account balance is not large enough to absorb his share of the loss, he is obligated to pay $1,500 into the partnership to cover the deficit, or debit balance. If Ottis is able to pay, this entry records the receipt:

Dec.	31	Cash.	1,500.00	
		Ottis, Capital		1,500.00
		To record the additional investment of Ottis to cover his *share of loss.*		

After the $1,500 is received, the partnership has $18,500 in cash. The following entries record the cash distributions to the proper parties:

Jan.	15	Accounts Payable	5,000.00	
		Cash		5,000.00
		To pay the partnership creditors.		
	15	Skinner, Capital.	4,000.00	
		Parr, Capital.	9,500.00	
		Cash		13,500.00
		To distribute the remaining cash to the partners *according to the balances of their capital accounts.*		

When a partnership's liquidation loss creates a debit balance in one partner's capital account balance, that partner may be unable to make up the deficit. In such cases, since each partner has unlimited liability, the deficit must be borne by the remaining partner or partners. For example, assume that Ottis is unable to pay the $1,500 necessary to cover the deficit in his capital account. If Ottis is unable to pay, his deficit must be shared by Skinner and Parr in their income-and-loss-sharing ratio. The partners share incomes and losses in the ratio of Ottis, 3; Skinner, 2; and Parr, 1. Therefore, Skinner and Parr share in a 2:1 ratio. This means that Skinner and Parr must share the $1,500 by which Ottis's share of the loss exceeded his capital account balance in a 2:1 ratio. Normally, the defaulting partner's deficit is transferred to the capital accounts of the remaining partners. This is accomplished for Ottis, Skinner, and Parr with the following entry:

Jan.	15	Skinner, Capital.	1,000.00	
		Parr, Capital.	500.00	
		Ottis, Capital		1,500.00
		To transfer the deficit of Ottis to the capital accounts of Skinner and Parr.		

After the deficit is transferred, the capital accounts of the partners appear as in Illustration 14–4. These entries record the final payments to creditors and distribution to the partners:

Jan.	15	Accounts Payable	5,000.00	
		Cash		5,000.00
		To pay the partnership creditors.		
	15	Skinner, Capital.	3,000.00	
		Parr, Capital.	9,000.00	
		Cash		12,000.00
		To distribute the remaining cash to the partners according to their capital account balances.		

Note that Ottis's inability to meet his loss share now does not relieve him of liability. If he becomes able to pay at some future time, Skinner and Parr may collect the full $1,500 from him. Skinner may collect $1,000, and Parr, $500.

The sharing of an insolvent partner's deficit by the remaining partners in their original income-and-loss-sharing is generally regarded as equitable. In England, however, in the case of *Garner* v. *Murray,* Judge Joyce ruled that the debit balance of the insolvent partner's capital account is a personal debt due to the other partners and to be borne by them in the ratio of their capital account balances immediately prior to liquidation.

While *Garner* v. *Murray* still appears to be good law, it is considered by most to be inequitable. The decision applies only when the partnership agreement does not cover this situation and, although rendered in 1904, has not been applied in Canada. It is common practice to provide in the partnership agreement for the sharing of a partner's debit balance by the remaining partners in their income-and-loss-sharing ratio.

ILLUSTRATION 14–4

Allocating Liquidation Loss and Partner's Deficit to Capital Accounts

Ottis, Capital

Date		Explanation	Debit	Credit	Balance
Dec.	31	Balance			15,000.00
Jan.	15	Share of loss on sale	16,500.00		1,500.00 dr.
	15	Deficit to Skinner and Parr		1,500.00	–0–

Skinner, Capital

Date		Explanation	Debit	Credit	Balance
Dec.	31	Balance			15,000.00
Jan.	15	Share of loss on sale	11,000.00		4,000.00
	15	Deficit to Skinner and Parr	1,000.00		3,000.00

Parr, Capital

Date		Explanation	Debit	Credit	Balance
Dec.	31	Balance			15,000.00
Jan.	15	Share of loss on sale	5,500.00		9,500.00
	15	Deficit to Skinner and Parr	500.00		9,000.00

Summary of the Chapter in Terms of Learning Objectives

LO 1. A partnership is a voluntary association between the partners that is based on a contract. The life of a partnership is limited by agreement or by the death or incapacity of a partner. Normally, each partner can act as an agent of the other partners and commit the partnership to any contract within the apparent scope of its business. All partners in a general partnership are personally liable for all the debts of the partnership. Limited partnerships include one or more general partners plus one or more (limited) partners whose liabilities are limited to the amount of their investments in the partnership. The risk of becoming a partner results in part from the fact that partnership characteristics include mutual agency and unlimited liability.

LO 2. A partnership's net incomes or losses are allocated to the partners according to the terms of the partnership agreement. The agreement may specify that each partner will receive a given fraction, or that the allocation of incomes and losses will reflect salary allowances and/or interest allowances. When salary and/or interest allowances are granted, the residual net income or loss usually is allocated equally or on a stated fractional basis.

LO 3. When a new partner buys a partnership interest directly from one or more of the existing partners, the amount of cash paid from one partner to another does not affect the total recorded equity of the partnership. The recorded equity of the selling partner(s) is simply transferred to the capital account of the new partner. Alternatively, a new partner may purchase an equity by investing additional assets in the partnership. When this occurs, part of the new partner's investment may be credited as a bonus to the capital accounts of the existing partners. Also, to gain the participation of the new partner, the existing partners may give the new partner a bonus whereby portions of the existing partners' capital balances are transferred to the new partner's capital account. Occasionally, goodwill is recorded when a new partner invests in a partnership.

LO 4. When a partnership is liquidated, losses and gains from selling the partnership assets are allocated to the partners according to their income-and-loss-sharing ratio. If a partner's capital account has a deficit balance that the partner cannot pay, the other partners must share the deficit in their relative income-and-loss-sharing ratio.

The following events affect the partner's capital accounts in several successive partnerships. On a work sheet with six money columns, one for each of five partners and a totals column, show the effects of the following events on the partners' capital accounts:

Demonstration Problem

13/4/89   Kelly and Emerson create K&E Co. Each invests $10,000, and they agree to share profits equally.

31/12/89 K&E Co. earns $15,000 in the year. Kelly withdraws $4,000 from the partnership, and Emerson withdraws $7,000.

1/1/90   Reed is made a partner in KE&R Co. after contributing $12,000 cash. The partners agree that each will get a 10% interest allowance on their beginning capital balances. In addition, Emerson and Reed are to receive $5,000 salary allowances. The remainder of the income is to be divided evenly.

31/12/90 The partnership's income for the year is $40,000, and these withdrawals occur: Kelly, $5,000; Emerson, $12,500; and Reed, $11,000.

1/1/91   For $20,000, Kelly sells her interest to Merritt, who is accepted by Emerson and Reed as a partner in the new ER&M Co. The profits are to be shared equally after Emerson and Reed each receive $25,000 salaries.

31/12/91 The partnership's income for the year is $35,000, and these withdrawals occur: Emerson, $2,500, and Reed, $2,000.

1/1/92   Davis is admitted as a partner after investing $60,000 cash in the new Davis & Associates partnership. Davis is given a 50% interest in capital after the other partners transfer $3,000 to his account from each of theirs. A 20% interest allowance (on the beginning-of-year capital balances) will be used in sharing profits,

	but there will be no salaries. Davis will get 40% of the remainder, and the other three partners will each get 20%.
31/12/92	Davis & Associates earns $127,600 for the year, and these withdrawals occur: Emerson, $25,000; Reed, $27,000; Merritt, $15,000; and Davis, $40,000.
1/1/93	Davis buys out Emerson and Reed for the balances of their capital accounts, after a revaluation of the partnership assets. The revaluation gain is $50,000, which is divided in the previous 1:1:1:2 ratio. Davis pays the others from personal funds. Merritt and Davis will share profits on a 1:9 ratio.
28/2/93	The partnership had $10,000 of income since the beginning of the year. Merritt retires and receives partnership cash equal to her capital balance. Davis takes possession of the partnership assets in his own name, and the company is dissolved.

Solution to Demonstration Problem

Planning the Solution

- Evaluate each transaction's effects on the capital accounts of the partners.
- Each time a new partner is admitted or a partner withdraws, allocate any bonus based on the income-or-loss-sharing agreement.
- Each time a new partner is admitted or a partner withdraws, allocate subsequent net incomes or losses in accordance with the new partnership agreement.

Event	Kelly	Emerson	Reed	Merritt	Davis	Total	Share of Income
13/4/89							
Initial investment	$10,000	$10,000				$ 20,000	
31/12/89							
Income (equal)	7,500	7,500				15,000	$ 15,000
Withdrawals	(4,000)	(7,000)				(11,000)	
Ending balance	$13,500	$10,500				$ 24,000	
1/1/90							
New investment			$12,000			12,000	
31/12/90							
10% interest	1,350	1,050	1,200			3,600	
Salaries		5,000	5,000			10,000	40,000
Remainder (equal)	8,800	8,800	8,800			26,400	
Withdrawals	(5,000)	(12,500)	(11,000)			(28,500)	
Ending balance	$18,650	$12,850	$16,000			$ 47,500	
1/1/91							
Transfer interest	(18,650)			$18,650		–0–	
31/12/91							
Salaries		25,000	25,000			50,000	35,000
Remainder (equal)		(5,000)	(5,000)	(5,000)		(15,000)	
Withdrawals		(2,500)	(2,000)			(4,500)	
Ending balance	$ –0–	$30,350	$34,000	$13,650		$ 78,000	
1/1/92							
New investment					$ 60,000	60,000	
Bonuses to Davis		(3,000)	(3,000)	(3,000)	9,000	–0–	
Adjusted balance		$27,350	$31,000	$10,650	$ 69,000	$138,000	
31/12/92							
20% interest		5,470	6,200	2,130	13,800	27,600	127,600
Remain. (1:1:1:2)		20,000	20,000	20,000	40,000	100,000	
Withdrawals		(25,000)	(27,000)	(15,000)	(40,000)	(107,000)	
Ending balance		$27,820	$30,200	$17,780	$82,800	$158,600	
1/1/93							
Gain (1:1:1:2)		10,000	10,000	10,000	20,000	50,000	
Adjusted balance		$37,820	$40,200	$27,780	$102,800	$208,600	
Transfer interests		(37,820)	(40,200)		78,020	–0–	
Adjusted balance		$ –0–	$ –0–	$27,780	$180,820	$208,600	
28/2/93							
Income (1:9)				1,000	9,000	10,000	10,000
Adjusted balance				$28,780	$189,820	$218,600	$227,600*
Settlements				(28,780)	(189,820)	(218,600)	(227,600)**
Final balance				$ –0–	$ –0–	$ –0–	$ –0–

* Total of reported net incomes.
** Total of allocated net incomes.

Glossary

General partner a partner who assumes unlimited liability for the debts of the partnership; the general partner in a limited partnership is usually responsible for its management. p. 692

General partnership a partnership in which all partners have unlimited liability for partnership debts. p. 692

Limited partners partners who have no personal liability for debts of the limited partnership beyond the amounts they have invested in the partnership. p. 692

Limited partnership a partnership that has two classes of partners, limited partners and one or more general partners. p. 692

Mutual agency the legal relationship among the partners whereby each partner is an agent of the partnership and is able to bind the partnership to contracts within the apparent scope of the partnership's business. p. 691

Partnership an unincorporated association of two or more persons to carry on a business for profit as co-owners. p. 690

Partnership contract the agreement between partners that sets forth the terms under which the affairs of the partnership will be conducted. p. 691

Partnership liquidations the winding up of a partnership business by converting its assets to cash and distributing the cash to the proper parties. pp. 705–11

Statement of changes in partners' equity a financial statement that shows the total capital balances at the beginning of the period, any additional investments by the partners, the net income or loss of the period, the partners' withdrawals during the period, and the ending capital balances. p. 697

Unlimited liability of partners the legal relationship among general partners of a partnership that makes each general partner responsible for paying all the debts of the partnership if the other partners are unable to pay their shares. p. 692

Objective Review

Answers to the following questions are listed at the end of this chapter. Be sure that you decide which is the one best answer to each question *before* you check the answers.

LO 1 Which of the following is a characteristic of a partnership?

a. A partnership is a voluntary association between two or more persons that is based on a contract.

b. All partners in a general partnership are personally liable for all partnership debts.

c. The life of a partnership is always limited.

d. Unless the partnership contract specifies otherwise, each partner can act on behalf of the other partners and commit the partnership to any contract within the scope of its business.

e. All of the above are characteristics of a partnership.

LO 2 Slim and Jim form a partnership with initial investments of $50,000 and $25,000, respectively. The partners agree to annual salary allowances of $30,000 to Slim and $20,000 to Jim. Also, they agree to an interest allowance equal to 12% of each partner's beginning-of-year capital balance. The remaining balance of income or loss is to be shared equally. How would a first-year net income of $45,000 be shared between Slim and Jim?

a. Slim, $30,000; Jim, $15,000.

b. Slim, $29,000; Jim, $16,000.

c. Slim, $28,100; Jim, $16,900.

d. Slim, $27,000; Jim, $18,000.

e. Slim, $22,500; Jim, $22,500.

LO 3 Davis and Travis operate a partnership and share earnings equally. Davis's recorded equity is $80,000, and Travis's recorded equity is $70,000. Davis and Travis agree to accept Caldwell's $60,000 investment in the business in return for a one-quarter share of the partnership's earnings and a one-quarter equity in net assets. The entry to record Caldwell's investment in the partnership would include:

a. A credit to Davis, Capital, for $7,500.

b. A credit to Travis, Capital, for $3,750.

c. A credit to Caldwell, Capital, for $52,500.

d. A credit to Caldwell, Capital, for $60,000.

e. Both (b) and (c) are correct.

LO 4 The balance sheet for the partnership of Rome, Steele, and Robb before liquidation is as follows:

Assets		Liabilities and Owners' Equity	
Cash.	$ 6,000	Accounts payable	$15,000
Merchandise inventory	42,000	Rome, capital	30,000
Other assets	27,000	Steele, capital	10,000
		Robb, capital	20,000
		Total liabilities and	
Total assets	$75,000	owners' equity	$75,000

The merchandise inventory and other assets are sold for a total of $60,000. If incomes and losses are shared in a 3:2:1 ratio, what amount of cash should Rome receive on distribution of the remaining cash?

a. $20,000.

b. $30,000.

c. $33,000.

d. $25,500.

e. $17,000.

LO 5 In a relationship between partners, the characteristic whereby each partner is able to bind the partnership to contracts within the apparent scope of the partnership's business is:

a. Limited life.

b. Unlimited liability.

c. Mutual agency.

d. Voluntary association.

e. General partnership.

---

1. Amey and Lacey are partners. Lacey dies, and her son claims the right to take his mother's place in the partnership. Does he have this right? Why?

2. If Roscoe cannot legally enter into a contract, can he become a partner?

3. If a partnership contract does not state the period of time the partnership is to exist, when does the partnership end?

Questions for Class Discussion

4. As applied to a partnership, what does the term *mutual agency* mean?

5. Kurt and Ellen are partners in operating a store. Without consulting Kurt, Ellen enters into a contract for the purchase of merchandise for the store. Kurt contends that he did not authorize the order and refuses to take delivery. The vendor sues the partners for the contract price of the merchandise. Will the partnership have to pay? Why?

6. Would your answer to Question 5 differ if Kurt and Ellen were partners in a public accounting firm?

7. Can partners limit the right of a partner to commit their partnership to contracts? Would the agreement be binding (*a*) on the partners and (*b*) on outsiders?

8. What does the term *unlimited liability* mean when it is applied to members of a partnership?

9. The partnership agreement of Barnes and Ardmore provides for a two-thirds, one-third sharing of income but says nothing about losses. The first year of partnership operations resulted in a loss and Barnes argues that the loss should be shared equally because the partnership agreement said nothing about sharing losses. What do you think?

10. Ace and Bud are partners who agree that Ace will receive a $50,000 salary allowance after which remaining incomes or losses will be shared equally. If Bud's capital account is credited $1,000 as his share of the net income in a given period, how much net income did the partnership earn?

11. Van, Wink, and York are partners with capital account balances of $7,000 each. Zack pays Van $8,000 for his one-third interest and is admitted to the partnership. The bookkeeper debits Van, Capital, and credits Zack, Capital, for $7,000. Zack objects; he wants his capital account to show an $8,000 balance, the amount he paid for his interest. Explain why Zack's capital account is credited for $7,000.

12. If the partners in Blume Partnership want the financial statements to show the procedures used to allocate the partnership income among the partners, on what financial statement should the allocation appear?

13. After all partnership assets are converted to cash and all liabilities have been paid, the remaining cash should equal the sum of the balances of the partners' capital accounts. Why?

14. Kay, Kat, and Kim are partners. In a liquidation, Kay's share of partnership losses exceeds her capital account balance. She is unable to meet the deficit from her personal assets, and the excess losses are shared by her partners. Does this relieve Kay of liability?

15. A partner withdraws from a partnership and receives assets of greater value than the book value of his equity. Should the remaining partners share the resulting reduction in their equities in the ratio of their relative capital balances or in their income-and-loss-sharing ratio?

Exercises

Exercise 14–1
Journalizing partnership entries
(LO 2)

On March 1, 1993, Reed and Vaughn formed a partnership. Reed contributed $88,000 cash and Vaughn contributed land valued at $70,000 and a building valued at $120,000. Also, the partnership assumed responsibility for Vaughn's $80,000 long-term note payable associated with the land and building. The partners agreed to share profits as follows: Reed is to receive an annual salary allowance of $30,000, both are to receive an annual interest allowance of 10% of their original capital investment, and any remaining profit or loss is to be shared equally. On October 20, 1993, Reed withdrew cash of $32,000 and Vaughn withdrew $25,000. After the adjusting entries and the closing entries to the revenue and expense accounts, the Income Summary account had a credit balance of $79,000. Present General Journal entries to record the initial capital investments of the partners, their cash withdrawals, and the December 31 closing of the withdrawals accounts. Finally, determine the balances of the partners' capital accounts as of the end of 1993.

Newton and Berry began a partnership by investing $50,000 and $75,000, respectively. During its first year, the partnership earned $165,000.

Exercise 14–2
Income allocation in a partnership
(LO 2)

Required

Prepare calculations showing how the income should be allocated to the partners under each of the following plans for sharing net incomes and losses:

a. The partners failed to agree on a method of sharing income.
b. The partners agreed to share incomes and losses in proportion to their initial investments.
c. The partners agreed to share income by allowing a $55,000 per year salary allowance to Newton, a $45,000 per year salary allowance to Berry, 10% interest on their initial investments, and the balance equally.

Assume that the partners of Exercise 14–2 agreed to share net incomes and losses by allowing yearly salary allowances of $55,000 to Newton and $45,000 to Berry, 10% interest allowances on their investments, and the balance equally. Determine (*a*) the shares of Newton and Berry in a first-year net income of $94,400, and (*b*) the partners' shares in a first-year net loss of $15,700.

Exercise 14–3
Income allocation in a partnership
(LO 2)

The partners in the Royal Partnership have agreed that partner Prince may sell his $90,000 equity in the partnership to Duke, for which Duke will pay Prince $75,000. Present the partnership's journal entry to record the sale on September 30.

Exercise 14–4
Sale of a partnership interest
(LO 3)

The E-O Partnership has total partners' equity of $510,000, which is made up of Elm, Capital, $400,000, and Oak, Capital, $110,000. The partners share net incomes and losses in a ratio of 80% to Elm and 20% to Oak. On November 1, Ash is admitted to the partnership and given a 15% interest in equity and in incomes and losses. Prepare the journal entry to record the entry of Ash under each of the following unrelated assumptions: Ash invests cash of (*a*) $90,000; (*b*) $125,000, and (*c*) $60,000.

Exercise 14–5
Admission of a new partner
(LO 3)

Holland, Flowers, and Wood have been partners sharing net incomes and losses in a 5:3:2 ratio. On January 31, the date Wood retires from the partnership, the equities of the partners are Holland, $350,000; Flowers, $240,000; and Wood, $180,000. Present General Journal entries to record Wood's retirement under each of the following unrelated assumptions:

Exercise 14–6
Retirement of a partner
(LO 3)

> *a.* Wood is paid $180,000 in partnership cash for his equity.
> *b.* Wood is paid $200,000 in partnership cash for his equity.
> *c.* Wood is paid $150,000 in partnership cash for his equity.

Exercise 14–7
Liquidation of a partnership
(LO 4)

The Red, White & Blue partnership was begun with investments by the partners as follows: Red, $175,000; White, $220,000; and Blue, $205,000. The first year of operations did not go well, and the partners finally decided to liquidate the partnership, sharing all losses equally. On August 31, after all assets were converted to cash and all creditors were paid, only $60,000 in partnership cash remained.

Required

1. Calculate the capital account balances of the partners after the liquidation of assets and payment of creditors.

2. Assume that any partner with a deficit pays cash to the partnership to cover the deficit. Then present the General Journal entries on August 31 to record the cash receipt from the deficient partner(s) and the final disbursement of cash to the partners.

3. Now make the contrary assumption that any partner with a deficit is not able to reimburse the partnership. Present journal entries (*a*) to transfer the deficit of any deficient partners to the other partners and (*b*) to record the final disbursement of cash to the partners.

Exercise 14–8
Liquidation of a partnership
(LO 4)

Sandburg, McArthur, and Cox are partners who share incomes and losses in a 1:4:5 ratio. After lengthy disagreements among the partners and several unprofitable periods, the partners decided to liquidate the partnership. Before the liquidation, the partnership balance sheet showed total assets, $116,000; total liabilities, $88,000; Sandburg, Capital, $1,200; McArthur, Capital, $11,700; and Cox, Capital, $15,100. The cash proceeds from selling the assets were sufficient to repay all but $24,000 to the creditors. Calculate the loss from selling the assets, allocate the loss to the partners, and determine how much of the remaining liability should be paid by each partner.

Exercise 14–9
Liquidation of a limited partnership
(LO 4)

Assume that the Sandburg, McArthur, and Cox partnership of Exercise 14–8 is a limited partnership. Sandburg and McArthur are general partners and Cox is a limited partner. How much of the remaining $24,000 liability should be paid by each partner?

Problems

Problem 14–1
Methods of allocating partnership income
(LO 2)

Tom Katz, Kaye Reeves, and Alice Troy invested $40,000, $56,000, and $64,000, respectively, in a partnership. During its first year, the firm earned $124,500.

Required

Prepare entries to close the firm's Income Summary account as of December 31 and to allocate the net income to the partners under each of the following assumptions:

a. The partners did not specify any special method of sharing incomes.

b. The partners agreed to share net incomes and losses in the ratio of their beginning investments.

c. The partners agreed to share income by providing annual salary allowances of $33,000 to Katz, $28,000 to Reeves, and $40,000 to Troy; allowing 10% interest on the partners' beginning investments; and sharing the remainder equally.

Linda Nuñez and Ray Parker are in the process of forming a partnership to which Nuñez will devote one-half time and Parker will devote full time. They have discussed the following alternative plans for sharing net incomes and losses:

Problem 14–2
Allocating partnership incomes and losses; sequential years
(LO 2)

a. In the ratio of their initial investments, which they have agreed will be $21,000 for Nuñez and $31,500 for Parker.

b. In proportion to the time devoted to the business.

c. A salary allowance of $3,000 per month to Parker and the balance in accordance with their initial investment ratio.

d. A $3,000 per month salary allowance to Parker, 10% interest on their initial investments, and the balance equally.

The partners expect the business to generate income as follows: year 1, $18,000 net loss; year 2, $45,000 net income; and year 3, $75,000 net income.

Required

1. Prepare three schedules with the following column headings:

Income/ Loss Sharing Plan	Year _____		
	Calculations	Nuñez	Parker

2. Complete a schedule for each of the first three years by showing how the partnership net income or loss for each year would be allocated to the partners under each of the four plans being considered. Round your answers to the nearest whole dollar.

Brad Marshall, Jon Spiller, and Leigh Rand formed the MSR Partnership by making capital contributions of $183,750, $131,250, and $210,000, respectively. They anticipate annual net incomes of $225,000 and are considering the following alternative plans of sharing net incomes and losses: (a) equally; (b) in the ratio of their initial investments; or (c) salary allowances of $40,000 to Marshall, $30,000 to Spiller, and $45,000 to Rand; interest allowances of 10% on initial investments, with any remaining balance shared equally.

Problem 14–3
Partnership income allocation, statement of changes in partners' equity, and closing entries
(LO 2)

Required

1. Prepare a schedule with the following column headings:

Income/Loss Sharing Plan	Calculations	Share to Marshall	Share to Spiller	Share to Rand	Totals

Use the schedule to show how a net income of $225,000 would be distributed under each of the alternative plans being considered. Round your answers to the nearest whole dollar.

2. Prepare a statement of changes in partners' equity showing the allocation of income to the partners, assuming they agree to use alternative *c* and the net income earned is $105,000. During the year, Marshall, Spiller, and Rand withdrew $17,000, $24,000, and $32,000, respectively.

3. Prepare the December 31 journal entry to close Income Summary assuming they agree to use alternative *c* and the net income is $105,000. Also, close the withdrawals accounts.

Problem 14–4
Withdrawal of a partner
(LO 3)

Part 1. Godfrey, Gully, and Speck are partners with capital balances as follows: Godfrey, $84,000; Gully, $69,000; and Speck, $147,000. The partners share incomes and losses in a 3:2:5 ratio. Gully decides to withdraw from the partnership, and the partners agree not to have the assets revalued on his retirement. Prepare General Journal entries to record the February 1 withdrawal of Gully from the partnership under each of the following unrelated assumptions:

a. Gully sells his interest to Goldman for $80,000 after Godfrey and Speck approve the entry of Goldman as a partner.

b. Gully gives his interest to a son-in-law, Spain. Godfrey and Speck accept Spain as a partner.

c. Gully is paid $69,000 in partnership cash for his equity.

d. Gully is paid $107,000 in partnership cash for his equity.

e. Gully is paid $15,000 in partnership cash plus computer equipment recorded on the partnership books at $35,000 less accumulated amortization of $11,600.

Part 2. Assume that Gully does not retire from the partnership described in Part 1. Instead, Hatch is admitted to the partnership on February 1 with a 25% equity. Prepare General Journal entries to record the entry of Hatch into the partnership under each of the following unrelated assumptions:

a. Hatch invests $100,000.

b. Hatch invests $72,500.

c. Hatch invests $131,000.

Problem 14–5
Liquidation of a
partnership
(LO 4)

Swanson, Chapel, and Page plan to liquidate their partnership. They have always shared losses and gains in a 3:2:1 ratio, and on the day of the liquidation their balance sheet appeared as follows:

SWANSON, CHAPEL, AND PAGE
Balance Sheet
May 31, 19—

Assets		Liabilities and Owners' Equity	
Cash	$ 90,400	Accounts payable	$122,750
Inventory	268,600	David Swanson, capital	46,500
		Annie Chapel, capital	106,250
		Maria Page, capital	83,500
		Total liabilities and	
Total assets	$359,000	owners' equity	$359,000

Required

Assume that the inventory is sold and the cash is distributed to the proper parties on May 31; prepare the General Journal entries for the sale, the gain or loss allocation, and the distribution of the cash in each of the following unrelated cases:

a. The inventory is sold for $300,000.

b. The inventory is sold for $250,000.

c. The inventory is sold for $160,000, and any partners with resulting deficits can and do pay in the amount of their deficits.

d. The inventory is sold for $125,000, and the partners have no assets other than those invested in the business.

Until November 16, 1993, Rohan, Kovak, and Keene were partners that shared incomes and losses in the ratio of their beginning-of-year capital account balances. On November 16, Rohan suffered a heart attack and died. Kovak and Keene immediately ended the business operations and prepared the following adjusted trial balance:

Problem 14–6
Withdrawal of a partner
(LO 3)

ROHAN, KOVAK, AND KEENE
Adjusted Trial Balance
November 16, 1993

Cash.	$ 10,625	
Accounts receivable.	30,415	
Allowance for doubtful accounts		$ 1,115
Supplies inventory	46,875	
Equipment	148,860	
Accumulated amortization, equipment		14,842
Building.	227,325	
Accumulated amortization, building.		56,850
Land	14,800	
Accounts payable		22,688
Note payable (secured by mortgage)		37,005
Tracy Rohan, capital		141,040
Tracy Rohan, withdrawals	5,700	
Jackie Kovak, capital		141,040
Jackie Kovak, withdrawals	5,700	
Kerry Keene, capital		70,520
Kerry Keene, withdrawals	16,200	
Services revenue		75,150
Operating expense.	53,750	
Totals	$560,250	$560,250

Required

1. Prepare the November 16 General Journal entries to close the revenue, expense, income summary, and withdrawals accounts of the partnership.

2. Assume the estate of Rohan agreed to accept the land and building and to assume the mortgage note thereon in settlement of its claim against the partnership assets, and that Kovak and Keene planned to continue the business and rent the building from the estate. Prepare the partnership's December 1 General Journal entry to transfer the land, building, and mortgage note in settlement with the estate.

3. Assume that, instead of the foregoing, the estate of Rohan demanded a cash settlement and the business had to be sold to a competitor, who gave $298,000 for the noncash assets and assumed the mortgage note but not the accounts payable. Prepare the December 1 General Journal entry to transfer the noncash assets and mortgage note to the competitor, and the entries to allocate the gain or loss to the partners and to distribute the partnership cash.

Janet Koppen and Beverly Spikes want to form a partnership and are considering two methods of sharing incomes and losses. Method *a* splits all incomes and losses in a 2:3 ratio, or 40% to Koppen and 60% to Spikes. Method *b* depends on the income or loss of

Problem 14–7
Analytical essay
(LO 2)

the partnership. If the partnership incurs a loss, the partners share it equally. If the income is in the range of $0 to $45,000, it is allocated based on an annual salary allowance of $15,000 to Koppen and $30,000 to Spikes. If the net income exceeds $45,000, the residual after the salary allowances is shared equally.

Koppen has retained you to write an evaluation of the two methods, indicating which is more favourable to her. Your discussion should include a comparison of the two methods at each of the three possible net income levels. Also discuss the importance of asking Koppen to estimate the partnership's future earnings.

Problem 14–8
Analytical essay
(LO 3)

Guido, DeVito, and Vanelli have been operating a successful partnership for several years. Even though business is good, DeVito and Vanelli have disagreed with Guido on several occasions regarding the business, and Guido is now withdrawing from the partnership. The partners agree that the book values of the assets are less than their market values. However, they do not want to change the recorded values at this time. As a result, the partners have agreed that Guido should withdraw cash in an amount greater than his capital account balance.

DeVito and Vanelli are not sure how to calculate the adjustments to their capital accounts (brought about by the difference between Guido's equity and the cash he is withdrawing). DeVito thinks they should split the difference in the ratio of their capital account balances. Vanelli thinks the adjustments should be calculated using their original income-and-loss-sharing ratio. Which partner do you think is correct? Explain the reasons for your answers.

Alternate Problems

Problem 14–1A
Methods of allocating
partnership income
(LO 1)

Paul Jones, Will Rogers, and Anne Thompson invested $82,000, $49,200, and $32,800, respectively, in a partnership. During its first year, the firm earned $135,000.

Required

Prepare entries to close the firm's Income Summary account as of December 31 and to allocate the net income to the partners under each of the following assumptions. (Round your answers to the nearest whole dollar.)

a.   The partners did not specify any special method of sharing incomes.
b.   The partners agreed to share net incomes and losses in the ratio of their beginning investments.
c.   The partners agreed to share income by providing annual salary allowances of $48,000 to Jones, $36,000 to Rogers, and $25,000 to Thompson; allowing 10% interest on the partners' beginning investments; and sharing the remainder equally.

Problem 14–2A
Allocating partnership
incomes and losses;
sequential years
(LO 1)

Jacob Jackson and K. D. Fletcher are in the process of forming a partnership to which Jackson will devote one-third time and Fletcher will devote full time. They have discussed the following alternative plans for sharing net incomes and losses:

a.   In the ratio of their initial investments, which they have agreed will be $52,000 for Jackson and $78,000 for Fletcher.
b.   In proportion to the time devoted to the business.
c.   A salary allowance of $2,000 per month to Fletcher and the balance in accordance with their initial investment ratio.

d. A $2,000 per month salary allowance to Fletcher, 10% interest on their initial investments, and the balance equally.

The partners expect the business to generate income as follows: year 1, $18,000 net loss; year 2, $38,000 net income; and year 3, $94,000 net income.

Required

1. Prepare three schedules with the following column headings:

Income/ Loss Sharing Plan	Year _____		
	Calculations	Jackson	Fletcher

2. Complete a schedule for each of the first three years by showing how the partnership income or loss for each year would be allocated to the partners under each of the four plans being considered. (Round your answers to the nearest whole dollar.)

Ella Phillips, Chet Fong, and Lou Campos formed the PFC Partnership by making capital contributions of $72,000, $108,000, and $60,000, respectively. They anticipate annual net incomes of $120,000 and are considering the following alternative plans of sharing net incomes and losses: (*a*) equally; (*b*) in the ratio of their initial investments; or (*c*) salary allowances of $20,000 to Phillips, $15,000 to Fong, and $40,000 to Campos; interest allowances of 12% on initial investments, with any remaining balance shared equally.

Problem 14–3A
Partnership income allocation, statement of changes in partners' equity, and closing entries
(LO 2)

Required

1. Prepare a schedule with the following column headings:

Inc./Loss Sharing Plan	Calculations	Share to Phillips	Share to Fong	Share to Campos	Totals

Use the schedule to show how a net income of $120,000 would be distributed under each of the alternative plans being considered. Round your answers to the nearest whole dollar.

2. Prepare a statement of changes in partners' equity showing the allocation of income to the partners, assuming they agree to use alternative *c* and the net income actually earned is $55,000. During the year, Phillips, Fong, and Campos withdrew $9,000, $19,000, and $12,000, respectively.

3. Prepare the December 31 journal entry to close Income Summary assuming they agree to use alternative *c* and the net income is $55,000. Also, close the withdrawals accounts.

Part 1. Soltani, Sugimoto, and Suza are partners with capital balances as follows: Soltani, $303,000; Sugimoto, $74,000; and Suza, $223,000. The partners share incomes and losses in a 5:1:4 ratio. Soltani decides to withdraw from the partnership, and the partners agree not to have the assets revalued on her retirement. Prepare General Journal entries to record the April 30 withdrawal of Soltani from the partnership under each of the following unrelated assumptions:

Problem 14–4A
Withdrawal of a partner
(LO 3)

a. Soltani sells her interest to Samba for $250,000 after Sugimoto and Suza approve the entry of Samba as a partner.

b. Soltani gives her interest to a daughter-in-law, Shulak; Sugimoto and Suza accept Shulak as a partner.

c. Soltani is paid $303,000 in partnership cash for her equity.

d. Soltani is paid $175,000 in partnership cash for her equity.

e. Soltani is paid $100,000 in partnership cash plus manufacturing equipment recorded on the partnership books at $269,000 less accumulated amortization of $168,000.

Part 2. Assume that Soltani does not retire from the partnership described in Part 1. Instead, Sung is admitted to the partnership on April 30 with a 20% equity. Prepare General Journal entries to record the entry of Sung under each of the following unrelated assumptions:

a. Sung invests $150,000.

b. Sung invests $98,000.

c. Sung invests $213,000.

Problem 14–5A
Liquidation of a partnership
(LO 4)

Huggins, Hart, and Love, who have always shared incomes and losses in a 2:1:2 ratio, plan to liquidate their partnership. Just prior to the liquidation their balance sheet appeared as follows:

HUGGINS, HART, AND LOVE
Balance Sheet
January 18, 19—

Assets		Liabilities and Owners' Equity	
Cash	$174,300	Accounts payable	$171,300
Equipment	308,600	C. J. Huggins, capital	150,200
		D. C. Hart, capital	97,900
		J. D. Love, capital	63,500
		Total liabilities and	
Total assets	$482,900	owners' equity	$482,900

Required

Under the assumption the equipment is sold and the cash is distributed to the proper parties on January 18, prepare General Journal entries for the sale, the gain or loss allocation, and the distribution of cash in each of the following unrelated cases:

a. The equipment is sold for $325,000.

b. The equipment is sold for $265,000.

c. The equipment is sold for $100,000, and any partners with resulting deficits can and do pay in the amount of their deficits.

d. The equipment is sold for $75,000, and the partners have no assets other than those invested in the business.

Problem 14–6A
Withdrawal of a partner
(LO 3)

Until July 3, 1993, Daily, Murray, and Dryer were partners that shared incomes and losses in the ratio of their beginning-of-year capital account balances. On July 3, Murray suffered a heart attack and died. Daily and Dryer immediately terminated the partnership and prepared the following adjusted trial balance:

DAILY, MURRAY, AND DRYER
Adjusted Trial Balance
July 3, 1993

Cash.	$ 31,418	
Accounts receivable.	18,322	
Allowance for doubtful accounts		$ 725
Supplies inventory	54,910	
Equipment	110,660	
Accumulated amortization, equipment		15,808
Building.	303,300	
Accumulated amortization, building.		68,390
Land	27,400	
Accounts payable.		25,975
Note payable (secured by mortgage)		64,012
Jess Daily, capital.		164,800
Jess Daily, withdrawals	21,700	
Mel Murray, capital.		206,000
Mel Murray, withdrawals	38,200	
Pat Dryer, capital.		41,200
Pat Dryer, withdrawals	10,500	
Services revenue		195,600
Operating expense.	166,100	
Totals	$782,510	$782,510

Required

1. Prepare the July 3 General Journal entries to close the revenue, expense, income summary, and withdrawals accounts of the partnership.

2. Assume the estate of Murray agreed to accept the land and building and to assume the mortgage note thereon in settlement of its claim against the partnership assets, and that Daily and Dryer planned to continue the business and rent the building from the estate. Prepare the partnership's July 16 General Journal entry to transfer the land, building, and mortgage note in settlement with the estate.

3. Assume that, instead of the foregoing, the estate of Murray demanded a cash settlement and the business had to be sold to a competitor, who gave $350,000 for the noncash assets and assumed the mortgage note but not the accounts payable. Prepare the July 16 General Journal entry to transfer the noncash assets and mortgage note to the competitor, and the entries to allocate the gain or loss to the partners and to distribute the partnership cash.

Janet Koppen and Beverly Spikes want to form a partnership and are considering two methods of sharing incomes and losses. Method *a* splits all profits and losses in a 2:3 ratio, or 40% to Koppen and 60% to Spikes. Method *b* depends on the income or loss of the partnership. If the partnership incurs a loss, the partners share it equally. If the income is in the range of $0 to $45,000, it is allocated based on an annual salary allowance of $15,000 to Koppen and $30,000 to Spikes. If the net income exceeds $45,000, the residual after the salary allowances is shared equally.

Problem 14–7A
Analytical essay
(LO 2)

   Spikes has retained you to write an evaluation of the two methods indicating which is most favourable to her. Your discussion should include a comparison of the two methods at each of the three possible net income levels. Also, discuss the importance of asking Spikes to estimate the partnership's future earnings.

Kay Doobie, Ed Foley, and Brian McKenzie have been operating a partnership for several years. Business has not been good recently, and Doobie is withdrawing from the partnership. The partners agree that the market values of the assets are less than

Problem 14–8A
Analytical essay
(LO 3)

their recorded book values. However, they do not want to change the recorded values at this time. As a result, the partners have agreed that Doobie should withdraw cash in an amount that is less than her capital account balance.

Foley and McKenzie are not sure how to calculate the adjustments to their capital accounts (brought about by the difference between Doobie's equity and the cash she is withdrawing). Foley thinks they should split the difference in the ratio of their capital account balances. McKenzie thinks the adjustments should be calculated using their income-and-loss-sharing ratio. Which partner do you think is correct? Explain why.

Provocative Problems

Provocative Problem 14–1
Hartel and Huitt
Partnership
(LO 1)

Keith Hartel and Todd Huitt agreed to share the annual net incomes or losses of their partnership as follows: if the partnership earns a net income, the first $60,000 is allocated 40% to Hartel and 60% to Huitt to reflect the time devoted to the business by each partner. Income in excess of $60,000 is shared equally. However, the partners have agreed to share any losses equally.

Required

1. Prepare a schedule showing how net income of $72,000 for 1993 should be allocated to the partners.

2. Sometime later in 1994, the partners discovered that $80,000 of accounts payable had existed on December 31, 1993, but had not been recorded. These accounts payable relate to expenses incurred by the business. They are now trying to determine the best way to correct their accounting records, particularly their capital accounts. Huitt suggests that they make a special entry crediting $80,000 to the liability account, and debiting their capital accounts for $40,000 each. Hartel, on the other hand, suggests that an entry should be made to record the accounts payable and retroactively correct the capital accounts to reflect the balance that they would have had if the expenses had been recognized in 1993. If they had been recognized, the partnership would have reported a loss of $8,000 instead of the $72,000 net income.
   (a) Present the journal entry suggested by Huitt for recording the accounts payable and allocating the loss to the partners.
   (b) Give the journal entry to record the accounts payable and correct the capital accounts according to Hartel's suggestion. Show how you calculated the amounts presented in the entry.

3. Which suggestion do you think complies with their partnership aggreement? Why?

Provocative Problem 14–2
The Med Mart
(LO 3)

Martha Emerson and Florence Knight are partners who own and operate The Med Mart, a medical supply store. Emerson's recorded equity in the business is $129,000 and Knight's recorded equity is $69,000. They share incomes and losses by allowing annual salary allowances of $55,000 to Emerson and $30,000 to Knight, with any remaining balance being shared 70% to Emerson and 30% to Knight.

Gail Emerson, Martha Emerson's daughter, has been working in the store on a salary basis. In addition to working in the store, Gail is a registered nurse and works part-time at a nearby hospital. Because Gail is well known and liked by many of the doctors, nurses, and other employees at the hospital, she attracts a great deal of business to the store. The partners believe that at least one third of the past three years' sales can be traced directly to Gail's association with the store, and it is reasonable to assume she was instrumental in attracting even more.

Gail is paid $2,000 per month, but feels this is not sufficient to induce her to remain with the store as an employee. However, she likes the work and plans to continue in the medical field. What she really wants is to become a partner in the business.

Her mother is anxious for her to remain in the business and proposes the following:

a. That Gail Emerson be admitted to the partnership with a 20% equity in the net assets.

b. That she, Martha Emerson, transfer from her capital account to Gail's capital account one half of the 20% interest; that Martha contribute cash to the firm for the other half of Gail's interest; and that Gail sign a note to Martha for the amount of cash paid by Martha.

c. That incomes and losses be shared by continuing the $55,000 and $30,000 salary allowances of the original partners and that Gail be given a $24,000 annual salary allowance, after which any remaining income or loss will be shared 50% to Martha Emerson, 30% to Florence Knight, and 20% to Gail Emerson.

Required

1. Prepare a schedule showing the partners' capital balances both before and immediately after Gail's admission to the partnership.

2. Assume the net incomes for the past three years were $87,600, $91,200, and $95,400, respectively. Prepare one schedule showing how net income was allocated during the past three years, and a second schedule showing how net income would have been allocated if Martha's proposal had been in effect all three years.

3. Describe how the admission of Gail would affect Florence's equity and share in future profits, and how the partnership might benefit from Gail's admission. Would you advise Florence to accept the proposal?

The balance sheet of the Baroque Partnership on December 31, 1993, is as follows:

Provocative Problem 14–3
Baroque Partnership
(LO 3)

Assets		Liabilities and Owners' Equity	
Cash	$ 20,000	Bonet, capital	$ 34,000
Other assets	80,500	Lebeaux, capital	50,500
Land	67,000	Dubois, capital	83,000
		Total liabilities and	
Total assets.	$167,500	owners' equity	$167,500

The income-and-loss-sharing percentages are Bonet, 20%; Lebeaux, 30%; and Dubois, 50%. Bonet wishes to withdraw from the partnership, and the partners finally agree that the land owned by the partnership should be transferred to Bonet in full payment for his equity. In reaching this decision, they recognize that the land has appreciated since it was purchased and is now worth $78,000. If Bonet retires on January 1, 1994, what journal entries should be made on that date?

Review the "As a Matter of Ethics" case on page 706. Then write a brief essay describing Janis Carpenter's engagement and the suggestions you would offer the partners. Your essay should include the reasons why your suggested settlement is fair.

Provocative Problem 14–4
As a Matter of Ethics:
Essay

Ethics

Analytical and Review Problems

A&R Problem 14-1

Max and Kasim entered into a partnership to carry on a business under the firm name of Maxim Sportsland. Prior to the final signing of the agreement Max asks you to evaluate the "income/loss distribution clause" contained in the agreement.

Your examination revealed that the agreement called for the following: Equal sharing of net income and losses after an initial allocation of $50,000 to Max and $20,000 to Kasim to reflect the difference in time and expertise devoted to the business by each partner. This allocation would be made regardless of the level of net income/loss.

Required

Prepare a report to Max on the particular clause of the agreement. Your report should show the consequence on each partner of operating results as follows: (*a*) net income of $100,000; (*b*) net income of $20,000; (*c*) operation at break-even, that is, no net income or loss; (*d*) loss of $20,000; (*e*) loss of $100,000.

A&R Problem 14-2

The summarized balance sheet of Dell, Funk, and Shield showed:

Assets		Equities	
Cash	$ 20,000	Liabilities	$ 60,000
Other assets	280,000	Dell, capital	80,000
		Funk, capital	120,000
		Shield, capital	40,000
Total assets.	$300,000	Total equities.	$300,000

The partnership has operated successfully for nearly 25 years, and Shield, because of his age and health, is pushing for sale of the business. In fact, he has found Arn, a buyer who is willing to pay $360,000 cash and take over the liabilities. Both Dell and Funk are not anxious to sell what they refer to as "our little gold mine."

Shield is adamant about getting out and has proposed the following:

1. Either sell to Arn, or Dell and Funk (a new partnership) should buy out Shield at an amount Shield would receive if the business was sold to Arn.

2. Admit Arn to partnership upon the purchase of Shield's share for an amount Shield and Arn will negotiate.

The present partnership agreement calls for a distribution of net income/loss on a 3:5:2 basis. If Arn is admitted to partnership the ratio would not change; he would be entitled to Shield's 20% share of net income/loss. If Dell and Funk buy out for an amount based on the Arn offer, Dell and Funk would continue to share net income/loss on the same relative basis. They would (the new partnership of Dell and Funk) have to borrow sufficient funds from the bank to retain a minimum cash balance of $10,000.

Required

1. Prepare the General Journal entry for admission of Arn to the partnership upon his purchase of Shield's interest for an undisclosed amount.

2. Prepare the necessary entries to record Shield's withdrawal from the partnership. The amount paid to Shield is equal to the amount he would have received if the partnership was sold to Arn.

Answers to Objective Review Questions

LO 1	(*e*)	LO 3	(*e*)	LO 5	(*c*)
LO 2	(*b*)	LO 4	(*d*)		

Accounting Principles, Conceptual Framework, and Alternative Valuation Methods

A ccounting principles or concepts are not laws of nature. They are broad ideas developed as a way of *describing* current accounting practices and *prescribing* new and improved practices. In studying Part V, you will learn about some new accounting concepts that the Accounting Standards Board (AcSB) developed in an effort to guide future changes and improvements in accounting. You also will learn about some major alternatives to the historical cost measurements reported in conventional financial statements. Studying these alternatives will help you understand the nature of the information that is contained in conventional statements. In addition, it will help you grasp the meaning of new reporting practices that may occur in future years.

Learning Objectives

After studying Part V, you should be able to:

1. Explain the difference between descriptive concepts and prescriptive concepts.
2. Explain the difference between bottom-up and top-down approaches to the development of accounting concepts.
3. Describe the major components in the Accounting Standards Board's "Financial Statement Concepts."
4. Explain why conventional financial statements fail to adequately account for price changes.
5. Use a price index to restate historical cost/nominal dollar costs into constant purchasing power amounts and to calculate purchasing power gains and losses.
6. Explain the current cost approach to valuation, including its effects on the income statement and balance sheet.
7. Explain the current selling price approach to valuation.
8. Define or explain the words and phrases listed in the Part V glossary.

ACCOUNTING PRINCIPLES AND CONCEPTUAL FRAMEWORK

Descriptive and Prescriptive Accounting Concepts

To fully understand the importance of financial accounting concepts or principles, you must realize that they serve two purposes. First, they provide general descriptions of existing accounting practices. In doing this, concepts and principles serve as guidelines that help you learn about accounting. Thus, after learning how the concepts or principles are applied in a few situations, you develop the ability to apply them in different situations. This is easier and more effective than memorizing a very long list of specific practices.

Second, these concepts or principles help accountants analyze unfamiliar situations and develop procedures to account for those situations. This purpose is especially important for the Accounting Standards Board, which is charged with developing uniform practices for financial reporting in Canada and with improving the quality of such reporting.

In prior chapters, we defined and illustrated several important accounting principles. Listed together here for convenience, these principles describe in general terms the practices currently used by accountants.

Generally Accepted Accounting Principles

Business entity principle	Full-disclosure principle	Objectivity principle
Conservatism principle	Going-concern principle	Realization or revenue principle
Consistency principle	Matching principle	Time-period principle
Cost principle	Materiality principle	Unit of measure*

*See p. 740.

The listed principles (defined on pages 737–40) are useful for teaching and learning about accounting practice and are helpful for dealing with some unfamiliar transactions. As business practices have evolved in recent years, however, these principles have become less useful as guides for accountants to follow in dealing with new and different types of transactions. This problem has occurred because the principles are intended to provide general descriptions of current accounting practices. In other words, they describe what accountants currently do; they do not necessarily describe what accountants should do. Also, since these principles do not identify weaknesses in accounting practices, they do not lead to major changes or improvements in accounting practices.

In order to improve accounting practices, principles or concepts should not merely *describe* what was being done, they should *prescribe* what ought to be done to make things better.

Before we examine the concepts enunciated in the conceptual framework, we need to look more closely at the differences between descriptive and prescriptive uses of accounting concepts.

LO 1 Explain the difference between descriptive concepts and prescriptive concepts.

The Processes of Developing Descriptive and Prescriptive Accounting Concepts

Sets of concepts differ in how they are developed and used. In general, when concepts are intended to describe current practice, they are developed by looking at accepted specific practices, and then making some general rules to encompass them. This bottom-up approach is diagrammed in Illustration V–1, which shows the arrows going from the practices to the concepts. The outcome of the process is a set of general rules that summarize practice and that can be used for education and for solving some new problems. For example, this approach leads to the concept that assets are recorded at cost. However, these kinds of concepts often fail to show how new problems should be solved. For example, the concept that assets are recorded at cost does not provide

ILLUSTRATION Ⅴ –1

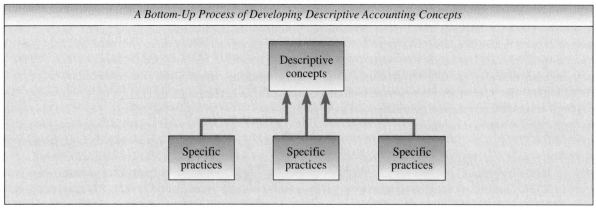

A Bottom-Up Process of Developing Descriptive Accounting Concepts

LO 2 Explain the difference between bottom-up and top-down approaches to the development of accounting concepts.

much direct guidance for situations in which assets have no cost because they are donated to a company by a local government. Further, because these concepts are based on the presumption that current practices are adequate, they do not lead to the development of new and improved accounting methods. To continue the example, the concept that assets are initially recorded at cost does not encourage asking the question of whether they should always be carried at that amount.

In contrast, if concepts are intended to *prescribe* improvements in accounting practices, they are likely to be designed by a top-down approach (Illustration V–2). Note that the top-down approach starts with broad accounting objectives. The process then generates broad concepts about the types of information that should be reported. Finally, these concepts should lead to specific practices that ought to be used. The advantage of this approach is that the concepts are good for solving new problems and evaluating old answers; its disadvantage is that the concepts may not be very descriptive of current practice. In fact, the suggested practices may not be in current use.

Since the AcSB uses accounting concepts to prescribe accounting practices, the Board uses a top-down approach to develop its conceptual framework. The Board's concepts are not necessarily more correct than the previously developed concepts. However, the new concepts are intended to provide better guidelines for developing new and improved accounting practices. The Board has stated that it will use them as a basis for its future actions, and already has used them to justify important changes in financial reporting.

The Conceptual Framework

LO 3 Describe the major components in the Accounting Standards Board's "Financial Statement Concepts."

During the 1970s the accounting profession in both Canada and the United States turned its attention to the apparent need for improvement in financial reporting. In 1980 *Corporate Reporting: Its Future Evolution,* a research study, was published by the Canadian Institute of Chartered Accountants, and in 1989 "Financial Statement Concepts," section 1000 of the *CICA Handbook,* was approved. In the United States the Financial Accounting Standards Board (FASB) published, in the 1978–85 period, six statements regarded as the most comprehensive pronouncement of the conceptual framework of accounting. FASB (*SFAC 1*) and Accounting Standards Board (*CICA Handbook,* section 1000) identified the broad objectives of financial reporting.

A Top-Down Process of Developing Prescriptive Accounting Concepts

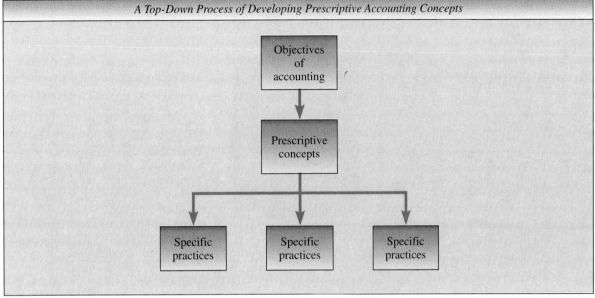

The Objectives of Financial Reporting

"Financial Statement Concepts" identified the broad objectives of financial reporting. The most general objective stated in the *CICA Handbook,* par. 1000.12, is to "communicate information that is useful to investors, creditors and other users in making resource allocation decisions and/or assessing management stewardship." From this beginning point the Accounting Standards Board (AcSB) expressed other, more specific objectives. These objectives recognize that (1) financial reporting should help users predict future cash flow and (2) in making such predictions, information about a company's resources and obligations is useful if it possesses certain qualities. All of the concepts in the "Financial Statement Concepts" are intended to be consistent with these general objectives. Of course, present accounting practice already provides information about a company's resources and obligations. Thus, although the conceptual framework is intended to be prescriptive of new and improved practices, the concepts in the framework are also descriptive of many current practices.

The Qualities of Useful Information

The AcSB discussed the fact that information can be useful only if it is understandable to users. However, the users are assumed to have the training, experience, and motivation to analyze financial reports. With this decision, the AcSB indicated that financial reporting should not try to meet the needs of unsophisticated or other casual report users.

The AcSB said that information is useful if it is (1) relevant, (2) reliable, and (3) comparable. Information is *relevant* if it can make a difference in a decision. Information has this quality when it helps users either predict the

Irene M. Gordon, CGA

Ms. Gordon received a B.A. in economics and commerce and both an M.A. and a Ph.D. in economics at Simon Fraser University, where she has been a member of the faculty of business administration since 1981. Ms. Gordon teaches financial accounting and is engaged in research in the areas of positive accounting theory, the accounting-economics interface, social responsibility accounting, and issues in accounting education. She has been a member of CGA-Canada Research Committee since 1984 and was president of the Canadian Academic Accounting Association for 1988–1989.

While my university degrees all carry economics in the title, my Ph.D. courses, thesis, and subsequent research have heavily emphasized accounting issues ranging from pensions to internal control to accounting theory. Accounting research is fundamentally interdisciplinary in character. It is this breadth of character that initially sparked my interest and has held it over time. Additionally, in a world where accounting standard setters' decisions are made which have an effect on differing cultures, societies, economic systems, and individuals, this interdisciplinary emphasis is vital. The link between the research of individual accounting academics and standard setting is both important and a "two-way street." Without continuing accounting research, the standard setting process might lack the background or new ways to view our rapidly changing world. As well this linkage gives a purpose to much of the ongoing accounting research.

future or evaluate the past, as long as it is received in time to affect their decisions.

Information is *reliable* if users can depend on it to be free from bias and error. Reliable information is verifiable and faithfully represents what is supposed to be described. In addition, users can depend on information only if it is neutral. This means that the rules used to produce information should not be designed so that they lead users to accept or reject any specific decision alternative.

Information is *comparable* if users can use it to identify differences and similarities between companies. Comparability is possible only if companies follow uniform practices. However, even if all companies uniformly follow the same practices, comparable reports do not result if the practices are not appropriate. For example, comparable information would not be provided if all companies were to ignore the useful lives of their assets and amortize all assets over two years.

Comparability also requires consistency, which means that a company should not change its accounting practices unless the change is justified as a reporting improvement. Another important principle discussed is materiality.

Elements of Financial Statements

Another important step was to determine the elements of financial statements. This involved defining the categories of information that should be contained in financial reports. The AcSB's discussion of financial statement elements includes definitions of important elements such as assets, liabilities, equity, revenues, expenses, gains, and losses. In earlier chapters we referred to many of these definitions when we explained various accounting procedures.

Recognition and Measurement

The AcSB, in paragraphs 36–47 of section 1000, established concepts for deciding (1) when items should be presented (or "recognized") in the financial statements and (2) how to assign numbers (or "measure") those items. In general, items should be recognized in the financial statements if they meet the following criteria:

1. Definitions—The item meets the definition of an element of financial statements.
2. Measurability—It has a relevant attribute measurable with sufficient reliability.
3. Relevance—The information about it is capable of making a difference in user decisions.
4. Reliability—The information is representationally faithful, verifiable, and neutral.

The question of how items should be measured raises the fundamental question of whether financial statements should be based on cost or on value. Since this question is quite controversial, the AcSB's discussion of this issue is perhaps more descriptive of current practice than it is prescriptive of new measurement methods. However, before we consider alternative accounting valuation systems, let us review and expand upon the accounting concepts or principles.

An understanding of accounting principles begins with the recognition of the broad concepts as to the nature of the economic setting in which accounting operates.

Accounting Principles

The Business Entity Principle

Every business unit or enterprise is treated in accounting as a separate entity, with the affairs of the business and those of the owner or owners being kept entirely separate.

The Going-Concern Principle

Unless there is strong evidence to the contrary, it is assumed that a business will continue to operate as a going concern, earning a reasonable profit for a period longer than the life expectancy of any of its assets.

The Time-Period Principle

The environment in which accounting operates—the business community and the government—requires that the life of a business be divided into relatively short periods and that changes be measured over these short periods. Yet, it is generally agreed that earnings cannot be measured precisely over a short period and that it is impossible to learn the exact earnings of a business until it has completed its last transaction and converted all its assets to cash.

Cost Principle

The cost principle specifies that cash-equivalent cost is the most useful basis for the initial accounting of the elements that are recorded in the accounts and reported on the financial statements. It is important to note that the cost principle applies to the initial recording of transactions and events.

The cost principle is supported by the fact that at the time of a completed arm's-length business transaction, the market value of the resources given up in the transaction provides reliable evidence of the valuation of the item acquired in the transaction.

When a noncash consideration is involved, cost is measured as the market value of the resources given or the market value of the item received, whichever is more reliably determinable. For example, an asset may be acquired with a debt given as settlement. Cost in this instance is the present value of the amount of cash to be paid in the future, as specified by the terms of the debt. The cost principle applies to all of the elements of financial statements, including liabilities.

The cost principle provides guidance at the original recognition date. However, the original cost of some items acquired is subject to depreciation, depletion, amortization, and write-down in conformity with the matching principle and the conservatism constraint (discussed in the sections that follow).

Realization or Revenue Principle

The realization or revenue principle specifies when revenue should be recognized in the accounts and reported in the financial statements. Revenue is measured as the market value of the resources received or the product or service given, whichever is the more reliably determinable.

Under the realization or revenue principle, revenue from the sale of goods is recognized according to the sales method (i.e., at the time of sale) because the earning process usually is complete at the time of sale. At that time, the relevant information about the asset inflows to the seller would be known with reliability.

Under the realization or revenue principle, revenue from the sale of services is recognized on the basis of performance because performance determines the extent to which the earning process is complete.

The realization or revenue principle requires accrual basis accounting rather than cash basis accounting for revenues. For example, completed transactions for the sale of goods or services on credit usually are recognized as revenue in the period in which the sale or service occurred rather than in the period in which the cash is eventually collected.

Matching Principle

A major objective of accounting is the determination of periodic net income by matching appropriate costs against revenues. The principle recognizes that streams of revenues continually flow into a business, and it requires (1) that there be a precise cutoff in these streams at the end of an accounting period, (2) that the inflows of the period be measured, (3) that the costs incurred in securing the inflows be determined, and (4) that the sum of the costs be deducted from the sum of the inflows to determine the period's net income.

The Objectivity Principle

The objectivity principle holds that changes in account balances should be supported to the fullest extent possible by objective evidence.

Bargained transactions supported by verifiable business documents originating outside the business are the best objective evidence obtainable, and whenever possible, accounting data should be supported by such documents.

Full-Disclosure Principle

The full-disclosure principle requires that the financial statements of a business clearly report all of the relevant information about the economic affairs of the enterprise. This principle rests upon the primary characteristic of relevance. Full disclosure requires (*a*) reporting of all information that can make a difference in a decision and (*b*) that the accounting information reported must be understandable (i.e., not susceptible to misleading inferences). Full disclosure also requires that the major accounting policies and any special accounting policies used by the company be explained in the notes to the financial statements.

The Consistency Principle

In many cases two or more methods or procedures have been derived in accounting practice to accomplish a particular accounting objective. While recognizing the validity of different methods under varying circumstances, it is still necessary, in order to ensure a high degree of comparability in any concern's accounting data, to insist on a consistent application in the company of any given accounting method, period after period. It is also necessary to insist that any departures from this doctrine of consistency be fully disclosed in the financial statements and the effects thereof on the statements be fully described.

The Principle of Conservatism

The principle of conservatism holds that the accountant should be conservative in his or her estimates and opinions and in the selection of procedures, choosing those that neither unduly understate nor overstate the situation.

The Principle of Materiality

A strict adherence to accounting principles is not required for items of little significance. Consequently, the accountant must always weigh the costs of complying with an accounting principle against the extra accuracy gained thereby, and in those situations where the cost is relatively great and the lack of compliance will have no material effect on the financial statements, compliance is not necessary.

There is no clear-cut distinction between material and immaterial items. Each situation must be individually judged, and an item is material or immaterial as it relates to other items. As a guide, the amount of an item is material if its omission, in the light of the surrounding circumstances, makes it probable that the judgment of a reasonable person would have been changed or influenced.

Implementation Constraints

Two of the principles listed, materiality and conservatism, are different from the other principles. In fact, some regard these as constraints which exert a modifying influence on financial accounting and reporting. The two other constraints are cost-benefit and industry peculiarities.

The cost of preparing and reporting accounting information should not exceed the value or usefulness of such information. Accounting focuses on usefulness and substance over form. Thus, pecularities and practices of an industry may warrant selective exceptions to accounting principles and practices. These exceptions are permitted for specific items where there is a clear precedent in the industry based on uniqueness and usefulness.

Departure from the strict application of accounting principles and concepts must be fully disclosed whether it be on the basis of (*a*) materiality, (*b*) conservatism, (*c*) cost-benefit, or (*d*) industry pecularity.

Unit-of-Measure Assumption

The unit-of-measure assumption specifies that accounting should measure and report the results of the entity's economic activities in terms of a monetary unit such as the Canadian dollar. The assumption recognizes that the monetary unit of measure is an effective means of communicating financial information. Thus, money is the common denominator—the yardstick used in accounting. Using money allows dissimilar things to be aggregated.

Unfortunately, use of a monetary unit for measurement purposes poses a dilemma. Unlike a yardstick which is always the same length, the dollar changes in value. Therefore, during times of inflation or deflation, dollars of different size are entered in the accounts and intermingled as if they possessed equal purchasing power. Because of the practice of ignoring changes in the purchasing power of a dollar, accounting implicitly assumes that the magnitude of change in the value of the monetary unit is not material. This is incorrect. The next section discusses this problem and the efforts of the accounting profession to develop alternative valuation systems that report the effects of changes in prices.

ALTERNATIVE ACCOUNTING VALUATION SYSTEMS

All accountants agree that conventional financial statements provide useful information for making economic decisions. However, many accountants also believe that conventional financial statements fail to adequately account for the impact of changing prices. Sometimes, this makes the statements misleading. That is, the statements may imply certain facts that are inconsistent with the real state of affairs. As a result, the information in the statements may lead decision makers to make decisions inconsistent with their objectives.

Conventional Financial Statements Fail to Account for Price Changes

LO 4 Explain why conventional financial statements fail to adequately account for price changes.

Failure to Account for Price Changes on the Balance Sheet

In what ways do conventional financial statements fail to account for changing prices? The general problem is that transactions are recorded in terms of the historical number of dollars paid. These amounts are not adjusted even though subsequent price changes may dramatically change the value of the purchased items. For example, Old Company purchased 10 acres of land for $25,000. Then, at the end of each accounting period, Old Company presented a balance sheet showing "Land . . . $25,000." Six years later, after price increases of 97%, New Company purchased 10 acres of land that was next to and nearly identical to Old Company's land. New Company paid $49,250 for the land. Comparing the conventional balance sheets of the two companies reveals the following balances:

	Old Company	New Company
Land	$25,000	$49,250

Without knowing the details that led to these balances, a statement reader is likely to conclude that either New Company has more land than Old Company or that New Company's land is more valuable. In reality, both companies own 10 acres that are of equal value. The entire difference between the prices paid by the two companies is explained by the 97% price increase between the two purchase dates. That is, $25,000 × 1.97 = $49,250.

Failure to Account for Price Changes on the Income Statement

The failure of conventional financial statements to adequately account for changing prices also shows up in the income statement. For example, assume that in the previous example, the companies purchased machines instead of land. Also, assume that the machines of Old Company and New Company are identical except for age; both are being amortized on a straight-line basis over a 10-year period with no salvage value. As a result, the annual income statements of the two companies show the following:

	Old Company	New Company
Amortization expense, machinery	$2,500	$4,925

Although assets of equal value are being amortized, the income statements show amortization expense for New Company that is 97% higher than Old Company's. This is inconsistent with the fact that both companies own identical machines affected by the same amortization factors. Furthermore, although Old Company appears more profitable, it must pay more income taxes due to the apparent extra profits. Also, if Old Company's selling prices are linked to its costs, it may not recover the full replacement cost of its machinery through the sale of its products.

Valuation Alternatives to Conventional Measurements of Cost

There are three basic alternatives to the historical cost measurements presented in conventional financial statements without adjustment for changing prices. These alternatives are:

1. Historical costs adjusted for changes in the general price level.
2. Current replacement cost valuations.
3. Current selling price valuations.

We discuss each of these in the remaining sections of Part V.

Adjusting Historical Costs for General Price Level Changes

LO 5 Use a price index to restate historical cost/ nominal dollar costs into constant purchasing power amounts and to calculate purchasing power gains and losses.

One alternative to conventional financial statements is to restate dollar amounts of cost incurred in earlier years to reflect changes in the general price level. In other words, a specific dollar amount of cost in a previous year can be restated as the number of dollars that would have been expended if the cost had been paid with dollars that have the current amount of purchasing power.

For example, assume the general price index shown at right for December of 1987 through 1993. Then, assume that a firm purchased assets for $1,000 in December 1987 and purchased assets for $1,500 in December 1988. The 1987 cost of $1,000 correctly states the number of monetary units (dollars) expended in 1987. Also, the 1988 cost of $1,500 correctly states the number of monetary units expended in 1988. However, in a very important way,

Year	Price Index
1987	92.5
1988	100.0
1989	109.5
1990	123.7
1991	135.0
1992	150.0
1993	168.0

the 1987 monetary units do not mean the same thing as the 1988 monetary units. A dollar (one monetary unit) in 1987 represented a different amount of purchasing power than a dollar in 1988. Both of these dollars represent different amounts of purchasing power than a dollar in 1993.

To communicate the total amount of purchasing power given up for the assets, the historical number of monetary units must be restated in dollars with the same amount of purchasing power. For example, the total amount of cost incurred during 1987 and 1988 may be stated in terms of the purchasing power

ILLUSTRATION V-3

Expressing Costs in Constant Purchasing Power

Year Cost Was Incurred	Monetary Units Expended (a)	Price Index Factor for Adjustment to 1988 Dollars (b)	Historical Cost Stated in 1988 Dollars (a × b = c)	Price Index Factor for Adjustment to 1993 Dollars (d)	Historical Cost Stated in 1993 Dollars (c × d)
1987	$1,000	100/92.5 = 1.08108	$1,081	168/100 = 1.68000	$1,816*
1988	1,500		1,500	168/100 = 1.68000	2,520
Total cost	$2,500		$2,581		$4,336

* An alternative calculation is $1,000 × (168.0/92.5) = $1,816.

of 1988 dollars or the purchasing power of 1993 dollars. These calculations are presented in Illustration V–3.

Conventional financial statements disclose revenues, expenses, assets, liabilities, and owners' equity in the historical monetary units exchanged when the transactions occurred. As such, they are sometimes called historical cost/ nominal dollar financial statements. This emphasizes the difference between conventional statements and historical cost/constant purchasing power statements. Historical cost/constant purchasing power accounting uses a general price index to restate the dollar amounts on conventional financial statements into amounts that represent current general purchasing power.

The same principles for determining amortization expense, cost of goods sold, accruals of revenue, and so forth, apply to both historical cost/nominal dollar statements and historical cost/constant purchasing power statements. The same generally accepted accounting principles apply to both. The only difference between the two is that constant purchasing power statements reflect adjustments for general price level changes, and nominal dollar statements do not.

The Impact of General Price Changes on Monetary Items

Some assets and liabilities are defined as monetary items. Monetary assets represent money or claims to receive a fixed amount of money. Monetary liabilities are obligations that are fixed in terms of the amount owed. The number of dollars to be received or paid does not change even though the purchasing power of the dollar may change. Examples of monetary items include cash, accounts receivable, accounts payable, and notes payable.

Because the amount of money that will be received or paid is fixed, a monetary item is not adjusted for general price level changes on a historical cost/constant purchasing power balance sheet. For example, assume that $800 in cash was owned at the end of 1993. Regardless of how the price level has changed since the cash was acquired, the amount to be reported on the December 31, 1993, historical cost/constant purchasing power balance sheet is $800.

Although monetary items are not adjusted on the balance sheet, they do involve special risks. When the general price level changes, monetary items create **purchasing power gains and losses.** Owning monetary assets during a period of inflation results in a loss of purchasing power. Owing monetary liabilities during a period of inflation results in a gain of purchasing power. During a period of deflation, the effects are just the opposite. Monetary assets result in purchasing power gains and monetary liabilities result in purchasing power losses.

For example, assume that a company has a cash balance of $800 on December 31, 1993, which resulted from the following:

Cash balance, December 31, 1992	$ 200
Cash receipts, assumed to have been received uniformly throughout the year	1,500
Cash disbursements, assumed to have been made uniformly throughout the year	(900)
Cash balance, December 31, 1993	$ 800

Also assume that the general price index was 150.0 at the end of 1992, that it averaged 160.0 throughout 1993, and was 168.0 at the end of that year. As the price level increased throughout 1993, the purchasing power of the cash declined. To calculate the loss during the year, the beginning cash balance and each receipt or disbursement must be adjusted for price changes to the end of the year. Then the adjusted balance is compared with the actual balance to determine the loss. The calculation is as follows:

	Nominal Dollar Amounts	Price Index Factor for Restatement to December 31, 1993	Restated to December 31, 1993	Gain or (Loss)
Beginning balance	$ 200	168.0/150.0 = 1.12000	$ 224	
Receipts	1,500	168.0/160.0 = 1.05000	1,575	
Disbursements	(900)	168.0/160.0 = 1.05000	(945)	
Ending balance, adjusted . .			$ 854	
Ending balance, actual . . .	$ 800		(800)	
Purchasing power loss. . . .				$(54)

Stated in terms of general purchasing power at year-end, the beginning cash balance plus receipts less disbursements was $854. Since the company has only $800 on hand, the $54 difference is a loss of general purchasing power.

In the preceding calculation, note that we adjusted the receipts and disbursements from the *average* price level during the year (160.0) to the ending price level (168.0). Because we assumed the receipts and disbursements occurred uniformly throughout the year, we used the average price level to approximate the price level at the time each receipt and disbursement took place. If receipts and disbursements do not occur uniformly, then we must separately adjust each receipt and each disbursement from the price level at the time of the receipt or disbursement to the price level at year-end.

The calculation of purchasing power gains and losses that result from owing monetary liabilities is the same as it is for monetary assets. Assume, for example, that a note payable for $300 was outstanding on December 31, 1992, when the price index was 150.0. On April 5, 1993, when the price index was 157.0, a $700 increase in the note resulted in a $1,000 balance that remained outstanding throughout the rest of 1993. On December 31, 1993, the price index was 168.0. On the historical cost/constant purchasing power balance sheet for December 31, 1993, the note payable is reported at $1,000. The purchasing power gain or loss during 1993 is calculated as follows:

	Nominal Dollar Amounts	Price Index Factor for Restatement to December 31, 1993	Restated to December 31, 1993	Gain or (Loss)
Beginning balance	$ 300	168.0/150.0 = 1.120	$ 336	
April 5 increase	700	168.0/157.0 = 1.070	749	
Ending balance, adjusted . .			$ 1,085	
Ending balance, actual . . .	$1,000		(1,000)	
Purchasing power gain . . .				$85

Stated in terms of general purchasing power at year-end, the amount borrowed was $1,085. Since the company can pay the note with $1,000, the $85 difference is a gain in general purchasing power earned by the firm.

To determine a company's total purchasing power gain or loss during a year, the accountant must analyze each monetary asset and each monetary liability. The final gain or loss is then described as the *purchasing power gain (or loss) on net monetary items owned or owed*.

The Impact of General Price Changes on Nonmonetary Items

Nonmonetary items include shareholders' equity and all assets and liabilities that are not fixed in terms of the number of monetary units to be received or paid. Land, equipment, intangible assets, and many product warranty liabilities are examples of nonmonetary items. The prices of **nonmonetary assets** tend to increase or decrease over time as the general price level increases or decreases. Similarly, the amounts needed to satisfy **nonmonetary liabilities** tend to change with changes in the general price level.

To reflect these changes on historical cost/constant purchasing power balance sheets, nonmonetary items are adjusted for price level changes that occur after the items were acquired. For example, assume that $500 was invested in land (a nonmonetary asset) at the end of 1987, and the investment was still held at the end of 1993. During this time, the general price index increased from 92.5 to 168.0. The historical cost/constant purchasing power balance sheets would disclose the following amounts:

ILLUSTRATION V–4

Reporting the Effects of Price Changes on Monetary and Nonmonetary Items

Financial Statement Item	When the General Price Level Rises (Inflation)		When the General Price Level Falls (Deflation)	
	Balance Sheet Adjustment Required	Income Statement Gain or Loss	Balance Sheet Adjustment Required	Income Statement Gain or Loss
Monetary assets	No	Loss	No	Gain
Nonmonetary assets	Yes	None	Yes	None
Monetary liabilities	No	Gain	No	Loss
Nonmonetary equities and liabilities . .	Yes	None	Yes	None

Asset	December 31, 1987, Historical Cost/Constant Purchasing Power Balance Sheet (a)	Price Index Factor for Adjustment to December 31, 1993 (b)	December 31, 1993, Historical Cost/Constant Purchasing Power Balance Sheet (a × b)
Land	$500	168.0/92.5 = 1.81622	$908

The $908 shown as the investment in land at the end of 1993 has the same amount of general purchasing power as $500 at the end of 1987. Thus, no change in general purchasing power is recognized from holding the land.

Illustration V–4 summarizes the impact of general price level changes on monetary and nonmonetary items. The illustration shows which items require adjustments to prepare a historical cost/constant purchasing power balance sheet. It also shows which items generate purchasing power gains and losses recognized on a constant purchasing power income statement.

Current Cost Valuations

LO 6 Explain the current cost approach to valuation, including its effects on the income statement and balance sheet.

As we said before, all prices do not change at the same rate. In fact, when the general price level is rising, some specific prices may be falling. If this were not so, if all prices changed at the same rate, then historical cost/constant purchasing power accounting would report current values on the financial statements.

For example, suppose that a company purchased land for $50,000 on January 1, 1992, when the general price index was 135.0. Then, the price level increased until December 1993, when the price index was 168.0. A historical cost/constant purchasing power balance sheet for this company on December 31, 1993, would report the land at $50,000 × 168.0/135.0 = $62,222. If all prices increased at the same rate during that period, the market value of the land would have increased from $50,000 to $62,222, and the company's historical cost/constant purchasing power balance sheet would coincidentally disclose the land at its current value.

Because all prices do not change at the same rate, however, the current value of the land may differ substantially from the historical cost/constant dollar amount of $62,222. For example, assume that the company had the land appraised and determined that its current value on December 31, 1993, was $80,000. The difference between the original purchase price of $50,000 and the current value of $80,000 is explained as follows:

Unrealized holding gain	$80,000 − $62,222 = $17,778
Adjustment for general price level increase	$62,222 − $50,000 = 12,222
Total change	$80,000 − $50,000 = $30,000

In this case, the historical cost/constant purchasing power balance sheet would report land at $62,222, which is $17,778 ($80,000 − $62,222) less than its current value. This illustrates an important fact about historical cost/constant purchasing power accounting; it does not attempt to report current value. Rather, historical cost/constant purchasing power accounting restates original transaction prices into equivalent amounts of current, *general* purchasing power. The balance sheets display current values only if current, *specific* purchasing power is the basis of valuation.

Current Costs on the Income Statement

When the current cost approach to accounting is used, the reported amount of each expense, or **current cost,** is the number of dollars that would have been needed at the time the expense was incurred to acquire the consumed resources. For example, assume that the annual sales of a company included an item sold in May for $1,500. The item had been acquired on January 1 for $500. Also, suppose that in May, at the time of the sale, the cost to replace this item was $700. Thus, the annual current cost income statement would show sales of $1,500 less cost of goods sold of $700. In other words, when an asset is acquired and then held for a time before it expires, the historical cost of the asset usually is different from its current cost at the time it expires. Current cost accounting measures the amount of expense as the cost to replace the asset at the time the asset expires or is sold.

The result of measuring expenses in current costs is that revenue is matched with the current (at the time of the sale) cost of the resources used to earn the revenue. Thus, operating profit is not greater than zero unless revenues are large enough to replace all of the resources consumed in the process of producing those revenues. Those who argue for current costs believe that operating profit measured in this fashion provides an improved basis for evaluating the effectiveness of operating activities.

Current Costs on the Balance Sheet

On the balance sheet, current cost accounting reports assets at the amounts that would have to be paid to purchase them as of the balance sheet date. Liabilities are reported at the amounts that would have to be paid to satisfy the liabilities as of the balance sheet date. Note that this valuation basis is similar to historical cost/constant purchasing power accounting in that a distinction exists between monetary and nonmonetary assets and liabilities. Monetary assets and liabilities are fixed in amount regardless of price changes. There-fore, monetary items are not adjusted for price changes. All of the nonmone-tary items, however, must be evaluated at each balance sheet date to deter-mine the best estimate of current cost.

For a moment, think about the large variety of assets reported on balance sheets. Given that there are so many different assets, you should not be sur-prised that accountants have difficulty obtaining reliable estimates of current costs. In some cases, they use price indexes that relate to specific categories of assets. Such specific price indexes may provide the most reliable source of current cost information. In other cases, when an asset is not new and has been partially amortized, its current cost can be estimated by determining the cost to acquire a similar but new asset. Amortization on the old asset is then based on the current cost of the new asset. Clearly, the accountant's professional judgment is an important factor in developing current cost data.

Current Selling Price Valuations

LO 7 Explain the current selling price approach to valuation.

In the previous discussion, you learned that conventional financial statements generally report historical costs in nominal dollars. That is, no adjustments are made for price changes. We also explained how accountants use a general price level index to adjust the nominal dollar amounts to measure the historical costs in terms of a constant purchasing power. Next, we discussed the alterna-tive of reporting current (replacement) costs in the financial statements.

The final alternative to be considered is the reporting of assets (and liabili-ties) at current selling prices. On the balance sheet, this means assets would be reported at the amounts that would be received if the assets were sold. Simi-larly, liabilities would be reported at the amounts that would have to be paid to settle or eliminate the liabilities.

The argument for reporting the current selling prices of assets is based on the idea that the alternative to owning an asset is to sell it. Thus, the sacrifice a business makes to hold an asset is the amount it would receive if the asset were sold. Further, the benefit derived from owing a liability is the amount the busi-ness avoids paying by not eliminating the liability. If these current selling prices are reported on the balance sheet, the shareholders' equity represents the net amount of cash that would be realized by liquidating the business. This net liquidation value is the amount that could be invested in other projects if the business were liquidated. Therefore, one can argue that net liquidation value is the most relevant basis for evaluating whether the income the com-pany earns is enough to justify remaining in business.

Some proponents of the current selling price approach believe that it should be applied to assets but not to liabilities. Others argue that it applies equally well to both. Still others believe that it should be applied only to assets held for sale. They would not apply it to assets held for use in the business.

A related issue is whether to report the adjustments to selling price as gains and losses in the income statement. Some businesses, especially banks, have expressed concern over the fact that reporting such gains or losses would cause large fluctuations in their reported net incomes. As an alternative to reporting the gains or losses on the income statement, they may be shown in shareholders' equity on the balance sheet as "unrealized gains and losses."

At the present time, a project is underway to evaluate the possibility of reporting the selling prices of marketable investments and marketable liabilities. A variety of individuals and groups have expressed both positive and negative opinions on the matter. The financial press describes the selling price approach to valuation as ''mark to market'' accounting.

Summary of Part V in Terms of Learning Objectives

LO 1. Some accounting concepts provide general descriptions of current accounting practices. Other concepts prescribe the practices accountants should follow. These prescriptive concepts are most useful in developing accounting procedures for new types of transactions and making improvements in accounting practice.

LO 2. A bottom-up approach to developing concepts examines current practices and then develops concepts to provide general descriptions of those practices. In contrast, a top-down approach begins by stating accounting objectives, and from there, develops concepts that prescribe the types of accounting practices accountants should follow.

LO 3. The AcSB's financial statement concepts identify the broad objectives of financial reporting and the qualitative characteristics accounting information should possess. The elements contained in financial reports are defined and the recognition and measurement criteria to be used are identified

LO 4. Conventional financial statements report transactions in the historical number of dollars received or paid. Therefore, the statements are not adjusted to reflect general price level changes or changes in the specific prices of the items reported.

LO 5. To restate a historical cost/nominal dollar cost in terms of constant purchasing power, multiply the nominal dollar cost by a factor that represents the change in the general price level since the cost was incurred. On the balance sheet, monetary assets and liabilities should not be adjusted for changes in prices. However, purchasing power gains or losses result from holding monetary assets and owing monetary liabilities during a period of general price changes.

LO 6. Current costs on the balance sheet are the dollar amounts that would be spent to purchase the assets at the balance sheet date. On the income statement, current costs are the dollar amounts that would be necessary to acquire the consumed assets on the date they were consumed.

LO 7. Reporting current selling prices of assets and liabilities is supported by those who believe the balance sheet should show the net cost of not selling the assets and settling the liabilities. Some argue for applying selling price valuations to all assets and liabilities, or to marketable investments and marketable liabilities only, or to assets only. The related gains and losses may be reported on the income statement, but some would show them as unrealized shareholders' equity items on the balance sheet.

Glossary

Current cost In general, the cost that would be required to acquire (or replace) an asset or service at the present time. On the income statement, the number of dollars that would be required, at the time the expense is incurred, to acquire the resources consumed. On the balance sheet, the amounts that would have to be paid to replace the assets or satisfy the liabilities as of the balance sheet date. pp. 747–48

Historical cost/constant purchasing power accounting an accounting system that adjusts historical cost/nominal dollar financial statements for changes in the general purchasing power of the dollar. pp. 743–46

Historical cost/nominal dollar financial statements conventional financial statements that disclose revenues, expenses, assets, liabilities, and owners' equity in terms of the historical monetary units exchanged at the time the transactions occurred. p. 743

Monetary assets money or claims to receive a fixed amount of money; the number of dollars to be received does not change regardless of changes in the purchasing power of the dollar. pp. 743–45

Monetary liabilities fixed amounts that are owed; the number of dollars to be paid does not change regardless of changes in the general price level. pp. 743–48

Nonmonetary assets assets that are not claims to a fixed number of monetary units, the prices of which therefore tend to fluctuate with changes in the general price level. p. 745

Nonmonetary liabilities obligations that are not fixed in terms of the number of monetary units needed to satisfy them, and that therefore tend to fluctuate in amount with changes in the general price level. p. 745

Purchasing power gains or losses the gains or losses that result from holding monetary assets and/or owing monetary liabilities during a period in which the general price level changes. p. 744

Synonymous Terms

Selling price valuation in accounting mark to market accounting.

Objective Review

Answers to the following questions are listed at the end of Part V. Be sure that you decide which is the one right answer to each question *before* you check the answers.

LO 1 The evolution of the conceptual framework is intended to:

a. Provide a historical analysis of accounting practice.
b. Describe current accounting practice.
c. Provide concepts that attempt to prescribe what should be done in accounting practice.
d. Describe every situation that may be encountered in accounting practice and prescribe an accounting principle for each one.
e. None of the above is correct.

LO 2 Which of the following statements is true?

a. A disadvantage of accounting concepts developed using the top-down approach is that they provide little guidance for solving new problems.

b. Gathering information from various practicing accountants and formulating accounting concepts based on current practice illustrates the use of the bottom-up developmental approach.

c. The major advantage of the top-down approach to developing new accounting concepts is that it provides a comprehensive description of current accounting practice.

d. Prescriptive concepts would most likely result from the use of the bottom-up developmental approach.

e. None of the above.

LO 3 That a business should be consistent from year to year in its accounting practices most directly relates to the concept that information reported in financial statements should be:

a. Relevant. b. Material. c. Reliable. d. Measurable. e. Comparable.

LO 4 The following selected information is from the conventional balance sheets of Company A and Company B:

	Company A	Company B
Cash	$ 24,000	$ 40,000
Equipment, net	96,000	102,200
Land	130,000	157,800
Total assets	$250,000	$300,000

Based on this information, which of the following statements is true?

a. Company B's assets are worth $50,000 more than Company A's assets.

b. Company A's assets are worth at least $16,000 less than Company B's assets.

c. If Company A and Company B own identical equipment and amortize the equipment on the same basis, Company A must have purchased its machinery at an earlier date than Company B.

d. If Company A and Company B own identical tracts of land, Company B must have purchased its land at a later date than Company A.

e. The relative values of Company A's and Company B's assets cannot be determined from this conventional balance sheet information.

LO 5 Foster Company purchased 150 acres of land for $100,000 in 1990 when the general price index was 145.0 and the specific price index for land was 142.0. In December 1993, the general price index was 150.0 and the specific price index for land was 140.0. The purchasing power gain (or loss) pertaining to land that would be reported on the 1993 historical cost/constant purchasing power income statement would be (rounded to the nearest dollar):

a. $ –0– . b. $ 3,448. c. $(3,448). d. $ 1,408. e. $(1,408).

LO 6 In the current cost approach to accounting:

a. All balance sheet items are restated to reflect general price level changes.

b. On the balance sheet, nonmonetary items are restated to reflect general price level changes.

c. On the balance sheet, monetary items are restated to reflect general price level changes.

d. Nonmonetary assets are reported at the amounts that would have to be paid to purchase them as of the balance sheet date.

e. None of the above is correct.

LO 7 If current selling price valuations were used to account for the assets and liabilities of a business:

a. Gains and losses from changing market values would not be recorded.

b. Losses from changing market values would be recorded but not gains.

c. All accountants agree that gains and losses from changes in market values would be reported on the income statement.

d. Some accountants believe that gains and losses from changes in market values should be accumulated and reported on the balance sheet as unrealized gains and losses.

e. None of the above is correct.

LO 8 Obligations that are not fixed in terms of the number of monetary units needed to satisfy them, and that therefore tend to fluctuate in amount with changes in the general price level, are called:

a. Monetary assets. *b.* Monetary liabilities. *c.* Nonmonetary assets.
d. Nonmonetary liabilities. *e.* Current liabilities.

Questions for Class Discussion

1. Why are concepts developed with a bottom-up approach less useful in leading to accounting improvements than those developed with a top-down approach?

2. What is the starting point in a top-down approach to developing accounting concepts?

3. What is the starting point in a bottom-up approach to developing accounting concepts?

4. What are the basic objectives of external financial reporting according to ''Financial Statement Concepts''?

5. What is implied by saying that financial information should have the qualitative characteristic of relevance?

6. What are the characteristics of accounting information that make it reliable?

7. Some people argue that conventional financial statements fail to adequately account for inflation. What general problem with conventional financial statements generates this argument?

8. What is the fundamental difference in the adjustments made under current cost accounting and under historical cost/constant purchasing power accounting?

9. What are historical cost/nominal dollar financial statements?

10. What is the difference between monetary and nonmonetary assets?

11. What is the difference between monetary liabilities and nonmonetary liabilities? Give examples of both.

12. If the monetary assets held by a firm exceed its monetary liabilities throughout a period in which prices are rising, which results, a purchasing power gain or loss? What if monetary liabilities exceed monetary assets during a period in which prices are falling?

13. If accountants preferred to display current values in the financial statements, would they use historical cost/constant purchasing power accounting or current cost valuations?

14. "The distinction between monetary assets and nonmonetary assets is just as important for current cost accounting as it is for historical cost/constant purchasing power accounting." Is this statement true? Why?

15. What is meant by the current selling price valuation of a liability?

Exercises

A company's plant and equipment consisted of land purchased in late 1987 for $225,000, machinery purchased in late 1989 for $85,000, and a building purchased in late 1991 for $330,000. Values of the general price index for December of 1987 through 1994 are as follows:

| 1987 . . . . | 100.0 | 1989 . . . . | 120.0 | 1991 | . . . | 150.0 | 1993 . . . . | 180.0 |
| 1988 . . . . | 112.0 | 1990 . . . . | 144.0 | 1992 . . . . | | 165.5 | 1994 . . . . | 192.0 |

Exercise V–1
Adjusting costs for historical cost/constant purchasing power statements
(LO 6)

Required

1. Assuming the preceding price index adequately represents end-of-year price levels, calculate the amount of each asset's cost that would be shown on a historical cost/constant purchasing power balance sheet for (*a*) December 31, 1993, and (*b*) December 31, 1994. Ignore any accumulated amortization.

2. Would the historical cost/constant purchasing power income statement for 1994 disclose any purchasing power gain or loss as a consequence of holding these assets? If so, how much?

Determine whether the following are monetary or nonmonetary items:

1. Wages payable. 2. Accounts payable. 3. Patents. 4. Preferred shares. 5. Product warranties liability. 6. Returnable deposits. 7. Notes receivable. 8. Prepaid rent. 9. Merchandise inventory. 10. Equipment. 11. Goodwill. 12. Retained earnings. 13. Savings accounts. 14. Prepaid insurance.

Exercise V–2
Classifying monetary and nonmonetary items
(LO 6, 7)

A company purchased land in 1991 at a cost of $245,000 and in 1992 at a cost of $120,000. What is the current cost of these land purchases in (*a*) 1993 and (*b*) 1994, given the following specific price index for land costs? (Round your answers to the nearest whole dollar.)

1991 . . . . 102.0   1992 . . . . 100.0   1993 . . . . 107.1   1994 . . . . 96.9

Exercise V–3
Calculating amounts for current cost statements
(LO 7)

Calculate the general purchasing power gain or loss in 1994 given the following price indexes: December 1993, 120.0; average during 1994, 125.0; and December 1994, 153.0

a. The cash balance on December 31, 1993, was $37,000. During 1994, cash sales occurred uniformly throughout the year and amounted to $235,500. Payments of expenses also occurred evenly throughout the year and amounted to $166,500. Accounts payable of $34,000 were paid in December.

b. Accounts payable amounted to $26,000 on December 31, 1993. Additional accounts payable amounting to $55,000 were recorded evenly throughout 1994. The only payment of accounts during the year was $34,000 in late December.

Exercise V–4
Calculating general purchasing power gain or loss
(LO 6)

Problems

Problem V–1
Adjusting costs to
historical cost/constant
purchasing power amounts
(LO 6)

Levine Supply Company purchased machinery for $237,000 on December 30, 1990. They expected the equipment to last six years and to have no salvage value; straight-line amortization was to be used. They sold the equipment on December 31, 1994, for $101,000. End-of-year general price index numbers were as follows:

1990	121.0	1992	138.2	1994	157.1
1991	135.3	1993	144.4		

Required

(Round all answers to the nearest whole dollar.)

1. What should be presented for the equipment and accumulated amortization on a historical cost/constant purchasing power balance sheet dated December 31, 1993? Hint: Amortization is the total amount of cost that has been allocated to expense. Therefore, the price index numbers used to adjust the nominal dollar cost of the asset should also be used to adjust the nominal dollar amount of amortization.

2. How much amortization expense should be shown on the historical cost/constant purchasing power income statement for 1993?

3. How much amortization expense should be shown on the historical cost/constant purchasing power income statement for 1994?

4. How much gain on the sale of equipment should be reported on the historical cost/nominal dollar income statement for 1994?

5. After adjusting the equipment's cost and accumulated amortization to the end-of-1994 price level, how much gain in (loss of) purchasing power was realized on the sale of the equipment?

Problem V–2
Calculating purchasing
power gain or loss
(LO 6)

Setlaff Printing Company had three monetary items during 1994, cash, accounts receivable, and accounts payable. The changes in these accounts during the year were as follows:

Cash:	
Beginning balance.	$ 45,250
Cash proceeds from sale of building (in	
March 1994).	25,600
Cash receipts from customers (spread evenly	
throughout the year)	179,700
Payments of accounts payable (spread evenly	
throughout the year)	(137,350)
Dividends declared and paid in June 1994.	(22,000)
Payments of other cash expenses during July 1994 . .	(38,900)
Ending balance	$ 52,300
Accounts receivable:	
Beginning balance.	$ 46,400
Sales to customers (spread evenly throughout	
the year)	187,800
Cash receipts from customers (spread evenly	
throughout the year)	(179,700)
Ending balance	$ 54,500

Accounts payable:
Beginning balance. . . . . $ 57,500
Merchandise purchases (spread evenly
   throughout the year) 115,800
Special purchase near end of December 1994 23,750
Payments of accounts payable (spread evenly
   throughout the year) . . . . (137,350)
Ending balance . . . . $ 59,700

General price index numbers at the end of 1993 and during 1994 are as follows:

Dec. 1993	. . . .	234.1	June 1994	. . . .	239.4	Avg. for 1994 . . . . 240.2	
Jan. 1994	. . . .	235.0	July 1994	. . . .	240.0		
Mar. 1994	. . . .	237.6	Dec. 1994	. . . .	245.8		

Required

Calculate the general purchasing power gain or loss experienced by Setlaff Printing Company in 1994. (Round all amounts to the nearest whole dollar.)

Suffex Corporation purchased a tract of land for $425,000 in 1987, when the general price index was 174.9. At the same time, a price index for land values in the area of Suffex's tract was 181.2. In 1988, when the general price index was 188.5 and the specific price index for land was 203.7, Suffex Corporation bought another tract of land for $320,500. In late 1994, the general price index is 242.0 and the price index for land values is 259.9.

Problem V–3
Historical cost/nominal dollars, historical cost/constant purchasing power, and current costs
(LO 5, 6, 7)

Required

1. In preparing a balance sheet at the end of 1994, show the amount that should be reported for land based on (*a*) historical cost/nominal dollars, (*b*) historical cost/constant purchasing power, and (*c*) current costs. (Round all amounts to the nearest whole dollar.)

2. In Suffex Corporation's December 1994 meeting of the board of directors, one director insists that Suffex has earned a gain in purchasing power as a result of owning the land. A second director argues that there could not have been a purchasing power gain or loss since land is a nonmonetary asset. Which director do you think is correct? Explain your answer.

Write a brief essay that explains the difference between descriptive and prescriptive concepts and that explains why the conceptual framework is designed to be prescriptive. Also discuss the question of whether specific concepts can be both descriptive and prescriptive.

Problem V–4
Analytical essay
(LO 1, 2, 3, 4)

Alternate Problems

Bolton & Sykes Corporation purchased machinery for $720,000 on December 30, 1989. They expected the equipment to last eight years and to have no salvage value; straight-line amortization was to be used. They sold the equipment on December 31, 1994, for $295,000. End-of-year general price index numbers were as follows:

Problem V–1A
Adjusting costs to historical cost/constant purchasing power amounts
(LO 6)

1989	. . . .	198.4	1991	. . . .	209.6	1993 . . . . 228.2	
1990	. . . .	202.0	1992	. . . .	220.3	1994 . . . . 234.7	

Required

(Round all answers to the nearest whole dollar.)

1. What should be presented for the equipment and accumulated amortization on a historical cost/constant purchasing power balance sheet dated December 31, 1992? *Hint:* Amortization is the total amount of cost that has been allocated to expense. Therefore, the price index numbers used to adjust the nominal dollar cost of the asset should also be used to adjust the nominal dollar amount of amortization.

2. How much amortization expense should be shown on the historical cost/constant purchasing power income statement for 1993?

3. How much amortization expense should be shown on the historical cost/constant purchasing power income statement for 1994?

4. How much gain on the sale of equipment should be reported on the historical cost/nominal dollar income statement for 1994?

5. After adjusting the equipment's cost and accumulated amortization to the end-of-1994 price level, how much gain in (loss of) general purchasing power was realized on the sale of the equipment?

Problem V–2A
Calculating purchasing
power gain or loss
(LO 6)

Pharmco, Inc., had three monetary items during 1994, cash, accounts receivable, and accounts payable. The changes in these accounts during the year were as follows:

Cash:
Beginning balance	$122,000
Cash proceeds from sale of machinery (in February 1994).	45,200
Cash receipts from customers (spread evenly throughout the year)	397,800
Payments of accounts payable (spread evenly throughout the year)	(217,200)
Payments of other cash expenses in August 1994. . .	(152,050)
Dividends declared and paid during October 1994 . .	(104,600)
Ending balance.	$ 91,150

Accounts receivable:
Beginning balance	$187,450
Sales to customers (spread evenly throughout the year)	462,500
Cash receipts from customers (spread evenly throughout the year)	(397,800)
Ending balance.	$252,150

Accounts payable:
Beginning balance	$ 91,100
Merchandise purchases (spread evenly throughout the year)	175,350
Special purchase near end of October 1994.	68,900
Payments of accounts payable (spread evenly throughout the year)	(217,200)
Ending balance.	$118,150

General price index numbers at the end of 1993 and during 1994 are as follows:

Dec. 1993	76.8	Aug. 1994	72.4	Dec. 1994	76.0
Jan. 1994	76.2	Oct. 1994	74.9	Avg. for 1994	73.3
Feb. 1994	74.7				

Required

Calculate the general purchasing power gain or loss experienced by Pharmco, Inc., in 1994. (Round all amounts to the nearest whole dollar.)

Beta Company purchased a tract of land for $78,500 in 1986, when the general price index was 100.6. At the same time, a price index for land values in the area of Beta's tract was 97.0. In 1987, when the general price index was 107.2 and the specific price index for land was 106.8, Beta Company bought another tract of land for $115,000. In late 1994, the general price index is 134.5 and the price index for land values is 127.0.

Problem V–3A
Historical cost/nominal dollars, historical cost/ constant purchasing power, and current costs (LO 1, 5, 6, 7)

Required

1. In preparing a balance sheet at the end of 1994, show the amount that should be reported based on (*a*) historical cost/nominal dollars; (*b*) historical cost/constant purchasing power; (*c*) current costs. (Round all amounts to the nearest whole dollar.)

2. In Beta Company's December 1994 meeting of the board of directors, one director insists that Beta has incurred a loss of purchasing power as a result of owning the land. A second director argues that there could not have been a purchasing power gain or loss since land is a nonmonetary asset. Which director do you think is correct? Explain your answer.

Write a brief essay that explains why a top-down approach to developing descriptive accounting concepts is not likely to be effective. Also explain why a bottom-up approach is more likely to be effective. Finally, explain why the conceptual framework reflects a top-down approach to developing concepts.

Problem V–4A
Analytical essay (LO 1, 2, 3, 4)

					Answers to Objective
LO 1 (*c*)		LO 4 (*e*)		LO 7 (*d*)	**Review Questions**
LO 2 (*e*)		LO 5 (*a*)		LO 8 (*d*)	
LO 3 (*e*)		LO 6 (*d*)			

Accounting for Corporations, Long-Term Installment Notes, and Bonds

Most students of business will at some time work for a corporation. Perhaps all students will own (either directly or indirectly through a retirement fund) some debt or share securities issued by corporations. For these reasons, you should have a basic understanding of corporations and the methods used to account for corporations and for shares and bonds.

These topics are discussed in Part VI, which consists of the following chapters:

Organization and Operation of Corporations

Business organizations that operate as corporations enjoy many advantages, including the ability to grow larger by selling stock to the public. The annual report presents accounting information that helps bridge the gap between a corporation's owners and its professional managers.

*T*here are three common types of business organizations: proprietorships, partnerships, and corporations. Corporations, however, transact more business than do the other two combined. Thus, from an overall economic point of view, corporations are clearly the most important form of business organization. As you study this chapter, you will learn how corporations are organized and operated, and some of the procedures used to account for corporations.

Learning Objectives

After studying Chapter 15, you should be able to:

1. Explain the advantages, disadvantages, and organization of corporations, and the differences in accounting for partnerships and corporations.
2. Record the issuance of no-par value shares and the issuance of par value shares.
3. Record transactions involving share subscriptions and explain the effects of subscribed shares on a corporation's assets and shareholders' equity.
4. State the differences between common and preferred shares, and allocate dividends between the common and preferred shares.
5. Explain convertible preferred shares and explain the meaning of the par, redemption, book, and market values of shares.
6. Define or explain the words and phrases listed in the chapter glossary.

Advantages of the Corporate Form

LO 1 Explain the advantages, disadvantages, and organization of corporations, and the differences in accounting for partnerships and corporations.

Corporations have become the dominant type of business because of the advantages created by the characteristics of this form of business organization. We describe these characteristics and their advantages next.

Corporations Are Separate Legal Entities

Unlike a proprietorship or partnership, a corporation is a separate legal entity. Separate and distinct from its owners, a corporation conducts its affairs with the same rights, duties, and responsibilities as a person. However, because it is not a real person, a corporation can act only through its agents, who are its officers and managers.

Shareholders Are Not Liable for the Corporation's Debts

As a separate legal entity, a corporation is responsible for its own acts and its own debts. Its shareholders are not liable for either. From the viewpoint of an investor, this lack of shareholders' liability is, perhaps, the most important advantage of the corporate form of business.

Ownership Rights of Corporations Are Easily Transferred

The ownership of a corporation is represented by shares that generally can be transferred and disposed of any time the owners wish to do so. Also, the transfer of shares from one shareholder to another usually has no effect on the corporation or its operations.[1]

Corporations Have Continuity of Life

A corporation's life may continue indefinitely because it is not tied to the physical lives of its owners. In some cases, a corporation's life may be initially limited by the laws of the jurisdiction of its incorporation. The corporation's articles of incorporation can be renewed, however, and the life extended when the stated time expires. Thus, a corporation may have a perpetual life as long as it continues to be successful.

Shareholders Do Not Have a Mutual Agency Relationship

The shareholders of a corporation do not have the mutual agency relationship that exists for partners. Thus, a shareholder who is not a manager does not have the power to bind the corporation to contracts. Instead, a shareholder's participation in the affairs of the corporation is limited to the right to vote in the shareholders' meetings. Therefore, if you become a shareholder in a corporation, you may not have to worry about the character of the other shareholders to the same extent that you would if the business were a partnership.

Ease of Capital Accumulation

Buying shares in a corporation is often more attractive to investors than investing in a partnership. Share investments are attractive because (1) shareholders are not liable for the corporation's actions and debts, (2) shares usually can be transferred easily, (3) the life of the corporation is not limited, and (4) shareholders do not have a relationship of mutual agency. These advantages make it possible for some corporations to accumulate large amounts of capital from the combined investments of many shareholders. In a sense, a corporation's capacity for raising capital is limited only by its ability to convince investors that it can use (and has used) their funds profitably. This situation is very different from the one faced by most partnerships, where mutual agency and unlimited liability reduce the number of investors who might be willing to become partners.

Governmental Regulation

Corporations are created by fulfilling the requirements of federal or provincial corporation laws. These laws subject a corporation to considerable regulation

Disadvantages of the Corporate Form

---

[1] However, a transfer of ownership can create significant effects if it brings about a change in who controls the company's activities.

and control. Single proprietorships and partnerships escape much of this regulation. In addition, they do not have to file many governmental reports required of corporations.

Taxation

As business units, corporations are subject to the same property and payroll taxes as single proprietorships and partnerships. In addition, corporations are subject to taxes that are not levied on either of the other two. The most burdensome of these are income taxes, which may amount to 50% of a corporation's pretax income. However, the tax burden does not end there. The income of a corporation is taxed *twice,* first as income of the corporation and again as personal income to the shareholders when cash is distributed to them as dividends. This differs from single proprietorships and partnerships, which are not subject to income taxes. Their income is taxed only as the personal income of their owners.

The tax situation of a corporation is generally viewed as a disadvantage. However, in some cases, it can work to the advantage of shareholders. Income taxes may be saved or at least delayed if a large amount of income is divided among two or more tax-paying entities. Thus, if an individual has a large personal income and pays taxes at a high rate, that person may benefit if some of the income is earned by a corporation that he or she owns, as long as the corporation avoids paying dividends. By not paying dividends, the corporation's income is taxed only once at the lower corporate rate, at least temporarily until dividends are paid. Additionally, the dividend tax credit gives some relief from the effects of double taxation.

Organizing a Corporation

A corporation is created by securing a certificate of incorporation or a charter from the federal or provincial government. The requirements that must be met to be incorporated vary among jurisdictions. Under the Canada Business Corporations Act, 1975, incorporation is a matter of right. One person, over 18, of sound mind, and not bankrupt, may incorporate by submitting completed articles of incorporation and other required documentation to the Director, Corporations Branch, Department of Consumer Affairs. Once the documentation is in order, the Director issues a certificate of incorporation, and a corporation comes into existence. The subscribers then purchase the corporation's shares, meet as shareholders, and elect a board of directors, who are responsible for guiding the company's business affairs.

Organization Costs

The costs of organizing a corporation, such as legal fees, promoters' fees, and amounts paid to secure articles of incorporation, are called **organization costs.** On the corporation's books, these costs are debited on incurrence to the Organization Costs account. In a sense, this intangible asset benefits the corporation throughout its life; thus, you could argue that the cost should be amortized over the life of the corporation, which may be unlimited. Nevertheless, a cor-

ILLUSTRATION 15–1

Alternative Structures of Authority in a Corporation

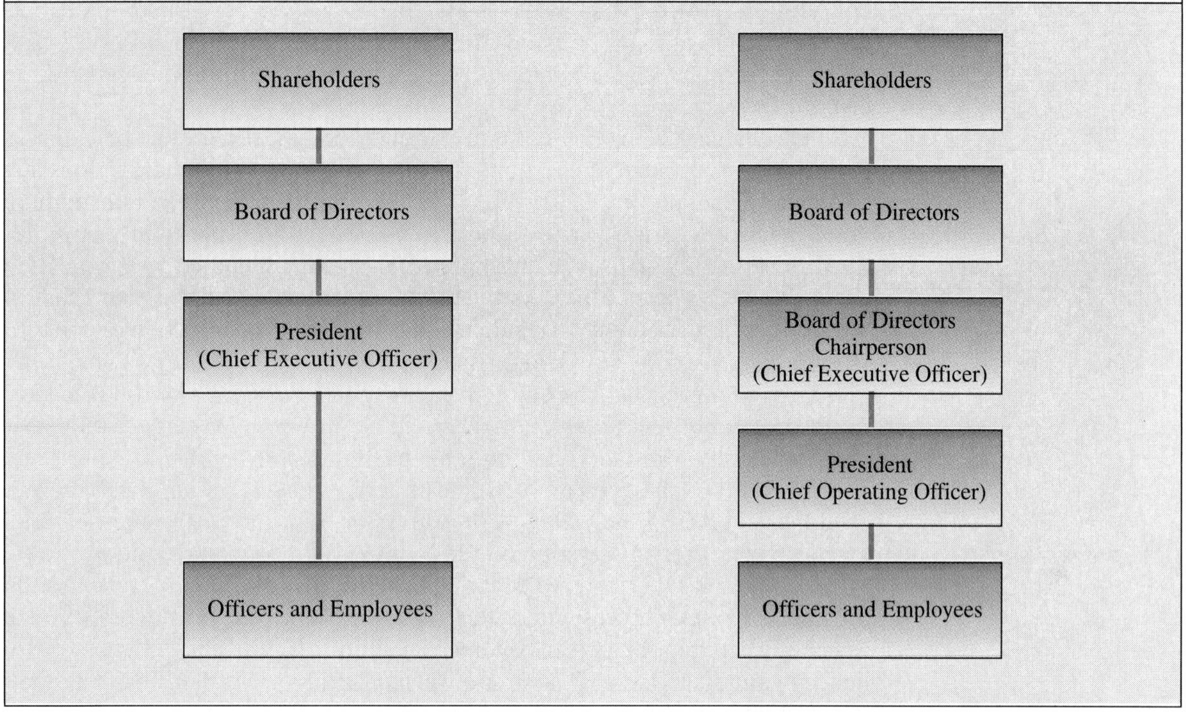

Shareholders	Shareholders
Board of Directors	Board of Directors
President (Chief Executive Officer)	Board of Directors Chairperson (Chief Executive Officer)
	President (Chief Operating Officer)
Officers and Employees	Officers and Employees

poration should make a reasonable estimate of the benefit period, which the CICA recommends should not exceed 40 years, and write off its organization costs over this period.

Although not necessarily related to the benefit period, income tax rules currently permit a corporation to write off 75% of organization costs as a tax-deductible expense at an annual 7% rate on a diminishing balance basis. Consequently, some corporations adopt the tax period over which to write off such costs. There is no theoretical justification for this, but it is widely used in practice. Also, because organization costs are usually not material in amount, the *materiality principle* supports the arbitrarily short amortization period.

Management of a Corporation

Although the organizational structures of all corporations are similar, they are not always the same. Illustration 15–1 diagrams two widely used alternatives. In all cases, the ultimate control of a corporation rests with its shareholders, but this control is exercised only indirectly through the election of the board of directors. Individual shareholders' rights to participate in management begin and end with a vote in the shareholders' meetings, where each of them has one vote for each share owned.

Normally, a corporation holds a shareholders' meeting once each year to elect directors and transact other business as required by the corporation's bylaws. A group of shareholders that owns or controls the votes of 50% plus one share of a corporation can easily elect the board and thereby control the corporation. However, in most companies, only a very few shareholders attend the annual meeting or even care about getting involved in the voting process. As a result, a much smaller percentage may be able to dominate the election of board members.

Shareholders who do not attend shareholders' meetings must be given an opportunity to delegate their voting rights to an agent. A shareholder does this by signing a document, called a **proxy,** that gives a designated agent the right to vote the shares. Prior to a shareholders' meeting, a corporation's board of directors typically mails to each shareholder an announcement of the meeting and a proxy that names the existing board chairperson as the voting agent of the shareholder. The announcement asks the shareholder to sign and return the proxy.

A corporation's board of directors is responsible for and has final authority for managing the corporation's activities. However, it can act only as a collective body. An individual director has no power to transact corporate business. Although the board has final authority, it usually limits its actions to establishing broad policy. Day-to-day direction of corporate business is delegated to executive officers appointed by the board to manage the business.

Traditionally, the chief executive officer (CEO) of the corporation is the president. Under the president, there may be several vice presidents who are assigned specific areas of management responsibility, such as finance, production, and marketing. In addition, the corporate secretary keeps the minutes of the meetings of the shareholders and directors and ensures that all legal responsibilities are fulfilled. In a small corporation, the secretary is also responsible for keeping a record of the shareholders and the transfer of shares among shareholders.

As shown on the right side of Illustration 15–1, many corporations have a different structure in which the chairperson of the board of directors also is the chief executive officer. With this arrangement, the president is usually designated the chief operating officer (COO), and the rest of the structure is essentially the same.

Share Certificates and the Transfer of Shares

When investors buy a corporation's shares, they usually receive a share certificate as proof that they purchased the shares. In many corporations, only one certificate is issued for each block of shares purchased. This certificate may be for any number of shares. For example, the certificate of Illustration 15–2 is for 50 shares. Other corporations may use preprinted certificates, each of which represents 100 shares, plus blank certificates that may be made out for any number of shares.

When selling shares of a corporation, a shareholder completes and signs a transfer endorsement on the back of the certificate and sends it to the corporation's secretary or the transfer agent. The secretary or agent cancels and files the old certificate and issues a new certificate to the new shareholder. If the old certificate represents more shares than were sold, the corporation issues two new certificates. One certificate goes to the new shareholder for the sold shares and the other to the original shareholder for the remaining unsold shares.

ILLUSTRATION 15–2

A Share Certificate

Transfer Agent and Registrar

If a corporation's shares are traded on a major stock exchange, the corporation must have a *registrar* and a *transfer agent*. The registrar keeps the shareholder records and prepares official lists of shareholders for shareholders' meetings and for dividend payments. Registrars and transfer agents usually are large banks or trust companies that have the computer facilities and staff to carry out this kind of work.

When a corporation has a transfer agent and a shareholder wants to transfer ownership of some shares to another party, the owner completes the transfer endorsement on the back of the share certificate and sends the certificate to the transfer agent, usually with the assistance of a stockbroker. The transfer agent cancels the old certificate and issues one or more new certificates and sends them to the registrar. The registrar enters the transfer in the shareholder records and sends the new certificate or certificates to the proper owners.

Corporation accounting was initially discussed in Chapter 4. In that discussion, we explained the entries to record several basic transactions of corporations. The entries included recording an issue of common shares for cash and closing a net income or a net loss from Income Summary to Retained Earnings. Also, the declaration and later payment of cash dividends were recorded. *At this point, you should review the Chapter 4 discussion of these entries on pages 199 through 201.* After completing that review, keep in mind that the

Corporation Accounting

shareholders' equity accounts of a corporation are divided into contributed capital accounts and retained earnings accounts. Also, remember that when a corporation's board of directors declares a cash dividend on the *date of declaration,* a legal liability of the corporation is incurred. The board of directors declares that on a specific future date, *the date of record,* the shareholders according to the corporation's records will be designated as those to receive the dividend. Shares purchased after the date of record are ex-dividend, that is, the purchaser is not entitled to the declared but unpaid dividend. Finally, on the *date of payment,* the liability for the declared cash dividend is paid by the corporation.

The financial statements of a corporation were first illustrated in Chapter 5. The income statement was shown in Illustration 5–2 on page 251, the retained earnings statement was shown in Illustration 5–4 on page 257, and the balance sheet was shown in Illustration 5–5 on page 257. When you review these illustrations, note that income taxes were deducted on the income statement as an expense. Recall that a business organized as a corporation must pay income taxes as a legal entity; a proprietorship or partnership does not pay income taxes, although the owners are taxed on their share of the reported incomes. Also, cash dividends to shareholders are not an expense of the corporation; they are not deducted on the income statement. Instead, dividends are a *distribution of* net income and are subtracted on the retained earnings statement. Finally, notice that the shareholders' equity in Illustration 5–4 is divided into common shares and retained earnings.

Shareholders' Equity Accounts Compared to Partnership Accounts

To demonstrate the use of separate accounts for contributed capital and retained earnings as found in corporation accounting and to contrast their use with the accounts used in partnership accounting, assume the following: On January 5, 1993, a partnership involving two partners and a corporation having five shareholders were formed. Also assume that $25,000 was invested in each. In the partnership, J. Olm invested $10,000 and A. Baker invested $15,000. In the corporation, each of the five shareholders bought 500 common shares at $10 per share. Without dates and explanations, General Journal entries to record the investments are:

Partnership			Corporation		
Cash	10,000		Cash	25,000	
J. Olm, Capital . . .		10,000	Common Shares . . .		25,000
Cash	15,000				
A. Baker, Capital . .		15,000			

After the entries are posted, the owners' equity accounts of the two companies appear as follows:

	Partnership					Corporation			
	J. Olm, Capital					Common Shares			
Date	Dr.	Cr.	Bal.		Date	Dr.	Cr.	Bal.
Jan. 5, 1993		10,000	10,000		Jan. 5, 1993		25,000	25,000

	A. Baker, Capital		
Date	Dr.	Cr.	Bal.
Jan. 5, 1993		15,000	15,000

To continue the illustration, assume that during 1993, each company earned a net income of $8,000 and also distributed $5,000 to its owners. According to the partnership agreement, incomes are allocated 40% to Olm and 60% to Baker. The cash distribution to the partners was divided equally. The corporation declared the dividends on December 20, 1993, and both companies made the cash payments to owners on December 25, 1993. The entries to record the distribution of cash to partners and the declaration and payments of dividends to shareholders are as follows:

Partnership			Corporation		
J. Olm, Withdrawals	2,500		Dividends Declared.	5,000	
A. Baker, Withdrawals . . .	2,500		Dividends Payable . . .		5,000
Cash		5,000	Dividends Payable	5,000	
			Cash		5,000

At the end of the year, the entries to close the Income Summary accounts are as follows:

Partnership			Corporation		
Income Summary.	8,000		Income Summary.	8,000	
J. Olm, Capital. . . .		3,200	Retained Earnings . . .		8,000
A. Baker, Capital . . .		4,800			

Finally, the entries to close the withdrawals accounts and the Dividends Declared account are:

Partnership			Corporation		
J. Olm, Capital	2,500		Retained Earnings	5,000	
A. Baker, Capital.	2,500		Dividends Declared . .		5,000
J. Olm, Withdrawals . .		2,500			
A. Baker, Withdrawals.		2,500			

After posting these entries, the owners' equity accounts of the two companies are as follows:

Partnership								

J. Olm, Capital

Date	Dr.	Cr.	Bal.
Jan.　5, 1993		10,000	10,000
Dec. 31, 1993		3,200	13,200
Dec. 31, 1993	2,500		10,700

Corporation

Common Shares

Date	Dr.	Cr.	Bal.
Jan.　5, 1993		25,000	25,000

A. Baker, Capital

Date	Dr.	Cr.	Bal.
Jan.　5, 1993		15,000	15,000
Dec. 31, 1993		4,800	19,800
Dec. 31, 1993	2,500		17,300

Retained Earnings

Date	Dr.	Cr.	Bal.	
Dec. 20, 1993	5,000		5,000	dr.
Dec. 31, 1993		8,000	3,000	

J. Olm, Withdrawals

Date	Dr.	Cr.	Bal.
Dec. 25, 1993	2,500		2,500
Dec. 31, 1993		2,500	–0–

Dividends Declared

Date	Dr.	Cr.	Bal.
Dec. 20, 1993	5,000		5,000
Dec. 31, 1993		5,000	–0–

A. Baker, Withdrawals

Date	Dr.	Cr.	Bal.
Dec. 25, 1993	2,500		2,500
Dec. 31, 1993		2,500	–0–

Observe that in the partnership, after all entries have been posted, the $28,000 equity of the owners appears in the capital accounts of the partners:

J. Olm, capital	$10,700
A. Baker, capital	17,300
Total owners' equity	$28,000

By comparison, the shareholders' equity of the corporation is divided between contributed capital and the Retained Earnings account, as follows:

Common shares	$25,000
Retained earnings	3,000
Total shareholders' equity	$28,000

Authorization and Issuance of Shares

When a corporation is organized, its articles authorize it to issue a desired number of shares. If all of the authorized shares have the same rights and characteristics, they are called **common shares.** However, a corporation may be authorized to issue both common and preferred shares. (We discuss preferred shares later in this chapter.) If a corporation chooses to place a limitation on the number of shares it may issue, such limitation must be stated in the articles, not in the by-laws. When a balance sheet is prepared, both the number of shares authorized and the number issued are shown.

LO 2 Record the issuance of no-par value shares.

Sale of Shares for Cash

When shares are sold for cash and immediately issued, an entry like the following is made to record the sale and issuance:

June	5	Cash	300,000.00	
		Common Shares		300,000.00
		Sold and issued 30,000 common shares at $10 per share.		

Exchanging Shares for Noncash Assets

A corporation may accept assets other than cash in exchange for its shares. In the process, the corporation also may assume some liabilities, such as a mortgage on some of the property. These transactions are recorded with an entry like this one:

June	10	Machinery.	10,000.00	
		Buildings	65,000.00	
		Land	15,000.00	
		Long-Term Notes Payable		50,000.00
		Common Shares		40,000.00
		Exchanged 4,000 common shares for machinery,		
		buildings, and land.		

A corporation also may give shares of its share capital to its promoters in exchange for their services in organizing the company. In this case, the corporation receives the intangible asset of being organized in exchange for its shares. Record this transaction as follows:

June	5	Organization Costs	5,000.00	
		Common Shares		5,000.00
		Gave the promotors 500 common shares in exchange for		
		their services in organizing the corporation.		

Usually, shares are sold for cash and immediately issued. However, corporations sometimes sell their shares through **subscriptions.** For example, when a new corporation is formed, the organizers may realize that the new business has limited immediate need for cash but will need additional cash in the future. To get the corporation started on a sound footing, the organizers may sell

Sale of Shares through Subscriptions

LO 3 Record transactions involving share subscriptions and explain the effects of subscribed shares on a corporation's assets and shareholders' equity.

shares to investors who agree to contribute some cash now and to make additional contributions in the future. When shares are sold through subscriptions, the investor agrees to buy a certain number of the shares at a specified price. The agreement also states when payments are to be made. When the subscription is accepted by the corporation, it becomes a contract and the corporation acquires an asset. The asset is the right to receive payment from subscribers. At the same time, subscribers gain an equity in the corporation.

To illustrate the sale of shares through subscriptions, assume that on May 6, Northgate Corporation accepted subscriptions to 5,000 common shares at $12 per share. The subscription contracts called for a 10% down payment to accompany the subscriptions with the balance to be paid in two equal installments due after three and six months. Northgate records the subscriptions with the following entry:

May	6	Subscriptions Receivable, Common Shares.	60,000.00	
		Common Shares Subscribed		60,000.00
		Accepted subscriptions to 5,000 common shares at $12 per share.		

At the time that subscriptions are accepted, the firm debits the Subscriptions Receivable account for the total amount of the subscription. This is the amount the subscribers agreed to pay. Notice that the **Common Shares Subscribed** account is credited for the same amount.

Later, the subscriptions receivable will be converted into cash when the subscribers pay for their shares. And when payment is completed, the subscribed shares will be issued. Receipt of the down payment and the two installment payments are recorded with these entries:

May	6	Cash	6,000.00	
		Subscriptions Receivable, Common Shares		6,000.00
		Collected 10% down payments on the common shares subscribed.		
Aug.	6	Cash	27,000.00	
		Subscriptions Receivable, Common Shares		27,000.00
		Collected the first installment payments on the common shares subscribed.		
Nov.	6	Cash	27,000.00	
		Subscriptions Receivable, Common Shares		27,000.00
		Collected the second installment payments on the common shares subscribed.		

In this case, the down payments accompanied the subscriptions. Therefore, the accountant could have combined the May 6 entries to record the receipt of the subscriptions and to record the down payments.

When shares are sold through subscriptions, the shares usually are not issued until the subscriptions are paid in full. Also, if dividends are declared before subscribed shares have been issued, the dividends go only to the holders of outstanding shares, not to the subscribed shares. However, as soon as the subscriptions are paid, the shares are issued. The entry to record the issuance of the Northgate common shares is as follows:

Aug.	5	Common Shares Subscribed	50,000.00	
		Common Shares		50,000.00
		Issued 5,000 common shares sold through subscriptions.		

Subscriptions are usually collected in full, but not always. Sometimes, a subscriber fails to pay the agreed amount. When this default happens, the subscription contract is canceled. If the subscriber has made a partial payment on the contract, the amount may be refunded. Or the company may issue a lesser number of shares. Or in some jurisdictions, the subscriber's partial payment may be kept by the corporation to compensate for damages suffered.

Subscriptions Receivable and Subscribed Shares on the Balance Sheet

Subscriptions receivable are reported on the balance sheet as current or long-term assets, depending on when collection is expected. If a corporation prepares a balance sheet after accepting subscriptions to its share capital but before the shares are issued, both the issued shares and the subscribed shares should be reported on the balance sheet as follows:

Common shares, unlimited number of shares authorized, 20,000 shares issued	$200,000
Common shares subscribed, 5,000 shares.	60,000
Total common shares issued and subscribed	$260,000

Par and No-Par Value

LO 2 Record the issuance of par value shares.

The Canada Business Corporations Act, 1975, as well as the more recently passed provincial counterparts, require that all shares be of **no-par** or nominal value. These acts also require the total consideration received by the corporation for each share issued must be added to the stated capital account maintained for the shares of that class or series. Some provinces still permit the issuance of par value shares. **Par value** is an arbitrary value a corporation places on a share of its share capital.

When a corporation issues par value shares, the par is printed on each certificate and is used in accounting for the share capital. If the shares are issued at par, the entry to record the issue is the same as if the shares were of no-par value. If, however, the shares are issued at a price above their par value, they are said to be issued at a **premium.** For example, if a corporation sells and issues its $10 par value common share capital at $12 per share, they are sold at a $2 per share premium. Although a premium is an amount in excess of par paid by purchasers of newly issued share capital, it is not considered a profit to the issuing corporation. Rather, a premium is part of the investment of shareholders who pay more than the par for the shares.

In accounting for shares sold at a premium, the premium is recorded separately from the par value shares to which it applies. For example, if a corporation sells and issues 10,000 shares of its $10 par value common shares for cash at $12 per share, the sale is recorded as follows:

Dec.	1	Cash	120,000.00	
		Common Shares		100,000.00
		Premium on Common Shares.		20,000.00
		Sold and issued 10,000 common shares of $10 par value		
		shares at $12 per share.		

When a balance sheet is prepared, the premium is disclosed under "Other Contributed Capital."

Rights of Common Shareholders

LO 4 State the differences between common and preferred shares, and allocate dividends between common and preferred shares.

When investors buy a corporation's common shares, they acquire all the *specific* rights granted by the corporation's articles to its common shareholders. They also acquire the *general* rights granted shareholders by the laws of the jurisdiction in which the company is incorporated. The laws vary, but common shareholders usually have the following general rights:

1. The right to vote at shareholders' meetings.
2. The right to sell or otherwise dispose of their shares.
3. The right to share pro rata with other common shareholders in any dividends declared.
4. The right to share equally in any assets that remain after creditors are paid when the corporation is liquidated.

In addition, if desired, the articles of incorporation may provide additional rights. For example, the articles may specifically provide for the **preemptive right,** which holds that no shares of a class shall be issued unless the shares have first been offered to the shareholders holding shares of that class, and that those shareholders have a first opportunity to acquire the offered shares in proportion to their holdings of the shares of that class, at such a price and on such terms as those shares are offered to others.

Classes of Shares

The Canada Business Corporations Act allows corporations to issue registered no-par-value shares by class and by series of the class so long as there exists one "residual" class of shares that may vote at all meetings of shareholders (except for meetings of specified classes of shareholders) and that may receive the remaining assets of a corporation upon dissolution. The act does not use the adjectives *common* and *preferred* but simply refers to shares in general. Classes of shares may continue to be designated common, preferred,

Class A, Class B, and so on; however, the act does require the articles to set out the rights, privileges, restrictions, and conditions attaching to each class and series of shares. Because of their widespread usage the terms *common* and *preferred* are used throughout this book.

Preferred Shares

As mentioned earlier in this chapter, a corporation may be authorized to issue more than one kind or class of share capital. If two classes are issued, one is generally called **preferred** and the other is called *common*.

The term *preferred* is used because the preferred shares have a higher priority (or senior status) relative to common shares in one or more ways. These typically include a preference for receiving dividends and a preference in the distribution of assets if the corporation is liquidated.

In addition to the preferences it receives, preferred share capital carries all the rights of common share capital, unless they are nullified in the articles of incorporation. For example, most preferred shares do not have the right to vote. In effect, this disadvantage is accepted in return for the preferences.

Preferred Dividends

A preference for dividends gives preferred shareholders the right to receive their dividends before the common shareholders receive a dividend. In other words, a dividend cannot be paid to common shareholders unless preferred shareholders also receive one. The amount of dividends that the preferred shareholders must receive is usually expressed as a dollar amount per share or as a percentage applied to the par value. For example, holders of 9%, $100 par value, preferred shares must be paid dividends at the rate of $9 per share per year before the common shareholders can receive any dividend. A preference for dividends does not, however, grant an absolute right to dividends. If the board of directors does not declare a dividend, neither the preferred nor the common shareholders receive one.

Cumulative and Noncumulative Preferred Shares

Preferred shares can be either **cumulative** or **noncumulative.** For cumulative, any undeclared dividends accumulate each year until they are received. For noncumulative, the right to receive dividends is forfeited in any year that the dividends are not declared.

When preferred shares are cumulative and the board of directors fails to declare a dividend to the preferred shareholders, the unpaid dividend is called a **dividend in arrears.** The accumulation of dividends in arrears on cumulative preferred shares does not guarantee that they will be paid. However, the cumulative preferred shareholders must be paid both the current dividend and all dividends in arrears before any dividend can be paid to the common shareholders.

To show the difference between cumulative and noncumulative preferred shares, assume that a corporation has outstanding 1,000 of $9 preferred shares issued at $100 per share and 4,000 common shares issued at $50 per share.

During the first two years of the corporation's operations, the board of directors declared cash dividends of $5,000 in 1993 and $42,000 in 1994. The allocations of the total dividends are as follows:

	Preferred	Common
Assuming noncumulative preferred:		
1993	$ 5,000	$ –0–
1994:		
First: current preferred dividend	$ 9,000	
Remainder to common		$33,000
* * * * *		
Assuming cumulative preferred:		
1993	$ 5,000	$ –0–
1994:		
First: dividends in arrears	$ 4,000	
Next: current preferred dividend	9,000	
Remainder to common		$29,000
Totals	$13,000	$29,000

Notice that the allocation of the 1994 dividends depends on whether the preferred shares are noncumulative or cumulative. With noncumulative preferred shares, the preferred shareholders never receive the $4,000 that was skipped in 1993. However, when the preferred shares are cumulative, the $4,000 in arrears is paid in 1994 before the common shareholders receive a dividend.

Disclosure of Dividends in Arrears in the Financial Statements

Dividends are not like interest expense, which is incurred as time passes and therefore must be accrued. A liability for a dividend does not come into existence until the dividend is declared by the board of directors. Thus, if a preferred dividend date passes and the corporation's board fails to declare the dividend on its cumulative preferred shares, the dividend in arrears is not a liability. Accordingly, it does not appear as a liability on the balance sheet. However, when preparing financial statements, the *full-disclosure principle* requires you to report the amount of preferred dividends in arrears as of the balance sheet date. Normally, this information is given in the notes to the financial statements. If there is no such disclosure, readers of the financial statements have the right to assume that preferred dividends are not in arrears.

Participating and Nonparticipating Preferred Shares

Dividends on preferred shares are generally limited each year to a stated amount or are determined by applying the preferred percentage to the par value. When preferred shares are so limited, they are called *nonparticipating preferred shares*. Most preferred shares are nonparticipating. However, holders of some preferred shares may be paid additional dividends in excess of the stated percentage or amount. Such preferred shares are called **participating preferred shares.**

Large corporations with publicly traded shares rarely issue participating preferred shares. However, smaller corporations needing to raise more capital than the organizers can provide sometimes issue these shares. If the organizers are not willing to share control, but are willing to share profits with other investors, the corporation may issue participating preferred shares that have limited voting rights.

To illustrate participating preferred shares, assume that the 1,000 shares of $9 preferred in the previous example are participating, and participation is based on an equal percentage of the average **stated** (average issue price) **value** of each class of shares. Also, assume that cash dividends of $48,000 are declared in 1995. The allocation between preferred and common shares is as follows:

	Preferred	Common
First, to preferred [9% × (1,000 × $100)]	$ 9,000	
Next, to common [9% × (4,000 × $50)]		$18,000
Remainder maintains equal percentage to preferred and common: ($48,000 − $9,000 − $18,000 = $21,000)		
$21,000 × ($100,000 ÷ $300,000)	7,000	
$21,000 × ($200,000 ÷ $300,000)		$14,000
Totals	$16,000	$32,000

Observe that the first step satisfies the preferred's right to $9 (9% of stated value) before any dividends are paid to the common shareholders. Next, the common shareholders receive 9% of stated value. Finally, any additional dividends are allocated on the basis of the relative stated value amounts outstanding. As a result, both preferred and common shares are paid the same percentage (16% of stated value in this case). This is confirmed by the following calculation:

	Total Stated Value	Total Dividend	Per cent of Stated Value
Preferred (1,000 × $100)	$100,000	$16,000	16
Common (4,000 × $50)	200,000	32,000	16
Totals.	$300,000	$48,000	16

In this example, no matter how large the total dividend might be, the preferred shares have the right to participate with common on an equal percentage basis. Therefore, the preferred shares in this example are called *fully participating preferred*. In other cases, the right to receive additional dividends beyond the basic preferred percentage is limited to a stated amount or percentage. For example, $9 preferred might have the right to participate in additional dividend declarations, up to an additional $2 per share or 2% of stated value. These types of shares are called *partially participating preferred*.

Why Preferred Shares Are Issued

A corporation might issue preferred shares for several reasons. One reason is to raise capital without sacrificing control of the corporation. For example, suppose that the organizers of a business have $100,000 cash to invest but wish to organize a corporation that needs $200,000 of capital to get off to a good start. If they sold $200,000 of common shares, they would have only 50% control and would have to negotiate extensively with the other shareholders in making policy. However, if they issue $100,000 of common to themselves and can sell to outsiders, at $100 per share, 1,000 shares of $8 cumulative preferred that have no voting rights, they retain control of the corporation.

A second reason for issuing preferred shares is to boost the return earned by the common shareholders. Using the previous example to illustrate, suppose that the corporation's organizers expect the new company to earn an annual after-tax income of $24,000. If they sell and issue $200,000 of common shares, this income produces a 12% return on the $200,000 of common shareholders' equity. However, if they sell and issue $100,000 of each kind of shares, retaining the common for themselves, their own return increases to 16% per year, as shown here:

Net after-tax income	$24,000
Less preferred dividends (1,000 × $8)	(8,000)
Balance to common shareholders (equal to 16% on their $100,000 investment)	$16,000

In this case, the common shareholders earn 16% because the assets contributed by the preferred shareholders are invested to earn $12,000 while the preferred dividend payments amount to only $8,000.

The use of preferred shares to increase the return to common shareholders is an example of **financial leverage.** Whenever the dividend rate on preferred shares is less than the rate that the corporation earns on its assets, the effect of issuing preferred shares is to increase (or *lever*) the rate earned by common shareholders. Financial leverage also occurs when debt is issued and paid an interest rate less than the rate earned from using the assets the creditors loaned to the corporation.

There are other reasons for issuing preferred shares. For example, a corporation's preferred shares may appeal to some investors who believe that its common shares are too risky or that the dividend rate on the common shares will be too low. Also, if a corporation's management wants to issue common shares but believes the current market price for the common shares is too low, the corporation may issue preferred shares that are convertible into common shares. Later, if and when the price of the common increases, the preferred shareholders can convert their shares into common shares.

As mentioned above, an issue of preferred shares can be made more attractive to some investors by giving them the right to exchange the preferred shares for a fixed number of common shares. **Convertible preferred shares** offer investors a higher potential return than do nonconvertible preferred shares. If the company prospers and its common shares increase in value, the convertible preferred shareholders can share in the prosperity by converting their preferred shares into the more valuable common shares.

To see how the conversion of preferred shares is recorded, assume that a corporation's outstanding shares include 1,000 shares of $10 convertible preferred. The shares were originally issued for $103 per share. Each preferred share is convertible into four shares of common. If all of the preferred shares are converted on May 1, the entry to record the conversion is:

May	1	Preferred Shares	103,000.00	
		Common Shares		103,000.00
		To record the conversion of preferred shares.		

When the preferred shares are converted into common shares, the balance in the preferred shares account is removed and replaced with an account balance related to common shares. No gain or loss is recorded.

In addition to a par value and average stated value, shares may have a redemption value, a market value, and a book value.

Convertible Preferred Shares

LO 5 Explain convertible preferred shares and explain the meaning of the par, redemption, book, and market values of shares.

Share Values

Redemption Value of Callable Preferred Shares

Some issues of preferred shares are callable. This means that the issuing corporation has the right to retire the **callable preferred shares** by paying a specified amount to the preferred shareholders. The amount that must be paid to call and retire a preferred share is its **call price,** or *redemption value.* This amount is set at the time the shares are issued. Normally, the call price includes the issue price of the shares plus a premium that provides the shareholders with some additional return on their investment. When the issuing corporation calls and retires preferred shares, it must pay not only the call price but also any dividends in arrears.

Market Value

The market value of a share is the price at which it can be bought or sold. Market values are influenced by a wide variety of factors, including expected future earnings, dividends, and events in the economy at large.

Book Value

The **book value of a share** is one share's portion of the corporation's net assets as recorded in its accounts. If a corporation has only common shares, divide

ILLUSTRATION 15–3

Shareholders' Equity with Preferred and Common Shares

Shareholders' Equity

Share capital:
Preferred, $7, cumulative and nonparticipating, 2,000
   shares authorized, 1,000 shares issued and outstanding $105,000
Common, no-par value, unlimited number of shares
   authorized, 10,000 shares issued and outstanding $260,000
Total contributed capital $365,000
Retained earnings   82,000
Total shareholders' equity $447,000

total shareholders' equity by the number of outstanding shares to determine book value. For example, if total shareholders' equity is $285,000 and there are 10,000 shares outstanding, the book value per share is $28.50 ($285,000/ 10,000 shares).

Computing the book values of shares is more complex when both common and preferred shares are outstanding. To calculate the book values of each class of shares, first allocate the total shareholders' equity between the two classes. The preferred shareholders' portion equals the preferred share's call price (average stated or par value if the preferred is not callable) plus any cumulative dividends in arrears. The remaining shareholders' equity is then allocated to the common shares. To determine the book value per share of preferred, divide the portion of shareholders' equity assigned to preferred by the number of preferred shares outstanding. Similarly, the book value per share of common is the shareholders' equity assigned to common divided by the number of outstanding common shares. For instance, assume a corporation has the shareholders' equity as shown in Illustration 15–3.

If the preferred shares are callable at $103 per share and two years of cumulative preferred dividends are in arrears, the book values of the corporation's shares are calculated as follows:

Total shareholders' equity.		$447,000
Less equity applicable to preferred shares:		
Redemption value	$103,000	
Cumulative dividends in arrears	14,000	(117,000)
Equity applicable to common shares		$330,000
Book value of preferred shares ($117,000/1,000) . .		$ 117.00
Book value of common shares ($330,000/10,000) . .		$ 33.00

In their annual reports to shareholders, corporations sometimes report the increase in the book value of the corporation's shares that has occurred during a year. Also, book value may have significance in contracts. For example, a shareholder may enter into a contract to sell shares at their book value at some future date. However, this agreement may not be wise because the shares are likely to have a market value that differs from its book value.

Similarly, book value should not be confused with the *liquidation value*. If a corporation is liquidated, its assets probably will sell at prices that are quite different from the amounts at which they are carried on the books.

LO 1. Advantages of the corporate form of business include the following: (*a*) status as separate legal entity, (*b*) lack of shareholder liability for the corporate debts, (*c*) a corporation's continuity of life, and (*d*) the fact shareholders are not agents of the corporation. A disadvantage is that corporations are closely regulated by government. Also, the taxable status of corporations is often a disadvantage but sometimes may be an advantage.

A corporation is governed by the shareholders through the board of directors. Officers who manage the corporation include a president, perhaps one or more vice presidents, and a secretary. The chief executive officer may be the president or the board of directors chairperson.

LO 2. When shares are issued, the par value is credited to the share capital account and any excess is credited to a separate contributed capital account. If the shares have no par value, the entire proceeds are credited to the share capital account.

LO 3. If a corporation sells shares through subscriptions, the right to receive payment is an asset of the corporation and the subscribers' equity is recorded in contributed capital accounts. The balance of the Common Shares Subscribed account is transferred to the Common Shares account when the shares are issued, which normally occurs after all payments are received.

LO 4. Preferred shares have a priority (or senior status) relative to common shares in one or more ways. Usually, this means that common shareholders cannot be paid dividends unless a specified amount of dividends is also paid to preferred shareholders. Preferred shares also may have a priority status if the corporation is liquidated. The dividend preference for many preferred shares is cumulative, and a few preferred shares also participate in dividends beyond the preferred amount.

LO 5. On the conversion of convertible preferred shares into common shares, the carrying value of the preferred shares is transferred to contributed capital accounts that relate to common shares. No gain or loss is recorded. Par value is an arbitrary amount assigned to a share when the class of shares is authorized. If preferred shares are callable, the amount that must be paid to retire the shares is its call price plus any dividends in arrears. Market value is the price that a share commands when it is bought or sold. The book value of a preferred share is any dividends in arrears plus its stated value, par value, or, if it is callable, its redemption price. The residual shareholders' equity is divided by the number of outstanding common shares to determine the book value per share of the common.

Summary of the Chapter in Terms of Learning Objectives

Demonstration Problem

Barton Corporation was created on January 1, 1993. The following transactions relating to shareholders' equity occurred during the first two years of the company's operations. Prepare the journal entries to record these transactions. Also prepare the balance sheet presentation of the organization costs, liabilities, and shareholders' equity as of December 31, 1993, and December 31, 1994. Include appropriate notes to the financial statements.

1993

Jan. 1 Authorized the issuance of unlimited number of shares of no-par-value common shares and 100,000 shares of no-par-value preferred shares. The preferred shares pay a $10 annual dividend, which is cumulative.

1 Issued 200,000 common shares at $12 per share.

1 Issued 100,000 common shares in exchange for a building valued at $820,000 and merchandise inventory valued at $380,000.

1 Accepted subscriptions for 150,000 commmon shares at $12 per share. The subscribers made no down payments, and the full purchase price was due on April 1, 1993.

1 Reimbursed the company's founders for $100,000 of organization costs, which are to be amortized over 10 years.

1 Issued 12,000 preferred shares for $110 per share.

Apr. 1 Collected the full subscription price for the January 1 common and issued the shares.

Dec. 31 The Income Summary account for 1993 had a $125,000 credit balance before being closed to Retained Earnings; no dividends were declared on either the common or preferred shares.

1994

June 4 Issued 100,000 common shares for $15 per share.

Dec. 10 Declared dividends payable on January 10, 1995, as follows:

To preferred shareholders for 1993	$120,000
To preferred shareholders for 1994	120,000
To common shareholders for 1994	300,000

31 The Income Summary account for 1994 had a $1 million credit balance before being closed to Retained Earnings.

Solution to Demonstration Problem

Planning the Solution

- Record journal entries for the events in 1993.
- Close the accounts related to retained earnings.
- Determine the balances for the 1993 balance sheet.
- Determine the following amounts to use in the balance sheet and the accompanying note:
  - *a.* The number of shares issued.
  - *b.* The amount of dividends in arrears.
  - *c.* The unamortized balance of organization costs.

- Prepare the specified portions of the 1993 balance sheet.
- Record journal entries for the events in 1994.
- Close the accounts related to retained earnings.
- Determine the balances for the 1994 balance sheet.
- Determine the following amounts to use in the balance sheet and the accompanying note:
  - *a.* The number of shares issued.
  - *b.* The unamortized balance of organization costs.
- Prepare the specified portions of the 1994 balance sheet.

1993				
Jan.	1	Cash	2,400,000.00	
		Common Shares		2,400,000.00
		Issued 200,000 common shares.		
	1	Building	820,000.00	
		Merchandise Inventory	380,000.00	
		Common Shares		1,200,000.00
		Issued 100,000 common shares.		
	1	Subscriptions Receivable	1,800,000.00	
		Common Shares Subscribed		1,800,000.00
		Accepted subscriptions for 150,000 common shares.		
	1	Organization Costs	100,000.00	
		Cash		100,000.00
		Reimbursed the founders for organization costs.		
	1	Cash	1,320,000.00	
		Preferred Shares		1,320,000.00
		Issued 12,000 preferred shares.		
Apr.	1	Cash	1,800,000.00	
		Subscriptions Receivable		1,800,000.00
		Collected balance due on subscribed common shares.		
	1	Common Shares Subscribed	1,800,000.00	
		Common Shares		1,800,000.00
		Issued 150,000 subscribed common shares.		
Dec.	31	Income Summary	125,000.00	
		Retained Earnings		125,000.00
		To close the Income Summary account and update Retained Earnings.		
1994				
June	4	Cash	1,500,000.00	
		Common Shares		1,500,000.00
		Issued 100,000 common shares.		
Dec.	10	Cash Dividends Declared	540,000.00	
		Dividends Payable, Common Shares		300,000.00
		Dividends Payable, Preferred Shares		240,000.00
		Declared current dividends and dividends in arrears to common and preferred shareholders, payable on January 10, 1995.		

Dec.	31	Income Summary	1,000,000.00	
		Retained Earnings		1,000,000.00
		To close the Income Summary account and update		
		Retained Earnings.		
	31	Retained Earnings	540,000.00	
		Cash Dividends Declared		540,000.00
		To close to Retained Earnings Cash Dividends		
		Declared.		

Balance sheet presentations:

	As of December 31	
	1993	**1994**
Assets		
Organization costs	$ 90,000	$ 80,000
Liabilities		
Dividends payable, common shares		$ 300,000
Dividends payable, preferred shares		240,000
Total liabilities		$ 540,000
Shareholders' Equity		
Share capital:		
Preferred, no par value, $10, cumulative, 100,000 shares		
authorized, 12,000 shares issued	$1,320,000	$1,320,000
Common, no par value, unlimited number of shares		
authorized, 450,000 shares issued in 1993, and 550,000		
shares in 1994	$5,400,000	$6,900,000
Total contributed capital	$6,720,000	$8,220,000
Retained earnings (see Note 1)	125,000	585,000
Total shareholders' equity	$6,845,000	$8,805,000

Note 1: As of December 31, 1993, there was $120,000 of dividends in arrears on the cumulative preferred shares.

Glossary

LO 6 Define or explain the words and phrases listed in the chapter glossary.

Book value of a share one share's portion of the issuing corporation's share capital recorded in its accounts. pp. 779–81

Call price of preferred shares another name for *redemption value*. p. 779

Callable preferred shares preferred shares that the issuing corporation, at its option, may retire by paying a specified amount (the call price) to the preferred shareholders plus any dividends in arrears. p. 779

Common shares shares of a corporation that has only one class of shares, or if there is more than one class, the class that has no preferences over the corporation's other classes of shares. p. 770

Common Shares Subscribed a shareholders' equity account in which a corporation records the par or stated value of unissued common share that investors have contracted to purchase. p. 772

Convertible preferred shares preferred shares that can be exchanged for shares of the issuing corporation's common shares at the option of the preferred shareholder. p. 779

Cumulative preferred shares preferred shares on which undeclared dividends accumulate until they are paid; common shareholders cannot receive a dividend until all cumulative dividends have been paid. p. 775

Dividend in arrears an unpaid dividend on cumulative preferred shares; it must be paid before any regular dividends on the preferred shares and before any dividends on the common shares. p. 775

Financial leverage the achievement of an increased return on common shares by paying dividends on preferred shares or interest at a rate that is less than the rate of return earned with the assets invested in the corporation by the preferred shareholders or creditors. p. 778

Noncumulative preferred shares preferred shares on which the right to receive dividends is forfeited for any year that the dividends are not declared. p. 775

No-par shares a class of shares that does not have a par value; no-par shares can be issued at any price without creating a discount liability. pp. 773–74

Organization costs the costs of bringing a corporation into existence, including legal fees, promoters' fees, and amounts paid to secure the charter. p. 764

Par value an arbitrary value assigned to a share when the shares are authorized. pp. 773–74

Participating preferred shares preferred shares that give their owners the right to share in dividends in excess of the stated percentage or amount. p. 777

Preemptive right the right of common shareholders to protect their proportionate interest in a corporation by having the first opportunity to buy additional common shares issued by the corporation. p. 774

Preferred shares shares that give their owners a priority status over common shareholders in one or more ways, such as the payment of dividends or the distribution of assets on liquidation. pp. 775–79

Premium on shares the difference between the par value of shares and its issue price when it is issued at a price above par value. pp. 773–74

Proxy a legal document that gives an agent of a shareholder the power to exercise the voting rights of that shareholder's shares. p. 766

Stated value the total proceeds of a share issue credited to the share capital account when the shares are issued. p. 777

Shares subscription a contractual commitment by an investor to purchase unissued shares and become a shareholder. pp. 771–73

Synonymous Terms

Call price redemption value.

Preferred senior status.

Subscribers incorporators; founders; promoters.

Objective Review

Answers to the following questions are listed at the end of this chapter. Be sure that you decide which is the one best answer to each question *before* you check the answers.

LO 1 An advantage of the corporate form of organization is:

a. That ownership rights are easily transferred.

b. That shareholders have a mutual agency relationship with the corporation.

c. The ease of capital assembly.

d. The lack of governmental regulation compared to single proprietorships and partnerships.

e. Both (*a*) and (*c*) are correct.

LO 2 Verde Corporation has an unlimited number of common shares authorized. The company issued 7,000 shares in exchange for some equipment valued at $105,000. (Note: the last time Verde issued shares was two years ago at $10 per share.) The entry to record the transaction would include:

a. A credit to Retained Earnings for $35,000.

b. A credit to Contributed Capital in Excess of Par Value for $35,000.

c. A debit to Equipment for $70,000.

d. A credit to Common Shares for $105,000.

e. None of the above.

LO 3 Sweeps Publishing Corporation accepted subscriptions for 9,000 common shares at $48 per share. A 10% down payment was made on the date of the subscription contract, and the balance was to be paid in full six months later. The entries to record receipt of the final balance and the issuance of the shares would include:

a. A credit to Common Shares Subscribed for $432,000.

b. A credit to Common Shares for $432,000.

c. A credit to Subscriptions Receivable, Common Shares for $432,000.

d. A debit to Subscriptions Receivable, Common Shares for $388,800.

e. None of the above.

LO 4 Bearcat Corporation has shareholders' equity as follows:

Preferred shares, $5, cumulative and nonparticipating, 10,000 shares authorized, 9,000 shares issued and outstanding . .	$ 500,000
Common shares, no-par value, 100,000 shares authorized, 27,000 shares issued and outstanding	810,000
Total contributed capital.	$1,310,000
Retained earnings	1,260,000
Total shareholders' equity.	$2,570,000

Dividends have not been declared for the past two years, but in the third year, Bearcat Corporation declared $288,000 of dividends distributable to both preferred and common shareholders. Determine the amount of dividends to be paid to the common shareholders.

a. $ 90,000.

b. $135,000.

c. $153,000.

d. $243,000.

e. $288,000.

LO 5 World Cinema Inc.'s callable preferred shares have a call price of $108 plus any dividends in arrears. The shareholders' equity of the company is as follows:

Preferred shares, $9, cumulative and nonparticipating, 5,000 shares authorized, 1,000 shares issued and outstanding (dividends are in arrears for two years) .	$ 96,000
Common shares, no-par value, 50,000 shares authorized, 12,000 shares issued and outstanding	$360,000
Total contributed capital	$456,000
Retained earnings	174,000
Total shareholders' equity.	$630,000

The book values per share of the preferred and common shares are:

a. Preferred, $126.00; common, $42.00.

b. Preferred, $96.00; common, $32.50.

c. Preferred, $90.00; common, $45.00.

d. Preferred, $108.00; common, $43.50.

e. Preferred, $114.00; common, $31.00.

LO 6 Preferred shares that can be exchanged for shares of its issuing corporation's common shares at the option of the shareholder are:

a. Participating preferred shares.

b. Noncumulative preferred shares.

c. Callable preferred shares.

d. Convertible preferred shares.

e. Cumulative preferred shares.

Questions for Class Discussion

1. What are the advantages and disadvantages of the corporate form of business organization?
2. Why is the income of a corporation said to be taxed twice?
3. Who is responsible for directing the affairs of a corporation?
4. What is a proxy?
5. What are organization costs? List several examples of these costs.
6. How are organization costs classified on the balance sheet?
7. What are the duties and responsibilities of a corporation's registrar and transfer agent?
8. List the general rights of common shareholders.
9. Laws place no limit on the amounts that partners can withdraw from a partnership. On the other hand, laws regulating corporations place definite limits on the amount of dividends that shareholders can receive from a corporation. Why do you think there is a difference?

10. What distinguishes preferred shares from common shares?

11. What is the difference between cumulative and noncumulative preferred shares?

12. What is the difference between participating and nonparticipating preferred shares?

13. What are the balance sheet classifications of these accounts: (*a*) Subscriptions Receivable, Common Shares, and (*b*) Common Shares Subscribed?

14. What is the difference between the market value and the book value of a share?

15. Why would an investor find convertible preferred shares attractive?

Mini Discussion Case

Case 15–1

James Gunn operated the Friendly Inn Motel and Restaurant as a sole proprietorship for five years. The business was successful, and he had two modest expansions since starting.

Gunn had reached a level of operation that required a major decision of sell or expand. After much deliberation and consultation with a close friend, Gunn decided to undertake a major expansion. Prior to proceeding with the expansion, he incorporated the business.

Carrying the plans for the expansion under his arm, he set out to keep an appointment with his banker. Gunn was somewhat annoyed with the banker's apparent lack of interest in the plans. It appeared to Gunn that the banker was more interested in obtaining James Gunn's and his wife's personal guarantees for the required loan than in his plans. On returning home he remarked to his wife that he couldn't understand the banker's attitude—in prior borrowings the banker had never asked for any sort of guarantees.

Required:

Discuss the banker's attitude.

Exercises

Exercise 15–1
Recording issuances of shares
(LO 2)

Prepare General Journal entries to record the following issuances of shares by three different corporations:

1. One thousand common shares are issued for $45,000 cash.

2. Two hundred common shares are issued to promoters in exchange for their efforts in organizing the corporation. The promoters' efforts are estimated to be worth $7,000.

3. Assume the same facts as in (2), except that the shares have a $20 par value.

Exercise 15–2
Comparative entries for partnership and corporation
(LO 1, 2)

Carl Tenbrink and Donna Mills began a new business on February 14 when each of them invested $125,000 in the company. On December 20, it was decided that $68,000 of the company's cash would be distributed equally between the owners. Two cheques for $34,000 were prepared and given to the owners on December 23. On December 31, the company reported a $96,000 net income.

Prepare two sets of journal entries to record the investments by the owners, the distribution of cash to the owners, the closing of the Income Summary account, and the withdrawals or dividends under these alternative assumptions: (*a*) the business is a partnership, and (*b*) the business is a corporation that issued 1,000 no-par-value common shares.

United Tire Corporation sold and issued 20,000 common shares for $840,000 on July 25. Give the entry to record the sale under each of the following independent assumptions: (*a*) the shares have no par value, (*b*) the shares have a $10 par value, and (*c*) the shares have a $20 par value.

Exercise 15–3
Accounting for par and no-par shares
(LO 2)

On May 15, Quality Dairy Corporation accepted subscriptions to 40,000 no-par-value common shares at $26.00 per share. The subscription contracts called for one fourth of the subscription price to accompany each contract as a down payment with the balance to be paid on November 15. Give the entries to record (*a*) the subscriptions, (*b*) the down payments, (*c*) receipt of the remaining amount due on the subscriptions, and (*d*) issuance of the shares.

Exercise 15–4
Share subscriptions
(LO 3)

The outstanding share capital of Cooper Realty Corporation includes 47,000 shares of $4 cumulative and nonparticipating preferred and 82,000 shares no-par value common. During its first four years of operation, the corporation declared and paid the following amounts in dividends: first year, $0; second year, $200,000; third year, $420,000; and fourth year, $200,000. Determine the total dividends paid in each year to each class of shareholders. Also determine the total dividends paid to each class over the four years.

Exercise 15–5
Allocating dividends between common and cumulative preferred shares
(LO 4)

Determine the total dividends paid in each year to each class of shareholders of the previous exercise under the assumption that the preferred shares are noncumulative. Also determine the total dividends paid to each class over the four years.

Exercise 15–6
Allocating dividends between common and noncumulative preferred shares
(LO 4)

The outstanding share capital of Chemco Corporation includes 8,000 shares of $6 cumulative and fully participating preferred shares and 16,000 shares of no-par-value common. It has regularly paid all dividends on the preferred. This year, the board of directors declared and paid a total of $96,000 in dividends to the two classes of shareholders. Determine the dividend per share to be paid to each class and the percent of average stated value to be paid to each class of shareholders. The preferred was issued at $100 per share and common at $10 per share.

Exercise 15–7
Allocating dividends between common and participating preferred shares
(LO 4)

Four individuals have agreed to begin a new business requiring a total investment of $600,000. Each of the four will contribute $100,000, and the remaining $200,000 will be raised from other investors. Two alternative plans for raising the money are being considered: (1) issue 6,000 common shares at $100 to all investors, or (2) issue 4,000 common shares at $100 to the four founders and 2,000 shares at $100, $7, cumulative and

Exercise 15–8
Effect of preferred shares on rates of return
(LO 4)

nonparticipating preferred to the remaining investors. If the business is expected to earn an after-tax net income of $84,000, what rate of return will the founders earn under each alternative? Which of the two plans will provide the higher return to the four founders?

Exercise 15–9
Effect of preferred shares
on rates of return
(LO 4)

How would your answers to Exercise 15–8 be changed if the business is expected to earn an after-tax net income of only $36,000?

Exercise 15–10
Convertible preferred
shares
(LO 5)

Camden Corporation has 8,000 outstanding shares of $8 preferred that is convertible into the corporation's no-par common at the rate of 5 shares of common for 1 share of preferred. The preferred shares were issued at $126 per share. Assume that all shares are presented for conversion.

Longview Manufacturing Corporation has issued 16,000 shares of $50 preferred at $500 per share. Each preferred share is convertible into 40 shares of the corporation's no-par-value common. Assume that one fourth of the convertible preferred shares were presented for conversion.

Present entries dated March 2 to record the conversions on the books of the two corporations.

Exercise 15–11
Per share book value
(LO 5)

The shareholders' equity section from HeadStart Software Corporation's balance sheet is as follows:

Shareholders' Equity

Share capital:
Preferred share capital, $8, cumulative and nonparticipating,
$110 call price, 6,000 shares issued and outstanding. . . . . . . $ 600,000
Common, no par value, 120,000 shares issued and outstanding . . 1,200,000
Retained earnings 780,000
Total shareholders' equity $2,580,000

Required

1. Determine the book value per share of the preferred and of the common under the assumption that there are no dividends in arrears on the preferred shares.

2. Determine the book value per share for each class of shares under the assumption that two years' dividends are in arrears on the preferred shares.

Problems

Problem 15–1
Share subscriptions
(LO 2, 3, 4)

Micron Corporation is authorized to issue 60,000 shares of $4 cumulative and nonparticipating preferred and an unlimited number of no-par-value common shares. Micron Corporation then completed these transactions:

July 6 Accepted subscriptions to 80,000 common shares at $18 per share. Down payments equal to 25% of the subscription price accompanied each subscription. The balance is due on August 10.

July   20   Gave the corporation's promoters 2,000 common shares for their services in getting the corporation organized. The board valued the services at $35,000.

Aug.   4   Accepted subscriptions to 6,000 shares of preferred at $65 per share. The subscriptions were accompanied by 50% down payments. The balance is due on September 5.

       10   Collected the balance due on the July 6 common subscriptions and issued the shares.

       30   Accepted subscriptions to 1,000 shares of preferred at $62 per share. The subscriptions were accompanied by 50% down payments. The balance is due on October 30.

Sept. 5   Collected the balance due on the August 4 preferred subscriptions and issued the shares.

Required

1. Prepare General Journal entries to record the transactions.
2. Prepare the shareholders' equity section of the corporation's balance sheet as of the close of business on September 30. Assume that retained earnings are $60,000.

Solar Energy Company is authorized to issue an unlimited number of common shares and 100,000 shares of $10, noncumulative and nonparticipating, convertible preferred. The company completed the following transactions:

Problem 15–2
Shareholders' equity transactions
(LO 2, 3, 4, 5)

1992

Feb.   5   Issued 70,000 common shares at $10 for cash.

       28   Gave the corporation's promoters 3,750 common shares for their services in organizing the corporation. The directors valued the services at $40,000.

Mar.   3   Issued 44,000 common shares in exchange for the following assets with the indicated reliable market values: land, $80,000; buildings, $210,000; and machinery, $155,000.

Dec. 31   Closed the Income Summary account. A $27,000 loss was incurred.

1993

Jan. 28   Issued 4,000 preferred shares at $100 for cash.

Dec. 15   Solar Energy Company's preferred shareholders submitted 2,500 of their convertible shares for conversion into common shares on this date. The convertible preferred shareholders accepted nine common shares for each preferred share.

      31   Closed the Income Summary account. A $98,000 net income was earned.

1994

Jan.   1   The board of directors declared a $10 cash dividend to preferred shares and $0.20 per share cash dividend to outstanding common shares, payable on February 5 to the January 24 shareholders of record.

Feb.   5   Paid the previously declared dividends.

Oct. 20   Accepted subscriptions to 4,000 common shares at $14.90 per share. Down payments of 40% accompanied the subscription contracts. The balance is due on January 20, 1995.

Dec. 31   Closed the Cash Dividends Declared and Income Summary accounts. A
$159,000 net income was earned.

Required

1. Prepare General Journal entries to record the transactions.
2. Prepare the shareholders' equity section of the balance sheet as of the close of
business on December 31, 1994.

Problem 15–3
Calculating book values;
allocating dividends
between preferred and
common shares
(LO 4, 5)

Part 1. The balance sheet of Desktop Services Corporation includes the following information:

Shareholders' Equity

Share capital:	
Preferred $8, cumulative and nonparticipating, 2,500 shares	
authorized and issued	$250,000
Common, no-par value, 40,000 shares authorized and issued . .	400,000
Retained earnings	192,500
Total shareholders' equity	$842,500

Required

Assume that the preferred has a call price of $105 plus any dividends in arrears. Calcu-
late the book value per share of the preferred and common under each of the following
assumptions:

a.   There are no dividends in arrears on the preferred.
b.   One year's dividends are in arrears on the preferred.
c.   Three years' dividends are in arrears on the preferred.

Part 2. Since its organization, TVP Corporation has had 14,000 outstanding shares of
$11 preferred and 235,000 shares of no-par-value common. No dividends have been
paid this year, and none were paid during either of the past two years. However, the
company has recently prospered, and the board of directors wants to know how much
cash would be required to provide a $1.50 per share dividend on the common. Preferred
was issued at $100 per share and the common at $10 per share.

Required

Prepare a schedule that shows the amounts of cash required for dividends to each class
of shareholders to provide the desired $1.50 per share dividend to the common share-
holders under each of the following assumptions:

a.   The preferred is noncumulative and nonparticipating.
b.   The preferred is cumulative and nonparticipating.
c.   The preferred is cumulative and fully participating based on stated value.
d.   The preferred is cumulative and participating to 14% based on stated value.

Problem 15–4
Allocating dividends in
sequential years between
preferred and common
shares
(LO 4)

Alphalon Cookware Company has 4,000 outstanding shares of $8 preferred and 56,000
shares of no-par-value common. During a seven-year period, the company paid out the
following amounts in dividends:

1990	. . . .	$ –0–
1991	. . . .	46,000
1992	. . . .	–0–
1993	. . . .	60,000
1994	. . . .	74,000
1995	. . . .	68,400
1996	. . . .	144,000

No dividends were in arrears for the years prior to 1990.

Required

1. Prepare three schedules with column headings as follows:

Year	Calculations	Preferred Dividend per Share	Common Dividend per Share

2. Complete schedules under each of the following assumptions. (Round your answers to the nearest cent.) Preferred was issued at $100 per share and common at $10 per share.
    a. The preferred is noncumulative and nonparticipating.
    b. The preferred is cumulative and nonparticipating.
    c. The preferred is cumulative and fully participating based on percentage of stated value.

Simplex Clock Corporation's common shares are selling on a stock exchange today at $16.45 per share, and a just-published balance sheet shows the following information about the shareholders' equity of the corporation:

Problem 15–5
Calculation of book values
(LO 5)

Shareholders' Equity

Share capital:
Preferred, $7.50, cumulative and nonparticipating, 3,000 shares
    authorized and outstanding . . . . $ 300,000
Common, no par value, 75,000 shares authorized and outstanding . .   750,000
Retained earnings   375,000
Total shareholders' equity $1,425,000

Required

Answer these questions: (1) What is the market value of the corporation's common shares? (2) If there are no dividends in arrears, what are the book values of (*a*) the preferred shares and (*b*) the common shares? (3) If two years' dividends are in arrears on the preferred shares, what are the book values of (*a*) the preferred shares and (*b*) the common shares? (Assume that the preferred is not callable.)

Daphne Thomas and Elizabeth White want to go into business as special event promoters. Both can contribute fairly large amounts of capital, but they will need to acquire additional equity capital from other investors in about a year. Thomas has the expertise to run the business, and White will handle the administrative details. They plan to hire about three employees initially and will distribute all profits annually. White wants to operate as a general partnership, but Thomas thinks they should form a corporation. Thomas asks you to write a brief essay supporting her view in favour of the corporate form. What would you include in your essay to convince White that a corporation would be preferable to a partnership in their situation?

Problem 15–6
Analytical essay
(LO 1)

Refer to the shareholders' equity section of the balance sheet in Problem 15–3. Assume, however, that an unlimited number of common shares are authorized instead of 40,000. Also, assume that the preferred is convertible into common at a rate of eight common shares for each share of preferred. If 1,000 shares of the preferred are converted into common, describe how this affects the shareholders' equity section of the balance sheet (immediately after the conversion). If you are a common shareholder in

Problem 15–7
Analytical essay
(LO 4, 5)

this company, and the company plans to pay total cash dividends of $300,000, does it make any difference to you whether or not the conversion takes place before the dividend declaration? Why?

Alternate Problems

Problem 15–1A
Share subscriptions
(LO 2, 3, 4)

Conran Corporation is authorized to issue 50,000 shares of $9 cumulative and nonparticipating preferred and an unlimited number of no-par-value common shares. Conran Corporation then completed these transactions:

Apr. 4   Accepted subscriptions to 65,000 common shares at $17 per share. Down payments equal to 25% of the subscription price accompanied each subscription. The balance is due on June 3.

      11   Gave the corporation's promoters 1,300 common shares for their services in organizing the corporation. The board valued the services at $26,000.

May   1   Accepted subscriptions to 5,000 preferred shares at $120 per share. The subscriptions were accompanied by 40% down payments. The balance is due on July 31.

June 3   Collected the balance due on the April 4 common subscriptions and issued the shares.

July 1   Accepted subscriptions to 2,000 preferred shares at $122 per share. The subscriptions were accompanied by 40% down payments. The balance is due on August 15.

      31   Collected the balance due on the May 1 preferred subscriptions and issued the shares.

Required

1. Prepare General Journal entries to record the transactions.
2. Prepare the shareholders' equity section of the corporation's balance sheet as of the close of business on July 31. Assume that retained earnings are $23,000.

Problem 15–2A
Shareholders' equity transactions
(LO 2, 3, 4, 5)

Coach Motor Company is authorized by its articles of incorporation to issue an unlimited number of common shares and 50,000 shares of $10, noncumulative and nonparticipating, convertible preferred. The company completed the following transactions:

1992

Feb.   2   Issued for cash 110,000 common shares at $1 per share.

      28   Gave the corporation's promoters 65,000 common shares for their services in organizing the corporation. The directors valued the services at $80,000.

Mar. 10   Issued 150,000 common shares in exchange for the following assets with the indicated reliable market values: land, $70,000; buildings, $130,000; and machinery, $89,000.

Dec. 31   Closed the Income Summary account. A $61,000 loss was incurred.

1993

Jan.   1   Issued for cash 6,000 preferred shares at $100 per share.

Dec.   1   Coach Motor Company's preferred shareholders submitted 750 shares of their convertible preferred for conversion into common shares on this date. The convertible preferred shareholders accepted 70 common shares for each share of preferred.

      31   Closed the Income Summary account. A $196,000 net income was earned.

1994

Jan.   1   The board of directors declared a $10 cash dividend to preferred shares and $0.20 per share cash dividend to outstanding common shares, payable on January 25 to the January 15 shareholders of record.

      25   Paid the previously declared dividends.

Nov. 15   Accepted subscriptions to 30,000 common shares at $3.20 per share. Down payments of 25% accompanied the subscription contracts. The balance is due on February 15, 1995.

Dec. 31   Closed the Cash Dividends Declared and Income Summary accounts. A $262,000 net income was earned.

Required

1. Prepare General Journal entries to record the transactions.
2. Prepare the shareholders' equity section of the balance sheet as of the close of business on December 31, 1994.

Part 1. The balance sheet of Global Filter Company includes the following information:

Problem 15–3A
Calculating book values; allocating dividends between preferred and common shares
(LO 4, 5)

Shareholders' Equity

Share capital:

Preferred, $11, cumulative and nonparticipating, 2,000 shares authorized and issued	$200,000
Common, no-par value, 60,000 shares authorized and issued . . .	600,000
Retained earnings	120,000
Total shareholders' equity	$920,000

Required

Assume that the preferred shares have a call price of $106 plus any dividends in arrears. Calculate the book value per share of the preferred and common under each of the following assumptions:

a. No dividends are in arrears on the preferred shares.

b. One year's dividends are in arrears on the preferred shares.

c. Three years' dividends are in arrears on the preferred shares.

Part 2. Since its organization, Newhouse Corporation has had 3,200 outstanding shares of $11 preferred and 64,000 shares of no-par-value common. No dividends have been paid this year, and none were paid during either of the past two years. However, the company has recently prospered and the board of directors wants to know how much cash would be required to provide a $1.50 per share dividend on the common. The preferred was issued at $100 per share and the common at $10 per share.

Required

Prepare a schedule that shows the amounts of cash required for dividends to each class of shareholders to provide the desired $1.50 per share dividend under each of the following assumptions:

a. The preferred is noncumulative and nonparticipating.

b. The preferred is cumulative and nonparticipating.

c. The preferred is cumulative and fully participating based on stated value.

d. The preferred is cumulative and participating to 13% of stated value.

Problem 15–4A
Allocating dividends in sequential years between preferred and common shares (LO 4)

Oxford Bros. Company has 2,000 outstanding shares of $12 preferred and 30,000 shares of no-par-value common. During a seven-year period, the company paid out the following amounts in dividends:

1990	$ –0–
1991	54,000
1992	–0–
1993	30,000
1994	39,000
1995	48,000
1996	90,000

No dividends were in arrears for the years prior to 1990.

Required

1. Prepare three schedules with column headings as follows:

Year	Calculations	Preferred Dividend per Share	Common Dividend per Share

2. Complete a schedule under each of the following assumptions. (Round your calculations of dividends per share to the nearest cent.) The preferred was issued at $100 per share and common at $10 per share.

a. The preferred is noncumulative and nonparticipating.

b. The preferred is cumulative and nonparticipating.

c. The preferred is cumulative and fully participating based on a percentage of stated value.

Problem 15–5A
Calculation of book values (LO 5)

Denver Plastics Corporation's common shares are selling on a stock exchange today at $12.80 per share, and a just-published balance sheet shows the following information about the shareholders' equity of the corporation:

Shareholders' Equity

Share capital:	
Preferred, $10.50, cumulative and nonparticipating,	
7,800 shares authorized and outstanding.	$ 780,000
Common, no par value, 165,000 shares authorized and	
outstanding	1,650,000
Retained earnings	330,000
Total shareholders' equity	$2,760,000

Required

Answer these questions: (1) What is the market value of the corporation's common shares? (2) If there are no dividends in arrears, what are the book values of (a) the preferred shares and (b) the common shares? (3) If two years' dividends are in arrears on the preferred, what are the book values of (a) the preferred shares and (b) the common shares? (Assume that the preferred shares are not callable.)

Daphne Thomas and Elizabeth White want to go into business as special-event promoters. Both can contribute fairly large amounts of capital, but they will need to acquire additional cash in about a year. Thomas has the expertise to run the business, and White will handle the administrative details. They plan to hire about three employees initially and will distribute all profits annually. White wants to operate as a partnership, but Thomas thinks they should form a corporation. White asks you to write a brief essay supporting her view in favour of the partnership form. What would you include in your essay to convince Thomas that a partnership might be preferable to a corporation in their situation?

Problem 15–6A
Analytical essay
(LO 1)

Refer to the shareholders' equity section of the balance sheet in Problem 15–3A. Assume, however, that the common has 100,000 shares authorized instead of 60,000. Also, assume that the preferred shares are convertible into common at a rate of eight common shares for each share of preferred. If 1,000 shares of the preferred are converted into common shares, describe how this affects the shareholders' equity section of the balance sheet (immediately after the conversion). If you are a common shareholder in this company, and cash dividends of $487,000 are to be paid out, does it make any difference to you whether or not the conversion takes place? Why?

Problem 15–7A
Analytical essay
(LO 4, 5)

Provocative Problems

Kara McLeod and Erin Morris have operated a clothing and tailoring company, M&M Fashions, for a number of years as partners sharing net incomes and losses in a three-to-two ratio. That is, McLeod gets three fifths (60%) while Morris gets two fifths (40%). Because the business is growing, the two partners entered into an agreement with Michael Lyon that includes converting their partnership into a corporation. The new corporation, M&M Fashions, Inc., is authorized to issue 65,000 shares of no-par-value common shares. On the date of the incorporation, July 31, 1993, a trial balance of the partnership ledger appears as follows:

Provocative Problem 15–1
M&M Fashions, Inc.
(LO 2)

M&M FASHIONS
Trial Balance
July 31, 1993

Cash	$ 26,600	
Accounts receivable	45,600	
Allowance for doubtful accounts		$ 1,450
Merchandise inventory	359,640	
Store equipment	91,100	
Accumulated amortization, store equipment		27,330
Buildings	410,000	
Accumulated amortization, buildings		123,000
Land	160,000	
Accounts payable		49,400
Notes payable		389,200
Kara McLeod, capital		288,800
Erin Morris, capital		213,760
Totals	$1,092,940	$1,092,940

The agreement between the partners and Lyon includes these provisions:

1. The partnership assets are to be revalued to reflect the following items. Changes in asset values should be allocated to the partners' capital accounts according to their income and loss ratio.

    a. The $1,100 account receivable of John O'Connell is known to be uncollectible and is to be written off as a bad debt.

    b. After writing off the O'Connell account, the allowance for doubtful accounts is to be increased to 4% of the remaining accounts receivable.

    c. The merchandise inventory is to be written down to $342,140 to allow for damaged and shopworn goods.

    d. Insufficient amortization has been taken on the store equipment. Therefore, its book value is to be decreased to $45,550 by increasing the balance of the accumulated amortization account.

    e. The building is to be written up to its replacement cost, $492,000, and the balance of the accumulated amortization account is to be increased to show the building to be three-tenths amortized.

2. After the partnership assets are revalued, the assets and liabilities are to be transferred to the corporation in exchange for its shares, with each partner accepting shares at $10 per share for her equity in the partnership.

3. Michael Lyon is to buy any remaining authorized shares for cash at $10 per share.

    When this agreement was finalized, you were hired as the accountant for the new corporation. Your first job is to determine the number of shares that each person should receive, and to prepare entries on the corporation's books to record the issuance of the shares in exchange for the partnership assets and liabilities and the issuance of the shares to Lyon for cash. In addition, prepare a balance sheet for the corporation as it should appear after all the adjustments have been recorded and the shares issued.

Provocative Problem 15–2
Sonora Corporation
(LO 4)

The management of Sonora Corporation is considering expanding its operations into an additional innovative line of business. It is expected that assets invested in this expansion can earn a rate of return of 20% per year. At present, Sonora Corporation's outstanding share capital includes only 40,000 shares of no-par-value common, issued at $20 each. There are no other contributed capital accounts, and retained earnings equal $385,000. Existing operations consistently earn approximately $210,000 each year. To finance the expansion, management is considering three alternatives:

    a. Issue 6,000 of $12, cumulative, nonparticipating, nonvoting preferred shares. Investment advisors for the company have concluded that these shares could be issued at $100 per share.

    b. Issue 3,000 of $12, cumulative, fully participating, nonvoting preferred shares. The investment advisors have concluded that these shares could be sold for $200 per share.

    c. Issue 15,000 common shares at $40 per share.

    In evaluating these three alternatives, Sonora Corporation management has asked you to calculate the dividends that would be distributed to each class of shareholder, assuming that the board of directors declares dividends each year equal to the total net income earned by the corporation. Your calculations should show the distribution of dividends to preferred and common shareholders under each of the three alternative financing plans. Also calculate dividends per share of preferred and dividends per share of common.

    As a second part of your analysis, assume that you own 1,500 of the common shares outstanding prior to the expansion and that you will not acquire or purchase any of the newly issued shares. Based on your analysis, would you prefer that the proposed expansion in operations be rejected? If not, comment on the relative merits of each alternative from your point of view as a common shareholder.

Having received a $150,000 lump sum of severance pay, Tom Campbell is thinking about investing the money in one of two securities: Tricom Corporation common or the preferred issued by Beltline Company. The companies manufacture competing products, and both have been in business about the same length of time—five years for Tricom and six years for Beltline. Also, the two companies have about the same amounts of shareholders' equity, as shown here:

Tricom Corporation

Share capital:
Common, 1 million shares authorized,
    400,000 shares issued $2,000,000
Retained earnings   900,000
Total shareholders' equity $2,900,000

Beltline Company

Share capital:
Preferred, $10, cumulative and nonparticipating,
    10,000 shares authorized and issued $1,000,000*
Common, no par value, 150,000 shares authorized
    and issued 1,500,000
Retained earnings   130,000
Total shareholders' equity $2,630,000

* The current and one prior year's dividends are in arrears on the preferred shares.

    Tricom did not pay a dividend on its common shares during its first year's operations; however, in each of the past four years, it has paid a cash dividend of $0.25 per share. The shares are currently selling for $7.75 per share. In contrast, the preferred shares of Beltline Company are selling for $96 per share. Campbell has told you that he favours these shares as an investment. He feels that they are a bargain because they are selling not only $4 below average stated value but also $24 below book value, and as he says, "The dividends are guaranteed because it is preferred share capital." He also believes that the common shares of Tricom are overpriced at 7% above book value and 55% above average stated value, while paying only a $0.25 per share dividend.

a. Are the preferred shares of Beltline Company actually selling at a price $24 below book value, and are the common shares of Tricom Corporation actually selling at a price 7% above book value and 55% above average stated value?

b. From an analysis of the shareholders' equity sections, express your opinion of the preferred and common as investments and describe some of the factors that Campbell should consider in choosing between the two.

Use the information provided in the financial statements of Bombardier Inc. and the notes (see Appendix I) to answer the following questions:

1. Does it appear that Bombardier has been authorized to issue any preferred shares? If so, are any outstanding as of January 31, 1992?

2. How many common shares have been authorized? How many shares are outstanding as of January 31, 1992?

3. What is the par value of the common shares? What is the total book value of both classes of common shares at January 31, 1992?

4. Are any common shares subscribed?

5. What was the highest market value of class A shares during 1992? What was the lowest?

6. What was the total amount of dividends paid to all classes of shares during 1992? During 1991?

Analytical and Review Problems

A&R Problems 15-1

Until March 2 of the current year, Knox, Lacy, and Mann were partners sharing losses and gains in a 4:4:2 ratio. On that date they received their certificate of incorporation of KLM Company, Limited. All the assets and liabilities of the partnership were taken over by the new corporation.

The trial balance of the partnership just before the transfer and the opening trial balance of the corporation appear below:

KNOX, LACY AND MANN
Post-Closing Trial Balance
March 2, 19—

Cash	$ 4,500	
Accounts receivable	20,500	
Allowance for doubtful accounts		$ 500
Merchandise inventory.	33,000	
Store equipment	13,500	
Accumulated amortization, store equipment.		3,500
Land	8,500	
Building	65,000	
Accumulated amortization, building		9,500
Accounts payable		15,500
Mortgage payable		12,000
John Knox, capital.		45,000
Robert Lacy, capital		40,000
George Mann, capital		19,000
	$145,000	$145,000

KLM COMPANY, LIMITED
Trial Balance
March 2, 19—

Cash	$ 4,500	
Accounts receivable	20,500	
Allowance for doubtful accounts		$ 1,500
Merchandise inventory.	25,000	
Store equipment	8,000	
Land	22,000	
Building	52,000	
Accounts payable		15,500
Mortgage payable		12,000
Share capital, common, no par value, 10,300 shares . .		103,000
	$132,000	$132,000

Required

How many shares did each shareholder receive? Support your answer.

A&R Problem 15-2

During the first year after incorporation, the following common share transactions were completed:

a. Immediately after incorporation sold 50,000 shares at $30 per share for cash.

b. Near mid-year received a subscription for 1,000 shares at $40 per share, collected 50% in cash, balance due in two equal installments within one year.

c. Two months later issued 500 shares for a used machine that would be used in operations. The machine had cost $20,000 new and was carried by the seller at a book value of $13,000. It was appraised at $21,000 six months previously by a reputable independent appraiser.

d. Collected half of the unpaid subscriptions in (*b*).

Required

Give entries for each of the above transactions.

The following was reported by the *Globe and Mail,* October 14, 1992, page 1:

Company directors charged

MONTREAL—In an unprecedented move, the federal government is prosecuting five directors of a chemical company, charging that their work endangered fish in the St. Lawrence River. Robert Dubé, a lawyer at Environment Canada, said five senior officials of Tioxide Canada Inc. of Tracy, Que., were charged yesterday with violating, between Oct. 15 and 20, 1991, a section of the Fisheries Act that makes it illegal to "deposit or permit the deposit of a deleterious substance . . . in water frequented by fish." Each director is liable to a fine of up to $1-million, and repeat offenders could face up to three years in jail.

Required

Corporation statutes grant limited liability to shareholders of a corporation. However, the directors do not appear to have the same protection with regard to certain acts of the corporation. Do you believe this is a double standard? Explain.

LO 1	(*e*)	LO 3	(*b*)	LO 5	(*a*)
LO 2	(*d*)	LO 4	(*c*)	LO 6	(*d*)

Answers to Objective Review Questions

Additional Corporate Transactions, Reporting of Income and Retained Earnings, and Earnings per Share

Astonishing growth of global markets is leading even small companies to customers and investors in other countries. In addition, today's complex world requires complex financial structures. In many cases, parent corporations control subsidiaries operating in different industries, provinces, or countries.

W̲ e begin this chapter with a discussion of dividends and other transactions between a corporation and its shareholders. In this section of the chapter, you will learn about stock dividends, stock splits, and repurchases of shares by the issuing corporation. The second section of the chapter explains how income and retained earnings information is classified and reported. The third section explains how accountants report the earnings per share of a corporation. Understanding these topics will help you interpret and evaluate corporate financial statements. Note: use of the term *shares* rather than *stock* is preferred in Canada, but in the case of dividends in shares of the issuing corporation, *stock dividend* is normally used instead of *share dividend*. Also, the terms *stock split, stock option,* and *treasury stock* are in common usage.

Learning Objectives

After studying Chapter 16, you should be able to:

1. Record cash dividends, stock dividends, and stock splits and explain their effects on the assets and shareholders' equity of a corporation.
2. Record retirement of shares and describe their effects on shareholders' equity.
3. Describe restrictions and appropriations of retained earnings and the disclosure of such items in the financial statements.
4. Explain how the income effects of discontinued operations, extraordinary items, changes in accounting principles, and prior period adjustments are reported.
5. Calculate earnings per share for companies with simple capital structures and explain the difference between basic and fully diluted earnings per share.
6. Record the purchases and sales of treasury shares (Appendix F).
7. Define or explain the words and phrases listed in the chapter glossary.

CORPORATE DIVIDENDS AND OTHER SHARE CAPITAL TRANSACTIONS

In Chapter 3, we first described a corporation's retained earnings as the total amount of its net incomes less its net losses and dividends declared since it began operations. Years ago, retained earnings were commonly called **earned surplus.** However, the term is rarely used anymore.

Retained Earnings and Dividends

Most jurisdictions require that a corporation not pay cash dividends unless retained earnings are available. However, the payment of a cash dividend reduces both cash and shareholders' equity. Therefore, a corporation cannot pay a cash dividend simply because it has a credit balance in Retained Earnings; it also must have enough cash on hand to pay the dividend. If cash or assets that will shortly become cash are not available, the board of directors may choose to avoid a dividend declaration even though the Retained Earnings balance is adequate. Even if a corporation has a large Retained Earnings balance, the board of directors may refuse to declare a dividend because the available cash is needed in the operations of the business.

In deciding whether to declare dividends, the board of directors must recognize that operating activities are a source of cash. Perhaps some cash from operating activities should be paid out in dividends and some should be retained for emergencies. In addition, some cash may be retained to pay dividends in years when current operating activities do not generate enough cash to pay normal dividends. Furthermore, management may want to retain some cash from operating activities to finance expanded operations. See page 769 for a discussion of entries for the declaration and distribution of a cash dividend.

As was noted in Chapter 15, shareholders enjoy limited liability. Consequently, corporation laws provide for the protection of creditors and others dependent on the continuity of the corporation. To this end, the more recently passed corporations acts include a solvency test. For example, the Canada Business Corporation Act 1975 provides the following in section 40:

> A corporation shall not declare or pay a dividend if there are responsible grounds for believing that
> (*a*) the corporation is, or would after the payment be, unable to pay its liabilities as they become due; or
> (*b*) the realizable value of the corporation's assets would thereby be less than the aggregate of its liabilities and stated capital of all classes.

Entries for the declaration and distribution of a cash dividend were presented earlier and need not be repeated here. It should be noted that asset distributions in excess of a credit balance in Retained Earnings are liquidating dividends—a return of original investment.

Stock Dividends

Sometimes, a corporation distributes its own unissued shares to its shareholders without receiving any consideration from the shareholders. This type of distribution is called a stock dividend. A stock dividend and a cash dividend are very different. A cash dividend transfers assets from the corporation to the shareholders. As a result, a cash dividend reduces the corporation's assets and its shareholders' equity. On the other hand, a stock dividend does not transfer assets from the corporation to the shareholders; it has no effect on assets and no effect on total shareholders' equity.

However, a stock dividend does have an effect on the components of shareholders' equity. To record a stock dividend, you must transfer some of the Retained Earnings balance to contributed capital accounts. For example, assume that Northwest Corporation's shareholders' equity is as follows:

LO 1 Record cash dividends, stock dividends, and stock splits and explain their effects on the assets and shareholders' equity of a corporation.

Shareholder's Equity

Share capital:	
Common shares, no-par value, unlimited number of shares authorized, 10,000 shares issued and outstanding	$108,000
Retained earnings	35,000
Total shareholders' equity	$143,000

On December 31, the directors of Northwest Corporation declared a 10% or 1,000-share stock dividend distributable on January 20 to the shareholders of record on January 15.

If the market value of Northwest Corporation's shares on December 31 is $15 per share, the dividend declaration is recorded as follows:

Dec.	31	Stock Dividends Declared.	15,000.00	
		Common Stock Dividend Distributables		15,000.00
		To record the declaration of a 1,000-share common stock dividend.		

Note that the debit is to Stock Dividends Declared. In previous chapters, when we discussed cash dividends, they were debited to Dividends Declared. However, since a corporation may declare stock dividends as well as cash dividends, a convenient system of accounts would include separate Cash Dividends Declared and Stock Dividends Declared accounts.

In the year-end closing process, close the Stock Dividends Declared account to Retained Earnings as follows:

Dec.	31	Retained Earnings	15,000.00	
		Stock Dividends Declared		15,000.00

On January 20 record the distribution of the shares as follows:

Jan.	20	Common Stock Dividend Distributable	15,000.00	
		Common Shares		15,000.00
		To record the distribution of 1,000 common shares.		

Note that these entries shift $15,000 of the shareholders' equity from retained earnings to contributed capital, or in other words, $15,000 of retained earnings is *capitalized*. Note also that the amount of retained earnings capitalized is equal to the market value of the 1,000 shares issued ($15 × 1,000 shares = $15,000).[1]

---

[1] The Canada Business Corporations Act requires that the value of a stock dividend be added to the stated capital account. In other jurisdictions, for example, Ontario, the amount to be capitalized is left to the board of directors.

ILLUSTRATION 16–1

The Effect of Northwest Corporation's Stock Dividend on Shareholders

Before the 10% stock dividend:

Share capital:

Common shares (10,000 shares)	$108,000
Retained earnings	35,000
Total contributed and retained capital	$143,000

$143,000/10,000 shares outstanding = $14.30 per share book value.
Book value of Johnson's 100 shares: $14.30 × 100 = $1,430.

After the 10% stock dividend is distributed:

Share capital:

Common shares (11,000 shares)	$123,000
Retained earnings	20,000
Total contributed and retained capital	$143,000

$143,000/11,000 shares outstanding = $13 per share book value.
Book value of Johnson's 110 shares: $13 × 110 = $1,430.

As you already learned, a stock dividend does not distribute assets to the shareholders; it has no effect on the corporation's assets. Also, it has no effect on total shareholders' equity and no effect on the percentage of the company owned by each individual shareholder. To illustrate these last points, assume that Johnson owned 100 shares of Northwest Corporation's outstanding shares prior to the stock dividend. The 10% stock dividend gave each shareholder 1 new share for each 10 shares previously held. Therefore, Johnson received 10 new shares.

Illustration 16–1 shows Northwest Corporation's total contributed and retained capital and the book value of Johnson's 100 shares before the dividend and after the dividend.

Illustration 16–1 shows that before the stock dividend, Johnson owned 100/10,000, or 1/100, of the Northwest Corporation shares, and his holdings had a $1,430 book value. After the dividend, he owns 110/11,000, or 1/100, of the corporation, and his holdings still have a $1,430 book value. In other words, there was no effect on Johnson's investment except that it was repackaged from 100 units into 110. Also, the only effect on the corporation's capital was a transfer of $15,000 from retained earnings to contributed capital. To summarize, there was no change in the corporation's total assets, no change in its total capital or equity, and no change in the percentage of that equity owned by Johnson.

Why Stock Dividends Are Distributed

If stock dividends have no effect on corporation assets and shareholders' equities other than to repackage the equities into more units, why are such dividends declared and distributed? The primary reason for stock dividends is related to the market price of a corporation's common shares. For example, if a profitable corporation grows by retaining earnings, the price of its common shares also tends to grow. Eventually, the price of a share may become high enough to discourage some investors from buying the shares. Thus, the corporation may declare stock dividends to keep the price of its shares from increasing too much. Yet another reason normally cited by management is to preserve cash. For these reasons, some corporations declare stock dividends each year.

Some shareholders may like stock dividends for another reason. Often, corporations that declare stock dividends continue to pay the same cash dividend per share after a stock dividend as before. The result is that shareholders receive more cash each time dividends are declared.

Amount of Retained Earnings Capitalized

If a corporation declares a stock dividend, the Canada Business Act requires that the corporation capitalize an amount of retained earnings that equals the market value of the shares to be distributed. A requirement to capitalize a specified amount of retained earnings is without justification. If the board of directors can decide the amount of cash dividends, then the power to decide the amount of retained earnings to be capitalized should also be left to their discretion. The authors therefore believe that the provision of the Ontario Corporations Act is correct. That is, the board of directors decides the amount of retained earnings to be capitalized. In the meantime, since there is not consistency in corporate laws in the amount of retained earnings to be capitalized, corporations must observe the requirements of the laws of the jurisdiction of incorporation.

Stock Dividends on the Balance Sheet

Since a stock dividend is "payable" in shares rather than in assets, it is not a liability of its issuing corporation. Therefore, if a balance sheet is prepared between the declaration and distribution dates of a stock dividend, the amount of the dividend distributable should appear on the balance sheet in the shareholders' equity section, as follows:

Share Capital:	
Common shares, no-par value, unlimited number of shares authorized, shares issued and outstanding	$108,000
Common stock dividend distributable, 1,000 shares	15,000
Total common shares issued and to be issued	$123,000
Retained earnings	20,000
Total shareholders' equity	$143,000

Stock Splits

Sometimes, when a corporation's shares are selling at a high price, the corporation calls it in and issues two, three, or more new shares in the place of each previously outstanding share. For example, a corporation that has shares selling for $375 a share may call in the old shares and issue to the shareholders 4 shares, 10 shares, or any number of shares in exchange for each share formerly held. In the case of par value shares, the par value of the new shares is propor-

AS A MATTER OF

Ethics

Falcon Corporation's board of directors and officers have been meeting to discuss and plan the agenda for the corporation's 1994 annual shareholders' meeting. The first item considered by the directors and officers was whether to report a large government contract that Falcon has just obtained. Although this contract will significantly increase income and cash flows in 1994 and beyond, management decided that there is no need to reveal the news at the shareholders' meeting. "After all," one officer said, "the meeting is intended to be the forum for describing the past year's activities, not the plans for the next year."

After concluding that the contract will not be mentioned, the group has moved on to the next topic for the shareholders' meeting. This topic is a motion for the shareholders to approve a compensation plan that will award the managers the rights to acquire large quantities of shares over the next several years. According to the plan, the managers will have a three-year option to buy shares at a fixed price that equals the market value of the shares as mea-sured 30 days after the upcoming shareholders' meeting. In other words, the managers will be able to buy shares in 1995, 1996, or 1997 by paying the 1994 market value. Obviously, if the shares increase in value over the next several years, the managers will realize large profits without having to invest any cash. The financial vice president asks the group whether they should reconsider the decision about the government contract in light of its possible relevance to the vote on the stock option plan.

tionately reduced. This is known as a **stock split.** The usual purpose of a stock split is to reduce the market price of the shares and thereby facilitate trading in the shares. Less frequently, a corporation may have a **reverse stock split.** In that case the corporation calls in the old shares and issues 1 new share for each 2 shares, 3 shares, 10 shares, or any number of shares previously held. The usual purpose of a reverse stock split is to cause an increase in the per share market value.

A stock split (or reverse split) has no effect on total shareholders' equity, and no effect on the equities of the individual shareholders. Also, the balances of the Contributed Capital and Retained Earnings accounts are not changed. Thus, a stock split (or reverse split) does not require a journal entry. All that is required is a memorandum entry in the share capital account reciting the facts of the split. For example, such a memorandum might read, "Issued 10 new common shares for each old share previously outstanding." When you prepare the balance sheet, the new number of shares outstanding must be used.

Retirement of Share Capital

Under the Canada Business Corporations Act, as well as under the more recently passed provincial acts, for example, Ontario, a corporation may purchase and retire shares of its own outstanding share capital if it can satisfy a solvency test applicable to cash dividends and cited earlier in this chapter.

When shares are purchased for retirement, the debit to the stated capital account is the product of the number of shares acquired multiplied by the weighted average per share invested by the shareholders. If the shares are purchased for less than the weighted average per share invested by the share-

LO 2 Record retirement of shares and describe their effects on shareholders' equity.

holders, the difference is credited to an account such as Contributed Capital from Retirement of Shares. On the other hand, if the shares are purchased for more than the weighted average per share invested by the shareholders, the difference is debited to contributed capital from previous credit balances of share retirement transactions to the extent of its balance with any remainder debited to Retained Earnings.

For example, assume a corporation originally issued its no-par-value common shares at an average price of $12 per share. If the corporation later purchased and retired 1,000 of these shares at the price for which they were issued, the entry to record the retirement is:

Apr.	12	Common Shares	12,000.00	
		Cash		12,000.00
		Purchased and retired 1,000 common shares at $12		
		per share.		

On the other hand, if the corporation paid $11 per share instead of $12, the entry for the retirement is:

Apr.	12	Common Shares	12,000.00	
		Cash		11,000.00
		Contributed Capital from the		
		Retirement of Common Shares		1,000.00
		Purchased and retired 1,000 common shares at $11		
		per share.		

If the corporation paid $15 per share, the entry for the purchase and retirement is:

Apr.	12	Common Shares	12,000.00	
		Retained Earnings	3,000.00	
		Cash		15,000.00
		Purchased and retired 1,000 common shares at $15		
		per share.		

In jurisdictions which have par values when such shares are reqcquired for cancelation, all capital items related to the shares being retired are removed from the accounts, and the difference between the purchase price and the weighted average per share invested by the shareholders is treated in a like manner to that illustrated above for no-par-value shares. In addition to the entry to record the reacquisition of shares, corporate statutes require the corporation to restrict or appropriate retained earnings equal to the cost of the reacquired shares. This requirement is based on a view that the reacquisition of shares has the same impact as the payment of a cash dividend. The restriction may be accomplished by a note (cross-referenced to the balance sheet) or by a journal entry such as the following:

Retained Earnings	12,000	
Restricted Retained Earnings—Reacquisition		
of Shares		12,000

A corporation may voluntarily designate an amount of retained earnings for some special purpose as a means of explaining to shareholders why dividends are not being declared. In contrast to retained earnings, which carry binding restrictions by law or by contract, **appropriated retained earnings** result from a voluntary action by the board of directors. In earlier years, such appropriations were recorded by transferring portions of retained earnings from the Retained Earnings account to another shareholders' equity account such as Retained Earnings Appropriated for Contingencies or Retained Earnings Appropriated for Plant Expansion. When the contingency or other reason for an appropriation was passed, the appropriation account was eliminated by returning its balance to the Retained Earnings account.

Voluntary Appropriations of Retained Earnings

LO 3 Describe restrictions and appropriations of retained earnings and the disclosure of such items in the financial statements.

REPORTING OF INCOME AND RETAINED EARNINGS INFORMATION

When the revenue and expense transactions of a company consist of routine, continuing operations, the company's single-step income statement shows revenues followed by a list of operating expenses and finally by net income. Often, however, the activities of a business include items not closely related to its continuing operations. In these cases, the income effects of such items should be separated from the revenues and expenses of continuing operations. Otherwise, the income statement fails to provide readers with clear information about the results of business activities.

To see how various income statement items should be classified, look at Illustration 16–2. Observe that the income statement is separated into four sections labeled 1 through 4. The first portion of the income statement (the portion labeled as 1) shows the revenues, expenses, and income generated by the company's continuing operations. This portion looks just like the single-step income statement we first discussed in Chapter 5. The next income statement section, labeled 2, relates to discontinued operations.

Income Statement Items Not Related to Continuing Operations

LO 4 Explain how the income effects of discontinued operations, extraordinary items, changes in accounting principles, and prior period adjustments are reported.

Large companies often have several different lines of business operations or have several different classes of customers. A company's operations that involve a particular line of business or class of customers may qualify as a **segment of the business.** To qualify as a segment of a business, the assets, activities, and financial results of operations involving a particular line of business or class of customers must be distinguished from other parts of the business.

Discontinued Operations

ILLUSTRATION 16–2

Income Statement for a Corporation

CONNELLY CORPORATION
Income Statement
For Year Ended December 31, 1993

1	Net sales		$8,443,000
	Gain on sale of old equipment		30,000
	Total		$8,473,000
	Costs and expenses:		
	Cost of goods sold	$5,950,000	
	Amortization expense	35,000	
	Other selling, general, and administrative expenses	515,000	
	Interest expense	20,000	
	Income taxes	792,000	(7,312,000)
	Unusual loss on sale of surplus land		(45,000)
	Infrequent gain on relocation of a plant		72,000
	Income from continuing operations		$1,188,000
2	**Discontinued operations:**		
	Income from operation of discontinued Division A		
	(net of $166,000 income taxes)	$ 400,000	
	Loss on disposal of Division A (net of $60,000 tax		
	benefit)	(150,000)	250,000
	Income before extraordinary items and cumulative		
	effect of a change in accounting principle		$1,438,000
3	**Extraordinary items:**		
	Gain on sale of unused land expropriated by the		
	state for a highway interchange (net of $35,000		
	income taxes)	$ 142,500	
	Loss from earthquake damage (net of $310,000		
	income taxes)	(670,000)	(527,500)
	Net income		$ 910,500
4	**Earnings per common share** (250,000 shares outstanding):		
	Income from continuing operations		$4.75
	Discontinued operations		1.00
	Extraordinary items		(2.11)
	Net income		$3.64

Separating Discontinued Operations on the Income Statement

Normally, the revenues and expenses of all business segments are added together and reported as the continuing operations of the business (as in section 1 of Illustration 16–2). However, when a business sells or disposes of a business segment, the results of that segment's operations must be separated and reported as you see in section 2 of Illustration 16–2. In the illustration, the results of the discontinued operations are completely separated from the results of other activities. This separation makes it easier for financial statement readers to evaluate the continuing operations of the business.

Separating the Results of Operating a Segment That Is Being Discontinued from the Gain or Loss on Disposal

Within section 2 of Illustration 16–2, note that the income from *operating* Division A (the operation that is being discontinued) during the period is reported separately from the loss on the final *disposal* of Division A. Also, the income tax effects of the discontinued operations are separated from the income tax expense shown in section 1 of Illustration 16–2. Thus, the results of the discontinued operations are reported net of tax. Also, the amount of tax or tax benefit related to each item is disclosed. Similarly, unusual items, items that do not qualify as extraordinary, should be reported separately. For example, an actual statement is presented in Illustration 16–3 which discloses separately an unusual item—write-down of oil and gas properties.

The above discussion summarizes the method of *reporting* the results of discontinued operations and unusual items on the income statement. The detailed requirements for *measuring* the income or losses of dicontinued operations are discussed in a more advanced accounting course.

Extraordinary Items

Section 3 of the income statement in Illustration 16–2 reports gains and losses that are extraordinary. The *CICA Handbook*[2] identifies extraordinary items as items which result from transactions or events that have all of the following characteristics: (*a*) they are not expected to occur frequently over several years, (*b*) they do not typify the normal business activities of the entity, and (*c*) they do not depend primarily on decisions or determinations by management or owners. Thus, the essential characteristics of extraordinary items are that they are infrequent and atypical, and they result primarily from nonmanagement decisions. Examples are government expropriation of property or natural disasters. Gains or losses resulting from the risks inherent in an entity's normal business activities, such as losses on accounts receivable or inventories and gains and losses on disposals of long-term assets, would not be considered extraordinary.

Each extraordinary item should be disclosed separately and adequately described to allow users of the financial statements to understand the nature of the transactions or events and the extent to which income has been affected.

Prior Period Adjustments

Prior period adjustments are accounted for and reported as direct charges (or credits, including disclosure of the applicable income tax) to Retained Earnings: they cause the opening balance of retained earnings to be restated. To qualify as prior period adjustments, items must be rare in occurrence and must meet the specific criteria set out in paragraphs 3600.02–.03 of the *CICA Handbook*. Settlement of lawsuits arising in prior periods and one-time income tax settlement are normally the only items that qualify as prior period adjustments.

---

[2] *CICA Handbook*, section 3480.

ILLUSTRATION 16–3

CANADA NORTHWEST ENERGY LIMITED
Consolidated Statement of Earnings and Retained Earnings
For Year Ended September 30, 1988
(With Comparative Figures for Year Ended September 30, 1987)
(In thousands of dollars except per share amounts)

	1988	1987
Revenue:		
Gross oil and gas sales	$ 107,736	$ 86,217
Less: Royalties—Crown and other	10,267	9,367
Net oil and gas sales	97,469	76,850
Other income (Note 6)	14,780	13,208
	112,249	90,058
Expenses:		
Operating	27,220	16,794
General and administrative (Note 2)	11,361	10,112
Interest on long-term debt (Note 2)	14,759	1,603
Depletion and depreciation	49,768	29,468
	103,108	57,977
	9,141	32,081
Earnings before the following:		
Income and other taxes:		
Current	6,387	7,061
Deferred	(199)	6,944
Provincial government royalty tax credits	(3,000)	(2,072)
	3,188	11,933
Earnings before unusual item	5,953	20,148
Unusual item (Note 10)	(118,000)	
Net earnings (loss)	(112,047)	20,148
Preferred share dividends	11,031	10,366
Net earnings (loss) attributable to common shares . .	(123,078)	9,782
Retained earnings, beginning of year	162,099	19,317
Reduction of stated capital (Note 5)		133,000
Retained earnings, end of year	$ 39,021	$ 162,099
Information per common share:		
Average number of common shares outstanding .	19,445,976	19,244,792
Earnings (loss) before unusual item	$ (0.26)	$ 0.51
Net earnings (loss) after unusual item	$ (6.32)	$ 0.51

Notes to Consolidated Financial Statements

10   Unusual Items

Write-down of oil and gas properties net of deferred
   income taxes of $8,800 . . . . $118,000

Future net revenues have been calculated based on average prices for the two months ended September 30, 1988, without escalation or discounting. If prices in effect at the Company's year-end had been used, the write-down of oil and gas properties, net of deferred income taxes of $8,800, would have been $186,000. If the average price for the year had been used, the write-down net of deferred income taxes of $2,000 would have been $22,000.

ILLUSTRATION 16–4

Single-Year Statement of Retained Earnings

CONNELLY CORPORATION
Statement of Retained Earnings
For Year Ended December 31, 1994

Retained earnings, January 1, 1994.	$4,745,000
Prior period adjustment for accounting error:	
Cost of the land that was incorrectly charged to expense	
(net of $60,000 income taxes)	130,000
Retained earnings, January 1, 1994, as restated	$4,875,000
Plus net income.	937,500
Less cash dividends declared.	(240,000)
Retained earnings, December 31, 1994	$5,572,500

Accounting Changes

Accounting changes (section 1506 of the *CICA Handbook*) include (*a*) accounting errors, (*b*) changes in accounting policy, and (*c*) changes in estimates. The first two types of items—accounting errors arising in prior periods and changes in accounting policy necessitated by a change in circumstances or the development of new accounting principles—receive parallel treatment to that described for prior period adjustments. That is, they are applied retroactively with a restatement of the opening Retained Earnings. The latter, change in estimate, is accorded prospective treatment. As a company gains more experience in such areas as estimating bad debts, warranty costs, and useful lives of capital assets, there is often a sound basis for revising previous estimates. Such changes affect only the present and future statements. A detailed discussion and comparative statement presentation of items that require retroactive adjustment are left to a more advanced textbook; however, a simple single-year illustration is to be found in Illustration 16–4.

Statement of Changes in Shareholders' Equity

In Chapter 5, we explained that some corporations do not present a separate statement of retained earnings. Instead, they present a combined statement of income and retained earnings, an example of which is shown in Illustration 16–5. Other corporations show the statement of retained earnings information in an expanded statement called a *statement of changes in shareholders' equity*. In that statement, the beginning and ending balances of each shareholders' equity account are reconciled by listing all changes that occurred during the year. For example, the annual report of Bombardier Inc. for the year ended January 31, 1992, included the financial statement shown in Illustration 16–5.

EARNINGS PER SHARE

Among the most commonly quoted statistics on the financial pages of daily newspapers is **earnings per share** of common shares. Investors use earnings per share data when they evaluate the past performance of a corporation, project its future earnings, and weigh investment opportunities.

ILLUSTRATION 16–5

Statement of Shareholders' Equity

BOMBARDIER INC.
Consolidated Statements of Shareholders' Equity
For Years Ended January 31, 1992 and 1991
(In millions of dollars)

	1992 Number	1992 Amount	1991 Number	1991 Amount
Share capital (Note 10):				
Preferred shares, series 1:				
Balance at beginning of year.	1,496,500	$ 37.4	1,566,300	$ 39.1
Purchased for cancellation.	(68,300)	(1.7)	(69,800)	(1.7)
Balance at end of year.	1,428,200	35.7	1,496,500	37.4
Class A shares (multiple voting):				
Balance at beginning of year.	45,284,694	50.4	50,082,296	55.7
Converted from class A to class B	(48,502)	(0.1)	(4,793,802)	(5.3)
Purchased for cancellation.	—	—	(3,800)	—
Balance at end of year.	45,236,192	50.3	45,284,694	50.4
Class B subordinate voting shares:				
Balance at beginning of year.	96,158,120	276.0	81,315,552	170.9
Issued for cash	10,000,000	126.2	10,000,000	97.5
Issued under the share option plan (Note 11)	594,750	2.4	306,500	1.1
Issued to employees for cash	298,966	3.9	470,866	3.3
Converted from class A to class B	48,502	0.1	4,793,802	5.3
Purchased for cancellation.	—	—	(728,600)	(2.1)
Balance at end of year.	107,100,338	408.6	96,158,120	276.0
Total—share capital		494.6		363.8
Retained earnings:				
Balance at beginning of year		309.4		242.0
Net income.		107.7		100.1
Net premium on shares purchased		—		(3.0)
Issuance costs for Class B shares (net of income taxes) . .		(3.1)		(2.7)
Dividends paid:				
Preferred shares		(2.9)		(4.0)
Common shares		(24.3)		(23.0)
Balance at end of year.		386.8		309.4
Deferred translation adjustments (Note 12)		17.9		21.0
Total—Shareholders' equity		**$899.3**		**$694.2**

Companies with Simple Capital Structures

Earnings per share calculations may be simple or complex. The calculations are not as difficult for companies that have simple capital structures. A company has a **simple capital structure** if it has only common share capital and perhaps nonconvertible preferred shares outstanding. In other words, to have a simple capital structure, the company cannot have any outstanding options or rights to purchase common shares at a specified price or any securities convertible into common shares.

Calculating Earnings per Share When the Number of Common Shares Outstanding Does Not Change

Consider a company that has only common shares and cumulative nonconvertible preferred shares outstanding. If the number of common shares outstanding does not change during the period, calculate earnings per share as follows:

$$\text{Earnings per share} = \frac{\text{Net income} - \text{Preferred dividends}^3}{\text{Common shares outstanding}}$$

For example, assume that in 1993, Blackwell Company earned a $40,000 net income and paid its preferred dividends of $7,500. On January 1, 1993, the company had 5,000 common shares outstanding and this number did not change during the year. Calculate earnings per share for 1993 as follows:

$$\text{Earnings per share} = \frac{\$40,000 - \$7,500}{5,000} = \$6.50$$

However, the calculation becomes more complex if the number of common shares outstanding changes during the period. The number of common shares outstanding may change (1) because the company sells additional shares or reacquires shares or (2) because of stock dividends and stock splits.

Adjusting the Denominator for Sales or Purchases of Common Shares

If additional shares are sold or shares are reacquired during the year, earnings per share is based on the weighted-average number of shares outstanding during the year. For example, suppose that in 1994, Blackwell Company again earned $40,000 and preferred dividends were $7,500. However, on July 1, 1994, Blackwell sold 4,000 additional common shares. Also, on November 1, 1994, Blackwell reacquired 3,000 shares. In other words, 5,000 shares were outstanding for six months; then 9,000 shares were outstanding for four months; then 6,000 shares were outstanding for two months. When such changes occur, calculate the weighted-average number of shares outstanding during 1994 as follows:

Time Period	Shares Outstanding	Weighted by Portion of Year Outstanding
January–June.	5,000	$(6/12) = 2,500$
July–October.	$(5,000 + 4,000)$	$(4/12) = 3,000$
November–December	$(9,000 - 3,000)$	$(2/12) = 1,000$
Weighted-average common shares outstanding		6,500

LO 5 Calculate earnings per share for companies with simple capital structures and explain the difference between primary and fully diluted earnings per share.

---

[3] If the preferred shares were noncumulative, the deduction from net income would be made only to the extent of the preferred dividends declared. In the case of cumulative preferred, one year's preferred dividends are deducted from net income whether declared or not.

The calculation of earnings per share for 1994 is:

$$\text{Earnings per share} = \frac{\$40,000 - \$7,500}{6,500} = \$5$$

Adjusting the Denominator for Stock Splits and Stock Dividends

A stock split or stock dividend is different from a sale of shares. When shares are sold, the company receives new assets that it uses to generate additional earnings. On the other hand, stock splits and stock dividends do not provide additional assets for the company. Instead, a stock split or stock dividend simply means that the company's earnings must be allocated to a larger number of outstanding shares.

Because of the nature of stock splits and stock dividends, they are treated differently from sales of shares when calculating the weighted-average number of shares outstanding. When a stock split or stock dividend occurs, the number of shares outstanding during previous portions of the year must be retroactively restated to reflect the stock split or dividend. For example, consider the previous example of Blackwell Company. Assume that the share transactions in 1994 included a stock split, as follows:

Jan. 1: 5,000 common shares were outstanding.
July 1: Blackwell sold 4,000 additional common shares.
Nov. 1: Blackwell purchased 3,000 common shares.
Dec. 1: Outstanding common shares were split **2 for 1.**

Given these changes in the number of shares outstanding during 1994, calculate the weighted-average number of shares outstanding as follows:

Time Period	Shares Outstanding	Restated for Stock Split	Weighted by Portion of Year Outstanding
January–June	5,000	2	$(6/12) =$ 5,000
July–October	(5,000 + 4,000)	2	$(4/12) =$ 6,000
November	(9,000 − 3,000)	2	$(1/12) =$ 1,000
December	12,000	—	$(1/12) =$ 1,000
Weighted-average common shares outstanding			13,000

Note that every time shares were sold or purchased, the resulting number of outstanding shares was restated for the subsequent stock split. The same type of restatement is required for stock dividends. If, for example, the two-for-one stock split on December 1 had been a 10% stock dividend, the previous amounts of outstanding shares would have been adjusted by a multiplier of 1.10 instead of 2. The calculation of Blackwell Company's earnings per share for 1994 is:

$$\text{Earnings per share} = \frac{\$40,000 - \$7,500}{13,000} = \$2.50$$

ILLUSTRATION 16–6

Reporting Basic and Fully Diluted Earnings per Share

BCE INC.
Earnings per Share

	1991	1990	1989
Continuing operations	4.01	3.50	3.91
Discontinued real estate operations (loss)	—	—	(1.48)
Earnings per common share (Notes 1 and 21) . .	4.01	3.50	2.43
Dividends declared per common share.	2.57	2.53	2.49
Average number of common shares outstanding (thousands)	307,649	303,813	297,508

BOMBARDIER INC.

	1992	1991
Net income per common share:		
Basic	$0.73	$0.71
Fully diluted	$0.70	$0.70
Average number of common shares outstanding during the year . . .	144,121,395	136,073,170

TRIDEL ENTERPRISES INC.

	1991	1990
Earnings (loss) per share (Note 16):		
Basic:		
From continuing operations . . .	$(1.21)	$0.97
Net income (loss)	$(0.75)	$1.09
Fully diluted:		
From continuing operations . . .	$(1.08)	$0.95
Net income (loss)	$(0.65)	$1.07

Companies with Complex Capital Structures

Companies with **complex capital structures** have outstanding securities such as bonds or preferred shares that are convertible into common shares. Earnings per share calculations for companies with complex capital structures are more complicated. Often, such companies must present two types of earnings per share calculations. One is called **basic earnings per share**, and the other is called **fully diluted earnings per share.**

Suppose that a corporation has convertible preferred shares outstanding throughout the current year. However, consider what the effects would have been if the preferred shares had been converted at the beginning of the year. The result of this assumed conversion would have been to increase the number of common shares outstanding and to reduce preferred dividends. The net result may have been to reduce earnings per share, or to increase earnings per share. When the assumed conversion of a security reduces earnings per share, the security is said to be **dilutive;** those that increase earnings per share are **antidilutive.** Fully diluted earnings per share is calculated as if all dilutive securities (antidilutive securities are excluded from the calculation) had already been converted. The complexities of fully diluted earnings per share are left for more advanced accounting courses.

Presentations of Earnings per Share on the Income Statement

Because of the importance attached to earnings per share data, generally accepted accounting principles require that you show this information on the face of published income statements or in the notes to the financial statements cross-referenced to the income statement. Separate earnings per share calculations are normally presented for (1) income before extraordinary items, (2) extraordinary items, and (3) net income. Some corporations provide additional calculations such as unusual items in Illustrations 16–2 and 16–3. Examples from published statements are presented in Illustration 16–6.

Summary of Chapter in Terms of Learning Objectives

LO 1. Whereas cash dividends transfer corporate assets to the shareholders, stock dividends do not. Stock dividends and stock splits have no effect on assets, no effect on total shareholders' equity, and no effect on the equity of each shareholder. Depending on the jurisdiction, stock dividends are recorded by capitalizing retained earnings equal to the market value of the distributed shares, or capitalizing an amount set by the board of directors.

LO 2. When outstanding shares are repurchased and retired, the stated capital account is debited for the weighted average per share invested by the shareholders. If the purchase price is more or less than the weighted average per share, the difference is debited to Retained Earnings (more) or credited to Contributed Capital, Share Retirements (less).

LO 3. In most jurisdictions, retained earnings are legally restricted by an amount equal to the cost of reacquired shares. Retained earnings also may be restricted by contract. Corporations may voluntarily appropriate retained earnings to inform shareholders why dividends are not larger in amount. More often, however, this information is expressed in a letter to the shareholders.

LO 4. If management has implemented a plan to discontinue a business segment, the net income or loss from operating the segment and the gain or loss on disposal are separately reported on the income statement below income from continuing operations. Next, extraordinary gains or losses are listed.

Prior period adjustments, which include the income effects of accounting errors made in prior periods and changes in accounting policy or principle, are reported on the statement of retained earnings.

Changes in accounting estimates are made because new information shows the old estimates to be invalid. When an accounting estimate is changed, the new estimate is used to calculate revenue or expense in the current and future periods.

LO 5. Companies with simple capital structures do not have outstanding securities convertible into common shares. For such companies, earnings per share is calculated by dividing net income less dividends to preferred shares by the weighted average number of outstanding common shares. In calculating the weighted average number of shares outstanding, the number of shares outstanding prior to a stock dividend or stock split must be restated to reflect the effect of the stock dividend or stock split.

Companies with complex capital structures have outstanding securities that are convertible into common shares. These companies may have to report both basic earnings per share and fully diluted earnings per share. In calculating basic earnings per share, the denominator is the weighted-average number of common shares outstanding. Fully diluted earnings per share assumes the conversion of all dilutive securities.

Part A

Maritime Corporation's books on January 31, 1993, showed the following balances (summarized):

Demonstration
Problem

Cash	$ 70,000
Other current assets	50,000
Capital assets (net).	470,000
Other assets	110,000
	$700,000
Current liabilities	$ 60,000
Long-term liabilities	120,000
Common, 40,000 shares	420,000
Retained earnings	100,000
	$700,000

The board of directors is considering a cash dividend, and you have been requested to provide certain assistance as the independent accountant. The following matters have been referred to you:

1. What is the maximum amount of cash dividends that can be paid at January 1? Explain.
2. What entries would be made assuming a $1 per share cash dividend is declared with the following dates specified: (*a*) declaration date, (*b*) date of record, and (*c*) date of payment.
3. Assuming a balance sheet is prepared between declaration date and payment date, how would the dividend declaration be reported?

Part B

The records of South Corporation showed the following balances on November 1, 1993:

Common 27,500 shares	$770,000
Retained earnings	390,000

On November 5, 1993, the board of directors declared a stock dividend of one additional share for each five shares outstanding; issue date. January 10, 1994. The market value immediately after the declaration was $36 per share.

Required

Give entries in parallel columns for the stock dividend assuming, for problem purposes, (*a*) market value is capitalized, (*b*) $110,000 is capitalized (amount decided by the board), and (*c*) average paid in is capitalized. Assume the company records the dividend on declaration and credits a Stock Dividends Distributable account (not a liability).

Part C

Complete the following matrix:

	Method of Reflecting the Effect	
	Prospective	**Retroactive**
a. Change in estimate	_____	_____
b. Change in principle or method	_____	_____
c. Correction of error	_____	_____

Part D

Eastern Corporation had outstanding 10,000 no-par common shares sold initially for $20 per share. The Retained Earnings balance is $31,600. The corporation purchased and retired 500 shares of its common at $25 per share.

Required

Give entries to record the reacquired share transactions.

Part E

A company split its common shares three for one on June 30 of its fiscal year ended December 31. Before the split, there were 4,000 common shares outstanding. How many common shares should be used in computing EPS? How many common shares should be used in computing a comparative EPS amount for the preceding year?

Solution to Demonstration Problem

Part A

Requirement 1

The maximum cash dividend that can be paid at January 1 depends in part on the statutory provisions (i.e., solvency test); however, the *cash* available is limiting in this situation. Possible alternatives are:

1. Limit to cash, $70,000.
2. Limit to retained earnings, $100,000. This would require property dividends, liability dividends, or generating additional cash through borrowing or other means.

Requirement 2

a.	Date of declaration:		
	Dividends Declared (Retained Earnings).	40,000	
	Dividends Payable.		40,000
b.	Record date. No entry; prepare list of shareholders.		
c.	Date of payment:		
	Dividends Payable	40,000	
	Cash.		40,000

Requirement 3

Between declaration and payment dates, dividends payable for whatever amount is declared ($40,000) would be reported as a current liability. Retained earnings would be reported as $100,000 − $40,000 = $60,000.

Part B

	Amount Capitalized		
	(a)	*(b)*	*(c)*
	Market Value	Decision of the Board	Average Paid in
November 5, 1993:			
To record declaration:			
Retained Earnings	198,000^b	110,000^c	154,000^d
Stock Dividends			
Distributable			
(5,500 shares)	198,000	110,000	154,000
January 10, 1994:			
To record the share issue:			
Stock Dividend			
Distributable	198,000	110,000	154,000
Common Shares			
(5,500 shares)	198,000	110,000	154,000

Note: Alternative accounting: An equally acceptable alternative manner of accounting and reporting the stock dividend would be to disclose the November 5, 1993, stock dividend declaration in the *notes* to the 1993 financial statements. Then the entry to record the January 10, 1994, issuance of the dividend shares would be the same as the declaration entry given above, except that Common Shares would be credited instead of Stock Dividends Distributable.
^{a}27,500 shares outstanding; 27,500 ÷ 5 = 5,500 shares issued for stock dividend.
^{b}Capitalize market value: 5,500 shares × $36 = $198,000.
^{c}Capitalize amount decided by the board = $110,000.
^{d}Capitalize average paid in: $770,000 ÷ 27,500 = $28 per share, average.
5,500 shares × $28 = $154,000.

Part C

	Method of Reflecting the Effect	
	Prospective	Retroactive
a. Change in estimate	✓	
b. Change in principle or method		✓
c. Correction of error		✓

Part D

Common Shares (500 shares @ $20)	10,000	
Retained Earnings	2,500	
Cash.		12,500

Note: Restriction of Retained Earnings (required by law) for $12,500 (the cost of the reacquired shares) may be recorded by journal entry or disclosed in a note.

Part E

In computing EPS for the year, 12,000 common shares should be used. The *CICA Handbook* prescribes retroactive treatment for stock dividends and stock splits for all periods presented. Therefore, 12,000 shares would also be used to compute EPS (restated) for the preceding year as well. The two EPS amounts are therefore (*a*) comparable and (*b*) both related to the current capital structure.

F

Treasury Stock

LO 6 Record purchases
and sales of treasury
shares.

Corporations often reacquire shares of their own stock. This is done for a variety of reasons. Some shares may be given to employees as a bonus. Others may be used to pay for the acquisition of another corporation. Sometimes. shares are repurchased to avoid a hostile takeover by an investor who seeks control of the company. Occasionally, shares are bought in order to maintain a favourable market for the stock.

Whatever the reason, if a corporation reacquires its own shares, the reacquired shares are called *treasury stock*. Treasury shares are a corporation's own shares that were issued and then reacquired by the issuing corporation. Notice that the acquired shares must be that of the issuing corporation. The acquisition of another corporation's shares does not create treasury stock. Also, treasury stock must have been issued and then reacquired. This distinguishes treasury stock from unissued share capital.

Although treasury stock differs from unissued shares in that it was previously issued, in other respects it has the same status as unissued shares. Neither is an asset. Both are subtracted from authorized shares to determine outstanding shares when such things as book values are calculated. Neither receives cash dividends nor has a vote in the shareholders' meetings.

Purchase of
Treasury Stock[4]

When a corporation purchases its own shares, it reduces in equal amounts both its assets and its shareholders' equity. To illustrate, assume that on May 1 of the current year, the condensed balance sheet of Curry Corporation appears as in Illustration F–1.

On May 1, Curry Corporation purchases 1,000 of its outstanding shares at $11.50 per share, and the transaction is recorded as follows:

May	1	Treasury Stock, Common	11,500.00	
		Cash		11,500.00
		Purchased 1,000 shares of treasury stock at $11.50		
		per share.		

---

[4] There are alternate ways of accounting for treasury stock transactions. This text will discuss the so-called cost basis or single transaction method. This method is recommended by the CICA.

ILLUSTRATION F–1

Curry Corporation's Balance Sheet Prior to the Purchase of Treasury Stock

CURRY CORPORATION
Balance Sheet
May 1, 1994

Assets		Shareholders' Equity	
Cash	$ 30,000	Share capital:	
Other assets	95,000	Common shares, no-par value, authorized and issued	
		10,000 shares	$100,000
		Retained earnings	25,000
Total assets	$125,000	Total shareholders' equity	$125,000

ILLUSTRATION F–2

Curry Corporation's Balance Sheet Immediately After the Purchase of Treasury Stock

CURRY CORPORATION
Balance Sheet
May 1, 1994

Assets		Shareholders' Equity	
Cash	$ 18,500	Share Capital:	
Other assets	95,000	Common shares, no-par value, authorized and issued 10,000 shares of which 1,000 are in the treasury	$100,000
		Retained earnings of which $11,500 is restricted by the purchase of treasury stock	25,000
		Total	$125,000
		Less cost of treasury stock	11,500
Total assets	$113,500	Total shareholders' equity	$113,500

The debit of the entry records a reduction in the equity of the shareholders. The credit records a reduction in assets. Both are equal to the cost of the treasury stock. After the entry is posted, a new balance sheet shows the reductions as in Illustration F–2.

In Illustration F–2 notice that the cost of the treasury stock appears in the shareholders' equity section as a deduction from common shares and retained earnings. In comparing the two balance sheets (Illustrations F–1 and F–2), you can see that the treasury stock purchase reduced both assets and shareholders' equity by the $11,500 cost of the shares. Also, the amount of *issued shares* is not changed by the purchase of treasury stock. The dollar amount of the issued shares remains at $100,000 and is unchanged from the first balance sheet. However, the purchase does reduce the amount of *outstanding shares*. Curry Corporation's outstanding share capital was reduced from 10,000 to 9,000 shares.

There is a distinction between issued shares and outstanding shares. Issued shares may or may not be outstanding. Outstanding shares were issued and remain currently in the hands of shareholders. Only outstanding shares receive cash dividends and have a vote in the meetings of shareholders.

Restricting Retained Earnings by the Purchase of Treasury Stock

The purchase of treasury stock by a corporation has the same effect on its assets and shareholders' equity as the payment of a cash dividend. Both transfer corporate assets to shareholders and thereby reduce assets and shareholders equity. Therefore, in jurisdictions which permit treasury stock, a corporation may purchase treasury stock or it may pay cash dividends, but the sum of both cannot exceed the amount of its retained earnings available for dividends. Tests of solvency also apply.

Unlike the payment of a cash dividend, the purchase of treasury stock does not reduce the balance of the Retained Earnings account. Instead, the purchase places a restriction on the amount of retained earnings available for dividends. Note how **restricted retained earnings** are shown in Illustration F–2. Usually, the restriction also is described in a note to the financial statements.

The restriction of retained earnings because of treasury stock purchases is a matter of law. Other types of legal restrictions on retained earnings may be imposed by law or by contract.

Reissuing Treasury Stock

Treasury stock may be reissued at cost, above cost, or below cost. If reissued at cost, the entry to record the transaction is the reverse of the entry used to record the purchase.

If treasury stock is sold at a price that is above cost, the amount received in excess of cost is credited to a contributed capital account, Contributed Capital, Treasury Stock Transactions. For example, if Curry Corporation sells for $12 per share 500 of the treasury shares purchased at $11.50 per share, the entry to record the transaction is as follows:

June	3	Cash	6,000.00	
		Treasury Stock, Common		5,750.000
		Contributed Capital, Treasury Stock Transactions . . .		250.00
		Sold at $12 per share 500 treasury shares that cost		
		$11.50 per share.		

When treasury stock is reissued at a price below cost, the entry to record the sale depends on whether there is a preexisting credit balance in the Contributed Capital, Treasury Stock Transactions, account. If none exists, the amount by which sales price is less than cost is debited to Retained Earnings. However, if the contributed capital account has a credit balance, the difference between sales price and cost is charged to the contributed capital account to the extent possible. After the credit balance in the contributed capital account is eliminated, any remaining difference between sales price and cost is debited to Retained Earnings. For example, if Curry Corporation sells its remaining 500 shares of treasury stock at $10 per share, the entry to record the sale is:

July	10	Cash	5,000.00	
		Contributed Capital, Treasury Stock Transactions	250.00	
		Retained Earnings.	500.00	
		Treasury Stock, Common		5,750.00
		Sold at $10 per share 500 treasury shares that cost		
		$11.50 per share.		

Glossary

LO 7 Define or explain the words and phrases listed in the chapter glossary.

Antidilutive securities convertible securities, the assumed conversion of which would have the effect of increasing earnings per share. p. 819

Appropriated retained earnings retained earnings voluntarily earmarked for a special use as a way of informing shareholders that assets from earnings equal to the appropriations are not available for dividends. p. 811

Basic earnings per share earnings per share statistics that are calculated for corporations with a simple capital structure and for corporations with complex capital structures before giving effect to the dilutive securities. p. 819

Changes in accounting estimates adjustments to previously made assumptions about the future such as salvage values and the length of useful lives of buildings and equipment. p. 815

Complex capital structure a capital structure that includes outstanding rights or options to purchase common shares or securities convertible into common shares. p. 819

Dilutive securities convertible securities the assumed conversion of which would have the effect of decreasing earnings per share. p. 819

Earned surplus a synonym for retained earnings, no longer in general use. p. 804

Earnings per share the amount of net income (or components of income) that accrues to common shares divided by the weighted-average number of common shares outstanding. pp. 815–19

Fully diluted earnings per share earnings per share statistics that are calculated as if all dilutive securities had already been converted. p. 819

Prior period adjustment items reported in the current statement of retained earnings as corrections to the beginning retained earnings balance; limited primarily to corrections of errors that were made in past years, settlement of lawsuits that originated in prior years, and one-time income tax settlements. p. 813

Prospective change affects current and future periods. p. 815

Restricted retained earnings retained earnings not available for dividends because of law or binding contract. pp. 811–12, 826

Retroactive change affects prior periods. p. 815

Reverse stock split the act of a corporation to call in its shares and issue one new share in the place of more than one share previously outstanding. p. 809

Segment of a business operations of a company that involve a particular line of business or class of customer, providing the assets, activities, and financial results of the operations can be distinguished from other parts of the business. p. 811

Simple capital structure a capital structure that does not include any rights or options to purchase common shares or any securities that are convertible into common shares. p. 816

Stock dividend a distribution by a corporation of its own shares to its shareholders without the receipt of any consideration in return. pp. 805–808

Stock split the act of a corporation to issue more than one new share in the place of each share previously outstanding. p. 809

Treasury stock issued shares that were reacquired and are currently held by the issuing corporation. pp. 824–27

Unusual gain or loss a gain or loss (that doesn't qualify as extraordinary) that is abnormal and unrelated or only incidentally related to the ordinary activities and environment of the business. p. 817

Synonymous Terms

Basic earnings per share   earnings per common share.

Retained earnings   earned surplus (no longer in use).

Statement of changes in shareholders' equity   statement of shareholders' equity.

Objective Review

Answers to the following questions are listed at the end of this chapter. Be sure that you decide which is the one best answer to each question *before* you check the answers.

LO 1   Which of the following statements is true with regard to stock dividends and stock splits?

a.   In a stock split, Retained Earnings is debited and the share account is credited for the average stated value of the issued shares.

b.   A corporation should capitalize an amount of retained earnings equal to the market value of the shares to be distributed.

c.   The effect of stock dividends and stock splits on the total assets of the issuing corporation is equal to their effect on total retained earnings.

d.   The distribution of stock dividends reduces both cash and shareholders' equity but a stock split reduces neither one.

e.   A stock dividend does not transfer assets from a corporation to the shareholders but requires that an amount of retained earnings be capitalized.

LO 2   The purchase and retirement of shares:

a.   Does not change the number of outstanding shares.

b.   Is recorded with a decrease in assets and a corresponding increase in assets.

c.   Necessarily requires a debit to Retained Earnings.

d.   Reduces in equal amounts both its total assets and its total shareholders' equity.

e.   Requires a credit to Retained Earnings.

LO 3   When a corporation appropriates retained earnings:

a.   The amount of the appropriation must be matched by available cash.

b.   The board of directors becomes permanently committed not to pay dividends from those appropriated amounts.

c.   The board of directors voluntarily allocates a portion of retained earnings for some special purpose, thereby indicating why dividends are not being declared.

d.   The appropriation is recorded by transferring the appropriated amount from Retained Earnings to a contributed capital account.

e.   None of the above.

LO 4   Which of the following qualifies as an extraordinary gain or loss?

a.   A loss of plant and equipment damaged as a result of a meteorite shower.

b.   A gain from the exchange of British pounds for dollars that resulted from credit sales of goods to British customers.

c. A loss incurred by a manufacturer of three-wheeled recreational vehicles as a result of a customer's lawsuit over injuries suffered from using the product.

d. A loss due to compensating a worker for injuries suffered while working at the company's plant.

e. None of the above are extraordinary items.

LO 5 Remington Corporation earned $250,000 in 1993, and preferred dividends were $70,000. On January 1, 1993, the company had 25,000 common shares outstanding. However, on July 1, 1993, Remington Corporation purchased and retired 5,000 shares. Earnings per share for 1993:

a. $7.20.

b. $8.00.

c. $9.00.

d. $10.00.

e. $11.11.

LO 6 The purchase of treasury stock by a corporation:

a. Does not change the amount of outstanding shares.

b. Is recorded with an increase to assets and a decrease to assets.

c. Decreases the amount of issued shares.

d. Reduces in equal amounts both its total assets and its total shareholders' equity.

e. Requires a debit to Retained Earnings.

A letter ᶠ identifies the questions, exercises, and problems based on Appendix F at the end of this chapter.

Questions for Class Discussion	1. What effect does the declaration of a cash dividend have on the assets, liabilities, and shareholders' equity of the corporation that declares the dividend? What is the effect of the subsequent payment of the cash dividend?

2. What effect does the declaration of a stock dividend have on the assets, liabilities, and total shareholders' equity of the corporation that declares the dividend? What is the effect of the subsequent distribution of the stock dividend?

3. What is the difference between a stock dividend and a stock split?

4. If a balance sheet is prepared between the date of declaration and the date of payment or distribution of a dividend, how should the dividend be shown if it is (*a*) a cash dividend, or (*b*) a stock dividend?

5. Why do laws place limitations on the reacquisition of a corporation's shares?

6. In the annual income statement of a corporation, what other sections of the statement might appear below income from continuing operations?

7. If a company operates one of its business segments at a loss during much of 1994, and then finds a buyer and disposes of that segment during November of that year, which two items concerning that segment should appear on the company's 1994 income statement?

8. Where on the income statement should a company disclose a gain that is abnormal and unrelated to the ordinary activities of the business and that is not expected to recur more often than once every several years and that occurs as a result of decisions or events outside the corporation?

9. Which of the following items would qualify as an extraordinary gain or loss: (*a*) operating losses resulting from a strike against a major supplier, (*b*) a gain from the sale of surplus equipment, or (*c*) a loss from damage to a building caused by a tornado (a type of storm that rarely occurs in the geographical region of the company's operations)?

10. In past years, Daley Company paid its sales personnel annual salaries without additional incentive payments. This year, a new policy is being instituted whereby they receive sales commissions rather than annual salaries. Does this new policy require a prior period adjustment? Explain why or why not.

11. After taking five years' straight-line amortization on an asset that was expected to have an eight-year life, a company concluded that the asset would last another six years. Does this decision involve a change in accounting principle? If not, how would you describe this change?

12. How is earnings per share calculated for a corporation with a simple capital structure?

13. In calculating the weighted-average number of common shares outstanding, how are stock splits and stock dividends treated?

14. What is the difference between basic earnings per share and fully diluted earnings per share?

15. What is the difference between simple capital structures and complex capital structures?

Mini Discussion Case

Case 16–1

The acquisition of previously issued shares, whether for retirement or for subsequent reissue, continues to be a controversial matter. Some argue that there is something unsavory about a corporation's trafficking, as an insider, in its own shares. But others believe that a corporation should have wide latitude in adjusting its capital structure.

Required
Discuss the pros and cons of a corporation's right to reacquire its own shares for:

a. Retirement.
b. Reissue at a future date.

Exercises

Exercise 16–1
Stock dividends
(LO 1)

Ritchfield Corporation's shareholders' equity appeared as follows on August 10:

Share capital:
Common shares, no-par value, 260,000 shares
    authorized, 80,000 shares issued $560,200
Retained earnings 235,000
Total shareholders' equity $795,200

On August 10, when the shares were selling at $9.00, the corporation's directors voted a 10% stock dividend distributable on September 2 to the August 17 shareholders of record. The shares were selling at $9.50 at the close of business on September 2.

Required

1. Prepare General Journal entries to record the declaration and distribution of the dividend.

2. Under the assumption that Cynthia McAllister owned 250 of the shares on August 10 and received her dividend shares on September 2, prepare a schedule showing the number of shares she held on August 10 and on September 2, with their total book values and total market values. Assume no change in total shareholders' equity from August 10 to September 2.

Exercise 16–2
Stock dividends and stock splits
(LO 1)

On March 31, 1993, Pacific Management Corporation's common shares were selling for $45 and the shareholders' equity section of the corporation's balance sheet appeared as follows:

Share capital:
Common shares, no-par value, unlimited number of shares
    authorized, 15,000 shares issued $670,450
Retained earnings. 298,900
Total shareholders' equity $969,350

Required

1. Assume the corporation declares and immediately issues a 50% stock dividend and capitalizes $30 per share of retained earnings. Answer the following questions about the shareholders' equity of the corporation after the new shares are issued:
   a. What is the retained earnings balance?
   b. What is the total amount of shareholders' equity?
   c. How many shares are outstanding?

2. Assume that instead of declaring a 50% stock dividend, the corporation effects a three-for-two stock split. Answer the following questions about the shareholders' equity of the corporation after the stock split takes place:
   a. What is the retained earnings balance?
   b. What is the total amount of shareholders' equity?
   c. How many shares are outstanding?

Exercise 16–3
Retirement of shares
(LO 2, 3)

On October 31, Reynold Corporation's shareholders' equity section appeared as follows:

Shareholders' Equity

Share capital:
Common shares, no-par value, unlimited number of shares
    authorized, 5,000 shares outstanding $250,000
Retained earnings. 220,100
Total shareholders' equity $470,100

On October 31, the corporation purchased and retired 900 shares at $50 per share. Give the entry to record the purchase and prepare a shareholders' equity section as it would appear immediately after the purchase and retirement.

The shareholders' equity section of Capital Vending, Inc.'s December 31, 1993, balance sheet is as follows:

Exercise 16–4
Retirement of shares
(LO 2)

Share capital:
Common shares, no-par value, 600,000 shares
 authorized, 30,000 shares issued $540,000
Retained earnings 105,800

Total shareholders' equity $645,800

 On the date of the balance sheet, the company purchased and retired 400 common shares. Prepare General Journal entries to record the purchase and retirement under each of the following independent assumptions: the shares were purchased for (*a*) $15 per share, (*b*) $18 per share, and (*c*) $25 per share.

The following list of items was extracted from the December 31, 1993, trial balance of Wesson Company. Using the information contained in this listing, prepare Wesson Company's income statement for 1993. You need not complete the earnings per share calculations.

Exercise 16–5
Income statement
categories
(LO 4)

	Debit	Credit
Salaries expense	$ 56,700	
Income tax expense (continuing operations)	48,380	
Loss from operating segment C (net of		
$10,200 tax benefit)	24,000	
Sales		$650,240
Total effect on prior years' income of		
change from declining-balance to		
straight-line amortization (net of		
$9,600 tax)		22,400
Extraordinary gain on provincial condemnation		
of land owned by Wesson Company (net of		
$24,800 tax)		58,000
Amortization expense	42,100	
Gain on sale of segment C (net of $19,700		
tax)		46,000
Cost of goods sold	390,200	

In preparing the annual financial statements for Metro Electronics Company, the correct manner of reporting the following items was not clear to the company's employees. Explain where each of the following items should appear in the financial statements.

Exercise 16–6
Classifying income items
not related to continuing
operations
(LO 4)

a. After amortizing office equipment for three years based on an expected useful life of eight years, the company decided this year that the office equipment should last seven more years. As a result, the amortization for the current year is $10,000 instead of $12,500.

b. This year, the accounting department of the company discovered that last year, an installment payment on their five-year note payable had been charged entirely to interest expense. The after-tax effect of the charge to interest expense was $13,400.

c. The company keeps its repair trucks for several years before disposing of the old trucks and buying new trucks. This year, for the first time in 10 years, it sold old trucks for a gain of $18,900 and then purchased new trucks.

Exercise 16–7
Weighted-average shares
outstanding and earnings
per share
(LO 5)

Comfort Footware Inc. reported $264,650 net income in 1993 and declared preferred
dividends of $43,000. The following changes in common shares outstanding occurred
during the year:

January 1:	60,000 common shares were outstanding.
June 1:	Sold 30,000 common shares.
September 1:	Declared and issued a 10% common stock dividend, or
	90,000 × 10% = 9,000 additional shares.

Calculate the weighted-average number of common shares outstanding during the year
and earnings per share.

Exercise 16–8
Weighted-average shares
outstanding and earnings
per share
(LO 5)

Cromwell Production Company reported $736,500 net income in 1993 and declared
preferred dividends of $66,500. The following changes in common shares outstanding
occurred during the year.

January 1:	120,000 common shares were outstanding.
March 1:	Sold 20,000 common shares.
September 1:	Purchased and retired 8,000 shares.
December 1:	Declared and issued a two-for-one stock split.

Calculate the weighted-average number of common shares outstanding during the year
and earnings per share.

Exercise 16–9
Reporting earnings per
share
(LO 5)

Southside Corporation's 1993 income statement, excluding the earnings per share portion of the statement, was as follows:

Sales		$475,000
Costs and expenses:		
Amortization	$ 51,900	
Income taxes	65,100	
Other expenses	205,000	322,000
Income from continuing operations		$153,000
Loss from operating discontinued business segment (net of		
$23,500 tax benefit)	$ 56,000	
Loss on sale of business segment (net of $9,400 tax benefit) . .	22,000	(78,000)
Income before extraordinary items		$ 75,000
Extraordinary gain (net of $18,400 taxes)		43,200
Net income		$118,200

  Throughout 1993, Southside had potentially dilutive securities outstanding. If
these particular securities had been converted, the number of common shares outstanding would have increased but the numerators in earnings per share calculations
would not have been affected. Assuming the dilutive securities had been converted at
the beginning of the year, the weighted-average number of common shares outstanding
during the year would have increased by 10,000 to 60,000. Present the earnings per
share portion of the 1993 income statement.

Problems

Problem 16–1
Cash dividend, stock
dividend, and stock
split
(LO 1)

Last April 30, Convenience Foods Corporation had an $862,500 credit balance in its
Retained Earnings account. On that date, the corporation's contributed capital consisted of 345,000 shares, which had been issued at $3 and were outstanding. It then
completed the following transactions:

May   10   The board of directors declared a $1.50 per share common dividend payable on June 16 to the May 31 shareholders of record.

June 16   Paid the dividend declared on May 10.

Aug.   5   The board declared a 1% stock dividend, distributable on September 2 to the August 20 shareholders of record. The shares were selling at $4.00 per share; this amount was used to capitalize retained earnings.

Sept. 2   Distributed the stock dividend declared on August 5.

      30   Because September 30 is the end of the company's fiscal year, closed the Income Summary account, which had a credit balance of $397,095. Also closed the Cash Dividends Declared and Stock Dividends Declared accounts.

Oct. 12   The board of directors voted to split the corporation's shares two for one. The split was completed on November 17.

Required:

1. Prepare General Journal entries to record these transactions and closings.

2. Under the assumption Phillip Bolton owned 5,000 shares on April 30 and neither bought nor sold any shares during the period of the transactions, prepare a schedule with columns for the date, supporting calculations, book value per share, and book value of Bolton's shares. Then complete the schedule by calculating the book value per share of the corporation's and of Bolton's shares at the close of business on April 30, May 10, June 16, September 2, September 30, and October 12. Assume that the only income earned by the company during these periods was the $397,095 earned and closed on September 30.

3. Prepare three shareholders' equity sections for the corporation, the first showing the shareholders' equity on April 30, the second on September 30, and the third on October 12.

The equity sections from the 1992 and 1993 balance sheets of Fairfax Corporation appeared as follows:

Problem 16–2
Calculating net income from balance sheet comparison
(LO 1, 2, 3)

Shareholders' Equity
(As of December 31, 1992)

Share capital:
Common shares, no-par value, unlimited number of shares
  authorized, 120,000 shares outstanding. . . . . $ 860,000
Retained earnings.   698,260

Total shareholders' equity $1,558,260

Shareholders' Equity
(As of December 31, 1993)

Share capital:
Common shares, no-par value, unlimited number of shares
  authorized, 125,000 shares are outstanding. . . . . $ 807,500
Retained earnings, of which $180,000 is restricted—
  retirement of shares   574,500

Total shareholders' equity $1,382,000

On March 16, June 25, September 5, and again on November 22, 1993, the board of directors declared $0.25 per share cash dividends on the outstanding common shares. And 20,000 shares were purchased and retired on May 14. On October 5, while the shares were selling for $9.50 per share, the corporation declared a 25% stock dividend on the outstanding shares. The new shares were issued on November 8.

Required

Under the assumption that there were no transactions affecting retained earnings other than the ones given, determine the 1993 net income of Fairfax Corporation. Show your calculations. (*Hint:* Remember the impact on retained of repurchase of shares at an amount greater than the per share weighted-average stated value.

Problem 16–3
Classifying income items in a published income statement
(LO 4)

Central Supply Company had several unusual transactions during 1993 and has prepared the following list of trial balance items. Select the appropriate items to use in constructing the 1993 income statement for the company.

	Debit	Credit
Accounts payable		$ 16,600
Loss from operation of Westside Division (net of $14,000 income tax benefit)	$ 42,000	
Sales		398,500
Cost of goods sold	175,600	
Loss on sale of office equipment (an unusual transaction for the company that occurs only when administrative offices are redecorated, which happens about every eight years)	6,300	
Amortization expense, buildings	35,620	
Amortization expense, office equipment	12,450	
Income tax expense	20,950	
Payment received in November of last year on customer account receivable incorrectly recorded in Sales account (net of $4,050 income tax benefit)	16,200	
Gain on sale of investment in land (The land was originally donated to Central Supply by a shareholder. Central Supply has never held land for investment purposes before and has no intention of doing so in the future.) (Net of $7,800 income taxes)		23,400
Loss on customer breach of contract (It is not unusual for companies in this industry, to be involved in breach of contract suits. However, the problem is not expected to arise in the foreseeable future.)	45,700	
Accumulated amortization, buildings		108,000
Accumulated amortization, office equipment		20,900
Gain on sale of Westside Division (net of $3,400 income taxes)		12,750
Interest earned		2,400
Other operating expenses	53,800	
Gain on payment from supplier to compensate for late delivery of materials purchased from supplier. (In this industry, such settlements with suppliers occur quite frequently.)		12,300
Effect on prior years' income of switching from straight-line amortization to accelerated amortization (net of $5,900 income tax benefit)	22,125	

Required

Prepare Central Supply Company's income statement for 1993, excluding the earnings per share statistics.

Problem 16–4
Changes in accounting principles
(LO 4)

On January 1, 1989, Fieldway Industries Inc. purchased a large piece of equipment for use in its manufacturing operations. The equipment cost $350,000 and was expected to have a salvage value of $40,000. Amortization was taken through 1992 on a declining-balance method at twice the straight-line rate, assuming an eight-year life. Early in 1993, the company concluded that given the economic conditions in the industry, a straight-line method would result in more meaningful financial statements. They argue that straight-line amortization would allow better comparisons with the financial results of other firms in the industry.

Required

1. Is Fieldway Industries allowed to change amortization methods in 1993?

2. Prepare a table that shows the amortization expense to be reported each year of the asset's life under both amortization methods and the cumulative effect of the change on prior years' incomes.

3. State the amount of amortization expense to be reported in 1993 and the cumulative effect of the change on prior years' incomes. How should the cumulative effect be reported? Does the cumulative effect increase or decrease net income?

4. Now assume that Fieldway Industries had used straight-line amortization through 1992 and justified a change to declining-balance amortization at twice the straight-line rate in 1993. What amount of amortization expense should be reported in 1993? Does the reporting of the cumulative effect of the change differ from your answer to requirement 3?

Except for the earnings per share statistics, the 1993, 1992, and 1991 income statements of Custom Printing Company were originally presented as follows:

Problem 16–5
Earnings per share calculations and presentation
(LO 5)

	1993	1992	1991
Sales.	$998,900	$687,040	$466,855
Costs and expenses	383,570	234,500	157,420
Income from continuing operations	$615,330	$452,540	$309,435
Loss on discontinued operations	(107,325)	—	—
Income (loss) before extraordinary items . .	$508,005	$452,540	$309,435
Extraordinary gains (losses)	—	80,410	(156,191)
Net income (loss)	$508,005	$532,950	$153,244

Information on common shares:

Shares outstanding on December 31, 1990.	12,000
Purchase and retirement of shares on March 1, 1991	− 1,200
Sale of shares on June 1, 1991	+ 5,200
Stock dividend of 5% on August 1, 1991.	+ 800
Shares outstanding on December 31, 1991.	16,800
Sale of shares on February 1, 1992	+ 2,400
Purchase and retirement of shares July 1, 1992	− 600
Shares outstanding on December 31, 1992	18,600
Sale of shares on March 1, 1993	+ 6,900
Purchase and retirement of shares on September 1, 1993 . .	− 1,500
Stock split of 3 for 1 on October 1, 1993.	+48,000
Shares outstanding on December 31, 1993.	72,000

Required

1. Calculate the weighted-average number of common shares outstanding during (*a*) 1991, (*b*) 1992, and (*c*) 1993.

2. Present the earnings per share portions of (*a*) the 1991 income statement, (*b*) the 1992 income statement, and (*c*) the 1993 income statement.

The shareholders' equity section of Wernli Corporation's balance sheet at April 30 is as follows:

Problem 16–6
Analytical essay
(LO 1)

Share capital:

Common shares, no-par value, unlimited number of shares authorized, 20,000 shares issued and outstanding	$360,000
Retained earnings.	148,000
Total shareholders' equity	$508,000

Wernli is considering increasing the number of outstanding common shares from 20,000 to 30,000 by one of the following alternative methods: (*a*) a three-for-two stock split or (*b*) declaring and issuing a 50% stock dividend.

Required

1. Describe the difference in how the declaration and issuance of the shares under the two alternative methods would be recorded in the accounting records of Wernli. Also, explain why the Common Shares account must be increased if one alternative is used but is not increased if the other alternative is used.

2. Describe the effects on Wernli's balance sheet of using one alternative versus the other.

Problem 16-7
Analytical essay
(LO 5)

Compusub Corporation has tentatively prepared its financial statements for the year ended December 31, 1993, and has submitted them to you for review. The shareholders' equity section of Compusub's balance sheet at December 31 is as follows:

Share capital:
Preferred shares, $2.50, cumulative
and nonparticipating, 30,000 shares authorized, 15,000
shares issued and outstanding . . . . $ 520,100
Common shares, no-par value, unlimited number of shares
authorized, 110,000 shares outstanding.   777,840
Retained earnings.   996,200
Total shareholders' equity. $2,294,140

Compusub Corporation's 1993 net income was $600,000 and no cash dividends were declared. The only share transaction that occurred during the year was the sale of 20,000 common shares on March 31, 1993. Earnings per share for 1993 was calculated as follows:

$$\frac{\text{Net income}}{\text{Common plus preferred shares outstanding as of Dec. 31}} = \frac{\$600,000}{110,000 + 15,000} = \$4.80$$

Required

1. Explain what is wrong with the earnings per share calculation, indicating what corrections should be made to both the numerator and the denominator.

2. Explain how your answer to requirement 1 would be different if the preferred shares were not cumulative and if the issuance of 20,000 shares had been a stock dividend.

FProblem 16-8
Treasury stock
transactions and stock
dividends
(LO 1, 6)

Southwest Publications, Inc.'s shareholders' equity on December 31, 1992, consisted of the following:

Share capital:
Common shares, no-par value, unlimited number of shares
authorized, 105,000 shares issued $603,750
Retained earnings   234,650
Total shareholders' equity. $838,400

During 1993, the company completed these transactions:

Mar. 6   Purchased 22,000 shares of treasury stock at $5.75 per share.

Apr. 17   The directors voted a $0.40 per share cash dividend payable on May 15 to the May 5 shareholders of record.

May 15 Paid the dividend declared on April 17.

Aug. 12 Sold 8,500 of the treasury shares at $6.00 per share.

Oct. 28 Sold 13,500 of the treasury shares at $5.00 per share.

Dec.   5 The directors voted a $0.30 per share cash dividend payable on January 3
         to the December 25 shareholders of record, and they voted a 10% stock
         dividend distributable on January 26 to the December 26 shareholders of
         record. The market value of $5.90 per share was the basis for capitalizing
         retained earnings.

      31 Closed the Income Summary account and carried the company's $100,250
         net income to Retained Earnings.

      31 Closed the Cash Dividends Declared and Stock Dividends Declared
         accounts.

Required

1. Prepare General Journal entries to record the transactions and closings for 1993.

2. Prepare a retained earnings statement for the year and the shareholders' equity
    section of the company's year-end balance sheet.

Alternate Problems

Last January 31, Richmond Corporation (federally incorporated) had a $3.5 million
credit balance in its Retained Earnings account. On that date, the corporation's contributed capital consisted of 50,000 shares, which had been issued at $75 and were
outstanding. It then completed the following transactions:

Feb. 13 The board of directors declared a $10 per share dividend, payable on
         March 14 to the March 1 shareholders of record.

Mar. 14 Paid the dividend declared on February 13.

May 22 The board declared a 25% stock dividend, distributable on June 18 to the
         June 4 shareholders of record. The shares were selling at $90 per share.

June 18 Distributed the stock dividend declared on May 22.

      30 Since June 30 is the end of the accounting year, closed the Income Sum-
         mary account, which had a credit balance of $1.5 million. Also closed the
         Cash Dividends Declared and Stock Dividends Declared accounts.

July   5 The board of directors voted to split the corporation's shares three for
         one. The shareholders voted approval of the split. The split was com-
         pleted on July 28.

Problem 16–1A
Cash dividend, stock
dividend, and stock
split
(LO 1)

Required

1. Prepare General Journal entries to record these transactions and to close the
    Income Summary account at year-end.

2. Under the assumption Denise Shay owned 2,500 shares on January 31 and nei-
    ther bought nor sold any shares during the period of the transactions, prepare a
    schedule with columns for the date, supporting calculations, book value per
    share, and book value of Shay's shares. Then complete the schedule by calculat-
    ing the book value per share of the corporation's and of Shay's shares at the
    close of business on January 31, February 13, March 14, June 18, June 30, and
    July 28. Assume that the only income earned by the company during these peri-
    ods was the $1.5 million which was earned and closed on June 30.

3. Prepare three shareholders' equity sections for the corporation, the first showing the shareholders' equity on January 31, the second on June 30, and the third on July 28.

Problem 16–2A
Calculating net income from balance sheet comparison
(LO 1, 2, 3)

The equity sections from the 1992 and 1993 balance sheets of Henneke Corporation appeared as follows:

Shareholders' Equity
(As of December 31, 1992)

Share capital:
Common shares, no-par value, unlimited number of shares
     authorized, 350,000 shares issued . . . . $ 8,750,000
Retained earnings. 1,960,720
Total shareholders' equity $10,710,720

Shareholders' Equity
(As of December 31, 1993)

Share capital:
Common shares, no-par value, unlimited number of shares
     authorized, 384,000 shares issued . . . . $ 9,384,000
Retained earnings, of which $270,000 is restricted 1,540,640
Total shareholders' equity $10,924,640

On February 11, May 24, August 13, and again on December 12, 1993, the board of directors declared $0.25 per share cash dividends on the outstanding shares; 10,000 shares were purchased at $27 per share and retired on July 6. On November 1, while the shares were selling for $26 per share, the corporation declared a 10% stock dividend on the outstanding shares. The new shares were issued on December 5.

Required

Under the assumption that there were no transactions affecting retained earnings other than the ones given, determine the 1993 net income of Henneke Corporation. Show your calculations.

Problem 16–3A
Classifying income items in a published income statement
(LO 4)

Systems Communications Corporation had several unusual transactions during 1993 and has prepared the following list of trial balance items. Select the appropriate items to use in constructing the 1993 income statement for the company.

	Debit	Credit
Cost of goods sold	$245,800	
Effect on prior years' income of switching from accelerated amortization to straight-line amortization (net of $24,500 income taxes)		$ 57,100
Gain on settlement with supplier to compensate for loss of major contract due to nondelivery of phone system from supplier. (In this industry, attempts to obtain such settlements with suppliers are not unusual but occur very infrequently.).		125,900
Accumulated amortization, buildings.		102,030
Income tax expense.	151,290	
Income from operating Products Division (net of $25,600 income taxes)		64,000
Three-year insurance policy paid in advance in January 1992 and recorded in prepaid insurance. No adjusting entry was made for expired portion in 1992. (net of $3,750 income tax benefit).	8,750	
Long-term note payable		86,500

	Debit	Credit
Gain on sale of telegraph displayed in main entrance (an unusual transaction for the company that occurs about once every three years when a new display is obtained).		4,700
Amortization expense	17,900	
Gain on sale of investment in shares (Systems Communications regularly maintains a large portfolio of share investments as part of its business activities, expecting to enhance the earnings of the company through purchases and sales of such securities.)		46,500
Other operating expenses.	235,680	
Gain on sale of Products Division (net of $45,800 income taxes)		106,900
Interest earned		36,200
Loss due to commercial plane crashing into warehouse (net of $16,200 income tax benefit)	37,800	
Sales		790,400

Required

Prepare Systems Communications Corporation's income statement for 1993, excluding the earnings per share statistics.

On January 1, 1989, the Blackwood Company purchased a major piece of equipment for use in its operations. The equipment cost $945,000 and was expected to have a salvage value of $105,000. Amortization was taken through 1992 using the straight-line method assuming an eight-year life. Early in 1993, the company concluded that, given the economic conditions in the industry, a declining-balance method at twice the straight-line method would result in more meaningful financial statements. They argue that declining-balance amortization would allow better comparisons with the financial results of other firms in the industry.

Problem 16–4A
Changes in accounting principles
(LO 4)

Required

1. Is Blackwood Company allowed to change amortization methods in 1993?

2. Prepare a table that shows the amortization expense to be reported each year of the asset's life under both amortization methods and the cumulative effect of the change on prior years' incomes.

3. State the amount of amortization expense to be reported in 1993 and the cumulative effect of the change on prior years' incomes. How should the cumulative effect be reported? Does the cumulative effect increase or decrease net income?

4. Now assume that Blackwood Company had used double-declining-balance amortization through 1992 and justified a change to straight-line amortization in 1993. What amount of amortization expense should be reported in 1993? Does the reporting of the cumulative effect of the change differ from your answer to requirement 3?

Except for the earnings per share statistics, the 1993, 1992, and 1991 income statements of Greggor Corporation were originally presented as follows:

Problem 16–5A
Earnings per share calculations and presentation
(LO 5)

	1993	1992	1991
Sales.	$661,843	$696,250	$455,600
Costs and expenses	237,760	245,800	168,725
Income from continuing operations	$424,083	$450,450	$286,875
Loss on discontinued operations	(42,408)	(18,018)	—
Income (loss) before extraordinary items . .	$381,675	$432,432	$286,875
Extraordinary gains (losses).	—	30,030	(33,750)
Net income (loss)	$381,675	$462,462	$253,125

Information on common share capital:

Shares outstanding on December 31, 1990	60,600
Sale of shares on March 1, 1991.	+10,800
Purchase and retirement of shares on July 1, 1991 . .	− 4,200
Shares outstanding on December 31, 1991	67,200
Sale of shares on May 1, 1992.	+18,000
Sale of shares on September 1, 1992	+ 2,640
Stock split of 3 for 2 on October 1, 1992.	+43,920
Shares outstanding on December 31, 1992	131,760
Purchase and retirement of shares on June 1, 1993 . .	−15,000
Sale of shares on July 1, 1993	+11,000
Stock dividend of 10% on October 1, 1993	+12,776
Shares outstanding on December 31, 1993	140,536

Required

1. Calculate the weighted-average number of common shares outstanding during (*a*) 1991, (*b*) 1992, and (*c*) 1993.

2. Present the earnings per share portions of (*a*) the 1991 income statement, (*b*) the 1992 income statement, and (*c*) the 1993 income statement.

Problem 16–6A
Analytical essay
(LO 1, 2)

The shareholders' equity section of Langhoffer Corporation's balance sheet at September 30 is as follows:

Share capital:

Common shares, no-par value, unlimited number of shares authorized, 50,000 shares outstanding	$ 650,000
Retained earnings	367,000
Total shareholders' equity.	$1,017,000

Assume now that an event occurs on October 1 that impacts Langhoffer's shareholders' equity section, but does not involve net income or additional investment of capital. The following are independent cases in which Langhoffer's shareholders' equity section has been revised to reflect that event.

	Case A	Case B	Case C
Common share capital:			
40,000 shares outstanding . .	$520,000		
65,000 shares outstanding . .		$ 800,000	
25,000 shares outstanding . .			$ 650,000
Retained earnings	317,000	217,000	367,000
Total shareholders' equity . . .	$837,000	$1,017,000	$1,017,000

Required

For each case, describe the differences in the September 30 and the October 1 shareholders' equity sections and state the event that must have occurred.

Problem 16–7A
Analytical essay
(LO 5)

Jaspin Company's financial statements for the year ended December 31, 1993, have been completed and submitted to you for review. The shareholders' equity section of Jaspin's balance sheet at December 31 is as follows:

Share capital:
  Preferred shares, $2.80 noncumulative and
    nonparticipating, 10,000 shares authorized, 10,000
    shares issued and outstanding . . . . $ 498,700
  Common shares, no-par value, unlimited number of shares authorized,
    60,000 shares outstanding.   946,900
  Retained earnings   450,530
  Total shareholders' equity $1,896,130

The only share transactions during 1993 were the purchase of 12,000 common shares on July 1 and the sale of 6,000 common shares on October 31. Jaspin's 1993 net income was $240,000. A cash dividend on the preferred shares was declared on December 1, but was not paid as of December 31. Earnings per share for 1993 was calculated as follows:

$$\frac{\text{Net income}}{\substack{\text{Common shares} \\ \text{outstanding on Dec. 31}}} = \frac{\$240,000}{60,000} = \$4.00$$

Required

1. Explain what is wrong with the earnings per share calculation, indicating what corrections should be made to both the numerator and the denominator.

2. Explain how your answer to requirement 1 would be different if there had not been a cash dividend declaration to preferred shares and if the purchase and retirement of 12,000 common shares had taken place on January 2, 1993.

Fairlane Corporation's shareholders' equity on December 31, 1992, consisted of the following:

Problem 16-8A
Treasury stock transactions and stock dividends
(LO 1, 6)

Share capital:
  Common shares, no-par value, unlimited number of shares
    authorized, 370,000 shares issued $5,642,500
  Retained earnings.   627,200
  Total shareholders' equity $6,269,700

During 1993, the company completed these transactions:

Feb. 12 Purchased 15,000 shares of treasury stock at $27 per share.
    18   The directors voted a $0.10 per share cash dividend payable on March 15 to the March 2 shareholders of record.

Mar. 15 Paid the dividend declared on February 18.

June 4 Sold 6,200 of the treasury shares at $34 per share.

Sept. 1 Sold 8,800 of the treasury shares at $22 per share.

Dec. 12 The directors voted a $0.20 per share cash dividend payable on January 19 to the January 2 shareholders of record, and they voted a 1% stock dividend distributable on February 4 to the January 22 shareholders of record. The market value of $25 per share was the basis for capitalizing retained earnings.

    31   Closed the Income Summary account and carried the company's $247,300 net income to Retained Earnings.

    31   Closed the Cash Dividends Declared and Stock Dividends Declared accounts.

Required

1. Prepare General Journal entries to record the transactions and closings for 1993.
2. Prepare a retained earnings statement for the year and the shareholders' equity section of the company's year-end balance sheet.

Provocative Problems

Provocative Problem 16–1
Valtech Corporation
(LO 1, 2, 3)

On January 1, 1991, Karen Martin purchased 500 common shares of Valtech Corporation at $17 per share. On that date, the corporation had the following shareholders' equity:

Share capital:	
Common shares, no-par value, unlimited number of shares authorized, 100,000 shares outstanding............	$1,600,000
Retained earnings......................	1,200,000
Total shareholders' equity	$2,800,000

Since purchasing the 500 shares, Ms. Martin has neither purchased nor sold any additional shares. On December 31 of each year, she has received dividends on the shares held as follows: 1991, $1,320; 1992, $1,440; and 1993, $2,280.

On March 1, 1991, at a time when its shares were selling for $17.50 per share, Valtech Corporation declared a 20% stock dividend that was distributed one month later. On August 10, 1992, the corporation split its shares four for one.

Assume that Valtech Corporation's outstanding shares had a book value of $38.50 per share on December 31, 1991, a book value of $10.50 per share on December 31, 1992, and a book value of $11.75 on December 31, 1993.

Required

1. Prepare statements that show the components and amounts of the shareholders' equity in the corporation at the end of 1991, 1992, and 1993.

2. Prepare a schedule that shows the amount of the corporation's net income each year for 1991, 1992, and 1993. Assume that the changes in the company's retained earnings during the three-year period resulted from earnings and dividends.

Provocative Problem 16–2
Burtland Publishing Company
(LO 1)

Burtland Publishing Company's shareholders' equity on March 31 consisted of the following amounts:

Share capital:	
Common shares, no-par value, unlimited number of shares authorized, 120,000 shares issued and outstanding......	$4,380,000
Retained earnings......................	4,700,400
Total shareholders' equity	$9,080,400

On March 31, when the shares were selling at $40 per share, the corporation's directors voted a 10% stock dividend, distributable on April 30 to the April 7 shareholders of record. The directors also voted an $8.90 per share annual cash dividend, payable on May 22 to the May 1 shareholders of record. The amount of the latter dividend was a disappointment to some shareholders, since the company had paid a $9.19 per share annual cash dividend for a number of years.

Ann Guerci owned 1,200 common shares of Burtland Publishing Company on April 7, received her stock dividend shares, and continued to hold all of her shares until after the May 22 cash dividend. She also observed that her shares had a $40 per share market value on March 31, a market value it held until the close of business on April 7, when the market value declined to $38.50 per share. Give Burtland's entries to record the declaration and distribution or payment of the dividends involved here and answer these questions:

a. What was the book value of Guerci's total shares on March 31 (after taking into consideration the cash dividend declared on that day)? What was the book value on April 30, after she received the dividend shares?
b. What fraction of the corporation did Guerci own on March 31? What fraction did she own on April 30?
c. What was the market value of Guerci's total shares on March 31? What was the market value at the close of business on April 7?
d. What did Guerci gain from the stock dividend?

Quality Products, Inc., had the following rather special transactions and events in 1993:

Provocative Problem 16–3
Quality Products, Inc.
(LO 4)

a. Quality Products has distribution outlets in several foreign countries, one of which has been subject to political unrest. After a sudden change in governments, the new ruling body resolved that the amount of foreign investment in the country was excessive. As a result, Quality Products was forced to transfer ownership in its facility in that country to the new government. Quality Products was able to continue operations in a neighbouring country and was allowed to transfer much of its inventory and equipment to the neighbouring country. Nevertheless, the price paid to Quality Products for its facility resulted in a significant loss.
b. Quality Products' continuing operations involve a high technology production process. Technical developments in this area occur regularly, and the production machinery becomes obsolete surprisingly often. Because such developments occurred recently, Quality Products decided that it was forced to sell certain items of machinery at a loss and replace those items with a different type of machinery. The problem is how to report the loss.
c. Three years earlier, Quality Products, Inc., purchased some highly specialized equipment that was to be used in the operations of a new division that Quality Products intended to acquire. The new division was in a separate line of business and would have been a separate segment of the business. After lengthy negotiations, the acquisition of the division was not accomplished and the company abandoned any hope of entering that line of business. Although the equipment had never been used, it was sold in 1993 at a loss. Quality Products does not have a history of expanding into new lines of business and has no plans of doing so in the future.
d. Early last year, Quality Products purchased a new type of equipment for use in its production process. Although much of the production equipment is amortized over four years, a careful analysis of the situation led the company to decide that the new equipment should be amortized over eight years. Nevertheless, in the rush of year-end activities, the new equipment was included with the older equipment and amortized on a four-year basis. In preparing adjustments at the end of 1993, the accountant discovered that $135,000 amortization was taken on the new equipment last year, when only $67,500 should have been taken. The company is subject to a 25% income tax rate.

Required

Examine Quality Products' special transactions and events and describe how each one should be reported on the income statement or statement of retained earnings. Also state the item's specific characteristics that support your decision.

Provocative Problem 16–4
Bombardier Inc.
(LO 1, 2, 3, 4, 5)

BBD

The financial statements and related disclosures from Bombardier Inc.'s 1992 annual report are presented in Appendix I. Based on your examination of this information, answer the following:

1. Does Bombardier have a simple capital structure or a complex capital structure?
2. What was Bombardier's earnings per share of Class B shares in the second quarter of the 1992 year?
3. What was the total dollar amount of cash dividends paid by Bombardier during 1992?
4. What was the total dollar amount of cash dividends paid for both classes of common shares during 1992?
5. What was the total amount of cash dividends per share for both classes of common shares declared in 1992?
6. What was the total earnings per share for both classes of shares for 1992?
7. Did Bombardier have any extraordinary gains or losses during 1992?
8. Did Bombardier have any gains or losses on the disposal of a business segment during 1992?
9. According to Bombardier's share option plan, what price does an employee have to pay for shares? How many share options were outstanding on January 31, 1992?

Provocative Problem 16–5
As a Matter of Ethics:
Essay

Ethics

Review the As a Matter of Ethics case on page 809. Discuss the ethical implications of the tentative decision to avoid announcing Falcon Corporation's new government contract. What actions would you take if you were the financial vice president?

Analytical and Review Problems

A&R Problem 16–1

Included with the most recent dividend cheque was the following statement.

> On behalf of the board of directors I regret to inform you that they (the board) found it necessary to reduce your latest quarterly dividend from 40 to 25 cents per share. However, to mitigate the impact the board also declared a 20% stock dividend. The board expects that future economic conditions will permit the maintenance of the quarterly dividends at the new amount and the eventual restoration to the previously established per share level.

Within a few days of payment of the dividend, the president was confronted by the following letter from an irate shareholder:

Dear Mr. President:

   I was extremely disappointed with the reduced dividend and with no guarantee
from you that even the reduced dividend will be maintained. Have you no compas-
sion? I am a widow dependent on the meagre pension and dividends on the few
shares I hold. Is it not enough that my income has been eroded by inflation? Why
must you add to my misery by reducing, by half, the dividend I was certain of
receiving?

   I think there is something funny going on: my granddaughter informs me that the
company has nearly $400 million of retained earnings, and reduction of the dividend
was just another example of corporate irresponsibility. I have always believed in fair
play and await your reply before agreeing or disagreeing with my granddaughter's
conclusion.

                                            Sincerely yours,
                                            M. Seems, concerned shareholder

P.S. There are a couple of questions I would like to ask you: 1. What good is a stock
dividend when it caused a 20% decline in the price of the shares? 2. How come retained earnings decreased from last year even though net income was greater than
the dividend price?

Required

The president has asked you to draft a reply letter and to be certain to address all the
issues M. Seems raised.

The following information was taken from a published annual report of a Canadian   A&R Problem 16–2
corporation.

Year Ended December 31	(000)
Earnings before unusual item	$137,790
Provision for loss on returnable bottles . .	35,200
Loss from discontinued operations	—
Earnings before extraordinary item	102,590
Extraordinary item	—
Net earnings	$102,590
Earnings per share:	
Before unusual item:	
Basic	$2.41
Fully diluted	$2.23
Before extraordinary item:	
Basic	$1.80
Fully diluted	$1.69
Net earnings:	
Basic	$1.80
Fully diluted	$1.69

Required

Determine (*a*) the weighted-average number of shares outstanding and (*b*) the number
of shares that would result from the conversion of convertible securities and/or exercise of stock purchase warrants.

As a Matter of Record

Record Case 16–1

The following announcement appeared in a number of financial publications the third week of July 1992.

Coke buying shares

Coca-Cola Co. says its board has authorized buying up to 100 million of the company's common shares by 2000, adding to the 400 million shares repurchased since 1984.

Board chairman Roberto Goizueta cited "the increasingly strong cash-generating nature of our business," which "positions us to continue using excess cash to repurchase our stock."

Required

1. Evaluate the company's policy of "the increasingly strong cash-generating nature of our business positions us to continue using excess cash to repurchase our stock."

2. What are the usual reasons given by companies to justify repurchase of their own shares?

3. Could a policy that many would deem "more equitable" be used by the Coca-Cola Co. to accomplish the same goal? Explain.

Answers to Objective Review Questions

LO 1 (*e*)	LO 3 (*c*)	LO 5 (*b*)
LO 2 (*d*)	LO 4 (*a*)	LO 6 (*d*)

Installment Notes Payable and Bonds

Companies and other organizations, including governments, frequently need to borrow money for large, long-term projects, such as building a stadium. Special accounting techniques are used to measure interest expense and the amount of the liabilities.

*I*n Chapter 12, you learned to account for notes payable that require a single payment on the date the note matures. In those cases, the single payment includes the entire amount borrowed plus interest. However, many notes require a series of payments that consist of interest plus a part of the amount borrowed. We begin this chapter with a discussion of these installment notes. Then we turn to a discussion of bonds, which are liabilities issued by corporations as well as a variety of governmental bodies. The chapter concludes with a brief discussion of bond investments.

Learning Objectives

After studying Chapter 17, you should be able to:

1. Calculate and record the payments on an installment note payable.
2. Describe the various characteristics of different types of bond issues and prepare entries to record bonds that are issued between interest dates.
3. Calculate the price of a bond issue that sells at a discount and prepare entries to account for bonds issued at a discount.
4. Prepare entries to account for bonds issued at a premium.
5. Explain the purpose and operation of a bond sinking fund and prepare entries for sinking fund activities, for the retirement of bonds, and for the conversion of bonds into shares.
6. Describe the procedures used to account for investments in bonds.
7. Define or explain the words and phrases listed in the chapter glossary.

Although some promissory notes require a single lump-sum payment of the amount borrowed plus interest, most long-term notes require a series of payments. These notes are called **installment notes.** Each payment on an installment note includes interest and usually includes a partial repayment of the amount originally borrowed.

Installment Notes Payable

LO 1 Calculate and record the payments on an installment note payable.

When an installment note is used to borrow money, the borrower records the note just like a single-payment note. For example, suppose a company borrows $60,000 by signing an 8% installment note that requires six annual payments. The borrower records the note as follows:

1993					
Dec.	31	Cash	60,000.00	
		Notes Payable		60,000.00
		Borrowed $60,000 by signing an 8% note.		

An installment note payable requires the borrower to pay back the debt in a series of periodic payments. Usually, each payment includes all of the interest accrued to the date of the payment plus some portion of the original amount borrowed (also called the *principal amount*). The terms of installment notes commonly call for one of two alternative payment patterns.

Installment Payments of Accrued Interest plus Equal Amounts of Principal

Some installment notes require payments that consist of interest accrued to date plus equal amounts of principal. Because each periodic payment reduces the amount owed, the next period's interest is reduced and the total amount of the next payment is smaller than the previous payment. For example, suppose that the $60,000, 8% note just recorded requires that the accrued interest plus $10,000 of principal be paid at the end of each year. To find the amount of interest accrued in each year, look at column *c* of the table at the top of Illustration 17–1. The table shows that the interest equals 8% of the principal of the note at the beginning of the year. It also shows that the unpaid principal balance is reduced by $10,000 each year.

The graph in Illustration 17–1 shows that (1) the amount of principal in each payment remains constant at $10,000, (2) the amount of interest included in each payment gets steadily smaller, and (3) the total payment also gets smaller. Notice that the total interest expense of $16,800 equals the difference between the $76,800 paid back and the $60,000 borrowed.

The entries to record the first and the second annual payments are as follows:

1993 Dec.	31	Notes Payable.	10,000.00	
		Interest Expense	4,800.00	
		Cash		14,800.00
		To record first installment payment.		
1994 Dec.	31	Notes Payable.	10,000.00	
		Interest Expense	4,000.00	
		Cash		14,000.00
		To record second installment payment.		

Installment Payments that Are Equal in Total Amount

At this point, if you are not confident of your understanding of the concept of present value, turn back to Chapter 12 and review this concept. Also, see Appendix G at the end of the book for an expanded analysis of present and future values.

Many other installment notes require a series of equal-sized payments. Even though the payments are equal, they consist of changing amounts of interest and principal. For example, assume that the preceding $60,000, 8%

ILLUSTRATION 17–1

Installment Note with Payments of Accrued Interest and Equal Amount of Principal

	(a)	*(b)*	*(c)*	*(d)*	*(e)*
Period Ending	Beginning Principal Balance	Periodic Payment	Interest Expense for the Period *(a) x 8%*	Portion of Payment that Is Principal *(b) – (c)*	Ending Principal Balance *(a) – (d)*
Dec. 31, 1993	$60,000	$14,800	$ 4,800	$10,000	$50,000
Dec. 31, 1994	50,000	14,000	4,000	10,000	40,000
Dec. 31, 1995	40,000	13,200	3,200	10,000	30,000
Dec. 31, 1996	30,000	12,400	2,400	10,000	20,000
Dec. 31, 1997	20,000	11,600	1,600	10,000	10,000
Dec. 31, 1998	10,000	10,800	800	10,000	–0–
Total		$76,800	$16,800	$60,000	

Each payment consists of accrued interest and $10,000 principal

Interest decreases with each payment

Each payment includes $10,000 toward principal

□ Interest   ▨ Principal

note requires a series of six equal payments to be made at the end of each year. Each payment is to be $12,979. The amount of each payment is $12,979 because $60,000 is the present value of six annual payments of $12,979, discounted at 8%. (In this chapter, all monetary amounts are rounded to the nearest whole dollar.)

Allocating Each Payment between Interest and Principal. Each payment of $12,979 includes both interest and principal. Illustration 17–2 shows the allocation of each payment between interest and principal. In the table at the top of the illustration, the amount of interest expense in each payment is calculated in column *c*. As you have seen before, the amount of interest expense is found by multiplying the rate of interest (8%) by the principal balance as of the beginning of the year. Notice that the amount of the payment in excess of the interest goes to repay the principal. For example, the interest on the first payment is $4,800. Because the payment is $12,979, the rest of the payment ($8,179) reduces the principal.

Observe that the amount of interest declines in 1994 to only $4,146 because the principal is smaller. Because the size of the payment remains constant at $12,979 and the interest decreases to $4,146, the repayment of principal increases to $8,833. This process continues until the full $60,000 of original principal has been paid back.

The graph in Illustration 17–2 shows that (1) the amount of interest declines each year, (2) the amount of principal repaid increases each year, and (3) the total payment remains constant. Because the tables in Illustrations 17–1 and 17–2 show how the principal balance is reduced through the periodic payments, they are often referred to as *installment note amortization schedules*.

The journal entries to record the first and second periodic payments are:

1993					
Dec.	31	Notes Payable.	8,179.00		
		Interest Expense	4,800.00		
		Cash			12,979.00
		To record first installment payment.			
1994					
Dec.	31	Notes Payable.	8,833.00		
		Interest Expense	4,146.00		
		Cash			12,979.00
		To record second installment payment.			

Similar entries record each of the remaining payments. Compare Illustration 17–1 with Illustration 17–2 to be sure that you understand the differences between the two payment patterns.

How to Calculate the Periodic Payments. In the example, the $60,000, 8% loan required six annual payments of $12,979. Illustration 17–2 shows that these payments are precisely the amounts needed to repay the loan. But, how do you know ahead of time that the $12,979 payment will work?

ILLUSTRATION 17–2

	(a)	(b)	(c)	(d)	(e)
			Installment Note with Equal Payments		
Period Ending	Beginning Principal Balance	Periodic Payment	Interest Expense for the Period (a) x 8%	Portion of Payment that Is Principal (b) – (c)	Ending Principal Balance (a) – (d)
Dec. 31, 1993	$60,000	$12,979	$ 4,800	$ 8,179	$51,821
Dec. 31, 1994	51,821	12,979	4,146	8,833	42,988
Dec. 31, 1995	42,988	12,979	3,439	9,540	33,448
Dec. 31, 1996	33,448	12,979	2,676	10,303	23,145
Dec. 31, 1997	23,145	12,979	1,852	11,127	12,018
Dec. 31, 1998	12,018	12,979	961	12,019	–0–
Total		$77,874	$17,874	$60,000	

We can calculate the size of each payment using a table for the present value of an annuity such as Table 12–2 on page 629. To use the table for this purpose, we begin with the following equation:

$$\text{Payment} \times \text{Table value} = \text{Present value of the annuity}$$

Then, we can manipulate the equation to get this formula:

$$\text{Payment} = \frac{\text{Present value of the annuity}}{\text{Table value}}$$

Because the principal balance of an installment note equals the present value of the series of payments, the formula can now be presented as:

$$\text{Payment} = \frac{\text{Note balance}}{\text{Table value}}$$

The appropriate table value is based on the note's interest rate and the number of payments. For our example, the loan balance is $60,000. The interest rate is 8% and there are six payments. Therefore, the value from Table 12–2 is 4.6229. These facts can now be combined in the formula to compute the size of the payment:

$$\text{Payment} = \frac{\$60,000}{4.6229} = \$12,979$$

Borrowing by Issuing Bonds

Corporations often borrow money by issuing **bonds.**[1] Similar to notes payable, bonds involve a written promise to pay interest at a stated annual rate and to pay the principal, or **par value of the bonds.** Most bonds require that the borrower pay interest semiannually and pay the par value or **face amount** of the bonds at a fixed future date called the *maturity date of the bonds*. The annual amount of interest that must be paid is determined by multiplying the par value of the bonds by a stated rate of interest that was established before the bonds were issued.

Difference between Notes Payable and Bonds

When a business borrows money by signing a note payable, the money is generally borrowed from a single lender such as a bank. In contrast to a note payable, a bond issue typically includes a large number of bonds, usually in denominations of $1,000, that are sold to many different lenders. After they are originally issued, bonds are frequently bought and sold by investors. Thus, any particular bond may actually be owned by a number of people before it matures.

---

[1] The federal government and other governmental units, such as cities, provinces, municipalities, and utilities, also issue bonds. Although the examples in this chapter deal with bonds issued by business corporations, the methods used to account for bonds are the same for all organizations.

Difference between Shares and Bonds

The phrase *shares and bonds* may appear on the financial pages of newspapers or it may come up as a topic of conversation. Shares and bonds are not the same things and you should understand the differences between them. A share represents an equity or ownership right in a corporation. For example, a person who owns 1,000 of a corporation's 10,000 outstanding shares has an equity in the corporation measured at one tenth of the total shareholders' equity. Also, the person has a one-tenth interest in the corporation's future earnings. On the other hand, if a person owns a $1,000, 11%, 20-year bond issued by a corporation, the bond represents a debt or a liability of the corporation. The owner of the bond has two rights: (1) to receive 11% (or $110) interest each year the bond is outstanding and (2) to receive $1,000 when the bond matures 20 years after its date of issue.

Why Bonds Are Issued Instead of Shares

A corporation that needs funds for a long time may consider issuing either bonds or additional shares. Each approach has its advantages and disadvantages. Present shareholders may see the issuance of additional shares as a disadvantage if the shares are issued to new shareholders. Because the new shareholders are owners, the additional shares potentially dilute ownership, control of management, and earnings. On the other hand, bondholders are creditors and do not share in either management or earnings. However, a disadvantage to the company of issuing bonds is that the interest on the bonds must be paid whether or not there are any earnings.

A potential advantage of issuing bonds is that doing so might increase earnings for the common shareholders. For example, assume that a corporation with 200,000 outstanding common shares needs $1 million to expand its operations. Management estimates that, after the expansion, the company can earn $900,000 annually before bond interest, if any, and before corporate income taxes. Two plans for securing the needed funds are proposed: Plan A calls for issuing 100,000 additional common shares at $10 per share. This plan increases the total outstanding shares to 300,000. Plan B calls for the sale of $1 million of 10% bonds at par. Illustration 17–3 shows how the plans would affect the corporation's earnings, under the assumption of a 40% income tax rate. Even though the projected total income under Plan B is smaller, the amount of income per share is larger.

Corporations must pay not only federal income taxes but also provincial income taxes. These taxes may amount to as much as 40% or more of the corporation's before-tax income. However, interest expense is deductible in arriving at income subject to taxes. Therefore, when we assume a combined tax rate of 40%, as in Illustration 17–3, the reduction in taxes from issuing bonds equals 40% of the annual interest on the bonds. In other words, the tax saving effectively pays 40% of the interest cost.

ILLUSTRATION 17–3

Financing with Shares or with Bonds		
	Plan A	**Plan B**
Earnings before bond interest and income taxes. . . .	$ 900,000	$ 900,000
Deduct interest expense.		(100,000)
Income before income taxes.	$ 900,000	$ 800,000
Deduct income taxes (40% rate).	(360,000)	(320,000)
Net income	$ 540,000	$ 480,000
Plan A income per share ($540,000/300,000 shares) . .	$1.80	
Plan B income per share ($480,000/200,000 shares) . .		$2.40

Characteristics of Bonds

Over the years, corporate lawyers and financial experts have created a wide variety of bonds with different combinations of characteristics. We describe some of the more common characteristics of various bond issues in the following paragraphs.

LO 2 Describe the various characteristics of different types of bond issues and prepare entries to record bonds that are issued between interest dates.

Serial Bonds

Some bond issues include bonds that mature at different dates. As a result, the entire bond issue is repaid gradually over a period of years. Bonds of this type are called **serial bonds.** For example, a $1 million issue of serial bonds might have $100,000 of the bonds mature each year from 6 to 15 years after the bonds were issued. In this case, the $1 million issue would consist of 10 groups, or series, of bonds, each of which would have a total value of $100,000. Each group, or series, would have a unique maturity date. One series would mature after six years, another after seven years, and another each successive year until the entire $1 million issue had matured.

Sinking Fund Bonds

In contrast to serial bonds, **sinking fund bonds** all mature on the same date. However, sinking fund bonds require that the issuing corporation establish a separate pool of assets (called a *sinking fund*) for the purpose of providing the cash necessary to retire the bonds at maturity. We discuss sinking funds later in this chapter.

Registered Bonds and Bearer Bonds

The issuing corporation records the names and addresses of the owners of **registered bonds.** Interest payments on registered bonds are usually made by cheques mailed to the registered owners. This arrangement also offers some protection from loss or theft.

Bonds that are not registered are called **bearer bonds;** they are payable to whoever holds them (the *bearer*). The holder of a bearer bond is presumed to be its rightful owner. Generally, bearer bonds are also **coupon bonds.** Coupon bonds get their name from the interest coupons attached to each bond. Each coupon calls for payment of the interest due on the bond on the interest payment date. The coupons are detached as they become due and are deposited with a bank for collection. At maturity, the holder, or bearer, usually follows the same process and deposits the bond certificates with a bank for collection.

Secured Bonds and Debentures

When bonds are secured, specific assets of the issuing corporation are pledged, or mortgaged, as security. This gives the bondholders additional protection. In the event the issuing corporation fails to make the required payments of interest or par value, the bondholders can demand that the mortgaged assets be sold and the proceeds used to repay the bondholders. In contrast to secured bonds, unsecured bonds depend on the general credit standing of the issuing corporation. Unsecured bonds are called **debentures.** A company generally must be financially strong if it is to successfully issue unsecured bonds at a favourable rate of interest.

The Process of Issuing Bonds

When a corporation issues bonds, it normally sells them to an investment firm called an *underwriter*. In turn, the underwriter resells the bonds to the public.

The legal document that states the rights and obligations of the bondholders and the issuer is called the **bond indenture.** In other words, the bond indenture is the written legal contract between the issuing company and the bondholders. Each bondholder may receive a bond certificate to serve as evidence of the corporation's debt to the bondholder. As a way to reduce costs, however, many corporations no longer issue bond certificates to registered bondholders. Instead, the ownership of the bonds is registered with the corporation or the trustee.

If a bond issue is sold to a large number of investors, they are represented by a *trustee*. The trustee monitors the corporation's actions to ensure that the corporation fulfills its obligations as stated in the bond indenture. In most cases, the trustee is a large bank or trust company that is selected by the issuing company and identified in the indenture.

Accounting for the Issuance of Bonds

When a corporation issues bonds, the bond certificates (if any) are printed and the indenture is drawn and presented to the trustee of the bondholders. At that point, a memorandum describing the bond issue is commonly entered in the Bonds Payable account. The memorandum might read, ''Authorized to issue $8 million of 9%, 20-year bonds dated January 1, 1993, due on December 31, 2012, with interest payable semiannually on each June 30 and December 31.'' The bonds in this example are typical of most bonds in that interest is paid twice each year.

After the bond indenture is deposited with the trustee of the bondholders, all or a portion of the bonds may be sold. If all are sold at their par or face value, this entry records the sale:

| 1993 Jan. | 31 | Cash. . . . . Bonds Payable . . . . *Sold 9%, 20-year bonds at par.* | 8,000,000.00 | 8,000,000.00 |

When the semiannual interest is paid on these bonds, the transaction is recorded as follows:

| 1993 June | 30 | Interest Expense . . . . Cash . . . . *Paid the semiannual interest on the bonds.* | 360,000.00 | 360,000.00 |

And when the bonds are paid at maturity, the entry is:

| 2012 Dec. | 31 | Bonds Payable. . . . . Cash . . . . *Paid bonds at maturity.* | 8,000,000.00 | 8,000,000.00 |

As in the previous example, bonds are often sold on their stated, or contract, date. However, bonds also may be sold after their contract date and between interest dates. When this happens, the issuing corporation charges and collects from the purchasers the interest that has accrued on the bonds since the contract date or the preceding interest payment date. This accrued interest is then refunded to the purchasers on the next interest date. For example, on March 1, a corporation sold $100,000 of 9% bonds at par. The interest on the bonds is payable semiannually on each June 30 and December 31. The entry to record the sale two months after the contract date is:

Bonds Sold between Interest Dates

| Mar. | 1 | Cash. . . . . Interest Payable. . . . . Bonds Payable . . . . *Sold $100,000 of 9%, 20-year bonds on which two months' interest has accrued.* | 101,500.00 | 1,500.00 100,000.00 |

The $1,500 equals two months' interest ($100,000 × 9% × $^2/_{12}$).

At the end of four months, on the June 30 semiannual interest date, the purchasers of these bonds are paid a full six months' interest of $4,500 ($100,000 × 9% × $^6/_{12}$). This payment includes four months' interest earned by the bondholders after March 1 and the two months' accrued interest collected from them at the time the bonds were sold. The entry to record the payment is:

June	30	Interest Payable	1,500.00	
		Interest Expense	3,000.00	
		Cash		4,500.00
		Paid the semiannual interest on the bonds.		

This practice of first collecting accrued interest from bond purchasers and then refunding it to them in the next interest payment may seem inefficient. However, bond transactions are executed on a plus-accrued-interest basis because it is easier for the bond issuer. For example, if a corporation were to sell bonds on a variety of dates during an interest period and not collect accrued interest, the amounts the bondholders would receive on the next payment date would vary depending on how long they owned the bonds. To make the correct payments, the issuing corporation would have to keep detailed records of the purchasers and the dates on which they bought their bonds. This extra record-keeping can be avoided if each buyer is charged for accrued interest at the time of purchase. Then the corporation simply pays a full six months' interest to all purchasers, regardless of when they bought their bonds.

Bond Interest Rates

The interest rate to be paid by a corporation on its bonds is specified in the bond indenture and on each bond certificate. This rate is called the **contract rate**.[2] The contract rate of interest is applied to the par value of the bonds to determine the amount of interest to be paid each year. Even though bond interest is paid semiannually, the contract rate is usually stated on an annual basis.

For example, if a corporation issues a $1,000, 8% bond on which interest is paid semiannually, $80 will be paid each year in two payments of $40 each. Although the contract rate establishes the amount of interest that a corporation pays in cash, the contract rate is not necessarily the rate of interest expense that the corporation incurs. The interest expense the corporation incurs depends on how lenders assess their risks in lending to the corporation. This perceived risk is reflected in the **market rate for bond interest** available to the corporation. The market rate for bond interest is the rate borrowers are willing to pay and lenders are willing to accept for the use of money at the level of risk involved. The rate may change daily as the supply and demand for loanable funds changes. The market rate goes up when the demand for bond money increases and the supply decreases, and it goes down when the supply increases and the demand decreases.

Note that the market rate for bond interest is not the same for all corporations. The market rate for a specific corporation's bonds depends on the level of risk investors assign to those bonds. As the level of risk increases, the rate increases.

In many cases, a corporation that issues bonds offers a contract rate of interest equal to the rate it estimates the market will demand on the day the bonds are issued. If the estimate is correct, and the contract rate and market rate coincide on the day the bonds are issued, the bonds sell at par, which is

---

[2] This rate is also known as the *coupon rate,* the *stated rate,* or the *nominal rate.*

their face value. However, if the estimate is incorrect, the contract rate will not coincide with the market rate. As a result, bonds may sell below or above their par value (at a discount or a premium). Sometimes, the issuing corporation offers a low contract rate that results in a very large discount. Some companies even issue *zero-coupon bonds,* which do not provide for any periodic interest payments.

A **discount on bonds payable** results when a corporation issues bonds that have a contract rate below the prevailing market rate. For the same level of risk, investors can get the market rate of interest elsewhere for the use of their money. Thus, they will buy the bonds only at a price that will yield the prevailing market rate on the investment. To estimate the expected market price of the bonds, find the *present value* of the expected cash flows by discounting the cash flows from the bond investment at the current market interest rate.

Bonds Sold at a Discount

LO 3 Calculate the price of a bond issue that sells at a discount and prepare entries to account for bonds issued at a discount.

To illustrate how bond prices are determined, assume that a corporation offers to issue bonds with a $100,000 par value, an 8% annual rate, and a five-year life. Also assume that the market rate of interest for this corporation's bonds is 10%.[3] In exchange for the purchase price, the buyers of these bonds obtain the right to receive two different future cash inflows:

1. The right to receive $100,000 at the end of the bond issue's five-year life.
2. The right to receive $4,000 in interest at the end of each six-month interest period throughout the five-year life of the bonds.

To determine the price at which the bonds will be issued, you must calculate the present value of the future cash flows by discounting the amounts to be received at the market rate of interest. Although the market rate is expressed as an annual rate of 10%, this is understood to mean 5% semiannually. In five years, there are 10 semiannual periods. Therefore, use the number in the 10th row and the 5% column of Table 12–1 (page 625) to discount the $100,000 receipt at maturity. Then use the number in the 10th row and the 5% column of Table 12–2 (page 629) to discount the series of $4,000 interest payments. Calculate the present value of these cash flows as follows:

Present value of $100,000 to be received after 10 periods, discounted at 5% per period ($100,000 × 0.6139)	$61,390
Present value of $4,000 to be received periodically for 10 periods, discounted at 5% ($4,000 × 7.7217)	30,887
Present value of the bonds	$92,277

Thus, the maximum price that informed buyers would offer for the bonds is $92,277.

If the corporation accepts $92,277 for its bonds and sells them on their date of issue (January 1, 1993), the sale is recorded with an entry like this:

---

[3] The spread between the contract rate and the market rate of interest on a new bond issue is seldom more than a fraction of a percent. However, we use a difference of 2% here to simplify the illustrations.

Jan.	1	Cash	92,277.00	
		Discount on Bonds Payable	7,723.00	
		Bonds Payable		100,000.00
		Sold 8%, 5-year bonds at a discount on their date of		
		issue.		

In the corporation's financial statements, the bonds will appear in the long-term liability section assuming a January 1, 1993, balance sheet as follows:

Long-term liabilities:
Bonds payable, 8%, due December 31, 1997. . . . . $100,000
Less unamortized discount based on the 10% market rate
   for bond interest prevailing on the date of issue. 7,723 $92,277

As shown above, any unamortized discount on bonds payable is deducted from the par value of the bonds on the balance sheet to show the **carrying amount of the bonds payable.** The carrying amount is the net amount at which the bonds are recorded in the accounts.

Amortizing the Discount

In the previous discussion, the corporation received $92,277 for its bonds, but, in five years, it must pay the bondholders $100,000. The difference, the $7,723 discount, is part of the cost of using the $92,277 for five years. The total interest cost is $47,723, which is the difference between the amount borrowed and the amount repaid:

Amount repaid:
   Ten payments of $4,000 . . . . $ 40,000
   Maturity amount.   100,000
   Total repaid $140,000
Less: Amount borrowed . . . . .   (92,277)
Total interest expense . . . . . . $ 47,723

This amount also equals the sum of the cash payments and the discount:

Ten payments of $4,000 . . . . $40,000
Discount.   7,723
Total interest expense $47,723

When accounting for these bonds, you must accomplish two things: First, the total interest expense must be allocated to the 10 six-month periods in the bonds' life. Second, the carrying value of the bonds must be determined on each balance sheet date. Two alternative accounting methods are used to accomplish these objectives. They are the straight-line method and the interest method.

ILLUSTRATION 17–4

Calculation of Interest Expense and Bond Discount Amortization: Staight-Line Method

	(a)	(b)	(c)	(d)	(e)	(f)
		Interest Expense for the	Interest to Be	Discount to Be	Unamortized Discount at	Ending Carrying
Period Ending	Beginning Carrying Amount	Period (c) + (d)	Paid the Bondholders	Amortized $7,723/10	End of Period	Amount $100,000 − (e)
Jan. 1, 1993					$7,723	$ 92,277
June 30, 1993	$92,277	$ 4,772	$ 4,000	$ 772	6,951	93,049
Dec. 31, 1993	93,049	4,772	4,000	772	6,179	93,821
June 30, 1994	93,821	4,772	4,000	772	5,407	94,593
Dec. 31, 1994	94,593	4,772	4,000	772	4,635	95,365
June 30, 1995	95,365	4,772	4,000	772	3,863	96,137
Dec. 31, 1995	96,137	4,772	4,000	772	3,091	96,909
June 30, 1996	96,909	4,772	4,000	772	2,319	97,681
Dec. 31, 1996	97,681	4,772	4,000	772	1,547	98,453
June 30, 1997	98,453	4,772	4,000	772	775	99,225
Dec. 31, 1997	99,225	4,775*	4,000	775	–0–	100,000
Total.		$47,723	$40,000	$7,723		

* Adjusted to compensate for accumulated rounding of amounts.

Straight-Line Method. The **straight-line method of amortizing bond discount or premium** is the simpler of the two methods. This method allocates an equal portion of the discount or premium (and the total interest expense) to each six-month interest period.

In applying the straight-line method in the present example, divide the $7,723 discount by 10, which is the number of interest periods in the life of the bond issue. The $772 answer ($7,723/10 = $772.30, or $772) is the amount of discount to be amortized at the end of each interest period.[4] Total interest expense for each interest period is the $4,772 sum of the $4,000 cash paid and the $772 amortized discount. This $4,772 amount is also equal to one tenth of the total expense of $47,723.

At the time of the semiannual cash payment, the following entry records the periodic interest expense:

June	30	Interest Expense	4,772.00	
		Discount on Bonds Payable		772.00
		Cash		4,000.00
		To record payment of six months' interest and amortization of the discount.		

Illustration 17–4 shows the interest expense to be recorded and the discount to be amortized each period when the straight-line method is applied to the present example. Notice the following points in Illustration 17–4:

---

[4] In this chapter and in the exercises and problems at the end of the chapter, all calculations involving bonds have been rounded to the nearest whole dollar.

1. In column *f* and *a*, the $92,277 beginning carrying amount equals the $100,000 face amount of the bonds less the $7,723 discount on the sale of the bonds.
2. The semiannual interest expense of $4,772 (column *b*) equals $4,000 paid to the bondholders (column *c*) plus the $772 discount amortization (column *d*).
3. Interest paid to bondholders each period (column *c*) is determined by multiplying the par value of the bonds by the semiannual contract rate of interest ($100,000 × 4% = $4,000).
4. The discount amortized each period is $772 (column *d*).
5. The unamortized discount at the end of each period (column *e*) is determined by subtracting the discount amortized that period from the unamortized discount at the beginning of the period.
6. The end-of-period carrying amount (column *f*) of the bonds is determined by subtracting the end-of-period amount of unamortized discount (column *e*) from the face amount of the bonds ($100,000). For example, at June 30, 1993: $100,000 − $6,951 = $93,049.

Interest Method. Straight-line amortization used to be widely applied in practice. However, generally accepted accounting principles now allow the straight-line method to be applied only when the results do not differ materially from those obtained by using the **interest method of amortizing bond discount or premium.**[5]

As you learned earlier in the case of installment notes with equal periodic payments, the amount of interest expense changes each period when the interest method is used. This is also true for bonds. To calculate the amount of interest expense allocated to each period, simply multiply the carrying amount of the bonds at the beginning of each period by the market rate for the bonds at the time they were issued.

After calculating interest expense for a period, you can determine the amount of discount to be amortized by subtracting the cash interest payment from the interest expense. Illustration 17–5 presents a table for applying the interest method to the bonds in the previous example. The table shows the interest expense to be recorded (column *b*), the cash interest payment (column *c*), the discount to be amortized (column *d*), and the remaining balance sheet amounts (columns *e* and *f*).

Compare Illustration 17–5 with Illustration 17–4 and note these points about the interest method:

1. The interest expense (column *b*) results from multiplying each beginning carrying amount by the 5% semiannual market rate that prevailed when the bonds were issued. For example, in the period ended June 30, 1993, the expense is $4,614 ($92,277 × 5%) and, in the period ended December 31, 1993, it is $4,645 ($92,891 × 5%).

---

[5] FASB, *Accounting Standards—Current Text* (Norwalk, Conn., 1990), sec. I69.108. First published in *APB Opinion No. 21*, par. 15. Also see CICA Exposure Draft *Financial Instruments* (Toronto, 1991), par. 074.

ILLUSTRATION 17–5

Calculation of Interest Expense and Bond Discount Amortization: Interest Method						
	(a)	*(b)*	*(c)*	*(d)*	*(e)*	*(f)*
		Interest Expense	**Interest**	**Discount**	**Unamortized**	**Ending**
	Beginning	**for the**	**to Be**	**to Be**	**Discount at**	**Carrying**
Period	**Carrying**	**Period**	**Paid the**	**Amortized**	**End of**	**Amount**
Ending	**Amount**	**(a) × 5%**	**Bondholders**	**(b) − (c)**	**Period**	**$100,000 − (e)**
Jan. 1, 1993					$7,723	$92,277
June 30, 1993	$92,277	$ 4,614	$ 4,000	$ 614	7,109	92,891
Dec. 31,1993	92,891	4,645	4,000	645	6,464	93,536
June 30, 1994	93,536	4,677	4,000	677	5,787	94,213
Dec. 31, 1994	94,213	4,711	4,000	711	5,076	94,924
June 30, 1995	94,924	4,746	4,000	746	4,330	95,670
Dec. 31, 1995	95,670	4,784	4,000	784	3,546	96,454
June 30, 1996	96,454	4,823	4,000	823	2,723	97,277
Dec. 31, 1996	97,277	4,864	4,000	864	1,859	98,141
June 30, 1997	98,141	4,907	4,000	907	952	99,048
Dec. 31, 1997	99,048	4,952	4,000	952	–0–	100,000
Total		$47,723	$40,000	$7,723		

2. The amount of discount to be amortized each period is determined by subtracting the cash interest paid to the bondholders from the reported interest expense.

When the interest method is used to amortize a discount, the periodic entries involve the same accounts as straight-line method entries. However, the dollar amounts are different. For example, the entry to record the payment to the bondholders and to amortize the discount at the end of the first semiannual interest period of the bond issue in Illustration 17–5 is:

1993				
June	30	Interest Expense	4,614.00	
		Discount on Bonds Payable.		614.00
		Cash		4,000.00
		To record payment to the bondholders and amortization of a portion of the discount.		

Similar entries, differing only in the amount of interest expense recorded and discount amortized, are made at the end of each semiannual interest period in the life of the bond issue.

Comparing the Straight-Line and Interest Methods. Now we can examine the differences between the interest method of amortizing a discount and the straight-line method. Illustration 17–6 presents useful information for observing the differences.

The first graph in Illustration 17–6 shows how the amounts of interest expense under straight-line are the same each period, while the amounts

ILLUSTRATION 17–6

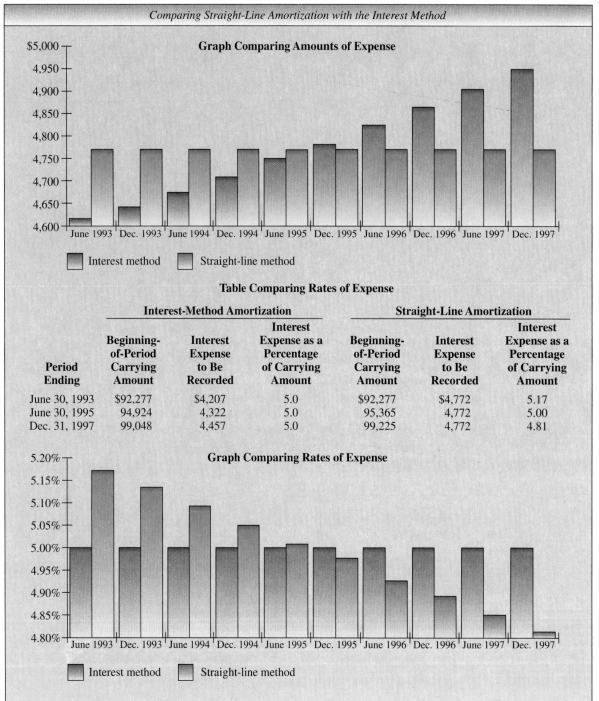

Comparing Straight-Line Amortization with the Interest Method

Graph Comparing Amounts of Expense

Table Comparing Rates of Expense

	Interest-Method Amortization			Straight-Line Amortization		
Period Ending	Beginning-of-Period Carrying Amount	Interest Expense to Be Recorded	Interest Expense as a Percentage of Carrying Amount	Beginning-of-Period Carrying Amount	Interest Expense to Be Recorded	Interest Expense as a Percentage of Carrying Amount
June 30, 1993	$92,277	$4,207	5.0	$92,277	$4,772	5.17
June 30, 1995	94,924	4,322	5.0	95,365	4,772	5.00
Dec. 31, 1997	99,048	4,457	5.0	99,225	4,772	4.81

Graph Comparing Rates of Expense

reported under the interest method increase each period. The table in the middle of Illustration 17–6 compares the two methods in three different interest periods. The table shows that when interest expense is expressed as a percentage of the beginning-of-period carrying value, the interest method results in the same percentages each period. On the other hand, when the straight-line method is used, the percentages change from period to period. This comparison extends to all 10 periods in the graph at the bottom of Illustration 17–6.

Recall that in this example, the corporation issued the bonds at a price that reflected a discounting of cash flows at 5% per six-month period. Thus, when the interest method is used, the amounts reported in the financial statements each period show an expense that is 5% of the beginning-of-period carrying value. For this reason, the interest method is preferred. In fact, the straight-line method can be used only where the results do not differ materially from those obtained through use of the interest method.

Bonds Sold at a Premium

LO 4 Prepare entries to account for bonds issued at a premium.

When a corporation offers to sell bonds carrying a contract rate of interest above the prevailing market rate for the risks involved, the bonds will sell at a **premium.** That is, buyers will bid up the price of the bonds, going as high, but no higher, than a price that will return the current market rate of interest on the investment. This price is the present value of the expected cash flows from the investment, determined by discounting these cash flows at the market rate of interest for the bonds.

For example, assume that a corporation offers to sell bonds that have a $100,000 par value and a five-year life. The interest is to be paid semiannually at a 12% annual rate. On the day of issue, the market rate of interest for the corporation's bonds is 10%. Buyers of these bonds discount the expected receipt of $100,000 after 10 six-month periods, and the expected receipt of $6,000 semiannually for 10 periods at the current market rate of 5% per six-month period. The calculation is:

Present value of $100,000 to be received after 10 periods, discounted at 5% per period ($100,000 × 0.6139)	$ 61,390
Present value of $6,000 to be received periodically for 10 periods, discounted at 5% ($6,000 × 7.7217).	46,330
Present value of the bonds	$107,720

If the bonds are sold for $107,720 on their issue date of May 1, 1993, the corporation records the sale as follows:

1993				
May	1	Cash	107,720.00	
		Premium on Bonds Payable		7,720.00
		Bonds Payable		100,000.00
		Sold bonds at a premium on their date of issue.		

When a balance sheet is prepared on May 1, 1993, the bonds appear as follows:

Long-term liabilities:
12% bonds payable, due May 1, 1998. . . . . $100,000
Add unamortized premium based on the 10% market
rate for bond interest prevailing on the date
of issue. 7,720 $107,720

As you can see, any unamortized premium on bonds payable is added to the par value of the bonds to show the carrying amount of the bonds on the balance sheet.

Amortizing the Premium

Over the life of these bonds, the issuing corporation will pay back $160,000, which consists of the 10 periodic interest payments of $6,000 plus the $100,000 par value. Because it borrowed $107,720, the total interest expense will be $52,280:

Amount repaid:
Ten payments of $6,000 . . . . $ 60,000
Maturity amount.   100,000
Total repaid . . . . $ 160,000
Less: Amount borrowed . . . . .   (107,720)
Total interest expense . . . . . . $ 52,280

This amount also equals the difference between the cash payments and the premium:

Ten payments of $6,000 . . . . $60,000
Premium. . . . .   (7,720)
Total interest expense $52,280

The allocation of this total interest expense over 10 semiannual periods is accomplished by amortizing the premium. Illustration 17–7 shows an amortization schedule for the bonds using the interest method.

Observe in Illustration 17–7 that the premium to be amortized each period (column *d*) is determined by subtracting the interest expense (column *b*) from the cash interest paid to the bondholders (column *c*). The ending carrying amount equals the sum of the $100,000 par value and the unamortized premium (column *e*).

Based on Illustration 17–7, the entry to record the first semiannual interest payment and premium amortization is:

ILLUSTRATION 17–7

Calculation of Interest Expense and Bond Premium Amortization: Interest Method

Period Ending	(a) Beginning Carrying Amount	(b) Interest Expense for the Period (a) × 5%	(c) Interest to Be Paid the Bondholders	(d) Discount to Be Amortized (c) − (b)	(e) Unamortized Premium at End of Period	(f) Ending Carrying Amount $100,000 + (e)
May 1, 1993					$7,720	$107,720
Nov. 1, 1993	$107,720	$ 5,386	$ 6,000	$ 614	7,106	107,106
May 1, 1994	107,106	5,355	6,000	645	6,461	106,461
Nov. 1, 1994	106,461	5,323	6,000	677	5,784	105,784
May 1, 1995	105,784	5,289	6,000	711	5,073	105,073
Nov. 1, 1995	105,073	5,254	6,000	746	4,327	104,327
May 1, 1996	104,327	5,216	6,000	784	3,543	103,543
Nov. 1, 1996	103,543	5,177	6,000	823	2,720	102,720
May 1, 1997	102,720	5,136	6,000	864	1,856	101,856
Nov. 1, 1997	101,856	5,093	6,000	907	949	100,949
May 1, 1998	100,949	5,051*	6,000	949	–0–	100,000
Total		$52,280	$60,000	$7,720		

* Adjusted to compensate for accumulated rounding of amounts.

1993 Nov.	1	Interest Expense	5,386.00	
		Premium on Bonds Payable	614.00	
		Cash		6,000.00
		To record payment to the bondholders and amortization of a portion of the premium.		

Similar entries, with decreasing amounts of interest expense and increasing amounts of premium amortization, are made at the end of the remaining periods in the life of the bond issue. Note that the amortization of the premium has the effect of reducing interest expense below the amount paid in cash. In effect, each cash payment retires part of the principal balance of the bonds. This process continues until the final payment, when the carrying value equals the par value of $100,000.

Accrued Interest Expense

When bonds are sold, the bond interest periods often do not coincide with the issuing company's accounting periods. In these cases, you must make an adjustment for accrued interest at the end of each accounting period. For example, the bonds described in Illustration 17–7 were issued on May 1, 1993, and interest was first recorded and paid on November 1 of that year. By December 31, 1993, two months' interest has accrued on these bonds. If the accounting period ends on that date, the following adjusting entry is required:

1993 Dec.	31	Interest Expense ($5,355 × 2/6)	1,785.00	
		Premium on Bonds Payable ($645 × 2/6)	215.00	
		Interest Payable ($6,000 × 2/6)		2,000.00
		To record two months' accrued interest and one third of the premium amortization applicable to the interest period.		

Two months are one third of a semiannual interest period. Therefore, the amounts in the entry are one third of the amounts applicable to the second interest period in the life of the bond issue. Similar entries will be made on each December 31 throughout the life of the issue. However, the amounts differ because the interest method of amortizing the premium produces a different measure of the expense in each interest period.

On May 1, 1994, this entry will record the semiannual payment of interest:

1994 May	1	Interest Payable	2,000.00	
		Interest Expense ($5,355 × 4/6)	3,570.00	
		Premium on Bonds Payable ($645 × 4/6)	430.00	
		Cash		6,000.00
		Paid the interest on the bonds, a portion of which was previously accrued, and amortized four months' premium.		

Retirement of Bonds

Bond indentures commonly include a provision that gives the issuing corporation the option of retiring the bonds prior to their maturity date. The provision states that the corporation can exercise an option to *call* the bonds before they mature by paying the par value plus a *call premium*. These bonds are known as **callable bonds.** One reason corporations insert call provisions into the bond indenture is to allow them to take action if market interest rates decline sharply. Specifically, the provisions permit the company to retire the old bonds that have a high interest rate with new bonds that pay a lower interest rate. Even if a particular issue of bonds is not callable, the issuing corporation may be able to retire its bonds by purchasing them on the open market.

Whether bonds are called or purchased in the open market, the price paid is not likely to equal the carrying value of the bonds. Because the market interest rate changes as economic conditions change, the market value of a bond's remaining cash flows also changes. Therefore, the price paid to purchase and retire bonds may result in a gain or loss. For example, assume that a company has $1 million of outstanding bonds. After interest is recorded on the April 1 interest payment date, $12,000 of unamortized premium remains. Because the market interest rate has increased, the bonds are selling at the quoted price of 98½, which stands for 98.5% of par value.[6] If the company buys and retires one tenth of the outstanding bonds at this price, the entry to record the purchase and retirement is:

Apr.	1	Bonds Payable	100,000.00	
		Premium on Bonds Payable	1,200.00	
		Gain on Retirement of Bonds.		2,700.00
		Cash		98,500.00
		To record the retirement of bonds.		

This retirement resulted in a $2,700 gain because the bonds were purchased for $2,700 below their carrying value.

Bond Sinking Fund

One reason investors buy bonds instead of shares is that bonds usually provide greater security than shares. To attract more investors, a corporation may give additional security to the bondholders by agreeing in the bond indenture to create a **bond sinking fund.** This fund consists of assets committed to be used for repaying the bondholders when the bonds mature.

LO 5 Explain the purpose and operation of a bond sinking fund and prepare entries for sinking fund activities, for the retirement of bonds, and for the conversion of bonds into shares.

A bond indenture that calls for a bond sinking fund to be created usually requires the issuing corporation to make regular periodic cash deposits with a sinking fund trustee. The trustee's duties are to safeguard the cash, invest it in securities of reasonably low risk, and add the earned interest and dividends to the accumulated balance in the sinking fund. When the bonds become due, the sinking fund trustee converts the sinking fund's investments to cash and pays the bondholders. Even though the sinking fund is in the custody of the trustee, it is the property of the bond issuer and should appear on its balance sheet in the long-term investments section.

The amounts that must be deposited to provide enough money to retire a bond issue at maturity depend on the net rate of return that can be earned on the invested funds. It is a net rate because the fee for the trustee's services is commonly deducted from the earnings.

To illustrate the accumulation of a sinking fund, assume that a corporation issues $1 million par value 10-year bonds on January 1, 1993. The bond indenture requires that the corporation make annual deposits with a sinking fund trustee on December 31 of each year in the bonds' life (1993 through 2002). Based on the assumption that the trustee will be able to earn an annual return of 8% on the invested assets, net of expenses, the corporation must deposit $69,029 each year.[7] Illustration 17–8 shows that these deposits and the earnings on the accumulated funds will generate enough cash to retire the bonds at maturity.

---

[6] Bond quotations are commonly expressed in this form. For example, a bond quoted at 101¼ can be bought or sold at 101.25% of its par value, plus accrued interest, if any. Broker's fees are added to this amount on purchases and deducted on sales.

[7] To understand how the periodic deposits to a sinking fund are calculated, study Appendix H at the end of the book. Using Table H–4, "Future Value of an Annuity of 1 per Period" in Appendix H, the payment of $69,029 is calculated as $1,000,000/14.4866 = $69,029.

ILLUSTRATION 17–8

	Expected Asset Accumulation of a Bond Sinking Fund that Earns 8%				
End of Year	Beginning-of-Period Sinking Fund Balance	8% Return Earned on Fund Balance	Amount Deposited	Total Increase in Sinking Fund	End-of-Period Sinking Fund Balance
1993	$ –0–	$ –0–	$ 69,029	$ 69,029	$ 69,029
1994	69,029	5,522	69,029	74,551	143,580
1995	143,580	11,486	69,029	80,515	224,095
1996	224,095	17,928	69,029	86,957	311,052
1997	311,052	24,884	69,029	93,913	404,965
1998	404,965	32,397	69,029	101,426	506,391
1999	506,391	40,511	69,029	109,540	615,931
2000	615,931	49,274	69,029	118,303	734,234
2001	734,234	58,739	69,029	127,768	862,002
2002	862,002	68,969*	69,029	137,998	1,000,000
Total		$309,710	$690,290	$1,000,000	

* Adjusted to compensate for accumulated rounding of amounts.

The entry to record the amount deposited each year appears as follows:

Dec.	31	Bond Sinking Fund	69,029.00	
		Cash		69,029.00
		To record the annual sinking fund deposit.		

The sinking fund trustee invests the deposits and sends the issuing corporation a report of the earnings on the investments at least once each year. The corporation then records the sinking fund earnings in its accounts and reports them on its income statement. For example, if 8% is earned during 1994, the corporation records the sinking fund earnings as follows:

1994 Dec.	31	Bond Sinking Fund	5,522.00	
		Sinking Fund Earnings		5,522.00
		To record the sinking fund earnings.		

When sinking fund bonds mature, the trustee converts the fund's assets into cash and pays the par value of the bonds to the bondholders. When the sinking fund assets are sold, the amount of cash generated is often a little more or a little less than is needed to pay the bondholders. If excess cash is produced, it is returned to the corporation. If there is not enough, the corporation must make up the deficiency.

For example, if the securities in the sinking fund of a $1 million bond issue produce $1,010,325 when converted to cash, the trustee uses $1 million to pay the bondholders and returns the extra $10,325 to the corporation. The corporation then records the payment of its bonds and the return of the extra cash with this entry:

Jan.	3	Cash.	10,325.00	
		Bonds Payable.	1,000,000.00	
		Bond Sinking Fund		1,010,325.00
		To record payment of bonds and the return of extra cash from the sinking fund.		

Restrictions on Dividends Due to Outstanding Bonds

To protect a corporation's financial position and the interests of its bondholders, a bond indenture may restrict the dividends the corporation may pay while its bonds are outstanding. Commonly, the restriction provides that the corporation may pay dividends in any year only to the extent that the year's earnings exceed sinking fund requirements.

Converting Bonds to Shares

To make a bond issue more attractive, bondholders may be given the right to exchange their bonds for a fixed number of shares of the issuing company's common shares. Such **convertible bonds** offer investors initial investment security, and if the issuing company prospers and its shares increase in price, an opportunity to share in the prosperity by converting their bonds to the more valuable shares. Conversion is at the bondholders' option and therefore does not take place unless it is to their advantage. However, most convertible bonds also are callable bonds. Thus, if the common share price rises enough to make conversion more attractive than being paid the call price, the issuing corporation can force bondholders to convert. To do this, the issuing corporation simply announces that the bonds are being called if the bondholders do not convert them without delay.

When bonds are converted into shares, the conversion changes a liability into owners' equity. The typical method of recording a conversion of bonds into shares transfers the carrying value of the converted bonds to contributed capital accounts. No gain or loss is recognized. For example, assume the following: (1) A company has outstanding $1 million of bonds on which there is $8,000 unamortized discount, (2) the bonds are convertible at the rate of a $1,000 bond for 90 shares of the company's no par value common stock, and (3) bonds with a par value of $100,000 have been presented for conversion on their interest date. The entry to record the conversion is:

May	1	Bonds Payable.	100,000.00	
		Discount on Bonds Payable.		800.00
		Common Shares		99,200.00
		To record the conversion of bonds.		

Note in this entry that the bonds' $99,200 carrying amount sets the accounting value for the capital contributed.

Ottawa Checking Out Index-Linked Bonds

On sale this week in London are items that may be copied on this side of the pond—index-linked bonds. The Bank of England has floated two bond issues of £104-million ($196-million), carrying rates of 2 percent and 2.5 percent.

Not an attractive return at first glance, but the point is that index-linked bonds compensate for inflation. If inflation is 5 percent, a 2-percent index-linked bond pays 7 percent.

Of course, most people would say that 2 percent is a poor real rate of return. But at higher rates, there is a good case for a bond that pays a fixed real return plus an adjustment for inflation.

This analysis now is being done in Ottawa, where the federal government is looking into starting a Canadian series of index-linked bonds. Naturally, private enterprise is able to do the job more quickly.

Ken Kelly, vice president for fixed income research at ScotiaMcLeod, has produced a report making the case in favour of index-linked bonds. He concludes that real rates of return in the 3- to 4-percent range would be attractive.

More to the point, his conclusion is that there is a measurable difference in the performance of an index-linked bond (ILB) and a nominal bond (the now-standard bond where the rate is fixed from the start).

Assuming that inflation will average 3.5 percent over the next 30 years, he estimates that a 4-percent ILB "would outperform a 30-year, 10-percent nominal bond if both bonds were held to maturity and all coupon payments were reinvested in treasury bills."

In designing an ILB, there are three general structures—a zero coupon, an indexed coupon, and an indexed principal.

The zero coupon bond offers the best inflation protection. It is bought at a discount and all the interest payments, including inflation adjustments, are paid at the end. (Ontario Hydro issued a zero coupon bond earlier this year that yielded about 11 percent. Only $20.30 was needed for each $1,000 that would be paid in 30 years.)

An indexed coupon bond has the most risk. Inflation adjustments are paid annually with the interest. Consequently, the investor has more money to reinvest and, thus, has less inflation protection. The reason for that is whenever the investor takes in cash, inflation starts to eat away at the value of that money.

Indexed principal bonds pay only the real return, and inflation is added onto the principal when that amount is paid out at the end of the term.

Mr. Kelly said the British government uses this structure for its bonds. He said Ottawa most likely will do the same, if it issues index-linked bonds.

Source: Bud Jorgensen, *The Globe & Mail,* October 9, 1991, p. B7. Reprinted by permission.

Investments in Bonds

LO 6 Describe the procedures used to account for investments in bonds.

So far in this chapter, our discussion of bonds has focused on the issuing corporation. We now shift our attention to the purchasers of bonds. Bonds purchased as an investment are recorded at cost, including any broker's fees. If interest has accrued at the date of purchase, the purchaser also pays for the accrued interest and records it with a debit to Interest Receivable. The following entry records a purchase of $50,000 of 9%, 10-year bonds on May 1, 1993, four months after their initial issuance, at the price of 92, plus $400 of broker's fees:

1993 May	1	Investment in AMCO Corporation Bonds.	46,400.00	
		Interest Receivable	1,500.00	
		Cash		47,900.00
		Purchased fifty $1,000, 9%, 10-year bonds dated		
		December 31, 1992, at a price of 92 plus a $400		
		broker's fee and accrued interest.		

The $46,400 cost of the bonds was their market value of $46,000 (92% × $50,000 par value) plus the $400 fee. This price created a discount of $3,600. Most bond investors do not record a discount (or a premium) in a separate account. The investment account is simply debited for the net cost. The accrued interest on May 1 was $1,500 ($50,000 × 9% × 4/12).

Short-Term Investments in Bonds

Assuming that AMCO Corporation pays interest semiannually on June 30 and December 31, the June 30, 1993, entry to record the receipt of interest from AMCO Corporation is as follows:

1993 June	30	Cash	2,250.00	
		Interest Receivable.		1,500.00
		Interest Earned.		750.00
		To record the first semiannual receipt of interest.		

This entry correctly reflects the fact that the purchaser owned the bonds for two months while the interest earned amounted to $750 ($50,000 × 9% × 2/12). However, recall that the bonds were purchased at a discount and then notice that this entry does not include any amortization of the discount. This practice is acceptable only if the bonds are held as a short-term investment. Under these conditions, the bond investment is reported at cost in the current asset section of the balance sheet. The market value of the bonds on the date of the balance sheet is also disclosed. For example, assume that the market value of the AMCO bonds is $49,000 on December 31, 1993. Thus, the investment would be reported as follows:

Current assets:
   Investment in AMCO Corporation bonds (market value is $49,000) . . $46,400

When the bonds are sold, the gain or loss on the sale is calculated as the difference between the sale proceeds and cost.

Long-Term Investments in Bonds

What if the bonds are held to maturity as a long-term investment? Over the holding period, the market value of the bonds generally moves toward par value as the maturity date approaches. In a similar fashion, any discount or premium should be amortized so that the carrying value at maturity will equal the bonds' par value. This process also means that the interest earned in each period will include some discount or premium amortization. The procedures for amortizing a discount or premium on bond investments parallel those discussed and applied previously to bonds payable. The only difference is that the amortized discount or premium is debited or credited directly to the investment account.

Sales of Bonds by Investors

An investor who buys a bond might later decide to sell it after several months or years. The price at which the bond is sold is determined by the market interest rate for the bonds on the day of the sale. The market interest rate on the day of the sale determines the price because the new investor could get this current rate elsewhere. Therefore, the new investor discounts the right to receive the bond's face amount at maturity and the right to receive its interest for the remaining periods of life at the current market rate to determine the price to pay for the bond. As a result, since bond interest rates vary over time, a bond that originally sold at a premium may later sell at a discount, and vice versa. The seller should report a gain or loss for the difference between the proceeds of the sale and the bonds' carrying value as of the date of the sale.

Mortgages as Security for Notes Payable and Bonds

Earlier in this chapter, we said that some bonds are secured and some are unsecured. These arrangements are also possible for notes payable. When bonds (or notes) are unsecured, the obligation to pay interest and par (or principal) is equal in standing with other unsecured liabilities of the issuing company. If the company becomes financially troubled and is unable to pay its debts in full, none of the unsecured creditors has preference over any other.

The ability of a company to borrow money by issuing unsecured bonds (or signing an unsecured note) depends on the company's general credit standing. In many cases, a company cannot obtain debt financing without providing security to the creditors. In other cases, the rate of interest that creditors would charge to provide unsecured debt is very high. As a result, many notes payable and bond issues are secured by mortgages.

A **mortgage** is a legal agreement that helps protect a lender if a borrower fails to make the payments required by a note payable or bond indenture. A mortgage gives the lender the right to be paid out of the cash proceeds from the sale of the borrower's assets identified in the mortgage.

A separate legal document, called the **mortgage contract,** contains the terms of a mortgage. The mortgage contract is given to the trustee of the bond issue or to the lender along with the note payable. A mortgage contract normally requires the borrower to pay all property taxes on the mortgaged property, to keep the mortgaged property repaired, and to be sure that it is adequately insured. In addition, the mortgage normally grants its holder (the lender) the right to foreclose if the borrower fails to pay. In a foreclosure, a court either sells the property or grants possession of the mortgaged property to the lender, who sells it. When the property is sold, the proceeds are first applied to court costs and then to the claims of the mortgage holder. The former owner of the property receives any cash that remains. This amount may be used to pay the debts of the unsecured creditors.

Summary of the
Chapter in Terms of
Learning Objectives

LO 1. Installment notes typically require either of two alternative payment plans: (*a*) payments that include accrued interest plus an equal amount of principal or (*b*) payments that are equal in amount but consist of a declining amount of interest and an increasing amount of principal. If the second pattern is used, the payments are determined by dividing the amount borrowed (the present value of the payments) by the annuity table value for the interest rate and the number of payments.

LO 2. An installment note usually is given when a company borrows money from a single creditor. A bond issue, on the other hand, is divided into bonds that have a par value of $1,000 each so that many investors can participate in the issue. Shares represent an equity interest in a corporation while bonds and installment notes are liabilities of the corporation. A bond issue may consist of serial bonds, which mature at different points in time, or of bonds that all mature on the same date. Some of the latter are sinking fund bonds, for which a fund of assets is established to pay the bondholders the par value of the bonds at the maturity date. If bonds are registered, the name and address of each bondholder is recorded with the issuing corporation. In contrast, bearer bonds are payable to whoever holds, or bears, the bonds. Interest on bearer bonds is paid when coupons are detached and presented for payment. Mortgages secure some bonds, and other bonds, called *debentures*, are unsecured.

When bonds are sold between interest dates, the accrued interest is charged to the purchaser, who is then repaid that amount on the next interest payment date.

LO 3. The contract rate of interest is applied to the par value of bonds to determine the annual cash payment of interest, which is usually paid in two installments. The present value of a bond is determined by adding the present value of the interest payments and the present value of the par value.

When bonds are issued at a discount, the Bonds Payable account is credited for the par value of the bonds and the difference between the cash proceeds and the par value is debited to Discount on Bonds Payable. Each time interest is paid, part of the discount is amortized, with the effect of increasing interest expense above the amount of cash paid. The interest method of amortization is required by generally accepted accounting principles, but the straight-line method may be used if the results are not materially different from the interest method.

LO 4. When the market interest rate for a corporation's bonds is less than the contract rate, the bonds sell at a premium. The premium is recorded by the issuer in a separate account and is amortized over the life of the bonds in a manner similar to the amortization of bond discount.

LO 5. A corporation that issues sinking fund bonds makes periodic deposits of cash with a sinking fund trustee. The trustee invests the assets, reports the earnings to the issuing corporation, and uses the accumulated sinking fund assets to repay the bondholders on the maturity date of the bonds.

When convertible bonds are converted into common shares, the carrying value of the bonds is transferred to contributed capital accounts that relate to common shares. Generally, no gain or loss is recorded.

LO 6. The cost of a bond investment (including brokerage fees) is usually debited to an Investment in Bonds account without separately identifying any premium or discount on the investment. If held as a short-term investment, cash receipts of interest are recorded as interest earned, and no attempt is made to amortize the premium or discount on the bond investment. However, if bonds are held as a long-term investment, the difference between the cost and par value of the investment must be amortized. The methods used to amortize premiums or discounts on bond investments parallel the amortization of premiums or discounts on bonds payable.

Demonstration Problem

The Stanley Tile Company patented and successfully test-marketed a new product. However, to expand its ability to produce and market the product, the company needed $4 million of additional financing. On January 1, 1993, the company borrowed the money in the following ways:

1. Stanley signed an $800,000, 10% installment note that is to be repaid in five annual payments. Each payment is to include principal of $160,000 plus accrued interest. The payments will be made on December 31, 1993–97.

2. Stanley also signed a second $800,000, 10% installment note calling for five annual installment payments that are equal in amount. The payments will be made on December 31, 1993–97.

3. Stanley also issued three separate groups of five-year bonds, each of which has a face amount of $800,000. On January 1, 1993, the market interest rate for all three groups of bonds was 10% per year.
    a. Group A will pay 10% annual interest on June 30 and December 31, 1993–97.
    b. Group B will pay 12% annual interest on June 30 and December 31, 1993–97.
    c. Group C will pay 8% annual interest on June 30 and December 31, 1993–97.

Required

1. For the first installment note: (*a*) prepare an amortization schedule and (*b*) present the entry for the first installment payment on December 31, 1993.

2. For the second installment note: (*a*) calculate the amount of each installment payment, (*b*) prepare an amortization schedule, and (*c*) present the entry for the first installment payment on December 31, 1993.

3. For the 10% (Group A) bonds: present (*a*) the January 1, 1993, entry to record the issuance of the bonds and (*b*) the June 30, 1993, entry to record the first payment of interest.

4. For the 12% (Group B) bonds: (*a*) calculate the issuance price of the bonds; (*b*) present the January 1, 1993, entry to record the issuance of the bonds; (*c*) prepare a schedule that shows periodic interest expense and premium amortization using the interest method; (*d*) present the June 30, 1993, entry to record the first payment of interest; and (*e*) present a January 1, 1995, entry to record the retirement of the bonds at the contractual call price of $832,000.

5. For the 8% (Group C) bonds: (*a*) calculate the issuance price of the bonds; (*b*) present the January 1, 1993, entry to record the issuance of the bonds; (*c*) prepare a schedule that shows periodic interest expense and discount amortization using the interest method; and (*d*) present the June 30, 1993, entry to record the first payment of interest.

Planning the Solution

Solution to Demonstration Problem

- For the first installment note, prepare a table similar to the one in Illustration 17–1 and take the numbers for the entry from the first line.

- For the second installment note, divide the amount borrowed by the annuity table factor for 10% and five payments. Prepare a table similar to Illustration 17–2 and take the numbers for the entry from the first line.

- For the bonds in Group A, prepare the entries using the par value and the contractual interest.

- For the bonds in Group B, first calculate the present value of the bonds' cash flows using the market interest rate. Next, use the result to record the issuance. Then, develop an amortization table similar to Illustration 17–7 and take from it the numbers needed for the journal entry. Finally, use the table to get the carrying value as of the date of the retirement of the bonds, and use it in the journal entry.

- For the bonds in Group C, first calculate the present value of the bonds' cash flows using the market interest rate. Next, use the result to record the issuance. Then, develop an amortization table similar to Illustration 17–5 and take from it the numbers needed for the journal entry.

1. *a.* The amortization schedule for the first installment note:

Period Ending	Beginning Principal Balance	Periodic Payment	Interest Expense for the Period	Portion of Payment that Is Principal	Ending Principal Balance
Dec. 31, 1993	$800,000	$ 240,000	$ 80,000	$160,000	$640,000
Dec. 31, 1994	640,000	224,000	64,000	160,000	480,000
Dec. 31, 1995	480,000	208,000	48,000	160,000	320,000
Dec. 31, 1996	320,000	192,000	32,000	160,000	160,000
Dec. 31, 1997	160,000	176,000	16,000	160,000	–0–
Total.		$1,040,000	$240,000	$800,000	

b. The entry for the first payment on this note on December 31, 1993:

1993				
Dec.	31	Interest Expense	80,000.00	
		Notes Payable.	160,000.00	
		Cash		240,000.00
		Made first payment on installment note.		

2. *a.* Calculation of the dollar amount of the five equal payments for the second installment note:

From Table 12–2, the present value of $1 to be paid annually for five years, discounted at 10%, is $3.7908. Therefore:

Periodic payment = $800,000/3.7908 = $211,037

b. The amortization schedule for the second installment note:

Period Ending	Beginning Principal Balance	Periodic Payment	Interest Expense for the Period	Portion of Payment that Is Principal	Ending Principal Balance
Dec. 31, 1993	$800,000	$ 211,037	$ 80,000	$131,037	$668,963
Dec. 31, 1994	668,963	211,037	66,896	144,141	524,822
Dec. 31, 1995	524,822	211,037	52,482	158,555	366,267
Dec. 31, 1996	366,267	211,037	32,627	174,410	191,857
Dec. 31, 1997	191,857	211,037	19,180*	191,857	–0–
Total		$1,055,185	$255,185	$800,000	

* Adjusted to compensate for rounding.

c. The entry for the first payment on this note on December 31, 1993:

1993				
Dec.	31	Interest Expense	80,000.00	
		Notes Payable.	131,037.00	
		Cash		211,037.00
		Made first payment on installment note.		

3. *a.* The entry for issuance of the 10% bonds on January 1, 1993:

1993				
Jan.	31	Cash	800,000.00	
		Bonds Payable, Group A		800,000.00
		Issued 10% bonds at face value.		

b. The entry for the first payment of interest on the bonds on June 30, 1993:

1993				
June	30	Interest Expense	40,000.00	
		Cash		40,000.00
		Paid interest on 10% bonds.		

4. *a.* Calculating the issue price of the 12% bonds:

Present value of $800,000 to be paid after 10 periods,
    discounted at 5% ($800,000 × 0.6139) $491,120
Present value of $48,000 to be paid periodically for
    10 periods, discounted at 5% ($48,000 × 7.7217)   370,642
Present value of the bonds $861,762

b. The entry for issuance of the 12% bonds on January 1, 1993:

1993				
Jan.	1	Cash	861,762.00	
		Bonds Payable, Group B		800,000.00
		Premium on Bonds Payable, Group B		61,762.00
		Issued 12% bonds at a premium.		

c. The premium amortization table for the 12% bonds (interest method):

Period Ending	Beginning Carrying Amount	Interest Expense for the Period	Interest to Be Paid the Bondholders	Premium to Be Amortized	Unamortized Premium at End of Period	Ending Carrying Amount
Jan. 1, 1993					$61,762	$861,762
June 30, 1993	$861,762	$ 43,088	$ 48,000	$ 4,912	56,850	856,850
Dec. 31, 1993	856,850	42,843	48,000	5,157	51,693	851,693
June 30, 1994	851,693	42,585	48,000	5,415	46,278	846,278
Dec. 31, 1994	846,278	42,314	48,000	5,686	40,592	840,592
June 30, 1995	840,592	42,030	48,000	5,970	34,622	834,622
Dec. 31, 1995	834,622	41,731	48,000	6,269	28,353	828,353
June 30, 1996	828,353	41,418	48,000	6,582	21,771	821,771
Dec. 31, 1996	821,771	41,089	48,000	6,911	14,860	814,860
June 30, 1997	814,860	40,743	48,000	7,257	7,603	807,603
Dec. 31, 1997	807,603	40,397*	48,000	7,603	–0–	800,000
Total		$418,238	$480,000	$61,762		

* Adjusted to compensate for accumulated rounding of amounts.

d. The entry for the first payment of interest of bonds on June 30, 1993:

1993				
June	30	Interest Expense	43,088.00	
		Premium on Bonds Payable, Group B.	4,912.00	
		Cash		48,000.00
		Paid interest on 12% bonds.		

e. The entry that would be made on January 1, 1995, for the retirement of the 12% bonds at the contractual call price of $832,000:

1995					
Jan.	1	Bonds Payable, Group B	800,000.00		
		Premium on Bonds Payable, Group B.	40,592.00		
		Gain on Retirement of Bonds.		8,592.00	
		Cash		832,000.00	
		Retired 12% bonds at contractual call price of			
		$832,000.			

5. *a.* Calculating the issue price of the 8% bonds:

> Present value of $800,000 to be paid after 10 periods,
> discounted at 5% ($800,000 × 0.6139) $491,120
> Present value of $32,000 to be paid periodically for
> 10 periods, discounted at 5% ($32,000 × 7.7217)   247,094
> Present value of the bonds $738,214

b. The entry for issuance of the 8% bonds on January 1, 1993:

1993				
Jan.	1	Cash.	738,214.00	
		Discount on Bonds Payable, Group C.	61,786.00	
		Bonds Payable, Group C		800,000.00
		Issued 8% bonds at a discount.		

c. The discount amortization table for the 8% bonds (interest method):

Period Ending	Beginning Carrying Amount	Interest Expense for the Period	Interest to Be Paid the Bondholders	Discount to Be Amortized	Unamortized Discount at End of Period	Ending Carrying Amount
Jan. 1, 1993					$61,786	$738,214
June 30, 1993	$738,214	$ 36,911	$ 32,000	$ 4,911	56,875	743,125
Dec. 31, 1993	743,125	37,156	32,000	5,156	51,719	748,281
June 30, 1994	748,281	37,414	32,000	5,414	46,305	753,695
Dec. 31, 1994	753,695	37,685	32,000	5,685	40,620	759,380
June 30, 1995	759,380	37,969	32,000	5,969	34,651	765,349
Dec. 31, 1995	765,349	38,267	32,000	6,267	28,384	771,616
June 30, 1996	771,616	38,581	32,000	6,581	21,803	778,197
Dec. 31, 1996	778,197	38,910	32,000	6,910	14,893	785,107
June 30, 1997	785,107	39,255	32,000	7,255	7,638	792,362
Dec. 31, 1997	792,362	39,638*	32,000	7,638	–0–	800,000
Totals		$381,786	$320,000	$61,786		

* Adjusted to compensate for accumulated rounding of amounts.

d. The entry for the first payment of interest on the bonds on June 30, 1993:

1993				
June	30	Interest Expense	36,911.00	
		Discount on Bonds Payable, Group C		4,911.00
		Cash		32,000.00
		Paid interest on 8% bonds.		

Bearer bond a bond that is made payable to whoever holds it (the bearer); this bond is not registered. p. 857

Glossary

LO 7 Define or explain the words and phrases listed in the chapter glossary.

Bond a long-term liability of a corporation or governmental unit, usually issued in denominations of $1,000, that requires periodic payments of interest and payment of its par value when it matures. p. 855

Bond indenture the contract between the corporation that issued bonds and the bondholders; it states the obligations and rights of each party. p. 858

Bond sinking fund assets that are committed to be used for repaying the holders of bonds covered by a bond indenture that requires the fund to be created; the issuing company makes deposits to the fund, which is managed by an independent trustee; the fund is established to provide cash for repaying the bondholders when the bonds mature. p. 871

Callable bond a bond that may be retired before maturity at the option of the issuing corporation. p. 870

Carrying amount of bonds payable the net amount at which bonds are recorded in the issuer's accounts; equals the par value of the bonds less any unamortized discount or plus any unamortized premium. p. 862

Contract rate of bond interest the rate of interest specified in the bond indenture; it is applied to the par value of the bonds to determine the amount of interest to be paid each year. p. 860

Convertible bond a bond that may be exchanged for shares of its issuing corporation at the option of the bondholder. p. 873

Coupon bond a bond that is issued with interest coupons attached to the bond certificate; the coupons are detached as they become due and are deposited with a bank for collection. p. 858

Debenture an unsecured bond that depends on the general credit standing of the issuing corporation. p. 858

Discount on bonds payable the difference between the par value of a bond and its issue price when the bond is sold for an amount less than its par value. p. 861

Face amount of a bond another term used to describe a bond's par value. p. 855

Installment notes promissory notes that require a series of payments, each of which consists of interest and a portion of the amount originally borrowed. p. 850

Interest method of amortizing bond discount or premium a method of calculating interest expense for a period; it multiplies the bonds' beginning carrying value by the market rate of interest from the date of issuance; the periodic amortization of discount or premium equals the difference between the cash interest paid and the interest expense. p. 864

Market rate for bond interest the rate borrowers are willing to pay and lenders are willing to accept for the use of money at the level of risk involved with that corporation's bonds. p. 860

Mortgage a legal agreement that helps protect a lender by giving the lender the right to be paid from the cash proceeds from the sale of the borrower's assets identified in the mortgage. p. 876

Mortgage contract a legal document that states the rights of the lender and the obligations of the borrower with respect to assets pledged as security for a bond or note payable. p. 876

Par value of a bond the amount that the borrower agrees to repay at maturity and the amount on which interest payments are based; also called the face amount of the bond. p. 855

Premium on bonds payable the difference between the par value of a bond and its issue price when the bond is sold for an amount greater than its par value. p. 867

Registered bonds bonds that have the names and addresses of their owners recorded by the issuing corporation; interest payments are distributed by cheques from the corporation to the owners. p. 857

Serial bonds an issue of bonds that mature at different dates, such that the total issue is repaid gradually over a period of years. p. 857

Sinking fund bonds bonds that require the issuing corporation to make deposits to a separate fund of assets during the life of the bonds; the bondholders are repaid at maturity from the assets in this fund. p. 857

Straight-line method of amortizing bond discount or premium a method that amortizes an equal amount of the original discount or premium in each accounting period in the life of the bonds. p. 863

Synonymous Terms

Contract interest rate coupon rate; stated rate; nominal rate.

Principal of a bond par value; face value.

Objective Review

Answers to the following questions are listed at the end of this chapter. Be sure that you decide which is the one best answer to each question *before* you check the answers.

LO 1 When an installment note requires a series of payments that are equal in amount:

a. The interest expense for a given period is calculated by multiplying the face amount of the note by the interest rate.

b. The payments consist of an increasing amount of interest and a decreasing amount of principal.

c. The payments consist of changing amounts of the principal portion of the payment, but the interest portion of the payment remains constant.

d. The payments consist of changing amounts of interest, but the principal amount remains constant.

e. The portion of the payment that reduces principal is determined by multiplying the beginning-of-period principal balance by the interest rate and deducting that amount of interest expense from the payment.

LO 2 On May 1, a corporation sold $500,000 of 9% bonds on which interest is payable semiannually on each January 1 and July 1. If the bonds were sold at par value plus accrued interest, the entry to record the first semiannual interest payment on July 1 would include:

a. A debit to Interest Payable for $15,000.

b. A credit to Cash for $45,000.

c. A debit to Bonds Payable for $22,500.

d. A debit to Interest Payable for $7,500.

e. A credit to Interest Payable for $15,000 and a debit to Interest Expense for $22,500.

LO 3 What would be the selling price of 10% bonds that have a $100,000 par value and an eight-year life if interest is to be paid semiannually? Assume the market rate of interest is 12% and the bonds were sold six months before the first interest payment.

a. $100,000.

b. $ 89,900.

c. $ 86,050.

d. $115,644.

e. $110,836.

LO 4 On December 31, 1993, Cello Corporation received $109,444 from the sale of 16% bonds payable, $100,000 par value, interest payable June 30 and December 31. The bonds were sold to yield a 14% market rate of interest. Using the interest method, the entry to record the second payment of interest on December 31, 1994, would include a debit to Premium on Bonds Payable in the amount of:

a. $7,661.

b. $ 339.

c. $ 678.

d. $7,637.

e. $ 363.

LO 5 When the bond indenture requires the issuing corporation to establish a bond sinking fund:

a. The issuing corporation is usually required to make periodic cash deposits with a sinking fund trustee.

b. Interest and dividends earned from investing the assets in the sinking fund are credited to Sinking Fund Earnings and reported on the income statement of the issuing corporation.

c. The issuing corporation reports the accumulated amount of assets in the fund on its balance sheet as a long-term investment.

d. The final entry to retire the bonds with sinking fund assets may include a debit or credit to Cash if the total amount of sinking fund assets differs from the par value of the bonds.

e. All of the above.

LO 6 When an investor purchases corporate bonds:

a. Interest accrued on the date of purchase should be reported by the investor as interest earned.

b. And the purchase price includes a premium, the amount of interest earned and recorded in later periods will exceed the amount of cash received each period.

c. And the bonds are held as a long-term investment, any premium or discount on the investment must be amortized in the process of recording interest income.

d. The investment should be recorded at cost, excluding any brokerage fees.

e. And the bonds are held as a short-term investment, any premium or discount on the investment must be amortized in the process of recording interest income.

LO 7 A bearer bond is:

a. A bond for which the name and address of the owner are recorded by the issuing corporation.

> *b.* An issue of bonds that mature at different points in time so that the entire bond issue is repaid gradually over a period of years.
>
> *c.* A bond that may be exchanged for shares of its issuing corporation's stock at the option of the bondholder.
>
> *d.* A bond that is not registered and is made payable to whoever holds the bond.
>
> *e.* None of the above.

Questions for Class Discussion

1. What are two common payment patterns on installment notes?
2. What is the difference between a note payable and a bond issue?
3. What is the primary distinction between a share of stock and a bond?
4. What advantages do bonds have over stock as a means of long-term financing?
5. What is a bond indenture? What are some of the provisions commonly included in an indenture?
6. Define or describe (*a*) registered bonds, (*b*) coupon bonds, (*c*) serial bonds, (*d*) sinking fund bonds, (*e*) callable bonds, and (*f*) debenture bonds.
7. Why does a corporation that issues bonds between interest dates collect accrued interest from the purchasers of the bonds?
8. What determines market interest rates for bonds?
9. When the straight-line method is used to amortize bond discount, how is the interest expense for each period calculated?
10. When the interest method is used to amortize bond discount or premium, how is the interest expense for each period calculated?
11. If the quoted price for a bond is 97¾, does this price include accrued interest?
12. Suppose that a bond issue matures when the sinking fund assets are insufficient for repaying the bondholders. Who makes up the deficiency before the bondholders are paid? If the sinking fund has more than enough cash to repay the bondholders at maturity, what happens to the excess?
13. Two legal documents are involved when a company borrows money in an arrangement secured by a mortgage. What are they and what is the purpose of each?
14. Why might a corporation issue convertible preferred shares or convertible bonds?
15. The financial statements for Bombardier Inc. are presented in Appendix I. What amount of Bombardier long-term debt is payable in 1992?

Mini Discussion Case

Case 17–1

The June 1986 issue of *Investment Research Overview* published by Richardson Greenshields of Canada Limited states:

> Strip bonds (or "zero-coupon" bonds, as they are called in the United States) began to sell in Canada in 1982. In the four years since that time an estimated $5 billion bonds have been "stripped" and sold by investment dealers in Canada. Harold B. Ehrlich, chairman, Berstein Macaulay Money Management Ltd., is quoted as saying, "When the history books are written, I am convinced zero-coupon bonds will be one of the great financial inventions of the 1970s and 1980s."

Required

Differentiate coupon and zero-coupon bonds and critically evaluate the claim made by Harold B. Ehrlich.

In solving the following exercises, round all dollar amounts to the nearest whole dollar. Also assume that none of the companies use reversing entries.

Exercises

On December 31, 1993, Cleveland Cutlery Company borrowed $130,000 by signing a four-year, 11% installment note. The note requires annual payments of accrued interest plus equal amounts of principal on December 31 of each year from 1994 through 1997. Prepare journal entries to record the first payment on December 31, 1994, and the last payment on December 31, 1997.

Exercise 17–1
Installment note with payments of accrued interest plus equal amounts of principal
(LO 1)

On December 31, 1993, Custom Window & Door Company borrowed $80,000 by signing a five-year, 12% installment note. The note requires annual payments of $22,193 to be made on December 31. Prepare journal entries to record the first payment on December 31, 1994, and the second payment on December 31, 1995.

Exercise 17–2
Installment note with equal payments
(LO 1)

Rainbow Roofing Company borrowed $350,000 by signing a 10-year, 14% installment note. The terms of the note require 10 annual payments of an equal amount, the first of which is due one year after the date of the note. Calculate the amount of the installment payments, based on the present values contained in Table 12–2, page 627.

Exercise 17–3
Calculating installment note payments
(LO 1)

On April 30 of the current year, Salmonson Corporation sold $3 million of its 8.9% bonds at par plus accrued interest. The bonds were dated January 1 of the current year, with interest payable on each June 30 and December 31; (*a*) how many months of interest had accrued on these bonds when they were sold? (*b*) give the entry to record the sale. (*c*) how many months of interest were paid on June 30 of the current year? (*d*) how many months of interest income did the bondholders earn during the first interest period? (*e*) give the entry to record the first interest payment.

Exercise 17–4
Bonds sold between interest dates
(LO 2)

On June 1 of the current year, Tricon Company sold $2 million of its 10.4%, 20-year bonds. The bonds were dated June 1 of the current year, with interest payable on each December 1 and June 1. Give the entries to record the sale at 98½ and the first semiannual interest payment, using straight-line amortization for the discount.

Exercise 17–5
Straight-line amortization of bond discount
(LO 3)

On September 1 of the current year, Computer Systems Corporation sold $1 million of its 10.5%, 10-year bonds at a price that reflected a 12% market rate for bond interest. Interest is payable each March 1 and September 1. Calculate the sales price of the bonds and prepare a General Journal entry to record the sale of the bonds. (Use present value Tables 12–1 and 12–2, pages 625 and 627.)

Exercise 17–6
Calculating sales price of bonds sold at discount
(LO 3)

Exercise 17–7
Interest method of amortizing bond discount
(LO 3)

Computer Systems Corporation of Exercise 17–6 uses the interest method of amortizing bond discount. Under the assumption that Computer Systems Corporation sold its bonds for $913,970 at the market rate of 12%, prepare a schedule with the column headings of Illustration 17–5 and present the amounts in the schedule for the first two interest periods. Also, prepare General Journal entries to record the first payment of interest to the bondholders, the adjusting entry as of December 31, and the second payment of interest.

Exercise 17–8
Calculating sales price of bonds sold at premium
(LO 4)

Mirror Image Corporation sold $780,000 of its own 12%, seven-year bonds on October 1, 1993, at a price that reflected a 10% market rate of bond interest. The bonds pay interest each April 1 and October 1. Calculate the selling price of the bonds and prepare a General Journal entry to record the sale. (Use present value Tables 12–1 and 12–2, pages 625 and 627.)

Exercise 17–9
Interest method of amortizing bond premium
(LO 4)

Assume that the bonds of Exercise 17–8 sold for $857,232 at the market interest rate of 10% and that Mirror Image Corporation uses the interest method to amortize the bond premium. Prepare General Journal entries to accrue interest on December 31, 1993, and to record the first payment of interest on April 1, 1994.

Exercise 17–10
Retirement of bonds
(LO 5)

Amstead Construction Company sold $1.2 million of its 9.9%, 20-year bonds at 97¾ on their date of issue, January 1, 1993. Five years later, on January 1, 1998, after the bond interest for the period had been paid and 25% of the original discount on the issue had been amortized with the straight-line method, the corporation purchased and retired bonds with $200,000 par value on the open market at 101¾. Give the entry to record the purchase and retirement.

Exercise 17–11
Bond sinking fund
(LO 5)

On January 1, 1993, Dayton Paper Company sold $1.5 million of 15-year sinking fund bonds. The corporation is required to deposit $47,211 with the trustee at the end of each year in the life of the bonds. It expects to earn 10% on the assets in the sinking fund: (a) prepare a General Journal entry to record the first deposit of $47,211 with the trustee on December 31, 1993; (b) prepare a General Journal entry on December 31, 1994, to record the $4,721 earnings for 1994 reported to the corporation by the trustee; (c) after the final payment to the trustee, the sinking fund had an accumulated balance of $1,501,945; prepare the General Journal entry to record the payment to the bondholders on January 1, 2008.

Exercise 17–12
Convertible bonds
(LO 5)

Piper Company has outstanding $20 million of 9%, 20-year bonds on which there is $350,000 of unamortized bond premium. The bonds are convertible into the corporation's common shares at the rate of one $1,000 bond for 200 shares, and $1 million of the bonds are presented for conversion.

Present an entry dated June 10 to record the conversion on the books of Piper Corporation.

On May 1, 1993, Blanton Company purchased 75 Unisam Company bonds dated December 31, 1992. Each bond has a par value of $1,000, a contract interest rate of 10%, and matures after 10 years. The bonds pay interest semiannually on June 30 and December 31. Blanton Company bought the bonds at 98½ plus accrued interest and a $1,000 brokerage fee. Blanton intends to hold the bonds as a temporary investment. Prepare journal entries for Blanton Company to record the purchase and the receipt of the interest payment on June 30, 1993.

Exercise 17–13
Bonds as temporary investments
(LO 6)

In solving the following problems, round all dollar amounts to the nearest whole dollar. Also assume that none of the companies use reversing entries.

Problems

On May 31, 1993, Myers Company borrowed $220,000 from a bank by signing a four-year, 14% installment note. The terms of the note require equal semiannual payments beginning on November 30, 1993.

Problem 17–1
Installment notes
(LO 1)

Required

1. Calculate the size of the installment payments. (Use Table 12–2 on page 627.)
2. Complete an installment note amortization schedule for the Myers Company note similar to Illustration 17–2.
3. Prepare General Journal entries to record the first and the last payments on the note.
4. Now assume that the note requires payments of accrued interest plus equal amounts of principal. Prepare General Journal entries to record the first and last payments on the note.

Norcom Drug Company sold $1.2 million of its own 9.5%, five-year bonds on their date of issue, December 31, 1992. Interest is payable on each June 30 and December 31, and the bonds were sold at a price to yield the buyers a 10% annual return. The corporation uses the straight-line method of amortizing the discount.

Problem 17–2
Straight-line method of amortizing bond discount
(LO 3)

Required

1. Calculate the price at which the bonds were sold. (Use present value Tables 12–1 and 12–2, pages 625 and 627.)
2. Prepare a bond discount amortization table similar to Illustration 17–4, but complete only the first two lines.
3. Prepare General Journal entries to record the sale of the bonds and the first two interest payments.

L&P Oil Corporation sold $5 million of its own 10%, 10-year bonds on December 31, 1992. The bonds were dated December 31, 1992, with interest payable on each June 30 and December 31, and were sold to yield the buyers a 9% annual return. The corporation uses the interest method of amortizing the premium.

Problem 17–3
Interest method of amortizing bond premium
(LO 4)

Required

1. Calculate the price at which the bonds were sold. (Use present value Tables 12–1 and 12–2, pages 625 and 627.)

2. Prepare a bond premium amortization table similar to Illustration 17–7, but complete only the first two lines.

3. Prepare General Journal entries to record the sale of the bonds and the first two interest payments.

Problem 17–4
Interest method of amortizing bond discount; bond sinking fund
(LO 3, 5)

Prepare General Journal entries to record the following transactions of Turner Communications Corporation. Use present value Tables 12–1 and 12–2 (pages 625 and 627) as necessary, to calculate the amounts in your entries.

1992

Dec. 31   Sold $3.1 million of its own 11.6%, 10-year bonds dated December 31, 1992, with interest payable on each June 30 and December 31. The bonds sold for a price that reflected a 12% market rate of bond interest.

1993

June 30   Paid the semiannual interest on the bonds and amortized a portion of the discount calculated by the interest method.

Dec. 31   Paid the semiannual interest on the bonds and amortized a portion of the discount calculated by the interest method.

      31   Deposited $160,312 with the sinking fund trustee to establish the sinking fund to repay the bonds.

1994

Dec. 31   Received a report from the sinking fund trustee that the sinking fund had earned $22,500.

2002

Dec. 31   Received a report from the sinking fund trustee that the bondholders had been paid $3.1 million on that day. Included was a $4,880 cheque for the excess cash accumulated in the sinking fund.

Problem 17–5
Straight-line method of amortizing bond premium; retirement of bonds
(LO 4, 5)

Prepare General Journal entries to record the following bond transactions of Standard Corporation:

1993

Dec. 1   Sold $1.5 million par value of its own 12.6%, 10-year bonds at a price to yield the buyers a 12% annual return. The bonds were dated December 1, 1993, with interest payable on each June 1 and December 1.

      31   Accrued interest on the bonds and amortized the premium for December 1993. Used the straight-line method to amortize the premium.

1994

June 1   Paid the semiannual interest on the bonds.

Dec. 1   Paid the semiannual interest on the bonds.

1995

Dec. 1   After paying the semiannual interest on the bonds on this date, Standard Corporation purchased one eighth of the bonds at 100½ and retired them. (Present only the entry to record the purchase and retirement of the bonds.)

On December 31, 1992, Geneva Corporation sold $4 million of 10-year, 13.2% bonds payable at a price that reflected a 14% market rate of bond interest. The bonds pay interest on June 30 and December 31. Use present value Tables 12–1 and 12–2 (pages 625 and 627) as needed in calculating your answers.

Problem 17–6
Comparison of straight-line and interest methods
(LO 3, 4)

Required

1. Present a General Journal entry to record the sale of the bonds.
2. Present General Journal entries to record the first and second payments of interest on June 30, 1993, and on December 31, 1993, using the straight-line method to amortize the premium or discount.
3. Present General Journal entries to record the first and second payments of interest on June 30, 1993, and on December 31, 1993, using the interest method to amortize the premium or discount.
4. Prepare a schedule similar to the table in Illustration 17–6 on page 866. It should have columns for the beginning-of-period carrying amount, interest expense to be recorded, and interest expense as a percentage of carrying amount, as calculated under (*a*) the interest method and (*b*) the straight-line method. In completing the schedule, present the amounts for the six-month periods ending on June 30, 1993, and December 31, 1993.

On January 1, 1993, the Palmgren Company entered into a bond covenant in which it agreed to accumulate $125,000 in a sinking fund by December 31, 1998. Management engaged the services of a trust company that agreed to pay 10% interest per year on the amount accumulated in the fund. The plan calls for six equal annual payments of $16,201 into the fund, starting on December 31, 1993, and ending on December 31, 1998.

Problem 17–7
Bond Sinking Fund
(LO 6)

Prepare a table similar to Illustration 17–8 showing the amount of annual earnings, the annual contribution, and the beginning and ending balances of the sinking fund for the years 1993 through 1998.

Review the transactions presented in Problem 17–4 for Turner Communications Corporation. Assume now that on December 31, 1992, the market rate of bond interest was 10% instead of 12%. Describe how the entries to record the sale of the bonds and the 1993 transactions are different as a result of this change in the facts.

Problem 17–8
Analytical essay
(LO 3, 4, 5)

Review the transactions presented in Problem 17–4 for Turner Communications Corporation. Assume now that on December 31, 1992, Turner sold $3.1 million of its own 12%, 5-year bonds instead of 11.6%, 10-year bonds. Describe how the entries to record the sale of the bonds and the 1993 transactions are different as a result of this change in the facts.

Problem 17–9
Analytical essay
(LO 3, 5)

Alternate Problems

In solving the following alternate problems, round all dollar amounts to the nearest whole dollar. Also assume that none of the companies use reversing entries.

Problem 17–1A
Installment notes
(LO 1)

Bisk Hardware Manufacturing Company financed a major expansion of its production capacity by borrowing $500,000 from a bank and signing an installment note. The five-year, 12%, $500,000 note is dated June 30, 1993, and requires equal semiannual payments beginning on December 31, 1993.

Required

1. Calculate the size of the installment payments. (Use Table 12–2 on page 627.)
2. Complete an installment note amortization schedule for the Bisk Hardware Manufacturing Company note similar to Illustration 17–2.
3. Prepare General Journal entries to record the first and last payments on the note.
4. Now assume that the note requires payments of accrued interest plus equal amounts of principal. Prepare General Journal entries to record the first and last payments on the note.

Problem 17–2A
Straight-line method of amortizing bond premium
(LO 4)

On December 31, 1992, SONOS Corporation sold $3.7 million of its own 12.9%, 10-year bonds. The bonds are dated December 31, 1992, with interest payable on each June 30 and December 31, and were sold to yield the buyers a 12% annual return. The corporation uses the straight-line method of amortizing the premium.

Required

1. Calculate the price at which the bonds were sold. (Use present value Tables 12–1 and 12–2, pages 625 and 627.)
2. Prepare a bond premium amortization table similar to Illustration 17–7, but complete only the first two lines.
3. Prepare General Journal entries to record the sale of the bonds and the first two interest payments.

Problem 17–3A
Interest method of amortizing bond discount
(LO 3)

JBC Corporation sold $800,000 of its own 9.7%, five-year bonds on their date of issue, December 31, 1992. Interest is payable on each June 30 and December 31, and the bonds were sold at a price to yield the buyers a 10% annual return. The corporation uses the interest method of amortizing the discount.

Required

1. Calculate the price at which the bonds were sold. (Use present value Tables 12–1 and 12–2, pages 625 and 627.)
2. Prepare a bond discount amortization table similar to Illustration 17–5, but complete only the first two lines.
3. Prepare General Journal entries to record the sale of the bonds and the first two interest payments.

Problem 17–4A
Straight-line method of amortizing bond discount; bond sinking fund
(LO 3, 5)

Prepare General Journal entries to record the following transactions of Dalcom Corporation. Use present value Tables 12–1 and 12–2 (pages 625 and 627), as necessary, to calculate the amounts in your entries.

1992

Dec. 31 Sold $1.4 million of its own 8.7%, six-year bonds dated December 31, 1992, with interest payable on each June 30 and December 31. The bonds sold for a price that reflected a 9% market rate of bond interest.

1993

June 30 Paid the semiannual interest on the bonds and amortized a portion of the discount calculated by the straight-line method.

Dec. 31 Paid the semiannual interest on the bonds and amortized a portion of the discount calculated by the straight-line method.

    31 Deposited $195,640 with the sinking fund trustee to establish the sinking fund to repay the bonds.

1994

Dec. 31 Received a report from the sinking fund trustee that the sinking fund had earned $19,600.

1998

Dec. 31 Received a report from the sinking fund trustee that the bondholders had been paid $1.4 million on that day. Included was a $4,770 cheque for the excess cash accumulated in the sinking fund.

Prepare General Journal entries to record the following bond transactions of Eco Paper Corporation:

Problem 17–5A
Interest method of amortizing bond premium; retirement of bonds
(LO 4, 5)

1993

Oct. 1 Sold $2.8 million par value of its own 10.7%, five-year bonds at a price to yield the buyers a 10% annual return. The bonds were dated October 1, 1993, with interest payable on each April 1 and October 1.

Dec. 31 Accrued interest on the bonds and amortized the premium for October through December 1993. The interest method was used to amortize the premium.

1994

Apr. 1 Paid the semiannual interest on the bonds.

Oct. 1 Paid the semiannual interest on the bonds.

1995

Oct. 1 After paying the semiannual interest on the bonds on this date, Eco Paper Corporation purchased one fourth of the bonds at 101¾ and retired them. (Present only the entry to record the purchase and retirement of the bonds.)

On December 31, 1992, Trask Chemical Company sold $7 million of 10-year, 12.5% bonds payable at a price that reflected a 12% market rate of bond interest. The bonds pay interest on June 30 and December 31. Use present value Tables 12–1 and 12–2 (pages 625 and 627) as needed in calculating your answers.

Problem 17–6A
Comparison of straight-line and interest methods
(LO 3, 4)

Required

1. Present a General Journal entry to record the sale of the bonds.
2. Present General Journal entries to record the first and second payments of interest on June 30, 1993, and on December 31, 1993, using the straight-line method to amortize the premium or discount.

3. Present General Journal entries to record the first and second payments of interest on June 30, 1993, and on December 31, 1993, using the interest method to amortize the premium or discount.

4. Prepare a schedule similar to the table in Illustration 17–6 on page 866. It should have columns for the beginning-of-period carrying amount, interest expense to be recorded, and interest expense as a percentage of carrying amount, as calculated under (*a*) the interest method, and (*b*) the straight-line method. In completing the schedule, present the amounts for the six-month periods ending on June 30, 1993, and December 31, 1993.

Problem 17–7A
Bond Sinking Fund
(LO 6)

On January 1, 1993, the Smith Company entered into a bond covenant in which it agreed to accumulate $400,000 in a sinking fund by December 31, 1999. Management engaged the services of a trust company that agreed to pay 15% interest per year on the amount accumulated in the fund. The plan calls for seven equal annual payments of $36,144 into the fund, starting on December 31, 1993, and ending on December 31, 1999.

Prepare a table similar to Illustration 17–8 showing the amount of annual earnings, the annual contribution, and the beginning and ending balances of the sinking fund for the years 1993 through 1999.

Problem 17–8A
Analytical essay
(LO 3, 4, 5)

Review the transactions presented in Problem 17–5A for Eco Paper Corporation. Assume now that on October 1, 1993, the market rate of bond interest was 13% instead of 10%. Describe how the entries to record the sale of the bonds and the December 31, 1993, accrual of interest are different as a result of this change in the facts.

Problem 17–9A
Analytical essay
(LO 4, 5)

Review the transactions presented in Problem 17–5A for Eco Paper Corporation. Assume now that on October 1, 1993, Eco sold $2.8 million of its own 10%, 10-year bonds instead of 10.7%, 5-year bonds. Describe how the entries to record the sale of the bonds and the December 31, 1993, accrual of interest are different as a result of this change in the facts.

Provocative Problems

In solving the following provocative problems, round all dollar amounts to the nearest whole dollar.

Provocative Problem 17–1
Sun Financial Company
(LO 2)

Sun Financial Company is planning major additions to its operating capacity and needs $4.5 million to finance the expansion. The company has been presented with three alternative proposals. Each involves issuing bonds that pay semiannual interest. The alternatives are

Plan A: Issue at par $4.5 million of 10-year, 12% bonds.
Plan B: Issue $5,094,000 of 10-year, 10% bonds.
Plan C: Issue $4,050,000 of 10-year, 14% bonds.

The market rate of interest for all of these bonds is expected to be 12%.

For each issue, calculate the expected cash outflow for interest for each six-month period, the expected cash proceeds from its sale, the interest expense for the first six-month period, and the amount that must be paid at maturity. Use the interest method to amortize bond premium or discount. Which plan has the smallest cash demands on the company prior to the final payment at maturity? Which requires the largest payment on maturity?

Provocative Problem 17–2
Capitol Tool Corporation
(LO 2)

The shareholders' equity of Capitol Tool Corporation includes 300,000 shares of outstanding common shares. Over the last three years, the corporation has earned an average of $0.60 per common share after taxes. To increase earnings, management is planning an expansion requiring the investment of an additional $1.8 million in the business. The cash is to be acquired either by selling an additional 180,000 common shares of the company at $10 per share or by selling $1.8 million of 10%, 10-year bonds at par. Management predicts that the expansion will double the company's earnings (before taxes and any bond interest) in the first year after it is completed. Later years' earnings are expected to exceed the first year's earnings by another 25%. The company expects to continue to pay provincial and federal income taxes of 40% on its pre-tax earnings (after any bond interest).

Capitol Tool Corporation's management wants to finance the expansion in a manner that will serve the best interests of the present shareholders and has asked you to analyze the two alternatives from this perspective. Your report should describe the relative merits and disadvantages of the two proposed methods of financing the expansion. Prepare a schedule that shows expected after-tax earnings per share of common shares under each method.

Provocative Problem 17–3
Clark Corporation
(LO 3)

The Clark Corporation issued $1 million of zero-coupon bonds on January 1, 1993. These bonds are scheduled to mature after eight years on December 31, 2000. Clark Corporation will not make any periodic interest payments, but will simply pay out $1 million to the bondholders on the maturity date.

Part 1. Assume that the market priced these bonds to yield an annual compounded interest rate of 8%:

a. Determine the proceeds that Clark would realize from issuing these bonds.
b. Present the journal entry that would be made to record the issuance of these bonds.
c. Prepare a table showing the amount of interest allocated to each year in the bonds' life (use the interest method).
d. Present the journal entry that would be made to record the interest expense accrued for these bonds at December 31, 1993.

Part 2. Assume that the market priced these bonds to yield an annual compounded interest rate of 12%:

a. Determine the proceeds that Clark would realize from issuing these bonds.
b. Present the journal entry that would be made to record the issuance of these bonds.
c. Prepare a table showing the amount of interest allocated to each year in the bonds' life (use the interest method).
d. Present the journal entry that would be made to record the interest expense accrued for these bonds at December 31, 1993.

Provocative Problem 17–4
Bombardier Inc.
(LO 2, 5)

BBD

Turn to the debt note to the financial statements for Bombardier Inc. in Appendix I. Use the information presented there to answer the following questions.

a. Has Bombardier issued any callable bonds? Any convertible bonds?

b. For the bonds and notes, what is the lowest interest rate? The highest?

c. For the bonds and notes, what is the earliest maturity date? The latest?

d. Are there any sinking fund bonds?

e. Were any new bonds issued during the year? Were any retired? How can you tell?

f. Identify bonds that were stated in currency from specific foreign countries. Which currencies are represented?

Analytical and Review Problems

A&R Problem 17–1

On June 30, 1993, Gorge Company issued $500,000 par value 8%, 10-year bonds convertible at the rate of a $1,000 bond for 50 common shares. The bonds were dated June 30, 1993, and were sold at a price to yield investors 10%. Interest was payable annually.

Required

1. Prepare entries on the following dates (Gorge uses straight-line to amortize discounts or premiums): June 30, 1993; December 31, 1993 (year-end); June 30, 1994; and June 30, 1995, to record conversion of 40 of the bonds.

2. On the assumption that Gorge used the interest method for amortization of discounts and premiums prepare entries on the following dates:
   a. December 31, 1993.
   b. June 30, 1994.
   c. June 30, 1995.

A&R Problem 17–2

On May 1, 1993, Tania Torres purchased as a long-term investment 20, $1,000 par value, 10% bonds, due 5½ years from date of purchase. Interest on the bonds is due and payable annually on November 1. Torres does not use discount or premium accounts related to investments of this nature and uses straight-line amortization.

Required

1. On the assumption that Torres' *total* cash outlay for the bonds was $17,040, prepare entries on the following 1993 dates:
   a. May 1, 1993.
   b. November 1, 1993.
   c. December 31, 1993 (year-end).

2. On the assumption that Torres' total cash outlay for the bonds was $22,520 prepare the entries on the following dates:
   a. May 1, 1993.
   b. November 1, 1993.
   c. December 31, 1993 (year-end).

Answers to Objective Review Questions

LO 1 (e)	LO 4 (e)	LO 6 (c)
LO 2 (a)	LO 5 (e)	LO 7 (d)
LO 3 (b)		

Financial Statements: Interpretation and Modifications

Your study of Part VII will contribute a great deal to your ability to understand and use financial statements. You will learn about the statement of changes in financial position, which is required in public financial reports. Also, you will learn some important techniques used in analyzing financial statements.

Statement of Changes in Financial Position

Cash flows in and out of a company as the company makes sales, collects receivables, pays expenses, buys and sells assets, borrows cash, issues stock, repays debt, and pays dividends. Information about the cash generated and spent is useful for evaluating the past and predicting the future.

C ash is the lifeblood of a business enterprise. In a sense, cash is the fuel that keeps a business alive. With cash, employees and suppliers can be paid, loans can be repaid, and owners can receive dividends. Without cash, however, none of these things can happen. In simple terms, a business must have an adequate amount of cash to operate. For these reasons, decision makers pay close attention to a company's cash position and the events and transactions causing that position to change. Information about the events and transactions that affect the cash position of a company is reported in a financial statement called the *statement of changes in financial position (SCFP)*. By studying this chapter, you will learn how to prepare and interpret an SCFP.

Learning Objectives

After studying Chapter 18, you should be able to:

1. Describe the information provided in a statement of changes in financial position and classify the cash flows of a company as operating, investing, or financing activities.

2. Identify for reporting on the SCFP any simultaneous investing and financing transactions.

3. Calculate cash inflows and outflows by inspecting the noncash account balances of a company and related information about its transactions.

4. Calculate the net cash provided or used by operating activities according to the direct approach and prepare the SCFP.

5. Prepare a working paper to identify changes in account balances and classify these changes as operating, investing, or financing activities.

6. Define or explain the words or phrases listed in the chapter glossary.

Why Cash Flow Information Is Important

Information about cash flows can influence decision makers in many ways. For example, if a company's regular operations bring in more cash than they use, investors will value the company higher than if property and equipment must be sold to finance operations. Information about cash flows can help creditors decide whether a company will have enough cash to pay its existing debts as they mature. And, investors, creditors, managers, and other users of financial statements use cash flow information to evaluate a company's ability to meet unexpected obligations. Cash flow information is also used to evaluate a company's ability to take advantage of new business opportunities that may arise. These are just a few of the many ways that different people use cash flow information.

The importance of cash flow information to decision makers has directly influenced the thinking of accounting authorities. For example, the CICA's "Financial Statement Concepts" clearly reflect the importance of cash flow information. The CICA stated that financial statements should include information about:

- How a business obtains and spends cash.
- Its borrowing and repayment activities.
- The sale and repurchase of its ownership securities.
- Dividend payments and other distributions to its owners.
- Other factors affecting a company's liquidity or solvency.[1]

To accomplish these objectives, a financial statement is needed to summarize, classify, and report the periodic cash inflows and outflows of a business. This information is provided in an SCFP.

In September 1985, the CICA's Accounting Standards Board revised section 1540 of the *Handbook*. This recommendation now requires businesses to include a **statement of changes in financial position** (SCFP), which is information about a company's cash receipts and disbursements during the reporting period.

Illustration 18–1 presents the SCFP for Grover Company. Note that the illustration groups cash flows in three categories: cash flows from operating activities, cash flows from investing activities, and cash flows from financing activities. The statement also reconciles the beginning-of-period and end-of-period balances of cash plus cash equivalents.

In the operating activities section of the statement, net income is adjusted to determine the **net cash provided (or used) by operating activities.** In the other two categories of cash flows reported on the statement—investing activities and financing activities—we subtract the cash outflows from the cash inflows to determine the net cash provided (or used).

Statement of Changes in Financial Position

LO 1 Describe the information provided in a statement of changes in financial position and classify the cash flows of a company as operating, investing, or financing activities.

Cash and Cash Equivalents

In section 1540 of the *CICA Handbook,* the Accounting Standards Board concluded that a statement of changes in financial position should explain the difference between the beginning and ending balances of cash, net of short-term borrowings, and **cash equivalents.** Prior to this new standard, cash equivalents were generally understood to be short-term, temporary investments of cash. However, not all short-term investments meet the CICA definition of cash equivalents. To qualify as a cash equivalent, an investment must satisfy these two criteria:

1. The investment must be readily convertible to a known amount of cash.
2. The investment must be sufficiently close to its maturity date so that its market value is relatively insensitive to interest rate changes.

Examples of cash equivalents include short-term investments in government Treasury Bills, commercial paper (short-term corporate notes payable), and money market funds.

---

[1] *CICA Handbook* (Toronto: The Canadian Institue of Chartered Accountants), par. 1540.01.

ILLUSTRATION 18–1

GROVER COMPANY
Statement of Changes in Financial Position
For Year Ended December 31, 1993

Cash flows from operating activities:		
Net income.		$38,000
Adjustments to reconcile net income to net		
cash provided by operating activities:		
Increase in accounts receivable	$(20,000)	
Increase in merchandise inventory.	(14,000)	
Increase in prepaid expenses.	(2,000)	
Decrease in accounts payable	(5,000)	
Decrease in interest payable	(1,000)	
Increase in income taxes payable	10,000	
Amortization expense	24,000	
Loss on sale of plant assets	6,000	
Gain on retirement of bonds	(16,000)	
Total adjustments		(18,000)
Net cash provided by operating activities . . .		$20,000
Cash flows from investing activities:		
Cash paid for purchase of plant assets	(70,000)	
Cash received from sale of plant assets.	12,000	
Net cash provided by investing activities. . . .		(58,000)
Cash flows from financing activities:		
Cash received from issuance of shares	15,000	
Cash received from issuance of bonds	60,000	
Cash paid to retire bonds.	(18,000)	
Cash paid for dividends.	(14,000)	
Net cash used in financing activities		43,000
Net increase in cash		5,000
Cash balance at beginning of 1993		12,000
Cash balance at end of 1993.		$17,000

The idea of classifying short-term, highly liquid investments as cash equivalents is based on the assumption that companies make these investments to earn a return on idle cash balances. However, some companies have other reasons for investing in items that meet the criteria of cash equivalents. For example, an investment company that specializes in the purchase and sale of securities may buy cash equivalents as part of its investing strategy.

Sometimes, items that meet the criteria of cash equivalents are not held as temporary investments of idle cash balances. Companies that have such investments are allowed to exclude them from the cash equivalents classification. However, the companies must develop a clear policy for determining which items to include and which to exclude. These policies must be disclosed in the notes to the financial statements and must be followed consistently from period to period.

On an SCFP cash receipts and payments are classified and reported on the statement as operating, investing, or financing activities. Within each category, individual cash receipts and payments are summarized in a manner that clearly describes the general nature of the company's cash transactions. Then the summarized cash receipts and payments within each category are netted against each other. A category provides a net cash flow if the receipts in the category exceed the payments. And if the payments in a category exceed the receipts, the category is a net use of cash during the period.

Classifying Cash Transactions

Operating Activities

Look at the cash flows classified as **operating activities** in Illustration 18–2. This illustration shows the reconciliation of Grover Company's net income to the cash provided by operating activities.

In Illustration 18–2, notice that the net cash provided by operating activities is $20,000. This same amount was reported on the SCFP in Illustration

ILLUSTRATION 18-2

Grover Company—Reconciliation of Net Income to Net Cash Provided by Operating Activities		
Net income		$38,000
Adjustments to reconcile net income to net cash provided by operating activities:		
(1) Increase in accounts receivable	$(20,000)	
Increase in merchandise inventory	(14,000)	
Increase in prepaid expenses	(2,000)	
Decrease in accounts payable	(5,000)	
Decrease in interest payable	(1,000)	
Increase in income taxes payable	10,000	
(2) (Amortization expense	24,000	
(3) Loss on sale of plant assets	6,000	
Gain on retirement of bonds	(16,000)	
Total adjustments		(18,000)
Net cash provided by operating activities		$20,000

18–1 on page 904. Illustration 18–2 shows three types of adjustments. The adjustments grouped under the section labeled (1) are for changes in noncash current assets and current liabilities that relate to operating activities. Adjustment (2) is for an item that relates to operating activities but that did not involve a cash inflow or outflow during the period. The adjustments grouped under (3) eliminate gains and losses that resulted from investing and financing activities. These gains and losses do *not* relate to operating activities.

Adjustments for Changes in Current Assets and Current Liabilities

To help you understand why adjustments for changes in noncash current assets and current liabilities are part of the reconciliation process, we use the transactions of a very simple company as an example. Assume that Simple Company's income statement shows only two items, as follows:

Sales	$20,000
Operating expenses	(12,000)
Net income	$ 8,000

For a moment, assume that all of Simple Company's sales and operating expenses are for cash. The company has no current assets other than cash and has no current liabilities. Given these assumptions, the net cash provided by operating activities during the period is $8,000, which is the cash received from customers less the cash paid for operating expenses. The net cash provided by operating activities also equals net income.

Adjustments for Changes in Noncash Current Assets

Now assume that Simple Company's sales are on account. Also assume that its Accounts Receivable balance was $2,000 at the beginning of the year and

$2,500 at the end of the year. Under these assumptions, cash receipts from customers equal sales of $20,000 minus the $500 increase in Accounts Receivable, or $19,500. Therefore, the net cash provided by operating activities is $7,500 ($19,500 − $12,000).

When we calculate the net cash flow, net income of $8,000 is adjusted for the $500 increase in accounts receivable to get $7,500 as the net amount of cash provided by operating activities. The calculations are as follows:

Receipts from customers ($20,000 − $500).	$19,500
Payments for operating expenses	(12,000)
Cash provided (or used) by operating activities . .	$ 7,500
Net income	$ 8.000
Less the increase in accounts receivable.	(500)
Cash provided (or used) by operating activities . .	$ 7,500

Notice that the increase in Accounts Receivable is subtracted from net income to determine cash provided.

As another example, assume instead that the Accounts Receivable balance decreased from $2,000 to $1,200. Under this assumption, cash receipts from customers equal sales of $20,000 plus the $800 decrease in Accounts Receivable, or $20,800. If we assume that sales and receipts from customers equal $20,000 and that payments for operating expenses equal $12,000, then net income and cash provided from operations will equal $8,000 ($20,000 − $12,000). If accounts receivable decrease by $800, then cash collected from customers is $20,800, not $20,000. That is, an additional $800 has been received from customers during this period, and cash provided by operations will be $8,800 ($8,000 + $800). The calculations are as follows:

Receipts from customers ($20,000 + $800).	$20,800
Payments for operating expenses	12,000
Cash provided (or used) by operating activities . .	$ 8,800
Net income	$ 8,000
Plus decrease in accounts receivable	800
Cash provided (or used) by operating activities . .	$ 8,800

The $800 decrease in Accounts Receivable is added to the $8,000 net income to get $8,800 net cash provided by operating activities.

Adjustments like these for Accounts Receivable are required for all noncash current assets related to operating activities. When a noncash current asset increases, part of the assets derived from operating activities goes into the increase. This leaves a smaller amount as the net cash inflow. For example, assume that the company purchases a two-year insurance policy for $1,800 at the beginning of year 1. Insurance expense for the year would be $900, and Prepaid Insurance would have a $900 closing balance. The increase in the noncash current asset, Prepaid Insurance, would be subtracted from net income because the cash outflow is $1,800, not $900. Thus, the $1,800 cash outflow for insurance is represented by the $900 insurance expense and the $900 deduction from net income as we calculate cash from operations.

When you calculate the net cash inflow, subtract the noncash current asset increase from net income. But when a noncash current asset decreases, additional cash is produced, and you should add this amount to net income. These modifications of income for changes in current assets related to operating activities are as follows:

Net income
Add: Decreases in current assets
Subtract: Increases in current assets

Net cash provided (or used) by operating activities

Adjustments for Changes in Current Liabilities

To illustrate the adjustments for changes in current liabilities, return to the original assumptions about Simple Company. Sales of $20,000 are for cash, and operating expenses are $12,000. However, assume now that Simple Company has Interest Payable as its only current liability. Also assume that the beginning-of-year balance in Interest Payable was $500 and the end-of-year balance was $900. This increase means that the operating expenses of $12,000 include $400 of interest that was not paid in cash during the period. Therefore, the cash payments for operating expenses were only $11,600, or $12,000 − $400. Under these assumptions, the calculation of net cash provided by operating activities is $8,400, or $20,000 in receipts from customers less $11,600 payments for expenses. Thus, the calculation of $8,400 is net income of $8,000 plus the $400 increase in Interest Payable.

Alternatively, if the Interest Payable balance decreased, for example by $300, the cash outflow for operating expenses would have been the $12,000 expense plus the $300 liability decrease, or $12,300. Thus, the calculation of net cash flow is $20,000 − $12,300 = $7,700. That is, $8,000 − $300 = $7,700. In other words, when determining cash flow subtract a decrease in Interest Payable from net income.

Adjustments like these for Interest Payable are required for all current liabilities related to operating activities. When a current liability decreases, part of the cash derived from operating activities pays for the decrease. Therefore, subtract the decrease from net income to determine the remaining net cash inflow. And when a current liability increases, it finances some operating expenses. In other words, cash was not used to pay for the expense, and the liability increase must be added to net income when you calculate cash provided by operating activities. These adjustments for changes in current liabilities related to operating activities are:

Net income
Add: Increases in current liabilities
Subtract: Decreases in current liabilities

Net cash provided (or used) by operating activities

One way to remember how to make these modifications to net income is to observe that a *debit* change in a noncash current asset or a current liability is *subtracted* from net income. And, a *credit* change in a noncash current asset or a current liability is *added* to net income.

Adjustments for Other Operating Items that Do Not Provide or Use Cash

Some operating items that appear on an income statement do not provide or use cash during the current period. One example is amortization; such as depreciation of plant and equipment, amortization of intangible assets, depletion of natural resources, amortization of bond discount or premium and bad debts expense.

These expenses are recorded with debits to expense accounts and credits to noncash accounts. They reduce net income but do not require cash outflows during the period. Therefore, when adjustments to net income are made, add these noncash expenses back to net income.

In addition to noncash expenses such as amortization, net income may include some revenues that do not provide cash inflows during the current period. An example is equity method earnings from an equity investment in another entity (see Appendix E, Chapter 8). If net income includes revenues that do not provide cash inflows, subtract the revenues from net income in the process of reconciling net income to the net cash provided by operating activities.

The adjustments for expenses and revenues that do not provide or use cash during the current period are as follows:

Net income
Add: Expenses that do not use cash
Subtract: Revenues that do not provide cash
Net cash provided (or used) by operating activities

Adjustments for Nonoperating Items

Some income statement items are not related to the operating activities of the company. These gains and losses result from investing and financing activities. Examples are gains or losses on the sale of plant assets and gains or losses on the retirement of bonds payable.

Remember that net income is reconciled to the net cash provided (or used) by operating activities. Therefore, net income must be modified to exclude gains and losses created by investing and financing activities. In making these modifications, subtract gains from financing and investing activities from net income and add losses back to net income:

Net income
Add: Losses from investing or financing activities
Subtract: Gains from investing or financing activities
Net cash provided (or used) by operating activities

ILLUSTRATION 18-3

Reconciliation of Net Income to Cash Flows from Operating Activities

Net Income or Net Loss

Plus	Minus
Decreases in noncash current assets. Increases in current liabilities.	Increases in noncash current assets. Decreases in current liabilities.
Expenses which do not require a cash outflow during the period.	Income which did not result in a cash inflow during the period.
Losses from investing and financing activities.	Gains from investing and financing activities.

ILLUSTRATION 18-4

Cash Flows from Investing Activities

Cash Inflows	Cash Outflows
Proceeds from selling productive assets (e.g., land, buildings, equipment, natural resources, and intangible assets).	Payments to purchase property, plant, and equipment or other productive assets (excluding merchandise inventory).
Proceeds from selling investments in the equity securities of other companies.	Payments to acquire equity securities of other companies.*
Proceeds from selling investments in the debt securities of other entities, except cash equivalents.	Payments to acquire debt securities of other entities, except cash equivalents.
Proceeds from collecting the principal amount of loans	Payments in the form of loans made to other parties.
Proceeds from the sale (discounting) of loans made by the enterprise.	

* Excluding those securities which are cash equivalents.

Illustration 18–3 summarizes the adjustments to net income or net loss required to determine net cash flows from operating activities.

Investing Activities

Transactions that involve making and collecting loans or that involve purchasing and selling capital assets, other productive assets, or investments (other than cash equivalents) are called **investing activities.** Usually, investing activities involve the purchase or sale of assets classified on the balance sheet as capital assets, i.e., plant and equipment and intangible assets, or long-term investments. However, the purchase and sale of short-term investments other than cash equivalents are also investing activities. Illustration 18–4 shows examples of cash flows from investing activities.

The fourth type of receipt listed in Illustration 18–4 involves proceeds from collecting the principal amount of loans. Regarding this item, carefully examine any cash receipts that relate to notes receivable. If the notes resulted

ILLUSTRATION 18-5

Cash Flows from Financing Activities

Cash Inflows	Cash Outflows
Proceeds from issuing equity securities (e.g., common and preferred shares).	Payments of cash dividends and other distributions to owners.*
Proceeds from issuing bonds and notes payable.	Repayments of cash loans.
Proceeds from other short- or long-term borrowing transactions.	Payments of the principal amounts involved in long-term credit arrangements.

* Some companies treat dividends as an operating activity outflow, while others disclose them in a separate category. Section 1540 of the *CICA Handbook* requires that dividends be disclosed but does not offer any guidance as to their category in the SCFP.

from sales to customers, classify the cash receipts as operating activities. Use this classification even if the notes are long-term notes. However, if a company loans money to other parties, classify the cash receipts from collecting the principal of the loans as inflows from investing activities. Nevertheless, the CICA concluded that collections of interest are not investing activities. Instead, they are reported as operating activities.

Financing Activities

The **financing activities** of a business include transactions with its owners and transactions with creditors to borrow money or to repay the principal amounts of loans. Financing activities include borrowing and repaying both short-term loans (except for those which are offset as part of determining the cash and cash equivalent balance) and long-term debt. However, cash payments to settle credit purchases of merchandise, whether on account or by note, are operating activities. Payments of interest expense are also operating activities. Illustration 18–5 shows examples of cash flows from financing activities.

Some important investing and financing activities do not involve cash receipts or payments during the current period. In the *CICA Handbook* the Accounting Standards Committee recognized that *noncash investing and financing activities* are important events that should be disclosed. For example, a company might purchase land and buildings and finance 100% of the purchase by giving a long-term note payable. Because this transaction clearly involves both investing and financing activities, it must be reported in both sections of the current period's SCFP even though no cash was received or paid. That is, the transaction is treated as if two cash transactions occurred simultaneously.

Other investing and financing activities may involve some cash receipt or payment but also involve giving or receiving other types of consideration. An example is if you purchase machinery valued at $12,000 by paying cash of $5,000 and trading in old machinery that has a market value of $7,000. In this

Noncash Investing and Financing Activities

LO 2 Identify for reporting on the SCFP any simultaneous investing and financing transactions.

ILLUSTRATION 18-6

Decco Company—Disclosure of Noncash Investing and Financing Activities

The company issued 1,000 common shares for the purchase of land and buildings with fair values of $5,000 and $15,000, respectively.

> Investing activity (outflow): Purchase of property for $20,000.
> Financing activity (inflow): Issue of common shares for $20,000.

The company entered into a capital lease obligation of $12,000 for new computer equipment.

> Investing activity (outflow): Acquisition of capital lease assets for $12,000.
> Financing activity (inflow): Capital lease obligation assumed for $12,000.

The company exchanged old machinery with a fair value of $7,000 and a book value of $8,000 for new machinery valued at $12,000. The balance of $5,000 was paid in cash.

> Investing activity (outflow): Acquisition of new machinery for $12,000.
> Investing activity (inflow): Disposal of old machinery for $7,000.

case, the SCFP reports a cash inflow of $7,000 from the sale of the old machine and a cash outflow of $12,000 on the purchase of the new machine. Illustration 18–6 shows an example of how a company might disclose its noncash investing and financing activities.

Examples of transactions that must be disclosed as noncash investing and financing activities include the following:

- The retirement of debt securities by issuing equity securities.
- The conversion of preferred shares to common shares.
- The leasing of assets in a transaction that qualifies as a capital lease.
- The purchase of long-term assets by issuing a note payable to the seller.
- The exchange of a noncash asset for other noncash assets.
- The purchase of noncash assets by issuing equity or debt securities.

Preparing a Statement of Changes in Financial Position

LO 3 Calculate cash inflows and outflows by inspecting the noncash account balances of a company and related information about its transactions.

The information you need to prepare a statement changes in financial position comes from a variety of sources. These include comparative balance sheets at the beginning and the end of the accounting period, an income statement for the period, and a careful analysis of each noncash balance sheet account in the General Ledger. However, because cash inflows and cash outflows are to be reported, you might wonder why we do not focus our attention on the Cash account. For the moment, we should at least consider this approach.

Analyzing the Cash Account

All of a company's cash receipts and cash payments are recorded in the Cash account in the General Ledger. Therefore, the Cash account would seem to be the logical place to look for information about cash flows from operating, investing, and financing activities. To demonstrate, review this summarized Cash account of Grover Company:

Summarized Cash Account

Balance, Dec 31, 1992	12,000		
Receipts from customers	570,000	Payments for merchandise	319,000
Proceeds from sale of plant		Payments for wages and other	
assets	12,000	operating expenses	218,000
Proceeds from issue of shares	15,000	Interest payments	8,000
		Tax payments	5,000
		Payments for purchase of	
		plant assets	10,000
		Payments to retire bonds	18,000
		Dividend payments	14,000
Balance, Dec 31, 1993	17,000		

In this account, the individual cash transactions are already summarized in major types of receipts and payments. For example, the account has only one debit entry for the total receipts from all customers. All that remains is to determine whether each type of cash inflow or outflow is an operating, investing, or financing activity and then place it in its proper category on the SCFP. The completed SCFP appears in Illustration 18–1 on page 904.

While an analysis of the Cash account may appear to be an easy way to prepare an SCFP, it has two serious drawbacks. First, most companies have so many individual cash receipts and disbursements that it is not practical to review them all. Imagine what a problem this analysis would present for Stelco, INCO, Loblaws, or Alcan, or even for a relatively small business. Second, the Cash account usually does not contain a description of each cash transaction. Therefore, even though the Cash account shows the amount of each debit and credit, you generally cannot determine the type of transaction by looking at the Cash account. Thus, the Cash account does not readily provide the information you need to prepare an SCFP. To obtain the necessary information, you must analyze the changes in the noncash accounts.

Analyzing Noncash Accounts to Determine Cash Flows

When a company records cash inflows and outflows with debits and credits to the Cash account, it also records credits and debits in other accounts. Some of these accounts are balance sheet accounts. Others are revenue and expense accounts that are closed to Retained Earnings, a balance sheet account. As a result, all cash transactions eventually affect noncash balance sheet accounts. Therefore, we can determine the nature of the cash inflows and outflows by examining the changes in the noncash balance sheet accounts. Illustration 18–7 shows this important relationship between the Cash account and the noncash balance sheet accounts.

In Illustration 18–7, notice that the balance sheet Equation 1 is expanded in 2 so that cash is separated from the other assets. Then the equation is rearranged in 3 so that cash is set equal to the sum of the liability and equity accounts less the noncash asset accounts. The illustration then points out in 4 that changes in one side of the equation (cash) must be equal to the changes in the other side (noncash accounts). Part 4 shows that you can fully explain the changes in cash by analyzing the changes in liabilities, owners' equity, and

ILLUSTRATION 18–7

Why an Analysis of the Noncash Accounts Explains the Change in Cash

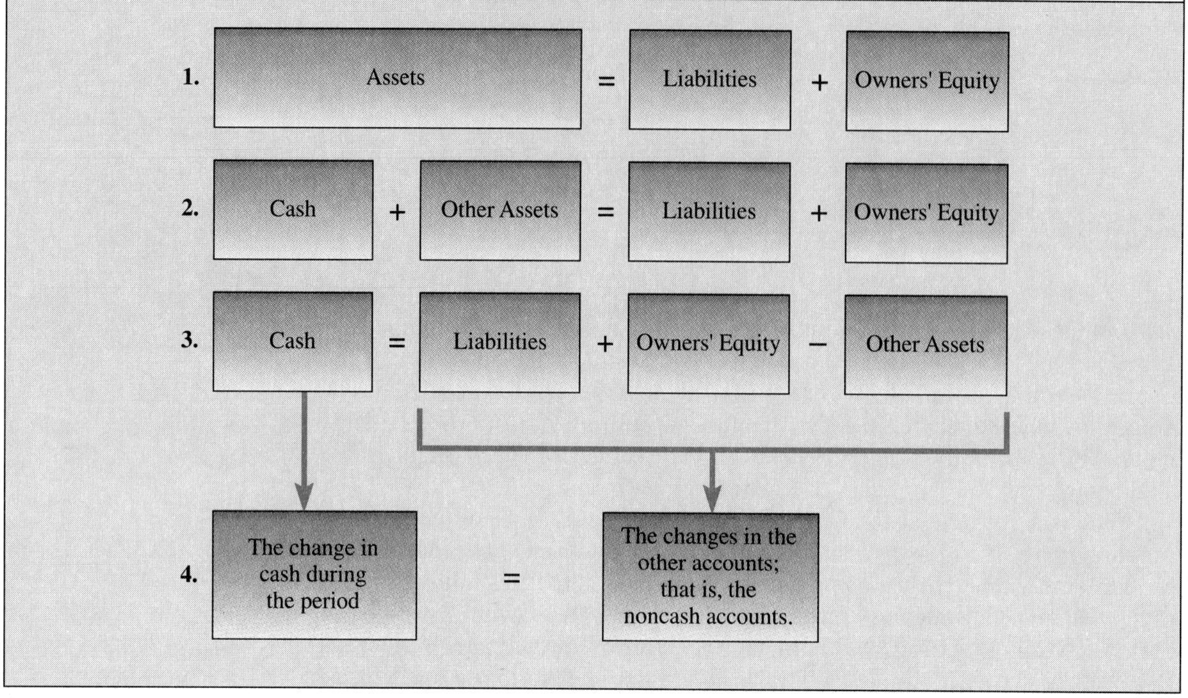

noncash assets. This information is all that is needed to prepare a statement of changes in financial position.

This overall process has another advantage. The examination of each noncash account also identifies any noncash investing and financing activities that occurred during the period. As you learned earlier, these noncash items must also be disclosed on the SCFP.

When beginning to analyze the changes in the noncash balance sheet accounts, recall that Retained Earnings is affected by revenues, expenses, and dividend declarations. Therefore, look at the income statement accounts to help explain the change in Retained Earnings. In fact, the income statement accounts provide important information that relates to the changes in several balance sheet accounts.

Illustration 18–8 summarizes some of these relationships between income statement accounts, balance sheet accounts, and possible cash flows. For example, to determine the cash receipts from customers during a period, adjust the amount of sales revenue for the increase or decrease in Accounts Receivable.[2] If the Accounts Receivable balance did not change, the cash collected

---

[2] This introductory explanation assumes that there is no bad debts expense. However, if bad debts occur and are written off directly to Accounts Receivable, the change in the Accounts Receivable balance will be due in part to the write-off. The remaining change results from credit sales and from cash receipts. This chapter does not discuss the allowance method of accounting for bad debts since it would make the analysis unnecessarily complex at this time.

ILLUSTRATION 18–8

Key Relationships between Income Statement Items and Balance Sheet Accounts

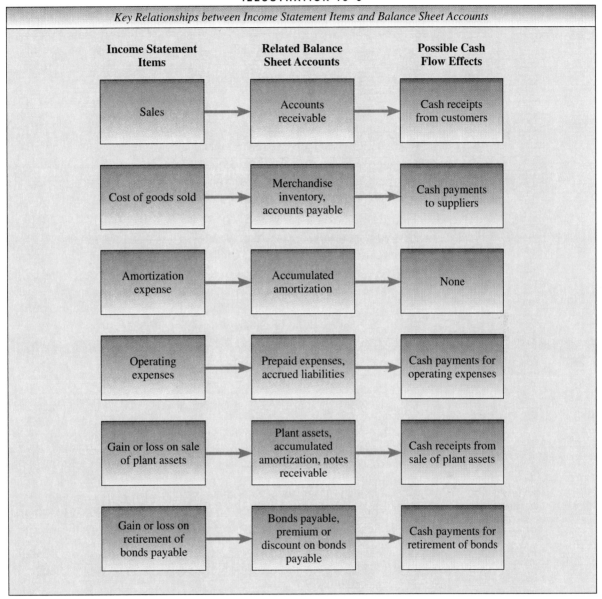

from customers is equal to sales revenue. On the other hand, if the Accounts Receivable balance decreased, cash collections must have been equal to sales revenue *plus* the reduction in Accounts Receivable. And if the Accounts Receivable balance increased, the cash collected from customers must have been equal to Sales *less* the increase in Accounts Receivable.

By analyzing all noncash balance sheet accounts and related income statement accounts in this fashion, you can obtain the necessary information for a statement of changes in financial position. So that you clearly understand this process, we illustrate it by examining the noncash accounts of Grover Company.

Grover Company: A Comprehensive Example

Grover Company's balance sheets for December 31, 1992 and 1993, and its 1993 income statement are presented in Illustration 18–9. Our objective is to prepare an SCFP that explains the $5,000 increase in cash, based on these financial statements and this additional information about the 1993 transactions:

a. Net income was $38,000.

b. Accounts receivable increased by $20,000.

c. Merchandise inventory increased by $14,000.

d. Prepaid expenses increased by $2,000.

e. Accounts payable decreased by $5,000.

f. Interest payable decreased by $1,000.

g. Income taxes payable increased by $10,000.

h. Amortization expense was $24,000.

i. Loss on sale of plant assets was $6,000; assets that cost $30,000 with accumulated amortization of $12,000 were sold for $12,000 cash.

j. Gain on retirement of bonds was $16,000; bonds with a book value of $34,000 were retired with a cash payment of $18,000.

k. Plant assets that cost $70,000 were purchased; the payment consisted of $10,000 cash and the issuance of a $60,000 note payable.

l. Sold 3,000 common shares for $15,000.

m. Paid cash dividends of $14,000.

Preparation of the SCFP

LO 4 Calculate the net cash provided or used by operating activities according to the direct approach and prepare the SCFP.

Direct Approach

The direct approach uses the comparative balance sheets, the income statement, and supplementary data to clarify certain transactions. To illustrate the direct approach, we use the financial statements in Illustration 18–10 and the information listed above. The comparative balance sheets show that cash increased by $5,000 during 1993. Therefore, $5,000 must be the amount on the last line before the cash balance at the beginning of 1993 on the SCFP (Illustration 18–1). This change is explained by examining and identifying the causes of the cash inflows and outflows.

Analysis of Cash Flows

In order to determine the cash flows from operations, we must adjust the net income figure from Illustration 18–10. First, we add or subtract the changes in the noncash current asset and current liability accounts.

Second, we adjust for the other operating items that do not provide or use cash. From the income statement we can determine that only amortization expense fits into this category. Therefore, we add back the amortization expense.

Third, we adjust for nonoperating items. In Illustration 18–10 these are the loss on sale of plant assets and the gain on retirement of debt.

The net cash provided by financing activities and by investing activities is taken from the additional information. Each item is identified with the corresponding letter from the above list of 1993 transactions, denoted *a* through *m*.

ILLUSTRATION 18–9

Financial Statements

GROVER COMPANY
Balance Sheet
December 31, 1993 and 1992

	1993		1992	
Assets				
Current assets:				
Cash		$ 17,000		$ 12,000
Accounts receivable		60,000		40,000
Merchandise inventory		84,000		70,000
Prepaid expenses		6,000		4,000
Total current assets		$167,000		$126,000
Long-term assets:				
Plant assets	$250,000		$210,000	
Less: Accumulated amortization . . .	60,000	190,000	48,000	162,000
Total assets		$357,000		$288,000
Liabilities				
Current liabilities:				
Accounts payable		$ 35,000		$ 40,000
Interest payable		3,000		4,000
Income taxes payable		22,000		12,000
Total current liabilities		$ 60,000		$ 56,000
Long-term liabilities:				
Bonds payable		90,000		64,000
		$150,000		$120,000
Shareholders' Equity				
Contributed capital:				
Common shares	$ 95,000		$ 80,000	
Retained earnings	112,000		88,000	
Total shareholders' equity		207,000		168,000
Total liabilities and shareholders' equity . .		$357,000		$288,000

Income Statement
For Year Ended December 31, 1993

Sales		$ 590,000
Cost of goods sold	$300,000	
Wages and other operating expenses	216,000	
Interest expense	7,000	
Income taxes expense	15,000	
Amortization expense	24,000	(562,000)
Loss on sale of plant assets		(6,000)
Gain on retirement of debt		16,000
Net income		$ 38,000

Although the direct approach technique may be adequate when doing relatively simple SCFPs, in many cases a more formal method is desirable. This is known as the *working paper approach,* which is illustrated and discussed on the next page.

ILLUSTRATION 18–10

GROVER COMPANY
Net Change in Cash—Direct Approach
For Year Ended December 31, 1993

	December 31 1993	December 31 1992	Increase (Decrease)
Cash flows from operating activities:			
Net income for 1993 (a)			$ 38,000
Adjustments to reconcile net income to cash provided by operating activities:			
1. Accounts receivable (b)	$60,000	$40,000	(20,000)
Merchandise inventory (c)	84,000	70,000	(14,000)
Prepaid expenses (d)	6,000	4,000	(2,000)
Accounts payable (e)	35,000	40,000	(5,000)
Interest payable (f)	3,000	4,000	(1,000)
Income taxes payable (g)	22,000	12,000	10,000
2. Amortization expense (h)			24,000
3. Loss on sale of plant assets (i)			6,000
Gain on retirement of debt (j)			(16,000)
Net adjustments			(18,000)
Cash provided by operating activities			20,000
Cash flows from investing activities:			
Cash received from sale of plant assets (i)			12,000
Cash paid for purchase of plant assets (k)			(70,000)
Net cash provided by investing activities			(58,000)
Cash flows from financing activities:			
Cash received from share issue (l)			15,000
Cash received from note issue (k)			60,000
Cash paid to retire bonds (j)			(18,000)
Cash paid for dividends (m)			(14,000)
Net cash provided by financing activities			43,000
Net increase in cash			$ 5,000

Preparing a Working Paper for an SCFP

LO 5 Prepare a working paper to identify changes in account balances and classify these changes as operating, investing, or financing activities.

When a company has a large number of accounts and many operating, investing, and financing transactions, the analysis of noncash accounts can be difficult and confusing. In these situations, a working paper can help organize the information needed to prepare an SCFP. A working paper also makes it easier to check the accuracy of your work.

Designing the Working Paper

Examine the working paper for Grover Company in Illustration 18–11. Observe that the balance sheet account balances at the beginning and end of the period are entered in the first and fourth money columns, respectively. The middle two columns are used for reconciling the differences in these balances and for developing the SCFP.

Following the balance sheets, we enter information in the Analysis of Changes columns about cash flows from operating, investing, and financing activities and about noncash investing and financing activities. Note that the working paper does *not* reconstruct the income statement. Instead, net income is entered as the first item used in computing the amount of cash flows from operating activities.

Entering the Analysis of Changes on the Working Paper

After the balance sheets are entered, we recommend using the following sequence of procedures to complete the working paper.

Operating Activities

1. Enter net income as an operating cash inflow (a debit) and as a credit to Retained Earnings, entry (*a1*); enter the difference in the cash balance, entry (*a2*).

2. In the statement of changes in financial position section, adjustments to net income are entered as debits if they increase cash inflows and as credits if they decrease cash inflows. Following this rule, adjust net income for the change in each noncash current asset and current liability related to operating activities. For each adjustment to net income, the offsetting debit or credit should reconcile the beginning and ending balances of a current asset or current liability (see entries *b* to *g*). For example, an increase in Accounts Receivable would be entered as a debit on the asset line and a credit in the operating activity section (see entry *b* in Illustration 18–11).

3. Enter the adjustments to net income for income statement items, such as amortization, that did not provide or use cash during the period (entry *h*). For each adjustment, the offsetting debit or credit should help reconcile a noncash balance sheet account.

4. Adjust net income to eliminate any gains or losses from investing and financing activities. Because the cash associated with a gain is excluded from operating activities, it is entered as a credit (entry *j*). On the other hand, losses are entered with debits (entry *i*). For each of these adjustments, the related debits and/or credits help reconcile balance sheet accounts and also involve entries to show the cash flow from investing or financing activities.

Investing Activities

Investing activities usually refer to transactions that affect long-term assets. Recall from the information that was provided about Grover Company's transactions that the company purchased plant assets and also sold plant assets. Both of these transactions are investing activities.

ILLUSTRATION 18–11

GROVER COMPANY Working Paper for Statement of Changes in Financial Position For Year Ended December 31, 1993				
	December 31, 1992	Analysis of Changes		December 31, 1993
		Debit	Credit	
Balance sheet—debits:				
Cash	12,000	(a2) 5,000		17,000
Accounts receivable	40,000	(b) 20,000		60,000
Merchandise inventory	70,000	(c) 14,000		84,000
Prepaid expenses	4,000	(d) 2,000		6,000
Plant assets	210,000	(k1) 70,000	(i) 30,000	250,000
	336,000			417,000
Balance sheet—credits:				
Accumulated amortization.	48,000	(i) 12,000	(h) 24,000	60,000
Accounts payable	40,000	(e) 5,000		35,000
Interest payable	4,000	(f) 1,000		3,000
Income taxes payable	12,000		(g) 10,000	22,000
Bonds payable.	64,000	(j) 34,000	(k2) 60,000	90,000
Common shares, no par value	80,000		(l) 15,000	95,000
Retained earnings	88,000	(m) 14,000	(a1) 38,000	112,000
	336,000			417,000
Statement of changes in financial position:				
Operating activities:				
Net income		(a1) 38,000		
Increase in accounts receivable			(b) 20,000 ⎫	
Increase in merchandise inventory. . . .			(c) 14,000 ⎪	
Increase in prepaid expenses			(d) 2,000 ⎪	
Decrease in accounts payable			(e) 5,000 ⎬	20,000
Decrease in interest payable			(f) 1,000 ⎪	
Increase in income taxes payable		(g) 10,000		
Amortization expense		(h) 24,000		
Loss on sale of plant assets		(i) 6,000		
Gain on retirement of bonds			(j) 16,000 ⎭	
Investing activities:				
Receipts from sale of plant assets		(i) 12,000		
Purchase of plant assets			(k1) 70,000 ⎫⎬	(58,000)
Financing activities:				
Payments to retire bonds			(j) 18,000 ⎫	
Receipts from issuance of stock		(l) 15,000	⎬	43,000
Payments of dividends.			(m) 14,000 ⎭	
Receipts from issuance of bonds.		(k2) 60,000		
Increase in cash balance			(a2) 5,000	5,000
		342,000	342,000	

Purchase of Plant Assets.   Grover Company purchased plant assets that cost $70,000 by issuing $60,000 of bonds payable to the seller and paying the $10,000 balance in cash. The effect of these transactions is similar to a cash inflow followed immediately by a cash outflow. Therefore, this transaction is reported as both a financing and an investing activity. That is, a financing cash inflow of $60,000 (entry *k2*) and an investing cash outflow of $70,000 (entry *k1*).

Sale of Plant Assets.   Grover Company sold plant assets that cost $30,000 and had accumulated amortization of $12,000. The result of the sale was a loss of $6,000 and a cash receipt of $12,000 (entry *i*). This cash receipt is reported in the statement of cash flows as a cash inflow from investing activities (see Illustration 18–1).

Recall from Grover Company's income statement that amortization expense was $24,000. Amortization does not use or provide cash. However, we should notice the effects of amortization expense, the plant asset purchase, and the plant asset sale on the Plant Assets and Accumulated Amortization accounts. These accounts are reconstructed, as follows:

Plant Assets				Accumulated Amortization			
Dec 31, 1992 Bal.	210,000					Dec 31, 1992 Bal.	48,000
Purchase	70,000	Sale	30,000	Sale	12,000	Amortization expense	24,000
Dec 31, 1993 Bal.	250,000					Dec 31, 1993 Bal.	60,000

The beginning and ending balances of these accounts were taken from Grover Company's balance sheets (Illustration 18–9). Reconstructing the accounts shows that the beginning and ending balances of both accounts are completely reconciled by the purchase, the sale, and the amortization expense. As a result, you can conclude that you did not omit any of the investing activities that relate to plant assets.

Financing Activities

Financing activities usually relate to a company's long-term debt and shareholders' equity accounts. In the information about Grover Company, there were four transactions that involved financing activities. One of these, the $60,000 issuance of bonds payable (entry *k2*) to purchase plant assets, was discussed above as a simultaneous investing and financing activity. The remaining three transactions were the retirement of bonds, the issuance of common shares, and the payment of cash dividends.

Payment to Retire Bonds Payable.   Grover Company's December 31, 1992, balance sheet showed bonds payable of $64,000, of which $34,000 were retired for $18,000 cash in 1993 (entry *j*). The income statement reports the $16,000 difference as a gain (entry *j*). The SCFP shows the $18,000 payment as a cash outflow from financing activities (see Illustration 18–1).

Notice that the beginning and ending balances of Bonds Payable are reconciled by the $60,000 issuance of new bonds and the retirement of $34,000 of old bonds. This is shown in the reconstructed Bonds Payable account that follows:

Bonds Payable

		Dec 31, 1992 Bal.	64,000
Retired bonds	34,000	Issued bonds	60,000
		Dec 31, 1993 Bal.	90,000

Receipt from Common Share Issuance. During 1993, Grover Company issued 3,000 common shares for $5 per share. This $15,000 cash receipt is reported on the SCFP as a financing activity (entry *l*). Look at the December 31, 1992 and 1993, balance sheets in Illustration 18–9. Notice that the Common Shares account balance increased from $80,000 at the beginning of 1993 to $95,000 at the end of 1993. Thus, the $15,000 share issue reconciles the change in the Common Shares account.

Payment of Cash Dividends. According to the facts provided about Grover Company's transactions, cash dividends of $14,000 were paid during 1993. This payment is reported as a cash outflow from financing activities (entry *m*). Also note that the effects of this $14,000 payment and the reported net income of $38,000 fully reconcile the beginning and ending balances of Retained Earnings. This is shown in the reconstructed Retained Earnings account that follows:

Retained Earnings

		Dec 31, 1992 Bal.	88,000
Cash dividend	14,000	Net income	38,000
		Dec 31, 1993 Bal.	112,000

All of Grover Company's cash inflows and outflows were described in the previous paragraphs. We also described one simultaneous investing and financing transaction. In the process of making these analyses, we reconciled the changes in all of the noncash balance sheet accounts. The change in the Cash account is reconciled by the statement of changes in financial position, as shown in Illustration 18–1.

Summary of Chapter in Terms of Learning Objectives

LO 1. The statement of changes in financial position reports cash receipts and disbursements as operating, investing, or financing activities. Operating activities include transactions related to producing or purchasing merchandise, selling goods and services to customers, and performing administrative functions. Investing activities include purchases and sales of noncurrent assets and short-term investments that are not cash equivalents. Financing activities include transactions with owners and transactions to borrow or repay the principal amounts of long-term and short-term debt.

LO 2. Those transactions that do not involve cash but are investing or financing activities must be disclosed in the SCFP and treated as if they were simultaneous cash transactions.

LO 3. Cash receipts and payments are recorded in the Cash account and in other *noncash* balance sheet accounts, or temporary accounts, such as revenues and expenses. The temporary accounts are closed to Retained Earnings. Therefore, to identify the cash receipts and cash payments, analyze the changes in the noncash balance sheet accounts created by income statement transactions and other events. For example, the amount of cash collected from customers is calculated by modifying sales revenues for the change in accounts receivable. Similarly, cash paid for interest is calculated by adjusting interest expense for the change in interest payable.

LO 4. To calculate the net cash provided (or used) by operating activities, first list the net income and then modify it for these three types of events: (*a*) changes in noncash current assets and current liabilities related to operating activities, (*b*) revenues and expenses that did not provide or use cash, and (*c*) gains and losses from investing and financing activities.

LO 5. To prepare an SCFP working paper, first enter the beginning and ending balances of the balance sheet accounts in columns 1 and 4. Then, establish the three sections of the SCFP. Enter net income as the first item in the operating activities section. Then adjust the net income for events *a* through *c*, identified in the preceding paragraph. This process reconciles the changes in the noncash current assets and current liabilities related to operations. Reconcile any remaining balance sheet account changes and report their cash effects in the appropriate sections. Enter noncash investing and financing activities at the bottom of the working paper.

Given the following condensed income statement and a partial list of account balances, calculate the cash provided by operating activities:

Demonstration
Problem

BUTTERFIELD COMPANY
Income Statement
For the Year Ended December 31, 1993

Sales		$225,000
Cost of goods sold		130,000
Gross profit from sales		$ 95,000
Operating expenses:		
Salaries and wages	$31,250	
Amortization expense	3,750	
Rent expense	9,000	
Amortization of patents	750	
Office expense	1,000	
Bond interest expense	3,375	49,125
Net income		$ 45,875

Butterfield Company's partial list of comparative account balances as of December 31, 1993 and 1992:

	1993	1992
Cash	$ 2,600	$ 2,200
Accounts receivable (net)	23,200	21,800
Inventory	17,900	19,300
Prepaid expenses	1,200	1,400
Accounts payable	11,400	12,100
Salaries and wages payable	250	650
Interest payable	1,500	750
Unamortized bond discount	500	875

Solution to
Demonstration
Problem

Planning the Solution

- Prepare a blank section of an SCFP for operating activities.
- Insert the net income figure at the beginning of the schedule.
- Examine each account balance to determine if it has increased or decreased during 1993.
- Adjust net income for increases and decreases in current assets and liabilities.
- Adjust net income for expenses which are not a decrease in cash.
- Compare your answer to the solution.

BUTTERFIELD COMPANY
Cash Provided by Operating Activities
For the Year Ended December 31, 1993

Cash provided by operating activities:		
Net income.		$45,875
Adjustments to reconcile net income to		
cash provided by operations:		
Increase in accounts receivable	$(1,400)	
Decrease in inventory	1,400	
Decrease in prepaid expenses	200	
Decrease in accounts payable	(700)	
Decrease in salaries and wages payable . .	(400)	
Increase in interest payable	750	
Amortization expense	3,750	
Amortization of patents	750	
Amortization of bond discount.	375	4,725
Cash provided by operating activities		$50,600

Glossary

LO 6 Define or explain
the words or phrases listed
in the chapter glossary.

Cash equivalent   an investment that is readily convertible to a known amount of cash. p. 903

Financing activities   transactions with the owners of a business or transactions with its creditors to borrow money or to repay the principal amounts of loans. p. 911

Investing activities   transactions that involve making and collecting loans or that involve purchasing and selling capital assets, other productive assets, or investments other than cash equivalents. p. 910

Net cash provided or used by operating activities   a calculation that begins with net income and then adjusts the net income amount by adding and subtracting items that are necessary to reconcile net income to the net cash provided or used by operating activities. p. 903

Operating activities   activities that involve the production or purchase of merchandise and the sale of goods and services to customers, including expenditures related to administering the business. p. 905

Statement of changes in financial position (SCFP)   a financial statement that reports the cash inflows and outflows for an accounting period, and that classifies those cash flows as operating activities, investing activities, and financing activities. p. 903

Glossary

LO 6 Define or explain
the words or phrases listed
in the chapter glossary.

Synonymous Terms

Cash inflow   source of cash
Cash outflow   use of cash

Objective Review

Answers to the following questions are listed at the end of this chapter. Be sure that you decide which is the one best answer to each question *before* you check the answers.

LO 1   A payment in the form of a loan made by a manufacturing company to another company is an example of:

a.   A cash flow from operating activities.
b.   A cash flow from investing activities.
c.   A cash flow from financing activities.
d.   A noncash investing and financing activity.
e.   A cash payment to purchase a cash equivalent.

LO 2   Outland Shirt Company purchased machines costing $24,000 and gave a three-year note payable for $20,000 and $4,000 cash as payment. On the SCFP this transaction would be reported as:

a.   A cash outflow from investing activities of $4,000.
b.   A cash outflow from investing activities of $20,000 and a cash inflow from financing activities for $20,000.
c.   A cash inflow from financing activities for $20,000 and a cash outflow from investing activities of $24,000.
d.   A cash inflow from investing activities of $4,000.
e.   A cash inflow from investing activities of $24,000 and a cash outflow from financing activities for $20,000.

LO 3 Snyder Company's Merchandise Inventory account balance decreased during a period from a beginning balance of $32,000 to an ending balance of $28,000. This change would be reported on the SCFP as:

a. A cash inflow from investing activities of $4,000.

b. A cash outflow from operating activities of $4,000.

c. A decrease in financing activities of $4,000.

d. An increase of cash provided by operations of $4,000.

e. A decrease in cash provided by operations of $4,000.

LO 4 Determine the net cash provided (or used) by operating activities based on the following data:

Net income	$74,900
Decrease in accounts receivable	4,600
Increase in inventory	11,700
Decrease in accounts payable.	1,000
Loss on sale of equipment	3,400
Payment of dividends.	21,500

a. $48,700.

b. $61,000.

c. $63,400.

d. $70,200.

e. $79,600.

LO 5 In preparing a working paper for an SCFP with the cash flows from operating activities reported according to the indirect method:

a. A decrease in accounts receivable is analyzed with a debit in the statement of changes in financial position section and a credit in the balance sheet section.

b. A cash dividend paid is analyzed with a debit to retained earnings and a credit in the investing activities section.

c. The analysis of a cash payment to retire bonds payable at a loss would require one debit and two credits.

d. Amortization expense would not require analysis on the working paper because there is no cash inflow or outflow.

e. None of the above is correct.

Questions for Class Discussion

1. What are the three categories of cash flows shown on a statement of changes in financial position (SCFP)?

2. What are some examples of items reported on an SCFP as investing activities?

3. What are some examples of items reported on an SCFP as financing activities?

4. A machine that was held as a long-term asset for use in business operations is sold for cash. Where should this cash flow appear on the SCFP?

5. A business increases its merchandise inventory. Where should this cash flow appear on the SCFP?

6. If a corporation pays cash dividends, where on the corporation's SCFP should the payment be reported?

7. A company purchases land for $200,000 and finances 100% of the purchase with a long-term note payable. Should this transaction be reported on an SCFP? If so, where on the statement should it be reported?

8. A company purchases land for $100,000, paying $20,000 cash and borrowing the remainder on a long-term note payable. How should this transaction be reported on an SCFP?

9. A company borrowed $50,000 by giving its bank a 60-day, 12% interest-bearing note. When the note was repaid, the company also paid interest of $1,000. On the SCFP, where would the $1,000 interest payment be reported?

10. When a working paper for the preparation of an SCFP is prepared, all changes in noncash balance sheet accounts are accounted for on the working paper. Why?

11. A company retired a long-term note payable by issuing common shares equal in value to the carrying amount of the note. How is this event analyzed on the SCFP working paper?

12. If a company reports a net income for the year, is it possible for the company to show a net cash outflow from operating activities? Explain your answer.

13. Why are expenses such as amortization of goodwill added to net income when cash flow from operations is calculated?

14. A company reports a net income of $15,000 that includes a $3,000 gain on sale of plant assets. Why is this gain subtracted from net income in the process of reconciling net income to the net cash provided or used by operating activities?

15. Refer to Bombardier Inc.'s consolidated statements of changes in financial position shown in Appendix I. What does Bombardier include in its definition of ''Cash position''?

Exercises

The following seven events occurred during the year. Place an *x* in one of the columns next to each event. If the item should appear in the SCFP in more than one section, place the *x* in the columns for the sections in which it would be presented.

Exercise 18–1
Classifying transactions on SCFP
(LO 1)

	SCFP		
	Operating Activities	Investing Activities	Financing Activities
a. Paid cash to purchase a trademark.	_____	_____	_____
b. Long-term bonds payable were retired by issuing common shares.	_____	_____	_____
c. A cash dividend that was declared in a previous period was paid in the current period.	_____	_____	_____
d. Surplus merchandise inventory was sold for cash.	_____	_____	_____
e. Borrowed cash from the bank by signing a six-month note payable.	_____	_____	_____
f. A six-month note receivable was accepted in exchange for a building that had been used in operations.	_____	_____	_____
g. Recorded amortization expense on all plant assets.	_____	_____	_____

Exercise 18–2
Organizing the SCFP and
supporting schedule
(LO 1, 2, 4)

Use the following information about the 1993 cash flows of Union Sales Company to
prepare a statement of changes in financial position.

Cash and cash equivalents balance, December 31, 1992 . . .	$ 20,000
Cash and cash equivalents balance, December 31, 1993 . . .	56,000
Cash paid to retire long-term notes payable	100,000
Cash received from sale of equipment	49,000
Increase in merchandise inventory	2,000
Cash paid for store equipment	19,000
Cash borrowed on six-month note payable	20,000
Cash dividends paid	12,000
Bonds payable retired by issuing common shares	
(there was no gain or loss on the retirement)	150,000
Increase in salaries payable	3,000
Land purchased and financed by long-term note payable . .	85,000
Increase in accounts receivable	8,000
Cash received as interest	2,000
Net income	73,000
Amortization expense	32,000

Exercise 18–3
Calculating cash flows
(LO 3)

In each of the following cases, use the information provided about the 1993 operations
of Dayton Window Company to calculate the indicated cash flow:

Case A:	Calculate cash paid for rent;	
	Rent expense	$11,400
	Prepaid rent, January 1	1,900
	Prepaid rent, December 31	2,850
Case B:	Calculate cash paid to employees:	
	Salaries expense	$34,000
	Salaries payable, January 1	2,100
	Salaries payable, December 31	2,500
Case C:	Calculate cash received from customers:	
	Sales revenue	$85,000
	Accounts receivable, January 1	4,200
	Accounts receivable, December 31	5,800

Exercise 18–4
Calculating cash flows
(LO 3)

In each of the following cases, use the information provided about the 1993 operations
of Greenleaf Company to calculate the indicated cash flow:

Case A:	Calculate cash received from interest:	
	Interest revenue	$17,000
	Interest receivable, January 1	1,500
	Interest receivable, December 31	1,800
Case B:	Calculate cash paid for utilities:	
	Utilities expense	$ 5,100
	Utilities payable, January 1	1,100
	Utilities payable, December 31	900
Case C:	Calculate cash paid for merchandise:	
	Cost of goods sold	$88,000
	Merchandise inventory, January 1	26,600
	Accounts payable, January 1	11,300
	Merchandise inventory, December 31 . .	21,900
	Accounts payable, December 31	14,000

Use the following income statement and information about changes in noncash current assets and current liabilities to present the cash flows from operating activities:

ACE SECURITY SYSTEMS COMPANY
Income Statement
For Year Ended December 31, 1993

Sales		$404,000
Cost of goods sold		198,000
Gross profit from sales		$206,000
Operating expenses:		
Salaries and wages	$55,230	
Amortization expense	9,600	
Rent expense.	10,800	
Amortization of goodwill. . . .	1,200	
Interest expense	4,250	81,080
Total		$124,920
Loss on sale of equipment		1,600
Net income.		$123,320

Changes in current asset and current liability accounts during the year, all of which related to operating activities, were as follows:

Accounts receivable	$9,000 increase
Merchandise inventory	6,000 increase
Accounts payable	3,000 decrease
Salaries and wages payable	1,000 decrease

REC Corporation's 1993 income statement showed the following: net income, $364,000; depreciation expense, $45,000; amortization expense, $8,200; and gain on sale of plant assets, $7,000. An examination of the company's current assets and current liabilities showed that the following changes occurred because of operating activities: accounts receivable decreased $18,100; merchandise inventory decreased $52,000; prepaid expenses increased $3,700; accounts payable decreased $9,200; other payables increased $1,400. Calculate the cash flow from operating activities.

Explain how the following transactions would be reported on the SCFP for Analog Corporation:

a. The income statement shows a $4,200 loss on exchange of machinery. The loss relates to an old machine that had a book value of $47,200 when it was exchanged for a new machine that had a cash price of $43,000.

b. Outstanding bonds payable carried on the books at $200,000 were retired by issuing 8,000 common shares that had a market value of $200,000.

c. A building valued at $430,000 was purchased by paying cash of $75,000 and signing a long-term note payable for the balance.

d. The income statement shows an $82,000 gain on the sale of land. The land had a book value of $90,000 and was sold for $172,000. Analog Corporation received $72,000 cash and accepted a long-term promissory note for the balance of the sales price.

Exercise 18–8
Statement of changes in
financial position
(LO 2, 3)

Dominion Company's 1993 and 1992 balance sheets presented the following
information:

	December 31	
	1993	**1992**
Debits		
Cash	$ 26,000	$ 31,000
Accounts receivable	16,000	14,000
Merchandise inventory	107,000	115,000
Equipment	98,000	78,000
Totals	$247,000	$238,000
Credits		
Accumulated amortization, equipment . .	$ 45,800	$ 31,200
Common stock, $10 par value	120,000	120,000
Retained earnings	81,200	86,800
Totals	$247,000	$238,000

An examination of the company's activities during 1993, including the income statement, reveals the following:

a. Sales (all on credit) $356,000
b. All credits to Accounts Receivable during the period
   were receipts from customers.
c. Cost of goods sold 182,000
d. All merchandise purchases were for cash.
e. Amortization expense 14,600
f. Other operating expenses 105,000
g. Net income 54,400
h. Equipment was purchased for $20,000 cash.
i. The company declared and paid $60,000 of cash
   dividends during the year.

Required

Prepare an SCFP that follows the direct approach to calculate the net cash provided (or
used) by operating activities. Do not prepare a working paper but show any supporting
calculations.

Problems

Problem 18–1
Statement of changes in
financial position (working
paper)
(LO 1, 2, 3, 5)

Montego Tool Corporation's 1993 and 1992 balance sheets carried the following items:

	December 31	
	1993	**1992**
Debits		
Cash	$ 58,000	$ 39,000
Accounts receivable	31,000	27,000
Merchandise inventory	203,000	178,000
Equipment	111,000	99,000
Totals	$403,000	$343,000

Credits

Accumulated amortization, equipment . . .	$ 52,000	$ 34,000
Accounts payable	23,000	32,000
Income taxes payable	9,000	8,000
Common shares	260,000	240,000
Retained earnings	59,000	29,000
Totals	$403,000	$343,000

An examination of the company's activities during 1993, including the income statement, shows the following:

a. Sales		$664,000
b. Cost of goods sold	$398,000	
c. Amortization expense	18,000	
d. Other operating expenses (paid with cash) . .	167,000	
e. Income taxes expense	14,000	597,000
f. Net income		$ 67,000

g. Equipment was purchased for $12,000 cash.
h. Eight hundred common shares were issued for cash at $25 per share.
i. The company declared and paid $37,000 of cash dividends during the year.

Required

Prepare an SCFP working paper.

Refer to the facts about Montego Tool Corporation presented in Problem 18–1. Prepare an SCFP. Do not prepare a working paper. Instead, prepare the statement directly from your examination of the balance sheets and the additional information provided about the income statement and other transactions of the company. Show your supporting calculations.

Problem 18–2
SCFP (direct approach)
(LO 1, 4)

Clarion Corporation's 1993 and 1992 balance sheets included the following items:

Problem 18–3
SCFP (working paper)
(LO 1, 2, 3, 5)

	December 31	
	1993	**1992**
Debits		
Cash	$ 43,100	$ 61,300
Accounts receivable	52,000	39,700
Merchandise inventory	219,000	202,000
Prepaid expenses	4,300	5,000
Equipment	127,600	88,000
Totals	$446,000	$396,000
Credits		
Accumulated amortization, equipment	$ 27,700	$ 35,200
Accounts payable	70,500	93,300
Short-term notes payable	8,000	5,000
Long-term notes payable	75,000	43,000
Common shares	161,000	125,000
Retained earnings	103,800	94,500
Totals	$446,000	$396,000

Additional information about the 1993 activities follows:

a.	Sales revenue		$397,000
b.	Cost of goods sold.	$200,000	
c.	Amortization expense	15,000	
d.	Other expenses	109,200	
e.	Income tax expense (paid with cash)	9,700	
f.	Loss on sale of equipment.	4,100	338,000

The equipment cost $37,500, was amortized
by $22,500, and was sold for $10,900.

g.	Net income		$ 59,000

h. Equipment that cost $77,100 was purchased by
paying cash of $20,000 and by signing a long-term note
payable for the balance.

i. Borrowed $3,000 by signing a short-term note payable.

j. Paid $25,100 to reduce a long-term note payable.

k. Issued 1,000 common shares for cash at $36 per share.

l. Declared and paid cash dividends of $49,700.

Required

Prepare a statement of changes in financial position working paper.

Problem 18–4
Statement of changes in
financial position
(LO 1, 4)

Refer to the information about Clarion Corporation presented in Problem 18–3. Prepare an SCFP. Do not prepare a working paper. Instead, prepare the statement directly from your examination of the balance sheets and the additional information provided about the income statement and other transactions of the company. Show your supporting calculations.

Problem 18–5
SCFP working paper
(LO 3, 4, 5)

Cambridge Company's 1993 and 1992 balance sheets carried the following items:

	December	
	1993	**1992**
Debits		
Cash	$ 4,892	$ 12,505
Temporary investments	3,879	1,840
Accounts receivable	82,806	88,174
Inventories.	63,989	62,577
Prepaid expenses	2,913	4,307
Long-term investments	8,722	4,748
Capital assets (net).	157,644	157,395
Totals	$324,845	$331,546
Credits		
Bank indebtedness.	$ 64,674	$ 44,679
Accounts payable	38,419	39,216
Property taxes payable	1,688	2,990
Income tax payable	10,094	6,318
Long-term debt	72,545	102,359
Share capital.	104,328	108,334
Retained earnings	33,097	27,650
Totals	$324,845	$331,546

An examination of the company's activities during 1993, including the income statement, shows the following:

Sales		$388,588
Cost of sales	$300,007	
General, selling, and administrative expenses . .	83,522	
Income tax expense	3,789	387,318
Income before the following		1,270
Gain on sale of capital assets.		10,977
Net income.		$ 12,247

Other information:

1. Amortization expense $15,921
2. Capital assets were purchased during the year at a cost of . .   31,693
3. Dividends paid during the year   6,800
4. During the year, capital assets with an original cost of $44,170 and accumulated amortization of $28,647 were sold for $26,500.
5. Cash and cash equivalents include cash and temporary investments net of bank indebtedness.

Required
Prepare an SCFP working paper.

Refer to the information about Cambridge Company presented in Problem 18–5. Prepare an SCFP. Do not prepare a working paper. Instead, prepare the statement directly from your examination of the balance sheets and the additional information provided about the income statement and other transactions of the company. Show your supporting calculations.

Problem 18–6
Statement of changes in financial position
(LO 3, 4, 5)

Write a brief essay explaining why, in preparing a statement of changes in financial position, it is generally better to determine the changes in cash by analyzing the changes in the noncash accounts rather than by examining the Cash account directly. You should include in your essay an explanation of why the changes in cash for the period equal the changes in the noncash balance sheet accounts.

Problem 18–7
Analytical essay
(LO 3)

Below are some items that might be found on a working paper for a SCFP. Write a brief essay describing where each item appears on a working paper for an SCFP. Also describe the nature of any debits and/or credits that should be entered in the Analysis of Changes columns next to each item.

Problem 18–8
Analytical essay
(LO 4, 7)

1. Accounts receivable.
2. Net income.
3. Amortization expense.
4. Payment to purchase equipment.

Alternate Problems

Problem 18–1A
Statement of changes in
financial position
(LO 1, 2, 3, 5)

Trilon Corporation's 1993 and 1992 balance sheets carried the following items:

	December 31	
	1993	**1992**
Debits		
Cash	$ 71,900	$ 42,400
Accounts receivable.	25,900	31,000
Merchandise inventory	233,800	186,500
Equipment	140,600	102,000
Totals	$472,200	$361,900
Credits		
Accumulated amortization, equipment	$ 64,400	$ 40,800
Accounts payable	51,300	47,500
Income taxes payable	6,000	9,000
Common shares	276,000	220,000
Retained earnings	74,500	44,600
Totals	$472,200	$361,900

An examination of the company's activities during 1993, including the income statement, shows the following:

a.	Sales (all on credit)		$813,000
b.	Cost of goods sold	$372,000	
c.	Amortization expense.	23,600	
d.	Other operating expenses (paid with cash)	239,700	
e.	Income tax expense.	59,800	695,100
f.	Net income		$117,900

g. Equipment was purchased for $38,600 cash.
h. Two thousand common shares were issued for cash at $28 per share.
i. The company declared and paid $88,000 of cash dividends during the year.

Required
Prepare an SCFP working paper.

Problem 18–2A
SCFP (direct approach)
(LO 1, 4)

Refer to the information about Trilon Corporation presented in Problem 18–1A. Prepare an SCFP. Do not prepare a working paper. Instead, prepare the statement directly from your examination of the balance sheets and the additional information provided about the income statement and other transactions of the company. Show your supporting calculations.

Systems Corporation's 1993 and 1992 balance sheets included the following items:

Problem 18–3A
SCFP (working paper)
(LO 1, 2, 3, 5)

	December 31	
	1993	**1992**
Debits		
Cash	$ 91,000	$ 47,700
Accounts receivable.	49,400	60,500
Merchandise inventory	303,000	326,800
Prepaid expenses	11,400	12,800
Equipment	185,500	144,000
Totals	$640,300	$591,800
Credits		
Accumulated amortization, equipment	$ 72,500	$ 62,000
Accounts payable	78,300	82,300
Short-term notes payable	11,500	7,500
Long-term notes payable	75,000	55,000
Common shares	322,000	300,000
Retained earnings	81,000	85,000
Totals	$640,300	$591,800

Additional information about the 1993 activities of the company is as follows:

a. Sales revenue		$722,000
b. Cost of goods sold	$390,000	
c. Amortization expense	24,400	
d. Other expenses	261,900	
e. Income taxes expense	6,300	
f. Loss on sale of equipment	1,400	684,000

The equipment cost $34,000, was amortized by $13,900, and was sold for $18,700.

g. Net income		$ 38,000

h. Equipment that cost $75,500 was purchased by paying cash of $25,500 and by signing a long-term note payable for the balance.

i. Borrowed $4,000 by signing a short-term note payable.

j. Paid $30,000 to reduce a long-term note payable.

k. Issued 2,000 common shares for cash at $11 per share.

l. Declared and paid cash dividends of $42,000.

Required

Prepare an SCFP.

Refer to the information about Systems Corporation presented in Problem 18–3A. Prepare an SCFP. Do not prepare a working paper. Instead, prepare the statement directly from your examination of the balance sheets and the additional information provided about the income statement and other transactions of the company. Show your supporting calculations.

Problem 18–4A
SCFP (direct approach)
(LO 1, 4)

Problem 18–5A
SCFP working paper
(LO 3, 4, 5)

Kamloop Company's 1993 and 1992 balance sheets carried the following items:

	December	
	1993	**1992**
Debits		
Cash	$ 26,604	$ 16,882
Temporary investments	5,397	2,484
Accounts receivable	111,628	109,035
Inventories.	126,385	114,479
Prepaid expenses	3,933	5,814
Long-term investments	11,775	6,410
Capital assets (net).	212,819	212,483
Totals	$498,541	$467,587
Credits		
Bank indebtedness.	$ 47,310	$ 40,317
Accounts payable	61,865	52,942
Property taxes payable.	12,279	4,035
Income tax payable	13,627	8,529
Long-term debt	97,936	138,185
Share capital	160,843	146,251
Retained earnings	104,681	77,328
Totals	$498,541	$467,587

An examination of the company's activities during 1993, including the income statement, shows the following:

Sales		$524,594
Cost of sales	$374,049	
General, selling, and administrative expenses . .	112,755	
Income tax expense	16,075	502,879
Income before the following		21,715
Gain on sale of capital assets.		14,818
Net income.		$ 36,533

Other information:

1. Amortization expense $21,493
2. Capital assets were purchased during the year at a cost of . .   42,786
3. Dividends paid during the year   9,180
4. During the year, capital assets with an original cost of $59,630 and accumulated amortization of $38,673 were sold for $35,775.
5. Cash and cash equivalents include cash and temporary investments net of bank indebtedness.

Required

Prepare an SCFP working paper.

Problem 18–6A
Statement of changes in
financial position
(LO 3, 4, 5)

Refer to the information about Kamloop Company presented in Problem 18–5A. Prepare an SCFP. Do not prepare a working paper. Instead, prepare the statement directly from your examination of the balance sheets and the additional information provided about the income statement and other transactions of the company. Show your supporting calculations.

When preparing a statement of changes in financial position, changes in noncash balance sheet accounts are analyzed to explain the changes in cash. Following are some income statement items that provide important information related to changes in noncash balance sheet accounts. Briefly explain how each of these income statement items and their related balance sheet accounts are used to identify specific cash inflows and outflows:

1. Sales.
2. Cost of goods sold.
3. Operating expenses.
4. Gain on sale of plant assets.

Below are some items that might be found on a working paper for an SCFP. Write a brief essay describing where each item appears on a working paper for an SCFP. Also describe the nature of any debits and/or credits that should be entered in the Analysis of Changes columns next to each item.

1. Accounts payable.
2. Inventories.
3. Loss on sale of equipment.
4. Payments of cash dividends.

Provocative Problems

Opticon Inc.'s 1993 statement of changes in financial position appeared as follows:

Cash flows from operating activities:		
Net income.		$ 80,200
Adjustments to reconcile net income to net cash provided by operating activities:		
Decrease in accounts receivable	$ 7,600	
Increase in merchandise inventory.	(12,700)	
Increase in prepaid expenses.	(2,600)	
Decrease in accounts payable	(6,600)	
Increase in income taxes payable	900	
Decrease in dividends payable	(6,000)	
Amortization expense	34,000	
Loss on sale of equipment	4,400	19,000
Net cash provided by operating activities . .		99,200
Cash flows from investing activities:		
Receipt from sale of office equipment	$ 9,300	
Purchase of store equipment.	(14,000)	
Net cash used by investing activities		(4,700)
Cash flows from financing activities:		
Payment to retire bonds payable.	$ (50,000)	
Dividends declared	(19,000)	
Net cash used by financing activities		(69,000)
Net increase in cash		$ 25,500
Cash balance at beginning of year		31,900
Cash balance at end of year		$ 57,400

Opticon Inc.'s beginning and ending balance sheets were as follows:

	December 31	
	1993	**1992**
Debits		
Cash	$ 57,400	$ 31,900
Accounts receivable	45,500	53,100
Merchandise inventory	208,000	195,300
Prepaid expenses	4,800	2,200
Equipment	181,100	195,600
Totals	$496,800	$478,100
Credits		
Accumulated amortization, equipment	$ 82,600	$ 63,400
Accounts payable	38,400	45,000
Income taxes payable	6,800	5,900
Dividends payable	–0–	6,000
Bonds payable	–0–	50,000
Common shares	225,000	225,000
Retained earnings	144,000	82,800
Totals	$496,800	$478,100

An examination of the company's statements and accounts showed:

a. All sales were made on credit.

b. All merchandise purchases were on credit.

c. Accounts Payable balances resulted from merchandise purchases.

d. Prepaid expenses relate to other operating expenses.

e. Equipment that cost $28,500 with accumulated amortization of $14,800 was sold for cash.

f. Equipment was purchased for cash.

g. The change in the balance of Accumulated Amortization resulted from amortization expense and from the sale of Equipment.

h. The change in the balance of Retained Earnings resulted from dividend declarations and net income.

i. Cash receipts from customers was $602,400.

j. Cash payments for merchandise inventory amounted to $315,700.

k. Cash payments for other operating expenses were $163,000.

l. Income taxes paid were $17,400.

Required

Present Opticon Inc.'s income statement for 1993. Show your supporting calculations.

The following items include the 1993 and 1992 balance sheets and the 1993 income statement of the St. Thomas Company. Additional information about the company's 1993 transactions is presented after the financial statements.

Provocative Problem 18–2
St. Thomas Company
(LO 1, 2, 3, 6)

ST. THOMAS COMPANY
Balance Sheet
December 31, 1993 and 1992

	1993		1992	
Assets				
Current assets:				
Cash and cash equivalents.	$ 3,100		$ 3,400	
Accounts receivable.	5,500		5,900	
Merchandise inventory	23,000		22,000	
Total current assets		$31,600		$31,300
Long-term investments:				
Straun Corporation				
common shares		8,000		10,000
Plant assets:				
Land.		12,000		9,000
Buildings	$50,000		$50,000	
Less: Accumulated amortization . .	25,000	25,000	22,500	27,500
Equipment.	$32,000		$26,000	
Less: Accumulated amortization . .	13,000	19,000	10,000	16,000
Total assets		$95,600		$93,800
Liabilities and Shareholders' Equity				
Liabilities				
Current liabilities:				
Notes payable	$14,000		$12,500	
Accounts payable	5,400		5,900	
Other accrued liabilities	3,900		4,300	
Interest payable	1,200		1,100	
Taxes payable	200		400	
Total current liabilities		$24,700		$24,200
Long-term liabilities:				
Bonds payable, due in 1999		25,000		20,000
Total liabilities		$49,700		$44,200
Shareholders' Equity				
Contributed capital:				
Common shares	$34,000		$30,000	
Retained earnings	13,500		19,600	
Total.	$47,500		$49,600	
Less: Cost of treasury shares	1,600		–0–	
Total shareholders' equity		45,900		49,600
Total liabilities and				
shareholders' equity.		$95,600		$93,800

ST. THOMAS COMPANY
Income Statement
For Year Ended December 31, 1993

Revenues:

Sales	$87,000	
Gain on sale of equity investment	400	
Dividend income	500	
Interest income.	100	$88,000

Expenses and losses:

Cost of goods sold	$38,200	
Other expenses.	19,800	
Interest expense	1,300	
Income tax expense	3,100	
Amortization expense, buildings	2,500	
Amortization expense, equipment	5,000	
Loss on sale of equipment	400	
Total expenses and losses.		70,300
Net income		$17,700

Additional information:

a. All the other expenses were initially credited to the Other Accrued Liabilities account.

b. Received $2,400 from the sale of Straun Corporation common shares, which originally cost $2,000

c. Received a cash dividend of $500 from the Straun Corporation.

d. Received $100 cash from the National Bank on December 31, 1993, as interest income.

e. Sold old equipment for $3,600. The old equipment originally cost $6,000 and had accumulated amortization of $2,000.

f. Purchased land costing $3,000 on December 31, 1993, in exchange for a note payable. Both principal and interest are due on June 30, 1994.

g. Purchased new equipment for $12,000 cash.

h. Purchased treasury stock for $1,600 cash.

i. Paid $1,500 of notes payable.

j. Sold additional bonds payable at par of $5,000 on January 1, 1993.

k. Issued 2,000 shares of common stock for cash at $2 per share.

l. Declared and paid a $23,800 cash dividend on October 1, 1993.

(The working papers that accompany the text include forms for this problem.)

Required

1. Prepare a working paper for St. Thomas Company's 1993 statement of changes in financial position.

2. Prepare the SCFP for 1993.

Look in Appendix I at the end of the book to find Bombardier Inc.'s Consolidated Statements of Changes in Financial Position. Based on your examination of that statement, answer the following questions:

1. During each of the years 1992 and 1991, was the cash provided from operating activities more or less than the cash paid for dividends?
2. In calculating the net cash provided from operating activities, which single item represented the largest addition to net income during 1992? During 1991?
3. What was the largest cash inflow from financing activities during 1992?
4. What was the largest cash outflow from investing activities during 1992?
5. Did the company issue any new shares for cash during the period? What were the proceeds?

Barrie Company earned $168,000 net income during 1993. Machinery was sold for $232,000, and a $48,000 loss on the sale was recorded. Machinery purchases totaled $660,000 including a July purchase for which a $160,000 promissory note was issued. Bonds were retired at their face value, and the issuance of new common shares produced an infusion of cash. Barrie's comparative balance sheets were as follows (in thousands):

	December 31	
	1993	**1992**
Cash	$ 208	$ 168
Receivables.	392	444
Inventory	648	620
Machinery	2,700	2,520
Accumulated amortization	(380)	(420)
Total assets	3,568	3,332
Accounts payable.	$ 476	$ 572
Notes payable	544	420
Dividends payable	64	40
Bonds payable	456	640
Common shares.	1,400	1,120
Retained earnings.	628	540
Total liabilities and shareholders' equity . .	$3,568	$3,332

a. What was Barrie's amortization expense in 1993?
b. What was the amount of cash flow from operations?
c. What was the amount of cash flow from investing activities?
d. What was the amount of the cash dividend declared? Paid?
e. By what amount would you expect the total sources of cash to differ from the total uses of cash?
f. What was the amount of cash flow from financing activities?

A&R Problem 18-2   The data below refers to the activities of Banff Limited.

Required

For each item, identify both the dollar amount and its classification—that is, whether it would appear as a positive or a negative adjustment to net income in the measurement of cash flow from operations or as some other source or use of cash.

1. Declared a $22,000 cash dividend; paid $19,000 during the year.
2. Sold for $120,000 cash land that had cost $95,000 two years earlier.
3. Sold for cash 2,000 shares for $14 a share.
4. Bought machinery for $37,000 in exchange for a note due in eight months.
5. Bought a computer which had fair value of $140,000 by giving in exchange real estate that had cost $95,000 in an earlier period.
6. Equipment amortization, $56,000.
7. Issued for cash on December 31, 1993, 10-year, 10% $500,000 par-value bonds at $24,000 discount.
8. Bought its own shares for $12,500 and immediately canceled them.
9. Paid a lawyer $13,500 for services performed, billed, and recorded correctly in 1992.
10. Reported net income of $86,000 for the year ended December 31, 1993.

Adjustments to derive cash flow from operations: A&R Problem 18–3

	Adjust By	
Income Element	**Adding**	**Subtracting**
1. Changes in current assets:		
a. Increases.	_____	_____
b. Decreases	_____	_____
2. Changes in current liabilities:		
a. Increases.	_____	_____
b. Decreases	_____	_____
3. Depreciation of plant assets	_____	_____
4. Amortization of intangible assets . .	_____	_____
5. Interest expense:		
a. Premium amortized	_____	_____
b. Discount amortized	_____	_____
6. Sale of noncurrent asset:		
a. Gain	_____	_____
b. Loss	_____	_____

Required

Indicate by an x in the appropriate column whether an item is added or subtracted to derive cash flow from operations.

LO 1 *(b)*		**LO 3** *(d)*		**LO 5** *(a)*	**Answers to Objective**
LO 2 *(c)*		**LO 4** *(d)*			**Review Questions**

CHAPTER 19

Analyzing Financial Statements

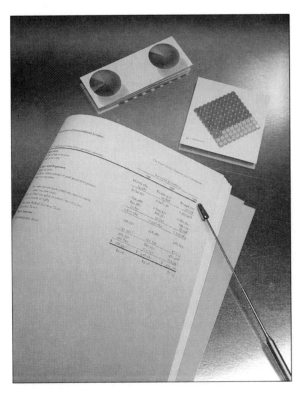

Financial reports are highly summarized descriptions of complex organizations. Analyzing and understanding the information they present requires a lot of effort; the people who prepare reports need to know what their readers are looking for and how to help them find it.

Learning Objectives

After studying Chapter 19 you should be able to:

1. Explain the relationship between financial reporting and general purpose financial statements.

2. Describe, prepare, and interpret comparative financial statements and common-size comparative statements.

3. Calculate and explain the interpretation of the ratios, turnover, and rates of return used to evaluate (*a*) short-term liquidity, (*b*) long-term risk and capital structure, and (*c*) operating efficiency and profitability.

4. State the limitations associated with using financial statement ratios and the sources from which standards for comparison may be obtained.

5. Describe the segment information disclosed in financial reports of large companies with operations in several lines of business and list the four basic issues faced by accountants in dealing with segment information.

6. Define or explain the words and phrases listed in the chapter glossary.

Financial Reporting

LO 1 Explain the relationship between financial reporting and general purpose financial statements.

Many people receive and analyze financial information about business firms. These people include managers, employees, directors, customers, suppliers, owners, lenders, potential investors, potential creditors, brokers, regulatory authorities, lawyers, economists, labour unions, financial advisors, and the financial press. Some of these groups, such as managers and some regulatory agencies, are able to gain access to specialized financial reports that meet their specific interests. However, the other groups usually must rely on the **general purpose financial statements** that companies publish periodically. General purpose financial statements include (1) an income statement, (2) a balance sheet, (3) a statement of retained earnings (or statement of changes in shareholders' equity), and (4) a statement of changes in financial position. In addition to the information contained in the body of general purpose financial statements, the information contained in the notes to the financial statements is an integral part of the statements.

Financial reporting is intended to provide useful information to investors, creditors, and others for making investment, credit, and similar decisions. The information should help the users assess the amounts, timing, and uncertainty of prospective cash inflows and outflows.

Financial reporting consists of the financial statements but is much broader. Financial reporting includes communicating information in a variety of ways. Some examples are annual reports filed with the appropriate securities commissions, news releases, and management letters or analyses included in annual reports. One such example is in Appendix I; look at the pages from Bombardier's annual report identified at the top as MANAGEMENT DISCUSSION.

The objectives of financial reporting were published in the CICA's "Financial Statement Concepts" (section 1000 of the *CICA Handbook*). The conceptual framework is intended to help accountants decide how accounting problems should be solved. (Part V provides a more in-depth discussion of the conceptual framework project.) In addition, the objectives provide important background information for those learning how to understand and analyze financial statements.

Some users of financial information may analyze statements for reasons that are not covered by the stated objectives. Even so, they should understand that, as the authoritative body for establishing accounting principles, the Accounting Standards Board intends that financial reporting (and financial statements) reflect these objectives. The primary idea is that financial reporting should help readers predict the amounts, timing, and uncertainty of future net cash inflows to the business. The methods of analysis and techniques explained in this chapter contribute to the process.

Comparative Statements

LO 2 Describe, prepare, and interpret comparative financial statements and common-size comparative statements.

When the financial information of a business is analyzed, individual items usually are not particularly significant in and of themselves. However, relationships between items and groups of items plus changes that occurred are significant. As a result, financial statement analysis involves identifying and describing relationships between items and groups of items and changes in items.

You can see changes in financial statement items more clearly when amounts for two or more successive accounting periods are placed side by side in columns on a single statement. Statements prepared in this manner are called **comparative statements.** Each financial statement can be presented in the comparative format.

In its simplest form, a comparative balance sheet consists of the amounts from two or more successive balance sheets arranged side by side so that you can see the changes in the amounts. However, the usefulness of the statement can be improved by also showing the changes in terms of absolute dollar amounts and as percentages. When this presentation is provided, as shown in Illustration 19–1, large dollar and large percentage changes are more readily apparent.

A comparative income statement is prepared in the same way. Income statement amounts for two or more successive periods are placed side by side, with dollar and percentage changes in additional columns. Illustration 19–2 shows such a statement.

ILLUSTRATION 19–1

Comparative Balance Sheet with Dollar and Percentage Changes

RANGER WHOLESALE COMPANY
Comparative Balance Sheet
December 31, 1994, and December 31, 1993

	December 31		Amount of Increase or (Decrease) during 1994	Percent of Increase or (Decrease) during 1994
	1994	1993		
Assets				
Current assets:				
Cash	$ 15,000	$ 20,500	$ (5,500)	(26.8)%
Temporary investments	3,000	70,000	(67,000)	(95.7)
Accounts receivable, net	68,000	64,000	4,000	6.3
Merchandise inventory	90,000	84,000	6,000	7.1
Prepaid expenses	5,800	6,000	(200)	(3.3)
Total current assets	$181,800	$244,500	$ (62,700)	(25.6)
Long-term investments:				
Real estate	$ –0–	$ 30,000	$ (30,000)	(100.0)
Apex Company common shares	–0–	50,000	(50,000)	(100.0)
Total long-term investments	$ –0–	$ 80,000	$ (80,000)	(100.0)
Plant and equipment:				
Office equipment, net	$ 3,500	$ 3,700	$ (200)	(5.4)
Store equipment, net	17,900	6,800	11,100	163.2
Buildings, net	176,800	28,000	148,800	531.4
Land	50,000	20,000	30,000	150.0
Total plant and equipment	$248,200	$ 58,500	$189,700	324.3
Total assets	$430,000	$383,000	$ 47,000	12.3
Liabilities				
Current liabilities:				
Accounts payable	$ 43,600	$ 55,000	$(11,400)	(20.7)
Wages payable	800	1,200	(400)	(33.3)
Taxes payable	4,800	5,000	(200)	(4.0)
Notes payable	5,000	–0–	5,000	N.A.
Total current liabilities	$ 54,200	$ 61,200	$ (7,000)	(11.4)
Long-term liabilities:				
Notes payable (secured by mortgage on land and buildings)	60,000	10,000	50,000	500.0
Total liabilities	$114,200	$ 71,200	$ 43,000	60.4
Shareholders' Equity				
Common—25,000 shares	$250,000	$250,000	$ –0–	–0–
Retained earnings	65,800	61,800	4,000	6.5
Total shareholders' equity	$315,800	$311,800	$ 4,000	1.3
Total liabilities and equity	$430,000	$383,000	$ 47,000	12.3

Note: N.A. = not applicable because there was no amount in 1993.

ILLUSTRATION 19–2

Comparative Income Statement with Dollar and Percentage Changes

RANGER WHOLESALE COMPANY
Comparative Income Statement
For Years Ended December 31, 1994 and 1993

	Years Ended December 31		Amount of Increase or (Decrease) during 1994	Percent of Increase or (Decrease) during 1994
	1994	**1993**		
Gross sales.	$973,500	$853,000	$120,500	14.1%
Sales returns and allowances.	13,500	10,200	3,300	32.4
Net sales.	$960,000	$842,800	$117,200	13.9
Cost of goods sold	715,000	622,500	92,500	14.9
Gross profit from sales	$245,000	$220,300	$ 24,700	11.2
Operating expenses:				
Selling expenses:				
Advertising expense.	$ 7,500	$ 5,000	$ 2,500	50.0
Sales salaries expense	109,500	97,500	12,000	12.3
Store supplies expense	3,200	2,800	400	14.3
Amortization expense, store equipment	2,400	1,700	700	41.2
Delivery expense	14,800	14,000	800	5.7
Total selling expenses	$137,400	$121,000	$ 16,400	13.6
General and administrative expenses:				
Office salaries expense	$ 41,000	$ 40,050	950	2.4
Office supplies expense	1,300	1,250	50	4.0
Insurance expense.	1,600	1,200	400	33.3
Amortization expense, office equipment	300	300	–0–	–0–
Amortization expense, buildings.	2,850	1,500	1,350	90.0
Bad debts expense.	2,250	2,200	50	2.3
Total general and administrative expenses.	$ 49,300	$ 46,500	$ 2,800	6.0
Total operating expenses.	$186,700	$167,500	$ 19,200	11.5
Operating income	$ 58,300	$ 52,800	$ 5,500	10.4
Less interest expense	6,300	1,500	4,800	320.0
Income before taxes	$ 52,000	$ 51,300	$ 700	1.4
Income taxes.	19,000	18,700	300	1.6
Net income.	$ 33,000	$ 32,600	$ 400	1.2
Earnings per share	$ 1.32	$ 1.30	$ 0.02	1.5

Analyzing and Interpreting Comparative Statements

In analyzing and interpreting comparative data, study any items that show significant dollar or percentage changes. Then try to identify the reasons for each change and, if possible, determine whether they are favourable or unfavourable. For example, in Illustration 19–1, the first item, "Cash," shows a decrease of $5,500. The next item, "Temporary investments," shows an extremely large decrease. Also, the "Long-term investments" were completely eliminated during the year. At first glance these changes appear to be unfavourable. However, these decreases must be evaluated in light of other changes that occurred. The increases in "Store equipment," "Buildings," and "Land," show that the company materially increased its plant assets between the two balance sheet dates. Further study suggests that the company has apparently constructed a new building on land that was held as an investment until needed for this expansion. Also, the company apparently paid for the new plant assets by reducing cash, selling the investment in Apex Company common shares, and issuing a $50,000 note payable.

In gaining control over operations, a comparative income statement can be especially useful to management. For example, in Illustration 19–2, "Gross sales" increased 14.1% and "Net sales" increased 13.9%. At the same time, "Sales returns and allowances" increased 32.4%, or at a rate more than twice that of gross sales. Returned sales usually represent wasted sales effort and dissatisfied customers. Therefore, the increased rate of "Sales returns and allowances" should be investigated, and the reason for the increase should be determined.

In addition to the large increase in the "Sales returns and allowances," note that the rate of increase of "Cost of goods sold" is greater than the rate of increase of "Net sales." This unfavourable trend should be corrected if possible.

In attempting to find reasons for Ranger Wholesale Company's increase in sales, the increases in advertising and in plant assets must be considered. For example, an increase in advertising may increase sales. Also, the increase in plant assets may have been necessary to support larger sales and production volumes.

Calculating Percentage Increases and Decreases

To calculate the percentage increases and decreases shown on comparative statements, divide the dollar increase or decrease of an item by the amount shown for the item in the base year. If no amount is shown in the base year, or if the base year amount is negative (such as a net loss) while the current year is positive, a percentage increase or decrease cannot be calculated. For example, in Illustration 19–1, there were no notes payable at the end of 1993, and a percentage change for this item cannot be calculated.

In this text, percentages and ratios typically are rounded to one or two decimal places. However, there is no uniform practice on this matter. In general, percentages should be carried out far enough to ensure that meaningful information is obtained. They should not be carried so far that the significance of relationships becomes lost in the length of the numbers.

Trend Percentages

Trend percentages (also known as *index numbers*) can be used to describe changes that have occurred from one period to the next. They are also used to compare data that cover a number of years. Calculate trend percentages as follows:

1. Select a base year and assign each item on the base year statement a weight of 100%.

2. Express each item from the statements for the years after the base year as a percentage of its base year amount. To determine these percentages, divide the amounts in the years after the base year by the amount of the item in the base year.

For example, if 1988 is selected as the base year for the following data, divide the amount of "Sales" in each year by $210,000 to get the trend percentages for sales. To get the trend percentages for cost of goods sold, divide the "Cost of goods sold" amount in each year by $145,000. And, the gross profit trend percentages equal the "Gross profit" amount in each year divided by $65,000.

	1993	1992	1991	1990	1989	1988
Sales	$400,000	$367,000	$320,000	$278,000	$241,500	$210,000
Cost of goods sold . .	260,000	212,000	190,000	165,000	159,500	145,000
Gross profit. . .	$140,000	$155,000	$130,000	$113,000	$ 82,000	$ 65,000

When the percentages are calculated, the trends for these three items appear as follows:

	1993	1992	1991	1990	1989	1988
Sales	190%	175%	152%	132%	115%	100%
Cost of goods sold . .	179	146	131	114	110	100
Gross profit. . .	215	238	200	174	126	100

Illustration 19–3 presents the same data in a graphical format. A graph can help identify trends and detect changes in their direction or growth rates. For example, note that although the trend for sales was consistently upward, the rate of increase declined slightly in 1993.

A graph also may help you identify and understand the relationships between items. For example, Illustration 19–3 shows that through 1992, cost of goods sold increased at a rate that was somewhat less than the increase in sales. Further, the differing trends in these two items had a pronounced effect on the percentage changes in gross profit. In 1993, while sales increased (at a slower rate), cost of goods sold increased at a much greater rate. The net effect of these 1993 changes was to sharply decrease gross profit, which reversed the trend of the past four years.

This presentation and analysis of the data suggest a problem that management needs to address. The graph also provides a warning to outside analysts that they should perhaps reconsider their past predictions of future cash flows.

The analysis of financial statement items may also include the relationships between items on different financial statements. For example, the combination of a downward sales trend with an upward trend for merchandise inventory, accounts receivable, and bad debts expense would indicate an unfavourable situation. On the other hand, an upward sales trend with a downward or a slower upward trend for accounts receivable, merchandise inventory, and selling expenses suggests an increase in operating efficiency.

ILLUSTRATION 19–3

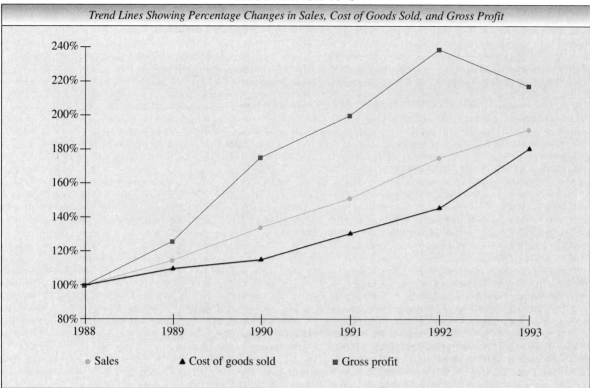

Trend Lines Showing Percentage Changes in Sales, Cost of Goods Sold, and Gross Profit

Common-Size Comparative Statements

Although the comparative statements illustrated so far show how each item has changed over time, they do not emphasize the relative importance of each item. Changes in the relative importance of each financial statement item are shown more clearly by **common-size comparative statements.**

In common-size statements, each item is expressed as a percentage of a *base amount.* For a common-size balance sheet, the base amount is usually the amount of total assets. This total is assigned a value of 100%. (Of course, the total amount of liabilities plus owners' equity also equals 100%.) Each asset, liability, and owners' equity item is then shown as a percentage of total assets (or total liabilities plus owners' equity). If you present a company's successive balance sheets in this way, changes in the mixture of the assets or liabilities and equity are more readily apparent.

For example, look at the common-size balance sheet presented in Illustration 19–4. Note that current assets represented more than 63% of total assets in 1993, whereas current assets amounted to less than 43% of total assets in 1994. Most of this change can be attributed to temporary investments, which fell from over 18% to less than 1% of total assets.

In producing a common-size income statement, the amount of net sales is usually the base amount and is also assigned a value of 100%. Then each statement item appears as a percentage of net sales. This format can be

ILLUSTRATION 19–4

Common-Size Comparative Balance Sheet

RANGER WHOLESALE COMPANY
Common-Size Comparative Balance Sheet
December 31, 1994, and December 31, 1993

	December 31		Common-Size Percentages	
	1994	1993	1994	1993
Assets				
Current assets:				
Cash	$ 15,000	$ 20,500	3.49%	5.35%
Temporary investments.	3,000	70,000	0.70	18.28
Accounts receivable, net	68,000	64,000	15.81	16.71
Merchandise inventory	90,000	84,000	20.93	21.93
Prepaid expenses	5,800	6,000	1.35	1.57
Total current assets	$181,800	$244,500	42.28	63.84
Long-term investments:				
Real estate	$ –0–	$ 30,000		7.83
Apex Company common shares	–0–	50,000		13.05
Total long-term investments	$ –0–	$ 80,000		20.88
Plant and equipment:				
Office equipment, net	$ 3,500	$ 3,700	0.81	0.97
Store equipment, net	17,900	6,800	4.16	1.78
Buildings, net	176,800	28,000	41.12	7.31
Land	50,000	20,000	11.63	5.22
Total plant and equipment	$248,200	$ 58,500	57.72	15.28
Total assets	$430,000	$383,000	100.00%	100.00%
Liabilities				
Current liabilities:				
Accounts payable	$ 43,600	$ 55,000	10.14%	14.36%
Wages payable	800	1,200	0.19	0.31
Taxes payable	4,800	5,000	1.12	1.31
Notes payable	5,000	–0–	1.16	
Total current liabilities	$ 54,200	$ 61,200	12.61	15.98
Long-term liabilities:				
Notes payable (secured by a mortgage on land and buildings)	60,000	10,000	13.95	2.61
Total liabilities	$114,200	$ 71,200	26.56	18.59
Shareholders' Equity				
Common—25,000 shares	$250,000	$250,000	58.14	65.27
Retained earnings	65,800	61,800	15.30	16.14
Total shareholders' equity	$315,800	$311,800	73.44	81.41
Total liabilities and equity	$430,000	$383,000	100.00%	100.00%

ILLUSTRATION 19–5

Common-Size Comparative Income Statement

RANGER WHOLESALE COMPANY
Common-Size Comparative Income Statement
For Years Ended December 31, 1994 and 1993

	Years Ended December 31		Common-Size Percentages	
	1994	1993	1994	1993
Gross sales	$973,500	$853,000	101.41%	101.21%
Sales returns and allowances	13,500	10,200	1.41	1.21
Net sales	$960,000	$842,800	100.00	100.00
Cost of goods sold.	715,000	622,500	74.48	73.86
Gross profit from sales	$245,000	$220,300	25.52	26.14
Operating expenses:				
Selling expenses:				
Advertising expense	$ 7,500	$ 5,000	0.78	0.59
Sales salaries expense	109,500	97,500	11.41	11.57
Store supplies expense	3,200	2,800	0.33	0.33
Amortization expense, store equipment	2,400	1,700	0.25	0.20
Delivery expense.	14,800	14,000	1.54	1.66
Total selling expenses.	$137,400	$121,000	14.31	14.35
General and administrative expenses:				
Office salaries expense	$ 41,000	$ 40,050	4.27	4.75
Office supplies expense.	1,300	1,250	0.14	0.15
Insurance expense	1,600	1,200	0.17	0.14
Amortization expense, office equipment	300	300	0.03	0.04
Amortization expense, buildings	2,850	1,500	0.30	0.18
Bad debts expense	2,250	2,200	0.23	0.26
Total general and administrative expenses	$ 49,300	$ 46,500	5.14	5.52
Total operating expenses	$186,700	$167,500	19.45	19.87
Operating income	$ 58,300	$ 52,800	6.07	6.27
Less interest expense.	6,300	1,500	0.66	0.18
Income before taxes.	$ 52,000	$ 51,300	5.41	6.09
Income taxes	19,000	18,700	1.98	2.22
Net income	$ 33,000	$ 32,600	3.43%	3.87%
Earnings per share	$ 1.32	$ 1.30	—	—

informative and useful. If you think of the 100% sales amount as representing one sales dollar, then the remaining items show how each sales dollar was distributed among costs, expenses, and profit. For example, the comparative income statement in Illustration 19–5 shows that the 1993 cost of goods sold consumed 73.86 cents of each sales dollar. In 1994, cost of goods sold consumed 74.48 cents of each sales dollar. While this increase is small, almost $6,000 of additional gross profit would have been earned if the cost of goods sold percentage in 1994 had remained at the 1993 level.

Common-size percentages help the analyst identify potential efficiencies and inefficiencies that may otherwise be difficult to see. To illustrate, even though the dollar amounts of office and sales salaries expense were greater in

ILLUSTRATION 19–6

Common Size Financial Statement Information

**Balance Sheet Information
(Composition of Total Assets)**
December 31, 1994

Other current assets (%)

Receivables (%)

Cash and temporary investments (%)

Plant and equipment (%)

**Income Statement Information
(Expenses and Net Income)**
For Year Ended December 31, 1994

Net income (%)

Operating expenses (%)

Interest and income taxes (%)

Cost of goods sold (%)

1994 than they were in 1993, both of these expenses represented smaller percentages of sales in 1994 than they did in 1993. These comparisons do not tell you why such changes took place, but they raise the possibility that the office and sales staffs were more productive in 1994 than in 1993.

Many corporate annual reports include graphic presentations of common-size information. Typical examples of these graphs appear in Illustration 19–6. The pie chart on the left side of the illustration shows the composition of Ranger Wholesale Company's assets on December 31, 1994. The chart on the right side shows the portions of each 1994 sales dollar that were consumed by cost of goods sold, operating expenses, and interest and tax expense. It also shows the portion that ended up as net income.

Analysis of Short-Term Liquidity

The amount of current assets less current liabilities is called the **working capital**, or *net working capital*, of a business. A business must maintain an adequate amount of working capital to meet current debts, carry sufficient inventories, and take advantage of cash discounts. Indeed, a business that runs out of working capital cannot continue its operations. Because current assets and current liabilities are so necessary for efficient operations, an important part of evaluating the financial position of a business involves the analysis of working capital.

When evaluating the working capital of a business, you must look beyond the simple dollar amount of the excess of the current assets over the current liabilities. Instead, you need to consider the amount of the excess in relation to the amount of current liabilities. To see why this is true, consider the following example of Ace Company and Brown Company:

LO 3 Calculate and explain the interpretation of the ratios, turnovers, and rates of return used to evaluate (*a*) short-term liquidity, (*b*) long-term risk and capital structure, and (*c*) operating efficiency and profitability.

	Ace Company	Brown Company
Current assets	$100,000	$20,000
Current liabilities . .	90,000	10,000
Working capital . . .	$ 10,000	$10,000

Ace and Brown both have the same $10,000 amount of working capital. However, Ace must be able to convert its current assets to at least 90% of their book value in order to pay the liabilities. On the other hand, Brown Company has a much greater cushion when it converts its current assets to cash. In theory, it could lose as much as 50% of the assets' book value and still be able to pay its liabilities. Thus, Brown faces a much less risky situation than Ace does.

As a general rule, the dollar amount of a company's working capital does not adequately describe the strength of its working capital position. The ratio of its current assets to its current liabilities is often a more useful description.

Current Ratio

The relationship between a company's current assets and its current liabilities can be expressed by the **current ratio.** To calculate the current ratio, simply divide total current assets by total current liabilities. For example, the current ratio of Brown Company is:

$$\frac{\text{Current assets, }\$20,000}{\text{Current liabilities, }\$10,000} = 2.0$$

In other words, Brown Company's current assets are two times its current liabilities, or the current ratio is 2 to 1. The current ratio of Ranger Wholesale Company at December 31, 1994, is:

$$\frac{\text{Current assets, }\$181,800}{\text{Current liabilities, }\$54,200} = 3.4$$

The current ratio expresses the relationship between current assets and current liabilities. A high current ratio generally indicates a stronger position because a higher ratio means the company is more capable of meeting its current obligations. On the other hand, a company might have a current ratio that is too high. This condition means that the company has invested too much in current assets compared to its needs. Normally, current assets do not generate very much additional revenue. Therefore, if a company invests too much in current assets, the investment is not being used efficiently.

Years ago, bankers and other creditors often used a current ratio of 2 to 1 as a rule of thumb in evaluating the debt-paying ability of a credit-seeking company. A company with a 2 to 1 current ratio was generally thought to be a good credit risk in the short run. However, most lenders realize that the 2 to 1 rule of thumb is not an adequate test of debt-paying ability. They realize that whether a company's current ratio is good or bad depends on at least three factors:

1. The nature of the company's business.
2. The composition of its current assets.
3. The turnover rate for some of its current assets.

In addition, the ratio can be affected by a company's choice of an inventory flow assumption. For example, a company that uses LIFO tends to have a smaller reported amount of current assets than if it uses FIFO. Therefore, consider the underlying factors before deciding that a given current ratio (or any other ratio, for that matter) is acceptable.

Whether a company's current ratio is adequate depends on the nature of its business. A service company that has no inventories other than supplies and that grants little or no credit may be able to operate on a current ratio of less than 1 to 1 if its sales generate enough cash to pay its current liabilities on time. On the other hand, a company that sells high-fashion clothing or furniture may occasionally misjudge future styles. If this happens, the company's inventory may not generate much cash until after a relatively long period of time. A company that faces risks like these may need a current ratio of much more than 2 to 1 to protect its liquidity.

Therefore, when you study the adequacy of working capital, consider the type of business under review. Before you decide that a company's current ratio is too low (or too high), compare the company's current ratio with ratios of other successful companies in the same industry. Another important source of insight is to observe how the ratio compares to its values in past periods.

Also consider the composition of a company's current assets when you evaluate its working capital position. Cash and temporary investments are more liquid than accounts and notes receivable. And, short-term receivables normally are more liquid than merchandise inventory. Cash can be used to pay current debts at once. But, accounts receivable and merchandise must be converted into cash before payments can be made. Therefore, an excessive amount of receivables and inventory could weaken the company's ability to pay its current liabilities.

Acid-Test Ratio

An easily calculated check on current asset composition is the **acid-test ratio,** also called the *quick ratio* because it is the ratio of quick assets to current liabilities. Quick assets are cash, temporary investments, accounts receivable, and notes receivable. These are the most liquid types of current assets. We calculate the acid-test ratio of Ranger Wholesale Company at the end of 1994 as follows:

Quick assets:		Current liabilities:	
Cash.	$15,000	Accounts payable.	$43,600
Temporary investments.	3,000	Wages payable	800
Accounts receivable.	68,000	Taxes payable.	4,800
		Notes payable.	5,000
Total	$86,000	Total	$54,200

$$\frac{\text{Quick assets, \$86,000}}{\text{Current liabilities, \$54,200}} = 1.59, \text{ or } 1.6 \text{ to } 1$$

A traditional rule of thumb for an acceptable acid-test ratio is 1 to 1. However, as is true for all financial ratios, you should be skeptical about rules of thumb.

The working capital requirements of a company are also affected by how frequently the company converts and replaces its current assets. For example, assume that Dash Company and Fox Company sell the same amounts of merchandise on credit each month. However, Dash Company grants 30-day terms to its customers, while Fox Company grants 60 days. Both collect their accounts at the end of these credit periods. As a result of the difference in terms, Dash Company turns over, or collects, its accounts twice as fast as Fox Company. Also, as a result of the more rapid turnover, Dash Company makes only one half the investment in accounts receivable that is required of Fox Company. Thus, Dash can operate successfully with smaller current and acid-test ratios.

Accounts Receivable Turnover

One way to measure how frequently a company converts its accounts receivable into cash is to calculate the **accounts receivable turnover.** To calculate the accounts receivable turnover, divide credit sales (or net sales, if the amount of credit sales is not readily available) for a year by the average accounts receivable balance during the year. The average balance can be approximated by averaging the beginning and ending balances. For example, calculate Ranger Wholesale Company's accounts receivable turnover for 1994 as follows:

a. December 31, 1993, accounts receivable . .	$ 64,000
b. December 31, 1994, accounts receivable . .	68,000
c. Average balance ($a + b$)/2.	66,000
d. Net sales for year	960,000

$$\frac{\text{Net sales, } \$960,000}{\text{Average accounts receivable, } \$66,000} = 14.5$$

Thus, it can be said that Ranger creates and collects its receivables approximately 14.5 times per year.

If accounts receivable are collected quickly, the accounts receivable turnover is high. In general, this situation is favourable because it means that the company does not have to commit large amounts of capital to accounts receivable. However, an accounts receivable turnover may be too high, especially if it results from the fact that credit terms are so restrictive that they have a negative effect on sales volume.

The ending accounts receivable balance is sometimes substituted for the average balance in calculating accounts receivable turnover. This approximation is suitable if the effect on the ratio is insignificant. If possible, credit sales should be used rather than the sum of cash and credit sales. Also, using gross accounts receivable (before subtracting the allowance for doubtful accounts) is more likely to provide helpful information. However, information about credit sales is seldom available in published financial statements. Likewise, published balance sheets may report accounts receivable at their net amount. Therefore, an external analyst may be forced to use total sales and net accounts receivable.

Days' Sales Uncollected

Accounts receivable turnover is only one way to measure how frequently a company collects its accounts. Another method is to calculate the **days' sales uncollected.** To illustrate the calculation of days' sales uncollected, assume that a company had credit sales of $250,000 during a year and $25,000 of accounts and short-term notes receivable at the year's end. Thus, one tenth of its credit sales are uncollected. In other words, the charge sales made during one tenth of a year, or 36.5 days ($\frac{1}{10} \times 365$ days in a year), are uncollected. In equation form, this calculation of days' sales uncollected is as follows:

$$\frac{\text{Accounts receivable, \$25,000}}{\text{Credit sales, \$250,000}} \times 365 = 36.5 \text{ day's sales uncollected*}$$

Days' sales uncollected has more meaning if you know the credit terms. According to a rule of thumb, a company's days' sales uncollected should not exceed one and one third times the days in its *credit* period if it does not offer discounts and one and one third times the days in its *discount* period if it does offer discounts. If the company offers 30-day terms without a discount, then 36.5 days is within the rule-of-thumb amount. However, if its terms are 2/10, n/30, the size of its days' sales uncollected seems excessive.

Turnover of Merchandise Inventory

Working capital requirements are also affected by how long a company holds merchandise inventory before selling it. This effect can be measured by calculating the **merchandise turnover,** which is the number of times the average inventory is sold during a reporting period. A high turnover generally indicates good merchandising. Also, from a working capital point of view, a company with a high turnover requires a smaller investment in inventory than one that produces the same sales with a low turnover. On the other hand, the merchandise turnover may be too high if a company keeps such a small inventory that sales volume is restricted.

To calculate merchandise turnover, divide the cost of goods sold during a period by the average inventory for the same period. Cost of goods sold measures the amount of merchandise (at cost) that was sold during an accounting period. Average inventory is the average amount of merchandise (at cost) on hand during the period. The 1994 merchandise turnover of Ranger Wholesale Company is calculated as follows:

$$\frac{\text{Cost of goods sold, \$715,000}}{\text{Average merchandise inventory, \$87,000}} = \frac{\text{Merchandise turnover}}{\text{of 8.2 times}}$$

In this calculation, the cost of goods sold was taken from the company's 1994 income statement. The average inventory was estimated by averaging the beginning inventory for 1994 ($84,000) and the ending inventory for 1994 ($90,000), which is $87,000 [($84,000 + $90,000)/2]. In case the beginning and

---

* Alternatively, the calculation may be 365 ÷ accounts receivable turnover.

ending inventories do not represent the amount of inventory normally on hand, a more accurate turnover may be computed by using the average of its monthly or quarterly inventories, if that information is readily available.

Standards of Comparison

LO 4 State the limitations associated with using financial statement ratios and the sources from which standards for comparison may be obtained.

After you compute ratios and turnovers in the process of analyzing financial statements, you then have to decide whether the calculated amounts suggest good, bad, or merely average performance by the company. To make these judgments, you must have some basis for comparison. The following are possibilities:

1. An experienced analyst may compare the ratios and turnovers of the company under review with *subjective* standards acquired from past experiences.
2. For purposes of comparison, an analyst may calculate the ratios and turnovers of a selected group of competing companies in the same *industry* as the one whose statements are under review.
3. *Published* ratios and turnovers (such as those provided by Dun & Bradstreet) may be used for comparison. Note that terminology may vary somewhat; for example, *acid-test ratio* may be called *quick ratio*.
4. Some local and national trade associations gather data from their members and publish *standard* or *average* ratios for their trade or industry. When available, these data can give the analyst a useful basis for comparison.
5. *Rule-of-thumb* standards can be used as a basis for comparison.

Of these five standards, the ratios and turnovers of a selected group of competing companies normally are the best bases for comparison. Rule-of-thumb standards should be applied with great care and then only if they seem reasonable in light of past experience and the industry's norms.

Analysis of Long-Term Risk and Capital Structure

LO 3 Calculate and explain the interpretation of the ratios, turnovers, and rates of return used to evaluate (*a*) short-term liquidity, (*b*) long-term risk and capital structure, and (*c*) operating efficiency and profitability.

An analysis of working capital evaluates the short-term liquidity of the company. However, analysts are also interested in a company's ability to meet its obligations and provide security to its creditors over the long-run. Indicators of this ability include *debt* and *equity* ratios, the relationship between *pledged plant assets and secured liabilities,* and the company's capacity to earn *sufficient income to pay its fixed interest charges.*

Debt and Equity Ratios

Financial analysts are always interested in the portion of a company's assets contributed by its owners and the portion contributed by creditors. This relationship is described by ratios that express (1) total liabilities as a percentage of total assets and (2) total shareholders' equity as a percentage of total assets. Calculate the debt and equity ratios of Ranger Wholesale Company as follows:

	1994	1993
a. Total liabilities.	$114,200	$ 71,200
b. Total owners' equity.	315,800	311,800
c. Total liabilities and shareholders' equity. . .	$430,000	$383,000
Percentages provided by creditors: (*a/c*) . .	26.6%	18.6%
Percentages provided by shareholders: (*b/c*) . .	73.4%	81.4%

In general, a company is less risky if it has only a small amount of debt in its capital structure. With a small amount of debt, the obligation to pay interest is less burdensome. Also, the greater the equity of the owners in relation to liabilities, the greater the losses that can be absorbed by the owners before the remaining assets become inadequate to satisfy the claims of creditors.

From the shareholders' point of view, however, including debt in the capital structure of a company may be desirable, so long as the risk is not too great. If a business can earn a return on borrowed capital that is higher than the cost of borrowing, the difference represents increased income to shareholders. Because debt can have the effect of increasing the return to shareholders, the inclusion of debt is sometimes described as *financial leverage*. Companies are said to be highly leveraged if a large portion of their assets are financed by debt.

Pledged Plant Assets to Secured Liabilities

Companies often borrow by issuing notes or bonds secured by mortgages on some of their plant assets. The ratio of pledged plant assets to secured liabilities is calculated to measure the protection provided to the secured creditors by the pledge of assets. To calculate this ratio, divide the book value of the pledged assets by the liabilities secured by the mortgages on those assets. The ratio for Ranger Wholesale Company is calculated as of the end of 1994 and 1993 as follows:

	1994	1993
Buildings, net	$176,800	$ 28,000
Land	50,000	20,000
a. Book value of pledged plant assets. . . .	$226,800	$ 48,000
b. Notes payable (secured by mortgage) . .	$ 60,000	$ 10,000
Ratio of pledged assets to secured liabilities (*a/b*)	3.8 to 1	4.8 to 1

The usual rule-of-thumb minimum value for this ratio is 2 to 1. However, the ratio needs careful interpretation because it is based on the book value of the pledged assets. As you know, book values are often unrelated to the amount that would be received for the assets in a foreclosure sale or other liquidation. Thus, estimated foreclosure or liquidation values are a better measure of the protection provided by pledged assets. Also, the long-term earning ability of the company with pledged assets is equally as important to secured creditors as the pledged assets' value because debts can be paid with cash generated by operating activities as well as cash obtained by selling assets.

Times Fixed Interest Charges Earned

The number of **times fixed interest charges were earned** is often calculated to describe the security of the return offered to creditors. The amount of income before the deduction of fixed interest charges and income taxes is the amount available to pay the fixed interest charges. To calculate the number of times fixed interest charges were earned, divide income *before* fixed interest charges and income taxes by the amount of fixed interest charges. The result is the number of times fixed interest charges were earned. The larger this number, the greater is the security for the lenders. A rule of thumb for this statistic is that creditors are reasonably safe if the company earns its fixed interest charges two or more times each year.

Calculate the number of times fixed interest charges were earned by Ranger Wholesale Company as follows:

		1994	1993
a.	Income before interest and taxes	$58,300	$52,800
b.	Interest expense	6,300	1,500
	Times fixed interest charges earned (*a/b*) . .	9.3	35.2

Thus, there would appear to be little risk for the creditors of this company. Although the ratio dropped substantially from 1993 to 1994, the cause of the increase was the change in the amount of interest, not the amount of income.

Analysis of Operating Efficiency and Profitability

Financial analysts are especially interested in the ability of a company to use its assets efficiently to produce profits for its owners and thus to provide cash flows to them. Several ratios are available to help you evaluate operating efficiency and profitability.

Profit Margin

The operating efficiency of a company can be expressed in terms of two components. The first is the company's **profit margin,** which describes the company's ability to earn a net income from sales. This quality is measured by expressing net income as a percentage of sales. For example, calculate the profit margin of Ranger Wholesale Company in 1994 as follows:

$$\frac{\text{Net income, } \$33,000}{\text{Net sales, } \$960,000} = 3.4\%$$

To evaluate the profit margin of a company, consider the nature of the industry in which the company operates. For example, a publishing company might be expected to have a profit margin between 10 and 15%, while a retail supermarket might have a normal profit margin of 1 or 2%. The profit margin is also affected by the marketing strategy that the company uses. That is, a low-margin strategy requires a high sales volume, while a high-margin strategy allows a lower volume of sales to be adequate.

Total Asset Turnover

The second component of operating efficiency is **total asset turnover**, which describes the ability of the company to use its assets to generate sales. To calculate this statistic, divide net sales by the average total assets employed in the business. For Ranger Wholesale Company, the total asset turnover is

$$\frac{\text{Net sales, \$960,000}}{\text{Average total assets, \$406,500}} = 2.4$$

The average total assets is usually estimated by averaging the total assets at the beginning ($383,000) and end ($430,000) of the period.

In general, the higher the total asset turnover, the more efficiently the company is using its assets. However, as in the case of profit margin, the evaluation of total asset turnover depends on the nature of the industry in which the company operates. The relationship between the assets' book value and their current market value should also be considered.

Both profit margin and total asset turnover describe the two basic components of operating efficiency. However, they also evaluate management performance because the management of a company is fundamentally responsible for its operating efficiency.

Return on Total Assets Employed

Because operating efficiency has two basic components (profit margin and total asset turnover), analysts frequently calculate a summary measure of these components. The summary measure is called the **return on total assets employed.** To calculate this measure, divide net income by the average total assets employed during the year. For example, calculate the return on the total assets employed by Ranger Wholesale Company during 1994 as follows:

a. Net income.	$ 33,000
b. Average total assets employed ($430,000 + $383,000)/2 . .	406,500
Return on total assets employed (*a/b*)	8.1%

The preceding calculation shows that Ranger Wholesale Company earned an 8.1% return on its average total assets employed in the business during 1994. However, you cannot tell whether this rate of return is good or bad without some basis for comparison. An especially useful basis for comparison is the rates of return earned by companies of similar size engaged in the same kind of business. You would also want to compare this rate with the rates produced on other kinds of investments. And, you should evaluate the trend in the rates of return earned by the company in recent years.

Earlier, we said that the return on total assets employed summarizes the two components of operating efficiency—profit margin and total asset turnover. The following calculation shows the relationship between these three measures. Notice that both profit margin and total asset turnover contribute to overall operating efficiency, as measured by return on total assets employed.

$$\text{Profit margin} \times \text{Total asset turnover} = \text{Return on total assets employed}$$

$$\frac{\text{Net Income}}{\text{Net Sales}} \times \frac{\text{Net Sales}}{\text{Average Total Assets}} = \frac{\text{Net Income}}{\text{Average Total Assets}}$$

For Ranger Wholesale Company:

$$3.4\% \quad \times \quad 2.4 \quad = \quad 8.1\%$$

Return on Common Shareholders' Equity

Perhaps the most important reason for operating a business is to earn a net income for its owners. The **return on common shareholders' equity** measures the success of a business in reaching this goal. Usually, you should use an average of the beginning-of-year and end-of-year amounts of common shareholders' equity in calculating the return. For Ranger Wholesale Company, the 1994 calculation is as follows:

	1994
a. Net income after taxes	$ 33,000
b. Average common shareholders' equity [($311,800 + $315,800)/2] . .	313,800
Rate of return on common shareholders' equity (*a/b*)	10.5%

When preferred shares are outstanding, subtract the preferred dividend requirements from net income to arrive at the common shareholders' share of income to be used in this calculation. And, the denominator of the ratio should be the average book value of the common shares.

Price-Earnings Ratio

A commonly used statistic in comparing investment opportunities in shares is the **price-earnings ratio.** To calculate the price earnings ratio, divide market price per share by earnings per share. For example, if Ranger Wholesale Company's common shares sold at $15 per share at the end of 1994, the end-of-year price-earnings ratio would be:

$$\frac{\text{Market price per share, \$15}}{\text{Earnings per share, \$1.32}} = 11.4$$

In comparing price-earnings ratios of different shares, remember that these ratios are likely to vary from industry to industry. For example, a price-earnings ratio of 8 to 10 is normal in the steel industry, while a price-earnings ratio of 20 might be expected in a growth industry, such as high-tech electronics.

Dividend Yield

When investors evaluate whether to buy shares at a given price per share, they often consider how much return they can expect to receive from cash dividends. **Dividend yield** is a statistic used to compare the dividend-paying performance of different investment alternatives. To calculate the dividend yield, divide the amount of dividends paid annually by the market price per share. For example, Ranger Wholesale Company paid cash dividends in 1994 of $29,000, which amounted to $1.16 per share. If the market price per share is $15, the dividend yield is:

$$\frac{\text{Annual dividends per share, \$1.16}}{\text{Recent market price per share, \$15}} = 7.7\%$$

To evaluate short-term liquidity, use these ratios:

$$\text{Current ratio} = \frac{\text{Current assets}}{\text{Current liabilities}}$$

$$\text{Acid-test ratio} = \frac{\text{Cash + Temporary investments + Current receivables}}{\text{Current liabilities}}$$

$$\text{Accounts receivable turnover} = \frac{\text{Credit sales}}{\text{Average accounts receivable}}$$

$$\text{Days' sales uncollected} = \frac{\text{Accounts Receivable}}{\text{Charge sales}} \times 365$$

$$\text{Merchandise turnover} = \frac{\text{Cost of goods sold}}{\text{Average merchandise inventory}}$$

To evaluate long-term risk and capital structure, use these ratios:

$$\text{Debt ratio} = \frac{\text{Total liabilities}}{\text{Total assets}}$$

$$\text{Equity ratio} = \frac{\text{Total shareholders' equity}}{\text{Total assets}}$$

$$\frac{\text{Pledged plant assets}}{\text{to secured liabilities}} = \frac{\text{Book value of pledged plant assets}}{\text{Total secured liabilities}}$$

$$\text{Times fixed interest charges earned} = \frac{\text{Income before interest and taxes}}{\text{Interest expense}}$$

To evaluate operating efficiency and profitability, use these ratios:

$$\text{Profit margin} = \frac{\text{Net income}}{\text{Net sales}}$$

$$\text{Total asset turnover} = \frac{\text{Net sales}}{\text{Average total assets}}$$

Review of Financial Statement Ratios and Statistics for Analysis

$$\text{Return on total assets employed} = \frac{\text{Net income}}{\text{Average total assets}}$$

$$\text{Return on common shareholders' equity} = \frac{\text{Net income} - \text{Preferred dividends}}{\text{Average common shareholders' equity}}$$

$$\text{Price earnings ratio} = \frac{\text{Market price per common share}}{\text{Earnings per share}}$$

$$\text{Dividend yield} = \frac{\text{Annual dividends declared}}{\text{Market price per share}}$$

Limitations of Ratio Analysis

The use of ratios requires prudence because certain of the ratios are subject to management or manipulation. For example, inventory turnover may be influenced by accelerating or holding back on purchases near the end of the fiscal period. Similarly, current ratio and acid-test ratio may be altered by payment of current liabilities just before the end of the fiscal period. Thus, caution should be exercised in the degree of reliance placed on certain of the ratios.

Reporting Information on Business Segments

LO 5 Describe the segment information disclosed in financial reports of large companies with operations in several lines of business and list the four basic issues faced by accountants in dealing with segment information.

Financial analysis is more complicated when a company is large and operates in more than one line of business. When information is provided about each **business segment** of the company, outside users of the financial statements can gain a better understanding of the overall business. A business segment is a portion of the company that can be separately identified by the products or services that it provides or a geographic market that it serves. The usefulness of segment information comes from the insight it provides about the relative performance of the segments and the dependence of the entire company on the profits derived from one or more of the segments.

Segment information must be published by certain companies, which are those that have issued securities (either shares or bonds) traded in public markets.[1] As an example, Illustration 19–7 shows segment information provided in the annual report of Northern Telecom Limited. The segment information is presented in a note to the financial statements.

Segment Information to Be Disclosed

In Illustration 19–7, observe that Northern Telecom has four segments: United States, Canada, Europe, and other geographic areas. Also notice that three items of information are presented for each segment:

1. Total revenues.
2. Operating earnings.
3. Identifiable assets.

---

[1] *CICA Handbook,* section 1700.

ILLUSTRATION 19-7

Segment Information for Northern Telecom Limited

Information on Business Segment by Geographic Areas

Business segment: The Corporation operates in one business segment, telecommunications equipment, which consists of the research and the design, development, manufacture, marketing, sale, installation, financing, and service of central office switching equipment, business communications systems and terminals, transmission equipment, cable, and outside plant products and other products and services.

Geographic area: The point of origin (the location of the selling organization) of revenues and the location of the assets determine the geographic areas.

The following table sets forth information by geographic area for the year ended December 31:

	1991	1990	1989
Total revenues:			
United States:			
Customers	$4,335.7	$3,938.3	$3,615.7
Transfers between geographic areas	309.9	205.3	165.1
	4,645.6	4,143.6	3,780.8
Canada:			
Customers	2,304.2	2,422.4	2,172.6
Transfers between geographic areas	865.5	771.6	605.3
	3,169.7	3,194.0	2,777.9
Europe:			
Customers	1,346.6	219.2	192.5
Transfers between geographic areas	4.3	.1	—
	1,350.9	219.3	192.5
Other:			
Customers	196.0	188.8	124.7
Transfers between geographic areas	77.1	68.6	75.0
	273.1	257.4	199.7
Elimination of transfers between geographic areas	(1,256.8)	(1,045.6)	(845.4)
Total customer revenues	$8,182.5	$6,768.7	$6,105.5
Operating earnings:			
United States	$1,211.6	$1,081.6	$ 899.7
Canada	705.8	678.4	625.4
Europe	223.6	(19.9)	(15.9)
Other	10.2	6.9	7.1
Operating earnings before research and development and general corporate expenses	2,151.2	1,747.0	1,516.3
Research and development expense	(948.3)	(773.7)	(729.8)
General corporate expenses	(371.9)	(324.2)	(277.6)
Operating earnings	831.0	649.1	508.9
Other income less non-operating expenses	(120.8)	(30.5)	6.2
Earnings before income taxes	$ 710.2	$ 618.6	$ 515.1
Identifiable assets:			
United States	$3,893.2	$3,141.8	$3,084.3
Canada	2,228.2	2,170.2	1,911.1
Europe	4,091.3	517.1	325.9
Other	332.2	243.3	176.0
Adjustments and eliminations	(1,565.9)	(706.6)	(429.3)
Identifiable assets	8,979.0	5,365.8	5,068.0
Investments	235.6	1,154.0	966.8
Corporate assets	319.6	322.5	274.7
Total assets	$9,534.2	$6,842.3	$6,309.5

Transfers between geographic areas are made at prices based on total cost of the product to the supplying segment.

ILLUSTRATION 19–7

concluded

Customer revenues by destination for the year ended December 31 were:

	1991	1990	1989
United States	$4,105.6	$3,747.3	$3,510.3
Canada	1,960.9	2,153.5	2,006.8
Europe	1,434.3	335.3	275.6
Other	681.7	532.6	312.8
Total	$8,182.5	$6,768.7	$6,105.5

Of the total customer revenues, including research and development, revenues from Bell Canada and other subsidiaries and associated companies of BCE, including associated companies of Northern Telecom, accounted for $1,478.1, $1,637.1, and $1,513.3, for 1991, 1990, and 1989, respectively.

Operating earnings represent total revenues less operating expenses. In computing operating earnings, none of the following items have been added or deducted: equity in net earnings of associated companies, investment and other income (net), interest charges, foreign currency exchange gains and losses, general corporate expenses, research and development expense, and provision for income taxes.

Identifiable assets are those assets of Northern Telecom that are identified with the operations in the geographic area. Corporate assets are principally cash and short-term investments and corporate plant and equipment.

Companies with material operations in more than one industry must disclose these items of information for each segment. In addition, they may be required to report (1) sales by major product lines and (2) sales to major customers. Notice that Northern Telecom identifies revenues from Bell Canada and transfer pricing between geographic areas.

Four Basic Segment Reporting Issues

Companies face four basic issues in compiling information about their segments. The *CICA Handbook,* section 1700, provides detailed guidelines for dealing with these issues. Although these guidelines are too complex to be fully explained at this introductory level, you should be aware of each basic issue.

Identifying Significant Segments. The operations of a business may not be neatly organized in segments that are important to financial statement readers. For purposes of segment reporting, the business must be divided into enough segments to show the basic industries in which it operates. On the other hand, it should not be divided into so many segments that the information becomes overwhelming.

Transfer Pricing between Segments. In many companies, one or more of their segments sell products or services to the other segments. Sales between seg-

AS A MATTER OF
Ethics

Diane Coleman is the manager of Lacto Corporation's Tech Division. Jay Smiley is the manager of the company's Salnic Division. Tech Division's product is not sold to the public but is transferred to Salnic Division, where it is added to other components to produce the finished product. Tech Division's profit equals the difference between its costs and the revenue that it earns on sales to Salnic Division. Salnic Division is also affected by this price, but in the opposite direction. That is, the transfer price paid to Tech Division is one of the costs incurred by Salnic Division. Several managers in each division are compensated in proportion to the profit that their divisions earn. As a result, Coleman and other Tech Division managers benefit if the transfer price is high. Smiley and the Salnic Division managers, on the other hand, benefit if the transfer price is low.

The components manufactured by Tech Division are also produced by outside companies. If Salnic Division were allowed to buy the components from other suppliers, it would have to pay approximately $5 million for next year's supply. However, the costs Tech Division will incur to produce the next year's components will be about $3.2 million. Because of this difference, top management will not let Salnic Division buy from outsiders.

In making plans for the upcoming year, Coleman is dealing with the issue of what price Salnic Division should be charged for Tech Division's components. Coleman is tempted to try for a price in excess of $5 million, because top management really will not let Smiley buy from outsiders. Coleman wonders how Smiley and top management will react to the price she will try to establish.

ments provide revenues to the selling segment and create costs for the purchasing segment. To avoid double counting them, these sales and costs are eliminated when preparing the financial statements for the entire business. However, sales between segments are not eliminated when describing the performance of each segment. The issue is how to determine a fair price (called a **transfer price**) for these sales that allows the profit of both the selling and the buying segments to be usefully measured.

Measuring Segment Profitability Even if each segment of a business operates as a highly independent unit, some general expenses of the business benefit more than one segment. Some of these **common expenses** can be allocated to the segments on a reasonable basis. Others may not be usefully allocated. When preparing segment profit information, you first must determine which expenses to allocate and which to leave unallocated. For these expenses to be allocated, you must then determine the most reasonable basis for allocation.

Identifying Segment Assets. Many assets are easily identified with specific segments because they are used by only one segment. Other assets are shared by more than one segment. To report the amount invested in the assets in each segment, you must determine reasonable bases for allocating the book value of shared assets among the segments that benefit from them. You will probably find that the cost of some assets cannot be allocated among the segments. For example, Northern Telecom identified nearly $319.6 million of assets as belonging to the corporate segment as of the end of 1991.

Summary of the Chapter in Terms of Learning Objectives

LO 1. Financial reporting is intended to provide information useful to investors, creditors, and others in making investment, credit, and similar decisions. The information is communicated in a variety of ways, including general purpose financial statements. These statements normally include an income statement, balance sheet, statement of retained earnings or statement of changes in shareholders' equity, and statement of changes in financial position.

LO 2. Comparative financial statements show amounts for two or more successive periods, sometimes with the changes in the items disclosed in absolute and percentage terms. In common-size statements, each item is expressed as a percentage of a base amount. The base amount for the balance sheet is usually total assets, and the base amount for the income statement is usually net sales.

LO 3. To evaluate the short-term liquidity of a company, calculate a current ratio, an acid-test ratio, the accounts receivable turnover, the days' sales uncollected, and the merchandise turnover.

In evaluating the long-term risk and capital structure of a company, calculate debt and equity ratios, pledged plant assets to secured liabilities, and the number of times fixed interest charges were earned.

In evaluating operating efficiency and profitability, calculate profit margin, total asset turnover, return on total assets employed, and return on common shareholders' equity. Other statistics used to evaluate the profitability of alternative investments include the price earnings ratio and the dividend yield.

LO 4. In deciding whether financial statement ratio values are satisfactory, too high, or too low, you must have some bases for comparison. These bases may come from past experience and personal judgment, from ratios of similar companies, or from ratios published by trade associations and other public sources. Traditional rules of thumb should be applied with great care and only if they seem reasonable in light of past experience.

LO 5. Large companies that operate in more than one industry disclose the following information on each industrial segment: revenues, operating profits (before interest and taxes), amortization expense, capital expenditures, and identifiable assets. They may also report a geographical distribution of sales and sales to major customers. The four problems accountants face in preparing segment information include identifying significant segments, transfer pricing between segments, measuring segment profitability, and identifying segment assets.

Demonstration Problem

Use the financial statements of Precision Company to satisfy the following requirements:

1. Prepare a comparative income statement showing the percentage increase or decrease for 1994 over 1993.
2. Prepare common-size comparative balance sheets for 1994 and 1993.

3. Compute the following ratios as of December 31, 1994, or for the year ended December 31, 1994:

   a. Current ratio.
   b. Acid-test ratio.
   c. Accounts receivable turnover.
   d. Days' sales uncollected.
   e. Merchandise turnover.
   f. Debt ratio.
   g. Pledged plant assets to secured liabilities.
   h. Times fixed interest charges earned.
   i. Profit margin.
   j. Total asset turnover.
   k. Return on total assets employed.
   l. Return on common shareholders' equity.

PRECISION COMPANY
Comparative Income Statement
For Years Ended December 31, 1994 and 1993

	1994	1993
Sales	$2,486,000	$2,075,000
Cost of goods sold	1,523,000	1,222,000
Gross profit from sales	$ 963,000	$ 853,000
Operating expenses:		
Advertising expense	$ 145,000	$ 100,000
Sales salaries expense	240,000	280,000
Office salaries expense	165,000	200,000
Insurance expense	100,000	45,000
Supplies expense	26,000	35,000
Amortization expense	85,000	75,000
Miscellaneous expense	17,000	15,000
Total operating expenses	$ 778,000	$ 750,000
Operating income	$ 185,000	$ 103,000
Less interest expense	44,000	46,000
Income before taxes	$ 141,000	$ 57,000
Income taxes	47,000	19,000
Net income	$ 94,000	$ 38,000
Earnings per share	$ 0.99	$ 0.40

PRECISION COMPANY
Comparative Balance Sheet
December 31, 1994, and December 31, 1993

	1994	1993
Assets		
Current assets:		
Cash	$ 79,000	$ 42,000
Temporary investments	65,000	96,000
Accounts receivable (net)	120,000	100,000
Merchandise inventory	250,000	265,000
Total current assets	$ 514,000	$ 503,000
Plant and equipment:		
Store equipment (net)	$ 400,000	$ 350,000
Office equipment (net)	45,000	50,000
Buildings (net)	625,000	675,000
Land	100,000	100,000
Total plant and equipment	$1,170,000	$1,175,000
Total assets	$1,684,000	$1,678,000

Liabilities	1994	1993
Current liabilities:		
Accounts payable	$ 164,000	$ 190,000
Short-term notes payable	75,000	90,000
Taxes payable	26,000	12,000
Total current liabilities.	$ 265,000	$ 292,000
Long-term liabilities:		
Notes payable (secured by		
mortgage on building and land) . .	400,000	420,000
Total liabilities	$ 665,000	$ 712,000
Shareholders' Equity		
Common—95,000 shares.	$ 475,000	$ 475,000
Retained earnings	544,000	491,000
Total shareholders' equity	$1,019,000	$966,000
Total liabilities and equity	$1,684,000	$1,678,000

Solution to Demonstration Problem

Planning the Solution

- Set up a four column income statement, enter the 1994 and 1993 amounts in the first two columns, and then enter the dollar change in the third column and the percentage change from 1993 in the fourth column.

- Set up a four-column balance sheet; enter the 1994 and 1993 amounts in the first two columns, and then compute and enter the amount of each item as a percent of total assets.

- Compute the given ratios using the provided numbers; be sure to use the average of the beginning and ending amounts where appropriate.

1.

PRECISION COMPANY
Comparative Income Statement
For Years Ended December 31, 1994 and 1993

	1994	1993	Increase (Decrease) in 1994 Amount	Percent
Sales.	$2,486,000	$2,075,000	$411,000	19.8
Cost of goods sold.	1,523,000	1,222,000	301,000	24.6
Gross profit from sales	$ 963,000	$ 853,000	$110,000	12.9
Operating expenses:				
Advertising expense.	$ 145,000	$ 100,000	$ 45,000	45.0
Sales salaries expense. . . .	240,000	280,000	(40,000)	(14.3)
Office salaries expense . . .	165,000	200,000	(35,000)	(17.5)
Insurance expense	100,000	45,000	55,000	122.2
Supplies expense	26,000	35,000	(9,000)	(25.7)
Amortization expense. . . .	85,000	75,000	10,000	13.3
Miscellaneous expense . . .	17,000	15,000	2,000	13.3
Total operating expenses . .	$ 778,000	$ 750,000	$ 28,000	3.7
Operating income	$ 185,000	$ 103,000	$ 82,000	79.6
Less interest expense	44,000	46,000	(2,000)	(4.3)
Income before taxes.	$ 141,000	$ 57,000	$ 84,000	147.4
Income taxes	47,000	19,000	28,000	147.4
Net income	$ 94,000	$ 38,000	$ 56,000	147.4
Earnings per share.	$ 0.99	$ 0.40	$ 0.59	147.5

2.

PRECISION COMPANY
Common-Size Comparative Balance Sheet
December 31, 1994, and December 31, 1993

Assets	December 31 1994	December 31 1993	Common-Size Percentages 1994	Common-Size Percentages 1993
Current assets:				
Cash	$ 79,000	$ 42,000	4.69%	2.50%
Temporary investments	65,000	96,000	3.86	5.72
Accounts receivable (net)	120,000	100,000	7.13	5.96
Merchandise inventory	250,000	265,000	14.85	15.79
Total current assets	$514,000	$ 503,000	30.53	29.97
Plant and equipment:				
Store equipment (net)	$ 400,000	$ 350,000	23.75	20.86
Office equipment (net).	45,000	50,000	2.67	2.98
Buildings (net).	625,000	675,000	37.11	40.23
Land.	100,000	100,000	5.94	5.96
Total plant and equipment	$1,170,000	$1,175,000	69.47	70.03
Total assets	$1,684,000	$1,678,000	100.00%	100.00%
Liabilities				
Current liabilities:				
Accounts payable	$ 164,000	$ 190,000	9.74%	11.32%
Short-term notes payable	75,000	90,000	4.45	5.36
Taxes payable	26,000	12,000	1.54	0.72
Total current liabilities.	$ 265,000	$ 292,000	15.73	17.40
Long-term liabilities:				
Notes payable (secured by mortgage on building and land)	400,000	420,000	23.75	25.03
Total liabilities	$ 665,000	$ 712,000	39.48	42.43
Shareholders' Equity				
Common—95,000 shares.	$ 475,000	$ 475,000	28.21	28.31
Retained earnings	544,000	491,000	32.31	29.26
Total shareholders' equity	$1,019,000	$ 966,000	60.52	57.57
Total liabilities and equity	$1,684,000	$1,678,000	100.00%	100.00%

3. Ratios for 1994:
   a. Current ratio: $514,000/$265,000 = 1.9
   b. Acid-test ratio: ($79,000 + $65,000 + $120,000)/$265,000 = 1.0
   c. Average receivables: ($120,000 + $100,000)/2 = $110,000
      Accounts receivable turnover: $2,486,000/$110,000 = 22.6
   d. Days' sales uncollected: ($120,000/$2,486,000) × 365 = 17.6 days
   e. Average inventory: ($250,000 + $265,000)/2 = $257,500
      Merchandise turnover: $1,523,000/$257,500 = 5.9 times
   f. Debt ratio: $665,000/$1,684,000 = 39.5%
   g. Pledged assets to secured liabilities:
      ($625,000 + $100,000)/$400,000 = 1.8
   h. Times fixed interest charges earned: $185,000/$44,000 = 4.2 times
   i. Profit margin: $94,000/$2,486,000 = 3.8%
   j. Average total assets: ($1,684,000 + $1,678,000)/2 = $1,681,000
      Total asset turnover: $2,486,000/$1,681,000 = 1.48
   k. Return on total assets employed: $94,000/$1,681,000 = 5.6% or
      3.8% × 1.48 = 5.6%
   l. Average total equity: ($1,019,000 + $966,000)/2 = $992,500
      Return on common shareholders' equity: $94,000/$992,500 = 9.5%

Glossary

LO 6 Define or explain the words and phrases listed in the chapter glossary.

Accounts receivable turnover a measure of how long it takes a company to collect its accounts, calculated by dividing credit sales (or net sales) by the average accounts receivable balance. p. 958

Acid-test ratio the relationship between quick assets (cash, temporary investments, accounts receivable, and notes receivable) and current liabilities, calculated as quick assets divided by current liabilities. p. 957

Business segment a portion of the business that can be separately identified by the products or services that it provides or a geographic market that it serves. p. 966

Common expenses expenses incurred for the benefit of more than one segment of a business; some common expenses can be allocated among the segments, while others cannot be allocated. p. 969

Common-size comparative statements comparative financial statements in which each amount is expressed as a percentage of a base amount. In the balance sheet, the amount of total assets is usually selected as the base amount and is expressed as 100%. In the income statement, net sales is usually selected as the base amount. pp. 952–55

Comparative statements financial statements with data for two or more successive accounting periods placed in columns side by side, sometimes with changes shown in dollar amounts and percentages. pp. 947–55

Current ratio the relationship of a company's current assets to its current liabilities, that is, current assets divided by current liabilities. pp. 956–57

Days' sales uncollected the number of days of average credit sales volume accumulated in the accounts receivable balance, calculated as the product of 365 times the accounts receivable balance divided by credit sales. p. 959

Dividend yield the annual cash dividends paid per share expressed as a percentage of the market price per share; used to compare the dividend paying performance of different investment alternatives. p. 965

Financial reporting the process of providing information that is useful to investors, creditors, and others in making investment, credit, and similar decisions. pp. 946–47

General purpose financial statements statements published periodically for use by a wide variety of interested parties; include the income statement, balance sheet, statement of retained earnings (or statement of changes in shareholders' equity), and statement of changes in financial position. p. 946

Merchandise turnover the average number of times a company's inventory is sold during an accounting period, calculated by dividing cost of goods sold by the average merchandise inventory balance. p. 959

Price-earnings ratio a measure used to evaluate the profitability of alternative common investments, calculated as market price per common share divided by earnings per share. p. 964

Profit margin a component of operating efficiency and profitability, calculated by expressing net income as a percentage of net sales. p. 962

Return on common shareholders' equity a measure of profitability in the use of assets provided by common shareholders, measured by expressing net income less preferred dividends as a percentage of average common shareholders' equity. p. 964

Return on total assets employed a summary measure of operating efficiency and management performance, calculated by expressing net income as a percentage of average total assets. p. 963

Times fixed interest charges earned a measure of a company's ability to satisfy fixed interest charges, calculated as income before interest and income taxes divided by fixed interest charges. p. 962

Total asset turnover a component of operating efficiency and profitability, calculated by dividing net sales by average total assets. p. 963

Transfer price a price assigned to products or services sold by one segment of a business to another. p. 969

Working capital current assets minus current liabilities. p. 955

Synonymous Terms

Acid-test ratio quick ratio.

Business segment line of business.

Trend percentages index numbers.

Working capital net working capital.

Objective Review

Answers to the following questions are listed at the end of this chapter. Be sure that you decide which is the one best answer to each question *before* you check the answers.

LO 1 Which of the following is not an objective of financial reporting?

a. Financial reporting includes reporting information in general purpose financial statements and in other ways such as news announcements and management discussions in annual reports.

b. Financial reporting should provide information that is useful primarily for meeting the needs of corporation managers.

c. Financial reporting should provide information that is useful to investors and creditors and other users in making investment, credit, and similar decisions.

d. Financial reporting should provide information to help users assess the amounts, timing, and uncertainty of prospective cash inflows and outflows.

e. Financial reporting should provide information to assess management's stewardship.

LO 2 Given the following information for Moyers Corporation, determine the common-size percentages for gross profit from sales.

	1994	1993
Net sales	$134,400	$114,800
Cost of goods sold	72,800	60,200

a. 45.8% in 1994; 47.6% in 1993.

b. 113% in 1994; 100% in 1993.

c. 12.8% increase during 1994.

d. 100% in 1994; 88.8% in 1993.

e. 54.2% in 1994; 52.4% in 1993.

LO 3 Times fixed interest charges earned describes:

a. How fast a company collects its accounts.

b. The security of the return offered to creditors.

c. Short-term liquidity.

d. Operating efficiency and profitability.

e. The protection provided to the secured creditors by the mortgages on the assets.

LO 4 Which of the following may be used as a standard for comparing ratios and turnovers computed in the process of analyzing financial statements?

a. Rule-of-thumb standards.

b. Past experience of the analyst with the company under review, as well as other companies.

c. Ratios and turnovers of a selected group of companies competing in the same industry as the one whose statements are under review.

d. Data gathered and published by local and national trade associations as standard or average ratios for their industry.

e. All of the above.

LO 5 Which of the following items of segment information is usually disclosed in the financial reports of large companies having operations in several lines of business?

a. Identifiable assets.

b. Transfer pricing between segments.

c. Operating earnings.

d. Revenues by major product line and/or geographic area.

e. All of the above are usually disclosed.

LO 6 A summary measure of operating efficiency and management performance, calculated by expressing net income as a percentage of average total assets, is called:

a. Times fixed interest charges earned.

b. Total asset turnover.

c. Return on total assets employed.

d. Price-earnings ratio.

e. Profit margin.

Questions for Class Discussion

1. Who are the intended users of general purpose financial statements?

2. What statements are usually included in the general purpose financial statements published by corporations?

3. Explain the difference between financial reporting and financial statements.

4. Financial reporting should help users make what kind of predictions?

5. When trends are calculated and compared, it is often informative to compare the trend of sales with the trends of several other financial statement items. What are some of the items that should be compared to sales in this fashion?

6. What items are usually assigned a value of 100% on (*a*) a common-size balance sheet and (*b*) a common-size income statement?

7. Why is working capital given special attention in the process of analyzing balance sheets?

8. Which ratio provides the better indication of a company's ability to meet its debt obligations in the very near future, the current ratio or the acid-test ratio? Why?

9. Suggest several reasons why a 2-to-1 current ratio may not be adequate for a particular company.

10. What is the significance of the number of days' sales uncollected?

11. Why does merchandise inventory turnover provide information about a company's short-term liquidity?

12. Why is the capital structure of a company, as measured by debt and equity ratios, of importance to financial statement analysts?

13. What ratios would you calculate for the purpose of evaluating management performance?

14. How can you use the information provided by the price-earnings ratio and dividend yield?

15. What insights are provided to financial statement users by segment information?

Mini Discussion Cases

Case 19–1

Analysts have often used working capital ratios to test for companies' financial health. Some years ago, however, there were several cases of companies with healthy working capital ratios which, shortly thereafter, were forced into bankruptcy apparently because they were unable to pay their debts as they became due.

Required

Discuss the shortcomings of working capital analysis. What other kinds of analyses might be used which would overcome these deficiencies? Why?

Case 19–2

A friend comes to you excitedly urging you to take advantage of an investment opportunity. As support for her recommendation the friend shows you the company's annual report and says, "This company has earnings per share of $3.23." She says that she has just purchased 500 of the company's shares at $21.25 and urges you to do the same before the price goes up any further.

Required

It is now 5:00 P.M. and the markets have closed for the day. Your friend has allowed you to borrow her copy of the annual report until tomorrow morning. What analyses are you going to use to evaluate this investment? What further information do you think you might require? Why?

Exercises

Exercise 19–1
Calculating trend percentages
(LO 2)

Calculate trend percentages for the following items, using 1990 as the base year. Then state whether the situation shown by the trends appears to be favourable or unfavourable:

	1994	1993	1992	1991	1990
Sales	$785,200	$742,920	$694,600	$646,280	$604,000
Cost of goods sold	359,040	337,280	315,520	293,760	272,000
Accounts receivable	52,800	50,000	47,200	44,000	40,000

Exercise 19–2
Reporting percentage
changes
(LO 2)

Where possible, calculate percentages of increase and decrease for the following items.
The parentheses indicate negative balances.

	1994	1993
Equipment, net	$70,400	$55,000
Notes receivable	8,000	16,000
Notes payable	20,000	–0–
Retained earnings	(3,000)	15,000
Cash	8,400	(2,100)

Exercise 19–3
Calculating common-size
percentages
(LO 2)

Express the following income statement information in common-size percentages and
assess whether the situation is favourable or unfavourable.

GRUNDFEST CORPORATION
Comparative Income Statement
For Years Ended December 31, 1993 and 1992

	1993	1992
Sales	$640,000	$490,000
Cost of goods sold.	352,000	257,250
Gross profit from sales	$288,000	$232,750
Operating expenses	181,760	125,440
Net income	$106,240	$107,310

Exercise 19–4
Evaluating short-term
liquidity
(LO 3)

Fitzwater Company's December 31 balance sheets included the following data:

	1993	1992	1991
Cash	$ 17,200	$ 28,500	$ 33,400
Accounts receivable, net.	69,000	54,000	48,000
Merchandise inventory.	81,000	46,000	29,000
Prepaid expenses	9,800	5,500	4,600
Plant assets, net	175,000	182,000	170,000
Total assets	$352,000	$316,000	$285,000
Accounts payable	$ 69,200	$ 44,600	$ 32,700
Long-term notes payable secured by mortgage on plant assets	85,000	85,000	75,000
Common—12,500 shares	125,000	125,000	125,000
Retained earnings	72,800	61,400	52,300
Total liabilities and shareholders' equity	$352,000	$316,000	$285,000

Required

Compare the short-term liquidity positions of the company at the end of 1993, 1992, and
1991, by calculating: (*a*) the current ratio and (*b*) the acid-test ratio. Comment on any
changes that occurred.

Exercise 19–5
Evaluating short-term
liquidity
(LO 3)

Refer to the information in Exercise 19–4 about Fitzwater Company. The company's
income statements for the years ended December 31, 1993, and 1992, included the
following data:

	1993	**1992**
Sales.	$610,000	$575,000
Cost of goods sold	$366,000	$352,000
Other operating expenses	201,000	185,000
Interest expense	10,200	10,200
Income taxes.	4,900	4,200
Total costs and expenses.	$582,100	$551,400
Net income	$ 27,900	$ 23,600
Earnings per share.	$ 2.23	$ 1.89

Required

For the years ended December 31, 1993, and 1992, calculate the following (assume all sales were on credit): (*a*) days' sales uncollected, (*b*) accounts receivable turnover, and (*c*) merchandise turnover. Comment on any changes that occurred from 1992 to 1993.

Refer to the information in Exercises 19–4 and 19–5 about Fitzwater Company. Compare the long-term risk and capital structure positions of the company at the end of 1993 and 1992 by calculating the following ratios: (*a*) debt and equity ratios, (*b*) pledged plant assets to secured liabilities, and (*c*) times fixed interest charges earned. Comment on any changes that occurred.

Exercise 19–6
Evaluating long-term risk and capital structure
(LO 3)

Refer to the financial statements of Fitzwater Company presented in Exercises 19–4 and 19–5. Evaluate the operating efficiency and profitability of the company by calculating the following: (*a*) profit margin, (*b*) total asset turnover, and (*c*) return on total assets employed. Comment on any changes that occurred.

Exercise 19–7
Evaluating operating efficiency and profitability
(LO 3)

Refer to the financial statements of Fitzwater Company presented in Exercises 19–4 and 19–5. This additional information about the company is known:

Exercise 19–8
Evaluating profitability
(LO 3)

Common share market price, December 31, 1993	$24.00
Common share market price, December 31, 1992	16.00
Annual cash dividends per share in 1993	1.32
Annual cash dividends per share in 1992	1.16

Required

To evaluate the profitability of the company, calculate the following for 1993 and 1992: (*a*) return on common shareholders' equity, (*b*) price-earnings ratio on December 31, and (*c*) dividend yield.

Common-size and trend percentages for a company's sales, cost of goods sold, and expenses follow:

Exercise 19–9
Determining income effects from common-size and trend percentages
(LO 3)

	Common-Size Percentages			**Trend Percentages**		
	1994	**1993**	**1992**	**1994**	**1993**	**1992**
Sales	100.0%	100.0%	100.0%	95.9%	98.0%	100.0%
Cost of goods sold	56.3	60.0	61.4	87.9	95.8	100.0
Expenses	28.8	28.7	28.8	95.8	97.6	100.0

Required

Determine whether the company's net income increased, decreased, or remained unchanged during this three-year period.

Exercise 19–10
Segment reporting with
sales between segments
(LO 5)

The following operating information is available about the two business segments of the York Corporation:

	Segment P	Segment Q
Sales to outside parties	$200,000	$520,000
Sales to Segment Q	?	
Purchases from Segment P		?
Other expenses of each segment	240,000	316,000

The items that Segment P sold to Segment Q were processed further and then sold by Q to outside parties. In measuring the intersegment sales, the manager of Segment P believes that they should be priced at $100,000, which is approximately the same price that would have been paid by outside buyers. The Segment Q manager argues that the price should be lower because Segment Q is part of the York Corporation family and is not an outside buyer. According to the Segment Q manager, a price of $50,000 would more than cover Segment P's cost.

Required

Prepare reports that show the sales, expenses, and income from operating each segment under the alternate assumptions that the intersegment sales are priced at (*a*) $100,000 and (*b*) $50,000. Then express each segment's income from operations as a percent of its sales. Comment on the importance of the transfer pricing decision in evaluating the performance of each segment.

Problems

Problem 19–1
Calculating ratios and
percentages
(LO 2, 3)

The condensed statements of Compton Car Company follow:

COMPTON CAR COMPANY
Comparative Income Statement
For Years Ended December 31, 1994, 1993, and 1992
($000)

	1994	1993	1992
Sales	$74,000	$68,000	$59,000
Cost of goods sold	45,658	40,052	33,866
Gross profit from sales	$28,342	$27,948	$25,134
Selling expenses	$12,306	$11,506	$10,095
Administrative expenses	8,658	8,262	7,304
Total expenses	$20,964	$19,768	$17,399
Income before taxes	$ 7,378	$ 8,180	$ 7,735
Income taxes	2,140	2,372	2,243
Net income	$ 5,238	$ 5,808	$ 5,492

COMPTON CAR COMPANY
Comparative Balance Sheet
December 31, 1994, 1993, and 1992
($000)

	1994	1993	1992
Assets			
Current assets	$12,780	$11,940	$14,140
Long-term investments	–0–	100	930
Plant and equipment (net)	19,150	20,000	16,250
Total assets	$31,930	$32,040	$31,320
Liabilities and Shareholders' Equity			
Current liabilities	$ 5,050	$ 4,990	$ 4,870
Common share capital	13,500	13,500	13,390
Other contributed capital	1,850	1,850	1,460
Retained earnings	11,530	11,700	11,600
Total liabilities and shareholders' equity	$31,930	$32,040	$31,320

Required

1. Calculate each year's current ratio.
2. Express the income statement data in common-size percentages.
3. Express the balance sheet data in trend percentages with 1992 as the base year.
4. Comment on any significant relationship revealed by the ratios and percentages.

The condensed comparative statements of Federal Stamp Corporation follow:

Problem 19–2
Calculation and analysis of trend percentages
(LO 2)

FEDERAL STAMP CORPORATION
Comparative Income Statement
For Years Ended December 31, 1995–1989
($000,000)

	1995	1994	1993	1992	1991	1990	1989
Sales	$500	$455	$416	$364	$334	$299	$260
Cost of goods sold	247	228	204	179	157	142	120
Gross profit from sales	$253	$227	$212	$185	$177	$157	$140
Operating expenses	203	170	147	102	100	87	75
Net income	$ 50	$ 57	$ 65	$ 83	$ 77	$ 70	$ 65

FEDERAL STAMP CORPORATION
Comparative Balance Sheet
December 31, 1995–1989
($000,000)

	1995	1994	1993	1992	1991	1990	1989
Assets							
Cash	$ 13	$ 17	$ 19	$ 22	$ 23	$ 20	$ 25
Accounts receivable, net	99	97	95	73	64	61	51
Merchandise inventory	250	243	230	194	174	148	130
Other current assets	6	8	5	9	8	8	5
Long-term investments	–0–	–0–	–0–	34	34	34	34
Plant and equipment, net	400	418	386	215	222	200	206
Total assets	$768	$783	$735	$547	$525	$471	$451

Liabilities and Equity	1995	1994	1993	1992	1991	1990	1989
Current liabilities.	$143	$147	$133	$107	$ 93	$ 77	$68
Long-term liabilities	179	202	215	98	100	104	99
Common share capital	200	200	200	175	175	160	160
Other contributed capital.	48	48	48	40	40	40	40
Retained earnings	198	186	139	127	117	90	84
Total liabilities and equity	$768	$783	$735	$547	$525	$471	$451

Required

1. Calculate trend percentages for the items of the statements using 1989 as the base year.

2. Analyze and comment on the situation shown in the statements.

Problem 19–3
Calculation of financial statement relationships (LO 3)

The 1993 financial statements of Karlin Corporation follow:

KARLIN CORPORATION
Income Statement
For Year Ended December 31, 1993

Sales		$888,700
Cost of goods sold:		
Merchandise inventory, December 31, 1992	$ 77,500	
Purchases.	410,900	
Goods available for sale	$488,400	
Merchandise inventory, December 31, 1993	52,000	
Cost of goods sold		436,400
Gross profit from sales		$452,300
Operating expenses.		267,400
Operating income.		$184,900
Interest expense		13,200
Income before taxes		$171,700
Income taxes		36,000
Net income		$135,700

KARLIN CORPORATION
Balance Sheet
December 31, 1993

Assets		Liabilities and Shareholders' Equity	
Cash	$ 29,100	Accounts payable	$ 48,900
Temporary investments	47,600	Accrued wages payable	5,400
Accounts receivable, net	55,500	Income taxes payable	7,100
Notes receivable (trade)	8,000	Long-term note payable,	
Merchandise inventory.	52,000	secured by mortgage on	
Prepaid expenses.	3,900	plant assets	120,000
Plant assets, net	383,200	Common—50,000 shares.	250,000
		Retained earnings	147,900
		Total liabilities and	
Total assets.	$579,300	shareholders' equity	$579,300

Assume that all sales were on credit. On the December 31, 1992, balance sheet, the assets totaled $480,300, common share capital was $250,000, and retained earnings were $103,800.

Required

Calculate the following: (*a*) current ratio, (*b*) acid-test ratio, (*c*) days' sales uncollected, (*d*) merchandise turnover, (*e*) ratio of pledged plant assets to secured liabilities, (*f*) times fixed interest charges earned, (*g*) profit margin, (*h*) total asset turnover, (*i*) return on total assets employed, and (*j*) return on common shareholders' equity.

Two companies that operate in the same industry as competitors are being evaluated by a bank that can lend money to only one of them. Summary information from the financial statements of the two companies follows.

Problem 19–4
Comparative analysis of financial statement ratios
(LO 3)

Data from the current year-end balance sheets:

	Monarch Company	Command Company
Assets		
Cash	$ 18,700	$ 33,000
Accounts receivable	34,500	53,800
Notes receivable (trade) . . .	8,500	6,000
Merchandise inventory. . . .	88,600	119,700
Prepaid expenses.	4,200	6,200
Plant and equipment, net. . .	284,100	288,600
Total assets.	$438,600	$507,300
Liabilities and Equity		
Current liabilities.	$ 60,300	$ 94,700
Long-term notes payable. . .	80,000	100,000
Common share capital* . . .	175,000	180,000
Retained earnings	123,300	132,600
Total liabilities and equity . .	$438,600	$507,300

Data from the current year's income statements:

	Monarch Company	Command Company
Sales	$625,000	$780,500
Cost of goods sold	372,500	465,200
Interest expense	8,000	11,000
Income tax expense	13,800	21,900
Net income.	75,300	95,800

Beginning-of-year data:

	Monarch Company	Command Company
Accounts receivable, net. . .	$ 28,800	$ 52,900
Notes receivable	–0–	–0–
Merchandise inventory. . . .	54,900	101,000
Total assets.	388,100	422,500
Common share capital* . . .	175,000	180,000
Retained earnings	100,500	90,800

* Common shares outstanding: Monarch, 17,500 shares; Command, 18,000 shares.

Required

1. Calculate current ratios, acid-test ratios, accounts (including notes) receivable turnovers, merchandise turnovers, and days' sales uncollected for the two companies. Then identify the company that you consider to be the better short-term credit risk and explain why.

2. Calculate profit margins, total asset turnovers, returns on total assets employed, and returns on common shareholders' equity. Assuming that each company paid cash dividends of $3.00 per share and each company's shares can be purchased at $40 per share, calculate their price-earnings ratios and the dividend yield. Also, identify which company's shares you would recommend as the better investment and explain why.

Problem 19–5
Analysis of working capital
(LO 3)

Davis Corporation began the month of October with $360,000 of current assets, a current ratio of 2.4 to 1, and an acid-test ratio of 1.4 to 1. During the month, it completed the following transactions:

Oct. 2 Bought $40,000 of merchandise on account. (The company uses a perpetual inventory system.)

4 Sold merchandise that cost $35,000 for $64,000.

10 Collected a $12,000 account receivable.

14 Paid a $14,000 account payable.

20 Wrote off a $6,000 bad debt against the Allowance for Doubtful Accounts account.

21 Declared a $0.50 per share cash dividend on the 50,000 outstanding common shares.

25 Paid the dividend declared on October 21.

27 Borrowed $50,000 by giving the bank a 60-day, 12% note.

30 Borrowed $75,000 by signing a long-term secured note.

31 Used the $125,000 proceeds of the notes to buy additional machinery.

Required

Prepare a schedule showing the company's current ratio, acid-test ratio, and working capital after each of the transactions. Round to two decimal places.

Problem 19–6
Analytical essay
(LO 3)

Visican Company and Stockton Company are similar companies that operate within the same industry. The following information is available:

	Visican			Stockton		
	1994	**1993**	**1992**	**1994**	**1993**	**1992**
Working capital	$105,000	$81,000	$60,000	$50,000	$45,000	$52,000
Current ratio	3.5	2.7	2.0	1.9	2.0	2.1
Acid test ratio.	2.7	2.2	1.6	1.0	1.1	1.2
Accounts receivable turnover. . . .	15.2	14.6	15.0	32.8	26.7	28.4
Merchandise inventory turnover . .	13.2	12.1	12.0	22.1	19.4	16.8

Required

Write a brief essay comparing Visican Company and Stockton Company based on the information provided. Your discussion should include their relative ability to meet current obligations and to use current assets efficiently.

Problem 19–7
Analytical essay
(LO 3)

Roster Company and Farleigh Company are similar companies that operate within the same industry. Roster Company began operations in 1992 and Farleigh Company in 1980. In 1994, both companies paid 7% interest to creditors. The following information is also available:

	Roster			Farleigh		
	1994	1993	1992	1994	1993	1992
Sales	$300,000	$220,000	$100,000	$600,000	$560,000	$578,000
Profit margin	3.2	3.4	3.3	2.7	2.9	2.6
Total asset turnover.	2.0	1.8	1.6	3.6	3.4	3.3
Return on total assets employed . .	6.4	6.1	5.3	9.7	9.9	8.6

Required

Write a brief essay comparing Roster Company and Farleigh Company based on the information provided. Your discussion should include their relative ability to use assets efficiently to produce profits. Also comment on their relative success in employing financial leverage in 1994.

Alternate Problems

The condensed statements of Stanton Corporation follow:

Problem 19–1A
Calculating ratios and percentages
(LO 2, 3)

STANTON CORPORATION
Comparative Income Statement
For Years Ended December 31, 1994, 1993, and 1992
($000)

	1994	1993	1992
Sales	$111,000	$95,500	$82,800
Cost of goods sold	61,100	49,700	39,500
Gross profit from sales . . .	$ 49,900	$45,800	$43,300
Selling expenses	$ 14,800	$11,700	$12,600
Administrative expenses . .	11,100	11,800	10,700
Total expenses	$ 25,900	$23,500	$23,300
Income before taxes	$ 24,000	$22,300	$20,000
Income taxes	3,600	3,300	3,000
Net income	$ 20,400	$19,000	$17,000

STANTON CORPORATION
Comparative Balance Sheet
December 31, 1994, 1993, and 1992
($000)

	1994	1993	1992
Assets			
Current assets.	$29,400	$18,700	$20,100
Long-term investments	–0–	1,500	6,600
Plant and equipment	59,900	61,200	47,400
Total assets	$89,300	$81,400	$74,100
Liabilities and Shareholders' Equity			
Current liabilities	$12,300	$10,100	$ 8,600
Common share capital	20,000	20,000	18,000
Other contributed capital	6,500	6,500	4,500
Retained earnings.	50,500	44,800	43,000
Total liabilities and shareholders' equity . .	$89,300	$81,400	$74,100

Required

1. Calculate each year's current ratio.
2. Express the income statement data in common-size percentages.
3. Express the balance sheet data in trend percentages with 1992 as the base year.
4. Comment on any significant relationships revealed by the ratios and percentages.

Problem 19–2A
Calculation and analysis of trend percentages
(LO 2)

The condensed comparative statements of Great Outdoors Company follow:

GREAT OUTDOORS COMPANY
Comparative Income Statement
For Years Ended December 31, 1995–1989
($000,000)

	1995	1994	1993	1992	1991	1990	1989
Sales	$500	$520	$510	$540	$580	$570	$610
Cost of goods sold.	210	217	214	228	239	232	234
Gross profit from sales	$290	$303	$296	$312	$341	$338	$376
Operating expenses	221	228	226	245	252	256	276
Net income	$ 69	$ 75	$ 70	$ 67	$ 89	$ 82	$100

GREAT OUTDOORS COMPANY
Comparative Balance Sheet
December 31, 1995–1989
($000,000)

	1995	1994	1993	1992	1991	1990	1989
Assets							
Cash.	$ 35	$ 38	$ 37	$ 41	$ 50	$ 47	$ 51
Accounts receivable, net	103	114	110	112	123	121	129
Merchandise inventory	157	163	161	160	173	183	176
Other current assets.	23	24	25	27	26	29	31
Long-term investments	87	67	47	94	94	94	97
Plant and equipment, net	398	404	408	323	328	333	338
Total assets	$803	$810	$788	$757	$794	$807	$822
Liabilities and Equity							
Current liabilities	$178	$185	$168	$135	$161	$187	$232
Long-term liabilities.	147	162	177	192	210	222	237
Common share capital.	160	160	160	160	160	160	160
Other contributed capital	65	65	65	65	65	65	65
Retained earnings	253	238	218	205	198	173	128
Total liabilities and equity	$803	$810	$788	$757	$794	$807	$822

Required

1. Calculate trend percentages for the items of the statements using 1989 as the base year.
2. Analyze and comment on the situation shown in the statements.

The 1994 financial statements of Heartland Corporation follow:

Problem 19–3A
Financial statement ratios
(LO 3)

HEARTLAND CORPORATION
Income Statement
For Year Ended December 31, 1994

Sales		$647,000
Cost of goods sold:		
Merchandise inventory, December 31, 1993	$ 50,100	
Purchases.	400,000	
Goods available for sale	$450,100	
Merchandise inventory, December 31, 1994	38,600	
Cost of goods sold		411,500
Gross profit from sales		$235,500
Operating expenses.		182,100
Operating income.		$ 53,400
Interest expense		7,500
Income before taxes		$ 45,900
Income taxes		8,100
Net income		$ 37,800

HEARTLAND CORPORATION
Balance Sheet
December 31, 1994

Assets		Liablities and Shareholders' Equity	
Cash	$ 13,800	Accounts payable	$ 32,500
Temporary investments	16,300	Accrued wages payable	4,100
Accounts receivable, net.	34,700	Income taxes payable	4,600
Notes receivable (trade)	7,000	Long-term note payable,	
Merchandise inventory.	38,600	secured by mortgage	
Prepaid expenses.	3,800	on plant assets	75,000
Plant assets, net	217,600	Common—12,500 shares.	125,000
		Retained earnings	90,600
		Total liabilities and	
Total assets.	$331,800	shareholders' equity	$331,800

Assume that all sales were on credit. On the December 31, 1993, balance sheet, the assets totaled $288,400, common share capital was $125,000, and retained earnings were $58,800.

Required

Calculate the following: (*a*) current ratio, (*b*) acid-test ratio, (*c*) days' sales uncollected, (*d*) merchandise turnover, (*e*) ratio of pledged plant assets to secured liabilities, (*f*) times fixed interest charges earned, (*g*) profit margin, (*h*) total asset turnover, (*i*) return on total assets employed, and (*j*) return on common shareholders' equity.

Two companies that operate in the same industry as competitors are being evaluated by a bank that can lend money to only one of them. Summary information from the financial statements of the two companies follows:

Problem 19–4A
Comparative analysis of
financial statement ratios
(LO 3)

Data from the current year-end balance sheets:

	Sun Company	Lakeway Company
Assets		
Cash	$ 22,600	$ 42,800
Accounts receivable	79,000	88,800
Notes receivable (trade)	13,500	12,300
Merchandise inventory	88,800	120,000
Prepaid expenses	11,800	13,400
Plant and equipment, net.	178,500	255,000
Total assets	$394,200	$532,300
Liabilities and Shareholders' Equity		
Current liabilities	$ 85,000	$106,300
Long-term notes payable	90,000	101,000
Common share capital*	136,500	159,000
Retained earnings	82,700	166,000
Total liabilities and equity	$394,200	$532,300

Data from the current year's income statements:

	Sun Company	Lakeway Company
Sales.	$527,500	$744,000
Cost of goods sold	388,500	529,000
Interest expense	10,600	13,200
Income tax expense	8,600	15,100
Net income	48,800	67,200

Beginning-of-year data:

	Sun Company	Lakeway Company
Accounts receivable, net.	$ 73,500	$ 75,300
Notes receivable.	–0–	–0–
Merchandise inventory	106,300	84,500
Total assets	385,700	450,000
Common share capital*	136,500	159,000
Retained earnings	47,550	114,700

* Common shares outstanding: Sun, 13,650 shares; Lakeway, 15,900 shares.

Required

1. Calculate current ratios, acid-test ratios, accounts (including notes) receivable turnovers, merchandise turnovers, and days' sales uncollected for the two companies. Then identify the company that you consider to be the better short-term credit risk and explain why.

2. Calculate profit margins, total asset turnovers, returns on total assets employed, and returns on common shareholders' equity. Assuming that each company paid cash dividends of $1 per share and each company's shares can be purchased at $33 per share, calculate their price-earnings ratios and dividend yield. Also, identify which company's shares you would recommend as the better investment and explain why.

Problem 19–5A
Analysis of working capital
(LO 3)

Country Comfort Corporation began the month of August with $845,000 of current assets, a current ratio of 2.6 to 1, and an acid-test ratio of 1.1 to 1. During the month, it completed the following transactions:

Aug. 2 Sold merchandise that cost $41,000 for $69,000.

    4 Collected a $53,000 account receivable.

Aug. 8 Bought $75,000 of merchandise on account. (The company uses a perpetual inventory system.)

10 Borrowed $50,000 by giving the bank a 60-day, 12% note.

14 Borrowed $100,000 by signing a long-term secured note.

20 Used the $150,000 proceeds of the notes to buy additional machinery.

22 Declared a $1.50 per share cash dividend on the 50,000 outstanding common shares.

25 Wrote off a $14,000 bad debt against Allowance for Doubtful Accounts.

27 Paid a $66,000 account payable.

31 Paid the dividend declared on August 22.

Required

Prepare a schedule showing the company's current ratio, acid-test ratio, and working capital after each of the transactions. Round to two decimal places.

Lamar Company and Guadalupe Company are similar companies that operate within the same industry. The following information is available:

Problem 19–6A
Analytical essay
(LO 3)

	Lamar			Guadalupe		
	1994	**1993**	**1992**	**1994**	**1993**	**1992**
Working capital	$240,000	$190,000	$195,000	$240,000	$190,000	$195,000
Current ratio	2.3	2.4	2.2	0.8	1.0	0.9
Acid test ratio.	1.2	1.1	1.3	0.4	0.5	0.6
Accounts receivable turnover.	16.7	16.4	15.9	6.9	7.8	14.7
Merchandise inventory turnover	10.5	11.2	16.7	10.2	11.8	16.1

Required

Write a brief essay comparing Lamar Company and Guadalupe Company based on the information provided. Your discussion should include their relative ability to meet current obligations and to use current assets efficiently.

Information pertaining to Gaynor Corporation's operation for the three-year period ending December 31, 1994, follows:

Problem 19–7A
Analytical essay
(LO 3)

	1994	**1993**	**1992**
Sales	$560,000	$400,000	$250,000
Income before taxes	100,000	90,000	50,000
Interest expense	50,000	30,000	15,000
Debt ratio	20.8%	28.4%	32.2%
Equity ratio	79.2%	71.6%	67.8%
Times fixed interest charges earned	3.0	4.0	4.3

Required

Based on the information provided, evaluate Gaynor Corporation's ability to meet obligations and provide security to its creditors. Would your answer be different if Gaynor's $100,000 income before taxes in 1994 included an extraordinary loss of $60,000? How?

Provocative Problems

Provocative Problem 19–1
The Ajax Company
(LO 2, 3)

The Ajax Company is a diversified firm that develops, manufactures, and markets premium-quality household products, architectural coatings, and food service products. In addition to the liquid bleach product from which it takes its name, the company markets the leading line of dry salad dressing mixes. Founded in 1913, the Ajax Company has become an international company with sales in excess of $1 billion. A recent annual report included a 10-year summary, from which the following information has been extracted: (in thousands, except per-share data)

	Year 4	Year 3	Year 2	Year 1
Operations				
Net sales.	**$1,089,070**	$1,054,847	$974,566	$913,807
Percent change	**+ 3.2**	+8.2	+ 6.6	+ 5.4
Net earnings.	**$95,610**	$86,124	$79,709	$65,507
Percent change	**+11.0**	+8.0	+21.7	+45.2
Common Share Capital				
Per share:				
Earnings from continuing operations . .	**$3.60**	$3.27	$3.09	$2.72
Earnings from discontinued operations.	**—**	—	—	—
Net earnings:				
Assuming no dilution	**$3.60**	$3.27	$3.09	$2.72
Assuming full dilution.	**$3.50**	$3.17	$3.01	$2.64
Dividends	**$1.40**	$1.24	$1.08	$0.95
Shareholders' equity at end of year	**20.61**	18.37	16.40	13.48
Other Data				
Working capital	**$240,180**	$203,011	$144,424	$117,333
Total assets	**849,225**	778,062	701,396	603,875
Long-term debt	**38,151**	38,945	43,174	72,597
Shareholders' equity.	**549,793**	485,856	431,313	325,998
Current ratio.	**2.4**	2.0	1.8	1.7
Percent return on net sales— continuing operations	**8.8**	8.2	8.2	7.2
Percent return on average shareholders' equity.	**18.5**	18.8	20.2	21.6

Courtesy of The Ajax Company.

Discuss the format of the Ajax Company's presentation relative to the illustrations in the chapter. Then evaluate the company's performance over the four-year period.

Provocative Problem 19–2
T. J. Topp Company
(LO 2, 3)

In your position as controller of T. J. Topp Company, you are responsible for keeping the board of directors informed about the financial activities and status of the company. In preparing for the next board meeting, you have calculated the following ratios, turnovers, and percentages to enable you to answer questions:

	1994	1993	1992
Current ratio.	2.6 to 1	2.4 to 1	2.1 to 1
Acid-test ratio	0.8 to 1	1.1 to 1	1.2 to 1
Merchandise turnover	7.5 times	8.7 times	9.9 times
Accounts receivable turnover	6.7 times	7.4 times	8.2 times
Return on shareholders' equity	9.75%	11.50%	12.25%
Profit margin.	3.3%	3.5%	3.7%
Total asset turnover	2.6 times	2.6 times	3.0 times
Return on total assets	8.8%	9.4%	10.1%
Sales to plant assets	3.8 to 1	3.6 to 1	3.3 to 1
Sales trend.	128.00	117.00	100.00
Selling expenses to net sales.	9.8%	13.7%	15.3%

Required

Use the given data to answer each of the following questions. Explain your answers.

1. Is it becoming easier for the company to meet its current debts on time and to take advantage of cash discounts?
2. Is the company collecting its accounts receivable more rapidly?
3. Is the company's investment in accounts receivable decreasing?
4. Are dollars invested in inventory increasing?
5. Is the company's investment in plant assets increasing?
6. Is the shareholders' investment becoming more profitable?
7. Is the company using its assets efficiently?
8. Did the dollar amount of selling expenses decrease during the three-year period?

Davis, Inc., and Crawford, Inc., are competing companies with similar backgrounds. The shares of each company can be purchased at book value. Joan Rogers has an opportunity to invest in only one of the companies; she is undecided as to which company is better managed and which shares are the better investment. Prepare a report for Rogers stating which company you think is better managed and which company's shares you think may be the better investment. Back your report with any ratios, turnovers, and other analyses that provide relevant information.

Provocative Problem 19–3
Davis, Inc., and Crawford, Inc.
(LO 3)

Balance Sheets
December 31, 1993

	Davis, Inc.	Crawford, Inc.
Assets		
Cash	$ 34,200	$ 34,900
Accounts receivable, net.	86,300	92,100
Merchandise inventory	119,600	126,200
Prepaid expenses	3,600	4,500
Plant and equipment, net.	392,900	376,700
Total assets	$ 636,600	$ 634,400
Liabilities and Shareholders' Equity		
Current liabilities	$ 110,700	$ 124,400
Long-term notes payable	128,200	117,000
Common share capital*	231,600	203,600
Retained earnings	166,100	189,400
Total liabilities and equity	$ 636,600	$ 634,400

Income Statements
For Year Ended December 31, 1993

	Davis, Inc.	Crawford, Inc.
Sales.	$1,657,500	$1,747,600
Cost of goods sold	1,147,800	1,235,400
Gross profit on sales	$ 509,700	$ 512,200
Operating expenses	439,100	469,500
Operating income	$ 70,600	$ 42,700
Interest expense	10,500	10,100
Income before taxes	$ 60,100	$ 32,600
Income taxes.	10,000	4,900
Net income	$ 50,100	$ 27,700

December 31, 1992, Data

	Davis, Inc.	Crawford, Inc.
Accounts receivable	$ 106,600	$ 144,800
Merchandise inventory	101,100	116,600
Total assets	595,500	563,000
Common share capital*	231,200	203,100
Retained earnings	150,700	162,000

* Common shares outstanding: Davis, Inc., 23,120 shares; Crawford, Inc., 20,310 shares.

Provocative Problem 19–4
Bombardier Inc.
(LO 5)

Use the financial statements and related notes of Bombardier Inc. shown in Appendix I to answer the following questions:

1. What revenue segments are identified by Bombardier?
2. What were the revenues and costs attributed to "Transportation equipment" in 1992?
3. What was the 1992 income (loss) of Bombardier's five identified segments for classes of products. Which one earned the largest income? Which earned the smallest?
4. Which geographic segments are identified by Bombardier?
5. Which geographic segment has the greatest revenue from customers for 1992? Which one has the smallest?
6. Which geographic segment has the most invested in assets at the end of 1992? Which one has the smallest?

Provocative Problem 19–5
As a Matter of Ethics:
Essay

Ethics

Review the "As a Matter of Ethics" case on page 969 and write a brief essay discussing Coleman's ethical responsibility as the manager of Tech Division. Your discussion should consider the possibility that Coleman has the ability to dominate the pricing decision and the alternative possibility that the division managers are expected to negotiate a price for top management's approval.

A&R Problem 19–1

DATA COMPANY, LTD.
Balance Sheet
As at December 31, 1994

Assets		Liabilities and Capital	
Cash	$_____	Current liabilities	$_____
Accounts receivable	_____	12% bonds payable	_____
Inventory.	_____	Common shares.	7,500
Capital assets.	_____	Retained earnings.	_____
		Total liabilities and	
Total assets.	$_____	capital	$_____

Required

Using the format shown above complete the balance sheet for Data Company, Ltd., from the following ratios (round amounts to $100):

Net income	$ 3,600
Sales (all on account)	$45,000
Current ratio	3 to 1
Liabilities to total assets	1 to 2
Inventory turnover	5 times
Average collection period.	60.83 days
Capital asset turnover	3 times
Total asset turnover.	1.5 times
Expenses (including income tax at 40%) . .	$11,400
Dividends paid during the year	1,800

A company began the month of May with $200,000 of current assets, a 2-to-1 current ratio, and a 1-to-1 acid-test (quick) ratio. During the month it completed the following transactions:

A&R Problem 19–2

	Current Ratio			Acid-Test Ratio		
	Inc.	Dcr.	No. Change	Inc.	Dcr.	No. Change
a. Bought $50,000 of merchandise on account (the company uses a perpetual inventory system).						
b. Sold for $70,000 merchandise that cost $40,000 (sales on account).						
c. Collected an $8,500 account receivable.						
d. Paid a $30,000 account payable.						
e. Wrote off a $2,000 bad debt against the allowance for doubtful accounts.						
f. Declared a $1 per share cash dividend on the 20,000 outstanding common shares.						
g. Paid the dividend declared in (*f*).						
h. Borrowed $25,000 by giving the bank a 60-day, 10% note.						
i. Borrowed $100,000 by placing a 10-year mortgage on the plant.						
j. Used $50,000 of proceeds of the mortgage to buy additional machinery.						

Required

1. Indicate the effect on (*a*) current ratio and (*b*) acid-test ratio of each transaction. Set up a chart in your answer similar to that shown above and use check marks to indicate your answers. (Working capital is defined as "current assets minus current liabilities.")

2. For the end of May, calculate the:
   a. Current ratio.
   b. Acid-test ratio.
   c. Working capital.

Answers to Objective
Review Questions

LO 1 (*b*)	**LO 3** (*b*)	**LO 5** (*e*)
LO 2 (*a*)	**LO 4** (*e*)	**LO 6** (*c*)

Appendixes

Nine appendixes supplement the regular topical coverage of *Fundamental Accounting Principles*. Appendixes A through F appear with the specific chapters related to their topics. The other three appendixes are presented in this section of the text. The titles of the nine appendixes are listed to the right.

A Recording Prepaid and Unearned Items in Income Statement Accounts (Chapter 3)

B Reversing Entries (Chapter 4)

C The Adjusting Entry Approach to Accounting for Merchandise Inventories (Chapter 5)

D Recording Vouchers: Manual System (Chapter 7)

E Investments in Equity Securities (Chapter 8)

F Treasury Stock (Chapter 16)

G Present and Future Values: An Expansion

H Accounting for Corporate Income Taxes

I Financial Statements and Related Disclosures from Bombardier Inc.'s 1992 Annual Report

Present and Future Values: An Expansion

Because of the time value of money, cash flows occurring at different times are not equivalent. The math techniques described in this appendix allow you to reach more informed decisions about future cash flows or to provide information to others so that they can make more informed decisions.

*T*he concept of present value is introduced and applied to accounting problems in Chapters 12 and 17. This appendix is designed to supplement those presentations with additional discussion, more complete tables, and additional homework exercises. In studying this appendix, you will also learn about the concept of future value.

Learning Objectives

After studying Appendix G, you should be able to:

1. Explain what is meant by the present value of a single amount and the present value of an annuity, and be able to use tables to solve present value problems.

2. Explain what is meant by the future value of a single amount and the future value of an annuity, and be able to use tables to solve future value problems.

The present value of a single amount to be received or paid at some future date may be expressed as:

$$p = \frac{f}{(1 + i)^n}$$

where:

p = Present value
f = Future value
i = Rate of interest per period
n = Number of periods

For example, assume that $2.20 is to be received one period from now. It would be useful to know how much must be invested now, for one period, at an interest rate of 10% to provide $2.20. We can calculate that amount with this formula:

$$p = \frac{f}{(1 + i)^n} = \frac{\$2.20}{(1 + .10)^1} = \$2.00$$

Alternatively, we can use the formula to find how much must be invested for two periods at 10% to provide $2.42:

$$p = \frac{f}{(1 + i)^n} = \frac{\$2.42}{(1 + .10)^2} = \$2.00$$

Note that the number of periods (n) does not have to be expressed in years. Any period of time, such as a day, a month, a quarter, or a year, may be used. However, whatever period is used, the interest rate (i) must be compounded for the same period. Thus, if a problem expresses n in months, and i equals 12% per year, then 1% of the amount invested at the beginning of each month is

Present Value of a Single Amount

LO 1 Explain what is meant by the present value of a single amount and the present value of an annuity, and be able to use tables to solve present value problems.

earned that month and added to the investment. Thus, the interest is compounded monthly.

A present value table shows present values for a variety of interest rates (i) and a variety of numbers of periods (n). Each present value is based on the assumption that the future value (f) is 1. The following formula is used to construct a table of present values of a single future amount:

$$p = \frac{1}{(1 + i)^n}$$

Table G–1 on page G-5 is a table of present values of a single future amount and is often called a *present value of 1* table.

Future Value of a Single Amount

LO 2 Explain what is meant by the future value of a single amount and the future value of an annuity, and be able to use tables to solve future value problems.

The following formula for the present value of a single amount can be modified to become the formula for the future value of a single amount with a simple step:

$$p = \frac{f}{(1 + i)^n}$$

By multiplying both sides of the equation by $(1 + i)^n$, the result is:

$$f = p \times (1 + i)^n$$

For example, we can use this formula to determine that $2.00 invested for one period at 10% will increase to a future value of $2.20:

$$f = p \times (1 + i)^n$$
$$= \$2.00 \times (1 + .10)^1$$
$$= \$2.20$$

Alternatively, assume that $2.00 will remain invested for three periods at 10%. The $2.662 amount that will be received after three periods is calculated with the formula as follows:

$$f = p \times (1 + i)^n$$
$$= \$2.00 \times (1 + .10)^3$$
$$= \$2.662$$

A future value table shows future values for a variety of interest rates (i) and a variety of numbers of periods (n). Each future value is based on the assumption that the present value (p) is 1. Thus the formula used to construct a table of future values of a single amount is

$$f = (1 + i)^n$$

Table G–2 on page G-6 is a table of future values of a single amount and is often called a *future value of 1* table.

In Table G–2, look at the row where $n = 0$ and observe that the future value is 1 for all interest rates because no interest is earned.

Observe that a table showing the present values of 1 and a table showing the future values of 1 contain exactly the same information because both tables are based on the same equation. As you have seen, this equation

TABLE G-1

Present Value of 1 Due in n Periods

Periods	1.0%	1.5%	3.0%	4.0%	8.0%	10.0%	12.0%	14.0%	16.0%	18.0%	20.0%
1	0.9901	0.9852	0.9709	0.9615	0.9259	0.9091	0.8929	0.8772	0.8621	0.8475	0.8333
2	0.9803	0.9707	0.9426	0.9246	0.8573	0.8264	0.7972	0.7695	0.7432	0.7182	0.6944
3	0.9706	0.9563	0.9151	0.8890	0.7938	0.7513	0.7118	0.6750	0.6407	0.6086	0.5787
4	0.9610	0.9422	0.8885	0.8548	0.7350	0.6830	0.6355	0.5921	0.5523	0.5158	0.4823
5	0.9515	0.9283	0.8626	0.8219	0.6806	0.6209	0.5674	0.5194	0.4761	0.4371	0.4019
6	0.9420	0.9145	0.8375	0.7903	0.6302	0.5645	0.5066	0.4556	0.4104	0.3704	0.3349
7	0.9327	0.9010	0.8131	0.7599	0.5835	0.5132	0.4523	0.3996	0.3538	0.3139	0.2791
8	0.9235	0.8877	0.7894	0.7307	0.5403	0.4665	0.4039	0.3506	0.3050	0.2660	0.2326
9	0.9143	0.8746	0.7664	0.7026	0.5002	0.4241	0.3606	0.3075	0.2630	0.2255	0.1938
10	0.9053	0.8617	0.7441	0.6756	0.4632	0.3855	0.3220	0.2697	0.2267	0.1911	0.1615
11	0.8963	0.8489	0.7224	0.6496	0.4289	0.3505	0.2875	0.2366	0.1954	0.1619	0.1346
12	0.8874	0.8364	0.7014	0.6246	0.3971	0.3186	0.2567	0.2076	0.1685	0.1372	0.1122
13	0.8787	0.8240	0.6810	0.6006	0.3677	0.2897	0.2292	0.1821	0.1452	0.1163	0.0935
14	0.8700	0.8118	0.6611	0.5775	0.3405	0.2633	0.2046	0.1597	0.1252	0.0985	0.0779
15	0.8613	0.7999	0.6419	0.5553	0.3152	0.2394	0.1827	0.1401	0.1079	0.0835	0.0649
16	0.8528	0.7880	0.6232	0.5339	0.2919	0.2176	0.1631	0.1229	0.0930	0.0708	0.0541
17	0.8444	0.7764	0.6050	0.5134	0.2703	0.1978	0.1456	0.1078	0.0802	0.0600	0.0451
18	0.8360	0.7649	0.5874	0.4936	0.2502	0.1799	0.1300	0.0946	0.0691	0.0508	0.0376
19	0.8277	0.7536	0.5703	0.4746	0.2317	0.1635	0.1161	0.0829	0.0596	0.0431	0.0313
20	0.8195	0.7425	0.5537	0.4564	0.2145	0.1486	0.1037	0.0728	0.0514	0.0365	0.0261
21	0.8114	0.7315	0.5375	0.4388	0.1987	0.1351	0.0926	0.0638	0.0443	0.0309	0.0217
22	0.8034	0.7207	0.5219	0.4220	0.1839	0.1228	0.0826	0.0560	0.0382	0.0262	0.0181
23	0.7954	0.7100	0.5067	0.4057	0.1703	0.1117	0.0738	0.0491	0.0329	0.0222	0.0151
24	0.7876	0.6995	0.4919	0.3901	0.1577	0.1015	0.0659	0.0431	0.0284	0.0188	0.0126
25	0.7798	0.6892	0.4776	0.3751	0.1460	0.0923	0.0588	0.0378	0.0245	0.0160	0.0105
26	0.7720	0.6790	0.4637	0.3607	0.1352	0.0839	0.0525	0.0331	0.0211	0.0135	0.0087
27	0.7644	0.6690	0.4502	0.3468	0.1252	0.0763	0.0469	0.0291	0.0182	0.0115	0.0073
28	0.7568	0.6591	0.4371	0.3335	0.1159	0.0693	0.0419	0.0255	0.0157	0.0097	0.0061
29	0.7493	0.6494	0.4243	0.3207	0.1073	0.0630	0.0374	0.0224	0.0135	0.0082	0.0051
30	0.7419	0.6398	0.4120	0.3083	0.0994	0.0573	0.0334	0.0196	0.0116	0.0070	0.0042
31	0.7346	0.6303	0.4000	0.2965	0.0920	0.0521	0.0298	0.0172	0.0100	0.0059	0.0035
32	0.7273	0.6210	0.3883	0.2851	0.0852	0.0474	0.0266	0.0151	0.0087	0.0050	0.0029
33	0.7201	0.6118	0.3770	0.2741	0.0789	0.0431	0.0238	0.0132	0.0075	0.0042	0.0024
34	0.7130	0.6028	0.3660	0.2636	0.0730	0.0391	0.0212	0.0116	0.0064	0.0036	0.0020
35	0.7059	0.5939	0.3554	0.2534	0.0676	0.0356	0.0189	0.0102	0.0055	0.0030	0.0017
36	0.6989	0.5851	0.3450	0.2437	0.0626	0.0323	0.0169	0.0089	0.0048	0.0026	0.0014
37	0.6920	0.5764	0.3350	0.2343	0.0580	0.0294	0.0151	0.0078	0.0041	0.0022	0.0012
38	0.6852	0.5679	0.3252	0.2253	0.0537	0.0267	0.0135	0.0069	0.0036	0.0019	0.0010
39	0.6784	0.5595	0.3158	0.2166	0.0497	0.0243	0.0120	0.0060	0.0031	0.0016	0.0008
40	0.6717	0.5513	0.3066	0.2083	0.0460	0.0221	0.0107	0.0053	0.0026	0.0013	0.0007
41	0.6650	0.5431	0.2976	0.2003	0.0426	0.0201	0.0096	0.0046	0.0023	0.0011	0.0006
42	0.6584	0.5351	0.2890	0.1926	0.0395	0.0183	0.0086	0.0041	0.0020	0.0010	0.0005
43	0.6519	0.5272	0.2805	0.1852	0.0365	0.0166	0.0076	0.0036	0.0017	0.0008	0.0004
44	0.6454	0.5194	0.2724	0.1780	0.0338	0.0151	0.0068	0.0031	0.0015	0.0007	0.0003
45	0.6391	0.5117	0.2644	0.1712	0.0313	0.0137	0.0061	0.0027	0.0013	0.0006	0.0003
46	0.6327	0.5042	0.2567	0.1646	0.0290	0.0125	0.0054	0.0024	0.0011	0.0005	0.0002
47	0.6265	0.4967	0.2493	0.1583	0.0269	0.0113	0.0049	0.0021	0.0009	0.0004	0.0002
48	0.6203	0.4894	0.2420	0.1522	0.0249	0.0103	0.0043	0.0019	0.0008	0.0004	0.0002
49	0.6141	0.4821	0.2350	0.1463	0.0230	0.0094	0.0039	0.0016	0.0007	0.0003	0.0001
50	0.6080	0.4750	0.2281	0.1407	0.0213	0.0085	0.0035	0.0014	0.0006	0.0003	0.0001

TABLE G–2

Future Value of 1 Due in n *Periods*

Periods	1.0%	1.5%	3.0%	4.0%	8.0%	10.0%	12.0%	14.0%	16.0%	18.0%	20.0%
0	1.0000	1.0000	1.0000	1.0000	1.0000	1.0000	1.0000	1.0000	1.0000	1.0000	1.0000
1	1.0100	1.0150	1.0300	1.0400	1.0800	1.1000	1.1200	1.1400	1.1600	1.1800	1.2000
2	1.0201	1.0302	1.0609	1.0816	1.1664	1.2100	1.2544	1.2996	1.3456	1.3924	1.4400
3	1.0303	1.0457	1.0927	1.1249	1.2597	1.3310	1.4049	1.4815	1.5609	1.6430	1.7280
4	1.0406	1.0614	1.1255	1.1699	1.3605	1.4641	1.5735	1.6890	1.8106	1.9388	2.0736
5	1.0510	1.0773	1.1593	1.2167	1.4693	1.6105	1.7623	1.9254	2.1003	2.2878	2.4883
6	1.0615	1.0934	1.1941	1.2653	1.5869	1.7716	1.9738	2.1950	2.4364	2.6996	2.9860
7	1.0721	1.1098	1.2299	1.3159	1.7138	1.9487	2.2107	2.5023	2.8262	3.1855	3.5832
8	1.0829	1.1265	1.2668	1.3686	1.8509	2.1436	2.4760	2.8526	3.2784	3.7589	4.2998
9	1.0937	1.1434	1.3048	1.4233	1.9990	2.3579	2.7731	3.2519	3.8030	4.4355	5.1598
10	1.1046	1.1605	1.3439	1.4802	2.1589	2.5937	3.1058	3.7072	4.4114	5.2338	6.1917
11	1.1157	1.1779	1.3842	1.5395	2.3316	2.8531	3.4785	4.2262	5.1173	6.1759	7.4301
12	1.1268	1.1956	1.4258	1.6010	2.5182	3.1384	3.8960	4.8179	5.9360	7.2876	8.9161
13	1.1381	1.2136	1.4685	1.6651	2.7196	3.4523	4.3635	5.4924	6.8858	8.5994	10.6993
14	1.1495	1.2318	1.5126	1.7317	2.9372	3.7975	4.8871	6.2613	7.9875	10.1472	12.8392
15	1.1610	1.2502	1.5580	1.8009	3.1722	4.1772	5.4736	7.1379	9.2655	11.9737	15.4070
16	1.1726	1.2690	1.6047	1.8730	3.4259	4.5950	6.1304	8.1372	10.7480	14.1290	18.4884
17	1.1843	1.2880	1.6528	1.9479	3.7000	5.0545	6.8660	9.2765	12.4677	16.6722	22.1861
18	1.1961	1.3073	1.7024	2.0258	3.9960	5.5599	7.6900	10.5752	14.4625	19.6733	26.6233
19	1.2081	1.3270	1.7535	2.1068	4.3157	6.1159	8.6128	12.0557	16.7765	23.2144	31.9480
20	1.2202	1.3469	1.8061	2.1911	4.6610	6.7275	9.6463	13.7435	19.4608	27.3930	38.3376
21	1.2324	1.3671	1.8603	2.2788	5.0338	7.4002	10.8038	15.6676	22.5745	32.3238	46.0051
22	1.2447	1.3876	1.9161	2.3699	5.4365	8.1403	12.1003	17.8610	26.1864	38.1421	55.2061
23	1.2572	1.4084	1.9736	2.4647	5.8715	8.9543	13.5523	20.3616	30.3762	45.0076	66.2474
24	1.2697	1.4295	2.0328	2.5633	6.3412	9.8497	15.1786	23.2122	35.2364	53.1090	79.4968
25	1.2824	1.4509	2.0938	2.6658	6.8485	10.8347	17.0001	26.4619	40.8742	62.6686	95.3962
26	1.2953	1.4727	2.1566	2.7725	7.3964	11.9182	19.0401	30.1666	47.4141	73.9490	114.4755
27	1.3082	1.4948	2.2213	2.8834	7.9881	13.1100	21.3249	34.3899	55.0004	87.2598	137.3706
28	1.3213	1.5172	2.2879	2.9987	8.6271	14.4210	23.8839	39.2045	63.8004	102.9666	164.8447
29	1.3345	1.5400	2.3566	3.1187	9.3173	15.8631	26.7499	44.6931	74.0085	121.5005	197.8136
30	1.3478	1.5631	2.4273	3.2434	10.0627	17.4494	29.9599	50.9502	85.8499	143.3706	237.3763
31	1.3613	1.5865	2.5001	3.3731	10.8677	19.1943	33.5551	58.0832	99.5859	169.1774	284.8516
32	1.3749	1.6103	2.5751	3.5081	11.7371	21.1138	37.5817	66.2148	115.5196	199.6293	341.8219
33	1.3887	1.6345	2.6523	3.6484	12.6760	23.2252	42.0915	75.4849	134.0027	235.5625	410.1863
34	1.4026	1.6590	2.7319	3.7943	13.6901	25.5477	47.1425	86.0528	155.4432	277.9638	492.2235
35	1.4166	1.6839	2.8139	3.9461	14.7853	28.1024	52.7996	98.1002	180.3141	327.9973	590.6682
36	1.4308	1.7091	2.8983	4.1039	15.9682	30.9127	59.1356	111.8342	209.1643	387.0368	708.8019
37	1.4451	1.7348	2.9852	4.2681	17.2456	34.0039	66.2318	127.4910	242.6306	456.7034	850.5622
38	1.4595	1.7608	3.0748	4.4388	18.6253	37.4043	74.1797	145.3397	281.4515	528.9100	1020.6747
39	1.4741	1.7872	3.1670	4.6164	20.1153	41.1448	83.0812	165.6873	326.4838	635.9139	1224.8096
40	1.4889	1.8140	3.2620	4.8010	21.7245	45.2593	93.0510	188.8835	378.7212	750.3783	1469.7716
41	1.5083	1.8412	3.3599	4.9931	23.4625	49.7852	104.2171	215.3272	439.3165	885.4464	1763.7259
42	1.5188	1.8688	3.4607	5.1928	25.3395	54.7637	116.7231	245.4730	509.6072	1044.8268	2116.4711
43	1.5340	1.8969	3.5645	5.4005	27.3666	60.2401	130.7299	279.8392	591.1443	1232.8956	2539.7653
44	1.5493	1.9253	3.6715	5.6165	29.5560	66.2641	146.4175	319.0167	685.7274	1454.8168	3047.7183
45	1.5648	1.9542	3.7816	5.8412	31.9204	72.8905	163.9876	363.6791	795.4438	1716.6839	3657.2620
46	1.5805	1.9835	3.8950	6.0748	34.4741	80.1795	183.6661	414.5941	922.7148	2025.6870	4388.7144
47	1.5963	2.0133	4.0119	6.3178	37.2320	88.1975	205.7061	472.6373	1070.3492	2390.3106	5266.4573
48	1.6122	2.0435	4.1323	6.5705	40.2106	97.0172	230.3908	538.8065	1241.6051	2820.5665	6319.7487
49	1.6283	2.0741	4.2562	6.8333	43.4274	106.7190	258.0377	614.2395	1440.2619	3328.2685	7583.6985
50	1.6446	2.1052	4.3839	7.1067	46.9016	117.3909	289.0022	700.2330	1670.7038	3927.3569	9100.4382

G *Present and Future Values: An Expansion*   G-7

$$p = \frac{f}{(1 + i)^n}$$

is nothing more than a reformulation of

$$f = p \times (1 + i)^n$$

Both tables reflect the same four variables p, f, i, and n. Therefore, any problem that can be solved with one of the two tables can also be solved with the other.

For example, suppose that a person invests $100 for a five-year period and expects to earn 12% per year. How much should the person receive after five years? To solve the problem using Table G–2, find the future value of 1, five periods from now, compounded at 12%. In the table, $f = 1.7623$. Thus, the amount to be accumulated over five years is $176.23 ($100 × 1.7623).

Table G–1 shows that the present value of 1, discounted five periods at 12% is 0.5674. Recall that the relationship between present value and future value may be expressed as:

$$p = \frac{f}{(1 + i)^n}$$

This formula can be restated as:

$$p = f \times \frac{1}{(1 + i)^n}$$

In turn, it can be restated as:

$$f = \frac{p}{\dfrac{1}{(1 + i)^n}}$$

Because we know from Table G–2 that $1/(1 + i)^n$ equals 0.5674, the future value of $100 invested for five periods at 12% is:

$$f = \frac{\$100}{0.5674} = \$176.24$$

In summary, the future value can be found two ways. First, we can multiply the amount invested by the future value found in Table G–1. Second, we can divide the amount invested by the present value found in Table G–2. As you can see in this problem, immaterial differences can occur between these two methods through rounding.

Present Value of an Annuity

An annuity is a series of equal payments occurring at equal intervals, such as three annual payments of $100 each. The present value of an annuity is defined as the present value of the payments one period prior to the first payment. This annuity and its present value (p) may be represented graphically as follows:

```
            $100   $100   $100
  o———————o——————o——————o
  p
```

LO 1 Explain what is meant by the present value of a single amount and the present value of an annuity, and be able to use tables to solve present value problems.

One way to calculate the present value of this annuity finds the present value of each payment with the formula and adds them together. For this example, assuming an interest rate of 18%, the calculation is

$$p = \frac{\$100}{(1 + .18)^1} + \frac{\$100}{(1 + .18)^2} + \frac{\$100}{(1 + .18)^3} = \$217.43$$

Another way calculates the present value of the annuity by using Table G–1 to compute the present value of each payment and then taking their sum:

First payment: $p = \$100 \times 0.8475 = \$\ 84.75$
Second payment: $p = \$100 \times 0.7182 = \ \ 71.82$
Third payment: $p = \$100 \times 0.6086 = \ \ 60.86$

Total: $p = \underline{\$217.43}$

We can also use Table G–1 to solve the problem by first adding the table values for the three payments and then multiplying this sum by the $100 amount of each payment:

From Table G–1: $i = 18\%, n = 1, p = \ \ 0.8475$
                     $i = 18\%, n = 2, p = \ \ 0.7182$
                     $i = 18\%, n = 3, p = \ \ \underline{0.6086}$
                                Sum $= \ \ \underline{2.1743}$

Present value $= 2.1743 \times \$100 = \underline{\$217.43}$

An easier way to solve the problem uses a different table that shows the present values of annuities, like Table G–3 on page G-9, which is often called a *present value of an annuity of 1* table. Look at Table G–3 on the row where $n = 3$ and $i = 18\%$ and observe that the present value is 2.1743. Thus, the present value of an annuity of 1 for three periods, discounted at 18%, is 2.1743.

Although a formula is used to construct a table showing the present values of an annuity, you can construct one by adding the amounts in a present value of 1 table.[1] Examine Table G–1 and Table G–3 to confirm that the following numbers were drawn from those tables:

From Table G–1		From Table G–3	
$i = 8\%, n = 1$	0.9259		
$i = 8\%, n = 2$	0.8573		
$i = 8\%, n = 3$	0.7938		
$i = 8\%, n = 4$	0.7350		
Total.	3.3120	$i = 8\%, n = 4$	3.3121

The minor difference in the results occurs because the numbers in the tables have been rounded.

---

[1] The formula for the present value of an annuity of 1 is:

$$p = \frac{1 - \dfrac{1}{(1 + i)^n}}{i}$$

TABLE G–3

Present Value of an Annuity of 1 per Period

Periods	1.0%	1.5%	3.0%	4.0%	8.0%	10.0%	12.0%	14.0%	16.0%	18.0%	20.0%
1	0.9901	0.9852	0.9709	0.9615	0.9259	0.9091	0.8929	0.8772	0.8621	0.8475	0.8333
2	1.9704	1.9559	1.9135	1.8861	1.7833	1.7355	1.6901	1.6467	1.6052	1.5656	1.5278
3	2.9410	2.9122	2.8286	2.7751	2.5771	2.4869	2.4018	2.3216	2.2459	2.1743	2.1065
4	3.9020	3.8544	3.7171	3.6299	3.3121	3.1699	3.0373	2.9137	2.7982	2.6901	2.5887
5	4.8534	4.7826	4.5797	4.4518	3.9927	3.7908	3.6048	3.4331	3.2743	3.1272	2.9906
6	5.7955	5.6972	5.4172	5.2421	4.6229	4.3553	4.1114	3.8887	3.6847	3.4976	3.3255
7	6.7282	6.5982	6.2303	6.0021	5.2064	4.8684	4.5638	4.2883	4.0386	3.8115	3.6046
8	7.6517	7.4859	7.0197	6.7327	5.7466	5.3349	4.9676	4.6389	4.3436	4.0776	3.8372
9	8.5660	8.3605	7.7861	7.4353	6.2469	5.7590	5.3282	4.9464	4.6065	4.3030	4.0310
10	9.4713	9.2222	8.5302	8.1109	6.7101	6.1446	5.6502	5.2161	4.8332	4.4941	4.1925
11	10.3676	10.0711	9.2526	8.7605	7.1390	6.4951	5.9377	5.4527	5.0286	4.6560	4.3271
12	11.2551	10.9075	9.9540	9.3851	7.5361	6.8137	6.1944	5.6603	5.1971	4.7932	4.4392
13	12.1337	11.7315	10.6350	9.9856	7.9038	7.1034	6.4235	5.8424	5.3423	4.9095	4.5327
14	13.0037	12.5434	11.2961	10.5631	8.2442	7.3667	6.6282	6.0021	5.4675	5.0081	4.6106
15	13.8651	13.3432	11.9379	11.1184	8.5595	7.6061	6.8109	6.1422	5.5755	5.0916	4.6755
16	14.7179	14.1313	12.5611	11.6523	8.8514	7.8237	6.9740	6.2651	5.6685	5.1624	4.7296
17	15.5623	14.9076	13.1661	12.1657	9.1216	8.0216	7.1196	6.3729	5.7487	5.2223	4.7746
18	16.3983	15.6726	13.7535	12.6593	9.3719	8.2014	7.2497	6.4674	5.8178	5.2732	4.8122
19	17.2260	16.4262	14.3238	13.1339	9.6036	8.3649	7.3658	6.5504	5.8775	5.3162	4.8435
20	18.0456	17.1686	14.8775	13.5903	9.8181	8.5136	7.4694	6.6231	5.9288	5.3527	4.8696
21	18.8570	17.9001	15.4150	14.0292	10.0168	8.6487	7.5620	6.6870	5.9731	5.3837	4.8913
22	19.6604	18.6208	15.9369	14.4511	10.2007	8.7715	7.6446	6.7429	6.0113	5.4099	4.9094
23	20.4558	19.3309	16.4436	14.8568	10.3711	8.8832	7.7184	6.7921	6.0442	5.4321	4.9245
24	21.2434	20.0304	16.9355	15.2470	10.5288	8.9847	7.7843	6.8351	6.0726	5.4509	4.9371
25	22.0232	20.7196	17.4131	15.6221	10.6748	9.0770	7.8431	6.8729	6.0971	5.4669	4.9476
26	22.7952	21.3986	17.8768	15.9828	10.8100	9.1609	7.8957	6.9061	6.1182	5.4804	4.9563
27	23.5596	22.0676	18.3270	16.3296	10.9352	9.2372	7.9426	6.9352	6.1364	5.4919	4.9636
28	24.3164	22.7267	18.7641	16.6631	11.0511	9.3066	7.9844	6.9607	6.1520	5.5016	4.9697
29	25.0658	23.3761	19.1885	16.9837	11.1584	9.3696	8.0218	6.9830	6.1656	5.5098	4.9747
30	25.8077	24.0158	19.6004	17.2920	11.2578	9.4269	8.0552	7.0027	6.1772	5.5168	4.9789
31	26.5423	24.6461	20.0004	17.5885	11.3498	9.4790	8.0850	7.0199	6.1872	5.5227	4.9824
32	27.2696	25.2671	20.3888	17.8736	11.4350	9.5264	8.1116	7.0350	6.1959	5.5277	4.9854
33	27.9897	25.8790	20.7658	18.1476	11.5139	9.5694	8.1354	7.0482	6.2034	5.5320	4.9878
34	28.7027	26.4817	21.1318	18.4112	11.5869	9.6086	8.1566	7.0599	6.2098	5.5356	4.9898
35	29.4086	27.0756	21.4872	18.6646	11.6546	9.6442	8.1755	7.0700	6.2153	5.5386	4.9915
36	30.1075	27.6607	21.8323	18.9083	11.7172	9.6765	8.1924	7.0790	6.2201	5.5412	4.9929
37	30.7995	28.2371	22.1672	19.1426	11.7752	9.7059	8.2075	7.0868	6.2242	5.5434	4.9941
38	31.4847	28.8051	22.4925	19.3679	11.8289	9.7327	8.2210	7.0937	6.2278	5.5452	4.9951
39	32.1630	29.3646	22.8082	19.5845	11.8786	9.7570	8.2330	7.0997	6.2309	5.5468	4.9959
40	32.8347	29.9158	23.1148	19.7928	11.9246	9.7791	8.2438	7.1050	6.2335	5.5482	4.9966
41	33.4997	30.4590	23.4124	19.9931	11.9672	9.7991	8.2534	7.1097	6.2358	5.5493	4.9972
42	34.1581	30.9941	23.7014	20.1856	12.0067	9.8174	8.2619	7.1138	6.2377	5.5502	4.9976
43	34.8100	31.5212	23.9819	20.3708	12.0432	9.8340	8.2696	7.1173	6.2394	5.5510	4.9980
44	35.4555	32.0406	24.2543	20.5488	12.0771	9.8491	8.2764	7.1205	6.2409	5.5517	4.9984
45	36.0945	32.5523	24.5187	20.7200	12.1084	9.8628	8.2825	7.1232	6.2421	5.5523	4.9986
46	36.7272	33.0565	24.7754	20.8847	12.1374	9.8753	8.2880	7.1256	6.2432	5.5528	4.9989
47	37.3537	33.5532	25.0247	21.0429	12.1643	9.8866	8.2928	7.1277	6.2442	5.5532	4.9991
48	37.9740	34.0426	25.2667	21.1951	12.1891	9.8969	8.2972	7.1296	6.2450	5.5536	4.9992
49	38.5881	34.5247	25.5017	21.3415	12.2122	9.9063	8.3010	7.1312	6.2457	5.5539	4.9993
50	39.1961	34.9997	25.7298	21.4822	12.2335	9.9148	8.3045	7.1327	6.2463	5.5541	4.9995

In addition to the preceding methods, you can use preprogrammed business calculators and spreadsheet computer programs to find the present value of annuities.

Future Value of an Annuity

LO 2 Explain what is meant by the future value of a single amount and the future value of an annuity, and be able to use tables to solve future value problems.

Just as an annuity has a present value, it also has a future value. The future value of an annuity is the accumulated value of the annuity payments and interest as of the date of the final payment. Consider the earlier annuity of three annual payments of $100. The points in time at which the present value (p) and the future value (f) occur are shown below:

$$\begin{array}{cccc} & \$100 & \$100 & \$100 \\ \circ & \!\!\!\!\!-\!\!\!\circ & \!\!\!\!\!-\!\!\!\circ & \!\!\!\!\!-\!\!\!\circ \\ p & & & f \end{array}$$

Note that the first payment is made two periods prior to the point at which the future value is determined. Therefore, for the first payment, $n = 2$. For the second payment, $n = 1$. Since the third payment occurs on the future value date, $n = 0$.

One way to calculate the future value of this annuity uses the formula to find the future value of each payment and adds them together. Assuming an interest rate of 18%, the calculation is:

$$f = \$100 \times (1 + .18)^2 + \$100 \times (1 + .18)^1 + \$100 \times (1 + .18)^0 = \$357.24$$

Another way calculates the future value of the annuity by using Table G–2 to find the sum of the future values of each payment:

First payment:	$f = \$100 \times 1.3924 = \$139.24$
Second payment:	$f = \$100 \times 1.1800 = 118.00$
Third payment:	$f = \$100 \times 1.0000 = 100.00$
Total:	$f = \$357.24$

A third approach adds the future values of three payments of 1 and multiplies the sum by $100:

From Table G–2:	$i = 18\%, n = 2, f = 1.3924$
	$i = 18\%, n = 1, f = 1.1800$
	$i = 18\%, n = 0, f = 1.0000$
	Sum = 3.5724

$$\text{Future value} = 3.5724 \times \$100 = \$357.24$$

A fourth and easier way to solve the problem uses a table that shows the future values of annuities, often called a *future value of an annuity of 1* table. Table G–4 on page G-11 is such a table. Note in Table G–4 that when $n = 1$, the future values are equal to 1 ($f = 1$) for all rates of interest because the annuity consists of only one payment and the future value is determined on the date of the payment. Thus, the future value equals the payment.

Although a formula is used to construct a table showing the future values of an annuity of 1, you can construct one by adding the amounts in a future

TABLE G–4

Future Value of an Annuity of 1 per Period

Periods	1.0%	1.5%	3.0%	4.0%	8.0%	10.0%	12.0%	14.0%	16.0%	18.0%	20.0%
1	1.0000	1.0000	1.0000	1.0000	1.0000	1.0000	1.0000	1.0000	1.0000	1.0000	1.0000
2	2.0100	2.0150	2.0300	2.0400	2.0800	2.1000	2.1200	2.1400	2.1600	2.1800	2.2000
3	3.0301	3.0452	3.0909	3.1216	3.2464	3.3100	3.3744	3.4396	3.5056	3.5724	3.6400
4	4.0604	4.0909	4.1836	4.2465	4.5061	4.6410	4.7793	4.9211	5.0665	5.2154	5.3680
5	5.1010	5.1523	5.3091	5.4163	5.8666	6.1051	6.3528	6.6101	6.8771	7.1542	7.4416
6	6.1520	6.2296	6.4684	6.6330	7.3359	7.7156	8.1152	8.5355	8.9775	9.4420	9.9299
7	7.2135	7.3230	7.6625	7.8983	8.9228	9.4872	10.0890	10.7305	11.4139	12.1415	12.9159
8	8.2857	8.4328	8.8923	9.2142	10.6366	11.4359	12.2997	13.2328	14.2401	15.3270	16.4991
9	9.3685	9.5593	10.1591	10.5828	12.4876	13.5795	14.7757	16.0853	17.5185	19.0859	20.7989
10	10.4622	10.7027	11.4639	12.0061	14.4866	15.9374	17.5487	19.3373	21.3215	23.5213	25.9587
11	11.5668	11.8633	12.8078	13.4864	16.6455	18.5312	20.6546	23.0445	25.7329	28.7551	32.1504
12	12.6825	13.0412	14.1920	15.0258	18.9771	21.3843	24.1331	27.2707	30.8502	34.9311	39.5805
13	13.8093	14.2368	15.6178	16.6268	21.4953	24.5227	28.0291	32.0887	36.7862	42.2187	48.4966
14	14.9474	15.4504	17.0863	18.2919	24.2149	27.9750	32.3926	37.5811	43.6720	50.8180	59.1959
15	16.0969	16.6821	18.5989	20.0236	27.1521	31.7725	37.2797	43.8424	51.6595	60.9653	72.0351
16	17.2579	17.9324	20.1569	21.8245	30.3243	35.9497	42.7533	50.9804	60.9250	72.9390	87.4421
17	18.4304	19.2014	21.7616	23.6975	33.7502	40.5447	48.8837	59.1176	71.6730	87.0680	105.9306
18	19.6147	20.4894	23.4144	25.6454	37.4502	45.5992	55.7497	68.3941	84.1407	103.7403	128.1167
19	20.8109	21.7967	25.1169	27.6712	41.4463	51.1591	63.4397	78.9692	98.6032	123.4135	154.7400
20	22.0190	23.1237	26.8704	29.7781	45.7620	57.2750	72.0524	91.0249	115.3797	146.6280	186.6880
21	23.2392	24.4705	28.6765	31.9692	50.4229	64.0025	81.6987	104.7684	134.8405	174.0210	225.0256
22	24.4716	25.8376	30.5368	34.2480	55.4568	71.4027	92.5026	120.4360	157.4150	206.3448	271.0307
23	25.7163	27.2251	32.4529	36.6179	60.8933	79.5430	104.6029	138.2970	183.6014	244.4868	326.2369
24	26.9735	28.6335	34.4265	39.0826	66.7648	88.4973	118.1552	158.6586	213.9776	289.4945	392.4842
25	28.2432	30.0630	36.4593	41.6459	73.1059	98.3471	133.3339	181.8708	249.2140	342.6035	471.9811
26	29.5256	31.5140	38.5530	44.3117	79.9544	109.1818	150.3339	208.3327	290.0883	405.2721	567.3773
27	30.8209	32.9867	40.7096	47.0842	87.3508	121.0999	169.3740	238.4993	337.5024	479.2211	681.8528
28	32.1291	34.4815	42.9309	49.9676	95.3388	134.2099	190.6989	272.8892	392.5028	566.4809	819.2233
29	33.4504	35.9987	45.2189	52.9663	103.9659	148.6309	214.5828	312.0937	456.3032	669.4475	984.0680
30	34.7849	37.5387	47.5754	56.0849	113.2832	164.4940	241.3327	356.7868	530.3117	790.9480	1181.8816
31	36.1327	39.1018	50.0027	59.3283	123.3459	181.9434	271.2926	407.7370	616.1616	934.3186	1419.2579
32	37.4941	40.6883	52.5028	62.7015	134.2135	201.1378	304.8477	465.8202	715.7475	1103.4960	1704.1095
33	38.8690	42.2986	55.0778	66.2095	145.9506	222.2515	342.4294	532.0350	831.2671	1303.1253	2045.9314
34	40.2577	43.9331	57.7302	69.8579	158.6267	245.4767	384.5210	607.5199	965.2698	1538.6878	2456.1176
35	41.6603	45.5921	60.4621	73.6522	172.3168	271.0244	431.6635	693.5727	1120.7130	1816.6516	2948.3411
36	43.0769	47.2760	63.2759	77.5983	187.1021	299.1268	484.4631	791.6729	1301.0270	2144.6489	3539.0094
37	44.5076	48.9851	66.1742	81.7022	203.0703	330.0395	543.5987	903.5071	1510.1914	2531.6857	4247.8112
38	45.9527	50.7199	69.1594	85.9703	220.3159	364.0434	609.8305	1030.9981	1752.8220	2988.3891	5098.3735
39	47.4123	52.4807	72.2342	90.4091	238.9412	401.4478	684.0102	1176.3378	2034.2735	3527.2992	6119.0482
40	48.8864	54.2679	75.4013	95.0255	259.0565	442.5926	767.0914	1342.0251	2360.7572	4163.2130	7343.8578
41	50.3752	56.0819	78.6633	99.8265	280.7810	487.8518	860.1424	1530.9086	2739.4784	4913.5914	8813.6294
42	51.8790	57.9231	82.0232	104.8196	304.2435	537.6370	964.3595	1746.2358	3178.7949	5799.0378	10577.3553
43	53.3978	59.7920	85.4839	110.0124	329.5830	592.4007	1081.0826	1991.7088	3688.4021	6843.8646	12693.8263
44	54.9318	61.6889	89.0484	115.4129	356.9496	652.6408	1211.8125	2271.5481	4279.5465	8076.7603	15233.5916
45	56.4811	63.6142	92.7199	121.0294	386.5056	718.9048	1358.2300	2590.5648	4965.2739	9531.5771	18281.3099
46	58.0459	65.5684	96.5015	126.8706	418.4261	791.7953	1522.2176	2954.2439	5760.7177	11248.2610	21938.5719
47	59.6263	67.5519	100.3965	132.9454	452.9002	871.9749	1705.8838	3368.8380	6683.4326	13273.9480	26327.2863
48	61.2226	69.5652	104.4084	139.2632	490.1322	960.1723	1911.5898	3841.4753	7753.7818	15664.2586	31593.7436
49	62.8348	71.6087	108.5406	145.8337	530.3427	1057.1896	2141.9806	4380.2819	8995.3869	18484.8251	37913.4923
50	64.4632	73.6828	112.7969	152.6671	573.7702	1163.9085	2400.0182	4994.5213	10435.6488	21813.0937	45497.1908

value of 1 table like Table G–2.[2] Examine Table G–2 and Table G–4 to confirm that the following numbers were drawn from those tables:

From Table G–2		From Table G–4	
$i = 8\%, n = 0$	1.0000		
$i = 8\%, n = 1$	1.0800		
$i = 8\%, n = 2$	1.1664		
$i = 8\%, n = 3$	1.2597		
Total.	4.5061	$i = 8\%, n = 4$	4.5061

Minor differences may occur because the numbers in the tables have been rounded.

You can also use business calculators and spreadsheet computer programs to find the future values of annuities.

Observe that the future value in Table G–2 is 1.0000 when $n = 0$ but the future value in Table G–4 is 1.0000 when $n = 1$. Why does this apparent contradiction arise? When $n = 0$ in Table G–2, the future value is determined on the date that the single payment occurs. Thus, no interest is earned and the future value equals the payment. However, Table G–4 describes annuities with equal payments occurring each period. When $n = 1$, the annuity has only one payment, and its future value also equals 1 on the date of its final and only payment.

Summary of the Appendix in Terms of Learning Objectives

LO 1. The present value of a single amount to be received at a future date is the amount that could be invested now at the specified interest rate to yield that future value. The present value of an annuity is the amount that could be invested now at the specified interest rate to yield that series of equal periodic payments. Present value tables and business calculators simplify calculating present values.

LO 2. The future value of a single amount invested at a specified rate of interest is the amount that would accumulate at a future date. The future value of an annuity to be invested at the specified rate of interest is the amount that would accumulate at the date of the final equal periodic payment. Future value tables and business calculators simplify calculating future values.

---

[2] The formula for the future value of an annuity of 1 is:

$$f = \frac{(1 + i)^n - 1}{i}$$

Answers to the following questions are listed at the end of this appendix. Be sure that you decide which is the one best answer to each question *before* you check the answers.

LO 1   Smith & Company is considering making an investment that would pay $10,000 every six months for three years. The first payment would be received in six months. If Smith & Company requires an annual return of 8%, which of the following statements is true?

a.   In determining the future value of the annuity, $n = 6$ and $i = 8\%$.
b.   In determining the present value of the annuity, $n = 3$ and $i = 8\%$.
c.   Smith & Company should be willing to invest no more than $25,771.
d.   Smith & Company should be willing to invest no more than $46,229.
e.   Smith & Company should be willing to invest no more than $52,421.

LO 2   On May 9, 1991, Frank and Cindy Huber received news that they had inherited $150,000 from one of Cindy's distant relatives. They decided to deposit the money in a savings account that yields an 8% annual rate of interest. They plan on quitting their jobs to travel around the country when the inheritance equals $299,850. In what year will Frank and Cindy be able to quit working?

a.   1993.
b.   1999.
c.   2000.
d.   2001.
e.   2002.

Velmar Products Inc. is considering an investment that is expected to return $345,000 after four years. If the company demands a 10% return, how much will it be willing to pay for this investment?

Exercise G–1
Present value of an amount
(LO 1)

Fairmont Corporation just invested $176,500 in a project expected to earn an 18% annual rate of return. The earnings will be reinvested in the project for 15 years. How much cash will accumulate over that period?

Exercise G–2
Future value of an amount
(LO 2)

Mantel Manufacturing Company is considering an investment that will return $103,500 at the end of each year for 14 years. If the company demands an annual return of 14%, how much should it be willing to pay?

Exercise G–3
Present value of an annuity
(LO 1)

Diane Belardi is planning to open an individual retirement account in which she will invest $2,100 annually at the end of each year. Belardi plans to retire after making 25 annual investments in a program that earns a return of 12%. How much will be in the account on the date of the final investment?

Exercise G–4
Future value of an annuity
(LO 2)

Exercise G–5
Interest rate on an
investment
(LO 1)

Mary Dolan has been offered the possibility of investing $0.3083 for 30 years, after which she will be paid $1. What annual rate of interest will she earn? (Use Table G–1 to find the answer.)

Exercise G–6
Number of periods of an
investment
(LO 1)

Conrad Wachs has been offered the possibility of investing $0.0431 at 18% per year. How many years must Wachs wait to receive $1? (Use Table G–1 to find the answer.)

Exercise G–7
Number of periods of an
investment
(LO 2)

Bruce Muldoon expects to invest $1 at 20% and hold the investment until it equals $850.5622. How many years will pass before it reaches that amount? (Use Table G–2 to find the answer.)

Exercise G–8
Interest rate on an
investment
(LO 2)

Mike Rooney expects to invest $1 and leave it on deposit for 28 years. At that time, he will receive $8.6271. What rate of interest will Rooney earn? (Use Table G–2 to find the answer.)

Exercise G–9
Interest rate on an
investment
(LO 1)

Diane Attebury expects an immediate investment of $5.6685 to return $1 annually for 16 years, with the first payment to be received after one year. What rate of interest will Attebury earn? (Use Table G–3 to find the answer.)

Exercise G–10
Number of periods of an
investment
(LO 1)

Michael Alper expects an investment of $7.0199 to return $1 annually for several years. If the investment earns a return of 14%, how many annual payments will he receive? (Use Table G–3 to find the answer.)

Exercise G–11
Interest rate on an
investment
(LO 2)

Pat Brenner expects to invest $1 annually for 35 years and have an accumulated value of $2,948.3411 on the date of the final payment. If this result occurs, what rate of interest will Brenner earn? (Use Table G–4 to find the answer.)

Exercise G–12
Number of periods of an
investment
(LO 2)

Sam Stanfield expects to invest $1 annually in a fund that will earn 12%. How many annual investments must Stanfield make to accumulate $1,911.5898 on the date of the final payment? (Use Table G–4 to find the answer.)

Exercise G–13
Present value of an
annuity
(LO 1)

Daphne Rankin financed a new automobile by paying $2,500 cash and agreeing to make 36 monthly payments of $500 each, with the first payment to be made one month after the purchase. The loan bears interest at an annual rate of 18% compounded monthly. What was the cost of the automobile?

David Jones deposited $8,500 in a savings account that earns interest at an annual rate of 16%, compounded quarterly. The $8,500 and its earned interest must remain in the account five years before they can be withdrawn. How much money will be in the account at the end of the five years?

Exercise G–14
Future value of an amount
(LO 2)

Jane Mitchell plans to have $145 withheld from her monthly paycheck and deposited in a savings account that earns 12% annually, compounded monthly. If Mitchell continues with her plan for three years, how much will accumulate in the account on the date of the final deposit?

Exercise G–15
Future value of an annuity
(LO 2)

Campton Company plans to issue 18%, 15-year, $500,000 par value bonds payable that pay interest semiannually on June 30 and December 31. The bonds are dated December 31, 1993, and will be issued on that date. If the market rate of interest for the bonds is 16% on the date of issue, how much cash will the company receive?

Exercise G–16
Present value of bonds
(LO 1)

Medical Equipment Company has decided to establish a fund that will be used after five years to replace a productive facility. The company makes an initial contribution of $230,000 to the fund and plans to make quarterly contributions of $75,000 beginning in three months. The fund is expected to earn 16%, compounded quarterly. How much will be in the fund after five years?

Exercise G–17
Future value of a single amount and an annuity
(LO 2)

Trevor Corporation expects to earn 20% per year on an investment that will pay back $1.2 million after eight years. Use Table G–2 to calculate the present value of the investment.

Exercise G–18
Present value of an amount
(LO 1)

Crawford Company invests $140,000 at 10% per year for 10 years. Use Table G–1 to calculate the future value of the investment after 10 years.

Exercise G–19
Future value of an amount
(LO 2)

LO 1 *(e)*   LO 2 *(c)*

Answers to Objective
Review Questions

Accounting for Corporate Income Taxes

Topical Coverage

Taxes are as unavoidable as tomorrow's sunrise. Business managers and owners need to know about income taxes so they can avoid paying more than the minimum required by the law without violating its requirements.

F inancial statements for a business should be prepared in accordance with generally accepted accounting principles. Income tax returns, on the other hand, must be prepared in accordance with income tax laws. As a result, a corporation's *income before taxes* measured in accordance with generally accepted accounting principles is almost never the same as *taxable income* calculated on income tax returns.

Learning Objectives

After studying Appendix H, you should be able to:

1. Explain why income taxes for accounting purposes may be different from income taxes for tax purposes.
2. Prepare an income tax schedule and journal entries for a company where timing differences exist between accounting and taxable income.

Accounting and Taxable Income

You have already learned how to determine net income under GAAP for a profit-oriented entity. However, the determination of taxable income for a corporation, while starting with the accounting net income, is done using the Canadian Income Tax Act. Almost always, this results in taxable income being different from the GAAP accounting income.

LO 1 Explain why income taxes for accounting purposes may be different from income taxes for tax purposes.

A major difference between accounting income and taxable income results from what are known as timing differences. These arise because some items are included as revenue or expense in one period under GAAP, whereas they are included in a different period under the income tax rules. For example:

1. The application of accounting principles for installment sales requires that gross profit on these sales is recognized in accounting income before it is recognized in taxable income under the income tax rules.
2. Accounting principles require an estimate of future costs, such as costs of making good on guarantees; they also require a deduction of such costs from revenue in the year the guaranteed goods are sold. However, tax rules do not permit the deduction of such costs until they are actually incurred.
3. Reported net income also differs from taxable income because the taxpayer uses a method or procedure believed to fairly reflect periodic net income for accounting purposes, but is required to use a different method of procedure for tax purposes. For example, the last-in, first-out inventory method of cost allocation may be used for accounting purposes, but is not permitted for tax purposes. Likewise, many companies use straight-line amortization for accounting purposes but are required to use a different procedure, called *capital cost allowances*, for tax purposes.

Capital Cost Allowances

Depreciation (amortization) accounting has been greatly influenced by income tax laws. The 1948 Income Tax Act replaced the complex body of rules that had developed for the purpose of limiting the amount of amortization allowed for tax purposes. The act defined and set a limit on amounts which could be deducted, for tax purposes, in respect to the cost of amortizable assets. These amounts are known as *capital cost allowances* (CCA).

The capital cost allowances are identical in nature and purpose with the accountants' concept of amortization and are based on the declining-balance method, discussed in Chapter 10. For tax purposes, the taxpayer may claim the maximum allowed or any part thereof in any year regardless of the amortization method and the amounts used in the accounting records.

Although capital cost allowances are based on the declining-balance method, certain procedures have been set out by the Regulations of the Act. The more important of these are as follows:

1. All amortizable assets are grouped into a comparatively small number of classes and a maximum rate allowed is prescribed for each group. The assets most commonly in use are set out below according to the class to which they belong, with the maximum rate of allowance for each such class (as at the time of writing).

    Class 1 (4%): Buildings or other structures.

    Class 7 (15%): Ships, scows, canoes, and rowboats.

    Class 8 (20%): Machinery, equipment, and furniture.

    Class 10 (30%): Automobiles, trucks, tractors, and computer hardware.

2. The assets of a designated class are considered to form a separate pool of costs. The costs of asset additions are added to their respective pools of unamortized capital cost. When assets are disposed of, the proceeds (up to the original cost) received from disposal are deducted from the proper pool. The balance of each pool of costs is also diminished by the accumulated capital cost allowance claimed. A capital cost allowance is claimed on the balance, referred to as the *unamortized capital cost* (UCC), in the pool at the end of the fiscal year. However, when there are net additions to the pool, only one half of the amount added is used in the calculation of CCA in the year of the net additions. The effect is that the assets are assumed to have been acquired halfway through the fiscal year.

3. "Losses" and "gains" on disposal of individual assets disappear into the pool of unamortized capital costs except when an asset is sold for more than its capital cost. In this case, proceeds of disposal in excess of the capital cost of the asset are normally treated as a capital gain. Where the proceeds of disposal (excluding the capital gain, if any) exceed the unamortized capital cost of the class immediately before the sale, the amount of the excess is treated as a "recapture" of capital cost allowances previously made. Such a recapture is considered as ordinary income. When all of the assets in a class are disposed of and the proceeds are less than the unamortized capital cost of the class immediately before the sale, the proceeds less the unamortized capital cost may be deducted in determining the year's taxable income.

Companies must, with few exceptions, use capital cost allowances for tax purposes, but commonly use straight-line amortization in their accounting records. A problem arising from this practice is discussed in the next section.

When one accounting procedure is required for tax purposes and a different procedure is used in the accounting records, a problem arises as to how much income tax expense should be deducted each year on the income statement. If the tax actually incurred in such situations is deducted, reported net income often varies from year to year due to the postponement and later payment of taxes. Consequently, in such cases, since shareholders may be misled by these variations, many accountants are of the opinion that income taxes should be allocated in such a way that any distortion resulting from postponing taxes is removed from the income statement.

Taxes and the Distortion of Net Income

LO 2 Prepare an income tax schedule and journal entries when timing differences exist.

To appreciate the problem involved here, assume that a corporation has installed a $100,000 machine, the product of which will produce a half-million dollars of revenue in each of the succeeding four years and $80,000 of income before amortization and taxes. Assume further that the company must pay income taxes at a 40% rate (round number assumed for easy calculation) and that it plans to use straight-line amortization in its records but the capital cost allowance for tax purposes. If the machine has a four-year life and a $10,000 salvage value and if the maximum permitted capital cost allowance rate on this particular machine is 50%, annual amortization calculated by each method will be as follows:

Year	Straight-Line	Capital Cost Allowance
1993	$22,500	$25,000
1994	22,500	37,500
1995	22,500	18,750
1996	22,500	8,750*
Totals	$90,000	$90,000

* Use $8,750 in order to match salvage value.
CCA allowed is $9,375.

In the year of acquisition, only one half of the CCA otherwise allowed may be claimed. In subsequent years, CCA may be claimed up to the maximum amounts allowed.

Since the company uses capital cost allowance for tax purposes, it will be liable for $22,000 of income tax on the first year's income, $17,000 on the second, $24,500 on the third, and $28,500 on the fourth. The calculation of these taxes is shown in Illustration H–1.

Furthermore, if the company were to deduct its actual tax payable each year in arriving at income to be reported to its shareholders, it would report the amounts shown in Illustration H–2.

Observe in Illustrations H–1 and H–2 that total amortization, $90,000, is the same whether calculated by the straight-line or the declining-balance method. Also note that the total tax paid over the four years, $92,000, is the same in each case. Then note the distortion of the final income figures in Illustration H–2 due to the postponement of taxes.

ILLUSTRATION H–1

Calculation of Income Taxes

Annual Income Taxes	1993	1994	1995	1996	Total
Income before amortization and income taxes	$80,000	$80,000	$80,000	$80,000	$320,000
Amortization for tax purposes (declining-balance)/CCA	25,000	37,500	18,750	8,750	90,000
Taxable income	$55,000	$42,500	$61,250	$71,250	$230,000
Annual income taxes (40% of taxable income).	$22,000	$17,000	$24,500	$28,500	$ 92,000

ILLUSTRATION H–2

Calculation of Remaining Income

Income after Deducting Actual Tax Liabilities	1993	1994	1995	1996	Total
Income before amortization and income taxes	$80,000	$80,000	$80,000	$80,000	$320,000
Amortization per books (straight-line) . .	22,500	22,500	22,500	22,500	90,000
Income before taxes	57,500	57,500	57,500	57,500	230,000
Income taxes (actual liability of each year)	22,000	17,000	24,500	28,500	92,000
Remaining income	$35,500	$40,500	$33,000	$29,000	$138,000

If this company should report successive annual income figures of $35,500, $40,500, $33,000, and then $29,000, some of its shareholders might be misled as to the company's earnings trend. Consequently, in cases such as this, many accountants think income taxes should be allocated so that the distortion caused by the postponement of taxes is removed from the income statement. These accountants advocate that

when one accounting procedure is used in the accounting records and a different procedure is used for tax purposes, the tax expense deducted on the income statement should not be the actual tax liability but the amount that would be payable if the procedure used in the records were also used in calculating the tax.

If the foregoing is applied in this case, the corporation will report to its shareholders in each of the four years the amounts of income shown in Illustration H–3.

In examining Illustration H–2, recall that the company's taxes payable are actually $22,000 in the first year, $17,000 in the second, $24,500 in the third, and $28,500 in the fourth, a total of $92,000. Then observe that when this $92,000 liability is allocated evenly over the four years, the distortion of the annual net incomes due to the postponement of taxes is removed from the published income statements.

ILLUSTRATION H–3

Tax Expense Based on Accounting Income					
Net Income That Should Be Reported to Shareholders	**1993**	**1994**	**1995**	**1996**	**Total**
Income before amortization and income taxes.	$80,000	$80,000	$80,000	$80,000	$320,000
Amortization per books (straight-line) . .	22,500	22,500	22,500	22,500	90,000
Income before taxes	57,500	57,500	57,500	57,500	230,000
Income taxes (amounts based on straight-line amortization)	23,000	23,000	23,000	23,000	92,000
Net income.	$34,500	$34,500	$34,500	$34,500	$138,000

When income taxes are allocated as in Illustration H–3, the tax payable for each year and the deferred income tax are recorded with an adjusting entry. The adjusting entries for the four years of Illustration H–2 and the entries in General Journal form for the payment of the taxes (without explanations) are as follows:

Entries for the Allocation of Taxes

1993	Income Tax Expense	23,000	
	Income Taxes Payable		22,000
	Deferred Income Tax		1,000
	Income Taxes Payable.	22,000	
	Cash		22,000
1994	Income Tax Expense	23,000	
	Income Taxes Payable		17,000
	Deferred Income Tax		6,000
	Income Taxes Payable.	17,000	
	Cash		17,000
1995	Income Tax Expense	23,000	
	Deferred Income Tax	1,500	
	Income Taxes Payable		24,500
	Income Taxes Payable.	24,500	
	Cash		24,500
1996	Income Tax Expense	23,000	
	Deferred Income Tax	5,500	
	Income Taxes Payable		28,500
	Income Taxes Payable.	28,500	
	Cash		28,500

Note: To simplify the illustration, it is assumed that the entire year's tax liability is paid at one time. However, corporations are usually required to pay estimated taxes on a monthly basis.

In the entries the $23,000 debited to Income Tax Expense each year is the amount that is deducted on the income statement in reporting annual net income. Also, the amount credited to Income Taxes Payable each year is the actual tax liability of that year.

Observe in the entries that since the actual tax payable in each of the first two years is less than the amount debited to Income Tax Expense, the difference is credited to *Deferred Income Tax*. Then note that in the last two years, because the actual liability each year is greater than the debit to Income Tax Expense, the difference is debited to Deferred Income Tax. Now observe in the following illustration of the company's Deferred Income Tax account that the debits and credits exactly balance each other out over the four-year period:

Deferred Income Tax

Year	Explanation	Debit	Credit	Balance
1993			1,000	1,000
1994			6,000	7,000
1995		1,500		5,500
1996		5,500		–0–

In passing, it should be observed that many accountants believe the interests of government, business, and the public would be better served if there were more uniformity between taxable income and reported net income. However, since the federal income tax is designed to serve other purposes in addition to raising revenue, it is apt to be some time before this is achieved.

Before concluding this appendix on income taxes, we should mention some additional features of the rules that govern accounting for income taxes.

1. In the example above, we assumed an income tax rate of 40% in each year. However, if the income tax rate changes, we use the rate in effect for that year. When the timing difference reverses, the average rate over the accumulation period should be used to avoid throwing the deferred tax amount into a debit balance (this point is covered more thoroughly in later courses).

2. In the example, 1993 income before taxes was *more than* taxable income because of a timing difference that was expected to reverse in 1995 or 1996. As a result, we recognized a deferred tax balance on the December 31, 1993, balance sheet. In other situations, just the opposite kind of timing difference may occur. In other words, a timing difference that will reverse in the future may cause income before taxes to be *less than* taxable income. These latter situations may, under certain conditions, result in the recognition of a deferred tax debit.

3. The Deferred Income Tax account balance may be reported as a long-term liability or as a current liability, depending on how far in the future the amount will reverse.

4. Federal tax laws generally require corporations to estimate their current year's tax liability and make advance payments of the estimated amount before the final tax return is filed. As a result, the end-of-year entries to record income taxes, such as those shown above, often have to be altered to take into consideration any previously recorded prepayments.

5. The income tax rate varies depending on the type of organization, small or large, and manufacturing or nonmanufacturing.

6. Intercorporation dividends are not taxable.

Exercises

Indicate which of the following items might cause timing differences for a corporation:

a. Sales on account.
b. Capital cost allowances.
c. Wages paid to employees.
d. Property taxes.
e. Installment sales.
f. Cost of goods sold.
g. Warranty expenses.
h. Rents received in advance.
i. Cash sales.

Exercise H–1
Timing differences
(LO 1)

a. Explain why accounting income is usually different from taxable income.
b. What reasons can you give for the two sets of rules?

Exercise H–2
Taxable vs. accounting income
(LO 1)

Vacon Inc. began operations on January 1, 1993. During 1993, Vacon's operations resulted in a current tax payable of $350,000. In addition, Vacon sold land for $210,000 that had cost $70,000. The sale qualified as an installment sale for tax purposes, so the gain was subject to tax as cash was received. The purchaser agreed to pay for the land on June 1, 1994. Present the December 31, 1993, entry to record Vacon Inc.'s income taxes. Assume a tax rate of 45% and that the profit on the land is fully taxable.

Exercise H–3
Recording corporate income tax expense
(LO 2)

Buster Corporation would have had identical accounting and taxable income for the three years 1993–1995 were it not for the fact that for tax purposes an operational asset that cost $24,000 was amortized ³⁄₆, ²⁄₆, ¹⁄₆ (assumed for problem purposes to be acceptable), whereas for accounting purposes, the straight-line method was used. The asset has a three-year operational life and no residual value. Income before amortization and income taxes for the years concerned follow:

Exercise H–4
Recording corporate income tax expense
(LO 2)

	1993	1994	1995
Pretax accounting income (before amortization)	$40,000	$45,000	$50,000

Assume an income tax rate of 40% for each year.

Required
1. Calculate the accounting and taxable income for each year.
2. Prepare journal entries to record the income tax expense for each year.

Exercise H-5
Analyze timing
differences; entries
(LO 2)

Castor Corporation reports the following information for the year ended December 31, 1993:

Revenue	$525,000
Expenses	390,000
Net income before tax	$135,000

Additional information:

a. Revenues (above) do not include $30,000 of rent which is taxable in 1993 but was unearned at the end of 1993.
b. Capital cost allowances for 1993 are $32,000 greater than the amortization expense included above.
c. Expenses (above) include $12,000 of estimated warranty expenses which are not deductible for tax purposes in 1993.
d. Assume an income tax rate of 40%.

Prepare a journal entry to record income taxes for Castor Corporation on December 31, 1993.

Exercise H-6
Timing differences; entries
(LO 2)

Income tax returns on Vastly Corporation reflected the following:

	Year Ended Dec. 31		
	1993	1994	1995
Royalty income	$180,000		
Investment income	30,000	$20,000	$40,000
Rent income	10,000	10,000	10,000
	$220,000	$30,000	$50,000
Deductible expenses	30,000	20,000	20,000
Taxable income	$190,000	$10,000	$30,000

Assume the average income tax rate for each year was 40%.

The only differences between taxable income on the tax returns and the pre-tax accounting income relate to royalty income. For accounting purposes, royalty income was recognized ratably (equally) over the three-year period.

Required

Give journal entries such as would appear at the end of each year to reflect income tax and allocation.

(CGA adapted)

Financial Statements and Related Disclosures from Bombardier Inc.'s 1992 Annual Report

Bombardier Inc. is a huge corporation. It seems impossible that a person could learn very much about it from only a few pages. But with the accounting knowledge you are learning, you will find a wealth of information in this annual report.

Report to Shareholders

Fifty years ago, on July 10, 1942, Joseph-Armand Bombardier founded *L'Auto-Neige Bombardier Limitée* to build and sell the B7, a tracked vehicle he had invented. He laid the foundation for a company that has not stopped growing, diversifying and expanding geographically — to become a recognized leader on the international scene.

We wish to highlight the half-century of unwavering effort which has enabled *Bombardier* to achieve technological, industrial and commercial leadership in three major manufacturing business segments: transportation equipment, aerospace and motorized consumer products.

As we account for the past year of operations, this is also an appropriate occasion to look back on the four major stages of our company's progress over the last five decades.

From 1942 to 1963, Joseph-Armand Bombardier established the company's foundation. This period marked the first successes of his large snowmobiles, followed by the development of a wide range of industrial tracked vehicles. Then came the 1959 launch of the Ski-Doo snowmobile, a recreational vehicle that would enjoy great popularity from the early 1960s onwards.

The second stage, from 1964 to 1973, saw the snowmobile market boom. *Bombardier* then pursued an aggressive commercial strategy and carried out a vertical integration which led to the 1970 acquisition of *Rotax*, of Austria. However, the 1973 energy crisis put an end to the snowmobile boom.

Between 1974 and 1986, our company sought to diversify. Starting with the Montréal subway car contract, *Bombardier* carved out a leading position in the transportation equipment industry. The 1982 New York subway contract confirmed beyond any doubt that the company had established itself firmly in this promising field.

With the purchase of *Canadair* in 1986, *Bombardier* made its debut in yet another key industry: aerospace. This fourth stage, still under way today, has seen our company vigorously expanding, through a series of strategic acquisitions: *BN* in Belgium, *ANF-Industrie* in France, *Shorts* in Northern Ireland, *Learjet* in the United States, *Prorail* in England, and lastly, in 1992, *UTDC* and *de Havilland* in Canada.

1991-92 was yet another important year in *Bombardier*'s progress. The rollout of the Canadair Regional Jet and the replacement of the French fleet of amphibious aircraft by our new CL-415 were major accomplishments. Two transactions completed in the current fiscal year with the Government of Ontario resulted in the purchase of transportation equipment manufacturer *UTDC* and aircraft manufacturer *de Havilland*, thereby broadening *Bombardier*'s Canadian industrial base.

The acquisition of *de Havilland* division of The Boeing Company fits perfectly with our growth strategy, which aims to reinforce our leadership position for specific products in specific markets. The de Havilland Dash 8 turboprop is an ideal counterpart to the Canadair Regional Jet airliner. In the 50-passenger-or-less category, *Bombardier* is now able to offer a complete family of regional aircraft. In addition, *Canadair* and *de Havilland* can now capitalize on technical and commercial synergies — in the same way that extremely productive synergies have been developed with *Shorts* and *Learjet*.

Business jets, regional aircraft and the manufacture of components for major engine and airframe manufacturers represent the three pillars of our progress in aerospace. Such diversification has given us greater staying power during difficult times, while allowing us to make the most of favourable market conditions as they emerge.

Maintaining this position requires a dynamic approach to the development of new programs and new-generation products. The development of the mid-size Learjet 60 and the Global Express project are two examples of this approach, in the business jet sector. They are consistent with our long-term vision, in which we seek to enlarge specific product lines to strengthen our lead in specific market niches.

**Laurent Beaudoin,
Chairman and
Chief Executive
Officer**

Bombardier has many other strengths in this high-technology field. We are the only main airframe manufacturer with integrated manufacturing facilities in several countries. The fact that we are established in Europe as well as in North America reinforces our present alliances, and enhances our ability to forge new partnerships on both sides of the Atlantic. Compared with most of its competitors, *Bombardier* also has the advantage of being less dependent on defence contracts for its financial stability. This is increasingly important in the current period of accelerated rationalization of military expenditures.

In aerospace, where achieving critical mass is necessary for companies who wish to successfully compete in increasingly globalized markets, *Bombardier* ranks seventh among the world's airframe manufacturers in the civilian aircraft market.

**Raymond Royer,
President and
Chief Operating
Officer**

Similar dynamics apply to transportation equipment. *Bombardier*, which is already the North American leader, has considerably strengthened its position with the purchase of *UTDC*. And overseas, a recent European Commission study ranks *Bombardier* among the ten largest European manufacturers.

Our company can match even its most diversified competitors in this field. Our product line ranges from push-pull commuter cars to shuttle-train cars for the English Channel tunnel, and from subway cars to self-propelled urban transit systems, including low-floor tramways. The *UTDC* acquisition enables *Bombardier* to offer an even wider product range in rolling stock, particularly in automatic light rail transit.

In this sector, we operate manufacturing plants in four European countries in addition to Canadian and American plants. This industrial base gives us greater flexibility and ability to adapt. Just as effective synergies have been established in aerospace, in the same way *Bombardier* can optimize the strengths of each of its transportation equipment divisions and subsidiaries in Europe, Canada and the United States.

These synergies are also evident in our research and development activities. This ability is increasingly important, as engineering becomes more and more the responsibility of the transportation equipment manufacturers. Building on its assembly expertise, *Bombardier* has become a designer as well, notably in the development of prototype and pre-production vehicles for the next generations of New York and Paris subway equipment. To maintain a leading position, *Bombardier* is going beyond technology transfers and product adaptation, to meet the more rigorous demands of transportation authori-

ties regarding performance, safety and environmental protection.

Generally speaking, 1991-92 was characterized by major research and development efforts in the majority of our current projects. For example, in building the shuttle trains for the English Channel tunnel, the *Mass Transit Division* together with *BN* and *ANF-Industrie* have had to face major challenges, given the unique conditions under which the vehicles will be operated.

While these efforts may weigh on *Bombardier*'s short-term profitability in this sector, it is clear that in the medium term the technological autonomy we are gaining will guarantee *Bombardier*'s growth in a rapidly changing market.

In the motorized consumer products segment, *Bombardier* has taken firm measures to rapidly re-establish its lead and to gain back its market share. Our first objective — to reduce the inventory of snowmobiles that had accumulated by the end of last year — has been met. The immediate effect of this is a considerable reduction in the operating deficit.

As for watercraft, *Bombardier* has achieved a significant increase of the market share with an innovative product which meets the most stringent demands of users. While snowmobiles are limited to snowy regions, the Sea-Doo watercraft enjoys a much wider market. Thus, our watercraft sales network now extends to some fifty countries.

For both snowmobiles and watercraft, *Bombardier* has pursued technical improvement programs that prepare the way for the future. In our watercraft business, we have followed a corporate responsibility strategy similar to our approach to the snowmobile business. As a manufacturer, we encourage prevention and the adoption of regulations to protect the consumer and the environment.

As the new year begins, *Bombardier* has a well-filled order book, and the company is strategically placed in all of its markets to take advantage of the economic recovery as soon as it firms up. With our geographic diversification and our manufacturing flexibility, we have weathered the recession of the past two years with very little difficulty. The consolidation of our existing assets and expansion based on a strategic vision have allowed us to maintain a healthy financial position.

The buoyancy of *Bombardier*'s stock is an excellent barometer of our financial strength. A new share issue made during the year to ensure stability was quickly sold, testifying to investor confidence in the future of our company.

To manage our recent North American expansion efficiently, to pursue our European growth, and to take full advantage of our geographic diversification in aerospace and transportation equipment, we have made changes in our management structure.

We have created the *Aerospace Group-North America* to oversee the activities of *Canadair*, *Learjet* and *de Havilland*. Mr. Robert E. Brown was appointed President of this group, and remains President of *Canadair*. European activities in aerospace will continue to be carried out by the *Shorts Group*, under Mr. Roy W.R. McNulty as President.

In transportation equipment, given the addition of *UTDC* and the growth prospects in North America — notably with the TGV — all North American activities now fall under Mr. Jean-Yves Leblanc, President of the *Transportation Equipment Group – North America*. This group includes *UTDC Systems*, *Auburn Technology*, *TGI*, and the La Pocatière, Thunder Bay and Barre plants. Mr. Michel de Lambert, Managing Director of *Bombardier Eurorail*, which includes *BN* Division, *ANF-Industrie*, *Bombardier Prorail* and *Bombardier-Wien*, is now directly responsible for European activities.

In conclusion, we wish to recognize the indispensable role of all our employees, both past and present, at every level of the company, in *Bombardier*'s growth through the years. Without their daily commitment and their staunch professionalism, it would have been impossible to go this far. Management fully recognizes this, and thanks the people of *Bombardier*.

As her term as Director comes to a close, we also wish to thank the Right Honourable Jeanne Sauvé for the exceptional contribution she has made to *Bombardier* over the years. Her judicious advice has been invaluable and we wish to express our deepest gratitude.

Bombardier can now rely in full confidence on the organization it has built. With the projects already under way, we can look forward optimistically to the decade ahead. We will continue to grow and innovate while remaining faithful to our strategic orientations and our fundamental objectives.

On behalf of the Board of Directors,

Laurent Beaudoin, FCA
Chairman and
Chief Executive Officer

Raymond Royer, CA
President and
Chief Operating Officer

Montréal, Canada
May 19, 1992

Historical Financial Summary

Revenues by continuing industry segments
[millions of dollars]

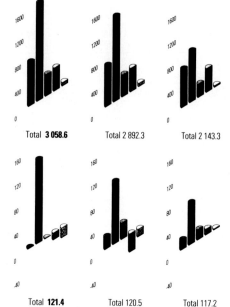

Total **3 058.6**   Total 2 892.3   Total 2 143.3

Income (loss) by continuing industry segments
[millions of dollars]

■ Transportation equipment
■ Aerospace
■ Defence
■ Motorized consumer products
▓ Bombardier Capital Group

Total **121.4**   Total 120.5   Total 117.2

Operations summary
[millions of dollars]

For the years ended January 31	1992	1991	1990
Revenues by continuing industry segments			
Transportation equipment	$ 725.6	$ 697.1	$ 639.5
Aerospace	1 519.1	1 382.9	840.6
Defence	366.2	358.3	214.7
Motorized consumer products	391.5	398.0	399.0
Bombardier Capital Group	56.2	56.0	49.5
Total	$ 3 058.6	$ 2 892.3	$ 2 143.3
Income (loss) by continuing industry segments			
Transportation equipment	$ 3.5	$ 20.1	$ 16.5
Aerospace	137.2	112.9	69.8
Defence	2.0	28.5	17.8
Motorized consumer products	(9.1)	(29.5)	10.1
Bombardier Capital Group	(12.2)	(11.5)	3.0
Total	121.4	120.5	117.2
Income taxes	13.7	20.4	25.7
Income from continuing operations	107.7	100.1	91.5
Income (loss) from discontinued operations	—	—	—
Net income	$ 107.7	$ 100.1	$ 91.5
Per common share (dollars)			
Income from continuing operations	0.73	0.71	0.68
Net income	0.73	0.71	0.68

Total 1 426.0 Total 1 405.8 Total 998.6 Total 554.9 Total 405.1 Total 395.8 Total 414.5

Total 108.8 Total 102.8 Total 54.2 Total 27.0 Total 40.6 Total 29.1 Total 11.6

1989	1988	1987	1986	1985	1984	1983
$ 311.3	$ 459.8	$ 374.2	$ 289.3	$ 197.3	$ 131.4	$ 173.9
630.7	554.7	287.6	—	—	—	—
143.9	100.8	92.0	64.7	33.7	132.8	90.5
310.3	273.8	235.7	194.7	169.7	130.2	148.4
29.8	16.7	9.1	6.2	4.4	1.4	1.7
$ 1 426.0	$ 1 405.8	$ 998.6	$ 554.9	$ 405.1	$ 395.8	$ 414.5
$ 46.3	$ 49.7	$ 34.1	$ 22.5	$ 32.5	$ 27.1	$ 20.2
34.8	39.7	15.4	—	—	—	—
7.4	0.6	0.4	2.5	3.5	15.3	8.7
14.6	10.7	5.1	0.6	3.7	(14.6)	(19.2)
5.7	2.1	(0.8)	1.4	0.9	1.3	1.9
108.8	102.8	54.2	27.0	40.6	29.1	11.6
19.9	23.8	11.4	10.8	16.2	11.4	5.2
88.9	79.0	42.8	16.2	24.4	17.7	6.4
(20.6)	(12.2)	3.3	(0.1)	(14.3)	(11.4)	(0.3)
$ 68.3	$ 66.8	$ 46.1	$ 16.1	$ 10.1	$ 6.3	$ 6.1
0.68	0.60	0.38	0.17	0.27	0.20	0.07
0.52	0.50	0.41	0.17	0.11	0.07	0.07

Historical Financial Summary (continued)

Consolidated balance sheets
[millions of dollars]

As at January 31	1992	1991	1990
Bombardier Inc. consolidated			
Cash and term deposits	$ 179.2	$ 87.5	$ 84.0
Accounts receivable	360.1	413.7	428.8
Financing receivables and property under leases	640.8	491.3	458.0
Inventories	1 215.7	992.7	583.5
Prepaid expenses	13.6	9.5	12.2
Fixed assets	626.8	533.5	335.7
Other assets	34.5	35.3	34.8
Total assets	**$ 3 070.7**	$ 2 563.5	$ 1 937.0
Short-term borrowings	$ 640.1	$ 558.2	$ 376.8
Accounts payable and accrued liabilities	883.2	818.1	671.1
Income taxes	18.2	13.7	13.3
Net advances on a contract	—	—	—
Long-term debt	381.2	265.9	147.0
Other long-term liabilities	54.9	68.0	55.6
Convertible notes	193.8	145.4	50.4
Preferred shares	35.7	37.4	157.7
Common shareholders' equity	863.6	656.8	465.1
Total liabilities and shareholders' equity	**$ 3 070.7**	$ 2 563.5	$ 1 937.0
Bombardier			
Cash and term deposits	$ 177.6	$ 87.2	$ 79.7
Accounts receivable	366.0	413.6	428.8
Inventories	1 215.7	992.7	583.5
Prepaid expenses	13.6	9.5	12.2
Fixed assets	603.8	514.7	327.5
Investment in BCG	87.0	68.5	60.4
Other assets	34.5	35.3	34.8
Total assets	**$ 2 498.2**	$ 2 121.5	$ 1 526.9
Short-term borrowings	$ 105.1	$ 135.6	$ 134.4
Accounts payable and accrued liabilities	846.2	799.2	622.0
Income taxes	17.7	13.2	13.3
Net advances on a contract	—	—	—
Long-term debt	381.2	265.9	147.0
Other long-term liabilities	54.9	68.0	55.6
Convertible notes	193.8	145.4	50.4
Preferred shares	35.7	37.4	39.1
Common shareholders' equity	863.6	656.8	465.1
Total liabilities and shareholders' equity	**$ 2 498.2**	$ 2 121.5	$ 1 526.9
Bombardier Capital Group			
Cash and term deposits	$ 1.6	$ 0.3	$ 4.3
Financing receivables and property under leases	640.8	491.4	458.0
Fixed assets	23.0	18.8	8.2
Total assets	**$ 665.4**	$ 510.5	$ 470.5
Short-term borrowings	$ 535.0	$ 422.6	$ 242.4
Accounts payable and accrued liabilities	42.9	18.9	49.1
Income taxes	0.5	0.5	—
Advances from related parties	31.3	23.9	14.6
Preferred shares	—	—	118.6
Common shareholders' equity	55.7	44.6	45.8
Total liabilities and shareholders' equity	**$ 665.4**	$ 510.5	$ 470.5

	1989	1988	1987	1986	1985	1984	1983
	$ 150.0	$ 116.7	$ 161.3	$ 6.9	$ 0.6	$ 2.5	$ 1.7
	174.0	119.1	144.6	111.3	100.9	90.8	72.8
	307.5	202.1	94.0	76.0	50.9	42.2	45.1
	220.2	247.3	114.9	152.3	167.5	117.2	149.0
	9.9	8.9	12.9	7.4	6.2	4.1	4.9
	262.1	200.6	181.0	111.8	124.3	98.8	87.7
	27.0	46.4	35.4	13.5	12.7	11.5	10.0
	$ 1 150.7	$ 941.1	$ 744.1	$ 479.2	$ 463.1	$ 367.1	$ 371.2
	$ 153.2	$ 48.6	$ 80.0	$ 63.2	$ 39.6	$ 35.8	$ 51.4
	341.5	314.1	252.5	136.0	108.2	74.9	97.4
	5.7	1.3	4.9	4.3	2.4	0.7	0.3
	—	—	—	65.8	132.6	77.0	32.6
	70.6	65.4	74.1	35.2	39.8	49.0	66.9
	54.5	9.5	8.2	7.4	6.6	6.2	5.8
	—	—	—	—	—	—	—
	158.3	167.5	40.0				
	366.9	334.7	284.4	167.3	133.9	123.5	116.8
	$ 1 150.7	$ 941.1	$ 744.1	$ 479.2	$ 463.1	$ 367.1	$ 371.2
	$ 150.0	$ 109.9	$ 161.3	$ 6.9	$ —	$ —	$ —
	174.0	119.1	144.6	111.3	100.9	90.8	72.8
	220.2	247.3	114.9	152.3	167.5	117.2	149.0
	9.9	8.9	12.9	7.4	6.2	4.1	4.9
	259.9	198.9	180.4	111.8	124.3	98.8	87.7
	30.4	22.7	19.1	16.8	15.6	14.9	13.7
	27.0	46.4	35.4	13.5	12.7	11.5	10.0
	$ 871.4	$ 753.2	$ 668.6	$ 420.0	$ 427.2	$ 337.3	$ 338.1
	$ 5.4	$ 5.1	$ 5.8	$ 5.3	$ 4.6	$ 7.6	$ 19.8
	328.3	297.2	251.2	134.7	107.3	73.3	95.9
	5.7	1.3	4.9	4.3	2.4	0.7	0.3
	—	—	—	65.8	132.6	77.0	32.6
	70.6	65.4	74.1	35.2	39.8	49.0	66.9
	54.5	9.5	8.2	7.4	6.6	6.2	5.8
	—	—	—	—	—	—	—
	40.0	40.0	40.0				
	366.9	334.7	284.4	167.3	133.9	123.5	116.8
	$ 871.4	$ 753.2	$ 668.6	$ 420.0	$ 427.2	$ 337.3	$ 338.1
	$ —	$ 6.8	$ —	$ —	$ 0.6	$ 2.5	$ 1.7
	307.5	202.1	94.0	76.0	50.9	42.2	45.1
	2.2	1.7	0.6	—	—	—	—
	$ 309.7	$ 210.6	$ 94.6	$ 76.0	$ 51.5	$ 44.7	$ 46.8
	$ 147.8	$ 43.5	$ 74.2	$ 57.9	$ 35.0	$ 28.2	$ 31.6
	13.2	16.9	1.3	1.3	0.9	1.6	1.5
	—	—	—	—	—	—	—
	7.0	2.7	8.6	5.3	3.9	3.9	2.5
	118.3	127.5	—	—	—	—	—
	23.4	20.0	10.5	11.5	11.7	11.0	11.2
	$ 309.7	$ 210.6	$ 94.6	$ 76.0	$ 51.5	$ 44.7	$ 46.8

Historical Financial Summary (continued)

General information
[millions of dollars]

January 31	1992	1991	1990
Export sales from Canada	$ 1 084.5	$ 975.8	$ 1 245.3
Additions to fixed assets	$ 166.6	$ 176.0	$ 93.1
Depreciation	$ 75.3	$ 76.8	$ 43.3
Dividend rate per common share (dollars)			
Class A	$ 0.16000	$ 0.16000	$ 0.12500
Class B	$ 0.17250	$ 0.17250	$ 0.13750
Book value per common share (dollars)	$ 5.67	$ 4.64	$ 3.54
Number of common shares (millions)	152.3	141.4	131.4
Shareholders of record	8 735	9 315	10 025

Market price range
[dollars]

For the years ended January 31	1992	1991	1990
Class A			
High	17.50	10.31	9.00
Low	8.38	7.25	5.56
Close	17.13	8.44	7.81
Class B			
High	17.25	10.31	9.00
Low	7.75	6.44	5.56
Close	17.13	7.88	7.63

Quarterly data
[unaudited]
[millions of dollars]

For the years ended January 31	1992	1991
	First Quarter	
Revenues[1]	$ 658.1	$ 558.5
Net income	$ 25.6	$ 23.4
Per common share (dollars)		
Net income	0.18	0.17
Dividend – Class B Share	0.0525	0.0525
Market price range of Class B Share		
High	$9\frac{1}{2}$	$8\frac{1}{8}$
Low	$7\frac{3}{4}$	$7\frac{1}{8}$

[1]Restated

	1989	1988	1987	1986	1985	1984	1983
	$ 782.0	$ 998.0	$ 715.0	$ 348.6	$ 182.0	$ 171.8	$ 215.2
	$ 52.7	$ 47.5	$ 40.8	$ 11.4	$ 19.4	$ 21.5	$ 13.9
	$ 40.1	$ 24.4	$ 18.1	$ 17.0	$ 11.2	$ 8.7	$ 9.7
	$ 0.11000	$ 0.07500	$ 0.04063	$ 0.02500	$ 0.00938	$ —	$ —
	$ 0.12250	$ 0.08750	$ 0.05313	$ 0.03750	$ 0.02188	$ —	$ —
	$ 2.92	$ 2.66	$ 2.26	$ 1.63	$ 1.50	$ 1.41	$ 1.34
	125.6	126.2	126.0	102.8	89.2	87.6	87.2
	10 707	12 194	10 017	6 306	5 430	6 613	7 786

	1989	1988	1987	1986	1985	1984	1983
	6.75	7.13	5.00	2.06	1.19	1.24	1.06
	3.94	3.50	1.97	1.20	0.98	0.79	0.48
	6.69	4.38	4.84	2.00	1.17	1.13	0.84
	6.81	7.13	4.91	2.06	1.17	1.17	0.97
	3.94	3.25	1.97	1.16	0.91	0.66	0.42
	6.69	4.31	4.72	2.00	1.16	1.09	0.67

1992	1991	1992	1991	1992	1991
	Second Quarter		Third Quarter		Fourth Quarter
$ 692.1	$ 734.5	$ 734.2	$ 791.6	$ 974.2	$ 807.7
$ 23.8	$ 22.0	$ 21.5	$ 21.4	$ 36.8	$ 33.3
0.16	0.16	0.15	0.14	0.24	0.24
0.0400	0.0400	0.0400	0.0400	0.0400	0.0400
11⅞	10¼	13½	9¾	17¼	8
9¼	7½	10¼	6⅝	12⅛	6½

Management Report

Bombardier Inc.'s Annual Report for the year ended January 31, 1992, and the financial statements included therein, were prepared by the Corporation's Management and approved by the Board of Directors. The Audit Committee of the Board is responsible for reviewing the financial statements in detail and for ensuring that the Corporation's internal control systems, management policies and accounting practices are adhered to.

The financial statements contained in this Annual Report have been prepared in accordance with the accounting policies which are enunciated in said report and which Management believes to be appropriate for the activities of the Corporation. The external auditors appointed by the Corporation's shareholders, Caron Bélanger Ernst & Young, have audited these financial statements and their report appears below.

All information given in this Annual Report is consistent with the financial statements included herein.

Pierre Poitras, CA
Vice-President and Treasurer

Paul H. Larose, CA
Vice-President, Finance

Auditors' Report

To the Shareholders of Bombardier Inc.

We have audited the consolidated balance sheets of Bombardier Inc. (a Canadian corporation) as at January 31, 1992 and 1991 and the consolidated statements of income, shareholders' equity and changes in financial position for the years then ended. These financial statements are the responsibility of the Corporation's Management. Our responsibility is to express an opinion on these financial statements based on our audits.

We conducted our audits in accordance with generally accepted auditing standards. Those standards require that we plan and perform an audit to obtain reasonable assurance whether the financial statements are free of material misstatement. An audit includes examining, on a test basis, evidence supporting the amounts and disclosures in the financial statements. An audit also includes assessing the accounting principles used and significant estimates made by Management, as well as evaluating the overall financial statement presentation.

In our opinion, these consolidated financial statements present fairly, in all material respects, the financial position of the Corporation as at January 31, 1992 and 1991 and the results of its operations and the changes in its financial position for the years then ended in accordance with generally accepted accounting principles.

Caron Bélanger Ernst & Young
Chartered Accountants
Montréal, Canada
March 6, 1992
(with the exception of notes 19b) and 19c) for which
the dates are respectively March 9 and April 9, 1992).

Consolidated Balance Sheets

As at January 31, 1992 and 1991
[millions of dollars]

	Notes	Bombardier Inc. consolidated 1992	1991	Bombardier 1992	1991	BCG 1992	1991
			(restated)				
Assets							
Cash and term deposits		$ **179.2**	$ 87.5	$ **177.6**	$ 87.2	$ **1.6**	$ 0.3
Accounts receivable		**360.1**	413.7	**366.0**	413.6	**—**	0.1
Financing receivables and property under leases	2	**640.8**	491.3	**—**	—	**640.8**	491.3
Inventories	3	**1 215.7**	992.7	**1 215.7**	992.7	**—**	—
Prepaid expenses		**13.6**	9.5	**13.6**	9.5	**—**	—
Fixed assets	4	**626.8**	533.5	**603.8**	514.7	**23.0**	18.8
Investment in BCG		**—**	—	**87.0**	68.5	**—**	—
Other assets	5	**34.5**	35.3	**34.5**	35.3	**—**	—
		$ **3 070.7**	$ 2 563.5	$ **2 498.2**	$ 2 121.5	$ **665.4**	$ 510.5
Liabilities							
Short-term borrowings	6	$ **640.1**	$ 558.2	$ **105.1**	$ 135.6	$ **535.0**	$ 422.6
Accounts payable and accrued liabilities		**883.2**	818.1	**846.2**	799.2	**42.9**	18.9
Income taxes		**18.2**	13.7	**17.7**	13.2	**0.5**	0.5
Advances from related parties		**—**	—	**—**	—	**31.3**	23.9
Long-term debt	7	**381.2**	265.9	**381.2**	265.9	**—**	—
Provision for pension costs	8	**41.3**	46.6	**41.3**	46.6	**—**	—
Deferred income taxes		**2.0**	7.2	**2.0**	7.2	**—**	—
Minority interest		**11.6**	14.2	**11.6**	14.2	**—**	—
		1 977.6	1 723.9	**1 405.1**	1 281.9	**609.7**	465.9
Convertible notes and shareholders' equity							
Convertible notes	9	**193.8**	145.4	**193.8**	145.4	**—**	—
Shareholders' equity		**899.3**	694.2	**899.3**	694.2	**55.7**	44.6
		1 093.1	839.6	**1 093.1**	839.6	**55.7**	44.6
		$ **3 070.7**	$ 2 563.5	$ **2 498.2**	$ 2 121.5	$ **665.4**	$ 510.5

The accompanying summary of significant accounting policies and notes are an integral part of these consolidated financial statements and discuss the financial statement presentation, the consolidation's eliminations and their restatement for 1991.

On behalf of the Board of Directors:

Director   Director

Consolidated Statements of Shareholders' Equity

For the years ended January 31, 1992 and 1991

[millions of dollars]

	Number	1992 Amount	Number	1991 Amount
Share capital (note 10)				
Preferred shares, series 1				
Balance at beginning of year	1 496 500	$ 37.4	1 566 300	$ 39.1
Purchased for cancellation	(68 300)	(1.7)	(69 800)	(1.7)
Balance at end of year	1 428 200	35.7	1 496 500	37.4
Class A shares (multiple voting)				
Balance at beginning of year	45 284 694	50.4	50 082 296	55.7
Converted from class A to class B	(48 502)	(0.1)	(4 793 802)	(5.3)
Purchased for cancellation	—	—	(3 800)	—
Balance at end of year	45 236 192	50.3	45 284 694	50.4
Class B subordinate voting shares				
Balance at beginning of year	96 158 120	276.0	81 315 552	170.9
Issued for cash	10 000 000	126.2	10 000 000	97.5
Issued under the share option plan (note 11)	594 750	2.4	306 500	1.1
Issued to employees for cash	298 966	3.9	470 866	3.3
Converted from class A to class B	48 502	0.1	4 793 802	5.3
Purchased for cancellation	—	—	(728 600)	(2.1)
Balance at end of year	107 100 338	408.6	96 158 120	276.0
Total — share capital		494.6		363.8
Retained earnings				
Balance at beginning of year		309.4		242.0
Net income		107.7		100.1
Net premium on shares purchased		—		(3.0)
Issuance costs for Class B shares (net of income taxes)		(3.1)		(2.7)
Dividends paid:				
Preferred shares		(2.9)		(4.0)
Common shares		(24.3)		(23.0)
Balance at end of year		386.8		309.4
Deferred translation adjustments (note 12)		17.9		21.0
Total — Shareholders' equity		$ 899.3		$ 694.2

The accompanying summary of significant accounting policies and notes are an integral part of these consolidated statements.

Consolidated Statements of Income

For the years ended January 31, 1992 and 1991

[millions of dollars except per share amounts]

	Notes	Bombardier Inc. consolidated 1992	1991	Bombardier 1992	1991	BCG 1992	1991
			(restated)				
Revenues							
Net sales		$ **3 002.4**	$ 2 836.3	$ **3 002.4**	$ 2 836.3	**$ —**	$ —
BCG revenues from operations		**56.2**	56.0	**—**	—	**63.3**	63.2
	21	**3 058.6**	2 892.3	**3 002.4**	2 836.3	**63.3**	63.2
Expenses							
Cost of sales and operating expenses	13	**2 828.2**	2 672.5	**2 835.3**	2 679.7	**—**	—
Interest on long-term debt		**28.7**	17.3	**28.7**	17.3	**—**	—
Interest expenses		**23.9**	35.9	**1.3**	8.6	**22.6**	27.3
Other expenses (income)	14	**56.4**	46.1	**3.5**	(1.3)	**52.9**	47.4
Operating loss from BCG		**—**	—	**12.2**	11.5	**—**	—
		2 937.2	2 771.8	**2 881.0**	2 715.8	**75.5**	74.7
Income (loss) before income taxes		**121.4**	120.5	**121.4**	120.5	**(12.2)**	(11.5)
Income taxes	15	**13.7**	20.4	**13.7**	20.4	**(0.6)**	0.5
Net income (loss)		$ **107.7**	$ 100.1	$ **107.7**	$ 100.1	$ **(11.6)**	$ (12.0)
Net income per common share:							
Basic		$ **0.73**	$ 0.71				
Fully diluted		$ **0.70**	$ 0.70				
Average number of common shares outstanding during the year		**144 121 395**	136 073 170				

The accompanying summary of significant accounting policies and notes are an integral part of these consolidated financial statements and discuss the financial statement presentation, the consolidation's eliminations and their restatement for 1991.

Consolidated Statements of Changes in Financial Position

For the years ended January 31, 1992 and 1991

[millions of dollars]

	Bombardier Inc. consolidated		Bombardier		BCG	
	1992	1991	**1992**	1991	**1992**	1991
Operating activities		(restated)				
Net income (loss)	$ **107.7**	$ 100.1	$ **107.7**	$ 100.1	$ **(11.6)**	$ (12.0)
Non-cash items:						
Depreciation and amortization	**75.3**	76.8	**74.3**	76.0	**1.0**	0.8
Net loss (income) of non-consolidated affiliate	**3.7**	(0.4)	**3.7**	(0.4)	—	—
Net loss from BCG	—	—	**11.6**	12.0	—	—
Provision for credit losses — BCG	**13.3**	7.5	—	—	**13.3**	7.5
Provision for pension costs	**(2.4)**	(6.2)	**(2.4)**	(6.2)	—	—
Deferred income taxes	**(5.2)**	7.2	**(5.2)**	7.2	—	—
Minority interest	**(1.0)**	0.8	**(1.0)**	0.8	—	—
Net changes in non-cash balances related to operations (note 16)	**(103.9)**	(171.5)	**(128.0)**	(141.7)	**24.1**	(29.8)
Cash provided by (used in) operating activities	**87.5**	14.3	**60.7**	47.8	**26.8**	(33.5)
Investing activities						
Additions to fixed assets	**(166.6)**	(176.0)	**(161.4)**	(159.0)	**(5.2)**	(17.0)
Investment in financing receivables and property under leases	**(162.8)**	(40.8)	—	—	**(162.8)**	(40.8)
Acquisition of minority interest in a subsidiary	**(0.9)**	(1.4)	**(0.9)**	(1.4)	—	—
Deferred translation adjustments	**(11.5)**	11.4	**(12.5)**	12.3	**1.0**	(0.9)
Acquisition of net assets of Learjet Corporation and assumption of bank loans	—	(125.4)	—	(125.4)	—	—
Acquisition of Procor Engineering Limited	—	(5.5)	—	(5.5)	—	—
Investment in BCG	—	—	**(29.1)**	(26.6)	—	—
Others	**(6.2)**	1.7	**(6.2)**	1.7	—	—
Cash used in investing activities	**(348.0)**	(336.0)	**(210.1)**	(303.9)	**(167.0)**	(58.7)
Financing activities						
Net variation in short-term borrowings	**83.4**	72.0	**(29.0)**	10.4	**112.4**	61.6
Proceeds from long-term debt	**141.2**	125.4	**141.2**	125.4	—	—
Reduction of long-term debt	**(18.9)**	(33.5)	**(18.9)**	(33.5)	—	—
Issues of convertible notes	**46.0**	95.9	**46.0**	95.9	—	—
Issues of shares net of issuance costs	**129.4**	99.2	**129.4**	99.2	**21.7**	11.7
Purchase of shares for cancellation	**(1.7)**	(6.8)	**(1.7)**	(6.8)	—	—
Dividends paid	**(27.2)**	(27.0)	**(27.2)**	(27.0)	—	—
Advances from related parties	—	—	—	—	**7.4**	14.9
Cash provided by financing activities	**352.2**	325.2	**239.8**	263.6	**141.5**	88.2
Increase (decrease) in cash	**91.7**	3.5	**90.4**	7.5	**1.3**	(4.0)
Cash position at beginning of year	**87.5**	84.0	**87.2**	79.7	**0.3**	4.3
Cash position at end of year	$ **179.2**	$ 87.5	$ **177.6**	$ 87.2	$ **1.6**	$ 0.3

Cash position represents cash and term deposits.

The accompanying summary of significant accounting policies and notes are an integral part of these consolidated financial statements and discuss the financial statement presentation, the consolidation's eliminations and their restatement for 1991.

Summary of Significant Accounting Policies

For the years ended January 31, 1992 and 1991

Financial statement presentation

In prior years, results of financial services subsidiaries were excluded from consolidation and were accounted for under the equity method. The Corporation has retroactively adopted the new requirement of the Canadian Institute of Chartered Accountants relating to consolidation of all subsidiaries as early as for the year ended January 31, 1992. Application of this new method of consolidation does not affect consolidated net income and shareholders' equity. However, because financial services operations are different in nature from the operations of the other Bombardier businesses, Management believes that the financial statements are more understandable if the information pertaining to financial services is shown separately. Accordingly, this financial information is shown as a separate column in the financial statements (BCG), together with the Real Estate Development activities essentially to be carried on land vacated by the Corporation, which Management believes also constitute a distinct operation from its principal businesses.

Beginning in 1992, the consolidated balance sheets are presented in an unclassified format because Management believes this presentation is more meaningful since the activities of the Corporation are concentrated in five main sectors each having its own normal operating cycle.

The descriptions of the columns shown in the financial statements are as follows:

Bombardier

This column represents essentially the activities of the manufacturing group concentrated in four main sectors, namely Transportation Equipment, Motorized Consumer Products, Aerospace and Defence. This group is referred to as "Bombardier" within these financial statements and uses a basis of presentation which is similar to that of previous years. The effect of intercompany transactions within this group has been eliminated.

BCG

Bombardier Capital Group ("BCG") represents the consolidation of the capital-intensive operations of the Corporation, namely the financial services and Real Estate Development activities. The effect of intercompany transactions within this group has been eliminated.

Bombardier Inc. consolidated

This column represents all the activities of the Corporation. The eliminations of transactions between Bombardier and BCG are summarized below:

Eliminations [millions of dollars]

	1992	1991
i) Consolidated balance sheets		
Accounts receivable	$ (5.9)	$ —
Investment in BCG	(87.0)	(68.5)
Total assets	$ (92.9)	$ (68.5)
Accounts payable and accrued liabilities	$ (5.9)	$ —
Advances from related parties	(31.3)	(23.9)
BCG equity	(55.7)	(44.6)
Total liabilities and equity	$ (92.9)	$ (68.5)
ii) Consolidated statements of income		
BCG revenues from operations	$ 7.1	$ 7.2
Cost of sales and operating expenses	(7.1)	(7.2)
Operating loss from BCG	(12.2)	(11.5)
Income taxes	0.6	(0.5)
Net loss	$ (11.6)	$ (12.0)
iii) Consolidated statements of changes in financial position		
Investing activities	$ 29.1	$ 26.6
Financing activities	(29.1)	(26.6)
	$ —	$ —

Bombardier Inc. consolidated – Accounting Policies

Basis of consolidation

The consolidated financial statements are expressed in Canadian dollars and include the accounts of the Corporation, its subsidiaries and its affiliate on the basis set out below:

Major corporate entities	Percentage owned	Basis of inclusion	Translation method
Bombardier			
Bombardier Inc. (Canada)			
Bombardier Corporation (U.S.)	100.0%	Consolidated	Integrated
Canadair Challenger, Inc. (U.S.)	100.0%	Consolidated	Integrated
Learjet Inc. (U.S.)	100.0%	Consolidated	Self-sustaining
Pullman Technology Inc. (U.S.)	100.0%	Consolidated	Integrated
Auburn Technology, Inc. (U.S.)	100.0%	Consolidated	Integrated
The Transportation Group Inc. (U.S.)	100.0%	Consolidated	Integrated
Short Brothers PLC (Northern Ireland)	100.0%	Consolidated	Self-sustaining
Bombardier Eurorail (Belgium)	91.7%	Consolidated	Self-sustaining
ANF-Industrie (France)	91.7%[1]	Consolidated	Self-sustaining
Bombardier Prorail Limited (England)	91.7%[1]	Consolidated	Self-sustaining
Bombardier-Rotax Wien (Austria)	91.7%[1]	Consolidated	Self-sustaining
Bombardier-Rotax GmbH (Austria)	100.0%	Consolidated	Self-sustaining
Canadair Aviation Services GmbH (Germany)	100.0%	Consolidated	Integrated
Scanhold OY (Finland)	50.0%	Equity accounted	Integrated
DBB Insurance Company Limited (Barbados)	100.0%	Consolidated	Self-sustaining
BCG			
Bombardier Capital Inc. (U.S.)	100.0%	Consolidated	Self-sustaining
Bombardier Credit Ltd. (Canada)	100.0%	Consolidated	
Bombardier Real Estate Ltd. (Canada)	100.0%	Consolidated	

[1] The ownership of these European subsidiaries in the Transportation Equipment Group was transferred during the year to Bombardier Eurorail (100% in 1991).

Translation of foreign currencies

Foreign operations are classified as integrated or self-sustaining.

a) Integrated foreign operations and accounts in foreign currencies

They have been translated into Canadian dollars using the temporal method. Under this method, monetary items of the balance sheet are translated at the rates of exchange in effect at year-end and non-monetary items are translated at historical exchange rates. Revenues and expenses (other than depreciation, which is translated at the same rates as the related fixed assets) are translated at the rates in effect on the transaction dates or at the average rates of exchange for the period. Translation gains or losses are included in the statement of income except those related to the translation of long-term debt, which are deferred and amortized over its remaining life on a straight-line basis.

b) Self-sustaining operations

All balance sheet items are translated at exchange rates in effect at year-end. The resulting gains or losses are shown under "Deferred translation adjustments" in the shareholders' equity. Revenues and expenses are translated at the average rates of exchange for the period.

Fixed assets

Fixed assets acquired through purchase or capital lease are recorded at cost. Depreciation is generally computed under the straight-line method over the following estimated useful lives:

Buildings	10 to 40 years
Equipment	3 to 15 years
Others	5 to 10 years

Income taxes

The Corporation follows the tax allocation method in providing for income taxes. Under this method, differences between income for accounting purposes and income for tax purposes, which result from the timing differences between revenues and expenses recorded for accounting as opposed to tax purposes, give rise to deferred income taxes.

Net income per common share

Basic net income per common share is calculated using the weighted average number of Class A and B shares outstanding during the year. Fully diluted net income per common share gives effect to the exercise of all potentially dilutive elements.

Pension costs and obligations

The Corporation and its subsidiaries maintain pension plans for the benefit of substantially all employees.

The pension obligations of the defined benefit pension plans are valued using an accrued benefit actuarial method and Management's best estimate assumptions. The assets of these pension plans are valued on the basis of market related values. Current service costs are expensed in the year. Adjustments arising from past service benefits and experience gains and losses are amortized on a straight-line basis over the average remaining service life of the employee groups covered by the plans.

Some European subsidiaries provide annually for pension costs based on the estimated amounts to be paid to their employees upon retirement. Any adjustment to this provision is charged to income.

Costs related to post-employment benefits other than pension costs offered to employees of some subsidiaries are recognized when incurred by retirees and paid by the employer.

Goodwill

Goodwill is amortized on a straight-line basis over periods not exceeding forty years.

**Bombardier –
Accounting Policies**

Inventory valuation and revenue recognition

a) Raw materials, work in process and finished products

Raw materials, work in process and finished products are valued at the lower of cost (actual cost, average cost or first-in, first-out depending on the sector) and net realizable value. The cost of work in process and finished products includes the cost of raw materials, direct labour and overhead.

b) Long-term contracts and program accounting

A significant portion of the Corporation's sales is related to long-term contracts and programs.

• Long-term contracts

Sales and income from long-term contracts are recognized in accordance with the percentage-of-completion method of accounting. Degree of completion is generally determined by comparing the costs incurred to date to the total cost anticipated for the entire contract.

The effect of changes to total estimated income for each contract is recognized in the period in which the determination is made and losses, if any, are recognized fully when anticipated.

• Programs

Sales of aircraft are recognized in accordance with the percentage-of-completion method of accounting in relation to units delivered, and income from those sales is determined under the program method of accounting. Under that method, the cost of the units delivered is estimated periodically for accounting purposes, taking into account factors such as the estimated number of aircraft to be manufactured under the program, anticipated total sales and estimated manufacturing costs. Any increase or decrease in income resulting from a change in the estimates is accounted for prospectively.

• Advances

Advances received on contracts and programs are deducted from inventories.

• Financing costs

Program for which specific financing is provided includes the related interest and borrowing costs.

Investment in BCG

The investment in BCG is equity accounted.

**BCG – Accounting
Policies**

Revenue recognition

Interest income related to finance receivables is recognized on an accrual basis computed on the average daily finance receivables balance outstanding. Accrual of interest income is suspended when collection of an account becomes doubtful, generally after the account becomes 90 days delinquent.

Provision for credit losses

BCG maintains a provision for credit losses on financing receivables at an amount that it believes to be sufficient to provide adequate protection against future losses in the portfolio. The provision for credit losses is determined principally on the basis of actual experience and further provisions are also provided to reflect Management's judgment of potential loss, including specific provisions for known troubled accounts.

Land held for development

Land held for development is stated at the lower of cost and net realizable value. Direct carrying costs and pre-development expenditures related to projects which are expected to be completed are capitalized.

Notes to Consolidated Financial Statements

For the years ended January 31, 1992 and 1991

[tabular figures in millions of dollars]

1. Acquisitions

a) Learjet Inc.

On June 29, 1990, the Corporation acquired the operations and substantially all of the net assets of Learjet Corporation, an American manufacturer of aerospace products, for a cash consideration of $91 100 000. This company is now operating under the name Learjet Inc. The accounts have been consolidated from April 9, 1990.

Net tangible assets acquired at attributed value

Working capital	$ 69.7
Fixed assets	66.8
	136.5
Long-term debt	5.2
Provision for pension costs	5.9
Acquisition cost	125.4
Bank loans assumed	34.3
Cash consideration	$ 91.1

b) Bombardier Prorail Limited

Effective November 16, 1990, the Corporation acquired, through its Belgian subsidiary Bombardier Eurorail, for a cash consideration of $5 537 000, all the share capital of Procor Engineering Limited, a manufacturer of rail-passenger-car body shells and locomotive body shells operating in United Kingdom. This company is now operating under the name Bombardier Prorail Limited. This acquisition has been accounted for by the purchase method.

Net tangible assets acquired at attributed value

Working capital	$ 2.9
Fixed assets	2.6
Acquisition cost	$ 5.5

2. Financing receivables and property under leases

	1992	1991
Finance receivables	$ 538.1	$ 495.4
Aircraft under operating leases	62.0	—
Receivables purchased from affiliates	61.7	1.2
Others	10.5	12.9
Provision for credit losses	(31.5)	(18.2)
	$ 640.8	$ 491.3

Finance receivables, arising from the financing of sales of equipment by manufacturers and distributors to dealers, are collateralized by the related inventory and secured by repurchase agreements. Under such agreements, BCG may repossess the equipment from a dealer within a time period specified in the agreement and may require the distributors or manufacturers to repurchase it for a cash consideration equal to the unpaid balance.

3. Inventories

	Transportation Equipment	Motorized Consumer Products	Aerospace	Defence	Total 1992	Total 1991
Raw materials and work in process	$ 18.4	$ 66.8	$ —	$ —	$ 85.2	$ 89.4
Contracts and programs	437.7	—	1 155.4	86.2	1 679.3	1 247.8
Finished products	4.1	36.3	113.9	—	154.3	170.3
	460.2	103.1	1 269.3	86.2	1 918.8	1 507.5
Advances received	(489.2)	(0.1)	(210.7)	(3.1)	(703.1)	(514.8)
Total net – 1992	$ (29.0)	$ 103.0	$ 1 058.6	$ 83.1	$ 1 215.7	
Total net – 1991	$ 79.2	$ 130.6	$ 730.8	$ 52.1		$ 992.7

Under certain contracts, the title to inventories is vested in the customer as the work is performed, in accordance with contractual arrangements and industry practice.

4. Fixed assets

	1992			1991		
	Cost	Accumulated depreciation	Net value	Cost	Accumulated depreciation	Net value
Bombardier						
Land and airport	$ 34.0	$ —	$ 34.0	$ 32.3	$ —	$ 32.3
Buildings	372.4	157.8	214.6	339.3	151.7	187.6
Equipment	715.7	386.1	329.6	689.7	408.0	281.7
Others	37.3	11.7	25.6	23.2	10.1	13.1
	1 159.4	555.6	603.8	1 084.5	569.8	514.7
BCG						
Land held for development	18.8	—	18.8	15.9	—	15.9
Equipment	6.4	2.7	3.7	4.1	1.7	2.4
Others	0.8	0.3	0.5	0.7	0.2	0.5
	26.0	3.0	23.0	20.7	1.9	18.8
Total	$ 1 185.4	$ 558.6	$ 626.8	$ 1 105.2	$ 571.7	$ 533.5

Fixed assets include equipment acquired through capital leases with a net value of $18 841 000 ($11 606 000 in 1991).

The Corporation leases buildings and equipment under long-term operating leases for which the total minimum lease payments amount to $114 015 000. The annual minimum payments for the next five years are as follows: 1993 – $33 083 000; 1994 – $25 472 000; 1995 – $14 930 000; 1996 – $8 422 000 and 1997 – $7 333 000.

5. Other assets

		1992		1991
Industrial designs and other assets	$	26.9	$	27.2
Deferred loss on translation of long-term debt		1.4		1.7
Goodwill		6.2		6.4
	$	34.5	$	35.3

6. Short-term borrowings

		1992		1991
Bombardier				
Bank loans	$	85.8	$	114.8
Current portion of long-term debt		19.3		20.8
		105.1		135.6
BCG				
Commercial paper		466.5		398.2
Bank loans		68.5		24.4
		535.0		422.6
Total	$	640.1	$	558.2

Commercial paper offerings, secured by an irrevocable letter of credit, which is guaranteed by Bombardier Capital Inc.'s group of banks, are authorized to a maximum of U.S. $400 000 000 as at January 31, 1992 and 1991 (outstanding amount of U.S. $397 100 000 and U.S. $339 100 000 was issued as at January 31, 1992 and 1991). The weighted average interest rate on commercial paper outstanding as at January 31, 1992 is 4.41% (7.3% as at January 31, 1991). The Corporation is committed to the group of banks to ensure that Bombardier Capital Inc. maintains certain financial ratios.

7. Long-term debt

	1992	1991
Bombardier Inc.		
• Debentures, 11.10%, maturing in May 2001, with a nominal value of $100 000 000	$ 100.0	$ —
• Bonds, 6%, maturing in April 1998, with a nominal value of 33 200 000 Swiss francs (35 625 000 Swiss francs as at January 31, 1991)	27.3	33.0
• Bonds, LIBOR rate plus at most 15/100 of 1%, with a nominal value of U.S. $25 000 000, maturing in September 1994, and a nominal value of U.S. $50 000 000 maturing in February 1995, 4.125% to 5.75% (6.6875% to 8.125% as at January 31, 1991)	88.1	87.2
• Bonds, 4 3/4% until July 1992, then 5% until due in July 1993, with a nominal value of 17 000 000 Swiss francs. Following an agreement with a financial institution, a portion of 5 000 000 Swiss francs of this debt is payable in U.S. dollars (8 000 000 Swiss francs as at January 31, 1991) with interest at LIBOR rate plus 5/8 of 1% (U.S. $2 272 727 and 7.25% as at January 31, 1992; U.S. $3 636 364 and 8.875% as at January 31, 1991)	14.0	15.7
• Bonds, 8.2%, maturing in April 1993, with a nominal value of 249 000 000 Belgian francs. Following an agreement with a financial institution, this debt is payable for U.S. $6 381 343 with interest at LIBOR rate plus 78/100 of 1% (6.405% as at January 31, 1992 and 9.0925% as at January 31, 1991)	8.8	9.5
• Bonds, 7 1/2%, maturing in February 1993, with a nominal value of 300 000 000 Luxembourg francs. Following an agreement with a financial institution, this debt is payable for U.S. $7 688 365, with interest at LIBOR rate plus 12/100 of 1% (6.38563% as at January 31, 1992 and 8.12% as at January 31, 1991)	10.7	11.5
Learjet Inc.		
• Loans, 9.02%, maturing in May 1998, with a nominal value of U.S. $25 000 000	29.4	—
• Bonds, 12.31%, maturing in November 1995. Following an agreement with a financial institution, this debt is payable for U.S. $25 000 000, with interest at 9.55%	29.2	29.2
Bombardier – Rotax GmbH		
• Loans, 3.5% to 8.75%, maturing from 1992 to 1998	27.3	26.3
Auburn Technology, Inc.		
• Bonds, 3% to 7.25%, maturing from 1997 to 2000	8.0	9.2
ANF-Industrie		
• Loans, 5% to 13%, maturing from 1992 to 1998	30.7	34.4
Amounts payable under capital leases, 6% to 16.6%, maturing from 1992 to 2006	17.1	26.2
Others, bearing interest up to 13%, maturing from 1992 to 2000	14.1	12.4
	404.7	294.6
Exchange adjustment arising from hedging foreign currencies to U.S. dollars	(4.2)	(7.9)
	400.5	286.7
Amounts due within one year	19.3	20.8
	$ 381.2	$ 265.9

The repayment requirements on the long-term debt during the next five fiscal years ending January 31 are as follows: 1993 – $19 323 000; 1994 – $50 627 000; 1995 – $51 204 000; 1996 – $106 485 000 and 1997 – $9 025 000.

8. Provision for pension costs

	1992	1991
Provision for pension costs – Europe	**$ 41.9**	$ 42.5
Pension costs – Canada and U.S.	**(0.6)**	4.1
	$ 41.3	$ 46.6

9. Convertible notes

The Corporation entered into an agreement with a financial institution in 1989 for the issue of convertible notes in order to partially finance the Canadair Regional Jet program. As at January 31, 1992, the Corporation had issued U.S. $165 000 000 of convertible notes (U.S. $125 000 000 as at January 31, 1991). These notes are unsecured, mature in October 2004 and bear interest at LIBOR rate plus 85/100 of 1% to October 1999 and thereafter at LIBOR rate plus 1.25% (6.2875% as at January 31, 1992 and 9.08438% as at January 31, 1991). Interest and borrowing costs for the fiscal year in the amount of $13 531 000 ($9 706 000 in 1991) are included in inventories of contracts and programs.

In October 1999, at the option of the Corporation or of the holders, these notes are redeemable prior to their maturity at their nominal value. The Corporation may then, at its option, repay the convertible notes in cash or with Class B Subordinate Voting Shares of the Corporation. The Corporation having the option to repay the notes with shares, these notes are shown under the heading "Convertible notes and shareholders' equity".

10. Share capital

On January 31, 1992, the share capital of the Corporation was modified by the subdivision of the Class A Shares (multiple voting) and the Class B Subordinate Voting Shares on a two-for-one basis and a change of the non cumulative preferential dividend rate on the Class B Subordinate Voting Shares from $0.025 to $0.0125 per share per annum. The following information has been adjusted to give effect to the stock split.

The authorized share capital of the Corporation is as follows:

An unlimited number of preferred shares, without nominal or par value, non-voting, issuable in series, of which one series consisting of 1 428 200 (1 496 500 as at January 31, 1991) Series 1 Cumulative Redeemable Preferred Shares is authorized. The quarterly dividend rate is equal to the greater of i) 1.875% and ii) one quarter of 75% of the average of the prime rates of three designated major Canadian banks for specified three-month periods;

224 000 000 Class A Shares (multiple voting), without nominal or par value, ten votes each, convertible at the option of the holder into one Class B Subordinate Voting Share; and

224 000 000 Class B Subordinate Voting Shares, without nominal or par value, one vote each with an annual non cumulative preferential dividend of $0.0125 per share, and convertible, at the option of the holder, into one Class A Share (multiple voting), after the occurrence of one of the following events: i) an offer made to Class A Shares (multiple voting) shareholders is accepted by the present controlling shareholder (the Bombardier family); ii) such controlling shareholder ceases to hold more than 50% of all outstanding Class A Shares (multiple voting) of the Corporation.

11. Share option plan

Under a share option plan, options are granted to key employees to purchase Class B Subordinate Voting Shares. The exercise price is equal to the average of the closing prices on the stock exchanges during the five trading days preceding the date on which the option was granted. The options are exercisable during a period commencing two years following the date of granting and ending not later than ten years after such date. The right to exercise is acquired gradually over this period.

Issued and outstanding options at year-end are as follows:

Date of granting	Exercise price	1992	1991
April 14, 1986	$ 2.48	1 564 000	1 873 000
December 12, 1986	4.13	745 000	815 000
February 17, 1987	4.86	160 000	160 000
June 8, 1987	6.19	90 500	241 750
May 2, 1988	4.88	14 000	21 000
August 30, 1988	5.83	212 250	367 750
February 21, 1989	6.12	125 000	160 000
March 20, 1989	6.54	20 000	20 000
April 30, 1989	6.31	50 000	50 000
December 21, 1989	7.88	1 300 000	1 300 000
February 1, 1990	7.66	50 000	50 000
January 18, 1991	7.08	550 000	550 000
December 2, 1991	12.45	20 000	—
January 6, 1992	14.12	40 000	—
January 20, 1992	15.25	30 000	—
		4 970 750	5 608 500

The number of options has varied as follows:

	1992	1991
Balance at beginning of year	5 608 500	5 407 000
Granted	90 000	600 000
Exercised	(594 750)	(306 500)
Cancelled	(133 000)	(92 000)
Balance at end of year	4 970 750	5 608 500

12. Deferred translation adjustments

	1992	1991
Bombardier		
Balance at beginning of year	$ **21.0**	$ (3.5)
Translation adjustments during the year	**(3.1)**	24.5
Balance at end of year	**17.9**	21.0
BCG		
Balance at beginning of year	**(2.2)**	(1.3)
Translation adjustments during the year	**1.0**	(0.9)
Balance at end of year	**(1.2)**	(2.2)
Eliminations	**1.2**	2.2
Total	$ **17.9**	$ 21.0

13. Cost of sales and operating expenses

Cost of sales and operating expenses include research expenses, excluding those incurred under contracts, amounting to $53 693 000 and $36 292 000 respectively for the years ended January 31, 1992 and 1991 net of various participative programs and related income tax credits.

14. Other expenses (income)

	1992	1991
Bombardier		
Loss (income) before income taxes of an affiliate	$ **4.3**	$ (1.0)
Loss (gain) on translation of foreign currencies	**0.2**	(1.1)
Minority interest	**(1.0)**	0.8
	3.5	(1.3)
BCG		
Credit losses on financing receivables and property under leases	**19.8**	18.2
Operating expenses	**33.1**	29.2
	52.9	47.4
Total	$ **56.4**	$ 46.1

15. Income taxes

The effective tax rate differs from the Canadian statutory rates for the following reasons:

	1992		1991	
	$	%	$	%
Income taxes calculated as statutory rates	**42.9**	**35.4**	42.4	35.2
Increase (decrease) resulting from:				
Manufacturing and processing credit	**(1.6)**	**(1.4)**	(0.8)	(0.7)
Net income taxes of foreign subsidiaries	**(9.1)**	**(7.4)**	(14.9)	(12.4)
Tax exempt items	**(8.2)**	**(6.7)**	(11.0)	(9.1)
Others	**4.0**	**3.2**	4.7	3.9
Recovery of income taxes arising from the use of unrecorded tax benefits (see below)	**(14.3)**	**(11.8)**	—	—
	13.7	**11.3**	20.4	16.9
Current income taxes	**18.1**		12.0	
Deferred income taxes	**(4.4)**		8.4	
	13.7		20.4	

During the year, agreements were reached with taxation authorities in various jurisdictions in Canada and abroad in which certain subsidiaries of the Corporation operate, pursuant to which it has been determined that further deductions totalling $615 000 000 are available to reduce taxable income, including the amounts of deferred losses and other deductions at the acquisition dates of the subsidiaries involved. The deductions are available in those jurisdictions to reduce future taxable income. Related deductions of $45 000 000 were utilized during the year ended January 31, 1992, for which the tax benefits amounted to $14 300 000. No tax benefits have been recorded in the accounts in relation to the remaining deductions, which total $570 000 000 as at January 31, 1992.

16. Net changes in non-cash balances related to operations

The net changes in non-cash balances related to operations are as follows:

	1992	1991
Bombardier		
Accounts receivable	$ **47.6**	$ 41.9
Prepaid expenses	**(4.1)**	4.2
Inventories	**(223.0)**	(299.2)
Accounts payable and accrued liabilities	**47.0**	111.5
Income taxes	**4.5**	(0.1)
	(128.0)	(141.7)
BCG		
Accounts receivable	**0.1**	(0.1)
Accounts payable and accrued liabilities	**24.0**	(29.6)
Income taxes	**—**	(0.1)
	24.1	(29.8)
Total	$ **(103.9)**	$ (171.5)

17. Pension plans

Based on actuarial valuations of defined benefit pension plans, the estimated present value of accrued pension benefits as at January 31, 1992 was $585 362 000 ($514 812 000 as at January 31, 1991) and the assets in these plans at market-related values were estimated at $671 456 000 ($594 840 000 as at January 31, 1991).

18. Contingencies

a) At the date of its acquisition by the Corporation in 1989, Short Brothers PLC had issued to the government of the United Kingdom 60 000 000 pounds sterling of 30-year non-interest-bearing loan stock. Repayment of the loan stock may be accelerated if the Corporation does not meet certain commitments under the Acquisition Agreement, which, on the other hand, also contains provisions for forgiveness of the loan after 1993 based on the level of certain expenditures (capital equipment, research and development, training and non-recurring costs on contracts and programs) made in Northern Ireland. As the Corporation anticipates satisfying the commitments made under the Acquisition Agreement and making the required expenditures, the loan stock is not recorded in the financial statements.

b) Under an agreement dated June 14, 1989, credits earned by the Corporation under a contract with Aerospatiale, Société Nationale Industrielle are sold to a joint venture corporation, 91 % of which is owned by a financial institution and 9 % by the Corporation. The joint venture corporation has a $152 000 000 credit facility. As at January 31, 1992, these credits amount to $150 000 000 ($123 727 000 as at January 31, 1991), in respect of which the Corporation remains contingently liable until their payment. Subsequent to year-end 1992, this credit agreement has been cancelled and the earned credits under the contract have been disposed of to another financial institution under a sale agreement whereby the Corporation is not contingently liable for their payment.

c) BCG has concluded an agreement with a financial institution whereby it can sell its finance receivables on an ongoing basis pursuant to a credit agreement of $120 000 000 ($100 000 000 as at January 31, 1991). As at January 31, 1992, pursuant to this agreement, the balance of these finance receivables sold was $102 320 000 ($88 865 000 as at January 31 ,1991). BCG remains liable for any finance receivables not collected by the financial institution, to an annual maximum of $12 000 000 ($10 000 000 as at January 31, 1991).

d) In the normal conduct of operations, there are pending claims by and against the Corporation. Any settlements or awards are reflected in income based on Management's best estimates. In addition, the Corporation is contingently liable for the usual contractor's obligations relating to product performance and contract completion, notably when the Corporation has sold certain credits earned under specific contracts to third parties.

19. Subsequent events

Subsequent to year-end, the Corporation concluded the following agreements relating to business acquisitions:

a) UTDC

On February 7, 1992, the Corporation acquired substantially all of the operations and net assets of UTDC Inc., a Canadian manufacturer of transportation equipment. The purchase price will be based on the audited adjusted book value of the net assets purchased. Pending final determination, the cash purchase price has been estimated by Management at $14 000 000, which amount has been paid. The accounts will be consolidated from the date of acquisition.

b) de Havilland

On March 9, 1992, through newly incorporated de Havilland Inc., the Corporation acquired a 51% interest in the net assets and operations of the de Havilland division of The Boeing Company. de Havilland is a Canadian manufacturer of aerospace products. The purchase price will be based on the audited adjusted book value of the net assets purchased. Pending final determination, Management has estimated the cash consideration to be $57 000 000, which amount will be paid following the completion of the audit. The accounts will be consolidated from the date of acquisition.

The remaining 49% ownership was simultaneously acquired by the Province of Ontario. As part of the acquisition, the Corporation obtained the right to buy, and the Province of Ontario obtained the right to sell to the Corporation, during the period from February 1, 1996 to January 31, 1997, all of Ontario's interest in de Havilland for a maximum amount of $49 000 000.

As part of this transaction, the Government of Canada and the Province of Ontario have agreed to provide the Corporation with various financial assistance programs, including the reimbursement of restructuring costs up to a maximum amount of $370 000 000 during the five-year period following the acquisition date.

c) Concarril

On April 9, 1992, the Corporation was selected by the Government of Mexico to acquire the operations and substantially all of the net assets of Constructora Nacional de Carros de Ferrocarril, S.A. of Mexico ("Concarril"), a Mexican manufacturer of transportation equipment, for a cash consideration estimated by the Management to be $27 000 000. The contractual agreement related to this acquisition is expected to be finalised shortly. The accounts will be consolidated from the date of acquisition.

20. Reclassification

Some 1991 figures have been reclassified to conform to the presentation adopted in 1992.

21. Segmented information

See chart on page 50.

Segmented Information
[millions of dollars]

	Bombardier Inc. consolidated	
	1992	1991
Industry segments		
Revenues		
Canada	**$ 273.0**	$ 277.5
United States	**960.0**	969.2
Europe	**1 651.7**	1 382.9
Other	**173.9**	262.7
Total	**$ 3 058.6**	$ 2 892.3
Income (loss) before income taxes	**$ 121.4**	$ 120.5
Identifiable assets	**$ 3 069.3**	$ 2 561.8
Corporate assets	**1.4**	1.7
Total assets	**$ 3 070.7**	$ 2 563.5
Additions to fixed assets	**$ 166.6**	$ 176.0
Depreciation of fixed assets	**$ 73.0**	$ 74.5
Export sales from Canada	**$ 1 084.5**	$ 975.8
Foreign sales of foreign subsidiaries	**1 701.1**	1 639.0
Total sales outside Canada	**$ 2 785.6**	$ 2 614.8

	Consolidated	
	1992	1991
Geographic segments		
Total revenue	**$ 3 266.0**	$ 3 044.1
Intercorporation transfers between geographic segments	**207.4**	151.8
Revenues	**$ 3 058.6**	$ 2 892.3
Income (loss) before income taxes	**$ 121.4**	$ 120.5
Identifiable assets	**$ 3 112.1**	$ 2 583.7
Intercorporation accounts receivable	**(42.8)**	(21.9)
Corporate assets	**1.4**	1.7
Total assets	**$ 3 070.7**	$ 2 563.5
Additions to fixed assets	**$ 166.6**	$ 176.0
Depreciation of fixed assets	**$ 73.0**	$ 74.5
Export sales		

	Transportation Equipment		Motorized Consumer Products		Aerospace		Defence		BCG	
	1992	1991	1992	1991	1992	1991	1992	1991	1992	1991
	$ 26.3	$ 44.9	$ 118.2	$ 126.9	$ 52.5	$ 38.3	$ 69.4	$ 60.5	$ 6.6	$ 6.9
	67.1	111.8	180.8	168.1	656.5	627.8	6.0	12.4	49.6	49.1
	627.9	536.3	72.4	94.8	660.6	466.4	290.8	285.4	—	—
	4.3	4.1	20.1	8.2	149.5	250.4	—	—	—	—
	$ 725.6	$ 697.1	$ 391.5	$ 398.0	$ 1 519.1	$ 1 382.9	$ 366.2	$ 358.3	$ 56.2	$ 56.0
	$ 3.5	$ 20.1	$ (9.1)	$ (29.5)	$ 137.2	$ 112.9	$ 2.0	$ 28.5	$ (12.2)	$ (11.5)
	$ 351.3	$ 424.3	$ 227.6	$ 306.1	$ 1 689.6	$ 1 203.3	$ 141.3	$ 117.6	$ 659.5	$ 510.5
	$ 45.9	$ 26.6	$ 14.9	$ 13.0	$ 97.8	$ 102.4	$ 2.8	$ 17.0	$ 5.2	$ 17.0
	$ 20.6	$ 23.3	$ 14.9	$ 15.4	$ 32.9	$ 32.9	$ 3.6	$ 2.1	$ 1.0	$ 0.8
	$ 133.3	$ 134.1	$ 219.5	$ 186.3	$ 613.8	$ 553.4	$ 117.9	$ 102.0	$ —	$ —
	566.0	518.1	53.8	84.7	852.8	791.3	178.9	195.8	49.6	49.1
	$ 699.3	$ 652.2	$ 273.3	$ 271.0	$ 1 466.6	$ 1 344.7	$ 296.8	$ 297.8	$ 49.6	$ 49.1

	Canada		United States		Europe	
	1992	1991	1992	1991	1992	1991
	$ 1 384.7	$ 1 250.8	$ 414.9	$ 394.0	$ 1 466.4	$ 1 399.3
	53.6	31.3	60.2	44.3	93.6	76.2
	$ 1 331.1	$ 1 219.5	$ 354.7	$ 349.7	$ 1 372.8	$ 1 323.1
	$ 50.3	$ 32.2	$ (16.0)	$ (6.5)	$ 87.1	$ 94.8
	$ 1 020.3	$ 902.3	$ 1 063.3	$ 815.6	$ 1 028.5	$ 865.8
	$ 46.9	$ 83.0	$ 21.1	$ 10.9	$ 98.6	$ 82.1
	$ 26.9	$ 24.9	$ 11.0	$ 8.2	$ 35.1	$ 41.4
	$ 1 084.5	$ 975.8				

Index

Comprehensive List of Accounts Used in
Exercises and Problems

Current Assets

101 Cash
102 Petty cash
103 Cash equivalents
104 Temporary investments
105 Allowance to reduce temporary investments to market
106 Accounts receivable
107 Allowance for doubtful accounts
108 Legal fees receivable
109 Interest receivable
110 Rent receivable
111 Notes receivable
115 Subscriptions receivable, common shares
116 Subscriptions receivable, preferred shares
119 Merchandise inventory
120 _____ inventory
121 _____ inventory
124 Office supplies
125 Store supplies
126 _____ supplies
128 Prepaid insurance
129 Prepaid interest
130 Prepaid property taxes
131 Prepaid rent
132 Raw materials inventory
133 Goods in process inventory, _____
134 Goods in process inventory, _____
135 Finished goods inventory

Long-Term Investments

141 Investment in _____ shares
142 Investment in _____ bonds
144 Investment in _____
145 Bond sinking fund

Capital Assets

151 Automobiles
152 Accumulated amortization, automobiles
153 Trucks
154 Accumulated amortization, trucks
155 Boats
156 Accumulated amortization, boats
157 Professional library
158 Accumulated amortization, professional library
159 Law library
160 Accumulated amortization, law library
163 Office equipment
164 Accumulated amortization, office equipment
165 Store equipment
166 Accumulated amortization, store equipment
167 _____ equipment
168 Accumulated amortization, _____ equipment
169 Machinery
170 Accumulated amortization, machinery
173 Building _____
174 Accumulated amortization, building _____
175 Building _____
176 Accumulated amortization, building _____
179 Land improvements _____
180 Accumulated amortization, land improvements _____
181 Land improvements _____
182 Accumulated amortization, land improvements _____
183 Land

Natural Resources

185 Mineral deposit
186 Accumulated depletion, mineral deposit

Intangible Assets

191 Patents
192 Leasehold
193 Franchise

194 Copyrights
195 Leasehold improvements
196 Organization costs
197 Deferred income tax debits

Current Liabilities

201 Accounts payable
202 Insurance payable
203 Interest payable
204 Legal fees payable
207 Office salaries payable
208 Rent payable
209 Salaries payable
210 Wages payable
211 Accrued payroll payable
213 Estimated property taxes payable
214 Estimated warranty liability
215 Income taxes payable
216 Common dividend payable
217 Preferred dividend payable
218 UI payable
219 CPP payable
220 Employees' income taxes payable
221 Employees' medical insurance payable
222 Employees' retirement program payable
223 Employees' union dues payable
224 PST payable
225 GST payable
226 Estimated vacation pay liability

Unearned Revenues

230 Unearned consulting fees
231 Unearned legal fees
232 Unearned property management fees
233 Unearned _____ fees
234 Unearned _____
235 Unearned janitorial revenue
236 Unearned _____ revenue
238 Unearned rent _____
240 Short-term notes payable
241 Discount on short-term notes payable

Unclassified Liabilities

245 Notes payable

Long-Term Liabilities

251 Long-term notes payable
252 Discount on notes payable
253 Long-term lease liability
254 Discount on lease financing
255 Bonds payable
256 Discount on bonds payable
257 Premium on bonds payable
258 Deferred income tax credit

Owner's Equity

301 _____ , capital
302 _____ , withdrawals
303 _____ , capital
304 _____ , withdrawals
305 _____ , capital
306 _____ , withdrawals

Corporate Contributed Capital

307 Common shares
309 Common shares subscribed
310 Common stock dividend distributable
313 Contributed capital from the retirement of common shares
314 Contributed capital, treasury stock transactions
315 Preferred shares
317 Preferred shares subscribed

Retained Earnings

318 Retained earnings
319 Cash dividends declared
320 Stock dividends declared

Other Owner's Equity

321 Treasury stock, common

Revenues

401 _____ fees earned
402 _____ fees earned
403 _____ services revenue
404 _____ services revenue
405 Commissions earned
406 Rent earned
407 Dividends earned
408 Earnings from investment in _____

409 Interest earned
410 Sinking fund earnings
413 Sales
414 Sales returns and allowances
415 Sales discounts

Cost of Goods Sold Items

501 Amortization of patents
502 Cost of goods sold
503 Depletion of mine deposit
505 Purchases
506 Purchases returns and allowances
507 Purchases discounts
508 Transportation-in

Manufacturing Accounts

520 Raw materials purchases
521 Freight-in on raw materials
530 Factory payroll
531 Direct labour
540 Factory overhead
541 Indirect materials
542 Indirect labour
543 Factory insurance expired
544 Factory supervision
545 Factory supplies used
546 Factory utilities
547 Miscellaneous production costs
548 Property taxes on factory building
550 Rent on factory building
551 Repairs, factory equipment
552 Small tools written off
560 Amortization of factory equipment
561 Amortization of factory building

Standard Cost Variance Accounts

580 Direct material quantity variance
581 Direct material price variance
582 Direct labour quantity variance
583 Direct labour price variance
584 Factory overhead volume variance
585 Factory overhead controllable variance

Expenses

Amortization and Depreciation Expenses

601 Amortization expense, _____
602 Amortization expense, copyrights
604 Amortization expense, boats
605 Amortization expense, automobiles
606 Amortization expense, building _____
607 Amortization expense, building _____
608 Amortization expense, land improvements _____
609 Amortization expense, land improvements _____
610 Amortization expense, law library
611 Amortization expense, trucks
612 Amortization expense, _____ equipment
613 Amortization expense, _____ equipment
614 Amortization expense, _____
615 Amortization expense, _____

Employee-related Expenses

620 Office salaries expense
621 Sales salaries expense
622 Salaries expense
623 _____ wages expense
624 Employees' benefits expense
625 Payroll taxes expense

Financial Expenses

630 Cash over and short
631 Discounts lost
633 Interest expense

Insurance Expenses

635 Insurance expense, delivery equipment
636 Insurance expense, office equipment
637 Insurance expense, _____

Rental Expenses

640 Rent expense
641 Rent expense, office space
642 Rent expense, selling space
643 Press rental expense
644 Truck rental expense
645 _____ rental expense

Supplies Expense

650 Office supplies expense

651 Store supplies expense
652 _____ supplies expense
653 _____ supplies expense

Miscellaneous Expenses

655 Advertising expense
656 Bad debts expense
657 Blueprinting expense
658 Boat expense
659 Collection expense
661 Concessions expense
662 Credit card expense
663 Delivery expense
664 Dumping expense
667 Equipment expense
668 Food and drinks expense
669 Gas, oil, and repairs expense
671 Gas and oil expense
672 General and administrative expense
673 Janitorial expense
674 Legal fees expense
676 Mileage expense
677 Miscellaneous expense
678 Mower and tools expense
679 Operating expenses
681 Permits expense
682 Postage expense
683 Property taxes expense
684 Repairs expense, _____

685 Repairs expense, _____
687 Selling expenses
688 Telephone expense
689 Travel and entertainment expense
690 Utilities expense
691 Warranty expense
695 Income taxes expense

Gains and Losses

701 Gain on retirement of bonds
702 Gain on sale of machinery
703 Gain on sale of temporary investments
704 Gain on sale of trucks
705 Gain on _____
801 Loss on disposal of machinery
802 Loss on exchange of equipment
803 Loss on exchange of _____
804 Loss on market decline of temporary investments
805 Loss on retirement of bonds
806 Loss on sale of investments
807 Loss on sale of machinery
808 Loss on sale of _____
809 Loss on _____
810 Loss or gain from liquidation

Clearing Accounts

901 Income summary
902 Manufacturing summary